Neural Networks and Soft Computing

Advances in Soft Computing

Editor-in-chief
Prof. Janusz Kacprzyk
Systems Research Institute
Polish Academy of Sciences
ul. Newelska 6
01-447 Warsaw, Poland
E-mail: kacprzyk@ibspan.waw.pl
http://www.springer.de/cgi-bin/search-bock.pl?series=4240

Esko Turunen
Mathematics Behind Fuzzy Logic
1999. ISBN 3-7908-1221-8

Robert Fullér
Introduction to Neuro-Fuzzy Systems
2000. ISBN 3-7908-1256-0

Robert John and Ralph Birkenhead (Eds.)
Soft Computing Techniques and Applications
2000. ISBN 3-7908-1257-9

Mieczysław Kłopotek, Maciej Michalewicz
and Sławomir T. Wierzchoń (Eds.)
Intelligent Information Systems
2000. ISBN 3-7908-1309-5

Peter Sinčák, Ján Vaščák, Vladimír Kvasnička
and Radko Mesiar (Eds.)
The State of the Art in Computational Intelligence
2000. ISBN 3-7908-1322-2

Bernd Reusch and Karl-Heinz Temme (Eds.)
Computational Intelligence in Theory and Practice
2001. ISBN 3-7908-1357-5

Robert John and Ralph Birkenhead (Eds.)
Developments in Soft Computing
2001. ISBN 3-7908-1361-3

Mieczysław A. Kłopotek, Maciej Michalewicz
and Sławomir T. Wierzchoń (Eds.)
Intelligent Information Systems 2001
2001. ISBN 3-7908-1407-5

Antonio Di Nola and Giangiacomo Gerla (Eds.)
Lectures on Soft Computing and Fuzzy Logic
2001. ISBN 3-7908-1396-6

Tadeusz Trzaskalik and Jerzy Michnik (Eds.)
Multiple Objective and Goal Programming
2002. ISBN 3-7908-1409-1

James J. Buckley and Esfandiar Eslami
An Introduction to Fuzzy Logic and Fuzzy Sets
2002. ISBN 3-7908-1447-4

Ajith Abraham and Mario Köppen (Eds.)
Hybrid Information Systems
2002. ISBN 3-7908-1480-6

Lech Polkowski
Rough Sets
2002. ISBN 3-7908-1510-1

Mieczysław A. Kłopotek, Sławomir T. Wierzchoń
and Maciej Michalewicz (Eds.)
Intelligent Information Systems 2002
2002. ISBN 3-7908-1509-8

Andrea Bonarini, Francesco Masulli
and Gabriella Pasi (Eds.)
Soft Computing Applications
2002. ISBN 3-7908-1544-6

Leszek Rutkowski
Janusz Kacprzyk
Editors

Neural Networks and Soft Computing

Proceedings of the Sixth International Conference on Neural Networks and Soft Computing, Zakopane, Poland, June 11–15, 2002

With 353 Figures
and 142 Tables

Physica-Verlag
A Springer-Verlag Company

Prof. Leszek Rutkowski
Department of Computer Engineering
Technical University Częstochowa
Al. Armii Krajowej 36
42-200 Częstochowa
Poland
lrutko@kik.pcz.czest.pl

Prof. Janusz Kacprzyk
Polish Academy of Sciences
Systems Research Institute
ul. Newelska 6
01-447 Warsaw
Poland
kacprzyk@ibspan.waw.pl

ISSN 1615-3871
ISBN 3-7908-0005-8 Physica-Verlag Heidelberg New York

Cataloging-in-Publication Data applied for
A catalog record for this book is available from the Library of Congress.
Bibliographic information published by Die Deutsche Bibliothek
Die Deutsche Bibliothek lists this publication in the Deutsche Nationalbibliografie; detailed bibliographic data is available in the Internet at <http://dnb.ddb.de>.

Physica-Verlag Heidelberg New York
a member of BertelsmannSpringer Science+Business Media GmbH

http://www.springer.de

Printed in Germany

Softcover Design: Erich Kirchner, Heidelberg

SPIN 10899922 88/3130/DK-5 4 3 2 1 0 – Printed on acid-free paper

Preface

This volume constitutes the proceedings of the 6th Conference on Neural Networks and Soft Computing, ICNNSC'2002, held in Zakopane, Poland in June 11-15, 2002. The Conference was organized by the Polish Neural Network Society in cooperation with the Department of Computer Engineering at the Technical University of Częstochowa. The previous conferences took place in Kule (1994), Szczyrk (1996), Kule (1997) and Zakopane (1999, 2000) and attracted a large number of papers and internationally recognized speakers like Prof. Robert Marks, Prof. Jacek Żurada, Prof. Ryszard Tadeusiewicz, Prof. Shiro Usui, Prof. Daniel Amit, Prof. Włodzisław Duch, Prof. Erkki Oja, Prof. Syozo Yasui, Prof. Enrique Ruspini, Prof. Witold Pedrycz, Prof. Janusz Kacprzyk and Prof. Lotfi A. Zadeh.
It was pointed out by Prof. Lotfi A. Zadeh that "Soft Computing (SC) is a coalition of methodologies which are oriented toward the conception and design of information/intelligent systems. The principal members of the coalition are: fuzzy logic (FL), neurocomputing (NC), evolutionary computing (EC), probabilistic computing (PC), chaotic computing (CC), and machine learning (ML). The constituent methodologies of SC are, for the most part, complementary and synergistic rather than competitive".
This volume presents most techniques and methodologies mentioned by Prof. Zadeh and, moreover, several interesting applications :

- Neural Networks
- Fuzzy Systems
- Evolutionary Algorithms
- Soft Computing in Classification and Pattern Recognition
- Medical Applications of Soft Computing
- Neuro-Fuzzy Systems
- Various Methods of Soft Computing
- Image Processing
- Soft Computing in Automatics
- Neural Networks for Signal Processing
- Economic Applications
- Mechanical Applications
- Various Applications

We are honored by participation of 17 distinguished professors who delivered invited talks in the area of the soft computing: Lotfi A. Zadeh, Zdzisław Bubnicki, Zdzisław Pawlak, Shun-ichi Amari, Ildar Batyrshin, Kaoru Hirota, Laszlo T. Koczy, Witold Kosiński, Vilém Novák, Soo-Young Lee, Šarunas Raudys, Rudy Setiono, Peter Sincak, Paweł Strumiłło, Hideyuki Takagi, Shiro Usui, Bogdan M. Wilamowski and Jacek Żurada. They significantly contributed to the success of the Conference.

I would like to thank our participants, invited speakers and reviewers of the papers for their scientific and personal contribution to the Conference. I also thank Prof. Janusz Kacprzyk – the co-editor and editor-in-chief of Advances in Soft Computing, and Mrs. Katharina Wetzel-Vandai from the Springer - Verlag Company for cooperation in preparation of this volume. Finally I thank my co-workers, especially dr Jarosław Bilski and Mr. Rafał Scherer for their enormous efforts to make the Conference a very successful event.

Częstochowa, June 2002

Leszek Rutkowski

President of the Polish Neural
Network Society

Table of Contents

Invited Papers

It is a Fundamental Limitation to Base Probability Theory on Bivalent Logic 1
Lotfi A. Zadeh

Soft Variables as a Generalization of Uncertain, Random and Fuzzy Variables 4
Zdzisław Bubnicki

Decision Algorithms, Bayes' Theorem and Flow Graphs 18
Zdzisław Pawlak

New Consideration on Criteria of Model Selection 25
Shun-ichi Amari

Generalized Conjunction, Disjunction and Negation Operations in Fuzzy Modeling 31
Ildar Batyrshin

Image Data Compression/Reconstruction by Fuzzy Relational Equation 40
Kaoru Hirota, Hajime Nobuhara, Witold Pedrycz

Interpolation in Hierarchical Rule Bases 48
László T. Kóczy, Leila Muresan, Kornél Csányi, Kaoru Hirota

On Algebraic Operations on Fuzzy Reals 54
Witold Kosiński, Piotr Prokopowicz, Dominik Ślęzak

Formal Fuzzy Logic and its Use in Modeling of Vagueness and Computing with Words 62
Vilém Novák

Independent Component Analysis for Simultaneous Active Noise Canceling and Blind Signal Separation 73
Hyung Min Park, Tae-Su Kim, Yoon-Kyung Choi, Soo-Young Lee

On The Universality of The Single-Layer Perceptron Model 79
Šarunas Raudys

A Hybrid Connectionist System for Multiple Regression 87
Rudy Setiono, Jacek M. Zurada

Financial Fraud Identification Using MF-ARTMAP Neural Network 95
Peter Sinčák, Marcel Hric, Richard Val'o, Pavol Horanský, Pavel Karel

Radial Basis Function Neural Networks: Theory and Applications 107
Paweł Strumiłło, Władysław Kamiński

Introduction of Interactive Evolutionary Computation and Its Application to CG Creativity 120
Hideyuki Takagi

Neuroinformatics Research in Vision 128
Shiro Usui

Soft Computing in Hardware Implementations 135
Bogdan M. Wilamowski, Okyay Kaynak

Neural Networks

On the Node Complexity of Threshold Gate Circuits with Sub-linear Fan-ins 143
Valeriu Beiu

Numerically Robust Learning Algorithms for Feed Forward Neural Networks 149
Jarosław Bilski, Leszek Rutkowski

A Neural Network Based Approach For Sensors Issued Data Fusion 155
Abdennasser Chebira, Kurosh Madani

Population Learning Metaheuristic for Neural Network Training 161
Ireneusz Czarnowski, Piotr Jędrzejowicz

A Penalty Function to Obtain Satisfactory Local Models of Complex Systems 167
Grzegorz Drałus, Jerzy Świątek

Feature Selection Based on Information Theory Filters 173
Włodzisław Duch, Jacek Biesiada, Tomasz Winiarski, Karol Grudziński, Krzysztof Grąbczewski

Neural Network Design without Learning 179
Ewa Dudek-Dyduch, Zbigniew Gomółka

New Ontogenic Neural Network Classificator Based on Probabilistic Reasoning 188
Adrian Horzyk

Discrete Quasi-gradient Features Weighting Algorithm 194
Norbert Jankowski

Input Ranking Revisited:A Theoretical Input Sensitivity Approach 200
Sanggil Kang, Can Isik, Steven Morphet

On the Influence of Synaptic Dilution on Memory Properties of Neural Networks 206
Robert Kosiński, Magdalena M. Sinołęcka

Evolutionary Algorithm vs. Other Methods for Constructive Optimisation of RBF Network Kernels 212
Jan Koszlaga, Paweł Strumiłło

Heuristic Dynamic Programming for Neural Networks Learning Part 1: Learning as a Control Problem 218
Maciej Krawczak

Heuristic Dynamic Programming for Neural Networks Learning Part 2: I-order Differential Dynamic Programming 224
Maciej Krawczak

Evaluation of Dipolar Neural Networks in Survival Time Prediction 230
Małgorzata Krętowska, Leon Bobrowski

A Synaptic Indicator Based Approach for Hidden Parameters Extraction In Industrial Environment 236
Kurosh Madani, Ion Berechet

Regression Hyper Surfaces with a Modified Neural Network Architecture 242
L. F. Mingo, P. Gisbert, J. D. Carrillo, C. Hernández

Response Surface Methodology at Irregular Grids Based on Voronoi Scheme with Neural Network Approximator 250
Jacek Pietraszek

Extended RBF Nets - Preliminary Studies 256
Ewaryst Rafajłowicz

How to Test Overfitting When There is not Enough Data for a Testing Set? 262
Izabela Rejer, Andrzej Piegat

On Very Large Scale Hamiltonian Neural Nets 268
Wieslaw Sienko, Wieslaw Citko

Fuzzy Systems

*On sup - * Compositions of Fuzzy Implications* 274
Michał Baczyński, Józef Drewniak, Jolanta Sobera

A New Approach to Fuzzy Constraints in Linear Programming 280
Joanna Banaś

On a Linguistic Description of Dependencies in Data 286
Ildar Batyrshin, Michael Wagenknecht

New Index of Significance for Inputs Selection 292
Joanna Chimiak-Opoka

Fuzzy Reliability Analysis 298
Jacek Mazurkiewicz, Tomasz Walkowiak

Variable Precision Rough Sets in Analysis of Inconsistent Decision Tables 304
Alicja Mieszkowicz-Rolka, Leszek Rolka

The Newton Interpolation Method with Fuzzy Numbers as the Entries 310
Elisabeth Rakus-Andersson

Fuzzy Optimization Using Direct Crisp and Fuzzy Interval Comparison 316
Pavel Sevastjanov, Paweł Róg

Membership Functions as Combination of Expert's Knowledge with Population Information 322
Ewa Straszecka, Joanna Straszecka

Towards More Human Consistent Reasoning via Intuitionistic Fuzzy Sets 328
Eulalia Szmidt, Janusz Kacprzyk

Fuzzy Relational Thesauri Expansion Using Categorized Textual Data 334
Domonkos Tikk, Jae Dong Yang

Evolutionary Algorithms

Investigation of the Neighborhood Attraction Evolutionary Algorithm Based on Neural Gas 340
Jutta Huhse, Thomas Villmann, Andreas Zell

A Fate of Two Evolutionary Walkers after the Departure from the Origin 346
Akira Imada

Genetic Algorithms with Adaptive Meta-heuristics for 2D Packing Problem 352
Romuald Jagielski

Genetic Decryption of Columnar Transposition Code 358
Anna Kleszczyńska, Piotr S. Szczepaniak

A Floating-Point Based Evolutionary Algorithm for Model Parameters Extraction and Optimization in HBT Device Simulation 364
Yiming Li, Chuen-Tsat Sun, Cheng-Kai Chen

Rule Extraction from Trained Neural Network with Evolutionary Algorithms 370
Urszula Markowska-Kaczmar, Marcin Chumieja

Genetic Algorithm for Observer Parameters Tuning in Sensorless Induction Motor Drive 376
Andrzej Przybył, Jerzy Jelonkiewicz

Moving Objects in the Problem of Path Planning by Evolutionary Computation 382
Roman Śmierzchalski, Andrzej Łebkowski

Soft Computing in Classification and Pattern Recognition

Determining Relevant Input Dimensions for the Self Organizing Map 388
Thorsten Bojer, Barbara Hammer, Marc Strickert, Thomas Villmann

The Use of Wide-frame Cepstrum in Speech Recognition 394
Justyna Brześcińska, Tomasz de Jastrzębiec Wykowski

Face Recognition/Detection by Clustering and Probabilistic Neural Networks 400
Giacomo Capizzi, Salvatore Coco, Cinzia Giuffrida, Antonio Laudani, Giuseppe Pappalardo

A Posteriori Corrections to Classification Methods 406
Włodzisław Duch, Łukasz Itert

Competent Undemocratic Committees 412
Włodzisław Duch, Łukasz Itert, Karol Grudziński

Reasoning in Structured Bayesian Networks 418
Mieczysław Alojzy Kłopotek

Machine Learning Methods for Improving Gender Recognition from Stop Consonants 424
Ewa Lukasik, Robert Susmaga

Sequential Classification 430
Agata Kołakowska, Witold Malina

Geometry and Logic in Pattern Classifiers 436
Witold Pedrycz, Nicolino Pizzi

Fuzzy Bayesian Classifier: a Multi-Agent System for Information Retrieval in the Web 444
José C Romero Cortés, Leonid B. Sheremetov

Medical Applications of Soft Computing

Can Neural Networks Be Used to Define the Rules of Cardiovascular Disease Prevention in the Nutrition Domain? 450
Agnieszka Borowiec, Krzysztof Fronczyk, Bohdan Macukow, Maciej Grzenda

A Practical Approach To Image Reconstruction From Projections Using Neural Networks Structure 456
Robert Cierniak

A Systolic Realisation of the Neuro-Tomograph 462
Robert Cierniak, Jacek Smoląg

An Investigation of Differential Skin Colonization of Neonates by Staphylococci, Using an Artificial Neural Network-based System 468
Diana R. Cundell, Les M. Sztandera, Alan Arbeter, Jean M. Morrone

Evolutionary Computing Techniques for Diagnosis of Urinary Tract Infections in Vivo, Using Gas Sensors 474
Vassilis Kodogiannis, Alexandros K. Pavlou, Panagiotis Chountas, Anthony P. F. Turner

Neural Expert System for Pharmaceutical Formulation Development - Focus on Solid Dispersions 480
Aleksander Mendyk, Renata Jachowicz, Anna Błasiak

Using Artificial Neural Network as a Tool for Epidemiological Data Analysis 486
Sebastian Polak, Aleksander Mendyk, Jerzy Brandys

A Neural Network Based Investigation of High Frequency Components of the ECG 492
Minija Tamošiūnaitė, Šarūnas Raudys

Automatic Ischemic Stroke Segmentation Using Various Techniques 498
Andrius Ušinskas, Erinija Pranckeviciene, Thomas Wittenberg, Peter Hastreiter, Bernd F. Tomandl

Neuro-Fuzzy Systems

Simple Modification of Takagi-Sugeno Model 504
Bohdan S. Butkiewicz

Applying Genetic Algorithm for Training Hybrid Neuro-Fuzzy Classifier - the nfgClass System 510
Piotr Grądzki

Fuzzy Calculus by RBF Neural Networks 516
Vojislav Kecman, Zhenquan Li

Extending Neuro-Fuzzy Classification to Semi-Supervised Learning 523
Aljoscha Klose, Daniela Girimonte, Rudolf Kruse

An ε-insensitive Learning in Neuro-Fuzzy Modeling 531
Jacek Łęski, Norbert Henzel

Soft Techniques for Bayesian Classification 537
Robert Nowicki, Leszek Rutkowski

Gradient Descent Based Optimization of Transparent Mamdani Systems 545
Andri Riid, Ennu Rüstern

A Neural Network Equivalent to a Neuro-Fuzzy System for Classification 551
Danuta Rutkowska

Compromise Weighted Neuro - Fuzzy Systems 557
Leszek Rutkowski, Krzysztof Cpałka

A Fuzzy Relational System with Linguistic Antecedent Certainty Factors 563
Rafał Scherer, Leszek Rutkowski

Interval Type 2 Neuro-Fuzzy Systems Based on Interval Consequents 570
Janusz Starczewski, Leszek Rutkowski

Generation of Fuzzy Neural Network Structure 578
Zbigniew Świątnicki, Vladimír Olej

Various Methods of Soft Computing

Regularization Background of Clustering Algorithms 584
Piotr Boguś, Katarzyna Lewandowska, Francesco Masulli

Simulated Annealing C-Means Clustering Algorithm Convergence Proof 590
Piotr Boguś, Anna Maria Massone, Francesco Masulli

Learning by Constraint Relaxation 596
John Day

Forests of Decision Trees 602
Krzysztof Grąbczewski, Włodzisław Duch

Agent Populations as Computational Intelligence 608
Marek Kisiel-Dorohinicki, Grzegorz Dobrowolski, Edward Nawarecki

Conditional Belief Functions Versus Proper Belief Functions 614
Mieczysław Alojzy Kłopotek, Sławomir Tadeusz Wierzchoń

Transformation Distances, Strings and Identification of DNA Promoters 620
Maciej Marczak, Włodzisław Duch, Karol Grudziński, Antoine Naud

Solving Stochastic Shortest Path Problem Using Monte Carlo Sampling Method: A Distributed Learning Automata Approach 626
Mohammad R. Meybodi, Hamid Beigy

Visualization of Large Data Sets Using MDS Combined with LVQ 632
Antoine Naud, Włodzisław Duch

Controlling the Asymptotic Level Density for Quantization Processes with Self-Organizing Maps 638
Ewa Skubalska-Rafajłowicz

Formal Neuro-Immune Network 644
Alexander Tarakanov, Georgy Penev, Kurosh Madani

Memory Management in Artificial Immune System 650
Krzysztof Trojanowski, Sławomir Tadeusz Wierzchoń

Image Processing

A Software Platform for Evaluation of Neural Algorithms for Stereo Image Processing 656
Bogusław Cyganek, Jan Borgosz

Sequential Analysis of Medical Images Using Neural Networks 662
Marek Czeleń, Grzegorz Wojtas, Zbigniew Mikrut

Medical Image Recognition Based on Fractal Features 668
Edward Kącki, Marcin Janaszewski

Improving Image Database Summarization by Automatic Image Feature Selection Using GA 674
Zoran Stejić, Eduardo M. Iyoda, Yasufumi Takama, Kaoru Hirota

Soft Computing in Automatics

System Identification Using Delaunay Tessellation of Self-Organizing Maps 680
Janos Abonyi, Ferenc Szeifert

Neural Network Reactive Navigation and Control of Wheeled Mobile Robot 686
Zenon Hendzel

Training of Neural Network Wiener Models with Recursive Prediction Error Algorithm 692
Andrzej Janczak

Dynamic GMDH Type Neural Networks 698
Marcin Mrugalski, Eugen Arinton, Józef Korbicz

Neural Networks for Signal Processing

Generalized Spectrum Analysis by Means of Neural Networks 704
Dariusz Grabowski, Janusz Walczak

Wavelet Network for Recursive Function Learning 710
Zygmunt Hasiewicz

Interpolation and Approximation of Models 716
Bruno Pelletier

Wavelet Network Estimating Regression Function 722
Przemysław Śliwiński

Economic Applications

Dynamic Programming with NAR Model Versus Q-learning - Case Study 728
Jarosław Chrobak, Andrzej Pacut

Evaluation of Economic Effectiveness of Provinces with Rough and Fuzzy Sets 734
Marcin Korzeń, Andrzej Piegat

Evolutionarily Developed Neural Networks for Investment Strategies Construction 742
Janusz Morajda

Credit Granting Procedure: Multilayer Perceptron And Classification Tree 748
Dorota Witkowska, Iwona Staniec

Mechanical Applications

Reliability Analysis of Structures by Neural Network Supported Monte Carlo Methods 754
Joanna Kaliszuk, Zenon Waszczyszyn

BP Neural Network Computation of Response Spectra Using a Subpicture Idea 760
Krystyna Kuźniar

Neural Networks in Updating of Dynamic Models with Experimental Verification 766
Bartosz Miller, Leonard Ziemiański

A Fuzzy Neural Network for the Analysis of Experimental Structural Mechanics Problems 772
Ewa Pabisek, Magdalena Jakubek, Zenon Waszczyszyn

Neural Network Identification of a Circular Hole in the Rectangular Plate 778
Grzegorz Piątkowski, Leonard Ziemiański

Neural Analysis of Concrete Shrinkage 784
Anna Urbańska, Zenon Waszczyszyn

Various Applications

Short-Term Load Forecasting for Energy Markets 790
Witold Bartkiewicz, Bożena Matusiak

Systolic architecture for Higher Order Neural Networks 796
Jarosław Bilski, Jacek Smoląg

Decomposition and Argument Reduction of Neural Networks 802
Piotr Buciak, Tadeusz Łuba, Hubert Niewiadomski, Michal Pleban, Piotr Sapiecha, Henry Selvaraj

Traffic Flow Simulation - Cellular Automata with Fuzzy Rules Approach 808
Marcin Burzyński, Waldemar Cudny, Witold Kosiński

An MLP Predictor of ELF Environmental Magnetic Fields Pollution 814
Giacomo Capizzi, Salvatore Coco, Cinzia Giuffrida, Antonio Laudani, Giuseppe Pappalardo, Roberto Pulvirenti

Forecasting of Meteorologic Data by Artificial Neural Networks 820
Kerem Cigizoglu

Artificial Neural Network Predictive System for Oxygen Steelmaking Converter 825
Jan Falkus, Piotr Pietrzkiewicz, Wojciech Pietrzyk, Jan Kusiak

Evaluation of a Helicopter Model Using Generalized Back Propagation Through Time 831
Krzysztof Fujarewicz

Correction of Non-linear Dynamic Properties of Temperature Sensors by the Use of ANN 837
Lidia Jackowska-Strumiłło

Short-Term Weather Forecasting with Neural Networks 843
Marcin Jaruszewicz, Jacek Mańdziuk

Method for Detection of Wheat Grain Damage with Application of Neural Networks 849
Aleksander Kubiak, Zbigniew Mikrut

The WWW Based Data Mining Toolbox Architecture 855
Łukasz Kurgan, Krzysztof Cios, Michael Trombley

Concept of Neural Model of the Sea Bottom Surface 861
Jacek Łubczonek, Andrzej Stateczny

Systolic Simulation of Hamming Neural Network 867
Jacek Mazurkiewicz

Neural Network Simulation of Energy Transfer Processes in a Membrane Protein System 873
Petr V. Nazarov, Vladimir V. Apanasovich, Vladimir M. Lutkovski, Marcus A. Hemminga, Rob B. M. Koehorst

Neural Network Modifiers of Nonlinear Dynamical Systems 879
Andrzej Ossowski

Probabilistic-Fuzzy Method of Ship Manoeuvre Safety Assessment in a Restricted Area 885
Zbigniew Pietrzykowski

Irregular Shape Particle Size Analysis Using Neural Network Approach 891
Edward Rój

Neural Classifier for Bottom Sediments 897
Dariusz Szulc, Mariusz Wąż

Performance of ROC Curves and LVQ Neural Networks in Detection of Middle Cerebral Artery Spasm 903
Mirosław Świercz, Zenon Mariak, Jarosław Krejza

Neural Network Approach to Acoustic Detection of Number of Vehicles 909
Tomasz Walkowiak, Paweł Żogał

It is a Fundamental Limitation to Base Probability Theory on Bivalent Logic*

Lotfi A. Zadeh

Professor in the Graduate School and Director
Berkeley Initiative in Soft Computing (BISC)
Computer Science Division and the Electronics Research Laboratory
Department of EECS
University of California, Berkeley, CA 94720-1776
Telephone: 510-642-4959; Fax: 510-642-1712
E-mail: zadeh@cs.berkeley.edu

Extended Abstract

Probability theory has long played—and is continuing to play—the role of the principal tool for dealing with problems in which uncertainty is a significant factor. The history of probability theory is a history of important advances in our understanding of decision-making in uncertain environments. But what we see alongside the brilliant successes are problem areas in which progress has been elusive. An example is the class of problems in which probabilities, utilities and relations are ill-defined in ways that put such problems well beyond the reach of existing methods.

A thesis that is put forth in this paper is that standard probability theory, call it PT, has fundamental limitations—limitations which are rooted in the fact that PT is based on bivalent logic. It is this thesis that underlies the radically-sounding title of the paper: It is a Fundamental Limitation to Base Probability Theory on Bivalent Logic.

The principal rationale for this thesis is that the conceptual structure of PT is directed at addressing the partiality of certainty but not the partiality of possibility and, most importantly, the partiality of truth. A direct consequence of these omissions is that PT lacks the capability to deal with information which is not just par-

---

* Research supported in part by ONR Contract N00014-00-1-0621, ONR Contract N00014-99-C-0298, NASA Contract NCC2-1006, NASA Grant NAC2-117, ONR Grant N00014-96-1-0556, ONR Grant FDN0014991035, ARO Grant DAAH 04-961-0341 and the BISC Program of UC Berkeley

tially certain but also partially possible and/or partially true. An example is: Most analysts believe that it is very unlikely that there will be a significant increase in the price of oil in the near future.

The principal negative consequences of basing PT on bivalent logic are the following.

1. Brittleness (discontinuity.) Almost all concepts in PT are bivalent in the sense that a concept, C, is either true or false, with no partiality of truth allowed. For example, events A and B are either independent or not independent. A process, P, is either stationary or nonstationary, and so on. An example of brittleness is: If all A's are B's and all B's are C's, then all A's are C's; but if almost all A's are B's and almost all B's are C's, then all that can be said is that the proportion of A's in C's is between 0 and 1. In particular, brittleness of independence creates serious problems in construction of Bayesian nets since only an epsilon separates independence from dependence.
2. The dilemma of "it is possible but not probable." A simple version of this dilemma is the following. Assume that A is a proper subset of B and that the Lebesgue measure of A is arbitrarily close to the Lebesgue measure of B. Now, what can be said about the probability measure, P(A), given the probability measure P(B)? The only assertion that can be made is that P(A) lies between 0 and P(B). The uniformativeness of this assessment of P(A) leads to counterintuitive conclusions. For example, suppose that with probability 0.99 Robert returns from work within one minute of 6pm. What is the probability that he is home at 6pm? Using PT, with no additional information or the use of the maximum entropy principle, the answer is: between 0 and 1. This simple example is an instance of a basic problem of what to do when we know what is possible but cannot assess the associated probabilities or probability distributions. A case in point relates to assessment of the probability of a worst case scenario.
3. Incapability to operate on perception-based information. This is the most serious limitation of PT. It is rooted in the fact that much of human knowledge is perception-based, e.g., "Most Swedes are tall;" "It is foggy in San Francisco during the summer," "It is unlikely to be warm tomorrow." and "Usually Robert returns from work at about 6pm."

Perceptions are intrinsically imprecise, reflecting the bounded ability of sensory organs and, ultimately, the brain, to resolve detail and store information. More concretely, perceptions are f-granular in the sense that (a) the boundaries of perceived classes are unsharp; and (b) the values of perceived attributes are granulated, with a granule being a clump of values drawn together by indistinguishability, similarity, proximity or functionality.

F-granularity of perceptions puts them well beyond the reach of conventional meaning-representation methods based on bivalent logic. As a consequence, PT, by itself, lacks the capability to operate on perception-based information: As an illustration, PT cannot provide an answer to the query: What is the probability that Robert is home at about t pm, given the perception-based information that (a) usually Robert leaves his office at about 5:30 pm; and (b) usually it takes about 30 minutes to reach home.

What can be done to endow probability theory with the capability to operate on perception-based information? In a recent paper entitled "Toward a Perception-Based Theory of Probabilistic Reasoning with Imprecise Probabilities," (Journal of Statistical Planning and Inference), I outlined an approach to a restructuring of probability theory which adds this capability to PT. Briefly, the proposed restructuring involves three stages of generalization: (a) f-generalization; (b) f.g-generalization; and (c) nl-generalization. More specifically:

a) F-generalization involves a progression from crisp sets to fuzzy sets in PT, leading to a generalization of PT which is denoted as PT^+. In PT^+, probabilities, functions, relations, measures and everything else are allowed to have fuzzy denotations, that is, be a matter of degree. In particular, probabilities described as low, high, not very high, etc. are interpreted as labels of fuzzy subsets of the unit interval or, equivalently, as possibility distributions of their numerical values.
b) F.g-generalization involves fuzzy granulation of variables, functions, relations, etc., leading to a generalization of PT which is denoted as PT^{++}. By fuzzy granulation of a variable, X is meant a partition of the range of X into fuzzy granules, with a granule being a clump of values of X which are drawn together by indistinguishability, similarity, proximity or functionality. Membership functions of such granules are usually assumed to be triangular or trapezoidal. Basically, granularity reflects the bounded ability of the human mind to resolve detail and store information.
c) Nl-generalization involves an addition to PT^{++} of a capability to operate on propositions expressed in a natural language, with the understanding that such propositions serve as descriptors of perceptions. Nl-generalization of PT leads to perception-based probability theory denoted as PTp. By construction, PTp is needed to answer the query in the Robert example: What is the probability that Robert is home at about t pm?

The principal thrust of what was said above may be viewed as a call for a recognition that standard probability theory has serious limitations—limitations which are rooted in its bivalent base and the fundamental conflict between bivalence and reality. What is needed to circumvent these limitations is a restructuring of the foundations of probability theory—a restructuring aimed principally at endowing probability theory with the capability to operate on perception-based information.

Soft Variables as a Generalization of Uncertain, Random and Fuzzy Variables

Z. Bubnicki

Institute of Control and Systems Engineering,
Wroclaw University of Technology
Wyspianskiego 27, 50-370 Wroclaw, POLAND

Summary. A concept of uncertain variables and their application in a class of uncertain systems has been developed. In this paper, after a short description of uncertain variables, nonparametric decision problems based on uncertain, random and fuzzy variables are presented. The analogies lead to the formulation of so called soft variables described by evaluating functions, introduced as a tool for a unification and generalization of decision problems based on uncertain knowledge representations. The application of the soft variables to a class of decision problems and a "principle of equivalency" concerning two different formulations of a knowledge given by an expert are presented.

1 Introduction

In recent years an idea of uncertain variables has been developed as a tool for decision problems in a class of uncertain systems described by traditional models or relational knowledge representations [1, 3, 5, 6, 8]. The uncertain variable is described by certainty distribution given by an expert and characterizing his / her knowledge concerning approximate values of the variable. The uncertain variables are related to random and fuzzy variables, but there are also essential differences. The uncertain, random and fuzzy variables may be considered as special cases of the more general description of uncertainty in the form of *soft variables* and *evaluating functions* [7, 8, 9].

In this paper, analogies between the descriptions based on uncertain, random and fuzzy variables, applied to nonparametric decision problems for static (memory less) systems will be presented (Sec. 3). These analogies will be used for a generalization in the form of a new (modified) version of the soft variables and their application to the decision problem (Sec. 4,5,6). We shall start with a very short description of uncertain variables (Sec. 2). Details and examples may be found in [5, 6, 8].

The main idea of the knowledge-based decision problem under consideration is illustrated in Fig.1. A nondeterministic knowledge of the plant KP and a requirement concerning y are used for the formulation of a nondeterministic knowledge of the decision making KD and via *determinization* of KD the deterministic decision algorithm $u_d = \Psi(z)$ in the open-loop decision system is obtained. Let us consider a nondeterministic plant with the input vector $u \in U$, the output vector $y \in Y$ and the vector of disturbances $z \in Z$, described by a relation $R(u,y,z) \subset U \times Y \times Z$ (a *relational knowledge representation*). For the given u and z we obtain the set of all possible outputs

$$D_y(u,z) = \{y \in Y : (u,y,z) \in R\}.$$

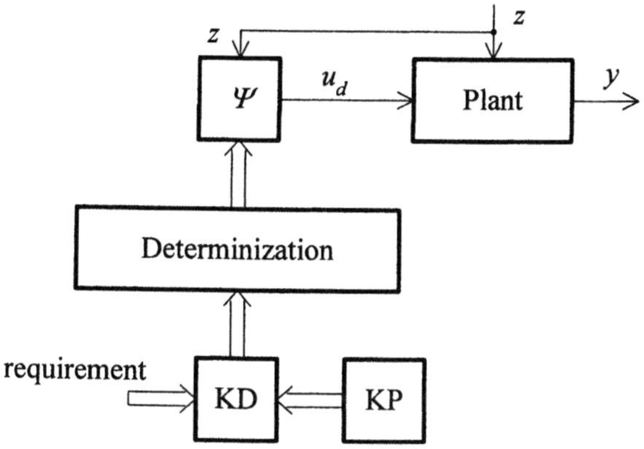

Fig.1. Block-scheme of a knowledge-based decision system

Assume that the property $z \in D_z$ is obtained as a result of observations and the property $y \in D_y$ is required by a user. The **decision problem** may be formulated as follows: For the given R, D_z and D_y one should determine the largest set $D_u \subset U$ for which the implication $u \in D_u \rightarrow y \in D_y$ is satisfied. Then

$$D_u = \{u \in U : \bigwedge_{z \in D_z} [D_y(u,z) \subseteq D_y]\}. \qquad (1)$$

In particular, if $D_z = \{z\}$ then we obtain

$$D_u(z) = \{u \in U : \ D_y(u,z) \subseteq D_y\}.$$

In this case KP $=< R(u,y,z) >$, KD $=< D_u(z) >$ and the determinization may consist in using the mean value

$$u_d = \int_{D_u(z)} u du \cdot [\int_{D_u(z)} du]^{-1} \triangleq \Psi(z).$$

This general approach to the decision problem will be used in the next sections for different descriptions of uncertainties.

2 Uncertain Logics and Variables

Consider a universal set Ω, $\omega \in \Omega$, a set $\overline{X} \subseteq R^k$, a function $g: \Omega \to \overline{X}$, a crisp property (predicate) $P(\overline{x})$ and the crisp property $\Psi(\omega, P)$ generated by P and g:

"For $\overline{x} = g(\omega) \triangleq \overline{x}(\omega)$ assigned to ω the property P is satisfied". Let us introduce the property $G_\omega(x) =$ " $\overline{x}(\omega) \cong x$ " for $x \in X \subseteq \overline{X}$, which means: " $\overline{x}$ is approximately equal to x " or " x is the approximate value of $\overline{x}$ ". The properties P and G_ω generate the soft property $\overline{\Psi}(\omega, P)$ in Ω: "the approximate value of $\overline{x}(\omega)$ satisfies P ", i.e.

$$\overline{\Psi}(\omega, P) = "\overline{x}(\omega) \,\tilde{\in}\, D_x", \qquad D_x = \{\overline{x} \in \overline{X} : P(\overline{x})\}, \tag{2}$$

which means: " $\overline{x}$ approximately belongs to D_x ". Denote by $h_\omega(x)$ the logic value of $G_\omega(x)$:

$$w[\overline{x}(\omega) \cong x] \triangleq h_\omega(x), \quad \bigwedge_{x \in X} h_\omega(x) \geq 0, \quad \max_{x \in X} h_\omega(x) = 1 \tag{3}$$

Definition 1. The *uncertain logic L* is defined by Ω, $\overline{X}$, X, crisp predicates $P(\overline{x})$, the properties $G_\omega(x)$ and the corresponding functions $h_\omega(x)$ for $\omega \in \Omega$. In this logic we consider soft properties (2) generated by P and G_ω. The logic value of $\overline{\Psi}$ is

$$w[\overline{\Psi}(\omega, P)] \triangleq v[\overline{\Psi}(\omega, P)] = \begin{cases} \max\limits_{x \in D_x} h_\omega(x) & \text{for } D_x \neq \varnothing \\ 0 & \text{for } D_x = \varnothing \end{cases}$$

and is called a *certainty index*. The operations are defined as follows:

$$v[\neg \overline{\Psi}(\omega, P)] = 1 - v[\overline{\Psi}(\omega, P)], \tag{4}$$

$$v[\Psi_1(\omega, P_1) \vee \Psi_2(\omega, P_2)] = \max\{v[\Psi_1(\omega, P_1), v[\Psi_2(\omega, P_2)]\}, \tag{5}$$

$$v[\Psi_1(\omega, P_1) \wedge \Psi_2(\omega, P_2)] = \begin{cases} 0 & \text{if for each } x \; w(P_1 \wedge P_2) = 0 \\ \min\{v[\Psi_1(\omega, P_1), v[\Psi_2(\omega, P_2)]\} & \text{otherwise} \end{cases} \tag{6}$$

where Ψ_1 is $\overline{\Psi}$ or $\neg\overline{\Psi}$, and Ψ_2 is $\overline{\Psi}$ or $\neg\overline{\Psi}$ □

For the logic L one can prove the following statements:

$$v[\overline{\Psi}(\omega, P_1 \vee P_2)] = v[\overline{\Psi}(\omega, P_1) \vee \overline{\Psi}(\omega, P_2)], \tag{7}$$

$$v[\overline{\Psi}(\omega, P_1 \wedge P_2)] \le \min\{v[\overline{\Psi}(\omega, P_1)], v[\overline{\Psi}(\omega, P_2)]\}, \tag{8}$$

$$v[\overline{\Psi}(\omega, \neg P)] \ge v[\neg \overline{\Psi}(\omega, P)]. \tag{9}$$

The interpretation (semantics) of the uncertain logic L is the following: The uncertain logic operates with crisp predicates P, but for the given ω it is not possible to state if P is true or false because the function g and consequently the value $\bar{x}$ is unknown. The function $h_\omega(x)$ is given by an expert, who "looking at" ω obtains some information concerning $\bar{x}$ and uses it to evaluate his opinion that $\bar{x} \cong x$.

Definition 2 (the *uncertain logic C*). The first part is the same as in Def.1. The certainty index of $\overline{\Psi}$ and the operations are defined as follows:

$$v_c[\overline{\Psi}(\omega, P) = \frac{1}{2}\{v[\overline{\Psi}(\omega, P)] + 1 - v[\overline{\Psi}(\omega, \neg P)]\}$$

$$\neg \overline{\Psi}(\omega, P) = \overline{\Psi}(\omega, \neg P), \tag{10}$$

$$\overline{\Psi}(\omega, P_1) \vee \overline{\Psi}(\omega, P_2) = \overline{\Psi}(\omega, P_1 \vee P_2), \tag{11}$$

$$\overline{\Psi}(\omega, P_1) \wedge \overline{\Psi}(\omega, P_2) = \overline{\Psi}(\omega, P_1 \wedge P_2) \qquad \square \tag{12}$$

For the logic C one can prove the following statements:

$$v_c[\overline{\Psi}(\omega, P_1 \vee P_2)] \ge \max\{v_c[\overline{\Psi}(\omega, P_1)], v_c[\overline{\Psi}(\omega, P_2)]\}, \tag{13}$$

$$v_c[\overline{\Psi}(\omega, P_1 \wedge P_2)] \le \min\{v_c[\overline{\Psi}(\omega, P_1)], v_c[\overline{\Psi}(\omega, P_2)]\}, \tag{14}$$

$$v_c[\neg \overline{\Psi}(\omega, P)] = 1 - v_c[\overline{\Psi}(\omega, P)]. \tag{15}$$

The variable $\bar{x}$ for a fixed ω will be called an uncertain variable. Two versions of uncertain variables will be defined by: $h(x)$ given by an expert and the definitions of certainty indexes $w(\bar{x} \mathrel{\tilde{\in}} D_x)$, $w(\bar{x} \mathrel{\tilde{\notin}} D_x)$, $w(\bar{x} \mathrel{\tilde{\in}} D_1 \vee \bar{x} \mathrel{\tilde{\in}} D_2)$, $w(\bar{x} \mathrel{\tilde{\in}} D_1 \wedge \bar{x} \mathrel{\tilde{\in}} D_2)$.

Definition 3. The *uncertain variable* $\bar{x}$ is defined by X, the function $h(x) = v(\bar{x} \cong x)$ given by an expert and the following definitions:

$$v(\bar{x} \mathrel{\tilde{\in}} D_x) = \max_{x \in D_x} h(x) \quad \text{for } D_x \ne \varnothing \quad \text{and} \quad 0 \text{ for } D_x = \varnothing, \tag{16}$$

$$v(\bar{x} \mathrel{\tilde{\notin}} D_x) = 1 - v(\bar{x} \mathrel{\tilde{\in}} D_x), \tag{17}$$

$$v(\bar{x} \mathrel{\tilde{\in}} D_1 \vee \bar{x} \mathrel{\tilde{\in}} D_2) = \max\{v(\bar{x} \mathrel{\tilde{\in}} D_1), v(\bar{x} \mathrel{\tilde{\in}} D_2)\}, \tag{18}$$

$$v(\bar{x} \mathrel{\tilde{\in}} D_1 \wedge \bar{x} \mathrel{\tilde{\in}} D_2) = \begin{cases} \min\{v(\bar{x} \mathrel{\tilde{\in}} D_1), v(\bar{x} \mathrel{\tilde{\in}} D_2)\} & \text{for } D_1 \cap D_2 \neq \varnothing \\ 0 & \text{for } D_1 \cap D_2 = \varnothing. \end{cases} \tag{19}$$

The function $h(x)$ will be called a *certainty distribution* □

The definition of the uncertain variable is based on logic L. Then for (2) the properties (7), (8), (9) are satisfied. In particular, (9) becomes $v(\bar{x} \mathrel{\tilde{\in}} \overline{D}_x) \geq v(\bar{x} \mathrel{\tilde{\notin}} D_x) = 1 - v(\bar{x} \mathrel{\tilde{\in}} D_x)$ where $\overline{D}_x = X - D_x$.

Definition 4. *C-uncertain variable* is defined by X, $h(x) = v(\bar{x} \cong x)$ given by an expert and the following definitions:

$$v_c(\bar{x} \mathrel{\tilde{\in}} D_x) = \frac{1}{2}[\max_{x \in D_x} h(x) + 1 - \max_{x \in X - D_x} h(x)], \tag{20}$$

$$v_c(\bar{x} \mathrel{\tilde{\notin}} D_x) = 1 - v_c(\bar{x} \mathrel{\tilde{\in}} D_x), \tag{21}$$

$$v_c(\bar{x} \mathrel{\tilde{\in}} D_1 \vee \bar{x} \mathrel{\tilde{\in}} D_2) = v_c(\bar{x} \mathrel{\tilde{\in}} D_1 \cup D_2), \tag{22}$$

$$v_c(\bar{x} \mathrel{\tilde{\in}} D_1 \wedge \bar{x} \mathrel{\tilde{\in}} D_2) = v_c(\bar{x} \mathrel{\tilde{\in}} D_1 \cap D_2) \quad \square \tag{23}$$

The definition of C-uncertain variable is based on logic C. Then for (2) the properties (13), (14), (15) are satisfied. According to (10) and (15) $v_c(\bar{x} \mathrel{\tilde{\notin}} D_x) = v_c(\bar{x} \mathrel{\tilde{\in}} X - D_x)$. The function $v_c(\bar{x} \cong x) \triangleq h_c(x)$ may be called *C-certainty distribution.* In the case of C-uncertain variable the expert's knowledge is used in a better way.

In a *continuous case* $h(x)$ is a continuous function in X and in a *discrete case* $X = \{x_1, x_2, ..., x_m\}$. The mean value of $\bar{x}$ is defined as follows:

$$M(\bar{x}) = \int_X x h(x) dx \cdot [\int_X h(x) dx]^{-1} \quad \text{or} \quad M(\bar{x}) = \sum_{i=1}^{m} x_i h(x_i) [\sum_{i=1}^{m} h(x_i)]^{-1} \tag{23a}$$

in a continuous case or a discrete case, respectively. For a pair of variables $(\bar{x}, \bar{y})$ described by $h(x, y) = v[(\bar{x}, \bar{y}) \cong (x, y)]$ we may consider marginal and conditional distributions with the following relationships:

$$h_x(x) = v(\bar{x} \cong x) = \max_{y \in Y} h(x, y), \quad h_y(y) = v(\bar{y} \cong y) = \max_{x \in X} h(x, y), \tag{24}$$

$$h(x, y) = \min\{h_x(x), h_y(y \mid x)\} = \min\{h_y(y), h_x(x \mid y)\} \tag{25}$$

where $h_y(y \mid x) = v[\bar{x} = x \rightarrow \bar{y} \cong y]$, $h_x(x \mid y) = v[\bar{y} = y \rightarrow \bar{x} \cong x]$.

Let us consider a plant described by a relation $R(u, y, z; x) \subset U \times Y \times Z$ where $x \in X$ is an unknown vector parameter which is assumed to be a value of an uncertain variable $\bar{x}$ described by $h_x(x)$ given by an expert. This is a parametric uncertainty and consequently we may formulate the following **parametric decision problem**: For the given *R*, *z*, $h_z(z)$ and D_y, find the decision u_d maximizing the certainty index of the property: For the approximate value of $\bar{x}$ the set of all possible outputs $D_y(u, z; x) = \{y \in Y : (u, y, z) \in R\}$ belongs to D_y given by a user. Then

$$u_d = \arg\max_{u \in U} v[D_y(u, z; \bar{x}) \tilde{\subseteq} D_y] = \arg\max_{u \in U} \max_{x \in D_x(u,z)} h_x(x)$$

where $D_x(u, z) = \{x \in X : D_y(u, z; x) \subseteq D_y\}$ and $u_d \triangleq \Psi(z)$ if u_d is a unique result of the maximization.

3 Nonparametric Decision Problems

The description of the uncertain plant in the form of the relation $R(u, y, z)$ may be extended and completed by using different descriptions of a nonparametric relationship between u, y and z.

A. Application of uncertain variables

Let us assume that (u, y, z) are values of uncertain variables $(\bar{u}, \bar{y}, \bar{z})$ and the knowledge of the plant has a form of the conditional certainty distribution $h_y(y \mid u, z)$, completed by the certainty distribution $h_z(z)$, i.e. KP $=< h_y(y \mid u, z), h_z(z) >$. The distributions $h_y(y \mid u, z)$ and $h_z(z)$ are given by an expert. The decision problem may consist in finding a conditional certainty distribution $h_u(u \mid z)$ for the given desirable certainty distribution $h_y(y)$ required by a user. The functions $f_y(y \mid u, z)$, $f_y(y)$ and $f_u(u \mid z)$ correspond to the sets $D_y(u, z)$, D_y and $D_u(z)$ introduced in Sec.1, respectively.

Decision problem: For the given $h_y(y \mid u, z)$, $h_z(z)$ and $h_y(y)$ one should determine $h_u(u \mid z)$.

According to (24) and (25)

$$h_y(y) = \max_{u \in U} \max_{z \in Z} \min\{h_y(y \mid u, z), h_{uz}(u, z)\} \tag{26}$$

and the joint certainty distribution

$$h_{uz}(u,z) = \min\{h_u(u \mid z), h_z(z)\}. \tag{27}$$

Finally

$$h_y(y) = \max_{u \in U} \max_{z \in Z} \min\{h_y(y \mid u,z), h_u(u \mid z), h_z(z)\}. \tag{28}$$

Any distribution $h_u(u \mid z)$ satisfying the equation (28) is a solution of our decision problem. It is easy to note that the solution of the equation (28) with respect to $h_u(u \mid z)$ is not unique. The distribution $h_u(u \mid z)$ describes the knowledge of the decision making KD and may be called an *uncertain decision algorithm*. Having $h_u(u \mid z)$ one can obtain the deterministic decision algorithm $u_d = \Psi(z)$ as a result of the determinization of the knowledge of the decision making KD $=< h_u(u \mid z) >$, which is determined from the knowledge of the plant KP for the requirement in the form of $f_y(y)$ (see Fig.1). The determinization may consist in using the mean value $u_{ad} = M_u(u \mid z) \triangleq \Psi_a(z)$ or the value $u_{bd} = \arg\max h_u(u \mid z) \triangleq \Psi_b(z)$. The determination of $h_u(u \mid z)$ may be decomposed into two steps. In the first step we determine the sets of the distributions $h_{uz}(u,z)$ satisfying the equation (26) and in the second step we determine $h_u(u \mid z)$ from the equation (27). In particular, as one of the solutions of the equation (27) we may accept $h_u(u \mid z) = h_{uz}(u,z)$. A theorem concerning the form of the solution and an example are presented in [7, 8, 9].

B. Application of random variables

Let us assume that (u, y, z) are values of random variables $(\tilde{u}, \tilde{y}, \tilde{z})$ which means that (u, y, z) are chosen randomly from the set $U \times Y \times Z$ according to a determined probability distribution. In the continuous case the knowledge of the plant given by an expert contains the conditional probability density $f_y(y \mid u,z)$ and the probability density $f_z(z)$ for $\tilde{z}$, i.e. KP $=< f_y(y \mid u,z), f_z(z) >$. The decision problem may consist in finding a conditional probability density $f_u(u \mid z)$ for the given desirable probability density $f_y(y)$ required by a user.

Decision problem: For the given $f_y(y \mid u,z)$, $f_z(z)$ and $f_y(y)$ one should determine $f_u(u \mid z)$.

The relationship between the probability densities $f_y(y)$, $f_y(y \mid u,z)$, $f_u(u \mid z)$ and $f_z(z)$ is as follows

$$f_y(y) = \int_U \int_Z f_y(y \mid u,z) f_u(u \mid z) f_z(z)\, du\, dz. \tag{29}$$

Any probability density $f_u(u \mid z)$ satisfying the equation (29) is a solution of our decision problem. It is easy to note that the solution of the equation (29) with respect to $f_u(u \mid z)$ may be not unique. The probability density $f_u(u \mid z)$ describes the knowledge of the decision making KD and may be called a *random decision algorithm*. Having $f_u(u \mid z)$ one can obtain the deterministic decision algorithm $u_d = \Psi(z)$ as a result of the determinization of KD $=< f_u(u \mid z) >$, which is determined from KP for the given requirement in the form of $f_y(y)$ (see Fig.1). Two versions of the determinization are the following:

$$u_{ad} = \mathrm{E}(\tilde{u} \mid z) = \int_U u f_u(u \mid z) du \triangleq \Psi_a(z),$$

$$u_{bd} = \arg\max_{u \in U} f_u(u \mid z) \triangleq \Psi_b(z).$$

C. Application of fuzzy variables

Let us consider two fuzzy variables (fuzzy numbers) $\hat{x}, \hat{y}$ defined by sets of values $X \subseteq R^1$, $Y \subseteq R^1$ and membership functions $\mu_x(x)$, $\mu_y(y)$, respectively. The membership function $\mu_x(x)$ is the logic value of the soft property $\varphi_x(x)=$ "if $\hat{x} = x$ then $\hat{x}$ is d_1" or shortly "$\hat{x}$ is d_1", and $\mu_y(y)$ is the logic value of the soft property $\varphi_y(y)=$ "$\hat{y}$ is d_2", i.e. $w[\varphi_x(x)] = \mu_x(x)$, $w[\varphi_y(y)] = \mu_y(y)$ where d_1 and d_2 denote the size of the number, e.g. $\varphi_x(x)=$ "$\hat{x}$ is small", $\varphi_y(y)=$ "$\hat{y}$ is large". Using φ_x and φ_y we can introduce the property $\varphi_x \to \varphi_y$ (e.g. if $\hat{x}$ is small then $\hat{y}$ is large) with the respective membership function $w[\varphi_x \to \varphi_y] \triangleq \mu_y(y \mid x)$ and the properties $\varphi_x \vee \varphi_y$, $\varphi_x \wedge \varphi_y$ for which the membership functions are defined as follows

$$w[\varphi_x \vee \varphi_y] = \max\{\mu_x(x), \mu_y(y)\}$$

$$w[\varphi_x \wedge \varphi_y] = \min\{\mu_x(x), \mu_y(y \mid x)\} \triangleq \mu_{xy}(x, y). \tag{30}$$

If we assume that $\varphi_x \wedge [\varphi_x \to \varphi_y] = \varphi_y \wedge [\varphi_y \to \varphi_x]$ then

$$\mu_{xy}(x, y) = \min\{\mu_x(x), \mu_y(y \mid x)\} = \min\{\mu_y(y), \mu_x(x \mid y)\}. \tag{31}$$

Using (31) it is easy to show that

$$\mu_x(x) = \max_{y \in Y} \mu_{xy}(x, y), \tag{32}$$

$$\mu_y(y) = \max_{x \in X} \mu_{xy}(x, y).$$

The equations (31) and (32) describe the relationships between μ_x, μ_y, μ_{xy}, $\mu_x(x \mid y)$ analogous to (24), (25) for uncertain variables. For the given $\mu_{xy}(x, y)$ the set of functions $\mu_y(y \mid x)$ is determined by (30) in which $\mu_x(x)$ is determined by (32). In particular, as one of the solutions of the equation (30) with respect to $\mu_y(y \mid x)$ (i.e. one of possible definitions of the membership function for an implication) we may accept $\mu_y(y \mid x) = \mu_{xy}(x, y)$.

The description concerning the pair of fuzzy variables may be directly applied to one-dimensional static plant with one input $u \in U$, one disturbance $z \in Z$ and one output $y \in Y$ $(U, Z, Y \subseteq R^1)$. The nonparametric description of the uncertain plant using fuzzy variables may be formulated by introducing three soft properties $\varphi_u(u)$, $\varphi_z(z)$ and $\varphi_y(y)$. The description is given by an expert and contains the membership functions

$$w[\varphi_u \wedge \varphi_z \rightarrow \varphi_y] = \mu_y(y \mid u, z), \qquad w[\varphi_z(z)] = \mu_z(z),$$

i.e. KP $= < \mu_y(y \mid u, z), \mu_z(z) >$.

For example, the expert says that "if $\hat{u}$ is large and $\hat{z}$ is medium then $\hat{y}$ is small", and gives the membership function $\mu_y(y \mid u, z)$ for this property and the membership function $\mu_z(z)$ for the property "$\hat{z}$ is medium". It is worth comparing with the description based on the uncertain variables: " if $\bar{u} = u$ and $\bar{z} = z$ then $\bar{y} \cong y$ ", characterized by the certainty distributions $h_y(y \mid u, z) = w[(\bar{u} = u) \wedge (\bar{z} = z) \rightarrow \bar{y} \cong y]$ and $h_z(z) = w[\bar{z} \cong z]$.

The decision problem may consist in finding such a membership function $\mu_u(u \mid z)$ for which the membership function for the output property $w[\varphi_y(y)] = \mu_y(y)$ will have a desirable form. This problem is analogous to that in point A for the uncertain variables and to that in point B for the random variables. The essential difference consists in the fact that the requirements in the form of $h_y(y)$ or $f_y(y)$ have been concerned directly with a *value of the output* and now the requirement in the form of $\mu_y(y)$ concerns the *output property* $\varphi_y(y)$.

Decision problem: For the given $\mu_y(y \mid u, z)$, $\mu_z(z)$ and $\mu_y(y)$ one should determine $\mu_u(u \mid z)$.

According to (32) and (31)

$$\mu_y(y) = \max_{u \in U} \max_{z \in Z} \min\{\mu_y(y \mid u, z), \mu_{uz}(u, z)\}, \tag{33}$$

$$\mu_{uz}(u, z) = \min\{\mu_u(u \mid z), \mu_z(z)\}, \tag{34}$$

$$\mu_y(y) = \max_{u \in U} \max_{z \in Z} \min\{\mu_y(y \mid u, z), \mu_u(u \mid z), \mu_z(z)\}. \tag{35}$$

Any membership function $\mu_u(u \mid z)$ satisfying (35) is a solution of our decision problem. The determination of $\mu_u(u \mid z)$ may be decomposed into two steps analogous to those for the uncertain variables. As one of the solution of the equation (34) with respect to $\mu_u(u \mid z)$ we may accept $\mu_u(u \mid z) = \mu_{uz}(u, z)$. The function $\mu_u(u \mid z)$ describes KD and may be called a *fuzzy decision algorithm* (a fuzzy controller in an open-loop control system). Having $\mu_u(u \mid z)$ one can obtain the deterministic decision algorithm $u_d = \Psi(z)$ via the determinization KD $=< \mu_u(u \mid z) >$, which is determined from KP for the given requirement in the form of $\mu_y(y)$ (see Fig.1). The determinization may consist in using the mean value $M(\hat{u} \mid z)$ defined in the some way as for an uncertain variable. A theorem concerning the form of the solution $\mu_u(u \mid z)$, an example and an extension to multi-dimensional case are presented in [7, 8, 9].

4 Soft Variables

It is easy to see the formal analogies between the relationships (28), (29) and (35), with the different interpretations. The uncertain, random and fuzzy variables may be considered as special cases of more general description of the uncertainty in the form of *soft variables* and *evaluating functions* [2, 7, 8] which may be introduced as a tool for a unification and generalization of decision problems based on the uncertain knowledge representation. The definition of a soft variable should be completed with the determination of relationships for the pair of soft variables.

Definition 5 (*soft variable and the pair of soft variables*): A soft variable $\check{x} =< X, g(x) >$ is defined by the set of values X and a bounded evaluating function $g : X \rightarrow R^+$, satisfying the following condition:

$$\int_X x g(x) < \infty$$

for the continuous case and

$$\sum_{i=1}^{\infty} x_i g(x_i) < \infty$$

for the discrete case.

Let us consider two soft variables $\check{x} = < X, g_x(x) >$, $\check{y} = < Y, g_y(y) >$ and the variable $(\check{x}, \check{y})$ described by $g_{xy}(x,y) : X \times Y \to R^+$. Denote by $g_y(y \mid x)$ the evaluating function of $\check{y}$ for the given value x (the conditional evaluating function). The pair $(\check{x}, \check{y})$ is defined by $g_{xy}(x,y)$ and two operations:

$$g_{xy}(x,y) = O_1[g_y(y \mid x), g_x(x)], \quad g_x(x) = O_2[g_{xy}(x,y)], \tag{36}$$

i.e.

$$O_1 : D_{gy} \times D_{gx} \to D_{g,xy}, \qquad O_2 : D_{g,xy} \to D_{g,x}$$

where D_{gx}, $D_{gy}(x)$ and $D_{g,xy}$ are sets of $g_x(x)$, $g_y(y \mid x)$ and $g_{xy}(x,y)$, respectively. The mean value $M(\check{x})$ is defined in the same way as for an uncertain variable, i.e. by (23a) with $g_x(x)$ in the place of $h_x(x)$ □

The evaluating function may have different practical interpretations. In the random case a soft variable is a random variable described by the probability density $g(x) = f(x)$ or by probabilities $g(x_i) = P(\tilde{x} = x_i)$, in the case of an uncertain variable $g(x) = h(x)$ is the certainty distribution and in the case of the fuzzy description a soft variable is a fuzzy variable described by the membership function $g(x) = \mu(x) = w[\varphi(x)]$ where w denotes a logic value of a given soft property $\varphi(x)$. In general, we can say that $g(x)$ describes an evaluation of the set of possible values X, characterizing for every value x its significance (importance or weight). This description presents a knowledge concerning the variable $\check{x}$ which may be given by an expert describing his / her subjective opinion or may have an objective character such as in the case of a random variable.

5 Application of Soft Variables to Decision Problem

The nonparametric decision problems considered in Sec. 3 may be generalized by using soft variables. Let us assume that (u, y, z) are values of soft variables $(\check{u}, \check{y}, \check{z})$ and KP $= < g_y(y \mid u, z), g_z(z) >$. The decision problem may consist in finding a conditional evaluating function $g_u(u \mid z)$ for the given desirable evaluating function $g_y(y)$ required by a user.

Decision problem: For the given $g_y(y \mid z)$, $g_z(z)$ and $g_y(y)$ one should determine $g_u(u \mid z)$.

According to (36)

$$g_y(y) = O_2\{O_1[g_y(y \mid u,z), O_1(g_u(u \mid z), g_z(z))]\}. \tag{37}$$

Any evaluating function $g_u(u,z)$ satisfying (37) is a solution of our decision problem. In the case of uncertain, random and fuzzy variables (37) has a form of (28), (29) and (35), respectively. The function $g_u(u \mid z)$ describes KD and may be called a *soft decision algorithm*. Having $g_u(u \mid z)$ one can obtain the deterministic decision algorithm $u_d = \Psi(z)$ via the determinization in the form of $u_{ad} = M(\hat{u} \mid z) \stackrel{\Delta}{=} \Psi_a(z)$ or $u_{bd} = \arg\max g_u(u \mid z) \stackrel{\Delta}{=} \Psi_b(z)$.

The formula (37) presents a relationship between $g_u(u \mid z)$, $g_y(y)$ and $g(z)$ for the given $g_y(y \mid u,z)$ describing the plant and the determined operations O_1, O_2. A generalization of this description may be presented as a relation (a relational knowledge representation)

$$R_g[g_u(u \mid z), g_y(y), g_z(z)] \subset D_{gu}(z) \times D_{gy} \times D_{gz}.$$

In the case (37) the relation R_g is reduced to an operation (a function) determined by $g_y(y \mid u,z)$ and the definitions of O_1, O_2. In general, the pair $g_u(u \mid z)$, $g_z(z)$ determines a set of possible functions $g_y(y)$:

$$\overline{D}_{gy} = \{g_y(y) \in D_{gy} : [g_u(u \mid z), g_y(y), g_z(z)] \in R_g\}.$$

If it is known that $g_z(z) \in \overline{D}_z$ and $g_y(y) \in \overline{D}_y$ denotes a user's requirement then the following decision problem may be formulated.

Generalized decision problem: For the given R_g, $\overline{D}_z$ and $\overline{D}_y$ find the largest set $\overline{D}_{gu}(z)$ such that the implication

$$g_u(u \mid z) \in \overline{D}_{gu}(z) \to g_y(y) \in \overline{D}_y$$

is satisfied. Then

$$\overline{D}_{gu}(z) = \{g_u(u \mid z) \in D_{gu}(z) : \bigwedge_{g_z \in \overline{D}_z} (\overline{D}_{gy} \subseteq \overline{D}_y)\}. \tag{38}$$

It is useful to see an analogy between this decision problem and the decision problem mentioned in Sec.1 for the relation R, and consequently an analogy between (38) and (1). Having $\overline{D}_{gu}(z)$ one can obtain a set of algorithms $\Psi(z)$ by using the determinization.

6 Principle of Equivalency

In the design of knowledge-based uncertain systems it may be important to investigate a relation between two cases concerning two different subjects of the knowledge given by an expert. In the first case (considered in this paper) an expert gives the knowledge of the plant KP, and the knowledge of the decision making KD is obtained from KP for the given requirement (*an approach* I). In the second case the knowledge of the decision making $\widetilde{\text{KD}}$ is given directly by an expert (*an approach* II). We can say that these two approaches are *equivalent* if $\widetilde{\text{KD}}$ is the same as KD or more generally, if $\widetilde{\text{KD}}$ belongs to the set of KD obtained from KP. The general formulation of a *principle of equivalency* [7, 8, 9] may be based on the description using the soft variables.

Principle of equivalency: If the knowledge of the decision making $\widetilde{\text{KD}}$ given by an expert has a form of a set of evaluating functions $\widetilde{D}_{gu}(z)$ and $\widetilde{D}_{gu}(z) \subseteq \overline{D}_{gu}(z)$ where $\overline{D}_{gu}(z)$ is determined by (38), then the approaches I and II are equivalent. In particular, if an expert gives one evaluating function $\widetilde{g}_u(u \mid z)$ and $\widetilde{g}_u(u \mid z) \in \overline{D}_{gu}(z)$ then the decision algorithm based on the knowledge of the decision making given by an expert is equivalent to one of the decision algorithms based on the knowledge of the plant □

In particular, for the cases A, B, C in Sec. 3 and the case (37) based on the soft variables the approaches I and II are equivalent if:

1. $\widetilde{h}_u(u \mid z)$ given by an expert satisfies the equation (28).
2. $\widetilde{f}_u(u \mid z)$ given by an expert satisfies the equation (29).
3. $\widetilde{\mu}_u(u \mid z)$ given by an expert satisfies the equation (35).
4. $\widetilde{g}_u(u \mid z)$ given by an expert satisfies the equation (37).

7 Conclusions

The soft variables described by the evaluating functions have been presented as a tool for a unification and generalization of decision problems based on uncertain knowledge representations. Such a generalization may be introduced in different cases based on descriptions using uncertain variables: for the stability analysis in uncertain systems, for the design of uncertain assembly processes, in multistage decision problems and in distributed systems [10, 12, 11, 4].

References

1. Bubnicki, Z. (1998) Uncertain variables and logic-algebraic method in knowledge based systems. In: Proc. of International Conference on Intelligent Systems and Control in Halifax. Acta Press, Zurich, pp 135–139
2. Bubnicki, Z. (2000) A unified approach to decision making and control in knowledge-based uncertain systems. In: Computing Anticipatory Systems: CASYS'00 – Fourth International Conference. American Institute of Physics, Melville N. York, pp 545–557
3. Bubnicki, Z. (2000) Uncertain variables in the computer aided analysis of uncertain systems. In: Computer Aided Systems Theory. Lecture Notes in Computer Science. Springer Verlag, Berlin, pp 528–542
4. Bubnicki, Z. (2000) Knowledge validation and updating in a class of uncertain distributed knowledge systems. In: Proc. of 16th IFIP World Computer Congress. Intelligent Information Processing. Publishing House of Electronics Industry, Beijing, pp 516–523
5. Bubnicki, Z. (2001) Uncertain variables and their applications for a class of uncertain systems. International Journal of Systems Science **32**, 651–659
6. Bubnicki, Z. (2001) Uncertain variables and their application to decision making. IEEE Trans. on SMC, Part A: Systems and Humans **31**, 587–596
7. Bubnicki, Z. (2001) A unified approach to descriptive and prescriptive concepts in uncertain decision systems. In: Proc. of the European Control Conference. Porto, Portugal, pp 2458–2463
8. Bubnicki, Z. (2002) Uncertain Logics, Variables and Systems. Springer-Verlag, Berlin London (in press)
9. Bubnicki, Z. (2002) A unified approach to descriptive and prescriptive concepts in uncertain decision systems. Systems Analysis Modelling Simulation **42**, 331–342
10. Bubnicki, Z. (2002) Stability and stabilization of discrete systems with random and uncertain parameters. In: Proc. of 15th IFAC World Congress. Barcelona, Spain
11. Bubnicki, Z. (2002) Uncertain variables and their application to decision making for a class of dynamical uncertain systems. In: Proc. of 15th International Conference on Systems Engineering. Las Vegas, USA
12. Bubnicki, Z. (2002) Application of uncertain variables for a class of intelligent knowledge-based assembly systems. Proc. of 7th International Symposium on Artificial Life and Robotics. Oita, Japan, vol 1, pp 98-101

Decision Algorithms, Bayes' Theorem and Flow Graphs

Zdzisław Pawlak

Institute of Theoretical and Applied Informatics, Polish Academy of Sciences, ul. Bałtycka 5, 44 100 Gliwice, Poland

Abstract. The paper concerns some relationships between decision algorithms, Bayes' theorem and flow graphs. It is shown it this paper that every decision algorithm reveals probabilistic properties, particularly it satisfies the total probability theorem and Bayes' theorem. This leads to a new look on Bayesian inference methodology, showing that Bayes' theorem can be used to reason directly from data without referring to prior and posterior probabilities, inherently associated with Bayesian inference. Besides, a new form of Bayes' theorem is introduced, based on the strength of decision rules, which simplifies essentially computations. Moreover it is shown that decision algorithms can be depicted in a form of a flow graph in which flow is ruled by the total probability theorem and Bayes' theorem. This leads to a new class of flow networks, unlike to those introduced by Ford and Fulkerson. Interpretation of flow graphs as a kind of neural network is briefly discussed.

1 Introduction

Decision algorithm is a finite set of "*if .. then*" decision rules. With every decision rule three probabilities are associated: the *strength*, the *certainty* and the *coverage* factors of the rule. The probabilities can be computed from the data or can be a subjective assignment. It is shown that the certainty and the coverage factors are related by Bayes' theorem. Besides, Bayes' theorem in the proposed setting can be presented in a very simple form, employing the strength of decision rules. This leads to a very simple computational algorithm, and furthermore it gives new look on Bayes' theorem and its applications [5].

It is shown later that with every decision algorithm a flow graph can be associated. The throughflow in the graph is related with the above mentioned probabilities and is ruled by the total probability theorem and Bayes' theorem. This leads to a new class of flow networks, unlike to those introduced by Ford and Fulkerson [2]. It seems that the introduced flow graphs may have many applications not necessarily associated with decision algorithms, but this requires further study.

A simple tutorial example given at the end of this paper is used to illustrate the basic ideas discussed in the paper.

2 Decision Algorithms

Let $\mathcal{L}$ be a formal language of formulas defined in a standard way, and called the *decision language.* We will not define exactly the language $\mathcal{L}$, and use it rather intuitively since for our considerations the exact definition is not necessary. We assume only that the set of formulas in $\mathcal{L}$ is partitioned into two classes, called *condition* and *decision formulas*, respectively.

A *decision rule* in $\mathcal{L}$ is an expression in the form $\Phi \rightarrow \Psi$, read "*if* Φ *then* Ψ", where Φ and Ψ are condition and decision formulas in $\mathcal{L}$ and call *predecessor* and *sucessor* of the rule, respectively.

Formulas Φ and Ψ are suposed to denote subsets of a finite set U, called the *universe.*

Let $||\Phi||$ denote the set of all objects from the universe U, having the property Φ.

If $\Phi \rightarrow \Psi$ is a decision rule then $supp\,(\Phi, \Psi) = card\,(||\Phi \wedge \Psi||)$ will be called the *support* of the decision rule and

$$\sigma\,(\Phi, \Psi) = \frac{supp\,(\Phi, \Psi)}{card\,(U)}$$

will be referred to as the *strength* of the decision rule.

With every decision rule $\Phi \rightarrow \Psi$ we associate a *certainty factor*

$$cer\,(\Phi, \Psi) = \frac{sup\,(\Phi, \Psi)}{card\,(||\Phi||)}$$

and a *coverage factor*

$$cov\,(\Phi, \Psi) = \frac{supp\,(\Phi, \Psi)}{card\,(||\Psi||)}$$

If $cer\,(\Phi, \Psi) = 1$, then the decision rule $\Phi \rightarrow \Psi$ will be called *certain*, otherwise the decision rule will be referred to as *uncertain*.

A set of decision rules $Dec\,(\Phi, \Psi) = \{\Phi_i \rightarrow \Psi_i\}_{i=1}^{n}$ $n \geq 2$, will be called a *decision algorithm* if all decision rules in the decision algorithm are:

1) *admissible*, i.e., $supp\,(\Phi_i, \Psi_i) \neq \emptyset$ for ever $1 \leq i \leq n$
2) *mutually exclusive* (*independent*), i.e., for every $\Phi_i \rightarrow \Psi_i$ and $\Phi_j \rightarrow \Psi_j$, $\Phi_i = \Phi_j$ or $\Phi_i \wedge \Phi_j = \emptyset$ and $\Psi_i = \Psi_j$ or $\Psi_i \wedge \Phi_j = \emptyset$
3) *cover* U, i.e., $||\bigvee_{i=1}^{n} \Phi_i|| = ||\bigvee_{i=1}^{n} \Psi_i|| = U$.

If $Dec\,(\Phi, \Psi) = \{\Phi_i \rightarrow \Psi_i\}_{i=1}^{n}$ is a decision algorithm, then $Dec\,(\Psi, \Phi) = \{\Psi_i \rightarrow \Phi_i\}_{i=1}^{n}$ is also a decision algorithm and will be called an *inverse decision algorithm* of $Dec\,(\Phi, \Psi)$.

$Dec\,(\Psi, \Phi)$ gives *reasons* (*explanations*) for decisions of the algorithm $Dec\,(\Phi, \Psi)$

3 Properties of Decision Algorithms

Let $Dec(\Phi, \Psi)_n$ be a decision algorithm and let $\Phi \to \Psi$ be a decision rule in the decision algorithm. By $D(\Phi)$ and $C(\Psi)$ we denote the set of all decisions of Φ and the set of all conditions of Ψ, respectively.

It can be shown that every decision algorithm has the following probabilistic properties.

$$\sum_{\Phi' \in C(\Psi)} cov(\Phi', \Psi) = 1 \tag{1}$$

$$\sum_{\Psi' \in D(\Phi)} cer(\Phi, \Psi') = 1 \tag{2}$$

$$\begin{aligned} \pi(\Psi) &= \sum_{\Phi' \in C(\Psi)} cer(\Phi', \Psi) \cdot \pi(\Phi') = \\ &= \sum_{\Phi' \in C(\Psi)} \sigma(\Phi', \Psi) \end{aligned} \tag{3}$$

$$\begin{aligned} \pi(\Phi) &= \sum_{\Psi' \in D(\Phi)} cov(\Phi, \Psi') \cdot \pi(\Psi') = \\ &= \sum_{\Psi' \in D(\Phi)} \sigma(\Phi, \Psi') \end{aligned} \tag{4}$$

$$\begin{aligned} cer(\Phi, \Psi) &= \frac{cov(\Phi, \Psi) \cdot \pi(\Psi)}{\sum_{\Psi' \in D(\Phi)} cov(\Phi, \Psi') \cdot \pi(\Psi')} = \\ &= \frac{\sigma(\Phi, \Psi)}{\sum_{\Psi' \in D(\Phi)} \sigma(\Phi, \Psi')} = \frac{\sigma(\Psi, \Phi)}{\pi(\Phi)} \end{aligned} \tag{5}$$

$$\begin{aligned} cov(\Phi, \Psi) &= \frac{cer(\Phi, \Psi) \cdot \pi(\Phi)}{\sum_{\Phi' \in C(\Psi)} cer(\Phi', \Psi) \cdot \pi(\Phi')} = \\ &= \frac{\sigma(\Phi, \Psi)}{\sum_{\Phi' \in C(\Psi)} \sigma(\Phi', \Psi)} = \frac{\sigma(\Phi, \Psi)}{\pi(\Psi)} \end{aligned} \tag{6}$$

where $\pi(\Phi) = \frac{card(||\Phi||)}{card(U)}$ and $\pi(\Psi) = \frac{card(||\Psi||)}{card(U)}$.

Obviously formulas 3) and 4) represent the total probability theorem, whereas formulas 5) and 6) are referring to Bayes' theorem. It is interesting to notice that the theorems have a new form in which the considered probabilities are expressed in terms of strength of decision rules. This simplifies essentially computations and also gives a new insight into both theorems.

4 Flow Graphs

With every decision algorithm we associate a directed, acyclic, connected graph defined in the following way: to every predecessor and successor of the decision rule in the decision algorithm we assocate a *node* of the graph. To every decision rule $\Phi \to \Psi$ we assign a directed *branch* connecting the *input node* Φ and the *output node* Ψ. Strength of the decision rule represents the *throughflow* of the corresponding branch.

The throughflow of the graph is governed by formulas (1),...,(6), and can be considered as a *flow conservation equation*, similar to that introduced by Ford and Fulkerson [4]. However, let us observe that flow graphs presented in this paper are different from flow networks of Ford and Fulkerson.

Formulas (1) and (2) are obvious. Formula (3) states that the outflow of the output node amounts to the sum of its inflows, whereas formula (4) says that the sum of outflows of the input node equals to its inflow. Finally, formulas (5) and (6) reveal how throughflow in the flow graph is distributed between its inputs and outputs.

It is obvious that the idea of flow graph can be also formulated more generally, independently of decision tables, but we will not consider this issue here.

5 An Illustrative Example

Let us conasider a set of 900 patients described by the decision algorithm below:

1) *if the patient is ill and old then the test is positive* (400)
2) *if the patient is ill and middle aged then the test is positive* (80)
3) *if the patient is healthy then the test is negative* (320)
4) *if the patient is ill and old then the test is negative* (40)
5) *if the patient is ill and middle aged then the test is negative* (60)

The number in parentheses at the end of each decision rule is the support of the rule, i.e., the number of patients displaying the properties indicated by the rule.

The decision algorithm represents the relationship between the patient status and the test result.

The certainty and coverage factors for the above algorithm are given in Table 1.

Table 1. Certainty and coverage factors

rule	*strength*	*certainty*	*coverage*
1	0.44	0.92	0.83
2	0.09	0.56	0.17
3	0.35	1.00	0.76
4	0.04	0.08	0.10
5	0.07	0.44	0.14

The certainty factors of the decision rules lead to the following conclusions:

- 92% ill and old patients have positive test result
- 56% ill and middle aged patients have positive test result
- all healthy patients have negative test result
- 8% ill and old patients have negative test result
- 44% ill and of middle aged have negative test result

In other words:

- ill and old patients most probably have positive test result (probability = 0.92)
- ill and middle aged patients most probably have positive test result (probability = 0.56)
- healthy patients have certainly negative test result (probability = 1.00)

The inverse decision algorithm is as follows:

1') *if the test result is positive then the patient is ill and old* (400)
2') *if the test result is positive then the patient is ill or middle aged* (80)
3') *if the test result is negative then the patient is healthy* (320)
4') *if the test result is negative then the patient is ill and old* (40)
5') *if the test result is negative then the patient is ill and middle aged* (60)

Employing the inverse decision algorithm and the coverage factors we get the following explanation of test result:

- reasons for positive test results are most probably disease and old age (probability = 0.83)
- reason for negative test result is most probably lack of the disease (probability = 0.76)

The flow graph for the decision algorithm is presented in Fig. 1.

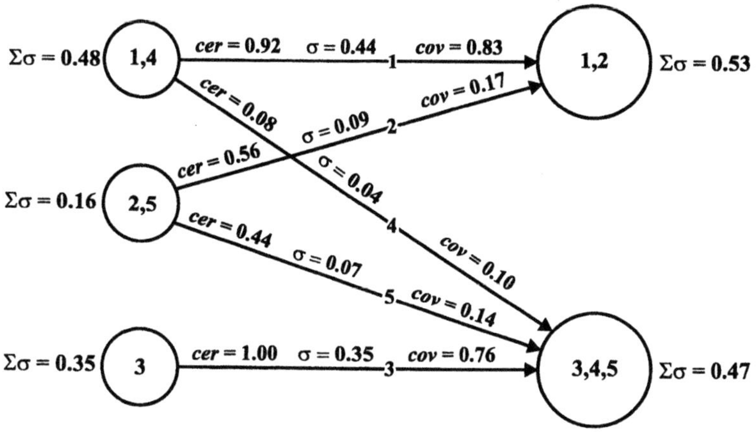

Fig. 1. Flow graph

Each input node of the flow graph represents a condition of corresponding decision rule, whereas each output node reveals decisions of the rules. The associated numbers are to be understood as probabilities of conditions and decisions respectively. Branches of the graph are labeled by strength of associated decision rules.

The flow graph of a decision algorithm shows how probabilities of decisions and conditions are related.

Each node of the graph satisties equations (1)...(6). Observe, that in order to compute all the conditional and total probabilities it is enough to know the strength of the decision rules only, which makes the computations very easy, and gives also clear insight into the structure of the decision algorithm.

It is also possible a completely different interpretation of the flow graph, which gives rise to many new applications, but this will be not discussed here and we leave it to another study.

It is clearly seen from the example the difference between Bayesian data analysis and the rough set approach. In the Bayesian inference the data is used to update prior probability (knowledge) into a posterior probability, whereas rough set based Bayesian inference is used to reason directly from data.

6 Flow Graphs and Neural Networks

Flow graphs can be also interpreted as a kind of neural network. Inputs and outputs of the flow graph correspond to inputs and outputs of the neural network, respectively, whereas branches represent connections in the network. Strength of decision rules is to be understood as weight of the corresponding connections. Moreover we assume that each input of the neural network is connected to every output of the network. In the initial stage strength of each connection is equal to zero. In the learning phase training examples are delivered to inputs of the neural network and are classified to outputs according to "tutor's" knowledge. In each example strength of connections and the certainty factors are computed. After the learning is completed the neural network gain "knowledge" acquired from training examples - which is represented as strength of connections and certainty factors. Now the neural network can be used to classify new examples without the tutor, according to maximal certainty factor, computed in the learning stage.

7 Conclusion

It has been shown in this paper that decision algorithms display interesting probabilistic featuers, i.e., they obey the total probability theorem and Bayes' theorem. This gives rise to a new perspective on Bayesian inference methodology, leads to new algorithms and new areas of applications.

Besides, representation of decison algorithms by flow graphs gives new insight into the decision processes. Interpretation of flow graphs as neural networks is outlined.

References

1. Bernardo, J. M., Smith,A. F. M.: Baysian Theory, Wiley Series in Probability and Mathematical Statistics. John Wiley & Sons, Chichester, New York, Brisbane, Toronto, Singapore (1994)
2. Ford, L.R., Fulkerson, D. R.: Flows in Networks. Princeton University Press, Princeton, New Jersey (1962)
3. Pawlak, Z.: Rough Sets – Theoretical Aspect of Reasoning about Data. Kluwer Academic Publishers, Boston Dordrech, London (1991)
4. Pawlak, Z.: Rough sets, decision algorithms and Bayes' theorem. European Journal of Operational Research 136, pp. 181 – 189 (2002)

New Consideration on Criteria of Model Selection

Shun-ichi Amari

Laboratory for Mathematical Neuroscience
RIKEN Brain Science Institute
Hirosawa 2-1, Wako-shi, Saitama 351-0198m Japan

Abstract. Model selection is an important problem for intelligent systems. We visit the well known criteria such as AIC, BIC and MDL, and show new remarkable facts which remain unexplored. When we compare two statistical models of which one is a submodel of the larger one, we show there is a better or more economic way of describing given data. This leads us a new criterion of model selection, which sits between MDL and AIC. We also point out that, for a hierarchical family of models such as neural networks or Gaussian mixtures, the classic theories of AIC, BIC and MDL do not hold. A new consideration is again necessary. We give some hints on this problem.

1 Introduction

When one uses a model for explaining observed data, it is a fundamental question how to choose a model. A complex model has a large capacity of representing a complex probability function or input output relation, by adjusting its parameters. However, given a finite number of data which include fluctuations, a complex model overfits the given specific data, and its behavior is not good for explaining or predicting new data compared with a simple model. Therefore, we need to choose an adequate model, depending on data.

Akaike [1] proposed an information based criterion named AIC, which tries to minimize the so-called the generalization error measured by the Kullback-Leibler divergence (KL divergence) from the true (unknown) distribution to the estimated best distribution in the underlying model. Schwarz [2] proposed a Bayesian criterion named BIC, which selects a model whose Baysian posterior probability is maximized.

A completely different idea was proposed by Rissanen [3], named MDL, which aims at minimizing the length of describing observed data by using a model, and the model that minimizes the description length is to be chosen. This principle is applicable to any data sequences irrespective of whether the underlying data generation mechanism is stochastic or not. The idea is developed further, and is defined in terms of the stochastic complexity [4] of data. The criterion is proved to be optimal in the minimax sense to predict further data.

Let us consider a regular statistical model $M_k = \{p(x, \boldsymbol{\theta})\}$, where x is a random variable, $p(x, \boldsymbol{\theta})$ is its probability density specified by k-dimensional parameter vector $\boldsymbol{\theta} = (\theta_1, \cdots, \theta_k)$. In the case of neural networks, x is replaced by a pair $(\boldsymbol{x}, y)$, input signal $\boldsymbol{x}$ and its output y. Given a set D of observed examples $x_1, \cdots x_n$, we search for the maximum likelihood estimator $\hat{\boldsymbol{\theta}}$. Then, the expected value of the KL divergence from the true distribution $q(x)$ to the estimated one, $p(x, \hat{\boldsymbol{\theta}})$, is given by

$$\text{AIC} = \text{Error} + k \tag{1}$$

where Error is

$$\text{Error} = -\sum \log p\left(x_i, \hat{\boldsymbol{\theta}}\right) \tag{2}$$

When one uses a more complex model with larger k, the Error decreases, while the second term penalizes a complex model, so that one can choose an adequate model by minimizing AIC.

By applying the MDL to the same problem, one can obtain a different criterion,

$$\text{MDL} = \text{Error} + \frac{k \log n}{2} \tag{3}$$

Here, the penalty term is different from the AIC. It is pointed out that, when the true model belongs to M_k, the AIC does not necessarily choose the model with the true k, while the MDL does, in the limit when n tends to infinity. This is the lack of consistency in statistics. However, the distribution $p(x, \hat{\boldsymbol{\theta}})$ selected by the AIC also converges to the true one, so that the consistency is kept in this sense.

The BIC preassumes a prior distribution π_k on the family $\{M_k\}$ of models, and prior distributions of $\pi(\boldsymbol{\theta}_k)$ on the parameters. It then calculates the posterior distribution

$$\text{Prob}\{M_k|D\} \tag{4}$$

given the data D, and selects the model that maximizes the posterior probability. This is based on a different philosophy, but by carrying out calculations, it turns out that the BIC criterion, applied to this problem, is the same as the MDL. The Baysian standpoint is generalized to give the stochastic complexity of Rissanen, which is optimal in the minimax sense.

A question still remains. Which is a better criterion to be used? The both criteria have respective theoretical bases with the optimality properties. Simulations show it depends on problems to be applied, and one cannot say any universal criteria to be used.

The present paper considers two new considerations on these criteria. One is reconsideration of minimizing the description length applied to the selection of models which are nested one another. This leads to a new criterion of

$$\text{MDL}' = \text{Error} + \frac{k \log \log n}{2}. \tag{5}$$

It is interesting to note that the penalty term sits between the MDL and the AIC, and the consistency of the order of the model is guaranteed.

The other point to be addressed is model selection among a family of hierarchical models, such as multilayer perceptrons, Gaussian mixtures of probability distributions, and many others. In such a family, a smaller model is embedded in a larger model as a subspace. When the true distribution lies in a smaller model, the parameters in a larger model loose identifiability. That is, the statistical model is unidentifiable, and the Fisher information degenerates in the larger model. The maximum likelihood estimator is no more asymptotically Gaussian. The analysis of the characteristics of the AIC and MDL heavily relied on the Gaussianity of the maximum likelihood estimator $\hat{\boldsymbol{\theta}}$ and the Cramer-Rao paradigm. When we apply the criteria to a hierarchical family, one should modify it. Estimation in such a singular statistical model is a very difficult problem. The Baysian estimator has an interesting behavior in such a case. We will point out this.

2 Minimum Description Length to Compare Two Nested Models

Let us consider a very simple model: Random variables X, Y are jointly normally distributed with mean μ_x and μ_y, respectively, and with the identity variance-covariance matrix. We consider two models,

$$M_2 : p(x, y, \mu_x, \mu_y) = \frac{1}{2\pi} \exp\left\{-\frac{1}{2}(x-\mu_x)^2 - \frac{1}{2}(y-\mu_y)^2\right\} \tag{6}$$

$$M_1 : p(x, y, \mu) = \frac{1}{2_1} \exp\left\{-\frac{1}{2}(x-\mu)^2 - \frac{1}{2}(y-\mu)^2\right\} \tag{7}$$

The M_2 is a submodel of M_1, where $\mu = \mu_x = \mu_y$ holds.

Given a set of observed data

$$D = \{(x_1, y_1), \cdots, (x_n, y_n)\}, \tag{8}$$

which model should one choose? We can easily generalize the consideration to general regular statistical models in which one is a submodel of the other, because the situation is the same asymptotically, from the point of view of information geometry [5].

We further simplify the problem. Putting

$$z = \frac{1}{\sqrt{2}}(x - y), \tag{9}$$

the random variable Z is subject to a Gaussian distribution with variance 1, and mean $\theta = (\mu_x - \mu_y)/\sqrt{2}$. This is a new larger model M_1. The smaller model M_0 is the Gaussian distribution with mean 0, that is $\theta = 0$. The problem reduces which model is better, M_1 or M_0.

We now consider the description length of data $D = \{z_1, \cdots, z_n\}$ with reference to model M_1 and M_0. The maximum likelihood estimator $\hat{\theta}$ in model M_1 is

$$\hat{\theta} = \frac{1}{n} \sum_i x_i = \bar{x} \tag{10}$$

In the present case, let us put

$$S = \frac{1}{n} \sum x_i^2 \tag{11}$$

Then, we have the error term in M_1 as

$$\text{Error} = n \left(S - \bar{x}^2\right) \tag{12}$$

while it is

$$\text{Error} = \frac{n}{2} S \tag{13}$$

in model M_0, because the mean is fixed to 0 in the latter simple model.

The MDL is given by

$$\text{MDL}\,(M) = \frac{n}{2} \left(S - \bar{x}^2\right) + \frac{1}{2} \log n \tag{14}$$

$$\text{MDL}\,(M) = \frac{n}{2} S. \tag{15}$$

It is clear that the error term is smaller by $n\bar{x}^2/2$ in the larger model M_1, while it has an additional penalty of $\log n/2$, since the number of parameter to be adjusted is larger by 1.

It is clear from (14) and (15) that, the larger model M_1 is better when $n\bar{x}^2 > \log n$ and M_0 is better otherwise. Therefore, by putting

$$c_n = \sqrt{\log n/n}, \tag{16}$$

the larger model is much better when $|\bar{x}| \gg c_n$, and the smaller model is much better when $|\bar{x}| \ll c_n$. The two models are comparable around $|\bar{x}| \approx c_n$.

We now consider a new method of describing the data in reference to M_1. Let us use a constant α, say $\alpha = 10$. When

$$|\bar{x}| > \alpha c_n \tag{17}$$

we encode $z^n = z_1 \cdots z_n$ by using the statistical model $p(z, \hat{\theta}) \in M_1$ whose description length is

$$\text{MDL}\,(M_1) = \frac{n}{2} \left(S - \bar{x}^2\right) + \frac{\log n}{2} \tag{18}$$

In order to send $\hat{\theta}$, we quantize it with accuracy $\delta = 1/\sqrt{n}$.

Then overall description length is,

$$\mathrm{MDL}\left(M_1, Z^n\right) = \frac{n}{2}\left(S - \bar{x}^2\right) + \frac{\log n}{2} + 1. \tag{19}$$

Here, one extra bit is needed to send if $|\bar{x}| > \alpha c_n$ or not.

When $|\bar{x}| < \alpha c_n$, the error part is the same, since we encode z^n by using $p\left(z, \hat{\theta}\right)$. In order to send z^n, we use one bit to show that $\bar{x}$ is within the interval of $\hat{\theta} = \bar{x} < |\alpha c_n|$. We then quantize the interval $[-\alpha c_n, \alpha c_n]$ whose accuracy is again $\delta = 1/\sqrt{n}$. Then, the length of describing $\hat{\theta}$ is

$$\frac{1}{2}\log\log n \tag{20}$$

Hence the description length in this new scheme is

$$\mathrm{MDL}^*\left(M_1, Z^n\right) = \frac{n}{2}\left(S - \bar{x}^2\right) + \frac{\log\log n}{2} + 1. \tag{21}$$

This gives the following theorem.

Theorem 1. Given a data set of length n, the description lengths comparing M_1 and M_0 are, respectively

$$\mathrm{MDL}^*(M_1) = \mathrm{Error} + \frac{1}{2}\log\log n \tag{22}$$

$$\mathrm{MDL}^*(M_0) = \mathrm{Error} \tag{23}$$

One can easily generalizes the above consideration to a more general case of comparing two models M_k and $M_{k'}$, $M_{k'} \subset M_k$.

Theorem 2. The description length comparing two models is

$$\mathrm{MDL}^*\left(M_k\right) = \mathrm{Error} + \frac{k}{2}\log\log n. \tag{24}$$

3 Hierarchical Models

Let us consider the set of multilayer perceptrons with h hidden units. When its output is disturbed by Gaussian noise, its behavior is described by a conditional probability of output y conditioned on input $\boldsymbol{x}$, and parameterized by $\boldsymbol{\theta}$ which consists of all the modifiable connection weights. Let M_h be the set of the conditional probability distributions of perceptrons with h hidden units. M_{h-1} is included as a submodel (subspace) in M_h.

When the true perceptron is in M_{h-1}, it also belongs to M_h. However, there are many parameters in M_h corresponding to the true one. As a simple example, let us consider the case with one hidden unit, and put

$$y = v\varphi(\boldsymbol{w} \cdot \boldsymbol{x}) + \varepsilon \tag{25}$$

where ε is the Gaussian noise. The parameters are $\boldsymbol{\theta} = (v, \boldsymbol{w})$. If the true model is $v = 0$, no hidden unit is necessary, and this belongs to M_0. However, this simple one is represented by the pair any points of the form $(0, \boldsymbol{w})$ or $(v, 0)$ in M_1. Hence, there is no unique point in M_1.

Given a set of input-output data D of size n, which model is better M_h or M_{h-1}? The ordinary methods of AIC and MDL use the assumption that the estimated parameter $\hat{\boldsymbol{\theta}}$ in any models is asymptotically subject to the Gaussian distribution, where the variance-covariance matrix is the inverse of the Fisher information matrix divided by n. This assumption does not hold in M_h. Because, when the true one is in M_{h-1}, the Fisher information matrix of M_h degenerates, and there is no inverse.

This opens a new interesting problem of model selection in hierarchical families of models such as multilayer perceptrons, Gaussian mixtures, ARMA models in time series, and so on. We have some preliminary studies [6], by using a simple toy model. The Bayesian approach to such a model family is also very interesting. The behavior heavily depends on the Bayes priors even in the asymptotic case.

4 Conclusions

Selection of an adequate model is an important problem for intelligent systems. In statistical models including neural networks, the problem has been studied intensively. There are a number of well known criteria such as AIC, BIC and MDL. However, there still remains which criterion one should use.

The present paper visited this problem, and pointed new ideas concerning these criteria.

References

1. Akaike, H. (1974) A new look at statistical model identification. IEEE Trans. on Automatic Control. **19**, 716–723
2. Schwarz, G. (1978) Estimating the dimension of a model. Annals of Statistics. **6**, 461–464
3. Rissanen, J. (1983) A universal data compression system. IEEE Trans. on Information Theory. **IT-29**, 656–664
4. Rissanen, J. (1986) Stochastic complexity and modeling. Annals of Statistics. **14**, 3, 1080–1100
5. Amari, S., Nagaoka, H. (2000) Methods of Information Geometry. AMS and Oxford University Press, New York
6. Amari, S., Ozeki, T. (2001) Differential and Algebraic Geometry of Multilayer Perceptrons. IEICE Trans. Fundamentals. E84-A, 1, 31–38

Generalized Conjunction, Disjunction and Negation Operations in Fuzzy Modeling

Ildar Batyrshin

Institute of Informatics Problems, Academy of Sciences of Tatarstan
Kazan State Technological University, K.Marx st., 68, Kazan, 420015, Russia
E-mail: batyr@emntu.kcn.ru

Abstract. Generalized operations of fuzzy logic are considered. New methods of generation of involutive, contracting and expanding negations are proposed. The methods of generation of simple parametric classes of non-associative conjunctions are discussed. The ways of embedding of strict monotonic conjunction and disjunction operations on ordinal scales based on the concept of lexicographic valuation (uncertainty with memory) and aimed to application in expert systems are described.

1 Introduction

A study of one or another type of conjunction, disjunction and negation operations (c-d-n-operations) is motivated by different reasons: a consideration of a class of operations defined by given properties, a suitability for the use in fuzzy models of quantitative data, a suitability for processing of qualitative experts information. From all these points of view c-d-operations of Zadeh $x \wedge y = min(x,y)$ and $x \vee y = max(x,y)$ [33] possess the maximum of useful properties and play the pivotal role in the construction of fuzzy logic. These operations are unique distributive c-d-operations [1,30]. The negation of Zadeh $\neg x = 1 - x$ is the simplest involutive negation on L =[0,1]. The algebra of fuzzy sets defined by c-d-n-operations of Zadeh is Kleene algebra [28]. Further, t-norms, t-conorms (t-operations for short) and involutive negations [24,29-31] are the most important classes of c-d-n-operations in fuzzy logic. The associativity determines the main properties of t-operations. Nevertheless, different generalizations of c-d-n-operations based on the change of the axioms of these operations or on the replacement of the set [0,1] by more general structure may be considered [2-14,16-22,27,30-32]. In the following several such generalizations of c-d-n-operations are discussed. New methods of generation of involutions, contracting and expanding negation [5,6,9] are considered in Sect. 2. The methods of generation of simple parametric non-associative c-d-operations suitable for tuning in fuzzy models [7,11-13] are discussed in Sect. 3. The strict monotonic c-d-operations suitable for processing of human estimates measured in ordinal scales [2,3,10] are considered in Sect. 4.

2 Involutive, Contracting and Expanding Negations

Suppose $L=[0,1]$. A negation is a non-increasing function $n:L \to L$ satisfying on L the conditions: $n(0)=1$, $n(1)=0$. Additional conditions on L define the following negations: $n(n(x))=x$ (involution or strong negation); $n(n(x)) \leq x$ (usual negation); $x \leq n(n(x))$ (weak negation); n is strictly decreasing and continuous (strict or bijective negation). Some of these negations are studied in [17,29-32].

Suppose n is a negation. An element $x \in L$ is called involutive, if $n(n(x))=x$, otherwise it is called non-involutive. An element $s \in L$, such that $n(s)=s$, is called a fixed point. A fixed point is unique if it exists. If n is a bijection then s exists. An increasing bijection from [0,1] onto itself is called an automorphism.

The following theorem is a modification of results from [29].

Theorem 1. A function $n:[0,1] \to [0,1]$ is an involution if and only if there exists an automorphism φ of [0,1] such that $n(x)=\varphi^{-1}(1-\varphi(x))$.

Sugeno negation $n(x)=(1-x)/(1+px)$, $(p>-1)$, is an example of involution.

Theorem 2. [5,6]. The functions $n_1, n_2:[0,1] \to [0,1]$ are involutions if and only if there exists an automorphism φ of [0,1] such that $n_1(x)=min\{1-\varphi(x), \varphi^{-1}(1-x)\}$ and $n_2(x)=max\{1-\varphi(x), \varphi^{-1}(1-x)\}$.

Theorem 3. [5,6]. The function $n:[0,1] \to [0,1]$ is an involution with fixed point s if and only if there exists an automorphism φ of the unit interval such that

$$n(x)=\begin{cases} 1-(1-s)\varphi\left(\dfrac{x}{s}\right), & if\ x \leq s \\ s\varphi^{-1}\left(\dfrac{1-x}{1-s}\right), & if\ s < x \end{cases}.$$

From theorems 2 and 3 with automorphism $\varphi(x)=x^p$ $(p>0)$ we get the following involutions: $n_1(x)=min\{1-x^p, (1-x)^{1/p}\}$, $n_2(x)=max\{1-x^p, (1-x)^{1/p}\}$ and $n(x)=1-(1-s)(x/s)^p$ if $x \leq s$, and $n(x)=s((1-x)/(1-s))^{1/p}$ if $s<x$.

Definition 4. [4]. A negation n is called a contracting negation in $x \in L$ if $x \wedge n(x) \leq n(n(x)) \leq x \vee n(x)$ and n is called contracting (on L) if it is contracting in all $x \in L$. A negation n is called an expanding negation in $x \in L$ if $n(x) \wedge n(n(x)) \leq x \leq n(x) \vee n(n(x))$ and n is called expanding (on L) if it is expanding in all $x \in L$.

It was shown that any negation n is contracting or expanding in any $x \in L$, and both properties are fulfilled in some $x \in L$ iff x is an involutive element of n. As result, a negation n is an involution iff it is contracting and expanding on L..

Denote $n^0(x)=x$, $n^1(x)=n(x)$, $n^{k+1}(x)=n(n^k(x))$, for $k=0,1,2,\ldots$. The set $G(x)=\bigcup_{k=0}^{\infty}\left\{n^k(x)\right\}$ is called a set generated by x. A rank of x is defined as $R(x)=$

$|G(x)|$ where $|\ldots|$ means cardinality. $R(x)=\infty$, if $G(x)$ is infinite . A rank of negation n is defined as $R(n)=\sup_{x\in L} R(x)$. Notation $n^{-k}(x)$ is used for n^{-1}.

Theorem 5. [8]. The set of noninvolutive elements of any bijective negation n on [0,1] has a unique representation as a union of non-intersected open intervals. On each of them n is contracting or expanding and for any element x from such an interval the sequences $a_k=n^{2k}(x)$ and $a_k^{-1}=n^{-2k}(x)$ belong to this interval and their limits are involutive elements coinciding with its borders.

Proposition 6. [9]. Suppose g and h are automorphisms of L, then the function

$$n(x)=\begin{cases}1-(1-s)g\left(\dfrac{x}{s}\right) & \text{if } x\le s\\ s-s\cdot h\left(\dfrac{x-s}{1-s}\right) & \text{if } s<x\end{cases}$$

where $s\in(0,1)$, defines a contracting negation n if $h(x)\le x\le g(x)$ on L and an expanding negation n if $g(x)\le x\le h(x)$ on L with fixed point s.

Theorem 7. [5,6]. Bijective negaion n with fixed point s is a contracting negation on L iff there exists an involution n_1 such that for all $x\in L$ it is fulfilled

$$n(x)\le n_1(x),\ \text{if } x<s; \qquad n_1(s)=n(s)=s; \qquad n_1(x)\le n(x),\ \text{if } x>s;$$

and n is expanding iff there exists an involution n_1 such that on L it is fulfilled

$$n_1(x)\le n(x),\ \text{if } x<s; \qquad n_1(s)=n(s)=s; \qquad n(x)\le n_1(x),\ \text{if } x>s.$$

Several methods of generation of negations may be based on this theorem [5,6].

Proposition 8. Suppose n_1 is an involutive negation with fixed point s and g, h are automorphisms of L, then the function

$$n(x)=\begin{cases}s+(1-s)g\left(\dfrac{n_1(x)-s}{1-s}\right) & \text{if } x\le s\\ s\cdot h\left(\dfrac{n_1(x)}{s}\right) & \text{if } s<x\end{cases}$$

is a contracting negation if $g(x)\le x\le h(x)$ on L and n is an expanding negation if $h(x)\le x\le g(x)$ on L.

Previous results may be easily extended on arbitrary automorphism φ of L if we take into account that $\min\{\varphi(x),\varphi^{-1}(x)\}\le x\le \max\{\varphi(x),\varphi^{-1}(x)\}$.

3 Non-Associative Conjunctions and Disjunctions

General classes of associative c-d-operations are given by *t*-norms and *t*-conorms, which play important role in fuzzy logic [24]. These operations are defined as functions $T,S{:}L\times L\rightarrow L$ satisfying on $L=[0,1]$ the following axioms: commutativity, associativity, monotonicity: $T(x,y)\leq T(x,z)$ and $S(x,y)\leq S(x,z)$, if $y\leq z$; and boundary conditions: $T(x,1)=x$, $S(x,0)=x$. *t*-operations may be obtained one from another as follows: $S(x,y)=n^{-1}(T(n(x),n(y)))$, and $T(x,y)=n^{-1}(S(n(x),n(y)))$, where n is a strict negation [31]. The simplest examples of *t*-operations mutually related by negation $n(x)=1-x$ are the following: $T_M(x,y)=min(x,y)$ and $S_M(x,y)=max(x,y)$, $T_P(x,y)=x\cdot y$ and $S_P(x,y)=x+y-xy$, $T_L(x,y)=max(x+y-1,0)$ and $S_L(x,y)=min(x+y,1)$. The methods of generation of *t*-operations are determined by the associativity property of these functions, e.g., $T(x,y)=\varphi^{-1}(T_1(\varphi(x),\varphi(y)))$ where T_1 is some *t*-norm, for example, T_P. Generalizations of *t*-operations given on $L=[0,1]$ may be based on the change of the system of axioms, on the replacement of the set $L=[0,1]$ by linguistic or finite scale, etc. [2,3,7,11,12,14,16,18–22,27].

Diverse applications of fuzzy logic are based on the rules of the following type: R_i: *If X is* A_i *and Y is* B_i *then Z is* C_i; and R_i: *If X is* A_i *and Y is* B_i *then* $z=f_i(x,y)$, known as Mamdani and Sugeno rules respectively, where X, Y, Z are fuzzy variables, e.g. *VOLUME, PRESSURE* etc., A_i, B_i, C_i are fuzzy terms, e.g. *LARGE, VERY LOW* etc., x, y, z and f_i are real valued variables and functions [23, 26]. For given crisp values of x and y the firing values w_i of rules are calculated as $w_i=T_1(A_i(x),B_i(y))$, where T_1 is some conjunction operation formalizing connective *"and"*, $A_i(x)$ and $B_i(y)$ are the membership values of x and y in fuzzy sets A_i and B_i. A conclusion of rules then may be calculated as $C_i(z)=T_2(w_i,C_i(z))$, and $z=T_2(w_i,f_i(x,y))$, respectively, where T_2 is a conjunction perhaps different from T_1. The aggregation of conclusions of rules (together with defuzzification in Mamdani models) gives real values to the output of the model.

The construction of optimal fuzzy models is traditionally based on a tuning of membership functions of fuzzy sets used in the rules. Instead of or additionally to the tuning of membership functions it may be used a tuning of operations given parametrically [7,15]. Such tuning gives possibility to keep expert knowledge stored in membership functions or to decrease the error of modeling when limitations on the number of rules and membership functions are given. But the known parametric classes of *t*-operations are sufficiently complicated for tuning [15] and hardware realization since the generation of these functions is based on the use of inverse functions φ^{-1}. For example, Yager *t*-norms have the form: $T(x,y)=1-min(1,((1-x)^p+(1-y)^p)^{1/p})$, $(p>0)$. Hence, for obtaining simpler parametric classes of c-d-operations it is necessary to delete the associativity from the definition of these operations [7]. Moreover, neither commutativity nor associativity of c-d-operations is needed in fuzzy models with two inputs, with fixed positions of variables in model, with fixed procedure of processing of model and so on. Non-commutativity of operations may be also desirable for taking into account different influence of input variables on the output of the system [7].

Conjunction T and disjunction S operations are defined in [7] as functions $T,S:[0,1]\times[0,1]\rightarrow[0,1]$ satisfying on [0,1] the following properties:

$$T(x,1) = T(1,x) = x, \quad S(x,0) = S(0,x) = x,$$

$$T(x,y) \leq T(u,v) \text{ if } x \leq u,\ y \leq v, \quad S(x,y) \leq S(u,v) \text{ if } x \leq u,\ y \leq v. \quad (1)$$

For these c-d-operations, the following properties are fulfilled:

$$T(0,0) = T(0,1) = T(1,0) = 0, \quad S(0,1) = S(1,0) = S(1,1) = 1, \quad (2)$$

$$T(1,1) = 1, \quad S(0,0) = 0, \quad (3)$$

$$T(x,0) = T(0,y) = 0, \quad S(1,y) = S(x,1) = 1. \quad (4)$$

Several methods of generation of such c-d-operations have been proposed in [7]. If T_1, T_2 are given conjunctions (e.g. simple t-norms), S_1 and S_2 are functions $S_i:[0,1]\times[0,1]\rightarrow[0,1]$ satisfying Eqs. (1) and (4) and h, g_1, $g_2:[0,1]\rightarrow[0,1]$ are non-decreasing functions such that $g_1(1)= g_2(1) = 1$ then conjunction T may be generated as follows: 1) $T(x,y) = T_2(T_1(x,y), S_1(g_1(x),g_2(y)))$; 2) $T(x,y) = T_2(T_1(x,y), g_1(S_1(x,y)))$; 3) $T(x,y) = T_2(T_1(x,y), S_2(h(x),S_1(x,y)))$. Disjunction operations may be generated dually or obtained from conjunctions by means of negation operation. The following are the examples of simple parametric conjunctions ($p,q \geq 0$): 1) $T(x,y)= min(x,y)(x^p + y^q - x^p y^q)$, 2) $T(x,y) = min(x,y)max(x^p,y^q)$.

More general G-conjunction and G-disjunction are considered in [11,12] as functions $T,S:[0,1]\times[0,1]\rightarrow[0,1]$ satisfying Eqs. (1)-(3). These c-d-operations may be generated as follows: $T(x,y) = f(T_1(g(x),h(y)))$ and $S(x,y) = f(S_1(g(x),h(y)))$, where T_1 is a G-conjunction, S_1 is a G-disjunction and f, g, $h:[0,1]\rightarrow[0,1]$ are non-decreasing functions such that $f(0)= g(0) = h(0) =0$, $f(1)= g(1) = h(1) = 1$. The following are the examples of the simplest G-conjunctions ($p,q \geq 0$): 1) $T(x,y)=(xy)^p(x + y - xy)^q$; 2) $T(x,y) =x^p y^q$; 3) $T(x,y)= min(x^p,y^q)$.

The parameters p, q used in the last two functions may be considered as modifiers of membership functions considered by Zadeh [13]. It was shown in several simulation examples [12,13] that the tuning of G-conjunctions can be successfully used in function approximation and in fuzzy systems identification.

4 Strict Monotonic Operations on Ordinal Scales

The operations of Zadeh may be easily extended on finite linearly ordered set of membership, true, plausibility values $L=\{a_1 < a_2 < \ldots < a_M\}$ with universal bounds $0 = a_1$ and $I = a_M$. Such scale may consist on linguistic grades like the following: $L=$ {*impossible* < *slightly possible* < *average possibility* < *very possible* < *sure*}. Involutive negation is uniquely defined as follows: $n(a_k) = n(a_{M-k+1})$, ($k=$

1,..., m). *min* and *max* are adequate c-d-operations on ordinal scales but they are not strict monotonic operations, e.g. $min(a,x)= a$ for all $x \geq a$. It is important to have strict monotonic c-d-operations or ordinal scales satisfying the conditions: 1) $T(x,y) < T(x,z)$ if $y< z$ and $x \neq 0$ *(strict monotonicity of T)*; and 2) $S(x,y)< S(x,z)$ if $y < z$ and $x \neq I$ *(strict monotonicity of S)*. But on finite scales it is impossible to introduce such operations. The solution of this problem was given in [2,3] where the result of operation $T(x,y)$ do not equal to one of the operands but to the string of operands ordered in a suitable way and called a lexicographic valuation [2,3].

Suppose $L= \{a_1 < a_2 < \ldots < a_M\}$. Let $J(l)$ denote the set $\{1, \ldots, l\}$. A $\wedge$-valuation on L is a string $f^\wedge(l)= (f_1, \ldots, f_l)$ of elements $f_j \in L$ such that if $l> 1$ then $0<f_j \leq f_{j+1} < I$ for all $j \in J(l-1)$. We also will write $f^\wedge$ instead of $f^\wedge(l)$. A $\wedge$-valuation $f^\wedge$ is considered as a result of conjunction of elements f_j from L such that $f_1= min_j\{f_j\}$ gives the result of *min* conjunction applied to operands f_j.

On the set of $\wedge$-valuations $F^\wedge$ the ordering relation $\leq$ is defined as follows: $f^\wedge(l) \leq g^\wedge(m)$ if $l \geq m$ and $f_j = g_j$ for all $j \in J(m)$ or if there exists $j \in J(l \wedge m)$ such that $f_j < g_j$ and $f_k = g_k$ for all $k < j$. This relation generalizes a lexicographic ordering of strings and the following property of fuzzy logic: $a \wedge b \leq a$. The relation $\leq$ defines a linear ordering on $F^\wedge$ with the minimal $0^\wedge= (0)$ and the maximal $I^\wedge= (I)$ elements.

Conjunction and disjunction operations on $F^\wedge$ are defined as follows. $S(f^\wedge, g^\wedge)= f^\wedge \vee g^\wedge$, where $\vee$ is a max operation defined by linear ordering relation $\leq$ on $F^\wedge$. $T(f^\wedge, g^\wedge) = (\wedge^*(f^\wedge g^\wedge))^\sim$, where $f^\wedge g^\wedge$ is a concatenation of $f^\wedge$ and $g^\wedge$, $\wedge^*$ is an operation sorting the elements of the string $f^\wedge g^\wedge$ in ascending order, and $\sim$ is a reduction operation transforming a string of ordered elements $f= (f_1, \ldots, f_l)$ in a $\wedge$-valuation $f^\wedge = f^\sim$ by: $f^\sim = (0)$ if $f_1 = 0$, $f^\sim = (I)$ if $f_1 = I$, otherwise $f^\sim = (f_1, \ldots, f_k)$ where k is the maximal index from $J(l)$ such that $f_k \neq I$. A reduction operation generalizes the following property of fuzzy logic: $a \wedge 0 = 0$, $a \wedge I = a$. It was proved that such conjunction T on $F^\wedge$ is a strict monotonic *t*-norm [3].

A generalization of disjunctive normal forms may be given as follows. A $(\vee,\wedge)$-valuation defined on L is a string $f^{\vee\wedge}(l) = [f_1^\wedge, \ldots, f_l^\wedge]$ of elements $f_j^\wedge$ from $F^\wedge$ such that if $l > 1$ then $I^\wedge > f_j^\wedge \geq f_{j+1}^\wedge > 0^\wedge$ for all $j \in J(l-1)$. A $(\vee,\wedge)$-valuation $f^{\vee\wedge}$ is considered as a result of disjunction of conjunctions $f_j^\wedge$ such that $f_1^\wedge = max_j\{f_j^\wedge\}$ gives the result of *max* disjunction applied to operands $f_j^\wedge$ with respect to ordering of these valuations. $F^{\vee\wedge}$ denotes the set of all $(\vee,\wedge)$-valuations on L. Ordering relation $\leq$ on $F^{\vee\wedge}$ is defined as follows: $f^{\vee\wedge}(l) \leq g^{\vee\wedge}(m)$ if $l \leq m$ and $f_j^\wedge = g_j^\wedge$ for all $j \in J(l)$ or if there exists $j \in J(l \wedge m)$ such that $f_j^\wedge < g_j^\wedge$ and $f_k^\wedge = g_k^\wedge$ for all $k <j$. This relation generalizes a lexicographic ordering of strings and the following property of fuzzy logic: $a \leq a \vee b$. The relation $\leq$ defines a linear ordering on $F^{\vee\wedge}$ with the minimal element $0^{\vee\wedge} = [0^\wedge] = [(0)]$ and the maximal element $I^{\vee\wedge} = [I^\wedge] = [(I)]$.

Conjunction and disjunction operations on $F^{\vee\wedge}$ are defined as follows:

$$T_1(f^{\vee\wedge}, g^{\vee\wedge}) = [\vee^*(T(f_1^{\wedge}, g_1^{\wedge}),\dots,T(f_i^{\wedge}, g_j^{\wedge}),\dots,T(f_l^{\wedge}, g_m^{\wedge}))]\sim, \quad i\in J(l), j\in J(m), \tag{5}$$

$$S_1(f^{\vee\wedge}, g^{\vee\wedge}) = [\vee^*(f^{\vee\wedge} g^{\vee\wedge})]\sim, \tag{6}$$

where T operations in the right side of Eq. (5) are conjunction operations on $F^{\wedge}$; $\vee^*(\dots)$ is an operation sorting the elements of string $(\dots)$ in descending order; ~ is a reduction operation transforming a string of ordered elements $h= [h_1^{\wedge},\dots,h_l^{\wedge}]$ in a $(\vee,\wedge)$-valuation $h^{\vee\wedge}= h\sim$ by: if $h_1^{\wedge} = 0^{\wedge}$ then $h^{\vee\wedge} = 0^{\vee\wedge} = [0^{\wedge}]$, if $h_1^{\wedge} = I^{\wedge}$ then $h^{\vee\wedge} = I^{\vee\wedge}= [I^{\wedge}]$, otherwise $h^{\vee\wedge}= [h_1^{\wedge},\dots,h_k^{\wedge}]$ where $h_k^{\wedge}$ is the maximal index from $J(l)$ such that $f_k \neq 0^{\wedge}$. $f^{\vee\wedge}g^{\vee\wedge}$ in Eq. (6) is a concatenation of $(\vee,\wedge)$-valuations $f^{\vee\wedge}$ and $g^{\vee\wedge}$: $f^{\vee\wedge}g^{\vee\wedge} =[f_1^{\wedge},\dots,f_l^{\wedge}, g_1^{\wedge},\dots,g_m^{\wedge}]$. A reduction operation on $F^{\vee\wedge}$ generalizes the following property of fuzzy logic: $a\vee 0= a$, $a\vee \mathrm{I} = \mathrm{I}$..

It was proved in [3] that operations T_1 and S_1 defined on $F^{\vee\wedge}$ are strict monotonic t-norm and t-conorm. These operations use only qualitative information about linear ordering of elements from L and hence they can be used for manipulation with information measured in ordinal scales. The negation operations on the sets on lexicographic valuations also may be introduced.

The algebra of lexicographic valuations with limited length was realized in expert systems shell LEXICO that was used in construction of intelligent tutoring system modeling chemical reactor and in several expert systems [10].

5 Conclusions

Distributivity of conjunction and disjunction operations of Zadeh is the most useful property of these operations, which gives possibility to transfer many results from crisp mathematics to fuzzy mathematics. But distributivity is very restrictive property because only *min* and *max* operations satisfy it. Moreover, these operations are not strict monotonic and not satisfy the excluded middle and the contradiction laws. Elimination of distributivity from the definition of c-d-operations deletes many useful properties of these operations but opens the door for wide class of associative t-norms and t-conorms. The class of t-operations is most general and interesting class of c-d-operations but the property of associativity is also restrictive for construction of simple parametric classes of operations suitable for tuning in fuzzy modeling. Moreover, associativity and commutativity are not necessary properties for c-d-operations used in popular fuzzy models. For this reason, non-associative and non-commutative c-d-operations should be studied better.

The structure of contracting and expanding negations is closely related with the structure of involutive negations that give us the better understanding of the nature of fuzzy negation operations. It would be interesting to study the influence of new concepts on the properties of fuzzy models based on negation operations.

The application of fuzzy logic to the modeling of human perceptions requires a development of operations suitable for processing of qualitative and linguistic information. From this point of view the generalization of the operations of Zadeh may be based on the replacement of the set of true values [0,1] by more general or specific structure. It may be the linearly or partially ordered set, the set of fuzzy sets of type 2, the set of lexicographic valuations etc. Many such generalizations have been studied but till nowadays it is an actual area of investigations. It may be supposed that the development of the theory of Precisiated Natural Language [34] will stimulate the development of generalized c-d-n-operations of fuzzy logic.

References

1. Alsina C, Trillas E, Valverde L (1983) On some logical connectives for fuzzy sets theory. J Math Anal Appl 93:15-26
2. Batyrshin IZ (1993) Uncertainties with memory in decision-making and expert systems. In: Fifth IFSA World Congress'93. Seoul, Korea, pp 737-740
3. Batyrshin IZ (1994) Lexicographic valuations of plausibility with universal bounds. I (in Russian). Techn Cybern, Izvestija Akademii Nauk 5:28-45
4. Batyrshin I (1995) Negation operations on a linearly ordered set of plausibility values. In: 3d European Congress on Intelligent Techniques and Soft Computing, EUFIT'95. Aachen, Germany, vol 2, pp 241-244
5. Batyrshin IZ (2002) On the structure of involutive, contracting and expanding negations. Fuzzy Sets and Systems (submitted)
6. Batyrshin IZ (2001) Basic Operations of Fuzzy Logic and Their Generalizations (in Russian). Otechestvo, Kazan
7. Batyrshin I, Kaynak O (1999) Parametric classes of generalized conjunction and disjunction operations for fuzzy modeling. IEEE Trans Fuzzy Syst 7:586-596
8. Batyrshin I, Wagenknecht M (1997) Noninvolutive negations on [0,1]. J Fuzzy Mathematics, 5:997-1010
9. Batyrshin I, Wagenknecht M (1998) Contracting and expanding negations on [0,1]. J Fuzzy Mathematics, 6:133-140
10. Batyrshin I, Zakuanov R, Bikushev G (1994) Expert system based on algebra of uncertainties with memory in process optimization. In: 1st Intern. FLINS Workshop, Mol, Belgium, World Scientific, pp 156-159
11. Batyrshin I, Kaynak O, Rudas I (1998) Generalized conjunction and disjunction operations for fuzzy control. In: EUFIT'98, Aachen, Germany, vol 1, pp 52-57
12. Batyrshin I, Kaynak O, Rudas I (2001) Fuzzy modeling based on generalized conjunction operations. IEEE Trans Fuzzy Syst (submitted)
13. Batyrshin I, Kaynak O, Rudas I (2001) Tuning of operations and modifiers in fuzzy models. In: First Intern. Conf. on Soft Computing and Computing with

Words in System Analysis, Decision and Control. Antalya, Turkey. Verlag b-Quadrat Verlag, pp 127–134
14.Berger M (1998) A new parametric family of fuzzy connectives and their application to fuzzy control. Fuzzy Sets Syst 93:1-16
15.Cervinka O (1997) Automatic tuning of parametric *T*-norms and *T*-conorms in fuzzy modeling. In: 7th IFSA World Congress. ACADEMIA, Prague, vol 1, 416-421
16.De Cooman G, Kerre EE (1994) Order norms on bounded partially ordered sets. J Fuzzy Mathematics 2:281-310
17.Esteva F, Trillas E, Domingo X (1981) Weak and strong negation functions for fuzzy set theory. In: 12th Int. Symp. on Multiple-Valued logic, Norman, 23-26
18.Fodor JC (1993) A new look at fuzzy connectives. Fuzzy Sets Syst 57:141- 148
19.Fodor JC (2001) Smooth associative operations on finite ordinal scales (submitted)
20.Godo LL, Lopez de Mantaras R, Sierra C, Verdaguer A (1988) Managing linguistically expressed uncertainty in MILORD application on medical diagnosis. AICOM 1:14-31
21.Goguen JA (1967) L-fuzzy sets. J Math Anal Appl 18:145-174
22.Herrera F, Herrera-Viedma E, Verdegay JL (1996) A model of consensus in group decision making under linguistic assessments. Fuzzy Sets Syst 78:73-87
23.Jang JSRoger, Sun CT, Mizutani E (1997) Neuro-Fuzzy and Soft Computing. A Computational Approach to Learning and Machine Intelligence. Prentice-Hall International, London
24.Klement EP, Mesiar R, Pap E (2000) Triangular Norms. Kluwer, Dordrecht
25.Klir GJ, Folger TA (1988) Fuzzy Sets, Uncertainty, and Information. Prentice-Hall International
26.Kosko B (1997) Fuzzy Engineering. Prentice-Hall, New Jersey
27.Mizumoto M, Tanaka K (1976) Some properties of fuzzy sets of type 2. Information and Control, 31:312-340
28.Skala HJ (1978) On many-valued logics, fuzzy sets, fuzzy logics and their applications. Fuzzy Sets Syst 1:129-149
29.Trillas E (1979) Sobre funciones de negacion en la teoria de conjunctos diffusos. Stochastica 3:47-59
30.Trillas E, Alsina C, Valverde L (1982) Do we need max, min and 1-*j* in fuzzy set theory? In: Yager RR (ed) Fuzzy Set and Possibility Theory. Pergamon Press, New York, pp 275-297
31.Weber S (1983) A general concept of fuzzy connectives, negations and implications based on *t*-norms and *t*-conorms. Fuzzy Sets Syst 11:115-134
32.Yager RR (1980) On the measure of fuzziness and negation. II. Lattices. Information and Control 44:236-260
33.Zadeh LA (1965) Fuzzy sets. Information and Control 8:338-353
34.Zadeh LA (1999) From computing with numbers to computing with words - from manipulation of measurements to manipulation of perceptions. IEEE Trans Circuits Systems - 1: Fundamental Theory and Applications 45:105-119

Image Data Compression/Reconstruction by Fuzzy Relational Equation

*Kaoru Hirota, *Hajime Nobuhara, and **Witold Pedrycz

*Department of Computational Intelligence and Systems Science, Tokyo Institute of Technology, 4259 Nagatsuta, Midoriku, Yokohama-city 226-8502, Japan
{hirota, nobuhara}@hrt.dis.titech.ac.jp

**Department of Electrical and Computer Engineering, University of Alberta, Edmonton, T6R, 2G7, Canada
pedrycz@ee.ualberta.ca

1. Introduction

Various image compression methods have been proposed to realize the easiness and relative inexpensiveness for obtaining and storing digital information, and the possibility to manipulate such information is almost unlimited [1][6][8]. As the number of image compression methods grows steadily, selecting appropriate methods is no longer a simple task. Now we face a stage in which we choose an appropriate method considering its applications (e.g. image database [5] and digital watermark [2] etc). An example of such image compression methods has been proposed by Hirota and Pedrycz, called Image Compression method based on Fuzzy relational equation [4]. In this paper, a fast image reconstruction method for ICF is proposed.

The ICF is formulated in Section 2 and a fast image reconstruction method for ICF is presented in section 3. Section 4 shows image compression and reconstruction experiments using 20 images (extracted from Standard Image DataBAse (SIDBA)).

2. Image Compression/Reconstruction Method Based on Fuzzy Relational Equation (ICF)

2.1 Image Compression

A method of lossy Image Compression/reconstruction method based on Fuzzy relational equation (ICF) has been proposed in [4]. In the ICF, a still gray scale image of size $M \times N$ is expressed as a fuzzy relation $R \in F(\mathbf{X} \times \mathbf{Y})$, $\mathbf{X} = \{x_1, x_2, \ldots, x_M\}$, $\mathbf{Y} = \{y_1, y_2, \ldots, y_N\}$ by normalizing the intensity range of each pixel into [0,1]. In the case of color image, an original image can be expressed by three fuzzy relations, i.e., $\mathbf{P} = \{P^{(R)}, P^{(G)}, P^{(B)}\} \subset F(\mathbf{X} \times \mathbf{Y})$, where, $P^{(R)}, P^{(G)}$, and $P^{(B)}$ denote the red, green and blue plane of the color image, respectively. Therefore, the ICF can also treat color images. For simplicity, in this paper, we consider only the case of gray scale images. The gray scale image $R \in F(\mathbf{X} \times \mathbf{Y})$ is compressed into $G \in F(\mathbf{I} \times \mathbf{J})$ by a max t-norm composite fuzzy relational equation,

$$G(i,j) = \max_{y \in Y} \left\{ B_j(y) \, t \max_{x \in X} \{ A_i(x) \, t R(x,y) \} \right\} \quad (\in [0,1]), \tag{1}$$

where t denotes a continuous t-norm, and $A_i \in \mathbf{A} = \{A_1, A_2, \ldots, A_I\} \subset F(\mathbf{X})$, $B_j \in \mathbf{B} = \{B_1, B_2, \ldots, B_J\} \subset F(\mathbf{Y})$, are called coders. The image compression process is shown in figure 1.

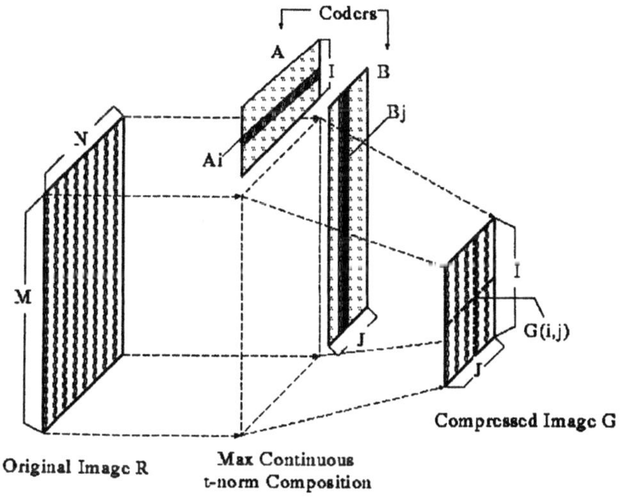

Figure 1. Image compression process

The coders $\mathbf{A}$ and $\mathbf{B}$ are defined by

$$\mathbf{A}=\{A_1,A_2,\ldots,A_I\},\ A_i(x_m)=\exp\left(-\mathrm{Sh}\left(\frac{iM}{I}-m\right)^2\right),\quad (m=1,2,\ldots,M), \tag{2}$$

and

$$\mathbf{B}=\{B_1,B_2,\ldots,B_J\},\ B_j(y_n)=\exp\left(-\mathrm{Sh}\left(\frac{jN}{J}-n\right)^2\right),\quad (n=1,2,\ldots,N), \tag{3}$$

where Sh denotes the sharpness of fuzzy sets A_i and B_j contained in coders $\mathbf{A}$ and $\mathbf{B}$. A preferable range of Sh depends on the compression rate, and it will be mentioned in the following image compression and reconstruction experiments. The shape of the fuzzy sets of coders is Gaussian-like, and it is preferable for the ICF. When the shape is triangle, a block noise will appear in the reconstructed images. The compression rate of ICF can be adjusted by the number of fuzzy sets contained in coders $\mathbf{A}$ and $\mathbf{B}$. The compression rate ρ is defined as

$$\rho=\frac{IJ}{MN}, \tag{4}$$

where IJ and MN denote the number of coefficients of compressed image and original one, respectively. In this paper, we take Yager's t-norm [3]

$$a t^{(p)} b = 1-\min\left\{1,\left\{(1-a)^p+(1-b)^p\right\}^{1/p}\right\},\quad (p\geq 1) \tag{5}$$

as the continuous t-norm appeared in fuzzy relational equation (1). Yager's t-norm can cover all continuous t-norms by changing the parameter p. Zadeh's t-norm and others cannot cover the all continuous t-norms. Frank's t-norm can also cover all continuous t-norms, but it has high computational complexity compared with Yager's one [3].

2.2 Image Reconstruction

The reconstruction of an image $R'\in F(\mathbf{X}\times\mathbf{Y})$ from the compressed image G is considered to be an inverse problem, under the condition that $\mathbf{A},\mathbf{B}$, and G are given. That is, the image reconstruction corresponds to the estimation of the solution R' that satisfies the fuzzy relational equation (1). In the case of max t-norm composite fuzzy relational equation, the structure of the solution set $\mathbf{R}\subset F(\mathbf{X}\times\mathbf{Y})$ is shown in figure 3 and the greatest solution and minimal solutions of $\mathbf{R}$ can be obtained analytically [3].

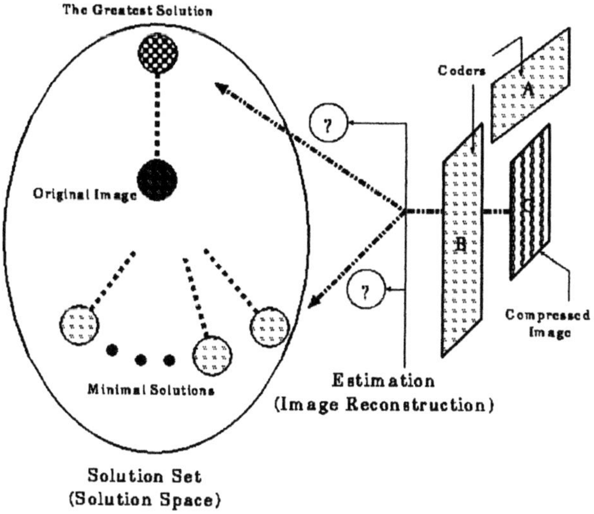

Figure 2. Image reconstruction process

Examples of reconstructed images (the greatest and one of the minimal solutions) and computation time are shown in figure 4 and table 1, respectively. The reconstructed images are obtained under the conditions that compression rate is 0.0625 (I x J = 64 x 64), Sh is 0.04, and Yager's t-norm parameter p is 1.0. As can be seen from figure 4, the minimal solutions presents bright pixels scattered on a black plane (background), yielding a meaningless result from the viewpoint of reconstructed image, whereas the greatest solution has quality comparable to the original image (figure 4). Therefore, only the greatest solution is considered as a reconstructed image in this paper. The greatest solution has been presented by Hirota and Pedrycz [4], and will be referred as H-P method. The greatest solution $\hat{R}$ of fuzzy relational equation (1) is given by

$$\hat{R}(x,y) = \min_{(i,j)\in I\times J}\left\{\left(A_i(x)tB_j(y)\right)\varphi_t G(i,j)\right\}, \tag{6}$$

$$a\varphi_t b = \sup\left\{c \in [0,1] \mid atc \le b\right\}. \tag{7}$$

In the case of H-P method, if Sh is a large value, the reconstructed image has high sharpness, but the white slit is more prominent in the image (see figure 5, left side image). Conversely, if Sh is small value, then the white slit is decreased, but the reconstructed image is blurred (see figure 5, right side image). Therefore, we employ a compromise value between such opposite sides. As can be seen from table 1, the reconstruction time of H-P method requires the large computation time. Therefore, in next section, we propose a fast image reconstruction of ICF.

Figure 3. Original image

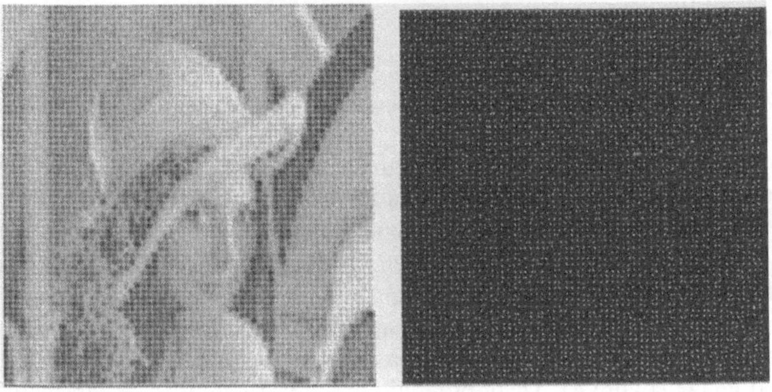

Figure 4. The greatest (let) and one of minimal solutions (right) (compression rate = 0.0625)

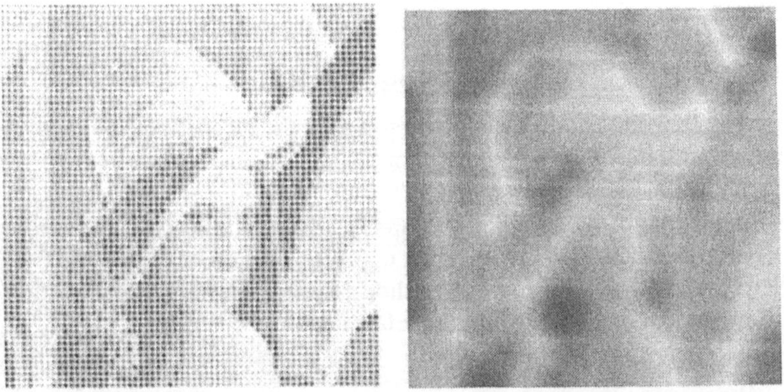

Figure 5. Left side image : the greatest, Sh = 0.2, right side image : the greatest, Sh = 0.001 (Compression rate = 0.0625)

Table 1. Computation time of ICF, computed using a Sun Ultra 10 (440MHz) workstation and 20 test images of SIDBA

Compression Rate	Compression Time (Average)	Reconstruction Time (Average)
$\rho = 0.0156$	0.93(s)	168.98(s)
$\rho = 0.0625$	1.43(s)	546.67(s)

3. Fast Image Reconstruction Method of ICF

In order to reduce the image reconstruction time of ICF, a fast image reconstruction method is proposed. The fast image reconstruction method is based on the following theorem [5]:

[Theorem 1] [5]

H-P method (eq. (6)) is equivalent to

$$\hat{R}(x,y) = \min_{j \in J}\left\{B_j(y)\varphi_t\left\{\min_{i \in I}\left\{A_i(x)\varphi_t G(i,j)\right\}\right\}\right\}. \tag{8}$$

Theorem 1 tells us the greatest solution obtained by the H-P method (eq. (6)) is the same one obtained by the proposed method (eq. (8)). The theoretical computation time of the H-P method and the proposed method correspond to

$$\text{H-P method: } IJMN(L+T+P), \tag{9}$$

$$\text{Proposed method: } JM(I+N)(L+P), \tag{10}$$

where, MN and IJ denote the size of original image R and compressed image G, respectively. The computation time min., t-norm, and relative pseudo-complement (eq. (7)) denote L, T, and P, respectively. The theoretical comparison shows that the computation time of the proposed method is shorter than that of the H-P method.

4. Experimental Comparison of Computation Time

A comparison of the proposed method with the H-P method from the viewpoint of reconstructed time is presented by image compression and reconstruction experiments using 20 images (extracted from SIDBA). The original images of size $M \times N = 256 \times 256$ pixels are compressed into images of size $I \times J = 32 \times 32$ and $I \times J = 64 \times 64$. The image reconstruction is performed by the H-P method and the proposed method, respectively. The result of comparison is shown in table 2. The decrease of the computation time to 1/132.02 and 1/382.29 are obtained, respectively.

Table 2. Image reconstruction time comparison of H-P method with proposed method, computed using Sun Ultra 10 workstation (440 MHz) and 20 test images of SIDBA

Compression Rate	H-P method (Average)	Proposed method (Average)
$\rho=0.0156$	168.98(s)	1.28(s)
$\rho=0.0625$	546.67(s)	1.62(s)

5. Conclusions

An Image Compression and reconstruction method based on Fuzzy relational Equation (ICF) is introduced. Furthermore, a fast image reconstruction method for ICF is proposed.

In image compression and reconstruction experiments using 20 images (extracted from SIDBA), the decrease of the image reconstruction time to 1/132.02 and 1/382.29 under compression rate of 0.0156 and 0.0625, respectively, is confirmed.

References

1. Antonini M, Barlaud M, Mathieu P, Daubchies I (1992) Image Coding using Wavelet Transform, IEEE Transaction on Image Processing, vol. 1, no. 2: 205-220
2. Barni M, Bartolini F, Piva A (2001) Improved Wavelet-Based Watermarking Through Pixel-Wise Masking, IEEE Transaction on Image Processing, vol. 10, no. 5: 783-791
3. DiNola A, Sessa S, Pedrycz W, Sanchez E, (1989) Fuzzy Relational Equation and their Applications to Knowledge Engineering, Kluwer Academic Publichers
4. Hirota K, Pedrycz W, (1999) Fuzzy Relational Compression, IEEE Transaction on Systems, Man, and Cybernetics, vol. 29, no. 3: 407-415
5. Liang KC, Jay Kuo CC (1999) WaveGuide: A Joint Wavelet-Based Image Representation and Description System, IEEE Transaction on Image Processing, vol. 8, no. 11: 1619-1629
6. Nasrabadi NM, King RA (1988) Image Coding using Vector Quantization: A Review, IEEE Transactions on Communications, vol. 3, no. 8: 957-971

7. Nobuhara H, Pedrycz W, Hirota K, (2000) Fast Solving Method of Fuzzy Relational Equation and Its Application to Lossy Image Compression/Reconstruction, IEEE Transactions on Fuzzy Systems, vol. 8, no.3: 325-334
8. Wallace GK (1991) The JPEG still picture compression standard, Communication ACM, vol. 34, no. 4 : 30-44

Interpolation in Hierarchical Rule Bases

László T. Kóczy[1,2], Leila Muresan[1,2], Kornél Csányi[1], Kaoru Hirota[2]

[1]Department of Telecommunication an Telematics, Technical University of Budapest, Magyar Tudósok körútja 2, 1117, Budapest, Hungary
[2]Széchenyi István University, Egyetem tér 1, 9026 Győr, Budapest, Hungary
[3]Dept. of Computational Intel.and Systems Sciences, Tokyo Institute of Technology, 4259 Nagatsuta, Midori–ku, Yokohama 226

Abstract.

In modelling complex systems one of the main difficulties is handling the curse of dimensionality. Our aim is to research the ways to cope with this problem in the special case of telecommunication supervision systems (TSS). Telecommunication networks are usually very large and complex, so the design of intelligent supervision systems raises the need of algorithms that can handle large amount of data, in high dimensional spaces in a user-friendly manner.
For this purpose, it seems suitable to use hierarchically structured fuzzy rule base systems, (for their descriptive power and their reduced complexity compared to classical fuzzy rule base systems). As inference algorithm for such rule base systems, the KH interpolation is suggested.

1 Introduction

The crucial aspect in applying artificial intelligence and soft computing systems to solve complex problems is to find a good balance between computational complexity (simplicity) and approximation accuracy of the approach. Fuzzy rule based systems and artificial neural nets offer an advantage in comparison to symbolic expert systems as the subsymbolic information contained in these models simplifies the model itself, however, still the upper limit of the number of variables that can be handled by these approaches in real time is around 5 to 10. An effective step forward was presented by Sugeno in the early 1990-s when he applied a hierarchical fuzzy model for his unmanned helicopter control experiment successfully.
Since then, the first commercial applications were introduced. The problem with general applications of this method is that in most complex problems there is no natural structure present in the system, and so, no hierarchical approach can be directly implemented.

For the structured approach of this method the essential point is that areas unsuitable for clear structuring can be "overbridged" with help of the interpolation technique extended to sub-rule bases.
Then, problematic parts of the primary model can be eliminated and so a clearly structured remainder can be effectively reduced by hierarchical structuring.
TSS (Telecommunication Supervision System) related problems in connection with this complex approach will illustrate these methods.

2 Hierarchical structures in TSS

One of the problems in TSS is the difficulty to integrate the data belonging to different hardware components. The rhytm of development of new hardware is increasing, new components may appear on monthly or even weekly basis. Information on the new hardware has to be added to the system without altering the already existing information or the functioning of the system.
The work of the human operator is characterized by the ability to process tenths of events per minute, to discriminate between important and insignificant events, and to make decision in a very short period of time in case that an important event occurrs. But in order to achieve all these goals, the amount of data to be presented to the operator has to be restricted (either to a specific geographical area, or a specific subset of events, etc.) so that the operator would not be overwhelmed.
On the other hand, complex tasks, such as configuring the system, predicting the ageing of hardware components, discovering the cause of certain flaws require a different approach, at a different level, taking into consideration all available data collected in a long period of time. For these tasks however, the immediate intervention is not required.
All these reasons lead to the idea of structuring knowledge in a hierarchical manner.
The hierarchy is formed from meta-level rules that look like:

If z_0 is D_i then use the sub-rulebase R_i

while in the lower levels, we deal with the usual type of rules:

If z_1 is A_{ij} then y is B_{ij} ,

A hierarchically structured fuzzy rule base will look like:

R_0 : **If** z_0 is D_1 **then use** R_1

If z_0 is D_2 **then use** R_2

...

If z_0 is D_n **then use** R_n

where $z_0 \in Z_0$ and represents the meta-level, and the sub-rule bases:

R_1 : **If** z_1 is A_{11} **then** y is B_{11}

If z_1 is A_{12} **then** y is B_{12}

...

If z_1 is A_{1m_1} **then** y is B_{1m_1}

where $Z_l \in X/Z_0$ (the projection to the dimensions which appear in Z_l)

R_2 : **If** z_1 **is** A_{21} **then** y is B_{21}

If z_1 **is** A_{22} **then** y is B_{22}

...

If z_1 **is** A_{2m_2} **then** y is B_{2m_2}

.....

R_n : **If** z_1 is A_{n1} **then** y is B_{n1}

If z_1 is A_{n2} **then** y is B_{n2}

...

If z_1 is A_{nm_n} **then** y is B_{nm_n}

The hierachical structure of fuzzy rule bases allows the division of data in manageable chunks, preserving in the meantime the interpretability of the information. So, for instance adding a new hardware component would result only in a new sub-rule base, which would not crush the functioning of the system. The characteristics of TSS - the type of events, the exact time of their occurence, the longitude and latitude of the affected equipment (wich inherently leads to the notions of geographical distance and neighborhood relationships), the alarm message, etc. form a mixture of categorical and numerical data, which can be organized in hierarchies in several ways, according to different reasonings. It is an open problem how to determine an optimal hierarchical organization.

3 Interpolation in TSS

A human operator cannot process very complex information (and this is even more difficult if the period of time to decide is extremely short). A method to simplify the task of the operator is to use a small number of linguistic terms instead to a whole range of numerical values. This corresponds to the choice of *T* fuzzy sets that describe an input domain.

Also, the work is further simplified if a reasoning based on similarity is applied, if knowledge in for of IF-THEN rules is available. This means that if it is known that IF x is A THEN y is *B*, then it is reasonable to presume that THE MORE x is similar to A THE MORE y is similar to *B*.

These arguments, and the need to use an inference for the hierarchical structures presented in the section above, lead us to the K-H interpolation in hierarchical fuzzy rule bases (see [5] for details). Moreover, the reasoning models also the regions for which more than one of the fuzzy terms in the meta-level apply (more than one sub-rule base is valid.)

The K-H interpolation uses the "horizontal representation" of the fuzzy sets, based on α-cuts, as introduced in [2], $\{A_\alpha : \alpha \in (0,1]\}$, where $A_\alpha = \{x : A(x) \geq \alpha\}$. For practical reasons, it is applied to CNF fuzzy sets. Moreover, the fuzzy set might be denoted in a vectorial way as:

$A \in \wp(X)$: left slope: $A_L = [a_{-m}, \ldots, a_{-1}]$, right slope: $A_U = [a_1, \ldots, a_m]$,

where $A_L(a_{-i}) = A_U(a_i) = \alpha_i$ (or $A = [a_{-m}, \ldots, a_{-1}, a_1, \ldots, a_m]$) and $a_{-1} = a_{-1} = 1$. The fuzzy distance used in the K-H interpolation is defined in [4] as the following fuzzy set:

Definition 2.1:

Fuzzy distance of two fuzzy sets:

$$\mu_{\tilde{d}_{L(A,B)}}(\delta) = \sum_{\alpha\in[0,1]} \alpha \mid D(\inf\{A_\alpha\}, \inf\{B_\alpha\}),$$

$$\mu_{\tilde{d}_{U(A,B)}}(\delta) = \sum_{\alpha\in[0,1]} \alpha \mid D(\inf\{A_\alpha\}, \inf\{B_\alpha\}),$$

$\delta \in [0,1]$, $\alpha \in \Lambda$

For multiple input problems we shall consider that all input domains are normalized (all inputs are scaled to [0,1]), which ensures that no input domain has greater impact/weight than the other.

Definition 2.2:

For two fuzzy sets A and B : $A \prec B$ holds if and only if $a_i \le b_i$, $i \in \{-m, \ldots -1, 1 \ldots m\}$.

Using the concept of fuzzy distance, the *Fundamental Equation of Rule Interpolation* can be written as:

$$d(A^*, A_1) : d(A^*, A_2) = d(B^*, B_1) : d(B^*, B_2)\,, \tag{1}$$

where $A_1 \rightarrow B_1$ and $A_2 \rightarrow B_2$ are the interpolating rules, A^* is the observation, B^* is the computed conclusion and the following conditions are satisfied:

$$A_1 \prec A^* \prec A_2 \quad \wedge \quad B_1 \prec B_2. \tag{2}$$

This can be written as :

$$b_i^* = \frac{\frac{1}{d(a_i^{(1)}, a_i^*)} b_i^{(1)} + \frac{1}{d(a_i^{(2)}, a_i^*)} b_i^{(2)}}{\frac{1}{d(a_i^{(1)}, a_i^*)} + \frac{1}{d(a_i^{(2)}, a_i^*)}}$$

If we denote the inverse distance $\frac{1}{d(a_i^{(1)}, a_i^*)}$ by h_i and we take into consideration not only two neighbours, but $|I|$ closest fuzzy sets, this becomes:

$$b^*_i = \frac{\sum_{i \in I} h_i b_i}{\sum_{j \in I} h_i}$$

By applying the K-H interpolation first in the sub-rule bases and then in the meta-level, the formula for hierarchically structured rule bases becomes:

$$b^*_{ij} = \frac{\sum_{i \in I} \sum_{j \in I_j} h_i h_{ij} b_{ij}}{\sum_{i \in I} \sum_{j \in I_j} h_i h_{ij}}$$

where h_i gives the similarity to the i'th rule in the meta-level, while h_{ij} is the similarity (inverse distance) between the corresponding projection of the antecedent and the antecedent of the j-th rule in the i-th sub- rule base.

Note that in order to apply the interpolation algorithm in hierarchical rule base, the consequents in the sub-rule base level must be proper fuzzy sets. In order to ensure this condition a modified version of the K-H interpolation has to be used, for instance MACI, which guarantees the normality of the conclusion. (See [1] for further details.)

4 Conclusion

In this paper we have presented a possible approach to deal with the typical, comlpex problems of TSS. Some of these problems suggest the usefulness of interpolation techniques, others lead to the idea of using hierarchical structures.

But the problem as a whole justifies the use of hierarchical rule-base systems, as presented in this paper, technique that mihgt handle a whole range of the so far unmanaged difficulties, specific to this domain. However, some aspects are still a matter of further research, as it is, for example, the use of both numerical and categorical data, or the best choice of the inputs for the upper and lower- level input dimensions of the hierarchy.

5 Acknowledgement

This research is supported by the Hungarian Scientific Research Fund Grants T034233 and T034212, IKTA 00207/2001, NKFP-2/0015/2002.

References

1. P. Baranyi , T. D. Gedeon and L. T. Kóczy, A general interpolation technique in fuzzy rule bases with arbitrary membership functions. Proc. of the IEEE Int. Conf. on System Man and Cybernetics (IEEE-SMC'96), Beijing, p. 510-515.1998.
2. D. Dubois, H. Prade, Fuzzy Sets, Probability and measurement, European J. of Operational Research, 40, p. 135-154, 1989
3. G. J. Klir, B. Yuan, Fuzzy Sets and Fuzzy Logic: Theory and Applications
4. L. T. Kóczy and K. Hirota, Ordering, distance and closeness of fuzzy sets. Fuzzy Sets and Systems 60, 281-293, 1993
5. L. T. Kóczy and K. Hirota, Approximate reasoning by linear rule interpolation and general approximation, Internat. J. Approx. Reason. 9, p. 197-225, 1993
6. L. T. Kóczy, L. Muresan, D. Tikk, Fuzzy systems with interpolation. An overview, IFSA/NAFIPS, Vancouver, 2001
7. L. Raman, Fundamentals of Telecommunications Network Management, 1999
8. D. Tikk and P. Baranyi, Comprehensive analysis of a new fuzzy rule interpolation method, IEEE Trans. on Fuzzy Systems 8 (3), p. 281-296,2000
9. H. Wang, Telecommunications Network Management, 1999

On Algebraic Operations on Fuzzy Reals

Witold Kosiński[1], Piotr Prokopowicz[2], and Dominik Ślęzak[1]

[1] Polish–Japanese Institute of Information Technology
ul. Koszykowa 86 , 02-008 Warszawa
[2] University of Bydgoszcz
Institute of Environmental Mechanics and Applied Computer Science
ul. Chodkiewicza 30, 85-064 Bydgoszcz, Poland
email: wkos@pjwstk.edu.pl, piotrekp@ab-byd.edu.pl, slezak@pjwstk.edu.pl

Abstract. Fuzzy counterpart of real numbers is investigated in order to algorithmise algebraic operations on fuzzy reals. Fuzzy membership functions satisfying conditions similar to the quasi–convexity are discussed. An extra feature, called the orientation of their graph, is added to the definition. Two operations: addition and subtraction between fuzzy numbers are proposed. They are programmed and implemented in the Delphi language for selected types of membership functions.

Keywords: fuzzy sets, fuzzy numbers, algebraic operations, quasi-convexity

1 Introduction

During the last four decades concepts of fuzzy sets and fuzzy logic have been developed and implemented to many industrial applications. Among various fields, the fuzzy logic based system and decision analysis seem to be the most known and common. Linguistic approach, where numbers are replaced by words as independent variables, is of great importance, especially in the applications to control processes.

In real-life problems both parameters and data used in mathematical modeling are vague. The vagueness can be described by fuzzy numbers and fuzzy sets. Fuzzy data analysis – understood in two different ways: the fuzzy analysis of data and the analysis of fuzzy data – requires more than fuzzy logic: it requires fuzzy arithmetic. Its development should be based on a well established theory of fuzzy sets defined on the real axis, in order to build a fuzzy counterpart of real numbers.

In the classical approach for numerical handling of fuzzy quantities the so–called extension principle is of fundamental importance. Formulated by Zadeh [1], [2], it provides a formal apparatus to carry over operations (e.g. arithmetic or algebraic) from sets to fuzzy sets. The commonly accepted theory of fuzzy reals is that set up by Dubois and Prade [3], who proposed a restricted class of membership functions, called (L, R)–numbers. However, if one wants to stay within this class while following the extension principle, approximations of fuzzy functions (and operations) are needed. Such approximations, unfortunately, may lead to large computational errors that cannot be further controlled when applying them repeatedly. Overcoming this drawback could be of a great help, e.g. in constructing fuzzy inference systems [4], fuzzy controllers, not mentioning an effective fuzzy calculus [5].

A number of attempts to introduce a non-standard operations fuzzy on fuzzy numbers has been made [6], [7], [8], [9], [10]. It was noticed that in order to construct operation algorithms for fuzzy numbers an invertibility in a weak sense of fuzzy number's membership functions is required. It turns out to be well modeled within the theory of quasi–convex functions [11]. Algebraic operations on the so-called convex fuzzy numbers, described e.g. by Drewniak [9], have close relations with the interval mathematics and the framework proposed in the present paper.

Comparing with the previous papers [12,13], we add an extra feature characterizing the direction in which the graph of the membership function should be drawn. It enables to cope another drawback, caused by the fact that in that the difference $A - A$ for a convex fuzzy number is usually a fuzzy zero – not the crisp zero. It also provides possibilities of novel interpretations of the fuzzy number based analysis. We introduce new operations of addition and subtraction of fuzzy numbers. They are programmed and implemented in the Delphi language for selected types of membership functions – triangular, trapezoidal and rectangular ones.

2 Definition of fuzzy number

Let us start with crisp or non–fuzzy real numbers. Let $r \in \mathbb{R}$, then its representation in the set–theoretical language is the characteristic function χ_r of the one–element set $\{r\}$, and its the classical definition

$$\chi_r(x) = \begin{cases} 1 \text{ if } & x = r \\ 0 \text{ if } & x \neq r \,. \end{cases} \tag{1}$$

In [12] the set of conditions distinguishing fuzzy membership functions corresponding to fuzzy reals is introduced. They are in some sense weaker than those proposed by Dubois and Prade, however similar to those given by Wagenknecht in [10]. The crucial condition is that assuming quasi-invertibility of membership functions. Thus, let us recall, by following [11], that $f : \mathbb{R} \to \mathbb{R}$ is **strictly quasi-convex**, iff for any $x, y, z \in \mathbb{R}$, $x < y < z$, we have

$$f(x) \leq f(z) \Rightarrow f(y) \leq f(z) \quad \text{and} \quad f(x) < f(z) \Rightarrow f(y) < f(z) \tag{2}$$

Together with the other requirements, the quasi-invertibility property enables to state quite an efficient calculus on fuzzy reals. In order to cope some drawbacks of this approach, we introduce the next feature to the definition of a fuzzy number – its orientation.

Let us consider a piecewise continuous and nonnegative function μ defined on $[a, b]$, where $a \leq b$, $\mu(a) = \mu(b) = 0$. If in $\mathbb{R}^2$ one adds points belonging to the segment $[a, b] \times \{0\}$ to the plot of μ, then the resulting set

$$C(\mu) = \{(x, y) \in \mathbb{R}^2 : y = \mu(x), x \in [a, b]\} \cup [a, b] \times \{0\} \qquad (3)$$

can be treated as a plane closed curve. Such a curve can possess two orientations: **positive** – if together with the increasing parameter of the curve its running point moves counterclockwise (compatible with the orientation of the coordinate vectors), and **negative** – in the opposite case. Fig. 1 shows an example of a curve with positive orientation.

By a **fuzzy number** we mean a triple $A = (\mathbb{R}, \mu, \mathsf{s})$, where $\mathsf{s} \in \{-1, 0, 1\}$ denotes the orientation. We distinguish two types of such numbers:

- **crisp** $A = (\mathbb{R}, \mu, \mathsf{s})$, where $\mathsf{s} = 0$ and μ is the characteristic function χ_r of a one–element set $\{r\}$, $r \in \mathbb{R}$.
- **genuinely fuzzy** $A = (\mathbb{R}, \mu, \mathsf{s})$, where $\mathsf{s} \in \{-1, 1\}$ corresponds to the orientation of C_μ and μ satisfies the following conditions: (1) μ is normal, i.e. $1 \in \mu(\mathbb{R})$, (2) the support of μ is a bounded interval, (3) $-\mu$ is strictly quasi–convex.

According to the fundamental theorem for strictly quasi–convex functions [11] fuzzy numbers are quasi-invertible, i.e. if support of A, dented by supp A is the interval (l_A, p_A) then there exist two points $1_A^-, 1_A^+ \in (l_A, p_A)$ such that μ is invertible (increasing) on $(l_A, 1_A^-)$, invertible (decreasing) on $(1_A^+, p_A)$, and constantly equal to 1 (because of normality) on $[1_A^-, 1_A^+]$.

The above function μ is called the **membership function** of fuzzy number A, and denoted by μ_A. We will also use the orientation function, denoted with the same letter s, i.e $\mathsf{s}(A) \in \{-1, 0, 1\}$. For simplicity, we will call $\mathsf{s}(A)$ the **orientation of fuzzy number** A.

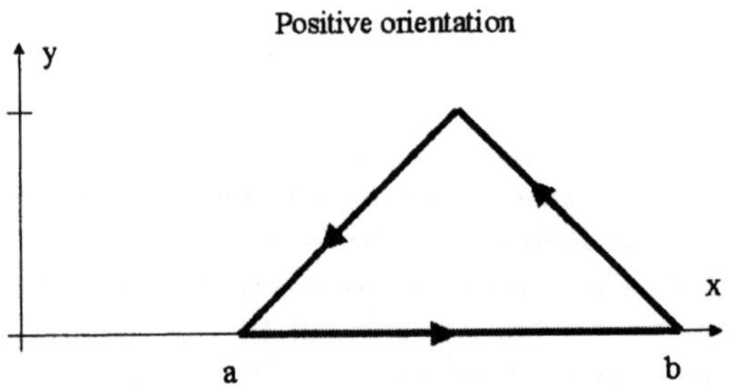

Fig. 1. Positive orientation of the curve of a triangular membership function

3 Fuzzy membership curves

The notion of a fuzzy number can be reformulated in terms of tuples $A = (C, \mathsf{s})$, for the closed curves. Because of the lack of space, let us express this idea in the following, a bit informal, way. Consider arbitrary $\mathcal{C} \subseteq \mathbb{R}^2$, which can be written as

$$\mathcal{C} = [l_A, p_A] \times \{0\} \cup [1_A^-, 1_A^+] \times \{1\} \cup \text{up}(\mathcal{C}) \cup \text{down}(\mathcal{C}) \tag{4}$$

where $\text{up}(\mathcal{C}), \text{down}(\mathcal{C}) \subseteq \mathbb{R}^2$ are the plots of some strictly monotonic functions. Abbreviations up and down do not correspond to the fact whether a given functions is increasing or decreasing but to the orientation of $A = (\mathcal{C}, \mathsf{s})$. Actually, they label the ascending and descending parts of the oriented curve. At Fig. 1, for instance, $\text{up}(\mathcal{C})$ corresponds to the decreasing part of membership function and $\text{down}(\mathcal{C})$ – to the increasing one.

In order to obtain a compact interpretation of both fuzzy and crisp reals, let $\mathcal{C}$ allow to take the form of $\mathcal{C}_r = r \times [0,1]$, by putting

$$l_A = 1_A^- = 1_A^+ = p_A = r \quad \text{and} \quad \text{up}(\mathcal{C}) = \text{down}(\mathcal{C}) = r \times [0,1] \tag{5}$$

Obviously, it corresponds to the function $\mu = \chi_r$ and – because of coincidence of up and down parts – should be labeled with neutral orientation $\mathsf{s} = 0$.

We call such interpreted subsets $\mathcal{C} \subseteq \mathbb{R}^2$ the **membership curves** of fuzzy numbers A, and denote them by $\mathcal{C}_A$. One can see that the obtained family of membership curves is richer than the family of fuzzy reals considered in the previous section. Actually, that former would be to poor to represent all possible results of arithmetic operations introduced below.

4 Arithmetic operations on fuzzy numbers

We are going to introduce new operations of addition and subtraction of fuzzy numbers. Let us, however, begin with an easier case, where one of fuzzy numbers is a crisp real. Let fuzzy number A and $r \in \mathbb{R}$ be given. For any $x \in \mathbb{R}$, we put:

Addition:

$$(A + \chi_r)(x) = A(x - r) \tag{6}$$

Subtraction:

$$(A - \chi_r)(x) = A(x + r) \tag{7}$$

The resulting fuzzy numbers have the same orientation as that of A, i.e.:

$$\mathsf{s}(\mathsf{A} + \chi_r) = \mathsf{s}(\mathsf{A} - \chi_r) = \mathsf{s}(\mathsf{A}) \tag{8}$$

Although in this particular paper we are going to discuss only addition and subtraction between fuzzy reals, the following is worth mentioning as well:

Multiplication:

$$(A \cdot \chi_r)(x) = A(x/r) \text{ iff } r \neq 0 \text{ and } 0 \text{ otherwise} \tag{9}$$

Division:

$$(A \div \chi_r)(x) = A(xr) \text{ for } x \in \mathbb{R} \text{ and } r \in \mathbb{R}^{++} = (0, \infty). \tag{10}$$

Here orientation of A changes according to the following law:

$$\mathsf{s}(\mathsf{A} \cdot \chi_\mathsf{r}) = \mathsf{sign}(\mathsf{r}) \cdot \mathsf{s}(\mathsf{A}) \tag{11}$$

where sign : $\mathbb{R} \to \{-1, 0, 1\}$ is the standard signum function. In particular, by using $r = -1$, we can relate to each A its opposite fuzzy number, which is a fuzzy number with support and orientation stated as follows:

$$\text{supp}(-A) = (-p_A, -l_A) \qquad \mathsf{s}(-\mathsf{A}) = -\mathsf{s}(\mathsf{A}) \tag{12}$$

Function $-A$ is the mirror reflection of A with respect to y, while the orientation of the curve $\mathcal{C}_{-A}$ is opposite to that of $\mathcal{C}_A$.

Now, let us consider the general case of the addition operation. In order to make it less complicated, let us note that it is enough to perform the addition operation on the strictly monotonic parts of the membership curves of fuzzy numbers. This is because the constant parts $[l_A, p_A] \times \{0\}$ and $[1_A^-, 1_A^+] \times \{1\}$ can be uniquely recovered by drawing connections between the points in which the plots of monotonic subfunctions of $\mathcal{C}_A$ reach the levels of 0 and 1, respectively.

By **the sum $A + B$ of two fuzzy numbers A and B**, we mean fuzzy real C with the membership curve satisfying

$$\begin{aligned} (C|\text{up}(C))^{-1} &= (A|\text{up}(A))^{-1} + (B|\text{up}(B))^{-1} \\ (C|\text{down}(C))^{-1} &= (A|\text{down}(A))^{-1} + (B|\text{down}(B))^{-1} \end{aligned} \tag{13}$$

and with orientation induced by local orientations of up(C) and down(C).

Let us consider some special cases to illustrate the meaning of the above definition. We begin with the case of membership function of B stated as χ_r, $r \in \mathbb{R}$. Then we obtain

$$(B|\text{up}(B))^{-1} = (B|\text{down}(B))^{-1} = [0, 1] \times r \tag{14}$$

Thus, the whole operation corresponds to addition of r to all values of inverses of $A|\text{up}(A)$ and $A|\text{down}(A)$. Obviously, orientation of A remains unchanged, because such a shift does not affect the shape of $\mathcal{C}_A$.

Another special case is illustrated at Fig. 2. Fuzzy number $C = A + B$ is there obtained for triangular numbers of the same orientation. In this case, by putting $1_X = 1_X^+ = 1_X^-$, for $X = A, B, C$, membership function of C is a prolongation of functions defined over intervals $(l_C, 1_C)$ and $(1_C, p_C)$, such that

$$\begin{aligned} (C|(l_C, 1_C))^{-1} &= (A|(l_A, 1_A))^{-1} + (B|(l_B, 1_B))^{-1} \\ (C|(1_C, p_C))^{-1} &= (A|(1_A, p_A))^{-1} + (B|(1_B, p_B))^{-1} \end{aligned} \tag{15}$$

where $l_C = l_A + l_B$, $1_C = 1_A + 1_B$ and $p_C = p_A + p_B$. Moreover, orientation of C is the same as that of A and B.

Now, let us define **the subtraction $A - B$ of two fuzzy numbers A and B**, by such fuzzy number C that

$$C = A + (-B) \quad \text{where} \quad -B = B \cdot \chi_{-1} \tag{16}$$

As the last example in this section, let us claim that for each fuzzy real A one obtains

$$A - A = A + (-A) = \chi_0 \tag{17}$$

This is obviously true for A corresponding to a characteristic functions χ_r, because then $-A$ corresponds to χ_{-r}. Now, let us recall that if A is a non-crisp real, then $-A$ has the opposite orientation. In a more general case, if numbers A and B have opposite orientations, the sum $C = A + B$ satisfies equalities

$$\begin{aligned} \left(C|(l_C, 1_C^-)\right)^{-1} &= \left(A|(l_A, 1_A^-)\right)^{-1} + \left(B|(1_B^+, p_B)\right)^{-1} \\ \left(C|(1_C^+, p_C)\right)^{-1} &= \left(A|(1_A^+, p_A)\right)^{-1} + \left(B|(l_B, 1_B^-)\right)^{-1} \end{aligned} \tag{18}$$

where $l_C = l_A + p_B$, $1_C^- = 1_A^- + 1_B^+$, $1_C^+ = 1_A^+ + 1_B^-$, $p_C = p_A + l_B$. Orientation of C is positive iff the line up(C) is above the interval $(1_C^+, p_C)$, negative it is above $(l_C, 1_C^-)$ and neutral iff $l_C = 1_C^- = 1_C^+ = p_C$.

One can see that if we substitute $B = -A$ to the above formulas, then $l_C = 1_C^- = 1_C^+ = p_C = 0$, so indeed, the result is χ_0, with orientation $\mathsf{s}(C) = 0$. One can also notice that such a definition of subtraction does not lead to errors while performing longer sequences of algebraic operations. In particular, one can see at Fig. 2 that $(A + B) - B = A$.

5 Conclusions

In the present paper the next modifications of the two algebraic operation on fuzzy numbers have been proposed, by introducing the next feature to any fuzzy number, namely the orientation of the graph of its membership function. In this way a fuzzy number should be regarded as a pair: membership function and orientation. Moreover, four algebraic operations between fuzzy and crisp numbers have been defined. The operation of subtraction of two fuzzy numbers lastly defined does fulfill the requirement $A - A = \chi_0$, in contrast to the previous definition which was giving rather $A - A = O$ where O is a fuzzy number "around zero". We see that the present definitions solves next drawbacks (cf. Fig. 2.) of the operations based on the Zadeh's extension principle. In the further publication we will try to define the next algebraic operations.

Acknowledgements The work on the paper has been conducted in the framework of the internal research grant No.19/4 of PJWSTK and an internal research project of IMSiIS of Bydgoszcz University, both partially supported by KBN.

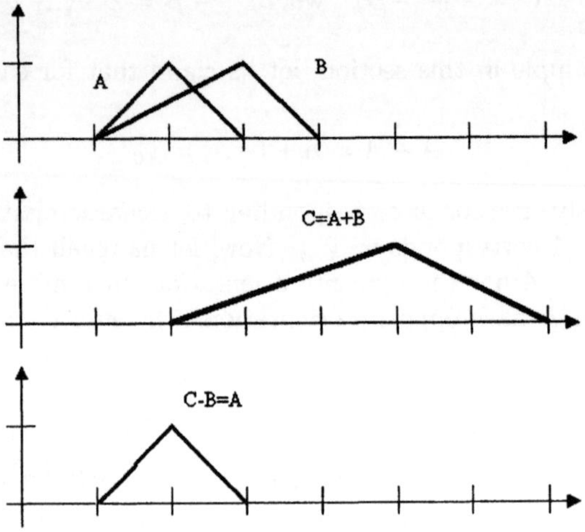

Fig. 2. Operations based on present definitions

References

1. Zadeh L.A., Fuzzy sets, *Information and Control*, **8** (1965) 338-353.
2. Zadeh L.A., The concept of a linguistic variable and its application to approximate reasoning, Part I, *Information Sciences*, **8** (1975) 199-249.
3. Dubois D., Prade H., Operations on fuzzy numbers, *Int. J. System Science*, **9** (1978) 576-578.
4. Kosiński W., Weigl M ., General mapping approximation problems solving by neural networks and fuzzy inference systems, *Systems Analysis Modelling Simulation*, **30/1** (1998) 11-28.
5. Weigl M., Neural networks and fuzzy inference systems in approximation problems (in Polish), Ph. D. Thesis , IPPT PAN, Warszawa (1995).
6. Sanchez E., Solutions of fuzzy equations with extended operations, *Fuzzy Sets and Systems*, **12** (1984) 237-248.
7. Czogała E., Pedrycz W., Elements and methods of fuzzy set theory (in Polish), PWN, Warszawa (1985).
8. Klir G.J., Fuzzy arithmetic with requisite constraints, *Fuzzy Sets and Systems*, **91** (1997) 165-175.
9. Drewniak J., Fuzzy numbers (in Polish), in: *Zbiory rozmyte i ich zastosowania*, J. Chojcan, J. Łęski (eds.), Wydawnictwo Politechniki Śląskiej, Gliwice (2001) 103-129.

10. Wagenknecht M., On the approximate treatment of fuzzy arithmetics by inclusion, linear regression and information content estimation, in: *Zbiory rozmyte i ich zastosowania*, J. Chojcan, J. Łęski (eds.), Wydawnictwo Politechniki Śląskiej, Gliwice (2001) 291-310.
11. Martos B., Nonlinear Programming - Theory and methods, (Polish translation of the English original published by Akadémiai Kiadó, Budapest, 1975) PWN, Warszawa (1983).
12. Kosiński W., Piechór K., Prokopowicz P., Tyburek K., On algorithmic approach to operations on fuzzy reals, in: *Methods of Artificial Intelligence in Mechanics and Mechanical Engineering*, T. Burczyński, W. Cholewa (eds.), PACM, Gliwice (2001) 95-98.
13. Kosiński W., Słysz P., Fuzzy reals and their quotient space with algebraic operations, *Bull. Polish Acad. Scien., Sèr. Techn. Scien.*, **41/3** (1993) 285-295.

Formal Fuzzy Logic and Its Use in Modeling of Vagueness and Computing with Words

Vilém Novák

University of Ostrava
Institute for Research and Applications of Fuzzy Modeling
30. dubna 22,
701 03 Ostrava 1, Czech Republic

Abstract. In this paper, a brief overview of fundamental concepts of the formal fuzzy logic are presented and some of its applications are pointed out.

1 Introduction

The last decade of the previous century have brought fuzzy logic to its maturity state. It has been demonstrated that fuzzy logic is much more than the "poor man's logic" — it is a well established sound formal system capable of explanation and modeling of a lot of phenomena in which vagueness plays a significant role. Moreover, it demonstrated its usefulness in the development of new approximation methods for continuous functions, clearly being closely connected with the artificial neural nets. For the applications, the most important is the predicate version of fuzzy logic and so, we will focus on it in this paper.

In general, fuzzy logic has profiled itself into a fuzzy logic in narrow sense (FLn) and that in broader sense (FLb). Informally, FLn is a special many-valued logic whose aim is to provide means, which can be used for modeling of various aspects of the vagueness phenomenon. The main characteristics of the latter is imperceptible change from its presence to non-presence. This can mathematically be captured by continuity. Therefore, it seems reasonable to consider structures of truth values based on the interval of real numbers $[0, 1]$ with continuous operations. The FLb logic is an extension of FLn towards capturing the meaning of some expressions of natural language and reasoning based on them.

A significant contribution to the metamathematics of fuzzy logic has been given by P. Hájek in [5]. According to him, we can distinguish three fundamental logics, namely Łukasiewicz, Gödel and product ones, all three of them being special cases of the so called basic fuzzy logic (BL-logic for short). All these logics have classical syntax which means that the syntax of classical predicate logic is used in fuzzy logic as well, possibly extended by some new specific connectives. Of course, the interpretation of all the connectives is based on the assumed structure of truth values.

This paper is a brief overview of some of the fundamental concepts and also of the potential of fuzzy logic for applications.

2 Fuzzy logic in narrow sense

2.1 Truth values

The set of truth values is in general considered to be a residuated lattice

$$\mathcal{L} = \langle L, \vee, \wedge, \otimes, \rightarrow, \mathbf{0}, \mathbf{1} \rangle,$$

where $\vee$ and $\wedge$ are lattice operations, $\mathbf{0}, \mathbf{1}$ are the smallest and the greatest elements $\langle L, \otimes, \mathbf{1} \rangle$ is a commutative monoid and the operations $\otimes$ (product) and $\rightarrow$ (residuum) fulfil the adjunction condition

$$a \otimes b \leq c \quad \text{iff} \quad a \leq b \rightarrow c \tag{1}$$

for all $a, b, c \in L$.

A more specific case is a BL-algebra, which is a residuated lattice fulfilling the conditions of prelinearity ($(a \rightarrow b) \vee (b \rightarrow a) = \mathbf{1}$) and divisibility ($a \otimes (a \rightarrow b) = a \wedge b$ for all $a, b \in L$).

Recall that a t-norm $\otimes$ is a binary operation on $[0, 1]$ which is commutative, associative, monotonous and 1 is a boundary element. The most important example of BL-algebra is obtained when $L = [0, 1]$ (unit interval of reals) and $\otimes$ is a continuous t-norm. Recall that due to famous Ling's representation, every continuous t-norm is isomorphic either to minimum, or product, or Łukasiewicz conjunction (2), or it is a "mixture" of some of them (see, e.g. [6]).

The richest structure is MV-algebra introduced by C. C. Chang in [2] and further intensively studied (cf. [7]). This is a generalization of boolean algebra. The most important example is the Łukasiewicz MV-algebra

$$\mathcal{L}_{\text{Ł}} = \langle [0, 1], \otimes, \oplus, \neg, \mathbf{0}, \mathbf{1} \rangle$$

where

$$a \otimes b = 0 \vee (a + b - 1), \tag{2}$$
$$a \oplus b = 1 \wedge (a + b), \tag{3}$$
$$\neg a = 1 - a, \tag{4}$$

$a, b \in [0, 1]$. Moreover, we define the residuation operation by $a \rightarrow b = 1 \wedge (1 - a + b)$ (i.e. MV-algebra is also a residuated lattice) .

2.2 Traditional and evaluated syntax

There are a lot of various kinds of logics based on the residuated lattice (monoidal, MTL-, SMTL-, BL-, SBL-, Gödel, product, Łukasiewicz, etc. logics). Below, we will mention only the basic fuzzy logic (briefly BL-logic). All these logics have traditional syntax, i.e. they have classical concepts of term and formula (possibly with some new connectives) and further, logical axioms, deduction rules of modus ponens and generalization and provability and formal theory are introduced in a standard way.

The semantics is nonstandard since the formulas are evaluated by truth values taken from L. Let us stress that all the mentioned logics are complete in the sense that a formula of a given theory is provable iff it is true in the degree $\mathbf{1}$ in all its models).

A more radical departure from classical logic is FLn with evaluated syntax, known also under the name *Pavelka logic.* In this logic, each formula is on syntactical level evaluated by some value $a \in L$, i.e. we may consider *fuzzy sets of axioms.* Then, we can introduce the concept of evaluated proof (a sequence of evaluated formulas) and *provability degree* of a formula in the given fuzzy theory. It can be demonstrated that this is a generalization of the classical concept of provability.

We will present this logic in more details below. Let us remark that FLn with evaluated syntax possesses a lot of properties which are generalizations of the corresponding properties of classical logic. Their proofs are mostly non-trivial and more complex but, besides other outcomes, they enable us to view classical logic from different point of view.

2.3 Basic fuzzy logic

This logic has been proposed by P. Hájek in [5], who established its syntax and semantics, characterized its main properties and proved its completeness.

A *predicate language* J of BL-logic consists of *predicates* $P, Q, \ldots$, each together with its *arity* and *object constants* $c, d, \ldots$.

Logical symbols are *object variables* $x, y, \ldots$, *connectives* $\&, \Rightarrow$, *logical constants* $\bot, \top$ (falsity and truth) and *quantifiers* $\forall, \exists$. *Terms* are object variables and object constants.

Atomic formulas have the form $P(t_1, \ldots, t_n)$ where P is a predicate of arity n and $t_1, \ldots, t_n$ are terms. If A, B are formulas and x is an object variable then $A \Rightarrow B$, $A \,\&\, B$, $(\forall x)B$, $(\exists x)A$ $\bot$, $\top$ are formulas. Each formula results from atomic formulas by iterated use of this rule. The set of all formulas for the given language J is denoted by F_J.

The following formulas are (schemes of) logical axioms of the BL-logic:

(A1) $(A \Rightarrow B) \Rightarrow ((B \Rightarrow C) \Rightarrow (A \Rightarrow C))$
(A2) $(A \,\&\, B) \Rightarrow A$
(A3) $(A \,\&\, B) \Rightarrow (B \,\&\, A)$

(A4) $(A \& (A \Rightarrow B)) \Rightarrow (B \& (B \Rightarrow A))$
(A5a) $(A \Rightarrow (B \Rightarrow C)) \Rightarrow ((A \& B) \Rightarrow C)$
(A5b) $((A \& B) \Rightarrow C) \Rightarrow (A \Rightarrow (B \Rightarrow C))$
(A6) $((A \Rightarrow B) \Rightarrow C) \Rightarrow (((B \Rightarrow A) \Rightarrow C) \Rightarrow C)$
(A7) $\bot \Rightarrow A$
($\forall$1) $(\forall x)A(x) \Rightarrow A(t)$ (t substitutable for x in $A(x)$)
($\exists$1) $A(t) \Rightarrow (\exists x)A(x)$ (t substitutable for x in $A(x)$)
($\forall$2) $(\forall x)(A \Rightarrow B) \Rightarrow (A \Rightarrow (\forall x)B)$ (x not free in A)
($\exists$2) $(\forall x)(A \Rightarrow B) \Rightarrow ((\exists x)A \Rightarrow B)$ (x not free in B)
($\forall$3) $(\forall x)(A \vee B) \Rightarrow (A \vee (\forall x)B)$ (x not free in A)

Further connectives are defined as follows:

$$\begin{aligned}
A \wedge B &:= A \& (A \Rightarrow B), \\
A \vee B &:= ((A \Rightarrow B) \Rightarrow B) \wedge ((B \Rightarrow A) \Rightarrow A), \\
\neg A &:= A \Rightarrow \bot, \\
A \nabla B &:= \neg(\neg A \& \neg B) \\
A \Leftrightarrow B &:= (A \Rightarrow B) \& (B \Rightarrow A), \\
A^n &:= \underbrace{A \& A \& \cdots \& A}_{n-\text{times}} .(n\text{-fold conjunction})
\end{aligned}$$

The *deduction rules* of BL-logic are modus ponens (from A and $A \Rightarrow B$ infer B) and generalization (from A infer $(\forall x)A$). Given this, the notions of a *proof* and of a *provable formula* in BL are defined in the obvious way.

A *theory* over BL is a set of formulas. A *proof* in a theory T is a sequence $A_1, \ldots, A_n$ of formulas whose each member is either an axiom of BL-logic or a member of T (special axiom) or follows from some preceding members of the sequence using the above deduction rule.

$T \vdash A$ means that A is *provable* in T, i.e. is the last member of of a proof in T. The deduction theorem for BL reads as follows:

Theorem 1 (Deduction theorem). *Let T be a theory and let A be a closed formula. Then to every formula $B \in F_{J(T)}$ there is $n \geq 1$ such that*

$$T \cup \{A\} \vdash B \quad \textit{iff} \quad T \vdash A^n \Rightarrow B.$$

Let $\mathcal{J}$ be a predicate language and let $\mathcal{L}$ be a BL-algebra. An *$\mathcal{L}$-structure* for $\mathcal{J}$ is

$$\mathcal{M} = \langle M, (r_P)_P, (m_c)_c \rangle$$

where $M \neq \emptyset$, $r_P \subsetapprox M^n$ is an n-ary fuzzy relation assigned to each n-ary predicate P and m_c is an element of M assigned to object constant c. *Values* of terms t in $\mathcal{M}$ are defined in an ordinary way. Values of formulas are defined as follows:

$$\begin{aligned}
\mathcal{M}(P(t_1,\dots,t_n)) &= r_P(\mathcal{M}(t_1),\dots,\mathcal{M}(t_n)),\\
\mathcal{M}(A \Rightarrow B) &= \mathcal{M}(A) \rightarrow \mathcal{M}(B),\\
\mathcal{M}(A \,\&\, B) &= \mathcal{M}(A) \otimes \mathcal{M}(B),\\
\mathcal{M}(\bot) &= 0; \qquad \mathcal{M}(\top) = 1,\\
\mathcal{M}((\forall x)A) &= \inf\{\mathcal{M}(A(v/x)) \mid v \in M\},\\
\mathcal{M}((\forall x)A) &= \sup\{\mathcal{M}(A(v/x)) \mid v \in M\}.
\end{aligned}$$

provided the infimum/supremum exists in the sense of $\mathbf{L}$. An $\mathcal{L}$-structure $\mathcal{M}$ is a standard model of a theory T if $\mathcal{L}$ is a BL-algebra on $[0,1]$ for some continuous t-norm $\otimes$.

Theorem 2 (Completeness). *Let T be a theory of BL-fuzzy predicate logic. For each formula A, T proves A iff $\mathcal{M}(A) = 1$ for each standard model of T.*

According to this theorem, which is a strengthening due to Cignoli et al. [3] of the original result of P. Hájek, BL-fuzzy logic is a general logic of fuzzy set theory, because the continuity assumption complies with the idea that fuzzy set theory is a mathematical theory of vagueness.

2.4 Fuzzy logic with evaluated syntax

The principal feature of this logic is the departure of its syntax from the traditional conception by admitting that formulas may be evaluated by values taken from the same set as is the set of truth values. Thus, we work with the concept of *evaluated formula* which is a couple ${}^{a}/A$ where A is a formula and $a \in L$. This can be viewed as a generalization of the classical concept of provability in logic, which then becomes its special case depending on the assumed structure of truth values. The latter is, in general, supposed to be the Łukasiewicz algebra $\mathcal{L}_{\mathrm{L}}$. For the detailed presentation of fuzzy logic with evaluated syntax — see [12].

Syntax. The language of this logic, J, is essentially the same as for BL-logic with one exception: it contains also logical (truth) constants being names of all the other truth values from L (besides falsity and truth). We will denote them by $\mathbf{a}$, $a \in L$.

The inference rules deal with evaluated formulas and have the following form: *modus ponens*

$$r_{MP}: \frac{{}^{a}/A, {}^{b}/A \Rightarrow B}{a \otimes {}^{b}/B}, \tag{5}$$

generalization

$$r_G: \frac{{}^{a}/A}{{}^{a}/(\forall x)A}, \tag{6}$$

logical constant introduction

$$r_{LC}: \frac{a/A}{a \to a/\mathbf{a} \Rightarrow A}. \tag{7}$$

The numerator of each of this scheme contains evaluated formulas being the hypotheses and the denominator contains a conclusion being an evaluated formula whose evaluation is computed from the evaluations of the hypotheses. Note that the rule r_{LC} makes possible to identify the evaluated formula with the formula $\mathbf{a} \Rightarrow A$.

An evaluated formal proof of a formula A from a fuzzy set $X \underset{\sim}{\subset} F_J$ of axioms is a finite sequence of evaluated formulas

$$w := a_0/A_0,\ a_1/A_1, \ldots,\ a_n/A_n \tag{8}$$

such that $A_n := A$ and for each $i \le n$, $a_i/A_i := X(A_i)/A_i$ where X is either a fuzzy set of logical or special axioms, or there is an inference rule r whose conclusion is an evaluated formula a_i/A_i from some hypotheses being evaluated formulas preceding it. The evaluation a_n of the last member in (8) is the *value* of the evaluated proof w and is denoted by $\mathrm{Val}(w)$.

Axioms in the graded formal systems are sets of evaluated formulas, or, in other words, *fuzzy sets of formulas*. We may thus introduce a formal fuzzy theory T in the language J of FLn, which is a triple

$$T = \langle \mathrm{LAx}, \mathrm{SAx}, R \rangle$$

where $\mathrm{LAx} \underset{\sim}{\subset} F_J$ is a fuzzy set of logical axioms, $\mathrm{SAx} \underset{\sim}{\subset} F_J$ is a fuzzy set of special axioms, and R is a set of inference rules (which contain, at least the above three ones).

A formula A is a theorem in the degree a (or provable in the degree a) in the fuzzy theory T, in symbols $T \vdash_a A$, if

$$a = \bigvee \{\mathrm{Val}(w) \mid w \text{ is a proof of } A \text{ from } \mathrm{LAx} \cup \mathrm{SAx}\}. \tag{9}$$

Note that unlike the classical syntax where finding one finite proof is sufficient, the situation here is not so simple. In general, a sequence (possibly infinite) of finite proofs must be considered, because maximum of their values does not need to exist, and so, we cannot confine ourselves to one proof only.

Theorem 3 (deduction theorem). *Let T be a fuzzy theory and A be a closed formula. Then to every formula $B \in F_{J(T)}$ there is $n \ge 1$ such that*

$$T \vdash_a A^n \Rightarrow B \quad \textit{iff} \quad T \cup \{\mathbf{1}/A\} \vdash_a B.$$

Logical axioms.

(R1) $A \Rightarrow (B \Rightarrow A)$.
(R2) $(A \Rightarrow B) \Rightarrow ((B \Rightarrow C) \Rightarrow (A \Rightarrow C))$.
(R3) $(\neg B \Rightarrow \neg A) \Rightarrow (A \Rightarrow B)$.
(R4) $((A \Rightarrow B) \Rightarrow B) \Rightarrow ((B \Rightarrow A) \Rightarrow A)$.
(B1) $(\mathbf{a} \Rightarrow \mathbf{b}) \Leftrightarrow (\overline{\mathbf{a} \to \mathbf{b}})$
where $\overline{\mathbf{a} \to \mathbf{b}}$ denotes the logical constant (atomic formula) for the truth value $a \to b$ when a and b are given.
(T1) $(\forall x)A \Rightarrow A_x[t]$
for any term t which is substitutible for x.
(T2) $(\forall x)(A \Rightarrow B) \Rightarrow (A \Rightarrow (\forall x)B)$
provided that x is not free in A.

The fuzzy set LAx of logical axioms is

$$\mathrm{LAx}(A) = \begin{cases} a \in L & \text{if } A := \mathbf{a}, \\ \mathbf{1} & \text{if } A \text{ has some of the forms (R1)–(R4), (B1), (T1)–(T2),} \\ \mathbf{0} & \text{otherwise.} \end{cases}$$

Semantics. This is defined in the same way as in the case of BL-logic. As a special case, if $\mathbf{a}$ is a logical constant for some $a \in L$ then $\mathcal{M}(\mathbf{a}) = a$.

The structure $\mathcal{M}$ is a *model* of the fuzzy theory T, $\mathcal{M} \models T$, if $\mathrm{SAx}(A) \leq \mathcal{M}(A)$ holds for all formulas $A \in F_J$.

Given a fuzzy theory T, we say that A is true in the degree a in the fuzzy theory T, in symbols $T \models_a A$, if

$$a = \bigwedge\{\mathcal{D}(A) \mid \mathcal{D} \models T\}. \tag{10}$$

The following theorem is a generalization of the Gödel completeness theorem for classical logic.

Theorem 4 (Completeness theorem I).

$$T \vdash_a A \quad \textit{iff} \quad T \models_a A$$

holds for every formula $A \in F_J$ and every consistent fuzzy theory T.

Let us remark that FLn with evaluated syntax is representable inside Łukasiewicz logic, and also vice-versa, Łukasiewicz logic can be understood as a special case of the former.

3 About applications of fuzzy logic

3.1 Sorites paradox in fuzzy logic

The following theorem is an application of the completeness theorem to the solution of the sorites paradox in fuzzy logic.

Theorem 5. *Let T be a fuzzy theory in which all Peano axioms are accepted in the degree 1. Furthermore, let $1 \geq \varepsilon > 0$ and $\mathbb{FN} \notin J(T)$ be a new predicate. Then the fuzzy theory*

$$T^+ = T \cup \{^1/\mathbb{FN}(0), {}^{1-\varepsilon}/(\forall x)(\mathbb{FN}(x) \Rightarrow \mathbb{FN}(x+1)), {}^1/(\exists x)\neg\mathbb{FN}(x)\}$$

is a conservative extension of T.

Let us put $\mathbb{FN}(x) :=$ "x is small". Then, by this theorem the theory of natural numbers in fuzzy logic can be extended by this predicate in such a way that the inference "if x is small then $x+1$ is also small" is practically valid and at the same time, the axiom $^1/(\exists x)\neg\mathbb{FN}(x)$ stating that "there are numbers not being small" does not cause a contradiction (this is impossible in classical logic).

3.2 Approximation abilities of fuzzy logic

Fuzzy logic is a powerful theory, using which the problem of approximation of functions can be studied. A significant contribution in this direction has been given by I. Perfilieva (e.g. [14,15]). This is possible either in BL-logic in simpler form, or we can extend FLn (with evaluated syntax) by a special product conjunction connective $\&_{\Pi}$ interpreted using an ordinary product.

We introduce the following three special formulas. Let $P_1, \ldots, P_k$ be unary predicate symbols and $E_{i_1 \ldots i_n}$, $1 \leq i_j \leq k$, $1 \leq j \leq n$, $n \geq 1$, be closed instances of some formula. The *disjunctive normal form* is

$$\mathrm{DNF}(x_1, \ldots, x_n) = \bigvee_{i_1, \ldots, i_n = 1}^{k} (P_{i_1}(x_1) \,\&\cdots\&\, P_{i_n}(x_n) \,\&\, E_{i_1 \ldots i_n}), \tag{11}$$

the *conjunctive normal form* is

$$\mathrm{CNF}(x_1, \ldots, x_n) = \bigwedge_{i_1, \ldots, i_n = 1}^{k} (P_{i_1}(x_1) \,\&\cdots\&\, P_{i_n}(x_n) \to E_{i_1 \ldots i_n}). \tag{12}$$

and the *additive normal form*

$$\mathrm{ANF}(x_1, \ldots, x_n) = \mathop{\nabla}_{i_1, \ldots, i_n = 1}^{k} ((P_{i_1}(x_1) \,\&_{\text{Ł}} \cdots \&_{\text{Ł}}\, P_{i_n}(x_n)) \,\&_{\Pi}\, E_{i_1 \ldots i_n}). \tag{13}$$

where $\&_{\text{Ł}}$ denotes Łukasiewicz conjunction and $\&_{\Pi}$ the product conjunction.

Furthermore, we have to introduce also a special binary predicate $\approx$ representing a fuzzy equality. Using it, a pseudometric can be introduced in every model. Finally, let $A(x_1, \ldots, x_n)$ be a, so called, extensional formula (informally, this means that it represents a continuous function in every structure with respect to topology generated by the mentioned pseudometric).

Theorem 6. *Let T be a fuzzy theory, $\mathbf{c}_1, \ldots, \mathbf{c}_k \in J(T)$ be object constants and $A(x_1, \ldots, x_n)$ be extensional. Then*

(a)

$$T \vdash \mathrm{DNF}(x_1, \ldots, x_n) \Rightarrow A(x_1, \ldots, x_n), \tag{14}$$

$$T \vdash A(x_1, \ldots, x_n) \Rightarrow \mathrm{CNF}(x_1, \ldots, x_n) \tag{15}$$

(b)

$$T \vdash \mathrm{DNF}(x_1, \ldots, x_n) \Rightarrow \mathrm{ANF}(x_1, \ldots, x_n) \tag{16}$$

$$T \vdash \mathrm{ANF}(x_1, \ldots, x_n) \Rightarrow \mathrm{CNF}(x_1, \ldots, x_n). \tag{17}$$

This theorem states that every continuous function can be approximated by a function represented by some normal form (whose structure we know) and that ANF can be the best.

I. Perfilieva in [15] has also demonstrated that a single layer network with n inputs and one output can be represented by a formula of fuzzy logic in the additive normal form. Moreover, the previous theorem theoretically substantiates the approximation ability of neural networks.

3.3 Formalization of computing with words in fuzzy logic

Fuzzy logic has abilities to model the meaning of a fragment of natural language consists. This leads to an extension of FLn, which is also referred to as *fuzzy logic in broader sense* (FLb).

The considered fragment of natural language consists of few proper *adjectives*, mostly forming an evaluation linguistic trichotomy of the type "small", "medium" and "big". and *linguistic hedges*, which form a special kind of the so called intensifying adverbs, such as "very, slightly, roughly", etc. These usually belong among *evaluating expressions*, which characterize a position on a bounded ordered scale (usually an interval of some numbers. Sometimes are included also *connectives* "and", "or" and *conditional clause* "if ... then ...".

It is clear that atomic evaluating expressions usually form pairs of antonyms, i.e. the pairs

"nominal adjective — antonym".

Of course, there are a lot of other examples, e.g. "young — old", "ugly — nice", "stupid — clever", etc.

The expressions of the form ⟨noun⟩ is $\mathcal{A}$ where $\mathcal{A}$ is an evaluating expression are called *evaluating predications.*

In the logical analysis of natural language a distinguished role is played by *intension* of a linguistic expression (this can be identified with the property denoted it) and *extension*, which a set of elements determined by an intension, which fall into the meaning of a expression in a *possible world* (a "particular state of affairs" which determine truth of a sentence).

In FLn, intension of a linguistic expression $\mathcal{A}$ can be formalized as follows. First, we assign it a formula $A(x) \in F_J$. Then intension of $\mathcal{A}$ is the set

$$\mathrm{Int}(\mathcal{A}) = \left\{ {}^{a_t}/A_x[t] \,\middle|\, t \in M_J \right\} \tag{18}$$

of evaluated formulas being closed instances of $A(x)$, where M_J is a set of closed terms.

Furthermore, we identify a structure $\mathcal{M}$ for J with a possible world. Then the extension of $\mathcal{A}$ in a given possible world is the fuzzy relation

$$\mathrm{Ext}_{\mathcal{M}}(\mathcal{A}) = \left\{ {}^{\mathcal{M}(A_x[t])}/\mathcal{M}(t) \,\middle|\, t \in M_J \right\}$$

where $\mathcal{M}(t) \in D$ is an interpretation of the terms t in $\mathcal{M}$.

Obviously, using these concepts, we can model the meaning of more complex expressions, and namely of conditional clauses known as fuzzy IF-THEN rules. Moreover, from their intensions we may construct fuzzy theories and thus obtain a mathematical model of natural human deduction, which is based on the use of vague expressions of natural language.

References

1. Black , M.(1937): Vagueness: An Exercise in Logical Analysis, Philosophy of Science 4, 427–455. Reprinted in Int. J. of General Systems 17(1990), 107–128.
2. Chang, C. C.(1958): Algebraic analysis of many valued logics, Trans. AMS, 93, 74–80.
3. Cignoli, R., Esteva, F., Godo, L. and A. Torrens (2000): Basic Fuzzy Logic is the logic of continuous t-norms and their residua. Soft Computing 4, 106–112.
4. Gottwald, S.(2001): A Treatise on Many-Valued Logics. Research Studies Press Ltd., Baldock, Herfordshire, UK.
5. Hájek, P.(1998): Metamathematics of fuzzy logic. Kluwer, Dordrecht.
6. Klement, E. P., Mesiar, R. and E. Pap (2000), Triangular Norms — Basic Properties and Representation Theorems. In [11], 63–81.
7. Mundici, D., Cignoli, R. and D'Ottaviano, I.M.L. (2000): Algebraic foundations of many-valued Reasoning, Kluwer, Dordrecht.
8. Novák, V. (1992): The Alternative Mathematical Model of Linguistic Semantics and Pragmatics. Plenum, New York.
9. Novák, V. (2001): Antonyms and Linguistic Quantifiers in Fuzzy Logic. Fuzzy Sets and Systems 124, 335-351.
10. Novák, V.: Joint consistency of fuzzy theories. Mathematical Logic Quaterly (to appear).
11. Novák, V. and I. Perfilieva (Eds.)(2000): Discovering World With Fuzzy Logic. Springer-Verlag, Heidelberg, (Studies in Fuzziness and Soft Computing, Vol. 57)
12. Novák, V., Perfilieva I. and J. Močkoř (1999): Mathematical Principles of Fuzzy Logic. Kluwer, Boston.

13. Novák, V. and I. Perfilieva (1999): Evaluating Linguistic Expressions and Functional Fuzzy Theories in Fuzzy Logic. In: L. A. Zadeh and J. Kacprzyk (eds.): Computing with Words in Information/Intelligent Systems 1. Springer-Verlag, Heidelberg, 383–406.
14. Perfilieva, I.(2001): Normal Forms for Fuzzy Logic Functions and Their Approximation Ability. Fuzzy Sets and Systems 124, 371–384.
15. Perfilieva, I. (2001): Neural Nets and Normal Forms from Fuzzy Logic Point of View. Neural Network World 6, 627–638.
16. Shoenfield, J. R. (1967): Mathematical Logic. New York: Addison–Wesley.
17. Zadeh, L.A. (1975): The concept of a linguistic variable and its application to approximate reasoning I, II, III, Inf. Sci., 8, 199–257, 301–357; 9, 43–80.

Independent Component Analysis for Simultaneous Active Noise Canceling and Blind Signal Separation

Hyung Min Park[1], Tae-Su Kim[1], Yoon-Kyung Choi[2], and Soo-Young Lee[1,2]

[1] Brain Science Research Center, Korea Advanced Institute of Science and Technology, Daejeon, Korea

[2] Extell Technology Corporation, Seoul, Korea

Abstract. A new algorithm is presented to perform active noise canceling and blind signal separation simultaneously. In many real-world problems speech signal is contaminated by noises, some of which are completely unknown while the other may be estimated by microphones located near the noise sources. Electric 'line' signals of audio equipments may also be used to estimate the noises. The active noise canceling removes the estimated noises with reverberation, while blind signal separation extracts speech signal from unknown noisy mixtures. Both algorithms are based on independent component analysis (ICA), which assumes statistical-independence among acoustic sources. The ICA-based active noise canceling utilizes higher-order statistics, and outperforms the standard least-mean-square (LMS) algorithm with quadratic statistics in real-world applications.

1 Introduction

Although current speech recognition technologies have been quite successful for clean speeches, the poor performance in real-world noisy environments prevents the speech recognition technology from popularity. To overcome this critical difficulty it is necessary to enhance speech signals by eliminating noises from speech-noise mixtures for robust speech recognition. The speech enhancement comes with two approaches, i.e., adaptive noise canceling (ANC) and blind signal separation (BSS). ANC is an approach to reduce noise based on reference noise signals, while no reference signal is known for BSS. The Least-Mean-Square (LMS) algorithm has been the popular choice for ANC.[1,2] With the assumption of linear mixing and statistical-independence among acoustic sources independent component analysis (ICA) has recently been developed for BSS.[3-6] In this paper we show that ICA is also applicable to ANC with much better performance than that of LMS algorithm. Also, the ICA results in an unified framework for simultaneous ANC and BSS for practical applications. The multi-path reverberation of speech signal and noise sources in office or car environment is well taken care of in this paper.

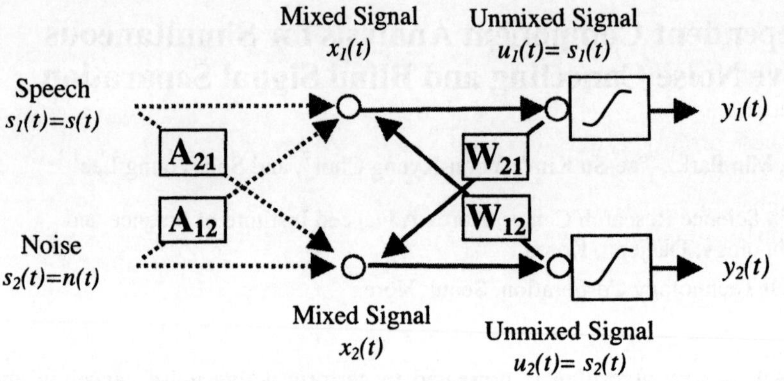

Fig. 1. Network architecture of the blind signal separation

2 ICA-based Blind Signal Separation

As shown in Fig.1, BSS attempts to separate unknown sources $\mathbf{s}(t)$=[$s_1(t)$, $s_2(t)$,,, $s_L(t)$] from linear mixtures of independent sources $\mathbf{x}(t)$=[$x_1(t)$, $x_2(t)$,, $x_L(t)$]. Here, the number of microphones and the number of sources are the same L. The measured mixed signal at the lth microphone at the jth sampling time may be represented as

$$x_l[j] = s_l[j] + \sum_{m \neq l}^{L} \sum_{k=0}^{K} A_{lmk} s_m[j-k], \quad \text{for } l = 1, 2, \ldots, L \tag{1}$$

$$u_l[j] = x_l[j] + \sum_{m \neq l}^{L} \sum_{k=0}^{K} W_{lmk} u_m[j-k], \quad \text{for } l = 1, 2, \ldots, L \tag{2}$$

where $s_m[j]$ denotes the mth source signal at the jth sampling time, and A_{lmk} is the convolutional mixing coefficient from the mth source to the lth microphone with the kth time delays for the multi-path reverberation. Also, W_{lmk} is the unmixing coefficient. Here, we do not attempt to deconvolve each source, and concentrate on the signal separation only. In this case the feedback architecture allows $\mathbf{W}= -\mathbf{A}$ for easy estimation of time delays. Only K time-delays are considered for simplicity. Depending upon acoustic environments and sampling frequency the maximum number of time-delays may be set between several hundreds and several thousands.

The BSS algorithm adaptively estimates the unknown mixing coefficients from examples of mixed signals $x_l(t)$(l=$1,2,\ldots,L$). In ICA-based BSS algorithm the adaptation is made toward the extraction of statistically-independent sources by maximizing entropy as [4,5]

$$\Delta W_{lmk} = -\eta\varphi(u_l[j])\, u_m[j-k], \qquad \varphi(u) = -(\partial p/\partial u)/p(u) \tag{3}$$

where η is a learning rate and $p(y_l)$ denotes the probability density function of y_l. The stochastic learning rule may be implemented as on-line or batch mode.

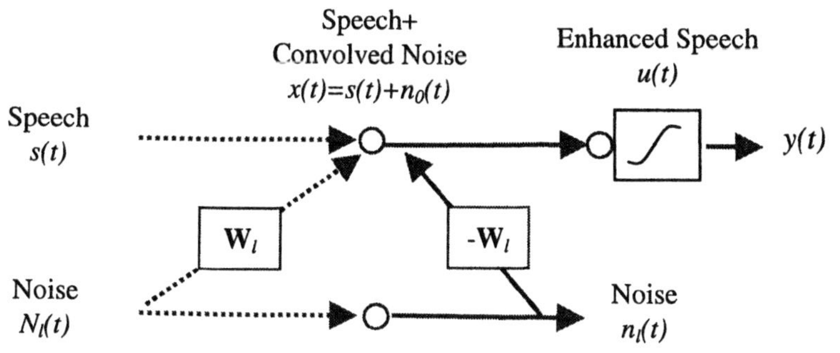

Fig. 2. Network architecture of the active noise canceling

3 ICA-based Active Noise Canceling

An adaptive noise canceling system is shown in Fig.2, where signal $s(t)$ is transmitted over a channel to a microphone and noise $n_0(t)$ is added from the noise source $n_l(t)$ (l=1,2,.., L) through convolution channels **W**s. Other sensors receive the noise signals $n_l(t)$ to form the reference signals. The goal is to get a system output $u(t)$ which is the best estimate of the signal $s(t)$ as

$$u[j] = s[j] + n_0[j] - \sum_{l=1}^{L}\sum_{k=0}^{K} W_{lk} n_l[j-k]. \tag{4}$$

The most popular algorithm for noise cancellation is Least-Mean-Square (LMS) algorithm, which minimizes the squared error and results in [1,2]

$$\Delta W_{lk} - \eta\, u[j]\, n_l[j-k], \tag{5}$$

where η is a learning rate. Eq.(5) decorrelates the output signal from the reference noise signal, and removes noise components of the primary input signal based on second-order statistics only. However, the speech and noise signals may depend upon in higher-order statistics.

Comparing Fig.1 and Fig.2, it is clear that ANC is a special case of BSS with zero values for some mixing coefficients. Therefore, we may derive an ANC algorithm based on ICA by minimizing entropy as

$$\Delta W_l = \eta\varphi(u[j])n_l[j-k], \qquad \varphi(u) = -(\partial p/\partial u)/p(u) \tag{6}$$

Comparing Eqs.(5) and (6), one notices that the LMS algorithm is a special case of the ICA-based algorithm for Gaussian signals. In Ref.6, the same adaptation rule was derived with linear approximation near convergence for i.i.d. signals. Also, the convergence property of Eq.(6) is similar to that of LMS algorithm.[7] However, only statistical-independence is assumed in this paper. The ICA-based ANC algorithm can remove noise components based on statistical independence, which incorporates both second-order and higher-order statistics.

4 Simultaneous ANC and BSS

Now we combine the BSS in Section 2 and ANC in Section 3. As shown in Fig.3, an array of microphones measures the mixed signals, which consist of multi-path convolutions of speech signal and several noise sources. Also, it is assumed that some of the noise sources may be approximately extracted by other means. For example, one may put several microphones in a running car to measure mixtures of speech, car audio music, engine noise, wind noise, etc., and the music signals may be extracted from the "line" jack of the car audio. By combining Eqs.(2) and (4) and applying the same maximum entropy concept simultaneously, one obtains adaptive learning rules similar to Eqs. (3) and (6). Also, it is possible to do sequentially, i.e., to conduct ICA first and perform BSS latter. Both the simultaneous and sequential methods result in good speech enhancement.

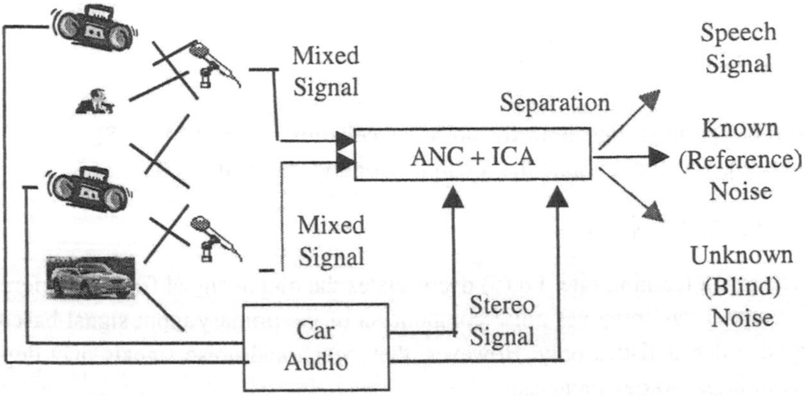

Fig. 3. Network architecture of the simultaneous active noise canceling and blind signal separation

5 Experimental Results

The developed algorithm is currently implemented with C++ in Pentium-based personal computers. For applications with only 2 sources one may utilize stereo inputs of standard sound cards in the personal computer. For applications with more sources a real-time data acquisition board may be required. We recommend 16-bits AD conversion and at least 11 kHz sampling rates.

In Fig.4 the waveforms of speech, noise, mixed signal, and enhanced speech are shown. The SNR improvements of the LMS and ICA-based algorithms arc also compared for car, speech, and music noises in Fig.5. The ICA-based algorithm outperforms the popular LMS algorithm, especially for the speech and music noises. Both speech and music have super-Gaussian probability distribution, and higher-order statistics are important in these signals.

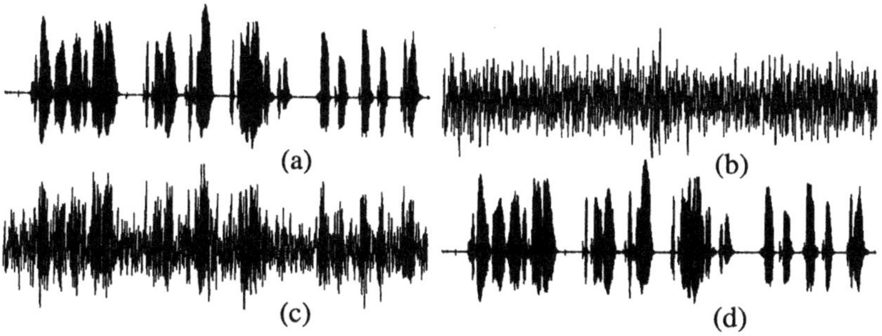

Fig.4 Results of an ANC experiments. (a) speech signal, (b) car noise, (c) mixed signal, and (d) enhanced speech signal

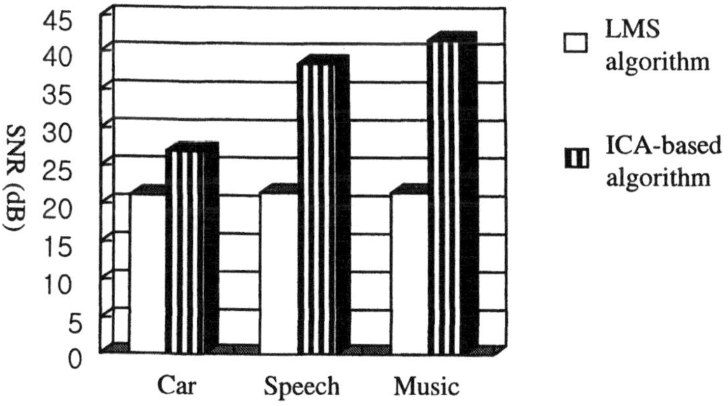

Fig.5 SNR enhancements of ANC experiments with different noises. Results of LMS and ICA-based algorithms are compared.

The ANC/BSS hybrid method is applied to a real-world problem with 2 microphones and 4 sources, of which 2 sources are extracted electronically from a car audio. Although exact SNR is not available for more than two unknown sources with reverberation, human perception is much more improved both in normal office environments and in heavily-reverberated rooms. No significant difference was found for the simultaneous and sequential methods.

6 Conclusion

In this paper we present a novel method to perform ANC and BSS simultaneously for speech enhancement. Both ANC and BSS methods are based on ICA, and easily integrated into a single mathematical framework. Also, the ICA-based ANC outperforms standard LMS algorithm. The results demonstrate usefulness of the developed technique as a front-end of robust speech recognition systems in real-world noisy environments. However, real-time processing with reasonable performance requires a special hardware, which will come out in the near future.

Acknowledgment: This research was partially supported by Korean Ministry of Science and Technology as the Brain Neuroinformatics Research Program.

References

1. Widrow, B., Glover, J.R., et. al. (1975) Adaptive noise canceling: principles and applications. Proceedings of the IEEE **63**, 1692–1716.
2. Haykin, H. (1996) Adaptive Filter Theory, Prentice-Hall, Eaglewood Cliffs, 3rd edition
3. Bell, A.J., Sejnowski, T.J. (1995) An information-maximization approach to blind separation and blind deconvolution. Neural Computation **7**, 1129–1159,
4. Lee, T.W., Bell, A.J., Lambert, R.L. (1997) Blind separation of delayed and convolved sources. Advances in Neural Information Processing Systems **9**, MIT Press, Cambridge, MA, 758–764,.
5. Torkkola, K. (1996) Blind separation of convolved sources based on information maximization. IEEE Workshop on Neural Networks for Signal Processing
6. Park, H.M., Jeong, H.Y., Lee, T.W., Lee, S.Y. (1999) Subband-based blind signal separation for noisy speech recognition. Electronics Letters **35**, 2011-2012
7. Douglas, S.C., Meng, T.H. (1994) Stochastic gradient adaptation under general error criteria. IEEE Transaction on Signal Processing **42**, 1335– 1351

On The Universality of The Single-Layer Perceptron Model

Šarūnas Raudys

Institute of Mathematics and Informatics
Akademijos 4, Vilnius LT-2100, Lithuania

Abstract. The Single Layer Perceptron (SLP) calculates a weighted sum of numerous inputs and produces output as a smooth non-linear two side bounded function of this sum. We show that this simple mathematical model, originally proposed to consider the information processing in brain cells, features much more universal principles. If appropriately trained, the SLP can implement many commonly known statistical classification and regression algorithms. The SLP training and retraining can be used to model aging processes in technology, biology and society. The SLP model can be utilized to simulate continuous and turbulent wave propagation in excitable medias.

1 The Single Layer Perceptron and its Training Algorithm

The non-linear single layer perceptron is a simplified mathematical model of elementary information processing cell in living organisms – a neuron. Animal and human brains are composed of billions of interconnected neurons. The first mathematical model of the neuron was suggested by McCulloch and Pitts [1] and later improved by a number of authors. According to Rumelhart *et al.* [2] the SLP has several inputs (say n), $x_1, x_2, \dots, x_p$ (an input vector X), and one output, o, which is calculated according to equation $o = f(VX^T + v_0)$, where $f(net)$ is a non-linear activation function, e.g. *a sigmoid function*, $f(net) = 1/(1+\exp(-net))$, and v_0, $V = (v_1, v_2, \dots, v_p)$ are the weights of the perceptron.

Single layer perceptrons are traditionally applied for classification and prediction. In classification, if sigmoid function (2) is used, one compares the output o with the threshold value of 0.5. The decision boundary is linear. To find the weights for the SLP, one minimizes a certain cost function. The most popular cost function is the sum of squares

$$cost = \frac{1}{N_1 + N_2} \sum_{i=1}^{2} \sum_{j=1}^{N_i} \left(y_j^{(i)} - f(V(X_j^{(i)})^T + v_0)\right)^2, \qquad (1)$$

where $y_j^{(i)}$ is a desired output (a target) for $X_j^{(i)}$, the j-th training observation of class ω_i, and N_i is the number of training vectors of class ω_i.

In the pattern classification, the desired outputs are associated with the class label. If the sigmoid function is used, one typically utilizes $t_j^{(1)} = 1$, $y_j^{(2)} = 0$ or $y_j^{(1)} = 0.9$, $y_j^{(2)} = 0.1$. Sigmoid activation function is smooth and can be differentiated.

Usually, to determine the weights v_0, v_1, v_2, ... , v_p, one minimizes cost function (1). In the gradient descent optimization algorithm (delta rule, back propagation), one calculates derivatives of the cost function and finds the weights in iterative manner. At step *t*, one updates the weight vector $V_{(t)}$ according to equations

$$V_{(t+1)} = V_{(t)} - \eta \frac{\partial cost_t}{\partial V}, \; v_{0(t+1)} = v_{0(t)} - \eta \frac{\partial cost_l}{\partial v_0}, \tag{2}$$

where η is the learning-step and $\partial cost_l / \partial V$ is the gradient of the cost function.

In 1960 Widrow and Hoff [3] proved that linear perceptron (one without the non-linearity in its output) can realize standard mean square regression and classification. In the second section we will explain that while training the SLP one can obtain seven known statistical classification algorithms or six regressions. In the third section, SLP is used to simulate and analyze an individual's aging process. We refer to the fact that in gradient descent (back-propagation) training, the weights are increasing permanently together with an increase in the number of iterations. We define the individual's age as the *capability to rapidly re-train in order to solve new task satisfactorily and survive in constantly changing environments.* I hypothesize that SLP model can be utilized to simulate aging processes in variety of fields. In the fourth section, utilization of SLP model to analyze and control signal propagation in 2-dimensional excitable media model is considered. Here each elementary cell (node) receives excitation signals from its neighbors. We can use the excitable media model to analyze and control signal propagation in chemistry, ecology, meteorology, heart muscle activation process, and even to investigate problems of interaction among humans in a community, where each individual can receive or transmit positive or negative influences from his nearest and farther neighbors.

2 SLP and Statistical Algorithms

In [4, 5, 6] the conditions were presented, under which a perceptron in the back propagation total gradient training would converge to seven different classification methods as well as to six different regressions. For classification, these conditions include:

E1) the center of training data have to be moved to the origin of coordinates;
E2) the training process is started from zero weights;
E3) if $N_2 = N_1$, symmetrical targets are used, i.e. y_{2j}=1-y_{1j} for sigmoid function;
E4) the total gradient training (batch mode) method is be used.

Then after the first iteration, one the Euclidean distance classifier. Only sample mean vectors are used to design classification rule here. In further iterations, one has a regularized discriminant analysis where to each element of the sample covariance matrix **S** a positive constant λ is added. Value of λ diminishes with an increase in the number of iterations. In the end one approaches a standard Fisher linear discriminant function. If the number of training vectors is very small and matrix **S** is singular, we approach the Fisher rule with a pseudo-inversion of matrix **S**. In further iterations, one has a robust discriminant analysis where atypical training vectors (outliers) are ignored. If one controls weights magnitudes, one can get a minimum empirical error classifier. In case one classifies training vectors without error, one can get the support vector machine.

Which classification method will be obtained depends on training parameters, first of all on the number of iterations. Other very important parameters are: target values, learning step, noise injection to training vectors, and regularization or anti-regularization term added to conventional cost function ([6], Section 4.6).

In regression, instead of requirement E3), a sample mean of variable y have to be shifted to zero. Then, if sample standard deviations of all variables are set to 1 and $\eta=1$, after the first iteration, one obtains a weight vector composed of correlation coefficients only. In further iterations, one has regularized regression and moves towards standard mean square regression with conventional or pseudo inverse of sample covariance matrix **S**. Conditions exist where in perceptron training one can obtain robust, as well as minimax (support vector) regressions [5]. In robust regression training, vectors that are predicted with large error are ignored. In the minimax regression, a maximal prediction error is minimized.

Considering the above, it is important to notice that in the SLP training, *no assumptions* about statistical structure of probability density function of the data is made, however, a variety of the statistical algorithms can be obtained.

3 SLP for Analyzing Aging in Technical Systems, Biology and Society

One of the important features of the SLP used as a classifier is the increase of weights with every iteration during the gradient descent (back-propagation) training. With this increase, the value of the cost function to be minimized "saturates" and its gradient diminishes. As a consequence, the gradient descent training slows down.

Let us suppose that the classification task changes abruptly and already trained SLP must be re-trained to solve a new task. In such situation, large weighs and saturation of the cost function impede re-training process. We can utilize this property of the perceptron in order to simulate the aging process of an individual.

To analyse aging processes we suggest exploiting a concept: *maturation and aging of system/individual/population are affected by external influences and are related with ability to learn, to adapt to sudden changes of the environment rapidly and survive* [7]. An essence of the "adaptation to the changed environment" model are two different classification tasks the perceptron ought to learn. Two tasks stand for an external influence that is varying in time. After T_{first} training iterations with the first data (the classification task to be learned), at some moment the task changes. During T_{first} iterations the perceptron learns the information accumulated in the first training set. After the task (external influence) changes, the perceptron ought to learn the new information accumulated in new training set.

Illustrating the idea in Fig. 1*a* we present an artificial example with 2 non-intersecting bi-variate Gaussian pattern classes, π_1 and π_2. The SLP is trained with this data at first. If a number of iterations, T_{first}, is sufficient, we obtain ideal discriminant line 1, $g(\mathbf{x}) = v_1x_1 + v_2x_2 + v_0 = 0$. Afterwards the data is shifted to the right and down (pattern classes π_{11} and π_{21}). To get separation of new classes, π_{11} and π_{21}, one only needs to change the threshold v_0. If SLP was trained for a long time, say T_{first} = 1000 iterations with η =1 and, t_{1j} = 0, the weighs turn out to be rather large. After training process terminates, the cost function has a deep minimum at $v_0 \approx 0$ in a space of threshold v_0 (curve 1 in Fig. 1*b*). For pattern classes π_{11} and π_{21} we have the minimum at $v_0 \approx 12$ (curve 2) in space of threshold v_0 (v_1 and v_2 are supposed to stay unchanged). However, at this point the cost function 1 is already flat. Hence, training is slow. After T_{second} =200 iterations the perceptron does not succeed to change a position of the discriminant line. We get very similar discriminant (line 2 in Fig.1*a*) that gives 50% error for classes π_{11} and π_{21}. If, however, in the first stage the SLP was trained short, e.g. T_{first} =250 iterations, the weights do not get so large. The minimum of the cost function is not very deep (curve 3 in Fig.1*b*). During subsequent T_{second} = 200 training iterations with pattern classes π_{11} and π_{21}, one can move to a minimum ($v_0 \approx 6$) of new cost function (curve 4). In Fig. 2 we have a graph, a probability of correct classification as a function of T_{first} (T_{second} =200). The graph has a "rise and fall" character: ability *to learn the new information* first increases and then decreases with T_{first}.

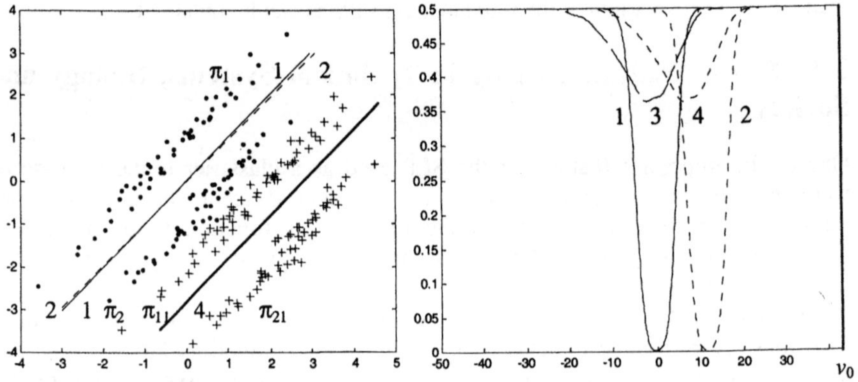

Fig. 1. *a* – original, π_1 and π_2, and shifted (π_{11} and π_{21}) classes and positions of discriminant boundaries; *b* – costs as the functions of threshold v_0 for original data (1, 3) and shifted data (2, 4): graphs 1, 2 – T_{first} =1000; 3, 4 – T_{first} =250.

In our model, we exploited the concept: an individual's age is a capability to rapidly re-train itself to solve new task satisfactorily, and survive in constantly changing environments. The word "individual" can mean a cell, biological population, technological equipment, economical unit, social organization. In technology, a tool in an enterprise, a new model of computer, the software have to be adapted to users at first, manufacturing rejects have to be detected and removed. Therefore, in the beginning, effectiveness of new products tends to increase with time. Later, new competing products appear, physical tear and wear become visible. Replacement of old parts does not pay off any more. In principle, moderately new computers, the software (say 4-6 years old) can be utilized to solve many everyday jobs. To solve state-of-the-art problems, however, they cannot be upgraded any more. The products get "old". Thus, a dependence of product's performance on time has a raise and fall character.

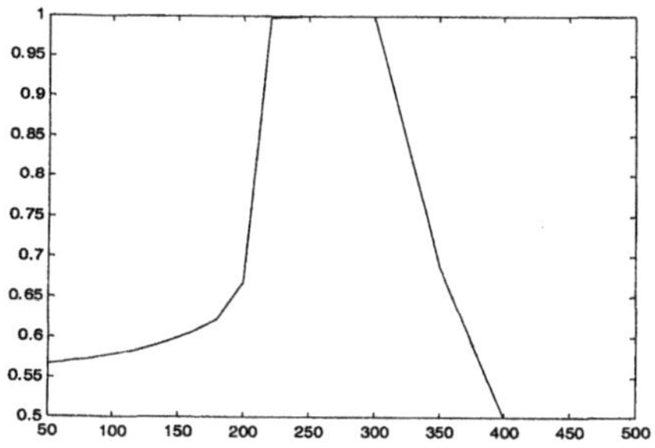

Fig. 2. A probability of correct classification as a function of T_{first} (T_{second} =200).

There are a large number of such examples in biology. Immune activity of mammals, from humans to mice, almost equals to zero in newborns. Later it increases with age (for humans this activity peaks at 11-15 years), after that slowly declines [8, 9]. Immune aging curves notably resemble the curve in Fig. 2 and variety of simulated "rise and fall" curves in [7]. The rise and fall behaviour, however, is also characteristic to enterprises, states and even civilizations (remember a well known saying from history textbooks "rise and fall of the Roman empire" and reasons of this phenomenon). In all cases, we have the maturation (learning) process, growth of the strength of connections between the perceptrons (weights), saturation (virtual decline in the slope of the activation function $f(arg)$) and gradual degradation (inability to learn new information quickly). An age distribution of new recipients of doctoral degrees in the USA, changes in distributions of the wages in post-communist countries resemble the "rise and fall" graphs.

Theoretical studies show that training and retraining of single layer perceptron classifier can be affected by a choice of the target values, learning step, noise injection to inputs and desired outputs of the perceptron [6, 7]. Shift of the target values t_{2j} and t_{1j} to each other, a noise injection slows down the weights growing process and make the adaptation to the new changed data faster. It means that these factors can be utilized to control *aging and rejuvenation processes* of the perceptrons. There are a number of factors in real life that perform similar regularization functions and can be utilized to affect maturing and aging.

4. Signal Propagation in Excitable Media

Wave propagation in excitable media is an important unsolved problem. The wave propagation is vital in auto-catalytic chemical reactions, biological cells and tissues, meteorology, cosmology and seismology [10]. Powerful stream of research in this direction is carried out for needs of cardiology where it can be used for prediction and treatment of atrial and ventricular fibrillation and tachycardias. Computer simulations and experiments performed *in numero* can yield information that cannot be obtained in any other way [11]. The underlying mathematical model to analyse ionic currents in cells is a system of first order differential equations. Unfortunately, the models based on differential equations are not yet computationally reasonable. A cellular network composed of single layer perceptrons with smooth soft limiting activation function in each node, however, can help to model the wave propagation task many times faster [12].

Like in other cellular models, in the new model, the output signals from one node (SLP) are transmitted to neighbouring ones. Transmitting moment is proportional to perceptron's output signal value. After transmitting the signal, the SLP remains quiet during certain time, T_{refr}, called refractory period. In simulation studies, calculations are performed in discrete time moments. Fig. 3 depicts a piece of rectangular 2D area of the model composed of 6×10 cells. In this model, each cell is connected to six neighbouring ones. The transfer weights, $(v_1, v_2, \ldots, v_6) = \boldsymbol{V}$, depend on the direction between two cells. As a consequence, the weighs determine *anisotropy of the media*. In the isotropic tissue model, we have the same transmitting strengths along all six directions. In the anisotropic model, some (or all) of the weights can differ. In each node, weighted summations of the inputs, $net = v_1x_1 + v_2x_2 + \ldots + v_6x_6 + v_0 = \boldsymbol{VX}^T + v_0$, are performed and each SLP transmits its output signal after a time proportional to $f(net)$. More complex models can be created easily.

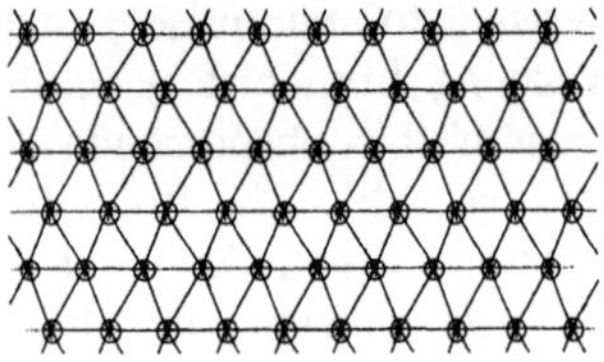

Fig. 3. The SLP based excitable media model.

Initial excitation, concrete shape of the activation function, $f(net)$, refractory period, T_{refr}, and especially magnitudes of the transfer weights, v_1, v_2, ... , v_6, determine different wave propagation patterns. If refractory period is lengthy, we have smooth uniform wave propagations without any additional waves births. A wave propagation pattern depends mainly on the values and mutual distribution of weighs in different directions. If refractory period is brief, however, we have additional waves arising even in case of homogeneous isotropic media.

In Fig. 4 we have two patterns of wave propagation in 2D excitable areas composed of 340×340 (*a*) and 200×200 (*b*) nodes for different sets of values of homogeneous isotropic excitable media model. In both examples, central nodes of the model were excited only once, however, multiple secondary waves were born later. Afterwards the waves propagate to the centre (*a*) and outside (*b*).

Excitable medias can contain inhomogenities, "high-resistance" connections. Often small obstacles do not affect the wave propagation. In certain cases, however, the spiral waves arise. In dependence on model parameters the obstacles cause new spontaneous waves, a reduction in a speed of the wave propagation, etc.

Fig. 4. Two patterns of wave propagation in 2D excitable areas composed of 340×340 (*a*) and 200×200 (*b*) nodes for different sets of values of media model.

In Fig. 5 we have the wave propagation in rectangular 2D isotropic homogeneous 200×200 area (lengthy refractory period, all weighs are equal to 0.9) with a small rectangular obstacle, A, composed of 2×10 non-conducting cells. After starting excitation the cell *S*, an angle shaped wave 1 broadens and propagates to the right and down. Here, for relative large weighs (0.9) and isotropic homogeneous tissue we have a rigorous shape of the wave (see the wave 1 after 270 propagation steps). Due to the obstacle unexcited cells appear behind the wave and trigger a spiral.

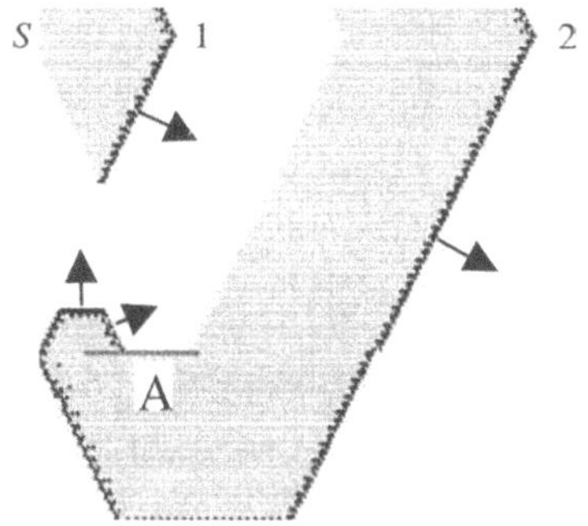

Fig. 5. The wave propagation in a rectangular 2D isotropic homogeneous 200 × 200 area with small rectangular obstacle, A, composed of 2 × 10 non-conducting elements: 1 - after $t = 270$ steps, 2 – after $t = 940$ steps.

As a result, the wave bends after it departs from obstacle. After initial bending at obstacle's edge, the wave begins to rotate around the obstacle and forms the spiral (wave 2 after 940 steps). The spiral rotates enduringly around the obstacle. The waves continue to rotate further even if *the obstacle is removed.*

The excitable media models can be developed further in different ways. One can design a network with different distances between the nodes and specify the "neighboring nodes" in a variety of ways. The impulses transmitted can be positive and negative. Each node (individual) can receive or transmit influences from its nearest and from farther neighbors. Such media model can be used to investigate problems of interaction among human beings, relations between large organizations, enterprises, etc.

Conclusion

The *model of the weighted sum with smooth soft-limiting output* was proposed to analyze the information processing in living organisms. The model, however, can be used for wider variety of tasks. This model can realize many famous statistical classification and regression algorithms. Its training and retraining can be used to simulate aging processes in technology, biology and society. It can be utilized to consider continuous and turbulent wave propagation in excitable medias. Future research possibly will reveal other advantageous areas of perceptron's application.

References

1. McCulloch W.S. and Pitts W. (1943). A logical calculus of the ideas immanent in nervous activity. *Bulletin of Mathematical Biophysics*, **5**:115-33
2. Rumelhart D.E., Hinton G.E., Williams R.J. (1986). Learning internal representations by error propagation. In: Rumelhart D.E., McClelland J.L. (Eds.), *Parallel Distributed Processing: Explorations in the microstructure of cognition.* Bradford Books, Cambridge, MA **I**:318–62
3. Widrow B. and Hoff M.E. (1960). Adaptive switching circuits. *WESCON Convention Record*, **4**:96–104
4. Raudys Š. (1998). Evolution and generalization of a single neurone. I. SLP as seven statistical classifiers. *Neural Networks*, **11**(2):283-296
5. Raudys Š. (2000). Evolution and generalization of a single neurone. III. Primitive, regularized, standard, robust and minimax regressions. *Neural Networks*, **13** :507-523
6. Raudys Š. (2001). *Statistical and Neural Classifiers: An integrated approach to design.* Springer. London.
7. Raudys Š. (2002). An adaptation model for simulation of aging process. *Int. J. of Modern Physics C* (2002, accepted)
8. Thomsen O. and Kettel K. (1927). Die Starke der menschlichen Isoagglutinine und entsprechende Blutkorperchenreceptoren in vershiedenen Lebensaltern. *Z. Immunitatsforsch.*, **63**:67-93
9. Makinodan T. and Yunis E., Eds. (1977). *Immunololgy and Aging*. Plenum Medical Book Company, New York & London.
10. Vinson M., Mironov S., Mulvey S., Pertsov A. (1997). Control of spatial orientation and lifetime of scroll rings in excitable media. *Nature*, **3886** (3):477-480.
11. Henriquez C.S. and Papazoglou A.A. (1996). Using computer models to understand the roles of tissue structure and membrane dynamics in arrhythmogenesis. *Proceedings of the IEEE*, **84** (3):334–354
12. Raudys Š. (2002). Neural network models of wave propagation in excitable media. *Proc. of IASTED Int. Conf. on Modelling, Identification and Control MIC'2002*, Feb. 18-21, 2002. Innsbruck, Austria (Hamsa M.H. ed.). Acta Press. Anaheim, Calgary: 352-357

A Hybrid Connectionist for Multiple Regression

Rudy Setiono[1] **and Jacek M. Zurada**[2]

[1] School of Computing
National University of Singapore
Singapore 117543
email: rudys@comp.nus.edu.sg

[2] Electrical and Computer Engineering Department
University of Louisville
Computational Intelligence Lab
Louisville, KY 40208, USA
email: jmzura02@athena.louisville.edu

Abstract. We present a hybrid system for generating multiple linear regression lines for the solution of a function approximation problem. The system consists of three components: (1) a neural network which is trained to fit the data samples; (2) a simple algorithm for splitting the input space of the data into subregions and (3) the traditional multiple regression technique for finding the coefficients of the regression lines. While neural networks work particularly well for nonlinear function approximation, their outputs are difficult to explain to a human user. Our proposed system predicts the network outputs as linear functions of the input attributes. In order to maintain the predictive accuracy of the networks, the system divides the space of the input data into several subspaces. In each of these subspaces, a linear equation is generated for predicting the target values for all samples that belong to the subspace. We illustrate the effectiveness of the system using two data sets, one is an artificial data set, while the other is a real world data set for predicting the fuel consumption of automobiles.

1 Introduction

Decisions are likely to hinge on estimated figures provided by a regression method applied on some available data. If the regression method is not done properly, forecast figures can turn out to be completely off their true values and thus lead to poor decisions.

Neural networks are natural candidates for solving regression problems because they are proven to be universal function approximators [1, 3]. This means that given sufficient and adequately chosen sample data points, a neural network can be trained to find suitable connection weights and biases that will compute the underlying function to any degree of precision desired.

In a wide variety of practical problems, neural networks have been known to be able to do regression with very high accuracy [8, 10]. However, they are not without important drawbacks. Foremost is their complex input-to-output mapping which is difficult for a human user to comprehend. Compared to the nonlinear mapping of neural networks, linear functions computed by traditional statistical techniques are much more comprehensible. The coefficients of a linear regression function indicate clearly the expected change in the output for every unit change in the associated inputs.

There are regression methods that restrict their solutions to linear functions of the inputs. Many are based on Quinlan's C4.5 decision-tree algorithm [9] which is a robust method originally designed for classification problems. In order to apply C4.5 to regression problems, the target variable is discretized so that estimating the output becomes a classification problem of finding the best output interval.

The RECLA system [12] discretizes the target variable and allows the user to choose from among 3 methods for sub-dividing the intervals of the target variable: (1) equally probable intervals, where each subinterval contains the same number of data samples; (2) equal width interval; and (3) k-means clustering, such that in each interval, the sum of the distances of all data samples to its center of gravity is minimized.

The Relative Unsupervized Discretization (RUDE) algorithm [7] discretizes not only the continuous target variable, but also all continuous input variables. Its key component is a clustering algorithm which regroups values of the target variables into subintervals that are characterized by similar values of some set of input attributes. Once the variables have been discretized, C4.5 can be applied for solving the original regression problem. The experimental results show that compared to the trees from the data sets discretized using equal width interval and k-means clustering methods, the decision trees generated from RUDE-discretized data have fewer nodes but suffer from lower regression accuracy.

The problem with casting a regression task as a classification task lies in the splitting of the continuous target variable. Splitting the interval into many fine subintervals leads to smaller deviations within each subinterval. But, too many subintervals requires numerous classes in the resulting classification task. This degrades the prediction accuracy of the classification tree. RECLA applies the wrapper approach [4] to overcome this problem. It is an iterative approach that tries varying number of intervals until the best estimated accuracy is found.

This paper describes a method for representing the input-output mapping of trained neural networks in terms of linear regression functions. Unlike RECLA and RUDE, our proposed method does not require discretization of the target variable, thus avoiding the difficulty associated with discretization. The neural networks have a single layer of hidden units with hyperbolic tangent activation function and a single output unit with linear activation function. The conditions of the rules generated by our method divide the input space of the data into subspaces, while the consequent of each rule is a linear regression function.

The crucial component in our proposed system is the approximation of the hidden unit activation function by a 3-piece linear function. This is done for each hidden unit left in the network after pruning. The nonlinear network output is then replaced by a weighted combination of the linearized activation functions. Relevant input variables are identified by network pruning. Statistical linear regression further removes variables that do not significantly contribute to the prediction.

2 Network training and pruning

We divide the available data samples $(\mathbf{x}^i, y^i), i = 1, 2, \ldots,$ where $\mathbf{x}^i \in \mathbb{R}^N$ and $y^i \in \mathbb{R}$, randomly into the training set, the cross-validation set and the test set. Using the training data set, a network with a single hidden layer consisting of H units. is trained so as to minimize the sum of squared errors $E(\mathbf{w}, \mathbf{v})$ augmented with a penalty term $P(\mathbf{w}, \mathbf{v})$:

$$E(\mathbf{w}, \mathbf{v}) = \sum_{i=1}^{K} \left(\tilde{y}^i - y^i\right)^2 + P(\mathbf{w}, \mathbf{v}) \quad (1)$$

$$P(\mathbf{w}, \mathbf{v}) = \epsilon_1 \left(\sum_{m=1}^{H} \sum_{\ell=1}^{N} \frac{\eta w_{m\ell}^2}{1 + \eta w_{m\ell}^2} + \sum_{m=1}^{H} \frac{\eta v_m^2}{1 + \eta v_m^2} \right) + \epsilon_2 \left(\sum_{m=1}^{H} \sum_{\ell=1}^{N} w_{m\ell}^2 + \sum_{m=1}^{H} v_m^2 \right) \quad (2)$$

where K is the number of samples in the training data set, $\epsilon_1, \epsilon_2, \eta$ are positive penalty parameters, and $\tilde{y}^i$ is the predicted function value for input sample $\mathbf{x}^i$

$$\tilde{y}^i = \sum_{m=1}^{H} \tanh\left(z_m^i\right) v_m + \tau = \sum_{m=1}^{H} \tanh\left((\mathbf{x}^i)^T \mathbf{w}_m\right) v_m + \tau, \quad (3)$$

$\mathbf{w}_m \in \mathbb{R}^N$ is the network weights from the input units to hidden unit m, $v_m \in \mathbb{R}$ is the network weight from hidden unit m to the output unit, $\tanh(\xi)$ is the hyperbolic tangent function, $z_m^i = (\mathbf{x}^i)^T \mathbf{w}_m$ is the scalar product of $\mathbf{x}^i$ and $\mathbf{w}_m$, and τ is the output unit's bias.

Once the network has been trained, irrelevant and redundant hidden units and input units are removed from the network by applying the algorithm N2PFA (Neural Network Pruning for Function Approximation) [10]. This algorithm checks the accuracy of the network on the cross-validation samples to determine if a unit can be removed. If the removal of an input or a hidden unit does not cause a deterioration in the network's accuracy on this set of samples, then the unit will be removed. The benefit of network pruning is two-fold. First, pruned networks are less likely to overfit the training data, and hence they generalize better than fully connected networks. Second, simplifying the network topology by pruning can be expected to result in fewer linear regression equations.

3 Linear approximation of tanh(z)

Once a trained network has been obtained, we fit the hidden unit activations of the samples using a piece-wise linear function. This is achieved by finding a 3-

piece linear approximating function for each of the network's hidden units. Since the hidden unit activation function tanh(z) is antisymmetric, it is sufficient to illustrate just for the nonnegative values of z. Suppose that the input z ranges from 0 to z_m. A simple and convenient approximation of $h(z)$ is to over-estimate it by the piecewise linear function $L(z)$ as shown in Figure 1. To ensure that

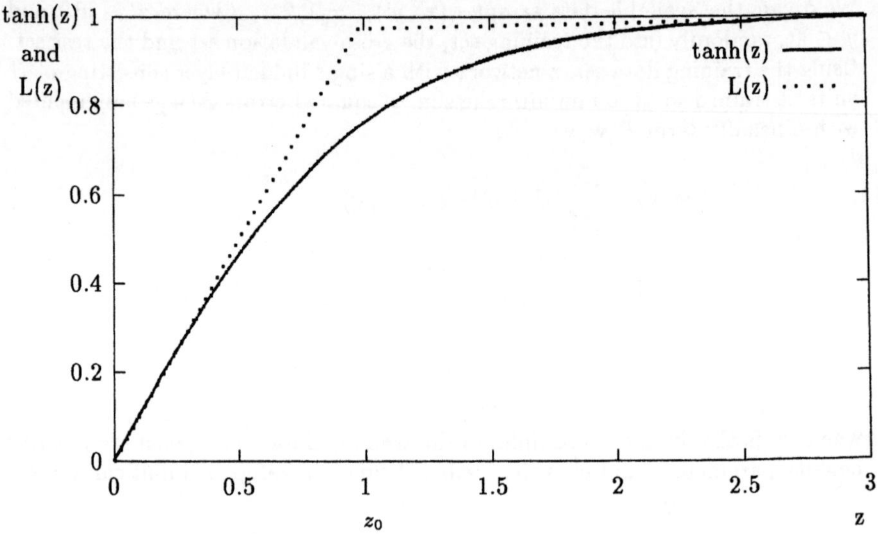

Fig. 1. The tanh(z) function (solid curve) for $z \in [0, 3]$ is approximated by a 2-piece linear function (dashed lines).

$L(z)$ is larger than $h(z)$ everywhere between 0 to z_m, the line on the left should intersect the coordinate (0, 0) with a gradient of $h'(0) = 1$, and the line on the right should intersect the coordinate $(z_m,\ h(z_m))$ with a gradient of $h'(z_m) = 1 - h^2(z_m)$. Thus, $L(z)$ can be written as

$$L(z) = \begin{cases} z & \text{if } 0 \le z \le z_0 \\ h(z_m) - (z_m - z)h'(z_m) & \text{if } z > z_0 \end{cases} \quad . \tag{4}$$

The point of intersection z_0 of the two lines is given by

$$z_0 = \frac{h(z_m) - z_m h'(z_m)}{(h(z_m))^2} \quad . \tag{5}$$

It can be shown [11] that the total error E_A of estimating $h(z)$ by $L(z)$ is bounded by $-\frac{1}{2} - \ln 0.5$. That is, the total error is bounded by a constant value.

4 Generating regression rules from neural network

A set of linear regression rules can be generated from a pruned network once the network hidden unit activation function tanh(z) has been approximated by 3-piece linear function as described in the previous section. The steps are:

1. For each hidden unit $m = 1, 2, \ldots, H$, generate the 3-piece linear approximation $L_m(z)$ (Eg. 4).
2. Using the pair of points $-z_{m0}$ and z_{m0} from function $L_m(z)$, divide the input space into 3^H subregions.
3. For each non-empty subregion, generate a rule as follows:
   (a) Generate the rule *condition*: $(C_1$ and C_2 and $\cdots C_H)$, where C_m is either $z_m^i < -z_{m0}$, $-z_{m0} \leq z_m^i \leq z_{m0}$, or $z_m^i > z_{m0}$.
   (b) Generate the rule *consequence* as follows:
      - Collect all training samples that satisfy this rule condition.
      - Compute the coefficients of the predicting equation by applying least squares multiple linear regression.
4. Apply C4.5 [9] to simplify the rule conditions.

The rule condition $(C_1$ and C_2 and ... and $C_H)$ defines intersections of half-spaces in the input space. As the boundaries of the region defined by such intersections involve the network weights, C4.5 may be applied to remove these weights from the rule conditions. The result will be a set of rules that can be much easier to understand and analyze.

5 Experimental results

5.1 2Dplane data set

The data set is downloaded from `http://www.ncc.up.pt/~ltorgo/Research/`. Each artificially generated sample has 10 discrete attributes $X_1, X_2, \ldots, X_{10}$ and the values of the attributes had been generated independently according to the following probabilities:

$$P(X_1 = 1) = P(X_1 = -1) = \frac{1}{2}$$
$$P(X_k = 1) = P(X_k = 0) = P(X_k = -1) = \frac{1}{3}, \quad k = 2, 3, \ldots 10$$

The target value y was obtained using the following rule:

- If $X_1 = 1$, then set $y = 3 + 3X_2 + 2X_3 + X_4 + e$
- If $X_1 = -1$, then set $y = -3 + 3X_5 + 2X_6 + X_7 + e$

where e is random error $N(0, 1)$.

Two-thousand samples were used for training and one thousand samples were used for testing the accuracy of the neural network and the extracted rules. The initial number of hidden units was 8. After pruning, 2 hidden units remained.

Of the 10 original input units, only the relevant 7 input units were still present in the pruned network. Since there are 2 hidden units the sample space could be divided up into $3 \times 3 = 9$ subregions. However, only 2 of of these subregions are not empty. The values of z_{10} and z_{20} are computed using the hidden unit activations of the training samples and they are 0.96 and 0.98, respectively. The rule conditions that define the boundaries of the non-empty subregions are:

- Region 1: C_1 and $C_2 \equiv (-0.96 \leq z_1^i \leq 0.96)$ and $(-0.98 < z_2^i)$.
- Region 2: C_1 and $C_2 \equiv (z_1^i > 0.96)$ and $(-0.98 \leq z_2^i \leq 0.98)$.

All training samples that fall in Region 1 were grouped into one group, and all the others were grouped into a second group. The SAS [5] package was applied twice to find the multiple regression equations for the data in the two regions. The 7 inputs found to be relevant by the network were used as SAS input, these were $X_1, X_2, \ldots X_7$. Since some of these inputs may not contribute significantly to the prediction of the output in a region, the SAS procedure stepwise regression with FORWARD option was applied to select those inputs that are significant at the significance level $\alpha = .10$. The results from SAS are as follows:

- If Region 1, then $\hat{y} = 2.99 + 3.01X_1 + 1.96X_2 + 1.02X_3$.
- If Region 2, then $\hat{y} = -2.97 + 2.97X_4 + 2.08X_5 + 0.96X_6$.

C4.5 was applied to simplify the rule conditions that describe the two regions, All training samples $\mathbf{x}^i$ that fall in Region 1 were labeled "1" and all those that fall in Region 2 were labeled "2". A very simple rule was discovered by C4.5:

- Rule 1: if $(X_1 = 1)$, then Region 1.
- Default rule: Region 2.

5.2 Auto-mpg data set

The target to be predicted in this problem is the city-cycle fuel consumption of different car models in miles per gallon [6]. The 3 discrete attributes of the data are (1) cylinders with possible values of 3, 4, 5, 6, and 8; (2) model with possible values of 70, 71, 72, 73, 74, 75, 76, 77, 78, 79, 80, 81, and 82; and (3) origin with possible values of 1, 2, and 3. The 4 continuous attributes are (1) displacement, (2) horsepower, (3) weight, and (4) acceleration.

The training data set contains 358 samples and the test set contains 40 samples. The binary-coded data required the neural network to have 25 input units. One network input is needed for each possible value of the discrete attributes. The two ordinal discrete attributes cylinders and model are encoded using the thermometer scheme. The first five network inputs I_1, I_2, I_3, I_4, I_5 are assigned the binary input values of $(0,0,0,0,1)$,$(0,0,0,1,1)$,$(0,0,1,1,1)$, $(0,1,1,1,1)$ and $(1,1,1,1,1)$ if the number of cylinders is 3,4,5,6, or 8, respectively. The attribute model requires 13 network inputs, $I_6, \ldots, I_{18}$. The network inputs I_{19}, I_{20} and I_{21} are used for the nominal discrete attribute origin. Their input values are $(0,0,1)$, $(0,1,0)$ and $(1,0,0)$, if origin of the car is 1, 2, or 3, respectively. The

Table 1. The average prediction error rates for the Auto-mpg data.

Predictor	Training data (358 samples)		Test data (40 samples)	
	MAE	MAPE	MAE	MAPE
Pruned network	2.18	9.30	1.91	7.77
NN Rule 1	1.24	8.39	0.42	2.91
NN Rule 2	2.27	8.41	1.85	7.12
NN Rules 1+2	1.93	8.40	1.60	6.38
Linear regression	2.12	9.53	2.20	9.46

range of the 4 continuous attributes are normalized to $[0, 1]$ and 4 network input units $I_{22}, I_{23}, I_{24}, I_{25}$ are assigned these normalized input values.

The pruned neural network has only one hidden unit left. Eight of the 25 input units remained. The relevant inputs are $I_3, I_4, I_9, I_{14}, I_{16}, I_{21}, I_{23}$ and I_{24}. After approximating the hidden unit activation function by the piecewise linear function, it is found that two linear regression functions were required.

NN Rule 1: if Region 1, then $\hat{y} = 23.12 + 1.49\, I_{14} - 3.39\, I_{23} - 9.72\, I_{24}$
NN Rule 2: if Region 2, then $\hat{y} = 26.98 + 6.83\, I_4 + 6.03\, I_9 + 3.84\, I_{14} - 1.82\, I_{16} - 2.09\, I_{21} - 9.11\, I_{23} - 26.17\, I_{24}$

The coefficients of the regression equations were obtained using SAS STEPWISE procedure with FORWARD option. A variable is included in the linear equations only if its coefficient is significantly different from 0 at $\alpha = .10$ level.

Table 1 summarizes the error rates of the extracted rules and multiple linear regression for this example. The error rates are computed as the Mean Absolute Error (MAE) and the Mean Absolute Percentage Error (MAPE):

$$\text{MAE} = \frac{1}{P}\sum_{i=1}^{P} |\hat{y}^i - y^i| \qquad \text{MAPE} = \frac{1}{P}\sum_{i=1}^{P} 100 \times |(\hat{y}^i - y^i)/y^i|$$

The figures in the table highlight the advantages of splitting the samples into two groups and having different regression equations for the samples in different groups. Fitting a single linear regression line on the entire training samples leads to the worst predictive accuracy. The error rates of the pruned neural network are less than those of the single regression equation due to the network's ability to fit the data using a more complex function. However, the error rates are reduced even further in this example by having two multiple linear regression equations. SAS found that different sets of inputs contribute significantly to the prediction of the samples in the different regions. For samples in the first region, only 3 inputs are significant, while for those in the second region 7 inputs are significant. Finally, when C4.5 was run to generate rules that separate samples in the first region from those in the second region, seven rules were generated. Input I_3 which was not pruned by the network pruning algorithm, but does not appear in both NN Rule1 and Rule2, turns out to be an important input for separating the samples in the two regions.

6 Conclusion

We have presented a hybrid method that combines neural networks, statistical regression, and decision tree classification method to represent nonlinear relationship between variables in a data set as compact sets of linear functions. Linear equations that provide predictions of the continuous target values of data samples are obtained by approximating each hidden unit activation by a 3-piece linear function. These linear approximating functions also divide the input space of the data into subregions, where target values all samples that are in the same subregion are predicted by the same linear regression function. C4.5 classification algorithm is applied to obtain rules that describe the decision boundaries of the regions and statistical multiple linear regression is applied to simplify the functions. Input attributes that do not contribute significantly to the prediction of the output are removed. Our preliminary experimental results show the effectiveness of our proposed methods on two problems, one artificially generated and one real world data.

References

1. Cybenko, G. (1989) Approximation by superpositions of a sigmoidal function. *Mathematics of Control, Signals, and Systems*, 2, 303-314.
2. Dennis Jr. J.E. and Schnabel, R.E. (1983) Numerical methods for unconstrained optimization and nonlinear equations. Englewood Cliffs, New Jersey: Prentice Halls.
3. Hornik, K. (1991) Approximation capabilities of multilayer feedforward networks. *Neural Networks*, 4, 251-257.
4. John, G., Kohavi, R. and Pfleger, K. (1994) Irrelevant features and the subset selection problem. In *Proc. of the 11th International Conference on Machine Learning*, Morgan Kaufman, San Mateo, 121-129.
5. Khattree, W. and Naik, D.N. Applied multivariate statistics with SAS software. SAS Institute, Carey, N.C., 1999.
6. Kilpatrick, D., and Cameron-Jones, M. Numeric prediction using instance-based learning with encoding length selection. *Progress in Connectionist-Based Information Systems* Singapore: Springer-Verlag, 1998.
7. Ludl, M-C. and Widmer, G. (2000) Relative unsupervised discretization for regression problems. In *Proc. of the 11th European Conf. on ML, ECML 2000*, Lecture Notes in AI 1810, Springer, R.A. Mantaras and E. Plaza (Eds), 246-253, Barcelona.
8. Meltser, M., Shoham, M. and Manevitz, L. (1997) Aproximations of functions by multi-layer perceptrons: a new approach. *Neural networks*, 10 (6), 1069-1081.
9. Quinlan, R. (1993) C4.5: Programs for machine learning. Morgan Kaufmann, San Meteo, CA.
10. Setiono, R. and Leow, W.K. (2000) Pruned neural networks for regression. In *Proc. of the 6th Pacific Rim Conference on Artificial Intelligence, PRICAI 2000*, Lecture Notes in AI 1886, Springer, R. Mizoguchi and J. Slaney (Eds), 500-509, Melbourne.
11. Setiono, R., Leow, W.K. and Zurada, J.M. (2002) Extraction of rules from artificial neural networks for nonlinear regression. In *IEEE Trans. on Neural Networks*, forthcoming.
12. Torgo, L. and Gama, J. (1997) Search-based class discretization. In *Proc. of the 9th European Conference on Machine Learning, ECML-97*, Lecture Notes in AI 1224, Springer, M. van Someren and G. Widmer (Eds), 266-273, Prague.

Financial Fraud Identification Using MF-ARTMAP Neural Network[α]

Peter Sinčák[2,1], Marcel Hric[1], Richard Val'o[1], Pavol Horanský[3], Pavel Karel[3]

[1]Center for Intelligent Technologies, Dcpartment of Cybernetics and AI
Faculty of EE and Infomatics, Technical University of Kosice, Slovakia
[2]Siemens PSE& I, AG Vienna, ECANSE Group, Austria
[3]Tatrabanka a.s. Bratislava, Slovakia

Summary : The paper deals with application of MF-ARTMAP neural network on financial fraud data. The focus was on classification of data into 5 types of fraud based on the expert knowledge with the aim to achieve the tool with highest classification accuracy. The fraud was characterized with 22 features and verbal features were encoded into numerical values to be able to used them in classification procedure. The results show that in case of sufficient data (fraud) representation neural networks could be used with success and in case if there are rather small examples expert generated rules are preferred.

Keywords: Neural Networks, ART neural networks, fuzzy logic, feature space, classification procedures, fuzzy cluster, fuzzy class, classification accuracy assessment

Introduction

Intelligent technologies play important role in decision systems. Decision procedure is very important part of any complex decision support system. Decision and pattern recognition are very close procedures and could be viewed as similar processes. Both are working with feature space and in both approaches is the final procedure a classification which makes the final decision or categorization. Even considering prediction could be viewed as trends classification in selected feature space where the final step is again classification with time series-like input and output value. In all cases the classification is

[α] This project is supported by Vega Project from Ministry of Education of Slovak Republic “Intelligent Technologies in Modeling Intelligent Systems”, partially by EU Maria-Curie Individual Fellowship and also by Tatrabanka a.s. Slovakia.

considered as unknown function approximation and if it is a function we can make decision, categorization or even prediction.

Classification is a very important procedure in the feature space with very high application potential. It is in fact clusters identification in the feature space and their association with classes of interest. The main problem is in definition of the cluster in the feature space which could be very complex and is leading to fuzzy approach to cluster identification and also frequent situation when two or more different clusters in the feature space are associated with the same class.

This fist problem is associated with a cluster shape determination that is in fact already given on training data and the problem is the overlap of two or more clusters in the feature space. Therefore the knowledge about fuzzy categorization of the unknown input could be a solution to increase accuracy of the classification system. The later problem is associated with the data nature and the fact that classes determined by experts could be represented by various clusters in the feature space in completely different locations of the feature space. The identification of such a classes is rather difficult with approaches like neural network based on BP approach which must design the approximation of rather complicated discrimination function. The approaches based on ART or ARTMAP technology are rather flexible and much more suitable for these situations when class is consisted of various clusters in the feature space. These two considerations let us to design a MF ARTMAP approach and work on its further development mainly for classification purposes.

Motivation of the project

Classification is mapping from feature space into space of classes. Considering supervised mode a determination of training sets is extremely important. Many times is a situation that the training sites produce non-homogeneous training data which are represented in the feature space as union of clusters in different locations in the feature space.

From this perspective the classification approach which uses labeled clustering is the most appropriate way of handling classification task. In Figure 1 is the basic concept of ARTMAP neural network which is approaching a problem as labeled clustering task. The role of the Mapfield neural layer is to associate the various clusters into the desired class. The coefficient ρ is adjusted in the training phase and reflects the plasticity of the system. Number of nodes in the recognition layer reflects number of identified clusters in the feature space. It very often happens that it is very difficult to decide if a certain point in feature space belongs to a certain class. Therefore an approach based on fuzzy sets has many advantages to reduce misclassification results. Sometimes it is more convenient to have results in the form of transparent information concerning relations of the observed point in the feature space to all classes of interest. Instead of the crisp classifier output we can be more satisfied with outputs based on fuzzy sets and namely on values of membership functions of observed input to fuzzy cluster and fuzzy classes. The notions of fuzzy clusters and fuzzy class are described in the next part of this paper. The motivation is to provide for the end-user a smaller number of misclassifications and higher readability of the classification results. The output of these classification results is a vector of values describing relation of the input to each class of interest. The desire is to have a highly parallel tool with incremental learning ability similar to ARTMAP family neural network.

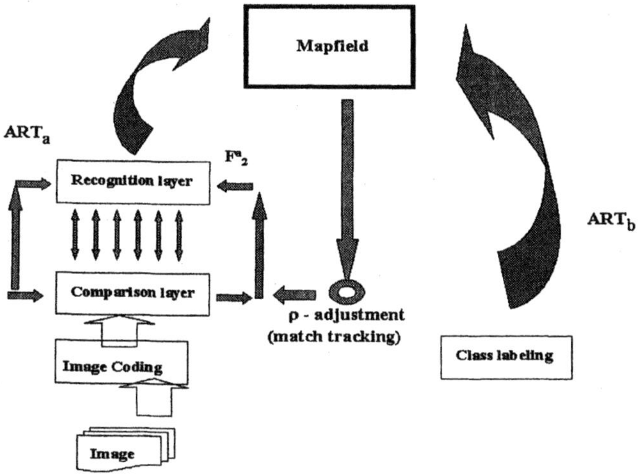

Figure 1 : The basic concept of ARTMAP neural network

Description of the method

The project is based on the assumption that data in feature space are organized in fuzzy clusters. Fuzzy cluster is considered as a fuzzy relation A in multidimensional feature space.

$$A(\bar{x}) = \int_Y \frac{1}{1 + \left| \left(\frac{\left| \bar{x}_S - \bar{x} \right|}{\bar{E}} \right)^{\bar{F}} \right|} / \bar{x} \qquad (1)$$

Where A is a fuzzy relation, Y is feature space, x is point in feature space and Xs, E, F are parameters of fuzzy relation. Each fuzzy relation A is defined by equation [2] as combination of partial functions f_i for each dimension.

$$A(\bar{x}) = \frac{1}{1 + \left| \frac{1}{\bar{f}(x)} - 1 \right|} \tag{2}$$

Partial funcion for each dimension is defined by equation [3].

$$f_i(x_i) = \frac{1}{1 + \left(\frac{|x_{S_i} - x_i|}{E_i} \right)^{F_i}} \tag{3}$$

There are many fuzzy clusters in feature space and a certain set of fuzzy clusters create a fuzzy class. Fuzzy class is the union of fuzzy clusters belonging to a considered class defined by training set e.g.

$$CL = \{\bigcup_{i=1}^{n} A_i\} \tag{4}$$

Generally we can consider fuzzy class as a set of fuzzy clusters Ai representing the variety of the numerical representation of the class. Relation between μCL (x) and μA(x) must be as follows:

$$\mu_{CL}(X) = \max_{i = 1, n}(\mu_{A_i}(X)) \tag{5}$$

where Ai is a fuzzy cluster which belongs to class CL and n is a number of fuzzy clusters creating class CL. The MF-ARTMAP is intended to be such a tool to calculate values of membership functions of X to each class of interest in feature space. In figure 2 we can find an example of 2-dimensional fuzzy relation with various parameters in single-dimensional directions in the space. The space is n+1 dimensional where n is number of features and (n+1)-st dimension is fuzzy relation value.

As it is clear from the basic equation of the membership function the influence of the shape is done by variables E and F. Basically these 2 variables influence the shape of the membership function of the cluster in the feature space. The membership function should be adapted to the cluster as it exists in the feature space, which means each cluster should have completely different shape of the membership function with ability to describe the non-linearity of the clusters in the feature space. Variable E and F are different in each cluster and even each dimension of the feature space could lead to the fitted shape of the membership function to each detected cluster. In Figure 3 are examples of the influence of E and F to the shape of the membership function. The representation in more than 2 dimensional space is rather complex and could lead to efficient description of the membership to the clusters which mean ability to reduce the number of nodes in the recognition layer of MF-ARTMAP neural network. The learning procedure on the training data is searching the proper values of E and F in every direction of the feature space and every cluster that is detected by MF-ARTMAP. The procedure is efficient and only few iterations are need to achieve stability and able to identify inputs from the training set into different fuzzy clusters and consequently to fuzzy classes. This gives possibility to have more complex view about categorization and relation of categories in feature space what is a non trivial information if we do have high dimensional feature space defined by interpreter for pattern recognition purposes. More details about MF-ARTMAP approach can be found in

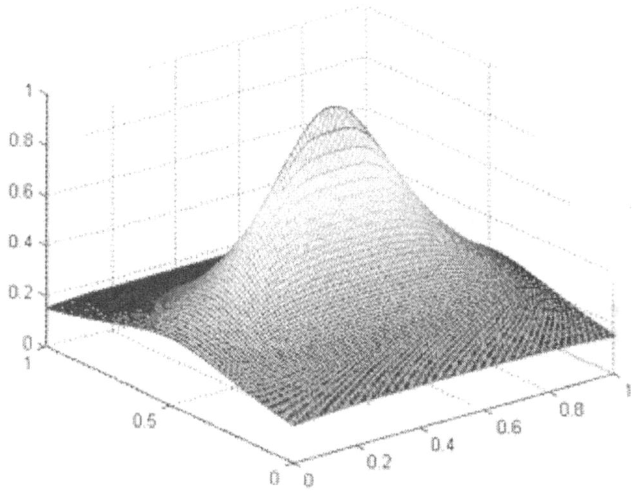

Figure 2 : Two dimensional membership value with various parameters

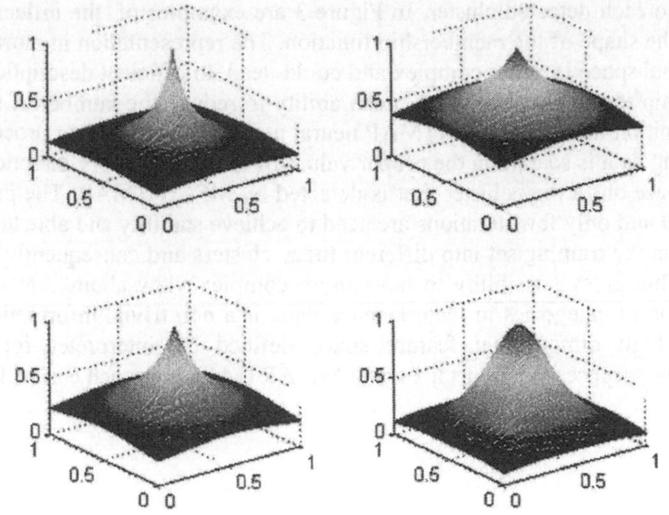

Figure 3 : The shapes of the membership functions when F=1, E=0.1, E=0.4 (top) and E=0.2, F=1, F=2 (bottom)

Experimental results

Experiments using real-world data were done during this project. The aim was to prove the suitability of these technologies for these types of data. Accuracy assessment was evaluated using contingency table analysis. A contingency table was used in a basic comparison study between all methods, which were investigated and developed. Some details about contingency table analysis for accuracy assessment of classification results can be found in [8].

Experiments on real-world data

The application of MF-ARTMAP in financial fraud transaction data is an interesting challenge of this approach. The theoretical advantage of this approach is to reveal relations between types of frauds and indication and recommendations to change a feature space with the aim to be able to discriminate the type of the fraud.

The financial fraud data consists of a training set of 9000 points in the feature space and of a test set of 9000 points of the feature space. A point in the feature space has 22 attributes, 10 real and 12 nominal, and 7 binary output values. The class of a fact is determined by the output which has a value of one; the other six output values are zero. Class "0" represents clear financial transaction, classes "1" – "6" represent some kinds of fraud financial transaction. The data represents 22 attributes of the financial transaction. The representation set was determined by financial fraud experts.

The pre-analysis of the data for processing was made in the following aspects:

1. analysis of the non-contradictory labeling of the data by expert – means the expert should not label similar data with different labels
2. analysis of statistical occurrences of the fraud types – if there is no sufficient data representation of the fraud type – there is difficult to make decision about fraud identification
3. way how to encode the linguistic features into the numerical form to be able to process the complex fraud description in 22 dimensional feature space.

The analysis of point 1 shows some problems which has been cleaned and some correction in representing set of fraud has been made. Concerning to the point 2 analysis shows that fraud type 2 and 6 had only 4 cases in representative set – that means we have removed them from the classification analysis and further processing. So for classification processing we have used classes 0 – no fraud, 1, 3, 4, 5 – these are selected frauds. The frauds type 2 and 6 has been not included into the classification because of non sufficient representation in representing set.

The classification has been made and tables 1 and 2 representing the classification results on financial fraud data with 2 randomly selected subsets of the representing sets. It is clear that both results are similar and if the representative set per fraud are sufficient is it possible to used these approaches for these type of data. In case if the representation of the fraud is poor – there are only few examples then the identification will be done using rule-base approach implemented into the overall classification approach. This will be a matter of further research to integrate the rule-base approach and neural technology into final decision support system. The complex system must also take into consideration the type of error so we have to take extreme care if the fraud is classified as non-fraud – which is more important problem if the non-fraud is classified as a fraud. These considerations will be included into the future research. The number of clusters associated with each class are interesting view of ART technology can easily handle non-uniform classes consisting of more different clusters and belonging according to the expert into one class. The table 3 shows number of clusters associated which each type of class after training procedure.

Predicted	Actual 1	2	3	4	5
1'	98.93	1.19	9.03	20.68	0.00
2'	0.76	98.80	0.00	0.00	0.00
3'	0.21	0.00	90.96	6.89	0.00
4'	0.08	0.00	0.00	72.41	0.00
5'	0.00	0.00	0.00	0.00	100.00

Table 1 : Financial fraud transaction classification on test data

The MF-ARTMAP reveals also relation of these frauds to the other types of the fraud and give more complex view to the classification procedure what is important for improvement of the overall process.

Predicted	Actual 1	2	3	4	5
1'	98.66	0.23	5.61	16.66	0.00
2'	0.80	99.52	1.12	0.00	0.00
3'	0.17	0.00	93.25	0.00	0.00
4'	0.10	0.00	0.00	83.33	0.00
5'	0.00	0.00	0.00	0.00	100.00

Table 2 : Financial fraud transaction classifications with changing training and test data (results on test data)

Regarding to the results presented in the tables 1 and 2 the values of the membership function of misclassification results belonging to the class 0 – but in fact (according to the expert identification) these frauds were not type 0 (non-fraud) w hich is a very serious problem. Therefore we did an analysis of the misclassifications patterns and values of the membership functions produced with the MF ARTMAP. There are 2 major results of this analysis to prevent an misclassifications as follows:

1. to give a feedback to the expert to re-evaluate the misclassified patterns and if pattern with high membership function to the non-fraud and is still a fraud according to the expert some further analysis must be done.
2. if the membership function of the misclassified patterns to class 'non-fraud' is the highest but not exceeding a certain thresholds e.g. 0.7 is probably a new type of fraud which does not belong to any of selected examples and should be classified as another type of cluster (class). This information should be discussed with the expert to confirm these considerations and implement it into the system.

The above consideration can be done only by MF-ARTMAP because of providing the values of membership function of the patterns to the fuzzy clusters or fuzzy classes. The ARTMAP technology does not provide this information and is not possible to make and feedback to the expect in this extend. The following values in the table 8 shows the values of membership functions of the patterns which were misclassified from fraud type 4 to class 0 (non-fraud). The values are in interval and could be a solid base for further discussion with the expert to improve the classification results and decrease the misclassification of fraud 4 to class 0.

Type of the class	0	1	3	4	5
Number of clusters in the class	763	30	16	5	2

Table 3 : Number of clusters in the feature space associated with type of fraud type

Class	Membership values of misclassified patterns to the class (interval) originally labeled by expert to class 4
Class 0	From 0.9801 To 0.9993
Class 4	From 0.9598 To 0.9890

Table 4: The table shows membership values of the patters to classes 0 and 4 which have been identified by expert as class 4. This table could inspiration for discussion with the expert to improve the classification results and decrease the misclassification of the frauds.

Conclusion

The paper presents further application of the MF-ARTMAP with F adaptation approach to the classification procedure. The advantage of this approach is higher readability of the neural network in providing the values of membership functions of input to fuzzy clusters or fuzzy classes identified by this approach.

The experiments on financial fraud data has been presented and MF ATRMAP is able to provide an useful feedback information to the expert in fraud identification to reconsider the fraud labeling. The expert should also provide explanation why the misclassified pattern have close metric distance to class _"non-fraud" and in this case some additional features should be under consideration to distinguish fraud from non-fraud transaction.

In the future research we will provide further development of MF-ARTMAP to be able to retrieve some explicit knowledge from the network topology as well as to be able to implement some apriory knowledge into the system. Also beside parallel MF-ARTMAP we will focus our attention to hierarchical classification system to achieve the highest classification accuracy in the form of classification modular complex. Also some implementation the MF-ARTMAP as an autonomous agent and a part of Intelligent Multi-Agent System.

References

[1] P.M. Atkinson and A.R.L. Tatnall, "Neural networks in remote sensing," *Int. J. Remote Sensing,* vol. 18, 4, 1997, 711-725.

[2] J. Richards, *Remote sensing digital image analysis: An introduction.* Springer Verlag: Berlin, 1993.

[3] B.G. Lees and K. Ritman, "Decision-tree and rule-induction approach to integration of remotely sensed and GIS data in mapping vegetation in disturbed or hilly environments," *Environmental Management,* vol. 15, 1991, pp. 823-831.

[4] C.H. Chen, "Trends on information processing for remote sensing," in Proceedings of the International Geoscience and Remote Sensing Symposium (IGARSS), vol. 3, Aug. 3-8 1997, pp. 1190-1192.

[5] P. Werbos, Beyond Regression: New Tools for Prediction and Analysis in the Behavioral Sciences, Ph.D. thesis, Harvard University, 1974.

[6] G.A. Carpenter, M.N. Gjaja, S. Gopal, and C.E. Woodcock, "ART neural networks for remote sensing" Vegetation classification from Landsat TM and terrain data," *IEEE Transactions on Geoscience and Remote Sensing,* vol. 35, no. 2, 1997, pp. 308-325.

[7] D. Rutkowska, R. Nowicki, „Implication-based neuro-fuzzy architectures" in International journal of applied mathematics and computer science, vol. 10, no. 4, 2000, pp. 675-701

[8] P. Sinčák, H. Veregin, and N. Kopčo, "Conflation techniques in multispectral image processing," *Geocarto Int,* March, pp. 11-19. 2000.

[9] S. Grossberg, "Adaptive pattern classification and universal recoding, I: Feedback, expectation, olfaction, and illusions," *Biological Cybernetics,* vol. 23, 1976, pp. 187-202.

[10] G.A. Carpenter, B.L. Milenova, and B.W. Noeske, "Distributed ARTMAP: a neural network for fast distributed supervised learning," *Neural Networks,* vol. 11, no. 5, Jul. 1998, pp. 793-813.

[11] J.R. Williamson, "Gaussian ARTMAP: A neural network for fast incremental learning of noisy multidimensional maps," *Neural Networks,* vol. 9, 1996, pp. 881-897.

[12] R.K. Cunningham, *Learning and recognizing patterns of visual motion, color, and form,* Unpublished Ph.D. thesis, Boston University, Boston, MA: 1998.

[13] R. Duda and P. Hart, *Pattern Classification and Scene Analysis,* Wiley, New York: 1973.

[14] Sinčák, Kopčo, Hric, Veregin: MF-ARTMAP to identify fuzzy clusters in feature space, accepted to IIZUKA 2000, 6-th International Conference on Computational Intelligence, IIZUKA - Japan, October 1-4, 2000 (1)

[15] Sinčák, Hric, Vaščák : Pattern Recognition with MF-ARTMAP Neural Networks, accepted to INTECH 2001, 2-nd International Conference on Intelligent Technologies, Bangkok – Thailand, November 27-29, 2001

[16] Ocelikova, E.-Nguyen Hong, T.: Diferential Equations for maximum entropy Image Restoration. In: Proc. of the 3rd International Conference „ Informatics and Algorithms ´99 „„ Prešov, september 9-10, 1999, pp. 214-218. . ISBN 80-88941-05-9

[17] Ocelikova, E.-Klimesova, D.: Clustering by Boundary Detection. In: Proc. of the 4th International Scientific Technical Conference "Process control – ŘÍP 2000", Pardubice , June 2000, pp. 108, ISBN 80-7194-271-5.

[18] D. Klimesova , E. Ocelikova,: GIS and Spatial Data Network. In: Proc. of International Conference "Agrarian Perspectives X-Sources of Sutainable Economic Growth in the Third Millenium. Globalisation versus Regionalism. sept. 18-19, 2001, Prague, Czech republic, ISBN 80-213-0799-4

Radial Basis Function Neural Networks: Theory and Applications

Paweł Strumiłło[1], Władysław Kamiński[2]

[1] Institute of Electronics, Technical University of Łódź,
18/22 Stefanowskiego, 90-924 Łódź, Poland, e-mail: pstrumil@ck-sg.p.lodz.pl
[2] Faculty of Process and Environmental Engineering, Technical University of Łódź, 213 Wólczańska, 93-005 Łódź, Poland, e-mail: kaminski@ck-sg.p.lodz.pl

Abstract. Essential theory and main applications of feed-forward connectionist structures termed radial basis function (RBF) neural networks are given. Universal approximation and Cover's theorems are outlined that justify powerful RBF network capabilities in function approximation and data classification tasks. The methods for regularising RBF generated mappings are addressed also. Links of these networks to kernel regression methods, density estimation, and nonlinear principal component analysis are pointed out. Particular attention is put on discussing different RBF network training schemes, e.g. the constructive method incorporating orthogonalisation of RBF kernels. Numerous, successful RBF networks applications in diverse fields such as signal modelling, non-linear time series prediction, identification of dynamic systems, pattern recognition, and knowledge discovery are outlined.

1 Introductory definitions

Radial basis function (RBF) neural networks are feed-forward connectionist structures comprising a single hidden layer of linearly independent functions $\{\phi_1, \phi_2, \ldots, \phi_m\}$ that form a basis for an m-dimensional function space [1]. A wide class of nonlinear mappings $f_m : R^N \to R$ belonging to so generated linear space, i.e., $f_m \in span\{\phi_1, \phi_2, \ldots, \phi_m\}$, can be obtained by means of RBF network structure (Fig. 1). Its transfer function is given by the following linear regression equation:

$$f_m(x) = \sum_{k=1}^{m} w_k \phi_k(x) + w_0 \tag{1}$$

where $\phi_k(x) = \phi(\|x - c_k\| / s_k)$ are the basis functions (also termed the kernels) being translated dilations of a radially-symmetric prototype function $\phi : R^N \to R$ and w_k, $k = 0, 1, \ldots, m$ are the adjustable weight coefficients of linear regression (1).

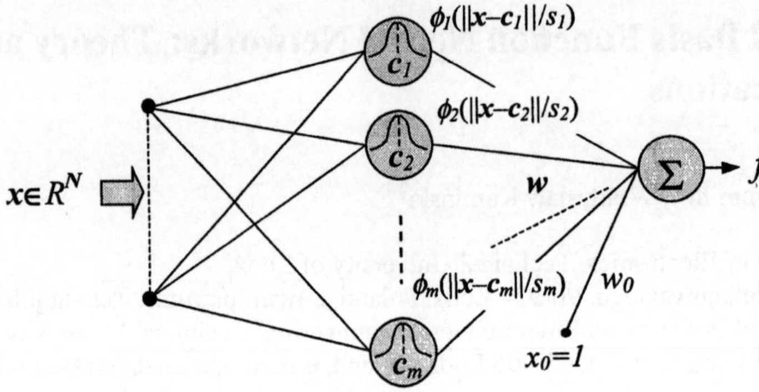

Fig. 1. Radial basis function (RBF) neural network

Due to radial-symmetry of the kernels constants, $c_k \in R^N$ are termed centres and $\|\cdot\|$ is a norm (not necessary Euclidean, e.g., Mahalonobis) on R^N defining distance $r = \|x - c_k\|$ between the input $x \in R^N$ and the centre c_k. The adopted norm can be additionally scaled by dilation factors $s_k \in R$ that are either assigned individually to each of the basis functions or made equal for all of them, i.e., $s_1 = s_2 = \ldots = s_m = s > 0$. A suitable choice of kernels for the basis functions was investigated by Micchelli [2]. For RBF networks the ones which are of particular interest are $\phi(r) = exp(-r^2)$ – Gaussian, $\phi(r) = 1/\sqrt{r^2+1}$ – inverse multiquadric, $\phi(r) = r$ – linear, $\phi(r) = r\,log\,r$ – thin plate spline, $\phi(r) = \sqrt{r^2+1}$ – multiquadric, $\phi(r) = r^3$ – cubic, etc. The Gaussian and the inverse multiquadric are termed localised functions since $\phi(r) \to 0$ for $r \to \infty$ while the remaining RBFs are considered as non-local (i.e., $\phi(r)$ is unbounded for $r \to \infty$). Localised kernels have important analogy to receptive fields observed in biological neuronal systems (e.g. in the retinal surface of the visual system) that are sensitive to stimuli located within a bounded range of the input space. However, Powell [3] indicates that non-local RBFs are more efficient in approximating smooth input–output mappings than localised RBFs (see also [4] for a comprehensive survey of neural networks transfer functions and the authors' work [5]).

The paradigm of approximating RBF neural networks comes from the theory of potential functions [6] and multivariate interpolation in high-dimensional spaces studied by Powell [3], who has shown that for a given set of P interpolation knots $\{(x_i, y_i) \in R^d \times R\}_{i=1}^{P}$, i.e., y_i scalar values given (e.g., measured) at x_i coordinates, there exists an interpolation function $f_m(x) = \sum_{i=1}^{m=P} w_i \phi(\|x\text{-}x_i\|)$ that satisfies the interpolation condition $f_m(\boldsymbol{x}_i)=y_i$, $i=1,2,\ldots, m=P$. Note, that the interpolation function is a linear superposition of a number of RBFs that is equal to the number of interpolation knots that coincide with the kernel centres $\boldsymbol{c}_i=\boldsymbol{x}_i$. By inserting the interpolation condition in the equation of the interpolation function one obtains $\boldsymbol{\Phi w}=\boldsymbol{y}$, where $\boldsymbol{w}=[w_1,w_2,\ldots,w_P]$, $\boldsymbol{y}=[y_1,y_2,\ldots,y_P]$ and the square matrix $\boldsymbol{\Phi}=\{\phi(\|\boldsymbol{x}_j-\boldsymbol{x}_i\|),(j,i)=1,2,\ldots,P\}$ (the interpolation matrix) is non-singular for distinct $\boldsymbol{x}_i$ and a class of suitably chosen RBFs [2]. Hence, the solution to the interpolation problem is readily obtained as $\boldsymbol{w}=\boldsymbol{\Phi}^{-1}\boldsymbol{y}$.

2 RBF networks are universal approximators

The underpinning idea proposed in [1] and [7] that led to the concept of RBF neural networks relied on reformulating the strict interpolation condition (with as many RBF kernels as data points) into the problem of function approximation, in which the number of RBF kernels is intentionally lower than the number of available data training points, i.e., $m<P$. Many signal and system modelling tasks (e.g., time-series prediction, identification of dynamic systems) can be defined in terms of function approximation [10], [11], [12].

Theoretical justification for using RBF networks as function approximators was given in [8] where the universal approximation theorem (similar to the one proposed earlier for the multilayer perceptron networks (MLP)) was formulated for RBF networks topologies (Fig. 1). Namely: *for any continuous input-output mapping function* $f(\boldsymbol{x})$, *there exists an RBF network with m integrable bounded kernels, such that the mapping function* $f_m(\boldsymbol{x})$ *given by* (1) *approximates* $f(\boldsymbol{x})$ *arbitrarily close in the* L^p *norm for every* $p\in[1,\infty)$ (*where* L^P *is a space of functions satisfying* $\int_{R^N}|f(\boldsymbol{x})|^p\,dx<\infty$). Note also, that multi-output RBF network can be split-up into a set of separate single-output networks, each sharing the same set of RBFs (such as defined in (1) and shown in Fig. 1). Hence, RBF networks can be considered as multi-input – multi-output universal approximators. Moreover, a functional equivalence between RBF networks and fuzzy inference systems was noted in [9] (each RBF kernel can serve as a fuzzy membership function).

Consider a task of recovering an underlying signal $f(\boldsymbol{x})$ from training samples $T=\{(\boldsymbol{x}_i,y_i)\in R^d\times R\}_{i=1}^{P}$, where $y_i=f(\boldsymbol{x}_i)+\eta_i$ contains an additive noise component or measurement error. Fig. 2 illustrates examples of possible solutions to such tasks and points out to capabilities of RBFNNs but also highlights the problems that can arise in such applications (see section 4 and discussion on regularisation theory).

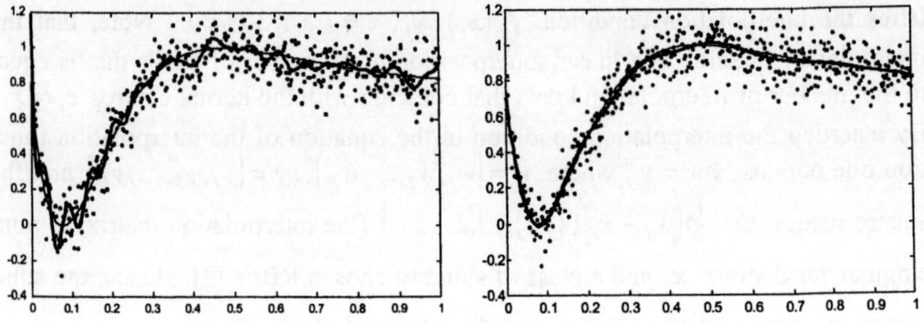

(a) (b)

Fig. 2. RBF networks applied to approximation of signal $f(t)=e^{-t}-4e^{-2t}+3e^{-3t}$ (thin solid line) contaminated with additive noise; (a) approximation with 100 RBF kernels (thick solid line) – see the over-fitting phenomenon, (b) approximation with 15 RBF kernels (thick solid line) – good fit to the noise-free signal is obtained (both networks were trained on noisy data)

An area of wide application of RBF networks approximating capabilities is identification of non-linear dynamic systems, control, and time-series prediction. Relationships between system inputs $u(t)$ and system responses $y(t)$ are modelled by one-step ahead prediction equation:

$$y(t+1)=S(y(t),y(t-1),\dots,y(t-k);\dots u(t+1),u(t),\dots,u(t-n)) \tag{2}$$

where $S(\cdot)$ is the multivariate function defined on $k+m+1$ dimensional vector inputs that needs to be approximated by the network. Such a system modelling approach cast into RBF network approximation task has been adopted in [12] for identification of stationary and time-varying nonlinear systems [13]. Other reported RBF applications in function approximation task are non-linear time series prediction [15], control [16, 17], non-parametric estimation [18] and telecommunications [19].

3 RBF networks are universal data classifiers

When discussing RBF network data classification capabilities it is useful to view the hidden RBF network layer as a nonlinear mapping of the *input data space* $X \in R^d$ into a new *m*-dimensional space spanned by the basis functions $\{\phi_1,\phi_2,\dots,\phi_m\}$ – termed *feature space.* In particular each input data point x is assigned an *m*-dimensional feature vector $\Phi(x)$ in this new space where:

$$\Phi(x)=[\phi_1(x),\phi_2(x),\dots,\phi_m(x)]^T \tag{3}$$

The question arises if there is any gain in applying such a nonlinear mapping to the input data patterns. Answer comes from the Cover's theorem on the separability of patterns [20]: "*a complex pattern classification problem cast in a high-dimensional space nonlinearly is more likely to be linearly separable than in a low dimensional space*". Hence, in practice, it is possible to construct a nonlinear mapping by means of a sufficiently high number of RBF kernels for which the originally given nonlinear data classification problem will become linearly separable. This is equivalent to finding a hyperplane $w^T \Phi(x) + w_0 = 0$ in the feature space that will ensure linear separation of features into different classes. In practice, however, due to the curse of dimensionality problem, dimensionality of the feature vector should be at least ten times smaller than the number of training samples P per class, i.e., $m/P < 10$ [21]. Thus, for applications in which an *a priori* knowledge can be incorporated into the data classification task, configuration of network receptive field should be sought for, as incrementation of the problem dimensionality is not required. To illustrate this point, consider a nonlinear data classification problem defined by the XOR (Exclusive OR) logical function [20]. By using an RBF network with two Gaussian kernels centred at $c_1 = [1, 1]$ and $c_2 = [0,0]$, four binary inputs $\{x_i\}_{i=1}^{4} = \{(0,0), (0,1), (1,0), (1,1)\}$ for the XOR can be linearly separated in the feature space $\phi_1 \times \phi_2$ of the same dimension, e.g., by the following decision boundary: $w_1\phi_1(x) + w_2\phi_2(x) + w_0 = exp(-\|x - c_1\|^2) + exp(-\|x - c_2\|^2) - 1 = 0$. Fig. 3 shows RBF generated mapping that linearises the XOR nonlinear data classification problem.

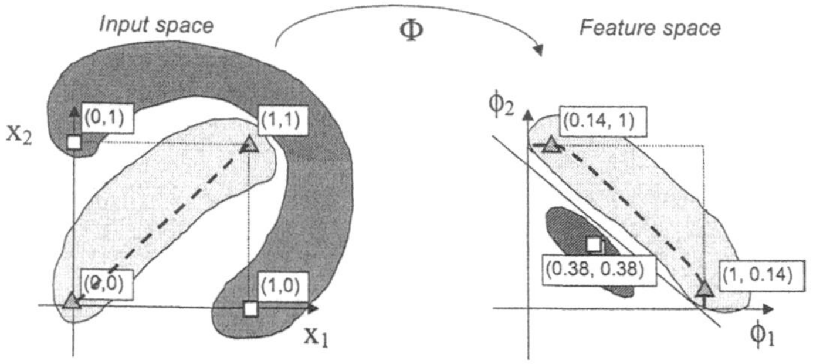

Fig. 3. Nonlinear mapping Φ of the input space onto feature space induced by RBF kernels that linearise data classification problem defined by the XOR logical function

RBF network capability for generating nonlinear transformations of input spaces into feature spaces can be effectively employed for feature extraction. Whereas the method of Principal Component Analysis (PCA) extracts the most expressive features in a linear manner, RBF network can perform more complex, nonlinear feature extraction tasks. Namely, instead of constructing the transformation matrix from eigenvectors of $N \times N$ correlation matrix $\boldsymbol{R} = E\left[xx^T\right]$ (as in PCA), another correlation matrix $\tilde{\boldsymbol{R}} = E\left[\Phi(x)\Phi^T(x)\right]$ of size $m \times m$ is computed in the feature space for the collection of *m*-dimensional features $\{\phi_k(x_i)\}_{i=1}^{P}$, $k = 1,2,\ldots,m$. Importantly, for RBF kernels that generate inner-product kernels, i.e., $K(x,x_i) = \sum_{k=1}^{m} \phi_k(x)\phi_k(x_i) = \Phi(x)\Phi^T(x_i)$, $i = 1,2,\ldots,P$ (e.g. for the Gaussian function) optimal classification hyperplanes in the feature space can be constructed without any need for explicit computation of this space itself [20]. Whereas PCA is limited to principal axis only, by using this concept, also termed Kernel PCA [22], it is possible to fit principal curves to probability distributions of data. An open issue is the choice of RBF kernels that would provide appropriate feature space construction. However, one of the proposed choices is maximisation of the variance of the obtained features [23].

RBF networks can be also viewed as a special case of the density estimation which is a statistical method referred to as the kernel-based density estimation [23], that first models statistical distributions $p(x|\omega_k)$ of the data within classes ω_k and undertakes the classification decision by using the Bayes decision theory. Namely, on the basis of *a priori* probability densities $p(x|\omega_k)$ the so called *a posteriori* probabilities $p(\omega_k|x)$ are computed for each of the classes $k = 1,2,\ldots,K$, by means of the Bayes rule:

$$p(\omega_k|x) = \frac{p(\omega_k)p(x|\omega_k)}{p(x)}, \tag{4}$$

where $p(\omega_k)$ is the unconditional probability of classes occurrences in an overall data distribution $p(x)$. It was shown that *a posteriori* probabilities can be expressed by RBF network with normalised kernels $\tilde{\phi}_k(x) = \phi_k(x) \Big/ \sum_{k=1}^{m} \phi_k(x)$ [23].

3.1 RBF networks applications in data classification tasks

Artificial neural networks have gained widespread applications in pattern classification tasks where no *a priori* knowledge about statistical structure of data is available. In these applications non-parametric approaches outperform other pattern classification schemes such as model-based (Bayesian classifiers) or rule-based (expert systems) methods [21]. In particular, RBF kernels use some norm $\phi(\|x_i - x_0\|)$ (e.g., Euclidean) rather than dot product $\phi(x_i \cdot w)$ (as for logistic functions) to measure the significance of an input pattern x_i. Accordingly, RBF networks generate cluster like decision surfaces in the input space whereas MLPs combine such surfaces from hyperplanes, e.g., a moderate size RBF network (64 weights) produces excellent result for the two-spiral classification benchmark for which a much larger MLP network would be required (see Fig. 4) [24].

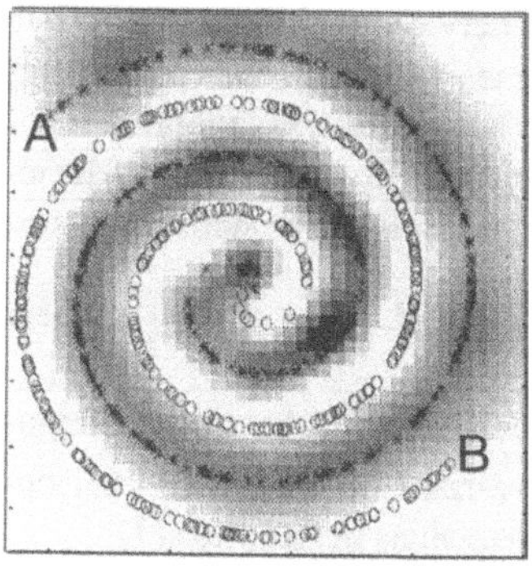

Fig. 4. Two spiral shaped classes marked by asterisks (class A) and circles (class B) are given; a suitably trained RBF network (with $m=64$ kernels placed at random locations) generates a spiral grayscale image that fits dark regions encompassing class A spiral indicated by asterisks whereas bright regions coincide with circles from class B spiral; grayscale thresholding of the RBF generated image provides accurate classification of the classes

There have been reported numerous applications of RBF networks in solving data classification problems, some of the recent ones are: classification of data from incomplete feature vectors [25], classification of UV-spectra [26], classification genetic code [27], econometry [28–29] and telecommunications [30].

Recently, an actively pursued research topic is data mining and knowledge discovery [31]. Among other approaches [31], RBF networks can be used for extraction of decision rules, because contribution of each kernel to the overall network output can be readily evaluated. In [32] a method of analysis of a pre-trained RBF network was proposed that allows discovering the rule base, coded in Boolean functions and acquiring rules for Iris flowers classification benchmark.

4 Training schemes for RBF networks

The task of optimising RBF neural network structure, known as network training, can be defined as the problem of finding the best basis $\{\phi_k\}_{k=1}^{m}$ and the best set of regression weight coefficients w that minimise the functional $\varepsilon(f_m)=\|f(x)-f_m(x)\|$ which is further termed the *generalisation error*. One of the popular method for providing good network generalisation properties is the *cross-validation technique*. Here, we point to another technique, referred to as *regularisation*, that relies on setting additional constraint criteria on the obtained solutions. In the case of RBF neural networks, the common choice is the Tikhonov regularisation, for which the network error is defined as the following functional:

$$\varepsilon(f_m)=\sum_{i=1}^{P}\|y_i-f_m(x_i)\|^2+\lambda\|Df_m\|^2 \tag{5}$$

i.e. the standard sum-square-error term is augmented by the regularising term $\|Df_m\|^2$ being a quadratic form of the differential operator D acting on f_m, and λ (a positive real number) controlling the trade-off between the two terms. While the first term in (2) enforces "goodness of fit" to the training data, the regularising term, on the contrary, enforces "smoothness" to the RBF network generated mapping (choice of a suitable λ, e.g. that can be combined with the cross-validation technique). As shown in [33], an approximation that minimises (5) with respect to f_m (i.e. for $m<P$) is given by linear expansion: $f_m(x)=\sum_{i=1}^{m} w_i\phi(\|x\text{-}c_i\|)$, where kernels $\phi(\cdot)$ are the so called Green functions associated with the selected regulariser D. In particular, the use of a rotationally invariant, linear differential operators for the regulariser D leads to Green functions such as defined for (1).

For a given finite dimensional expansion f_m, minimisation of (5) with regard to the weight vector $\boldsymbol{w}$ leads to the result [33]:

$$\left(\boldsymbol{\Phi}^T\boldsymbol{\Phi}+\lambda\boldsymbol{\Phi}_0\right)\boldsymbol{w}=\boldsymbol{\Phi}\boldsymbol{y} \tag{6}$$

where $y=[y_1,y_2,\dots,y_P]^T$, $\boldsymbol{\Phi}$ and $\boldsymbol{\Phi}_0$ are P-by-m and m-by-m matrices correspondingly:

$$\boldsymbol{\Phi}=\begin{bmatrix}\phi(x_1,c_1) & \phi(x_1,c_2) & \cdots & \phi(x_1,c_m)\\ \phi(x_2,c_1) & \phi(x_2,c_2) & \cdots & \phi(x_2,c_m)\\ \vdots & \vdots & \cdots & \vdots\\ \phi(x_P,c_1) & \phi(x_P,c_2) & \cdots & \phi(x_P,c_m)\end{bmatrix},\ \boldsymbol{\Phi}_0=\begin{bmatrix}\phi(c_1,c_1) & \phi(c_1,c_2) & \cdots & \phi(c_1,c_m)\\ \phi(c_2,c_1) & \phi(c_2,c_2) & \cdots & \phi(c_2,c_m)\\ \vdots & \vdots & \cdots & \vdots\\ \phi(c_m,c_1) & \phi(c_m,c_2) & \cdots & \phi(c_m,c_m)\end{bmatrix} \tag{7}$$

and where the simplified notation $\phi(\alpha,\beta)=\phi(\|\alpha-\beta\|)$ is used for the radial basis.

Note, that for $\lambda=0$ (i.e. no regularisation) the weight vector is readily given by $\boldsymbol{w}=\boldsymbol{\Phi}^+y$, where $\boldsymbol{\Phi}^+=\left(\boldsymbol{\Phi}^T\boldsymbol{\Phi}\right)^{-1}\boldsymbol{\Phi}^T$ is the pseudo-inverse of matrix $\boldsymbol{\Phi}$. This is the minimum length vector solving the over-determined least-squares data fitting problem (more data points than kernel weights, i.e., $P>m$).

Clearly, RBF network structures can be regarded as tools, for which non-linear mapping problems can be simply re-formulated into problems of linear optimisation. This viewpoint, that concentrates on optimising network regression weights only, has in fact earned a bad name for RBF networks, since in some applications they generate disappointing results, e.g., much worse than popular MLP networks with adaptable sigmoidal neurons $\varphi(x)=1/(1+exp(\beta w\cdot x-\theta))$ i.e., with slopes

βw and activation thresholds θ adjusted in the course of an iterative gradient descent learning scheme.

In training RBF networks two sets of parameters need be optimised:

- network receptive field (i.e., kernel functions ϕ, their number, and their arrangement within the input data space) – termed *input training*,
- network weights w – termed *output training*.

Input training is a nonlinear training problem with respect to parameters of the kernels functions (their scaling parameters s_k and centres c_k). It can be enhanced by exploiting an *a priori* knowledge about distribution of the input training data $\{x_i\}_{i=1}^{P}$ (an approach not possible for MLP training), e.g. kernel centres can be selected from the input training data. Other more advanced schemes are: the self-organised choice of centres that groups kernel centres at statistically important regions of input data, the orthogonal least squares (OLS) learning procedure that searches for an optimum number of centres in an incremental manner [34], and optimisation of centres by genetic programming (GP) [35]. Finally, excellent RBF training results have been achieved in a method combining the OLS and GP for designing network receptive field [36].

Note, however, that output training may have to be performed many times (e.g. for an increasing number of kernel nodes) because the quality of input "data perception" by means of the selected kernels can only be evaluated after the output layer weights are determined. Thus, output training can become the main factor determining an overall demand on computing time (e.g., for each tested version of the network $O(Pm^2 + 5m^3)$ summations and multiplications are required for matrix pseudoinversing).

4.1 Orthogonalisation of kernels for constructive network training

Search for a suitable neural approximator for the application at hand can be effectively organised in a constructive training manner, i.e., the one in which the number of network processing elements is incremented in each training run until the network error converges to a predefined margin. However, a new set of weights coefficients w needs to be computed for each augmented network version. This is because the RBF kernels (or sigmoids) do not form an orthogonal set of functions. There exists, however, a simple equivalence between linearly independent functions and orthogonal basis defined in a normed space of functions, as given by the Schmidt theorem: *for a set of linearly independent functions $\{\phi_k\}_{k=1}^{m}$ defined in Hilbert space (a complete inner product function space), there exists a set of orthogonal functions $\{u_k\}_{k=1}^{m}$, such that any function u_k is a linear combination of $\{\phi\}_{k=1}^{m}$ and vice versa, any ϕ_k is a linear combination of orthogonal functions $\{u_k\}_{k=1}^{m}$*. Application of this theorem to artificial neural network training has been proposed for kernel othonormalisation [24] and orthogonalisation of any nonlinear network basis function [14]. The training procedure involving orthogonalisation of the basis functions is the following:

1. ***Start** from a single basis function network, i.e.* $\phi_{m=1}$.
2. *Orthogonalise the m-th basis function using the formula:* $u_m(x) = \phi_m(x) + \sum_{k=1}^{m-1} a_{m,k} u_k(x)$ *(for the first kernel* $u_1 = \phi_1$*), where* $a_{m,k} = -\frac{\langle \phi_m(x), u_k(x) \rangle}{\langle u_k(x), u_k(x) \rangle}$, $k = 1, 2, \ldots, m-1$.
3. *Compute new weight using:* $w'_m = \frac{\langle y, u_m \rangle}{\|u_m\|^2}$, *where* $y = [y_1, y_2, \ldots, y_P]^T$.
4. *Compute response of the orthogonal basis network to the training inputs* $f_m(x_i) = \sum_{k=1}^{m} w'_k u_k(x_i)$, $i = 1, 2, \ldots, P$.
5. *Check network error.*
6. *If the error is too large increment network basis (m=m+1) by a function and go to step 2.*
7. *"De-orthogonalise" network basis back to the initial basis* $\{\phi_i\}_{i=1}^{m}$ *by using linear transformation of orthogonal basis weights* w'_k *to "non-orthogonal basis" weights* w_k*: starting from* $w_m = w'_m$ *and using the recursive formula* $w_k = w'_k + \sum_{j=k+1}^{m} w_j a_{jk}$ *to obtain* $f_m(x) = \sum_{k=1}^{m} w_k \phi_k(x)$ *and **stop**.*

Computation cost involved in incremental construction of a network with m orthogonal kernels is $O\left(\frac{m(m+1)(2P+1)}{2}\right)$ of floating point additions and multiplications, where P is the number of training patterns. This is a considerably low computing cost in comparison to the SVD method. For orthogonal set of basis there is no requirement for re-computation of other network weights for a new added kernel (in the final step 7., network weights are computed only once at the cost of $O\left(\frac{m(m-1)}{2}\right)$). For example, in a constructive RBF network training scheme that starts from a single kernel and stops at 30 kernel network size, the orthogonalisation training procedure outperforms the SVD method by a factor of 20.

It has been proved that the sequence of RBF network generated mappings with an incremented basis, can be constructed, that approximate functions belonging to the Sobolev space (i.e., functions satisfying $\int_{R^N} |f(x)|^p \, dx < \infty$) with a rate of convergence proportional to $O(1/\sqrt{m})$. That is the error is not dependent on function dimension [37]. Considerable results on this subject are included in [38]. In [10] a matching pursuit of kernels has been proposed for adaptive selection of RBF kernels in ECG signal modelling application. It was also shown [39], that for an incremental training scheme using genetic based optimisation of RBF kernels three are sufficient for achieving average classification accuracy for the Iris classification benchmark at the level of 98%.

A competing approach to network constructive training concepts is the minimal resource allocation network (MRAN) algorithm proposed in [13]. This training scheme is capable of growing or pruning the hidden layer of the RBF network in an on line manner so that network size is matched to the time-varying complexity of the problem. Finally, it is worth noting that application of a gradient descent training to all RBF network parameters yielded mappings that outperformed generalisation performance of MLP in the NETtalk speech synthesis task [20], [40].

5 Concluding remarks

As opposed to MLP networks, that instantly have become the most popular ANN architectures, the progress in RBF neural networks research interest has experienced steady but firm growth. There is a number of reasons for that. Firstly, RBF networks need more design decisions about their configuration (i.e., their initialisation) whereas for MLPs, the entire control is taken over by back-propagation (BP) or its variants. The BP is simple to deploy if *a priori* knowledge about the solved problem is not available. On the other hand, RBFs can perform much better than MLPs, if input training phase can fit network receptive field to input data structure. MLP training gives no option for such network pre-tuning. Secondly, as pointed out in this paper, constructive RBF training methods are particularly effective, because optimum network output weights can be computed fast in a "one-shot" manner, avoiding error correcting iterative learning rules. Thirdly, the single non-linear hidden layer structure of RBF networks has a strong background in the theory of functional normed spaces, hence analytical tools for investigation of their properties are readily accessible. Moreover, RBF networks display links to statistical methods such as kernel regression, density estimation, nonlinear principal component analysis, and are functionally equivalent to fuzzy systems. Such a collection of concepts into a single framework, not to mention the analogy of RBF kernels to tuned cortical neurons, calls for further, studies that seem far from being exhausted.

References

1. Broomhead D.S., Lowe D. (1988) Multivariable functional interpolation and adaptive networks, Complex Systems, **2**, 321–355
2. Micchelli C.A. (1986) Interpolation of scattered data: distance matrices and conditionally positive definite functions, Constructive Approximation, **2**, 11–22

3. Powell M.J.D. (1985) Radial basis functions for multivariable interpolation: a review, IMA Conference on Algorithms for the Approximation of Functions and Data, Shrievenham, U.K., 143–167
4. Duch W., Jankowski N. (1999) Survey of neural network transfer functions, Neural Computing Surveys, **2**, 163–212
5. Strumiłło P., Kamiński W. (2001) Neural networks with orthogonal transfer functions, 9th European Symposium on Artificial Neural Networks", ESANN'2001, Bruges, Belgium, April 25–27 2001, 95–100
6. Ajzerman M.A., Browerman E.M., Rozonoer L.I. (1976) Image recognition: the method of potential functions, WNT, Warszawa (in Polish)
7. Moody J.E., Darken, C.J. (1989) Fast learning in networks of locally-tuned processing units, Neural Computation, **1**, 281–294
8. Park J., Sandberg L.W. (1993) Approximation and radial-basis-function networks, Neural Computation, **5**, 305–316.
9. Hunt K.J., Haas R., Murray-Smith R.M. (1996) Extending the functional equivalence of radial basis function neural networks and fuzzy inference systems, IEEE Trans. Neural Networks, **7**, 3, 776–781
10. Strumiłło P. (2002) Matching pursuit of basis in two–layer neural networks for signal approximation, accepted for publication in the International Journal of Computers, Systems and Signals.
11. Strumiłło P., Kamiński W. (1999) Evaluation of air pollution field in urban area using regularised RBF neural networks, Proceedings of the IVth Conference on neural networks and their application, Zakopane, 716–721
12. Whitehead B.A., Choate T.D. (1996) Cooperative-competitive genetic evolution of radial basis function centers and widths for time series prediction, IEEE Trans. Neural Networks, **7**, 4, 869–880
13. Yingwei L., Saratchandran P., Sundararajan N. (1998) Performance evaluation of sequential minimal radial basis function neural network learning algorithm, IEEE Trans. Neural Networks, **9**, 2, 308–318
14. Strumiłło P., Kamiński W. (2001) Orthogonalisation procedure for training radial basis functions neural networks, Bulletin of the Polish Academy of Sciences, Technical Sciences, **49**, No. 3, 479–491
15. Cheng E.S., Chen S., Mulgrew M. (1996) Gradient radial basis function networks for nonstationary nonlinear time series prediction, IEEE Trans. Neural Networks, **7**, 1, 190–194
16. Fabri S., Kadirkamanathan V. (1996) Dynamic structure neural networks for stable adaptive control of nonlinear systems, IEEE Trans. Neural Networks, **7**, 5, 1151–1167
17. Luo W. Moris A.J, Martin, E.B., Karim, M.N. (1996) Control relevant identification of a pH waste water neutralisation process using adaptive radial basis function networks, Computer and Chemical Engineering, **20**, 2, S1017–S1022
18. Krzyżak A., Lindner T., Lugosi G. (1996) Nonparametric estimation and classification using radial basis function nets and empirical risk minimization, IEEE Trans. Neural Networks, **7**, 2, 475–487
19. Chen S., Mulgrew B., Grant P.M. (1993) A clustering algorithm for digital communications channel equalization using radial basis function networks, IEEE Trans. Neural Networks, **3**, 4, 570–579
20. Haykin S. (1999) Neural networks, a comprehensive foundation, Prentice Hall.

21. Jain A.K., R.P.W. Duin, J. Mao (2000) Statistical pattern recognition: a review, IEEE Trans. Pattern Analysis and Machine Intelligence, **22**, 1, 4–37
22. Scholkopf B., Smola A., Muller K.R. (1998) Nonlinear component analysis as a kernel eigenvalue problem, Neural Computation, **10**, 1299–1319
23. Lowe D. (1999) Radial basis networks and statistics, Ch. 3, 65-95, in Statistics and neural networks, Ed. Kay J.W., Titterington D.M., Oxford University Press, Oxford
24. Kamiński W., Strumiłło P. (1997) Kernel Orthonormalisation in Radial Basis Function Neural Networks", IEEE Trans. Neural Networks, **8**, no. 5, 1177–1183
25. Rybowski R. (1998) Classification of incomplete feature vector by radial basis function networks, Pattern Recognition Letters, **19**, 14, 1257–1264
26. Pulido A., Ruisanchez, Rius F.X. (1999) Radial basis function applied to the classification of UV-visible spectra, Analitycal Chemica Acta, **388**, 3, 273–281
27. Musavi M.T., Bryant R.J. et al. (1998) Mouse chromosome classification by radial basis function network with fast orthogonal search, **11**, 4, 769–777
28. West D. (2000) Neural network credit scoring models, Computers and Operations Research, **27**, 11-12, 1131–1152
29. Kamiński W., Witkowska D. (2001) Firm classification: Artificial Neural Network, Approach, 10th International Conference on System Modeling Control, Zakopane, Poland, **1**, 362–368
30. Kumar P.C., Saratchandran P., Sundararajan N. (2000) Minimal radial basis function neural networks for nonlinear channel equalisation, IEE Proc.–Vis. Image Process. **147**, 5, 428–435
31. Cichosz P. (2000) Systems that learn (in Polish), WNT, Warszawa
32. Koszlaga J., Strumiłło P. (2000) Rule extraction from trained radial basis function neural networks, Colloquia in Artificial Intelligence, 2000, Lodz, Poland, 97–106
33. Girosi F., Jones M., Poggio T. (1995) Regularization theory and neural network architectures, Neural Computations, **7**, 219–269
34. Chen S., Cowan C.F.N., Grant P.M. (1991) Orthogonal least squares learning algorithm for radial basis function networks, IEEE Trans. Neural Networks, **2**, 2, 302–309
35. Billings S.A., Zheng G.L. (1995) Radial basis network configuration using genetic algorithms, Neural Networks, **8**, 6, 877–890
36. Chen S., Wu Y., Luk B.L. (1999) Combined genetic algorithm optimisation and regularised orthogonal least squares learning for radial basis function networks, IEEE Trans. Neural Networks, **10**, 5, 1239–1243
37. Girosi F., Anzelotti G. (1994) Rates of convergence for radial basis functions and neural networks", in Artificial neural networks for Speech and Vision, R. Mammone (Ed.), Chapman & Hall, 97–114
38. Beliczyński B. (2000) Incremental function approximation by neural networks (in Polish), WPW, Warszawa
39. Koszlaga J., Strumiłło P. (2002) Evolutionary algorithms vs. other methods for constructive optimisation of RBF network kernels, accepted for presentation at the Sixth International Conference on Neural Networks and Soft Computing
40. Karayannis N. B., Mi G.W. (1997) Growing radial basis neural networks: merging supervised and unsupervised learning with network growth techniques, IEEE Trans. Neural Networks, **8**, 6, 1492–1505

Introduction of Interactive Evolutionary Computation and Its Applications to CG Creativity

Hideyuki Takagi

Kyushu Institute of Design
4-9-1, Shiobaru, Minami-ku, Fukuoka, 815-8540 Japan
Tel&Fax: +81-92-553-4555, E-mail: takagi@kyushu-id.ac.jp

Abstract. We summarize the outline of Interactive Evolutionary Computation (IEC) and discuss its research directions. Then, we introduce four IEC-based educational systems for artistic creativity for CG beginners. They are for CG lighting design, virtual aquarium, figurative education, and fireworks animation.

1 Introduction

One of technologies that optimizes a target system to obtain better system outputs based on our preference or knowledge, such as Figure 1, is Interactive Evolutionary Computation (IEC). The IEC can be said as system optimization based on human subjective evaluation.

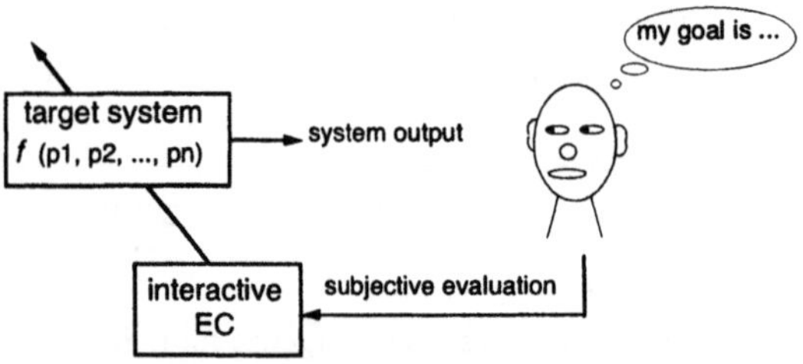

Fig. 1. General framework of IEC systems: system optimization based on human subjective evaluation.

For example, suppose to design a building or a bridge that well matches to the scene around, fit a hearing aid to user's hearing, or retrieve an image from an image database that matches given design concept. The IEC system displays the outputs of CAD, hearing aid sound, or images to an IEC user and make the user evaluate the system outputs. The IEC inputs the user's subjective evaluation as fitness values and optimizes the parameters of the CAD system, hearing aid, and retrieval engine (see Fig. 1). As a concrete EC technology, genetic algorithms (GA), genetic programming (GP), evolutionary strategy, and evolutionary programming are used for the IEC.

From the optimization search point of view, the IEC searches out the coordinate that maximizes user's subjective evaluation in the parameter space of the target system. An IEC user compares the real outputs from the target system with the ideal target in mind and evaluates the system outputs with the psychological distance between two. The EC searches the global optimum that corresponds to the ideal target in mind in a searching space consisting of parameter axes of the target system and one axis of the user's psychological distance (see Figure 2).

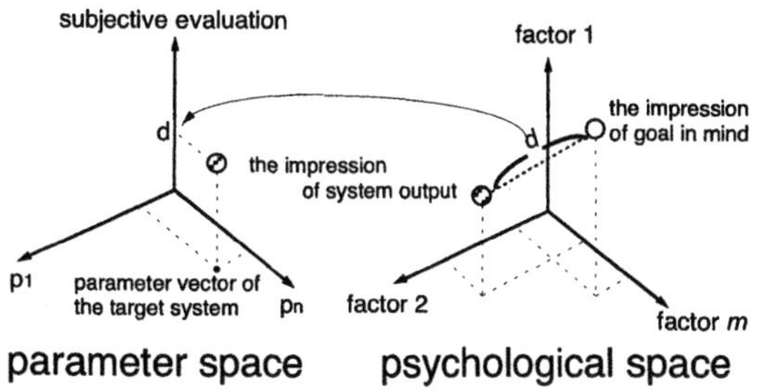

Fig. 2. Psychological distance between target in our psychological spaces and actual system outputs becomes the fitness axis of a feature parameter space where EC searches the global optimum in an IEC system.

There might be doubt whether the EC can search out the global optimum based on human evaluation whose precision is far from that of a mathematical fitness function. Unlike normal EC search with a fitness function, the role of EC for the IEC tasks is not to find out a pinpoint of the global optimum but global optimum area. If all parameter sets in the global optimum area cannot be distinguished by an IEC user, all of them are identical for the human user and are global optima. Due to this characteristics of the IEC, the EC search generation number to reach to the global optima of the IEC tasks is comparatively quite fewer than that of normal EC numerical or combinatorial optimization in general.

Following the general introduction of the IEC in this section, we discuss the direction of the IEC research in section 2. We leave the detail survey of IEC researches to the reference [11] but introduce our IEC research on computer graphics (CG) in section 3 as the examples of the IEC applications.

2 Research Direction of IEC

There are two IEC research directions; one is application oriented research whose objective is to expand IEC application fields and evaluate the usefulness of the IEC in each field, and another is interface research to reduce IEC user's fatigue that all human-machine interaction systems cannot avoid more or less.

The first research direction is expansion of IEC application fields and their evaluation. The IEC has been applied to wide variety of fields from artistic fields in early time to engineering and education fields. Some of applications includes: graphic arts and animation, 3-D CG lighting, music, editorial design, industrial design, facial image generation, speech processing and synthesis, hearing aid fitting, virtual reality, media database retrieval, data mining, image processing, control and robotics, food industry, geophysics, education, entertainment, social system, and so on. The direction of developing new IEC fields should be continued.

Evaluation is essential for any research. Unfortunately, there were a few researches that just applied the IEC without evaluation. Subjective tests are frequently requested to evaluate systems having a human factor, and management technique of psychological experiments and statistical tests are necessary for the subjective tests. Although it is understandable that researchers in artistic and engineering field may not be familiar to psychological experiments, IEC technology cannot be grown without the evaluation.

The second research direction is the IEC interface research to reduce human fatigue problem and make it practical. As a human user must be included in an IEC system, human fatigue problem cannot be avoided. Negative features of the IEC include that (1) the EC in the IEC has to have less population size and generation numbers than normal EC, (2) time sequential display is requested for sound, for example, which increases psychological fatigue of an IEC user, and others. Improvement of interactive user interface is a key to solve these problems.

Some of our IEC interface researches are: discrete subjective fitness value input method, prediction of human subjective evaluation characteristics, GA acceleration in early generations, on-line knowledge embedding, and visualization of EC search space [11].

3 IEC-based Computer Graphics

CG is the most popular IEC application. The IEC started from the *biomorph* that was CG in 1986 [5], and several IEC-based CG followed it. One type of CG application is drawing concrete images such as plants, animals, airplanes, faces, and so on, and other are abstract graphics. Most of them are math equation-based CG, and the coefficients of the equations are parametrically changed by the IEC or new equations are generated by Interactive GP (IGP). Now, the quality level of the IEC-based CG exceeds that of laboratory and reaches to the level of professional art.

In this section, we introduce our four CG applications.

3.1 3-D CG Lighting

3-D CG is a simulation of photograph, and its impression is dramatically changed by lighting as same as photography. Although many people can evaluate how the CG lighting matches to the given design concept, they can not always have CG lighting technique. We applied IEC to the CG lighting design that not only professional CG designers but also amateurs came to handle [1–3].

GA determines the attributes of three lights of our experimental 3-D CG system; they are type of the light source, ON/OFF, lightness level, color, and the spherical coordinate of its location or direction in a 3-D space. These parameters are encoded into 90 or 114 bits chromosomes for monochrome or color lighting, respectively, are interactively optimized based on lighting designer's taste, and are adjusted to let the lighting impression match to the given design concept. As what an IEC user does is ony to subjectively evaluate how CG lighting images generated by the EC are close to the given concept, even unskilled amateurs can design CG lighting.

Five subjects tried to bring the lighting impression of a CG woman close to the given design concept with two lighting methods: manual lighting design based on try-and-error and Interactive GA (IGA)-based lighting design. Lighting examples of one subject are shown in Figure 3. Four given design concepts are shown with the figures. The former two figures are with monochrome lighting, and the latter two figures are with color lighting whose searching complexity is higher than that of the former ones. These pair lighting images designed by the five subjects were evaluated by other subjects with Sheffé's method of paired comparisons. Through this subjective test, we found that the IGA-based CG lighting was not effective for skilled CG users but CG amateurs [1,2].

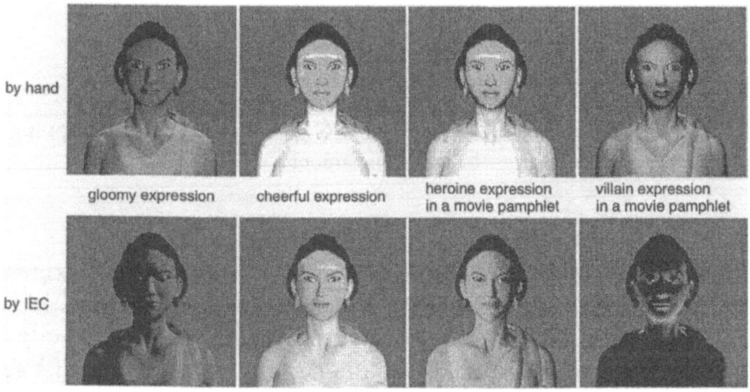

Fig. 3. Lighting design examples of one CG beginner for four given design motives by hand (upper) and IGA (lower). Color lights are used for right two concepts.

3.2 Virtual Aquarium

Virtual aquarium is our edutainment project to let CG amateurs including those who have no CG experience freely create several varieties of 3-D CG fish shapes and let the created CG fishes autonomously swim in a 3-D virtual reality (VR) space. The final image of the system usage is to let students in an art class imagine *fishes on Mars*, for example, realize their shapes using this IEC-based fish CG creation system through Internet, and enjoy to see them swimming in a 3-D VR aquarium when the students visit the aquarium theater some day.

Since the role of an IEC user is not to directly create CG fishes but to evaluate the created CG fishes, even inexperienced students can create several varieties of CG fishes with the help of this system. In orthodox art education, education to grow the capability of artistic imagination is mainly conducted through artistic skill such as drawing, carving, or forming artistic works. In other words, student's imagination which is expressed in his or her artistic works to be filtered by his/her skill. The IEC-based CG systems in sections 3 allow us to educate students' artistic imagination with very few or no influence of their artistic skill.

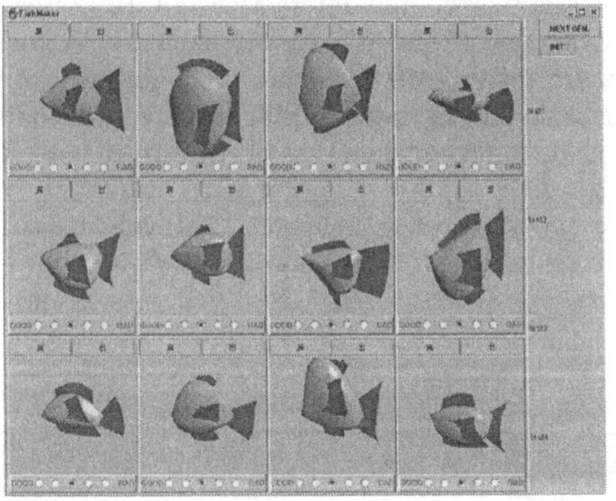

Fig. 4. User interface of an IEC-based fish CG generator. Texture mapping is conducted after this shape design in this experiment.

Fundamental techniques used in this project are parametric expression of 3-D fish shapes for the IEC, Internet version of an IEC interface, and an autonomous fish behavior model. Parametric expression of the fish body shapes is realized by the combination of equations, $f(x) = a(x - X_L)^p(X_R - x)^q$, and that of fins is expressed using Bézier curves [4]. The coefficients of these functions are tuned by GA. The Internet use of this system is realized by Java programming. The IEC interface and CG drawing parts run at a client computer, and GA part runs at a server computer. The user's subjective fitness values and coefficients of the functions for fish shapes are communicated between the client and server sides. The autonomous fish behavior is realized based on Boid model used in Artificial Life field. We embed not only normal Bold model that forms a fish shoal but also a predation model that predators pursue weaker fishes in certain distance and the weaker fishes try to escape from the attack.

3.3 3-D Figurative Education

We are conducting more generic 3-D figurative education project that expands function-based CG modeling from only fish shape in section 3.2 to general shapes. A hyper-quadratic function is used as a fundamental model, and any 3-D shapes are formed by combining multiple hyper-quadratic functions. Users who has no or less CG experience can use this figurative education system by adjusting the coefficient parameters of the hyper-quadratic functions.

The IEC is used to determine these parameter values [8]. According to the increase of the number of the hyper-quadratic functions, the number of adjusting parameters increases; it becomes difficult to manually adjust these parameters. Essentially important point in figurative education is not paying attention to the parameter adjustment but the imagination of creative shape. This is why the IEC is introduced.

Subjective test showed that the IEC approach is better to imagine novel design, and manual adjustment is better when we clearly know how to modify the shape [7]. This result suggests us that it is one effective usage that we use the IEC in early stage to imagine novel forms and then manually adjust after concrete shape is fixed.

3.4 Fireworks CG Animation

Our other project is an IEC-based fireworks CG animation where 3-D fish CG creation in section 3.2 is replaced by the creation of fireworks CG animation. The project purpose is education of artistic sense through Internet as same as that of the IEC-based 3-D fish CG project.

The structure of a typical Japanese fireworks shell mainly consists of the lumps of powder called as *HOSHI* (or Star as direct translation) that are arranged in concentric circles and burst charge that scatters the *HOSHI* all around. The combination of the number of layers, the types of the *HOSHI*, and amount of power creates several types, colors, and color change of fireworks as if a large spherical bloom of burning colors is open.

To create fireworks CG animation, (1) structure design that the number of layers in a fireworks shell, the arrangement of *HOSHI*, and types of the *HOSHI* are determined and (2) temporal simulation of physical characteristics that are determined by parameters such as powder explosion, burning time, and scattered direction depending on the type of the *HOSHI* are necessary. We adopt Interactive GP (IGP) to design the former structure and IGA to optimize the parameters of the latter simulation in our system. As the best values of the parameters that GA optimizes varies according to the former structure, it is need to use the GA that can dynamically change its chromosome when the GA runs.

Currently, we have developed a temporal version of the fireworks CG animation system that the former structure is designed manually and the latter parameters are optimized by IGA. First, an IEC user determines the fireworks structure manually and then pushes the start bottom of each small window to start physical simulation of the shooting up of fireworks and the exploration of powder and evaluates the CG animation of the simulation. The CG animation is drawn based on particle system [10]. These subjective fitness values are used for GA optimization to create new fireworks animation. Figure 5 shows one shot examples generated by a student who has no CG experience using this system.

Fig. 5. One shot examples of CG fireworks animation generated by our IEC-based system.

Since several physical factors such as burning time, scattered direction and distance, gravity, and so on, are parametrized, we can make several simulations. At this moment, real fireworks cannot be automatically made from the data obtained by this fireworks simulation because we do not know the real correspondence of the amount of physical factors, for example, relationship between the amount of powder and its burning time or explosion force. However, it may not need for professional fireworks designers; some of them told that what they need is not such physical parameters but a design support system that provides them artistic design inspiration.

4 Discussion and Conclusion

We introduced our four educational IEC applications to increase creativity using CG applications. Anyone who create artistic images in mind can be educationally amused to reinforce his/her imagination regardless his/her CG skill. Subjective test results for some of these IEC systems supported its effectiveness for our objectives. The Internet version of these systems must increase its applicability to pupils and students in the world. We hope that the IEC technology further spread into education.

References

1. Aoki K. Takagi H., and Fujimura N. (1996) "Interactive GA-based design support system for lighting design in computer graphics," in *Int. Conf. on Soft Computing (IIZUKA'96)*, Iizuka, Fukuoka, Japan, World Scientific, Singapore, 533–536.
2. Aoki K. and Takagi H., (1997) "3-D CG lighting with an interactive GA," in *1st Int. Conf. on Conventional and Knowledge-based Intelligent Electronic Systems (KES'97)*, Adelaide, Australia, 296–301.
3. Aoki K. and Takagi H., (1998) "Interactive GA-based design support system for lighting design in 3-D computer graphics," Trans. of IEICE, **J81-DII**(7), 1601–1608, (*in Japanese*).
4. Bézier, P. (1972) Numerical Control: Mathematics and Applications, Wiley.
5. Dawkins, R. (1986) The Blind Watchmaker, Essex: Longman.
6. Hayashida N. and Takagi H., (2002) "Acceleration of EC Convergence with Landscape Visualization and Human Intervention," Applied Soft Computing, Elsevier Science, (*will appear*).
7. Nishino H., Takagi H., Cho S. B., and Utsumiya K., (2001) "A 3D Modeling System for Creative Design," in *15th Int. Conf. on Information Networking (ICOIN-15)*, Beppu, Japan, 479–486.
8. Nishino, H., Takagi, H. and Utsumiya, K., (2001) "Implementation and Evaluation of an IEC-Based 3D Modeling System," in *IEEE Int. Conf. on Systems, Man, and Cybernetics Conference (SMC2001)*, Tucson, AZ, USA, 1047–1052.
9. Poli A. and Cagnoni S., (1997) "Genetic programming with user-driven selection: Experiments on the evolution of algorithms for image enhancement," in *2nd Annual Conf. on Genetic Programming*, 269–277.
10. Reeves W. T., (1983) "Particle System - A Technique for Modeling a Class of Fuzzy Objects", Computer Graphics **17**(3), SIGGRAPH'83, 359–376.
11. Takagi H., (2001) "Interactive Evolutionary Computation: Fusion of the Capacities of EC Optimization and Human Evaluation," Proceedings of the IEEE, **89**(9), 1275–1296.
12. Watanabe T. and Takagi H., (1995) "Recovering system of the distorted speech using interactive genetic algorithms," in *IEEE Int. Conf. on Systems, Man and Cybernetics (SMC'95)*, Vancouver, Canada, **1**, 684–689.

Neuroinformatics Research in Vision

Shiro Usui

Department of Information and Computer Sciences, Toyohashi University of Technology, Toyohashi, 441-8580 Japan

Abstract. The NRV project (Neuroinformatics Research in Vision) is the first project in Japan started in 1999 under the Science and Technology Agency of Japan, aimed at building the foundation of neuroinformatics research. Because of the wealth of data on the visual system, the NRV project will use vision research to promote experimental, theoretical and technical research as a pilot study on neuroinformatics. Details can be found at: http://www.neuroinformatics.gr.jp/.

1. Introduction

Recalling the origins - in a recent report from the OECD Megascience Forum [1] the new field of neuroinformatics was defined as "the combination of neuroscience and information sciences to develop and apply advanced tools and approaches essential for a major advancement in understanding the structure and function of the brain". An emerging trend in modeling and understanding brain processes is that understanding brain at one level can be greatly enhanced by considering the process embedded in its context. Equally important is consideration of complexities of neuronal processes operating in much detailed sub-systems. Significant goal is to explore how abstractions at different levels are related, e.g. the pathways from molecular to system levels. Another critical goal is to discuss the disposition of the computational approach to support effective modeling across abstractions and sub-systems.

2. NRV Project

One of the frontiers of the 21st century is the elucidation of the complicated and elaborate functions of the brain, such as sensory perception, recognition, memory, emotion, etc. The specialization and segmentation of advanced research topics make it very difficult to integrate related evidence so as to understand the functions of the brain. The introduction of information science technology in the analysis, processing, transmission, storage, integration, and utilization of information is indispensable.

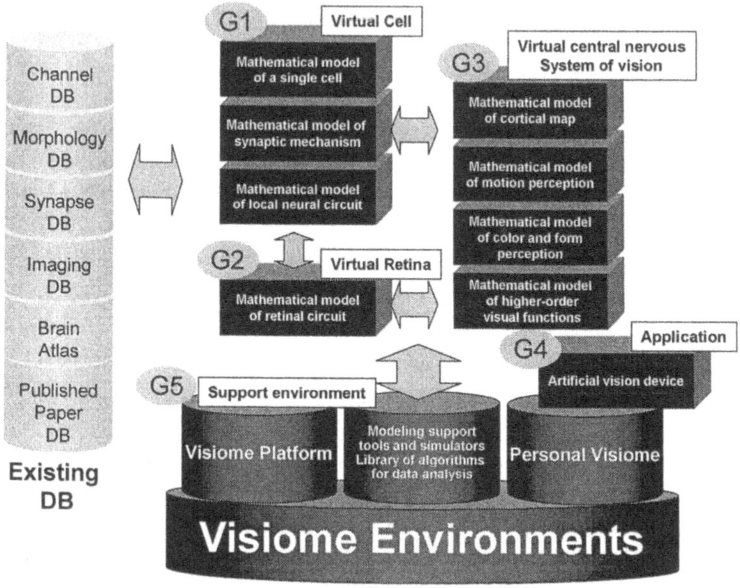

Fig. 1. NRV Project Concepts

Neuroinformatics is the new research paradigm for the 21st century, which fuses the experimental techniques with the mathematical and information science techniques. In particular, mathematical models are used to describe and integrate data and results obtained from a number of research fields. These mathematical models can be regarded as the platform that supports the simulation experiment indispensable for studying and understanding the function and mechanism of the human brain. In general, Neuroinformatics should construct the support environment that integrates the databases devoted to various research fields with the data analysis techniques. This should promote research relying on mathematical models, and advance the comprehension and knowledge of brain neuronal systems. If the research of each conventional field is a warp, neuroinformatics is the woof which links them.

The NRV project is the first project in Japan started in 1999 under the Science and Technology Agency of Japan, aimed at building the foundation of neuroinformatics research in Japan[2]. Because of the wealth of data on the visual system, the NRV project will use vision research to promote experimental, theoretical and technical research in neuroinformatics.

The first goal of the project is to construct mathematical models for each level of visual system (single neuron, retinal neural circuit, visual function). The second goal is to build resources for neuroinformatics utilizing information science technologies and the research support environment which integrates them. The third goal is to realize a new vision device based on the brain-type information processing principle. The NRV Project has the following research groups and topics at this present fiscle year of 2001:

Group1: Modeling a single neuron by mathematical reconstruction

Intracellular information processing mechanism between nerve cells are described by mathematical models. This group carries out the construction of "virtual nerve cell" by integrating knowledge obtained from molecular biology, biophysics, electrophysiology and anatomy, to produce models of single neurons. Such mathematical models can reproduce behavior of realistic neurons on a scale of molecular to simple neural circuit, spatially, and sub-millisecond to year, temporally. They are considered as the smallest functional units of a model family.

Group2: Realization of virtual retina based on cell physiology

The retina is an ideal preparation for studying brain structure and function as well as neural signal processing in the brain, partly because it is a very accessible and self-contained part of the brain. Consequently there is a considerable amount of research results on all aspects of retinal visual information processing. A mathematical model of a retinal neural circuit will be constructed from neurophysiological experimental data and from the characteristics of single neurons obtained from G1. This retinal neural circuit will form the base for "virtual retina". Multiple cellular functions will be integrated into a mathematical model of the retinal-neural-circuit information processing mechanism that encompasses everything from the light energy conversion mechanism in a photoreceptor, which is the input, to the encoding mechanism of impulse sequence in a ganglion cell, which is the output cell of a retina.

Group3: Study on the visual function by computational and systems' approach

Two kinds of information flow exist in the visual system: One part of the visual system processes information related to intrinsic object properties or discrimination of objects, such as color and shape. Another part is concerned with the discrimination of motion and position (spatial vision). This group evaluates the information processing mechanisms in both the object discrimination and motion perception, and constructs mathematical models for these visual functions.

Group4: Realization of artificial vision devices and utilization of silicon technology for recording and stimulation

Movement detection is based on the spatio-temporal information processing in vision. It is one of the most basic and important functions of human and other living creatures. This study carries out research on the realization of new devices, circuits, and networks which fuse the visual information processing mechanisms of movement detection with semiconductor devices or circuit functions. It aims at the development of the analog-digital hybrid vision device with the ability that exceeds human's vision (for example, ultra-high speed). In order to record signals form nerve cells, or stimulate nerve cells, we utilize silicon growth technology and aim at developing multi-channel electrode array, which could be implanted on intact visual neural system.

Group5: Fundamental neuroinformatics research and development

The total support environment for experimental data analysis, model parameter estimation, simulations, etc. will be developed. The results of this project will be made available on the internet in a database: VISIOME (= Vision + ome) Platform that integrates morphological and physiological knowledge, mathematical models, related studies, and references.

3. Retina for Example: Neuroinformatics Study on the Vertebrate Retina

The vertebrate retina has been intensively studied over the past decades using physiological, morphological and pharmacological techniques. Since the retina is a unique and interesting neural system from the viewpoints not only of neuroscience but also of engineering, which has been thought to be a window to the brain because of its accessibility and suitability for the investigation. The retina is an ideal model of neural network system and neural information processing system. Since the early 1980s, enzymatic dissociation techniques have been employed for the isolation of a variety of retinal cells, including photoreceptors, horizontal cells and bipolar cells. Using isolated cell preparations, membrane ionic currents of solitary retinal cells have been studied in a quantitative fashion using the voltage-clamp techniques. These data provide information concerning the functional role of the ionic currents in generating and shaping the light response of the retinal neurons. However, the detailed experimental data alone are not enough to understand how the retinal neurons work. A combination of experimental work and mathematical modeling is necessary to clarify the complicated retinal functions. We believe mathematical modeling and simulation analysis with the advanced computer system have a potential to understand the relationships between the microscopic characteristics and its integrative functions of the neural system including the brain.

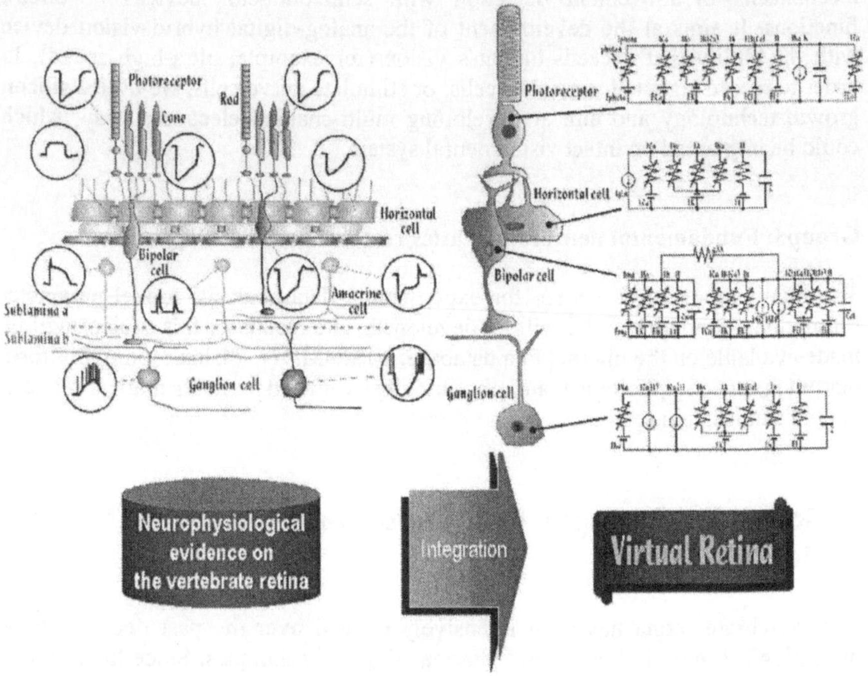

Fig. 2. Ionic currents based retinal model

The purpose of this study is to develop a realistic model of the retina which replicates the detailed neurophysiological structures and retinal functions. This approach allows the exploration of the computational functions performed by retinal neurons including the role and interaction of ionic channles and receptors, and the subcellular events such as transmitter release, binding and uptake.

In the present study, mathematical descriptions of the membrane ionic currents in the retinal neurons, photoreceptors, horizontal cells, bipolar cells and ganglion cells are realized as shown in Figure 2. Electrical properties of each neuron is described by a parallel conductance circuit. The voltage- and time-dependent characteristics of ionic conductance is modeled by Hodgkin-Huxley types of equations. The developed model is capable of accurately reproducing the voltage- and current-clamp responses of retinal neurons. Any electrical response including light response which depends on the dynamic balance of different ionic currents is quantitatively analyzed by the model. Therefore, hypotheses on how the retina processes visual information are understood at the cellular and subcellular level. Neuroinformatics model can be used to summarize what we know and what we need to find out on the retina [3].

4. VISIOME Platform : A Neuroinformatics Database and Environment for Vision Science

Understanding the brain function requires integration of many and diverse information from the level of molecule to the level of neuronal networks. However, the huge amount of information is making it almost impossible for any individual researcher to make an integrated view of the brain. To solve this problem, it will be required to make useful neuroinformatics tools for information storing, maintenance and sharing. In the present study, we constructed a database system for neuronal visual system named "Visiome Platform" as a test bed for useful neuroinformatics environment as shown in Figure 3.

The basic concept of the Visiome Platform is to make a web site integrating mathematical models, experimental data and related information. The Visiome Platform has two major characteristic features. First, it will allow researchers to reuse the models and experimental data in the database. Researchers can see how the models work or compare their own results with other experimental data, improve or integrate models, and formulate their own hypothesis into a model. Second, it will provide novel index system (Visiome Index) of research field of the visual system specially oriented to the model studies. The Visiome Index is

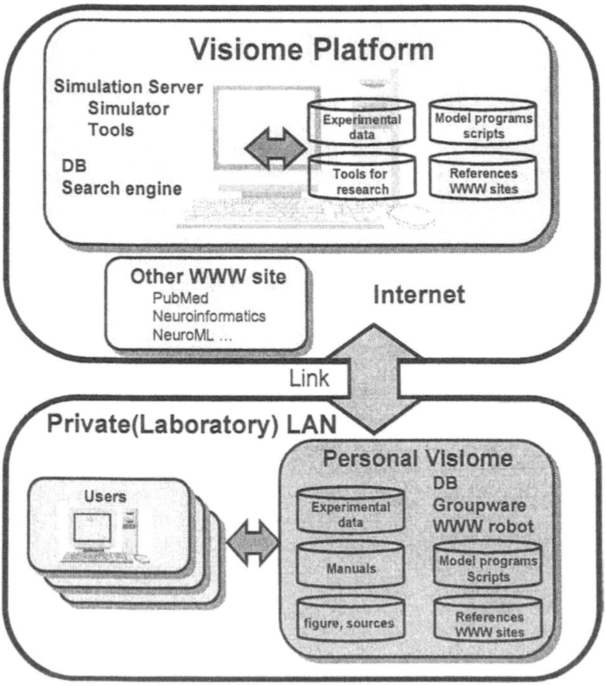

Fig. 3. Visiome environment.

based on neuronal and cognitive functions that are important targets of modeling studies. The Visiome Index will help researchers to understand the visual system from the aspect of visual functions and to construct models formulating their own hypotheses.

The Visiome Platform will provide more than just a database of models and data. Powerful analysis libraries and simulation tools will be also available on the platform including the Personal Visiome. The Visiome Platform will realize a virtual environment for global electronic collaborations by making available to researchers useful tools for simulation and data analysis with reusable models and data.

Acknowledgements

The author thanks Drs. Masao Ito, Shun-ichi Amari at RIKEN BSI and each member of NRV project for their supports and collaborations.

References

1. Final report of the OECD Megascience Forum: Working Group on Biological Informatics, January 1999. http://www.oecd.org/pdf/M000014000/M00014759.pdf
2. Shiro Usui and Shun-ichi Amari, Trends and scope of neuroinformatics Research. Brain Science 24(1):11-17, 2002. (In Japanese).
3. Usui, S., Kamiyama, Y., Ishii, H., Ogura, T. and Ishihara, A., "Ionic current model of the outer retinal cells", Modeling in the Neurosciences (Edited by. R. R. Poznanski), Harwood Academic Publishers, 293-319 (1999)

Soft Computing in Hardware Implementations

Bogdan. M. Wilamowski[1] and Okyay M. Kaynak[2]

[1] University of Idaho, College of Engr., 800 Park Blvd. Boise ID 83712, USA
[2] Bogazici University, EEE Department, Bebek, 80815 Istanbul, Turkey

Summary. Several VLSI implementations for soft computing are described, including piecewise approximation and nonlinear signal processing using MOS device characteristics. Both fuzzy and neural technologies are investigated. Fuzzy controllers are the most popular choice for hardware implementation of complex control surfaces because they are easy to design. Neural controllers are more complex and hard to train, but provide an outstanding control surface with much less error than that of a fuzzy controller.

1 Introduction

The mathematical power of machine intelligence is commonly attributed to their neural-like system architecture and the fault tolerance arising from their massively interconnected structure and parallel processing. Another feature of soft computing systems is that instead of "zero" and "one" digital levels they use fuzzy/continuous levels and in this way much more information is passed through the system at a given time. Analog signal processing is usually much faster than digital [1-3]. Several computation processes can be done simultaneously, and AD and DA conversion is not required. Analog integration or differentiation has already been used for many years. Analog summation and multiplication are also quite common. For computational intelligence, more sophisticated nonlinear functions are required such as WTA fuzzy membership functions , normalization circuits, MIN and MAX operators, division circuits, analog memory, neural circuits, and others [4-12]. In realizing such nonlinear signal processing, the nonlinear characteristics of MOS devices can provide an advantage.

2 Dynamic system modeling

All nonlinear dynamic systems can be described by a set of nonlinear differential equations. This set can always be written in state variable form where the number of equations is equal to the number of the state variables and each equation is of the first order. Such a system on the VLSI chip would require several integrators and nonlinear terms as shown in Fig. 1.

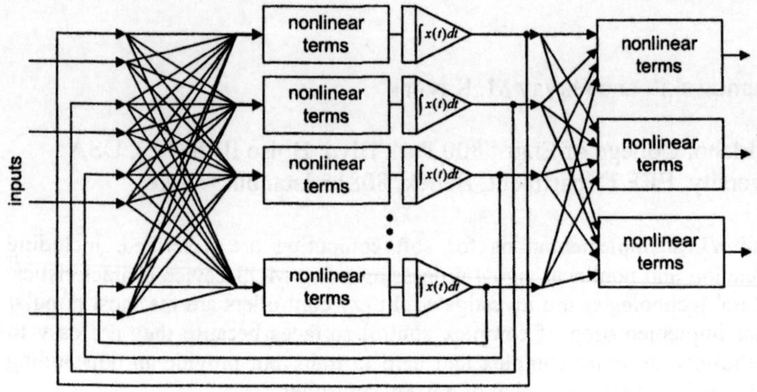

Fig. 1. Block diagram of an nonlinear dynamic system

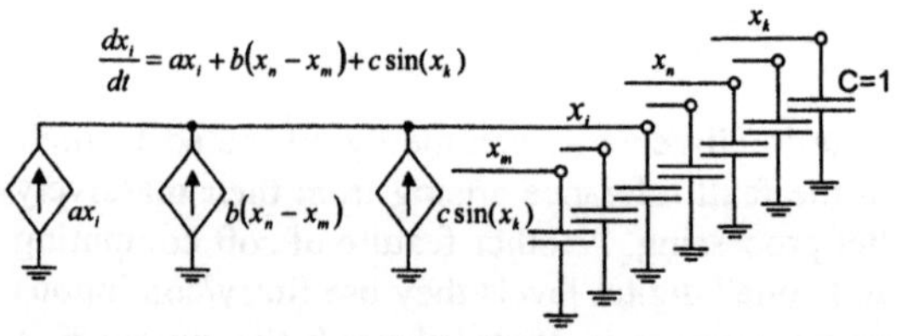

Fig. 2. Equivalent diagram for differential equation used in SPICE program. Voltage on each capacitor represents one state variable

It is not easy to simulate very large set of nonlinear differential equations. Instead of developing dedicated code in MATLAB, FORTRAN, or in C the entire system can be simulated using the SPICE program, which was developed to handle very stiff, highly nonlinear, electronic systems. The SPICE program uses with second order Gear integration scheme and it can easily handle any other dynamic systems. An example of an equivalent circuit for an *i*-th differential equation for the state variable x_i is shown on Fig. 2. Note that in the case shown in Fig. 2 three dependent current sources could be combined into one, controlled by a nonlinear expression of many variables.

For example relatively complex system of oil well [15], described by 25 nonlinear differential equations, was initially simulated in MATLAB and with standard libraries each simulation requires 8 to 12 hours of a the computer time. The SPICE program uses an implicit integration scheme, the computation time is almost independent on the observation time. When the same system was simulated on SPICE the results was obtained in matter of seconds.

3 Microprocessor implementation of neuro-fuzzy systems

In hardware, fuzzy systems dominate current trends in both microprocessor applications [13] and in custom designed VLSI chips [14]. Control surfaces obtained from fuzzy controllers are rough, which can cause unstable control. On other hand neural networks usually require a computation of tangent hyperbolic activation functions. This tasks it often too complex for simple microprocessors. When tangent hyperbolic function is replaced by Elliott function

$$f(net) = \tanh(net) = \frac{2}{1-\exp(-2net)} - 1 \quad \Rightarrow \quad f(net) = \frac{net}{1+|net|} \qquad (1)$$

then the computations are relatively simple and the results are almost as good as in the case of sigmoidal function. With this approach neural network implementations resulted with shorter code, faster operation, and much more accurate results. Fig. 3 shows comparison of several controllers for the same desired control surface implemented in the popular HC11 micro-controller using various fuzzy and neural network architectures. Table 1 shows comparison of errors, processing times and lengths of the code.

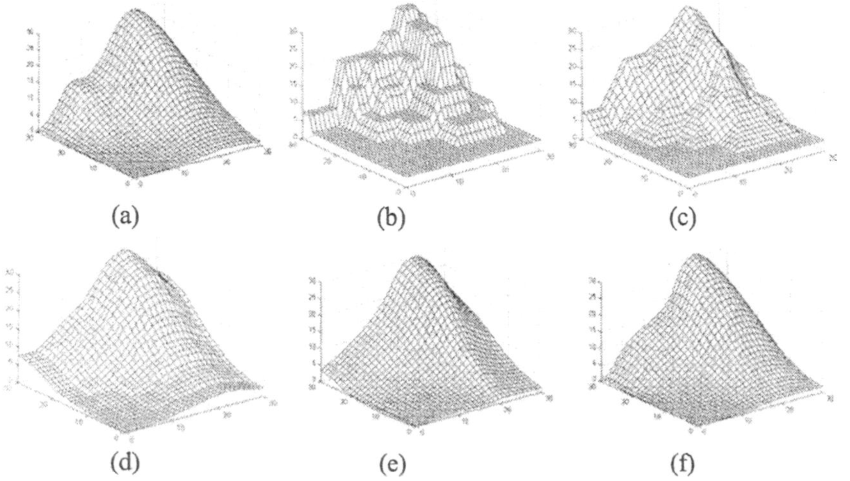

Fig. 3. Control surfaces for various controllers. (a). Required control surface, (b) Fuzzy Zadeh type with trapezoidal, (c) Fuzzy Zadeh type with triangular, (d) Fuzzy Tagagi-Sugeno type with triangular, (e) neural controller with four neurons 2-1-1-1-1 architecture, (e) neural controller with six neurons 2-1-1-1-1-1-1 architecture.

4 FPGA implementation of fuzzy systems

The design of an FPGA-based fuzzy controller can be very simple. It consists of an FPGA, analog-to-digital (A/D) converters for the inputs, a digital-to-analog (D/A) converter for the output and a ROM chip.

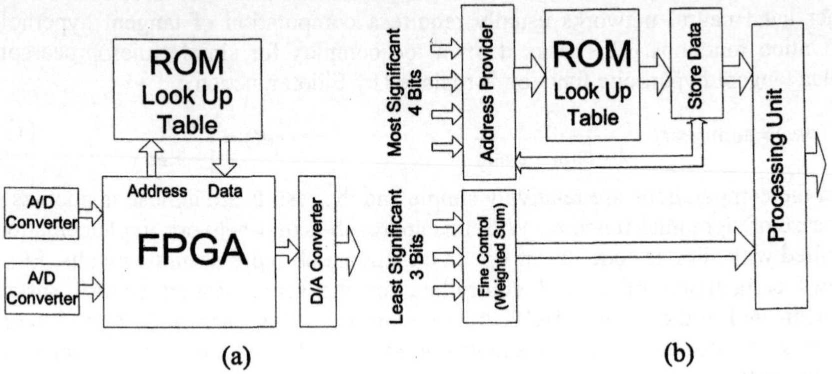

Fig. 4. FPGA implemented fuzzy controller (a) Simple look-up table approach (b) Modified look-up table approach with reduced memory requirement.

The size of the LUT grows exponentially as number of inputs increases. This is the downfall of the solution of Fig. 4(a). The size of ROM can be significantly reduced if the concept presented in Fig. 4(b) is used. In this approach only three or four most significant bits of each input to determine the address for the lookup table. A weighted average of least significant bits are used to eliminate rawness (Fig. 5).

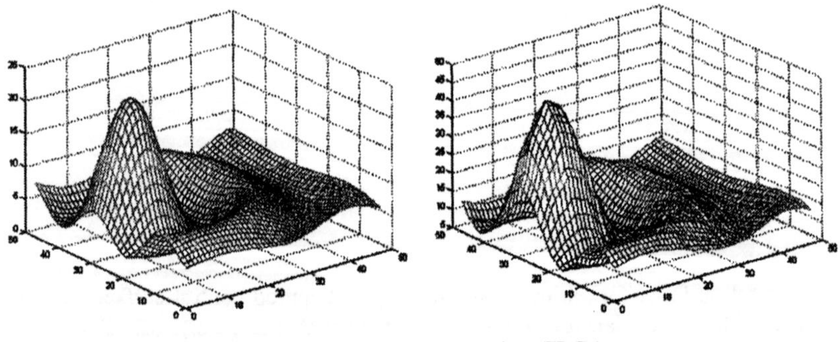

Fig. 5. Control surfaces (a) required, (b) implemented on FPGA

5 Custom VLSI implementation

5.1 Synthesis of arbitrary piecewise function using CMOS current mirrors

In normal operation VLSI current mirrors are operating in linear mode and the output current is proportional to the input current. But the same circuits, used out of normal operating range, can be used as nonlinear building blocks for piecewise approximations (Fig 6).

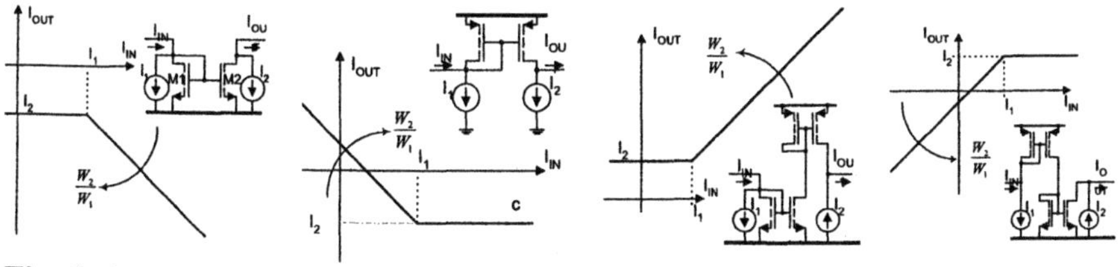

Fig. 6. Current mirrors as nonlinear elements

Using a combination of circuits from Figure 6 any arbitrary piecewise-linear function can be synthesized. An example of such function is in Fig. 7. Adding constant current sources at the input and output can change the location of the break points. Slops are controlled by W/L ratios of transistors pairs.

5.2 Using properties of silicon devices to implement complex nonlinear systems

Nonlinear blocks can be implemented using neural networks, fuzzy systems, or nonlinear functions such as multiplication, division, root, etc. There are several examples, described in the following subsections, illustrates how to create arbitrary nonlinear blocks using nonlinear characteristics of MOS transistors.

5.2.1 VLSI implementation of fuzzifiers

The fuzzifier block must convert crisp analog values into several fuzzy variables. The conversion takes place using membership functions of triangular, trapezoidal or Gaussian type shapes. Several different circuits have been already proposed [4-12]. In the circuit shown in Fig. 8 only one differential pair is required per membership function and one current source per fuzzifier. Note that several different shapes of the membership function can be obtained by selecting different W/L ratios of MOS transistors.

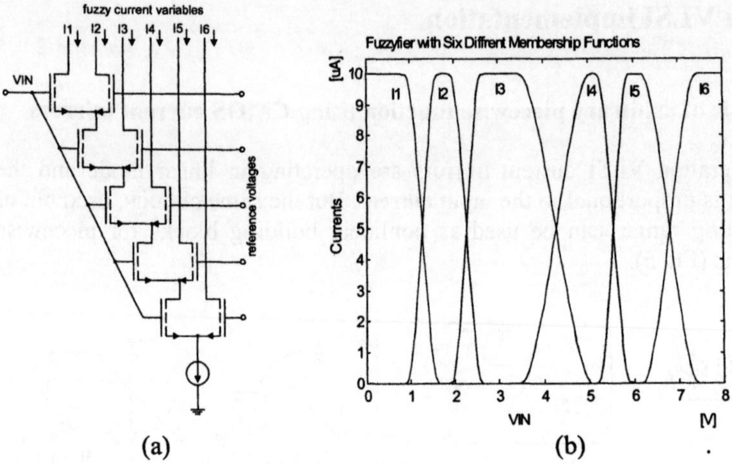

Fig. 7. Fuzzifier circuit with four differential pairs creating five membership functions: (a) circuit diagram and (b) fuzzifier characteristics.

5.2.2 MIN and MAX circuits

Current mode MIN/MAX circuits operate correctly over several orders of magnitude of signal change. Baturone et al [10] proposed a current mode MAX1 operator with relatively high accuracy. The one proposed in Fig. 9 MAX2 operator, is equally simple and a higher accuracy can be obtained Using DeMorgan theorem, each MAX circuit can be easily converted into a MIN circuit by introducing additional biasing currents.

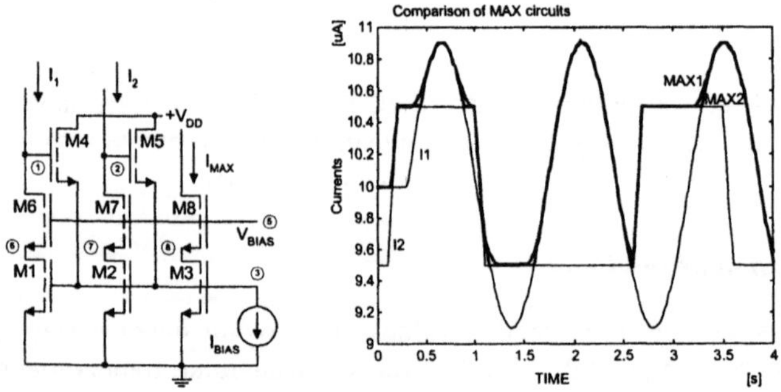

Fig. 8. Current mode MAX operator (a) circuit diagram and (b) simulation results for MAX1 [29] and for the proposed MAX2.

5.2.3 VLSI implementation of neurons

Neural networks could be implemented on the VLSI chip in several ways. The circuit of Fig. 10 works as nonlinear transconductance amplifier where inputs and outputs are currents. Weights are implemented by selecting different W/L ratios. With positive and negative outputs of the differential pair both positive and negative weights can be implemented.

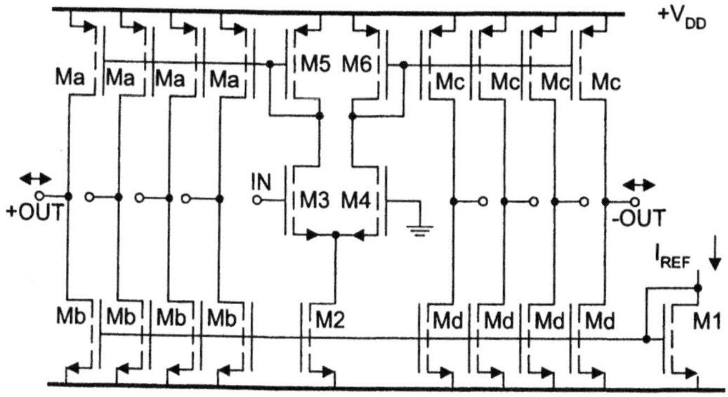

Fig. 9. Neuron circuit

6 Conclusion

A drawback of neural controllers is that the design process is more complicated than that of fuzzy controllers. However, this difficulty can be easily overcome with proper design tools. One severe disadvantage of a fuzzy system is its limited ability of handling problems with multiple inputs. This is not a serious limitation of neural networks. Control surfaces obtained from neural controllers also do not exhibit the roughness of fuzzy controllers that can lead to unstable or raw control. The analog signal processing is usually much faster. Several computation processes can be done simultaneously and AD and DA conversion is not required.

There are also some problems that have to be solved before the networks can be implemented on VLSI chips. First, an approximation function needs to be developed because CMOS neural networks have an activation function different than any function used in neural network software. Next, this function has to be used to train the network. Finally, the last problem for VLSI designers is the quantization effect caused by discrete values of the channel length (L) and width (W) of MOS transistor geometries.

Acknowledgment

This work was supported by NSF international grant NSF INT-9906233; and by NSF-Idaho EPSCoR and National Science Foundation grant EPS-0132626

References

1. Zurada, J., *Introduction to Artificial Neural Systems*, West Publishing Company, 1992.
2. Wilamowski B. M. (1998) "Neuro-Fuzzy Systems and its applications" tutorial at 24th IEEE International Industrial Electronics Conference (IECON'98) August 31 - September 4, 1998, Aachen, Germany, vol. 1, pp. t35-t49.
3. Wilamowski, B. M., "Neural Networks and Fuzzy Systems" The Mechatronics Handbook. CRC Press 2002, pp. 32-1 to 32-26
4. Choi J., B.J.Sheu, and J.C.F. Chang, (1994) A Gaussian Synapse Circuit for Analog VLSI Neural Networks. *IEEE Trans. on Very Large Scale Integration (VLSI) Systems*, vol. 2, no. 1, pp. 129-133.
5. Rodriguez-Vazquez A. and F. Vidal-Verdu, Learning in Neuro/Fuzzy Analog Chips, *IEEE International Symposium on Circuits and Systems*, Seattle WA, vol. 3, pp. 2325-2328, April 30-May 3 1995.
6. Yamakawa, A fuzzy Inference Engine in Nonlinear Analog Mode and its Application to a Fuzzy Logic Control, *IEEE Trans. on Neural Networks*, vol. 4, pp. 496-522, 1993.
7. Ota, Y. and B. M. Wilamowski, " CMOS Implementation of a Voltage-Mode Fuzzy Min-Max Controller", *Journal of Circuits, Systems and Computers*, vol. 6, No 2, pp. 171-184, April 1996.
8. Ahmadi S., L. Sellami, and R. W. Newcomb, A CMOS PWL Fuzzy Membership Function, *IEEE International Symposium on Circuits and Systems*, Seattle WA, vol. 3, pp. 2321-2324, April 30-May 3 1995
9. Angulo J.R., (1995) A BiCMOS Universal Membership Function Circuit with Fully Independent, Adjustable Parameters, *Proc. IEEE International Symposium on Circuits and Systems*, pp. 275-278.
10. Baturone I., A. Barriga, and J. L. Huertas, "Multi-input Voltage and Current-Mode Min/Max Circuits," *Proceedings: 3rd Int. Conf. on Fuzzy Logic, Neural Networks and Soft Computing*, Iizuka, Japan, 1994.
11. Ota Y. and B. Wilamowski, Current-Mode CMOS Implementation of a Fuzzy Min-Max Network, *World Congress on Neural Nerworks* vol. II, pp. 480-483, 1995.
12. Yamakawa T., "A Fuzzy Inference Engine in Nonlinear Analog Mode and its Application to a Fuzzy Logic Control," *IEEE Trans. on Neural Networks*, vol. 4, no. 3, pp. 496-522, May 1993.
13. Wilamowski B.M. and J. Binfet, "Do Fuzzy Controllers Have Advantages over Neural Controllers in Microprocessor Implementation" Proc. of. 2-nd *International Conference on Recent Advances in Mechatronics - ICRAM'99*, Istanbul, Turkey, pp. 342-347, May 24-26, 1999.
14. Wilamowski, B. M. , R. C. Jaeger, and M. O. Kaynak, "Neuro-Fuzzy Architecture for CMOS Implementation" *IEEE Transaction on Industrial Electronics*, vol. 46, No. 6, pp. 1132-1136, Dec. 1999.
15. B. M. Wilamowski and O. Kaynak, "Oil Well Diagnosis by sensing Terminal Characteristics of the Induction Motor," *IEEE Transactions on Industrial Electronics,* Vol 47, No 5, pp. 1100-1107, October 2000

On the Node Complexity of Threshold Gate Circuits with Sub-linear Fan-ins

Valeriu Beiu

Washington State University, School of Electrical Engineering & Computer Science
102 Spokane Str. (EME), PO Box 642752, Pullman, WA 99164-2752, USA

Abstract. This paper discusses *size*-optimal solutions for implementing arbitrary Boolean functions using threshold gates. After presenting the state-of-the-art, we start from the result of Horne and Hush [12], which shows that threshold gate circuits restricted to *fan-in* 2 can implement arbitrary Boolean functions, but require $O(2^n/n)$ gates in $2n$ layers. This result will be generalized to arbitrary *fan-ins* (Δ), lowering the *depth* to $n/\log\Delta + n/\Delta$, and proving that all the (relative) minimums of *size* are obtained for sub-linear *fan-ins* ($\Delta < n - \log n$). The fact that *size*-optimal solutions have sub-linear *fan-ins* is encouraging, as the *area* and the *delay* of VLSI implementations are related to the *fan-in* of the gates.

1 Introduction

The model we shall discuss is made of neurons composed of a cell body and many outgrowths: the *axon* (the 'output' of the neuron), and the *dendrites*. Formally, a *network* is a graph having several input nodes, and some (at least one) output nodes. If a synaptic *weight* is associated with each edge, and each node computes the *weighted sum* of its inputs to which a nonlinear activation function is then applied: $f(\mathbf{x}) = f(x_1, \ldots, x_\Delta) = \sigma\left(\sum_{i=1}^{\Delta} w_i x_i + \theta\right)$, the network is a *neural network* (NN), with $w_i \in \mathbb{R}$ the synaptic *weights*, $\theta \in \mathbb{R}$ known as the *threshold*, Δ being the *fan-in*, and σ a non-linear activation function. If the underlying graph is acyclic, the NN does not have feedback, and can be layered. Two cost functions have been used to characterize such NNs: (i) *depth* (*i.e.*, number of edges on the longest input-to-output path, or number of layers); and (ii) *size* (*i.e.*, number of neurons).

In the last decade the impetus of VLSI technology has made neurocomputer design a really lively topic. Hundreds of designs have been build, while several are available as commercial products [9]. For VLSI implementations the *area* of the connections counts, and the *area* of one neuron can be related to its associated *weights* [21]. That is why several authors have taken into account cost functions which can be linked to a VLSI implementation by the assumptions one makes on how the *area* scales with the *weights* and the *thresholds* [6]. It is worth emphasizing that it is anyhow desirable to limit the range of parameter values [22], because: (*i*) the maximum value of the *fan-in* [10]; and (*ii*) the maximal ratio between the largest and the smallest *weight* cannot grow over a certain (technological) limit [8].

The paper will start by overviewing results detailing upper and lower bounds on the *size* of *threshold gate* (TG) *circuits* (TGCs). We will show that TGCs require exponential *size* for implementing arbitrary *Boolean functions* (BFs), while there are *size*-optimal TGCs having sub-linear *fan-ins*. Such results are encouraging for hardware (VLSI) implementations where the *fan-ins* are limited.

2 Previous Results

NNs have been experimentally shown to be quite effective in many applications [2, 9]. This success has led researchers to undertake a rigorous analysis of their mathematical properties and has generated two directions of research for finding: (*i*) existence/constructive proofs for the 'universal approximation problem'; (*ii*) tight bounds on the *size* of the NNs solving the approximation problem. Only the second aspect will be shortly discussed, restricting the results to TGCs [13, 16].

The particular case of BFs has been intensively studied [18]. The first lower bound on the *size* of a TGC for 'almost all' *n*-ary BFs ($f: \mathbb{B}^n \to \mathbb{B}$, where $\mathbb{B} = \{0, 1\}$) was given by Neciporuk [17]: $size \geq 2\,(2^n/n)^{1/2}$. A very tight upper bound of $size \leq 2\,(2^n/n)^{1/2} \times \{1 + \Omega\,[(2^n/n)^{1/2}]\}$ was proven in $depth = 4$ [15]. A similar existence lower bound of $\Omega\,(2^{n/3})$ for arbitrary BFs was detailed in [20]. For classification problems ($f: \mathbb{R}^n \to \mathbb{B}^k$) specified by a set of m examples (Remark: for arbitrary BF $m = 2^n$), the first result was that a NN of $depth = 3$ and $size = m - 1$ could compute an arbitrary dichotomy ($k = 1$). The main improvements have been:

- Baum [3] presented a TGC with one hidden layer having *size* $\lceil m/n \rceil$ [1], capable of realizing an arbitrary dichotomy on a set of m points *in general position* in $\mathbb{R}^n$ (if the points are on the corners of the n-dimensional hypercube, $m - 1$ nodes are still needed);
- a slightly tighter bound of only $\lceil 1 + (m - 2)/n \rceil$ TGs in the hidden layer for realizing an arbitrary dichotomy on a set of m points was proven in [14]; the $m - 1$ nodes condition was shown to be the least upper bound needed;
- Arai [1] showed that $m - 1$ hidden neurons are necessary for arbitrary separability, but improved the bound for the dichotomy problem to $m/3$;
- Beiu [4] has detailed existence lower and upper bounds: $2m\log m/n^2 < size < 2m\log m/n^2 \log n$ (by estimating the entropy of the data-set);
- Beiu and De Pauw [7] have improved on the previous results, by proving two new bounds $2m/(n\log n) < size < 1.44m/n$.

Other existence lower bounds for the arbitrary dichotomy problem are [11]: a *depth*-2 solution of $m/\{n\log(m/n)\}$ TGs; a *depth*-3 solution of $2(m/\log m)^{1/2}$ TGs (if $m \gg n^2$); while arbitrarily interconnected TGCs need $(2m/\log m)^{1/2}$ TGs (if $m \gg n^2$). A general solution for multioutput BFs was given by Horne & Hush [12].

Proposition 1 *Arbitrary BFs of the form* $f: \{0, 1\}^n \to \{0, 1\}^\mu$ *can be implemented by TGCs restricted to fan-in 2 with a node complexity of* $\Theta\,\{\mu\, 2^n / (n + \log\mu)\}$ *and requiring* $O\,(n)$ *layers.*

Proof Decompose each BF into two subfunctions using Shannon's decomposition $f(x_1, x_2, \ldots, x_n) = \bar{x}_1 f_0\,(x_2, \ldots, x_n) + x_1 f_1\,(x_2, \ldots, x_n)$. By doing this recursively, the output BFs will be implemented by binary trees. To eliminate most of the lower level nodes, replace them with a subnetwork that computes *all the possible* BFs

[1] In this paper $\lceil x \rceil$ is the ceiling of x, and $\lfloor x \rfloor$ is the floor of x; all the logarithms are taken to base 2 (except explicitly mentioned otherwise).

needed by the higher level nodes. Each subcircuit eliminates one variable and has three nodes (one OR and two ANDs). Thus, the upper tree has:

$$size_{upper} = 3\mu \cdot \sum_{i=0}^{n-q-1} 2^{i} = 3\mu\,(2^{n-q} - 1), \tag{1}$$

and $depth_{upper} = 2(n-q)$. The subfunctions now depend on q variables, and the lower subnetwork that computes all the possible BFs of q variables has:

$$size_{lower} = 3 \cdot \sum_{i=1}^{q} 2^{2^{i}} < 4 \cdot 2^{2^{q}}, \tag{2}$$

and $depth_{lower} = 2q$ (for details see Fig. 2 from [12]). That q which minimizes the $size_{BFs} = size_{upper} + size_{lower}$ is determined by solving $d\,(size_{BFs})\,/\,dq = 0$, and gives:

$$q \approx \log\{n + \log\mu - 2\log(n + \log\mu)\}. \tag{3}$$

By substituting (3) in (1) and (2), the minimum *size*:

$$size^{*}_{BFs}(n, \mu) \approx 3\mu \cdot 2^{n-q} = 3\mu \cdot 2^{n} / (n + \log\mu)$$

is determined. □

3 Computing Arbitrary BFs with Arbitrary Fan-in TGs

It is well known that implementing arbitrary BFs using classical Boolean gates requires exponential *size* circuits [18]. The bounds for *size* (mentioned before) are also exponential if TGCs are used to solve arbitrary BFs. Still, there are *exponential gaps*, suggesting that there might be *size*-optimal TGCs having $depth \neq$ constant. We shall generalize *Proposition 1* to arbitrary *fan-ins* determining the number of layers, and subsequently finding the critical points establishing the *size* minimums.

Proposition 2 *Arbitrary BFs of the form* $f : \{0, 1\}^{n} \rightarrow \{0, 1\}^{\mu}$ *can be implemented by TGCs restricted to fan-in* Δ *in* $\boldsymbol{O}(n/\log\Delta)$ *layers.*

Proof We use the approach from [12] and limit the *fan-in* to Δ. Each output BF can be decomposed in $2^{\Delta-1}$ subfunctions ($2^{\Delta-1}$ AND gates). The OR gate has $2^{\Delta-1}$ inputs. We decompose this OR function in a tree of *fan-in* $= \Delta$ OR gates. This first decomposition step eliminates $\Delta-1$ variables and generates a tree of:

$$depth = 1 + \lceil(\Delta - 1) / \log\Delta\rceil,$$
$$size = 2^{\Delta-1} + \lceil(2^{\Delta-1} - 1) / (\Delta - 1)\rceil.$$

Repeating this procedure recursively k times, we have:

$$depth_{upper} = k \cdot \{1 + \lceil(\Delta - 1) / \log\Delta\rceil\} \tag{4}$$

$$\begin{aligned} size_{upper} &= \{2^{\Delta-1} + \lceil(2^{\Delta-1} - 1) / (\Delta - 1)\rceil\} \cdot \sum_{i=0}^{k-1} 2^{i(\Delta-1)} \\ &= size \cdot \{2^{k(\Delta-1)} - 1\} / (2^{\Delta-1} - 1) \\ &\cong 2^{k(\Delta-1)}(1 + 1/\Delta) \approx 2^{k\Delta-k}, \end{aligned} \tag{5}$$

where the subfunctions depend only on $q = n - k\Delta$ variables. We now generate all the possible subfunctions of q variables with a subnetwork of:

$$depth_{lower} = \lfloor (n-k\Delta)/\Delta \rfloor \cdot \{1+\lceil (\Delta-1)/\log\Delta \rceil\} \tag{6}$$

$$\begin{aligned} size_{lower} &= \{2^{\Delta-1}+\lceil (2^{\Delta-1}-1)/(\Delta-1)\rceil\} \cdot \textstyle\sum_{i=1}^{\lfloor n/\Delta\rfloor-k} 2^{2^{n-k\Delta-i\Delta}} \\ &= size \cdot \{2^{2^{0}}+2^{2^{\Delta}}+\ldots+2^{2^{n-(k+1)\Delta}}\} \\ &< (size+1)\cdot 2^{2^{n-(k+1)\Delta}} \approx 2^{\Delta}\cdot 2^{2^{n-k\Delta-\Delta}} . \end{aligned} \tag{7}$$

The inequality (7) can be proved by induction. Clearly:

$$size \cdot 2^{2^{0}} < (size+1)\cdot 2^{2^{0}} .$$

Let us consider the statement true for α; we shall prove it for $\alpha+1$:

$$size \cdot \{2^{2^{0}}+\ldots+2^{2^{\alpha\Delta}}\} + size \cdot 2^{2^{(\alpha+1)\Delta}} < size \cdot 2^{2^{(\alpha+1)\Delta}} + 2^{2^{(\alpha+1)\Delta}}$$

$$size \cdot \{2^{2^{0}}+\ldots+2^{2^{\alpha\Delta}}\} < (size+1)\cdot 2^{2^{\alpha\Delta}} < 2^{2^{(\alpha+1)\Delta}}$$

and computing the logarithm:

$$\begin{aligned} 2^{\alpha\Delta} + \log(size+1) &= 2^{\alpha\Delta} + \log\{2^{\Delta-1}+\lceil (2^{\Delta-1}-1)/(\Delta-1)\rceil\} \\ &< 2^{\alpha\Delta} + \log\{2^{\Delta-1}+2^{\Delta-1}/\Delta+1\} \\ &< 2^{\alpha\Delta} + \Delta < 2^{(\alpha+1)\Delta}. \end{aligned}$$

From (4) and (6) we can estimate $depth_{BFs}$:

$$\begin{aligned} depth_{BFs} &= \{k+\lfloor (n-k\Delta)/\Delta \rfloor\} \cdot \{1+\lceil (\Delta-1)/\log\Delta \rceil\} \\ &\approx (n/\Delta)\cdot(\Delta/\log\Delta+1) = n/\log\Delta + n/\Delta = \boldsymbol{O}(n/\log\Delta) \end{aligned}$$

and from (5) and (7) we estimate $size_{BFs}$ as:

$$\begin{aligned} size_{BFs} &= \mu \cdot size \cdot \{2^{k(\Delta-1)}-1\}/(\Delta-1) + (size+1)\cdot 2^{2^{n-(k+1)\Delta}} \\ &\approx \mu \cdot 2^{k\Delta-k} + 2^{\Delta}\cdot 2^{2^{n-k\Delta-\Delta}} \end{aligned} \tag{8}$$

concluding the proof. ❑

Proposition 3 *Arbitrary BFs of the form* $f: \{0,1\}^n \to \{0,1\}^{\mu}$ *can be implemented by TGCs, where all the critical points of* $size_{BFs}(\mu, n, k, \Delta)$ *are relative minimums situated in the vicinity of the parabola* $k\Delta \approx n - \log(n+\log\mu)$.

Proof To determine the critical points, we equate the partial derivatives to zero. Starting from (8) we compute $\partial size_{BFs}/\partial k = 0$:

$$\mu \cdot 2^{k\Delta-k}(\ln 2)(\Delta-1) + 2^{\Delta} 2^{2^{n-k\Delta-\Delta}} (\ln 2)\, 2^{n-k\Delta-\Delta}(\ln 2)(-\Delta) = 0$$

$$\{\mu(\Delta-1)/\Delta/(\ln 2)\}\cdot 2^{2k\Delta-k-n} = 2^{2^{n-k\Delta-\Delta}}$$

and using the notations $k\Delta = \gamma$, $\beta = \mu(\Delta-1)/(\Delta \ln 2)$, and taking logarithms:

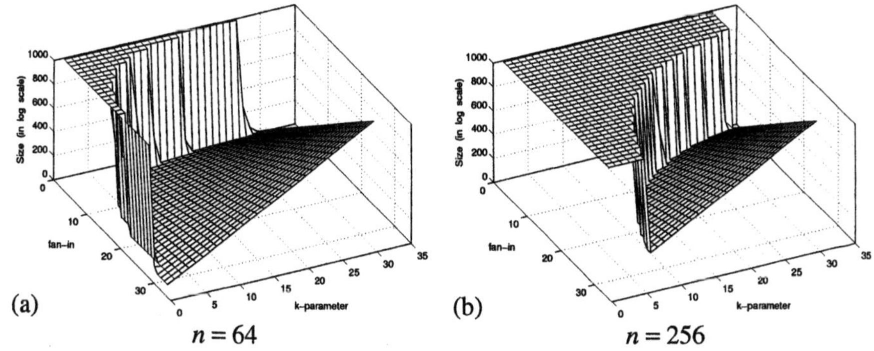

Fig. 1. The *size* of NNs implementing arbitrary BFs: (a) $n = 64$; (b) $n = 256$.

$$\log\beta + 2\gamma - k - n = 2^{n-\gamma-\Delta} \tag{9}$$

which has an approximate solution $\gamma = k\Delta \approx n - \log(n + \log\mu)$.

Starting again from (8), we compute $\partial size_{BFs} / \partial\Delta = 0$:

$$\mu 2^{k\Delta - k}(\ln 2)\, k + 2^{\Delta}(\ln 2)\, 2^{2^{n-k\Delta-\Delta}} + 2^{\Delta}\, 2^{2^{n-k\Delta-\Delta}} (\ln 2)\, 2^{n-k\Delta-\Delta}(\ln 2)(-k) = 0$$

$$\mu k \cdot 2^{\gamma-k} = k(\ln 2)\cdot 2^{n-\gamma}\cdot 2^{2^{n-\gamma-\Delta}} - 2^{\Delta}\cdot 2^{2^{n-\gamma-\Delta}}$$

$$\mu k \cdot 2^{\gamma-k}\cdot 2^{\gamma-n} = k(\ln 2)\cdot 2^{2^{n-\gamma-\Delta}} - 2^{\Delta}\cdot 2^{\gamma-n}\cdot 2^{2^{n-\gamma-\Delta}}$$

$$(\mu/\ln 2)\cdot 2^{2\gamma-k-n} = \{1 - 2^{\gamma+\Delta-n}/(k\ln 2)\}\cdot 2^{2^{n-\gamma-\Delta}}$$

which—by neglecting $2^{\gamma+\Delta}/\{k(\ln 2)\cdot 2^{n}\}$—gives $\log\beta + 2\gamma - k - n = 2^{n-\gamma-\Delta}$ *i.e.* the same equation as (9).

All of these show that the critical points are situated in the (close) vicinity of the parabola $k\Delta \approx n - \log(n + \log\mu)$. It follows that *size*-optimal TGCs can be obtained for $\Delta \approx [n - \log(n + \log\mu)] / k$, *i.e.* ranging from constant to at most $n - \log n$. ❑

The exact values of $size_{BFs} \approx \mu \cdot 2^{n-\log(n+\log\mu)-k} + 2^{\Delta}\cdot 2^{2^{\log(n+\log\mu)-\Delta}}$ have been computed for many different values of n, μ, Δ and k. Figure 1 reveals the $k\Delta \approx n - \log n$ parabolas ($\mu = 1$), k and Δ having the same influence on $size_{BFs}$. It is to be mentioned that the (relative) minimums (on, or in the vicinity of the parabola), should be of *practical interest* as leading to *size*-optimal circuits having fewer layers: $n/\log\Delta + n/\Delta$ instead of $2n$ (as in [12]).

4 Conclusions

The main conclusion is that *size*-optimal TGCs for implementing arbitrary BFs have sub-linear *fan-ins*. In general, arbitrary BFs can be implemented using classical Boolean or TGs. In both cases, the *size* is exponential, but there is an exponential gap in between them. All of these show that in the space of all possible solutions, there are interesting *fan-in* dependent *depth-size* tradeoffs. These results also show that removing the analog behavior of the neurons (by substituting the nonlinear activation function with a hard limiter), reduces their computational abilities.

References

1. Arai, M. (1993) Bounds on the Number of Hidden Units in Binary-Valued Three-Layer Neural Networks. Neural Networks **6**, 855–860
2. Arbib, M.A. (1995) The Handbook of Brain Theory and Neural Networks. MIT Press, Cambridge
3. Baum, E.B. (1988) On the Capabilities of Multilayer Perceptrons. J. Complexity **4**, 193–215
4. Beiu, V. (1996) Entropy Bounds for Classification Algorithms. Neural Network World **6**, 497–505
5. Beiu, V. (1996) Digital Integrated Circuit Implementations. Chapter E1.4 in [9]
6. Beiu, V. (1998) On the Circuit and VLSI Complexity of Threshold Gate COMPARISON. Neurocomputing **19**, 77–98
7. Beiu, V., De Pauw, T. (1997) Tight Bounds on the Size of Neural Networks for Classification Problems. In: Mira, J., Moreno-Díaz, R., Cabestany, J. (eds.) Biological and Artificial Computation. Springer-Verlag, Berlin, pp. 743–752
8. Bruck, J., Goodmann, J.W. (1990) On the Power of Neural Networks for Solving Hard Problems. J. Complexity **6**, 129–135
9. Fiesler, E., Beale, R. (1996) Handbook of Neural Computation. I*o*P, New York
10. Hammerstrom, D. (1988) The Connectivity Analysis of Simple Association –or– How Many Connections Do You Need. In: Anderson, D.Z. (ed.) Neural Information Processing Systems. AIPress, New York, pp. 338–347
11. Hassoun, M.H. (1995) Fundamentals of Artificial Neural Networks. MIT Press, Cambridge
12. Horne, B.G., Hush, D.R. (1994) On the Node Complexity of Neural Networks. Neural Networks **7**, 1413–1426
13. Hu, S. (1965) Threshold Logic. Univ. California Press, Berkeley
14. Huang, S.-C., Huang, Y.-F. (1991) Bounds on the Number of Hidden Neurons of Multilayer Perceptrons in Classification and Recognition. IEEE Trans. Neural Networks **2**, 47–55
15. Lupanov, O.B. (1973) The Synthesis of Circuits from Threshold Elements. Problemy Kibernetiki **20**, 109–140
16. Minnik, R.C. (1961) Linear-Input Logic. IRE Trans. Electr. Comp. **10**, 6–16
17. Neciporuk, E.I. (1964) The Synthesis of Networks from Threshold Elements. Soviet Mathematics **5**, 163–166. English transl. (1964) Automation Express **7**, 27–32 & 35–39
18. Parberry, I. (1994) Circuit Complexity and Neural Networks, MIT Press, Cambridge
19. Shannon, C. (1949) The Synthesis of Two-Terminal Switching Circuits. Bell Sys. Tech. J. **28**, 59–98
20. Siu, K.-Y., Roychowdhury, V.P., Kailath, T. (1991) Depth-Size Tradeoffs for Neural Computations. IEEE Trans. Comp. **40**, 1402–1412
21. Williamson, R.C. (1990) ε-Entropy and the Complexity of Feedforward Neural Networks. In: Lippmann, R.P., Moody, J.E., Touretzky, D.S. (eds.) Advances in Neural Information Processing Systems. Morgan Kaufmann, San Mateo, pp. 946–952
22. Wray, J., Green, G.G.R. (1995) Neural Networks, Approximation Theory, and Finite Precision Computation. Neural Networks **8**, 31–372

Numerically Robust Learning Algorithms for Feed Forward Neural Networks

Jarosław Bilski, Leszek Rutkowski

Department of computer Engineering, Technical University of Częstochowa,
Al. Armii Krajowej 36, 42-200 Częstochowa, Poland,
e-mail: bilski{lrutko}@kik.pcz.czest.pl

Keywords. Neural networks, RLS learning algorithms, QR decomposition.

Summary. In recent years several neural networks learning algorithms have been developed by making use of the RLS recursion. These algorithms are based on the matrix inversion lemma and in some cases can be numerically ill-conditioned. For example the rounding errors can accumulate and cause errors to occur in both the estimated parameters and the covariance matrix. In this paper we present numerically robust learning algorithms based on the QR decomposition – a well known technique in the linear prediction theory.

1. Introduction

In recent years several fast neural networks learning algorithms have been developed. The RLS-based procedures (see [1, 4 ,5]) rely on the analogy between adaptive filters and neural networks. It is well known that in adaptive filtering the RLS algorithm is typically an order of magnitude faster than the LMS algorithm. This is the main motivation to study the RLS procedures which are based on the matrix inversion lemma. Unfortunately, in some cases the matrix inversion lemma version of RLS can be numerically ill-conditioned For example the rounding errors can accumulate and cause errors to occur in both the estimated parameters and the covariance matrix.

Consider the following equation:

$$\mathbf{A}\mathbf{w} = \mathbf{h} \tag{1}$$

There are several methods to develop numerically robust algorithms in order to solve equation (1).

i) The symmetric covariance matrix can be factored in the form

$$\mathbf{A} = \mathbf{Q}\mathbf{Q}^T \tag{2}$$

where Q is a triangular matrix, see e.g. [2].

ii) Let

$$\mathbf{P} = \mathbf{A}^{-1} \tag{3}$$

The UD factorisation takes the form

$$\mathbf{P} = \mathbf{UDU}^{T} \tag{4}$$

where U is an upper triangular matrix and D is a diagonal matrix, see e.g. [3]

iii) The QR decomposition is based on assumption that the following representation of equation (1) is valid:

$$\mathbf{A} = \mathbf{QR} \tag{5}$$

where R is a square, upper triangular matrix and Q is the orthogonal matrix, see e.g. [6, 7, 8].

Various neural network learning algorithms based on representations (2) and (4) have been developed in [2, 3]. In this paper we implement the idea of the QR decomposition (5) to train multilayer neural networks.

2. QR decomposition for neural network learning

In our implementations of the method we introduce a performance measure

$$J(n) = \sum_{t=1}^{n} \lambda^{n-t} \sum_{j=1}^{N_L} e_j^{(L)2}(t) = \sum_{t=1}^{n} \lambda^{n-t} \sum_{j=1}^{N_L} \left[b_j^{(L)}(t) - \mathbf{x}^{(L)T}(t) \mathbf{w}_j^{(L)}(n) \right]^2 \tag{6}$$

where λ is a positive constant, called forgetting factor, close to but less then 1. In Fig. 1 we show a model of the i-th neuron in the k-th layer. For the terminology consult [5] and Fig.1.

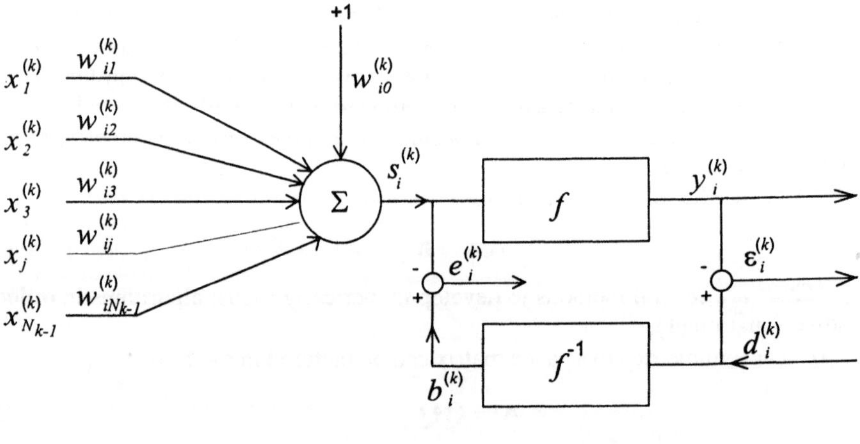

Fig. 1. Model of the i-th neuron in the k-th layer

The performance index (6) is minimized by taking the partial derivative of $J(n)$ with respect to $\mathbf{w}_i^{(k)}(n)$ and setting it equal to zero, i.e.

$$
\begin{aligned}
\frac{\partial J(n)}{\partial \mathbf{w}_i^{(k)}(n)} &= -2\sum_{t=1}^{n} \lambda^{n-t}\left(-\tfrac{1}{2}\right)\sum_{j=1}^{N_L} \frac{\partial\, e_j^{(L)2}(t)}{\partial \mathbf{w}_i^{(k)}(n)} = \\
&= -2\sum_{t=1}^{n} \lambda^{n-t}\left(-\tfrac{1}{2}\right)\sum_{j=1}^{N_L} \frac{\partial e_j^{(L)2}(t)}{\partial s_i^{(k)}(n)} \frac{\partial s_i^{(k)}(n)}{\partial \mathbf{w}_i^{(k)}(n)} = \mathbf{0}
\end{aligned}
\tag{7}
$$

By defining

$$
e_i^{(k)}(n) \hat{=} -\frac{1}{2}\frac{\partial \sum_{i=1}^{N_L} e_i^{(L)2}(n)}{\partial s_i^{(k)}(n)} \tag{8}
$$

We obtain

$$
\begin{aligned}
e_i^{(k)}(n) &= -\frac{1}{2}\frac{\partial \sum_{i=1}^{N_L} e_i^{(L)2}(n)}{\partial s_i^{(k)}(n)} = -\frac{1}{2}\sum_{l=k+1}^{L}\sum_{m=1}^{N_l} \frac{\partial \sum_{i=1}^{N_L} e_i^{(L)2}(n)}{\partial s_m^{(l)}(n)} \frac{\partial s_m^{(l)}(n)}{\partial s_i^{(k)}(n)} = \\
&= \sum_{l=k+1}^{L}\sum_{m=1}^{N_l} e_m^{(l)}(n) w_{mi}^{(lk)}(n) f'\left(s_i^{(k)}(n)\right) = f'\left(s_i^{(k)}(n)\right) \sum_{l=k+1}^{L}\sum_{m=1}^{N_l} e_m^{(l)}(n) w_{mi}^{(lk)}(n)
\end{aligned}
\tag{9}
$$

where $w_{mi}^{(lk)}$ connects the m-th neuron from l-th layer with output of the i-th neuron from k-th layer.

In result the equation (7) is converted to

$$
\sum_{t=1}^{n} \lambda^{n-t} e_i^{(k)}(t)\mathbf{x}^{(k)}(t) = \mathbf{0} \tag{10}
$$

or to the normal equation in the form

$$
\sum_{t=1}^{n} \lambda^{n-t}\left[b_i^{(k)}(t) - \mathbf{x}^{(k)T}(t)\mathbf{w}_i^{(k)}(n)\right]\mathbf{x}^{(k)}(t) = \mathbf{0} \tag{11}
$$

where

$$b_i^{(k)}(n)=\begin{cases} b_i^{(L)}(n)=f^{-1}\left(d_i^{(L)}(n)\right) & for\, k=L \\ s_i^{(k)}(n)+e_i^{(k)}(n) & for\, k=1\ldots L-1 \end{cases} \tag{12}$$

Equation (11) can be presented in the vector form

$$\mathbf{h}_i^{(k)}(n)=\mathbf{A}^{(k)}(n)\mathbf{w}_i^{(k)}(n) \tag{13}$$

where

$$\mathbf{A}^{(k)}(n)=\sum_{t=1}^{n}\lambda^{n-t}\mathbf{x}^{(k)}(t)\mathbf{x}^{(k)T}(t) \tag{14}$$

$$\mathbf{h}_i^{(k)}(n)=\sum_{t=1}^{n}\lambda^{n-t}b_i^{(k)}(t)\mathbf{x}^{(k)}(t) \tag{15}$$

The equation (13) can be solved recursively by the QR algorithm:

$$e_i^{(k)}(n)=\begin{cases} b_i^{(L)}(n)-s_i^{(L)}(n)=f^{-1}\left(d_i^{(L)}(n)\right)-s_i^{(L)}(n) & for\, k=L \\ f'\left(s_i^{(k)}(n)\right)\sum_{l=k+1}^{L}\sum_{m=1}^{N_l}w_{mi}^{(lk)}(n)e_m^{(l)}(n) & for\, k<L \end{cases} \tag{16}$$

$$b_i^{(k)}(n)=\begin{cases} b_i^{(L)}(n)=f^{-1}\left(d_i^{(L)}(n)\right) & for\, k=L \\ s_i^{(k)}(n)+e_i^{(k)}(n) & for\, k=1\ldots L-1 \end{cases} \tag{17}$$

$$\hat{\mathbf{w}}_i^{(k)}(n)=\mathbf{R}^{(k)-1}(n)\mathbf{Q}^{(k)T}(n)\mathbf{h}_i^{(k)}(n) \tag{18}$$

$$\mathbf{w}_i^{(k)}(n)=(1-\eta)\mathbf{w}_i^{(k)}(n-1)+\eta\,\hat{\mathbf{w}}_i^{(k)}(n) \tag{19}$$

where $\mathbf{Q}^{(k)}(n)$, $\mathbf{R}^{(k)}(n)$ and $\mathbf{A}^{(k)}(n)$ are related by

$$\mathbf{A}^{(k)}(n)=\mathbf{Q}^{(k)}(n)\mathbf{R}^{(k)}(n) \tag{20}$$

and vector $\hat{\mathbf{w}}_i^{(k)}(n)$ is a temporary solution while η is a learning factor.

The initial values of the weight vector $\mathbf{w}_i^{(k)}(n)$ can be chosen as small random numbers.

3. Simulations

First, the performance of the QR algorithm was tested on the XOR logic scheme. We use a simple neural network with sigmoidal functions *f*. As a stopping criterion we take

$$\sum_{j=1}^{N_L} \left[d_j^{(L)}(t) - y_j^{(L)}(t) \right]^2 \leq \gamma \tag{21}$$

where γ is arbitrary chosen threshold and $N_L=1$. One epoch consists of 4 iterations. The structure of the neural network consists of 2 inputs, 2 neurons in the hidden layer and a single output. The threshold $\gamma=0.01$. Four pairs of input and desired output patterns are used for its training: (0.1, 0.1; 0.1), (0.1, 0.9; 0.9), (0.9, 0.1; 0.9), (0.9, 0.9; 0.1). Exemplary learning curves for the momentum BP and QR algorithms are shown in Fig. 2.

Moreover, we examined the QR algorithm (comparing with momentum BP) on the approximation of the logistic mapping given by

$$x_{n+1} = 4x_n(1 - x_n), 0 \leq x_n \leq 1 \tag{22}$$

which generates a chaotic time series. The analogue approximator, with sigmoidal functions *f*, is based on 1 input, 3 neurons in the hidden layer and a single output. The learning curves for the momentum BP and QR algorithms are given in Fig. 3.

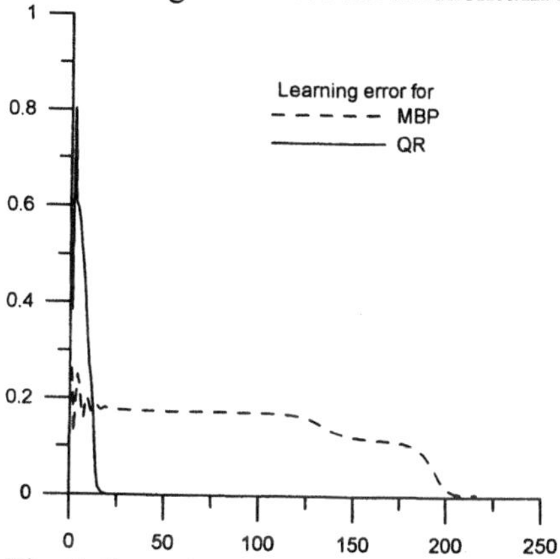

Fig. 2. Learning curve – XOR function: a) backpropagation, b) QR method

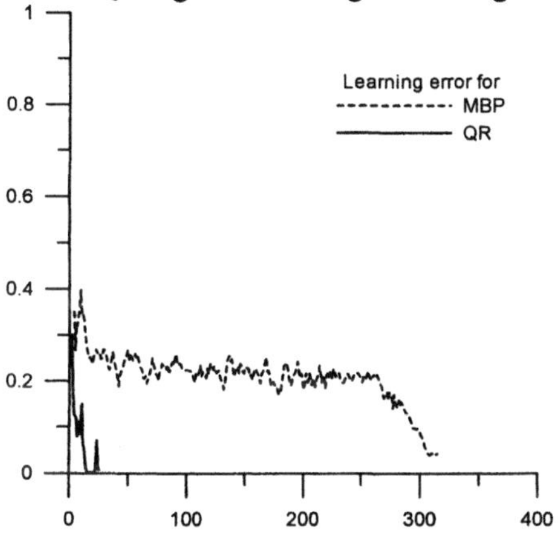

Fig. 3. Learning curve - function approximation: a) backpropagation, b) QR method

4. Conclusion

In this paper we developed the QR learning algorithm which is more powerful than the conventional backpropagation. Simulations indicate at least tenfold increase in the training efficiency comparing with the conventional momentum backpropagation.

References

[1] R. Azimi-Sadjadi, R.-J. Liou (1992) Fast learning process of multilayer neural networks using recursive least squares method, IEEE Transactions on Signal Processing, vol. 40, no. 2

[2] J. Bilski (1996) The modified RLS algorithm for learning of the feedforward neural networks, II KSNiIZ, Szczyrk, pp. 32-38

[3] J. Bilski (1996) New algorithms for learning of the feedforward neural networks, II KSNiIZ, Szczyrk, pp. 39-45

[4] J. Bilski, K. Cpałka (1997) The extended RLS algorithm for neural network learning, III KSNiIZ, Kule, pp. 77-84

[5] J. Bilski, L. Rutkowski (1998) A Fast Training Algorithm for Neural Networks, IEEE Transaction on Circuits and Systems – II, vol. 45,no. 6, June 1998: 749-753

[6] P. Strobach (1990) Linear Prediction Theory - A Mathematical Basis for Adaptive Systems, Springer-Verlag, New York

[7] P.E. Wellstead, M.B. Zarrop (1991) Self-tuning Systems – Control and Signal Processing, Wiley

[8] T. Söderström, P. Stoica (1989) System Identification, Prentice Hall International

A Neural Network Based Approach For Sensors Issued Data Fusion

Abdennasser Chebira and Kourosh Madani

Intelligence in Instrumentation and Systems Lab. (I^2S)
SENART Institute of Technology - University PARIS XII
Avenue Pierre POINT, F-77127 LIEUSAINT - FRANCE

E-Mail : {chebira ; madani}@univ-paris12.fr

Abstract: In this paper, we present a Functional Link Network (FLN) based neural technique for sensors issued data fusion. Thanks to a pruning algorithm, we build dynamically the internal layer of the FLN, constructing an optimal architecture of the FLN neural network defining an optimal fusion policy. As the neural FLN minimize the mean square error (MSE) during the learning step, an optimal fusion policy is reached in the sense of the MSE. Experimental results related to performances enhancement of metric sensors have been reported validating our approach.

1 Introduction

When facing a practical data fusion problem, the main difficulties are related on the one hand, to information sources modeling, and on the other hand, to the choice (definition) of appropriated fusion policy. A large number of fusion operators are available in the literature and the system designer's experience is the main basis in choosing and defining an appropriated fusion policy ([1] and [2]). However, such choice operation remains subjective.

Among enticing property of Neural Networks (NNs) are their learning and generalization capabilities ([3] to [5]). These properties makes such techniques suitable for non linear optimization problems. Among neural models which are well adapted to perform optimization task is Functional Link Network (FLN) like neural model. It's universal approximation property and it's sufficient flexibility, allows to design an efficient recursive algorithm that formally defines an optimal fusion policy [2]. In this paper we present a pruning concept and an algorithm based on such concept, designed for FLN (PAFLN), that optimizes the FLN's internal layer using minimum square error (MSE) criterion. Using fusion operators within the FLN's internal layer makes such optimized FLN based NN acting as an optimal universal fusion operator in the sense of MSE criterion optimization [5].

Section 2 presents some of the main fusion operators and especially those used within the frame of fuzzy set theory. Section 3 present the FLN's structure and based pruning algorithm. The section 4 presents application of the FLN structure to the sensor's issued data fusion where an example dealing with metric information issues from asymmetric position sensors will be reported. Finally section 5 will conclude this paper.

2 Fusion operators

This section discusses some current data fusion operators, that are used in conventional data fusion approaches. Several authors have introduced various classes of fusion operators ([1] and [6]). These classes of operators have different actions, depending on the problem's framework: possibility theory, fuzzy set theory, etc.. Following notations will be used: $\sigma(.,.)$ represents the fusion operator, D^n is a n dimensional decision space, and d_i designates decision variables to be fused. So, we suppose here that each sensing process provides a set of events and to each event i it is associated a variable d_i, value of which belongs to the range $[0,1]$ representing some confidence rate related to the influence of that event.

2.1 Context independent, constant behavior operators (CICB)

In this case, two hypothesis are considered:

- The acquisition context does not influence the sensing process.
- The fusion operator is independent of the sensing process.

Context Independent Constant Behavior (CICB) operators may belong to strictest operator (T-norms) or to the most indulgent operators (T-conorms). Compromise operators lie in the range $[min(d_i,d_j), max(d_i,d_j)]$:

$$\forall(d_1,d_2) \in D^2, \; min(d_1,d_2) \le \sigma(d_1,d_2) \le max(d_1,d_2) \cdot \tag{1}$$

Some of the most popular CICB like operators are given below:

$$\forall(d_1,d_2) \in D^2, \sigma(d_1,d_2) = \max(0, d_1 + d_2 - 1) \tag{2}$$

$$\forall(d_1,d_2) \in D^2, \sigma(d_1,d_2) = d_1 \times d_2 \tag{3}$$

$$\forall(d_1,d_2) \in D^2, \sigma(d_1,d_2) = \frac{2 d_1 \times d_2}{d_1 + d_2} \tag{4}$$

$$\forall(d_1,d_2) \in D^2, \sigma(d_1,d_2) = \frac{d_1 + d_2}{2} \tag{5}$$

$$\forall(d_1,d_2) \in D^2, \sigma(d_1,d_2) = d_1 + d_2 - d_1 \times d_2 \tag{6}$$

$$\forall(d_1,d_2) \in D^2, \sigma(d_1,d_2) = \min(d_1, d_2) \tag{7}$$

$$\forall(d_1,d_2) \in D^2, \sigma(d_1,d_2) = \max(d_1, d_2) \tag{8}$$

$$\forall(d_1,d_2) \in D^2, \sigma(d_1,d_2) = \sqrt{d_1 \times d_2} \tag{9}$$

$$\forall(d_1,d_2) \in D^2, \sigma(d_1,d_2) = \max(1,\ d_1 + d_2) \tag{10}$$

2.2 Context dependent, variable behavior operators (CDVB)

Two hypothesis are also considered:

- The acquisition context does not influence the sensing process.
- The semantic associated to the value provided by sensing process is significant.

Depending on context, strictness operators are used if decision thresholds are high and indulgence is suggested if decision values are low (the scholar exam notation dilemma could be an example). As in the case of CICB operators, one may use the following operator:

$$\sigma(d_1,d_2)=\begin{cases}\dfrac{min(d_1,d_2)}{1-|d_1-d_2|} & if \quad d_1+d_2\le 1\\ \dfrac{max(d_1,d_2)}{1+|d_1-d_2|} & if \quad d_1+d_2>1\end{cases} \tag{11}$$

2.3 Context dependent operators (CD)

Using this class of operators, supposes that each sensing process have been modeled (even if not formally). For real word problems, modeling sensing process may be complex. Some global knowledge and some measure of the sensing processes to be fused should be available. One of the following policies are used:

- Cooperative fusion is used when fusion operators have a conjunctive behavior (T-conorms).
- Competitive fusion is used when fusion operators have a disjunctive behavior, T-norms.
- Complementary fusion is used when fusion operators have a compromise behavior, means.

One can use the following operator, where α_i represents the confidence associated to the information source *i*.

$$\sigma(x,y)=\sum_{i=1}^{2}\alpha_i d_i \qquad \text{with} \qquad \alpha_i\in[0,1] \tag{12}$$

3 FLN structure and based pruning algorithm

The FLN architecture is depicted in Figure 1, including an input layer, an output layer and a hidden layer achieving a functional expansion. Transposition of a *n* dimensional input space (R^n) to a *m* dimensional space (R^m), with *m>n*, is the main function that FLN performs. Such transposition can use non-linear functions. The FLN's output is then a linear weighted combination of the m input components. Such transposition (from R^n to R^m) is deterministic and invariable. The output can be written as (13), where $\mathbf{x}$ is an *n* by 1 input vector, $\mathrm{f_i}(.)$, with $1\le i\le m$, is an arbitrary function, and $\bar{\alpha}$ is a m by 1 column vector of unknown weights (weight vector): $O=\sum_{i=1}^{m}\alpha_i f_i(\mathbf{x})=\bar{\alpha}\ \bar{f}(\mathbf{x})$ (13).

The learning step consists of finding the weight vector $\bar{\alpha}$ that minimizes some criterion. This may be done with a standard square root algorithm or one of its fast and/or recursive versions. If the least square criterion is used, $\bar{\alpha}$ is given by (14), where *A* is a *p* by *m* matrix, which represents the learning input data base, *p* is the number of patterns in the learning data base. Fast algorithms can be used to solve the equation (14).

$$\overline{\alpha} = (A^T A)^{-1} A\mathbf{O} \quad (14)$$

where: $A=[\ Y_1^T, Y_2^T, \ldots, Y_p^T\ ]^T$, $\mathbf{Y}_i^T = \overline{f}(x_i)$, $\mathbf{O} = [O_1^T, O_2^T, \ldots, O_p^T]^T$.

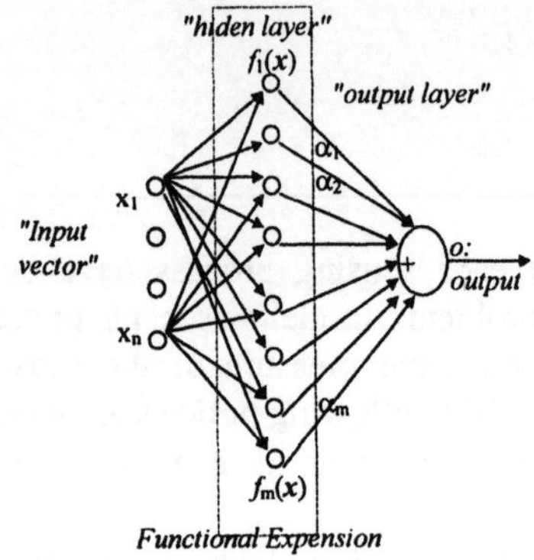

Fig. 1. Bloc diagram of the FLN structure.

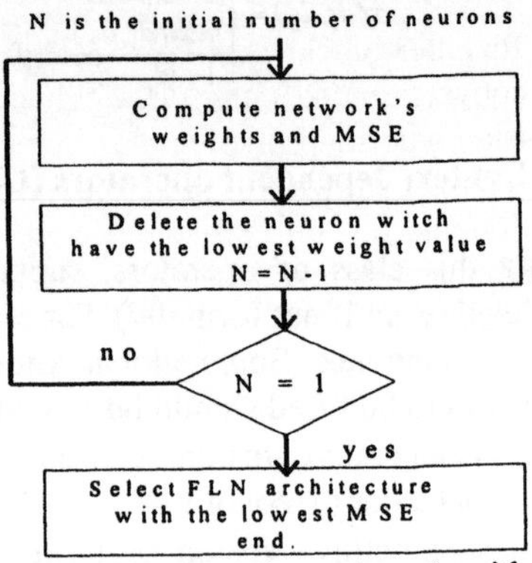

Fig. 2. FLN based pruning algorithm.

It has been proved that FLN can approximate any continuous function [6]. The main difficulty when using FLN in practice is the choice of the transposition functions set and the appropriated dimension of the space R^m. The set of transposition functions $\{ fi \}$ can be chosen in different ways. One can choose polynomial expansion or trigonometric functions, makes the network acting then as a polynomial approximator or a Fourier analysis device. Note that $f_i(\mathbf{x})$ could be chosen conform to (15), where $\overline{n_j}$, $\overline{\mathbf{c}_j}$ and $\overline{\rho_j}$ are constant vectors. In this case, FLN acts as a special case of Radial Basis Functions (RBF) NNs. Other choice of $f_i(\mathbf{x})$ makes the FLN a particular case of Multi-Layers Perceptron (MLP).

$$fi(\mathbf{x}) = \sum_{j=1}^{q} \overline{n_j}\Theta(\|\mathbf{x} - \overline{\mathbf{c}_j}\|, \overline{\rho_j}) \quad \text{with } \Theta(z,\rho) = (z^2 + \rho^2)^{1/2} \quad (15)$$

As FLN may use fast least square algorithm to achieve learning, one can easily add a pruning algorithm to the FLN paradigm: beginning with a large number of transposition functions, network's weights are computed, then neurons with the lowest weight values are removed. This operation is repeated until removing all insignificant neurons in the hidden layer. In each step, the network's MSE is computed and finally the optimal structure with the lowest MSE is retained.

4 Application to sensors issued data fusion

Using data fusion operators as the set of transposition functions (see figure 3), the FLN could then be seen as a universal data fusion operator. The weight vector $\overline{\alpha}$ defines the particular fusion policy which has been learned by the network (we assume, of course, that a learning database is available). Computing the weight vector $\overline{\alpha}$ is achieved by minimizing the mean square error, it defines the optimal fusion policy according to MSE criterion.

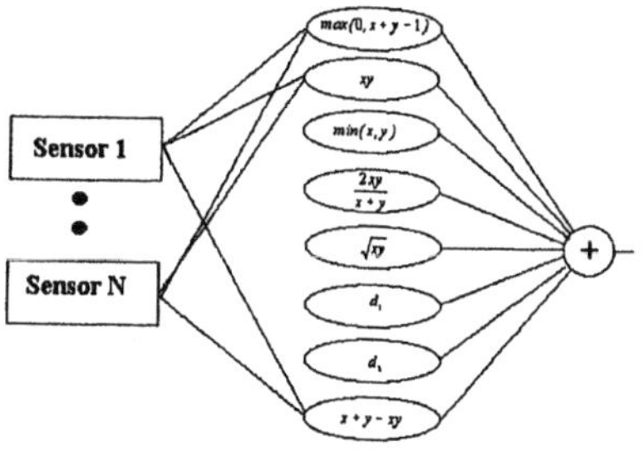

Fig. 3. FLN used as universal data fusion operator.

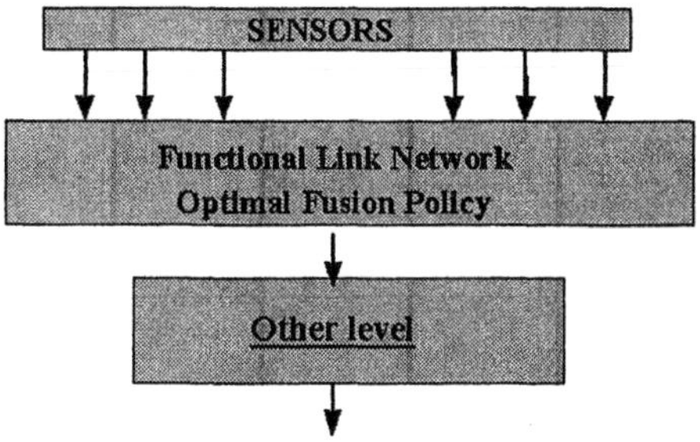

Fig. 4. Bloc diagram of the FLN based sensors issued data Fusion architecture.

Let us to consider a validation example related to metric measurement. It should be noted that metric sensors are central devices in numerous industrial production processes[7]. Thus, we consider here a metric data provided by two sensors. The first sensor provides a distance measure for witch the relative error increases as the distance increase. The second one provides a distance measure for witch the relative error decreases as the distance increase. So the first sensor is well adapted to short distance measurement, whereas the second one is more appropriated to long distance measurement. Thus, in the case of middle range measurement, both of two sensors provide imprecise values. The goal here is to enhance the middle range measurement precision. For that, we use the PAFLN algorithm to determine an optimal fusion policy, which will be used to construct a neural based smart sensor including the set of two sensors and the neural fusion operator.

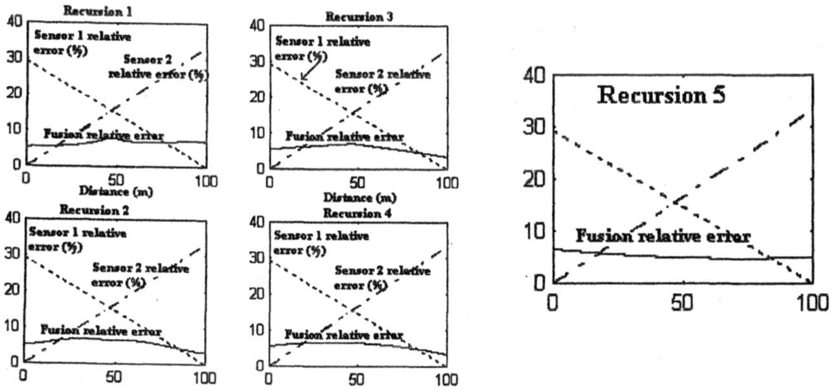

Fig. 5. Measurement relative error as function of measured distance for each sensor and the neural based smart sensor's. The five successive graphs, labeled "Recursion 1" to "Recursion 5" give the measurement relative error'sevolution.

To validate our concepts, we have built a learning database and a generalization database including respectively 100 and 500 patterns. Results are shown in figure 5. This figure shows the individual relative errors for each sensor (1 and 2) and the neural based smart sensor's one. One can note that for middle range distances, the neural based sensor leads to more reliable measurement. Initial FLN includes 5 neurons in it's hidden layer. The optimal FLN's structure for this fusion problem uses 4 neurons, which corresponds to the lowest global MSE. So, the neural based smart sensor will operate as following: for short and far distances, the appropriated individual sensors will be used, whereas, for intermediate distances, the neural based fusion policy will be used. Referring to the section 2, one can note that this global fusion corresponds to a Context Independent Variable Behavior (CIVB) like operator.

5 Conclusion

In this paper, we have presented a neural network based method that allows the optimal selection of a data fusion policy. The internal layer of a FLN is built dynamically, by adding a pruning algorithm (PAFLN) to the conventional FLN structure, leading to an optimal architecture defining an optimal fusion policy. Such dynamical adaptive fusion operator construction algorithm gives a solution to the difficult dilemma of fusion operator choice as well as to the expansion functions choice in conventional FLN structures. An application example dealing with metric sensors issued data fusion has been presented validating our PAFLN approach, enhancing the distance measurement process.

References

1. I. Bloch (1996), "Information Combination Operators for Data Fusion : A Comparative Review with Classification". IEEE Transaction On SMC, part A,Vol. 26, N°1, pp 52-67, 1996.
2. Y. Cheng and R. L. Kashyap (1992), "Recursive Fusion Operators : Desirable properties and illustrations". Data Fusion in Robotics and Machine Intelligence", Ed. M. A. Abidi and R. C. Gonzalez, Academic Press inc, 1992.
3. Brown M & Harris C.J, "Neural Networks for Modeling and Control" in Advances in Intelligent Control, Taylor & Francis Lts, pp. 17-57, ISBN 0-7484-0066-4.
4. A. Sachenko, V. Kochan, V. Turchenko, V. Golovko, J. Savitsky, A. Dunets, T. Laopoulos (2000), "Sensor errors prediction using neural networks", Proceedings of the IJCNN'2000 Conf., Jul 24-Jul 27 2000, 2000, Como, Italy, p 441-446.
5. K. Madani, A. Chebira, R. Reynaud, T. Maurin and K. Bouchefra (1998), "Hybrid neural-based decision level fusion architecture: application to road traffic collision avoidance", Optical Engineering 37(2), 1998.
6. Nageswara S. V. Rao (1997), "Fusion Rule Estimation Using Vector Space Methods" Proceedings of SPIE, Sensor Fusion : Architectures, Algorithms, and Applications, volume 3067, pp 130-135, 24-24 April 1997, Orlando, Florida.
7. A. Sachenko (1999), "IMCS development on the basis of distributed sensor networks", IEEE AFRICON Conference, v1, 1999 IEEE, Piscataway, NJ, USA, p 345-350.

Population Learning Metaheuristic for Neural Network Training

Ireneusz Czarnowski and Piotr Jędrzejowicz

Department of Information Systems, Gdynia Maritime University
Morska 83, 81-225 Gdynia, Poland
{irek, pj}@wsm.gdynia.pl

Abstract. Population based methods handle a population of individuals that evolves with the help of information exchange and self-improvement procedures. In this paper an application of a new metaheuristic called population learning algorithm (PLA) to ANN is investigated. The paper proposes several implementations of the PLA to training feed-forward artificial neural networks. The approach is validated by means of computational experiment in which PLA algorithm is used to train ANN solving a variety of benchmarking problems. Results of the experiment prove that PLA can be considered as a useful and effective tool for training ANN.

1 Introduction

Artificial neural networks are, nowadays, being used for solving a wide variety of real-life problems like, for example, pattern recognition, prediction, control, combinatorial optimization or classification. Main advantages of the approach include ability to tolerate imprecision and uncertainty and still achieving tractability, robustness, and low cost in practical applications. Since training a neural network for practical application is often very times consuming, an extensive research work is being carried in order to accelerate this process. Another problem with ANN training methods is danger of being caught in a local optimum. Hence, researchers look not only for algorithms that train neural networks quickly but rather for quick algorithms that are not likely, or less likely, to get trapped in a local optimum [1,3,10].

In this paper we investigate application of the recently proposed population-based metaheurictic known as the population-learning algorithm (PLA) [4]. To test and evaluate application of the PLA to training neural networks several benchmark problems have been chosen.

The paper briefly presents an idea of the population learning algorithm and gives a detailed description of the PLA implementation designed for training ANN solving the two spirals problem, 10 - parity problem and several medical and management problems.

The research has been supported by the KBN, grant no. 8T11F020 19 2000

2 Population Learning Algorithm

Population learning algorithms (PLA) handle population of individuals. An individual represents a coded solution of the considered problem. Initially, a massive population of individuals, known as the initial population, is generated. The number of individuals in the initial population should be sufficient to represent adequately the whole space of feasible solutions. Sufficient number of individuals relates to the need of covering the neighbourhood of all of the local optima. Adequate representation of these neighbourhoods is related to the need of assuring that the improvement process, originated at the initial stage should be effective enough to carry at least some individuals to the highest stages of learning. The number of individuals for the particular PLA implementation is, usually, set at the fine-tuning phase.

Generating the initial population could be, simply, based on some random mechanism assuring the required representation of the whole feasible solution space. Once the initial population has been generated, individuals enter the first learning stage. It involves applying some, possibly basic and elementary, improvement schemes or conducting simple learning sessions. The improved individuals are then evaluated and better ones pass to the subsequent stage. A strategy of selecting better or more promising individuals must be defined and duly applied. At the following stages the whole cycle is repeated. Individuals are subject to improvement and learning, either individually or through information exchange, and the selected ones are again promoted to a higher stage with the remaining ones dropped out from the process. At the final stage the remaining individuals are reviewed with a view to selecting a solution to the problem at hand.

Learning process at early stage can be run in parallel. Individuals are then grouped into classes with possibly different curricula, which are different improvement schemes. At certain level the best from all groups join together to from higher-level groups where improvement and learning process are still carried in parallel. At some stage selected individuals are brought together to complete education.

At different stages of the process, different improvement schemes and learning procedures are applied. These gradually become more and more sophisticated and time consuming as there are less and less individuals to be taught.

3 PLA Implementations for ANN Training

In this paper we propose using population-learning algorithm to train artificial neural networks. PLA implementations for training ANN solving classification problems are based on the following assumptions:

- An individual is a vector of real numbers from the predefined interval, each representing a value of weight of the respective link between neurons in the considered ANN.

- The initial population of individuals is generated randomly.
- There are five learning/improvement procedures - standard mutation, local search, non-uniform mutation, gradient mutation and application of the gradient adjustment operator.
- There is a common selection criterion for all stages. At each stage, individuals with fitness below the current average are rejected.

The proposed approach involves the following steps executed sequentially: generation of the initial population, application of the respective learning/improvement procedure, selection of individuals, entering the next stage with another learning/improvement procedure, continuation until all stages have been completed. The above scheme implemented as a sequential algorithm called seq-PLA can be run in a single processor environment.

The parallel-PLA scheme is based on the cooperation between the master worker (server) whose task is to manage computations and a number of slave workers, who act in parallel, performing computations as requested by the master. The approach allows a lot of freedom in designing population-learning process. The master worker is managing communication flow during the population learning. It allocates computational tasks in terms of the required population size and number of iterations as well as oversees information exchange between slaves. The latter involves upgrading, at various learning stages, current populations maintained by all slaves with globally best individuals.

The following features characterize the proposed parallel-PLA:

- Master worker defines number of slave workers and size of the initial population for each of them.
- Each slave worker uses identical learning/improvement procedures.
- Master worker activates parallel processing.
- After completing each stage workers inform master about the best solution found so far.
- Master worker compares the received values and sends out the best solution to all the workers replacing their current worst individual.
- Master worker can stop computations if the desired quality level of the objective function has been achieved. This level is defined at the beginning of computations through setting the desired value of the mean squared error on a given set of training patterns.
- Slave workers can also stop computations if the above condition has been met.
- The computations are carried out for the predefined number of iterations (number of stages).

A variant of the above approach, called parallel-PLAs, differs with respect to the strategy of using the best solution send to slaves from the master. Now the best solution is used to produce offspring by applying two types of the crossover operators - a single point crossover and a position crossover. Both are applied in turn to generate offspring from all of the current individuals for each slave

4 Experiment Layout and Results

The described implementations of the PLA algorithm have been used to train several neural networks applied to solving popular benchmarking classification problems - two spirals, 10-parity, Wisconsin breast cancer, Cleveland heart disease and credit approval.

ANN solving the two spirals problem has two real-valued inputs corresponding to the x and y coordinates of the point, and one binary target output that classifies the point as belonging to either of the two spirals coiling three times around the origin. The two spirals are constructed from 97 points given by the respective coordinates from the training set. Solving the two spirals problem appears to be a very difficult task for back-propagation networks [5,9]. The topology of the network for this problem has been adopted from [2] where also an efficient constructive training algorithm called CASCOR was proposed. This so-called "shortcut" topology has four hidden units and 25 links with 25 weights.

In 10-parity problem ANN has to be trained to produce the Boolean "Exclusive OR" function of ten variables. A two-layer neural network with 10, 10 and 1 neurons in layers 1, 2 and 3, respectively is used.

Diagnosis of breast cancer involves classifying a tumor as either benign or malignant based on cell descriptions gathered by microscopic examination. Breast cancer databases was obtained from Dr. William H. Wolberg, University of Wisconsin Hospitals, Madison [6]. It includes 699 examples, 9 inputs and 2 outputs each. The corresponding ANN has 9, 9 and 1 neurons in layers 1, 2 and 3.

Cleveland heart disease problem involves predicting heart disease, that is deciding whether at least one of four major vessels is reduced in diameter by more than 50%. The binary decision is made based on personal data. The data set includes 303 examples with 13 inputs and 2 outputs and the corresponding ANN has 13, 13 and 1 neurons in layers 1, 2 and 3.

Credit card approval involves predicting the approval or rejection of a credit card to a customer. The data set consists of 690 examples with 15 inputs and two outputs with a good mix of attributes. The corresponding ANN to be trained has 15, 15 and 1 neurons in layers 1, 2 and 3.

All data sets for the described problems are available at the UCI repository [7] and are often used to compare various techniques for ANN training. Data set for the 2-spiral problem is available and have been obtained from the home page http://www.cae.wisc.edu/~ece602/data/CMUbenchmark.

Computational experiment carried to evaluate the proposed PLA implementations has been based on the following quality measures: correct classification ratio for the "10 cross validation" (10CV) approach, correct classification ratio for the training, test and validation sets constructed using the 50%-25%-25% (TTV) principle [8], mean squared error - MSE, and mean relative error - MRE.

All artificial neural networks used in the experiment have sigmoid activation function with the sigmoid gain equal 1. Average size of the initial population in all PLA impementations has been set to 200. A maximum number of repetitions for each learning/improvement procedure has been set to 20 except for the 2-spiral problem in both - sequential and parallel versions where it has been set to 40. Each benchmarking problem has been solved 50 times and the reported values of the quality measures have been averaged over these 50 runs. All computations have been carried on the Sun Challenge R4400 and, additionally, for parallel-PLA and parallel-PLAs in PVM environment. Experiment results are shown in Table 1. In Table 2 performance of the PLA implementations is compared with some reported results from the literature.

It can be observed that PLA implementations guarantee good or even competitive level of training quality. It seems that the approach is also interesting in terms of computational time requirements. The authors have not been able to find comparable data on time performace of alternative approaches. Some conclusions can be drawn from the information on time performance of the Novel algorithm, which required 900 minutes to train ANN solving 2-spiral problem and 35 minutes to train ANN solving 10-parity problem [10].

5 Conclusion

Main contribution of the paper is seen as successfully applying the population based metaheuristic to training feed forward ANN. This application has resulted in proposing a new training algorithm that, in several instances, outperforms previously reported ones. It is impressively effective with respect to training ANN solving difficult 2-spiral problem as well as some other benchmarking classification problems considered difficult.

The proposed PLA seems to be a worthy and flexible training tool, which application to ANN training should be further investigated and refined. The approach seems promising in term of producing good or even excellent quality training in a reasonable time. Future research should concentrate on analysis of the PLA characteristics with a view to finding rules for effective algorithm configuration and fine-tuning, as well as on search for efficient learning/improvement procedures.

References

1. Duch, W., Korczak, J. (1998): Optimization and Global Minimization Methods Suitable for Neural Network, Neural Computing Surveys 2, http://www.icsi.berkeley.edu/~jagopta/CNS

Table 1. Computational experiment results averaged over 50 runs

Problem	Approach	TTV	10CV	MRE	MSE	training time [min]
Two spirals	seq-PLA	71.6%	74.7%	0.29	0.25	45
Two spirals	parallel-PLA	89.2%	88.4%	0.07	0.04	20
Two spirals	parallel-PLAs	91.7%	92.0%	0.07	0.04	18
10 parity	parallel-PLA	93.6%	92.2%	0.06	0.04	3.5
Breast	seq-PLA	95.4%	96.4%	0.02	0.01	1.5
Heart	seq-PLA	81.0%	81.3%	0.21	0.17	1.5
Credit	seq-PLA	82.0%	82.6%	0.20	0.17	2.5

Table 2. PLA versus the reported accuracy of training algorithms. Source for the best reported: http://www.phys.uni.torun.pl/kmk/projects/datasets.html

Problem	Approach	Literature reported accuracy	Best achieved PLA accuracy
Two spirals	Novel	94.0% [10]	91.7%
Two spirals	Simulated Annealing	84.8% [9]	91.7%
Two spirals	Back Propagation	52.0% [10]	91.7%
Breast	Back Propagation	96.7%	96.4%
Breast	C 4.5	94.7%	96.4%
Heart	Back Propagation	81.3%	81.3%
Credit	Cal5	0.132 (training error)	0.174

2. Fahlman, S.E., Lebiere, C. (1990): The Cascade-Corelation Learning Architecture, in Touretzky (Ed.) Advances in Neural Information Processing Systems **2**, Morgan Kaufmann
3. Hertz, J., Krogh, A., Palmer, R.G. (1995): Introduction to the Theory of Neural Computation, WNT, Warsaw (In Polish)
4. Jędrzejowicz, P. (1999): Social Learning Algorithm as a Tool for Solving Some Difficult Scheduling Problems, Foundation of Computing and Decision Sciences **24**, 51-66
5. Kevin, J., Witbrock, L., Witbrock, M.J. (1998): Learning to Tell Two Spirals Adapt, in Proceedings of the Connectionist Models Summer School, Morgan Kaufmann
6. Mangasarian, O.L., Wolberg, W.H. (1990): Cancer Diagnosis via Linear Programming, SIAM News, vol. 23, Number 5, 1-18
7. Merz, C.J., Murphy. P.M. (1998): UCI Repository of machine learning databases [http://www.ics.uci.edu/ mlearn/MLRepository.html]. Irvine, CA: University of California, Department of Information and Computer Science
8. Prechelt, L. (1994): Proben 1 - A Set of Benchmark and Benchmarking Rules for Neural Network Training Algorithm, Technical Report 21/94, Fakultt fr Informatik, Universitt Karlsruhe, D-76128 Karlsruhe, Germany, Anonymous /pub/papers/techraports/1994/1994-21.ps.Z. on ftp.ira.uka.de
9. Wah, B.W., Minglun Qian (2000): Constrained Formulations for Neural Network Training and Their Applications to Solve the Two-Spiral Problem, Proc. of Fifth Int'l Conference on Computer Science and Informatics, ICIS, **1**, 598-601
10. Yi Shang, Wah, B.W. (1996): A Global Optimization Method for Neural Network Training, Conference of Neural Networks, IEEE Computer **29**, 45-54

A Penalty Function to Obtain Satisfactory Local Models of Complex Systems

Grzegorz Drałus[1], Jerzy Świątek[2]

[1] Rzeszow University of Technology, Department of Electrical and Computer Engineering Fundamentals ul. Pola 2, 35-959 Rzeszów, Poland, e-mail: gregor@prz.rzeszow.pl
[2] Wroclaw University of Technology, Institute of Control and Systems Engineering Wyb.Wyspiańskiego 27, 50-370 Wrocław, Poland, e-mail: prodyd@ac.pwr.wroc.pl

Summary: In this paper using a penalty function to obtain satisfactory local models in global modeling of complex systems using neural networks are discussed. Complex systems consist of several subsystems in a cascade structure. As models, non-typical neural multilayer feedforward networks were used. To formulate the global performance index the global resultant criterion, which consist a global error criterion and a penalty function for local errors, approach is proposed. Global resultant criterion required developing of a new backpropagation learning algorithm. The computer simulation results of modelling of the chosen complex system are presented.

1 Introduction

In complex industrial processes there exist a number of situation for which model developing is necessary. Simple plant models are sufficient for control of continuous processes, given fixed output values, and for optimization of static processes, given a determined quality criterion. For complex control of industry processes it is necessary to specify control algorithm for different phases of the process. The necessity for developing models of complex systems is forced by the need for complex control of complex industrial systems [1].

The traditional task of complex systems modelling is based on optimal parameter finding based on some quality criterion adopted [1, 8]. Mathematical methods of complex systems modelling are usually based on optimization and modelling of subsystems. Subsequently, a complex system model is derived from optimal component system models.

Nowadays neural networks have many applications in science. Neural networks can be used for modelling and for identification of "simple" plants [6, 9] owing to their ability to approximate nonlinear functions [7]. Lately, neural networks have been also used for complex system modelling [11].

In this paper using a penalty function to obtain satisfactory local models in global modeling of complex systems using neural networks are discussed.

A complex system consists of several subsystems. Models have the same structure as the complex systems to be modeled [4]. Non-typical neural multilayer feedforward networks were used as the models [2,3,5]. On the base of internal and output signals a global model may be constructed. A globally optimal model is desired, but also the local sub-model ought to be good enough. When errors between local models and local sub-systems are closely limited is to use the penalty function method. By optimization of a resultant quality criterion, which consists of global error criterion and a penalty function for local errors of global model, which accounts for the quality of submodels is obtained. Consequently, a globally optimal model is generated, whereas the local errors do not exceeds the limits. Globally optimal models, which take into consideration local model quality required developing of a new backpropagation learning algorithms for non-typical multilayer neural networks.

2 The global model with taking into account quality local models

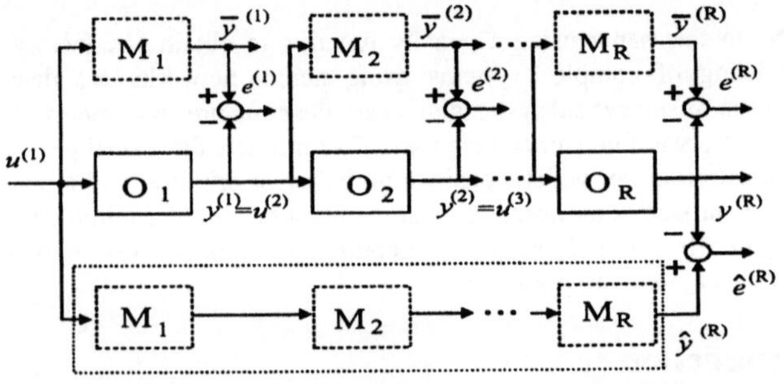

Fig. 1. The structure of a complex system and their model

Let us consider the complex system shown in Fig.1, for which an appropriate complex model is built. The structures of the model and of the complex system are the same. The complex model consists of R local models, which are denoted as M_r. The outputs $\bar{y}^{(r)}$ of the local models are described by the formula:

$$\bar{y}^{(r)} = \boldsymbol{\Phi}_r\left(\boldsymbol{u}^{(r)}, \boldsymbol{w}^{(r)}\right) \tag{1}$$

The output $\hat{y}^{(R)}$ of the global model is described by

$$\hat{y}^{(R)} = \boldsymbol{\Phi}_R\left(\boldsymbol{\Phi}_{R-1}\left(\cdots\boldsymbol{\Phi}_1\left(\boldsymbol{u}^{(1)},\boldsymbol{w}^{(1)}\right),\cdots,\boldsymbol{w}^{(R-1)}\right),\boldsymbol{w}^{(R)}\right) = \hat{\boldsymbol{\Phi}}_R\left(\boldsymbol{u}^{(1)},\boldsymbol{w}^{(1)},\ldots,\boldsymbol{w}^{(R)}\right) = \hat{\boldsymbol{\Phi}}_R\left(\boldsymbol{u}^{(1)},\boldsymbol{W}\right) \tag{2}$$

where $\boldsymbol{W} = \left\{\boldsymbol{w}^{(1)}, \boldsymbol{w}^{(2)}, \cdots, \boldsymbol{w}^{(R)}\right\}$ is a set of parameters of a global model and $\boldsymbol{w}^{(r)}$ is a matrix of parameters of the r-th local model.

The global quality criterion [3] for all K patterns and for all J_R errors, as a difference between the actual response of the j-th (j=1,2,…, J_R) outputs signals of global model $\hat{y}_j^{(R),k}$ and the complex system $y_j^{(R),k}$ is:

$$Q_u(\boldsymbol{W}) = \frac{1}{2}\sum_{k=1}^{K}\sum_{j=1}^{J_R}\left(\hat{y}_j^{(R),k} - y_j^{(R),k}\right)^2 \tag{3}$$

The local quality criterion [4] for the r-th submodel for all J_r errors is:

$$Q_r(w^{(r)}) = \frac{1}{2}\sum_{k=1}^{K}\sum_{j=1}^{J_r}\left(\overline{y}_j^{(r),k} - y_j^{(r),k}\right)^2 \tag{4}$$

2.1 Satisfactory local models

In global modelling with regard to quality of local models of sub-systems an optimal set of parameters for global quality criterion $Q_u(W)$ is to be found. Also, the constraints for local quality criterions $Q_r(w^{(r)})$ have to be taken into account

$$\widetilde{W} \to Q_u(\widetilde{W}) = \min_{W \in D_W} Q_u(W) \tag{5}$$

$$D_W = \left\{w^{(1)}, \ldots, w^{(R)} : Q_1(w^{(1)}) \le \lambda_1, Q_2(w^{(2)}) \le \lambda_2, \ldots, Q_R(w^{(R)}) \le \lambda_R\right\} \tag{6}$$

The vector $\lambda = [\lambda_1\ \lambda_2\ \ldots\ \lambda_R]$ includes the positive factors of admissible quality criteria of respective local models.

The limiting functions h_r are introduced, which results from the limitations on the quality criteria of the local models for all (r=1,2,..., R) subsystems:

$$h_r(w^{(r)}) = \frac{1}{2}\sum_{k=1}^{K}\sum_{j=1}^{J_r}\left(\overline{y}_j^{(r),k} - y_j^{(r),k}\right)^2 - \lambda_r \le 0 \tag{7}$$

One way of solving the problem of searching for a global minimum of multi-quality criterion with limits is the use of penalty functions [10]. In the method of the penalty function, the modified quality criterion is created by addition of a function called the penalty function to the quality criterion Q_u. The resultant quality criterion is:

$$T(W,p) \equiv Q_u(W) + G(W,p), \qquad p \in (0,+\infty) \tag{8}$$

where: p – the parameter [10], $G(W,p)$ – a function of penalty.

2.2 Method of the external penalty function

The external penalty function [10] often can by written as:

$$G(W,p) = pK(W) = p\sum_{r=1}^{R} K_r(w^{(r)}) \qquad p \in (0,+\infty) \tag{9}$$

where: the function $K(W)$ is equal to zero when constraints are not exceeded. Otherwise, $K(W)$ is not equal to zero.

In the particular case the penalty function of K_r can by presented as:

$$K_r(w^{(r)}) = \max\left(0, h_r(w^{(r)})\right) \tag{10}$$

where: $$\max\left(0, h_r(w^{(r)})\right) \equiv \begin{cases} 0, & \text{if } h_r(w^{(r)}) \le 0 \\ h_r(w^{(r)}), & \text{if } h_r(w^{(r)}) > 0 \end{cases} \tag{11}$$

Then the resultant quality criterion is:

$$T(\boldsymbol{W},p) \equiv Q_u(\boldsymbol{W}) + G(\boldsymbol{W},p) = \frac{1}{2}\sum_{k=1}^{K}\sum_{j=1}^{J_R}\left(\hat{y}_j^{(R),k} - y_j^{(R),k}\right)^2 + p\sum_{r=1}^{R} K_r(\boldsymbol{w}^{(r)}) \qquad (12)$$

2.3 The new backpropagation learning algorithm for the resultant quality criterion

One of the most common learning algorithms for multilayer neural networks uses the gradient search technique [6, 9] to find the network parameters that minimize a criterion function. The algorithm should minimize the criterion function $T(\boldsymbol{W},p)$, for which the gradient descent method was used. The modification parameters of the network are determined iteratively according to:

$$\Delta w_{ji} = -\eta\frac{\partial T(\boldsymbol{W},p)}{\partial w_{ji}} = -\eta\sum_{k=1}^{K}\frac{\partial Q_u(\boldsymbol{W})}{\partial z_j^k}\frac{\partial z_j^k}{\partial w_{ji}} - \eta\sum_{k=1}^{K}\frac{\partial G(\boldsymbol{W},p)}{\partial z_j^k}\frac{\partial z_j^k}{\partial w_{ji}} \qquad (13)$$

Let's consider a M-layer network with the same neurons with activation function. Developing the formula (13), the adjustment of the parameters in the modified gradient method can be done as follows: For the output layer ($m=M$):

$$\Delta w_{ji}^{(r),m} = -\eta\sum_{k=1}^{K} f'(z_j^{M,k})\left(\left(\hat{y}_j^{(R),k} - y_j^{(R),k}\right) + \begin{cases} 0, & \text{if } h_R(\boldsymbol{w}^{(R)}) \le 0 \\ p\dfrac{\partial K_R(\boldsymbol{w}^{(r)})}{\partial \bar{y}_j^{(R),k}}, & \text{if } h_R(\boldsymbol{w}^{(R)}) > 0 \end{cases}\right)\tilde{u}_i^{m-1,k} \qquad (14)$$

For normal hidden layers (m=1, 2, ..., M-1, where $\tilde{u}_j^{m,k}$, $\bar{y}_j^{(r),k}$ are not available)

$$\Delta w_{ji}^{(r),m} = -\eta\sum_{k=1}^{K} f'(z_j^{m,k})\sum_{l=1}^{I_{m+1}}\delta_l^{(r),m+1,k}\, w_{lj}^{(r),m+1}\,\tilde{u}_i^{m-1,k} \qquad (15)$$

For additional hidden layers (r=1,...,R-1, where $\tilde{u}_j^{m,k}$, $\bar{y}_j^{(r),k}$ are available)

$$\Delta w_{ji}^{(r),m} = -\eta\sum_{k=1}^{K} f'(z_j^{m,k})\left(\sum_{l=1}^{I_{m+1}}\delta_l^{(r+1),m+1,k}\, w_{lj}^{(r+1),m+1} + \begin{cases} 0, & \text{if } h_r(\boldsymbol{w}^{(r)}) \le 0 \\ p\dfrac{\partial K_r(\boldsymbol{w}^{(r)})}{\partial \bar{y}_j^{(r),k}}, & \text{if } h_r(\boldsymbol{w}^{(r)}) > 0 \end{cases}\right)\cdot\tilde{u}_i^{m-1,k} \qquad (16)$$

3 Simulation results

The static complex system that has been modeled is shown in Fig.2. The input of the complex system is denoted by $\boldsymbol{u}$. Signal $\boldsymbol{v}$ is the output from the first simple system, as well as the input for the second simple system. The output of the second simple system is $\boldsymbol{y}$ signal, which is also the output of the complex system.

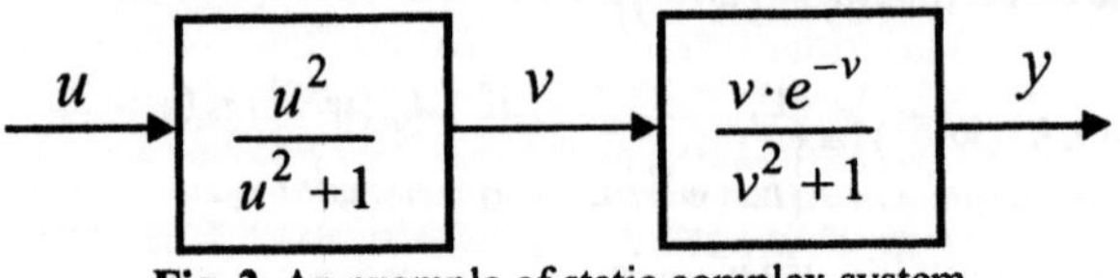

Fig. 2. An example of static complex system

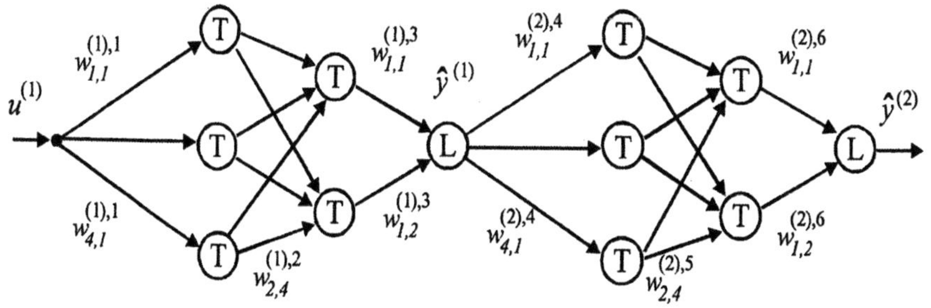

Fig. 3. Structure of the neural network for complex system modeling

Taking into consideration all the three signals, a neural network representing the complex system is shown in Fig.3. The model has the following structure: 1-4T-2T-1L-4T-2T-1L. The following numbers means: the number of network inputs, the number of neurons in first hidden layer, etc., "T" - tangent transfer function, "L" - the linear transfer function. As shown in Fig.3, the number of neurons in the third hidden layer is equal to the number of outputs in the first local subsystem.
The vectors of the learning input data includes 101 points uniformly distributed in the interval <0,5>. The vectors of the testing data includes 101 points distributed regularly in the interval <0,0.05,...,5> with the step 0.05.
The initial weights of the network were generated, by Nguyen-Widrow algorithm [12]. A modified *Rprop* learning algorithm was used [3]. The simulation program written by the author in the Pascal programming language was used. The results of learning of global model using the external penalty function (10) after 200 and 800 epochs are shown in tab.1. The following values of the factors λ in the formula (6) were accepted: λ_1=500 x10^{-6} λ_2=100 x10^{-6}. The results of testing the model are shown in tab.2.

Table 1. Values of quality criteria for learning data

	After 200	epochs		After 800	epochs	
Model	Q_u x10^{-6}	Q_2 x10^{-6}	Q_1 x10^{-6}	Q_u x10^{-6}	Q_2 x10^{-6}	Q_1 x10^{-6}
p=1	128	88	520	33	9	500
p=10	236	204	533	32	13	500
p=100	146	93	428	24	34	500
p=1000	522	195	498	218	100	500

Table 2. Values of quality criteria for testing data

	After 200	epochs		After 800	epochs	
Model	Q_u x10^{-6}	Q_2 x10^{-6}	Q_1 x10^{-6}	Q_u x10^{-6}	Q_2 x10^{-6}	Q_1 x10^{-6}
p=1	144	85	653	42	10	611
p=10	261	211	671	43	13	619
p=100	179	99	576	30	40	526
p=1000	645	206	544	214	101	527

Where: Q_u – the global criterion (3), Q_1, Q_2 - the local quality criteria (4).

4 Conclusions

The method of global modelling, with taking into account quality of local models of static complex system was presented. Based on of global quality criterion and constrain for local quality criterions using external penalty function the common gradient backpropagation learning algorithm was modified. The considered method and modified learning algorithm needed developing suitable simulating program. The new method gives possibility to build globally optimal models for complex systems with regard to quality of local models. An example of the static non-linear complex system considered. Computer simulations confirm correctness of the proposed method. There were obtained the global models of the complex system in which values of local quality criterions Q_1, Q_2 not exceed the suitable limits: λ_1, λ_2, for all values of the *p*-parameter after 800 epochs of learning.

The presented method by the modified learning algorithm, and the simulations program can also to model complex systems with many number of inputs, internal signals, many number of outputs with many number of subsystems.

References

1. Bubnicki Z. (1980) Identification of Control Plants. Oxford, Amsterdam. N. York. Elsevier.
2. Drałus G., Świątek J. (2000) A Modified Backpropagation Algorithm for Modelling Static Complex Systems Using Neural Networks. The 5th International Conference Neural Networks and Soft Computing, Zakopane, Poland, pp. 463-468.
3. Drałus G., Świątek J. (2000) Static neural network in global modelling of complex systems. The 14th Internat. Conf. on Systems Engineering, Coventry, UK, pp.547-551.
4. Drałus G., Świątek J. (2001) Globally Optimal Models of Complex Systems with Regard to Quality Local Models. Proc. of the 14th International Conference on Systems Science, Wroclaw, Poland, vol.1. pp. 217-226.
5. Drałus G., Świątek J. (2002) Global Modelling of Complex Systems by Neural Networks. Proc. of 7th International Symposium on Artificial Life and Robotics, Beeppu, Oita, Japan, vol. 2, pp. 618–621.
6. Duch W., Korbicz J., Rutkowski L., Tadeusiewicz R. (2000) Neural Networks. Academic Publisher House Exit, Warsaw (in Polish)
7. Horink K. (1989), Multilayer Feedforward Networks Are Universal Approximators. Neural Networks, 2, pp.359-366.
8. Mańczak K., Nahorski Z. (1983) Computer's Identification of Control Plants, PWN.
9. Osowski S. (1996) Neural Networks. WNT. Warsaw (in Polish)
10. Seidler J., Badach A., Molisz W. (1980) Methods of Solving the Optimization Tasks. WNT, Warsaw (in Polish)
11. Venkatesh S.R., Dahleh M.A. (1997) System Identification of Complex Systems - Problem Formulation and Results. Proc. of the 36th IEEE Conference on Decision and Control, IEEE, vol.3, pp.2441-6.
12. Zell A. (1993) SNNS – Stuttgart Neural Network Simulator, User Manual. Stuttgart.

Feature Selection Based on Information Theory Filters

Włodzisław Duch[1], Jacek Biesiada[2], Tomasz Winiarski[1], Karol Grudziński[1], and Krzysztof Grąbczewski[1]

[1] Department of Informatics, Nicholas Copernicus University, Grudziądzka 5, 87-100 Toruń, Poland. http://www.phys.uni.torun.pl/kmk

[2] The Silesian University of Technology, Department of Electrotechnology, Division of Computer Methods, ul. Krasińskiego 8, 40-019 Katowice, Poland.

Abstract. Feature selection is an essential component in all data mining applications. Ranking of futures was made by several inexpensive methods based on information theory. Accuracy of neural, similarity based and decision tree classifiers calculated with reduced number of features. Comparison with computationally more expensive feature elimination methods was made.

1 Introduction

Recent data mining applications in bioinformatics, chemistry and commercial domains are very challenging. In case of bioinformatics a very large ($\sim 10^4 - 10^5$)) number of features are associated with activity of genes (up to 30.000 in humans and even more in some plants), while properties of proteins may be described by more than 100.000 features. All these features may be important for some problems, but for a given task only a small subset of these features is relevant. In commercial applications the situation is similar. Therefore computationally inexpensive methods of filtering features are urgently needed.

Methods of feature selection may be divided into three broad categories. Methods that require evaluation of each potentially useful subset of features by a classifier, called "wrapper methods" [5]. This name is also used for a large class of methods for parameter adaptation. Wrapper methods treat computational intelligence (CI) algorithms as black boxes with some parameters to be determined on the basis of test runs. Finding subsets of features is equivalent to assigning binary weights to inputs. The problem is NP-complete since the number of all subsets 2^N grows exponentially with the number of features N. Second group of feature selection methods is based on specific properties of CI methods. Neural networks allow to compute gradients in respect to internal parameters, allowing for feature selection methods based on regularization techniques that may be more efficient than the blind wrapper approach. The third group of methods is based on evaluation of individual features in respect to the task performed, or filtering features that potentially carry useful information, independently from the final CI method used.

Correlation coefficients and other methods for evaluation of the usefulness of features are usually variants of information-theoretical approaches. Computational complexity of this approach may be much lower than in the case of wrapper approach, depending on the degree to which interaction among features is taken into account. Several filter methods based on information theory are compared here with k-nearest neighbor (kNN) wrapper method. Two question we attempt to answer are: are filters competitive to computationally more demanding wrapper methods, and are all filters equally good for all methods? CI systems that have been selected include neural network, decision tree and kNN method. First a few information theory filters are described and then results of experimental simulations presented.

2 Filters and wrappers

The simplest wrapper approach based on successive elimination (or addition) of features, leaving those features that lead to highest accuracy, is quite effective [1]. It is equivalent to the best-first search, requiring $N(N-1)/2$ evaluations using CI algorithm on the training set. Obvious variants of the simplest approach include evaluation of results by crossvalidation, and using beam search to avoid local minima.

Ranking methods based on information theory filters evaluate single features, neglecting possible interactions. Setiono [4] has used the concept of normalized information gains G_i' for feature f_i. These information gains can be calculated in the following way. First, information contained in the whole training set is:

$$I(S) = -\sum_{j=1}^{K} p(C_j)\log_2 p(C_j) \tag{1}$$

where $p(C_j) = n_j/n$ is the fraction of samples $\mathbf{X}$ from class C_j, $j = 1..K$. Continuous features are discretized to compute information associated with a single feature. Let n_{ik} be the number of samples for which features f_i takes a value inside the interval $r_k(f_i)$ and n_{ikj} be the number of such samples $\mathbf{X}$ for which $\mathbf{X} \in C_j$. Information contained in the subset S_{ik} of samples with f_i in the interval $r_k(f_i)$ is:

$$I(S_{ik}) = -\sum_{j=1}^{K} p_{ikj}\log_2 p_{ikj}; \quad p_{ikj} = n_{ikj}/n_{ik} \tag{2}$$

Summing (or integrating) $I(S_{ik})$ over all M intervals information E_i contained in all subsets of feature f_i is computed; this information may also be computed directly

$$E_i = \sum_{k=1}^{M} p_{ik} I(S_{ik}); \quad I_i = -\sum_{k=1}^{M} p_{ik}\log_2 p_{ik}; \quad p_{ik} = \frac{n_{ik}}{n} \tag{3}$$

Information gain and normalized information gain is

$$G_i = I(S) - E_i; \quad G_i' = G_i/I_i \tag{4}$$

A feature is more important if its normalized information gain is larger. This method, referred to as “info gain” or IG, treats all features as independent.

Another method, based on mutual information, includes possible interactions between features has been proposed by Battiti [2] and is called BA in the rest of the paper. Let $p(r_k(f)) = p(f \in r_k(f))$ be the probability of finding samples with feature f in the interval $r_k(f)$. Mutual information between two features f, s is defined as:

$$I(f,s) = \sum_{k=1}^{N}\sum_{j=1}^{N} p(r_k(f) \wedge r_j(s)) \cdot \log_2 \frac{p(r_k(f) \wedge r_j(s))}{\cdot p(r_j(s))\, p(r_k(f))} \tag{5}$$

The mutual information between feature f and the set of classes is:

$$I(C,f) = \sum_{i=1}^{K}\sum_{k=1}^{M} p(C_i \wedge r_k(f)) \cdot \log_2 \frac{p(C_i \wedge r_k(f))}{p(C_i) \cdot p(r_k(f))} \tag{6}$$

where $r_1(f), r_2(f), \ldots, r_N(f)$ is a partition of the range of f values into equal intervals and $p(C_i \wedge r_k(f))$ is the probability that vector X from class C_i has feature f in the interval r_k. The sum runs over all these intervals and all the classes. The recommended number of intervals is usually between 16 and 32 [2]. $M = 24$ was used in our experiments, but results may differ significantly for small numbers of intervals. The algorithm for finding the best subset of k features goes as follows:

1. Set F to the whole set of N features and set S to an empty set.
2. Compute the mutual information $I(C,f)$ for every feature $f \in F$ and the set of classes $C = \{C_1, \ldots C_K\}$.
3. Find the feature f that maximizes $I(C,f)$. Move f from the set F to the set in S, $S = S \cap f, F = F - f$.
4. Repeat the following until set S will have k features:
   (a) Compute the mutual information $F(f,s)$ between features $f \in F$ and $s \in S$.
   (b) Choose g as the feature that maximizes $I(C,f) - \beta \sum_{s \in S} I(f,s)$, where β is a parameter in the interval [0.5,1] (as recommended in [2]).
   (c) Move g from F to S.

Small values stress the importance of high mutual information between the feature and set of classes; large values stress more the mutual information with the features already included in the set S.

Pruning decision trees allows to rank features, with the most important features near the root of the tree, and the least important pruned first. In particular the Separability Split Value (SSV) criterion [7] selects features that give the largest gain in separability test, hence it may be used for feature ranking.

3 Numerical experiments

Two datasets were used in numerical experiments: hepatobiliary disorders and hypothyroid problems (these datasets are described in [6]). Feature ranking was determined on the training set using the IG (4), BA for 6 β values (6) and SSV algorithms.

Using these rankings the kNN [1], the IncNet neural network [3], the Feature Space Mapping (FSM) neurofuzzy system [8], and the K* classification method [9] were used to calculate accuracy on the test set, adding consecutively the most important features in a given ranking to the pool of features used. Since results for different β values do not differ significantly accuracy curves have been ploted only for $\beta = 0.5$.

The **hepatobiliary disorders** dataset contains 4 classes, 9 continuous and one binary feature. 373 cases were used for training and feature selection, 163 cases as the test data. This dataset is noisy, has strongly overlapping classes and is rather difficult to classify [6]. The kNN ranking (Table 3) has been done by dropping features [1] on standardized data with k=1, and Minkowski distance function with exp = 0.6, optimized for all features. Some differences in ranking are found, but feature 3 and 4 are in all rankings among the most important while features 8 and 9 are the least significant.

Method	**Most – Least Important**								
IG	3	1	8	4	6	7	5	2	9
SSV best-first	3	7	4	5	1	2	6	8	9
BA $\beta = 0.5 - 0.6$	4	3	7	1	5	2	9	8	6
BA $\beta = 0.7$	4	3	7	1	2	9	5	8	6
BA $\beta = 0.8 - 1.0$	4	3	1	7	2	9	5	8	6
SBL Ranking	1	4	6	7	5	8	9	2	3

Table 1. Results of feature ranking on the hepatobiliary disorders data; see description in text.

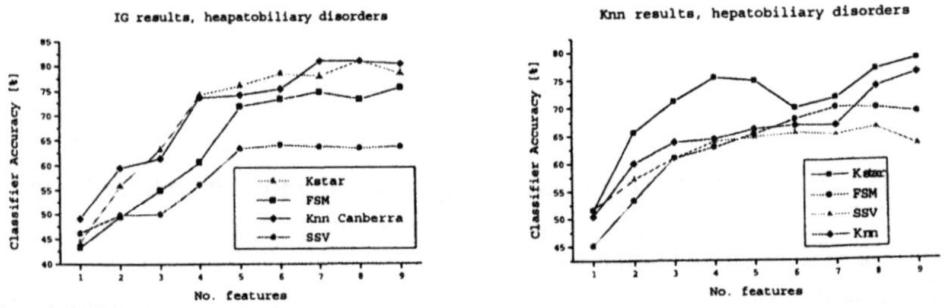

Fig. 1. Left figure: feature selection using normalized information gains; right figure: SBL ranking, Minkowski $exp = 0.6$, $k = 1$.

The same approach was used for the **hypothyroid dataset** (see description in [6]). A total of 3772 cases are used for training (results from one year) and 3428 cases for testing (results from the next year). There are 3 classes but one dominates, with almost 93% of cases. The IG and the SSV with best first search, both computationally the least expensive methods, have correctly identified the most important features. Interaction of features included in BA has missed important features 18-20, treating them as least important. This has degraded results of all classification methods completely (Fig. 2).

Method	Most – Least Important																				
Info gain	17	21	19	18	3	7	13	10	8	15	6	16	5	4	20	12	1	2	11	9	14
SSV best-first	17	21	3	19	18	8	1	20	12	13	15	16	14	11	10	9	7	6	5	3	2
Info interacting $\beta = 0.5$	21	17	13	7	15	12	9	5	8	4	6	16	10	14	2	11	3	18	1	20	19
Info interacting $\beta = 0.7 - 0.8$	21	17	13	15	5	12	9	14	8	4	6	16	7	10	2	11	3	18	1	20	19
Info interacting $\beta = 1.0$	21	17	15	13	5	12	9	14	4	8	6	16	7	10	2	11	3	1	20	18	19
SBL Ranking	17	3	19	8	21	20	18	10	15	13	7	16	9	4	11	5	12	14	6	1	2

Table 2. Results of feature ranking on the hypothyroid dataset; see description in text.

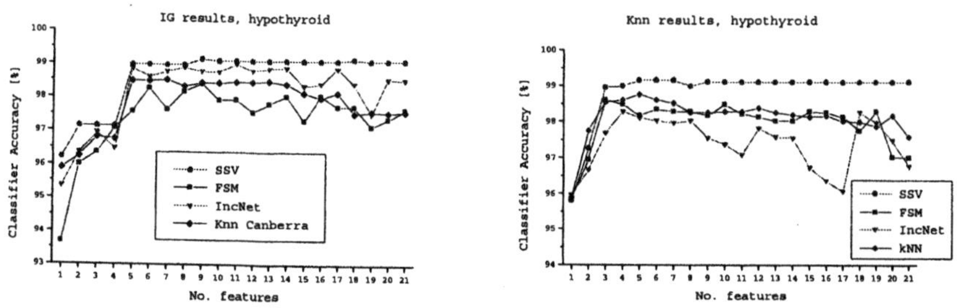

Fig. 2. Hypothyroid data set. Left figure: normalized information gains; right figure: SBL ranking, Canberra, $k = 4$.

4 Conclusions

Several conclusions may be drawn from our study (many results could not be presented in the limited space of this article). Accuracy obtained on wrapper ranking has not been higher than accuracy that may be achieved with filters; in Table 2 features 21 has been placed at the end by the wrapper approach, leading to a serious degradation of performance. Inexpensive filter methods based on information theory may reduce the feature space quite effectively, selecting most important features, but they have several problems. Results may strongly depend on discretization of continuous features and calculation of probabilities. Methods that treat each feature separately are computationally most efficient, but sometimes leave redundant features. Methods that take feature interaction into account are slower, but in principle should allow to select smaller subsets of important features. Unfortunately (see Fig.

2) such methods may rank low important features since their mutual information with those already selected is high. In multiclass problems, especially with classes that have small percentage of the total number of vectors, feature selection for discrimination of a single class against the rest may give quite different results.

Decision trees allow for independent feature ranking as well as hierarchical ranking including interactions with previous features. This type of methods seem to be competitive with filters based on information theory. After analysis of IG and BA failures we have proposed a new feature selection method that includes feature interaction using a consistency index (in preparation).

Evaluation of the quality of a classifier using overall accuracy only is not sufficient. Much more information is derived from the Receiver Operating Curves [9]. It may also be easier to aggregate (for example by linear combination) several features rather than select them. This is the next step, going beyond feature selection methods. Dependence on the choice of the number of intervals for calculation of information may partially be removed if Gaussian overlapping windows are used instead of intervals.

Acknowledgments: Support by the Polish Committee for Scientific Research, grant 8 T11C 006 19, is gratefully acknowledged.

References

1. Duch W, Grudziński K (1999) The weighted k-NN method with selection of features and its neural realization, 4th Conference on Neural Networks and Their Applications, Zakopane, May 1999, pp. 191-196
2. Battiti R. (1991) Using mutual information for selecting features in supervised neural net learning. IEEE Transaction on Neural Networks **5**, 537-550
3. Jankowski N, Kadirkamanathan V. (1997) Statistical control of RBF-like networks for classification. 7th Int. Conf. on Artificial Neural Networks, Lausanne, Switzerland, Springer Verlag, pp. 385-390
4. Setiono R, Liu H. (1996) Improving Backpropagation learning with feature selection. Applied Intelligence: The International Journal of Artifical Intelligence, *Neural Networks, and Complex Problem-Solving Technologies* **6**, 129-139
5. Kohavi R. (1995) Wrappers for performance enhancement and oblivious decision graphs. PhD thesis, Dept. of Computer Science, Stanford University
6. Duch W, Adamczak R, Grąbczewski K, A new methodology of extraction, optimization and application of crisp and fuzzy logical rules. IEEE Transactions on Neural Networks 12 (2001) 277-306
7. Grąbczewski K. Duch W. (2000) The Separability of Split Value Criterion, *5th Conference on Neural Networks and Soft Computing*, Zakopane, Poland, pp. 201-208
8. Duch W, Diercksen G.H.F. (1995) Feature Space Mapping as a universal adaptive system, Computer Physics Communications **87**, 341–371
9. Witten I.H, Frank E. (2000) Data mining. Morgan Kaufmann Publishers, San Francisco
10. Swets J.A. (1988) Measuring the accuracy of diagnostic systems. Science **240**, 1285-93

Neural Network Design without Learning

E.Dudek-Dyduch; Z.Gomółka–

- - University of Mining and Metallurgy Cracow, Poland
al. Mickiewicza 30, 30-059 Kraków,
E-mail: edd@ia.agh.edu.pl,
– - Rzeszów University, Institute of Technology
ul.Rejtana 16 A, 35-310 Rzeszów.
E-mail: zgomolka@atena.univ.rzeszow.pl,

Abstract:
The paper deals with homogeneous neural networks of the feed-forward type. Contrary to the classical learning methods, the authors present a theoretical approach to a new method of neural network design. As an example, the designing of the neural network for ridges detection in interferometry images has been presented. To ensure the correctness of theoretical considerations, several results of experiments obtained with real images have been presented as well.

1. Introduction

In order to bring to the fore interferometry techniques, we briefly recall that this is one of the modern techniques of restitution of three dimensional shapes of the observed object on the basis of two dimensional "flat like images" registered by a CCD camera. Further questions about the nature of interferometry images and their wide applications can be answered in [1]. The preliminary stage of this process is conducted with ridges detection, and to solve this computational task, the discussed neural network was applied. To find out an answer to the main question stated in this paper, let's briefly recall the properties of homogenous feed-forward networks. In these networks, the connections of each neuron belonging to the same layer with neurons of the preceding layers are the same. Consequently, there is the same neuron's weight distribution function in one layer.

This kind of architecture reminds a biological visual system of a crab *limulus*, see Fig.1. Simple, homogeneous excitation and decay weights system enable a crab to detect edge lines in his visual surroundings. The comprehensive description of homogeneous networks in task of ridges detection may be found in earlier works [2], [3], [4], [5], [6].

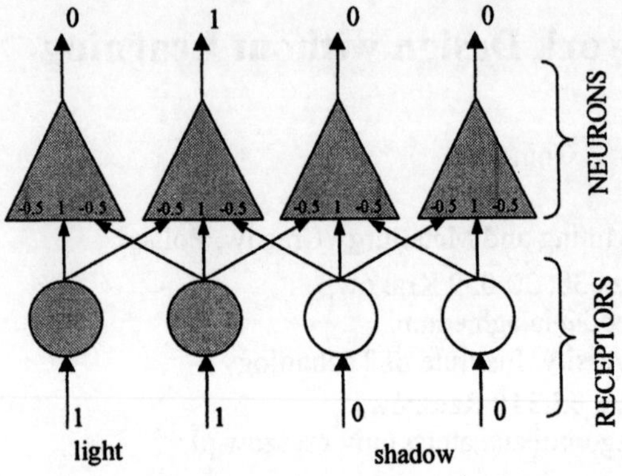

Fig. 1. The model of a crab visual system

Now we will briefly recall of the assumptions. The major skeleton of the network consists of one-dimensional homogeneous networks that indicate local maxima distribution for particular directions, as it is shown in Fig.2. Generally, for one-dimensional homogenous networks, the following relations occur. The input function of the j-th layer $e_j(n)$ might be expressed by means of the weight distribution function $w_j(i)$:

$$e_j(n) = \sum_{i=-\infty}^{+\infty} w_j(i) f_{j-1}(n+i) = \sum_{i=-q_j}^{q_j} w_j(i) f_{j-1}(n+i) \qquad (1)$$

where f_j, q_j denote the output function and range of weight distribution function of the j-th layer, respectively. By taking advantage of the above equation, we may write the flow equation:

$$f_j(n) = h_j\left(e_j(n)\right) = h_j\left(\sum_{i=-q_j}^{q_j} w_j(i) f_{j-1}(n+i)\right) \qquad (2)$$

$$f_{j+1}(n) = h_{j+1}\left(e_{j+1}(n)\right) = h_{j+1}\left(\sum_{i=-q_{j+1}}^{q_{j+1}} w_{j+1}(i) h_j\left(\sum_{l=-q_j}^{q_j} w_j(l) f_{j-1}(n+i+l)\right)\right) \qquad (3)$$

where h_j stands for transfer function of the j-th layer. For the network given in Fig. 2, formulas (4-8) are fulfilled.

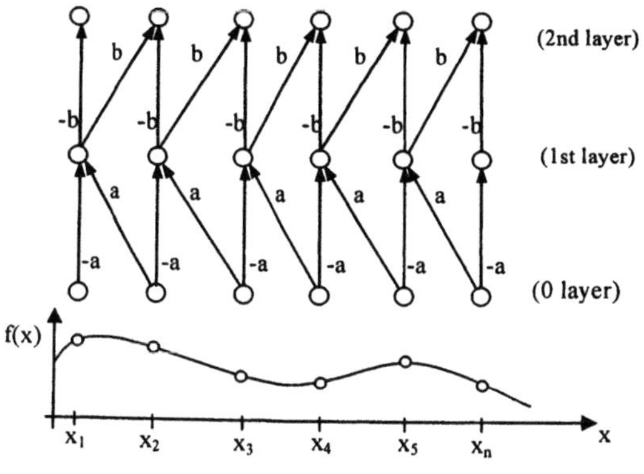

Fig.2. The network architecture.

The weight distribution function of the first layer $w_1(i)$ and the second layer $w_2(i)$ is of the form:

$$w_1(i)=\begin{cases}-a & for \quad i=0\\ a & for \quad i=1\\ 0 & for \quad i\neq 0, i\neq 1\end{cases} \qquad (4) \qquad w_2(i)=\begin{cases}b & for \quad i=0\\ -b & for \quad i=1\\ 0 & for \quad i\neq 0, i\neq 1\end{cases}$$

where parameters $\boldsymbol{a} > 0$ and $\boldsymbol{b} > 0$. The transfer function $h(e)$ in the first and the second layer has the form:

$$h_1(e)=\begin{cases}0 & for \quad e<-p\\ k(e+p)/2p & for \quad -p\leq e\leq p\\ k & for \quad e>p\end{cases} \qquad h_2(e)=\begin{cases}0 & for \quad e<p_d\\ \dfrac{e-p_d}{(p_g-p_d)} & for \quad p_d\leq e\leq p_g\\ 1 & for \quad e>p_g\end{cases} \qquad (5)$$

respectively, where p and k are parameters of positive values. The slopes of both function are shown in the Fig. 3.

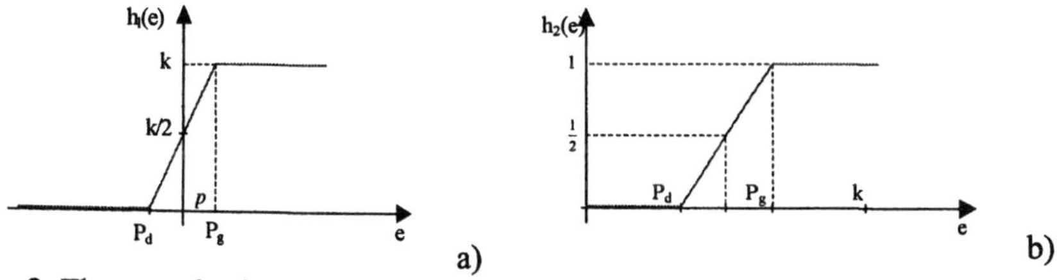

Fig. 3. The transfer functions in the first layer a), and in the second layer b).

Assuming homogenous weighting of the signal in the first layer by $\boldsymbol{a}$ value and in the second layer by $\boldsymbol{b}$, we have:

$$e_1(n)=\sum_{i=-q}^{q} w_1(i)\cdot f_0(n+i)=-af_0(n)+af_0(n+1)=a\Delta^1 f_0(n) \qquad (6)$$

and:

$$e_2(n)=\sum_{i=-q}^{q} w_2(i)\cdot f_1(n+i)=bf_1(n-1)-bf_1(n)=-b\Delta^1 f_1(n-1) \qquad (7)$$

While the network works on the linear part of transfer function h_1, we obtain

$$e_2(n)=-b\Delta^1 f_1(n-1)=-b\frac{ak}{2p}\Delta^2 f_0(n-1)=-\alpha\Delta^2 f_0(n-1) \qquad (8)$$

$$\text{for} \quad \Delta^1 f_0(n)\in[-p,p] \quad \text{where} \quad \alpha=\frac{abk}{2p}$$

These equations may be called a "neuron-like" version of convolution in the signal analysis theory.

2. Neural network performing image processing

Let us briefly recall that we are in the progress of designing a neural network for image processing while looking for similarities to biological systems. Keeping on this way of thinking, we extended the network from Fig. 2 to the two dimensional case and we got an architecture presented in Fig. 4, which might be successfully applied to image processing. It consists of two subsystems working on two perpendicular directions *X* and *Y*, respectively.

In general, the function describing weights of connections of neurons $N_0(i,j)$ and $N_1(l,k)$ is a function of all four co-ordinates. In the case of homogeneous network, this function depends only on the differences of co-ordinates of neurons:

$w_1(i,j,l,k) = f(i-l,j-k)$

Moreover, in our one-directional separate subsystems, the connections link only parallel rows or columns of equal co-ordinates of the two following layers:

$w^x(i,j,l,k) = f(j-k) \wedge i=l$ we will denote later as $w^x(k,j)$

$w^y(i,j,l,k) = f(i-l) \wedge j=k$ we will denote later as $w^y(l,i)$

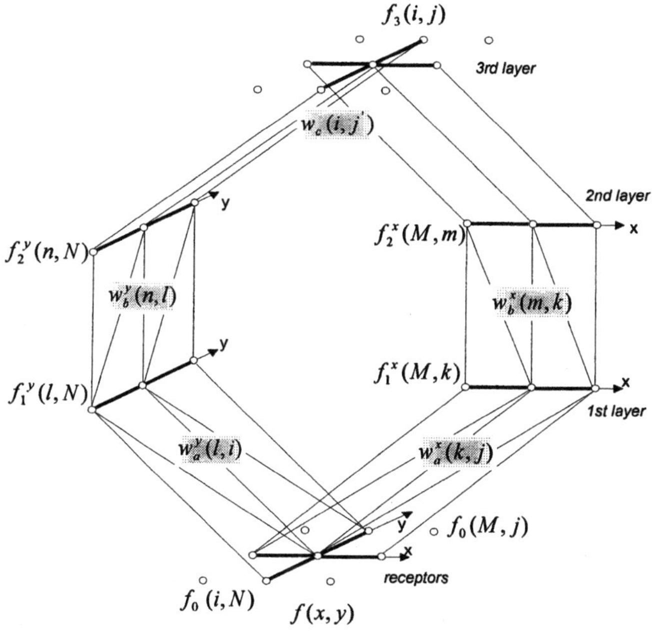

Fig.4. The extended network for image analysis.

The extended form of the weight distribution given by the matrix W_1, W_2 may be rewritten in the form (for the first and the second layer in the *X* and *Y* direction, respectively):

$$w_1^x(k,j) = \begin{cases} a(-1)^{(j-k)}\binom{1}{k-j+1} & for \quad k,j \in [0, M_x - 1] \\ 0 & for \quad k,j \notin [0, M_x - 1] \end{cases} \tag{9}$$

and:

$$w_1^y(l,i) = \begin{cases} a(-1)^{(i-l)}\binom{1}{l-i+1} & for \quad l,i \in [0, M_y - 1] \\ 0 & for \quad l,i \notin [0, M_y - 1] \end{cases} \tag{10}$$

where *(i, j)* , *(l, k)* coordinates of elements (neurons), M_x, M_y stand for the number of neurons in the subsystem *X* and *Y*, respectively.

Let us consider the performance of a network on two presumed perpendicular intersections of the image M and N. Transfer functions for both directions are the same $h_1(e_1)$. Function $f_1^x(M, k)$ can be written in the form:

$$f_1^x(M,k) = h_1(e_1(M,k)) = h_1\left(\sum_{j=0}^{M_x-1} w_1^x(k,j) f_0(M,j)\right) \tag{11}$$

and consequently for the perpendicular direction:

$$f_1^y(l,N) = h_1(e_1(l,N)) = h_1\left(\sum_{i=0}^{M_y-1} w_1^y(l,i) f_0(i,N)\right) \tag{12}$$

The weights distribution functions in the second layer can be formulated as follows:

$$w_2^x(m,k) = \begin{cases} b(-1)^{(k-m)}\begin{pmatrix} 1 \\ m-k+2 \end{pmatrix} & \text{for } k,m \in [0, M_x - 1] \\ 0 & \text{for } k,m \notin [0, M_x - 1] \end{cases} \tag{13}$$

$$w_2^y(n,l) = \begin{cases} b(-1)^{(l-n)}\begin{pmatrix} 1 \\ n-l+2 \end{pmatrix} & \text{for } l,n \in [0, M_y - 1] \\ 0 & \text{for } l,n \notin [0, M_y - 1] \end{cases} \tag{14}$$

Consequently, the output signals in the second layer can be written in the form:

$$f_2^x(M,m) = h_2(e_2(M,m)) = h_2\left(\sum_{k=0}^{M_x-1} w_2^x(m,k) f_1^x(M,k)\right) \tag{15}$$

$$f_2^y(n,N) = h_2(e_2(n,N)) = h_2\left(\sum_{l=0}^{M_y-1} w_2^y(n,l) f_1^y(l,N)\right) \tag{16}$$

By further extending both last equations, we can get a global form of the second layer outputs (not only M and N intersections):

$$f_2^x(i,m) = h_2(e_2(i,m)) = h_2\left(\sum_{k=0}^{M_x-1} w_2^x(m,k) f_1^x(i,k)\right) \tag{17}$$

$$f_2^y(n,j) = h_2(e_2(n,j)) = h_2\left(\sum_{l=0}^{M_y-1} w_2^y(n,l) f_1^y(l,j)\right) \tag{18}$$

The output signals of the second layers $f_2^x(i,m)$ and $f_2^y(n,j)$, have to be accumulated by the third layer. As both matrixes of the output signals F_2^x and F_2^y are of the same size, we can build a matrix F_2:

$$F_2 = \begin{bmatrix} F_2^x \\ F_2^y \end{bmatrix} \tag{19}$$

The particular elements of that matrix F_2 are described as:

$$f_2(j',j) = \begin{cases} f_2^x(j',j) & \text{for } j' < M_x \wedge j \in [0, M_x - 1] \\ f_2^y(j' - M_x, j) & \text{for } j' \ge M_x \wedge j \in [0, M_x - 1] \end{cases} \tag{20}$$

where $j' \in [0, \{2(M_x - 1)\}]$.

The last third layer accumulates signals from both directions so its weights may be written as:

$$W_3 = c\begin{bmatrix} 1 & 0 & 0 & \dots & 0 & 1 & 0 & 0 & \dots & 0 \\ 0 & 1 & 0 & \dots & 0 & 0 & 1 & 0 & \dots & 0 \\ 0 & 0 & 1 & \dots & 0 & 0 & 0 & 1 & \dots & 0 \\ \vdots & \vdots & \vdots & \dots & \vdots & \vdots & \vdots & \vdots & \vdots & \vdots \\ 0 & 0 & 0 & \dots & 1_{(i,j'=M_x-1)} & 0 & 0 & 0 & \dots & 1_{(i,j'=2(M_x-1))} \end{bmatrix} \quad (21)$$

where c denotes positive weight coefficient of the output layer. This notation refers in some details to the multi-diagonal matrix notation described in [7]. The input signal to the particular neuron in this layer may be expressed as:

$$e_3(i,j) = \sum_{j'=0}^{2(M_x-1)} w_3(i,j')f_2(j',j) \quad (22)$$

In other words, a particular neuron of the third layer is supplied by:

$$e_3(i,j) = f_2^x(i,j) + f_2^y(i,j) \quad (23)$$

thus we can additionally write that e_3 varies in the range:

$$0 \le e_3(i,j) \le 2 \quad (24)$$

Now we have to consider the shape of the last transfer function in the third layer i.e. $h_3(e_3)$. This problem can be solved by formulating three different states of signals $f_2^x(i,j)$ and $f_2^y(i,j)$, respectively, in the second layer:

- $f_2^x(i,j) = f_2^y(i,j) = 0 \quad \Rightarrow \quad e_3(i,j) = 0$, considered point in the input signal/image does not belong to the ridge line,
- $f_2^x(i,j) \ge \frac{1}{2} \vee f_2^y(i,j) \ge \frac{1}{2} \quad \Rightarrow \quad e_3(i,j) \ge \frac{1}{2}$, considered point belongs to the ridge line,
- $f_2^x(i,j) = f_2^y(i,j) = 1 \quad \Rightarrow \quad e_3(i,j) = 2$, investigated point might be qualified as a part of the ridge line. Probability exists that this point is a result of pepper noise only (possibility of misclassification.)

Bearing this in mind, we can build a "threshold" transfer function in the last layer as depicted on the Fig. 5.

The values of k and p_o are assumed as: $k = 1$, $p_o = 1$, thus for $e_3(i,j) \ge p_o$ we have $f_3(i,j) = 1$.

Now, since we have finished the review of the network equations, we can start considerations on how to impose a two-dimensional net onto a task of interferometry image processing.

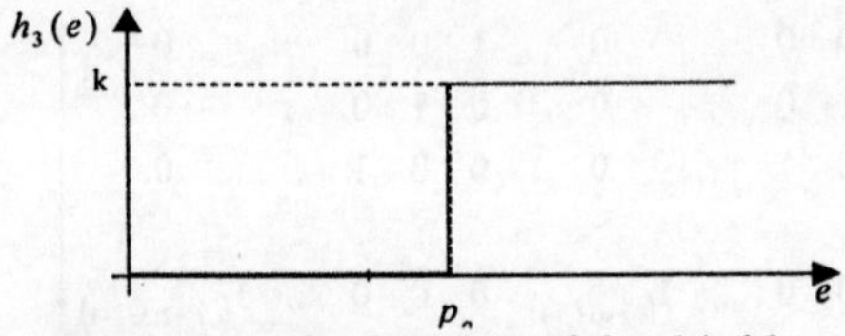

Fig.5. Transfer function of the third layer.

3. Experiments and results

To ensure the reader that the proposed network might be successfully tested with real signals we provided a number of experiments, which are related to other classical methods employed in known image processing techniques. Images obtained from the moiré projector, i.e. the matrix of the intensity function have been supplied to the zero layer of the network. Examples of the input images and obtained results have been shown in Fig. 6.

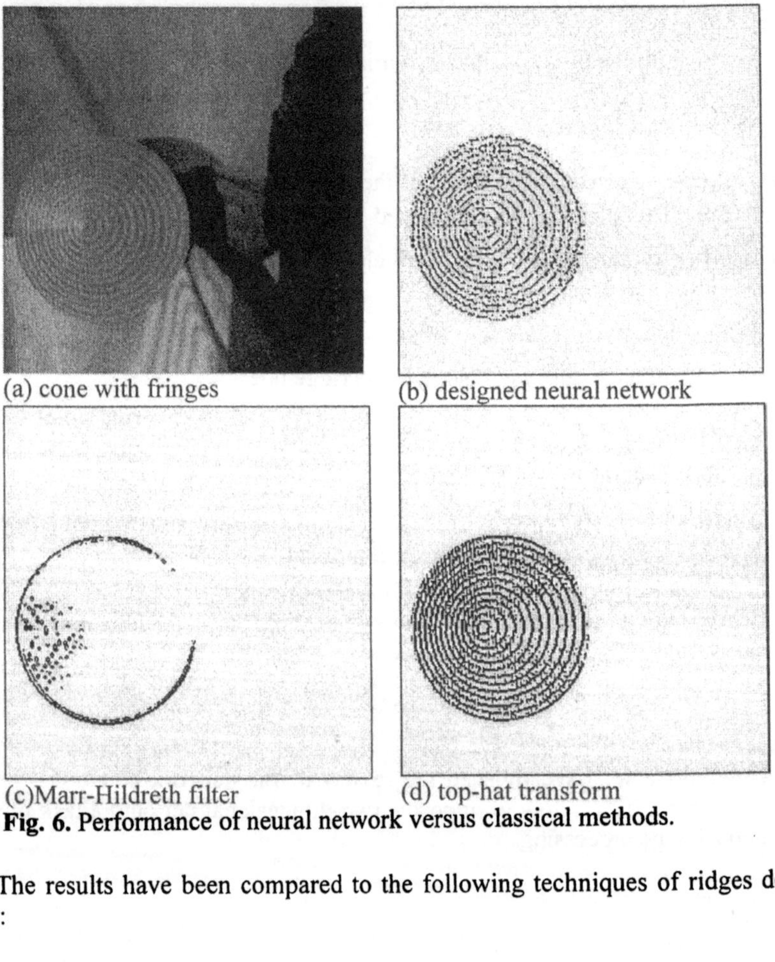

(a) cone with fringes (b) designed neural network

(c)Marr-Hildreth filter (d) top-hat transform

Fig. 6. Performance of neural network versus classical methods.

The results have been compared to the following techniques of ridges detection:

- Top-hat transform: known morphological technique of skeletoning commonly applied in image processing described by [8],
- Marr-Hildreth: adopted method of edge detection by means of a new kind filtering prepared to the task of ridge detection.

4. Conclusions

The major aim of this work is a presentation of a new method of neural network design as opposed to the classical approach. This circumvention tightly merges the structure of the network (i.e. size and weights distribution) with the network purpose, so consequently, the optimal number of neurons and layers will be exploited. The authors presented consecutive stages of the neural networks design process for ridges indication in interferometry images, as the example. The network consists of several one-dimensional sub-networks for maxima detection, which resemble biological nets mentioned in the preface to this work.

Designed slopes of neurons from the third layer gave us the expected results, i.e. map of the ridges. The crucial advantage of such a network lies in the periodicity of weights distribution, so the net can be imposed on the highly parallel computational platforms [9]. This property of the network makes performing of the task of ridges detection possible in a real time, which is obviously an advantage. Analogously, we may design an additional network, which will be able to solve other tasks in image processing. Regarding the above conclusions, the final answer to the initial question of this paper seems to be unequivocally positive.

References

[1] Gomolka Z. (2000),"Neural Networks for Interferometry Image Processing", PhD thesis, AGH Cracow, (In Polish).

[2] Dudek-Dyduch E. (1986), „Cybernetics of Neuron like Systems, – Parallel Signal Processing; ", Polish Cybernetics Society Presss, Cracow (In Polish).

[3] Dudek-Dyduch E., Gomolka Z. (1996)"Adjusting parameters of two dimensional neural network", Proc. Of the Second Conference of Polish Neural Society,

[4] Dudek-Dyduch E., Dyduch T. (1996), "On feed forward homogenous layer neural nets", Proc. Of the Second Conference of Polish Neural Society, Szczyrk.

[5] Dyduch T., Dudek-Dyduch E., (1998) "Application of neural networks in 3D object recognition system", International Journal of Pattern Recognition and Artificial Intelligence Vol. 12 No. 4 ,491-504.

[6] Dudek-Dyduch E., Gomolka Z. (2000), "Hybrid System - Wavelet Decomposition and Hierarchical Neural networks, Fifth International Conference Neural Networks and Soft Computing- Zakopane , June 6-10 2000 , 186-195.

[7] Gawronski R. (1975), „Bionic Problems in the Wide Systems"", Department of National Defense Presss, Warsaw1975, (In Polish).

[8] Klette R., Zamperoni P. (1996), "Handbook of image processing operators", John Wiley&sons 1996.

[9] Dyduch T., Gomolka Z. (2000), "Implementation of homogeneous neural network on highly parallel CNAPS platform", Fifth International Conference Neural Networks and Soft Computing- Zakopane , June 6-10 2000 , 186-195.

New Ontogenic Neural Network Classificator Based on Probabilistic Reasoning

Adrian Horzyk

University of Mining and Metallurgy, Faculty of Electrical Engineering, Automatics, Computer Science and Electronics, Mickiewicza Av. 30, 30-059 Cracow, Poland, horzyk@uci.agh.edu.pl.

ABSTRACT. Many training and configuration methods of today suffer from imprecisely defined training parameters and difficult configuration manners. The determination of a neural network topology and all training parameters is sometimes very difficult and only experts can take advantageous of them. This paper introduces a new ontogenic method for fully automatic configuration of neural network topology and all parameters of thus network. The method enables us to create a universal neural network classificator fully automatically. The presented method uses some probabilistic estimations of training data to create minimal 3-layer partially connected neural network topology that fully satisfies training data requirements. Optionally, this method can automatically carry out some reductions of minor features of training data without loosing correct classification and good generalization properties of the neural network. Finally, the described configuration method is very fast, user-independent, efficient and economical in comparison to other methods of today.

1. Introduction

Neural networks are a very powerful computational tool that enables us to solve different problems in a similar way. One of the main strength of artificial neural networks is their ability to adapt their interconnection weights (by changing them according to a given learning rule) to solve problems. Moreover, the superiority of neural computations is in their ability to generalize the knowledge collected in the training process. On the other hand, one of the main drawbacks of the neural networks is the lack of knowledge for determining the topology of the network. The difficulties of preprocessing the learning data or choosing the most efficient learning method and its training parameters are well-known [1, 2, 4]. That is why the use of neural networks is difficult for non-neural-experts today. In order to overcome these difficulties many researchers have proposed some methods that can help to answer some of these questions and make the use of neural networks more easy. A relatively new class of neural networks tries to overcome some part of these problems by letting the network also automatically adapt its topology to the problem. These are the so-called ontogenic neural networks [1, 2]. What distinguishes ontogenic algorithms from other neural network training algorithms is that they are used not only to train the weights, but also to learn the topology needed to correctly learn the training data. The proper determination of the topology is very important, because the topology affects many important characteristics of the network's learning, such as training time and generalization capability.

This paper introduces a new ontogenic method for automatic configuration of non-linear neural classificator (MAC-NM). The configuration of the neural network is based on some probabilistic analysis of the training data that should be somehow similar to each other for each training class. The presented method creates 3-layer partially connected neural network topology with inter- and supralayer connections. One of the most powerful aspects of the presented method is its ability to create the appropriate topology very quickly and economically. Firstly, the topology is built up (fig. 1) and then it is reduced (fig. 2). During the reduction phase of the method only the minor connections and neurons are reduced thanks to the described probabilistic estimations. Furthermore, what distinguishes the method is its ability to automatically and correctly classify negatives of the training input vectors. The main drawback of the method is the lack of ability to work on non-binary training data. On the other hand, the created and configured network can easily classify non-binary input vectors. Finally, the non-linearity of the neural network enables us to adapt it to almost any training data.

2. Description of the Method

In this paper, the training data set consists of *N* couples (u^n, C_m), where (u^n, C_m) means that $u^n \in C_m$, $n = 1,\dots,N$, *N* is also the total number of training patterns, $m \in \{1,\dots,M\}$, *M* is the number of all training classes. Training patterns $u^n = [u_1^n,\dots,u_K^n]$ always consist of bipolar values, i.e. $u_k^n \in \{-1,+1\}$. In the following considerations all binary features for each training pattern are treated independently. The goal of "pure" classification [2] is to assign an input vector $v = [v_1,\dots,v_K]$ to one of *M* classes C_m. In contrast, the introduced method creates the neural network that is able not only to classify input patterns but also to answer the question about the degree of input vector similarity to all *M* classes! Though training data must be bipolar the classified input vector $v = [v_1,\dots,v_K]$ can be analog (continuous), i.e. $v_k \in \langle -1,+1 \rangle$. This feature is very useful when we have to do with some noisy input vectors.

Training data can be characterized by some distributions of their binary features. These distributions are used to define the **probability of correct classification** (Laplace's probability [3]) of *k*-th binary feature of the training pattern u^n:

$$p_k^n = \frac{\breve{N}_k^m}{\breve{N}_k} \; if \; u_k^n = +1 \;\&\; p_k^n = \frac{N^m - \breve{N}_k^m}{N - \breve{N}_k} \; if \; u_k^n = -1 \;\Rightarrow\; p_k^n = \frac{2\breve{N}_k^m - N^m(1-u_k^n)}{2\breve{N}_k - N(1-u_k^n)},$$

where $N^m = \left\| \{u^n : u^n \in C_m \;\&\; n = 1,\dots,N\} \right\|$, $N = \sum_{m=1}^{M} N^m$,

$$\breve{N}_k^m = \left\| \{u_k^n : u_k^n = +1 \,\&\, n = 1,...,N \,\&\, u^n \in C_m\} \right\|, \breve{N}_k = \left\| \{u_k^n : u_k^n = +1 \,\&\, n = 1,...,N\} \right\|.$$

In this way, the **probability vectors of correct classification** are for every training pattern u^n defined: $p^n = [p_1^n,...,p_K^n]$. The vectors of probabilities of correct classification are used to define the **discrimination vectors** (d^n) for all training patterns u^n as follows:

$$d^n = [d_1^n,...,d_K^n] = \left[\frac{p_1^n \cdot u_1^n}{N^m},...,\frac{p_K^n \cdot u_K^n}{N^m} \right]$$

The probabilities of correct classification and the binary features of training patterns are used in order to achieve the maximal discrimination of training patterns as a result of the neural network configuration process.

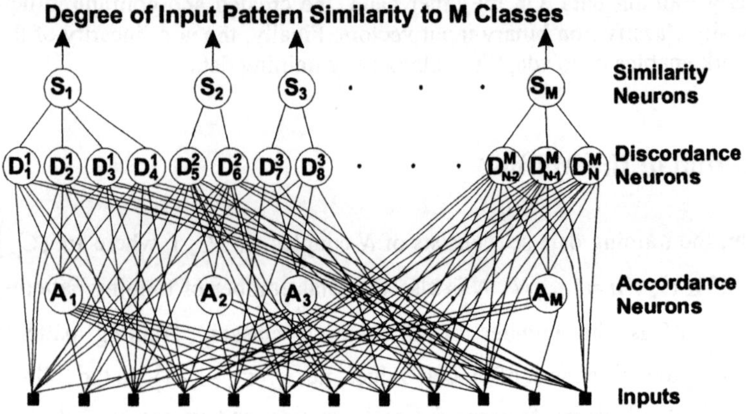

Figure 1. The network topology after growing phase of the method. There are shown: A_m – the accordance neurons, D_n^m – the discordance neurons and S_m – the similarity neurons

The process of automatic configuration of the non-linear 3-layer partially connected neural network topology with supra- and interlayer connections (fig. 1) is nearly joined with the process of weights computation after the appropriate discrimination vectors. Firstly, the probability vectors of correct classification of all training patterns p^n (n=1,...,N) must be computed. Next, the discrimination vectors d^n are for every training pattern calculated. Accordant binary features ($K^m = \{k : k \in \{1,...K\} \,\&\, \forall u^{n_1}, u^{n_2} \in C^m : u_k^{n_1} = u_k^{n_2}\}$) of each m-th class are separated and converted into connections of the appropriate accordance neurons A_m. On the other hand, the discordant binary features are a basis to create the discordance neurons D_n^m (fig. 1) for each class C_m.

The main drawback of the created topology in the growing phase of the method is its size. In the reduction phase of the method, the minor connections (weights) and neurons will be reduced. The minor connections are selected after the discrimination coefficients d_k^n associated with them. Practical applications show that the reduction of minor connections (up to 30-70% of all created connections) [5] and minor neurons (up to 20-40% of all created neurons) do not disturb correct classification and good generalization properties of the neural network. The natural feature of the described reductions is the ability to diminish sensitiveness on artifacts and strengthen similar features of all training patterns.

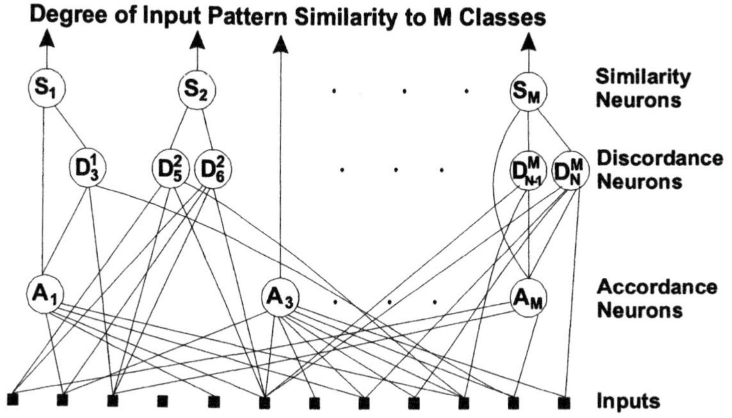

Figure 2. The neural network topology after reduction phase of the method

The reduction phase of the presented method is divided into 6 stages:

1. Reduction of minor supralayer connections of discordance and interlayer connection of accordance neurons after their discrimination values.
2. Removal of neurons that have no more input connections.
3. Reduction of discordance neurons that have only interlayer connections and no more supralayer connections. In this case, the associated accordance neurons are directly connected to the appropriate (for these classes) similarity neurons.
4. Removal of duplicated discordance neurons.
5. Reduction of single discordance neurons of classes if there are no direct supralayer connections between their accordance and similarity neurons. In case of reduction all supralayer connections of these removed discordance neurons are switched over to the appropriate accordance neurons.
6. Reduction of similarity neurons of classes without discordance neurons. In this case, the outputs of the appropriate accordance neurons become the outputs of the neural network.

As a result of such reductions, the hybrid partially-connected neural network architecture is achieved (fig. 2). The reduction phase can be repeated independently of the previous growing phase. In this way, the presented method enables us to gradually adapt the neural network topology to the demands of whichever application.

After the network topology configuration, the weights can be established. The interconnection weights $\hat{w}_k^m$ of the accordance neurons A_m are computed as follows:

$$\hat{w}_k^m = \frac{d_k^{n_m}}{\sum_{j\in K^m}\left|d_j^{n_m}\right|} \quad if\ k \in K^m \quad \& \quad \hat{w}_k^m = 0 \quad otherwise$$

where $n_m \in \{n : n = 1,...,N \,\&\, u^n \in C^m\}$

The supralayer connection weights w_k^n of the discordance neurons D_n^m are computed as follows:

$$w_k^n = \frac{d_k^n}{\sum_{j=1}^{K}\left|d_j^n\right|} \quad if\ k \notin K^m \quad \& \quad w_k^n = 0 \quad otherwise$$

The null value of any weight corresponds with the lack of connection.
The outputs values of the accordance and discordance neurons are computed as weighted sums of their inputs $x = [x_1,...,x_K]$ (respectively):

$\hat{y}^m = \sum_{k\in K^m} \hat{w}_k^m x_k$ is the output value of the accordance neuron A_m,

$y^n = \sum_{k\in\{1,...,K\}\setminus K^m} w_k^n x_k + \breve{w}_n^m \hat{y}^m$ is the output value of the discordance neuron D_n^m associated with the m-th class C_m where $\breve{w}_n^m = 1 - \sum_{j\in\{1,...K\}\setminus K^m}\left|w_j^n\right|$ is the interlayer connection weight such that the source neuron of this interconnection is the accordance neuron A_m and the sink neuron is the discordance neuron D_n^m (fig. 1).

The interlayer connection weights $\dot{w}_j^m$ of similarity neurons S_m play no role in classification and are all set to 1, i.e.: $\dot{w}_j^m = 1$. On the other hand, the non-linear activation function of these similarity neurons plays important role in final classification and is defined as follows:

$$\dot{y}^m = f_{SGNMAX}\left(\{y^n : n \in \{1,2,...,N\} \,\&\, u^n \in C_m\}\right)$$

where

$$f_{SGMMAX}(X) = \begin{cases} x_{MIN} & if\ |x_{MAX}| < |x_{MIN}| \\ x_{MAX} & if\ |x_{MAX}| \geq |x_{MIN}| \end{cases}$$

where

$X = [x_1,...,x_L]$, $x_{MAX} = \max\{x_1,...,x_L\}$, $x_{MIN} = \min\{x_1,...,x_L\}$.

The output value $\dot{y}^m$ of the similarity neuron S_m is the output value of the neural network as well (fig. 1). This m-th output value is the measure of the degree of similarity of the given input pattern (even of negatives) to the m-th class C_m.

3. Conclusion

This paper introduces a new ontogenic method for fully automatic configuration of 3-layer partially connected neural network topologies with inter- and supralayer connections. The method enables us to create a universal neural network classificator without user guidance. All parameters of the network (except the level of reduction) are computed automatically. This feature makes the introduced method easy to use even for non-neural-experts. The presented method uses the described probabilistic estimation of training data to create neural network topology and to configure its weights. Optionally, this method enables us to do impressive reduction of minor weights and neurons so that the generalization ability of the reduced network is still good enough. Moreover, the created neural network classifies all the training patterns with an expected 100% degree of similarity to the appropriate classes. Furthermore, the network can automatically classify negatives of the training patterns indicating the inverse of them by the negative signs of the output values corresponding to the degrees of similarity of the appropriate classes. Finally, the described configuration method is very fast and efficient in comparison to other method used today [1, 2]. Even huge data bases can be work out very fast, because the method needs to look over the training data only a few times. Moreover, the huge data bases can lead to impressive reduction of weights and neurons in the reduction phase of the method producing the compact neural network topologies that correctly classifies input data.

The main limitation of the presented method is that it can use only binary data patterns (vectors) for training. Moreover, all binary features of training data are treated as independent though they need not to be sometimes. Though the dependency of binary features of training data do not matter, the method is in this case not most effective. In spite of some limitations of the presented method, it creates a universal ontogenic classificator that can be used to lot's of various applications.

References

1. Duch W., Korbicz J., Rutkowski L., Tadeusiewicz R. (eds) (2000) Biocybernetics and biomedical engineering. Neural networks, vol. 6, EXIT, Warsaw
2. Fiesler E., Beale R. (eds) (1997) Handbook of neural computation, IOP Publishing Ltd and Oxford University Press, Bristol & New York
3. Hellwig Z. (1993) Elements of calculus of probability and mathematical statistics, PWN, Warsaw
4. Horzyk A. (2001) New methods for training the feedforward networks, PhD Work at the University of Mining and Metallurgy, Cracow
5. Horzyk A. (2001), Fast Automatic Configuration of Artificial Neural Networks Used for Binary Patterns Recognition, Biocybernetics and Biomedical Engineering, vol. 21(1), PWN, Warsaw, pp 25-36

Discrete Quasi-gradient Features Weighting Algorithm

Norbert Jankowski

Department of Informatics, Nicholas Copernicus University
ul. Grudziadzka 5, 87-100 Toruń, Poland, http://www.phys.uni.torun.pl/~norbert

Abstract. A new method of feature weighting, useful also for feature extraction has been described. It is quite efficient and gives quite accurate results. Weighting algorithm may be used with any kind of learning algorithm. The weighting algorithm with k-nearest neighbors model was used to estimate the best feature base for a given distance measure. Results obtained with this algorithm clearly show its superior performance in several benchmark tests.

1 Introduction

It is well known [1,2] that initial feature set of data sets/databases used for classification or approximation is not the *optimal information source* and the feature analysis may be very helpful in further processing of data. Several methods which use different strategy of feature extraction and weighting were already presented in books and articles [3,4,1,5]. Some of them measure amount of information belonging to a given attribute (or a subset[1]) using information theory or statistics. Other methods use learning models to observe accuracy changes what help to estimate weights in the next phase of feature weighting (or extraction) process [6,7,4]. Such type of feature weighting may be used with several learning models types. Algorithm presented in this article belongs to the second type of feature weighting/extracting algorithms, and will be presented in conjunction with k-nearest neighbors model [8], although algorithm itself may be used with any learning model.

2 Feature weighting algorithm

General idea of a Discrete quasi-gradient algorithm is based on *looking for optimal* vector of weight changes in given state of weighting procedure. The process is repeated as long as any improvement of accuracy may be done. In parallel some control parameters change to stimulate quasi-gradient directions of weights changes. Another goal of this algorithm was to create stable feature weighting algorithm. It means that new (weighted) set of features should never significantly decrease accuracy of the final model. Of course it is impossible to expect any progres if original feature set is optimal. Next,

[1] But if subset become bigger the complexity grow exponentially.

repeating the whole procedurc of weighting a few distinguishable solutions may be found. This is not an error, it is nature of some databases. Such information may be important in propagation of this information (separate weighted sets of features) to other models and it may help to obtain different final models.

The main loop of the algorithm consists of cross-validation (CV) as a learning technic. This means that a whole data set is divided in n equal (if possible) parts (commonly called folds) $\mathcal{S}_i$, $i = 1, \ldots, n$. In each CV–iteration procedure *FindWeights* is called. *FindWeights* use two sets $\hat{\mathcal{S}}_i$ ($\hat{\mathcal{S}}_i = \bigcup_{k=1,\ldots,n,\ k\neq i} \mathcal{S}_k$) as a learning set, and $\mathcal{S}_i$ as a validation set. As a result procedure *FindWeights* returns vector of feature weights $\mathbf{w}_i$. Lets define:

$$\mathbf{w}_i = FindWeights(\hat{\mathcal{S}}_i, \mathcal{S}_i) \tag{1}$$

Each weight of $\mathbf{w}_i$ is in $[0, 1]$ interval. Details of procedure *FindWeights* will be presented later. Vectors $\mathbf{w}_i$ consist of weights for each feature $k = 1, \ldots, d$, where d is the dimension of data set $\mathcal{S}$. Now the sum of weights vectors is calculated and the final weights vector is obtained through normalization:

$$\tilde{\mathbf{w}} = \mathbf{w} / \max_{k=1,\ldots,d} w_k \qquad \mathbf{w} = \textstyle\sum_{i=1}^{n} \tilde{\mathbf{w}}_i \tag{2}$$

where $\mathbf{w} = [w_1, \ldots, w_d]$. The above part of CV learning is really simple: if all CV iterations are completed, the final model is estimated as a *consequence* of intermediate models. Now the *FindWeights* as the heart of whole algorithm will be described.

Procedure *FindWeights***.** First, the initial values are assigned to weights: $w_k = 1, \quad k = 1, \ldots, d$. In this case the algorithm starts from full feature set. It may be useful sometimes to start from $w_k = 0$, what mean that algorithm starts from an empty feature set and tries to add feature by feature — this strategy may be more efficient, computationally, if working with highly dimensional data sets. The main loop (one of three) is repeated as long as any progress in the maximization of accuracy on validation set may be done. The contents of that loop is called *main phase.* The goal of the *main phase* is to observe changes, determining which features may help to improve the accuracy by changing current weights by Δ, and next to apply positive/progresive changes and simultaneously coordinating the change of Δ. In the inner loop for each feature two quantities v_i^+ and v_i^- are computed:

$$v_i^+ = validate(\mathbf{w}^+, i) \qquad v_i^- = validate(\mathbf{w}^-, i) \tag{3}$$

where $\mathbf{w}^{\pm} = [w_1, \ldots, w_{i-1}, w_i \pm \Delta, w_{i+1}, \ldots, w_d]$. *validate*$(\mathbf{w})$ is a function which compute the accuracy on validation set $\mathcal{S}$ (see eq. 1) for the learning model $\mathcal{M}$ which is trained on a data set $\hat{\mathcal{S}}$. To obtain results presented in section 3 the k-nearest neighbor model was used as $\mathcal{M}$.

Vectors $\mathbf{v}^+$ and $\mathbf{v}^-$ contain information about weight changes by step Δ that may help to improve results. If any $v_i^{\pm}$ indicate that given change may help the new set of weights is defined according to:

$$w_i' = w_i - \theta\Delta \quad \text{if} \quad v_i^- > v \tag{4}$$
$$w_i' = w_i + \theta\Delta \quad \text{if} \quad v_i^+ > v \wedge v_i^- <= v \tag{5}$$

where θ defines the speed (I like $\theta = 1$ – really fast!), and $v = validate(\mathbf{w})$.

The above equation says that all features which may help if they are changed, are indeed changed. If for new weights $v_{new} = validate(\mathbf{w}')$ is smaller than $v = validate(\mathbf{w})$ the procedure goes back to weights $\mathbf{w}$, else $\mathbf{w}'$ become the new weight vector.

As long as the current parameter Δ leads to a better accuracy, weight changes are made and the inner loop is continued. Usually the starting Δ is equal to 1. The step Δ is decreased if no progress in maximization of accuracy on validation set is done: $\Delta = \Delta/2$. After that if Δ is still bigger (or equal to) than Δ_{min}, the second loop is repeated again. If Δ is smaller than Δ_{min} (for example 0.01) loop is broken and weights are normalized:

$$\tilde{\mathbf{w}} = \mathbf{w} / \max_{k=1,\dots,d} w_k \tag{6}$$

The *main phase* loop is repeated (with initial $\Delta = 1$) as long as the weighting algorithm gives with better accuracy on a validation test. Since the main phase loop is repeated the algorithm is able to jump out from local minima keeping the best solution found so far. Without that loop the performance of the algorithm was average or even worst.

Outline of this algorithm may be found at my WWW page.

3 Results

The performance on several databases was checked to test the stability of the algorithm and to test whether feature weighting helps or may destroy the generalization ability. All test were performed on databases from Machine Learning Database Repository at the UCI [9] using 10-fold CV test, except that data sets which have original testing sets. All results were averaged from 10 runs. Standardization of most database was performed before the learning phase. Each table with results have four parts. First presents results which were obtained with feature weighting algorithm for kNN, second without feature weighting, and third show default accuracy – percentage of most majority class. Fourth shows results obtained by other models. This part contains only the best models for a given database[2]. Note that k-weight [10] and GIBL [7] are algorithms which estimate feature influence. It is common that some models have really good accuracy for one benchmark giving much worst results for other data sets. In tables with results the notation is used:

[2] If you want to browse more results see WWW pages of my LAB: http://www.phys.uni.torun.pl/kmk/projects/datasets.html.

`kNN [CVx] [M]`. `k` defines the number of neighbors. CVx if exists means that weighting algorithm was used, and x defines the number of folds in CV. If M occurs non-Euclidian metric was used, such as the Manhattan, Minkovsky or Canberra[3]. For some data set significant improvement of accuracy on test sets is observed, and for others data sets the accuracy is not (essentially) changed while for others the classification model decreases its accuracy.

Thyroid disease is one of the best known benchmark data sets, as well one really nontrivial for classification. The training set has 3772 cases, and testing set has 3428 cases. There are 3 classes, and the most frequent has 92.71% of all cases. Number of attributes is 21 (15 binary, 6 continuous). The accuracy on test set of plain 1NN (kNN with 1 neighbor) is really poor, just 93.14% (see tab. 1). For 3NN with Manhattan distance the accuracy is 94.4%, but using weighted features 98.36%. The best results were obtained for 3NN with the Canberra metric – 98.56%. This very good results were obtained only because irrelevant features were removed – see figure 1.

Flags classification problem have 193 vectors, 28 attributes, and each vector may be assigned to one of 8 classes. Feature weighting for this data set was very efficient (see tab. 2). For 1NN CV3 with Manhattan metric accuracy in test was 62.04% and without weighting 50.91%. For 3NN with weighting 61.51% and 48.07% without. The best non-weighted kNN have accuracy 52.56% and this is nearly 10% less than for the best plain kNN.

Glass data contains 214 vectors, each vector has 9 attributes and may be classified to one of the 6 classes. For this benchmark weighting looks very important, and the improvement may be really large (see tab. 3). The best results were obtained for 1NN CV3 with Manhattan metric giving 80.81% accuracy, and the plain version finished with just 73.50%. For 3 neighbors (3NN CV3 Manh) weighted version has 78.04%, and non-weighted 72.06%.

The number of Δ changes change from 25 to 40 for glass data set and from 25 to 50 for flags data set (it is around 1 minute on Pentium 4).

For the following data sets results of feature weighting were not significant (around 0.3-2%): australian credit, appendicitis, cleveland heart, wine.

4 Conclusions

Discrete quasi-gradient weighting algorithm presented in this paper is really efficient and results have good accuracy on several tests. Sometimes the improvement was around 10% of accuracy. This algorithm may be used as feature extraction tool. The starting feature set may be full or empty, and because of that it may be useful for huge dimensional data sets. Also alternative weighting sets may be obtained, what may be very important in further analysis. Using this feature weighting algorithm the kNN model was placed at the top of ranking of the best methods for presented data sets. Sometimes the

[3] Canberra metric: $canb(\mathbf{x}, \mathbf{y}) = \sum_{i=1}^{d} |x_i - y_i|/|x_i + y_i|$.

Model	test	train
3NN CV3 Camberra	98.56	99.37
3NN CV2 Manh	98.36	99.28
1NN CV2 Manh	98.26	100.00
3NN CV2	98.28	99.24
1NN CV2	98.26	100.00
2NN CV2	98.36	99.28
3NN Camberra	96.30	98.49
3NN Manh	94.40	96.58
1NN Manh	93.76	100.00
1NN	93.14	100.00
default	92.71	-
C-MLP2LN+ASA [11]	99.36	99.90
CART [12]	99.36	99.80
PVM [12]	99.36	99.80
SSV [13]	99.36	99.76
IncNet [14]	99.24	99.68
MLP a,b opt. [11]	99.36	99.90
MLP2LN [11]	99.00	99.70
Cascade correlation [15]	98.50	100.00
BP+genetic [15]	98.40	99.40
Quickprop [15]	98.30	99.60
kNN+weights [10]	98.22	98.89
RProp [15]	98.00	99.60
kNN+weights [10]	97.96	98.89...

Table 1. Accuracy for thyroid data set.

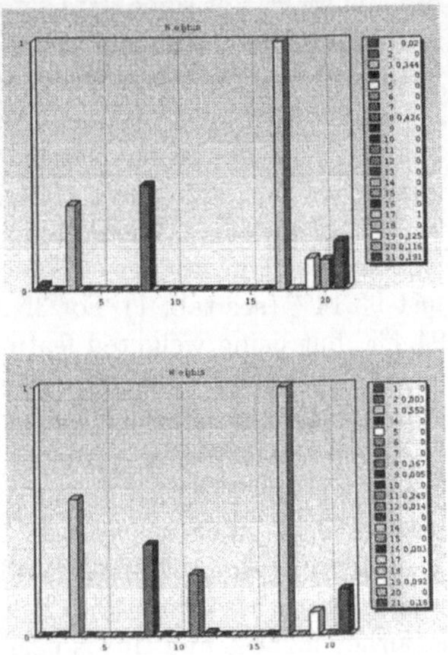

Fig. 1. Feature weights for thyroid data set.

Model	test	train
1NN CV3 Manh	62.04	100.0
3NN CV3 Manh	61.51	76.07
7NN CV3 Manh	58.30	68.28
27NN CV3 Manh	56.19	59.78
27NN Manh	52.56	56.53
7NN Manh	52.03	63.57
1NN Manh	50.91	100.00
17NN Manh	50.25	57.97
3NN Manh	48.07	72.53
27NN	46.76	51.75
1NN	48,52	100,00
default	31.09	-
CART [16]	62.40	-
IB1 [16]	56.60	-
C 4.5 [16]	56.20	-
GIBL [7]	55.11	-
IBL [7]	48.29	- ...

Table 2. Accuracy for flags data set.

Model	test	train
1NN CV3 Manh	80.81	100.00
3NN CV3 Manh	78.04	87.64
3NN CV3 Mink–0.7	77.97	88.78
3NN CV2 Manh	77.49	87.53
3NN CV2	75.00	85.11
1NN Manh	73.50	100.00
3NN Manh	72.06	84.98
3NN	70.85	83.63
1NN	70.45	100.00
default	35.51	-
GIBL [7]	78.55	-
Bayes [16]	71.80	-
CART	71.40	-
IB1 [16]	71.10	-
ID3 [16]	69.10	-
IBL [7]	70.52	-

Table 3. Accuracy for glass data set.

accuracy on testing and training parts were very similar, which means that solution found are close to optimum for a given model. It is important that algorithm may be used not only for kNN, but for several machine learning models, including artificial neural networks.

References

1. C. M. Bishop. *Neural Networks for Pattern Recognition.* Oxford University Press, 1995.
2. R. O. Duda, P. E. Hart, and D. G. Stork. *Patter Classification and Scene Analysis.* Wiley, 2nd ed. edition, 1997.
3. M. Dash and H. Liu. Feature selection for classification. *Intelligent Data Analysis*, 1(3), 1997.
4. M. Fernández and C. Hernández. How to select the inputs for a multilayer feedforward by using the training set. In *5th International Work Conference on Artificial an Natural Neural Networks*, pages 477–486, Alicante, Spain, 1999.
5. H. Almuallim and T. G. Dietterich. Efficient algorithms for identifying relevant features. In *Proceedings of the Ninth Canadian Conference on Artificial Intelligence*, pages 38–45, Vancouver, 1992. Morgan Kaufmann.
6. D. R. Wilson and T. R. Martinez. Instance-based learning with genetically derived attribute weights. In *International Conference on Artificial Intelligence, Expert Systems and Neural Networks*, pages 11–14, 1996.
7. D. R. Wilson. *Advances in Instance-Based Learning Algorithms.* PhD thesis, Department of Computer Science Brigham Young University, 1997.
8. T. M. Cover and P. E. Hart. Nearest neighbor pattern classification. *Institute of Electrical and Electronics Engineers Transactions on Information Theory*, 13(1):21–27, jan 1967.
9. C. J. Merz and P. M. Murphy. UCI repository of machine learning databases, 1998. http://www.ics.uci.edu/~mlearn/MLRepository.html.
10. W. Duch and K. Grudziński. Search and global minimization in similarity-based methods. In *International Joint Conference on Neural Networks*, page 742, Washington, 1999.
11. W. Duch, R. Adamczak, and K. Grabczewski. Extraction of logical rules from backpropagation networks. *Neural Processing Letters*, 7:1–9, 1998.
12. S.M. Weiss and I. Kapouleas. An empirical comparison of pattern recognition, neural nets and machine learning classification methods. In J.W. Shavlik and T.G. Dietterich, editors, *Readings in Machine Learning.* Morgan Kauffman, 1990.
13. K. Grabczewski and Włodzisław Duch. The separability of split value criterion. In L. Rutkowski and R. Tadeusiewicz, editors, *Neural Networks and Soft Computing*, pages 202–208, Zakopane, Poland, June 2000.
14. N. Jankowski. *Ontogenic neural networks and their applications to classification of medical data.* PhD thesis, Department of Computer Methods, Nicholas Copernicus University, Toruń, Poland, 1999.
15. W. Schiffman, M. Joost, and R. Werner. Comparison of optimized backpropagation algorithms. In *Proceedings of ESANN'93*, pages 97–104, Brussels, 1993.
16. Frederick Zarndt. A comprehensive case study: An examination of machine learning and connectionist algorithms. Master's thesis, Department of Computer Science Brigham Young University, 1995.

Input Ranking Revisited: A Theoretical Input Sensitivity Approach

Sanggil Kang[1], Can Isik[1], and Steven Morphet[1, 2]

[1] Department of Electrical Engineering and Computer Science, Syracuse University, Syracuse, NY 13244, USA
[2] Syracuse Research Corporation, North Syracuse, NY 13212, USA

Abstract. In feedforward neural networks, all inputs contribute to a greater or lesser extent when calculating the outputs. Therefore, inputs may be ordered from the greatest contributor to the least. Input ranking is non-trivial – cursory examination of the weight and bias matrices fails to reveal ranking. Solving the ranking issue allows for elimination of inputs with little influence on output. This paper presents a new method of determining the input sensitivity of three-layer feedforward neural networks. Specifically, sensitivity of an input is independent of the magnitudes of the remaining inputs, providing an unambiguous ranking of input importance. Small changes to influential inputs will result in great changes to output. This concept motivated the theoretical approach to input ranking. Examination of theoretical results will demonstrate the correctness of this approach.

1 Introduction

Neural networks are [typically] non-linear systems, as such, the sensitivity of an output with respect to an input *i* may depend on the magnitude of input *i* as well as other inputs. The issue of input sensitivity ranking, in one form or another, has been addressed in the literature since the late 1980's.

Choi *et al* [1] address neural network robustness by analyzing weight sensitivity. Engelbrecht *et al* [2] address the difficulty domain experts have identifying input parameters having significant influence on system output. Zurada *et al* [6] address deleting unimportant inputs from neural network training sets leading to [potentially] smaller neural networks and reduced data vector sizes. Piche [4] attempts to understand the effects of errors on neural networks. He *et al* [3] address improving neural network accuracy and reducing training time.

Sung [5] addresses reducing size, shortening training times, and achieving higher accuracy in neural networks. As such, [5] employed input ranking to identify prunable inputs. Specifically, three different input ranking methods are compared – sensitivity analysis; fuzzy curves; and changes in MSE. Sung compared these methods for effectiveness on backpropagation neural networks trained to model simple nonlinear functions. Sung derives a sensitivity analysis formula for backpropagation neural networks with two hidden layers.

Several concerns arise when examining the related literature. Specifically, the sensitivity of an input is dependent on the magnitude of all inputs; thus, the actual ranking becomes problematic. Also, [4] requires neural networks with [statistically] large input to hidden neuron ratios. Many approaches require the omission of bias terms in neural networks. In [1], sensitivity is calculated at specific points in the input space (which will most likely vary when different points are evaluated). Many approaches also require the training of many neural networks in order to evaluate sensitivity.

Our method addresses many of these issues. For instance, in our approach, the sensitivity of an input is independent of the magnitudes of the remaining inputs. Our method decouples the inputs from each other, avoiding problems associated with calculating the joint probability density function. The ratio of hidden neurons to inputs is of no concern, and the derived equations include bias terms. Our method averages input sensitivity across the input range, and requires only one trained neural network to determine input sensitivity. In addition, to identify dependent inputs, only two trained neural networks are required.

2 Theory

The following is an analytical formulation of input sensitivity in systems whose inputs contribute to the output in a decoupled fashion. Outputs may be thought of as the sum of functions of individual inputs. For instance, $y = y_1(x_1) + y_2(x_2) + \ldots + y_n(x_n)$. Such systems may be modeled via feedforward, partially connected neural networks (PCNNs) in which no hidden neuron is connected to more than one input neuron. The structure of the PCNN is depicted in Fig. 1.

Each hidden neuron is assumed to have a non-linear transfer function. Each output neuron is assumed to have a linear transfer function. This derivation assumes neural networks with three layers (input, hidden, output).

2.1 Architecture Justification

Fig. 1 implies that the sensitivity of an input is not effected when changes are introduced to the remaining inputs (the input sensitivity of an input i is measured in isolation by adding disturbance to input i only). Thus, calculating input sensitivities in PCNNs is computationally inexpensive. Also, the joint density function of input and noise is easily derived.

Typically, PCNNs will have larger mean squared errors (MSE) than fully connected FFNNs when trained on coupled input/output mappings. However, ranking results from PCNNs and fully connected FFNNs are very similar.

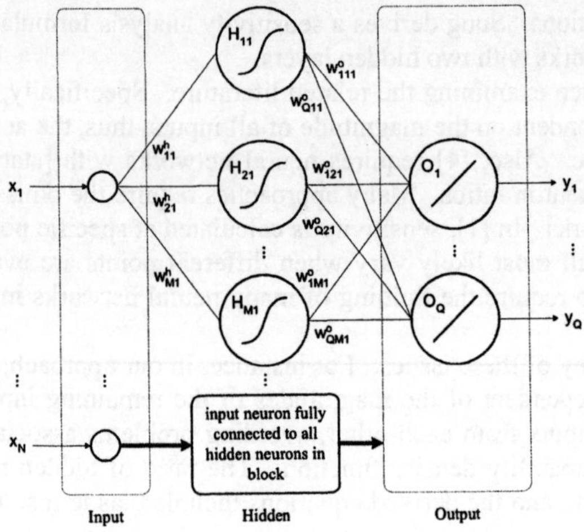

Fig. 1. Feedforward partially connected neural network

2.2 Notation and Assumptions

- Input i is denoted as x_i (i=1,2,…,N (the number of input neurons)).
- x_i is a uniformly distributed random variable in the range [K_1,K_2] (i=1,2,…,N).
- Input disturbance Δx is normally distributed with zero mean and σ^2 variance.
- Δx is independent of x_i (i=1,2,…,N).
- σ is assumed small (allowing for approximation in the derivation section).
- M is the number of hidden neurons in each hidden neuron block.
- The output of the jth hidden neuron connected to the ith input neuron is denoted as z_{ji} (i=1,2,…,N and j=1,2,…,M).
- Output q is denoted as y_q (q=1,2,…,Q (the number of output neurons)).
- The weight connecting the ith input neuron and the jth hidden neuron is denoted as w^h_{ji} (i=1,2,…,N and j=1,2,…,M).
- The weight connecting the jth hidden neuron and the qth output neuron in hidden block i is denoted as w^o_{qji} (i=1,2,…,N; j=1,2,…,M and q=1,2,…,Q).
- Biases at the hidden and output layers are denoted as b^h_{ji} and b^o_q respectively.

2.3 Derivation of Theoretical Input Sensitivity

After training, the sensitivity of the ith input is calculated by introducing disturbance to [only] input i. The output error of each hidden neuron (denoted as Δz_{ji}) is (t denotes the hidden neuron transfer function)

$$\Delta z_{ji} = t\left(w_{ji}^{h}(x_i + \Delta x) + b_{ji}^{h}\right) - t\left(w_{ji}^{h} x_i + b_{ji}^{h}\right) \tag{1}$$

The 2nd moment and the mean of Δz_{ji} (denoted as $E[\Delta z_{ji}^2]$ and $E[\Delta z_{ji}]$ respectively) are obtained using the joint probability density function of x_i and Δx.

$$E\left[\Delta z_{ji}^{2}\right] = \int_{-\infty}^{\infty}\int_{-\infty}^{\infty} \Delta z_{ji}^{2} f(x_i, \Delta x) d\Delta x dx_i \tag{2}$$

$$E\left[\Delta z_{ji}\right] = \int_{-\infty}^{\infty}\int_{-\infty}^{\infty} \Delta z_{ji} f(x_i, \Delta x) d\Delta x dx_i \tag{3}$$

The output error of the qth output neuron (denoted as Δy_q^i) is

$$\Delta y_q^i = \sum_{j=1}^{M} w_{qji}^{o} \Delta z_{ji} \tag{4}$$

Therefore, the mean and 2nd moment of Δy_q^i are

$$E\left[\Delta y_q^i\right] = \sum_{j=1}^{M} w_{qji}^{o} E\left[\Delta z_{ji}\right] \tag{5}$$

$$E\left[\Delta y_q^{i\,2}\right] = \sum_{j=1}^{M} w_{qji}^{o\,2} E\left[\Delta z_{ji}^{2}\right] + 2\cdot\left(\sum_{j=1}^{M-1}\sum_{m=j+1}^{M} w_{qji}^{o} w_{qmi}^{o} E\left[\Delta z_{ji}\right]E\left[\Delta z_{mi}\right]\right) \tag{6}$$

From Eqs. 5 and 6, the standard deviation of the output error is

$$STD\left(\Delta y_q^i\right) = \sqrt{E\left[\Delta y_q^{i\,2}\right] - E\left[\Delta y_q^i\right]^2} \tag{7}$$

The sensitivity of output neuron q with respect to input i is

$$S_q(x_i) = STD\left(\Delta y_q^i\right) / STD(disturbance) \tag{8}$$

Thus, the sensitivity of input i (denoted as $S(x_i)$) is

$$S(x_i) = (1/Q)\sum_{q=1}^{Q} S_q(x_i) \tag{9}$$

2.4 Hyper-Tangent Derivation

By replacing the transfer function in Eq. 1 with 'tanh' (the hyper-tangent function), the output error of each hidden neuron yields

$$\Delta z_{ji} = \tanh\left(w_{ji}^{h}(x_i + \Delta x) + b_{ji}^{h}\right) - \tanh\left(w_{ji}^{h} x_i + b_{ji}^{h}\right) \tag{10}$$

Since Δx is small, Eq. 10 is approximated by

$$\Delta z_{ji} = \tanh\left(w_{ji}^{h}(x_i + (\Delta x/2)) + b_{ji}^{h}\right) - \tanh\left(w_{ji}^{h}(x_i - (\Delta x/2)) + b_{ji}^{h}\right) \tag{11}$$

$$\Delta z_{ji} = \left(2\sinh\left(w_{ji}^{h}\Delta x\right)\right) / \left(\cosh\left(w_{ji}^{h}\Delta x\right) + \cosh\left(2w_{ji}^{h} x_i + 2b_{ji}^{h}\right)\right) \tag{12}$$

Assuming $w_{ji}^{h}\Delta x$ is small, $\sinh\left(w_{ji}^{h}\Delta x\right)$ approximates $w_{ji}^{h}\Delta x$ and $\cosh\left(w_{ji}^{h}\Delta x\right)$ approximates 1. Rewriting Eq. 12 yields

$$\Delta z_{ji} = \left(2w_{ji}^{h}\Delta x\right) / \left(1 + \cosh\left(2w_{ji}^{h} x_i + 2b_{ji}^{h}\right)\right) \tag{13}$$

Further, the density functions of x_i and Δx are respectively (where $K_1 \le x_i \le K_2$; $-\Delta x_i \le \Delta x \le \Delta x_i$; and $\sigma \le 0.01$)

$$f(x_i) = 1/(K_2 - K_1) \tag{14}$$

$$f(\Delta x) = \exp\left(\left(-\Delta x^2\right)/\left(2\sigma^2\right)\right)/\left(\sqrt{2\pi}\sigma\right) \tag{15}$$

Therefore, the joint density function of random variables x_i and Δx is

$$f(x_i, \Delta x) = \exp\left(\left(-\Delta x^2\right)/\left(2\sigma^2\right)\right)/\left((K_2 - K_1)\sqrt{2\pi}\sigma\right) \tag{16}$$

The equation for input sensitivity is derived by simple substitution. Repeat the above calculations for all inputs to obtain the order of input importance.

3 Theoretical Results

Example 1, from Sung's work, presents the input rankings of partially and fully connected neural networks. The networks are trained on the decoupled equation $y = (x_1 + 2)^2 + \sin(2\pi x_2)$, where $0 \le x_1, x_2 \le 1$. An additional input (denoted as x_3, $0 \le x_3 \le 1$) having no bearing on the value of y is introduced. Calculating the mathematical input sensitivity using the derivative of the output in terms of the inputs yields $\delta y/\delta x_1$=5, $\delta y/\delta x_2$=4.03 and $\delta y/\delta x_3$=0. Therefore, the ranking is $x_1 > x_2 > x_3$.

Table 1. Statistical and theoretical input sensitivities for example 1.

NN		Statistical Sensitivity			Theoretical Sensitivity			Input
Type	Inputs	x_1	x_2	x_3	x_1	x_2	x_3	Ranking
PCNN	x_1,x_2	1.00	0.72	NA	1.00	0.68	NA	$x_1>x_2$
PCNN	x_1,x_2,x_3	0.96	0.69	0.08	0.93	0.66	0.08	$x_1>x_2>x_3$
FCNN	x_1,x_2	0.70	0.58	NA	0.69	0.55	NA	$x_1>x_2$
FCNN	x_1,x_2,x_3	0.69	0.47	0.05	0.67	0.45	0.05	$x_1>x_2>x_3$

Example 2 presents the input rankings of partially and fully connected neural networks. The networks are trained on the coupled equation $y = \log(x_1) \times \exp(x_2)$. The noisy input from example 1 is also introduced. Calculating the mathematical input sensitivity using the derivative of the output in terms of the inputs yields $\delta y/\delta x_1$=12.05, $\delta y/\delta x_2$=1.67 and $\delta y/\delta x_3$=0. Therefore, the ranking is $x_1 > x_2 > x_3$.

Table 2. Statistical and theoretical input sensitivities for example 2.

NN		Statistical Sensitivity			Theoretical Sensitivity			Input
Type	Inputs	x_1	x_2	x_3	x_1	x_2	x_3	Ranking
PCNN	x_1,x_2	1.39	0.16	NA	1.34	0.15	NA	$x_1>x_2$
PCNN	x_1,x_2,x_3	1.39	0.15	0.07	1.35	0.14	0.07	$x_1>x_2>x_3$
FCNN	x_1,x_2	0.36	0.61	NA	0.35	0.61	NA	$x_2>x_1$
FCNN	x_1,x_2,x_3	0.43	0.56	0.03	0.41	0.56	0.03	$x_2>x_1>x_3$

In both examples, statistical and theoretical results are in close agreement (a trend that continued with additional experiments). In example 1, the rankings are as anticipated for both the PCNNs and FCNNs. In example 2, the rankings are as anticipated only for the PCNNs. Neither our method nor statistical simulation computes the correct ranking for FCNNs. When FCNNs are trained, the network weight updates are dependent on the magnitude of all inputs. Our equations assume weight updates are dependent only on the magnitude of the considered input (motivating the use of PCNNs). FCNNs violate this essential requirement, resulting in incorrect ranking.

4 Conclusions

This paper illustrates a new approach for determining input sensitivity ranking. The model has several advantages undisclosed in related literature. Specifically, the sensitivity of an input is independent of the magnitudes of other inputs. Calculating the sensitivity of input i is explicit since only input i is perturbed. When removing inputs from fully trained, partially connected neural networks, retraining is unnecessary. The theoretical model produces reliable input rankings when applied to PCNNs trained on either coupled or decoupled mappings. Moreover, the theoretical model strongly agrees with statistical results.

Future work includes extending the theoretical derivation to four-layers; examining correlated and dependent mappings; and exploring application areas.

References

1. Choi, J. Y.; Choi, C. H. *Sensitivity Analysis of Multilayer Perceptron with Differentiable Activation Functions.* IEEE Transactions on Neural Networks. vol. 3, no. 1, 1992, pp. 101-107.
2. Engelbrecht, A. P.; Cloete, I.; Zurada, J. M. *Determining the Significance of Input Parameters Using Sensitivity Analysis.* Proceedings 1995 International Workshop on Artificial Neural Networks. pp. 382-388.
3. He, F.; Sung, A. H.; Guo, B. *A Neural Network Model for Prediction of Oil Well Cement Bonding Quality.* Proceedings 1997 IASTED International Conference on Control. pp. 417-420.
4. Piche, S. *Robustness of Feedforward Neural Networks.* International Joint Conference on Neural Networks. vol. 2, 1992, pp. 346-351.
5. Sung, A. H. *Ranking Input Importance in Neural Network Modeling of Engineering Problems.* Proceedings 1998 IEEE International Joint Conference on Neural Networks. vol. 1, pp. 316-321.
6. Zurada, J. M.; Malinowski, A.; Cloete, I. *Sensitivity Analysis for Minimization of Input Data Dimension for Feedforward Neural Network.* Proceedings 1994 IEEE International Symposium on Circuits and Systems. vol. 6, pp. 447-450.

On the Influence of Synaptic Dilution on Memory Properties of Neural Networks

Robert A. Kosiński [a,b] **and Magdalena M. Sinołęcka** [c]

[a] Faculty of Physics, Warsaw Technical University, 00-662 Warsaw
[b] Central Institute for Labor Protection, 00-701 Warsaw, Poland
[c] Institute of Physics of Polish Academy of Sciences, 02-438 Warsaw, Poland

Abstract. Memory properties of two kinds of artificial neural networks – Hopfield and cellular – with four different types of dilution of synaptic connections, are investigated. Dilution of synaptic connections inside blocks forming the whole Hopfield network, dilution outside blocks, random dilution and dilution due to a specific cloning template of a cellular network are applied. A comparison of the number of stored patterns per neuron and per synapse is made for the networks under consideration.

1 A model of a neural network

Memory properties of artificial neural networks (ANN) are connected with one of their most important applications (see e.g. [1]). In Hopfield networks, full connection between neurons, convenient for analytical computations, is assumed. This assumption, however, does not correspond to the situation in the human brain, where each of $N \approx 10^{11}$ neurons has (on average) 10^4 synaptic connections with other neurons. On the other hand, in hardware applications of ANN it is easier to increase the number of neurons (e.g. semiconductor junctions) than the number of synaptic connections (i.e. the number of conducting paths), because of problems with the topology of paths. Thus, the idea of diluting synaptic connections without a significant decrease of the memory capacity of the network is clear.

In the present work, memory properties of a Hopfield network with new types of dilution of synaptic connections are investigated and discussed. Also, memory properties of cellular neural networks [2], widely applied in pattern recognition (see e.g. [2,3]) and investigations of complex phenomena like chaos or pattern formation [2,4,7], are investigated.

Our network consists of N neurons $S_i = \pm 1$ with synaptic connections $J_{ij} \in [-1,+1]$ designed according to Hebb's rule. In the network, p random patterns $\{\xi^\mu_i\}$ are stored and the effectiveness of the retrieval process is controlled, using overlap $m^\mu = N^{-1}\sum_i \xi_i^\mu S_i$, where $\mu = 1,2,3,\ldots p$ and $\{S_i\}$ is the current network state. Recognition of the pattern is correct if the final value of the overlap is $m^\mu > 0.97$. Patterns with 10% of flipped neurons are used as a starting configuration. Zero temperature of the network is assumed – neurons are updated asynchronically according to

$$S_i(t+1) = sign\,[\sum_j J_{ij} S_j(t)]\,. \tag{1}$$

Computations have been performed for the network of different sizes with N from 1024 to 14400 neurons and maximal network capacity $\alpha_c = p_+/N$, where p_+ denotes the maximal number of patterns which can be stored and successfully retrieved.

Two types of the structure of neural networks are investigated: 1) the Hopfield type with three different types of dilution of synaptic connections; 2) the cellular network where two indices i, j, indicating the row and the column of the neuron's location, with the cloning template containing connections only between all neurons in the same row and column, i.e. with dilution of synaptic connections.

2 Types of dilution of synaptic connections

In the case of the Hopfield network, the following three types of dilution of synaptic connections are examined. In the first type (dilution inside blocks) the network is divided into n blocks, each consisting of V neurons. All synaptic connections inside the blocks are cut, while connections between blocks have Hebb's form, which gives in the present case:

$$J_{ij}^{ab} = \begin{cases} \frac{1}{(n-1)V} \sum_{\mu=1}^{V} \xi_{ia}^{\mu} \xi_{jb}^{\mu} & a \neq b \\ 0 & a = b \end{cases} \tag{2}$$

where indices i, j indicate the neurons inside the blocks; a, b are indices locating a block in the network. For example, the matrix of synaptic connections $[J]$ for n = 4 blocks has the form

$$\begin{pmatrix} [0] & & & [J_{ij}] \\ & [0] & \ddots & \\ & \ddots & [0] & \\ [J_{ij}] & & & [0] \end{pmatrix}, \tag{3}$$

where $[0]$ denotes a matrix containing zeroes and $[J_{ij}]$ is a matrix resulting from Hebb's rule [5]. Choosing the size of the network N = 1260 neurons, there can be n = 2,3,4,5,6,7,9 blocks.

In the second type of dilution (dilution outside blocks), the network is divided into n blocks, similarly as above, but now all synaptic connections between the blocks are diluted in the following way: all connections between blocks are cut except connections between neurons with the same indices inside the blocks. Thus, the synaptic connections have the form

$$J_{ij}^{ab}=\begin{cases}\dfrac{1}{(n-1)V}\sum_{\mu=1}^{p}\xi_{ia}^{\mu}\xi_{jb}^{\mu} & a\neq b,\quad i=j\\ \dfrac{1}{(n-1)V}\sum_{\mu=1}^{p}\xi_{ia}^{\mu}\xi_{jb}^{\mu} & a=b,\quad i\neq j\\ 0 & other\end{cases}, \tag{4}$$

where *i, j, a* and *b* have the same meaning as earlier. Now matrix *[J]* for the whole network has the form

$$[J]=\begin{pmatrix}[J'] & [0'] & [0'] & [0']\\ [0'] & [J'] & [0'] & [0']\\ [0'] & [0'] & [J'] & [0']\\ [0'] & [0'] & [0'] & [J']\end{pmatrix} \tag{5}$$

where *[J']* is a matrix with 0 diagonal and other elements equal J_{ij} . *[0']* is a matrix with diagonal elements equal J_{ij} and other elements equal 0.

For comparison calculations for the standard, random dilution has been performed, with synaptic connections of the form:

$$J_{ij}=\frac{c_{ij}}{NC}\sum_{\mu=1}^{p}\xi_i^{\mu}\xi_j^{\mu} \tag{6}$$

where $c_{ij}=1$ with probability C, or 0 with probability $1-C$.

In the case of cellular network, synaptic connections of neuron S_{ij} are limited to connections with neurons in the same *i* (row) and *j* (column). They have Hebb's form, while other connections are equal zero. Matrix *[A]* of the cloning template for each neuron has the form

$$A=\begin{pmatrix}0 & \cdots & 1 & \cdots & 0\\ \cdots & \cdots & \cdots & \cdots & \cdots\\ 1 & \cdots & 1 & \cdots & 1\\ \cdots & \cdots & \cdots & \cdots & \cdots\\ 0 & \cdots & 1 & \cdots & 0\end{pmatrix}. \tag{7}$$

The neurons at the edges of the network have a reduced number of respective neighbours. Thus, the number l_{cd} of synaptic connections in the N-neuron network equals $l_{cd}=N(N^{1/2}-1)$, the number of synaptic connections in the case of a fully connected Hopfield network is $l_{fc}=N(N-1)/2$, hence the rate of dilution is given by the difference

$$\Delta l = l_{fc} - l_{cd} = \frac{N}{2}(N-1) - N(\sqrt{N}-1) = \frac{N}{2}(\sqrt{N}-1)^2 . \tag{8}$$

Thus, the reduction of synaptic connections with respect to fully connected network δ equals:

$$\delta = \Delta l / l_{cd} = (\sqrt{N}-1)/(\sqrt{N}+1) . \tag{9}$$

Calculating δ for a cellular network with $N = 1000$ neurons, we obtain a reduction of 93.86% of synaptic connections in the network.

3 Results and discussion

For an infinite Hopfield network, the maximal memory capacity is given by $\alpha_c = 0.138$ (see e.g. [1]), which means that when we try to store the next pattern, after pattern $p_+ = \alpha_c N$, a blackout catastrophe occurs, i.e. all the stored patterns are forgotten. This is due to the interference of other patterns in the process of retrieving one of them. This phenomenon is not observed for a finite size networks, as results e.g. from Fig.1, which shows maximal storage capacities of an infinite Hopfield network (Fig.1.a) and a network with $N = 1024$ neurons (Fig.1.b), as a function of the number of patterns per neuron $\alpha \equiv p/N$.

Fig.2 illustrates maximal storage capacity α_c as a function of dilution parameter C for dilution inside blocks (triangles), dilution outside blocks (circles) and random dilution (squares), for a network with $N = 1260$ neurons. Note that an increase in the number of blocks causes a reduction of storage capacity for both the cases – dilution inside and outside blocks. This is due to the fact that with the increase of the number of blocks i.e. $n \to N$, the network tends to a fully disconnected network.

It is interesting to observe maximal storage capacity per synapse α_c/C as a function of dilution parameter C for the types of dilution of the Hopfield network under consideration (Fig.3). It can be seen that this quantity, also measuring memory capabilities of the network, increases for all three types of dilution. Comparing these three types of dilution of the Hopfield network (Fig.2, Fig.3) it can be seen that the dilution inside the blocks is most effective. Moreover, it seems to be easier to perform this type of dilution in the hardware implementation of the network than random dilution with a definite value of C parameter.

Memory properties of diluted cellular networks have been examined for networks with N up to 14400. The maximal number of effectively stored patterns p_+ for such networks with the networks having the dilutions described above is shown in Fig.4. In this case, the maximal storage capacity of the network with N neurons can be approximated by the relation [6]:

$$\alpha_c = 0.332\ N^{-0.464} \quad . \tag{10}$$

As we can see, the storage capacity of this network, with such extreme dilution of synaptic connections for a rather large network with $N = 10\ 000$ neurons, equals $\alpha_c \approx 0.005$. This is approximately 28 times less than for a infinite, fully connected Hopfield network ($\alpha_c = 0.138$). In this case, too, blackout catastrophe is not observed.

By comparing memory capacity of the cellular network and the randomly diluted network we obtain $\alpha_c = 0.332 \times 1260^{-0.464} = 0.012$ for $N = 1260$ and the cellular network, while for the randomly diluted network with the same dilution, i.e. $C = \delta = 0.945$, according to Fig.2, we obtain $\alpha_c \approx 0.011$. Thus, we can notice that memory capacities of both types of networks are approximately the same, although the cellular network seems to have a simpler internal structure from the point of view of the topology of synaptic connections.

Let us consider a maximal number of effectively stored patterns p_+ per number of synaptic connections per neuron q, for a fully connected Hopfield network and the diluted cellular network under consideration in the limit $N \rightarrow \infty$. In our cellular network, the number of synaptic connections per neuron is $q = 2(N^{1/2} - 1)$. As results from our computations, for networks with $N > 2000$, the relation p_+/q can be approximated with $p_+/q \approx 0.23$, while for the infinite Hopfield network $p_+/q = 0.138$. Thus, this quantity shows that the diluted cellular network has better memory properties than the fully connected Hopfield network.

It can be concluded that the diluted networks under considerations, with respect to some quantifiers important in hardware implementations, have better memory properties than fully connected Hopfield networks. Moreover, it seems that new types of dilution present a more effective way of simplifying the internal network structure, than random dilution of synaptic connections. It should be remembered, however, that the present investigations concerned some networks of specific sizes and the *size effect* may limit some of the present conclusions. Interesting results concern memory properties of the cellular neural network with a simple topology of synaptic connections. In this case, the rate of dilution of synaptic connections is of the order of 93%, however, the memory capacity of such a network is still reasonable.

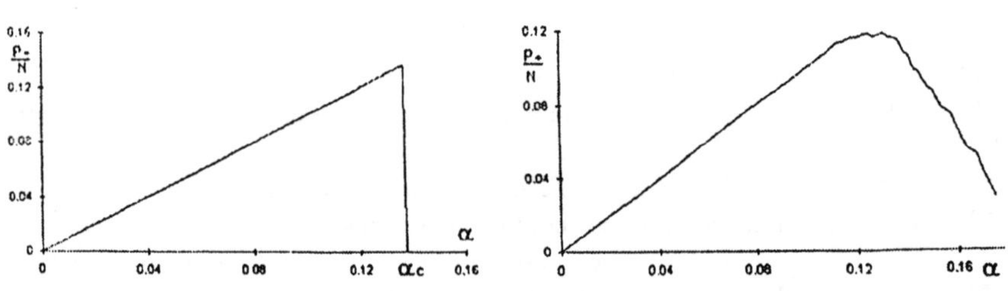

Fig.1.Maximal number of effectively stored patterns p_+/N as a function of the relative number of learned patterns $\alpha = p/N$, for a fully connected Hopfield network (left) and a network with $N = 1024$ neurons (right).

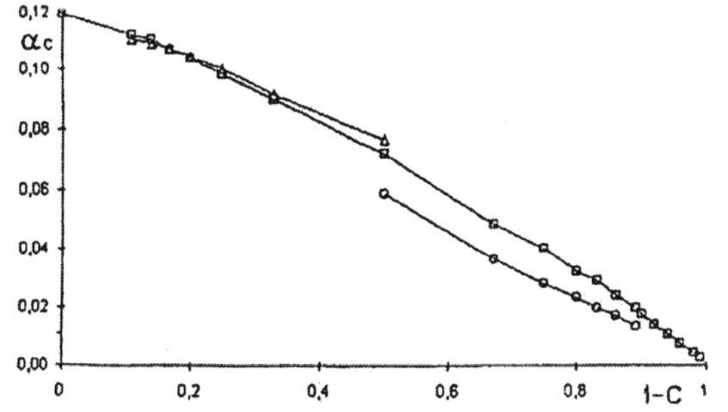

Fig.2. Maximal storage capacity α_c as a function of dilution parameter $1 - C$ for a network with $N = 1260$ neurons. Dilution inside blocks – triangles, dilution outside blocks – circles, random dilution – squares.

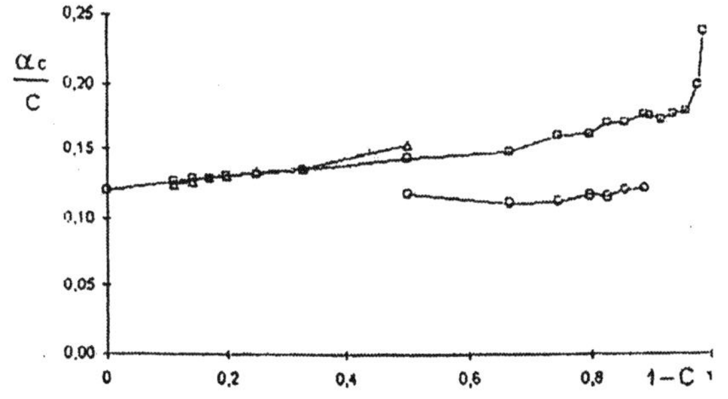

Fig.3. Maximal storage capacity per synapse α_c/C as a function of dilution parameter $1 - C$. The symbols on the curve are the same as in Fig.2.

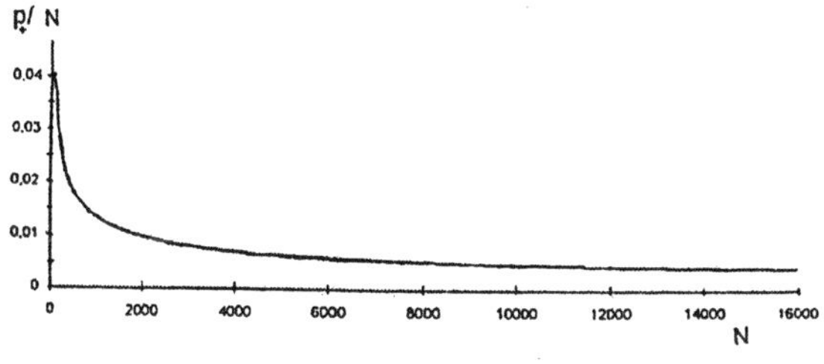

Fig.4. Maximal storage capacity p_+/N as a function of the number of neurons N in the diluted cellular network.

References

[1] P. Peretto, *An Introduction to the Modeling of Neural Networks*, Cambridge, Univ. Press, NY (1992)

[2] L.O. Chua and T. Roska, IEEE Trans. on Circuits and Systems, 40, 163 (1988)

[3] L.O. Chua, *CNN: a Paradigm for Complexity,* World Sci. Singapore (1998)

[4] J. Ito and K. Kaneko, Neural Net. 13, 275 (2000)

[5] R.A. Kosiński and M. Sinołęcka, Acta Phys. Polon. B 8, 2589 (1999)

[6] A. Popiołkiewicz and R.A. Kosiński, unpublished

[7] A.Krawiecki, A.Sukiennicki, R.A.Kosinski, Phys.Rev. E. 62,7683 (2000)

Evolutionary Algorithm vs. Other Methods for Constructive Optimisation of RBF Network Kernels

Jan Koszlaga, Paweł Strumiłło

Institute of Electronics, Technical University of Łódź, 18/22 Stefanowskiego, 90-924 Łódź, Poland, e-mail: koszlaga@ck-sg.p.lodz.pl, pstrumil@ck-sg.p.lodz.pl

Abstract. Three methods for optimising Radial Basis Function (RBF) neural network receptive field are compared in the paper, namely: gradient descent, simulation annealing, and evolutionary algorithm. An incremental RBF network training scheme is considered, i.e., in which RBF kernels are added one at the time and individually optimised. Algorithmic implementations of the tested optimisation methods for configuring the RBF receptive field are shown and their computation costs are compared. The considered optimisation methods yield excellent results for the classification benchmark of Iris flowers. For the genetic optimisation scheme three RBF Gaussian kernels are sufficient to achieve average classification accuracy of the Irises at the level of 98%.

1 Introduction

Radial Basis Function (RBF) neural network is a feedforward structure with one hidden layer composed of radial kernels $\varphi_j = \varphi(\|x - c_j\|)$, $j = 1, 2, \ldots, m$, where: $x \in X$ is the network input vector, c_j indicate radial functions positions in the input space $X \in R^N$ and $\|\cdot\|$ denotes a norm, e.g. Euclidean. From a wide class of admissible RBF kernels the Gaussian $\varphi(x) = exp(-x^2/\sigma^2)$ (where σ is its spread) is the most frequently used RBF kernel. Single output RBF network transfer function f_m comprising m-hidden kernels φ_j is given by a linear superposition:

$$f_m(x) = \sum_{j=1}^{m} w_j \varphi_j(x) = w^T \varphi(x) \tag{1}$$

This mapping turns out to offer powerful capabilities both in function approximation and data classification tasks [1], e.g., modelling of signals and systems, control, and telecommunications. A key to successful applications of RBF networks is suitable design of the receptive field that is defined by the set of basis kernels and finding best weight set w minimising network error, e.g., the sum-squared error that is usually used for testing network performance:

$$\varepsilon(c,\sigma,w)=\sum_{i=1}^{P}\left[d_i - f_m(x_i)\right]^2 \quad (2)$$

where: $\{x_i, d_i\}_{i=1}^{P}$ is the network training set (i.e., a subset of an entire available data with another, disjoined subset reserved for network testing). For a predefined number of network kernels m, it can be seen from (1) and (2), that computation of weights w can be realised by means of a linear method, whereas optimisation of kernel parameters, i.e.: kernel centres (c_j) and kernel widths (σ_j) for $j = 1,2,\ldots,m$ requires a nonlinear optimisation strategy. If these kernels parameters are fixed (or guessed) a priori disappointing results are usually obtained. Thus, there have been many supervised and unsupervised schemes developed for optimisation of RBF network receptive field [1]. Optimisation of centres by genetic programming was proposed in [2] and more recently in [3] for non-linear time-series prediction. Also, excellent results have been obtained in a method combining the orthogonal least squares and genetic algorithms for designing network receptive field [4].

In this study three optimisation algorithms are compared for optimising RBF network receptive field: gradient descent, simulation annealing, and an evolutionary algorithm. Once the receptive field is optimised, computation of network output weights is performed for evaluation of receptive field fit to the training data. Network weights are calculated by means of matrix pseudo-inverse method [1].

2 Optimisation of RBF network receptive field

The following incremental RBF network training scheme is proposed (Fig. 1). Kernels are added one at a time $m = m+1$ (starting from a single kernel) then, in each incrementation step, nonlinear optimisation of the current kernel parameters (by means of the tested optimisation algorithms) is carried out, and finally network output weights are computed so that network error can be evaluated.

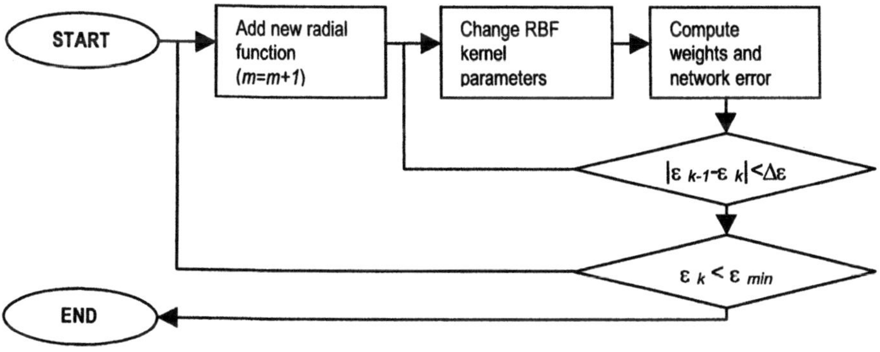

Fig. 1. Incremental training scheme for optimising RBF network receptive field

Two parameters of each new added Gaussian kernel are optimised, its centre c_m and its width σ_m. Within the kernel optimisation loop network output weights and network error ε_k are computed. The criterion for abandoning further optimisation of kernel parameters is $\Delta\varepsilon_k = |\varepsilon_{k-1} - \varepsilon_k| < \Delta\varepsilon^*$, i.e., for a predefined number of iterations there is no larger drop of the error than $\Delta\varepsilon^*$ (Fig. 1). If this criterion is satisfied, current kernel parameters are frozen and, if the network error margin ε_{min} is still not met, new kernel is added and its parameters optimised.

2.1 The method of steepest descent

There exist several versions of steepest descent methods [5]. The rules adopted for optimisation of kernel parameters are the following:

- optimisation of centres: $c_{t+1} = c_t + (rand(0..1) - 0.5) \cdot \sigma \cdot \eta_c$ (3)
- optimisation of widths: $\sigma_{t+1} = \sigma_t + (rand(0..1) - 0.5) \cdot \sigma \cdot \eta_\sigma$ (4)

where: *rand(0...1)* denotes a random number in the range [*0, 1*] and η_c, η_σ are coefficients defining step size of the steepest descent algorithm.

2.2 The method of simulated annealing

Simulated annealing is similar to steepest descent method. It has, however, a higher probability that network error (2) will achieve global minimum [5]. This is because an additional coefficient is added that introduces hazarding into the simulation annealing method. The simulated annealing method is a counterpart to physical annealing process. "Temperature" *T* represents the parameter that influences the probability of achieving the objective function. The pseudo-code of the procedure that is proposed for optimisation of RBF kernels is the following:

```
Repeat
  m=m+1, T = initial temperature
  Create radial function
    Repeat
      Change parameters using equations (3,4)
      Decrease temperature
      Calculate R = exp(-Δε_k / T)
    Until Δε_i = |ε_(k-1) - ε_k| < Δε* OR (rand(0..1) > R)
Until (ε_k < ε_min)
```

An example illustrating RBF network learning curves for three different rates at which the annealing parameter is decreased are shown in Fig. 2.

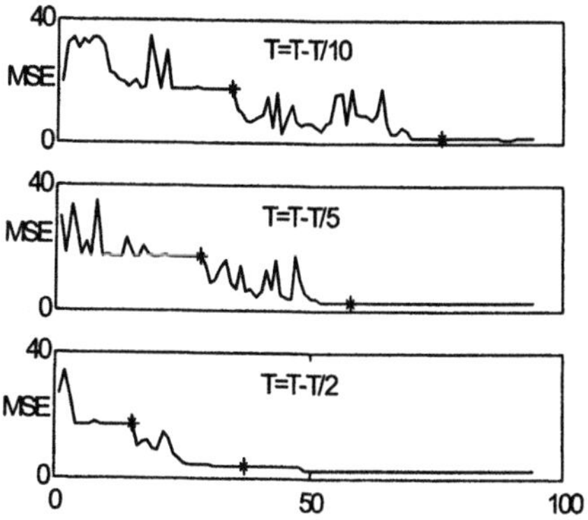

Fig. 2. Network mean square errors (MSE) vs. iteration number of the simulated annealing optimisation of the RBF receptive filed for three different schemes of changing the annealing parameter (the Iris classification benchmark)

2.3 Evolutionary optimisation

A general framework for this population based optimisation method is as follows [5]:

1. Generate initial population of random individuals.
2. Use genetic operators on the current population (crossover and mutation).
3. Selection a new population.
4. Check network performance by using the optimised parameters in the current RBF kernel.

Individuals S^i contain $N+1$ parameters to be optimised, namely kernel centre in N-dimensional input data space and its width:

$$S^i = \{c^i, \sigma^i\} = \{p_1^i, p_2^i, \ldots, p_{N+1}^i\} \tag{5}$$

In the crossover operation (taking place with the probability P_c) two individuals are selected. After the crossover operation the produced offsprings (new individuals) are:

$$S^i = \{p_1^i, p_2^i, \ldots, p_k^i, p_{k+1}^j, \ldots, p_{N+1}^j\} \tag{6a}$$

$$S^j = \{p_1^j, p_2^j, \ldots, p_k^j, p_{k+1}^i, \ldots, p_{N+1}^i\} \tag{6b}$$

where k is the crossover point chosen at random. Individuals are mutated with probability P_m using equations (3, 4).

Fig. 3a illustrates how the network learning curve depends on the size of the population and Fig. 3b proves that genetic search is much more efficient than random search for optimum RBF network parameters (computation example explained in section 3).

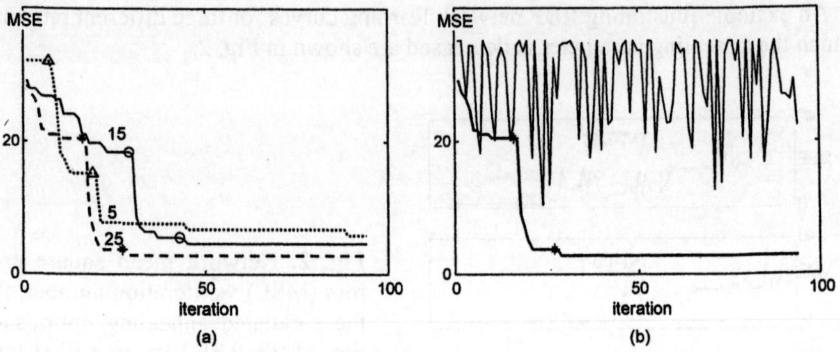

Fig. 3. (a) influence of the population size on the training rate of the RBF network, (b) comparison of random search and genetic search (thick line) for optimum RBF receptive filed (the Iris classification benchmark)

3 Computing results

A popular data classification benchmark of Iris flowers served for testing the optimisation methods on the task of configuring RBF receptive field. There are three classes of Irises (i.e., Setosa, Versicolor, and Virginica) to be classified on the basis of four flower features $\{x_1, x_2, x_3, x_4\}$, i.e., sepal length and width and petal length and width correspondingly. There are 50 feature vectors for each class of flowers. Thirty-five vectors were chosen for RBF network training and 15 left for network testing. RBF networks with 4 inputs and 3 outputs, trained according to the proposed incremental manner (Fig. 1), gave classification results shown in Table 1. These are averaged values for 50 different network training runs. Values presented in Table 1 do not change significantly for more than three basis functions.

Table 1. Confusion matrix for the Iris classification problem; presented results were obtained for RBF networks trained incrementally up to three hidden RBF Gaussian kernels

		Accuracy of RBF generated classification in [%]		
		Setosa	Versicolor	Virginica
Iris class	Setosa	100[a] / 100[b] / 100[c]	0	0
	Versicolor	0	97[a] / 95[b] / 97[c]	3[a] / 5[b] / 3[c]
	Virginica	0	8[a] / 8[b] / 3[c]	92[a] / 92[b] / 97[c]

[a] Method of steepest descent,
[b] Method of simulation annealing,
[c] Evolutionary structure optimisation

The optimisation methods were also compared in terms of computation cost. Number of floating point operations (FLOPS) required in each iteration of these methods is listed in Table 2. The listed computation costs represent average values due to statistical nature of the tested algorithms.

Table 2. Numbers of FLOPS for one iteration of the tested optimisation algorithms

Steepest descent	Simulated annealing	Evolutionary programming
~250.000 flops	~250.000 flops	~190.000[a] flops ~310.000[b] flops

[a] 15 individuals in population, [b] 25 individuals in population

4 Conclusions

Evolutionary programming, simulation annealing and the steepest descent method have been applied to configuring RBF neural network receptor field. All three tested methods proved very efficient in this task and are comparable in terms of the computing cost involved. Compact size RBF network trained by means of these algorithms was obtained. From the three tested methods, the best result was obtained by applying the evolutionary programming methods, for which only three RBF kernels were sufficient to achieve average classification accuracy of Iris flowers at the level of 98%. The presented study is a part of the research leading towards using RBF neural networks as knowledge extractors [6]. Compact size networks simplify the procedure of constructing rule bases.

References

1. Haykin S. (1994) Neural networks, a comprehensive foundation, Prentice Hall.
2. Whitehead B.A., Choate T.D. (1996) Cooperative-competitive genetic evolution of radial basis function centers and widths for time series prediction, IEEE Trans. Neural Networks, **7**, 4, 869–880
3. Hong S,-G., Oh S.-K., Kim M.-S., Lee J.-J. (2001) Nonlinear time series modelling and prediction using Gaussian RBF network with evolutionary structure optimization, Electronics Letters, **37**, 10, 639–640
4. Chen S., Wu Y., Luk B.L. (1999) Combined genetic algorithm optimisation and regularised orthogonal least squares learning for radial basis function networks, IEEE Trans. Neural Networks, **10**, 5, 1239–1243
5. Michalewicz Z. (1996) Genetic algorithms + data structures = evolution programs (in Polish), WNT, Warszawa
6. Koszlaga J., Strumiłło P. (2000) Rule extraction from trained Radial Basis Function neural networks, Colloquia in Artificial Intelligence, Poland, October 2000, 97–106

Heuristic Dynamic Programming for Neural Networks Learning Part 1: Learning as a Control Problem

Maciej Krawczak[1, 2]

[1] Systems Research Institute, Polish Academy of Sciences
[2] Warsaw School of Information Technology,
Newelska 6, 01-447 Warsaw, Poland

Summary. The learning process of multilayer neural networks can be considered as a multistage optimal control process. We introduce a gain parameter into the models of neurons. Setting the parameter to a small value makes the neuron model "almost linear", and the learning process problem can be solved using computational tools specified for *linear-quadratic* systems optimization. In Part 1 the continuation methodology is applied for changing the gain parameter in order to reach 1.0. In Part 2, by considering the gain parameter as an additional control variable, the optimal value of the parameter can be found. The methodology we propose to call the *heuristic dynamic programming*.

1 Introduction

Learning of a neural network is meant to adjust connections between layers (connections between neurons) in order to minimize the performance index of learning. For this, the backpropagation algorithm with various modifications is usually used. At the same time, the learning process of multilayer neural networks can be considered as a particular multistage optimal control problem, and can be naturally treated by the dynamic programming approach [4, 5, 7].

In this paper we introduce a gain parameter into the models of neurons. The value of this parameter is tacitly assumed to be 1.0 in almost all learning algorithms used. Note that setting the parameter to a small value makes the neuron model "almost linear". Thus, the learning process problem can be solved using computational tools specified for *linear-quadratic* systems optimization, like the first order differential dynamic programming methodology. Using the continuation methodology [6] the value of the gain parameter may be changed in order to reach 1.0.

2 Neuron Models with Parameters

Let us consider an artificial neuron model which is a nonlinear processing unit performing the operation $f(net)$ by means of the activation function, where *net* is the input to the neuron. There are two typical activation functions, commonly used, described by the sigmoidal functions:

unipolar

$$f(net,\lambda)=\frac{1}{1+\exp(-\lambda\; net)}, \tag{1}$$

and *bipolar*

$$f(net,\lambda)=\frac{2}{1+\exp(-\lambda\; net)}-1, \tag{2}$$

where $\lambda>0$ is the gain parameter, $1/\lambda$ being called sometimes the temperature of the system. This parameter describes the slope of the activation functions. These functions are shown in the following Fig. 1 and 2.

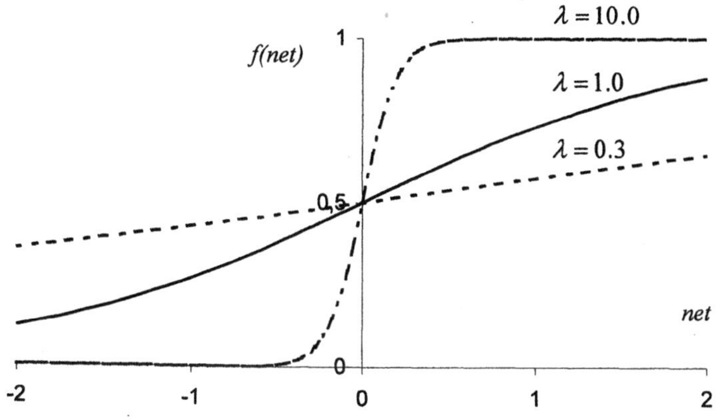

Fig. 1. A unipolar sigmoidal function with different gain values

We can observe how a curve changes with respect to the gain parameter λ. Assuming reasonable values of the input, for large value of the gain parameter the sigmoidal function terns into the Heaviside's function (the step function), while for small values of the parameter the sigmoidal function becomes an "almost linear" function.

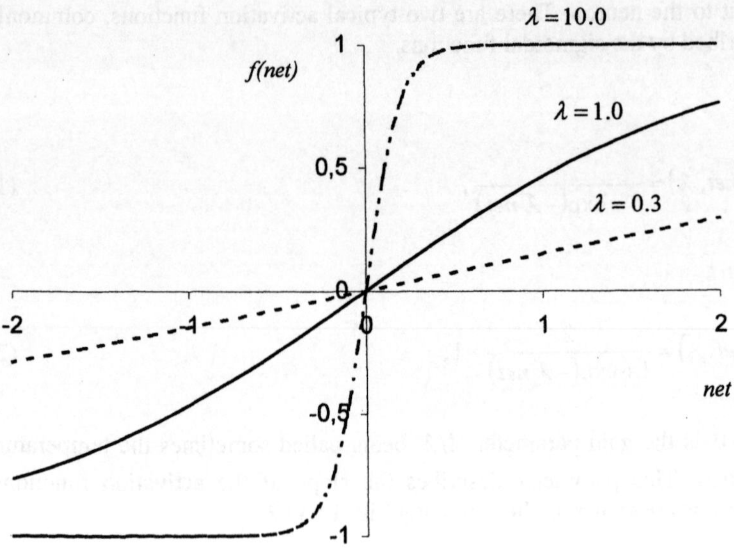

Fig. 2. A bipolar sigmoidal function with different gain values

3 The Continuation Method

In the literature on nonlinear optimization one can find a little known methodology called the *continuation method* [2], which allows finding *near optimal* solutions. The method is usually presented in terms of finding zeroes of a mapping $G : R^n \to R$, and it can be generalized for findings fixed points [9].

Following the papers of the present author [5, 6] we will consider the learning of the neural networks problem as the optimization problem

$$\min_{W[0,\,L-1]} \left\{ E = \frac{1}{2} \sum_{p=1}^{P} \left\| D_p - X_p(L) \right\|^2 \right\}, \tag{3}$$

subject to

$$X(l+1) = F[W(l),\, X(l)] \quad \text{for } l = 0,1,\ldots,L-1, \tag{4}$$

where $F(l)$ is an aggregated function of transition from one layer to another. Let $\widetilde{W}[0, L-1]$ be a solution of the problem (3)-(4). Now, let us consider the following homotopy

$$\min_{W[0, L-1]}\left\{E = \frac{1}{2}\sum_{p=1}^{P}\left\|D_p - X_p(L)\right\|^2\right\}, \tag{5}$$

subject to

$$X(l+1) = F[W(l), X(l), \lambda], \quad \text{for } l = 0,1,\ldots,L-1, \tag{6}$$

such that for $\lambda = 1$ the problem (5)-(6) is equivalent to (3)-(4). It is assumed that the problem (5)-(6) has some trivial, or easy to compute, solution for $\lambda = \lambda_0$. The value of the parameter λ_0 is treated as the starting point. Additionally, due to the "almost" linear-quadratic form of the considered problem, it is assumed that the solution obtained for $\lambda = \lambda_0$ is the global one. This assumption is based on the properties of the first order differential dynamic methodology described in [8].

Next, the problem can be imbedded into a family of problems with the parameter λ. Usually we do not consider the gain parameter, which means that we assume that the parameter is equal 1. The basic idea is as follows, if for all $\lambda \in [\lambda_0, 1]$ there exist weights $W(\lambda, [0, L-1])$ such that there are the solutions of (5)-(6), then the curve $W(\lambda, [0, L-1])$ can be found numerically starting at the point

$$W(\lambda_0, [0, L-1]) \text{ and ending at } W(1, [0, L-1]) = \widetilde{W}(1, [0, L-1]).$$

In the above expressions we use a special notation for describing a sequence of values, namely $W(\lambda, [l, r-1]) = [W(\lambda, (l)), W(\lambda, (l+1)), \ldots, W(\lambda, (r-1))]$.

In the case of the linear-quadratic optimization problem, like the neural netwoks learning, it is obvious that there does exist a solution of (5)-(6) for any $\lambda \in [\lambda_0, 1]$, where $0 < \lambda_0 \leq 1$. It is assumed that the curve $W(\lambda, [0, L-1])$ is continuous and has first derivatives.

This kind of approach is known in the literature as the continuation or homotopy method [2]. Due to the continuous differentiability of the considered sigmoidal activation functions, it is obvious that the function $W(\lambda, [0, L-1])$ is continuous and differentiable with respect to the gain parameter $0 < \lambda < +\infty$.

There are two main methods of finding the solution curve $W(\lambda, [0, L-1])$: the first is the discrete method [2] and the second – is the Davidenko's method [3].

Discrete method

The interval $[\lambda_0, 1]$ should be divided into several segments

$$\lambda_0 < \lambda_1 < \lambda_2 < \cdots \lambda_N = 1$$

and the corresponding partial problems

$$\min_{W[0,\,L-1]} \left\{ E = \frac{1}{2} \sum_{p=1}^{P} \left\| D_p - X_p(L) \right\|^2 \right\}, \tag{7}$$

subject to

$$X(l+1) = F[W(l), X(l), \lambda_k], \quad l = 0,1,\ldots,L-1, \tag{8}$$

for $k = 0,1,\ldots,N$, should be solved.

Starting with the known solution $W(\lambda_0, [0, L-1])$, obtained by applying the first order differential dynamic programming method, the new weights $W(\lambda_1, [0, L-1])$ are computed. The procedure is performed sequentially for all $\lambda_0 < \lambda_1 < \lambda_2 < \cdots \lambda_N = 1$ until the point $\lambda_N = 1$ is reached. The main problem is to determine the conditions of existence of the partition $\lambda_0 < \lambda_1 < \lambda_2 < \cdots \lambda_N = 1$ and the iterative process

$$\lambda_{k+1} = I(\lambda_k, W(k, [0, L-1])), \quad k = 0,1,\ldots,N. \tag{9}$$

According to [9], for linear-quadratic optimization problems the relationship (9) exists, and the problem of the partition of the range $[\lambda_0, 1]$ must ensure that the reachable sets of the obtained solution of (7)-(8)

$$\{W(\lambda_k, [0, L-1]), W(\lambda_{k+1}, [0, L-1])\}$$

and

$$\{W(\lambda_{k+1}, [0, L-1]), W(\lambda_{k+2}, [0, L-1])\},$$

for $k = 1, 2,\ldots, N-2$ overlap for each pair $\{\lambda_k, \lambda_{k+1}\}$, $k = 0,1,\ldots,N-1$.

Davidenko's method

The method requires writing the optimization problem in the following way

$$H(W(\lambda, [0, L-1]), \lambda) = 0 . \tag{10}$$

By differentiating (10) with respect to λ one can get the following Davidenko's differential equation

$$\begin{aligned} &H_W(W(\lambda, [0, L-1], \lambda))\frac{dW(\lambda, [0, L-1], \lambda)}{d\lambda} \\ &+ H_W(W(\lambda, [0, L-1], \lambda)) = 0 \end{aligned} \tag{11}$$

with $W(\lambda_0, [0, L-1], \lambda_0)$ as the initial conditions, and by numerical integration from λ_0 to 1.0 - the solution $\widetilde{W}[0, L-1] = W(1, [0, L-1])$. The main difficulty is the implicit nature of this equation for such complex problems as the neural network learning.

4 Conclusions

The proposed application of the continuation method combined with the first order differential dynamic optimization approach gives the new possibility of finding the global optimal value of the performance index of the learning process for the multilayer feedforward neural networks. In some sense the approach is similar to the idea of simulated annealing methodology [1].

References

1. AARTS, E., LAARHOVEN, P. (1987). Simulated Annealing: Theory and Practice. Wiley and sons, N-Y.
2. AVILA, J. H., (1974). The Feasibility of Continuation Methods for Nonlinear Equations. *SIAM J. Numer. Anal.*, vol. 11, No. 1.
3. DAVIDENKO, D. (1953). *On the Approximate Solution of a System of Nonlinear Equations*. Dokl. Akad. SSSR, 88, 601-604. (in Russian).
4. KRAWCZAK, M. AND MIZUKAMI, K. (1994). The control theory approach to perceptron learning process. *IEE of Japan*, Okayama.
5. KRAWCZAK, M. (2000a). Backpropagation versus dynamic programming approach. *Bulletin of Polish Academy of Sciences*. Vol. 48, No. 2, pp. 167-180.
6. KRAWCZAK, M. (2000b). Feedforward neural networks learning by continuation method. *Proc. IIZUKA'2000*. Fukuoka - Japan, October 2000.
7. KRAWCZAK, M. (2001a). Parameterization of neural networks learning. *Proc. 14th Int. Conference on Systems Science*, Wrocław, Poland, September 2001.
8. KRAWCZAK, M. (2001b). Neural networks learning as a particular optimal control problem. *Proc. 7th Int. Conference on Methods and Models in Automation and Robotics,* IEEE, Międzyzdroje, Poland, August 2001.
9. ORTEGA J. M., RHEINBOLDT, W. C. (1970). *Iterative Solution of Nonlinear Equations in Several Variables*. Academic Pres, N-Y, S. Francisco, London.

Heuristic Dynamic Programming for Neural Networks Learning Part 2: I-order Differential Dynamic Programming

Maciej Krawczak[1, 2]

[1] Systems Research Institute, Polish Academy of Sciences
[2] Warsaw School of Information Technology,
Newelska 6, 01-447 Warsaw, Poland

Summary. The learning process of multilayer neural networks is considered as a multistage optimal control process. For small values of the gain parameter of used neurons for the learning differential dynamic programming of first order can be applied. Adjustment of the gain parameters can be done by continuation methodology as was described in [1]. In this paper by considering the gain parameter as an additional control variable,, starting form a small value of the parameter, the optimal value of the parameter is found. The methodology we propose to call the *heuristic dynamic programming.*

1 Introduction

The learning process of a neural network is considered as a special case of optimal control problem. The layers can be treated as stages, weights of neuron connection correspond to controls. In [1] a gain parameter of used neurons was considered, for a small value of the parameter the optimization problem becomes an *"almost linear" – quadratic* optimal control problem. This kind of problems can be solved by e.g. differential dynamic programming approach [3, 4, 5]. By including the gain parameter to control parameters the same procedure (differential dynamic programming) we are ready to find the optimal value of this parameter.

The application of methodology based on dynamic programming we can assume that if there exist optimal solution of the neural network learning problem then the found solution, both weights and the gain parameter are optimal.

This paper is a continuation of [1] and the used notation here is exactly the same, and the reader is ask for reading first Part 1.

2 Differential Dynamic Programming

Let us rewrite the considered first order differential dynamic programming method, and introduce the gain parameter into the neuron models, as follows.

The return function has the form of a multi stage system, a like feedforward neural network, has the form

$$V(X(0), W[0, L-1], \lambda) = \frac{1}{2}\sum_{p=1}^{P}\|D_p - X_p(L)\|^2 . \qquad (1)$$

The first order expansion of the return function for the whole network $V(X(0), W[0, L-1], \lambda)$ about some nominal weights $\overline{W}[0, L-1]$ and a nominal parameter $\overline{\lambda}$ can be written as

$$\begin{aligned} & V(X'(0), W'[0, L-1], \lambda') \\ & = V(\overline{X}(0), \overline{W}[0, L-1], \overline{\lambda}) \\ & + \frac{\partial V(\overline{X}(0), \overline{W}[0, L-1], \overline{\lambda})}{\partial W[0, L-1]} \delta W[0, L-1] \\ & + \frac{\partial V(\overline{X}(0), \overline{W}[0, L-1], \overline{\lambda})}{\partial \lambda[0, L-1]} \delta\lambda . \end{aligned} \qquad (2)$$

The variations in the weight variables $\delta W = W' - \overline{W}$ and the parameter $\delta\lambda = \lambda' - \overline{\lambda}$ must be small enough to ensure the validity of the expansion. Choosing δW and $\delta\lambda$ as

$$\delta W[0, L-1] = \eta \left[\frac{\partial V(\overline{X}(0), \overline{W}[0, L-1], \overline{\lambda})}{\partial W[0, L-1]} \right]^T \qquad (3)$$

and

$$\delta\lambda = \eta \left[\frac{\partial V(\overline{X}(0), \overline{W}[0, L-1], \overline{\lambda})}{\partial \lambda} \right]^T \qquad (4)$$

where η is the learning parameter, we obtain that the return function

$$V(X'(0), W'[0, L-1], \overline{\lambda})$$

will be smaller than

$$V(\overline{X}(0), \overline{W}[0, L-1], \overline{\lambda}).$$

Instead of consideration of the return function for the whole network $V(X(0, W[0, L-1], \lambda))$, the backward form can be calculated

$$V(X(l), W[l, L-1], \lambda) = V(X(l+1), W[l+1, L-1], \lambda) \tag{5}$$

for l, $l = 1,2,\ldots, L-1$, with the condition for the last layer

$$V(X(L), W[L-1, L-1], \lambda) = \frac{1}{2}\sum_{p=1}^{P} \|D_p - X_p(L)\|^2 . \tag{6}$$

The partial derivative of the return function (5) takes the form

$$V_W(l) = F_W^T(l) V_X(l+1, \lambda) F_W(l). \tag{7}$$

In order to obtain (7) the expression must be calculated $V_X(l, \lambda)$, which can be calculated using the following sequential relations

$$V_X(L, \lambda) = -\sum_{p=1}^{P} \|D_p - X_p(L)\| . \tag{8}$$

$$V_X(l, \lambda) = F_X(l) V_X(l+1, \lambda). \tag{9}$$

The derivative of the return function $V(X(0, W[0, L-1], \lambda))$ with respect to λ is obtained in a similar manner, as

$$V_\lambda(L, \lambda) = -\sum_{p=1}^{P} \|D_p - X_p(L)\| \tag{10}$$

$$V_\lambda(l, \lambda) = V_\lambda(l+1, \lambda) + F_\lambda(l) V_X(l+1, \lambda) \tag{11}$$

where $V_X(l+1, \lambda)$ is given by (8) and (9).

Using Equations 8 - 10, the gradients of the return functions, which are required for Equations 9 and 11, can be computed from the sequence of the equations solved from the last layer back to the inputs.

The parameter λ can be found at the input layer by minimizing the optimal return function $V'(X'(0), W'[0, L-1], \bar{\lambda})$ with respect to λ.

3 The Heuristic Dynamic Programming Algorithm

The heuristic differential dynamic programming algorithm for the learning of multilayer neural networks can be formulated in the following steps:

1. Initialise weights: $W(l) = \overline{W}(l), \quad l = 0, 1, 2, \ldots, L-1$
   $\overline{\lambda}$ as a small value, e.g. 0.1

2. Set: $E = 0$

3. Set: $p = 0$ (p denotes the index of the pattern's number)

4. Submit a pattern: $(X_p(0), D_p), \quad p = p+1$

5. Compute the layers' outputs: $X(l) = \overline{X}(l), \quad l = 1, 2, \ldots, L$ from the system equation and the nominal weights and parameter
6. Compute the performance index of learning:

$$E = E + \frac{1}{2}\left\|D_p - \overline{X}_p(L)\right\|^2, \tag{12}$$

7. Compute the partial derivatives:

$V_X(l) = V_X(\overline{X}(l), \overline{W}[l, L-1], \overline{\lambda})$ for $l = L, L-1, \ldots, 0$ from

$$V_X(l) = F_X(l)\, V_X(l+1) \tag{13}$$

$$V_X(L) = -\left\|D_p - X_p(L)\right\|$$

$$V_\lambda(l) = V_\lambda(l+1) + F_\lambda(l)\, V_X(l+1) \tag{14}$$

$$V_\lambda(L) = -\sum_{p=1}^{P}\left\|D_p - X_p(L)\right\|$$

8. Compute the gradient of the return function with respect to the weights for each level:

$$\frac{\partial V(\overline{X}(l), \overline{W}[l, L-1], \overline{\lambda})}{\partial \overline{W}(l)}$$

$$= \left[\frac{\partial F(\overline{X}(l), \overline{W}(l))}{\partial \overline{W}(l)} \right]^T \frac{\partial V(\overline{X}(l+1), \overline{W}[l+1, L-1], \overline{\lambda})}{\partial \overline{X}(l+1)} \tag{15}$$

for $l = L-1,,...,0$

9. Choose the learning parameter $\eta > 0$ and compute the new weight values

$$W'(l) = \overline{W}(l) - \eta \left[\frac{\partial V(\overline{X}(l), \overline{W}[l, L-1], \overline{\lambda})}{\partial \overline{W}(l)} \right]^T \tag{16}$$

10. If $p = P$ then goto Step 3 else goto Step 11

11. If $l = 0$ then compute the new value of the gain parameter

$$\lambda' = \overline{\lambda} - \eta \left[\frac{\partial V(\overline{X}(0), \overline{W}[0, L-1], \overline{\lambda})}{\partial \lambda} \right]^T \tag{17}$$

12. Set

$$\overline{W}[0, L-1] = W'[0, L-1]$$

$$\overline{W}[0, L-1] = W'[0, L-1]$$

$$\overline{X}[1, L] = X'[1, L]$$

$$\overline{\lambda} = \lambda'$$

13. If $E < E_{MAX}$ then goto STOP else goto Step 3

STOP

4 Conclusions

The first order differential dynamic programming algorithm can ensure global optimisation of the learning process for the neural networks with the linearized models of neurons. By introducing the approach to the optimisation of the gain parameter the methodology allows for finding the global optimum of the learning index performance. We will call this method the heuristic dynamic programming for the multilayer neural networks learning.

The methodology can be extended for a case where each neuron in the network is characterized by an individual gain parameter.

4 References

1. KRAWCZAK, M., (2002). Heuristic Dynamic Programming for Neural Network Learning, Part 1: Learning as a Control Problem.
2. AVILA, J. H., (1974). The Feasibility of Continuation Methods for Nonlinear Equations. *SIAM J. Numer. Anal.*, vol. 11, No. 1.
3. KRAWCZAK, M. AND MIZUKAMI, K. (1994). The control theory approach to perceptron learning process. *IEE of Japan*, Okayama.
4. KRAWCZAK, M. (1995). Differential dynamic programming of first order as backpropagation interpretation. *Proc. 12th Int. Conference on Systems Science*, Wrocław, Poland, September 1995.
5. KRAWCZAK, M. (1999). Dynamic learning for feedforward neural networks. *Proc. ICONIP'99 ANZIIS'99&ANNES'99 &ACNN'99*, Perth, Australia, November 1999.
6. KRAWCZAK, M. (2000a). Backpropagation versus dynamic programming approach. *Bulletin of Polish Academy of Sciences*. Vol. 48, No. 2, pp. 167-180.
7. KRAWCZAK, M. (2001a). Parameterization of neural networks learning. *Proc. 14th Int. Conference on Systems Science*, Wrocław, Poland, September 2001.
8. KRAWCZAK, M. (2001b). Neural networks learning as a particular optimal control problem. *Proc. 7th Int. Conference on Methods and Models in Automation and Robotics*, IEEE, Międzyzdroje, Poland, August 2001.
9. ORTEGA J. M., RHEINBOLDT, W. C. (1970). *Iterative Solution of Nonlinear Equations in Several Variables*. Academic Pres, N-Y, S. Francisco, London.
10. RICHTER S., R., DE CARLO, R. (1984). A Homotopy Method for Eigenvalue Assignment Using Decentralized State Feedback. *IEEE Transactions on Automatic Control*, Vol. AC-29, 2.

Evaluation of Dipolar Neural Networks in Survival Time Prediction

Małgorzata Krętowska[1] and Leon Bobrowski[1,2]

[1] Faculty of Computer Science, Technical University of Białystok, Wiejska 45a, 15-351 Białystok, Poland
[2] Institute of Biocybernetics and Biomedical Engineering PAS, Ks. Trojdena 4, Warsaw, Poland
e-mail: mmac@ii.pb.bialystok.pl; leon.bobrowski@ibib.waw.pl

Abstract. In this paper a dipolar neural network designed for prediction of survival time is presented. The proposed method is based on minimization of piece-wise linear criterion functions. Basis exchange algorithms are exploited as an optimization technique. The method allows estimation of discrete hazards as conditional probabilities of failure occurrence. The prediction capacity of neural network models is evaluated by accuracy, sensitivity, and specificity measures, which are compared to results of logistic regression.

1 Introduction

Artificial neural networks can be regarded as an alternative method to the statistical models [4,11], which often require some prior assumptions. In this paper a neural network application for prediction of the time of a specific event occurrence (survival time) is considered. Survival data [5] are a set of covariates vectors with an additional variable. In case of patients, for whom the event of interest (e.g. death, disease relapse) occurred, the variable represents failure time. If the event did not occur, the variable expresses follow-up time. For the latter, so called censored cases, we do not know the exact failure time, we only know that it is no less than their follow-up time. Such incomplete information causes several problems in analysis of survival data. As ignoring the information from censored cases may bias the outcome, techniques which are able to cope with censoring are needed.

Several approaches to adapt artificial neural networks to the analysis of survival data have been proposed so far. The most common idea is to divide the survival time into disjoint intervals and train a neural network model to classify patients failure times into appropriate time intervals. Depending on the structure of a neural network, the output may be regarded as failure probability [7], hazard function [1], or cumulative failure probability [8] in ordered time intervals.

In this paper we evaluate the capacity of dipolar neural networks [6] for prediction of discrete hazards as conditional probabilities of failure. The approach is compared to logistic regression, which is widely used in medical applications.

2 Grouped survival data

Grouped survival time is considered in the paper. The failure time is divided into K disjoint intervals I_k $(k = 1, 2, \ldots, K)$, where $I_k = [t_{k-1}, t_k)$ and $0 < t_1 < t_2 < \ldots < t_K$, $t_0 = 0$, $t_K < \infty$. Each patient O_i $(i = 1, 2, \ldots, M)$ is described by $(\mathbf{x}_i, \delta_i, t_i)$, where $\mathbf{x}_i$ is N-dimensional covariates vector, δ_i - failure indicator (is equal to 1 for uncensored cases and 0 otherwise) and t_i - survival time.

The analysis is focused on prediction of the conditional failure probabilities (dicrete hazards), in separate time intervals. The hazard rate in the k-th time interval is defined as $h_k = P(t \in I_k / t > t_{k-1})$. Taking into account the likelihood function built on a given data set we receive:

$$-\log L = -\sum_{i=1}^{M} \sum_{k=1}^{K_i} \{d_{ki} \log h_{ki} + (1 - d_{ki}) \log(1 - h_{ki})\} \tag{1}$$

where K_i specifies the last time interval in which the subject O_i was observed, d_{ki} is a censoring indicator, which is equal to 1 for time interval I_{K_i} for uncensored subject O_i and equal to 0 otherwise. The equation shows that the censoring indicator d_{ki} can be treated as an estimator of the hazard h_{ki}.

3 Modular neural network

Prediction of the conditional failure probabilities is done by using a modular neural network [6]. The network consists of $K - 1$ ordered neural networks NN_k (Fig. 1). Each network NN_k is trained to differentiate patients with the failure time belonging to the k-th time interval (the output equal to 1) from other patients being at risk in this time interval (0 at the output).

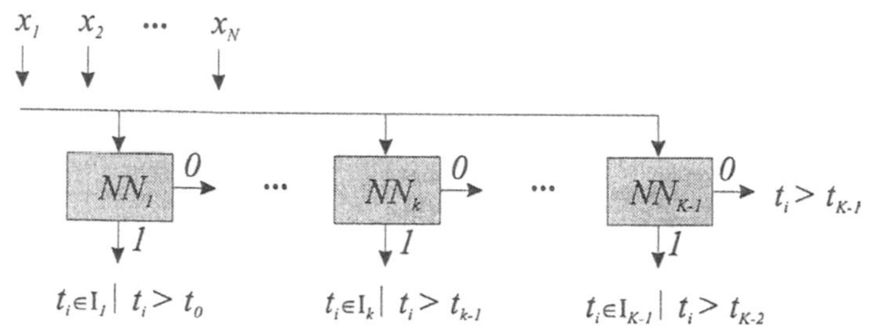

Fig. 1. The structure of modular neural network

A rule for prediction of the hazard rates for a new patient O_i is shown in Fig. 1. A new covariates vector $\mathbf{x}_i$ (describing the patients O_i) is given for the input of the network NN_1. If the module returns 1, the patient is supposed to fail in the first time interval. The output equal to 0 means, that the patient survives the first interval. and the vector $\mathbf{x}_i$ is given for the input of the next network. The procedure is repeated until one of the modules returns 1 or the last network NN_K is reached.

3.1 Learning of dipolar neural network

Each dipolar neural network NN_k consists of three layers: input, hidden and output layer. The hidden layer is built from neurons with the binary activation function.

The proposed learning procedure is based on the concept of dipoles [2]. The dipole is a pair of different covariates vectors $(\mathbf{x}_i, \mathbf{x}_j)$ from the learning set. We distinguish mixed and pure dipoles. Mixed dipoles are formed between objects, which should be separated while pure ones between objects which are similar from the point of view of an analyzed criterion.

Considering the k-th time interval we take into account only those patients, who are at risk in this interval. The main goal is to separate patients who are supposed to fail in the k-th time interval from those, who fail later. In this case the mixed dipoles are formed between each two objects O_i and O_j with $d_{ki} \neq d_{kj}$. If $d_{ki} = d_{kj}$ objects O_i and O_j constitute a pure dipole.

Let us introduce two types of piece-wise linear and convex (CPL) penalty functions $\varphi_j^+(\mathbf{v})$ and $\varphi_j^+(\mathbf{v})$:

$$\varphi_j^+(\mathbf{v}) = \begin{cases} \delta_j - <\mathbf{v}, \mathbf{y}_j> & \text{if } <\mathbf{v}, \mathbf{y}_j> \leq \delta_j \\ 0 & \text{if } <\mathbf{v}, \mathbf{y}_j> > \delta_j \end{cases} \quad (2)$$

$$\varphi_j^-(\mathbf{v}) = \begin{cases} \delta_j + <\mathbf{v}, \mathbf{y}_j> & \text{if } <\mathbf{v}, \mathbf{y}_j> \geq -\delta_j \\ 0 & \text{if } <\mathbf{v}, \mathbf{y}_j> < -\delta_j \end{cases} \quad (3)$$

where $\mathbf{y}_j = [1, x_1, \ldots, x_N]^T$ is an augmented covariates vector and $\mathbf{v} = [-\theta, w_1, \ldots, w_N]^T$ is an augmented weight vector. Each mixed dipole $(\mathbf{y}_i, \mathbf{y}_j)$, which should be divided, is associated with a function $\varphi_{ij}^m(\mathbf{v})$ being a sum of two function with opposite signs ($\varphi_{ij}^m(\mathbf{v}) = \varphi_j^+(\mathbf{v}) + \varphi_i^-(\mathbf{v})$ or $\varphi_{ij}^m(\mathbf{v}) = \varphi_j^-(\mathbf{v}) + \varphi_i^+(\mathbf{v})$). For pure dipoles, which should stay undivided, we associate a function $\varphi_{ij}^p(\mathbf{v})$ ($\varphi_{ij}^p(\mathbf{v}) = \varphi_j^+(\mathbf{v}) + \varphi_i^+(\mathbf{v})$ or $\varphi_{ij}^c(\mathbf{v}) = \varphi_j^-(\mathbf{v}) + \varphi_i^-(\mathbf{v})$). A dipolar criterion function is a sum of penalty functions associated with each dipole:

$$\Psi_d(\mathbf{v}) = \sum_{(j,i)\in I_p} \alpha_{ij}\varphi_{ij}^p(\mathbf{v}) + \sum_{(j,i)\in I_m} \alpha_{ij}\varphi_{ij}^m(\mathbf{v}) \quad (4)$$

where α_{ij} determines relative importance (price) of the dipole $(\mathbf{y}_i, \mathbf{y}_j)$, I_p and I_m are the sets of pure and mixed dipoles, respectively. The parameters of neurons in a hidden layer are obtain by sequential minimization of the dipolar criterion function. The minimization is done by using basis exchange algorithms [3], similar to linear programming. The hidden layer divides the whole N-dimensional feature space into disjoint areas. Each area is connected with one of the two distinguished classes: patients who fail in the k-th interval, and patients who survive. A decision element in the output layer returns 1 if the input vector belongs to the area connected with first class and 0 otherwise.

4 Logistic regression

One of the most common methods used in medical applications for classification is logistic regression [11]. It can be also used to predict hazard rates for sequential time intervals I_k. For each module NN_k we could calculate (if the assumptions are fulfilled) an alternative logistic regression model LR_k:

$$\frac{P(t \in I_k | \mathbf{y}, t > t_{k-1})}{P(t > t_k | \mathbf{y}, t > t_{k-1})} = \exp(\beta^T \mathbf{y}) \qquad (5)$$

where $\beta = [\beta_0, \beta_1, \ldots, \beta_N]^T$ is a vector of regression coefficients. The LR_k model should separate patients with different d_{ki} values. Thus only patients who are at risk in the k-th time interval are taken into account while calculating the regression coefficients.

5 Experimental results

The data set from the Veteran's Administration (VA) lung cancer study [5] is considered. In this trial, male patients with advanced inoperable tumors were randomized to either standard (69 subjects) or test chemotherapy (68 subjects). Only 9 subjects from 137 were censored. Information on performance status at baseline (Karnofsky rating - KPS), disease duration in months, age in years at randomization, prior therapy (yes, no), and cell type (large, squamous, small, adeno), was available. The survival time was divided into three intervals (see table 1).

Table 1. Description of survival time intervals

Time interval	Uncensored cases (n)	Censored cases (n)
$I_1 : \langle 0, 31)$	39	1
$I_2 : \langle 31, 100)$	39	3
$I_3 : \langle 100, \ldots)$	50	5

The quality of the models is evaluated by accuracy, sensitivity and specificity measures. A comparison of the above measures was done by using McNemar's test for no association for matched pairs [10].

Logistic regression analysis and McNemar's test were performed using SAS STAT package. A p-value of less than 0.05 was regarded as statistically significant. Selection of the appropriate structure of the NN_k networks (the number of neurons in hidden layers) was done by using a nested cross-validation method [9]. We received three neurons for NN_1 module and four neurons for NN_2.

Table 2. Evaluation of quality of dipolar neural networks NN_k and logistic regression LR_k

	NN_1	LR_1	NN_2	LR_2
TP (n)	30	26	23	19
FN (n)	11	15	15	19
FP (n)	18	9	17	9
TN (n)	78	87	40	48
Accuracy (%)	78.8	82.5	66.3	70.5
(95% CI)	(71.1; 85.4)	(75; 88.5)	(55.9; 75.7)	(60.3; 79.4)
Sensitivity (%)	73.2	63.4	60.5	50
(95% CI)	(57.1; 85.8)	(46.9; 77.9)	(43.4; 75.9)	(33.4; 66.6)
Specificity (%)	81.3	90.6	70.2	84.2
(95% CI)	(72; 88.5)	(83; 96)	(56.6; 81.5)	(72.1; 92.5)
McNemar's test (p)	0.194	0.004	0.724	0.059

The quality measures of dipolar neural networks and logistic regression models are shown in table 2. Taking into consideration dipolar neural networks, the differences between capacity for failures and survivors prediction are not significant ($p = 0.194$ and $p = 0.724$). In case of logistic regression models the differences are significant for LR_1 ($p = 0.004$) and marginally significant for LR_2 ($p = 0.059$).

Table 3. Comparison of dipolar neural networks NN_k to the results obtained for logistic regression models LR_k (p-values for McNemar's test)

	NN_1 vs. LR_1	NN_2 vs. LR_2
Accuracy	0.166	0.346
Sensitivity	0.046*	0.206
Specificity	0.003*	0.005*

* - statistically significant differences at 0.05 significance level

The accuracy of neural network modules is lower than logistic regression models (table 2), but the differences are not statistically significant (see table 3: $p = 0.166$ and $p = 0.206$). Statistically significant differences are between sensitivity, of NN_1 and LR_1 models ($p = 0.046$) and between specificity of two approaches ($p = 0.003$ and $p = 0.005$ for NN_1 vs. LR_1 and NN_2 vs. LR_2 respectively).

6 Conclusions

The artificial neural network approach was proposed for prediction of discrete hazards as conditional probabilities of failure occurrence. Prediction quality of each single dipolar neural network, which is included in a modular network, was compared to a relative logistic regression model. The accuracy of the models was comparable. Statistically significant differences were found between sensitivity and specificity for the two approaches. The capacity of correct failures prediction (sensitivity) of logistic regression models was worse than the capacity of dipolar neural networks. On the other hand, the ability of correct survivors prediction (specificity) was better for logistic regression models. The differences between specificity and sensitivity for dipolar neural networks models were not very high (about 10%). In case of logistic regression models the sensitivity was about 30% lower than specificity. As from medical point of view correct failures prediction is more important, the modular neural network can be regarded as a useful tool for survival time prediction.

Acknowledgements This work was supported by the grant W/WI/1/02 from Technical University of Białystok.

References

1. Biganzoli E., Boracchi P., Mariani L., Marubini E. (1998) Feed forward neural networks for the analysis of censored survival data: a partial logistic regression approach. Statistics in Medicine **17**(10), 1169–1186
2. Bobrowski L., Krętowska M., Krętowski M. (1997) Design of neural classifying networks by using dipolar criterions. Proc. of the Third Conference on Neural Networks and Their Applications, 689–694
3. Bobrowski L., Niemiro W. (1984) A method of synthesis of linear discriminant function in the case of nonseparability. Pattern Recognition **17**, 205–210
4. Cheng B., Titterington D. M. (1994) Neural Networks: A Review from a Statistical Perspective. Statistical Science **9**(1), 2–30
5. Kalbfleisch J. D., Prentice R. L. (1980) The Statistical Analysis of Failure Time Data. John Wiley & Sons
6. Krętowska M. (2001) Dipolar neural networks applied to censored survival data. Biocybernetics and Biomedical Engineering **21**(2), 55–65
7. Ohno-Machado L. (1997) A comparison of Cox proportional hazards and artificial neural network models for medical prognosis. Comput. Biol. Med. **27**(1)
8. Ohno-Machado L., Musen M. (1997) Modular neural networks for medical prognosis: Quantifying the benefits of combining neural networks for survival prediction. Connection Science **9**, 71–96.
9. Ripley R. M. (1998) Neural networks for breast cancer prognosis. PhD Thesis, Department of Engineering Science, University of Oxford
10. SAS Institute Inc. (1996) SAS/STAT Software: Changes and Enhancements Release 6.11. Cary, NC: SAS Institute Inc.
11. Schumacher M., Rossner R., Vach W. (1996) Neural networks and logistic regression: Part I. Computational Statistics & Data Analysis **21**, 661–682

A Synaptic Indicator Based Approach For Hidden Parameters Extraction In Industrial Environment

Kurosh Madani[1] and Ion Berechet[2]

[1] Intelligence in Instrumentation and Systems Lab. (I^{2}S) - SENART Institute of Technology - University PARIS XII, Avenue Pierre POINT, F-77127 Lieusaint - France

[2] CREATA Holding SA - Puits Godet 10 - CH 2000 Neuchâtel- Switzerland

Abstract: In the case of a large number of applications, especially complex industrial ones, the knowledge on system's (process, plant, etc.) parameters during the operation of the system is of major importance. However, in real cases, there are always parameters, which are not accessible. In the present work, we focus our interest around the extraction possibility of information relative to inaccessible parameters, which is a difficult problem in a general context. We will discuss some realistic and especially, realizable conditions for which a solution could be approached. In proposed approach, we use the neural network's learning and a synaptic weight based indicator to detect changes related to system's inaccessible parameters. Experimental results relative to a real industrial process have been reported validating our approach.

1 Introduction

In the case of a large number of applications, especially complex industrial ones, the knowledge on system's (process, plant, etc.) parameters during the operation of the system is of major importance. The knowledge of such parameters (especially internal parameters) is a chief condition to predict the system's evolution and related decisions. In theory, such parameters could be obtained by implementation of as many as needed appropriated sensors. However, in real cases (real systems), only a very limited number of sensors could be implemented. The limitation of sensors number is related to several reasons among which are: cost constraints, implementation difficulty, monitoring or supervision difficulties, etc..

In the present work, we focus our interest around the following question: is it possible to extract information relative to inaccessible parameters during the plant's operation ? Our approach is based on use of Artificial Neural Networks (ANN) and especially their learning and generalization capabilities. The mentioned property of ANN makes such techniques suitable for design new solutions overcoming limitations of conventional techniques [1], [2], [3], [4]. The problem we are interested in here deals with several domains as Intelligent Measurement, Identification and Behavior Prediction. Concerning the use of ANN in the above-mentioned topics, a number of advances has been accomplished in each area ([5] to [7]). To approach a solution to the above posed problem, we propose a different slant using a synaptic weight based indicator (which will be defined later) to detect changes related to system's inaccessible parameters. We use the neural network's learning to sample the behavior of those inaccessible parameters.

The paper is organized as follow: in section 2, we formulate the problem, discussing supposed conditions, and we expose our solution to the posed problem. In section 3, we present and discuss experimental results validating the proposed approach. In the last section we give the conclusion and future perspectives.

2 Problem Formulation and Proposed Solution

Let us consider a system with a given number of inputs, outputs and internal parameters. We suppose system inputs and outputs to be always accessible. However, concerning the system's internal parameters, if they may be accessible for a limited period then, they become inaccessible during the operation phase. Thus, we suppose that these parameters may be accessible for a given period and then, they will be supposed to be inaccessible. We emphasize that the internal parameter's accessibility during some determined period is a realistic condition, which could be realizable in a large number of real world industrial environments: accessibility during maintenance of the plant, parameters characterization during the test phase of the plant's (or system) manufacturing, etc.. The posed question is: *is it possible to extract information relative to inaccessible parameters?*.

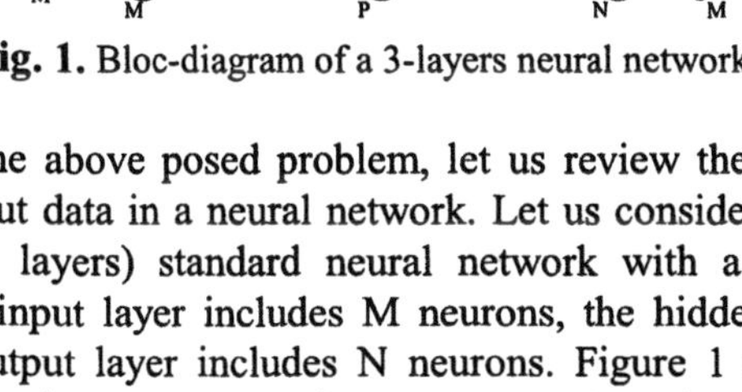

Fig. 1. Bloc-diagram of a 3-layers neural network.

Before analyzing the above posed problem, let us review the consequence of a perturbation on input data in a neural network. Let us consider a 3 layers (input, hidden and output layers) standard neural network with a Back-Propagation learning rule. The input layer includes M neurons, the hidden layer includes P neurons and the output layer includes N neurons. Figure 1 shows such neural network, where $\mathbf{X} = (X_1, \ldots, X_j, \ldots, X_M)^T$ represents the input vectors, with $j \in \{1, \cdots, M\}$, $\mathbf{h} = (h_1, \ldots, h_k, \ldots, h_P)^T$ with $k \in \{1, \cdots, P\}$ represents the hidden layers output and $\mathbf{S} = (S_1, \ldots, S_i, \ldots, S_N)^T$ the output vector with $i \in \{1, \cdots, N\}$. We note W_{kj}^{H} and W_{ik}^{S} synaptic matrixes elements, corresponding to input-hidden layers and hidden-output layers respectively. Neurons of the hidden layer are supposed to have a non-linear activation function F(.) and the activation function of the output layer's neurons is supposed to be linear. Finally, V_k^H and V_i^S, defined by relation (1), represent the synaptic potential (activity) vectors components of hidden and output neurons, respectively (e.g. vectors V^H and V^S components).

$$V_k^H = \sum_{j=1}^{j=M} W_{kj}^H . x_j \quad \text{and} \quad V_i^S = \sum_{k=1}^{k=P} W_{ik}^H . h_k \qquad (1)$$

We suppose that synaptic weights of the neural network have been adjusted thank to a learning process. Taking into account such considerations, the k-th hidden and the i-th output neurons outputs will be given by relations (2) where λ is a real.

$$h_k = F(V_k^H) \quad \text{and} \quad s_i = \lambda V_i^S \qquad (2)$$

Let us now consider some perturbation ΔX on j-th input: the j-th input component would thus become $X_j + \Delta X$. This perturbation will modify the hidden and output neuron's responses. Using Taylor approximation, the k-th hidden neuron's output will be subject to a modification expressed by relation (3), where F'(.) represents the derivative of the activation function F(.). In the same way, the i-th output neuron will generate an output error expressed by relation (4).

$$\Delta h = F(V_k^H + W_{kj}^H \Delta x) - F(V_k^H) = F'(V_k^H) W_{kj}^H \Delta x \qquad (3)$$

$$\Delta S_i = \varepsilon_i = \sum_{k=1}^{P} W_{ik}^S \Delta h_k \qquad (4)$$

A new training of the neural net will modify synaptic weights of both input-hidden and hidden-output synaptic matrixes ($\mathbf{W}^H$ and $\mathbf{W}^S$ matrixes). According to the standard Back-Propagation rule expressed by relation (5), giving the modification of synaptic weight connecting the j-th neuron to the i-th neuron of two adjacent layers in a network, one can write relations (6). These relations show that synaptic weights will be modified proportionally to the input perturbation.

$$\Delta W_{i,j} = -\eta \frac{\partial \varepsilon_i}{\partial W_{i,j}} \qquad (5)$$

$$\Delta W_{i,k}^S \propto -\eta\, F'(V_k) W_{k,j}^H \Delta X \quad \text{and} \quad \Delta W_{k,j}^H \propto -\eta\, F'(V_k)\, \Delta X \qquad (6)$$

2.1 Definition and Interpretation of a Synaptic Indicator

So, the synaptic matrix relative to a pair of layers will contain information relative to all changes on input data of the concerned pair of layers. Let us define an indicator, that we call Synaptic Indicator (SI) conform to relation (7). Note that for a pair of adjacent layers, if the input layer includes M neurons, then M Synaptic Indicators could be available. On the other hand, note that the j-th indicator will contain information relative to changes corresponding to the j-th input neuron (j-th parameter).

$$I_j = \sum_{i=1}^{i=N} W_{i,j} \qquad (7)$$

Let us now interpret the Synaptic Indicator, defined-above. After a learning process, the considered pair of layers will act as some non-linear function identifier minimizing the output neurons errors. If G(.) is the learned transfer function, then the considered pair of layers will realize Y = G (X). On the other hand, the relation (7) could also be written as: $I_j = \sum_{i=1}^{i=N} W_{i,j} \cdot 1$. It could be remarked that this relation corresponds to the outputs computation in a two layers neural network with linear activation function, where the input vector is identity vector **1**. So, the above-defined synaptic indicator could be interpreted as the response of a linear neural network, which approximates the function $G^{-1}(.)$ (representing the G(.) inverse function), to some normalized input stimulus (see figure 2).

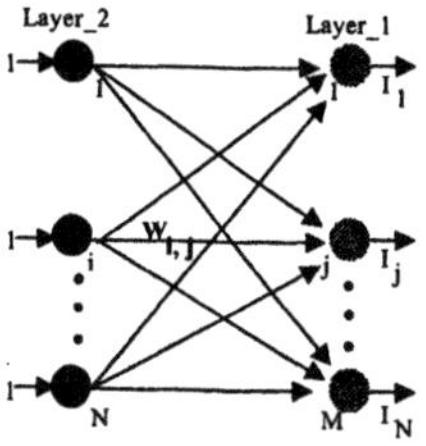

$$\begin{pmatrix} I_1 = \sum_{i=1}^{i=N} W_{i,1} \\ \vdots \\ I_j = \sum_{i=1}^{i=N} W_{i,j} \\ \vdots \\ I_M = \sum_{i=1}^{i=N} W_{i,M} \end{pmatrix} = \begin{pmatrix} W_{1,1} & \cdots & W_{i,1} & \cdots & W_{N,1} \\ \vdots & \ddots & \vdots & \iddots & \vdots \\ W_{1,j} & \cdots & W_{i,j} & \cdots & W_{N,j} \\ \vdots & \iddots & \vdots & \ddots & \vdots \\ W_{1,M} & \cdots & W_{i,M} & \cdots & W_{N,M} \end{pmatrix} \bullet \begin{pmatrix} 1 \\ \vdots \\ 1 \\ \vdots \\ 1 \end{pmatrix}$$

$$\mathbf{I} = (I_1 \ \cdots \ I_j \ \cdots \ I_M)^T = G^{-1}(1)$$

Fig. 2. Interpretation of Synaptic Indicator.

2.2 Inaccessible Parameters Monitoring Using Synaptic Indicator

Let us now consider a system with a given number of inputs, outputs and internal parameters and with conditions (hypothesis) mentioned at the beginning of the section 2. Let us also consider a 3 layers neural network (designated by ANN_N°1 and in conformity with figure 1) identifying such system. That means that the mentioned neural network pre-learns some appropriated database, including data relative to system (or plant) inputs, outputs and internal parameters behavior. Then, a reference set of synaptic indicators relative to system's internal parameters is generated. The same ANN is then used as the plant's model to generate database relative to the system's response to the normalized input stimulus (vector **1**). This first ANN will be used to generate SI during the monitoring phase. Then a second ANN, acting as a neural identifier, model the hidden parameter's behavior. Figure 3 shows the learning bloc diagram of such identifier.

Figure 4 presents bloc diagram of the complete inaccessible parameters monitoring system. After the pre-learning phase, such system, acting as a virtual sensor, could be used to detect changes related to system's internal parameters. In monitoring operation mode, the neural network learns periodically accessible data (inputs and outputs) leading to a new synaptic matrix. This new synaptic matrix is then used to generate a new set of synaptic indicators, which is compared to the reference set of synaptic indicators (obtained from pre-learning phase). One can remark that in our technique, we use the ANN learning capability to sample changes related to inaccessible parameters.

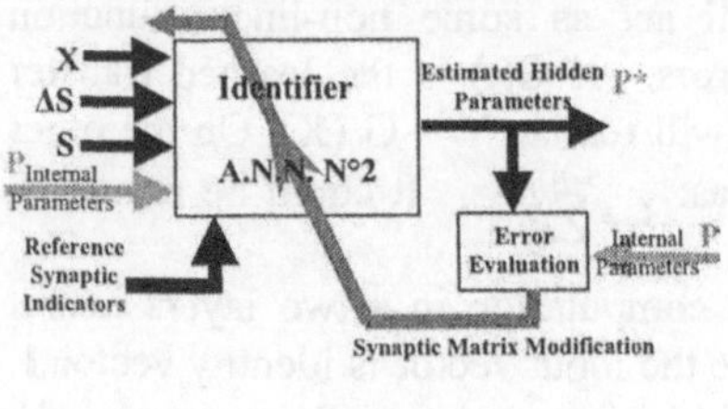

Fig. 3. Hidden parameters estimation module.

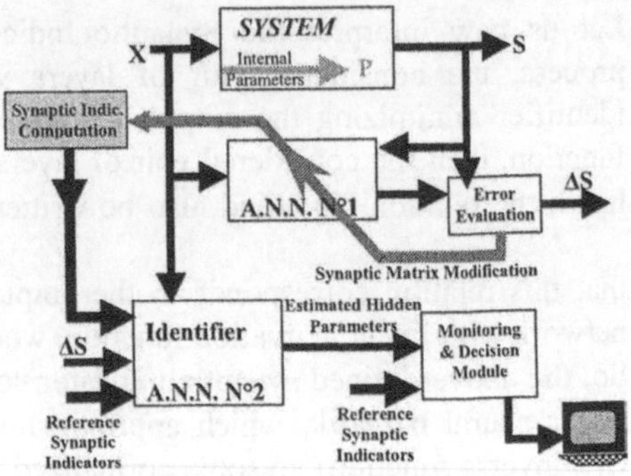

Fig. 4. Inaccessible parameters monitoring phase bloc-diagram.

3 Experimental Results

To validate the above exposed concept, we have used our technique in the case of real world industrial process internal parameters monitoring. The industrial process is a drilling rubber plant, which is used to manufacture a set of products with complex profiles (for car industry) needing several different kinds of plastics. Because of industrial confidentiality, we will not give the nature of parameters. The input of the process corresponds to some angular speed and the output of the process is related to some linear speed of produced plastic matter. The final product's quality (profile, mechanical and acoustic properties) is correlated to internal parameters, which are not directly accessible during process operation. A normalized database, including input, output and internal parameter's variations, has been constructed during the plant's testing period. This database has been divided in two databases: one used for pre-learning phase, and the other one for validation. Figure 5 shows the experimental database used for validation. It also shows results relatives to the pre-learning phase plotting the evolution of synaptic indicators (SI). Figure 6 gives experimental results relative to the hidden parameter behavior monitoring (estimated by the SI based virtual sensor).

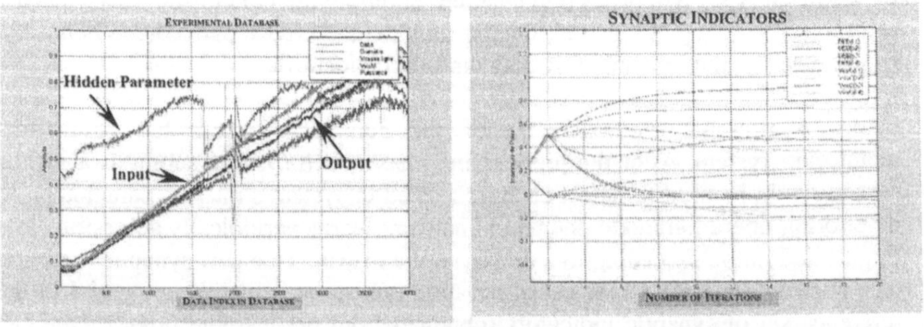

(a) (b)

Fig. 5. (a): Experimental database including , input, output internal parameters. (b): Evolution of Synaptic Indicators (SI) during the pre-learning phase.

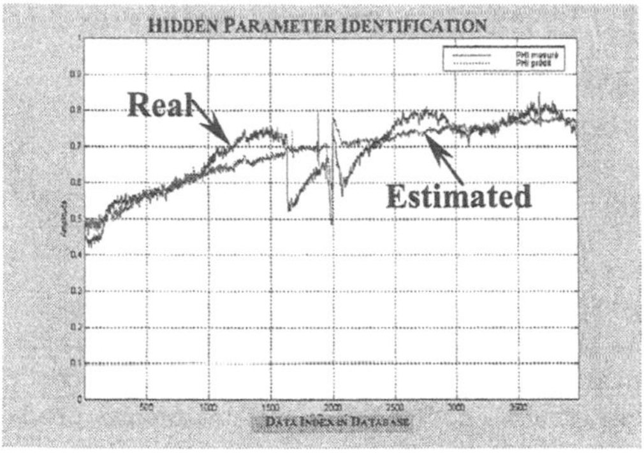

Fig. 6. (a): hidden parameter behavior monitoring by the SI based virtual sensor.

4 Conclusion

In the present work, we focus our interest around the extraction possibility of information relative to inaccessible parameters. We discussed some realistic (and especially, realizable) conditions for which a solution has been approached. In our approach, we use the neural network's learning and a synaptic indicator to detect changes related to system's inaccessible parameters. The obtained results show feasibility and efficiency of the presented approach offering solution to a difficult problem for which conventional techniques haven't been able to propose a viable solution. However, several problems are still open: fine quantification and fine identification of inaccessible internal parameter's behavior. We are working now to understand dependencies on process nature and other related problems.

References

[1] M. Mayoubi, M. Schafer, S. Sinsel 1995), "Dynamic Neural Units for Non-linear Dynamic Systems Identification", LNCS Vol. 930, Springer Verlag, 1995, pp.1045-1051.

[2] Faller W., Schreck S. (1995), "Real-Time Prediction Of Unsteady Aerodynamics : Application for Aircraft Control and Maneuverability Enhancement", IEEE Transactions on Neural Networks, Vol. 6, N¡ 6, Nov. 1995.

[3] Y. Maidon, B. W. Jervis, N. Dutton, S. Lesage (1996), "Multifault Diagnosis of Analogue Circuits Using Multilayer Perceptrons," IEEE European Test Workshop 96, Montpellier, June 12-14,1996.

[4] I. Grabec (1997), "Continuation of Chaotic Fields by RBFNN", LNCS Vol. 1240 - Springer Verlag 1997, pp. 597-606.

[5] A. Sachenko, V. Kochan, V. Turchenko, V. Golovko, J. Savitsky, A. Dunets, T. Laopoulos (2000), "Sensor errors prediction using neural networks", Proceedings IJCNN'2000, Jul 24-Jul 27 2000, Como, Italy, pp. 441-446.

[6] A. Sachenko (1999), "IMCS development on the basis of distributed sensor networks", IEEE AFRICON Conference, v1, 1999 IEEE, Piscataway, NJ, USA, p 345-350.

[7] Y. Zhang, Y. MA (1997), "CGHA for Principal Component extraction in the complex domain", IEEE Trans. On Neural Networks, Vol. 8, No. 5, 1997, pp. 1031-1036.

Regression Hyper Surfaces with a Modified Neural Network Architecture

Mingo L.F.[1], Gisbert P.[2], Carrillo J.D.[2], and Hernández C.[2]

[1] Dept. de Organización y Estructura de la Información
Escuela de Informática, Universidad Politécnica de Madrid
Crta. de Valencia km. 7, 28031 Madrid, Spain. lfmingo@eui.upm.es

[2] Facultad de Informática, Universidad Politécnica de Madrid
Campus de Montegancedo, 28660 Boadilla del Monte, Madrid, Spain.
{gisbert, jcarrillo}@fi.upm.es

Abstract. This paper describes the application of Enhanced Neural Networks (*ENN*) to the regression analysis problem. This architecture permits to have different weights for each pattern once the network has been trained, in such a way that the Mean Square Error *MSE* is lower than classical Multilayer Perceptrons. These nets are employed as universal approximator of continuous mappings. The training algorithm is introduced same way as the mathematical proof of the aproximation capabilities of this architecture. Finally, several results are shown, among them, the two-spirals problem, with a comparison with other methods that have tried to solve this problem. In short, *ENN* have a better behaviour than the backpropagation networks, and they improveb the *MSE* ratio.

1 Introduction

Multilayer neural networks are based on the property that the pattern set has the same weights for the connections once the network has been trained. It does not matter what pattern is the input to the net, the weights will be allways the same. This property gives a global generalization for the pattern set and the regression surfaces generated by the net can be global to all the patterns. The architecture *ENN* is characterized for having different weights for each different pattern which is introduced to the net [1,2]. To achieve such idea, two neural networks have been combined in order to simulate axo-axonic connections. One network (assistant) will compute weights belonging to the other network (principal) depending on the input pattern. That is, each pattern produces a set of weights that is employed in the neural network to output the desired response, see figure 1.

Such behaviour seems very logic from a neuropsicological point of view. Barbizet [3] proposes that connections among the neurons propagate the input signal to different neurons increasing or decreasing the power of the signal, depending of the features of the connections. But such behaviour also accepts that the connection features depend on the output signal of a neuron. Mathematically [1,4], the previous idea could be expressed as: $w_{ji} = o_k$, beeing w_{ji} a weight of the principal network and o_k the output of a neuron of the assistant network. Such idea permits to introduce cuadratic terms in the output equations of the network where they were lineal equations using *MLP* if the activation function is a lineal one.

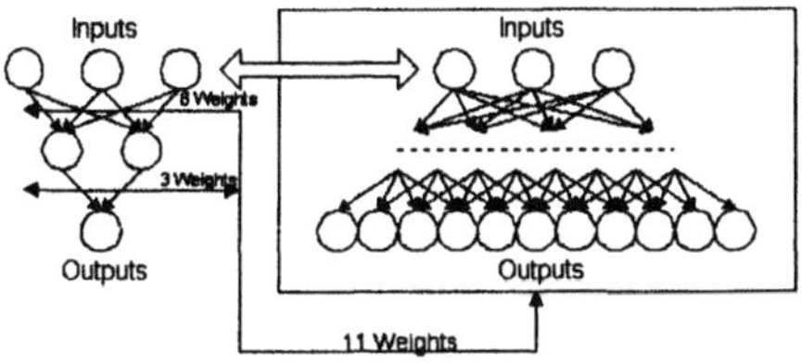

Fig. 1. *ENN* Architecture

A two input neurons network with lineal activation functions and no hidden layer generates the equation (1) as output of the net. This is a quadratic equation computed by a lineal neural network. Therefore such net can make a regression analysis using quadratic polynomials [2]. And moreover, if the principal network has n hidden layers, then the output equation is a $n-2$ degree polynomial. So we can say that this architecture performs a regression analysis with polynomial hypersurfaces provided the activation function belongs to the bclass of lineal functions [2,5].

$$o = w_{11}x^2 + w_{22}y^2 + (w_{12} + w_{21})xy + (w_{31+b_1})x + (w_{32} + b_2)y + b_3 \quad (1)$$

In order to overcome the problem of having a high number of hidden layers when a good approximation is found, the lineality of the architecture is transformed into a *Non Lineal Enhanced Neural Networks.* In this case all activation functions of the main network are lineal ones, and only the output neurons of assistant network have an activation function $g(x)$. When the net has been trained, assistant network outputs a functional basis of functions $g(x)$, and the main network uses such basis in order to compute the best approximation based in the non lineal combination of functions $g(x)$ [4,5].

2 *ENN* as Universal Approximator

Funahashi [6] stated that any continuous mapping function can be approximated with a multilayer neural network with at least one hidden layer whose activation functions must be sigmoidals. The starting point of the proof of this theorem, in case we have only one hidden layer, is the integral formula proposed by Irie and Miyake [7]. It is easy to prove the theorem for a multilayer network (more than 1 hidden layer) by induction.

Let $\phi(x)$ be a noconstant, bounded and monotone increasing continuous function. Let K be a compact subset (bounded closed subset) of R^n and

$f(x_1, \cdots, x_n)$ be a real valued continuous function on K. Then for an arbitrary $\epsilon > 0$, there exists an integer N and real constants $c_i, \omega_i (i = 1, \cdots, N)$, $w_{ij} (i = 1, \cdots, N; j = 1, \cdots, n)$ such that:

$$\hat{f}(x_1, \cdots, x_n) = \sum_{i=1}^{N} c_i \phi (\sum_{j=1}^{n} w_{ij} x_j - \omega_i) \tag{2}$$

In other words, for an arbitrary $\epsilon > 0$, there exists a three-layer network whose output functions for input and output layers are linear and which has an input-output mapping $\hat{f}(x_1, \cdots, x_n)$ such that:

$$max_{x \in K} |f(x_1, \cdots, x_n) - \hat{f}(x_1, \cdots, x_n)| < \epsilon \tag{3}$$

Previous theorem can be applied to *ENN*. Given an assistant network with activation function φ in the hidden neurons, the output equation of a given neuron k in the assistant network is:

$$o_k = \varphi \left(\sum_{l=1}^{n} w_{kl} x_l \right) \tag{4}$$

where n is the number of input neurons, x_l is the input value of neuron l and w_{kl} is the weight from neuron l to neuron k.

Given a one hidden layer perceptron with activation function ϕ in the hidden layer, the output equation of the net is:

$$o = \sum_{i=1}^{N} c_i \phi \left(\sum_{j=1}^{n} w_{ij} x_j - \theta_i \right) \tag{5}$$

where n is the number of inputs, N is the number of hidden neurons, and c_i are the weights from hidden neuron i to output neuron.

ENN architecture is based on the idea that weight connections of the principal net are computed by an assistant net. If we consider an one output neuron network with one hidden layer the equation of its output is very similar to (5), except that weights are outputs of assistant network (4).

Taking equations (5) and (4) the output of principal net is:

$$o = \sum_{i=1}^{N} c_i \phi \left(\sum_{k=1}^{n} x_k \varphi \left(\sum_{l=1}^{n} w_{b'l} x_l \right) - \varphi \left(\sum_{l=1}^{n} w_{\hat{b}l} x_l \right) \right) \tag{6}$$

$$c_i = \varphi \left(\sum_{l=1}^{n} w_{bl} x_l \right) \tag{7}$$

where N is the number of hidden neurons in the principal net and n is the number of inputs.

Output equation of an output neuron of principal net (6) is quite similar to equation (2) used to proof the approximation capabilities of a neural network. In this equation the parameters b, b' y $\hat{b}$ have the following constraints concerning the network architecture:

- $b = \{1, \cdots, N\}$
- $b' = \{N+1, \cdots, nN+N+1\}$
- $\hat{b} = \{nN+N+2, \cdots, nN+2N+2\}$

Besides, there must exist a matrix C with dimensions $(n+1) \times N(n+1)$ in such a way that the following system $w_{ij} = C^b \boldsymbol{x}$ must have a solution. There exist a valid solution provided the following constraints are made (direct application of Funahashi's Theorem):

- If the input $\boldsymbol{x}$ is a normalized vector, that is, the sum of its components is equal to 1, then $C^b = (w_{kh}, \cdots, w_{kh})$. That is, all assistant weights connected to an output neuron have the same values. In this case the neural net will behave in a *MLP* manner (*ENN* simulates *MLP*).
- The system also has a solution if input is not normalized. Applying Funahashi [6] some weights w_{ij} in the principal net can be computed in order to optimize the problem. Such values are the desired patterns of assistant network. In the same way and appliying Funahashi, weights of assistant network can be estimated with an error $\epsilon > 0$. *ENN* under such situation are powerful than *MLP*.

The application of neural networks to the fields of engineering has been done using the classical multilayer neural networks "with two or more hidden layers", the proposed theorem above establishes that *ENN* with n-hidden layers is able to perform a $n+2$-degree polynomial approximation if lineal functions are implemented, and a $n+2$-degree general approximation with no lineal activation function, that is, *ENN* behave like universal approximators.

3 Application to Regression Problems

When checking the behavior of this network, several examples described next have been performed. All of this will be a helpful tool to observe the behavior of this network against the problems that have yet been studied with different kind of networks.

3.1 XOR Function

The first example is the classic *XOR*, this problem is usefull to show how the input space is divided using the enhanced neural networks. The architecture employed has been a principal network 2 - 1 - 1 (full) with an perceptron assistant network. The absolute error obtained after 50 epochs is lower than 0.03, what means that there exists a good behaviour.

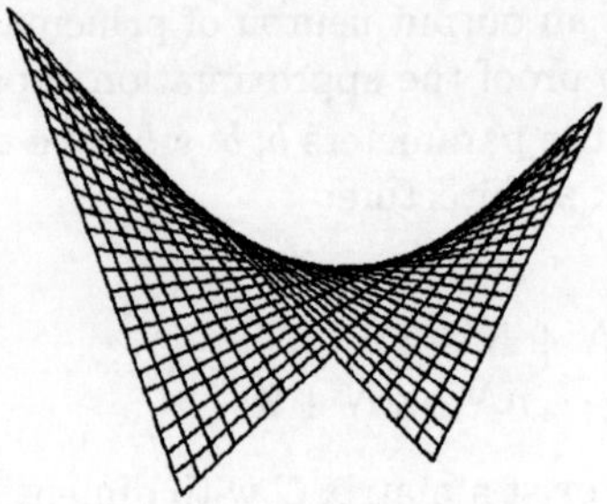

Fig. 2. Input Space of the *XOR ENN*

Figure 2 shows the division of the input space, taking into account only negative or positive outputs. It can be seeing a logical division, if we consider the pattern structure.

The log that the simulator traces, has provided the information about the values of the weights of the assistant network (table 1) and the weights of the principal network (table 2) that the assistant network outputs for each input pattern.

Table 1. Assistant Net Weights for the *XOR* problem

Weight Values			
w_{11}	w_{12}	w_{10}	
-0.000107	3.229842	0.001012	x_0
-3.230230	0.002078	-0.002761	x_1
-0.000882	0.002416	-0.001904	*Bias*

Table 2. Principal Net Weights for the *XOR* problem

Input Pattern		Weights Values		
-1	-1	3.229455	3.230180	-0.000156
1	1	-3.231220	-3.225348	-0.003653
-1	1	-3.231005	3.234336	-0.005678
1	-1	3.229241	-3.229504	0.001869

According to [4,5], any boolean function of n variables can be expressed by a n degree polynomial and therefore such expression can be approximated by an *ENN* with no error at all provided the number of hiddes layer was $n-2$.

3.2 Two Spirals Problem

Next problem consists on learnig the two-spiral problem. Figure 3 shows the graphic representation of the problem. The task to perform is to learn to separate between two sets of points that lie into two different spirals in the $x - y$ plane. This is a complex task for back propagation neural networks. It is also recomended to check the generalization of the network with other sets of points along the whole input space, once the network has been succesfully trained.

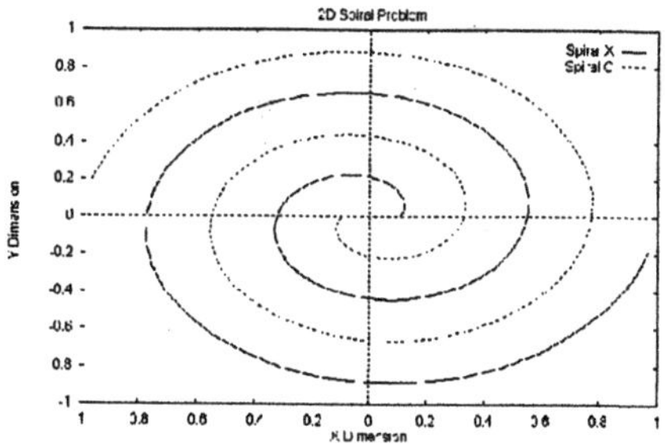

Fig. 3. 2D two-spirals problem illustration

Lang and Witbrock [10] obtained good results with a network 2 - 5 - 5 - 5 - 1, in which each neuron is connected to all the neurons of all the previous layers. It takes the network 11.000 epochs to train. Fahlman [11] and Lebiere [12], using the quickprop algorithm, decreased the number of epochs till 7.900; same way using the correlation cascade neural networks, the number of epochs is 1.700, creating 15 hidden neurons.

In other paper, Claudio Moraga proposes a solution with only three neurons that get a perfect generalization. The two first neurons are able to compute the module of the input vector and the arctangent of the inputs, the third neuron only performs a lineal separation of the data processed by the two frist neurons.

Table 4 shows the obtained results when solving the two-spirals problem, using an enhanced neural network *ENN*. The employed architecture has been a principal network with the following layer configuration: 2 - 13 -1, and an assistant network with 2 - 39 neurons in each one of the two layers. The total number of weights to adjust is 131. The number of epochs employed to get the last configuration has been 10.000 epochs.

First of all, looking at the images, it can be seen that the performance is 100not correct, there exist some points that are wrong classified but, in general, the result obtained for this problem using *ENN* is very good (see table 3).

The obtained results improve the previous work concerning this problem, that is based on the use of the back propagation algorithm. In this example,

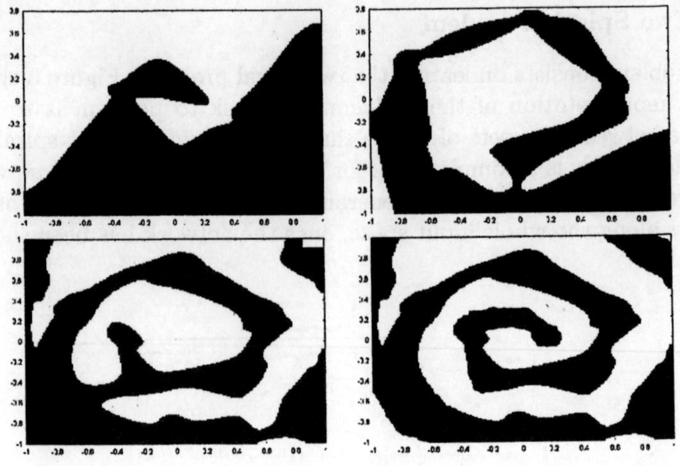

Fig. 4. Generation of regression surfaces in the two spirals problem.

Table 3. Performance of several methods dealing the two-spirals problem.

–	Witbrock	Fahlman	Lebiere	Moraga	ENN
Algorithm	BP	QuickProp	Cascade Correlation	BP	ENN
Architecture	2-5-5-5-1		15 Hiddens	2-2-1	2-13-1
Iterations	11.000	7.900	1.500		10.000
Weights	318	318	59	9	131
Generalization	Fair	Fair	Fair	Perfect	Fair

ENN only employ one hidden layer, and almost in all the papers that deal with this problem [11,12] the neural network architecture has more than one hidden layers, obtaining a similar generalization.

4 Conclusions

This kind of neural networks *ENN* have the advantage of knowing the degree of approximation (output equation) just regarding the number of hidden layers, assistant network simulates, in a certain way, a pre-processing of input data. Same way as all the networks, the generalization power of the network can also be increased adding hidden layers and neurons.

Obtained results improve the performance of the back propagation, since *BPNN* needs more hidden layers to achieve similar results. *ENN* can work with only one hidden layer same way as the *BPNN* can work with more than one hidden layer. The two-spirals problem needs three hidden layers with a *BPNN* to achieve a solution similar to the *ENN* with a hidden layer.

Seeing the *ENN* architecture, it can be noticed that the assistant network function is to pre-proccess the input data, but this data are not incorporated to the principal network as inputs, they are incorporated as weights of the principal network, and are employed to compute the desired output in order to minimize the *MSE.*

References

1. Mingo L.F., Arroyo F., Luengo C., Castellanos J.: **Learning HyperSurfaces with Neural Networks**. The 11th Scandinavian Conference on Image Analysis. Kangerlussuaq, Greenland. June 7-11. ISBN: 87-88306-42-9. Pp.: 731-737. (1999).
2. Mingo L.F., Giménez V., Castellanos J.: **Interpolation of Boolean Functions with Enhanced Neural Networks**. Second Conference on Computer Science and Information Technologies. CSIT 1999. Yerevan, Armenia. August 17-22. Pp.: 247-251. (1999).
3. Barbizet J., Duizabo Ph.: *Manual de Neuropsicología.* Toray-Masson S.A. Translation from *Abrege de Neuropsychologie.* Pp.: 17-21. (1978).
4. Mingo L.F., Martínez A., Giménez V., Castellanos J.: **Paramtric Bivariate Surfaces with Neural Networks.** Machine Graphics and Vision Journal. Vol.: 9. No.: 1. ISSN 1230-0535. Pp.: 41-46. (2000).
5. Luis Fernando de Mingo López: **Non-Linear Combination of Neurocomputed Basis to Approximate Functions.** International Journal of Computation Research. Vol.: 1. No.: 2. (2000).
6. Funahashi K.: **On the Approximate Realization of Continuous Mappings by Neural Networks.** Neural Networks, Vol. 2. Pp.: 183-192. (1989).
7. Irie B., Miyake S.: **Capabilities of Three-layered Perceptrons.** IEEE International Conference on Neural Networks. Vol. 1. Pp.: 641-648. (1988).
8. Lapedes A. & Farber R.: **Nonlinear Signal Processing Using Neural Networks: Prediction and System Modeling**. Los Alamos National Laboratory, Los Alamos, N.M., LA-UR-87-2662. (1987).
9. Lapedes A. & Farber R.: **How Neural Networks Work.** Los Alamos National Laboratory, Los Alamos, N.M., LA-UR-88-418. (1988).
10. Kevin J.L., Michael J., Witbrock: **Learning to tell two spirals apart.** Proceedings of th 1988 Connectionist Models Summer Scholl, Morgan Kaufmann. (1988).
11. Scott E.F.: **Faster learning variations on Backpropagation: An empirical study.** Proceedings of th 1988 Connectionist Models Summer Scholl, Morgan Kaufmann. (1988).
12. Scott E.F., Christian L.: **The Cascade-Correlation Learning Architecture.** Touretzky (ed.) Advances in Neural Information Processing Systems 2, Morgan Kaufmann. (1990).

Response Surface Methodology at Irregular Grids Based on Voronoi Scheme with Neural Network Approximator

Jacek Pietraszek

Cracow University of Technology, PL-31-864 Kraków, Al. Jana Pawła II 37
email: pmpietra@mech.pk.edu.pl

Summary

Traditional response surface methodology is based on polynomial approximators and designs prepared according to statistical requirements. In those cases when response surface cannot be modelled with single polynomial plane, a neural network approximator should be used. These approximators require a different design identification procedure. The author proposes to apply well-known Voronoi scheme to construct iteratively a new design.

1. Traditional design of experiment methodology

Traditional design of experiments (DOE) methodology, as described in [1–2,5–11] is a set of treatment procedures where the investigation unit is treated as a black-box with some quantitative or qualitative inputs and one or more outputs which may be measured. The theoretical fundamentals of this methodology were founded by Robbins and Monro [12], Kiefer and Wolfowitz [3] investigations on stochastic approximation.

It is very useful in industrial applications where theoretical model is unavailable or too complex to be effectively applied. Academic methodology initially developed for industrial utilization was formalized in the last years and coded as ISO 3534. This code has two editions: in the year 1993 and 2000.

1.1. The aim of experimental design

Two goals occur most often: (a) find minima or maxima of the unit response or (b) identify the function model of the unit response. The first case is based implicitly on the first-order (two-level designs) or the second-order (three-level designs) polynomial model. It is very popular in industrial practice, if qualitative inputs of the investigated unit are considered. This also includes quantitative inputs discriminated by nominal values [6,7].

The second case is based on the same polynomials but explicitly. In particular investigations the model may be constructed on other functions but it requires more difficult statistical analysis than in standard cases. It requires only quantitative inputs of the investigated unit [6].

1.2. Response surface methodology

There are two especially exposed cases, if the model is defined explicitly. The first one is a central composite design being composition (hence the name) of three-level fractional factorial design and so called star points. In this case there are not any additional conditions.

The second case describes a situation when input values must sum to a constant. This appears most often if a mixture is considered, hence the name: mixture design. These designs may be applied with or without additional conditions formulated by linear equalities and inequalities.

Both cases are often named response surface methodology (RSM) because they are strongly focused on explicit model and extensive visualization of the investigated unit's answer as 2D or 3D plots. Industrial usage is concentrated on model's utilization in control system and searching optimal settings (in the sense of the defined criterion). The response surface methodology based on polynomial models and regular grids is described in [1,2,8,].

1.3. Structure of experimental design

The structure of the input data set is the fundamental property of experimental design. Available values of inputs are coded and restricted: $\{-1, +1\}$ for two-level designs, $\{-1, 0, +1\}$ for three level designs and $\{-\alpha, -1, 0, +1, \alpha\}$ for composite designs where α is the so-called star point value. Mixture designs have values specially generated by simplex-centroid or simplex-lattice scheme [13].

The most of canonical designs have orthogonal design matrices. It is a very useful property: all calculated main effects are not correlated. Unfortunately not all of the required treatments may be set in industrial practice. The design loses the orthogonal property in this case and the structure of data set becomes irregular.

2. Iterative design generator based on Voronoi scheme

If data obtained from model do not satisfy the assumed error level in comparison to measures from verification experiments, it is necessary to enhance the experiment design by new treatments addition. There are a lot of procedures e.g. classical composite procedure leading from two-level design (linear model) through three-level design (verification of curvature) to five-level composite design (full quadratic model) [6,8] or the so-called *design improving* implemented by Statsoft in their statistical package *Statistica* [13] based on D-optimal criterion. Most of enhancing procedures are based on linear or quadratic approximation model.

Author proposes to use procedure of area splitting based on Voronoi scheme. This scheme was first described by Voronoi in year 1908 [15]. The area is divided into subareas bounded by envelope of midperpendiculars of segments between existing nodes. This way every node has an assigned area bounded by a broken line. The example of the composite design for 2 variables and its splitting into Voronoi's areas is presented in Fig.1.

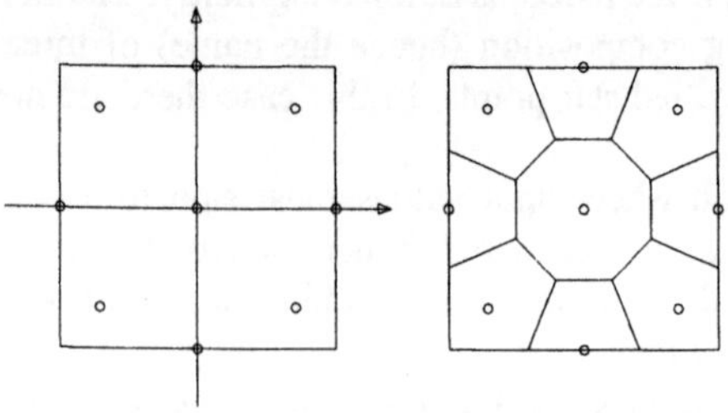

Fig. 1. Composite design for 2 variables and its Voronoi's areas

The original design has 9 treatments: one central, four belonged to $2^{(2-0)}$ fractional factorial and four as star points. The corners of boundaries should be treated as new nodes. There are 8 internal corners and 8 corners placed on the external boundary defined by limits of input variables. It may be done in two ways: (a) including internal corners placed inside of the total area or (b) including all corners with the ones placed on the external boundary also. If only internal corners are used, the new treatments in all steps of iteration will be placed within area bounded by the envelope of original design, but if all corners are used, the new treatments will fill the total area defined by limits of input variables. The choice is left to the researcher. It may depend on technical possibilities of investigated unit also. Both cases of the enhancement after the first step of iteration are presented in Fig.2.

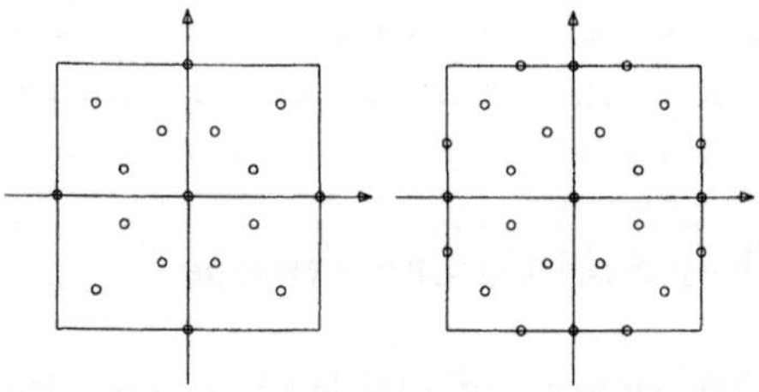

Fig.2. Two kinds of the design enhancement

3. Numerical tests of Voronoi based design

As a test for proposed procedure author used simulated unit with two inputs and one output. The reference function of the unit was quadratic polynomial:

$$z = x_1^2 + x_2^2, \tag{1}$$

where x_1, x_2 were input variables and z was output variable. The square limited by −1,4142 and +1.4142 was a domain.

Then five designs were prepared: (a) two-level two-variable full factorial $2^{(2-0)}$ and its two Voronoi's iterations and (b) five level two-variable composite design and its one Voronoi's iteration. There were calculated simulated measures for the all designs.

As an approximator a multi-layer perceptron (MLP) was used. Its topology was in scheme 2-5-5-1. There were 16 instances of MLP identified for every design due to statistical requirements. A statistical package STATISTICA Neural Network [14] was used as a neural network simulator.

Two comparative criterions were established: root mean squared error (RMS) and maximum error (MAXERR). All criterions were calculated over whole domain of design (not only in nodes) for every identified network.

There were values of average and standard error calculated for both criterions (Table 1). Then an analysis of variance was performed: its results were statistically significant (at significance level 0.05) i.e. effect of Voronoi's iteration is significant and cannot be omitted. A statistical package STATISTICA [13] was used to all required statistical analysis.

Table 1. Criterion's values

Design	No of treatments	RMS Average	RMS Std.err.	MAXERR Average	MAXERR Std.err.
2V	16	1.0742	0.0012	2.0035	0.0030
2V+VOR1	16	0.7039	0.0827	2.0398	0.2840
2V+VOR2	16	0.2281	0.1111	1.3482	0.3685
COMP	16	0.6540	0.3285	2.1865	0.6108
COMP+VOR1	16	0.1256	0.1499	0.8936	0.4402

2V – two-level two-variable full factorial design; *2V+VOR1* – (2V) design after the first Voronoi's iteration; *2V+VOR2* – (2V) design after the second Voronoi's iteration; *COMP* – two-variable composite design; *COMP+VOR1* – composite design after the first Voronoi's iteration

Good visualization of the analysis results is box plot, where averages, standard errors and 95% confidence interval are plotted. There is presented RMS box plot only due to limited space (Fig.3). As may be observed, the Voronoi's iterations leads to improve of prediction accuracy.

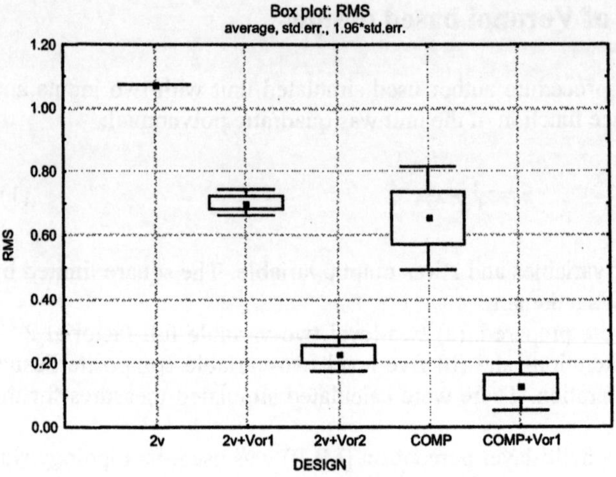

Fig.3. Root mean squared error in different designs

One of the most important economic criterions of design usability is a number of required treatments. The purpose of DOE is to obtain the best information at number of treatments as small as possible. This way a scatter plot is appropriate visualization: error versus number of treatments (Fig.4). It is very interested that full factorial design after two Voronoi's iterations has over three times better RMS value than composition design at the same number of treatments.

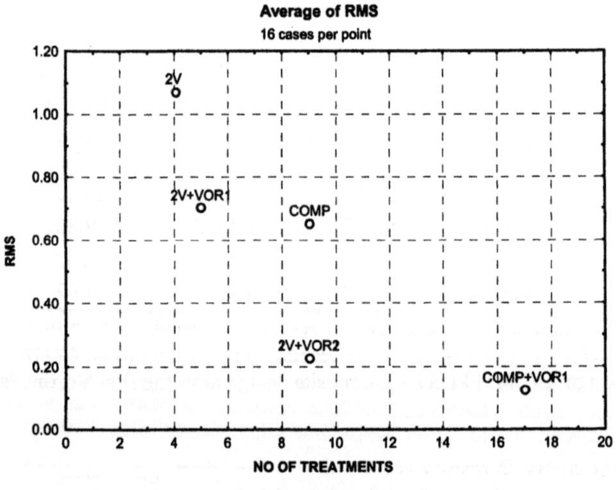

Fig.4. Economic value of different designs

4. Conclusions

The author proposed the iterative procedure of DOE design construction based on Voronoi's splitting scheme. The procedure was tested on some two variables examples and the obtained results were strongly positive. It seems profitable to test this procedure on other examples with more input variables and other more complex reference function.

While every precaution has been taken in the preparation of this article, the author cannot assume that presented idea is absolutely unique all over the world.

References

1. Box GEP, Draper NR (1987), Empirical Model-Building and Response Surfaces, John Wiley & Sons, New York
2. Draper NR, Smith H (1981), Applied Regression Analysis, John Wiley & Sons, New York
3. Kiefer J, Wolfowitz J (1952) Stochastic Estimation of the Maximum of a Regression Function. Ann Math Statist 23:462–466
4. Koronacki J (1989), Stochastic Approximation: Optimisation Methods in Probabilistic Treatments, WNT Publishing House, Warsaw (In Polish)
5. Mańczak K (1976), Experimental Design Methodology, WNT Publishing House, Warsaw (In Polish)
6. Mason RL, Gunst RF, Hess JL (1989), Statistical Design and Analysis of Experiments: with Applications to Engineering and Science, John Wiley & Sons, New York
7. McLean RA, Anderson VL (1984), Applied Factorial and Fractional Designs, Marcel Dekker, New York
8. Myers RH, Montgomery DC (1995), Response Surface Methodology: Process and Product Optimization Using Designed Experiments. John Wiley & Sons, New York
9. Phadke MS (1989), Quality Engineering Using Robust Design, Prentice-Hall International, New York
10. Polański Z (1984), Design of Experiments in Technology, PWN Publishing House, Warsaw (In Polish)
11. Rafajłowicz E (1996), Design of Experiments Algorithms with Implementations in Mathematica. PLJ Academic Publishing House, Warsaw (In Polish)
12. Robbins H, Monro S (1951), A Stochastic Approximation Method. Ann Math Statist 22:400–407
13. StatSoft Inc. (2001), STATISTICA (Data Analysis Software System), Version 6. www.statsoft.com.
14. StatSoft Inc. (2000), STATISTICA Neural Networks, Version 4.0F. www.statsoft.com.
15. Voronoi G (1908), A New Applications of the Continuous Parameters in the Theory of Quadratic Forms, The Research of Parallel Primitives, J Reine angew Math 134 (In French)

Extended RBF Nets – Preliminary Studies

Ewaryst Rafajłowicz[1]

Institute of Engineering Cybernetis, Wrocław University of Technology, Wybrzeże Wyspiańskiego 27, 50 370 Wrocław, Poland

Abstract. Our aim is to propose an extension of RBF networks, which reduces oversmoothing when a surface with a discontinuity or sharp changes is fitted by the net. If a learning sequence contains random errors, then they smoothed in flat areas, while sufficiently large jumps are preserved.

1 Introduction

Our starting point is the well known class of radial basis function (RBF) networks of the form

$$y = \sum_{j=1}^{r} w_j \cdot K\left(\frac{||x - x_j^*||}{h_x}\right), \tag{1}$$

where $y \in R$ is the net output for input vector $x \in R^d$, which is transformed to the output by a nonnegative kernel function $K : R \to R$ (typically taken to be Gaussian or other hat-like function). Each kernel in (1) is shifted to one of net's centers x_j^*, $j = 1, 2, \ldots r$ and scaled by $h_x > 0$, which, for simplicity, is assumed to be the same for all the basis functions. h_x is called the smoothing parameter. $||.||$ is a norm in R^d and w_j's are weights of the net.

This class of networks has growing popularity among researchers and practitioners due to its large capacity of approximating functions and decisions in pattern recognition (see [1], [2] [3], [4], [8] for an excerpt of contributions where also extensive bibliographies can be found).

There is, however, one drawback of RBF nets limiting their performance, namely, RBF networks usually produce too smooth approximations of surfaces and decision functions (see Fig. 1, where a stair-like function is approximated by Gaussian RBF with centers at each each observation points).

2 Net structure

Our aim in this paper is to propose an extension of RBF networks, which aims to reduce these drawbacks An example of performance of the extended RBF net is shown in Fig.4 for the same data as in Fig. 1. Lack of space and preliminary stage of of our studies forces us to present extended RBF nets at a moderate level of generality. The proposed extension of RBF nets has following two new ingredients:

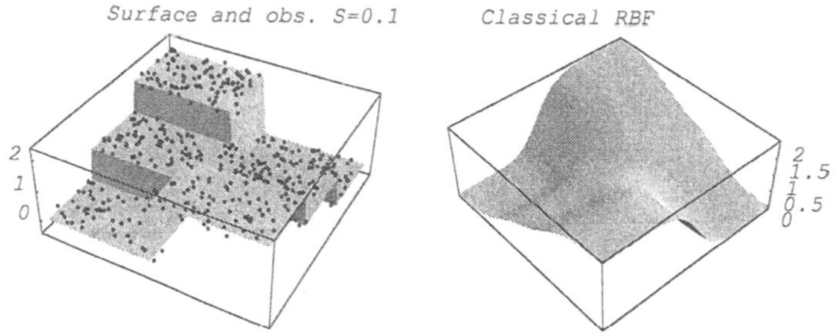

Fig. 1. Left panel – plot of the original surface and observations with random $N(0, 0.1)$ errors (dots). Right panel – classical RBF net performance. Visible degradation of edges, although oversmoothing was avoided by selecting smoothing parameter at small level $h = 0.1$).

- a feedback from the net output to its weights (see Fig. 2),
- an additional RBF factors, which act in the output space, i.e., the centers of these factors are selected from (possibly transformed) output observations.

These ingredients are introduced in the next subsection. Although the net shown in Fig. 2 is not as general as possible (h_x and x_j^*'s do not depend on the net output), it is still too general for investigating recurrent feedback processes. Fortunately, for our purposes it suffices to consider more specific class of weights. Namely, selecting in (1) the weights as follows $w_j = \omega_j(m, x) \cdot V((m - y_j^*)/H)$ we arrive to extended RBF net

$$m^* = \sum_{j=1}^{r} \omega_j(m^*, x) \cdot V\left(\frac{(m^* - y_j^*)}{H}\right) \cdot K\left(\frac{||x - x_j^*||}{h_x}\right), \tag{2}$$

which describes a steady state of the following iterations

$$m^{(k+1)} = \sum_{j=1}^{r} \omega_j(m^{(k)}, x) \cdot V\left(\frac{(m^{(k)} - y_j^*)}{H}\right) \cdot K\left(\frac{||x - x_j^*||}{h_x}\right), \quad k = 0, 1, \ldots, \tag{3}$$

provided that they are convergent. $\omega_j(m, x)$'s are new weights.

The output of the net $y = m^*$, but in practice y is taken to be $m^{(k)}$, after sufficiently many iterations of (3), when subsequent $m^{(k)}$'s do not change essentially.

Concerning function $V : R \to R$, we impose the same general conditions as those, which are usually required from kernels $K(.)$, i.e.,

$$V(t) \geq 0, \quad \int_{-\infty}^{\infty} V(t)dt = 1, \quad \int_{-\infty}^{\infty} tV(t)dt = 0, \quad \int_{-\infty}^{\infty} t^2 V(t)dt < \infty, \tag{4}$$

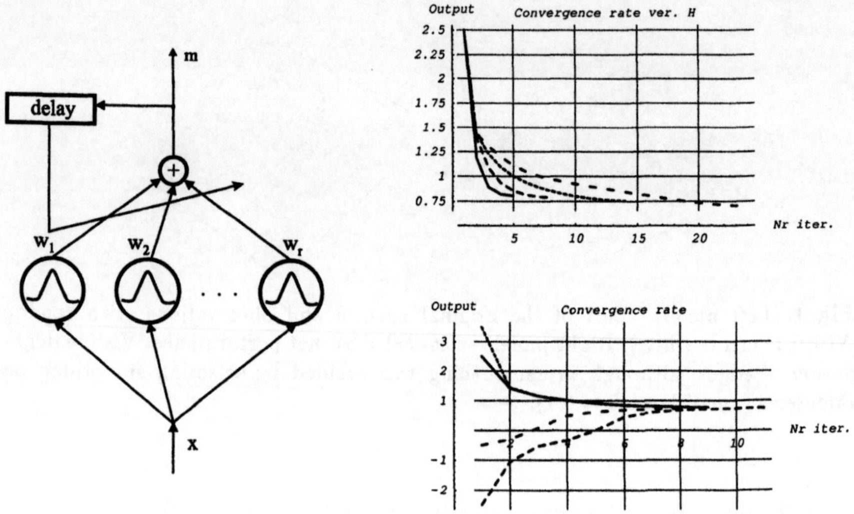

Fig. 2. Left panel – Structure of RBF net with feedback. Right panel – convergence rate of output feedback recurrent process for different starting points (lower plot) and for different widths of vertical RBF's (upper plot).

Analysis of (2) reveals that the extension of RBF nets proposed in this paper is in the presence of a new factor $V\left(\frac{(m^*-y_j^*)}{H}\right)$ in radial basis functions. This factor is different in spirit than the traditional RBF's $K\left(\frac{||x-x_j^*||}{h_x}\right)$, since also output centers y_j^*'s and kernel V are present. The difference is, however, not only formal, but also in the role played by the factors $V\left(\frac{(m^*-y_j^*)}{H}\right)$. Selecting carefully $H > 0$, y_j^*'s and V, one can obtain jump preserving smoothing RBF nets and our main topic in this paper is to show how to choose these ingredients.

3 Learning

A training sequence consists of pairs of input-output observations (x_i, y_i), where either $y_i = F(x_i)$ or

$$y_i = F(x_i) + \varepsilon_i, \quad i = 1, 2, \ldots n. \tag{5}$$

In the above, $F : R^d \to R$ denotes a surface to be approximated or estimated by our net. In the latter case F is unknown and ε_i's random errors with zero mean.

Selecting weights as follows

$$\omega_j(m,x) = \frac{y_j^*}{\sum_{l=1}^{r} V\left(\frac{(m-y_l^*)}{H}\right) \cdot K\left(\frac{||x-x_l^*||}{h_x}\right)} \tag{6}$$

we remain m, H and h_x and RBFs' centers x_l^*, y_l^*, $l = 1, 2, \ldots r$ to be chosen in a learning process.

For preliminary studies we select the centers at the observation points, i.e., $x_i^* = x_i$, $y_i^* = y_i$, $i = 1, 2, \ldots n$.

Remark 31 *From our simulation studies, which are not reported in this paper, it follows that one should carefully and simultaneously select both x_i^*'s and y_i^*'s. Otherwise, one can spoil jump preserving properties of the extended net.*

Substituting the above chosen centers into (2) we get

$$m^* = \frac{\sum_{j=1}^{n} y_j \cdot V\left(\frac{(m^*-y_j)}{H}\right) \cdot K\left(\frac{||x-x_j||}{h_x}\right)}{\sum_{l=1}^{n} V\left(\frac{(m^*-y_l)}{H}\right) \cdot K\left(\frac{||x-x_l||}{h_x}\right)}, \tag{7}$$

The attempt of solving this equation by feedback iterations provides (compare also (3))

$$m^{(k+1)} = \frac{\sum_{j=1}^{n} y_j \cdot V\left(\frac{(m^{(k)}-y_j)}{H}\right) \cdot K\left(\frac{||x-x_j||}{h_x}\right)}{\sum_{l=1}^{n} V\left(\frac{(m^{(k)}-y_l)}{H}\right) \cdot K\left(\frac{||x-x_l||}{h_x}\right)}, \quad k = 0, 1, \ldots. \tag{8}$$

As a staring point it is reasonable to take

$$m^{(0)} = y_{i_*}, \quad \text{where} \quad i_* = arg \min_{1 \le i \le n} ||x - x_i||. \tag{9}$$

By the lack of space we can not provide the proof of convergence of (8) here. Roughly speaking, the proof is based on the fixed point theorem and it reveals that for H larger than a certain H_{min} the iterations (8) are convergent with probability one, if n sufficiently large (but still finite). The rate of convergence is sufficient for practical applications. Usually, it is enough to use 5-6 iterations (see the right panel in Fig. 2, where the rate of convergence is investigated for different H and different starting points).

The r.h.s. of (7) has a very similar structure as algorithms for estimating a vertically weighted regression discussed in [7], [5] and [6]. The main difference is in introducing the recurrent process (8), which is convergent to m^*.

4 Results of simulations

To verify the performance of (8) $n = 500$ observations of the following surface

$$F(x) = \begin{cases} \exp\left[-20\left((x^{(1)} - 1/4)^2 + (x^{(2)} - 3/4)^2\right)\right] + 0.3, & \text{if } x^{(1)} < x^{(2)}, \\ \exp\left[-20\left((x^{(1)} - 3/4)^2 + (x^{(2)} - 1/4)^2\right)\right] - 0.3, & \text{otherwise.} \end{cases}$$

were generated according to (5) (see also left panel in Fig. 3) with x_i's being uniformly distributed in $[0,1] \times [0,1]$. The results of extended RBF net

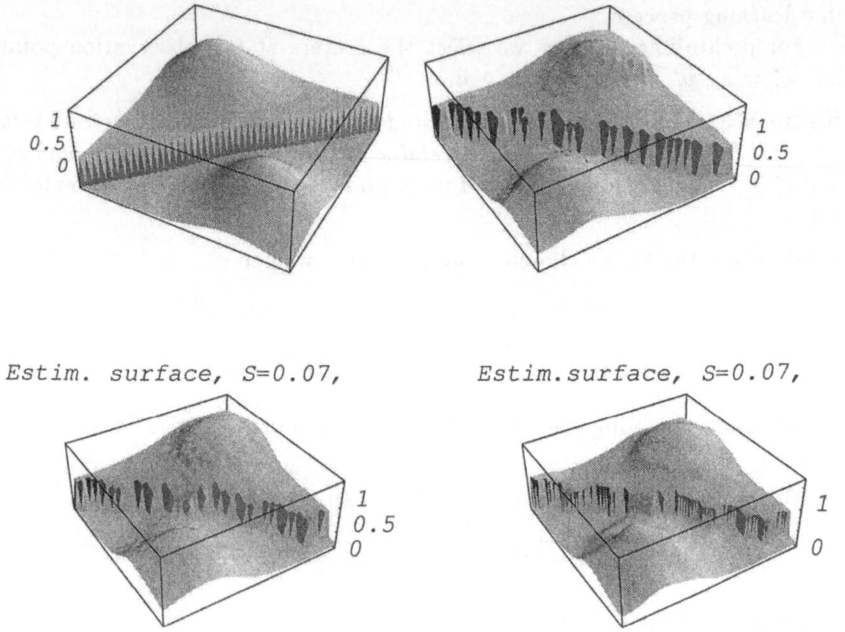

Fig. 3. Extended RBF net performance: upper plots – in the presence of additive errors distributed uniformly in $[-0.1, 0.1]$. $H = 0.4$; lower plots – in the presence of additive errors with $N(0, 0.07)$ distribution. RBF parameters $H = 0.25$ and $h = 0.012$ (lower left panel), $h = 0.07$ (lower right panel).

learning are shown in Fig. 3 (uuper plot) for ε_i's being uniformly distributed while Fig. 3 (lower plots) was obtained when errors were normally distributed. Analogously, Fig. 4 was obtained by applying extended RBF net learning to $n = 1000$ observations of the stairs-like function corrupted by $N(0, 0.1)$ errors.

Conclusions. Good jump preserving properties of the proposed extension of RBF nets, which can be observed from the above mentioned simulations, makes it promising that also similar nets with carefully selected RBF centers would have the jump preserving properties.

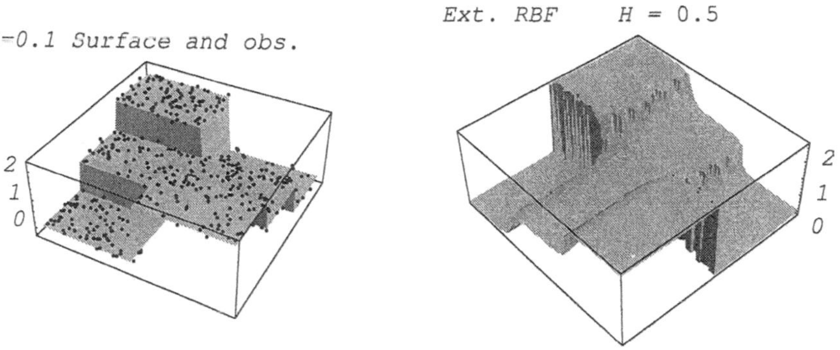

Fig. 4. Left panel – plot of the original surface plus errors. Right panel – ERBF net performance - $H = 0.25$, $h = 0.06$.

References

1. F. Girosi (1992). Regularization theory, radial basis functions and networks. In V. Cherkassky, J. H. Friedman, and H. Wechsler, editors, *From Statistics to Neural Networks. Theory and Pattern recognition Applications*, pages **166–187. Springer-Verlag, Berlin.
2. F. Girosi and G. Anzellotti (1993). Rates of convergence for radial basis functions and neural networks. In R. J. Mammone, editor, *Artificial Neural Networks for Speech and Vision*, pages 97–113. Chapman & Hall, London.
3. F. Girosi, M. Jones, and T. Poggio (1995). Regularization theory and neural network architectures. *Neural Computation*, **7**, 219–267.
4. A. Krzyżak, T. Linder, and G. Lugosi (1996). Nonparametric estimation and classification using radial basis function nets and empirical risk minimization. *IEEE Transactions on Neural Networks*, **7**, 475–487.
5. Pawlak, M. and Rafajłowicz, E. (1999). Vertically weighted regression - a tool for nonlinear data analysis and constructing control charts. *Journal of the German Statistical Association*, **84**, 367-388.
6. Pawlak, M. and Rafajłowicz, E. (2001). Jump preserving signal reconstruction using vertical weighting. *Nonlinear Analysis*, **47**, 327-338.
7. Rafajłowicz, E. (1996). Model free control charts for continuous time production processes. *Preprint, Institute of Engineering Cybernetics, Wrocław University of Technology, also presented at Seminar of Department of Statistics, European University Viadrina, July 1996.*
8. L. Xu, A. Krzyżak, and E. Oja (1993) Rival penalized competitive learning for clustering analysis, RBF net and curve detection. *IEEE Transactions on Neural Networks*, **4**, 636–649.

How to Test Overfitting When There is not Enough Data for a Testing Set?

Izabela Rejer[1], Andrzej Piegat[2]

The University of Szczecin, Mickiewicza 64, Szczecin, Poland
[1] i_rejer@uoo.univ.szczecin.pl
[2] Andrzej.Piegat@wi.tuniv.szczecin.pl

Abstract. A good neural network has to produce precise results not only when dealing with training data but also when it is used for cases which has not been presented during a process of training. It means that in order to test a neural network's performance you have to possess more examples than you use to train it. But what should you do if you have even a problem with gathering enough data for training? Where can you find new examples? This problem, in one of two possible kinds of overfitting, can be solved by using a method which will be presented in this article.

Introduction

All neural networks, regardless of kind, need data to be trained. In average, the more training parameters are in a network the more training examples should be gathered. It is very difficult to define exactly how much data are required because it depends on the amount and characteristics of input variables. Generally, it can be said that the higher dimension of an input vector and the higher nonlinearity of a problem, the more complicated surface of a model and the larger amount of data are required to train a network. It means that, when you have a large input vector you need more training parameters and of course more training data. Unfortunately, when you deal with neural networks you need not one but at least two sets of data: training set and testing set. The first one is used to train a network and the second – to test its capabilities for a generalisation [2]. A proper classification of data for sets that are mentioned above is a really complicated task [3], but generally it can be said that in most cases both sets should be about the same size. This means that you have to collect twice the amount of data that is used for training.

Not always you have the possibility to gather enough data. This is a common situation when you deal with economic problems of time series. It isn't so often when you consider microeconomic issues which are related "to relatively small units, an individual, a firm, an industry, a single market" like, for example, stock market, but is normal in macroeconomic issues which are related "to highly aggregate markets or the entire economy" [1]. The main cause of problems with gathering enough amount of data in macroeconomic situations is that researcher has to use data sources which were prepared by external institutions. Unfortunately such institutions publish their data yearly, quarterly or in the best case – monthly. It means that when you want to examine a development of a real macroeconomic problem for the last five years you have only 60 pieces of monthly data. And on the other hand you can not examine macroeconomic issues in a much longer period because economic situation is not so stable. That is an answer why when you deal with macroeconomic problems you can hardly collect enough data to train a network, not to mention testing it. So what can you do in such situation, how can you test the capabilities for a generalisation of a created model?

1. The unemployment rate model

Authors of this article met the above problem during a study of an unemployment rate in Poland in years: 1992-1999. The most important goal of the study was to create a neural network model which indicated causal dependencies between main macroeconomic factors and the unemployment rate. The first step of this research was to build a very precise model showing which factors could be used to replace unemployment rate in a specific moment of time. The survey had started with 28 different factors which were suspected to influence on the unemployment rate. During a research the input vector was reduced to five variables which were: number of inhabitants, money supply, number of graduates, interest rate of bill rediscount and exchange rate of 100 USD. All partial models which had to be produced in order to find a final model (which is presented in Fig. 1) were built as a perceptron neural networks with one hidden layer composed of ten hidden sigmoidal neurons.

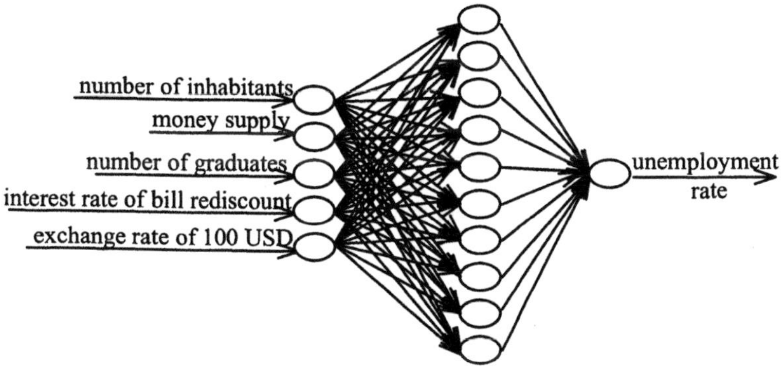

Fig. 1. A perceptron model of the unemployment rate in a specific moment of time

Unfortunately only 96 pieces of data (monthly data from 01.1992 to 12.1999) were possible to get what was hardly enough to train such big networks. As there was no possibility to gather more data and rather little sense to divide full set of training examples into two subsets, it was clear that another way of building a testing set had to be found.

2. Two kinds of overfitting

You have to test neural network models in order to check theirs capabilities for a generalisation. It means you have to check whether answers of a neural network model for new examples are as good as for these which were presented during a process of training. When the test is positive you have well-learned network which can be used in a normal work. It can be said that such network has proper capabilities for a generalisation or it is good fitted to the examined system. Sometimes after process of training you can receive a network which is, as it is called, "overfitted". It means that the network produces excellent results when deals with the examples from the training set but very poor results when deals with the examples from the testing set. The term "overfitting" has two slightly different meanings that depend on kind of data describing the examined system [3]. First meaning of the "overfitting" is connected with systems which are described by rather noisy data [4]. When you deal with noisy data you use a neural network to find a general rule of an examined system. In such situation you will say your model is overfitted when it fits to single pieces of data instead of giving a general approximation of all of them. In the Fig. 2 are shown two neural network models of the same noisy system.

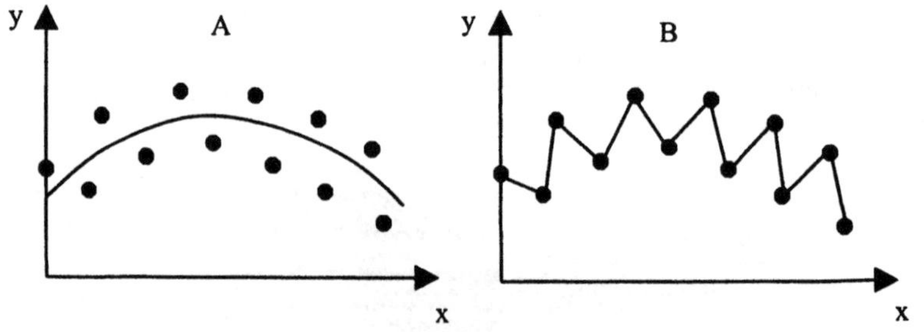

Fig. 2. Overfitting of a neural network model of a noisy system

The model presented in the Fig. 2A is a good example of the approximation while the second one is overfitted because there is a possibility that it does not illustrate a general rule of a system but a noise which exists in data. Of course only the knowledge whether you deal with noisy or unnoisy data allows you to find out which one of these two models is correct. Such situation is a consequence of other requirements which have to be met by a model of an unnoisy system. When you have unnoisy data you want to receive a neural network model which can be not only a good reflection of a general rule of a system but which can also fit the data in the most precise way. In such case you would rather prefer a model presented in the Fig. 2B than this presented in the Fig. 2A. But how about the overfitting in such situation? Is it possible to talk about the overfitting when there is only a little or even none noise in data? The answer is 'yes', but this time overfitting is connected with neural network capabilities for an interpolation. In the Fig. 3 are presented two different neural network models of the same unnoisy system.

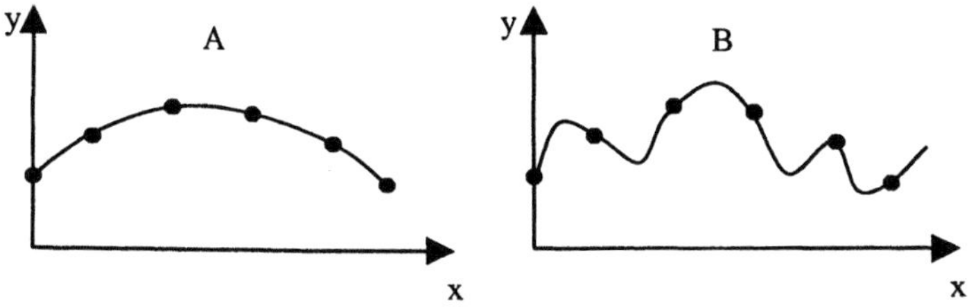

Fig. 3. Overfitting of a neural network model of an unnoisy system

Both presented models are fitted to the training data with the same rate of precision. However, the second model has no capabilities for the interpolation so its answers for the examples, which have not been presented during a process of training, will be as bad as they can.

As it was said in the first chapter the goal of the authors' research was to find variables which can replace the unemployment rate in a specific moment of time. This means that the authors looked for the most precise model with good capabilities for interpolation so they had to deal with the second kind of overfitting.

3. A method of generating testing examples

A method which will be presented in this chapter seems to be not very complicated but according to the knowledge of the authors of this article has not been published or proposed before.

Looking carefully in the Fig. 3 you can observe that the only possibility for the overfitting in such system exists between two pieces of training data following one after the other. If you want your model to have good interpolation capabilities, the only thing you have to do is to check its performance in response to values put between training data. If the results do not meet your expectations (like in the Fig. 4), it means the model is overfitted. The situation shown in the Fig. 4 is quite simply because system presented there is described only by one input variable. But what can be done when there is a larger dimension of an input vector? The authors' proposal of dealing with such situations is quite similar to this mentioned above.

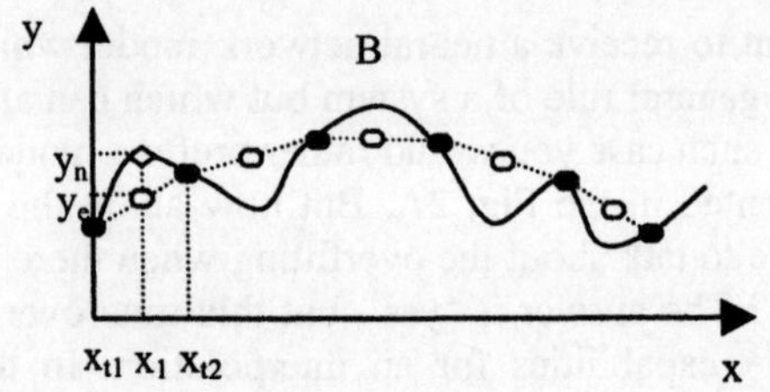

Fig. 4. Testing an overfitting in one input system; x – an input variable; x_{t1}, x_{t2} – two examples of training data; x_1 – an example of testing data; y – an output variable; y_n – a network response for value x_1; y_e – an expected response for value x_1.

The problem which has to be solved is to find a way of generating new examples which can be used to test the overfitting of the neural model. The method proposed by the authors is based on the fact that the examined problem is connected with time series. This means that both input and output variables can be presented in regard of time. Now, the assumption can be made that all variables (input and output) are changing steadily between two moments of time: from t to $t+1$. According to this assumption the model should produce correct results not only for values of all input variables in moments t and $t+1$ but also in moment $t+0,5$.

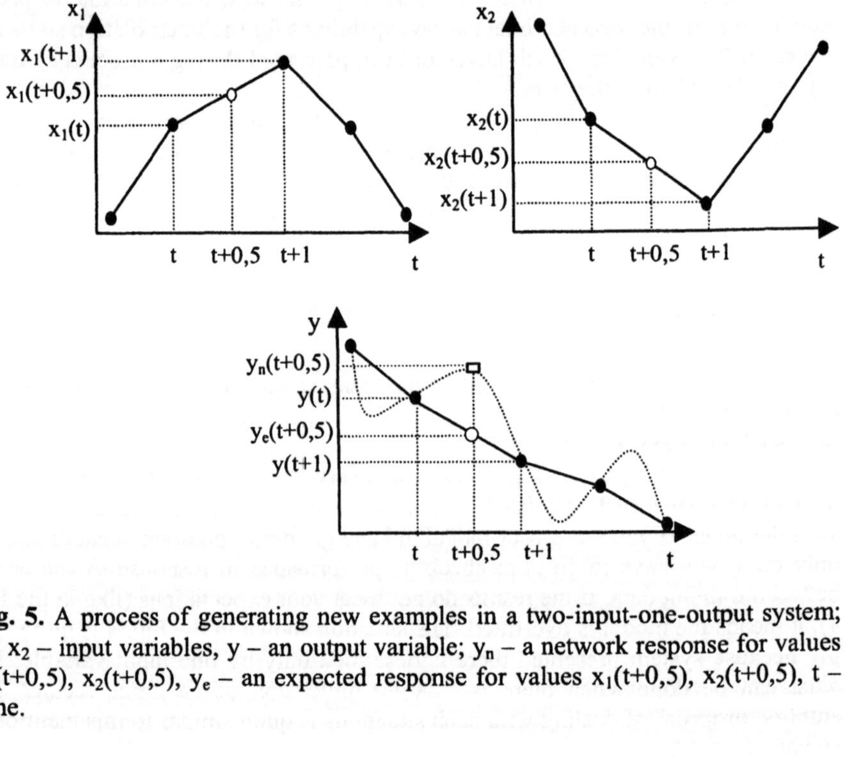

Fig. 5. A process of generating new examples in a two-input-one-output system; x_1, x_2 – input variables, y – an output variable; y_n – a network response for values $x_1(t+0,5)$, $x_2(t+0,5)$, y_e – an expected response for values $x_1(t+0,5)$, $x_2(t+0,5)$, t – time.

The values of input (and output) variables in moment $t+0,5$ can be calculated as a normal arithmetic average:

$$x_i(t+0,5) = \frac{x_i(t) + x_i(t+1)}{2} \tag{1}$$

where:

x_i – input variable i (i=1 ... n)

$x_i(t)$ – a value of an input variable i in a moment of time

A process of generating new examples in two-inputs/one-output system can be illustrated as in the Fig. 5. In that figure you can see two training examples: $\{x_1(t), x_2(t), y(t)\}$, $\{x_1(t+1), x_2(t+1), y(t+1)\}$ and one new-generated testing example: $\{x_1(t+0,5), x_2(t+0,5), y(t+0,5)\}$. As in one-input system it can be said that a neural model is overfitted when its response for values of all input variables (in this case two) in the moment $t+0,5$: $y_n(t+0,5)$ considerably differs from $y_e(t+0,5)$.

4. Final remarks

The method which was described in the previous chapter is very useful because it allows to keep all known data in the training set. This is important not only when there is not enough data to separate a testing set but also when the input vector of the problem consists of many input variables. Sometimes, in such situations, it is difficult to choose a proper method for including data into training or testing set and on the other hand it is easy to leave empty spaces in training set what can be the direct cause of a poor performance of a network. An additional advantage of proposed method is that always the rate of overfitting can be checked visually on a chart, no matter how many input variables exist.

The method proposed in this article is dedicated, in a present form, especially for time series systems. The problem is how to expand it also for other kinds of systems. One of the authors of this article leads a research which aim is to answer above question. The results of this research will be presented soon.

References

1. Arnold R. A. (1996) Economics. West Publishing Company, USA
2. Masters T. (1996) Practical Neural Network Recipes in C++. Scientific-Technical Publishing Company, Warsaw
3. Piegat A. (2001) Fuzzy Modeling and Control. A Springer - Verlag Company, Heidelberg - New York
4. Zieliński J. S. (2000) Intelligence systems in management, Theory and practice. Scientific Publishing Company PWN, Warsaw

On Very Large Scale Hamiltonian Neural Nets

Wieslaw Sienko, Wieslaw Citko

Department of Electrical Engineering, Gdynia Maritime Academy, 81-225 Gdynia, Morska 83, Poland, Email: wcitko@am.gdynia.pl

Abstract. This paper presents how to design very large scale lossless neural nets (LONN), which can be used as Walsh-spectrum analyzer. This analysis relies on the orthogonality of weight matrix **W**, where **W** is Hurwitz-Radon matrix. The unique feature of the LONN is the possibility to treat them either as algorithms or as Hamiltonian physical objects (Walsh Transformation Processors).

1 Introduction

It has been pointed out that very large scale neural nets should be passive or particularly lossless [1,2,3]. These technical notions mean that from mathematical point of view they should be Hamiltonian systems. The purpose of this paper is to present some very universal properties of Hamiltonian neural nets in particular to show how to treat such nets as spectral analyzers, function approximators and orthogonal filters. A comment on quantum computing will be given as well.

2 Hamiltonian Neural Nets

A general description form of an autonomous Hamiltonian system is given by the following state-space equation:

$$\dot{\mathbf{x}} = \mathbf{J}\mathbf{H}'(\mathbf{x}) \tag{1}$$

where:

$$-\mathbf{J} = \mathbf{J}^{\mathbf{T}} = \mathbf{J}^{-1} \tag{2}$$

There is such a basis in R^{2n}, where matrix **J** has a form:

$$\mathbf{J} = \begin{bmatrix} \mathbf{0} & \mathbf{1} \\ -\mathbf{1} & \mathbf{0} \end{bmatrix} \text{ ; } \mathbf{0, 1, -1} \text{ are n x n diagonal matrices} \tag{3}$$

Function **H(x)** is a Hamiltonian (energy) of system. Since in Hamiltonian systems there is no dissipation of energy, their trajectories can be very complicated for $t \rightarrow \pm \infty$. Therefore, the basic method of their movement description is to find periodic solutions (using for example the Maupertuis principle). The equation (1) has constant solutions i.e. every point $\mathbf{x}_0 \in R^{2n}$ such that $\mathbf{H}'(\mathbf{x}_0) = \mathbf{0}$ is the equilibrium and $\mathbf{x}(t) \equiv \mathbf{x}_0$ is the solution. The structure of Passive Neural Networks has been proposed as a compatible connection of passive neurons [3]. For completeness of this presentation let us review some basic features of Lossless Neural Nets. First of all, a model of the lossless neuron in the form of signal (information) flow network is given in Fig.1.

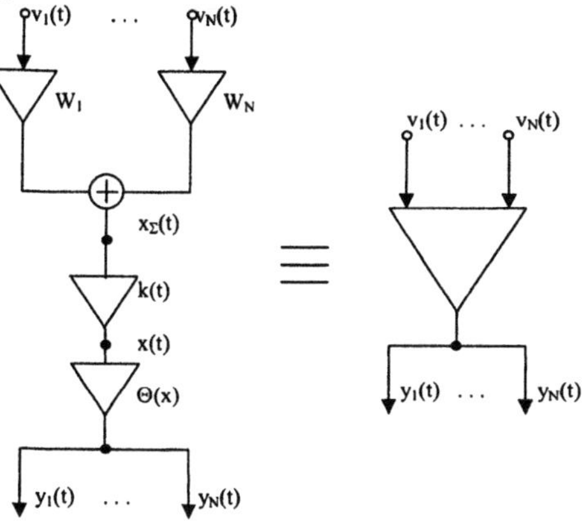

Fig. 1. A model of lossless neuron as a signal-flow network..

Basic features of lossless neuron are as follows:

1.
$$x(t) = k(t) * x_{\Sigma}(t) \quad \text{(linear block)} \tag{4}$$

where: $k(t) = L^{-1}\{K(s)\}$,

$K(s)$ – transmittance belonging to a class of lossless real functions.

2. $\Theta(x)$ belongs to class M of nonlinearities i.e.:

$$\mu_1 \le \frac{\Theta(x)}{x} \le \mu_2 \quad \mu_1, \mu_2 \in [0, \infty] \tag{5}$$

Sigmoidal activation function also belongs to this class.

3. Energy absorbed by neuron:

$$E = \sum_{i=1}^{N} \int_{-\infty}^{t} v_i(\tau) y_i(\tau) d\tau = \int_{-\infty}^{t} x_{\Sigma}(\tau)\Theta(x(\tau)) d\tau \ge 0, \forall t \tag{6}$$

For a first order neuron i.e. under the assumption that the linear block k(t) is an ideal integrator, one obtains:

$$x_{\Sigma}(t) = \dot{x}(t) \tag{7}$$

and the energy (6) can be seen as a Hamiltonian function of the neuron. Hence:

$$E = H(x) \quad \text{and} \quad H'(x) = \Theta(x) \tag{8}$$

Structure of lossless neural net can be obtained as compatible connections of N lossless neurons i.e. compatibility of connection preserves the losslessness of the net. An example of two neuron net is shown in Fig.2.

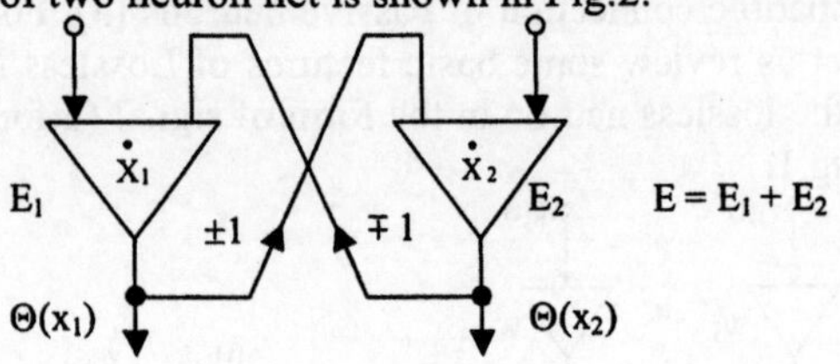

Fig. 2. Two lossless neurons compatible connected-two neuron lossless net.

It can be seen that the state-space description of the net from Fig.2 is as follows:

$$\begin{bmatrix} \dot{x}_1 \\ \dot{x}_2 \end{bmatrix} = \begin{bmatrix} 0 & \pm 1 \\ \mp 1 & 0 \end{bmatrix} \begin{bmatrix} \Theta(x_1) \\ \Theta(x_2) \end{bmatrix} \tag{9}$$

It is a Hamiltonian system with Hamiltonian function given by:

$$E = \sum_{i=1}^{N} E_i \tag{10}$$

where: E_i – energy (6) absorbed by i-th neuron.

The two neuron lossless net from Fig.2 can be treated as an elementary building block to create very large scale neural networks. Generally, lossless neural net composed of N neurons is described by the following state-space equation:

$$\dot{\mathbf{x}} = \mathbf{W}\boldsymbol{\Theta}(\mathbf{x}) \tag{11}$$

where: **W**- matrix of information flow connections (weight matrix) and $\mathbf{W} = -\mathbf{W}^T$ (skew-symmetry).

A neural net composed of N elementary neuron pairs from Fig.2 is called Lossless-Orthogonal Neural Net (LONN) if weight matrix **W** in Eq. (11) is orthogonal i.e.

$$\mathbf{W} \cdot \mathbf{W}^T = \mathbf{1} \tag{12}$$

Hence

$$\mathbf{W}^2 = -\mathbf{1} \text{ i.e. } \mathbf{W}^{-1} = \mathbf{W}^T = -\mathbf{W} \text{ (an involution)} \tag{13}$$

Thus, LONN is a Hamiltonian system with activation function $\boldsymbol{\Theta}(\mathbf{x}) = \mathbf{H}'(\mathbf{x})$, where $\mathbf{H}(\mathbf{x})$ – Hamiltonian function.

The weight matrix of LONN can be formulated as follows:

$$\mathbf{W}_{2^n} = \begin{bmatrix} \mathbf{W}_{2^{n-1}} & \mathbf{W}_C \\ -\mathbf{W}_C^T & -\mathbf{W}_{2^{n-1}} \end{bmatrix}; n = 1, 2, \ldots \tag{14}$$

where:

$$\mathbf{W}_1 = \begin{bmatrix} 0 & 1 \\ -1 & 0 \end{bmatrix} \tag{15}$$

and

$$\mathbf{W_C} \cdot \mathbf{W_C^T} = \mathbf{1} \quad \left(\dim \mathbf{W_C} = \dim \mathbf{W}_{2^{n-1}}\right)$$

$$\mathbf{W}_{2^{n-1}} \cdot \mathbf{W_C} - \mathbf{W_C} \cdot \mathbf{W}_{2^{n-1}} = \mathbf{0}$$

The simplest solution of (15) is: $\mathbf{W_C} = \mathbf{1}$.

Another solution of (15) is: $\mathbf{W_C} = \mathbf{W}_{2^{n-1}} + \mathbf{1}$

Thus for example:

$$\mathbf{W}_2 = \frac{1}{\sqrt{2}} \begin{bmatrix} 0 & 1 & 1 & 0 \\ -1 & 0 & 0 & 1 \\ -1 & 0 & 0 & -1 \\ 0 & -1 & 1 & 0 \end{bmatrix} \text{ or } \mathbf{W}_2 = \frac{1}{\sqrt{3}} \begin{bmatrix} 0 & 1 & 1 & 1 \\ -1 & 0 & -1 & 1 \\ -1 & 1 & 0 & -1 \\ -1 & -1 & 1 & 0 \end{bmatrix}$$

3 Lossless-Orthogonal Neural Net as a Spectrum Analyzer

Some basic properties of the LONN can be derived from Eq.(11). First, the structure of such a net creates a nonlinear vector field: $\mathbf{W\Theta(x)}=\mathrm{v}(\mathbf{x})$ with a single equilibrium point for $\mathbf{x} = \mathbf{0}$. Any LONN determines a type of orthogonal transformation, namely:

$$\mathbf{W} \cdot \mathbf{\Theta(x)} + \mathbf{I_{in}} = \mathbf{0} \tag{16}$$

where: $\mathbf{I}_{in}$ – input vector (input data or signal)
It is worth noting that Eq.(16) gives the steady state solution of the net under constant excitation. Hence, output of the net i.e.

$$\mathbf{\Theta(x)} = \mathbf{W I_{in}} \tag{17}$$

can be seen as a Walsh spectrum of input vector. Since, however $\mathbf{\Theta(x)}$ is output of nonlinear, dynamical Hamiltonian system, Eq.(17) is true only for such a bounded input that $|\mathbf{\Theta(x)}| \leq 1$ (for sigmoidal (±1) activation functions).
Since $\mathbf{W}^2 = \mathbf{-1}$ it is clear that, this Walsh analysis sets up the following relationships:

a) $(\mathbf{\Theta}, \mathbf{I}_{in}) = 0$, where (. , .) scalar product in L_2
b) The components of vector $\mathbf{\Theta(x)}$ are Fourier coefficients. Thus the LONN performs an expansion of input vector in the sum of orthogonal patterns

(columns or rows of weight matrix **W**). If input vector consists of discrete samples of a real function, then these patterns can be treated as Haar-like wavelets.

c) If for given input data set there are the large Fourier coefficients, then spectrum analysis fixes a number of principal components of the input data.

4 LONN as an Orthogonal Filter

Orthogonal filtering is one of basic operations in modern signal processing. For example in digital communication transmitted messages are encoded in the form of orthogonal symbols. Thus the transmitted signal consists of the symbols corrupted by additive noise. Hence, the main function of any receiver is to perform such an orthogonal filtering. A basic structure of an orthogonal filter using the structure of the LONN is shown in Fig.3.

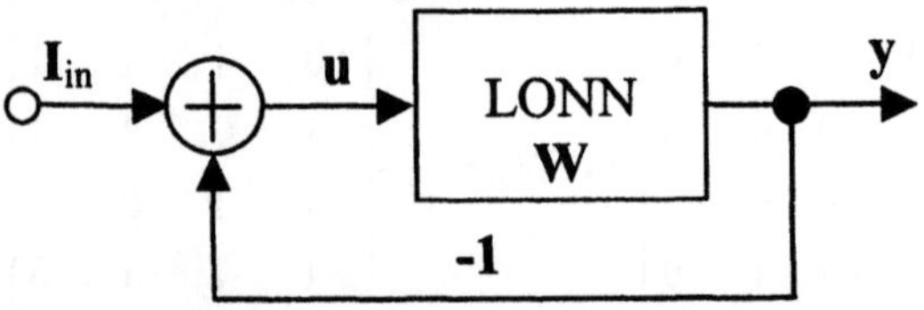

Fig. 3. Structure of an orthogonal filter.

It can be seen that such a filter performs the following expansion:

$$\mathbf{I}_{in} = \mathbf{u} + \mathbf{y} \tag{18}$$

where: **u** and **y** are orthogonal i.e. $\mathbf{y} = \mathbf{W}\mathbf{u}$.
At the same time Eq.(18) sets up two types of orthogonal transformations:

$$\mathbf{y} = 0{,}5 \cdot (\mathbf{1} + \mathbf{W})\mathbf{I}_{in} \tag{19}$$

$$\mathbf{u} = 0{,}5 \cdot (\mathbf{1} - \mathbf{W})\mathbf{I}_{in} \tag{20}$$

Hence, assuming that considered symbols are encoded by columns or rows of weight matrix (**1** + **W**), the largest Fourier coefficient of spectrum at output of orthogonal filter can be used as a measure of presence of hidden in noise information. Indeed, one obtains

$$\mathbf{I}_{in} = \mathbf{w}_i + \mathbf{n} = \mathbf{u} + \mathbf{y} \tag{21}$$

where: $\mathbf{w}_i$ - a symbol (a column or row of matrix (**1** + **W**)), $i \in [1, \ldots, N]$,
n - additive noise, $N = \dim \mathbf{W}$

Hence, there is such a minimal S/N ratio, that

$$\Theta_i = (\mathbf{w}_i + \mathbf{n}, \mathbf{w}_i) > \Theta_k = (\mathbf{w}_i + \mathbf{n}, \mathbf{w}_k), \forall k \neq i \quad (22)$$

where: Θ_i – the largest Fourier coefficient of the output spectrum.

Moreover, the absorbed and reflected signals **y** and **u** can be used for spectrum analysis, similarly as in Fettweis Digital Wave Filters Theory.

5 Concluding Remarks

In this paper we have presented how to design very large scale neural networks (LONN) which can be used as Walsh-spectrum analyzer. This analysis relies on the orthogonality of weight matrix **W** ($\mathbf{W}^2 = \mathbf{-1}$), where **W** can be classified as one of Hurwitz-Radon matrices. On the other hand it is worth noting that LONN can also be seen as a model of odd quantum systems containing half spin particles [4]. The unique feature of LONN, however, seems to be the fact that they can either be treated as algorithms or Hamiltonian physical devices (implementable for example in the VLSI technology). Parity functions, known from the literature [5,6] are an alternative tool for Walsh analysis and may create a framework for the so called quantum computing [7].

References

[1] Sienko W., Zurada J. (1990) Neural Signal-Flow Networks. Proc. of Neuronet'90. Conf., Prague, Czechoslovakia.

[2] Sienko W., Zurada J. (1991) Pseudopassive Neural Networks. Proc. IEEE ISCAS 1991, Singapore, p. 2495.

[3] Sienko W., Luksza A, Citko W. (1993) On Properties of Passive Neural Networks. Scientific Journal of Gdynia Maritime Academy, No. 25, p. 5, Gdynia.

[4] Sienko W. (2001) On Modeling the Quantum and Anticipatory Systems by Passive Neural Nets, International Journal of Computing Anticipatory Systems Edited by D. M. Dubois, Vol. 10, p. 218, CHAOS, Liege, Belgium.

[5] Roychowdhury V., Kai-Yeung Siu, Orlitsky A. (1994) Neural Models and Spectral Methods, in Theoretical Advances in Neural Computing and Learning. p. 3, Kluwer Academic Publishers Boston, London, Dordrecht.

[6] Mansour Y. (1994) Learning Boolean Functions via the Fourier Transform. in Theoretical Advances in Neural Computing and Learning. p. 391, Kluwer Academic Publishers Boston, London, Dordrecht.

[7] Ventura D., Martinez T. A Quantum Computational Learning Algorithm. quant-ph/9807052 18 July 1998.

On $sup-*$ Compositions of Fuzzy Implications

Michał Baczyński[1], Józef Drewniak[1,2], and Jolanta Sobera[1]

[1] Institute of Mathematics, University of Silesia,
40-007 Katowice, ul. Bankowa 14, Poland
E-mail: {michal,drewniak,jsobera}@ux2.math.us.edu.pl

[2] Institute of Mathematics, University of Rzeszów,
35-310 Rzeszów, ul. Rejtana 16a, Poland
E-mail: jdrewnia@univ.rzeszow.pl

Abstract. Recently we have examined properties of sup-min compositions of fuzzy implications [3]. However, in many applications, another connectives are used for composition of fuzzy implications. Now, we generalize these results to the case of sup $-*$ composition with a triangular norm $*$.

1 Introduction

The examination of compositions of fuzzy implications is very important in multistage decision making by approximate reasoning. It suffices to consider fuzzy implications as a particular case of fuzzy relations in $[0,1]$ which was initiated by Baldwin, Pilsworth [4]. They were generating new fuzzy implications as sup – min compositions of given ones. We are going to continue this way for the monotonic fuzzy implications (cf. Fodor, Roubens [7]).

Definition 1 ([1]). A function $I\colon [0,1]^2 \to [0,1]$ is called fuzzy implication if it is decreasing with respect to the first variable, increasing with respect to the second one and fulfils the binary implication truth table:

$$I(0,0) = I(0,1) = I(1,1) = 1\,, \qquad I(1,0) = 0\,. \tag{1}$$

The set of all fuzzy implications is denoted by FI.

By monotonicity assumption we get

$$I(0,x) = I(x,1) = 1\,, \qquad x \in [0,1]\,. \tag{2}$$

Example 1 ([2]). The family FI has the least element I_0 and the greatest element I_1:

$$I_0(x,y) = \begin{cases} 1, & \text{if } x = 0 \text{ or } y = 1 \\ 0, & \text{elsewhere} \end{cases}, \quad I_1(x,y) = \begin{cases} 0, & \text{if } x = 1 \text{ and } y = 0 \\ 1, & \text{elsewhere} \end{cases} \tag{3}$$

for $x, y \in [0,1]$.

The above defined family FI is possibly the most general, however, it not contains many fuzzy implication functions considered in the literature.

Example 2 (cf. [6]). The function $I(x,y) = \max(1-x, \min(x,y))$, $x, y \in [0,1]$ is not decreasing under x. The function $I(x,y) = \max(0, y-x)$, $x, y \in [0,1]$ does not fulfil (1) (since $I(0,0) = I(1,1) = 0$).

Another examples of fuzzy implications will be presented later.

2 Triangular norms

A wide class of binary operations is used as fuzzy conjunctions.

Definition 2 (cf. Klement et al. [9]). An associative, commutative operation $*\colon [0,1]^2 \to [0,1]$ is called triangular norm (t-norm) if it is increasing and has neutral element $e = 1$:

$$\forall_{x\in[0,1]} \ (x * 1 = 1 * x = x) \ . \tag{4}$$

Directly from this definition we get

$$\forall_{x\in[0,1]} \ (x * 0 = 0 * x = 0) \ , \tag{5}$$

and operation $*$ fulfils the conjunction truth table

$$0 * 0 = 0 * 1 = 1 * 0 = 0 \ , \qquad\qquad 1 * 1 = 1 \ . \tag{6}$$

Corollary 1. *Any t-norm $*$ forms a commutative semigroup $([0,1], *)$ with the neutral element $e = 1$ and the zero element $z = 0$.*

Example 3 (see [10]). Family of t-norms has the greatest element $* = \wedge$ and the least element $* = \triangle$ where

$$x \wedge y = \min(x,y), \quad x \triangle y = \begin{cases} x \wedge y, & \text{if } x = 1 \text{ or } y = 1 \\ 0, & \text{elsewhere} \end{cases} , \quad x, y \in [0,1] \ . \tag{7}$$

However, a great meaning have another pair of t-norms: the product t-norm $* = \cdot$ and the Łukasiewicz t-norm $* = \odot$, where

$$x \cdot y = xy \ , \qquad x \odot y = \max(x + y - 1, 0) \ , \qquad x, y \in [0,1] \ . \tag{8}$$

Example 4. Many useful binary operations do not belong to the family of t-norms. E.g. means

$$x * y = \frac{x+y}{2} \ , \qquad x * y = \sqrt{xy} \ , \qquad x, y \in [0,1]$$

are not associative. Operations

$$x * y = x + y \ , \qquad x * y = \sqrt{x^2 + y^2} \ , \qquad x, y \in [0,1]$$

have values beyond interval $[0,1]$ and do not fulfil (6).

Lemma 1 (see [9]). *Triangular norm $*$ is left-continuous if it is supremum preserving:*

$$\forall_{T\neq\emptyset} \ \forall_{x,y_t\in[0,1]} \quad x * (\sup_{t\in T} y_t) = \sup_{t\in T} (x * y_t) \ . \tag{9}$$

In other words operation $*$ in (9) is distributive with respect to the supremum.

Example 5. Triangular norm $* = \Delta$ is not left-continuous since for $x, y < 1$ we have

$$x = x \,\Delta\, 1 = x \,\Delta\, (\sup_{y\in[0,1)} y) \neq \sup_{y\in[0,1)} (x \,\Delta\, y) = 0 \ .$$

3 Relation compositions

The composition of fuzzy relations introduced by Zadeh [11] is called sup – min one. In more general setting for fuzzy relations in [0, 1] we have

Definition 3 (cf. Goguen [8]). The sup $-*$ composition of fuzzy relations $I, J \in FI$ is given by the formula

$$(I \circ J)(x, z) = \sup_{y\in[0,1]} (I(x, y) * J(y, z)) \ , \qquad x, z \in [0, 1] \ , \tag{10}$$

where $*$ is a binary operation in [0, 1].

We use here formula (10) with t-norm $*$. It can be proved that the composition $\circ$ obtains many properties from the operation $*$.

Theorem 1 ([5]). *For any t-norm $*$ the composition* (10) *is increasing, has the neutral element (identity fuzzy relation), and the zero element (empty fuzzy relation). Moreover, if t-norm is left-continuous, then the composition* (10) *is associative.*

In general, the composition (10) is not commutative.

Example 6. Let $z \in (0, 1)$. Using formulas (3) we get

$$(I_1 \circ I_0)(1, z) = 0 \neq 1 = (I_0 \circ I_1)(1, z) \ .$$

We must observe that the operation (10) is not internal in FI. The result of composition is a fuzzy relation but not necessary it is a fuzzy implication.

Example 7. Using the implication I_1 from (3) we see that (cf. (1), (6))

$$\begin{aligned}(I_1 \circ I_1)(1, 0) =& I_1(1, 0) * I_1(0, 0) \vee \sup_{y\in(0,1)} (I_1(1, y) * I_1(y, 0)) \\ & \vee I_1(1, 1) * I_1(1, 0) = 0 \vee 1 \vee 0 = 1 \neq 0 \ ,\end{aligned}$$

i.e., the composition $I_1 \circ I_1$ does not fulfil the condition (1).

By Theorem 1, similarly as in Baczyński et al. [3], we get

Theorem 2. *For every t-norm $*$ we have*

$$\forall_{I,J\in FI} \quad (I \circ J \in FI \Longleftrightarrow (I \circ J)(1, 0) = 0) \ . \tag{11}$$

4 Semigroups of fuzzy implications

The condition (11) is good for checking the composition of concrete fuzzy implications. However, we look for subfamilies of FI which are closed under the composition (10). After [3] we can describe three such subfamilies

$$FI_L = \left\{ I \in FI : \underset{x\in[0,1)}{\forall} I(1,x) = 0 \right\} \qquad \text{(left ideal)}, \tag{12}$$

$$FI_R = \left\{ I \in FI : \underset{x\in(0,1]}{\forall} I(x,0) = 0 \right\} \qquad \text{(right ideal)}, \tag{13}$$

$$FI_C = FI_L \cap FI_R \qquad \text{(central ideal)}. \tag{14}$$

Lemma 2. *Families* (12)-(14) *are closed with respect to composition* (10).

Proof. If $I, J \in FI_L$, $z \in [0,1)$, then by (4), (5) and (10)

$$(I \circ J)(1,z) = \sup_{y\in[0,1)} (I(1,y) * J(y,z)) \vee I(1,1) * J(1,z) = J(1,z) = 0 ,$$

i.e. $I \circ J \in FI_L$. Similarly, for $I, J \in FI_R$, $x \in (0,1]$ we get

$$(I \circ J)(x,0) = I(x,0) * J(0,0) \vee \sup_{y\in(0,1]} (I(x,y) * J(y,0)) = I(x,0) = 0 ,$$

i.e. $I \circ J \in FI_R$. Thus FI_C is also closed under $\circ$.

Directly from the above proof we get an explanation of notations (12)-(14).

Corollary 2. *Families* (12)-(14) *fulfil*

$$FI \circ FI_L \subset FI_L, \quad FI_R \circ FI \subset FI_R, \quad FI \circ FI_C \subset FI_C, \quad FI_C \circ FI \subset FI_C.$$

Theorem 3. *If t-norm $*$ is left-continuous, then $(FI_L, \circ, \leq)$, $(FI_R, \circ, \leq)$, $(FI_C, \circ, \leq)$ are ordered semigroups of fuzzy implications, where*

$$I \leq J \iff \underset{x,y\in[0,1]}{\forall} (I(x,y) \leq J(x,y)) . \tag{15}$$

Families (12)-(14) *are also complete, distributive lattices.*

Proof. The first part is a direct consequence of Lemma 2 and Theorem 1. Now, by [2], Theorem 2, $(FI, \leq)$ is a complete, distributive lattice. Moreover, conditions in (12) and (13) are preserved by lattice operations. E.g., if $I(1,x) = 0$, $J(1,x) = 0$, then $(I \vee J)(1,x) = 0$, $(I \wedge J)(1,x) = 0$. Therefore, families (12)-(14) are sublattices of $(FI, \leq)$.

A comparison of (1) with (12), (13) leads to

Corollary 3. *All implications from families* (12)-(14) *are discontinous.*

Example 8 (cf. [2]). Known continuous fuzzy implications of Dienes, Łukasiewicz and Reichenbach:

$$I_{DN}(x,y) = (1-x) \vee y\ , \qquad I_{LK}(x,y) = 1 \wedge (1-x+y)\ ,$$
$$I_{RC}(x,y) = 1 - x + xy\ , \qquad x,y \in [0,1]$$

are not from families (12)-(14) and condition (11) must be checked separately. For discontinous implications of Gödel, Goguen and Rescher:

$$I_{\mathrm{GD}}(x,y) = \begin{cases} 1, & \text{if } x \le y \\ y, & \text{if } x > y \end{cases}, \qquad I'_{\mathrm{GD}}(x,y) = \begin{cases} 1, & \text{if } x \le y \\ 1-x, & \text{if } x > y \end{cases},$$

$$I_{\mathrm{GG}}(x,y) = \begin{cases} 1, & \text{if } x \le y \\ \frac{y}{x}, & \text{if } x > y \end{cases}, \qquad I'_{\mathrm{GG}}(x,y) = \begin{cases} 1, & \text{if } x \le y \\ \frac{1-x}{1-y}, & \text{if } x > y \end{cases},$$

$$I_{\mathrm{RS}}(x,y) = \begin{cases} 1, & \text{if } x \le y \\ 0, & \text{if } x > y \end{cases}, \qquad x,y \in [0,1]$$

we have I_{GD}, $I_{GG} \in FI_R \setminus FI_L$, I'_{GD}, $I'_{GG} \in FI_L \setminus FI_R$, $I_{RS} \in FI_C$. Therefore, these implications can be also used in multiple compositions (without additional checking).

Example 9. Semigroups from Theorem 3 are bounded (as complete lattices) and we describe their bounds:

$$\min FI_L = \min FI_R = \min FI_C = \min FI = I_0\ ,$$
$$\max FI_L = I_L\ , \qquad \max FI_R = I_R\ , \qquad \max FI_C = I_L \wedge I_R\ ,$$

where, for $x, y \in [0,1]$

$$I_L(x,y) = \begin{cases} 1, & \text{if } x < 1 \text{ or } y = 1 \\ 0, & \text{elsewhere} \end{cases}, \qquad I_R(x,y) = \begin{cases} 1, & \text{if } x = 0 \text{ or } y > 0 \\ 0, & \text{elsewhere} \end{cases}.$$

From Theorem 1 we see that the relation composition has the neutral element, but the identity relation is not an implication. The family of implications has its own neutral element of composition (10).

Theorem 4. *For arbitrary t-norm* $*$, *the Rescher implication* I_{RS} *is the neutral element of the composition* (10) *in* FI. *Moreover, if operation* $*$ *is left-continuous, then semigroups from Theorem 3 have the neutral element* I_{RS}.

Proof. For arbitrary $I \in FI$, $x, z \in [0,1]$ we have

$$(I \circ I_{RS})(x,z) = \sup_{y \le z} I(x,y) = I(x,z)\ ,$$
$$(I_{RS} \circ I)(x,z) = \sup_{y \ge x} I(y,z) = I(x,z)\ ,$$

which proves that $I \circ I_{RS} = I_{RS} \circ I = I$. The rest is a consequence of Theorem 3.

Theorem 5. *The implication* I_0 *is the zero element in* FI_C*, the right zero in* FI_R*, and the left zero in* FI_L.

Proof. Let $I \in FI$, $x \in (0,1]$, $z \in [0,1)$. After (1)-(5) we have

$$(I_0 \circ I)(x,z) = \sup_{y \in [0,1)} (I_0(x,y) * I(y,z)) \vee I_0(x,1) * I(1,z) = I(1,z) ,$$

$$(I \circ I_0)(x,z) = I(x,0) * I_0(0,z) \vee \sup_{y \in (0,1]} (I(x,y) * I_0(y,z)) = I(x,0) .$$

If $I \in FI_L$, then $(I_0 \circ I)(x,z) = 0 = I_0(x,z)$. If $I \in FI_R$, then $(I \circ I_0)(x,z) = 0 = I_0(x,z)$. For $x = 0$ or $z = 1$ we can use the property (2) and we get $I_0 \circ I = I_0$ in FI_L, $I \circ I_0 = I_0$ in FI_R, which finishes the proof.

5 Conclusion

The above theorems precise conditions for associativity of implication compositions which is necessary in multiple repetition of implications (e.g. in multistage decision making). We see, that used t-norm $*$ cannot be arbitrary but assumption on left-continuity suffice for "regular" properties of composition (10). In particular, the most commonly used t-norms (8) are continuous which guarantee semigroup properties of composition (10). Further investigations of implications composition with additional assumptions on t-norms and concrete examples of fuzzy implications will be presented later.

References

1. Baczyński, M., Drewniak, J. (1999): Conjugacy classes of fuzzy implication, In: Reusch, B. (Eds.): Computational Intelligence: Theory and Applications, Springer-Verlag, Berlin, (LNCS Vol. **1625**), 287-298.
2. Baczyński, M., Drewniak, J. (2000): Monotonic fuzzy implications, In: Szczepaniak, P., Lisboa, P., Kacprzyk, J. (Eds.): Fuzzy Systems in Medicine, Physica-Verlag, Heidelberg, (Studies in Fuzzines and Soft Computing, Vol. **41**), 90-111.
3. Baczyński, M., Drewniak, J., Sobera, J. (2001): Semigroups of fuzzy implications, Tatra Mt. Math. Publ. **21**, 61-71.
4. Baldwin, J.F., Pilsworth, B.W. (1980): Axiomatic approach to implication for approximate reasoning with fuzzy logic, Fuzzy Sets Syst. **3**, 193-219.
5. Drewniak, J., Kula, K. (2002): Generalized compositions of fuzzy relations, Presented in FSTA 2002, Liptovsky Jan, Slovakia.
6. Cordón, O., Herrera, F., Peregrin, A. (1997): Applicability of the fuzzy operators in the design of fuzzy logic controllers, Fuzzy Sets Syst. **86**, 15-41.
7. Fodor, J.C., Roubens, M.C. (1994): Fuzzy Preference Modelling and Multicriteria Decision Support, Kluwer, Dordrecht.
8. Goguen, J.A. (1967): L-fuzzy sets, J. Math. Anal. Appl. **18**, 145-174.
9. Klement, E.P., Mesiar, R., Pap, E. (2000): Triangular Norms, Kluwer, Dordrecht.
10. Schweizer, B., Sklar, A. (1961): Associative functions and statistical triangle inequalities, Publ. Math. Debrecen **8**, 169-186.
11. Zadeh, L.A. (1965): Fuzzy sets, Inform. Control **8**, 338-353.

A New Approach to Fuzzy Constraints in Linear Programming

Joanna Banaś

Faculty of Computer Science & Information Systems, Technical University of Szczecin, 49, Żołnierska st., 71-210 Szczecin, Poland, e-mail: jbanas.dyda.ii.@ii.tuniv.szczecin.pl

Abstract. In the article it is described a new proposal of the transformation of fuzzy constraints in linear programming problem with fuzzy coefficients for hard constraints using triparametric approach. As regards constraint coefficients, it is assumed that they are flat fuzzy numbers on the *L-R* representation. The method is a trial of generalization of possibilistic approach based on the Zadeh's extension principle so that the nature of interpretation of fuzzy inequality can be graduated from the most optimistic to the most pessimistic interpretation. The proposed parameters of feasibility enable the person who decides to differentiate preferences in relation to particular constraints.

1 Introduction

The linear programming problem is the foundation of practically each matter of mathematical programming and therefore it is applied widely at many problems of deciding where this tool is used, for example at operation research. Sometimes the results of the verification of a model show a constant discrepancy against expected results, and this can be caused by objective non-uniqueness of parameters of a model. One of the proposals to make optimization models more flexible is introducing some elements of fuzzy set theory, by making the right sides of constraints fuzzy, introducing fuzzy goals, or, more generally, by fuzzying all coefficients of a model. Reviews of the methods can be found for example in the works of Kacprzyk [8] as well as Rommeltanger and Słowiński [15].

The fuzzy linear programming problem considered in the article can be formulated as follows:

$$c_1x_1 + c_2x_2 + \cdots + c_nx_n \to \max\ , \tag{1}$$

subject to the constraints:

$$\tilde{a}_{i1}x_1 \tilde{+} \tilde{a}_{i2}x_2 \tilde{+} \cdots \tilde{+} \tilde{a}_{in}x_n \le \tilde{b}_i,\ i \in \{1,\ldots,m\}, \tag{2}$$

$$\mathbf{x} = [x_1\ x_2 \ldots x_n]^T \ge \mathbf{0}, \tag{3}$$

or briefly:

$$\tilde{\text{Max}}\{\mathbf{c}^T\mathbf{x} : \tilde{\mathbf{A}}(\mathbf{x}) \le \tilde{\mathbf{b}}, \mathbf{x} \ge \mathbf{0}\}, \tag{4}$$

where the coefficients $\tilde{\mathbf{A}} = [\tilde{a}_{ij}]_{m\times n}$ and $\tilde{\mathbf{b}} = [\tilde{b}_1 \dots \tilde{b}_m]^T$ are flat fuzzy numbers [6,7,8,16] with the intervals of a continuous membership function.

2 The method of the transformation of constraints

The presence of fuzzy coefficients at both sides of constraints contribute to arising the following problems connected with fuzzy numbers theory

- modeling membership functions
- fuzzy numbers arithmetic (in the range of fuzzy numbers addition and multiplication by non-negative real number)
- comparison of two fuzzy numbers

It is assumed that the fuzzy numbers in the constraints (2) will be recorded in the *L-R* notation [6], i.e. $\tilde{a}_{ij} = (a_{ij}^L, a_{ij}^R, \alpha_{ij}^L, \alpha_{ij}^R)_{LR}$, $i \in \{1,\dots,m\}$, $j \in \{1,\dots,n\}$ on the left side of the constraints and $\tilde{b}_i = (b_i, 0, \beta_i)_{LR}$, $i \in \{1,\dots,m\}$ on their right side. The omission of the left spreads of the right sides of constraints will still be justifiable because it results from the nature of the inequality under consideration.

The rules over fuzzy numbers are defined in compliance with *the Zadeh's extension theory* [19]. Assuming that the reference functions *L*, *R* are defined identically for all coefficients $\tilde{a}_{ij}$, then we will receive:

$$\tilde{a}_{i1}x_1 \tilde{+} \tilde{a}_{i2}x_2 \tilde{+} \cdots \tilde{+} \tilde{a}_{in}x_n = (\mathbf{a}_i^L(\mathbf{x}), \mathbf{a}_i^R(\mathbf{x}), \alpha_i^L(\mathbf{x}), \alpha_i^R(\mathbf{x}))_{LR} = \tilde{\mathbf{a}}_i(\mathbf{x}), \tag{5}$$

where for $S \in \{L, R\}$ and $i \in \{1,\dots,m\}$

$$\mathbf{a}_i^S(\mathbf{x}) = \sum_{j=1}^n a_{ij}^S x_j, \quad \alpha_i^S(\mathbf{x}) = \sum_{j=1}^n \alpha_{ij}^S x_j . \tag{6}$$

Using the aggregation (5)–(6), the constraints (2) can be recorded briefly:

$$\tilde{\mathbf{a}}_i(\mathbf{x}) \le \tilde{b}_i . \tag{7}$$

Many scientists who are engaged in the problem (4) noted some faults of the approach based on the extension principle [19]. Although it constitutes the foundation of general fuzzy set theory and possibilistic linear programming (the degree of possibility Poss), some trials appeared to make this very optimistic approach more rigorous. This tendency can be observed at authors of both intuitive [11,12,13,14,18] and possibility [1,2,3,4,5,9,10,16,17] approaches to interpreting fuzzy constraints of the problem (4). However, it should be noticed that the indexes of certainty (Nec) proposed by Dubois i Prade [7] take into account the position of "the left arm" of fuzzy number $\tilde{b}_i$, considered by many authors who are engaged in interpreting the constraints (2) to be unessential. This results from the nature of the inequality (7), where practically only the biggest number of the stabilized "right arm" with the degree of membership 1 is essential. To what end it is to consider elements of the set $\tilde{b}_i$ less than the least upper bound of the core, since they reduce the set of admissible solutions? Contrary to "the left arm", "the right arm" of the number $\tilde{b}_i$ is very important because it interprets the fuzzying of the degree of satisfying the i-th constraint which constitutes the basis of a flexible linear programming – the set of feasible solutions increases at the cost of the certainty of satisfying the constraint, and vice versa. Therefore in compliance with the previous findings the right side of the inequality (7) for each $i \in \{1,\ldots,m\}$ will be considered by us as a fuzzy number with a decreasing membership function.

Notice that the degree of satisfying the inequality (7) calculated in accordance with the extension principle depends on the position of the number $\tilde{b}_i$ in relation to "the left arm" of the number $\tilde{\mathbf{a}}_i(\mathbf{x})$ and is equal to 0 for the position 7, 0.5 for the position 6 and finally 1 for the cases of 1 to 5 illustrated in Fig. 1. As far as it can still be understood at the position 1, 2 or 3, then the degree at the position 4 and 5 seems to be intuitively incorrect.

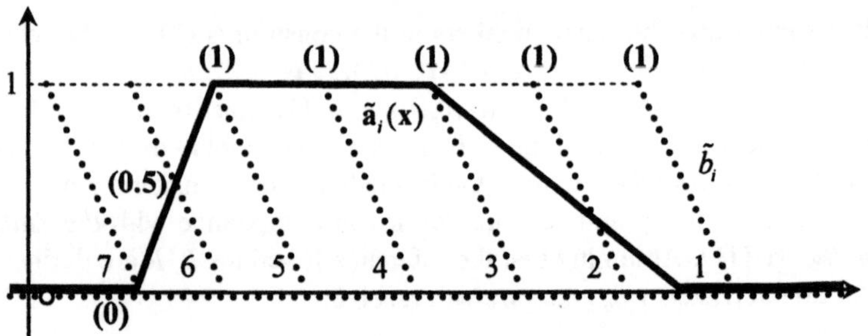

Fig. 1. Degrees of satisfying the inequality (7) calculated by Zadeh's extension principle

The problem results from that the membership function $\mu_{\tilde{\mathbf{a}}_i(\mathbf{x})}$ of the fuzzy number $\tilde{\mathbf{a}}_i(\mathbf{x})$ represented in Fig. 1 is not heterovalued on the core. Since the degree 1 at the position 5 is weakly trustworthy and its correctness is the better the closer by the least upper bound of the core of the number $\tilde{\mathbf{a}}_i(\mathbf{x})$ it is situated the core of the number $\tilde{b}_i$, so one proposes to consider the degrees of satisfying the inequality (7) as fuzzy numbers. Where "the left arm" of the membership function $\mu_{\tilde{\mathbf{a}}_i(\mathbf{x})}$ is heterovalued, the possibility of satisfying the inequality will be crisp as before (for example at the position 6 the possibility of satisfying the inequality (7) amounts to 0.5 with the degree of membership 1). However, when the core of the number $\tilde{b}_i$ is situated on the core of the number $\tilde{\mathbf{a}}_i(\mathbf{x})$, the possibility of satisfying the inequality will amount to 1, whereas the degree of membership in the fuzzy 1 will amount to (see Fig. 2): 0 at the position 5 – very weak 1, 0.5 at the position 4 – mean 1, 1 at the positions 3, 2 and 1 – very strong 1.

As we are not interested in determining the distance between fuzzy numbers, so the position 7 and all positions situated left from it will have the possibility of satisfying the inequality 0 with the degree of membership 1 (crisp zero). The possibility of satisfying the inequality τ (as meant in the extension principle [19]) and the degree of membership υ found for it will be recorded briefly (τ, υ). To simplify the interpretation we will resign the symbol „~" over the fuzzy degree of membership τ.

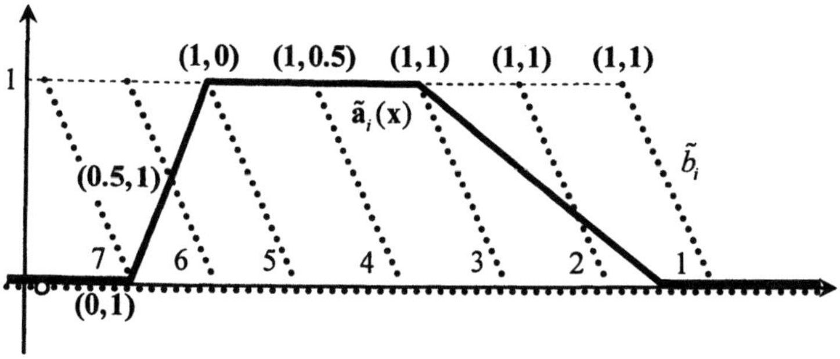

Fig. 2. Fuzzy degrees of satisfying the inequality (7)

Let notice that υ can be different from 1 only when τ will be equal to 1. If we agree that it will be introduced the lexicographical order in a set of the degrees of membership (τ, υ), it will be possible to grade the possibility of satisfying the inequality (7) in compliance with the intuition (see Fig. 2). Finally the inequality (7), $i \in \{1,\ldots,m\}$ will be satisfied at the level (τ_i, υ_i) at least, if

$$\begin{aligned} &\mathbf{a}_i^L(\mathbf{x}) - \alpha_i^L(\mathbf{x}) L^{-1}(\tau_i) \le b_i + \beta_i R^{-1}(\tau_i) && \text{if} \quad \tau_i \in \langle 0,1) \text{ i } \upsilon_i = 1, \\ &\mathbf{a}_i^L(\mathbf{x}) + \left(\mathbf{a}_i^R(\mathbf{x}) - \mathbf{a}_i^L(\mathbf{x})\right)\upsilon_i \le b_i && \text{if} \quad \tau_i = 1 \text{ i } \upsilon_i \in \langle 0,1 \rangle. \end{aligned} \tag{8}$$

One can notice that the suggested parameterization makes it possible to arrange exactly the number $\tilde{b}_i$ in relation to these elements of the number $\tilde{\mathbf{a}}_i(\mathbf{x})$, which do not exceed the least upper bound of its core. The parameter υ_i for $\tau_i = 1$ determines which part of the core is situated left from the number b_i. This approach is surely sufficiently good for many investigators of the problem (4), but some people could have some reservations as regards the total omission of the influence of "the left arm" of the number $\tilde{\mathbf{a}}_i(\mathbf{x})$. In so far as the degree $(1,1)$ does not arouse reservations at the position 1, so some doubts can arise at the positions 2 and 3.

In order to allow a more pessimistic approach to the inequality (7), one proposes to introduce the third parameter ω, which will be responsible for the trustworthiness of satisfying the inequality at the level $(1,1)$. The parameter $\omega \in \langle 0,1 \rangle$ determines the interval of values of the membership function $\langle 1-\omega, 1 \rangle$, where the "right arm" of the number $\tilde{\mathbf{a}}_i(\mathbf{x})$ is situated left from "the right arm" of the number $\tilde{b}_i$ provided, that we always start to arrange in accordance with the relationship "$\le$" from the upper parts of both sides. Consequently we assume for the position 3 the trustworthiness ω of the degree of satisfying $(1,1)$ of the inequality (7) to be equal to 0, for the position 2 ω will amount approximately to 0.7, and for the variant 1, ω will obviously be equal to 1 (see Fig. 3).

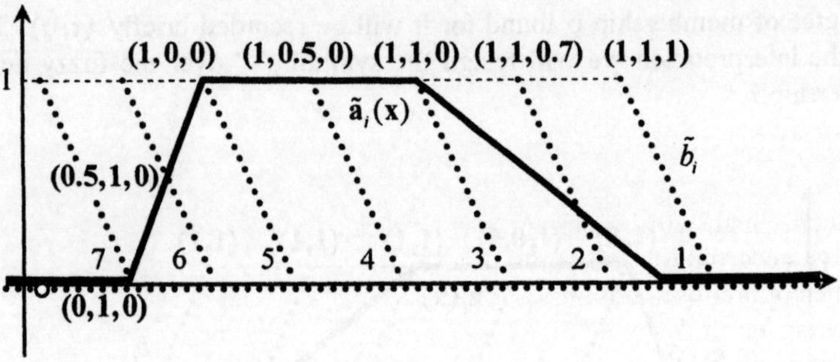

Fig. 3. Triparametric degrees of satisfying the inequality (7)

The triparametric degree of satisfying the inequality (7) will be recorded by us in form of (τ, υ, ω), but we assume $\omega = 0$ for $(\tau, \upsilon) \neq (1,1)$ (see Fig. 3). At the given interpretation the inequality (7), $i \in \{1,\dots,m\}$ will be satisfied at the level $(\tau_i, \upsilon_i, \omega_i)$ at least, when

$$
\begin{aligned}
&\mathbf{a}_i^L(\mathbf{x}) - \alpha_i^L(\mathbf{x}) L^{-1}(\tau_i) \le b_i + \beta_i R^{-1}(\tau_i) && \text{if} \quad \tau_i \in \langle 0,1),\ \upsilon_i = 1 \text{ i } \omega_i = 0, \\
&\mathbf{a}_i^L(\mathbf{x}) + \left(\mathbf{a}_i^R(\mathbf{x}) - \mathbf{a}_i^L(\mathbf{x})\right)\upsilon_i \le b_i && \text{if} \quad \tau_i = 1,\ \upsilon_i \in \langle 0,1\rangle \text{ i } \omega_i = 0, \\
&\begin{cases} \mathbf{a}_i^R(\mathbf{x}) \le b_i \\ \mathbf{a}_i^R(\mathbf{x}) + \alpha_i^R(\mathbf{x}) R^{-1}(1-\omega_i) \\ \qquad \le b_i + \beta_i R^{-1}(1-\omega_i) \end{cases} && \text{if} \quad \tau_i = 1,\ \upsilon_i = 1 \text{ i } \omega_i \in \langle 0,1\rangle.
\end{aligned}
\tag{9}
$$

3 Final remarks

Indexes $(\tau_i, \upsilon_i, \omega_i)$ can be called *parameters of feasibility of the i-th constraint*, $i \in \{1,\dots,m\}$. They make it possible to select the nature of interpretations of the inequality (7) from very optimistic to very pessimistic ones. If one has a little practice, this is very simple and very useful when an interactive procedure is used. A decision maker can express his/her preferences regarding fuzzy constraints and use various triparametric degrees of satisfying them for different *i*. In such way he/she can create his/her own hierarchy of significance of all constraints and on this basis to take risks where consequences of this will be least of all.

At the triparametric approach the parameter ω can serve determining the significance of the right spreads. When we find that the right spread of the number $\tilde{\mathbf{a}}_i(\mathbf{x})$ increases unfavourably at a big correlation of the coefficients $\tilde{a}_{ij}$, $j \in \{1,\dots,n\}$, then we can decrease the value of the parameter ω and intuitively, prevent the loss of some feasible solutions.

References

1. Buckley J.J (1988) Possibilistic linear programming with triangular fuzzy numbers. Fuzzy Sets and Systems **26**, 135–138
2. Buckley J.J (1989) Solving possibilistic linear programming problems. Fuzzy Sets and Systems **31**, 329–341
3. Buckley J.J (1995) Joint solution to fuzzy programming problems. Fuzzy Sets and Systems **72**, 215–220
4. Carlsson C., Korhonen P. (1986) A parametric approach to fuzzy linear programming. Fuzzy Sets and Systems **20**, 17–30
5. Dubois D. (1987) Linear programming with fuzzy data. In: Bezdek J.C. (ed) Analysis of Fuzzy Information **3**. CRC Press, Inc., Florida, 241–263
6. Dubois D., Prade H. (1978) Operations on fuzzy numbers. International Journal of Systems Science **9**, 613–626
7. Dubois D., Prade H. (1983) Ranking fuzzy numbers in the setting of possibility theory. Information Science **30**, New York, 183–224
8. Kacprzyk J. (1986) Fuzzy sets in system analysis. PWN, Warsaw (in polish)
9. Lee E.S., Li R.J. (1993) Fuzzy multiple objective programming and compromise programming with Pareto optimum. Fuzzy Sets and Systems **53**, North-Holland, 275–288
10. Luhandjula M.K. (1987) Multiple objective programming with possibilistic coefficients. Fuzzy Sets and Systems **21**, 135–146
11. Ramik J., Rimanek J. (1985) Inequality between fuzzy numbers and its use in fuzzy optimization. Fuzzy Sets and Systems **16**, 123–138
12. Ramik J., Rommelfanger H. (1996) Fuzzy mathematical programming based on some new inequality relations. Fuzzy Sets and Systems **81**, 77–87
13. Rommelfanger H. (1989) Inequality relations in fuzzy constraint and its use in linear fuzzy optimization. In: Verdegay J.L., Delgado M. (eds) The interface between artificial intelligence and operational research in fuzzy environment. Verlag TÜV Rheinland, Köln, 195–211
14. Rommelfanger H., Keresztfalvi T. (1991) Multicriteria fuzzy optimization based no Yager's parametrized t-norm. Foundations of Computing and Decision Sciences **16**, 99–110
15. Rommelfanger H., Słowiński R. (1998) Fuzzy linear programming with single or multiple objective functions. In: Słowiński R. (ed) Fuzzy sets in decision analysis, operation research and statistics. KAP, Boston/Dordrecht/London, 179–213
16. Sakawa M. (1993) Fuzzy sets and interactive multiobjective optimization. Plenum Press, New York
17. Sakawa M., Yano H. (1990c) Feasibility and Pareto optimality for multiobjective linear and linear fractional programming problems with fuzzy parameters. In: Verdegay J.L., Delgado M. (eds) The interface between artificial intelligence and operational research in fuzzy environment. Verlag TÜV Rheinland, Köln, 213–232
18. Słowiński R. (1986) A multicriteria fuzzy linear programming method for water supply system development planning. Fuzzy Sets and System **19**, 217–237.
19. Zadeh L.A. (1965) Fuzzy sets. Information and Control **8**, 338–353

On a Linguistic Description of Dependencies in Data

Ildar Batyrshin[1], Michael Wagenknecht[2]

[1] Institute of Problems of Informatics, Academy of Sciences of Tatarstan and Kazan State Technological University, K.Marx st., 68, Kazan, 420015, Russia
email: *batyr@emntu.kcn.ru*

[2] University of Applied Sciences Zittau/Goerlitz, IPM Theodor-Koerner-Allee 16, 02763 Zittau, Germany
email: *m.wagenknecht@hs-zigr.de*

Summary. The problem of linguistic description of dependencies in data by a set of rules R_k:"*If X is* T_k *then Y is* S_k" is considered, where T_k are linguistic terms like *SMALL, BETWEEN 5 AND 7* describing some fuzzy intervals A_k. The S_k are linguistic terms like *DECREASING* and *QUICKLY INCREASING* describing the slopes p_k of linear functions $y_k=p_kx+q_k$ approximating data on A_k. The decision of this problem is obtained as result of fuzzy partition of the domain of X on fuzzy intervals A_k, approximation of given data $\{x_i,y_i\},(i=1,\ldots,n)$ by linear functions $y_k=p_kx+q_k$ on these intervals and by re-translation of obtained results into linguistic form. The methods are illustrated by examples and potential applications of proposed methods are discussed.

1. Introduction

The problem of linguistic description of dependencies in data arise in such areas as process monitoring, diagnosis and control, data mining, qualitative reasoning about processes, etc. [1,4,6-8,14,20-24]. Here we consider the problem of linguistic description of dependencies in given data $\{x_i,y_i\},(i=1,\ldots,n)$ by a set of rules R_k:"*If X is* T_k *then Y is* S_k", where T_k are linguistic terms like *SMALL, LARGE, BETWEEN 5 AND 7* describing some fuzzy intervals A_k on X. The S_k are linguistic terms like *DECREASING* and *QUICKLY INCREASING* that characterize the speed of change of y on these intervals.
Fuzzy rules with such right-hand sides were considered in [2,3] where the methods of representation of such rules by fuzzy relations were proposed. In the following, we consider the inverse problem: How to generate such set of fuzzy rules based on given numerical data $\{x_i,y_i\},(i=1,\ldots,n)$. We propose that the solution of this problem may be obtained as result of approximation of given data by linear functions $y_k=p_kx+q_k$ on fuzzy intervals A_k (defining an optimal fuzzy partition of the domain of X) and by subsequent re-translation into linguistic form. For the construction of the optimal fuzzy partition a genetic algorithm is applied. Approximating functions are analytically calculated. Re-translation functions describe linguistically the fuzzy intervals A_k and the slopes p_k of approximating linear functions $y_k=p_kx+q_k$ on these intervals. As result, the rule base is constructed.
The considered problem can be divided in two mutually related parts: 1) the construction of fuzzy partition of the domain of input variable X on fuzzy intervals with optimal linear approximation of given data on these intervals, and 2) the lin-

guistic interpretation of the obtained fuzzy intervals and lines. The first problem is connected with the fuzzy piece-wise linear approximation of data, approximation by polygons and splines, shape analysis, fuzzy trend analysis and regression analysis, approximation of data by fuzzy Sugeno models etc. [1,5,9-14,16-19]. The second problem is related to the theory of fuzzy information granulation and computing with words [3,23,24]. The proposed approach to construction of rule bases from given data may be also considered as a calculation of granular derivatives [2].

These problems shell be discussed in the following sections. The tackling of the first problem is based on step-wise applications of genetic algorithm for finding knots, i.e. the points of intersection of fuzzy sets constituting the partition of fuzzy sets, and the parameters of these sets optimizing given fitness function. Initially, a partition with sufficiently large number of fuzzy sets is chosen which is sequentially reduced untill some final optimal partition is found. There are three reasons for applying the reduction approach. First, small fuzzy intervals which are not meaningful for linguistic interpretation are deleted. Second, intervals with small number of given points are deleted since small errors in initial data in such intervals may cause large deviations in slopes. Third, the neighbor intervals with similar linguistic interpretation of dependencies are merged. The application of a universal genetic algorithm enables a sufficiently fast solution of the considered problem with easy handling of penalties, criteria and other components.

In the following sections we describe more detailed the formulation of the problem and methods applied for its solution and illustrate them on examples of linguistic interpretation of given data.

2. Notations and Formulation of Problem

Suppose $D=\{(x_i,y_i)\}$, $x_i\in X$, $y_i\in Y$, $(i=1,\dots,n)$ to be a given set of data where X and Y are real intervals: $X=[x_l,x_r]$, $x_l<x_r$, $Y=[y_l,y_r]$, $y_l<y_r$. Denote $X_D=\{x_i\}$, $(i=1,\dots,n)$ and $Y_D=\{y_i\}$, $(i=1,\dots,n)$. Our goal is to approximate the underlying crisp dependence between input x and output y by a set of rules

R_k: *If X is* T_k *then Y is* S_k,

where T_k are linguistic terms like *SMALL, LARGE* and *BETWEEN 5 AND 10* describing some fuzzy intervals (normal and convex fuzzy sets A_k:$X\to[0,1]$). The S_k are linguistic terms like *DECREASING, CONSTANT* and *QUICKLY INCREASING* which describe the speed of the change of function y on A_k. We will suppose that the linguistic term S_k characterizes the slope p_k of the function $y_k = p_k x + q_k$ that approximates the given data Y_D on A_k.

We will suppose that the membership functions of A_k are continuous, strictly increasing on the left of the kernels $K(A_k)$ and strictly decreasing on the right of the kernels of A_k what takes place for most of popular membership functions [12,15]. As result, all α-cuts and, particularly, the kernels of fuzzy intervals are closed crisp intervals. Denote α-cut of fuzzy set A by $A_\alpha = [x_{\alpha l}, x_{\alpha r}]$. The value $h_a = x_{\alpha r}$ -

x_{α_l} will be called the **spread** of A_α or the spread of A at level α. A fuzzy set will be called a **singleton** at $x_0 \in X$ if $A(x) = 1$ at $x = x_0$ and $A(x) = 0$ otherwise.
We say that the set $P = \{A_k\}$, $(k=1,\dots,m)$, of fuzzy intervals on X defines an **(α,β)-fuzzy partition** of X, if $\sup_{j\neq k}(\sup_{x\in X}((A_j \cap A_k)(x))) = \alpha$ and $\inf_{x\in X}((\bigcup_{k=1}^{m} A_k)(x)) = \beta$, where $0 \le \alpha < 1$, $0 < \beta \le 1$. (α,β)-fuzzy partitions will be simply called fuzzy partitions. An (α,α)-partition will be denoted as α-partition. It follows that the intersection of kernels of fuzzy sets in fuzzy partitions are empty and hence they may be ordered. We will say that fuzzy interval A_j is located on the left-hand side of fuzzy interval A_k if $A_j(x_u) < A_k(x_v)$ for some $x_u \in K(A_j)$ and $x_v \in K(A_k)$. Such ordering relation will be denoted by $A_j \prec A_k$. Obviously, this ordering defines a linear strict ordering relation on the classes of fuzzy partition. We will suppose that in any fuzzy partition $P = \{A_k\}$, $(k=1,\dots,m)$, the numeration of fuzzy intervals corresponds to their ordering, i.e. $A_k \prec A_{k+1}$ for all $k=1,\dots,m-1$.
We suppose that for all $k=1,\dots,m-1$ and for all points x located between the kernel points of A_k and A_{k+1} it is fulfilled $(A_k \cup A_{k+1})(x) > 0$. From strict monotonicity of membership functions on both sides of the kernels of fuzzy intervals it follows that the membership function of intersection $A_k \cap A_{k+1}$ of two neighboring intervals of partition P attains its maximal value in some unique point x_{0k} located between the kernel points of these fuzzy intervals. Such point will be called a **knot.** The borders of the set $X=[x_l, x_r]$ also will be denoted as knots: $x_{00} = x_l$ and $x_{0m} = x_r$.
We call a partition P **normal** if for all $k,j = 1,\dots,m$ and $k \neq j$ we have $A_k(x) > A_j(x)$ if $x \in (x_{0k-1}, x_{0k})$. It is clear that any α-partition is normal.
We say that the fuzzy interval A_k "contains" the points x_i from the initially given data X_D if $x_i \in [x_{0k-1}, x_{0k})$ for $k=1,\dots,m-1$ and $x_i \in (x_{0k-1}, x_{0k}]$ for $k=m$. In these cases we will also say that x_i "belongs" to fuzzy interval A_k. The set of points from X_D belonging to A_k will be denoted by $X_D(A_k)$. The distance between knots $W(A_k) = x_{0k} - x_{0k-1}$ will be called the **spread of fuzzy set A_k in the fuzzy partition P.**
Let $L_X = \{T_1, T_2, \dots\}$ is a set of elements called terms. L_X will be called **a linguistic variable** and its elements will be called values of L_X. We will suppose that L_X contains a special element λ denoting the term **"meaningless"**. A function $N_X: F(X) \to L_X$, where $F(X)$ is a set of all fuzzy subsets of X, will be called **a re-translation function** and $N_X(A)$ will be called **a name** of fuzzy set A on X. For example, the set $TEMPERATURE_T = \{SMALL, LARGE, 100°, BETWEEN\ 30°\ AND\ 40°, NORMAL, VERY\ HOT, \lambda\}$ defines the values of linguistic variable *TEMPERATURE* which may be used for linguistic re-translation of fuzzy sets defined on a set of numerical values of temperature T.
We suppose that the set of values of linguistic variable L_X depends on the possible granulation of the set X which may be determined for example by possible size and locations of fuzzy granules on the set X. The elements of L_X may be generated by some grammar and the re-translation function may be defined by some re-translation procedure. We will say that A is **a meaningless** fuzzy set if $N_X(A) = \lambda$ otherwise it will be called **meaningful.** For example, a fuzzy sets may be considered as meaningless if their size or location does not match with possible sizes and locations of fuzzy sets defined by granulation of X in considered problem.

We call a function $y=px+q$ a **linear approximation of** $D=\{(x_i,y_i)\}$, $x_i\in X$, $y_i\in Y$, $(i=1,\ldots,n)$ on the **fuzzy set** $A:X\rightarrow[0,1]$ if it minimizes the following function

$$Q(p,q)=\sum_{i=1}^{n}\left[y_i-y(x_i)\right]^2\cdot A(x_i) \tag{1}$$

for all possible p,q. The parameters p and q may be obtained similarly to the solution of least-square approximation problem.

Suppose $Z=[p_l,p_r]$ to be a set of possible values of slopes p for $y=px+q$ and $L_Z=\{S_1,\ldots,S_t\}$ to be a set of terms used for notation of slopes. For example, we may have $L_Z=$ {*QUICKLY DECREASING, DECREASING, SLOWLY DECREASING, CONSTANT, SLOWLY INCREASING, INCREASING, QUICKLY INCREASING*}, or in short form $L_Z=$ {*QDE, DEC, SDE, CON, SIN, INC, QIN*}. The re-translation function $N_Z:F(Z)\rightarrow L_Z$ defined on the set of all fuzzy subsets of Z will translate numerical values of slopes into linguistic values if these numerical values are considered as singletons.

We call an (α,β)-fuzzy partition **admissible** if it is normal and satisfies the following conditions

$$K(A_k)\cap X\neq\varnothing,\qquad (k=1,\ldots,m) \tag{2}$$

$$\alpha\leq\alpha^* \tag{3}$$

$$\beta\geq\beta^* \tag{4}$$

$$W(A_k)\geq W\qquad (k=1,\ldots,m) \tag{5}$$

$$\mathrm{card}(X_D(A_k))>C,\qquad (k=1,\ldots,m) \tag{6}$$

$$N_Z(p_k)\neq N_Z(p_{k+1}),\qquad (k=1,\ldots,m-1), \tag{7}$$

Condition (2) requires that at least one kernel point of each fuzzy interval belongs to the interval $X=[x_l,x_r]$. Conditions (3) and (4) require the intersection of neighboring fuzzy intervals to be not greater than a given threshold α^*, and the union of fuzzy intervals cover domain X at least at level β^*, where α^*, β^* are fixed numbers from [0,1] such that $\alpha^*<1$ and $\beta^*>0$. Condition (5) is determined by restrictions on possible granulation of X. If the width of a fuzzy interval is less than the possible width of minimal granule W then such fuzzy interval is considered as meaningless. Condition (6) means that each fuzzy interval contains a sufficient amount of initial data. In the opposite case small random fluctuations in data may cause large deviations of the slope value p_k in the approximating functions $y_k=p_kx+q_k$. Finally, (7) requires that the linguistic interpretation of slope values on neighboring fuzzy intervals obtained by the re-translation function should be discriminative.

Suppose re-translation functions N_X and N_Z to be defined in a suitable way, admissible partition $P=\{A_k\}$, $(k=1,\ldots,m)$ of X is constructed and approximation functions $y_k=p_kx+q_k$ on A_k are determined. Then re-translation functions defines the following rule base

R_k: *If X is* $N_x(A_k)$ *then Y is* $N_z(p_k)$.

That is, the problem of linguistic description of data D is reduced to the problem of finding an optimal admissible partition of given set X with respect to some criteria of optimality.
We are led to the following problem: Find an admissible fuzzy partition $\{A_k\}$, $(k=1,...,m)$ of X minimizing the fitness function

$$Q_t = \sum_{k=1}^{m} \frac{\sum_{i=1}^{n} [y_i - y_k(x_i)]^{2t} A_k(x_i)}{\sum_{i=1}^{n} A_k(x_i)}, \tag{8}$$

where y_k are linear approximations of given data $D=\{(x_i,y_i)\}$, $x_i \in X$, $y_i \in Y$, $(i=1,...,n)$, on fuzzy intervals A_k, m is unknown number of fuzzy sets and t is some fixed real number used for obtaining better fitting of given data. We used in our simulations $t=2$.
This problem may be considered as a problem of constraint optimization if conditions (2) - (7) are handled as constraints in the optimization problem. Another approach to this optimization problem is to consider the class of fuzzy partitions satisfying some of the conditions (2) - (7) and to use other conditions as constraints. In the following sections we describe the approach to solve the optimization problem in the class of fuzzy partitions satisfying conditions (2) – (4). We consider 0.5-fuzzy partitions with fuzzy intervals defined by bell membership functions such that the centers of the first and the last membership functions coincide with the left and the right borders of interval $X=[x_l,x_r]$ and neighboring membership functions intersect at level 0.5. A genetic algorithm is used for obtaining the optimal fuzzy partition minimizing criterion (8). If conditions (5) - (7) are not fulfilled for some fuzzy interval then this interval is merged with one of the neighbor intervals, the number of classes is reduced and genetic algorithm is applied again. Initially, a partition with sufficiently large number of fuzzy intervals is obtained which is sequentially reduced till some final optimal partition satisfying (5)-(7) is found.

References

1. Babuska R. (1998) Fuzzy Modeling for Control. Kluwer, Boston.
2. Batyrshin I. (2002) On granular derivatives and solution of granular initial value problem. International Journal of Applied Mathematics and Computer Science. (Submitted for publication).
3. Batyrshin I. and Panova A. (2001) On granular description of dependencies. In: Proceedings of 9th Zittau Fuzzy Colloquium, Zittau, Germany, 1-8.
4. Batyrshin I., Zakuanov R. and Bikushev G. (1994) Expert system based on algebra of uncertainties with memory in process optimization. In: Fuzzy Logic and Intelligent

Technologies in Nuclear Science. Proceedings of the 1st International FLINS Workshop, Mol, Belgium. World Scientific, 156-159.
5. De Boor C. (1978) A Practical Guide to Splines. Springer, New York.
6. De Kleer J. and Brawn J. (1984) A qualitative physics based on confluences. Artificial Intelligence **24**, 7-83.
7. Deogun J.S., Raghavan V. V., Sarkar A. and Sever H. (1997) Data mining: Research trends, challenges, and applications. In: Roughs Sets and Data Mining: Analysis of Imprecise Data (T. Y. Lin and N. Cercone, Eds.), 9-45. Kluwer, Boston.
8. Forbus K.D. (1984) Qualitative process theory. Artificial Intelligence **24**, 85-168.
9. Friedman J. H. (1991): Multivariate adaptive regression splines. Annals of Statistics **19**, 1.
10. Goodrich M.T. (1994) Efficient piecewise-linear function approximation using the uniform metric. Proc. 10th ACM Symp. on Computational Geometry (SCG), 322-331.
11. Huarng K. (2001) Effective lengths of intervals to improve forecasting in fuzzy time series. Fuzzy Sets and Systems **123**, 387-394.
12. Jang J.S.R., Sun C.T. and Mizutani E. (1997) Neuro-Fuzzy and Soft Computing. A Computational Approach to Learning and Machine Intelligence. Prentice Hall, N.Y.
13. J. Kacprzyk and M. Fedrizzi (Eds) (1992) Fuzzy Regression Analysis. Omnitech Press, Warsaw.
14. Kivikunnas S. (1999) Overview of process trend analysis methods and applications. In: Proceedings of Workshop on Applications in Chemical and Biochemical Industry, Aachen, Germany.
15. Klir G.J. and Folger T.A. (1988) Fuzzy Sets, Uncertainty, and Information. Prentice-Hall, London.
16. Kosko B. (1997) Fuzzy Engineering. Prentice-Hall, N.J.
17. Loncaric S. (1998) A survey of shape analysis techniques. Pattern Recognition.**31**, No.8, 983-1001.
18. Wang Li-X. (1997) A Course in Fuzzy Systems and Control. Prentice Hall, N.J.
19. Yu J.-R., Tzeng G.-H., Li H.-L. (2001) General fuzzy piecewise regression analysis with automatic change-point detection. Fuzzy Sets and Systems **119**, 247-257.
20. Zadeh L.A. (1973) Outline of a new approach to the analysis of complex systems and decision processes. IEEE Trans. Syst. Man. Cybern. **1**, 28-44.
21. Zadeh L.A. (1975) The concept of a linguistic variable and its application to approximate reasoning, Part I. Inf. Sci. Vol. **8**, 199-249. Part II. Inf. Sci. **8**, 301-357. Part III. Inf. Sci. **9**, 43-80.
22. Zadeh L.A. (1996) Fuzzy logic = computing with words. IEEE Trans. on Fuzzy Systems **4**, No. 2, 103-111.
23. Zadeh L.A. (1997) Toward a theory of fuzzy information granulation and its centrality in human reasoning and fuzzy logic. Fuzzy Sets and Systems **90**, 111-127.
24. Zadeh L.A. (1999) From computing with numbers to computing with words - from manipulation of measurements to manipulation of perceptions. IEEE Trans. on Circuits and Systems - 1: Fundamental Theory and Applications **45**, No.1, 105-119.

New Index of Significance for Inputs Selection

Joanna Chimiak–Opoka

Technical University of Szczecin, Faculty of Computer Science & Information Systems, ul. Zolnierska 49, 71-210 Szczecin, Poland,
e-mail: <jchimiak@wi.ps.pl> website: http://ksir.wi.ps.pl/

Abstract. The reduction of dimensionality should be performed before applying any modelling tool. In the process of inputs selection we need an index to order the inputs according to their significance. In the paper a new index of significance is presented and the algorithm of its estimation in full–dimensional input–space is proposed. The algorithm subdivides space into cells and computes membership function for each of them. The experimental results, which were obtained using the proposed method, are very promising. Finally a benchmark example demonstrates how the process of inputs selection is applied.

1 Introduction

The higher is the amount of input variables, the more complicated model will be necessary to solve the problem. This phenomenon is known as a *curse of dimensionality* [1]. Many methods were developed to avoid the problem. Previous methods were based on mathematical or statistical tools (e.g. [9]). Subsequent methods used AI techniques such as neural network (e.g. [11]), fuzzy logic (e.g. [5,6]) and rough sets (e.g. [8]). A number of techniques for inputs selection have been presented in literature [7,9]. Although there are many papers about dimension reduction, the problem is often neglected and treated as a problem of minor importance. Study of known methods showed they had some disadvantages: analysis is often conducted in reduced input–space (even two-dimensional); data point distribution and non-linear dependencies[1] are taken into consideration rather seldom; an exact significance criterion is not specified — for more details see [3,2].

The method presented in the paper is sensitive to non-linear dependencies between input and output variables. The algorithm works in full–dimension of a problem and takes into consideration the distribution of data points. The advantages mentioned above make the method innovative and attractive for future development.

2 New methodology for inputs selection

Suppose that problem has k possible inputs $X = \{x_1, x_2, \ldots, x_k\}$ and one output y. Some of k inputs are less significant and can be eliminated from

[1] particularly statistical methods

modelling process. A criterion of input variable's significance is needed for inputs selection process. Let the significance of input variable x_i be equivalent to the strength of its influence on output surface shape (see def. 1). We need some numerical index of significance to select and order input variables (see def. 2).

Definition 1 (Significant Input). The output variable depends on significant input variables. The more influence on output space's curvature the variable has, the more significant it is.

Definition 2 (Index of Significance). The index of significance which is calculated for the input variable describes the influence of the variable on directional curvature of output–space.

Fig. 1. 2D and 3D examples of the significance index calculation

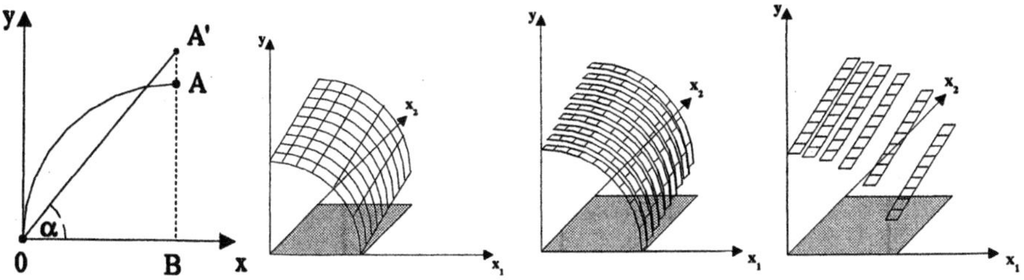

a) 2D: $\mathcal{W}(x)$ b) 3D: $y(x_1, x_2)$ c) 3D: $\mathcal{W}(x_1)$ d) 3D: $\mathcal{W}(x_2)$

Let's consider SISO (single input — single output) model: $y(x)$ defined on D (fig. 1.a: $D = \langle 0, B\rangle$). x influence on y is calculated as a ratio of the range of x ($\Delta x = |\overline{0B}|$) to the length of the curve $y(x)$ ($L = |\widehat{0A}| = |\overline{0A'}|$). Therefore the normalised index of significance is evaluated as follows:

$$\mathcal{W}(x) = 1 - \cos\alpha = 1 - \frac{\Delta x}{L} = 1 - \frac{\int\limits_D \mathrm{d}x}{\int\limits_D \sqrt{1 + \left(\frac{\mathrm{d}y(x)}{\mathrm{d}x}\right)^2}\,\mathrm{d}x} \tag{1}$$

The idea of the trigonometrical measure for SISO systems, named arc-angle significance index (AAS-index, α_i), was suggested by A. Piegat [10], p. 415–417. The equation (1) is generalised for two-inputs model: $y(X) = y(x_1, x_2)$ defined on $D = D_1 \times D_2$ (fig. 1.b), as follows:

$$\mathcal{W}(x_i) = 1 - \frac{\iint\limits_D \mathrm{d}X}{\iint\limits_D \sqrt{1 + \left(\frac{\partial y(X)}{\partial x_i}\right)^2}\,\mathrm{d}X} \tag{2}$$

where $\iint\limits_D \mathrm{d}X$ denotes double integral of all variables of $X = \{x_1, x_2\}$.

The equation (2) is interpreted as the ratio of reduced-curvature surface area to area of the projection of the surface on the input domain (see fig. 1.c-1.d). The index of significance for k-input models is calculated analogously [4].

A special grid of cells is created for data points and the index calculations are based on lengths of lines connecting centres of cells. A Gaussian membership function $\mu(X) = \exp\left[\sum_{i=1}^{k} \left|(x_i - m_i)\,(w_i c_{i1} + (1 - w_i)c_{i2})^{-1}\right|^2\right]$ located in the centre of gravity $(m_1, \ldots, m_k)$ of all points in the cell area and scaled (widths c_{ij}) according to cell size is used to estimate the mean value of the cell (see example in fig. 2).

Fig. 2. The grid construction and the index calculation by example

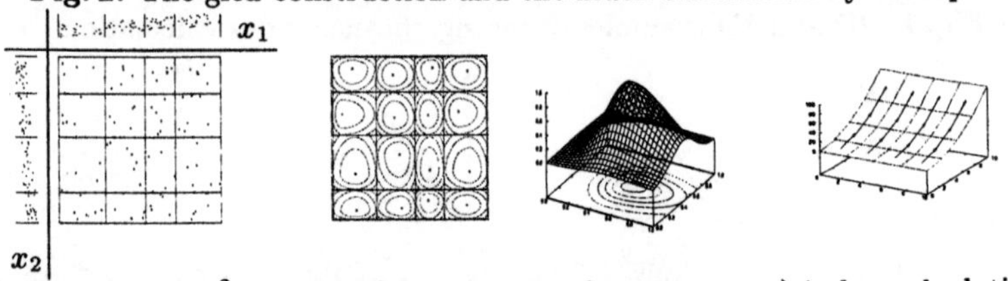

a) division into 4^2 cells b) membership functions c) index calculation

3 Calculation example

The new method was applied in three stages: i. the preliminary dimension reduction; ii. the elimination of dependent inputs; iii. the detection of significant inputs' sequence. As an example a function (3) was chosen which was also examined in [6] (*B. A Second Example*, page 683):

$$y = \sin(6x_1)\sin(4x_2)\sin(2x_3)\sin(5.4x_4)\sin(5.4x_5)\sin(3.5x_6) \tag{3}$$

where inputs $\{x_1, x_4, x_6, x_7, x_8, x_9\}$ and random noise R are defined on $\langle -1, 1\rangle$ and the other inputs are defined as $x_5 = \cos(x_1)$, $x_3 = \sin(x_4^2)$, $x_2 = 0.5(\sin(x_6) + R)$. Values of variables were randomly generated according to equation (3). The experiment was repeated 50 times for different sets of 10 000 data points.

i. The preliminary dimension reduction. The indices for all inputs $X = \{x_1, \ldots, x_k\}$, $(k = 9)$ were calculated using the grid with $g^k = 2^9$ cells. The mean values of $\mathcal{W}(x_i)$ obtained for 50 different data sets are shown in table 1. The mean indices $\mathcal{W}(x_7)$, $\mathcal{W}(x_8)$ and $\mathcal{W}(x_9)$ are much lower than the others.

This observation is confirmed for every single data set where the variables x_7, x_8 and x_9 are the last ones in all sequences of inputs obtained. Based on this result we can eliminate these variables x_7, x_8, x_9 as insignificant and begin next stage with reduced inputs set $X = \{x_1, \ldots, x_k\}$ $(k = 6)$.

ii. The elimination of dependent inputs. Each variable from previously obtained reduced set $X = \{x_1, \ldots, x_6\}$ we treat as an output variable and compute indices for the remaining ones, therefore we operate in 5-dimensional input–space. Let's analyse the distributions of indices' values shown in figure 3. For variables x_1 (fig. 3.a) and x_4 (fig. 3.d) we obtained similar values of indices for all inputs, so we can suspect these variables are independent. Hence, we should take into consideration these variables (x_1, x_4). The situation for variables x_3 and x_5 is clear too — the variables are dependent. When we consider x_3 as output (fig. 3.c), the index for x_4 is much higher then the others, which means x_3 is dependent on x_4. By analogy, x_5 is dependent on x_1 (fig. 3.e). With last two variables (x_2 and x_6) situation is unclear. The analysis of variables' index value distribution (fig. 3.b, fig. 3.f) suggests that variables x_2 and x_6 depend on each other. In situation like this we can not eliminate any of them (x_2, x_6). After the second stage we obtained reduced set $X = \{x_1, x_2, x_4, x_6\}$ of 4 variables $(k = 4)$.

iii. The detection of significant inputs' sequence. As the last stage we ordered 4 significant variables according to their indices' significance. We tested data sets in 12 different grids ($g^k = \{2^4, \ldots, 13^4\}$, see tab. 2). Sparse grids were inaccurate in case of linearisation, dense grids had too many empty cells. The most accurate results were obtained for medium–size grids ($g^k = \{5^4, \ldots, 8^4\}$) for which we obtained $x_1 x_2 \{x_4 x_6\}$ order in each of 200 cases. The values $\mathcal{W}(x_4)$ and $\mathcal{W}(x_6)$ were similar and these variables alternately appeared at the last position. For most cases (57%) we obtained $x_1 x_2 x_6 x_4$ order. Therefore, as the result of the algorithm we obtained reduced set of 4 variables:

$$X = \{x_1, x_2, x_6, x_4\} \tag{4}$$

Case study. The results obtained for function (3) differ. In article [6], after first stage fuzzy curves analysis (described in [5]), input set was reduced to $X = \{x_3, x_4, x_6, x_1, x_5, x_2\}$ and after second stage final input set was as follows: $X = \{x_3, x_5, x_6, x_2\}$. There is no possibility of verification of above results, because there is no significance criterion specified in [6].

Distinct results follow the meaning of variables' significance. If by significance we mean, for example, the value of linear correlation we could compute correlation coefficient and then we obtain yet another sequence of variables $(x_3 x_4 x_9 x_8 x_7 x_1 x_2 x_5 x_6)$.

Analytical study of single factors of function (3) reduced as much as possible gives the same significant inputs (5) as experiment with proposed algorithm (4).

Table 1. Mean results of 50 data sets of 10 000 points of function (3) tested in full–dimensional input–space

g^k	2^9
$\mathcal{W}(x_1)$	0.020660
$\mathcal{W}(x_2)$	0.039927
$\mathcal{W}(x_3)$	0.008085
$\mathcal{W}(x_4)$	0.009825
$\mathcal{W}(x_5)$	0.012401
$\mathcal{W}(x_6)$	0.016625
$\mathcal{W}(x_7)$	0.001084
$\mathcal{W}(x_8)$	0.001103
$\mathcal{W}(x_9)$	0.001064

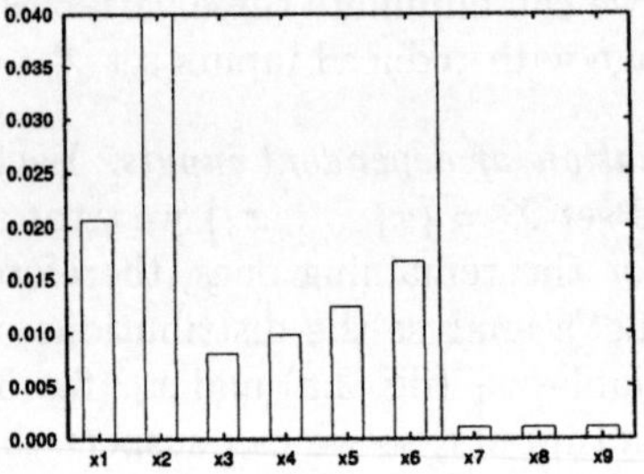

Fig. 3. Mean results of 50 data sets of 10 000 points of function (3) for each of $\{x_1, \ldots, x_6\}$ variables treated as output and tested in 4 grids ($g^k = \{2^5, \ldots, 5^5\}$)

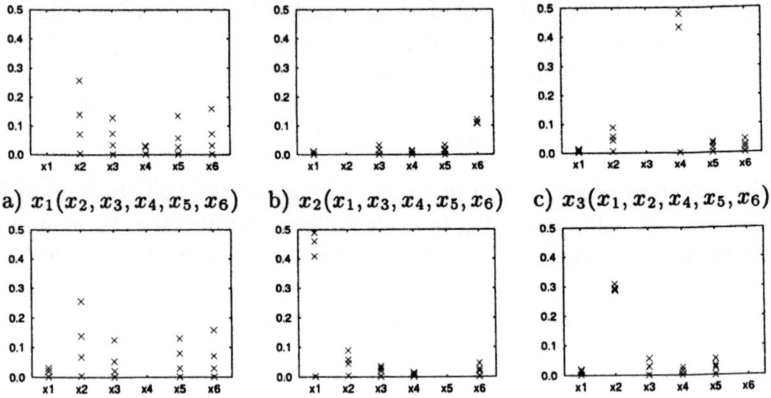

a) $x_1(x_2, x_3, x_4, x_5, x_6)$ b) $x_2(x_1, x_3, x_4, x_5, x_6)$ c) $x_3(x_1, x_2, x_4, x_5, x_6)$

d) $x_4(x_1, x_2, x_3, x_5, x_6)$ e) $x_5(x_1, x_2, x_3, x_4, x_6)$ f) $x_6(x_1, x_2, x_3, x_4, x_5)$

Table 2. Mean results of 50 data sets of 10 000 points of function (3) in reduced 4-dimensional input–space

g^k	non-empty	$\mathcal{W}(x_1)$	$\mathcal{W}(x_2)$	$\mathcal{W}(x_4)$	$\mathcal{W}(x_6)$	order
2^4	100.00%	0.000214	0.000687	0.000216	0.000269	$x_2x_6x_4x_1$
3^4	100.00%	0.002814	0.008074	0.002033	0.002887	$x_2x_6x_1x_4$
4^4	87.50%	0.060839	0.042951	0.030926	0.040439	$x_1x_2x_6x_4$
5^4	86.96%	0.061518	0.052739	0.040841	0.040264	$x_1x_2x_4x_6$
6^4	82.03%	0.088486	0.069421	0.059350	0.052344	$x_1x_2x_4x_6$
7^4	78.65%	0.110316	0.082807	0.067490	0.067015	$x_1x_2x_4x_6$
8^4	72.33%	0.105994	0.083347	0.069575	0.073291	$x_1x_2x_4x_6$
9^4	63.72%	0.095417	0.072719	0.061532	0.069282	$x_1x_2x_6x_4$
10^4	53.24%	0.080974	0.062431	0.053366	0.068705	$x_1x_2x_6x_4$
11^4	43.16%	0.062354	0.056943	0.044813	0.071851	$x_6x_1x_2x_4$
12^4	34.36%	0.044083	0.050369	0.031337	0.067629	$x_6x_2x_1x_4$
13^4	27.12%	0.027331	0.043326	0.023497	0.067171	$x_6x_2x_1x_4$

$$
\begin{array}{lll}
x_1 \Rightarrow & \varphi = \sin(6x_1)\cdot\sin(5.4\cos(x_1)) & \Rightarrow \mathcal{W}(x_1) = 0.72 \\
x_2 \Rightarrow & \varphi = \sin(4x_2) : x_2 = 0.5(\sin(x_6) + R) & \Rightarrow \mathcal{W}(x_2) = 0.66 \\
x_6 \Rightarrow & \varphi = \sin(3.5x_6) & \Rightarrow \mathcal{W}(x_6) = 0.62 \\
x_4 \Rightarrow & \varphi = \sin(5.4x_4)\cdot\sin(2\sin(x_4^2)) & \Rightarrow \mathcal{W}(x_4) = 0.53
\end{array} \quad (5)
$$

4 Conclusion

The new index of significance was introduced. This index can be used for selection of significant inputs from possible inputs set. An example of the method's application was presented. The method has also been verified for systems of known analytical form (linear/non-linear, additive/multiplicative functions) with cloud-like data point distribution (e.g. [4]). Recent results were consistent with analytical analysis of functions. The other results and papers devoted to the method proposed in this paper can be obtained from the website: `http://ksir.wi.ps.pl/`.

References

1. R. Bellman, *Dynamic programming*, Princeton University Press, 1957.
2. J. Chimiak, *Analysis of Cunningham's methods used for variable reduction of MISO systems*, 5th Session on Computer Science, Tech. Univ. of Szczecin, Faculty of Computer Science & Information Systems 2000, pp. 315–320 (In Polish).
3. ———, *Analysis of inputs significance in MISO systems. Part I. Comparative analysis of correlation coefficient and new arc-angle index*, Annuals of Appliable Informatics, Tech. Univ. of Szczecin, **8** (2001), pp. 37–62 (In Polish).
4. J. Chimiak–Opoka, *New method for variables selection in MISO systems — testing in ideal experimental environment*, 6th Session on Computer Science, Tech. Univ. of Szczecin, Faculty of Computer Science & Information Systems 2001, pp. 425–430 (In Polish).
5. Y. Lin and G.A. Cunningham III, *A new approach to fuzzy-neural system modeling*, IEEE Trans. on Fuzzy Systems **3** (1995), no. 2, 190–197.
6. Y. Lin, G.A. Cunningham III, S.V. Coggeshall, and R.D. Jones, *Nonlinear system input structure identyfication: Two stage fuzzy curves and surfaces*, IEEE Trans. on System, Man and Cybernetics **28** (1998), no. 5, 678–684.
7. H. Liu and H. Motoda, *Feature selection for knowledge discovery and data mining*, Kuwer Academic Publisher, 1998.
8. A. Mrozek and L. Plonka, *Data analysis using rought sets, Economic, medical and control application*, PLJ Academic Publishing Hause, Warsaw, 1999 (In Polish).
9. E. Nowak, *Problems of variables' selection in economometric models*, Polish Scientific Publishers, Warsaw, 1984 (In Polish).
10. A. Piegat, *Fuzzy modeling and control*, Springer-Verlag, Berlin/Heidelberg, Germany, 2001.
11. M. Sugeno and T. Yasukawa, *A fuzzy-logic-based approach to qualitive modeling*, IEEE Trans. on Fuzzy Systems **1** (1993), no. 1, 7–31.

Fuzzy Reliability Analysis

Jacek Mazurkiewicz[1], Tomasz Walkowiak[1]

[1] Institute of Engineering Cybernetics, Wroclaw University of Technology,
ul. Janiszewskiego 11/17, 50-372 Wroclaw, Poland
e-mail: jmazur@ict.pwr.wroc.pl, twalkow@ict.pwr.wroc.pl

Abstract. The paper describes an idea of using fuzzy sets approach to reliability analysis for transport systems. The main goal is to find the average number of working trucks. The fuzzy approach is used for better estimation of these reliability parameters related to trucks which are mainly described by experts. Different membership functions and different fuzzy approaches are used and the obtained results are compared. The Mulitilayer Perceptron is used as the approximation tool.

1 Introduction

Decisions related to technical systems ought to be taken based on different and sometimes contradictory conditions. The reliability - in a wide sense - is one of the main factors, which are taken into consideration during a decision process. The reliability maybe isn't the most important factor but is of a great weight as a support criterion. So a quantitative information related to the reliability characteristics is important and can be used as a decision-aided system if it is necessary to discuss different economic aspects. The models used for reliability analysis are mainly based on Markov or Semi-Markov processes [1] which are idealized and it is hard to reconcile them with practice. The typical reliability analysis uses very strict assumptions related to the life or repair time and random variables distributions of the analyzed system elements. On the other hand modern devices are characterized by very screwed up reliability parameters - sometimes they are completely unmeasured or the population of analyzed elements is too limited to find such general information. So - the reliability parameters are fixed based on the experts' experience. This fact is the reason why fuzzy approach to reliability parameters description is justifiable. We expect that such description can be find as a proper way to find the reliability analysis more accurate.

2 Reliability Case Study

One of the simplest reliability model is a set of n independent elements for which we have a given mean times between failures (MTBF): $m_{\lambda i}$ and a mean repair time

m_μ. Assuming that failure and renewal processes are governed by exponential distribution the Markov based reliability analysis could be used [1]. The real example of such system could be a transport system with n trucks. An important question, which could be answered within a help of Markov models, is how many trucks are working (let denote is as *ks*) in average. If we assume, that we have, one repair crew, one mean value of the repair time and possibly n different MTBFs we can build a Markov model which allows to calculate a probability of being in a given state. Hence, the average number of trucks is given as an expected value of non-fault trucks in a given state [1] (similar to equation 1). The main problem is the calculation of the stationary probability of being in a given state. The solution is given be a set of linear equations. The equations describes the intensities (therefore probabilities) of passing from one state to the other (so called pass matrix). Therefore from the computational point of view this is equal to the inversion of the matrix.

We have developed a simple software for calculation of *ks* for a given set of $m_{\lambda i}$ and the mean repair time m_μ for a case when only one repair crew exist (this fact has an influence on the pass matrix values). However, we have found that a number of states is growing very fast in a function of a truck number. It makes the process of the average truck number calculation very time consuming (i.e. for n = 6 there are 1957 states, where n = 7 there are 13700 states).

2.1 Neural Networks as Approximation Tool

In one of our previous researches we have found that neural networks are a very capable tool of speeding up reliability parameters calculations [5]. Therefore, we have decided to use the Multilayer Perceptron to estimate the mean number of working trucks. The network has n+1 input neurons: corresponding to each of system parameters: mean time to failures and mean time to repair and one output (estimated value of *ks*). Outputs of the network where normalized to (0,1) range – simply using division by n. Moreover, the network has a single hidden layer and the sigmoidal transfer functions. The network was trained by Levenberg-Marquardt [2] algorithm using MATLAB package [3]. A fast calculation of *ks* realized by neural network was possible due to a training data set. The data set was calculated by the Markov model for random mean time values (inputs to the net).

2.2 Simplified Approach

We have also tried to simplify the Markov model, by assumption that the failure process is described by one parameter, one MTBF denoted as m_λ. It could be understand that we have n identical, independent trucks. In such case, we have only n+1 Markov states corresponding to numbers of non-fault elements (0,1,..., n faults are possible). For a stationary state, the average number of running trucks is equal to:

$$ks = \sum_{i=0}^{n} (n-i)P_i \qquad (1)$$

P_i , probabilities of being in a given state, are calculated as a solution of matrix equation:

$$\mathbf{P} = \mathbf{P}\,\mathbf{Q} \text{ with constraint } \sum_{i=0}^{n} P_i = 1 \qquad (2)$$

where:

$$\mathbf{P} = [P_0\, P_1 \ldots P_i \ldots P_n] \qquad (3)$$

is a vector of probability of state occupation and Q is a pass transition matrix:

$$\mathbf{Q} = \begin{bmatrix} -n\lambda & n\lambda & 0 & 0 & \ldots \\ \mu & -(\mu+(n-1)\lambda) & (n-1)\lambda & 0 & \ldots \\ 0 & \mu & -(\mu+(n-2)\lambda) & (n-2)\lambda & \ldots \\ 0 & 0 & \mu & -(\mu+(n-3)\lambda) & \ldots \\ \ldots & \ldots & \ldots & \ldots & \ldots \end{bmatrix} \qquad (4)$$

Such approach simplifies the *ks* calculation, but bounds the possible applications.

3 Fuzzy Approach to Reliability Analysis

Modern devices – trucks including - are characterized by very screwed up reliability parameters. It is very hard to find the proper universal values related to reliability description of these devices. Sometimes the parameters are completely unmeasured or the population of analyzed elements is too limited to find such general information. So - the reliability parameters are fixed based on experts' experience. Therefore we propose to use fuzzy approach to reliability parameters descriptions.

It is necessary to remember, that only values which are close to physical parameters can be described by experts. Therefore, we propose to discuss a fuzzy representation of inverse of intensities – the mean values. We think that such approach is justified because it is more natural to talk about time parameters than the classical reliability values (intensities).

3.1 Membership Functions

There are different membership functions. It is rather hard to say which type of them is the most suitable for the analyzed problem. This is the reason why we decided to apply four - most classical - types of unsymmetrical membership functions: Gaussian, Π-shape, trapezoidal, triangular [4,6].

The unsymmetrical triangular membership function (illustrated at Fig. 1(a)) is a function of x, and depends on three scalar parameters a, b, and c, as given by:

$$f(x;a,b,c) = \max\left(\min\left(\frac{x-a}{b-a}, \frac{c-x}{c-b}\right), 0\right). \tag{5}$$

The unsymmetrical trapezoidal membership function is a function of a vector, x, and depends on four scalar parameters a, b, c and d (Fig. 1(b)):

$$f(x;a,b,c,d) = \max\left(\min\left(\frac{x-a}{b-a}, 1, \frac{d-x}{d-c}\right), 0\right). \tag{6}$$

The Gaussian membership function depends on parameters σ and c:

$$f(x;\sigma,c) = e^{\frac{-(x-c)^2}{2\sigma^2}} \tag{7}$$

We used the unsymmetrical Gaussian membership function which is a combination of two of Gaussian (illustrated at Fig. 1(c)).

The Π-shape unsymmetrical membership function is a spline-based curve illustrated at Fig. 1(d).

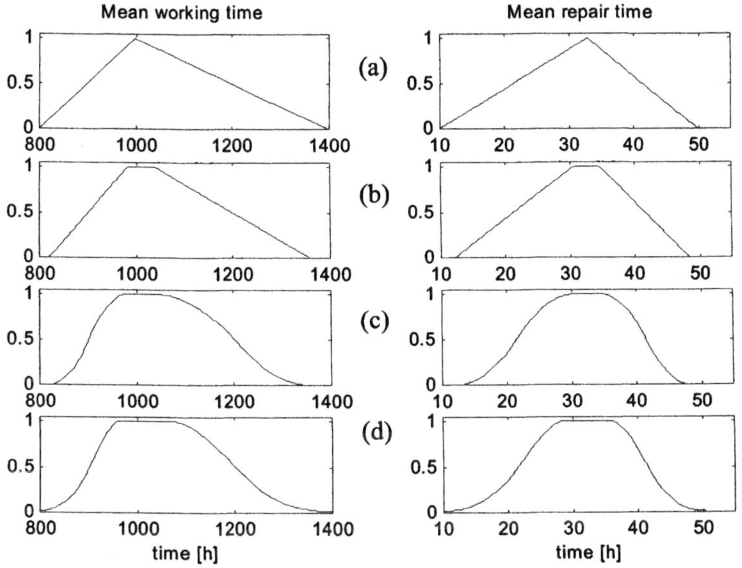

Fig. 1. Fuzzification methods – membership functions. **(a)** Triangular. **(b)** Trapezoidal. **(c)** Gaussian. **(d)** Π-shape

3.2 Fuzzy Detailed Approach

In general we propose the analysis of average number of trucks *ks* as a function of fuzzy mean value of intensities:

$$ks = g(m_{\lambda_1}, m_{\lambda_2}, ..., m_{\lambda n}, m_{\mu}) \tag{8}$$

This function creates a MISO system with *n+1* inputs. The calculation of output membership function based on a definition of MISO output for min/max operators:

$$f_{ks}(y) = \underset{y=g(x_1,x_2,x_n,x_{n+1})}{\text{MAX}} \{\text{MIN}(f_{m_\lambda}(x_1), f_{m_\lambda}(x_2), ..., f_{m_\lambda}(x_n), f_{m_\mu}(x_2))\} \tag{9}$$

where f(.) are fuzzy membership functions. The calculation of above are complicated and time consuming. Therefore, we tried to simplify it.

3.3 Fuzzy Simplified Approach

As it was stated in 2.2 it is possible to approximate the real situation by a simpler system in which we have only two inputs: the mean working time and the mean repair time. It results in a two inputs MISO system, with outputs given by:

$$f_{ks}(y) = \underset{y=g'(x_1,x_2)}{\text{MAX}} \{\text{MIN}(f_{m_\lambda}(x_1), f_{m_\mu}(x_2))\} \forall x_1, x_2, y \in R \tag{10}$$

where function g'( ) is described in 2.2 (equations (1) to (4)). The exact calculation of above function as in previous case (3.2) is not trivial and very time consuming task. However, due to features of function g'( ) it could be simplified:

$$g'(m_\lambda, m_\mu) = g'(m_\lambda / m_\mu, 1) = g''(m_\lambda / m_\mu) \tag{11}$$

So we can simply calculate the membership function related to a ratio of two fuzzy values [4,6]. Let's denote it as $f_{m\lambda m\mu}$. Since the function g''( ) is monotonic the output membership function could be calculated as:

$$f_{ks}(g''(x)) = f_{m_\lambda m_\mu}(x), \tag{12}$$

3.4 Fuzzy L-R Approach

The last approach produces the output membership function based on L-R representation [6] of mean time values: the mean working time and the mean repair time of trucks. So it's a simplified version of the previous approach. The L-R representation describes each parameter using triple of data – the "mean" value, and two offsets which allow to describe the range of the parameter. And only these parameters are further processed to achieve the L-R representation of the output function. Such representation guarantees a really simple and fast calculation of fuzzy output values but it gives only the approximation of fuzzy function of outputs values.

4 Results and Summary

The results of the researches are presented at Fig. 2. The analysis was realized for transport system equipped with $n = 6$ trucks. We used four membership functions described in section 3.1 and illustrated at Fig. 1. We can easily notice that fuzzy detailed and fuzzy simplified approaches generate very similar results. We think that the most interested results are related to fuzzy L-R approach. In this case, the results are very close to previous ones but achieved by method which is much faster than the previous two.

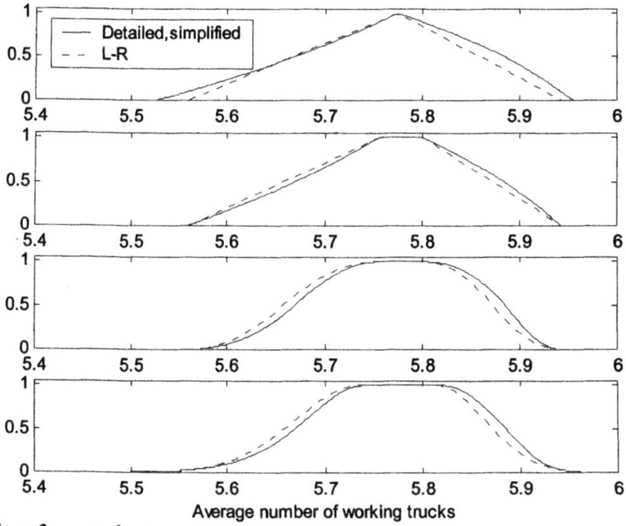

Fig. 2. Results of researches

This work has been supported by the Polish Council for Scientific Research, Grant No. 9 T12C 072 17.

References

1. Barlow R., Proschan F. (1996) Mathematical Theory of Reliability, Society for Industrial and Applied Mathematics, Philadelphia
2. Bishop Ch. (1995) Neural Networks for Pattern Recognition, Clarendon Press, Oxford
3. Demuth H., Beale M. (1998) Neural Networks Toolbox. The MathWorks Inc.
4. MATLAB, (1999) Fuzzy Logic Toolbox User's Guide. The MathWorks Inc.
5. Mazurkiewicz J., Walkowiak T. (2000) Neural Network for Reliability Parameters Analysis – Case Study. 5th Conference: Neural Networks and Soft Computing, Zakopane, Technical University of Czestochowa, 687 - 692
6. Piegat A. (1999) Fuzzy Modeling and Control, EXIT Academic Publishing House, Warsaw (in Polish)

Variable Precision Rough Sets in Analysis of Inconsistent Decision Tables

Alicja Mieszkowicz-Rolka [1], Leszek Rolka[1]

[1]Rzeszów University of Technology, Department of Avionics and Control, ul.W. Pola 2, 35-959 Rzeszów, Poland,
alicjamr@prz.rzeszow.pl, leszekr@prz.rzeszow.pl

Abstract. This paper discusses the idea of variable precision rough sets, which can be viewed as an extension of the basic rough set notion. A new definition of the positive area of classification is proposed and investigated. This approach leads to a change of properties of the approximation quality, which then becomes a more suitable measure for assessment of dependencies between condition and decision attributes in decision tables obtained from real processes. It was shown that the approximation quality can be equally obtained by using the notion of filling error of a set. The conclusions of the paper concern the admissible inclusion error α and present the comparison of the investigated measures. The propositions can be effectively applied to analysis of information systems in case of dynamic processes controlled by a human operator.

1 Introduction

The Rough Sets Theory introduced by Pawlak [1, 2] is an effective tool for analysing information systems expressed in form of decision tables. The elements of the universe of discourse U are expressed as decision rules. The attributes are divided into a set of condition attributes C and a set of decision attributes D. For comparing the elements of the universe an indiscernibility relation R is used, which generates a family of equivalence classes in the universe U. The consistency of a decision table can be evaluated using the measure of approximation quality $k = \gamma_c(D^*)$. In order to calculate the value of k the family C^* of equivalence classes obtained with respect to conditions attributes C is used to approximate the family D^* of equivalence classes generated with respect to decision attributes D. In case of inconsistent rules some equivalence classes of C^* must be omitted in calculation, no matter how many rules are contradictory and not considering the cardinality of the correspondent equivalence classes. That is why the basic model of a rough set (RS) appeared to be too restrictive in some applications [3]. When analysing dynamic processes controlled by a human operator the value of approximation quality could be nearly equal to zero. This would mean that the reasoning model of the operator is not constant and his decisions are inconsistent and random. The concept of Variable Precision Rough Sets was proposed by Ziarko in [3]. VPRS help to enlarge the application area especially towards those information systems, which describe the human control actions in dynamic processes. In such situations there always exists possibility of errors and the decision rules are gradually adapted.

2 Fundamentals of VPRS

The set inclusion relation α

The basic proposition of VPRS is a changed relation of set inclusion defined in (1) and (2) [3].

Let X, Y be nonempty subsets of the universal set U. We say that the set X is included in the set Y with an admissible error α

$$X \overset{\alpha}{\subseteq} Y \Leftrightarrow e(X,Y) \leq \alpha \tag{1}$$

where:

$$e(X, Y) = 1 - card(X \cap Y)/card(X). \tag{2}$$

We call the quantity $e(X, Y)$ the inclusion error of X in Y.

The value of α should be limited: $0 \leq \alpha < 0.5$.

α-approximation of a set

As a consequence of the former proposition a new notion of α-approximation of sets was introduced [3].

Let $A = <U, R>$ be an approximation space and $X \subseteq U$ any set,

where: U is a finite set of elements called the universe,

$R \subseteq U \times U$ is a binary relation called the indiscernibility relation.

Definition 1:

α-lower approximation of X by R, denoted as $\underline{R}X$ is a set

$$\underline{R}_{\alpha}X = \{x \in U : [x]_R \overset{\alpha}{\subseteq} X\} \tag{3}$$

which is equivalent to

$$\underline{R}_{\alpha}X = \{\, x \in U : e(\,[x]_R\,, X\,) \leq \alpha\,\}. \tag{4}$$

Definition 2:

α-upper approximation of X by R, denoted as $\overline{R}X$ is a set

$$\overline{R}_{\alpha}X = \{ x \in U : e([x]_R, X) \leq 1 - \alpha \}. \tag{5}$$

Definition 3:

α-boundary is a set

$$B_{\alpha R}X = \{ x \in U: \alpha < e([x]_R, X) < 1 - \alpha \}. \tag{6}$$

Following the definitions given above we formulate here, by analogy to RS, the notions of the α-lower approximation of a family X^* by R, α-positive area of X^* and γ_R-α-approximation quality of X^* by R.

If we consider an information system S, then we get:

Definition 4:

Let $X^* = \{ X_1, X_2, \ldots, X_n \}$ be a classification of the universe U.

α-positive classification area of X^*, with respect to a set of attributes P, in the system S is defined as follows:

$$Pos_P^{\alpha}(X^*) = \bigcup_{i=1}^{n} \underline{P}_{\alpha}(X_i). \tag{7}$$

Definition 5:

If $X^* = \{ X_1, X_2, \ldots, X_n \}$ is a classification of the universe U, then

$$\gamma_P^{\alpha}(X^*) = \frac{card\, Pos_P^{\alpha}(X^*)}{card\, U} = \frac{\sum_{i=1}^{n} card(\underline{P}_{\alpha}X_i)}{card\, U} \tag{8}$$

is called α-approximation quality of X^* by P.

For a decision table we get a measure denoted by k_{WZ} for the α-dependence of the decision attributes D on the condition attributes C:

$$k_{WZ} = \gamma_C^{\alpha}(D^*) = \frac{\text{card}\, Pos_C^{\alpha}(D^*)}{card\, U} = \frac{\sum_{i=1}^{m} card(\underline{C}_{\alpha}D_i)}{card\, U} \tag{9}$$

where: $0 \leq k_{WZ} \leq 1$, and $D^* = \{ D_1, D_2, \ldots, D_m \}$.

3 Positive area of classification

We propose a different definition of the α-positive area of a set X.

Definition 6:

$$PosR_{\alpha}(X) = \{\, x \in U: x \in ([x]_R \cap X) \text{ and } e([x]_R, X) \le \alpha \,\} \tag{10}$$

The notion $PosR_{\alpha}(X)$ can be applied to a family of sets. By using it to equivalence classes obtained from a decision table we get a new measure instead of k_{WZ}, denoted by k_{AR}.

Definition 7:
α-approximation quality of D^* by C is expressed as follows:

$$k_{AR} = \frac{card\, Pos_C^{\alpha}(D^*)}{card\, U} = \frac{\sum_{i=1}^{n}\sum_{j=1}^{m} \partial_{ij} \cdot card(C_i \cap D_j)}{card\, U} \tag{11}$$

$$\text{where } \partial_{ij} = \begin{cases} 1 & \text{if } e(C_i, D_j) \le \alpha \\ 0 & \text{otherwise} \end{cases}$$

where:
n - number of equivalence classes for decision attributes C,
m - number of equivalence classes for condition attributes D,
α - acceptable inclusion error; $0 \le \alpha < 0.5$.

It is easy to show that $R(C \cup D) = R(C) \cap R(D)$. The equivalence classes of Q^* for the sum $Q = C \cup D$ of condition and decision attributes are always included in the equivalence classes of C^* for condition attributes C. This is due to the properties of information systems [1]. For a consistent decision rule (in the sense of RS) one equivalence class for the attributes C will include exactly one equivalence class for the attributes Q.

Definition 8:
If X and Y are nonempty subsets of U and $X \subseteq Y$, then let us denote $f(X, Y)$ the filling error of Y by X

$$f(X, Y) = 1 - d(X, Y) \tag{12}$$

where:

$$d(X, Y) = \frac{card(X \cap Y)}{card\, Y} = \frac{card\, X}{card\, Y} \tag{13}$$

One have to determine the filling errors of the equivalence classes obtained for condition attributes C by the equivalence classes obtained for the sum of the attributes $Q = C \cup D$.

Using the introduced quantities we can now express the measure k_{AR} as follows:

$$k_{AR} = \frac{\sum_{i=1}^{n} \sum_{j=1}^{l} \omega_{ij} \cdot card\, Q_j}{card\, U} \tag{14}$$

$$\text{where } \omega_{ij} = \begin{cases} 1 & \text{for } \mathrm{Q_j} \subseteq C_i \quad \text{and} \quad f(\mathrm{Q_j}, C_i) \le \lambda \\ 0 & \text{otherwise} \end{cases}$$

n - number of equivalence classes for the condition attributes C
l - number of equivalence classes for the attributes $Q = C \cup D$
λ - acceptable filling error; $0 \le \lambda < 0.5$.

It can be shown that the acceptable filling error λ of the equivalence classes of C^* by the equivalence classes of Q^* is equal to α - the acceptable inclusion error of the equivalence classes of C^* in the equivalence classes of D^*.

Due to simplicity of calculation the equation (14) was used in a computer algorithm for determining the value of k_{AR}.

4 Conclusions

It was important to check the influence of the acceptable inclusion error α on the value of k_{WZ} and k_{AR} and on the properties of information system after removing (omitting) the condition attributes. Some of the obtained results are given in the Table 1. Basing on experimental investigations we have found that the value of k_{WZ} increased in some cases after removing a condition attribute and this fact makes a difference between VPRS and RS. Many decision tables, obtained from recording control action of a human operator (pilot), who controlled a dynamic plant (aircraft), were analysed. The investigations led to the following conclusions:

1. The acceptable inclusion error α, which is not greater than 0.25, allows to assess correctly the influence of particular condition attributes on the decisions undertaken by human operator controlling a dynamic plant.
2. Generally the value of k_{AR} is slightly lower than the correspondent value of k_{WZ} but it gives more information about the significance of individual condition attributes in the decision process. The property of increasing approximation

quality (k_{WZ}) after removing condition attributes is nearly eliminated for k_{AR} (see Table 1).

3. If the cardinality of particular equivalence classes for condition attributes is small, then the obtained results ($\alpha \in <0, 0.2>$) for VPRS (k_{AR} and k_{WZ}) and RS (k) are similar.
4. For large equivalence classes the differences between RS and VPRS are significant. It is possible, in an extreme case, to obtain the value of $k=\gamma_c(D^*)$ equal to 0 (RS), but the values of k_{WZ} and k_{AR} equal to 1. Therefore, VPRS and the proposed modification help to alleviate the restrictive character of RS.

Summarising, the proposed definition of positive area of classification leads to a new measure of approximation quality k_{AR}, which is not so "restrictive" as the original measure k of RS and not so "tolerant" as the measure k_{WZ} of VPRS.

Table 1. Analysis of experimental data

α	Measure	Removed attribute					
		none	1	2	3	4	5
0.34	k_{WZ}	0.607	0.607	0.787	0.607	0.607	0.590
	k_{AR}	0.574	0.574	0.574	0.541	0.574	0.525
0.25	k_{WZ}	0.607	0.607	0.393	0.557	0.607	0.443
	k_{AR}	0.574	0.574	0.574	0.541	0.574	0.525
0.2	k_{WZ}	0.541	0.541	0.328	0.426	0.510	0.377
	k_{AR}	0.525	0.525	0.328	0.410	0.525	0.377
0.15	k_{WZ}	0.459	0.459	0.328	0.410	0.459	0.377
	k_{AR}	0.459	0.459	0.328	0.410	0.459	0.377
0	k_{WZ}	0.459	0.459	0.328	0.410	0.459	0.377
	k_{AR}	0.459	0.459	0.328	0.410	0.459	0.377

References

1. Pawlak Z. (1991) Rough Sets. Theoretical Aspects of Reasoning about Data, Kluwer Academic Publishers, Dordrecht, Boston, London
2. Słowiński R. ed. (1992) Intelligent Decision Support. Handbook of Applications and Advances of the Rough Sets. Kluwer Academic Publishers
3. Ziarko W. (1992) Analysis of uncertain information in the framework of variable precision rough sets modeling. Proceedings of Workshop. Rough Sets. State of art and perspective, Kiekrz

The Newton Interpolation Method with Fuzzy Numbers as the Entries

Elisabeth Rakus-Andersson

Blekinge Institute of Technology, Department of Health, Science and Mathematics, S-37179 Karlskrona, Sweden
E-mail: Elisabeth.Andersson@bth.se

Summary. It is typical of some medical experiments, leading to measures regarded as the coordinates of points in the plane, that imprecise data can occur. In spite of it we still would like to derive a formula of the function that interpolates these points. We thus test the Newton interpolation method with divided differences when supposing that the entries will be fuzzy numbers in the L-R form. The equation describing the fuzzy function, which goes through the points, can be used as a prognosis in the case of other points that have only one coordinate known.

1 Newton Polynomials

At the beginning of the interpolating process we state the most important assumptions which concern the classical Newton method. Suppose that the function $y = f(x)$ is known at the $n+1$ points $(x_0, y_0), (x_1, y_1), \ldots, (x_n, y_n)$ with non-fuzzy coordinates, where the values x_k are spread out over the interval $[a, b]$ and satisfy the connections $y_k = f(x_k), k = 0, 1, \ldots, n$. A polynomial $p(x)$ of degree n shall be constructed which passes through these $n+1$ points. In the construction, only the numerical values x_k and y_k are needed. The polynomial $p(x)$ can be used to approximate $f(x)$ over the entire interval $[a, b]$.

We note that the polynomial $p_n(x)$ has a common form

$$p_n(x) = c_0 + c_1 x + c_2 x^2 + \cdots + c_n x^n \tag{1}$$

but it is more convenient to construct the Newton polynomial as [5]

$$p_n(x) = a_0 + a_1(x-x_0) + a_2(x-x_0)(x-x_1) + \cdots + a_n(x-x_0)(x-x_1)\cdots(x-x_{n-1}). \tag{2}$$

Following the physicians' advice we decide that it is no use constructing the polynomials of the degree greater than $n = 4$, that demand at least 5 points as the input data. Therefore we can concentrate on the polynomials which have $n \leq 4$. To find the coefficients of, e.g., $p_3(x)$ we propose the following scheme [5]

$$\begin{array}{llllll}
x_k & y_k & f[\ ] & f[\ ,\ ] & f[\ ,\ ,\ ] & f[\ ,\ ,\ ,\ ] \\
x_0 & y_0 & f[x_0]=a_0 & & & \\
 & & & f[x_0,x_1]=a_1 & & \\
x_1 & y_1 & f[x_1] & & f[x_0,x_1,x_2]=a_2 & \\
 & & & f[x_1,x_2] & & f[x_0,x_1,x_2,x_3]=a_3 \\
x_2 & y_2 & f[x_2] & & f[x_1,x_2,x_3] & \\
 & & & f[x_2,x_3] & & \\
x_3 & y_3 & f[x_3] & & &
\end{array} \tag{3}$$

in which the values $f[\ ]$, $f[\ ,\ ]$, $f[\ ,\ ,\ ]$, $f[\ ,\ ,\ ,\ ]$, called divided differences, are computed in accordance with the formulas below

$$\begin{aligned}
f[x_0,x_1] &= \frac{f[x_1]-f[x_0]}{x_1-x_0}, f[x_1,x_2]=\frac{f[x_2]-f[x_1]}{x_2-x_1}, \\
f[x_2,x_3] &= \frac{f[x_3]-f[x_2]}{x_3-x_2}, \text{ for } f[x_i]=y_i, i=0,1,2,3; \\
f[x_0,x_1,x_2] &= \frac{f[x_1,x_2]-f[x_0,x_1]}{x_2-x_0}, \\
f[x_1,x_2,x_3] &= \frac{f[x_2,x_3]-f[x_1,x_2]}{x_3-x_1}, \\
f[x_0,x_1,x_2,x_3] &= \frac{f[x_1,x_2,x_3]-f[x_0,x_1,x_2]}{x_3-x_0}.
\end{aligned} \tag{4}$$

The coefficients a_0, a_1, a_2, a_3 are the numbers from the upper diagonal in 3 calculated due to the formulas included in 4. They are applied to 2 for $n=3$.

Example 1 *Let us test the action of the method discussed above by taking into consideration three points $(3,14),(4,22),(6,44)$ with non-fuzzy coordinates. We will find the polynomial $p_2(x)=a_0+a_1(x-x_0)+a_2(x-x_0)(x-x_1)$ which interpolates these points provided that $y_k=p(x_k), k=0,1,2$.*

To solve the problem we begin with the scheme described by 3

$$\begin{array}{llll}
x_k\ y_k\ f[\ ] & f[\ ,\ ] & f[\ ,\ ,\ ] \\
3 \quad 14 \quad 14=a_0 & & \\
 & f[x_0,x_1]=\dfrac{22-14}{4-3}=8=a_1 & \\
4 \quad 22 \quad 22 & & f[x_0,x_1,x_2]=\dfrac{11-8}{6-3}=1=a_2 \\
 & f[x_1,x_2]=\dfrac{44-22}{6-4}=11 & \\
6 \quad 44 \quad 44 & &
\end{array}$$

The associated Newton polynomial is now expanded as

$$p_2(x) = 14 + 8(x-3) + (x-3)(x-4) = x^2 + x + 2.$$

In the further investigations of the subject taken up we assume that the numbers, included in the algorithm, are fuzzy.

2 A New Approach to the Operations on Fuzzy Numbers

Some medical experiments carried out on a sample of objects lead to imprecise values. The physicians are often interested in finding an equation of the function which approximates the pairs of vague informations in the best way. It is also desirable that these pairs, treated as the points, satisfy the equation of the approximating function. We can now prove an adaptation of the Newton method on condition that the data is not known exactly. To solve the task, we decide to introduce fuzzy numbers into the algorithm revealed above.

Let us recall the conception of a fuzzy number M in L-R representation as the following definition [1, 4, 6].

Definition 2 *A fuzzy number M is of L-R type if there exist reference functions L (for left) and R (for right), and scalars $\alpha > 0, \beta > 0$ with*

$$\mu_M(z) = \begin{cases} L\left(\dfrac{m-z}{\alpha}\right) & \text{for } z \le m \\ R\left(\dfrac{z-m}{\beta}\right) & \text{for } z \ge m, \end{cases} \tag{5}$$

where m, called the mean value of M, is a real number, and α and β are called the left and right spreads, respectively. Symbolically, M is denoted by (m, α, β).

Suppose that $M = (m, \alpha, \beta)$ represents the fuzzy number named as, e.g., "close to m" or "very close to m". We try to designate the difference between "close" and "very close" by establishing the appropriate values of the spreads α and β for both fuzzy numbers. Let us suggest a list containing the most popular, verbal expressions which are used by physicians for the imprecise numbers. We denote the list by $LIST$ and state its contents as

$$\begin{aligned} LIST = \{M_0 = \text{ exactly } m,\ M_1 = \text{almost exactly } m,\ M_2 = \text{very close to } m, \\ M_3 = \text{close to } m,\ M_4 = \text{approximately } m,\ M_5 = \text{perhaps } m\}. \end{aligned} \tag{6}$$

Each notion of the list is proposed to have an L-R representation suggested as

$$M_i = (m, i, i), i = 0, 1, 2, 3, 4, 5. \tag{7}$$

By accepting that $L(z) = R(z) = -z+1$ we derive new formulas of the membership functions for M_i, $i = 1,2,3,4,5$, expanded as

$$\mu_{M_i}(z) = \begin{cases} L\left(\dfrac{m-z}{i}\right) = -\dfrac{m-z}{i} + 1 = \dfrac{z+i-m}{i} & \text{for } z \in [m-i, m] \\ R\left(\dfrac{z-m}{i}\right) = -\dfrac{z-m}{i} + 1 = \dfrac{i+m-z}{i} & \text{for } z \in [m, m+i]. \end{cases} \tag{8}$$

If we use the fuzzy numbers $M_i, i = 0,1,2,3,4,5$, defined by 7 and 8 as the data in the Newton method of approximation we will cause the appearance of a fuzzy function which yields the value of y for any $x \in LIST$. We expect that y should belong to the class of numbers specified by 6. By performing the well known operations on fuzzy numbers due to [1, 4, 6] or [2, 3] we recognize that we never get the result y with the spreads satisfying the condition 7. To demonstrate this assertion let us add "very close to 5" to "perhaps 3" when using the classical definition of addition of two fuzzy numbers [1, 4, 6]. Hence, $(5,2,2)+(3,5,5) = (8,7,7)$. The result of the addition is the number with large spreads, that is not a member of $LIST$, either. The multiplication of these numbers will bring the effect $(5,2,2)\cdot(3,5,5) = (15, 5\cdot5+3\cdot2, 5\cdot5+3\cdot2) = (15,31,31)$ as the very imprecise number with the huge values of α and β despite of the fact that neither $(5,2,2)$ nor $(3,5,5)$ are spread so widely. Moreover, we are not sure how to express verbally such a number. Even testing the operations, recommended by [2, 3], we get the result $(5,2,2)\cdot(3,5,5) = (5\cdot3, \max(2\cdot3, 5\cdot5), \max(2\cdot3, 5\cdot5)) = (15,25,25)$ which still preserves the large values of the spreads, and we note that both α and β also will exceed the borders of the numbers placed in 7.

Let us consider the universes X and Y of positive fuzzy numbers x_k respective y_k of the type $M_i, i = 0,1,2,3,4,5$. By performing the operations of addition, subtraction, multiplication and division we wish to obtain other numbers looking like M_i. We thus propose the following operations on the fuzzy numbers from $LIST$ by defining them as

$$\begin{aligned} M_i + M_j &= (m_i,i,i) + (m_j,j,j) = (m_i + m_j, \max(i,j), \max(i,j)); \\ M_i - M_j &= (m_i,i,i) - (m_j,j,j) = (m_i - m_j, \max(i,j), \max(i,j)); \\ M_i \cdot M_j &= (m_i,i,i) \cdot (m_j,j,j) = (m_i \cdot m_j, \min(i,j), \min(i,j)); \\ M_i \div M_j &= (m_i,i,i) \div (m_j,j,j) = (m_i \div m_j, \min(i,j), \min(i,j)) \\ \text{for } i,j &= 0,1,2,3,4,5. \end{aligned} \tag{9}$$

These operations, which intuitively are interpreted as similar to the operations occurring in the case of the largest t-norm for multiplication (min) and the smallest s-norm for addition (max) [6], warrant that their results always will be the fuzzy numbers from 6. Let us note that the list of M_i has been created according to the physicians' advice. Hence, the users who define the entries of data in the way which is comfortable for them - in other words by choosing any description belonging to the *LIST* - expect that they obtain a result y as another fuzzy number from *LIST*.

To sum up, we ascertain that the classical model of finding a polynomial that interpolates the set of points has been adapted to the medical experiment with fuzzy data. If we accept the fuzzy numbers 7 in the Newton algorithm 3 performing the operations given by 9, we will model the fuzzy function which goes through the given points. To check that the function passes through the points (x_k, y_k), we compare if $m_{y_k} = m_{p_n(x_k)}$ for either $\mu_{y_k} \leq \mu_{p_n(x_k)}$ or $\mu_{y_k} \geq \mu_{p_n(x_k)}$, $n \leq 4$.

3 The Medical Example

During the experiment showing effects of three cultivations of the microorganisms, the relationship between the amount of culture medium liquid and the number of bacteria (in special units) has been determined as (almost exactly 3, close to 14), (very close to four, almost exactly 22) and (close to 6, very close to 44). We wish to express the connection between the amount of liquid and the number of bacteria for every value of liquid belonging to the interval $[3, 6]$ by means of a polynomial $p_2(x) = a_0 + a_1(x - x_0)(x - x_1)$.

In order to compute the coefficients a_0, a_1 and a_2 we build the table by making a practice of the pattern 3 with the operations performed in accordance with definitions 9 as follows

x_k	y_k	$f[\ ]$
$(3,1,1)$	$(14,3,3)$	$(14,,3,3) = a_0$
$(4,2,2)$	$(22,1,1)$	$(22,1,1)$
$(6,3,3)$	$(44,2,2)$	$(44,2,2)$

$$f[\ ,\ ]$$

$$\frac{(22,1,1)-(14,3,3)}{(4,2,2)-(3,1,1)} = \frac{(8,3,3)}{(1,2,2)} = (8,2,2) = a_1$$
$$\frac{(44,2,2)-(22,1,1)}{(6,3,3)-(4,2,2)} = \frac{(22,2,2)}{(2,3,3)} = (11,2,2)$$

$$f[\ ,\ ,\ ]$$

$$\frac{(11,2,2)-(8,2,2)}{(6,3,3)-(3,1,1)} = \frac{(3,2,2)}{(3,3,3)} = (1,2,2) = a_2.$$

The interpolating polynomial $p_2(x)$, provided that $x = (x, i, i)$, is obtained as the function

$$\begin{aligned} p_2(x) &= (14,3,3) + (8,2,2)\,[(x,i,i) - (3,1,1)] \\ &\quad +(1,2,2)\,\{[(x,i,i) - (3,1,1)]\,[(x,i,i) - (4,2,2)]\} \\ &= (x^2 + x + 2, l, l) \end{aligned}$$

where $l = \max(\max(3, \min(2, \max(i,1))), \max(2, \min(\max(i,1), \max(i,2))))$.

If $x = (5,2,2)$, the corresponding value of y will be computed as $y = (32,3,3)$ and expressed as the number "close to 32" with the membership function

$$\mu_y(z) = \begin{cases} L\left(\frac{32-z}{3}\right) = -\frac{32-z}{3} + 1 = \frac{z-29}{3} & \text{for } z \in [29, 32] \\ R\left(\frac{z-32}{3}\right) = -\frac{z-32}{3} + 1 = \frac{35-z}{3} & \text{for } z \in [32, 35]. \end{cases}$$

4 Conclusions

The method suggested in the paper should assist in the physicians' efforts to approximate a value of the dependent biological parameter if a number representing the independent feature is known. We base on vague observations which are composed as a set of points. These are interpolated by a Newton polynomial which comprises fuzzy numbers as coefficients. The polynomial is provided by the implementation of a new approach to the operations on fuzzy numbers, which make possible to keep both the coefficients and the values of the dependent variable within the set of fuzzy numbers determined verbally by an experienced physician. The algorithm with the numbers, calculated as a result of max and min operations, is very simple and can be applied by medical staff without any professional, mathematical help.

References

[1] Dubois D., Prade H. (1978), Fuzzy Real Algebra. Some Results, Fuzzy Sets and Systems 2, 327-348

[2] Dug Hun Hong, Sungho Lee and Hae Young Do (2001), Fuzzy Linear Regression Analysis for Fuzzy Input-Output Data Using Shape-Preserving Operations, Fuzzy Sets and Systems 122(3), 513-526

[3] Dug Hun Hong (2001), Shape Preserving Multiplications of Fuzzy Numbers, Fuzzy Sets and Systems 123, 81-84

[4] Kacprzyk J. (1986), Fuzzy Sets in System Analysis, Polish Scientific Publishing House, Warsaw (in Polish)

[5] Mathew J. H. (1992), Numerical Methods for Mathematics, Science and Engineering, 2nd Edition, Prentice Hall, Englewood Cliffs, New Jersey

[6] Zimmermann H. J. (1996), Fuzzy Set Theory and Its Applications, 3rd Edition, Kluwer Academic Publish, Boston

Fuzzy Optimization Using Direct Crisp and Fuzzy Interval Comparison

Pavel V. Sevastjanov and Paweł Róg

Institute of Math. & Comp. Sci., Technical University of Czestochowa,
Dabrowskiego st. 73, 42-201 Czestochowa, Poland, ph/fax. (+4834) 3250331
e-mail: sevast@k2.pcz.czest.pl

Abstract. In real optimization tasks, always there are two main groups of criteria: requirements of outcomes increasing or expenses decreasing and demands of uncertainty reduction, in other words, risk minimization. Therefore, it seems advisable to formulate optimization problem under conditions of uncertainty as, at least, two-objective on the basis of local criteria of benefits increasing or expenses reduction and risk minimization. Generally, risk may be treated as the uncertainty of result obtained. In a situation considered, the degree of risk (uncertainty) may be defined in natural way as width of final interval of target function at the point of obtained optimum. To solve the problem briefly described above, the technique of two-objective crisp and fuzzy interval comparison has been developed on the base of probability approach to interval comparison taking into account the relation of compared intervals widths. To illustrate the efficiency of method proposed, the simple example of minimization in the case of interval double-extreme discontinuous cost function of real argument is presented.

1 Introduction

In practice, there are many problems of optimization that formulated using imprecision parameters. Frequently, such parameters may be considered as intervals or fuzzy number. As the consequence, the optimization tasks with interval or fuzzy interval cost function of real arguments are obtained. The procedure of direct numerical optimization can generally be presented as a sequence of searching steps, on each of which we try to receive the smaller/greater target function value, than on previous one. It is clear, that in the case of interval or fuzzy interval target function we are faced with a problem of consecutive interval reduction. Unfortunately, even in case of successful resolving of optimization problem there are no any guarantee that the obtained result have sufficiently small uncertainty. It is easy to see that in our case such an uncertainty can be in natural way presented as the width of minimized/maximized interval target function. In a nutshell, in the case considered we deal with two local criteria. In general, simultaneous satisfaction the such criteria in a maximal degree is usually impossible. Thereby, there is a problem to construct a compromise criterion, which may be performed as the some aggregation of local criteria. To permit it, at first we must built the local criterion for quantitative assessment of degree in which one interval —

crisp or fuzzy — is large than another one. The problem of crisp and fuzzy intervals (numbers) ordering is of perennial interest, because of its direct relevance in practical modeling and optimization of real world processes. There exist numerous definition of the ordering relation over fuzzy quantities (as well as crisp intervals) [1]–[9]. In most cases the authors use some quantitative indices. The values of such indices presents degree to which one interval (fuzzy or crisp) is large/less than another interval. In some cases, even several indices are used simultaneously. For example, in [7] four indices of inequality and three of equality indices had been proposed. It was noted in review [9] of most known approaches, that although some of these methods have shown more consistency and better performance in difficult cases, no single method of fuzzy interval comparison may be putted forward as the best. Therefore, in this article we present new method for crisp and fuzzy interval comparison based on α-level representation of fuzzy intervals and probability estimation of fact that certain interval is large/equal than another one. The method allows to compare interval and real number and to take into account (implicitly) the widths of intervals ordered. Also we present the general method for optimization in the case or crisp or fuzzy interval cost function based on probability estimation of interval inequality and local criterion expressed explicitly the widths of intervals compared as measure of result's uncertainty and which therefore may be considered as criterion of risk minimization.

2 Crisp Interval Relation Expressions

Since the method proposed is based on the representation of fuzzy number as α-level sets, the main problem is to compare the crisp intervals. Let $A = [a_1, a_2]$ and $B = [b_1, b_2]$ be independent intervals and $a \in [a_1, a_2]$, $b \in [b_1, b_2]$ be random values distributed on these intervals. Since we deal with the crisp (non-fuzzy) intervals, the natural assumption is the random values a and b are distributed uniformly. In the cases of intervals intersection there are some subintervals, which play an important role in our analysis. For example (see Figure 1), the hitting of random values $a \in [a_1, a_2]$, $b \in [b_1, b_2]$ in the subintervals $[a_1, b_1]$, $[b_1, a_2]$, $[b_1, a_2]$ may be interpreted as the set of some independent random events. Let us define the events H_k: $a \in A_i, b \in B_j$ where A_i and B_j are some subintervals of intervals A and B, respectively, where $A = \bigcup\limits_m A_i$, $B = \bigcup\limits_l B_j$. It easy to see that events H_k form the complete set of events, describing all the cases of hitting random values a and b in the various subintervals A_i and B_j, respectively. Let $P(H_k)$ be probability of event H_k and $P(B > A/H_k)$ be conditional probability of $B > A$. Hence, for composite probability we get

$$P(B > A) = \sum_{k}^{n} P(H_k) P(B > A/H_k). \tag{1}$$

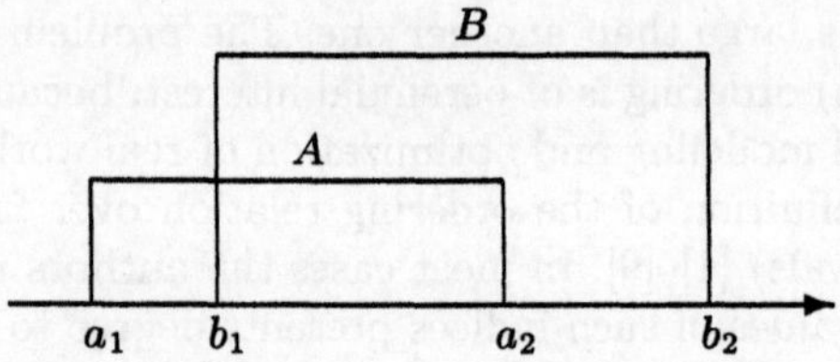

Fig. 1. Example of intervals intersection.

Becouse we deal with the uniform distributions of random values a and b in the given subintervals, the probabilities $P(H_k)$, $P(B > A/H_k)$ can be easily obtained from the simple geometrical reasons. For case, presented in fig. 1 we obtain

$$P(B > A) = 1 - \frac{1}{2}\frac{(a_2 - b_1)^2}{(a_2 - a_1)(b_2 - b_1)}.$$

In similar way, the expressions for the all possible cases of interval intersection as well as intersection of intervals and real numbers have been inferred. To complete the set of expressions for interval relations the formulae for probabilities of intervals equality have been obtained too. Of course, in all cases we have $P(B > A) + P(A > B) = 1$ and $P(A = B) + P(A \neq B) = 1$. Thus, if the probability $P(B > A) < 0.5$ the opposite event $A > B$ is more probable, since $P(B > A) + P(A > B) = 1$.

3 Fuzzy Interval Ordering

Let A and B be fuzzy intervals (numbers), $A_\alpha = \{x, \mu_A(x) \geq \alpha\}$ and $B_\alpha = \{y, \mu_B(y) \geq \alpha\}$ be α-levels sets of A and B accordingly. Since A and B are crisp intervals, the probability $P(B > A)$ for each pair A_α and B_α of A and B can be calculated by the way described in previous section. The set $P_\alpha(\alpha \in (0, 1])$ may be considered as the support of fuzzy subset

$$P(B > A) = \{\alpha / P_\alpha(B > A)\}, \tag{2}$$

where values α represent the membership degrees for fuzzy interval $P(B > A)$. In this way the fuzzy subset $P(B = A)$ may be easily built too. The result obtained is simple enough and reflects in some sense the nature of fuzzy arithmetic. Resulting "fuzzy probabilities" can be used directly. For instance, let A, B, C be fuzzy intervals and $P(A > B)$, $P(A > C)$ be fuzzy intervals, expressing the probabilities $A > B$ and $A > C$ respectively. Then the probability $PP = P(P(A > B) > P(A > C))$ gets the sense of probabilities comparison and is expressed in form of fuzzy interval as well. Such fuzzy calculations may be useful on the intermediate stages of analyze, since they preserve the fuzzy information uniformly. But as the practical result, the real number indices for fuzzy intervals ordering are needed. For this purpose, it seems more natural to use the simplest defuzzification:

$$\overline{P}(B > A) = \frac{\sum_{\alpha} P_{\alpha}(B_{\alpha} > A_{\alpha})}{\sum_{\alpha} \alpha}. \tag{3}$$

The results of testing are in good agreement with our intuition.

4 Two-objective Approach to Fuzzy Optimization

As it is noted in the section 1, on each step of direct numerical optimization there are at least two main local criteria which reflect our intention to minimize/maximize the target function and simultaneously to minimize the uncertainty of result obtained. Obviously, in our case criterion of interval target function minimization/maximization may be presented using probabilistic approach described in the previous sections. On the other hand, local criterion of uncertainty minimization may be performed in natural way through the relation of widths of compared intervals. Let's consider the local criteria of interval comparison that can be introduced as the some mathematical formalization of the above inexact reasoning. Let A and B be comparing intervals. As the first criterion it is possible to accept directly the probability that one of comparing intervals is less (at minimization) than another one

$$\mu_P^A = P(A < B), \quad \mu_P^B = P(B < A). \tag{4}$$

The method for calculation of such probabilities was described above. To define the second criterion, the relations of intervals widths were considered

$$X_W^A = \frac{W_A}{max(W_A, W_B)}, \quad X_W^A = \frac{W_B}{max(W_A, W_B)}, \tag{5}$$

where W_A, W_B are the widths of intervals A and B, respectively. Parameters x_p, x_w may be used for introducing the criteria that explicitly reflect our intention to decrease the uncertainty (width of interval target function) on the successive stages of numerical optimization procedure:

$$\mu_W^A = \begin{cases} 1 - X_W^A & \text{if } X_W^A < 1, \\ 0 & \text{otherwise} \end{cases} \quad \mu_W^B = \begin{cases} 1 - X_W^B & \text{if } X_W^B < 1, \\ 0 & \text{otherwise} \end{cases} \tag{6}$$

Obviously, for estimation of possibility $A < B$ it is necessary to use the pair of criteria μ_P^A, μ_W^A but for the appreciation of possibility $B < A$ the local criteria μ_P^B, μ_W^B must be considered too. It is easy to see, that some situations can exist when, for instance, on a certain step of numerical optimization we have

$\mu_P^A > 0.5$, $\mu_W^A = 0$. In other words, in such cases the width of smaller (in the probabilistic sense) interval A is more than width of greater interval B. It is clear, that to continue the optimization process in such cases we are compelled to recognize that $A < B$. So, the satisfaction a local criterion μ_W^A or μ_W^B in the optimization tasks may be rather desirable, however it is not necessary. Thereby, the general criteria for evaluation of interval inequality degree may be performed in forms:

$$D_{A<B} = \frac{1}{2}\left(r_p \mu_p^A(x_p) + r_w \mu_W^A(x_W)\right), \quad D_{B<A} = \frac{1}{2}\left(r_p \mu_p^B(x_p) + r_w \mu_W^B(x_W)\right),$$

where r_p, r_w are ranks or parameters of relative importance of considered local criteria. Of course, there are no problems to find the ranks r_p, r_w in such a simple case of only two local criteria, but usual restriction $(r_p + r_w)/2 = 1$ must be fulfilled. It is easy to see, that in any case $0 \leq D_{A<B}, D_{B<A} \leq 1$. In the procedure of optimization, using direct search methods, on each n's step of an algorithm some interval B characterizing an interval cost function is obtained. If A is an interval of cost function on the next possible step, then in the case of minimization we can qualify it as a good step, when $A < B$. The problem is to estimate the degree of possibility of $A < B$. For this purpose, introduced general criteria $D_{A<B}$, $D_{B<A}$ can be used. Of course, if $D_{A<B} < D_{B<A}$ then $B < A$ and in other case $B > A$. We note, that similar approach also had been used to built the general criterion $D_{A=B}$, which can be useful for mathematical formalization of interval equality constrains.

5 Illustrative example

To illustrate the developed technique of optimization, let's consider the specially constructed interval double-extreme discontinuous function:

$$F(x) = [\underline{f}, \overline{f}] \begin{cases} -\frac{[4.05,4.95]}{x} - 0.5x - 0.04, & x < 0, \\ \frac{[4.275,4.725]}{x} + 0.5x, & x > 0, \end{cases} \tag{7}$$

Introduced interval test function $F(x)$ has two local minima at points $x = -3$ and $x = 3$. It can be seen (see Tabl. 1) that at point $x = -3$ we have the greater width of interval $[\underline{f}, \overline{f}]$ and the lower mean value of f in this interval then at point $x = 3$. Hence, we have a typical situation when we must choose the point of global optimum under condition of competiting local criteria of cost function minimization and result certainty presented by width of interval cost function at points examined. The results of global minimization of interval test function F(x) for different ranking parameters are collected in Table 1. The testing has shown, that with the increasing of the relative importance of "width" criterion (rising r_w) at first the only slight growth of mean values of interval minimized test function and simultaneously reduction of its width at points of minimum are observed. The results obtained are in a

Table 1. The of global minimization of interval test function $F(x)$

Characteristics of global minimum	$r_p = 2$ $r_w = 0$	$r_p = 1.3$ $r_w = 0.7$	$r_p = 1.25$ $r_w = 0.75$	$r_p = 0.4$ $r_w = 1.6$
$F(x)$	$[2.81, 3.11]$	$[2.815, 3.107]$	$[2.926, 3.074]$	$[2.944, 3.081]$
Mean value of interval $F(x)$	2.96	2.961	3.0	3.012
Width of interval $F(x)$	0.3	0.292	0.148	0.137
Points of global minimum	−3	−3.08	3.045	3.286

good accordance with our intuitive imaginations. One of important features of method developed is that there is an opportunity to estimate the degrees of equalities and inequalities by the different quantitative ways. In practice, some restrictions (frequently, equality restrictions) can require almost absolute performance. In these cases we require the execution of corresponding interval relations with probability 0.95–0.99. For others, not such strict (important) restrictions, the probabilities of only a little more than 0.5 may be used. Of course, there are no problems to generalize the method presented in this section to the case of fuzzy intervals using α-cuts technique. It must be emphasized that to realize the proposed method the software on base of C++ had been elaborated that can be successfully used not only in optimization but for the spread range of decision making problems and at last in interval arithmetic and fuzzy arithmetic.

References

1. Baas S.M., Kwakernaak H. (1977) Rating and ranking multiple-aspect alternatives using fuzzy sets. Automatica **13**, 47–58
2. Ishihichi H., Tanaka M. (1990) Multiobjective programming in optimization of the Interval Objective Function. European Journal of Operational Research **48**, 219–225
3. Chanas S., Kuchta D. (1996) Multiobjective Programming in optimization of the Interval Objective Functions – a generalized approach. European Journal of Operational Research **94**, 594–598
4. Moore R.E. (1966) Interval analysis, Englewood Cliffs. N.J.: Prentice-Hall
5. Kulpa Z. (1997) Diagrammatic representation for a space of intervals. Machine Graphics and Vision **6**, 5–24
6. Helpern S. (1997) Representation and application of fuzzy numbers. Fuzzy sets and Systems **91**, 259–268
7. Dibois D., Prade H. (1983) Ranking of Fuzzy Numbers in the Setting of Possibility Theory. Information Sciences **30**, 183–224
8. Yager R. R., DetynieckiM. (2000) Ranking fuzzy numbers using α-weighted valuations. International Journal of Uncertainty, Fuzziness and Knowledge-based Systems **8**, 573–591
9. Wang X., Kerre E. E. (2001) Reasonable properties for the ordering of fuzzy quantities (I), (II). Fuzzy Sets and Systems **122**, 375–385, 387–405

Membership Functions as Combination of Expert's Knowledge with Population Information

Ewa Straszecka[1], Joanna Straszecka[2]
[1] Div. of Biomedical Engineering, Institute of Electronics, Silesian University of Technology, 16 Akademicka St., 44-100 Gliwice, Poland, phone (48)(32)2371725, fax (48)(32)2372225, e-mail ewa@boss.iele.polsl.gliwice.pl
[2] Department of Internal Diseases, Medical University of Silesia, 102 Edukacji St., 43-100 Tychy, Poland

Abstract. The paper aims at recommending an interpretation of medical indices with fuzzy rules. Advantages of expert's knowledge combination with population information are observed. A simple method of performance estimation of fuzzy diagnosis support systems by a change of rules firing threshold is proposed. Results of three methods of membership function determination are compared. Conclusions can be useful indications for membership function defining.

1 Introduction

Fuzzy sets are widely used in medical decision support systems. Natural language expressions like 'high blood pressure' or 'low heart rate' are typical for medical diagnosis. Therefore fuzzy rules in medical knowledge-based systems seem to be the best representation of diagnosis principles. However, the rules formulation involves defining fuzzy sets, precisely: their membership functions. Methods suggested in this field vary form neural networks [1] to statistics [2, 3, 4], but expert's knowledge is always be used in the process. Question arises to what extent the knowledge is sufficient for membership function shape determination and whether it can be considered as universal, regardless of a population treated. It is obvious that frequency of some diseases can depend on the inhabited region or living behaviours of a population. Examples of the former are thyroid gland diseases while the latter are coronary diseases. The diseases must be recognised by general practitioners as early as possible to send a patient to a specialist. The early diagnoses comprise many symptoms, sometimes not clearly manifested. The symptoms are easy obtainable information, as they are found during observation, patient's inquire and physical examination. Still they are numerous and their join interpretation is difficult. Medical indices are supporting tools in such cases. A medical index is a score test in which a disease risk is estimated on numerous health parameters. The parameters are evaluated according to score functions relating the risk with parameters values. The algebraic sum of scores for all the parameters characterises the disease risk for a chosen patient.

The score functions are step functions. The sum of scores resulting from the evaluation is next compared with critical values for 'healthy', 'ill' and sometimes 'not-determined' conclusions. However the critical values are difficult to define. The more numerous are symptoms the more difficult is their join estimation by the algebraic sum, as it is impossible to analyse all combinations of parameters values to find out the critical sums. Another difficulty is that unknown symptoms are treated in the same way as parameters of normal values (for which score equals zero), and so the sum is groundless lowered. The disadvantages do not appear in case of an alternative of fuzzy sets. That is why an interpretation of the score test by fuzzy rules should work better. Still, it is not obvious if fuzzy sets can manage better with diagnostic conclusion formulation than the original indices.

A construction of fuzzy rules on the basis of a score test is possible in three ways. Firstly – using an approximation of score functions secondly – constructing membership functions as an interpretation of step functions. In the third method Takagi-Sugeno rules can be transformed for joint representation of population and expert's knowledge. An example of INFARCTEST [8] interpretation by fuzzy rules using a database of 1225 factory workers provides interesting observations on the performance of the three methods of membership functions designing.

2 Membership Functions Designing

In the INFARCTEST [8] heart infarct risk is estimated on multiple health parameters. The parameters are evaluated according to step functions relating the infarct risk with parameters values (e.g. Fig.1*a*)). The algebraic sum of scores for all the parameters characterises the infarct risk for a chosen patient.

The simplest method of translating the step-function knowledge into fuzzy rules representation is lower (solid line without point markers in Fig. 1) or upper (dashed line) approximation of the score function. The approximation provides the membership function for high systolic blood pressure. Next its complement for low systolic blood pressure can be easily found (Fig. 2*a*)). Similarly the membership functions for risk can be defined. We can also determine three membership functions assuming that medium area of the step function is relevant to the medium risk. Such an approach is represented in Fig.2*b*). Finally a fuzzy identification using a database (i.e. population information) can be used. The classical Takagi-Sugeno algorithm of fuzzy identification [7] was transformed [5] to obtain one-premise rules of the form:

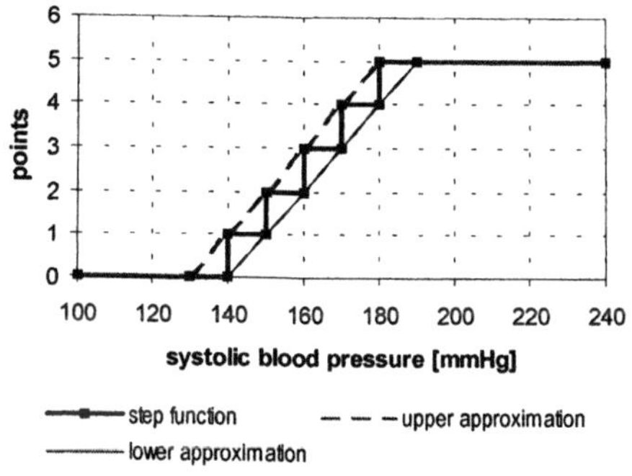

Fig.1. Original score step function for systolic blood pressure in INFARCTEST.

$$IF\ X_l\ is\ \mu_l^{(i)}\ THEN\ Y\ is\ \mu_{cl}^{(i)} \quad i = 1,\ldots,n \tag{1}$$

where X_l is a linguistic variable, $\mu_l^{(i)}$ - the membership function of the l-th variable in the (i)-th implication premise, $\mu_{cl}^{(i)}$ is the membership function of infarct risk in the (i)-th implication.

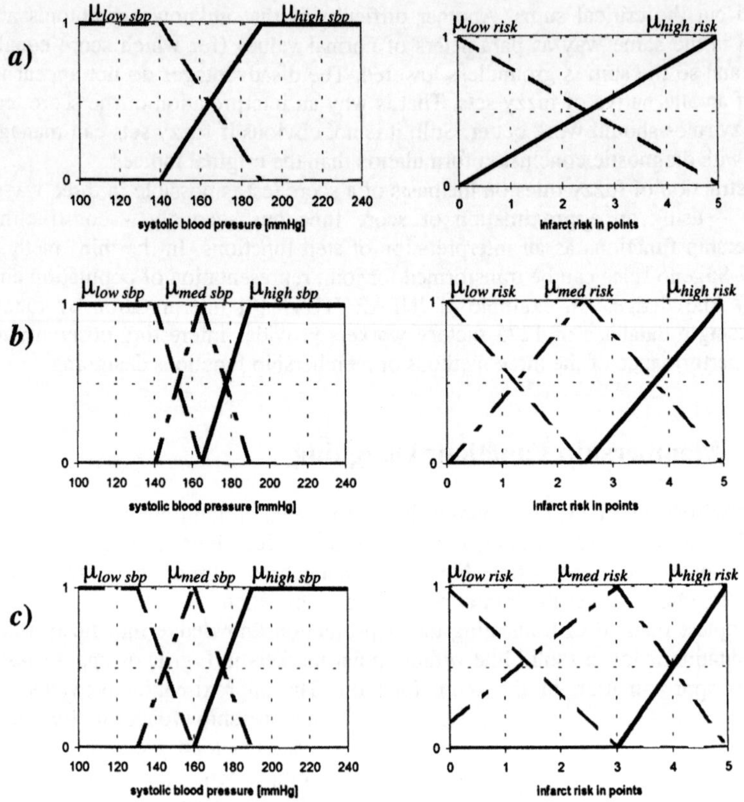

Fig.2. Three methods of membership functions determination for INFARCTEST representation, *sbp = systolic blood pressure, med = medium.*

The fuzzy identification was adopted to model INFARCTEST by fuzzy rules. A database of factory workers was used in the procedure [6]. From the identification a knowledge base of 27 rules for 9 most reliable symptoms was found. An example of membership functions obtained is given in Fig.2*c*). The same parameters were chosen to construct a knowledge base for the first method of membership functions designing, which resulted in 18 rules. In the similar way 27 rules were constructed for the second method.

3 Verification of Performance

The database was used to test the performance of the three methods. Mamdani algorithm of inference was used for the rule-based methods. The rules were fired at different thresholds η:

$$\mu_l^{(i)}(x_0) = \min(\mu_{pl}^{(i)}(x_{l0}), \delta_{x_l, x_{l0}})$$

$$\mu_c(y) = \max_{\substack{i=1,..n \\ \mu_l^{(i)}(x_0) \geq \eta}} \min(\mu_{cl}^{(i)}(y), \mu_l^{(i)}(x_0)) \tag{2}$$

where: x_{l0} – the value of the l-th parameter observed with a chosen patient,
$\delta_{x_l, x_{l0}}$ - the singleton relevant to the observed value.

Obviously, a number of fired rules decreased while η increased. Centres of gravity y_c for resulting fuzzy sets of infarct risk $\mu_c(y)$ were determined for each patient of the database.

It is evident that in the database of factory workers healthy persons as well as people at different infarct risk are represented. It should be manifested by an empirical distribution of score results and centres of gravity. Original INFARCTEST score results form a distribution [6] in which no border value can be determined. Now let's consider the proposed methods of fuzzy rules construction. A detailed statistical investigation of the results would be too extensive for the extended abstract size. Therefore only a quality analysis by a comparison of histograms is given.

As methods aim at medical diagnosis they should provide a differentiation of patients' results at least for two groups: healthy and at disease risk. Such a distinction is noticeable for the histograms η=0.9 (i)-(iii), η=0.8 (i)-(iii) in Fig.3. Only the most sure symptoms of the infarct risk are taken into account in these histograms as only rules with premise membership equal or greater than η take part in conclusion formulation. As the firing level diminishes, more doubtful symptoms are considered, and so the conclusions are less clear (η=0.6 (i)-(iii), η=0.5 (i)-(iii) in Fig.3). So proceeds the 'fuzzification of decision' together with firing level decrease, until 0.5 threshold is achieved. It is unreasonable to expect distinctive groups below this level as premise membership functions for all health parameters reach maximum of conjunction at this value (Fig.2). For η<0.5 groups separation is as difficult as with the original algebraic sum of scores. For all threshold values considered in Fig.3 it is evident that the second method of membership function designing, that most 'artificially' interpret expert's knowledge provides the worst results. Fuzzy identification shows the most appropriate differentiation among groups, but the first method, with only two membership functions for each health parameter is not much worse.

The method of inference results analysis based on η change can be useful for the right membership function determination. Indeed we should not aim at the best distinction among diagnoses, as in such a case we consider only absolutely evident symptoms which can lead to a wrong conclusion. However a method that cannot show a visible classification border is useless. It might be concluded from the histograms that the threshold in the interval [0.5, 0.9] is a reasonable choice for the first method and identification-based method, while the second method is always more deceptive than the others.

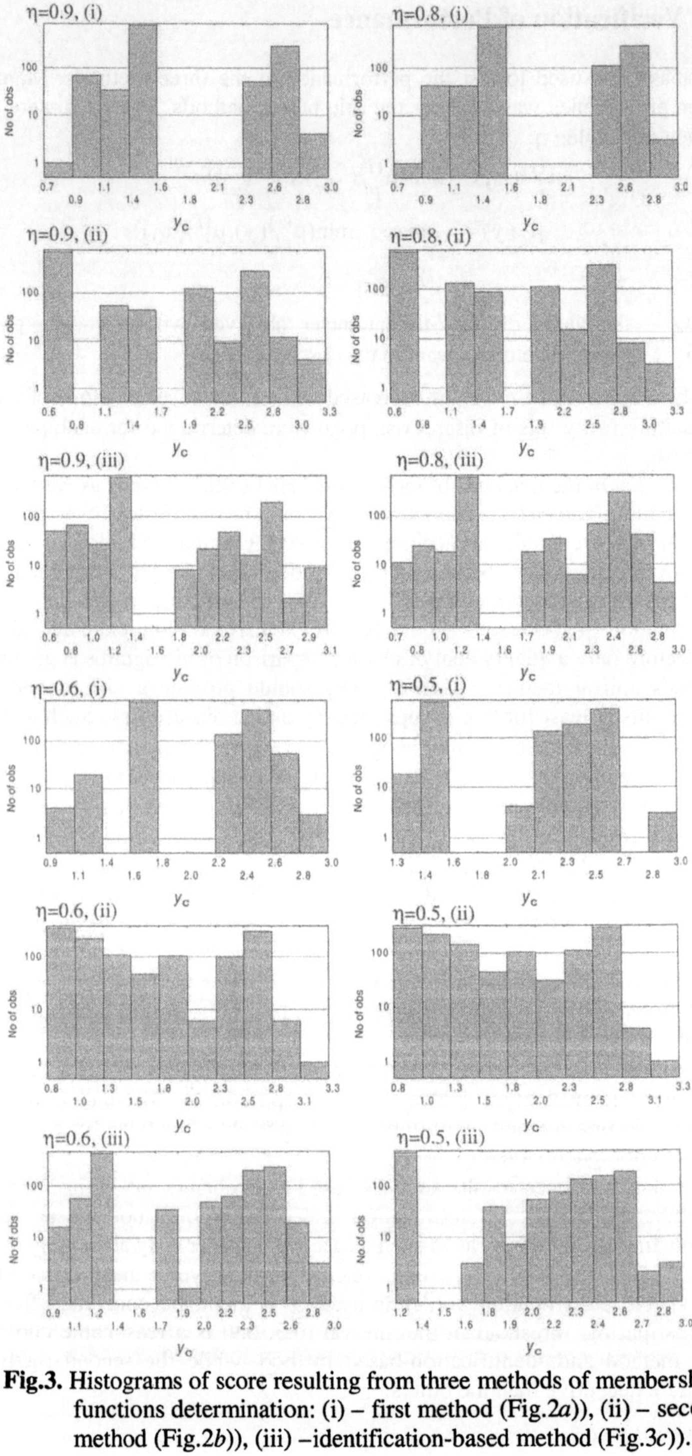

Fig.3. Histograms of score resulting from three methods of membership functions determination: (i) – first method (Fig.2*a*)), (ii) – second method (Fig.2*b*)), (iii) –identification-based method (Fig.3*c*)).

Certainly, if we use another way of inferencc, with different norms and implication operators, an improvement of results without a change of threshold level is possible. Nevertheless the investigation shows that in any case fuzzy rules should better classify patients than the score indices.

4 Conclusions

The algebraic sum that is the basis of most medical indices, is not an appropriate tool for representing joint influence of many symptoms on a diagnosis. It is impossible to determine a border for groups of healthy and ill people on the score sum. A more suitable representation of expert's knowledge consists in translating step functions defined by medical experts into IF-THEN fuzzy rules. To this end membership functions must be determined using population data whenever possible. If the latter are not available, membership functions can be: an approximation of the step function and a negation of it. More complex interpretations of expert's knowledge will probably result in deterioration of inference performance.
The knowledge of experts, though highly reliable is not universal. Membership functions shapes can be improved if a database of a specific population treated by a physician is available. Combining two kinds of information: experts' knowledge form score tests and population adequate features improves diagnosis support.
The right determination of membership functions is crucial for the performance of expert systems with fuzzy inference. In the lack of reliable information from a database it's better to use barely sufficient, but trustworthy knowledge from experts than to construct our own interpretation.
As new diagnostic procedures cause a rapid growth of examined symptoms, computer support should aim at a comprehension of the parameters and a reduction of everyday physician burden, which is provided by the fuzzy sets application.

References

[1] Boston J. R. (1997) Effects of Membership Function Parameters on the Performance of a fuzzy Signal Detector. IEEE Transactions on Fuzzy Systems **5**, No. 2, 249-255

[2] Civanlar M. R., Trussell H. J. (1986) Constructing membership functions using statistical data. Fuzzy Sets and Systems **18**, 1-13

[3] Rojas I., Pomares H., Ros E., Pietro A.(1998) Automatic construction of fuzzy rules and membership functions from training examples. Proc. EUFIT'98, 618-622

[4] Schuerz M. & oth, (2000) An assesment of different approaches to defi-ning fuzzy membership functions semi-automatically: Proc. ERUDIT-Workshop, 129-137

[5] Straszecka E.(2000) Fuzzy Systems in Medicine, P.S. Szczepaniak, P.J.G. Lisboa, J.Kacprzyk edts. Physica-Verlag, Springer Verlag Company, Chapter: Defining Membership Functions of fuzzy sets in medical decision support, Physica-Verlag Heidelberg, New York, 32-47

[6] Straszecka E. (in print) Building Membership Functions for Medical Knowledge Representation, Journal of Applied Computer Science

[7] Takagi T., Sugeno M.(1985) Fuzzy Identification of Systems and Its Applications to Modeling and Control, IEEE Trans. on Sys., Man & Cybernetics, **SMC-15**, 116-132

[8] Wydrzyński L.: (1990) INFARCTEST – Computer Test of Heart Infarct Risk and an Early Detection of Coronary Disease, Hypertension and Diabetes, POLGAT Gliwice, Poland (in Polish)

Towards More Human Consistent Reasoning via Intuitionistic Fuzzy Sets

Eulalia Szmidt and Janusz Kacprzyk

Systems Research Institute, Polish Academy of Sciences
ul. Newelska 6, 01–447 Warsaw, Poland
E-mail: {szmidt, kacprzyk }@ibspan.waw.pl

Abstract. Intuitionistic fuzzy sets (Atanassov [1], [2]), due to of an additional degree of freedom, can be viewed as a generalization of fuzzy sets. The additional degree of freedom makes a better modelling of imperfect information possible. We propose the use of intuitionistic fuzzy sets for a more human consistent reasoning under imprecise knowledge. An example of a medical database is considered. Employing intuitionistic fuzzy sets, we can express a hesitation concerning both the patients and illnesses. An illness for each patient is found by looking for the smallest distance [cf. Szmidt and Kacprzyk [5], [8]] between symptoms that are characteristic for a patient, and symptoms describing illnesses. Our new approach can help avoid drawbacks of the max-min-max rule that is usually employed [cf. De, Biswas and Roy [3]].

1 Introduction

To view intuitionistic fuzzy sets in a proper perspective, it may be expedient to look at a more general issue of fuzzy sets. Fuzzy sets theory was proposed by Zadeh in 1965 as a simple and efficient tool for the representation and processing of imprecise concepts and quantities (*tall* men, *large* numbers, ...) which fall beyond the scope of conventional precise mathematics because of a gradual (not abrupt) transition between the membership and non-membership of their elements. Zadeh replaced the conventional characteristic function of a crisp set, with values in $\{0, 1\}$, by a so-called membership function, with values in $[0, 1]$, allowing for a representation of the membership to a degree.

So, for each element of a fuzzy set a real value from $[0, 1]$ should be specified which denotes the membership degree of that element. Clearly, this requirement may be too strict. For example, in decision making problems, particularly in the cases of medical diagnosis, sales analyses, new product marketing, financial services, etc. there may exist some hesitation during the evaluation of an unknown object.

Intuitionistic fuzzy sets (Atanassov [1], [2]) can be viewed as a proper tool for representing hesitation concerning the (degree of) membership. To be more precise, a basic assumption of fuzzy set theory that if we specify the degree of membership of an element in a fuzzy set as a real number from

$[0,1]$, say a, then the degree of its non-membership is $1-a$, need not hold for intuitionistic fuzzy sets; it is assumed that the non-membership should be no more than $1-a$. Therefore, we can express a lack of knowledge (hesitation concerning both the membership and non-membership), and we can better model imperfect information, in particular of a linguistic form (cf. Zadeh and Kacprzyk's volume [12])

We will present here intuitionistic fuzzy sets as a tool for reasoning under imperfect facts and imprecise knowledge. An example of medical diagnosis will be presented assuming that there is a database, i.e. a description of a set of symptoms S, and a set of diagnoses D. We will describe a state of a patient knowing results of his/her medical tests. The problem description uses the concept of an intuitionistic fuzzy set to render two important facts: values of symptoms change for each patient as, e.g., temperature goes up and down, pain increases and decreases, etc., and in a medical database describing illnesses for different patients it should be taken into account that for different patients suffering from the same illness, values of the same symptom can be different.

The proposed method of diagnosis involves intuitionistic fuzzy distances as introduced in (Szmidt and Kacprzyk [5], [8]). For each patient the distances from his/her particular set of symptoms to a set of symptoms characteristic for each diagnosis are calculated. The lowest obtained distance points out a proper diagnosis.

2 Brief Introduction to Intuitionistic Fuzzy Sets

As opposed to a fuzzy set (Zadeh [11]) in X, given by $A' = \{< x, \mu_{A'}(x) > |x \in X\}$, where $\mu_{A'} : X \to [0,1]$ is the membership function of the fuzzy set A', $\mu_{A'}(x) \in [0,1]$, an *intuitionistic fuzzy set* (Atanassov [1], [2]) $A \in X$ is given by

$$A = \{< x, \mu_A(x), \nu_A(x) > |x \in X\} \tag{1}$$

where: $\mu_A : X \to [0,1]$ and $\nu_A : X \to [0,1]$ such that $0 \leq \mu_A(x) + \nu_A(x) \leq 1$, and $\mu_A(x)$, $\nu_A(x) \in [0,1]$ denote the degree of membership and non-membership of $x \in A$, respectively.

Obviously, each fuzzy set corresponds to the following intuitionistic fuzzy set $A = \{< x, \mu_{A'}(x), 1 - \mu_{A'}(x) > |x \in X\}$.

For each intuitionistic fuzzy set in X, we will call

$$\pi_A(x) = 1 - \mu_A(x) - \nu_A(x) \tag{2}$$

a *hesitation margin* (or an *intuitionistic fuzzy index*) of $x \in A$ and it is a hesitation degree of whether x belongs to A or not (cf. Atanassov [1], [2]). It is obvious that $0 \leq \pi_A(x) \leq 1$, for each $x \in X$.

On the other hand, for each fuzzy set A' in X, we evidently have $\pi_{A'}(x) = 1 - \mu_{A'}(x) - [1 - \mu_{A'}(x)] = 0$, for each $x \in X$.

Therefore, if we want to fully describe an intuitionistic fuzzy set, we must use any two functions from the triplet: membership function, non-membership function, and hesitation margin.

In other words, the application of intuitionistic fuzzy sets instead of fuzzy sets means the introduction of another degree of freedom into a set description (i.e. in addition to μ_A we also have ν_A or π_A).

Since the intuitionistic fuzzy sets, that from the perspective mentioned above, may be considered as a generalisation of fuzzy sets, give us an additional possibility to represent imperfect knowledge, they can make it possible to descibe many real problems in a more adequate and human-consistent way (for details and examples we refer the reader to Szmidt and Kacprzyk [6], [7], [9], [10]).

Basically, intuitionistic fuzzy sets based models may be adequate in situations when we face human testimonies, opinions, etc. involving two (or more) answers of the type: yes, no, I do not know, I am not sure, etc.

Voting can be a good example of such a situation as human voters may be divided into three groups of those who: vote for, vote against, abstain or give invalid votes. This third, "grey" area is of a great interest from the point of view of, say, customer behaviour analysis, voter behaviour analysis, etc. because people from this third, undecided group can finally become sure, i.e. become persons voting for (or against), customers wishing to buy products advertised, etc., after a proper enhancement (e.g., different marketing activities). This may be illustrated by the following example.

Example 1. A director of a factory is going to enlarge the assortment of production. The factory can start producing one of three new items only. Three experts are asked to point out the best option. Each solution has advantages and disadvantages. But experts are also aware that there are several important factors (relevant for the profit) which can not be either measured or foreseen properly at present. Whether the option chosen will be the most profitable depends on, e.g., the behaviour of other similar factories (maybe offering a cheaper product), costs of raw materials (different for each option) can change dramatically, etc. In such a case it seems quite reasonable that experts, while considering the three options, describe not only their pure preferences (expressed via membership functions) but also a hesitation as to each option. In real life people are very often faced with making decision in situations when there are "threads and opportunities" – a grey area that can finally support a chosen decision, or in an opposite case – turn it finally into a failure. Intuitionistic fuzzy sets are here a good tool. □

3 Medical Diagnostic Reasoning via Distances for Intuitionistic Fuzzy Sets

We consider the same data as those of De, Biswas and Roy [3]. Let the set of diagnoses be $D = \{$ *Viral fever, Malaria, Typhoid, Stomach problem, Chest problem*}. The considered set of symptoms is S = {*temperature, headache, stomach pain, cough, chest-pain*}.

The data are given in Table 1 – each symptom is described by three numbers: membership μ, non-membership ν, hesition margin π. For example, for malaria, we have: the temperature is high ($\mu = 0.7$, $\nu = 0$, $\pi = 0.3$), while for the chest problem, we have: temperature is low ($\mu = 0.1$, $\nu = 0.8$, $\pi = 0.1$).

Table 1. Symptoms characteristic for the diagnoses considered

	Viral fever	Malaria	Typhoid	Stomach problem	Chest problem
Temperature	(0.4, 0.0, 0.6)	(0.7, 0.0, 0.3)	(0.3, 0.3, 0.4)	(0.1, 0.7, 0.2)	(0.1, 0.8, 0.1)
Headache	(0.3, 0.5, 0.2)	(0.2, 0.6, 0.2)	(0.6, 0.1, 0.3)	(0.2, 0.4, 0.4)	(0.0, 0.8, 0.2)
Stomach *pain*	(0.1, 0.7, 0.2)	(0.0, 0.9, 0.1)	(0.2, 0.7, 0.1)	(0.8, 0.0, 0.2)	(0.2, 0.8, 0.0)
Cough	(0.4, 0.3, 0.3)	(0.7, 0.0, 0.3)	(0.2, 0.6, 0.2)	(0.2, 0.7, 0.1)	(0.2, 0.8, 0.0)
Chest *pain*	(0.1, 0.7, 0.2)	(0.1, 0.8, 0.1)	(0.1, 0.9, 0.0)	(0.2, 0.7, 0.1)	(0.8, 0.1, 0.1)

The set of patients is P = {*Al, Bob, Joe, Ted*}. The symptoms characteristic for the patients are given in Table 2 – as before, we need all three parameters (μ,ν,π) to describe each symptom. We look for a proper diagnosis

Table 2. Symptoms characteristic for the patients considered

	Temperature	Headache	Stomach pain	Cough	Chest pain
Al	(0.8, 0.1, 0.1)	(0.6, 0.1, 0.3)	(0.2, 0.8, 0.0)	(0.6, 0.1, 0.3)	(0.1, 0.6, 0.3)
Bob	(0.0, 0.8, 0.2)	(0.4, 0.4, 0.2)	(0.6, 0.1, 0.3)	(0.1, 0.7, 0.2)	(0.1, 0.8, 0.1)
Joe	(0.8, 0.1, 0.1)	(0.8, 0.1, 0.1)	(0.0, 0.6, 0.4)	(0.2, 0.7, 0.1)	(0.0, 0.5, 0.5)
Ted	(0.6, 0.1, 0.3)	(0.5, 0.4, 0.1)	(0.3, 0.4, 0.3)	(0.7, 0.2, 0.1)	(0.3, 0.4, 0.3)

for each patient p_i, $i = 1, \ldots, 4$, and we propose to:

- calculate for each patient p_i a distance of his symptoms (Table 2) from a set of symptoms s_j, $j = 1, \ldots, 5$ characteristic for each diagnosis d_k, $k = 1, \ldots, 5$ (Table 1),
- single out the lowest obtained distance which points out a proper diagnosis.

In Szmidt and Kacprzyk's works [5], [8] we proved that to properly calculate distances for intuitionistic fuzzy sets one should take into account all three parameters: membership, non-membership, and hesitation. To be more specific, the normalised Hamming distance for all symptoms of patient i from diagnosis k is equal to

$$l(s(p_i), d_k) =$$

$$= \frac{1}{10} \sum_{j=1}^{5} (|\mu_j(p_i) - \mu_j(d_k)| + |\nu_j(p_i) - \nu_j(d_k)| + |\pi_j(p_i) - \pi_j(d_k)|) \quad (3)$$

The distances (3) for each patient from the set of possible diagnoses are given in Table 3. The lowest distance points out a proper diagnosis: Al suffers from malaria, Bob from stomach problem, Joe from typhoid, whereas Ted from fever. We obtained the same results while applying the normalized

Table 3. The normalized Hamming distances for each patient from the set of possible diagnoses

	Viral fever	Malaria	Typhoid	Stomach problem	Chest problem
Al	0.28	0.24	0.28	0.54	0.56
Bob	0.40	0.50	0.31	0.14	0.42
Joe	0.38	0.44	0.32	0.50	0.55
Ted	0.28	0.30	0.38	0.44	0.54

Euclidean distance [cf. Szmidt and Kacprzyk [5], [8]]:

$$q(s(p_i), d_k) = (\frac{1}{10} \sum_{j=1}^{5} (\mu_j(p_i) - \mu_j(d_k))^2 + (\nu_j(p_i) - \nu_j(d_k))^2 +$$
$$+ (\pi_j(p_i) - \pi_j(d_k))^2)^{\frac{1}{2}} \quad (4)$$

The results are given in Table 4 – the lowest distance for each patient p_i from possible diagnosis D indicates the solution sought. As before, Al suffers from malaria, Bob from stomach problem, Joe from typhoid, whereas Ted from fever. Notice that the proposed approach differs in spirit from Sanchez's

Table 4. The normalized Euclidean distances for each patient from the set of possible diagnoses

R	Viral fever	Malaria	Typhoid	Stomach problem	Chest problem
Al	0.29	0.25	0.32	0.53	0.58
Bob	0.43	0.56	0.33	0.14	0.46
Joe	0.36	0.41	0.32	0.52	0.57
Ted	0.25	0.29	0.35	0.43	0.50

fuzzy relation based approach [4], and – in particular – from its intuitionistic counterpart by De, Biswas and Roy [3] that employs the max-min-max composition of intuitionistic fuzzy relations, with all their drawbacks. Here, values of all symptoms have an influence on the final solution. Moreover, symptoms can be additionally weighted, if necessary.

4 Conclusions

By employing intuitionistic fuzzy sets to express a hesitation, we propose a method for performing medical diagnosis based on the calculation of distances between a case considered and all illnesses included, taking into account values of all symptoms. Our approach makes it possible to introduce weights for all symptoms (for instance, for some illnesses some symptoms can be more important) that is impossible in the method proposed by De, Biswas and Roy [3] because the max-min-max rule "neglects" all values except for the extreme ones.

References

1. Atanassov K. (1986) Intuitionistic fuzzy sets, Fuzzy Sets and Systems, 20 (1986) 87-96.
2. Atanassov K. (1999) Intuitionistic Fuzzy Sets: Theory and Applications. Physica-Verlag.
3. De S.K., Biswas R. and Roy A.R. (2001) An application of intuitionistic fuzzy sets in medical diagnosis. Fuzzy Sets and Systems, Vol. 117, No.2, pp. 209-213.
4. Sanchez E. (1976) Resolution of composition fuzzy relation equations. Inform. Control, Vol. 30, pp. 38-48.
5. Szmidt E. and Kacprzyk J. (1997) On measuring distances between intuitionistic fuzzy sets, Notes on IFS, Vol.3, No.4, pp.1-13.
6. Szmidt E. and Kacprzyk J. (1998b) Group Decision Making under Intuitionistic Fuzzy Preference Relations. Proceedings of the 7th Int. Conference IPMU'98 (Paris, La Sorbonne, July 6-10), pp. 172-178.
7. Szmidt E. and Kacprzyk J. (1998c) Applications of Intuitionistic Fuzzy Sets in Decision Making. Proceedings of the 8th Congreso EUSFLAT'99 (Pamplona, Univ. De Navarra, September 8-10), pp. 150-158.
8. Szmidt E. and J. Kacprzyk J. (2000) Distances between intuitionistic fuzzy sets, Fuzzy Sets and Systems, Vol.114, No.3, pp.505-518.
9. Szmidt E. and Kacprzyk J. (2000) On Measures on Consensus Under Intuitionistic Fuzzy Relations. Proc. of Eight Int. Conf. on Information Processing and Management of Uncertainty in Knowledge-based Systems IPMU 2000, Madrid, July 3-7, 2000, pp. 1454-1461.
10. Szmidt E. and Kacprzyk J. (2001) Distance from consensus under Intuitionistic Fuzzy Preferences. In: Proc. on Eurofuse Workshop on Preference Modelling and Applications, Granada, Spain, April 25-27, 2001, pp. 73-77.
11. Zadeh L.A. (1965) Fuzzy sets. Information and Control Vol.8, pp. 338-353.
12. Zadeh L.A. and Kacprzyk J. (1999) (Eds.) Computing with words in information/intelligent systems. 1. Foundations. 2. Applications. Physica-Verlag. Heidelberg, New York.

Fuzzy Relational Thesauri Expansion Using Categorized Textual Data *

Domonkos Tikk[1] and Jae Dong Yang[2]

[1] Dept. of Telecom. & Telematics, Budapest University of Technology and Economics, 1117 Budapest, Magyar Tudósok Körútja 2., Hungary, e-mail: tikk@ttt.bme.hu

[2] Dept. of Computer Science, Chonbuk National University, Chonju 561–756, Korea, e-mail: jdyang@cs.chonbuk.ac.kr

Abstract. In our ongoing project we develop a tool that provides domain engineers with a facility to create fuzzy relational thesauri (FRTi) describing subject domains. The created FRTi can be used as knowledge base in information retrieval, e.g. for text search on the web. However, the manual creation of thesauri is quite tedious process if the source of data from which the domain engineer may select concepts for the thesaurus is not well organized. That is the typical case of textual databases. In order to ease FRT creation process we make use of a small starting FRT and our text categorization technique. The latter expands the starting FRT when doing the supervised learning phase of text categorization. This by-product of categorization is then used for enlarging automatically or semi-automatically FRT.

1 Introduction

The build-up of a fuzzy relational thesaurus (FRT) is considerably tedious process when the knowledge engineer has to take into account all the important concepts (in our approach: terms) of the actual domain, together with their possible synonyms and associated words. In order to facilitate this procedure we retrieve important terms from a sample text archive. The text archive can be the collection of documents selected by a domain expert, or obtained as the result of web searches. The next step is the categorization of the archive by means of our FRT based hierarchical (or structured) text categorization method [8]. This approach requires

- a small starting FRT typically consisting of the major concepts of the subject domain;
- labelling the documents for the supervised learning with category names corresponding to the concepts of the starting FRT;
- one-to-one correspondence between category names and FRT terms.

The categorization process uses FRT as the implementation of the hierarchical category system (often called taxonomy), i.e. the categories are

* This research was supported by the Chonbuk National University, and by the Hungarian Scientific Research Fund (OTKA) Grants No. D034614 and T34212.

represented by terms (concepts) in FRT. In order to prevent FRT from being incoherent and far from the view of its creator, categorization is proceeded on a copy of the starting FRT. The approach assigns to every category a set of terms, so-called local dictionaries, which contains words being typical for the category in the text corpus and are stored in FRT. From the aspect of categorization local dictionaries are useful to discriminate documents belonging to different categories. From the aspect of FRT creation, local dictionaries, being in fact a by-product of the categorization approach, collect the most frequent words of categories and so describe them efficiently. The size, contents and the preparation technique of the local dictionaries vary depending on various parameters of the categorization.

For the final expansion of the starting FRT, elements of local dictionaries can be inserted permanently to FRT. We provide an option for the knowledge engineer to supervise, filter and modify elements of local dictionaries before added to the thesaurus. Thus, FRT is maintained in accordance with the knowledge of the domain expert and reflecting his/her view on the domain.

This paper is organized as follows. Section 2 describes the basic concept of FRT and our project. Section 3 provides a brief description of our FRT based text categorization approach with special emphasize on the creation of local dictionaries. In section 4 we present the utilization of the local dictionaries, and finally section 5 summarizes the paper.

2 Fuzzy relational thesauri in information retrieval

A thesaurus in an information retrieval system (IRS) can be considered as a *knowledge base* that represents the conceptual model of certain subject domain [5]. The thesaurus has similar role in an IRS as a knowledge base in expert systems.

In what follows we assume that the knowledge base represented by the thesaurus is in term-centered form, which is maintained by the domain expert. A fuzzy relational thesaurus (FRT) [5], is a particular representation form, which is an extension of traditional thesauri schemes enriched by the strength of the term relationships and a richer set of binary relations. In FRT every term relation has a strength represented by a weight $\in (0,1]$. The term relation may comprise e.g. the following possibilities: *General relations*: *RT* – related term; *ST* – synonym term; *BT* – broader term; *NT* – narrower term. *Abstraction relations*: *KO* – kind of (specialization of, subclass of); *IO* – instance of; *FO* – has feature object [5]. These relations are organized in a partial ordering based on their specificity. The ordering is exploited, e.g. in the construction of FRT. Originally, the domain engineer determines the strength of actual term relations. In order to calculate the strength of relation between two arbitrary terms, the transitive closure of the term relations are computed using the partial ordering of the relations.

In [5] the authors assumed that the domain expert is assisted by a software tool, a kind of "FRT management system" which help him in the construction task. In the next we describe our ongoing project at which aims at developing this software. Because of the lack of space we give a brief description. Further details are in [3] (available online).

This approach provides an object-oriented mechanism to assist domain experts in constructing thesauri; it determines a considerable part of relationship degrees between terms by inheritance and supplies domain experts with information available from a thesaurus being constructed. It enables domain experts to incrementally construct the thesaurus as well, since the automatically determined degree of relationships can be refined whenever a more sophisticated thesaurus is needed. It may minimize domain expert's burden caused from the exhaustive specification of individual relationship.

For example, BT/NT relationship is redefined as a generalization hierarchy, while a vague relationship, RT is refined into aggregation and association that have more concrete semantics. The aggregation and association of a concept acts here as a property in the generalization hierarchy that its sub-concept inherits. We assign default strength to each relationship type. We worked out a mechanism to calculate the strength of a relationship between any arbitrary pair of concepts based on object-oriented paradigm, and a technique to resolve multiple inheritance situations. See more details in [3].

3 FRT based text categorization

Without any facility for preprocessing, the domain engineer should create the domain descriptive FRT based on raw textual data and/or his/her experience. Our goal is to facilitate this work thereby providing categorized textual data and the set of frequent words assigned to each category.

Automatic text categorization is a thriving research topic in the area of information retrieval. The objective is to assign a document to an appropriate category selected from a finite set. In the last decades the exponential increase of online available textual data stimulated developments of automated approaches. For a survey see [1]. These methods are usually based on a probabilistic model or learning strategies. For learning purpose a set of training documents with manually assigned class labels is assumed to be available.

As we mentioned earlier, our FRT based approach is applicable if categories are organized in *taxonomy.* Document categorization in taxonomy is a recently emerged field of text mining [2,6,4]. On the internet, topics are often organized in hierarchy (e.g. `www.yahoo.com`, `www.ibm.com/patents`), because it improves the perspicuity of the domain if the number of categories at a level is kept under a certain threshold.

Now we describe shortly our FRT based text categorization method [8]. The FRT is basically the implementation of the taxonomy, which stores and maintains adaptive local dictionary for each category. For categorization the type relationship is uniform, but their strength has importance when learning. In graph theory, digraphs can represent term hierarchy of FRT and taxonomy. An FRT can be applied to categorize documents belonging to the topic hierarchy of a taxonomy, if there exist a subgraph of FRT, which is isomorphic with the digraph of the taxonomy. Therefore each category is represented by an FRT term.

We use the most common representation framework, the *vector space* model, where a document D is described by a vector of word frequency values, $\mathbf{W}_D$, and vector of FRT terms appearing in the document $\mathbf{T}_D$, respectively:

$$\mathbf{W}_D = (w_1^D, \cdots, w_p^D); \qquad \mathbf{T}_D = (t_1^D, \ldots, t_q^D), \tag{1}$$

where p is the total number of unique terms appearing in the document collection, and q is the number of terms in FRT.

The set of unique terms is determined automatically by removing the stopwords from the total term set (like e.g. "the" in English) and then applying stemming on the remaining set. The value of w_i is the tf×idf weight of the ith term [7], and t_j is the number of appearance of jth FRT-term in the document D.

The categorization is done iteratively, alternating two phases. First, the vector $\mathbf{T}_D$ is used to infer the category (or categories) of D (see [8]). In the beginning of the categorization process FRT contains only few terms, therefore the categorization is usually not efficient. In order to endow FRT with good categorizing ability, in the second (learning) phase terms being typical for the category/ies of D are added to FRT. These two phases proceed alternatively, while the performance of categorization achieves a certain level or cannot be improved significantly.

For the purpose of FRT expansion one of the most important issue of the categorization is the determination of terms assigned to a category of a document, called local dictionary $L_D(C)$, inserted to FRT in the learning phase. The selection employs the K-nearest neighbour technique. First, the K nearest neighbours of D is selected in the sense of a similarity measure (usually cosine). Let then J denote the index set of documents among the neighbours of D being classified also in C, and containing common words with C. $L_D(C)$ is an importance ordered set of words appearing in D and in the documents of J, D_J. The importance value of the ith word is determined as the sum of frequency value in D and in D_J: $\sum_{j \in D_J \cup D} w_i^j$. The size of $L_D(C)$ can be controlled by two parameters, p_1 the maximum number of words, and α_1 the minimum (cumulated) frequency value of a word ($p_1 \in \mathbf{N}$, $\alpha_1 \in [0, 1]$). Thus, the final $L_D(C)$ is an ordered set with cardinality at most $|p_1|$, where every word has at least α_1 weight.

The classifier can commit two kinds of mistake. It can incorrectly assign a category to a document and hence reduce the *precision*, or it can reject incorrectly a category and hence degrade the *recall* of the classifier. The performance of the categorization depends on the above two quantities to be maximized. In the first case our approach decreases the relationship wait along the *topic path*, i.e. between the erroneously selected category C and the terms in $\mathbf{T}_D$ which supported C. In the latter case new terms are inserted to FRT in order to enhance the classification performance. The insertion is proceeded in such a way that the new terms are forced to be as deep in the taxonomy as possible. This is because a term deep in the hierarchy supports all the categories along the path between the term and the root. For more details see [8].

4 Expansion of FRT

The text categorization helps the knowledge engineers to create an FRT describing the subject domain efficiently in two ways. First, local dictionaries are provided to each category. The user is offered options to filter the words, modify the weight and to specify the kind of relationship according to his/her view about the subject domain. Second, new documents can be classified and thus new data are provided for further investigation and consideration.

We illustrate the described method on a simple example. We collected documents in the domain of *electronic appliances* from the web. The created a 211- and a 327-element document sets. We performed tests on both document sets. The unique term set (p in Eq. (1)) consisted of 3731, and 5793 words, respectively. The FRT was created by a semi-automatic thesaurus construction software [3]. In our application the depth of the taxonomy is three. The collected documents were classified into the following six top level topic: Audio, Computer, Computer Components, Computer Peripheral Device, House-Hold Appliances, Office Communications Appliances. We had 30 (31) 2nd level, and 40 (58) 3rd level topics in the case of 211 (327) document set. Each category had at least two training examples.

The size of the total number of inserted terms depends on the parameter p_1 and α_1. The content of the local dictionaries can be modified if the stemming is omitted, or if other preprocession is performed on the corpus. The classifier applies different methods assigning categories, which may also influence the size and contents of the local dictionaries. Table 1 shows the total number of inserted words in terms of the above parameters.

Table 1. Total number of inserted words in terms of p_1, α_1 and iterations

327-element document set				211-element document set			
P_1	α_1	inserted words	*it*	P_1	α_1	inserted words	*it*
5	0.1	1069~1198	10	7	0.05	766~769	12
5	0.25	630	3	5	0.1	708~723	10
5	0.2	796	15	10	0.02	860	10
7	0.05	1139~1204	12	7	0.05	1139~1204	12

The starting FRT contains 584, and 1779 terms in case of 211- and 327-element document set, resp. The total number of inserted words is comparable with these quantities. When stemming is proceeded in the preparation phase, a list of original versions is also provided to the user as synonyms of stemmed words. This option allows the user to select the best possible term to be inserted. The presented facility greatly reduces the required time for FRT creation even at the final insertion the user is prompted at each word.

5 Conclusion

We develop a fuzzy relational thesaurus management system. The aim of the system is to create a knowledge base for intelligent agent. FRT creation is a tedious process, which may be ease if the majority of data for the construction is supplied in a structured form. Therefore, we provide categorized textual data and local dictionaries assigned to categories to help the knowledge engineer in the build-up.

The information is retrieved by means of an FRT based text categorization approach that classifies documents into hierarchical topic taxonomies. The categorization process creates local dictionaries as a by-product while improving its classification performance.

References

1. L. Aas and L. Eikvil. Text categorisation: A survey. Raport NR 941, Norwegian Computing Center, 1999.
2. S. Chakrabarti, B. Dom, R. Agrawal, and P. Raghavan. Scalable feature selection, classification and signature generation for organizing large text databases into hierarchical topic taxonomies. *The VLDB Journal*, 7(3):163–178, 1998.
3. J. H. Choi, J. J. Park, J. D. Yang, and D. K. Lee. An object-based approach to managing domain specific thesauri: semiautomatic thesaurus construction and query-based browsing. Technical Report TR 98/11, Dept. of Computer Science, Chonbuk National University, 1998. http://cs.chonbuk.ac.kr/~jdyang/publication/techpaper.html.
4. W. Chuang, A. Tiyyagura, J. Yang, and G. Giuffrida. A fast algorithm for hierarchical text classification. In *Proc. of the 2nd Int. Conf. on Data Warehousing and Knowledge Discovery (DaWaK'00)*, pages 409–418, London, UK, 2000.
5. H. L. Larsen and R. R. Yager. The use of fuzzy relational thesaurus for classificatory problem solving in information retrieval and expert systems. *IEEE Trans. on Systems, Man, and Cybernetics*, 23(1), 1993.
6. A. McCallum, R. Rosenfeld, T. Mitchell, and A. Ng. Improving text classification by srinkage in a hierarchy of classes. In *Proc. of the ICML-98*, 1998. http://www-2.cs.cmu.edu/~mccallum/papers/hier-icml98.ps.gz.
7. G. Salton and M. J. McGill. *An Introduction to Modern Information Retrieval.* McGraw-Hill, 1983.
8. D. Tikk, J. D. Yang, and S. L. Bang. Text categorization using fuzzy relational thesauri. Submitted to *IEEE Trans. on Knowledge and Data Engineering.*

Investigation of the Neighborhood Attraction Evolutionary Algorithm Based on Neural Gas

Jutta Huhse, Thomas Villmann* and Andreas Zell
University Tübingen, Inst. of Computer Science
email: [huhse|zell]@informatik.uni-tuebingen.de
D–72076 Tübingen, Sand 1, Germany
*University Leipzig, Clinic for Psychotherapy and Psychosomatic Medicine
D–04107 Leipzig, Karl–Tauchnitz–Str.25, Germany
email: villmann@informatik.uni-leipzig.de

Summary. In this contribution we present a new approach to involve the idea of neighborhood cooperation during adaptation known from neural maps in evolutionary algorithms. Thereby we focus on application of cooperativeness according to the neural gas network and present first parameter studies for this NG-neighborhood attraction EA.

1 Introduction

Evolutionary algorithms (EAs) are stochastic search algorithms inspired by principles of biological evolution working simultaneously on a large number of *potential* problem solutions [9]. The combination of neural networks and EAs offers new possibilities to increase the power of adaptive approaches. Two main directions can be identified: the first one is to apply EAs to optimize a neural network whereas the second one deals with the transfer of methods from neural networks onto the framework of EAs. In this paper we want to study a *neighborhood attraction EA based on the neural gas network (NG)*. For this purpose we first clarify notations and concepts in evolution strategies (ESs), which are a special class of EAs. After this we take a closer look at neighborhood cooperativeness in neural networks (section 3.1) and first approaches to involve such ideas in EAs (section 3.2). Then we outline the new approach of incorporating cooperativeness in EA adaptation according to the NG (section 3.3) followed by parameter studies (section 4).

2 Basics of ESs

In EAs potential solutions are called individuals. All individuals (strings) $\mathbf{s}$ constitute the population $\mathbf{\Pi}$. In a *multiple population approach* the population $\mathbf{\Pi}$ is divided into subpopulations $\mathbf{\Pi}_i$. Each individual is judged by a *fitness function* F which plays the role of the assessing environment. There are two basic variation operators: *mutation* and *recombination* of individuals. Recombination of two randomly selected individuals $\mathbf{s}$ and $\mathbf{s}'$ can be generally described as $\mathbf{s}^{rec} = \eta(\mathbf{s}, \mathbf{s}')$ whereby η is the recombination operator. The (generalized) *intermediate* recombination operator in ES works on real values using the difference $\boldsymbol{\delta} = \mathbf{s}' - \mathbf{s}$ [2]:

$$\mathbf{s}^{rec} = \eta_{\theta}(\mathbf{s}, \mathbf{s}') = \mathbf{s} + \mathbf{\Theta} \cdot \boldsymbol{\delta}^{\mathrm{T}} \quad (1)$$

whereby $\mathbf{\Theta}$ is a diagonal matrix with diagonal elements $\boldsymbol{\theta} = (\theta_1, \ldots, \theta_N)$ with $\theta_i \in [0, 1]$. Mutation is realized as small random changes of the components of the individuals. In ES the mutation operator ϕ is usually given by

$$\mathbf{s}^{mut} = \phi_{\mathbf{z}}(\mathbf{s}) = \mathbf{s} + \mathbf{z}(\boldsymbol{\xi}) \tag{2}$$

with $\mathbf{z} = (z_1(\xi_1), \ldots, z_N(\xi_N))$ and z_i being normally distributed random variables with zero mean and variances ξ_i.

In one adaptation step, μ individuals of $\mathbf{\Pi}$ generate λ new ones with $\lambda > \mu$ by application of these operators. After these manipulations F judges how proper the individuals fulfill the considered task. If in one time step all individuals have gone under variation and evaluation, the *selection operator* extracts a new generation, which, in fact, gives the direction of evolution.

Two basic selection schemes are known in ES: the (μ, λ)– and the $(\mu + \lambda)$–strategy [10]: While in the (μ, λ)–strategy, where μ individuals produce λ children with $\mu < \lambda$, only the μ best of the λ children form the new population, in the $(\mu + \lambda)$–strategy all $\mu + \lambda$ individuals are allowed for the selection process. Whereas in the second strategy the best solution is preserved but the evolution tends to stagnate in a local minimum, in the first one the convergence is decelerated to allow reaching deeper minima (near the global minimum) but good solutions may be lost during the evolution. Balancing the advantages of both strategies the $(\mu * \lambda)$–approach is obtained. Here again μ individuals produce the λ preliminary offspring. However, in the selection step only the μ_t best individuals of the old generation and the λ new ones are allowed for selection [11]. Thereby μ_t depends on time t of evolution appearing as the number of generations performed: $\mu_t = \text{int}\left[(\mu - \mu_\tau) \cdot \gamma(t)\right] + \mu_\tau$, with $\text{int}[x]$ denoting the integer value of x. The function $\gamma(t)$ is of decreasing sigmoid type with $0 \leq \gamma(t) \leq 1$. In the investigations presented below, another type of selection is used which resembles to brood selection known from genetic programming [1]: *parental selection*. Here, each of the μ parent individuals generates λ offspring, the fittest of which replaces its parent. In this way, each parent individual contributes to the offspring generation which maintains the population diversity in comparison with the above mentioned strategies. This remaining diversity may be important if the convergence process of the EA strongly tends to homogeneity.

3 EAs and Neighborhood Cooperativeness

3.1 Neighborhood Cooperativeness in Neural Maps

Neural maps, as tools for (unsupervised) topographic vector quantization, project data from some (possibly high-dimensional) input space $\mathcal{V} \subseteq \Re^{D_\mathcal{V}}$ onto a position in some output space (neural map) $\mathcal{A}$, such that a continuous change of a parameter of the input data should lead to a continuous change of the position of a localized excitation in the neural map. This property is called *neighborhood preserving* (topographic) mapping. In the most widely used neural map algorithm, the *self-organizing map* (SOM) [7], the neurons are arranged *a priori* on a fixed grid $\mathcal{A}$. Other algorithms, such as the *neural gas* (NG) [8] dynamically adapt the neighborhood structure according to the data distribution during learning. Associated with each neuron $\mathbf{r} \in \mathcal{A}$ is a weight vector. The mapping is realized by

$\Psi_{\mathcal{V}\to\mathcal{A}} : \mathbf{v} \mapsto \mathbf{s}(\mathbf{v}) = \mathrm{argmin}_{\mathbf{r}\in\mathcal{A}}\, d(\mathbf{v}, \mathbf{w_r})$ where $d(\mathbf{v}, \mathbf{w_r})$ is the Euclidean distance. The neuron $\mathbf{s}$ is called *winner* or *best–matching unit*. During learning the weight vectors are adapted according to $\triangle \mathbf{w_r} = \epsilon h_\sigma^{NN}(\mathbf{r}, \mathbf{s}, \mathbf{v})(\mathbf{v} - \mathbf{w_r})$. Thereby $h_\sigma(\mathbf{r}, \mathbf{s}, \mathbf{v})$ is the neighborhood function usually chosen to be of Gaussian shape

$$h_\sigma^{NN}(\mathbf{r}, \mathbf{s}, \mathbf{v}) = \exp\left(-\frac{(d_{\mathcal{A}}(\mathbf{r}, \mathbf{s}(\mathbf{v})))^2}{2\sigma^2}\right) \tag{3}$$

where $d_{\mathcal{A}}(\mathbf{r}, \mathbf{s}(\mathbf{v}))$ is a certain distance measure defined on the set $\mathcal{A}$. For SOM $d_{\mathcal{A}}(\mathbf{r}, \mathbf{s}(\mathbf{v}))$ is evaluated in (the grid) $\mathcal{A}$ whereas for NG it is evaluated in the input (problem) space $\mathcal{V}$. During learning the neighborhood range σ and the learning rate ϵ decrease to small values referred to as remaining cooperativeness σ_{final} and learnability ϵ_{final} which corresponds to a *rough but fast learning* in the beginning replaced by a *fine tuning* in the convergence phase.

3.2 Neighborhood Cooperativeness in EAs according to SOM

Let $\mathbf{\Pi}$ be a set of subpopulations Π_i together with a *topological structure* Ω on $\mathbf{\Pi}$ defined by connectivity graph $\mathcal{G}_\Omega$. To each node i in $\mathcal{G}_\Omega$ is assigned a subpopulation Π_i. Usually, in the most approaches Ω is to be chosen agreement with biological migration systems (island model). During the evaluation individuals can *migrate*[1] to subpopulations within a certain fixed neighborhood range according to Ω, usually chosen as direct neighbors topology. The small migration rate is always constant.

In the *SOM-like migration* scheme [13,12] the individuals can migrate according to a time dependent neighborhood function h which is evaluated in $\mathcal{G}_\Omega$. Let $r_{i^*,k}^{\Omega} = \mathrm{rank}(\Pi_{i^*}, \Pi_k, \Omega)$ be the rank of neighborhood in $\mathcal{G}_\Omega$ defined as the minimal path length $\mathcal{G}_\Omega$. Then, in analogy to the SOM neighborhood function (3), we define:

$$h_{i^*}(t,k) = (1.0 - \epsilon_h) \cdot \exp\left(-\frac{r_{i^*,k}^{\Omega}}{2(\sigma_h(t))^2}\right) + \epsilon_h \tag{4}$$

with ϵ_h being a small positive constant. Because of $h_{i^*}(t,k) \in (0,1]$ we immediately can interpret $h_{i^*}(t,k)$ as a *probability of migration* of an individual of the subpopulation Π_k into the currently evaluated Π_{i^*}. At the beginning t_0 of the evolution process the range σ_h of the neighborhood nearly comprises the complete set of subpopulations and decreases during time, determined by $\sigma_h(t) \underset{t\to\infty}{\to} 0$. In this way, σ_h determines a characteristic scale for the range of the information flow. Following this approach, one can take the individuals of all subpopulations at the beginning as a uniform population which performs a first rough adaptation process. During the further development the various subpopulations become more and more separated from each other. Thus, *different regions* of the solution space are investigated. On the other hand, ϵ_h in (4) preserves a *remaining probability of migration*. In this way, one has a non–vanishing information flow through the topological ordered set $\mathbf{\Pi}$ of subpopulations. Hence, this SOM-like migration approach of first

[1] Thereby, migration means in our approach that an individual of one subpopulation visits another subpopulation for a short time (one or few generation steps) to share the genetic information during this time with the members of the visited subpopulation [9].

rough adaptation of neighboring subpopulations together with a more fine tuning in the further process by more and more but not completely independent subpopulations arranged on a topological structure according to a neighborhood function is in complete analogy to the learning strategy in neural maps. The *Neighborhood Attraction-ES* proposed by HUHSE AND ZELL [4] shows resemblance to the SOM-like migration. In this approach the topological structure Ω defines a rectangular lattice $\mathcal{A} = \mathcal{G}_{\Omega}$ of single individuals. Migration means here the following procedure: A new variation operator, called *neighborhood attraction operator*, is applied which carries out an *oriented variation* of one individual into direction to its fittest neighbor [6]. In detail, during one generation, each individual s is successively selected. Among all *direct* grid neighbors $\mathcal{N}(\mathbf{s})$ in $\mathcal{A}$ the fittest individual $\mathbf{s}^*$ is chosen. If the fitness value $F(\mathbf{s}^*)$ is better then $F(\mathbf{s})$, both individuals are varied according to $\eta_{\theta}(\mathbf{s}^*, \mathbf{s})$ in the recombination rule (1) whereby θ plays the role of the neighborhood attraction factor. In fact, this strategy leads to a concentration of individuals in regions with high fitness values. For this special variation, it is important that θ is of small values such that the offspring are placed near by the parent, following ES-mutation (see [4], [6]). Thus, this operator bears aspects of recombination as well as mutation. If s has no better neighbors, a special ES-mutation operation (2) is applied, taking also the neighborhood information into account: $\mathbf{s}^{mut} = \mathbf{s} + \frac{d_{\min}(\mathbf{s}', \mathbf{s})}{N} \cdot \mathbf{z}(\boldsymbol{\xi})$ with $d_{\min}(\mathbf{s}', \mathbf{s}) = \min_{i=1\ldots N} \|\mathbf{s}'_i - \mathbf{s}_i\|$ being the distance between $\mathbf{s}'$ and s based on the Euclidean norm. As pointed out in [6] due to the scaling factor $\boldsymbol{\delta} = \frac{d_{\min}(\mathbf{s}', \mathbf{s})}{N} \cdot \mathbf{z}(\boldsymbol{\xi})$ (N is the dimension of the problem space) of the mutation rule, such mutations which would jump over a grid neighbor without scaling, become less likely. During the contraction phase the values for $d_{\min}$ decrease on average and therefore, the effective step size of mutation is reduced.

3.3 NG-Neighborhood Attraction EA

We now propose a new attraction scheme. According to the idea in the NG mentioned above, we define the topological neighborhood for the individuals depending on their distances in the problem space [3]. The neighborhood radius for one individual s is determined by its averaged distance $\hat{d_E}$ to all other individuals. All individuals $\mathbf{s}'$ inside this radius belong to the neighborhood set $\mathcal{N}(\mathbf{s})$ of s. Now the neighborhood attraction is modified by ideas of NG:

Let $rank_{\mathbf{s}}(\mathbf{s}') = \#\{\tilde{\mathbf{s}} \in \mathcal{N}(\mathbf{s}) \,|\, d(\mathbf{s}, \tilde{\mathbf{s}}) < d(\mathbf{s}, \mathbf{s}')\}$ be the rank index of distances. Then s produces λ offspring: Offspring $\mathbf{s}_i$ is placed in direction to the neighbor $\mathbf{s}'_i$ according to

$$\mathbf{s}_i^{\text{offspring}}(\mathbf{s}) = \mathbf{s} + \epsilon h_{\sigma}(\mathbf{s}, \mathbf{s}'_i)(\mathbf{s} - \mathbf{s}'_i) \tag{5}$$

with

$$h_{\sigma}(\mathbf{s}, \mathbf{s}'_i) = \exp\left(-\frac{rank_{\mathbf{s}}(\mathbf{s}'_i)}{2\sigma^2}\right) \tag{6}$$

and decreasing cooperativeness parameter $\sigma(t) = \sigma_{init} \cdot (\sigma_{final}/\sigma_{init})^{(t/t_{max})}$ and adaptation strength $\epsilon(t) = \epsilon_{init} \cdot (\epsilon_{final}/\epsilon_{init})^{(t/t_{max})}$. Thereby, (6) is equivalent to the neighborhood learning in NG [8]. This attraction is performed only if s is not better judged than its neighbors. Otherwise the special ES-mutation operator mentioned above is applied.

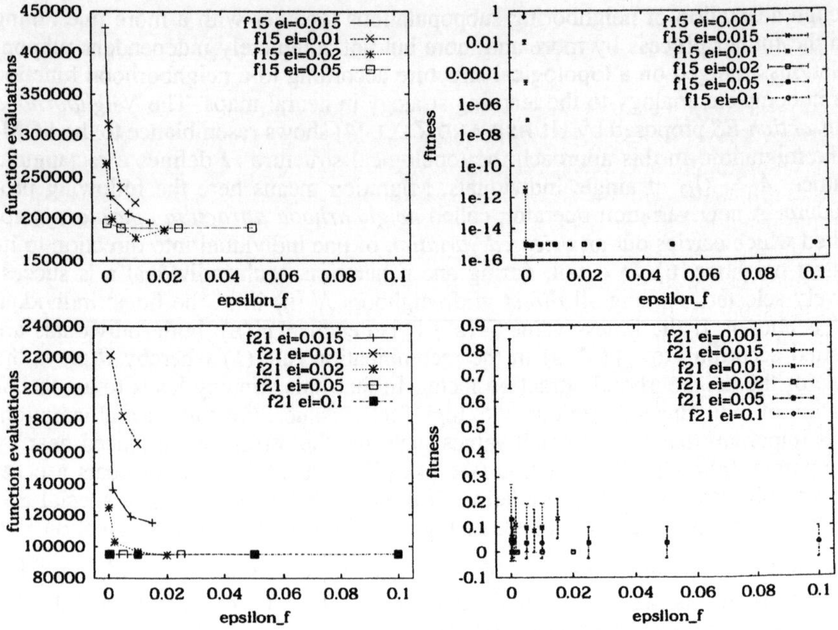

Fig. 1. Results of the parameter study for the adaptation strength ϵ. For details see text.

4 Parameter Studies for NG-Neighborhood Attraction EA

First tests led to the result that the new NG-attraction approach is able to solve the optimization tasks f_1, f_3, f_6, f_9, f_{15}, f_{16}, f_{18}, f_{19}, f_{20}, f_{21}, f_{22}, f_{23}, f_{24} known from [4,5] with a higher performance than the SOM-attraction approach[3]. Here we are interested in the influence of the adaptation strength ϵ.[2] For this purpose, we simplify $h_\sigma(\mathbf{s}, \mathbf{s}'_i)$ such that $h_\sigma(\mathbf{s}, \mathbf{s}'_i) = 1$ if $\mathbf{s}'_i \in \mathcal{N}(\mathbf{s})$. We varied both the initial values ϵ_{init} and final ones ϵ_{final}. The results for function f_{15} (*weighted sphere model*) as well as f_{21} (*Griewangk-function*) are depicted in Figure 1 – upper line and lower line, respectively. For each configuration we determined the number of evaluations needed to reach the optimum $f_{opt} = 0$ to assess the convergence speed (left) and the fitness (including deviations) at a certain time point to rate the robustness (right). If $\epsilon_{init} \leq 0.001$, for both functions convergence speed is too small and the optimum is not found in time (right). For $\epsilon_{init} \geq 0.01$, the robustness is much better (smaller deviations in finding the optimum, see right column). However, the convergence speed also crucially depends on ϵ_{final}. Fig.1, left shows for different ϵ_{init} that the number of function evaluations needed to reach the optimum decreases with increasing ϵ_{final}, which means an increase in convergence speed. These results are in agreement with the role of the learning parameter in neural network environments. Hence, a careful selection of the parameter regime is needed in advance for

[2] We also studied the influence of σ in h_σ. However, the influence was not critical. Because of the lack of space we omit the detailed description of the tests.

successful application of this strategy which can be obtained by analyzing the respective test suites.

5 Concluding remarks

The NG-neighborhood attraction EA combines ideas of topological neighborhood oriented cooperativeness in NG with migration strategies in EAs. The choice of topological neighbors offers the possibility to optimize the adaptation process according to the, possibly very complex, structure of the fitness function. It overcomes the fixed lattice structures of previous schemes (island model, SOM-like migration), which may lead to a decelerated convergence and decreased performance [11]. Thereby it is necessary that a careful parameter regime of the adaptation strength is applied whereas the setting of the cooperativeness parameter is not critical.

References

1. L. Altenberg. The evolution of evolvability in genetic programming. In K. E. Kinnear, editor, *Advances in Genetic Programming*, Complex Adaptive Systems, pages 47–74, Cambridge, 1994. MIT Press.
2. T. Bäck. *Evolutionary Algorithms in Theory and Practice*. Oxford University Press, New York - Oxford, 1996.
3. J. Huhse, T. Villmann, P. Merz, and A. Zell. Evolution strategies with neighborhood attraction using a neural gas approach. *Parallel Problem Solving from Nature*,submitted, 2002.
4. J. Huhse and A. Zell. Evolutionary strategy with neighborhood attraction. In H. Bothe and R.Rojas, editors, *Neural Computation 2000*, pages 363–369, Zürich, 2000. ICSC Academic Press.
5. J. Huhse and A. Zell. Evolution strategy with neighborhood attraction - A robust evolution strategy. In L. Spector, E. D. Goodman, A. Wu, W. B. Langdon, H.-M. Voigt, M. Gen, S. Sen, M. Dorigo, S. Pezeshk, M. H. Garzon, and E. Burke, editors, *Proceedings of the Genetic and Evolutionary Computation Conference (GECCO-2001)*, pages 1026–1033, San Francisco, California, USA, 7-11 2001. San Francisco, CA 94104, USA.
6. J. Huhse and A. Zell. Investigating the influence of the neighborhood attraction factor to the evolution strategies with neighborhood attraction. In M. Verleysen, editor, *Proc. Of European Symposium on Artificial Neural Networks (ESANN'2001)*, pages 179–184, Brussels, Belgium, 2001. D facto publications.
7. T. Kohonen. *Self-Organizing Maps*, volume 30 of *Springer Series in Information Sciences*. Springer, Berlin, Heidelberg, 1995. (Second Extended Edition 1997).
8. T. Martinetz and K. Schulten. Topology representing networks. *Neural Networks*, 7(3):507–522, 1994.
9. Z. Michalewicz. *Genetic Algorithms + Data Structures = Evolution Programs*. Springer–Verlag Berlin Heidelberg New York, third, revised and extended edition, 1996.
10. H.-P. Schwefel. *Numerical Optimization of Computer Models*. Wiley and Sons, 1981.
11. T. Villmann. Evolutionary algorithms and neural networks in hybrid systems. In *Proc. Of European Symposium on Artificial Neural Networks (ESANN'2001)*, pages 137–152, Brussels, Belgium, 2001. D facto publications.
12. T. Villmann. Evolutionary algorithms with subpopulations using a neural network like migration scheme and its application to real world problems. *Integrated Computer-Aided Engineering*, 9(1):25–36, 2002.
13. T. Villmann, R. Haupt, K. Hering, and H. Schulze. Parallel evolutionary algorithms with som-like migration. In A. Dobnikar, N. Steele, D. W. Pearson, and R. Albrecht, editors, *Artificial Neural Networks and Genetic Algorithms (Proc. Of ICANNGA'99)*, pages 274–279, Wien - New York, 1999. Springer-Verlag.

A Fate of Two Evolutionary Walkers after the Departure from the Origin

Akira Imada

Brest State Technical University
Moskowskaja, 267, Brest, 224017 Republic of Belarus
ai@brpi.unibel.by

Abstract. Using Sammon mappings, a method to visualize multidimensional space, we observe a strange difference between two evolutionary searches: Evolutionary Programming and Breeder Genetic Algorithm, when they search for weight solutions of fully connected neural network model of associative memory.

1 Introduction

We have been searching for weight configurations that store a set of bipolar patterns to a fully connected neural network model as associative memory by using evolutionary computations. In usual evolutionary computations, in most cases, a search starts with a population of candidate solutions distributed at random over the search space, and those candidate solutions eventually converge to one of real solutions. Usually, we can regard the solution as a top of a peak in the fitness landscape. However, our solutions of the fully-connected neural network model of associative memory constructs *ridges*, instead of *peaks*, emanating from the origin of the search space. Our search starts with all candidate solutions being at the Origin, that is, with all weights being zero at the start. In his book, Kauffman (1993) pointed out that "*In short, the landscape is very smooth for small synaptic weights, and hence the optimum is easily sought.*" We doubt, however, this is because the origin is the cross point of all ridges of solutions, though the Origin itself is a singular point. To tackle this issue, we analyze solutions obtained by two different evolutionary searches, Evolutionary Programming (EP) and Breeder Genetic Algorithm (BGA). Solutions located by multiple runs of each of the two evolutionary computations are visualized by using Sammon mapping. And we found quite a different phenomena between EP and BGA. That is, the solutions found by EP are almost uniformly distributed, while the ones found by BGA occupies almost a similar location.

2 Associative Memory

Associative memory is a dynamical system which has a number of stable states with a domain of attraction around them (Komlós and Paturi 1988). If the system starts at any state in the domain, it will converge to the stable state.

Hopfield (1982) proposed a fully connected neural network model of associative memory in which information is stored by being distributed among neurons, and retrieved from dynamically relaxed neurons' states. In the model, some of the appropriate configurations of synaptic weights give the network a function of associative memory.

The Hopfield model consists of N neurons and N^2 synapses. Each neuron state is either active (+1) or quiescent (−1). When an arbitrary N-bit *bipolar pattern*, a sequence of +1 and −1, is given to the network as an initial state, the dynamical behavior of neurons' states afterwards are characterized by the strengths of the N^2 synapses. The synaptic strengths are called *weights*, and the weight from neuron j to neuron i is denoted as w_{ij} in this paper. Provided the synaptic weights are determined appropriately, network can store some number of patterns as attractors. Hopfield employed the so-called Hebb's (1949) rule to prescribe the weights.

In analyzing the Hopfield model, there have been basically two different approaches: one is to explore *pattern space* searching for attractors under a specific weight configuration, and the other is to explore *weight space* searching for an appropriate weight configuration that stores a given set of patterns. The former approach searches for the optimal pattern configurations which minimize the Hamiltonian energy *in pattern space* with the weights being fixed, while the latter searches for the weight configurations *in weight space* that optimally store a set of given fixed patterns.

In this paper, our concern is on weight space where some points give a network a capability to store a fixed set of patterns, and we call these points solutions.

3 Evolutionary Searches

Our search is started with all individuals in the first population being initialized at the origin, and we found that this is very efficient initialization compared to usual randomized one. In this simulation, a set of p random bipolar patterns ξ^ν ($\nu = 1, 2, \cdots, p$) are produced before each run. The goal is to search for a weight configuration which stores all of these patterns as fixed points. Chromosome is a real-valued N^2-dimensional vector which represents a set of synaptic weights of an individual network, i.e.,

$$(w_{11}, w_{12}, \cdots, w_{1N}, w_{21}, \cdots\cdots, w_{NN}).$$

In each generation, these chromosomes are modified through evolutionary operations. Specific details of these operations are as follows.

3.1 Fitness evaluation

In both searches, when one of memorized patterns ξ^ν is given to the network as an initial state, the state of neurons varies from time to time afterwards (unless ξ^ν is a fixed point). In order for the network to function as an associative memory, the instantaneous network state must be similar to the input pattern ξ^ν. The similarity is defined by,

$$m^\nu(t) = \frac{1}{N}\sum_{i=1}^{N} \xi_i^\nu s_i^\nu(t),$$

where $s_i^\nu(t)$ is the state of neuron i at time t. This $m^\nu(t)$ is referred to as *overlap*. The quality of retrieval of memorized patterns are represented by $\langle m^\mu \rangle$, a temporal average of $m^\nu(t)$ over certain time interval t_0. We evaluate the fitness value of each network by further averaging these $\langle m^\mu \rangle$'s over all memorized patterns. Namely, the fitness f is

$$f = \frac{1}{t_0 \cdot p}\sum_{t=1}^{t_0}\sum_{\nu=1}^{p} m^\nu(t).$$

In this paper, t_0 is set to $2N$, twice the number of neurons. Note that the fitness 1 implies all the p patterns are stored as fixed points, while all other cases have a fitness less than 1.

3.2 EP

Our EP proceeds as follows. A population is constructed by μ points each of which has N^2 coordinates x_i $(i = 1, 2, \cdots, N^2)$ representing weight values of a network. Each point has additional N^2 variables σ_i $(i = 1, 2, \cdots, N^2)$ which are used to mutate the point itself. In this paper, all the x_i are initialized to zero and all the σ_i are initialized to 0.002. Each of these μ points is mutated by adding a Gaussian random variable of a standard deviation σ_i to each x_i. That is,

$$x_i^{\mathrm{new}} = x_i^{\mathrm{old}} + \sigma_i \cdot N_i(0,1).$$

This mutation produces μ mutants. After the mutation, these σ_i are also modified as:

$$\sigma_i^{\mathrm{new}} = \sigma_i^{\mathrm{old}} + 0.01 \cdot \sigma_i^{\mathrm{old}} \cdot N_i(0,1).$$

We now have the original μ points and their μ mutants. The fitness value of each of the 2μ points are compared to those of q points which are chosen randomly at every time of the comparison from the whole 2μ points. Then the 2μ points are ranked according to the number of wins, and the best μ points survive (q-tournament selection). The cycle of reconstructing the new population with better fitness points and restarting the search are repeated until one of the global optima is found or a set maximum number of generation has been reached. In this paper, μ are set to 200 and q is chosen to be 10.

3.3 BGA

The BGA uses the truncation selection (Mühlenbein et al. 1995), that is, two parent chromosomes are chosen *randomly* from the best $T\%$ of the population, and mated randomly (except for itself) to produce one offspring. This is repeated until the number of offspring is equal to the size of the population.

Recombination is made with discrete crossover (Mühlenbein et al. 1995), which is similar to *uniform crossover* (Syswerda 1989) in binary chromosomes. It operates on alleles of the selected parents' chromosomes. Two parents, $(u_1, \cdots, u_n)$ and $(v_1, \cdots, v_n)$, produce an offspring $(w_1, \cdots, w_n)$ so that w_i is either u_i or v_i with equal probability.

Then an allele x_i is chosen with probability p_m to be mutated. The BGA mutation is to give a small perturbation $\Delta x_i \times \delta$ on a variable x_i, where Δx_i is a mutation range for the variable x_i, and δ is calculated as

$$\delta = \alpha_0 + \frac{1}{2}\alpha_1 + \frac{1}{2^2}\alpha_2 + \cdots + \frac{1}{2^{15}}\alpha_{15}.$$

Each α_k takes the value 1 with probability 1/16, and otherwise takes the value 0. Then mutated new allele is

$$x_i \pm \Delta_i \times \delta,$$

with the sign $+/-$ being chosen with equal probability.

4 Sammon Mapping

As Collins (1997) wrote, the dimension reduction has been an important technique for visualization of the space of high dimensionality. The Sammon Mapping (Sammon 1969) is one of these techniques. This enables us to map a set of $\mathcal{N}$ points in n-dimensional space to 2D location data so that the distance information is preserved as much as possible, or as Shine et al. (1997) wrote *"so that the n-dimensional distances are approximated by 2 dimensional distances with a minimal error."* This problem is an optimization problem.

Shine et al. (1997) and Collins (1997) proposed a method to solve this problem by a GA, as follows. First, the distance matrix whose entries are Euclidean distances between all possible pairs of $\mathcal{N}$ points in the n-dimensional space is calculated. Then tentative $\mathcal{N}$ points in the 2-dimensional space are determined representing the original $\mathcal{N}$ points in the n-dimensional space. The distance matrix of these $\mathcal{N}$ points in the 2D space is also calculated, which then will be subtracted from the original n-dimensional distance matrix, yielding an error matrix. A GA is used to minimize this error matrix.

5 Experiments

Simulations were carried out on a network with 25 neurons. A fixed set of some random bipolar patterns is given to the network to be stored as associative memory. The configurations of 25^2 weights that allow the network to store these patterns as associative memory correspond to the peaks on the landscape. They are searched for by an EP and BGA.

6 Results and Discussion

Although w_{ij} can take an arbitrary real value, two different solutions on one of the hyper-lines emanating from the origin are identical since they differ only by scaling factor. In other words, $\kappa \cdot w_{ij}$ works exactly in the same way as w_{ij} for any scaling factor κ. Therefore, as Gardner (1988) did, all the solutions are normalized on the surface of hyper-sphere of radius one whose center is at the origin, by regarding points on a hyper-line as the point where the line crosses the hyper-sphere surface. These normalized points are very well visualized by Sammon mapping. For example Figure 1 is a mapping of 100 solutions on the $25^2 = 625$ dimensional hyper-sphere, each of which stores $p = 1$ pattern, onto two-dimensional space. It is important to note here that we made it possible by adding additional 100 random points very close to the origin in order to maintain the difference relation between the points in the 625-dimensions.

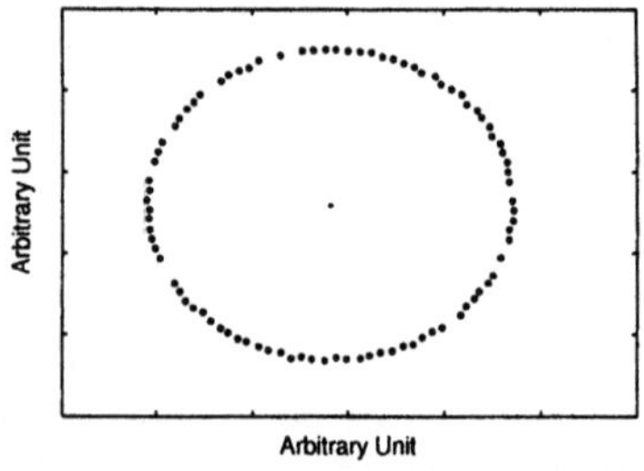

Fig. 1. Sammon mapping of 100 solutions ($p = 1$) located by EP.

Then a pair of 30 different solutions for $p = 6$ located by 30 runs of EP and BGA, respectively, are visualized. The results are shown in Figure 2.
Mühlenbein et al. (Mühlenbein et al. 1995), concluded that "*the BGA mutation scheme is able to optimize many multi-modal functions.*" However our observation was opposite, that is, BGA converges always to a similar solution while EP converges to different solutions for each run. We also started BGA with a randomly distributed first generation, instead of all zero population, but the results were the same. They always converged to one solution.

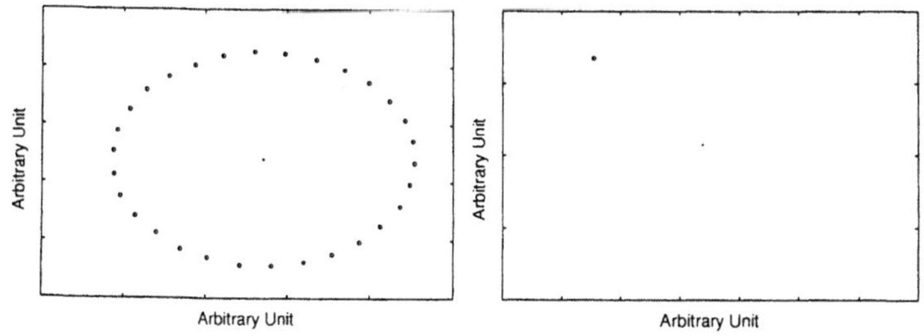

Fig. 2. Sammon mapping of 30 solutions ($p = 6$) located by EP (left) and BGA (right)

7 Conclusion

We have observed solutions of the fully connected neural network model those located by two different evolutionary searches, EP and BGA, and found that multiple runs of EP locates multiple solutions while BGA locates a single solution out of them. The reason awaits our further analysis.

References

Collins, T. D. (1997) *Using Software Visualization Technology to Help Evolutionary Algorithm Users Validate their Solutions.* Proceedings of the 7th International Conference on Genetic Algorithms, pp.307–314.

Gardner, E. (1988) *The Phase Space of Interactions in Neural Network Models.* Journal of Physics, 21A, pp.257-270.

Hopfield, J. J. (1982) *Neural Networks and Physical Systems with Emergent Collective Computational Abilities.* Proc. of the National Academy of Sciences, USA 79, pp.2554-2558.

Hebb, D. O. (1949) *The Organization of Behavior.* Wiley.

Komlós, J., and R. Paturi (1988) *Convergence Results in an Associative Memory Model.* Neural Networks 1, pp.239–250.

Mühlenbein, H. and D. Schlierkamp-Voosen (1995) *Predictive Models for the Breeder Genetic Algorithm I. Continuous Parameter Optimization.* Evolutionary Computation Vol.1 (1996), pp.25–49.

Sammon, J. W. (1969) *A Nonlinear Mapping for Data Structure Analysis.* IEEE Transactions on Computers. C-18(5), pp.401–408.

Shine, W. B. and C. F. Eick (1997) *Visualizing the Evolution of Genetic Algorithm Search Processes.* Proceedings of the IEEE International Conference on Evolutionary Computation, pp.367–372.

Syswerda, G. (1989) *Uniform Crossover in Genetic Algorithms.* Proceedings of the 3rd International Conference on Genetic Algorithms, pp.2–9.

Genetic Algorithms with Adaptive Meta-heuristics for 2D Packing Problem

Romuald Jagielski

School of Information Technology, Swinburne University of Technology, PO Box 218 Hawthorn, Melbourne, Australia

RJagielski@swin.edu.au

Abstract.

In this paper we have proposed meta-heuristics for 2D packing problem. These heuristics are based on quasi-ordering and are adaptive. The meta-heuristics combined together with genetic algorithms supplied with appropriate parameters produce considerably improved, optimal or near-optimal, results.

1 Introduction

The packing problem is a difficult standard problem with many practical applications. Broadly speaking, it is a problem of finding an optimal way of placing a set of objects in a container (a bin) of a minimal space. We will focus our interest only on the two-dimensional (2D) orthogonal packing of rectangles on a rectangular board or strip. This is problem belongs to the same class as the cutting problem, where the goal is to cut a strip of stock into required pieces, with a minimal waste of the material. Such problems occur in manufacturing and industry, and have some practical relevance.

Strip packing is a NP- hard problem. There exist many variations of the packing problem and a large number of approximate solutions have been offered. In this paper we discuss evolutionary approach to the 2D strip packing problem, and in particular some novel heuristics for genetic algorithms will be proposed.

2 The problem and its representation

The problem can be defined as follow: a set of *n* rectangles, r_i, i=0,…,*n-1* and a rectangular board of certain width and undetermined height are given. The objective is to place all the rectangles on board without overlaps in such a way that edges of r_i are parallel to x- and y-axes, respectively and the height is minimal.

A solution of the problem will consist two elements:

- □ A permutation all integers i, $0 <= i <= n-1$, where i represents the index of a rectangle. A permutation establishes the order of placing rectangles on the board;
- □ A strategy of placing rectangles on the board (in the order determined by the permutation). In this paper we will use a variation of so called BL algorithm (the name refers to a bin which we will fill with objects starting from bottom (**B**) left (**L**) corner, placing the object next to each other, filling the bin a layer by layer), commonly used by other researchers [1 – 4].

Let us assume that the board is represented by a matrix s[0:m-1, 0:n-1]. According to our algorithm (which seems to be equivalent to BLF strategy described in [1]), the first rectangle is put into the left corner of the board, s[0,0]. Then the algorithm finds the points of insertion for the each successive rectangle r_i, scanning the board in the order: s[0,0], s[0,1], s[0,2],…,s[0,n],s[1,0], s[1,1], s[1,2],…,s[1,n], s[2,0], s[2,1], s[2,2],…,s[2,n], …. A rectangle r_i with sides <*a*, *b*> will be inserted onto the board if the following conditions are satisfied:
(1) The rectangle can be placed without overlapping;
(2) One edge of the rectangle is parallel to x-axes, and the other edge to y-axes;
(3) The rectangle is allocated with disregard to its orientation, that is, if a rectangle with sides <*a*, *b*> cannot be placed then the 90^0 rotated rectangle <*b*, *a* > is considered for placement.

All problems we consider here have optimal solutions. For example the problem with 16 rectangles (we will refer to it as a problem of size 16) has board of the optimal size 20 x 20, and is defined as set of rectangles <*a*, *b*>:

0	1	2	3	4	5	6	7	8	9	10	11	12	13	14	15	// rectangle index
2	4	8	3	3	5	3	3	5	2	3	4	3	7	9	11	// side *a*
12	4	6	6	5	5	12	7	7	6	2	2	4	12	2	2	// side *b*

One possible solution of this problem is the following permutation:
14 2 13 3 9 15 6 4 0 5 8 7 1 12 10 11

3 The partial-order meta-heuristics

The idea of placing big objects at first is appealing. Rather then leaving small objects for placing on the board to the final stage of the allocation, one may expect that the task will be simplified, since it is easier to place successfully rather smaller rectangles than bigger, and to end up with an optimal arrangement. Consequently, pre-sorting of rectangles, according to their width or/and height, was used [1, 3]. Regrettably, this approach leads to extremely small diversity of the initial population. In this paper we propose including a partial order in the initial population of solutions.

Let us say set S is a solution of the problem, in a form of a permutation of rectangles, as we discussed it above. We will create a partition $\mathcal{P}$ of a set S as a collection of nonempty subsets of S such that

(1) For all $A \in \mathcal{P}$ and $B \in \mathcal{P}$, either $A = B$ or $A \cap B = \acute{\emptyset}$

(2) $S = \bigcup_{A \in \mathcal{P}} A$

That is, a partition of the set S is a collection of nonempty and pairwise disjoint subsets of S which exhaust the set S. The element of a partition is called a block, and the number of blocks in a partition is the rank of the partition. Partitioning is naturally induced by an equivalence relation. Since for the problem discussed in this paper we want to deal with solutions in form of partially ordered sets with regard to the size of rectangles, each solution will be a partition of S induced by the equivalence: given two rectangles *i* and *j*, they are in the same block (they are indiscernible with respect to the area) if

$$rectangle\_area_i \,/\, k = rectangle\_area_j \,/\, k$$

where "/" is an integer division operator, *k* – constant. The constant k (let us call it a granule) determines the rank of the partition – we assume here that *k* is between 2 and the average, for the given problem, rectangle area.

Such a partitioning results with a rough sorting. The following is a sample of a solution – a partition with rank 6, $k = 12$ (the first row shows the indices of the rectangles, the second shows the area of the corresponding rectangles):

13	2	6	5	0	8	15	4	12	3	9	14	7	1	11
84	48	36	25	24	35	22	15	12	18	12	18	21	16	8

It is impossible to know a priori the best value of the granule *k*, therefore in the initial population this value is generated randomly for each individual. As the process of evolution proceeds the optimal values for granules emerge. For example, the Figure 1 shows the distribution of granules in the population of 1000 individuals after 26 generations, when the optimal solution of the problem 16, described in previous section, was obtained. The graphic shows that mainly individuals with granule 5 and 9 survived, and indeed, one with $k = 9$ is the optimal solution.

Beside the type of ordering described above, that we will call a *simple partitioning* (P1), another meta-heuristic has been considered (P2). Let us divide each sequence of rectangles representing a solution into *n* equal (with the exception of the last one) groups – for convenience they can be called shelves. After that, the simple partitioning is applied for each shelf. In this meta-heuristic we use two parameters: *n* –number of shelves, and *k* – granule size. This is an example of ordered permutation of rectangles, as a possible solution to the problem 25, with $n = 5$, $k = 25$:

9	**7**	**6**	**19**	**22**	**18**	20	0	13	17	12	5	**21**	**1**	**2**	**23**	**3**	**15**	8	4	11	24	10	14	**16**
52	**26**	**22**	**15**	**4**	**2**	65	33	33	24	4	21	**48**	**39**	**18**	**10**	**14**	**20**	44	27	22	12	15	6	**24**

(The first row shows the indices of the rectangles, the second shows the area of the corresponding rectangles, bold fond is used to distinguish five shelves).

4 The implementation of genetic algorithms

Though the standard genetic algorithm is used here, many problem specific decisions have to be made considering the implementation of the genetic operators and choice of parameters. The following sections describe the details of the implementation.

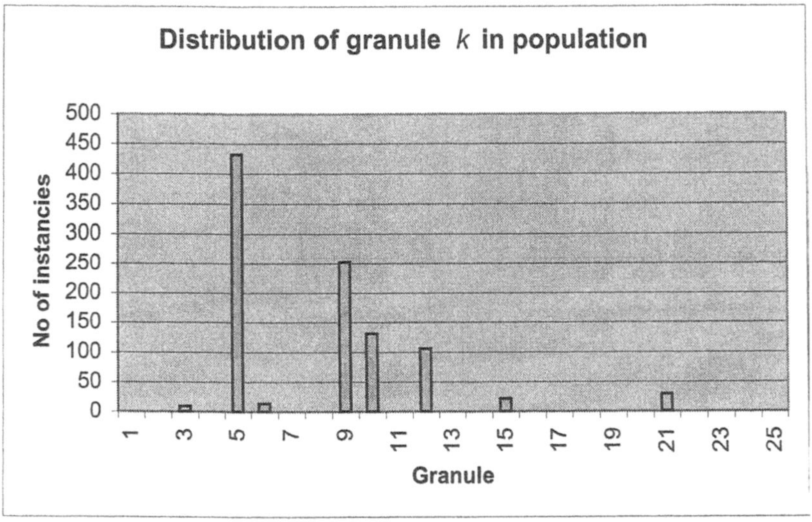

Figure 1. Distribution of ordering parameter *k* in a population.

4.1 Fitness function

The objective function is determined by the minimal height of the board (or length of the strip) after placing all objects. Following Hopper and Turton [1], we measure the packing quality as relative distance between the minimal packing height obtained by a genetic algorithm and the height in the optimal solution. We call this measure fitness f_H. However this fitness does not reflect the density of packing. For this reason a better function would be one that takes into account the total uncovered area of the optimal board (total wasted material). This fitness, f_W, can be expressed as a number of elementary units used in the problem definition (for example the problem of size 16, mentioned above, has optimal board 20 x 20, that is 400 units). This function can be improved by including a "punishment for holes" – the uncovered units on the board that cannot be utilized at all (because the process of placing rectangles went to far and is not reversible) have greater weight than the units at the end of the strip. This function we denote as f_P, and finally, the fitness f used by the genetic algorithms we take as:

$$f = f_H + a\ f_P$$

- where a is a constant, assumed as $a = 1/optimal\text{-}hight$.

4.2 Genetic operators

The mutation used here is a simple *order-based mutation*, where two randomly selected objects in a randomly selected permutation, are swapped.

As the crossover operator *order crossover* has been chosen. The experiments show, however, that the positive impact of crossover is noticeable only if it is used with low probability.

For selection the *tournament algorithm* is used, with a tournament group of size three.

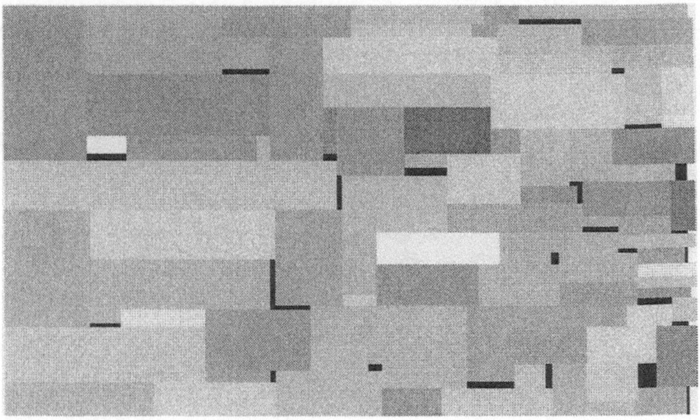

Figure 2. An example of a best solution of a problem of size 97 (rectangles are represented with different grade of shading)

5. Experimental results

The propositions described above were testing on data provided by Hopper [1]. All problems are divided into seven categories with different number of rectangles and size of the board. We used one problem from each category (with size 16, 25, 28, 49, 73, 97 and 196). All problems are known to have an optimal height.

For each problem the experiment was run five times, and the average results were taken. The essential parameters are following:

population size - 2000;
probability of crossover - 0.05
probability of mutation – 0.86
maximal number of generations – 60.

Figure 2 shows, as an example, the best solution of the problem size 97. The average best results, obtained for three different methods, are presented in Figure 3. The results are expressed as a relative distance of the best solution to the optimum height in %. The outcome of the method that did not use meta-heuristic (BLF) roughly repeats the results in [1] (the packing heights are between 0.2% -8%), however the results of the adaptive partitioning presented here are significantly closer to the optimum (between 0% and 3.3%). The results for simple partitioning (P1) are slightly better than partitioning with shelves (P2).

Conclusion

In this paper we have proposed new meta-heuristics for strip packing problem. These heuristics are based on partitioning and quasi-ordering and are adaptive. The meta-heuristics together with a carefully designed fitness function produce considerably improved results.

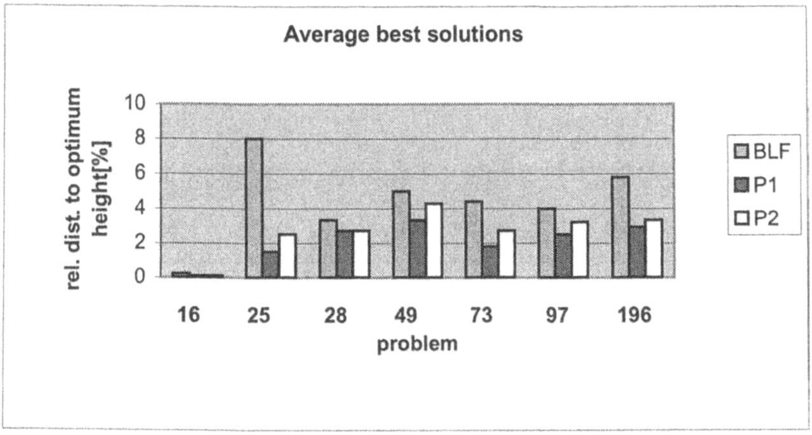

Figure 3. Average best solutions as relative distance to optimum height.

References

[1] Hopper, E. B.C.H. Turton An empirical investigation of meta-heuristic and heuristic algorithms for 2D packing problem, European Journal of Operational Research 128 (2001) 34-57

[2] Jakobs, S. On genetic algorithms for the packing of polygons, European Journal of Operational Research 88 (1996) 165 – 181

[3] Khuri, S. Evolutionary Heuristics for the Bin Packing Problem, Artificial Neural Nets and Genetic Algorithms, Proceeding of the International Conference, Ales, France, 1995

[4] Liu, D., Hongfei Teng An improved BL-algorithm for genetic algorithm of the orthogonal packing of rectangles, European Journal of Operational Research 112 (1999) 413-420

Genetic Decryption of Columnar Transposition Code

Anna Kleszczyńska [1)], Piotr S. Szczepaniak [1, 2)]

[1)] Institute of Computer Science, Technical University of Lodz
Sterlinga 16/18, 90-217 Lodz, Poland
[2)] Systems Research Institute, Polish Academy of Sciences
Newelska 6, 01-447 Warsaw, Poland

Abstract. Genetic algorithm proves to be a powerful tool in many diverse situations. Here its ability for decryption of the text coded using columnar transposition is presented. To this aim the basic genetic operations – crossover and mutation, as well as the fitness function obtain specific forms. Practical observations made during cryptoanalytical experiments complete the work.

Keywords. Cryptoanalysis, transposition code, genetic algorithm, genetic decryption

1 Columnar transposition

Columnar transposition is used in many current codes, for example in the Data Encryption Standard (DES) algorithm. The idea of this type of transposition is to change the order of bits within a bit string. In its earlier version it is the order of characters within the text which is changed. To perform the secret writing a given plaintext is first written row by row, each having d elements. Then, the columns of the resulting matrix are interchanged according to some rule, and finally the cryptotext is read from the rows of the new matrix [1,4].

Example.
Let the columnar transposition be performed for rows of length $d = 4$ and according to the permutation p: 2 4 1 3 .

```
plaintext -    H E L E N  P L A Y S  C H E S S
coding -             1 2 3 4     →     2 4 1 3
                     -------           -------
                     H E L E           E E H L
                     N P L A           P A N L
                     Y S C H           S H Y C
                     E S S             S   E S
cryptotext -   E E H L P A N L S H Y C S E S
```

□

Another type of transposition used in cryptography is the blocktransposition, also called complete-unit transposition or "*variante de Richelieu*" in French. It is cryptoanalytically equivalent to the columnar transposition, i.e. both of them assure the same cryptoanalytic security. With this in mind, the method involving columnar transposition has been chosen to be in the focus of the paper. Although the decoding is relatively simple as the frequency of letters is not changed [1,4], the code, being not trivial, proves to be a very grateful object to use in order to show clearly the specificity of the genetic mechanism when applied to cryptoanalysis.

2 Method

2.1 Assumptions

For the simplicity of consideration it is assumed that the encryption method and the length d are known. Of course, this may not be true in many practical situations but such an assumption is reasonable when presenting a novel method. Thus let the cryptotext to be decrypted be given as well as the dictionary – a few words in plaintext which are known to be present in the encrypted document but whose precise placement is unknown. It is worth having such information in order to be successful in cryptoanalysis.
Adapting here the nomenclature of genetic algorithms [2,3] an individual is defined as the candidate solution of the decryption problem – it is a pattern which reflects the order of the columns in the candidate decryption matrix. When the correct solution has been found, the pattern enables reading of the whole document under interest. It is assumed to be possible if for each word in the dictionary its decryption exists and can be located.

The goal is to find the rule according to which the columns of the coding matrix have been rearranged. Note that the classic algorithm of Holland is useless in this case. Let us explain it in detail.
Each individual of the initial population involves information about the order of columns within the matrix, more exactly: each number identifying a particular column is present in reality once and only once. For example, if d=4, then only sequences of the form 1,2,4,3 or 4,1,3,2 , or 4,2,1,3 , etc. are admissible. Application of the crossover exactly like it is in Hollands' method may create an individual with the same column number twice by simultaneous absence of another column. Moreover, it would be possible to obtain an individual possessing a number out of the admissible range. This is the reason why crossover and mutation should be defined anew. Another important question is the proper form of the function evaluating the candidate solutions.

2.2 Fitness

Each individual is a string of numbers that represent the candidate pattern, i.e. the rule for transposition of columns. The searched solution is the (right) order of numbers, and not a certain value as it is in classic problems of other fields.

Consequently, the proposed fitness uses a binary distance function. In other words, it is of importance whether the known word from the dictionary is different from the encoded one, and not to what extent it is different or similar. Thus, the distance is computed according to the following rule: if two considered letters differ, then the distance is "1"; if they are identical – the distance becomes "0". The distance values of considered letters are added and the result is divided by the length of the considered sequence (word). The steps in computing the fitness are:

1. Decode the whole cryptotext using the candidate pattern represented by the given individual.
2. Compute the distance between the considered word from the dictionary and the obtained decrypted text. The distance is computed according to the method described above.
3. Repeat step 2 moving the word along the text position by position; the computed distance is subtracted from number 1. Choose the maximal result.

Subtraction assures that the fitness is a positive definite and increasing function; in other words it is correctly defined for the problem at hand. The maximal value of the function reflects the minimal distance of the word to the text, and is the fitness of the considered individual (candidate solution).
When more words are considered, the procedure is repeated for each of them and the fitness is assumed to be the result of dividing the sum of the maximal values by the number of examined words from the dictionary.

2.3 Selection mechanism

Selection is the process of choosing individuals for the next generation from the set of individuals existing in the current population. Different methods reported in the literature are applicable. Here, the classic roulette wheel has been used.
The entire roulette wheel corresponds to the total value of fitness functions summed over all individuals of the considered population. Each individual is assigned a segment of the wheel proportional in size to the value of its fitness function. The higher the value, the greater the segment and the greater the likelihood that the given individual will find itself in the selected set.

2.4 Creation of new individuals

Because of the specificity of the considered problem single-parent operations seem to be a reasonable proposition here, and *inversion* is the basic one. Creation of a new population as a result of many inversions is similar to inbreeding. In the botany, inbred crossover is the pollination of a plant by itself, where no exchange with another individual takes place. The inversion works as follows. First, two positions determining different columns of the encryption matrix are randomly chosen. Then, the chosen columns are interchanged.

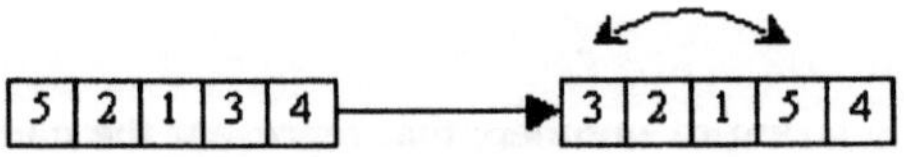

Fig.1. Scheme of inversion

As a result, new individuals always belong to the admissible population.

Example 1.

Let a given individual determine the order of columns 5,2,1,3,4 for the code of length d=5. Assuming that the 1st and 4th positions have randomly been chosen, the order of columns of the offspring individual is: 3,2,1,5,4.

□

The operation of mutation usually works by changing the value (e.g. inverting bit) on one chosen position of the solution with some small probability (mutation rate). In view of the already mentioned restrictions the mutation-like operation should also obtain a specific form, and the proposed computational steps are:

- random choice of two different positions;
- insertion of the first selected number to the position occupied by the second number;
- shift of all the numbers placed between the two selected (the second including) to fill the empty position left by the number pulled out first.

The proposed procedure assures that all the columns of the encryption matrix remain present.

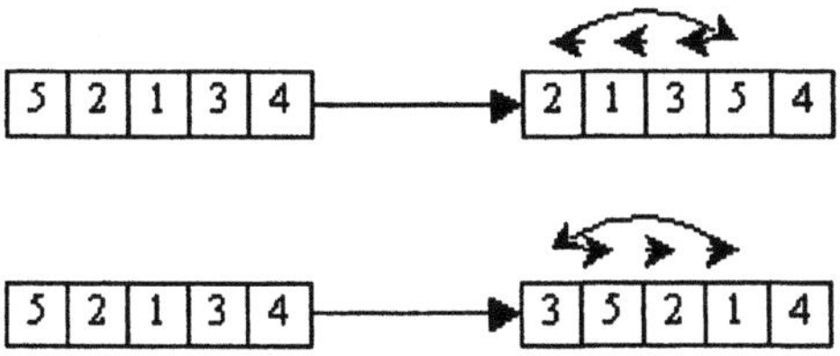

a)

b)

Fig.2. Insertion and shifting

Example 2.

Let the current situation be as in Example 1, i.e. d=5 and the individual is 5,2,1,3,4. If the random choice indicates the 1st and 4th positions, then the resulting order will be: 2,1,3,5,4 (Fig.2.a).

If the chosen order was reversed (4th and 1st), then the result would be: 3,5,2,1,4 (Fig.2b).

□

Obviously, both described operations may be analogously performed when the parameters of the individuals have binary coding.

3 Results and comments

The method has been tested by changing both cryptographic technique and parameters of the genetic algorithm. At the present stage of the study the results for the following set of parameters are well recorded and analysed:

1) number of columns d=5 and d=8;
2) number of individuals within population n=10 and n=30;

3) mutation rate for individual η=0.01, η=0.05 and η=0.1.

The number of individuals is reasonable for research testing. If more than 30 individuals were considered, with unnatural frequency could then the solution be within the initial population for the assumed 5 columns of the matrix. This is because the sets of numbers of possible solutions for the considered two cases consist of 5!=120 and 8!=40320 elements, respectively. Note that the attacked tasks should respect the capacities of personal computers available in our case. The situation changes significantly if one can make use of more powerful computing machines.

As reported in literature, the probability of mutation is usually estimated to be about 0.001. While solving the decryption task under testing it turned out, however, that significantly bigger values yield better efficiency. This is caused by both the definition of the problem and the specific form of mutation.

The efficiency of the decryption method was also evaluated with respect to the number of transposed columns, in other words in relation to the increased safety and complication of the coding method. The results are presented in Table 1. They are mean results obtained for three different cases of the cryptotext and one word from the dictionary but different for each of these cases.

Table 1. Percentage of successful decryption

%		*d*=5			*d*=8	
η	0,01	0,05	0,1	0,01	0,05	0,1
n						
10	99	100	100	20	20	17
30	100	100	100	59	63	64

It is evident that for *d*=5 the algorithm is always or almost always successful for the population sets of the two studied powers. The method proves more effective for bigger values of the mutation rate. With the increase of *d* (complication of coding) the method becomes less successful, particularly if the population of individuals is small (here *n*=10). This small number of individuals makes the influence of mutation rate η non-visible. The situation becomes clearer and the results are more satisfactory if the size of the population set is increased. The disproportion between the chosen number of individuals (*n*=30) and the number of possible situations (40320) remains disadvantageous but the method works well. The significance of parameter η becomes evident: the increase of η leads to a higher rate of successful cryptoanalyses. However, this higher rate of success is not equivalent to shorter decryption time measured in the value of *g* – the number of generations involved. The number of generations needed for successful decoding depends on both the number of individuals within the population and the number of columns in the matrix (Table 2).

It is worth looking (theoretically or experimentally) for a formula to determine an approximate number of required iterations. In the reported experiments, computations were arbitrarily stopped if after 200 generations no success was achieved. For d=5 the number is too high as only exceptionally morc than 100 iterations has had to be performed. For d=8 the limit may lie a little above the chosen 200.

Table 2. Mean number of generations needed to find the solution

g	d=5			d=8		
η	0,01	0,05	0,1	0,01	0,5	0,1
n						
10	25	25	25	102	117	104
30	9	9	9	83	87	91

4 Summary

Columnar transposition belongs to rather old cryptographic methods, and the analytic procedures for its decryption are well known. The goals of the presented work have been:

- search for a novel cryptographic method based on adaptation of the genetic algorithm;
- verification of the usefulness of the genetic method for decryption performed on an exemplary code not trivial to solve;
- gaining of experience related to the efficiency (in terms of speed) of the new method.

The general summarising statement is that the proposed version of the genetic algorithm is able to perform decryption of the columnar transposition code. Of course, the increase of the number of columns in the encryption matrix makes the code safer; the algorithm needs more generations to achieve success. To acquire the exhaustive knowledge of the properties of the method one needs to undertake the tremendous work of hundreds of decryption attempts with the use of powerful computers. The significance of collaboration with mathematicians in the task can hardly be overestimated. Other experiments not reported here show that the genetic method is able to perform cryptoanalysis of other codes as well but this subject lies beyond the scope of this paper.

References

1. Bauer F.L. (1997). *Decrypted Secrets. Methods and Maxims of Cryptology.* Springer Verlag, Berlin, Heidelberg.
2. Goldberg D.E. (1989). *Genetic Algorithms in Search, Optimization, and Machine Learning*. Addisson-Wesley Publ. Company, Reading, MA.
3. Michalewicz Z. (1996). *Genetic Algorithms + Data Structures = Evolution Programs*. 3rd edition, Springer-Verlag, Berlin.
4. Robling Denning D.E. (1982). *Cryptography and Data Security.* Addison Wesley Publ. Company Inc., Reading, MA.

A Floating-Point Based Evolutionary Algorithm for Model Parameters Extraction and Optimization in HBT Device Simulation

Yiming Li[1,2], Chuen-Tast Sun[3], and Cheng-Kai Chen[3]

[1] National Nano Device Laboratories, Hsinchu 300, Taiwan
[2] Microelectronics and Information Systems Research Center*
[3] Department Computer and Information Science*
* National Chiao Tung University, 1001 Ta Hsueh Rd., Hsinchu 300, Taiwan

Abstract. In this paper, we extract the HBT model parameters with a computational intelligence algorithm for the optimal VLSI device characterization. For a specified VLSI circuit, the proposed method to solve the HBT equivalent model and to extract parameters is based on the monotone iterative (MI) method and the genetic algorithm (GA) with floating-point operators. First, a set of nonlinear equations is solved with the MI method, and the solved results are used for the optimization with the GA method. The iteration will be stopped when the self-consistent convergent solution is obtained. Our simulation results demonstrate this method has excellent convergent property and highly computational efficiency. The approach not only provides a novel alternative for optimal VLSI circuit and device design but also has many practical applications in nanodevice I-V characterization, RF circuit optimization and system-on-a-chip function design.

1 Introduction

To study various VLSI devices, such as heterojunction bipolar transistors (HBTs) characteristics, a robust and automatic technology CAD (TCAD) tool is necessary both in academic research and industry applications. The genetic algorithm is a global optimal strategy for a wide rage of applications [1] [2] [3]. Especially, in microelectronics it has been applied to various aspects in the VLSI designs, such as cell placement, channel routing, test pattern generation and design for test. In this work we applied the GA in optimal I-V curves characterization, optimization, and model parameters extraction for semiconductor device models.
In conventional VLSI circuit design process, the circuit designer defines a target set of specified I-V curves for a specified device firstly, such as HBT, metal oxide semiconductor field effect transistor (MOSFET),... etc, and then finds out the set of parameters in the device model manually. It is a time-consuming task in microelectronic industry. Our method proposed here provides a novel alternative to solve this complex problem automatically by applying the GA and MI methods. The MI method was proposed and implemented successfully for various semiconductor devices and VLSI circuit simulation by us recently

[4] [5]. We apply it to solve nonlinear equations of the circuit model, and the GA is utilized to extract the parameters. The GA is based on floating-point operators and suitable for solving this numerical optimization problem. This paper is organized as follows. Sect. 2 states the HBT circuit model and the MI solution scheme. Sect. 3 discusses the GA applied in the extraction and optimization. Sect. 4 presents the computed results for the HBT device optimization. Sect. 5 draws conclusions and suggests the future works.

2 A HBT Circuit Model and Solution Method

A HBT device is an important semiconductor active device in high frequency circuit applications. Figure 1 shows a steady state VLSI circuit with HBT device, where the Gummal-Poon model for HBT is applied. Equations (1)-(5) are the governing nonlinear equations to be solved for the circuit operated at the steady state condition (DC). The current models I_1, I_2, I_{BL1}, I_{BL2}, I_{CT} are the functions of V_B, V_C, and V_E, respectively.

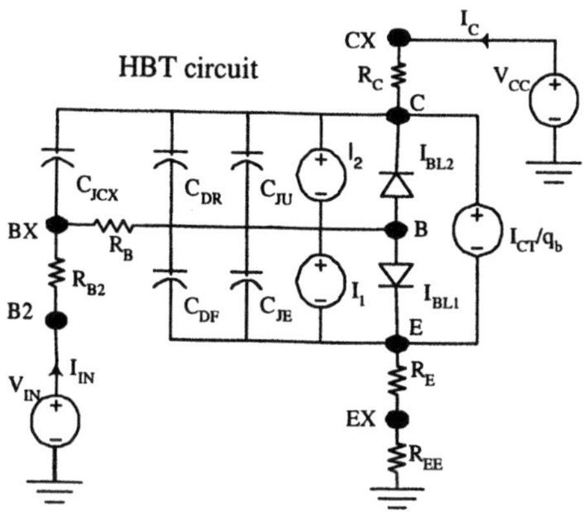

Fig. 1. A HBT circuit with the Gummal-Poon model for the DC analysis.

$$I_1 + I_{BL1} + \frac{I_{CT}}{q_b} + \frac{(V_{EX} - V_E)}{R_E} = 0 \tag{1}$$

$$I_2 + I_{BL2} - \frac{I_{CT}}{q_b} + \frac{(V_{CX} - V_C)}{R_C} = 0 \tag{2}$$

$$I_1 + I_{BL1} + I_2 + I_{BL2} + \frac{(V_B - V_{BX})}{R_B} = 0 \tag{3}$$

$$\frac{(V_B - V_{BX})}{R_B} + I_{IN} = 0 \tag{4}$$

$$\frac{(V_E - V_{EX})}{R_E} - \frac{V_{EX}}{R_{EE}} = 0 \tag{5}$$

The conventional circuit simulator, such as SPICE, applied the Newton's iteration (NI) method to solve this nonlinear model. However, the NI method is a local method and is sensitive in initial guesses. For this reason, the conventional VLSI circuit simulation is difficult to be automatized without applying a robust nonlinear solver. In this work, we apply the MI method to solve the problem. The MI method is a class of global methods. It is fast convergent and highly accurate. The computational procedure of the MI method for the HBT device simulation is as follows: (1) We decouple the system of nonlinear equations; (2) We solve each decoupled equation with the MI method sequentially [4] [5] [6]; and (3) The iteration loops will be terminated when the final self-consistent solution is convergent. The final result is a set of DC I-V curves as shown in Fig. 2. For a given set of parameters there is a corresponding set of I-V curves. The device modeling engineers examine at least 15 parameters to obtain a set of I-V curves. Table 1 shows a part of parameters to be extracted. The parameters resolution and numeric range are also included. We perform the floating-point based GA simulation for the device optimization and 15 model parameters extraction.

Table 1. A list of parameters (with its range and resolution) to be extracted.

Variable	Range	Resolution	Unit
R_B	$2.0 \sim 6.0$	0.00001	*Ohm*
I_S	$1.0e^{-25} \sim 1.0e^{-24}$	$1.0e^{-25}$	*A*
B_R	$0.2 \sim 0.3$	0.02	–
N_R	$1.0 \sim 1.1$	0.001	–

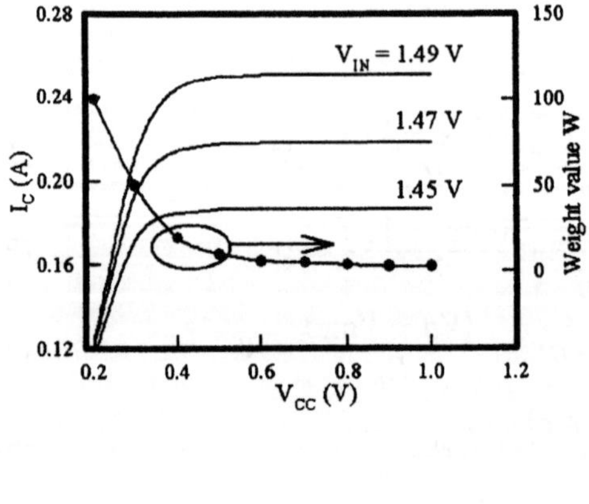

Fig. 2. HBT I-V curves, and the proposed weight function.

3 Genetic Algorithm

A genetic algorithm is a self-adaptive optimization strategy that mimics a living system. We briefly state the GA method for the HBT circuit characterization.

Step 1: *Problem Definition.* The relationship between modeling input parameter (V_{CC} and V_{IN}) and simulated result I_C can be written as follows:

$$f(V_{CC}, V_{IN}, \boldsymbol{P}) = I_C \tag{6}$$

The function f can be regarded as a nonlinear equations solver, and $\boldsymbol{P}$ contains all parameters to be extracted. The set of I_C points represents an I-V curve. The goal of evolvement is to minimize the difference between a set of targets and simulated I-V curves, and to find out their corresponding model parameters.

Step 2: *Encoding Method.* The design of gene encoding strategy depends on the property of problem. In this problem model, there are totally 15 parameters and all variables are floating-point numbers. We transform the floating-point numbers into bit strings instead of real numbers. The bit string has strongly combinatorial property, and we have found this representing has better results in crossover and mutation.

Step 3: *Fitness function (F) Calculation.* We consider the following function:

$$F = W * \sqrt{(I_{C_T} - I_{C_S})^2}, \tag{7}$$

where the W is weight function shown in Fig. 2. I_{C_T} and I_{C_S} are the sets for target and simulated I-V points,respectively. Because the linear region of the I-V curve is rather sensitive, we define W to emphasize the relative importance of each I-V point. It decreases as the applied voltage V_{CC} increases. We evaluate the discrepancy for two I-V sets with the F.

Step 4: *Reproduction.* We adopt the *tournament selection* with floating-point operators as the selection strategy and this hybrid strategy not only selects better chromosomes but also keeps weak ones for few generations to achieve higher population diversity. For the crossover scheme, in HBT device model, all parameters to be optimized can be classified into four categories which represent different numerical constraints. We take an uniform crossover scheme [7]; and based on our simulation experience, it is more effective than single and two-point crossover schemes. Finally, the mutation strategy changes the mutation rate dynamically to keep the population diversity.

4 Solution Results and Discussion

Figure 3 shows the comparison between multiple I-V curves evolution with and without the weight function after 300 generations. The evolutionary I-V curves with applying weight function achieve the target I-V curves rapidly, and it has a good evolution behavior. The importance of weight function introduced here not only redirects the evolution trend to better direction but also reduces the searching space in this multiple objective evolution problem, and the efficiency can be obtained.

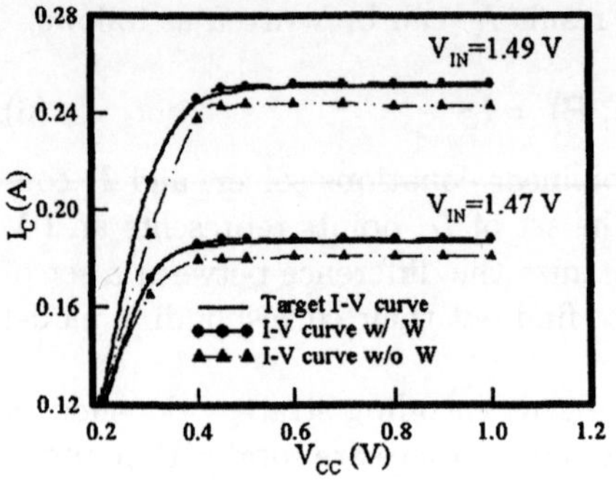

Fig. 3. A comparison of the method with and without the proposed weight function for multiple I-V curves optimization.

In addition, Fig. 4. shows the fitness score convergence behavior for the multiple I-V curves evolution with or without the dynamic mutation technique. The results suggest that the dynamic mutation scheme with floating-point operators keeps the population diversity and finally has better evolutionary results.

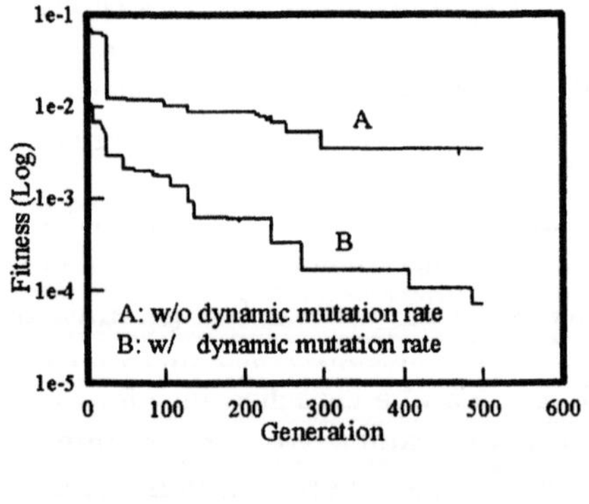

Fig. 4. A comparison of the method with and without the proposed dynamic mutation rate scheme.

Figure 5 shows the evolutions of the I-V curve. We start from an arbitrary I-V curves and it will approach to the desired final I-V curve step by step. Based on the MI and GA methods, the above process, from a given I-V curve to the final optimal I-V curve, is solved and evolved automatically. Compared with the conventional trial and error methodology to extract optimal parameters of the circuit model, our novel approach successfully reduces the complex procedures and simulation time significantly.

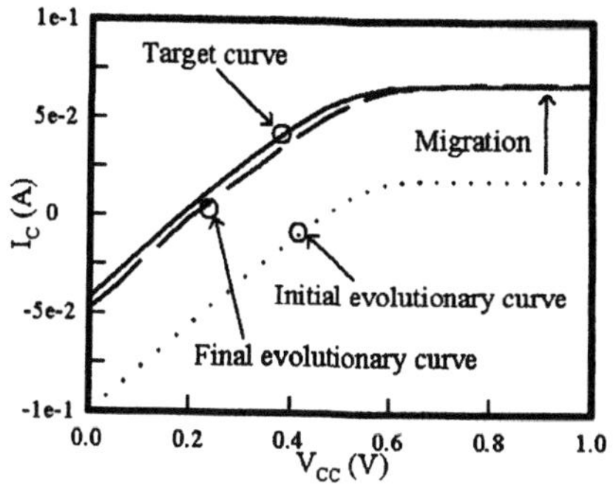

Fig. 5. An illustration for the migration processes of the I-V curve optimization.

5 Conclusions

In this paper, we have successfully developed a semiconductor device parameters extraction methodology with the MI method and GA methods. This simulation approach for a HBT device has been developed for its operation in the DC condition. The proposed method relies on the robust MI and the intelligence of the GA methods proposed here. Numerical results, fitness, and convergent behavior for HBT device characterization are presented to show the robustness and efficiency of this method. In the future work, we will extend this method for advanced VLSI devices and RF circuit simulation.

References

1. K. F. Man, et al., (1998) Genetic Algorithm for Control and Signal Processing. Springer.
2. R. Menozzi, et al., (1996) Small signal modeling for microwave FET linear circuits based on a genetic algorithm. IEEE Trans. Circ. Syst. -I, vol. 43, pp. **839-847**.
3. D. R. Pehlke and D. Pavlidis, (1992) Evaluation of the factors determining HBT high-frequency performance by direct analysis of S-parameter data. IEEE Trans. Microwave Theory Techn., vol. 40, pp. **2367-2373**.
4. Y. Li, et al., (2001) A New Parallel Adaptive Finite Volume Method for the Numerical Simulation of Semiconductor Devices. Comput. Physics Commun. **142**, 285-289.
5. Y. Li, et al., (1999) A Novel Approach for the Two-Dimensional Simulation of Submicron MOSFET's Using Monotone Iterative Method. IEEE International Symposium of VLSI Technology, Systems, and Applications, Taipei, June, 1999, **27-30**.
6. K.-Y. Huang, et al., (2001) A Computational Efficient Method for HBT Intermodulation Distortions and Two-Tone Characteristics Simulation. Simulation of Semiconductor Processes and Devices. Springer, Verlag Wien, **226-229**.
7. W. M. Spears and K. De Jong. (1991) One the Virtues of Parameterized Uniform Crossover. The Fourth International Conference on Genetic Algorithm, **230-236**.

Rule Extraction from Trained Neural Network with Evolutionary Algorithms

Urszula Markowska–Kaczmar[1], Marcin Chumieja[2]

[1,2]Wrocław University of Technology,Wyb.Wyspiańskiego 27, 50–270 Wrocław, Poland
Kaczmar@ci.pwr.wroc.pl

Abstract This paper describes a solution to the problem of incomprehensibility of the neural network by introducing simultaneously working Evolutionary Algorithms as a tool for extracting set of rules in the form of *if – then*. Each Evolutionary Algorithm is working for searching rules describing one class, which is recognized by a Neural Network. The proposed method has been tested on real domains in order to analyze its behavior under various conditions. A comparison with other rule extraction methods is presented as well.

1 Introduction

The knowledge embedded in the neural network (NN) is generally considered incomprehensible. This can be seen as a big limitation of NN because real applications need the integration of symbolic and connectionist approach. To solve this problem several approaches have been suggested in the literature. They can be divided into three groups. Local methods try to analyse behaviour of a single neuron in the hidden and output layers and they describe it in a form of rules defining the neuron activity (KT [3], Subset, M of N [2]). Different approach is used in global methods (black box methods). They do not investigate an activity of single neuron in a NN but they concentrate on behaviour of a whole network treating it as a black box (BRE [7], VIA [6]). Third possibility is called eclectic method. It combines some features from both of previous methods [4]. This paper describes a method to the problem of a knowledge extraction from trained NN by introducing Evolutionary Algorithm (EA). Presented solution belongs to the global methods. It means that rules are evaluated only on the basis of the input patterns and the NN answers. There are not special limitations on a type of NN, although described later experiments were made with MLP solving a classification problem.

2 Problem Formulation

The main objective of our research is to develop evolutionary algorithm (called GEX) to generate a set of crisp rules describing internal representation of mapping learned by a neural network solving a classification task. A typical classification problem made by NN can be described as follows. A set of examples or patterns is described by a vector of attributes $x=[x_1, \ldots x_k]$. Each attribute x_i is an important feature of an example. Each attribute is associated with one of NN input. At the moment we limited the type of an attribute to continuous values from a given range. Each pattern is classified by NN into one of the mutually exclusive class from a set of classes $C=\{C_1, \ldots, C_N\}$. The class is shown by the NN output vector $y=[y_1,..,y_k]$, where only one y_j is equal to 1 and it corresponds to class C_j. Others y_i are equal to 0. The role of EAs is search of a set of rule describing the way of classification made by NN. Each rule has a form given by (1):

$$IF\ condition(x_1)\ AND\ \ldots\ AND\ condition(x_k)\ THEN\ C_j \quad (1)$$

where part *condition* (x_i) can take one of the following form: x_i belongs to the range (X_b, X_h), x_i does not belong to the range (X_b, X_h), x_i is greater than X, x_i is less than X. Symbol x_i is an input of NN corresponding to the given attribute, X_b, X_h and X are limit values, C_j is a class.

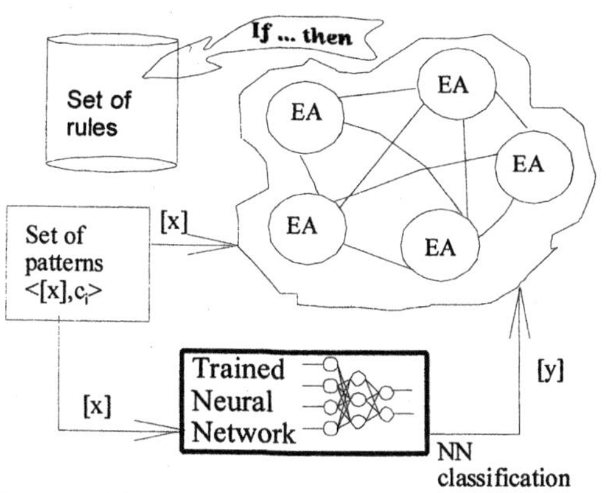

Fig. 1. Schema of the data flow in the GEX system

An extraction of the set of rules describing NN can be seen as a multimodal search for EA. In our approach there are many simultaneously working EAs (fig. 1), where each of them searches for rules describing one class recognized by a NN. From time to time some individuals with a small fitness function migrate to another population. After each generation rules are evaluated. To realize this task input patterns *[x]* are sequentially passed to the rules received in a given generation. For each pattern one looks for the fired rule. The consistency between the answer *[y]* of NN and the conclusion part C_i of fired rule for a given input pattern is the basis of the rule evaluation for EA (fig.1). The best rules from each generation update the set of extracted rules. At each step of evolution the set of extracted rules can be assessed on the basis of fidelity and the patterns covering.

3 Evolutionary Algorithm

In our approach one individual of EA represents one rule. A population is a set of rules (individuals), which have the same class in the conclusion part. The number of populations (EAs) is equal to the number of classes in the training set of NN. The evolution of each population proceeds independently. In each population operators of selection, crossover and mutation are applied. Mechanism of migration is implemented as well. It moves week individuals from one population to another.

During this process the conclusion of individual is changed for the class of the population, where it lands up.

A chromosome consists of genes (fig.2) describing conditions and one gene representing a conclusion of the rule indicating a class of individual. The number of genes designating the conditions is constant and equal to the number of NN inputs. Successive gene corresponds to the condition referring to the successive input of NN. A special flag before each gene with the condition informs about its activity. In such a way each individual phenotype (the rule) has variable length. This approach allows acquiring more general rules with a less number of conditions. Each gene representing a condition includes the following elements:

- *a flag of activity* – if set to one, it means that this condition takes a part in the rule,
- X_b, X_h – limit values defining a range,
- *operator of comparison* – which in combination with limit values gives one of the form of condition described in the previous section.

All elements have different way of coding. Operator of comparison is integer coded, flag is binary coded while limit values are real coded. Owing to this assumption, with reference to the applied algorithm the term evolutionary algorithm is being used in this paper. Mutation and crossover do not act to the gene describing the conclusion part. It represents the population, where the individual is living and it is changed only during a migration.

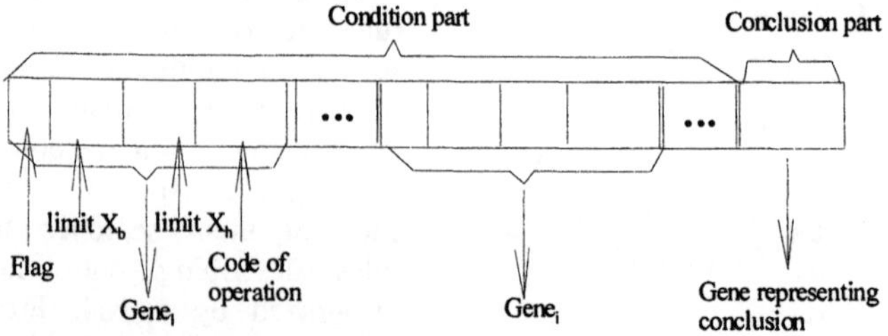

Fig. 2. Representation of a chromosome

Evaluation of rules is based on *accuracy* of rule which is defined by relation: *correctFires / Fires. Fires* describes how many times the rule was fired during the presentation of the patterns set, *CorrectFires* says how many times the rule was fired and the conclusion of the rule was identical with the NN answer on the pattern which caused the firing of rule. In the rule evaluation an answer of NN serves as an oracle. We assumed that extracted set of rules has to imitate as faithful as possible NN. The NN training to a satisfactory level is an important first step of rule extraction. According to [8] the fitness function of individual is calculated as follows (2):

$$eval = accuracy - 1.96 * \sqrt{\frac{accuracy'*(1.0 - accuracy')}{fires + 1}} \qquad (2)$$

where *accuracy'* is defined by *correctFires / (fires+1)*.

In our system three types of crossover operators are implemented: one-point, two-points and uniform. The mutation operator is used for each gene representing a condition. Each element creating such gene is mutated in a different way. Flag *activity* is mutated in a standard way. Limits X_b, X_h are random increased or decreased in a random value. Mutation of the comparison operator consists in random choosing a new operator. Each population of rules is evaluated on the basis of consistency with an answer of NN for all patterns in the set of patterns. Roulette wheel is applied to the selection of individuals to the new population. In the next step, the candidates to the crossover operation are chosen and crossover operator is initiated. Then in a new population individuals are mutated and at the end, if it is necessary, their genes are repaired.

4 Set of Extracted Rules

After each generation the best individuals (rules) update a set of rules (fig.1). A high coefficient of *accuracy* and *classCovering* characterizes a candidate to update the set of rules. The latter coefficient is defined by relation *correctFires / classPatternsCount*. In this relation *classPatternsCount* is the number of patterns for which an answer of NN is equal to a conclusion of the evaluated rule. *CorrectFires*, *accuracy* have the same meaning like in the section 3. Given rule r_l is added to the actual set of rules if it does not contain more general rule according to the definition 1. If a new rule is added to the set of rules all less general rules are removed from it.

Definition 1: Rule *r1* is more general than *r2* if the set of examples covered by *r2* is a subset of examples covered by *r1*.

In order to receive a classification of a given pattern, inference engine examines the set of rules in a predefined sequential order. All fired rules are identified. Next, the rule with the biggest fitness function from active rules is chosen. A conclusion of this rule is a result of classification made by the set of rules.

To evaluate a set of extracted rules two coefficients are defined: *covering* and *fidelity*, respectively in (3) and (4):

$$covering = classifiedCount\,/\,patternsCount \tag{3}$$

where *patternsCount* is the number of examples in the set of patterns while *classifiedCount* is the number of patterns from this set, which were classified by the set of extracted rules. In eq.4 *CorrectClassified* is the number of correct classification of patterns made by the set of rules in the meaning that they have the same result as the neural network classification.

$$fidelity = correctClassified\,/\,classifiedCount \tag{4}$$

These two coefficients evaluate a quality of the set of extracted rules in the presented bellow experiments.

5 Experimental Results

The proposed method was tested on the well known data sets: *Iris*, *Breast Cancer* and *Wine* from UCI Repository. The results are shown in Table 1. The experiments were made using 10-*fold cross-validation* method. In all experiments MLP was used with learning coefficient = 0.01 and momentum = 0.5. The error and the architecture of the

NN (in the following scheme: input – hidden – output number of neurons) for each experiment are shown separately for each database in Table 1.

Table 1. The results of experiments evaluating GEX method of the rule extraction

	Iris		Breast-cancer		Wine	
Number of patterns	50/50/50		456/227		59/71/46	
Input/output attributes	4/3		9/2		13/3	
The NN architecture	*4 – 4 – 3*		*9 –5 – 2*		*13 – 7 – 3*	
The NN Train error	0.003		0.005		*0.0005*	
	Avg	*StdDev*	*Avg*	*StdDev*	*Avg*	*StdDev*
Training set covering	100.0%	0.0%	99.2%	1.3%	100.0%	0.0%
Training set fidelity	97.5%	1.3%	97.1%	1.3%	94.5%	4.3%
Test set covering	99.7%	1.5%	99.4%	1.2%	99.7%	1.3%
Test set fidelity	99.0%	2.4%	97.0%	2.0%	91.6%	7.4%
Rule Number (*avg*)	4.7	1.3	11.2	3.6	55.9	11.48

The number of individuals in each population was equal to 30. The probability of mutation for activity = 0.1, for limits = 0.15, for operation = 0.1. In the experiments only uniform crossover operator was used with probability = 0.2 and the probability of change = 0.2. Each experiment consists of 50 generations of EA. The results are presented as an average from 25 experiments for each database. In Table 1 are given also the number of patterns in database with splitting for each class. The number of input attributes is equal to the number of the NN inputs. The number of output attributes of database is equal to the number of classes and to the number of the NN outputs. In Table 2 there is one of the best sets of rules received for *Iris* database. One can notice that the number of rules is small and rules are very comprehensible.

Table 2. An example of the set of rules for Iris database

IF (PetalLen>=4.76) THEN **Virginica**

IF (PetalLen>=2.08 and PetalLen<=5.02) AND (PetalW>=0.85 and PetalW<=2.49) THEN **Versicolour**

IF (PetalLen<=2.18) THEN **Setosa**

We compared the GEX method of the rule extraction with results received by another approaches *A.Mozer* [1] and *FullRe* [5] that use continuous values as well. In these papers the quality of extracted set of rules was evaluated by the *performance* coefficient which is defined by *correct number classification / number of all patterns*. This coefficient can be easily received by (6):

$$performance = covering * fidelity \quad (6)$$

Table 3. The comparison of GEX method with other rule extraction techniques

	Iris		Breast-cancer		Breast-cancer	
Proportion of train / test patterns	90/60		50%/50%		10-fold cross-validation	
Method	*FullRE*	*GEX*	*FullRE*	*GEX*	*A. Mozer*	*GEX*
Training set performance	96.63%	98.85%	96.77%	92.03%	96.3%	96.3%
Test set performance	98.36%	98.14%	95.61%	91.38%	95.2%	96.4%

In Table 3 there are results of comparison to other cited methods. In order to compare methods on the same basis we assumed the same proportion of patterns in the training and testing sets as authors reported in their papers. It can be observed that GEX has comparable *performance* to other methods and in some cases even better.

6 Summary

In the paper we described a new rule extraction technique performing on the basis of simultaneously working EAs. Rule extraction is very intensive search especially for continuous input variables so the use of evolutionary algorithm seemed to be a very good idea. All presented experiments have confirmed this hypothesis. The method can be used to all architectures of the NN. It does not depend nor on the NN complexity either the nature of application. It was able to extract rules for the well known *Iris*, *Breast Cancer* and *Wine* databases with satisfying results, comparable with other reported techniques. It can deal with continuous data values without any binarization or discretization. It does not need predefined rule. At the moment it is dedicated only to continuous input variables what seems to be more difficult case for rule extraction. From other point of view it can be seen as a limitation of described approach because it is difficult to find database containing only continuous data. To avoid this obstacle we plan to develop our system to process other than continuous data as well. More experiments are needed to evaluate a scalability of the proposed method.

References

1. Alexander, J.A., Mozer, M.C.: Template-based procedures for neural network interpretation, Neural Networks 12 (1999) 479–498
2. Andrews, R.: Survey and critique of techniques for extracting rules from trained artificial neural networks. Knowledge–Based Systems, Volume: 8, Issue: 6, December, (1995) 373–389
3. Fu L., M.: Rule Generation from neural network. IEEE Transactions on Systems, Man and Cybernetics vol. 24, No. 8. August (1994) 1114–1124
4. Setiono, R.: Extracting rules from pruned neural networks for breast cancer diagnosis. Artificial Intelligence in Medicine, Volume: 8, Issue: 1, February, (1996) 37– 51
5. Taha, I., Gosh, J.: Symbolic interpretation of artificial neural networks, Tech. Report TR-97-01-106, the Computer and Vision Research Center, University of Texas, Austin, 1996.
6. Thrun, S.: Extracting rules from artificial neural networks with distributed representation. Proceedings of the Eleventh International Conference on Machine Learning, New Brunswick, NJ. Morgan Kaufman
7. Tickle, A., Orlowski, M., Diedrich, J.: A methodology for extracting rules from trained neural networks. Rules and Networks: Proceedings of the Rule Extraction From Trained Artificial Neural Networks Workshop, Queensland University of Technology, Neurocomputing Research Center QUT NRC, April (1996) 90–102
8. Weiters T., Paredis J.: Genetic Rule Induction at an Intermediate Level. Knowledge Based Systems 15 (2002) 85–94

Genetic Algorithm for Observer Parameters Tuning in Sensorless Induction Motor Drive

Andrzej Przybył, przybyl@kik.pcz.czest.pl, Jerzy Jelonkiewicz jelon@kik.pcz.czest.pl

Technical University of Częstochowa, Department of Computer Engineering

Keywords. Genetic Algorithms, Flux Observer, Induction Motor

Abstract. The paper presents an example of genetic algorithm applied to speed adaptive flux observer parameters tuning in sensorless induction motor drive. The algorithm concerns an optimal gain matrix and PI controller gain coefficients tuning. The gain matrix is implemented in a neural network. Two methods of weights obtaining in the network is proposed. Presented approach selects an optimal operating point of the observer in the presence of measurement noise and inaccurate knowledge of mathematical model parameters.

1 Introduction

Induction motors are used in modern drive systems quite often because of very good dynamics and reliability. However to achieve this dynamics, the knowledge about non-measurable internal state of the machine is required e.g. rotor magnetic flux. State observers are often used to obtain information about the flux and rotor speed allowing the elimination of expensive and delicate speed sensor, e.g. optical encoder. Such an observer, like speed-adaptive flux observer, seems to be very attractive to apply in sensorless induction motor drive. Unfortunately practical realization meets many problems like long processing time and difficult tuning of gain matrix and gain coefficient values of PI controller [7]. This paper proposes the method of optimal parameters tuning in the specified work condition i.e. assumed value of measurement noise and difference between considered and real motor parameters.

2 Problem formulation

The description of induction motor uses well known mathematical model [4]. The model is represented by the state equation (1.1) with stator current and rotor flux as state variables. All values are represented in relative quantities fixed to the stationary reference frame. The block diagram of such an observer is presented in fig.1.

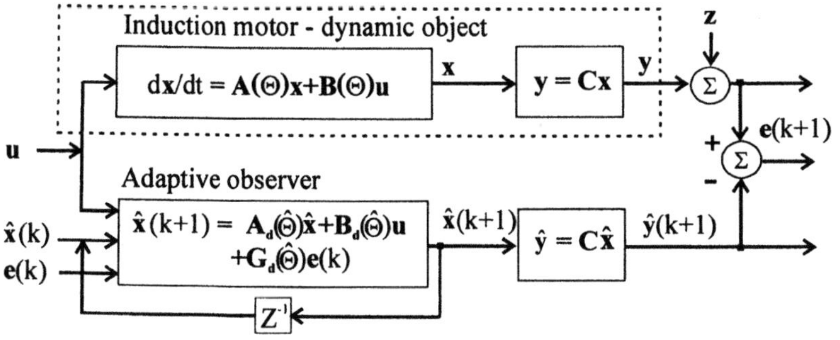

Fig. 1. Block diagram of the observer

$$\hat{\mathbf{x}}(k+1) = \mathbf{A}_d(\hat{\Theta})\hat{\mathbf{x}}(k) + \mathbf{B}_d(\hat{\Theta})\mathbf{u}(k) + \mathbf{G}_d(\hat{\Theta})\mathbf{e}(k) \qquad (1.1)$$

$$\hat{\mathbf{y}}_{k+1} = \mathbf{C}\hat{\mathbf{x}}_{k+1}$$

$$\hat{\omega}_m(k) = K_I \sum_{i=0}^{k} \varepsilon_\omega(i)T + K_P \varepsilon_\omega(k)T \qquad (1.2)$$

$$\varepsilon_\omega(i) = e_{1\alpha}(i)\hat{\psi}_{r\beta}(i) - e_{1\beta}(i)\hat{\psi}_{r\alpha}(i)$$

where $\mathbf{A}_d(\mathbf{\Theta}) = \begin{bmatrix} \mathbf{a}_{11} & \mathbf{a}_{12} \\ \mathbf{a}_{21} & \mathbf{a}_{22} \end{bmatrix}, \mathbf{B}_d(\mathbf{\Theta}) = \begin{bmatrix} \mathbf{b}_{11} \\ \mathbf{b}_{21} \end{bmatrix}, \mathbf{C} = \begin{bmatrix} 1 & 0 \end{bmatrix}, \mathbf{G}_d(\hat{\mathbf{\Theta}}) = \begin{bmatrix} \mathbf{g}_{1,1} \\ \mathbf{g}_{2,1} \end{bmatrix}$

are system, input, output and gain matrix respectively,
$\mathbf{u} = [\mathbf{u}_1] = [u_{s\alpha} + j \cdot u_{s\beta}], \mathbf{x} = [\mathbf{x}_1 \quad \mathbf{x}_2]^T = [i_{s\alpha} + j \cdot i_{s\beta} \quad \psi_{r\alpha} + j \cdot \psi_{r\beta}]^T$ are input and state vector and $\mathbf{\Theta} = \{\omega_m, r_s, r_r, x_s, x_M, x_r\}$ - induction motor model parameters. All matrix and vectors have complex elements.

The observer is represented by the linear non-stationary matrix equation (1.1) and by equation (1.2) that describe the adaptation process of the rotor speed. The equation is presented in the discrete form with the time constant T=409.6us.

The errors that appear on the observer output are generated mainly by: difference between considered and real motor parameters $\mathbf{\Theta} \neq \hat{\mathbf{\Theta}}$, measurement noise and finally differences in starting condition for the object and the observer.

If the observer works properly, the error caused by the last factor fades to zero after a short time. The other factors are still present and could cause incorrect operation of the system. However there is a feedback in the observer with a gain matrix that corrects state variables values every processing step. The output error is minimized if gain matrix and PI controller are properly tuned. The optimal gain matrix needs to be a function of changeable motor parameters $\mathbf{G}_d = \mathbf{G}_d(\hat{\mathbf{\Theta}})$.

3 Genetic algorithm in parameters tuning

Optimal gain matrix is a function of estimated parameters $\mathbf{G}_d=\mathbf{G}_d(\hat{\Theta})$ which may change in time, particularly $\hat{\omega}_m$ and sometimes $\hat{r}_s$ or $\hat{r}_r$. A simple neural network (fig.2) is proposed to realize this function. The inputs to the network are only these parameters which changeability in time can be estimated e.g. $\hat{\omega}_m$, $\hat{r}_r$.

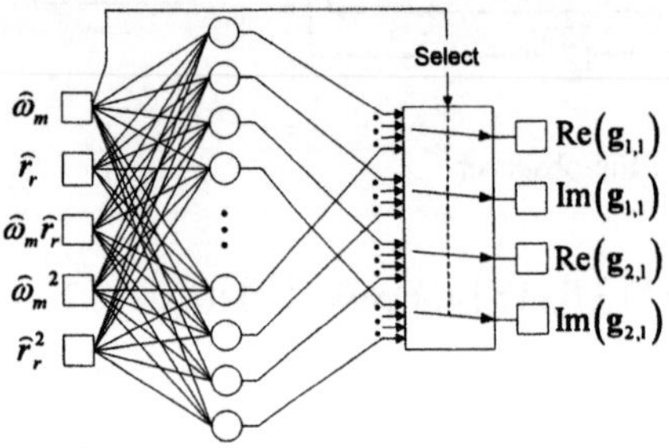

Fig. 2. Neural networks for the function $G_d = G_d(\hat{\Theta})$

The value of $\hat{r}_r$ can be estimated by the external thermal observer or its averaged values may be used. In the project the second approach is considered however there is a possibility to add the thermal observer to the system in the future. Presented neural network is based on the GMDH method [3] in which good accuracy is achieved even with one layer of linear neurons. Several groups of neurons approximate nonlinear function locally in different $\hat{\omega}_m$ value space regions. A kind of fuzzy-multiplexer, on the output, selects one of the group of neurons smoothly on the basis of $\hat{\omega}_m$ value. This is necessary because of very wide range of this parameter. Of course, there is also possible to use different kind of neural networks.

Two methods for such gain matrix parameters tuning are proposed:

- direct – it consist in fitness function calculation for various neural networks weights $\mathbf{W}^i$ and PI gain coefficients $\mathbf{K}^i$: $Q^i=Q(\mathbf{W}^i,\mathbf{K}^i)$ (2.1,2.2a)
- indirect – it consist in fitness function calculation for various observer pole locations that are specified by $\mathbf{P}^i$ parameters (fig.3) and various $\mathbf{K}^i$ values : $Q^i=Q(\mathbf{P}^i,\mathbf{K}^i)$ (2.1,2.2a). After tuning process, the required gain matrix can be determined on the basis of obtained parameters. Finally, neural networks weights $\mathbf{W}^i$ can be determined by the back-propagation algorithm. In this method only this pole locations are considered which guarantee stability of the observer without adaptation. This can be considered as necessary condition for stability of the speed-adaptive observer [2].
  Indirect method is found faster comparing to the first one.

In the indirect method $\mathbf{P^i} = \{m^i_{1,0}, m^i_{1,1}, a^i_1, m^i_{2,0}, m^i_{2,1}, a^i_2\}$ contains the factors of the observer pole locations in the z-complex co-ordinate system (fig 3).

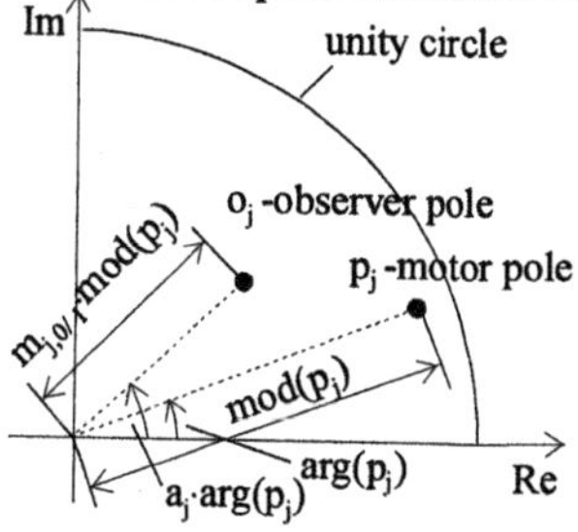

Fig. 3. Observer pole locations as a function of motor pole locations and $\mathbf{P^i}$ factors in the z-complex co-ordinate system; $m^i_{j,0}, m^i_{j,1}$ =0...1 - j-pole module ratio, (j=1,2) for $|\omega_m|$=0 and $|\omega_m|$=1 respectively; $a^i_{j,1}$ =0...2 - j-pole argument ratio constant for all ω_m values; i –index of a chromosome in a population

Moreover PI controller gain is defined as $\mathbf{K^i} = \{K_P, K_I\}$ and finally neural networks weights are $\mathbf{W^i}$; i- index of a chromosome in genetic algorithm where i=1..P ; P is the population size.

The first method is easier to implement however it needs longer processing time to find the satisfactory solution. The drawback of this method is that the pole locations are tested in all possible regions, even non-stabile ones. Whereas in the indirect method, searching is limited only to the probable, stable regions of the pole locations. Moreover indirect method does not consider the error caused by neural network implementation of $\mathbf{G}_d(\hat{\Theta})$ so its accuracy should be as high as possible.

The second method is selected in the paper. Sufficient accuracy of the NN (neural network) realization is obtained with the help of the GMDH method, which was confirmed in many simulations.

A fitness function which is required by genetic algorithm is defined in the form (2.1). Their values varies from 0 to 100 for the worst and the best parameters set.

$$\mathrm{ff}^i = 100 \cdot 0.01 / \left(0.01 + \sqrt{Q^i / C_1}\right) \tag{2.1}$$

$$Q^i = \sum_{l=1}^{L} \left(\sum_{k=1}^{N} \left(\mathbf{e}(k)^T \mathbf{e}(k) + \mathbf{e}^{\Theta}(k)^T \mathbf{e}^{\Theta}(k) \right) \right) \tag{2.2a}$$

$$\mathbf{e}(k) = \mathbf{x}(k) - \hat{\mathbf{x}}(k), \qquad \mathbf{e}^{\Theta}(k) = \omega_m{}^i(k) - \hat{\omega}_m{}^i(k) \tag{2.2b}$$

where C_1 is positive constant, N – number of time steps in simulation; l=1..L – index of simulation for successively tested extreme values of observer parameters and measurement errors; $L=2^{(2+4)}=64$ - multiplicity of simulation, results from system outputs number ($i_{s\alpha}$, $i_{s\beta}$) and number of modified parameters (r_s, r_r, x_s, x_r); $\mathbf{W^i}$, $\mathbf{P^i}$, $\mathbf{K^i}$ – successively tested parameters sets.

Performed simulations include ramp acceleration of the motor with constant U/f and deceleration down to ω_m=0.1 (fig. 4, 5). The tests are carried out for all combination of extreme values in the (2+4)-dimensional space created by observer parameters variations and measurement errors. Used approach can detect the sen-

sitivity of the observer to motor parameters changes. In the experiment the parameters varied $\pm 25\%$ for $\hat{r}_s, \hat{r}_r$ and $\pm 5\%$ for $\hat{x}_s$ and $\hat{x}_r$ which is well known assumption for this type of motor [7]. The value added to the output simulates measurement error and noise. Its value is $\pm 2\%$ of the rated signal.
A parameters tuning process was divided into two stages. The first one was the classical genetic algorithm repeated tens times for population with fifty chromosomes. In the second stage the best chromosome was exposed to the process of simulated annealing [3], where approximately 50% genes in the chromosome were modified, only a fraction of percent around their actual value. This approach speeds up the process of parameters tuning considerably and even after a few hundred iterations it can be stopped with satisfactory results.

4 Results

Obtained results of simulations confirmed that observer works better if measurement noises and motor parameters inaccuracy in tuning process is taken into account. Especially the motor parameters inaccuracy influences much the observer stability (fig.4b,c). System which parameters were tuned with the help of proposed method works satisfactory even with the presence of disturbances (fig.5).

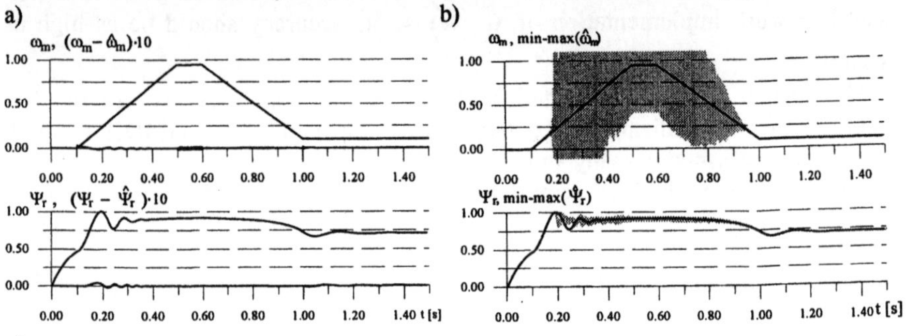

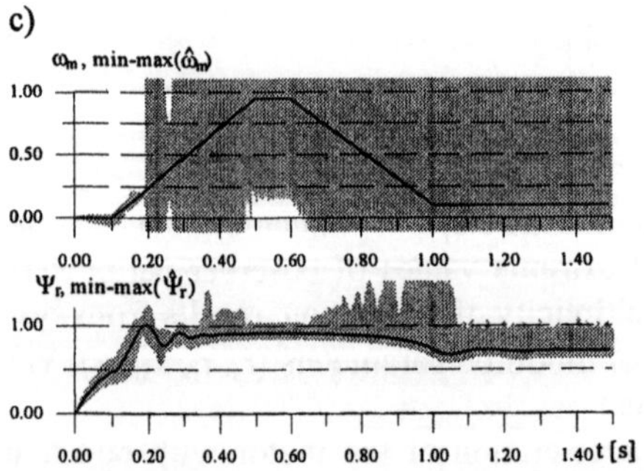

$$\mathbf{P}^i = \{m^i_{1,0}, m^i_{1,1}, a^i_1, m^i_{2,0}, m^i_{2,1}, a^i_2\} =$$
$$\{\ 0.331, 0.202, 1.714, 1.000, 0.995, 0.642\ \}$$
$$\mathbf{K}^i = \{K_P, K_I\} = \{\ 10.9, 49.4\ \}$$

Fig. 4. Transients of observer for parameters tuned for ideal case (no noises, accurately known motor model parameters): a) ideal case transient – ff=99.78; b) simulation with measurement noises –ff=65.29; c) simulation with motor model parameters detuned – ff=53.43. Black curve – reference transients, grey curve – observer min-max bands (l=1..L)

Static errors are the results of assumed range of motor parameters changes and are typical for this kind of observer, particularly in the low speed region [7]. Moreover in the tests the worst cases of motor parameter distortion were considered, which do not exist in real systems.

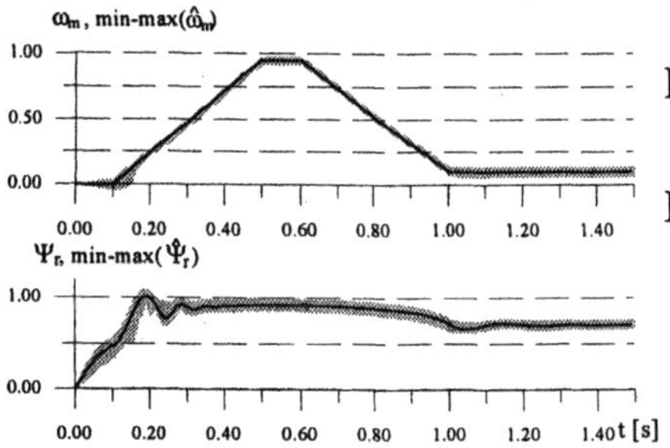

$$\mathbf{P}^{\mathrm{i}} = \left\{ m_{1,0}^{i}, m_{1,1}^{i}, a_{1}^{i}, m_{2,0}^{i}, m_{2,1}^{i}, a_{2}^{i} \right\} =$$

{ 0.285, 0.320, 1.588, 0.996, 0.84 0.224 }

$$\mathbf{K}^{\mathrm{i}} = \left\{ K_{P}, K_{I} \right\} = \{\ 10.0,\ 16.7\ \}$$

Fig. 5. Transients of observer for parameters tuned with proposed method including noises and inaccuracy of motor model parameters – ff=95.22. Black curve – reference transients, grey curve – observer min-max bands (l=1..L)

5 Conclusions

In the paper a method of parameters tuning in the speed-adaptive flux observer has been proposed. This method, using genetic algorithm, minimizes negative influence of measurement noise and motor parameters spread into performance of the system. As proved in the tests described approach improves the state observer design.

Presented solution has also general aspect and can be used in an observer of any other physical process.

References

1. Ogata K. (1987) Discrete-Time Control Systems, Prentice-Hall
2. Vas P. (1998) Sensorless Vector and Direct Torque Control, Oxford University Press
3. Duch W., Korbicz J., Rutkowski L., Tadeusiewicz R. (2000) Neural Networks. Biocybernetics and Biomedical Engineering (in Polish) vol. 6, AOW EXIT, Warsaw
4. Tunia H., Kaźmierkowski M. (1987), Converter Drive Automatics (in Polish), PWN, Warsaw
5. Mrugalski M., Janczak A. (2000), Evolutionary programming-based observers for nonlinear systems, Neural Networks And Soft Computing, Zakopane.
6. Kaczorek (1981), Control Theory (in Polish) vol.2, PWN , Warsaw
7. P.Wojsznis (2001), Analysis of Rotor Flux Estimators in Sensorless Induction Motor Vector Control (in Polish), Doctoral Dissertation, Wrocław

This work was sponsored by KBN, under grant 8 T10A 019 21.

MOVING OBJECTS IN THE PROBLEM OF PATH PLANNING BY EVOLUTIONARY COMPUTATION

Roman Śmierzchalski*, Andrzej Łebkowski**

*Gdynia Maritime University, Morska st. 83, 81-225 Gdynia, Poland,
** Technical University of Gdansk, Faculty of Electrical and Control Engineering

Abstract. A modified, new version of the evolutionary algorithm (of the EP/N - Evolutionary Planner /Navigator) has been used for computing the optimum path of a moving object in a given dynamic environment. The program estimating a safe path of the object in collision was developed. By taking into account certain boundaries of the manoeuvring region, along with obstacles and other moving objects, the problem of avoiding collisions was reduced to a dynamic optimisation task with static and dynamic constrains. The introduction of a time parameter and moving constrains representing the objects is the main distinction of the new system. Results of using the program for estimating the object in dynamic environment are given for example of avoiding collision at sea.

1 Introduction

In the problem of safe path for the movable objects, we look for a route that is a compromise between the cost of necessary deviation from a given route, or from the optimum route leading to a target point, and the safety of passing round all static and dynamic obstacles, here bearing the name of strange movable objects. All paths, which meet the condition of avoiding the risk of collision to a satisfactory degree, make a set of permissible paths. Thus the task of determining the safe path is reduced to the choice of an optimum solution, or a subset of optimum solutions from the set of permissible paths, taking into account certain cost criteria and the need to satisfy, in any circumstances, the safety conditions for example safety distance.

In earlier work (R. Śmierzchalski [6][7][8]) the problem of path planing to avoid collisions with moved objects was formulated as the multi-criterion optimisation task. The attempt to estimate the safe path using genetic algorithms was presented by Furuhashi T. *et al.* [2]. In the overwhelming majority of the reviewed publications on automatic object guidance, the navigational process in the areas of intensive traffic was supported using expert systems. Widening the problem and on the basis of the evolutionary path guidance concept Michalewicz Z. [4], Michalewicz Z. and Xiao J. [5], Xiao J. *et al.* [17], Lin H-S *et al.* [3], Trojanowski K. and Michalewicz Z. [16], a modified version evolutionary planer was developed which took into consideration the specifics of the object guidance in difficult navigational passages by including the motion of other objects, using the evolutionary technique R. Śmierzchalski [9][11][12][13][14], Śmierzchalski R., Z. Michalewicz [10] [15]. In the present work, the authors perform a new version of the EP/N (Evolutionary Planner /Navigator) algorithm, in which especial attention is paid to the path planing for fixed and moved constraints of the navigational area.

2 Selecting path by evolutionary algorithm

The compromise has to be reached between the costs of the diversion from an assumed, or the shortest route, and the acceptable safety of passing round static and dynamic constraints. Due to those contrasting criteria the problem can be reduced to a multi-criterion task for optimum path planning. In a sea variant, all paths whose vector of echo motion in a relative visualisation obtained from the radar system do not cross the area of danger defined by a safe distance D_b around the actual position of the object. The optimisation problem consists in selecting the optimum path from the permissible paths with respect to an assumed fitness function. The introduced changes include different types of constraints resulting from the new environment in which the objects move, especially dynamic constraints representing other moving objects. In the software they also include new genetic operators, and time parameter for covering the assumed path. The most recent change made in the programme is the option of *on-line* path planing.

2.1 Environment – dynamic and static constraints

Kinetic modelling of the objects motion was used in the programme. The environment in the system EP/N consists of static and dynamic constraints. The static constraints represent land, channels, and other navigational constraints like as areas of traffic separation. Those areas are modelled by fixed polygons. Dynamic constraints represent the areas of danger around approaching objects. These areas are called domains and are modelled by hexagons. Their areas depend on the current navigational situation and assumed safety conditions – safety distance. In modelling the environment the dimension of the own object is neglected as very small compared to the dimensions of the domains of strange objects. The dynamics of the object is taken into consideration in the stage of steering along the already calculated safe path.

All strange objects are attributed moving domains (at course and speed determined by the radar system), although only some of them represent real collision threat. The distance of danger is selected by the operator depending on navigational conditions.

In the previous version of the programme the own object was assumed to move at a constant speed V along the entire path, and at the initial time instant t_0 the motion of strange objects was assumed steady. The present version makes it possible to introduce changes to the parameters of motion of the dynamic constraints. It also includes the mutation operator for the own object speed. The speed parameters of the dynamic objects, as determined by the radar system, include: bearing, distance, course and speed. In the evolutionary algorithm each path is attributed an instantaneous dynamic area connected with each individual moving strange object. The instantaneous position of the dynamic area with respect to the passing path is evaluated by time t, determined from the crossing point (x_{int}, y_{int}) of the path of the own object S with the path of the strange object. This crossing point (x_{int}, y_{int}) is considered the point of collision threat. The time needed for covering the distance from the starting point (x_0, y_0) to the crossing point (x_{int}, y_{int}) by the own object moving at speed V along path S is t. For the same time t the position of the domain of the strange object is calculated in a similar way and taken into account via its path. The static constraints are seen in the same way from all paths and do not have to be re-calculated. In the programme EP/N a new position of the domain is only calculated for the best individual in each population. The level of collision danger is determined using the depth of penetration of the constraint by the path.

2.2 Population individuals – chromosomes, genetic operators, fitness function and evolutionary algorithm

It was assumed that the passing path S is represented by a single individual - a chromosome. Each individual consists of genes, specified by co-ordinates (x_i, y_i), being the line segment s_i turning points. Linked, the line segments s_i determine the passing path S. All individuals in the population have common beginning and end points. The population consists of m individuals. Each individual, apart from the co-ordinates turning point (x_i, y_i) of the particular line segments is attributed the data int_i informing whether the next segment of the path is safe and whether the turning point does not enter the restricted dangerous areas. The first population is generated in a random way.. The individuals are reproduced by the genetic operators, this reproduction leading to their modification and possible creation of better offsprings.

In the evolutionary procedure suggest using nine genetic operators. Basing on three basic operations, as the reproduction, crossover, and mutation, they develop modified operators which execute specific functions modifying the passing path - the chromosome. This list of operators includes: soft mutation, mutation, adding a gene, swapping gene locations, crossing, smoothing, deleting a gene and individual repair, mutation of the speed.

In the evaluation procedure, each individual - path is attributed its fitness function, being its value for the examined problem. Such an evaluation of particular solutions in the population makes it possible to recognise and make a distinction between better and worse paths for the actual steering goal in the examined environment. The fitness function must include both the safety conditions, and the economic conditions resulting from the change in the route. The safety conditions are satisfied for a given path if it does not cross the constraints.

Evolutionary algorithms create a class of algorithms with adaptational random search (Goldberg (1989), Michalewicz (1996), Arabas (2001)). Their operation bases on probabilistic methods for creating a population of solutions. In the present case of the safe paths estimation, they are used for creating the population of passing paths, and finding the optimum solution within this population, i.e. the best possible path with respect to the fitness function. The list below shows an operational concept of the adaptation algorithm estimating the safe paths with moved objects, using the C++ language convention.

```
Evolutionary_algorithm()
{ int T; /*T - generation counter variable*/
    T = 0;
    input_data_for_parametrising_operation_of_evolutionary_algorithm();
    input_data_for_defining_environment();
    P(T) = creation_of_initial_chromosome_population();
    building_dynamic_obstacles();
    population_evaluation ( P(T) );
    while ( != terminating_conditions() )
   {T = T + 1;
    Op = operator_selection();
    Par = selection_of_parents_or_parent();
    offspring_creation_and_ introduction( Op, Par );
    building_dynamic_obstacles();
    population_evaluation ( P(T) );
    introduction_of_new_individual();
    selection_of_best_individual ( P(T) );
   } }
```

The multiple iteration process of transforming and creating new individuals, accompanied by the creation of new populations is carried on until the „stop" tests in the program are fulfilled.

3 Simulation studies

The simulation test were divided into three phases. In the first phase, passing paths obtained in the *off-line* mode were tested. Then the real motion was studied of the own object travelling along the assumed path and passing other objects. The level of identity was assessed with which the positions of passed objects – domains were calculated with respect to the own object. For the *on-line* version, a quality assessment was made for the calculated path on the basis of *on-line* calculations performed after changing parameters of motion of one or more dynamic constraints. The comparison was made for two environments characterised by a relatively high level of complexity.

The first case (Fig. 1) presents the situation in which the own object passes round four islands and four objects moving from different directions and at different speeds. Input parameters for the simulation, in which the population number was equal to 40, are shown in Fig. 1.

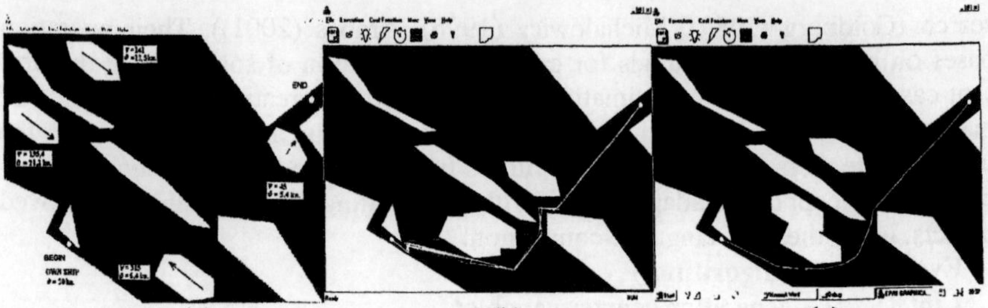

(a) (b) (c)

Fig. 1. Test environment No. 1. Mode: off-line. Generation=0 (a) Generation=500 (b), 2000 (c). Mode: off-line

Object path adaptations, made in the off-line mode after the own object has met four moving objects in a collision situation, are shown in **Fig. 1**, after 500, 2000 generations, respectively. The solution obtained after 2000 generations made it possible to pass round the islands, at the same time leaving aside the moving objects. Current speeds of the own object were individually calculated for each path segment which allowed the object to reach the target point in a safe way and the shortest possible time. The realisation of the proposed path optimised the object passage cost with respect both to safety and economic conditions, eliminating the risk of excessive approach to the passed objects.

4 Conclusions

The evolutionary method of evaluating the safe and optimum path of the own object in the environment with static and dynamic constraints is a new approach to the problem of avoiding collisions at sea. The performed tests lead to the following conclusions: evolutionary algorithms can be used for solving problems of avoiding collisions at sea, with the environment modelled in the form of polygons representing navigational constraints and strange object moving at changing speed and course, the evolutionary task of evaluating the object path in a collision situation is substituted by an adaptive search for a set of safe paths in the permissible space X and choosing from them the best possible path with respect to the adaptation function.

Acknowledgements

The research reported in this paper was supported by the DS 221 from the Polish State Committee for Scientific Research.

References

[1] Arabas J. Lectures of evolutionary algorytms (in polish) WNT, 2001.

[2] Furuhashi T, Nakaoka K., Uchikawa Y.; *A Study on Classifier System for Finding Control Knowledge of Multi-Input Systems.* (F. Herrera, J.L.Verdegay Editors) Genetic Algorithms and Soft Computing, Phisica-Verlang, 1996.

[3] Lin H.-S., Xiao, J., Michalewicz Z.; *Evolutionary Algorithm for Path Planning in Mobile Robot Environment.* Proc. IEEE Int. Conf. Evolutionary Computation, Orlando, Florida 1994.

[4] Michalewicz Z.; *Genetic Algorithms + Data structures = Evolution Programs.* Spriger-Verlang, 3rd edition 1996.

[5] Michalewicz Z., Xiao J.; *Evaluation of Paths in Evolutionary Planner/Navigator.* Proceedings of the 1995 International Workshop on Biologically Inspired Evolutionary Systems, Tokyo, Japan 1995.

[6] Śmierzchalski R.; *The Application of the Dynamic Interactive Decision Analysis System to the Problem of Avoiding Collisions at the Sea.* (in Polish) 1st Conference Awioniki, Science Work no 45, Vol. 2, pp. 139-148, Jawor, Poland 1995.

[7] Śmierzchalski R; *The Decision Support System to Design the Safe Maneuver Avoiding Collision at Sea.* ISAS'96, pp. 95-103, Orlando, USA 1996.

[8] Śmierzchalski R.; *Multi-Criterion Modeling the Collision Situation at Sea for Application in Decision Support.* 5th International Symposium on Methods and Models in Automation and Robotics, Vol. 2, pp. 699-704, Międzyzdroje, Poland 1996.

[9] Śmierzchalski R.; *Path planning for object in collision situations at sea by evolutionary computation.* 4th IFAC Conference on Manoeuvring and Control of Marine, pp.693-698, Brijuni, Croatia 1997.

[10] Śmierzchalski R.; Michalewicz Z.; *Adaptive Modelling of a Object Path in Collision Situations.* Proc. 2nd IEEE World Congress on Computational Intelligence, ICEC'98, pp. 806-811, Alaska 1998.

[11] Śmierzchalski R.; *Speed Mutation Evolutionary Object Path Planning in Navigation Traffic Areas.* Proc. IFAC Conference Control Applications in Marine Systems 98, pp. 187-192, Fukuoka 1998.

[12] Śmierzchalski R.; *Static and Dynamic Constrains in Evolutionary Problem of Object's Path Planning at Sea.* Proc. 3rd World Multiconference on Systemics, Cybernetics and Informatics (SCI'99), pp. 1124-1130, Orlando 1999.

[13] Śmierzchalski R.; *Evolutionary path planning of object in navigation traffic areas.* Journal of Marine Sciences and Technology, Vol. 4, No 1, Springer, pp. 1-6, 1999.

[14] Śmierzchalski R.; *An Evolutionary Method of Object's Path Planning at Sea.* Proc. International Conference IEEE Intelligent Transportation System, pp. 907-912, Tokyo 1999.

[15] Śmierzchalski R., Michalewicz Z.; *Modeling of a Object Path in Collision Situations at Sea by Evolutionary Algorithm.* IEEE Transaction on Evolutionary Computation No. 3 Vol. 4, pp. 227-241, 2000.

[16] Trojanowski K., Michalewicz Z.; *Planning Path of Mobil Robot.* (in Polish) 1st Conference Evolutionary Algorithms, Międzyzdroje, Poland 1996.

[17] Xiao J.; Michalewicz Z., Zhang, L.; *Evolutionary Planner/Navigator: Operator Performance and Self-Tuning.* Proc. IEEE Int. Conf. Evolutionary Computation, Nagoya, Japan, May1996.

Determining Relevant Input Dimensions for the Self Organizing Map

Thorsten Bojer[1], Barbara Hammer[1], Marc Strickert[1], and Thomas Villmann[2]

[1] Department of Mathematics/Computer Science,
University of Osnabrück
D-49069 Osnabrück, Germany
[2] Clinic for Psychotherapy and Psychosomatic Medicine,
University of Leipzig, Karl-Tauchnitz-Straße 25, D-04107 Leipzig, Germany,

Abstract. We propose a method to determine the relevance of the different input dimensions for a self organizing map (SOM). First, a growing self organizing map is adapted to the data. Afterwards, the effect of the input dimensions on the clustering or the topology of the SOM, respectively, is computed and the data dimensions which are ranked low are pruned. The algorithm is applied to real life satellite image data. The results are verified via visualizing the data in RGB-images as well as explicitely computing the classification error.

1 Introduction

Kohonen's self organizing map provides a powerful and biologically motivated tool which computes a topologically adequate clustering of training data [8]. For this purpose, a lattice of neurons is adapted to the data such that the lattice which is chosen a priori fits the unknown topology of the data as good as possible. There exist various possibilities of further processing the SOM's output: a classification can be approximated by means of attaching labels or local linear maps to the single neurons; substituting the data by their nearest neurons provides a compact representation of the data; the lattice of the SOM allows data visualization as well as structured data mining [6–8,11,13]. Hence SOMs are widely used for both, supervised and unsupervised learning tasks in robotics, image processing, data mining, and other areas of applications. One crucial property of SOMs consists in the fact that they compute a topologically adequate representation of the data assumed the lattice is chosen appropriately. Hence various adaptations and modifications of the standard SOM exist in order to measure the degree of topology preservation or to adapt the lattice structure to the data [1–3,9,14].

Often, data are high dimensional. Satellite remote sensing image data comprise $5-7$ dimensions according to the spectra provided by the Landsat Thematic Mapper up to several hundred dimensions for hyperspectral imagers. The larger the dimensionality, the more storing capacities and processing time are required for data processing. Furthermore, adequate visualization and data mining become difficult for high dimensional data. Hence input pruning, i.e. determining relevant data dimensions, is a highly interesting topic [15]. This task is particularly challenging if unsupervised training methods like SOMs are considered. They do not provide a clear objective like the prediction error. It is necessary to find intrinsic characteristics of the unsupervised network instead. We will deal with pruning methods for SOMs and their application to Landsat TM data in the following. We use a growing

SOM (GSOM) for training in order to guarantee an adequate topology. We measure the importance of the input dimensions on the clustering or the topological structure, respectively. Afterwards, we prune the irrelevant dimensions in labeled satellite data for which the error can be quantified.

2 The Self Organizing Map

Assume a finite set of training data $X = \{x^1, \ldots, x^m\} \subset \mathbb{R}^n$ is given. We denote the components of a vector x by $(x_1, \ldots, x_n)$. A SOM as proposed by Kohonen [8] consists of a set of codebooks $w^1, \ldots, w^K \in \mathbb{R}^n$ together with a neighborhood structure. We write $i \leftrightarrow j$ iff codebooks w^i and w^j are neighbored. Denote by $N(i,j)$ the minimum length of a path from w^i to w^j in this graph. Often, the neighborhood graph has a regular low dimensional grid structure which can be specified by a tuple $n_1 \times \ldots \times n_d$, where d is the grid dimensionality and n_i is the number of neurons in the respective grid dimension. Denote by $R_i = \{x^j \mid |x^j - w^i| \leq |x^j - w^k| \; \forall k \neq i\}$ the receptive field of the i th codebook. After determining a neighborhood graph, the codebooks are trained with the recursive update

$$\textit{for all } i : w^i := w^i + \eta \cdot \mathrm{e}^{-\lambda \cdot N(i,i_0)}(x^j - w^i)$$

where $x^j \in X$ is chosen at random, i_0 denotes the winner neuron, i.e. $x^j \in R_{i_0}$, and η and λ are positive learning rates which are often decreased during training in order to ensure convergence. This algorithm spreads the codebooks onto the data such that the topology of the data matches the topology of the lattice of neurons.

Roughly speaking, topology preservation means that neurons number i and j are neighbored in the lattice of neurons, i.e. $i \leftrightarrow j$, iff the codebooks w^i and w^j are neighbored codebooks in the data manifold, i.e. $R_i \cap R_j \neq \emptyset$. There exist various approaches in order to state an exact definition or to compute the degree of neighborhood preservation in an efficient way [1–3,9,14]. Obviously, a faithful representation is possible iff the lattice of neurons which is chosen a priori fits the unknown topology of the training data. The GSOM generalizes the above learning algorithm such that the lattice is determined during training [2]. Starting from a minimum lattice, codebooks are added to an already existing lattice dimension or a new lattice dimension is attached during training depending on the observed deviation of the training data from the codebooks. GSOM has the advantage of preserving a regular grid structure whereby guaranteeing a maximum degree of topology preservation.

3 Relevance Measures

The experiments in [5,7,10] indicate that a considerable reduction of the input dimensionality is possible without loosing much information in several applications. At the same time, theoretical results as proved in [12] restrict the possibility of efficiently finding reduced representations for general data. Hence we have to rely on heuristics adapted to the specific situation we are dealing with. We propose pruning algorithms for SOM which are related to methods proposed for the neural gas algorithm and successfully applied to artificial data in [5]. We define a relevance function $F : \{1, \ldots, n\} \to \mathbb{R}$ such that a high value $F(I)$ indicates that dimension I is relevant, a low value $F(I)$ indicates that dimension I could be pruned. There exist various possibilities of defining F:

Dispersion: We measure to which extend the variation around the codebook vectors is reduced in the respective dimension; if the variation is considerably reduced then the respective input dimension is important:

$$F^1(I) = 1 - \frac{1}{K} \cdot \sum_{j=1}^{K} \frac{\sum_{x^l \in R_j} |x_I^l - w_I^j| / |R_j|}{\sum_{x^l \in X} |x_I^l - w_I^j| / |X|}.$$

Weight function: The SOM is described by the mapping of an input vector to the winning codebook vector; this mapping can be approximated using softmin via

$$\sum_{j=1}^{K} w^j \cdot \frac{e^{-|x-w^j|^2/\beta}}{\sum_{o=1}^{K} e^{-|x-w^o|^2/\beta}}$$

where $\beta > 0$. The effect of dimension I concerning this mapping can be measured via the derivative with respect to the I th input dimension. The larger this value, the more important is the respective dimension. We denote this measure by $F^2(I)$.
Topology preservation: The fact that the receptive fields of w^i and w^j intersect is – for reasonably well behaved data – equivalent to the fact that the point in between, $(w^i + w^j)/2$, is closest to w^i and w^j. This test can be approximated by the test

$$\sum_{i \leftrightarrow j, k \neq i,j} \text{sgd}(|w^k|^2 - w^k(w^i + w^j) + w^i w^j) \approx 0,$$

sgd being the standard sigmodial function. Hence those dimensions are not important which change the above value only slightly. In this case, only those receptive fields intersect which neurons are neighbored in the lattice of neurons. Hence the I th component is important if the derivative of the above term with respect to the I th input dimension is large. We denote this measure by $F^3(I)$. Note that it only depends on the lattice of the SOM and not on the training data. Hence it can be computed very efficiently. Moreover, we can further reduce the above sum to only those neurons $k \neq i, j$ which are close to the neurons i or j, since a change in the topology will most likely manifest in local changes of the neighborhood structure. We refer to F_D^3 where D denotes the maximum distance of neuron k from neurons i and j in the neighborhood graph N.

4 Application to Satellite Data

Note that the above measures for the significance of the different input dimensions do not refer to a supervised learning task but rely on intrinsic characteristics of the SOM. We test these methods on a LANDSAT-TM satellite image from the Colorado area, U.S.A., for which a complete labeling of the inputs into 14 different classes of vegetation is available[1]. Hence we can compare the results obtained via unsupervised methods explicitely with the classification error on the data. The data comprises six input dimensions and about 3 mio. data points.

Since the above methods crucially depend on the fact that the topology of the SOM fits the data topology, we use a GSOM approach which leads to a lattice with

[1] Thanks to M.Augusteijn (University of Colorado) for providing the data

Table 1. Ranking of the input dimensions induced by the various significance measures.

	1	2	3	4	5	6	ranking
E	0.81	0.82	0.82	0.66	0.81	0.84	2 4 4 1 2 6
F^1	0.09	0.15	0.15	0.62	0.12	0.11	6 2 2 1 4 5
F^2	0.49	0.46	0.48	1.0	0.54	0.5	4 6 5 1 2 3
F^3	1.12	0.69	0.53	3.0	1.79	1.25	4 5 6 1 2 3
F_1^3	1.04	0.64	0.49	3.0	1.62	1.12	4 5 6 1 2 3
F_2^3	1.12	0.69	0.53	3.0	1.79	1.25	4 5 6 1 2 3

$12 \times 7 \times 3$ neurons. The topographic product for the degree of topology preservation (a value 0 indicates perfect agreement) yields a value of 0.0095 hence a nearly perfect fit [1]. This finding agrees with the results of a Grassberger-Procaccia analysis which yields an intrinsic data dimension of 3.14. A standard PCA computes the eigenvalues $(4.93, 0.68, 0.29, 0.05, 0.02, 0.02)$ [4]. Hence one intrinsic data dimension is dominant, $2-3$ dimensions contain further relevant information, where these intrinsic dimensions do not necessarily coincide with the Euclidian coordinates. Fig. 1 displays the labeled image and a RGB-representation based on the unsupervised SOM – each neuron in the SOM represents one color with RGB values according to the position in the 3-D lattice; all data points in the receptive field of a neuron are displayed in the same color as the neuron. Although no label information has been used for the second image one can observe a good agreement.

We compute a posterior labeling of the codebooks depending on the data: w^i is equipped with the vector $Y^i \in [0,1]^{14}$, 14 denoting the number of different labels, where $Y_j^i = |\{x^i \in X \,|\, x^i \in R_j \wedge y^i = j\}|/|R_j|$ denotes the percentage of points in the receptive field of w^i labeled with j. Those label j with maximum Y_j^i is attached to the codebook w^j. Hence the SOM induces a mapping which maps an input to the label of the closest codebook vector. This function misclassifies a percentage of 0.83 of the data. We refer to this accuracy via E. Note that a large number of misclassifications is due to the fact that the class boundaries lie within the receptive fields of the codebooks since no label information is used for training.

Additionally to the above relevance functions F^1, F^2, F^3, F_1^3, and F_2^3, we further measure the effect of pruning the I th input dimension on the labeling function if the percentage of misclassifications is measured according to E. The results together with the induced ranking of the input dimensions are collected in Tab. 1. All methods indicate that dimension 4 is most important. An RGB image based on this dimension only is shown in Fig. 1. Moreover, the induced ranking does not differ much between the various relevance measures. In particular, the very efficient measure F_1^3, which depends on neighbored neurons and their immediate neighborhood only, provides an accurate estimation of F^3, which depends on the whole neighborhood, as well as F^2, which additionally depends on the data. Iteratively pruning the dimensions ranked low allows us to drop all but two dimensions and still obtaining an accuracy of more than 0.6 as depicted in Fig. 1. The RGB-images obtained after pruning some of the input dimensions are displayed in Fig. 1.

Since an explicit labeling is usually not available for unsupervised methods, we need an adequate stopping criterion for input pruning. Note that the relevance factors according to F^3 form 4 well separated clusters: dimensions $\{1,6\}$, $\{2,3\}$, $\{4\}$, and $\{5\}$, hence stopping after pruning all dimensions from a specific cluster together with some prior estimation of the intrinsic dimensionality of the data could be a reasonable and efficient strategy for a pruning method.

5 Conclusions

The presented pruning methods provide a robust tool for efficiently determining relevant input dimension for an unsupervised SOM. They rely on intrinsic characteristics of the SOM and hence do not require explicit label information of the data. Therefore they are particularly suitable for data mining applications or visualization of data with an unknown structure. An application to real life satellite data for which an additional labeling is available showed promising results. In particular, pruning according to topology preservation is a very effective method which, additionally, proposed a natural stopping point in combination with prior dimensionality estimations. Further work has to be done on general stopping criteria.

References

1. H.-U. Bauer and K. R. Pawelzik. Quantifying the neighborhood preservation of Self-Organizing Feature Maps. *IEEE Trans. on Neural Networks*, 3(4):570–579, 1992.
2. H.-U. Bauer and T. Villmann. Growing a Hypercubical Output Space in a Self–Organizing Feature Map. *IEEE Transactions on Neural Networks*, 8(2):218–226, 1997.
3. B. Fritzke. Growing grid: a self-organizing network wirh constant neighborhood range and adaptation strength. *Neural Processing Letters*, 2(5):9–13, 1995.
4. P. Grassberger and I. Procaccia. Measuring the strangeness of strange attractors. *Physica*, 9D:189–208, 1983.
5. B. Hammer and T. Villmann. Input pruning for neural gas architectures. In: M.Verleysen, editro, *ESANN'2001*, pages 271-276, 2001.
6. T. Honkela, S. Kaski, T. Kohonen, and K. Lagus. Self-organizing maps of very large document collections: Justification for the WEBSOM method. In I. Balderjahn, R. Mathar, and M. Schader, editors, *Classification, Data Analysis, and Data Highways*, pages 245–252. Springer, Berlin, 1998.
7. S. Kaski. Dimensionality reduction by random mapping: fast similarity computation for clustering. In *Proceedings of IJCNN'92*, pages 413–418, 1998.
8. T. Kohonen. *Self-Organizing Maps*. Springer, 1997.
9. T. Martinetz and K. Schulten. Topology representing networks. *Neural Networks*, 7(3):507–522, 1993.
10. U. Matecki. *Automatische Merkmalsauswahl für Neuronale Netze mit Anwendung in der pixelbezogenen Klassifikation von Bildern*. Shaker, 1999.
11. A. Meyering and H. Ritter. Learning 3D-shape-perception with local linear maps. In *Proceedings of IJCNN'92*, pages 432–436, 1992.
12. R. Nock and M. Sebban. Sharper bounds for the hardness of prototype and feature selection. In H. Arimura, S. Jain, and A. Sharma, editors, *Algorihmic Learning Theory*, pages 224–237. Springer, 2000.
13. A. Ultsch. Self-organizing neural networks for visualization and classification. In O. Opitz, B. Lausen, and R. Klar, editors, *Information and Classification*, pages 307–313, London, UK, 1993. Springer.
14. T. Villmann, R. Der, M. Herrmann, and T. Martinetz. Topology Preservation in Self–Organizing Feature Maps: Exact Definition and Measurement. *IEEE Transactions on Neural Networks*, 8(2):256–266, 1997.
15. T. Villmann and E. Merenyi. Extensions and modifications of SOM and its application in satellite remote sensoring processing. In H. Bothe and R.Rojas, editors, *Neural Computation 2000*, pages 765–771, Zürich, 2000. ICSC Academic Press.

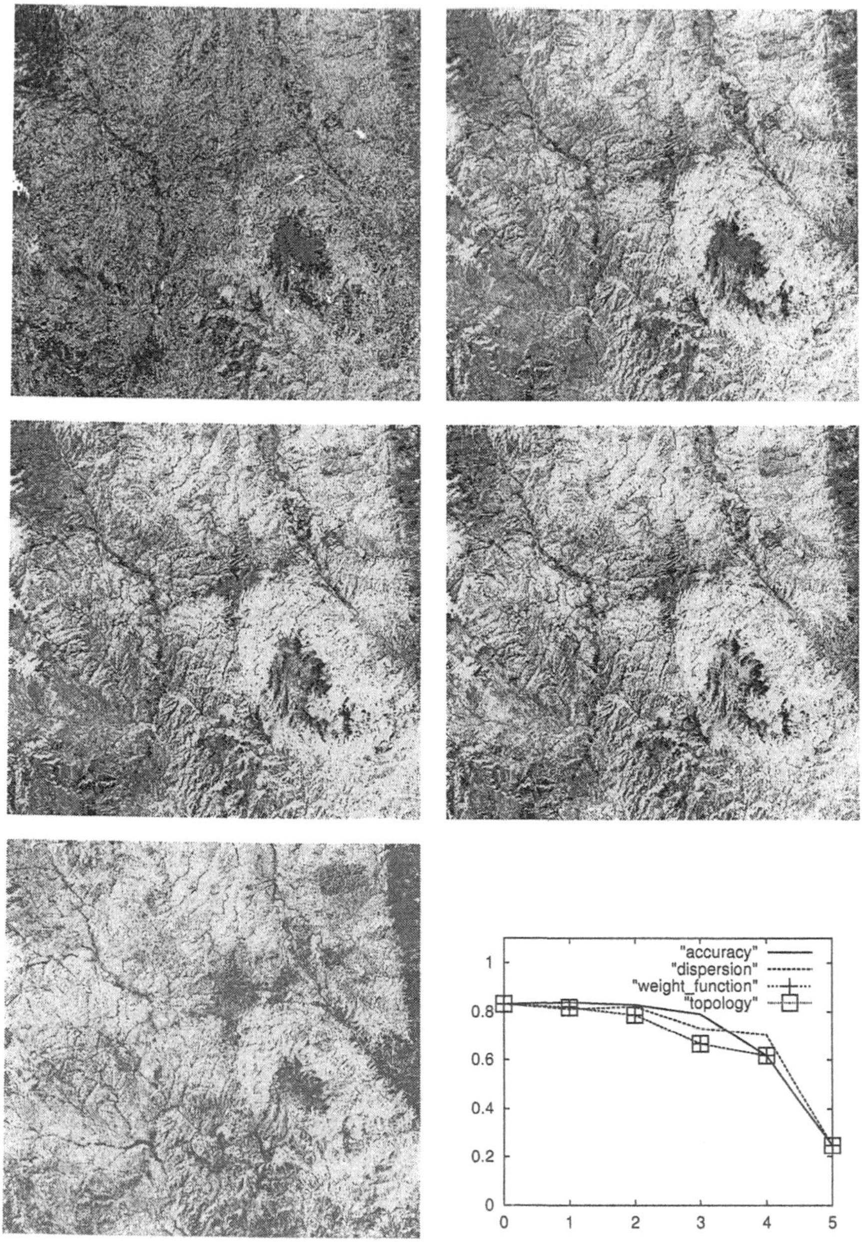

Fig. 1. First row - left: Classification according to the labeling, colors result from a specific color map; first row - right: RGB-visualization according to the SOM; second row - left: RGB-visualization with pruned dimensions 2 and 3; second row - right: RGB-visualization with pruned dimensions 1, 2, 3, and 6; third row - left: RGB-visualization based on dimension 4, only; third row - right: decrease of the accuracy if the input dimensions according to the various measures are pruned.

The Use of Wide–frame Cepstrum in Speech Recognition

Justyna Brześcińska, Tomasz de Jastrzębiec Wykowski

University of Mining and Metallurgy, Krakow,
brzescin@student.uci.agh.edu.pl,
wykowski@student.uci.agh.edu.pl

Abstract. The paper presents a new approach to speech recognition using cepstral analysis. Cepstrum is being counted in just two wide frames for each syllable in word. The algorithm is discussed and example of application using backpropagation neural network is given.

1 Cepstral Analysis

One of the methods often used in speech recognition is *cepstral analysis*. It is based on a theory that speech is a convolution of excitation signal and vocal tract impulse response (fig. 1). Therefore by using several transformations (fig. 2) it is possible to obtain information only about the sense of statement, discarding one about the speaker [2, 5].

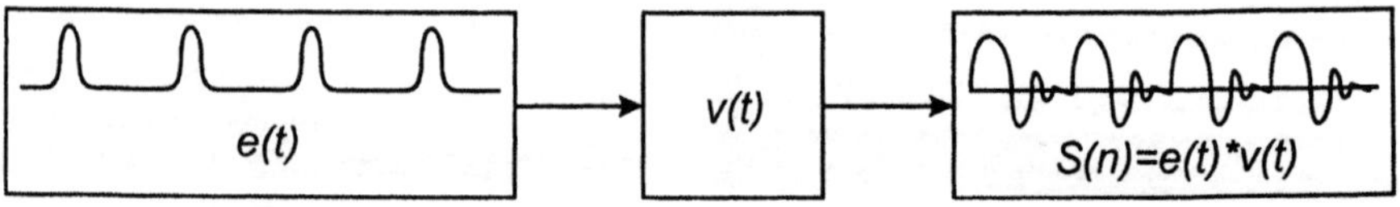

Fig. 1. Model of speech forming, *e(t)* — excitation signal, *v(t)* — vocal tract impulse response, *s(t)* — speech (convolution of excitation signal and vocal tract impulse response)

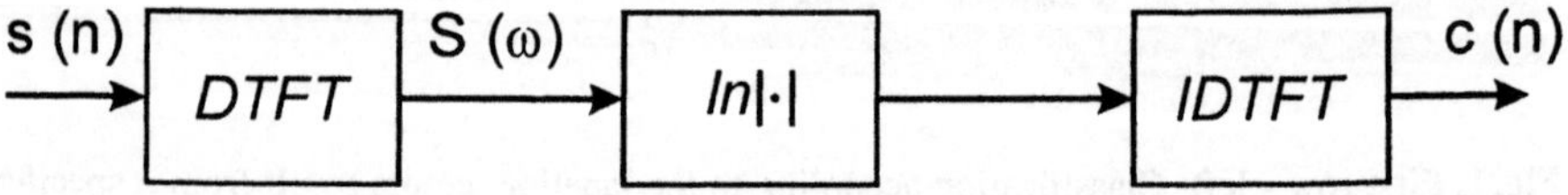

Fig. 2. Scheme of cepstrum counting, *DTFT* — discrete time Fourier transform, *ln*|·| — natural logarithm of absolute value, *IDTFT* — inverse discrete time Fourier transform

Obviously, there are many methods which reduce the computational complexity, concentrating on information distinguished by human's hearing system, and rejecting all other. One of these methods is processing the data with set of frequency filters which usually decrease length of the data vector to 16-20 values [6].

2 Common Approach

In most publications authors count cepstrum on successive frames of rather short length. The 128, 256, and 512 – elements frames are mostly used. Each frame usually contains information about one phoneme. Using this method an array build from consecutive cepstral vectors is obtained. Next, it is possible to reduce further amount of information, or to recognize every phoneme in utterance.

First method allows to classify utterance to one of pre-defined classes, usually by comparing information contained in obtained array with those patterns (one can consider artificial neural networks as a kind of comparing, with patterns encoded in neurons' weights). Unfortunately, the number of frames in an array is not constant as it depends on the length of utterance. To avoid problems with operating on arrays of different size they are usually normalized to some standard length through rejecting some of their vectors or adding empty ones (containing zeros). The other problem in this method is the amount of data. It is usually too big to be used without large computational power, so the need to reduce it appears. As a result, the computational complexity grows [4].

The second method is useful when high precision in phonemes recognition is needed. System tries to identify spoken word by comparing the phonemes sequence with vocabulary database. This method is used in systems with thousand and more words in dictionary. The precision in word recognition substitute the humans natural ability to distinguish words basing on context. Unfortunately, these systems needs very precise equipment (microphones, A/D convector), and process of sound acquisition is usually held in special, anechoic chamber. This makes these systems sensitive to distortion, and disabled them from being used in natural environment. High prices of equipments also decrease the number of potential users [3, 7].

3 Problem Solution

Presented method is based on recognition of whole syllables. Acquired syllable is divided into two parts: one of raising power (RP), and one of decreasing (DP), where power is described by (Eq. 1).

$$P(i)=\sum_{k=1}^{win} s(i*ovr+k)^2 \qquad (1)$$

where:

i – sample index

s(n) –signal

win – number of samples used to compute power, usually $win \in (200,500)$

ovr – number of overlapping samples in successive windows, $ovr < win$

The highest value of power mostly falls into utterance of vowel. Therefore both parts of the syllable contain, beside their own consonant, part of shared vowel.

Next, both parts are resized to vector of a constant length — *N*. The value of N should be high enough to ensure that the lengths of 80% of RP and DP are less than, or equal to it. If the part's length is shorter than *N*, it is widened by adding the same amount of zeros to both sides of it, thus putting non-zero values in the middle of new vector. In case when part's length is longer than *N*, it is reduced by removing samples of lower power index (from left side in case of RP, and from right side in case of DP). Example is shown on figure 3.

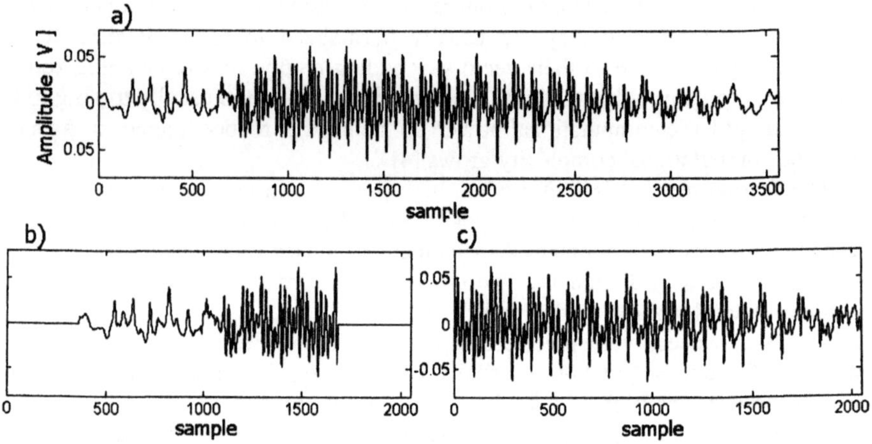

Fig. 3. Dividing syllable into two parts, with *N*=2048 **(a)** whole syllable, **(b)** RP shorter than *N* samples, widened to 2048, **(c)** DP containing more than 2048 samples, reduced to *N*.

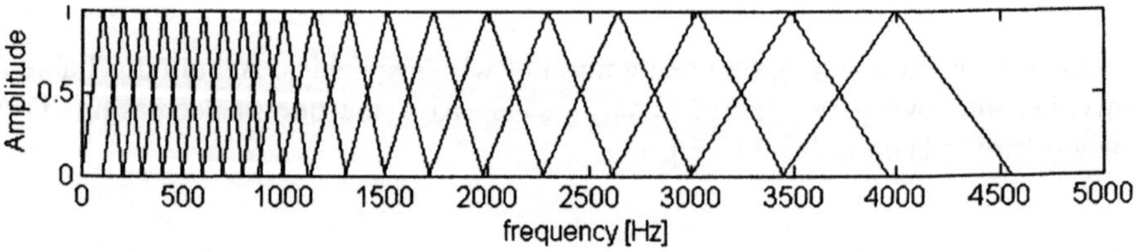

Fig. 4. Triangle filters in Mel scale

On so prepared vector following steps are made:

- normalization of signal by dividing it by sum of power of utterance:

$$s'(n) = \frac{s(n)}{\sum P(i)} \tag{2}$$

- preemphasis filter:

$$s''(n) = s'(n) - s(n-1) \tag{3}$$

- Hamming window:

$$s'''(n) = s''(n) * H(n) \tag{4}$$

where:

$$H(n) = \left[0{,}54 - 0{,}46\cos\left(\frac{2\pi(n-1)}{N-1}\right)\right] \tag{5}$$

- absolute value of FFT:

$$S(z) = \left|fft(s'''(n))\right| \tag{6}$$

- mapping to *mel* scale:

$$Mel(f) = 2595\ln\left(1 + \frac{f}{700}\right) \tag{7}$$

- set of K=20 bandpass triangle filters (fig. 4.)

$$m(i) = \sum_{z=1}^{N} f(i,z) * S(z) \tag{8}$$

- cepstral coefficients

$$c(n) = \sum_{i=1}^{K} m(i)\cos\left(\frac{\pi n}{K}(i - 0{,}5)\right) \tag{9}$$

Note: In most publication [3, 6] cepstral coefficients are multiplied by constant:

$$c'(n) = ac(n) \tag{10}$$

where:

$a = \frac{2}{K}$, or $a = \sqrt{\frac{2}{K}}$ depending on sources.

Performance of one more step, called *liftering* is also suggested:

$$c''(n) = \left(1 + \frac{L}{2}\sin\frac{\pi n}{L}\right)c'(n) \tag{11}$$

where L is a liftering constant

In the presented application cepstral coefficients are passed to the backpropagation neural network (Chap. 4). Before that, they are normalized to values from -1 to 1. For this reason authors omitted applying equations 9 and 10, which are just calibrations of cepstral coefficients. Nevertheless, these equations are mentioned here to present complete view on cepstrum issue.

4 Example of Application

Algorithm described above was tested in application which goal was to recognize a set of ten Polish words. These words were divided into two groups: of one, and two syllables. Both groups contained five words. Two backpropagation neural networks were created, one for each of group. Both networks contained:

- 43 input neurons,
- two hidden layers containing 15 neurons in first, and 10 in second,
- 5 output neurons, one for each word.

The input vector for neural network recognizing one–syllable words consisted of the following:

- 19 cepstral coefficients from both RP and DP
- length of word
- lengths of RP and DP
- slopes of power in RP and DP

The following data constituted an input vector for second network:

- 10 cepstral coefficients from both RP and DP of each syllable
- length of word
- lengths of syllables

Algorithm which locates syllables in utterance is precisely described in [1].

The system's aim was to achieve best performance, basing on small teaching set, consisting of just 5 utterances of each word. There were no validation set.

Tests were carried out for two speakers, one male and one female. This gave four neural networks, two for each person. Test sets consisted of 45 utterances of each word for male and of 20 for female.

Authors distinguished two types of errors:

1. unrecognized utterances, when none of network outputs' activation passed level of 0,5,
2. incorrectly recognized utterances, when other than expected neuron obtain highest value, over 0,5.

To ensure that obtained results were not coincidental, every network was trained five times. Mean, percentage values of each kind of errors are given in table I.

Sound for test and teaching sets was acquired in natural condition, using Sound Blaster Live! card and cheap monophonic microphone. The sampling frequency was 11 KHz and the value of N was 2048.

Table 1. Mean error rate for carried out tests

words	speaker	network error rate		
		unrecognized	incorrectly recognized	sum
one syllable	male	1,4 %	0,7 %	2,1 %
	female	1,2 %	1,0 %	2,1 %
two syllable	male	0,7 %	0,5 %	1,2 %
	female	1,2 %	1,0 %	2,1 %

5 Conclusion

Presented application shows great efficiency of described method. Despite of the high level of noise, and low standard of used equipment neural networks had almost no difficulty with recognizing and classifying acquired utterances. Used transformations, and backpropagation networks enable this system to work in real-time even on simple personal computers. Also because of employed neural networks application can adapt to current user.

References

[1] Brześcińska J., de Jastrzębiec Wykowski T. "Computer Usage's Support for Disabled", Metallurgy and Foundry Engineering — Special Edition, Krakow 2001, pp. 99-106 (in Polish)

[2] Deller J. Jr., Hansen J., Proakis J."Discrete — Time Processing of Speech Signal", IEEE Press, New York 2000

[3] Grocholewski S. "Statistical Foundations of ARM System For Polish Language", Poznań University of Technology Printing House, Poznań 2001 (in Polish)

[4] Hsiao-Fen Pois, Hsiao-chuan Wang „A Study of the Two-Dimensional Cepstrum Approach for Speech Recognition", Computer Speech and Language (1992), 6, pp. 361–375

[5] Oppenheim A.V. and al. "Applications of Digital Signal Processing“, Prentice-Hall, Inc. Englewood Cliffs, New Jersey USA 1978

[6] Picone J. "Signal Modelling Techniques in Speech Recognition", Proceedings of the IEEE, vol. 81, no 9, September 1993, pp. 1215-1247

[7]. Tadeusiewicz R. „Speech Signals", Transport and Communication Publishers, Warsaw 1988 (in Polish)

Face Recognition/Detection by Clustering and Probabilistic Neural Networks

Giacomo Capizzi[1], Salvatore Coco[1], Cinzia Giuffrida[1], Antonio Laudani[1], and Giuseppe Pappalardo[2]

[1] Department of Electrical, Electronic and Systems Engineering,
[2] Department of Mathematics and Informatics,
University of Catania, Viale A.Doria 6, Catania I-95125, Italy

Abstract. In this paper a face recognition/detection system is presented, composed out of three main blocks: a face extraction block, which identifies and extracts individual faces from the input image; a feature extraction block, which converts each face identified into a suitable set of features; and a PNN classifier, which recognizes the face presented to it as a feature set. Experiments carried out on a large set of images achieved excellent results in terms of speed and precision, compared with typical figures featured by most state-of-the-art systems.

1 Introduction

Research on face recognition has been particularly active in recent years, and several techniques have been devised, including those based upon: spatial image invariants [11], correlation matrices [6], eigenspace of the faces [10], features and templates [1]. Neural network (NN) classification has been employed in [8,9]. In a recent work [4], we have proposed a new recognition methodology which combines Probabilistic NN (PNN) classification, with feature extraction based on wavelets and the pseudo-spectral Gram transform. The results obtained improve upon the state-of-the-art.

In the typical face recognition problem, the input image consists of a single face in the foreground. In this paper, we tackle the more complex problem of recognizing faces when they occur in groups within the input image (see e.g. Fig. 3). The approach proposed achieves excellent results in terms of speed and precision, by building upon the feature extraction techniques of [4], which deals with single face recognition.

As shown in Fig. 1, the system proposed is composed out of three main blocks: the *face extraction block*, which identifies and extracts individual faces from the input image; the *feature extraction block*, which converts each face identified into a suitable set of features; and the *PNN classifier*, which ultimately recognizes the face presented to it as a feature set.

The face extraction block is dealt with in Section 2. The feature extraction block is based on wavelet transforms, least squares approximation and Gram polynomials expansion; the set of features it outputs, for each input image processed, includes the most significant Gram polynomial coefficients (about sixty); the interested reader is referred to our work [4] for further details. The PNN classifier, featuring a "One Class One Network" (OCON) architecture, is described in Section 3.

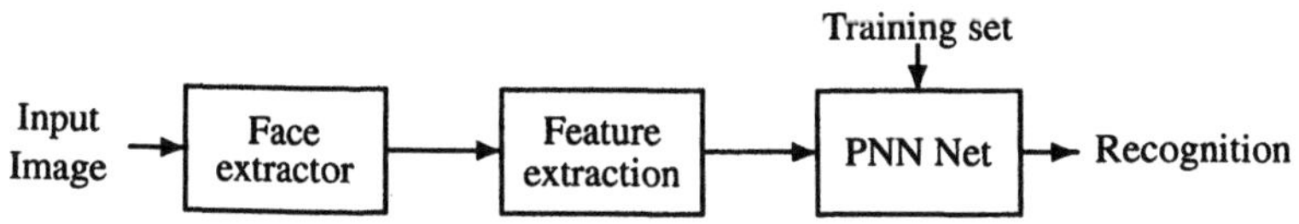

Fig. 1. Block diagram of the recognition system.

2 Extracting Faces from a Group

The face extraction block carries out an algorithm by which individual faces are identified within the input image. The algorithm presupposes the selection of suitable elements, which necessarily occur in any face, and therefore characterize the notion of a face as distinct from other graphical objects. Accordingly, the algorithm is carried out in two steps:

1. identification of the noted *characteristic elements* of each face within the input image;
2. extraction of individual faces based on the positions of the characteristic elements identified in the previous phase.

Carrying out step (1) amounts to clustering together pixel sets satisfying the visual properties expected of the desired characteristic elements. In the application at hand, the elements employed are each face's *eye pairs*; these enjoy the property that their aspect is scarcely variable with lighting conditions and facial expressions (see Section 2.1). Eyes are detected by means of the efficient clusterer proposed by us in [3]; in order to further improve its performance, the input image is preprocessed in such a way to make eye pixels stand out even more distinctly against the rest of the input image. Further details about step (1) are provided in Section 2.1.

Step (2) of the face extraction algorithm exploits a knowledge of the average metric properties of faces in order to infer which pixels, among those surrounding the eyes, constitute the entire face. Specifically, since the clusterer returns eyes individually, rather than in pairs, together with other spots which are not eyes, a suitable `eye_couple()` function carries out the task of finding real eye pairs. Finally, around each eye pair, function `face_extractor()` determines the minimum rectangle enclosing the face.

2.1 Eye Enhancement and Detection

It would be possible to try to characterize, hence identify, human eyes in terms of their geometrical, rather than luminance, properties. However, from the extensive experiments performed, it has turned out that such a characterization would not be very effective, at least for the low resolution images normally processed by face recognition systems. We have therefore turned to a luminance-based characterization of the eyes.

In this approach, eye pixels are not too difficult to detect within a group of faces, since their luminance patterns are rather insensitive to lighting and expression of the face. Typically, such patterns resemble those plotted in Fig. 2 for the example face shown. It can be noticed that, along the mid-eye columns (78,145), vertical luminance exhibits two dark peaks corresponding to the eyebrow and the pupil (row 75); and, along mid-eye rows (71,75,79), horizontal luminance gets darker at the right and left pupils (column 78 and 145 respectively).

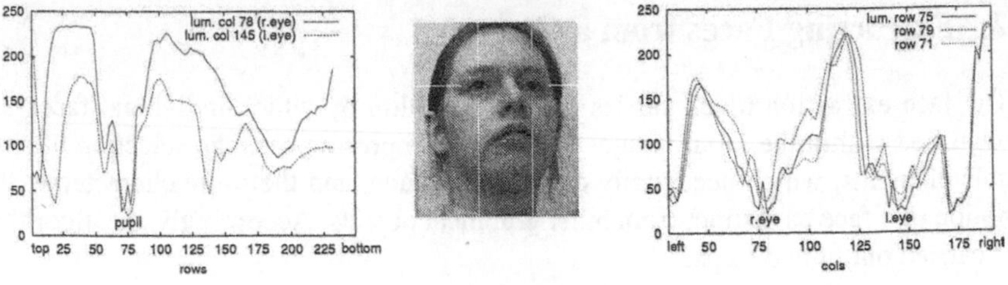

Fig. 2. Eye luminance patterns. In the face, columns 78,145, and row 75 are marked white.

The task of identifying the eyes within the image is performed by the clustering subsystem, which has been designed in accordance with the ideas put forward in [3]. In the standard approach to clustering, the image is scanned by looking directly for objects possessing the desired features (e.g. of shape or luminance). In contrast, greater simplicity and manageability, from a computational point of view, are afforded by the approach of [3]; in this, objects to be identified are viewed and sought as sets of pixels exhibiting relatively uniform local properties. These properties are selected by the user of the clusterer, depending on the specific application. In our face extraction system, a pixel (i, j) is assumed to be part of a cluster if the average luminance of its 3×5 rectangular neighbourhood is 'dark enough' (i.e. falls below a given threshold). The clusterer implementation is based on conventionally programmed luminance comparison routines rather th¡an neural computation.

Fig. 3. Input (top) and output (bottom) of the clusterer.

The performance of the clusterer is boosted by conveniently preprocessing the input image in such a way to increase its contrast, thus making the eyes within it even more conspicuous. Besides some shifting, scaling and normalization, preprocessing is essentially based on a quadratic filter which updates the luminance l_{ij} of image pixel (i,j) as: $l_{ij} \leftarrow l_{ij}^2 \times (L_M + L_m)/2L_{av}{}^2$, where L_M, L_m, L_{av} are the maximum, minimum and average luminance over the image.

2.2 Face Detection Based on Eye Position

In order to characterize a human face, distinguishing it effectively from other visual structures, fifteen key points have been identified in the literature (see e.g. [5]). Of these, six are localized near the face contour, and the others are used to characterize mouth angles (2 points), the eyebrows (3), the nose (1), and the eyes (4). However, all these points are needed to *identify* faces (in our approach, this is done differently, in a suitable feature space, cf. Fig. 1); for the simpler purposes of *extracting* faces, it is enough to identify the distances which define the rectangle enclosing the face.

The work [5] has shown that distances between the characteristic points of a human face satisfy fixed average proportions. Those useful for our purposes are shown in Table 1, where face height, minus forehead, has been normalized to 100.

Table 1. Some average distances in a face.

Distance	*Normalized Value*
face width	73.6
face height, excluding forehead	100.0
inter-eye distance	35.8
pupil radius	7.5

The clusters output by the clusterer are candidate eyes, for each of which the center and the radius are known. The face extraction algorithm includes two main functions, `eye_couple()` and `face_extractor()`. The former exploits the proportions given by Table 1 for the pupil radius and eye distance, in order to pair up the eyes correctly. The latter computes the eye distances and, based again on the table, uses them to determine the minimum rectangle enclosing each face.

Eye coupling Let $e_1, \ldots, e_M$ be the candidate eyes output by the clusterer. The main, mth $(1 \leq m \leq M)$ loop of function `eye_couple()` tests e_m for possible matching with $e_{m+1}, \ldots, e_M$. The matching test is passed by pair (e_m, e_n) if all of the following three conditions are satisfied:

1. *the radii of* (e_m, e_n) *must not differ by more than* 20%; this criterion avoids matching eyes lying in different planes, e.g. an eye in the foreground with one in the background; it cannot discriminate eyes in the same plane but belonging to different faces (for their radii would not differ much); the 20% tolerance takes into account small differences affecting a real eye couple due to slight head rotations;

2. *the ratio between the inter-eye distance of* (e_m, e_n) *and their mean radius must be consistent with Table 1, up to a 20% tolerance*;
3. *the line from* e_m *to* e_n *must not deviate from the horizontal by more than* 30° (this tolerance takes into account potential head inclinations).

It is worth noting that, in general, the real eyes will be less than the *M* clusters found by the clusterer, and in any case not all pairs returned by `eye_couple()` will be actual eye pairs. However, the would-be face extracted from a false eye pair is certain to be so unlike a real one that the PNN classifier will have no difficulty discarding it. On the other hand, as experiments have ascertained, the chance of `eye_pair()` failing to catch a real eye pair is virtually nil.

Face Extraction Function `face_extractor()` receives an eye pair as input and returns the minimum rectangle enclosing the relevant face. The (normalized) face width and height are derived with the help of Table 1. In fact, the tabular width is increased by 21% on each side to avoid cutting the ears, and (following [5]) the tabular height is extended by 60% at the top to capture the forehead.

3 The PNN Classifier

The output from the feature extractor block is fed to the PNN classifier (see Fig. 1). Since the former block extracts a feature set which proves well-suited to recognition [4], the choice of a neural network architecture is not too constrained by precision needs, and can address modularity, speed and robustness concerns.

In this light, following the approach of [8], the most appropriate architecture appears to be the OCON (One-Class-One-Network) one. In the OCON net employed, a thirty-neurons, single-layer subnet is provided for each class (i.e. face) to be recognized. All subnets are assembled together and share the inputs. The *n*th subnet outputs an estimated probability P_n that the input face belongs to class *n*. Estimated probabilities are then compared by the `MaxNet` component, which outputs the *n* that maximizes P_n, provided $P_n > 0.8$. This threshold avoids "intruders" (faces outside the database) to be mistakenly recognized.

OCON PNNs are non-supervised. The basis functions employed are of the Gaussian type. Their training set is taken from the same face databases employed as test sets for the recognition experiments. However, no image has been employed for both the training and the test set. More specifically, the subnet for each class has been trained by two groups of faces, belonging, respectively, to the class and its complement (all the other classes). Experimentally, the best ratio between the two groups has been found to be $2/3$.

The PNN architecture adopted has proved robust in recognizing faces even when deployed in a noisy environment. It can cope well with image modifications due to different lighting and head position or orientation. Altogether, no appreciable performance degradation has been observed, even in the presence of poor-quality images. In addition, the OCON architecture enjoys the virtue of *modularity*: varying the face database can be simply accomplished by adding/training or removing (as appropriate) the relevant subnets; and, most importantly, this does not require the entire network to be retrained. Finally, the classification tasks performed by the various subnets can be parallelized, thus obtaining substantial savings of computing time.

4 Conclusions

We have carried out experiments mainly on the UMIST and ORL databases, which contain large sets of low resolution, 256 gray level images Faces within the images belong to individuals of different race, age, sex, facial expressions (partially open eyes, smiling/non-smiling), facial details (glasses/no glasses), scale (up to 10%), and orientation (up to 20 degrees).

A positive classification rate of 99.5% average has been obtained. This should be contrasted with the 96% typical figures featured by most state-of-the-art detection/recognition systems (see e.g. [7] for more specific figures).

Processing times allow the proposed system to be employed in real-time applications. In experiments carried out on a Pentium III 800 PC, running under the Linux operating system, the recognition delay is below two seconds for a database holding about one thousand faces.

References

1. Brunelli R. and Poggio T. "Face Recognition: Features Versus Templates", IEEE Transaction on Pattern Analysis and Machine Intelligence, Vol. 15, pages 1042-1045, 1993.
2. Capizzi G., Coco S., and Pappalardo G. "Image Recognition By Wavelet Transform", Proceedings of SOCO '99, pages 492-496. Genova, June 1999.
3. Capizzi G., Coco S., and Pappalardo G. "A New Clustering Based System For Automated Object Recognition", Proceedings of SOCO '99, pages 503-507. Genova, June 1999.
4. Capizzi G., Coco S., and Pappalardo G. "Face Recognition by Pseudo-Spectral Transform and PNN Classification", Proceedings of SCS 2001, pages 297-300. IEEE. Iasi, Romania. July 2001.
5. Kelly M. D. "Visual identification of people by computer", Stanford AI Project, Stanford, CA, Tech. Rep. AI-130, 1970.
6. Kohonen T. "Correlation Matrix Memories", IEEE Transactions on Computers, Vol. C21, no. 4, Apr 1972.
7. Lawrance S., Giles C.L., Tsoi A.C., and Back A.D. "Face Recognition: A Convolutional Approach", NEC Res. Inst., Princeton, NJ Tech. Rep. 1995.
8. Lin S.H., Kung S.Y., and Lin L.J. "Face Recognition/Detection by Probabilistic Decision-Based Neural Network", IEEE Transactions on Neural Networks, Vol. 8, no. 1, pages 114-132. Jan. 1997.
9. Ranganath S., and Arun K. "Face Recognition Using Transform Features and Neural Networks", IEEE Transactions on Pattern Recognition, Vol. 30, pages 1615-1622, 1997.
10. Turk M. and Pentland A. "Eigenfaces for Recognition", J. Cognitive Neuroscience, Vol. 3, pages 71-86, 1991.
11. Zhang J., Yan Y., and Lades M. "Face Recognition: Eigenfaces, Elastic Matching, and Neural Networks", Proc. IEEE, Vol. 85, pages 1423-1435, 1997.

A Posteriori Corrections to Classification Methods

Włodzisław Duch and Łukasz Itert

Department of Informatics, Nicholas Copernicus University,
Grudziądzka 5, 87-100 Toruń, Poland; http://www.phys.uni.torun.pl/kmk

Abstract. *A posteriori* corrections are computational inexpensive and may improve accuracy, confidence, sensitivity or specificity of the model, or correct for the differences between a priori training and real (test) class distributions. Such corrections are applicable to neural and any other classification models.

1 Introduction

Training neural networks and other classification models may be time consuming, therefore one should try to derive as much information from the final model as possible. In pathological cases neural and other classifiers may lead to results that are below the base rates, i.e. below the values obtained by majority classifier. This may happen especially in case of strong imbalance between the number of samples from different classes. Another problem arises when the data available for training has different *a priori* probabilities than the test data. This problem arises frequently in biostatistics and medical statistics where controlled experiments do not reflect the true class distributions, in use of stratified cross-validation for training (see [2] for more examples). The overall accuracy may be not so important as the sensitivity, specificity or the confidence in the results that should be increased.

A posteriori procedures may frequently correct such problems. Correction increasing overall accuracy, accounting for differences in class distribution and increasing the desired aspects of the classification process are presented in subsequent sections.

2 Corrections increasing overall accuracy

Most classifiers, neural networks included, do not estimated rigorously probabilities. However, normalizing the classifier's outputs in such a way that they sum to unity some estimate of probabilities $p(C_i|\mathbf{X})$ that a vector $\mathbf{X}$ belongs to the class $C_i, i = 1..K$, is obtained. Suppose that the majority of samples belong to the last class C_K. Introducing $K-1$ linear scaling parameters:

$$P(C_i|\mathbf{X}) = \kappa_i p(C_i|\mathbf{X}), i = 1 \dots K-1; \quad P(C_K|\mathbf{X}) = 1 - \sum_{i=1}^{K-1} P(C_i|\mathbf{X}) \qquad (1)$$

it is easy to assure that even a very bad classifier will perform at least at the level of the majority classifier. This is achieved when all $\kappa_i = 0$. If all $\kappa_i = 1$ then nothing will change. If the coefficients $\kappa_i \in [0,1]$ normalization is preserved, but the probability of the majority class may only grow. In some situations it may be of advantage to decrease this probability. For that reason assume that $\kappa_i \in [0,+\infty], i = 1 \dots K-1$, and $\kappa_K = 1$, and the final probabilities are obtained from the softmax transformation instead of the linear rescaling:

$$P(C_i|\mathbf{X};\kappa) = \exp\left(\kappa_i p(C_i|\mathbf{X})\right/ \exp\left(\sum_{j=1}^{K} \kappa_j p(C_i|\mathbf{X})\right), \; i = 1 \dots K \tag{2}$$

If all $\kappa_i = 1$ the softmax transformation "flattens" probabilities while linear transformation does not change anything. For example, if there are two classes and $p(C_1|\mathbf{X}) + p(C_2|\mathbf{X}) = 1, p(C_i|\mathbf{X}) \in [0,1]$ the softmax transformed probabilities belong to $P(C_1|\mathbf{X}) \in [(1+e^{-1})^{-1}, (1+e^{+1})^{-1}]$, or approximately [0.27,0.73].

Rescaled probabilities depend on the κ coefficients. For the linear transformation the quadratic cost function may be taken as:

$$E(\kappa) = \sum_{\mathbf{X}} \sum_{i=1}^{K} \left(P(C_i|\mathbf{X};\kappa) - P_i(\mathbf{X})\right)^2 \tag{3}$$

where $P_i(\mathbf{X})$ are true probabilities that vector $\mathbf{X}$ belongs to the class C_i. In most cases only the class label is given instead of $P_i(\mathbf{X})$ probabilities, therefore $P_i(\mathbf{X}) = 1$ if the label of the training vector $\mathbf{X}$ is C_i, and 0 otherwise. Most classifiers minimize this error so there will be little to correct, but there are systems (for example Kohonen networks, rough set classifiers or decision trees) that do not minimize cost function directly. Adding such corrections may be regarded as the simplest form of stacking, i.e. training one classifier on the outputs of another [1].

The error function is quadratic in κ parameters:

$$E(\kappa) = \sum_{\mathbf{X}} \sum_{i=1}^{K} \left(\kappa_i p(C_i|\mathbf{X}) - P_i(\mathbf{X})\right)^2 \tag{4}$$

If linear rescaling is used and $\kappa_i \in [0,1], i = 1 \dots K-1$ then due to normalization (1) the cost function is:

$$E(\kappa) = \sum_{\mathbf{X}} \sum_{i=1}^{K-1} \left(\kappa_i p(C_i|\mathbf{X}) - P_i(\mathbf{X})\right)^2 + \sum_{\mathbf{X}} \left(1 - \sum_{i=1}^{K-1} \kappa_i p(C_i|\mathbf{X}) - P_K(\mathbf{X})\right)^2 \tag{5}$$

Minimum of this function is obtained from a solution of linear equation:

$$\mathbf{P}\cdot\kappa = \mathbf{Q}; \;\; \mathbf{P}_{ij} = \sum_{\mathbf{X}} (1+\delta_{ij}) p(C_i|\mathbf{X}) p(C_j|\mathbf{X}), \quad i,j = 1 \dots K-1; \tag{6}$$

$$\mathbf{Q}_i = \sum_{\mathbf{X}} p(C_i|\mathbf{X})\left(1 + P_i(\mathbf{X}) - P_K(\mathbf{X})\right) \tag{7}$$

Note that for the perfect classifier all $\kappa_i = 1$ since there is nothing to correct. For the majority classifier all $\kappa_i = 0$ because all probabilities except $p(C_K|\mathbf{X})$ are zero and no scaling of other classes will change it. However, if softmax transformation is used rescaling becomes possible. Starting from $p_K(C_i|\mathbf{X}) = 1$ and all other probabilities equal to zero, minimization of the cost function (4) with softmax transformed probabilities (2) leads to $P(C_K|\mathbf{X}) = N_K/N$ and all other probabilities $P(C_i|\mathbf{X}) = (N - N_K)/N(K-1)$. These probabilities may further be corrected by rescaling them and applying the softmax transformation iteratively. For 2-class problems there is only one scaling parameter κ, therefore it is easy to plot the number of errors as a function of κ. The number of errors is discontinuous and for more than two classes a minimum should be found using a global minimization method.

The primate splice-junction gene sequences (DNA) was used in the Statlog project [3]. It contains a set of 3190 sequences composed of 60 nucleotides. The task is to distinguish if there is an "intron => exon" or "exon => intron" boundary in the string, or neither. 2000 strings are used for training and 1190 for testing. The k nearest neighbor (kNN) classifer used for this task gave 85.4% on the test data. Optimizing k and the distance metric (using crossvalidation on the training data) only a slight improvement was obtained: with k=11 and Manhattan distance function accuracy reached 85.8% on training and 85.7% on the test data. After optimization of the κ parameters ($\kappa_1 = 1,0282$, $\kappa_1 = 0,8785$ the results improved on the training set to 86.4% and on the test set to 86.9%. Many probabilities of wrongly classified vectors became close to the threshold of predicting correct class, therefore comparison of an area under the ROC curves shows even more significant improvement. Similar improvements of the kNN results were noticed on several other datasets. More tests should be conducted with other data and classification methods but since calculation of such corrections does not cost anything they may be worthwhile to implement.

2.1 Changes in the a priori class distribution

Another type of corrections is useful if the a priori class distribution in the training data differs from the test data. If both the training and the test data represent the same process underlying data generation the densities $p(\mathbf{X}|C_i)$ in each class should remain constant, but the a posteriori probabilities $p(C_i|\mathbf{X})$ may change. According to the Bayes theorem:

$$p(\mathbf{X}|C_i) = p(C_i|\mathbf{X})p(\mathbf{X})/p(C_i) \tag{8}$$

An estimate of the a priori probabilities $p(C_i)$ should be made on the test data. This may be done naively by sampling the new data or in a more sophisticated way using iterative Expectation Maximization algorithm [2]. As usually the classification model is created on the training data, providing priors $p_t(C_i)$ and posteriors $p_t(C_i|\mathbf{X})$. Using Bayes theorem for the probabilities p_t estimated on the training set and using the assumption that the a posteriori probabilities do not change $p_t(\mathbf{X}|C_i) = p(\mathbf{X}|C_i)$ we obtain:

$$p(C_i|\mathbf{X})p(\mathbf{X})/p(C_i) = p(\mathbf{X}|C_i) = p_t(C_i|\mathbf{X})p_t(\mathbf{X})/p_t(C_i) \tag{9}$$

To eliminate $p(\mathbf{X})$ and $p_t(\mathbf{X})$ note that the $p(C_i|\mathbf{X})$ probabilities sum to 1 over all classes. Therefore

$$p(C_i|\mathbf{X}) = \frac{p_t(C_i|\mathbf{X})p(C_i)/p_t(C_i)}{\sum_j p_t(C_j|\mathbf{X})p(C_j)/p_t(C_j)} \tag{10}$$

i.e. the new posterior probabilities are simply corrected by the ratio of new priors $p(C_i)$ to the old priors $p_t(C_i)$ estimated on the training set, and renormalized to sum to one. A model estimated on the training data set may thus be applied to new data that has different a priori probabilities. For example, a model trained on data from controlled clinical experiments (with $p_t(disease)$ usually around 0.5) may be used in real world situations, when prior probabilities may be different (when $p_t(disease) \ll 0.5$).

Tests on several two-class medical data that were used in the Statlog project [3] showed that if the training data has $p(C_1)/p(C_2) = 1$ (typical for controlled experiments) and the class distribution is changed to $p(C_1)/p(C_2) = 5$ (even higher difference may be observed in real applications) this correction frequently increases accuracy by more than 10%.

2.2 Rejection rate, confidence, sensitivity and specificity

Frequently there is a need to improve confidence in the classification model. This may be done at a cost of rejecting some cases, i.e. assigning them to the "unknown" class. After training neural network or other classifiers outputs from these models are interpreted as probabilities. Suppose that the confusion matrix $P(C_i,C_j|M)$ for the two-class problem is known:

$$P(C_i,C_j|M) = \frac{1}{n}\left(\begin{array}{c|ccc|c} & C_+ & C_- & C_r & \\ C_+ & n_{++} & n_{+-} & n_{+r} & n_+ \\ C_- & n_{-+} & n_{--} & n_{-r} & n_- \end{array}\right) = \left(\begin{array}{c|ccc|c} & C_+ & C_- & C_r & \\ C_+ & p_{++} & p_{+-} & p_{+r} & p_+ \\ C_- & p_{-+} & p_{--} & p_{-r} & p_- \end{array}\right) \tag{11}$$

with rows corresponding to true classes, columns to predicted classes, and p_{ij} computed for a model M on $n = n_+ + n_-$ samples. The $p_{ij} = p(C_i,C_j|M)$ quantities are the training set estimations of joint probabilities of finding true class C_i and the predicted class C_j in the results; the model may also reject some cases as unpredictable, assigning them to the class C_r. The $p_\pm = p(C_\pm) = n_\pm/n$ are the a priori probabilities for the two classes, $p_\pm = p_{\pm+} + p_{\pm-} + p_{\pm r}$, and $p_+ + p_- = 1$.

To increase confidence in the decision of the model the errors on the test set may be decreased at the cost of rejection of some vectors. In neural networks this is done by defining minimum and maximum thresholds for the activity of output units. In models estimating probability similar thresholds may be introduced. For crisp logical rules confidence optimization is also possible if uncertainty of inputs are taken into account [4]. The following error function may be used for corrections after training of the model to set these thresholds:

$$E(M;\gamma) = \gamma \sum_{i \neq j} P(C_i,C_j|M) - \mathrm{Tr}\, P(C_i,C_j|M) \geq -1 \tag{12}$$

It should be minimized over model parameters M without constraints. Several quantities are used to evaluate classification models M created to distinguish C_+ class:

- Overall accuracy $A(M) = p_{++}(M) + p_{--}(M)$
- Overall error rate $L(M) = p_{-+}(M) + p_{+-}(M)$
- Overall rejection rate $R(M) = p_{+r}(M) + p_{-r}(M) = 1 - L(M) - A(M)$
- Sensitivity $S_+(M) = p_{+|+}(M) = p_{++}(M)/p_+$, or conditional probability of predicting class C_+ when the vector was indeed from this class.
- Specificity $S_-(M) = p_{-|-}(M) = p_{--}(M)/p_-$ (same for class C_-).

Note that the overall accuracy is equal to a combination of sensitivity and specificity weighted by the a priori probabilities:

$$A(M) = p_+S_+(M) + p_-S_-(M) \tag{13}$$

Thus sensitivity (specificity) plays the role of accuracy of the model for the C_+ (C_-) class only, with p_+ (p_-) being the fraction of samples from this class (other classes) in the training set. In the K-class problem one can always use a separate model to distinguish between a single class C_+ and all other classes C_-. The cost function for the model M_+ is (all $p_{ij} = p_{ij}(M_+)$):

$$E(M_+;\gamma) = \gamma L(M_+) - A(M_+) = \gamma\,(p_{+-} + p_{-+}) - (p_{++} + p_{--}) \tag{14}$$

should be minimized over parameters of the M_+ model created for the C_+ class. For large γ only the error is important and it may decrease at the expense of the rejection rate, for example by making the rule intervals more tight or the thresholds for neural activity closer to 1 and 0. In extreme case no errors will be made on the training set since the classifier will reject all such cases. For $\gamma = 0$ only accuracy is maximized, leading to less rejections. Using the error (loss) and the rejection rate the formula (14) becomes:

$$\min_M E(M;\gamma) \Leftrightarrow \min_M \{(1+\gamma)L(M) + R(M)\} \tag{15}$$

For $\gamma = 0$ a sum of the overall error and rejection rate is minimized, while for large γ the error term dominates, allowing the rejection rate to grow. In many applications it is important to achieve highest sensitivity or specificity. The error function (15) distinguishes only one of these quantities. Introduction of relative costs should be used instead. If the cost of assigning vectors from true class C_- to the predicted class C_+ is set to 1, and the cost of making an opposite error is α, the cost function is:

$$\min_M E(M;\alpha) = \min_M \{p_{+-}(M) + \alpha p_{-+}(M)\} \tag{16}$$

$$= \min_M \{p_+(1 - S_+(M)) - p_{+r}(M) + \alpha\,[p_-(1 - S_-(M)) - p_{-r}(M)]\} \tag{17}$$

For $\alpha = 0$ this is equivalent to maximization of $p_{++}(M) + p_{+r}(M)$ and for large α to maximization of $p_{--}(M) + p_{-r}(M)$.

Receiver Operator Characteristic (ROC) curves show the S_+ values as a function of $1 - S_-$, allowing for another way of adjusting the rejection thresholds. The approach described here allows for optimization with explicit costs; we have used it to optimize logical rules [4] where all predictions are binary and ROC approach is not so convenient.

3 Conclusions

Three types of corrections that can be applied *a posteriori*, i.e. after the model has already been trained, has been described in this paper. Some of these corrections may also be applied during the training process. They are aimed either at:
1) the overall increase of accuracy by scaling the probabilities on the training set and adding linear or nonlinear (softmax) scaling factors,
2) restoring the balance between the training and the test set if the distributions are quite different, or
3) improving confidence of classification, selectivity or specificity of results.

The first of these corrections is similar (although simpler) to the effect of adding an additional linear or non-linear perceptron trained on results obtained from other models, a procedure known as stacking [1]. Tests with the kNN method on DNA splice data set and other datasets show that this correction may improve results with no computational cost. The second correction is useful in real-world situations, when real distribution of classes in the data does not match the distribution in the data given for training. Finally the overall accuracy is not always the most important parameter. Relations between costs, selectivity, specificity and error functions have been investigated. We found them especially useful for optimization of logical rules.

More empirical tests are needed to evaluate usefulness of these corrections in practice, but our preliminary results are encouraging.

Acknowledgments: Support by the Polish Committee for Scientific Research, grant 8 T11C 006 19, is gratefully acknowledged.

References

1. Wolpert D.H. (1992) Stacked generalization. Neural Networks **5**, 241-259
2. Saerens M, Lattinne P, Decaestecker C. (2002) Adjusting the outputs of a classifier to new a priori probabilities: a simple procedure. Neural Computations (in press).
3. D. Michie, D.J. Spiegelhalter and C.C. Taylor, "Machine learning, neural and statistical classification". Elis Horwood, London 1994
4. Duch W, Adamczak R. and Grźbczewski K. (2001) Methodology of extraction, optimization and application of crisp and fuzzy logical rules. *IEEE Transactions on Neural Networks* **12**: 277-306

Competent Undemocratic Committees

Włodzisław Duch, Łukasz Itert, and Karol Grudziński

Department of Informatics, Nicholas Copernicus University,
Grudziądzka 5, 87-100 Toruń, Poland. http://www.phys.uni.torun.pl/kmk

Abstract. Committees of models are frequently employed to improve accuracy and decrease the variance of individual models. Each model has an equal right to vote (democratic procedure), despite obvious differences in model competence in different regions of the feature space. Adding competence factors to different models before calculation of the committee decision (undemocratic procedure) improves the quality of the committee. A method for creation of a committee of competent models is described and empirical tests presented.

1 Introduction

Combining information from different classifiers is an important and quite popular subject in machine learning. Whole conferences and special issues of journals are devoted to this subject (see references in [1]), know as ensemble learning, mixture of experts, voting classification algorithms, or committees of models [2]. Ortega, Koppel and Argamon [1] point out that there are problems, such as predicting the glucose levels of diabetic patients, that a large number of different learning algorithms have been applied.

Mixture of models may not only improve the accuracy of a single model, but also may decrease the variance, stabilizing and improving generalization of the whole system [3]. Two sources contribute to the variability of models created for use in a committee: different samples taken from the same data, for example in crossvalidation training or in such methods as boosting, bagging or arcing [2,3] and different bias of models due to the change of their complexity, such as the number of neurons or other parameters. Recently we have developed a framework for similarity based methods (SBM) [4] and used some methods that belong to this framework to create voting committees [5], obtaining significant improvements of results and decrease of variance of committee errors.

Typical voting techniques follow the democratic majority decision, linear combination or selecting the most confident models. In the mixture of experts neural architecture Jacobs [6] has introduced a gating network to select the most competent model. Very recently Ortega et al [1] used similar idea, a "referee meta-model" deciding which model should contribute to the final decision. These undemocratic procedures exploit the fact that different models may have different areas of competence. The idea of competent voting was also mentioned in [7] but has not been developed further. Global selection of competent models has recently been introduced [8]. Instead of training a meta-model each area of the input space in which a given model makes a number of errors is identified and a penalty factor is used to decrease the influence of this model during the voting.

In the next section methods for model combination are briefly discussed and algorithms for creating committees of competent models are described. In the third section results of a numerical experiment are presented. Finally some conclusions and plans for further work are given.

2 Combining models

Individual models are frequently unstable [3], i.e. quite different models are created as a result of repeated training (if learning algorithms are stochastic) or if the training set is slightly perturbed [9]. The mixture of models allows to approximate complicated probability distributions quite accurately. With $l = 1..m$ models providing estimation of probabilities $P(C_i|\mathbf{X};M_l)$ for $i = 1..K$ classes, one can use the majority voting, average results of all models, select one model that has highest confidence (i.e. gives the largest probability), set a threshold to select a subset of models with highest confidence and use majority voting for these models.

An empirical comparison of voting algorithms, including bagging and boosting, has been published by Bauer and Kohavi [10]. Tests were made using decision trees and naive Bayes method. The bagging algorithm uses classifiers trained on bootstrap samples, created by randomly drawing a fixed number of training data vectors from the pool which always contains all training vectors (i.e. drawing does not remove them from the pool). Results are aggregated by voting. AdaBoost (Adaptive Boosting) creates a sequence of training sets and determines weights of the training instances, with higher weights for those that are incorrectly classified. The arcing method uses a simplified procedure for weighting of the training vectors. Bauer and Kohavi [10] provided an interesting decomposition of bias and variance components of errors for these algorithms. Renormalized product of different predictors has been advocated recently by Hinton [11] in context of unsupervised probability density estimation.

A linear meta-model

$$p(C_i|\mathbf{X};M) = \sum_{l=1}^{m} W_{i,l} P(C_i|\mathbf{X};M_l) \tag{1}$$

provides additional mK linear parameters for model combination, determined using the standard Least Mean Squares (LMS) procedure.

3 Committees of Competent Models (CCM)

So far all models selected to the ensemble were allowed to vote on the final result. Krogh and Vedelsby [12] showed that ensemble generalization error is small if highly accurate classifiers disagreeing with each other are used. Contrary to this idea Xin Yao has used averaging of results with negative correlation between individual models to diversify their pool [13]. Each model does not need to be accurate for all data, but should account well for a different (overlapping) subset of data.

The Similarity Based Models [4] use reference vectors (selected from a training set) and it is relatively easy to determine the areas of the input space where a given model is competent (makes a few errors) and where it fails. Vectors that cannot be correctly classified show up as errors that all model make, but some vectors that are erroneously classified by one model may be correctly handled by another. This information may be used in several ways. A simple algorithm that includes information on the competence of different models is presented below.

1. Optimize parameters for all models $M_l, l = 1 \dots m$ on the training set using a cross-validation procedure.
2. For each model $l = 1 \dots m$
   (a) for all training vectors $\mathbf{R}_i$ generate predicted classes $C_l(\mathbf{R}_i)$;
   (b) if $C_l(\mathbf{R}_i) \neq C(\mathbf{R}_i)$, i.e. model M_l makes an error for vector R_i, determine the area of incompetence of the model, finding the distance $d_{i,j}$ to the nearest vector that M_l has correctly classified;
   (c) set parameters of the incompetence factor $F(||\mathbf{X}-\mathbf{R}_i||; M_l)$ in such a way that its value decreases significantly for $||\mathbf{X}-\mathbf{R}_i|| \geq d_{i,j}/2$.
3. The incompetence function for the model $F(\mathbf{X}; M_l)$ is a product of factors $F(||\mathbf{X}-\mathbf{R}_i||; M_l)$ for all training vectors that have been incorrectly handled.

The incompetence function $F(\mathbf{X}; M_l) \approx 1$ in all areas where the model has worked well and $F(\mathbf{X}; M_l) \approx 0$ near the training vectors where errors were made. A number of functions may be used for that purpose: a Gaussian function $F(||\mathbf{X}-\mathbf{R}_i||; M_l) = 1 - G(||\mathbf{X}-\mathbf{R}_i||^a; \sigma_i)$, where $a \geq 1$ coefficient is used to flatten the function, a simpler $F(||\mathbf{X}-\mathbf{R}_i||; M_l) = 1/(1+||\mathbf{X}-\mathbf{R}_i||^{-a})$ function or a sum of two logistic functions $\sigma(-||\mathbf{X}-\mathbf{R}_i|| - d_{i,j}/2) + \sigma(||\mathbf{X}-\mathbf{R}_i|| - d_{i,j}/2)$. Since a number of factors enters the incompetence function of the model each factor should quickly reach 1 outside the incompetence area. This is achieved either by using large a values, high slopes of sigmoids or defining a cut-off values where a value 1 is taken.

Such committee of competent models may be used in several ways. In the voting phase nearest neighbor reference vectors should be determined and only those classifiers that are competent should be included in the voting procedure. If no competent models are found the vector given for classification is probably an outlier and should be left as 'rejected' or 'impossible to classify'. Sometimes it helps if all such vectors are removed from the training set, but this is achieved automatically by competent classifiers.

Even simpler way of creating competent committee is introduced if linear combinations are used instead of majority voting. For class C_i coefficients of linear combination are determined from the least-mean square solution of:

$$p(C_i|\mathbf{X}; M) = \sum_{l=1}^{m} \sum_{m} W_{i,l} F(\mathbf{X}; M_l) P(C_i|\mathbf{X}; M_l) \quad (2)$$

The incompetence factors simply modify probabilities $F(\mathbf{X}; M_l)P(C_i|\mathbf{X}; M_l)$ that are used to set linear equations for all training vectors $\mathbf{X}$, therefore the solution is done in the same way as before. After renormalization $p(C_i|\mathbf{X}; M)/\sum_j P(C_j|\mathbf{X}; M)$ give final probability of classification. In contrast to AdaBoost and similar procedures [2] explicit information about competence, or quality of classifier performance in different feature space areas, is used here.

4 Numerical experiments

Numerical experiments were made on Telugu vowel data [14] containing intensities of 3 formants, for 6 vowels. The classes overlap strongly and 871 samples are given in the dataset. The results of different tests are collected in Table 1. Other methods discussed in ref. [14] gave worse results.

Table 1. Comparison of results on Telugu vowel data. 2xCV means 2-fold stratified crossvalidation test.

System	Accuracy	Remarks
CUC committee	88.2± 0.6%	2xCV (our calculation)
kNN	86.1± 0.6%	k=3, Euclidean, 2xCV (our calculation)
MLP	84.6 %	2xCV, 10 neurons [14]
Fuzzy MLP	84.2 %	2xCV, 10 neurons [14]
Bayes Classifier	79.2 %	2xCV, [14]
Fuzzy Kohonen	73.5 %	2xCV, [14]

Since our calculations with the nearest neighbor classifier gave quite promising results we have divided the dataset randomly into two parts and trained a committee of kNN models on each part, treating the other part as test data. The committee included the following models: M_1 with k=10, Euclidean, M_2 with k=13, Manhatan, M_3 with k=5, Euclidean and M_4 with k=5 and Manhatan.

Table 2. Accuracy of 4 models for each class, in %.

Class	M_1	M_2	M_3	M_4
C_1	50.0	45.8	65.3	62.5
C_2	88.8	91.0	87.6	89.9
C_3	84.3	84.3	84.9	84.7
C_4	85.4	84.8	90.1	88.1
C_5	91.3	88.4	90.3	90.1
C_6	90.6	92.8	90.1	90.4
Average	85.1	84.6	86.1	86.0

Accuracy of each model is given in Table 2. Although the overall accuracy may be similar these models significantly differ in the accuracy for different classes. If one could select the best model for a given class, for example model 3 for class 1, accuracy would grow to 87.9%, but of course the class cannot be selected, it should be predicted. 86 vectors were assigned to their classes incorrectly by all 4 models, giving a chance to account correctly for the remaining 785 vectors, or 90.1 % of all vectors.

The Table 3 contains results obtained from 4 types of committees, created by majority voting, selecting the model with highest confidence, linear combination (1) and a linear combination with competence factors (2). Results obtained with committees are usually better than results of a single model, with majority voting is the worst, the highest confidence and linear combination on the same level (slightly better) and a significant improvement for the linear combination of competent models.

Table 3. Results from committees created in 4 ways: by majority voting, highest confidence, linear combination and a linear combination with competence factors.

Class	Majority	Confidence	Combination	+ Competence
C_1	54.2	58.3	62.5	65.3
C_2	88.8	88.8	88.8	89.9
C_3	84.3	84.9	84.3	84.9
C_4	86.8	88.1	88.1	88.1
C_5	92.3	92.8	92.3	93.8
C_6	90.6	92.2	91.7	93.3
Average	85.9	87.0	87.0	88.2

5 Conclusions

Although more empirical tests are needed, assigning incompetence factors in various voting procedures, including linear combination of models, is an attractive idea that may significantly improve analysis of difficult problems. Since there is no need to create a single model that handles all data correctly learning may become modular, with each model specializing in different subproblems. A constructive approach to committee growth may be used: after creating initial committee by combining competent models created so far new models should be searched that classify correctly just those vectors, that the committee has still problems with.

Ideas presented here may be developed in a number of directions. So far we have tried to aggregate only a few models generated with different parameters. The same procedure may be applied to models generated using adaptive boosting or similar algorithms [2]. An interesting possibility is to train a neural network, providing input vectors and predicting competent models. A combination of classifiers gives Receiver Operator Characteristic (ROC) curves that cover a convex combination of all individual ROC curves, allowing to reach better operating points, i.e. detection rates for a given false alarm rate [17]. Models that end up with small effective coefficients for all training data may be pruned. Diversification of models by adding explicit negative correlation is also worth considering [13]. A lot of other options remains to be investigated.

Acknowledgments: Support by the Polish Committee for Scientific Research, grant 8 T11C 006 19, is gratefully acknowledged.

References

1. Ortega J, Koppel M, Argamon S. (2001) Arbitrating Among Competing Classifiers Using Learned Referees. Knowledge and Information Systems **3**, 470-490
2. Bauer E, Kohavi R. (1999) An empirical comparison of voting classification algorithms: bagging, boosting and variants. *Machine learning* **36**, 105-142
3. Breiman, L. (1998): Bias-Variance, regularization, instability and stabilization. In: Bishop, C. (Ed.) Neural Networks and Machine Learning. Springer, Berlin, Heidelberg, New York
4. Duch W. (2000) Similarity based methods: a general framework for classification, approximation and association, Control and Cybernetics **29**, 937-968
5. Duch W, Grudziński K. (2001) Ensembles of Similarity-Based Models. Inteligent Information Systems 2001, Advances in Soft Computing, Physica Verlag (Springer), pp. 75-85
6. Jacobs R. A. (1997) Bias/Variance Analyses of Mixtures-of-Experts Architectures. Neural Computation **9**, 369-383
7. Duch W, Adamczak R, Diercksen G.H.F. (2000) Classification, Association and Pattern Completion using Neural Similarity Based Methods. Applied Mathematics and Computer Science **10**, 101-120
8. Giacinto G, Roli F. Dynamic Classifier Selection Based on Multiple Classifier Behaviour. Pattern Recognition, 34 (2001) 179-181
9. Avnimelech R, Intrator N. (1999) Boosted Mixture of Experts: An Ensemble Learning Scheme. Neural Computation **11**, 483-497
10. Bauer E, Kohavi R. (1999) An empirical comparison of voting classification algorithms: Bagging, Boosting and variants. Machine Learning 36, 105-139
11. Hinton, G. (2000): *Training products of experts by minimizing contrastive divergence.* Gatsby Computational Neuroscience Unit Technical Report 2000-004
12. Krogh A, Vedelsby J. (1995) Neural Network Ensembles, Cross Validation, and Active Learning. Advances in Neural Information Processing Systems, MIT Press, **7**, 231–238.
13. Yao, X., Liu, Y. (1997): A New Evolutionary System for Evolving Artificial Neural Networks. IEEE Transaction on Neural Networks 8, 694–713
14. Pal, S.K. and Mitra S. (1999) *Neuro-Fuzzy Pattern Recognition.* J. Wiley, New York
15. Duch W, Adamczak R, Grabczewski K, A new methodology of extraction, optimization and application of crisp and fuzzy logical rules. IEEE Transactions on Neural Networks 12 (2001) 277-306
16. D. Michie, D.J. Spiegelhalter and C.C. Taylor, "Machine learning, neural and statistical classification". Elis Horwood, London 1994
17. Swets J.A. (1988) Measuring the accuracy of diagnostic systems. Science **240**, 1285-93

Reasoning in Structured Bayesian Networks

Mieczysław A. Kłopotek[1,2)]

[1)] Institute of Computer Science, Polish Academy of Sciences
[2)] Dept. of Computer Science, Warsaw University of Technology
e-mail: klopotek@ipipan.waw.pl

Abstract: The paper proposes a new type of Bayesian networks, so-called Structured Bayesian Networks (SBN). A new reasoning paradigm is proposed for SBN that is much simpler than for the general type Bayesian networks because the NP hard transformation to Markov trees can be avoided.

1. Introduction

Already for years, Bayesian networks [Pearl, 1988] appear to be a quite popular method of representation of uncertain knowledge. A Bayesian network is an acyclic directed graph (dag) nodes of which are labeled with variables and conditional probability tables of the node variable given its parents in the graph. The joint probability distribution is then expressed by the formula:

$$P(x_1,\ldots\ldots\ldots,x_n) = \prod_{i=1\ldots n} P(x_i \mid pa(x_i)) \qquad (1)$$

where $pa(X_i)$ is the set of parents of the variable (node) X_i.

Bayesian networks allow for efficient reasoning [Laurizen, 1988]. They contain information on conditional independences among variables [Geiger, 1990]. If edges of a network reflect causal relationships among variables, then the network is minimal. Hence Bayesian network can be reconstructed if at least part of conditional independence properties is known. Methods of discovery of Bayesian networks from data based on this suggestion have been elaborated in the past, e.g. algorithms by Spirtes, Glymour and Scheines [1993]: SGS, PC, PC+, CI and FCI.

However, for efficient reasoning, the Bayesian Networks need to be transformed to a special representation of so-called Markov trees (hyper-trees) e.g. via the triangulation process (consult [Shafer, 1996] for details). Transformation of a general Bayesian network to an optimal Markov tree is a NP hard task. Hence special learning procedures were developed to learn Markov-tree-like Bayesian networks directly from data [Cercone et al., 1997]. Markov-trees may ignore quite a large number of conditional independences, losing compactness of representation. General-type Bayesian networks are NP hard for reasoning [Cooper, 1990]. Hence new BN types to keep tractable both reasoning and learning are needed.

In this paper we propose a new class of Bayesian Networks – the structured Bayesian networks - for which efficient reasoning mechanism exist, and which are not as restrictive for learning and Markov trees and offer knowledge representation similar to hierarchical Bayesian networks [Koller, Pfeffer, 1997]).

2. Hypertrees and reasoning in Bayesian Networks

In the approach of Laurizen and Spiegelhalter [1988] to reasoning in Bayesian networks a transformation from a BN (Fig.1a) to a junction tree (called also Markov tree, Fig.2b) is needed. In brief, the stages of this transformation are as follows: first BN is transformed to a moral graph (Fig.1b), that is a graph where arcs of BN get unoriented and the parents of a node get connected (edge SY). Then the moral graph is triangulated (Fig1c) that is edges are added so that in any loop of more than tree nodes two non-neighboring are connected in the graph (edge SZ). This stage is the most time-consuming and a heuristic one.

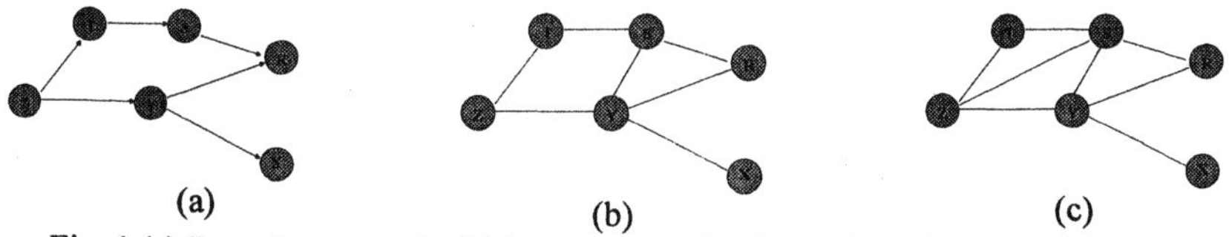

Fig. 1 (a) Bayesian network, (b) its moral graph, (c) its triangulated graph

Then maximal cliques (completely connected subgraphs) are sought. The cliques are called "hypernodes" of a hypertree (Fig.2a). In a hypertree we can find and order < of hypernodes such that for each given hypernode Hk a hypernode Hj can be assigned (j<k) such that for any Hi with i<k $Hi \cap Hk \subseteq Hj \cap Hk$. Node Hk is said to be a twig on the branch Hj. We define a Markov tree or junction tree in such a way that nodes of the tree are the hypernodes and edges connect the corresponding branches and twigs. The edges are labeled with so-called separators, that is sets of nodes common to the twig and the branch (Fig.2b).

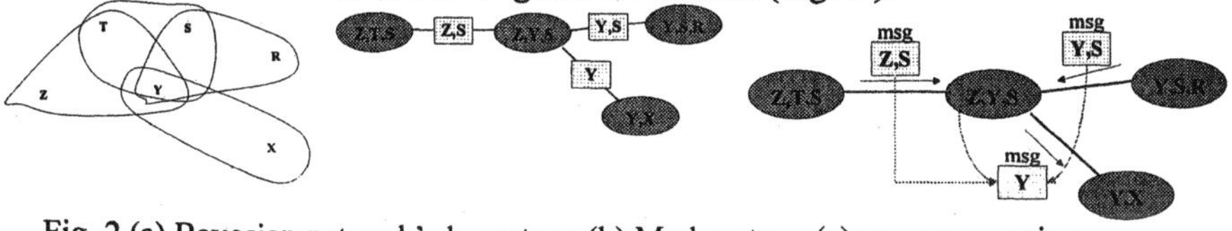

Fig. 2 (a) Bayesian network's hypertree, (b) Markov tree, (c) message passing

For purposes of reasoning each hypernode is assigned a potential. For this purpose the product $\prod_{i=1\ldots n} P(x_i \mid pa(x_i))$ is distributed over the hypernodes in such a way that a hypernode can get $P(X_i \mid pa(X_i))$ only if it contains both X_i and $pa(X_i)$.the potential Pot(Hk) is just the combination of all $P(X_i \mid pa(X_i))$ assigned to it. The potential can include also so-called "indicators" (see below) that will facilitate reasoning in the Bayesian networks.

Reasoning consists in message-passing in Markov tree.. A hypernode sends a message msg to its neighbour, given it receives messages from all the other neighbours. A message consists of combination of the potential and received messages from the other nodes projected onto the separator (Fig.2c). A joint probability distribution of a hypernode is the combination of its potential and the messages of all its neighbours. The complexity of the reasoning process depends on the sizes of the hypernodes (the cardinality of nodes contained in them).

3. Structured Bayesian Networks

A Structured Bayesian Network (SBN, Fig.4) is a Bayesian Network possessing the "collapsing property", illustrated in Fig. 3. A SBN has nodes with 0,1 or 2 ingoing and outgoing arrows. We distinguish two collapsing operators: (1) collapsing a sequence of two nodes where the first has only one ingoing and one outgoing arrow (Fig.3 right), (2) collapsing an "alternative" of nodes, where the first node has two outgoing arrows, the last two ingoing arrows and two nodes between exactly one ingoing and one outgoing arrow (Fig.3 left). The collapsing property means that by application of these collapsing operators we get a network consisting of a single node. Hence there exists a single root node and a single leave node.

We shall call the nodes with two outgoing arrows "branching nodes", and those with two ingoing arrows – "junction nodes". It is obvious that the number of branching nodes must be equal to the number of junction nodes. The junction node and the branching node participating in a single collapsing operation shall be called "corresponding nodes".

The collapsing operator may be viewed as elimination of the nodes preceding the last one on a given scheme by marginalizing them out.

$$P(\{x_1,\dots\dots,x_n\}\text{-pa}(x_k)) = \Sigma_{\text{pa}(xk)} \prod_{i=1\dots n} P(x_i \,|\text{pa}(x_i)) \tag{2}$$

Due to the specific structure of the network, the whole elimination process may be run locally:

$$P(\{x_1,\dots\dots,x_n\}\text{-pa}(x_k)) = \tag{3}$$
$$= \prod_{\{x1,\dots\dots,xn\}\text{-}\{xk\}\text{-pa}(xk)} P(x_i \,|\text{pa}(x_i))\ \Sigma_{\text{pa}(xk)} P(x_k \,|\text{pa}(x_k)) \prod_{y\in \text{pa}(xk)} P(y \,|\text{pa}(y))$$

It is important to see that any collapsing operation involves at most 4 nodes. This limits the space complexity of the operation to the respective dimensions.

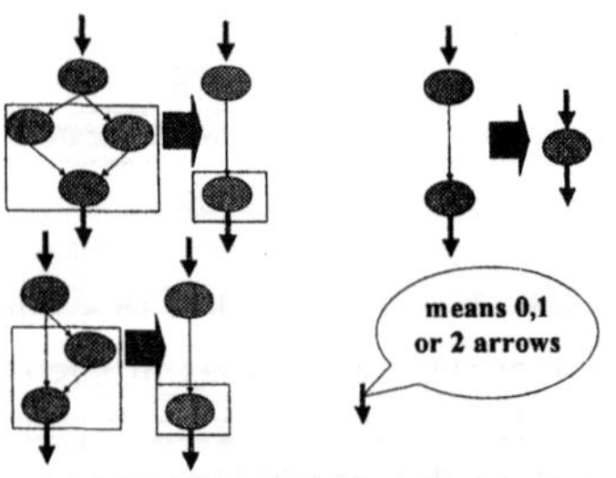

Fig. 3 Collapsing property

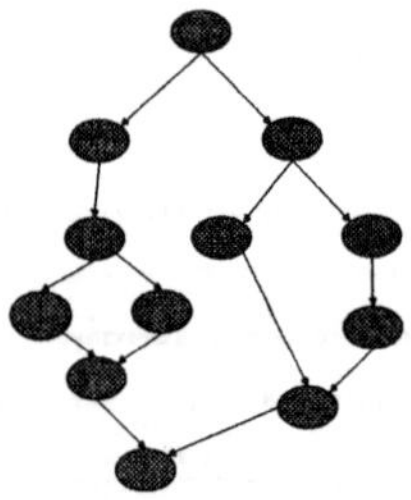

Fig. 4 A structured Bayesian network

A SBN is similar to the concept of hierarchical Bayesian networks: with collapsed nodes representing subnetworks. Any tree structured and polytree structured Bayesian network can be turned to an SBN by adding some supplementary nodes and splitting nodes with more than two in- or outgoing edges[1]. If for a network the collapsing operators would lead to a tree or a polytree (instead to a single

[1] In fact, any Bayesian network can be transformed to SBN in a systematic way [Klopotek, 2002].

node), we would see that we have to do with extended SBN. Handling an extended SBN is similar to the pure SBN, hence we will concentrate on the pure SBN below.

4. Margins in Structured Bayesian Networks

Let us concentrate first on marginal distribution calculations. Given an SBN, if we want to calculate the margin of a variable, then we do not need to take into account any node that is neither direct nor indirect predecessor of the node. It is a matter of simple formula (1) transformations. After eliminating those nodes that are not needed, we can apply many times the collapsing operators and we will obtain finally the margin for this node. Remember that at each collapsing operations at most 4 nodes will be involved so that the amount of memory needed for margin calculation is limited and linear in the size of the network whatever the size of the network. For general type BNs the amount of memory may grow exponentially with the number of nodes.

We can also easily derive a local computations procedure for calculation of margins for all variables, with nodes collecting information from their direct neighbors and – in case of "junction nodes"- information from the corresponding branching node. A node with only one predecessor would require only the marginal distribution of its predecessor to calculate its own marginal. A node with two predecessors ("junction" node) would require conditional distributions of its predecessors on the corresponding branching node and the marginal of that branching node. This would imply propagation of conditional and marginal distributions over the net (twice the effort of Markov tress) which is still tractable during reasoning.

5. Reasoning in Structured Bayesian Networks

In Bayesian networks, "reasoning" means calculating conditional probabilities of nodes given other nodes take on some particular values. In practice, this is achieved modifying the joint probability distribution with so-called "indicator" multipliers. "Unnormalized" conditional margins are calculated. When conditioning on X_k, the indicator multiplier $P_I(x_k)$ takes on the value 1 if the variable X_k takes the value x_k and is equal 0 otherwise. For the sake of uniformity, for all the variables X_i on which we do not condition, we assume that $P_I(x_i)$ has value 1 for every value x_i of the variable X_i.

With this assumption in mind we have a modified "joint probability distribution":

$$P(x_1,\ldots\ldots\ldots,x_n) \prod_{i=1\ldots n} P_I(x_i) = \prod_{i=1\ldots n} P_I(x_i) P(x_i \,|pa(x_i)) \qquad (4)$$

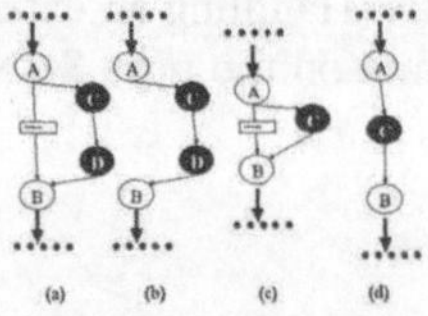

Fig. 5 the four cases

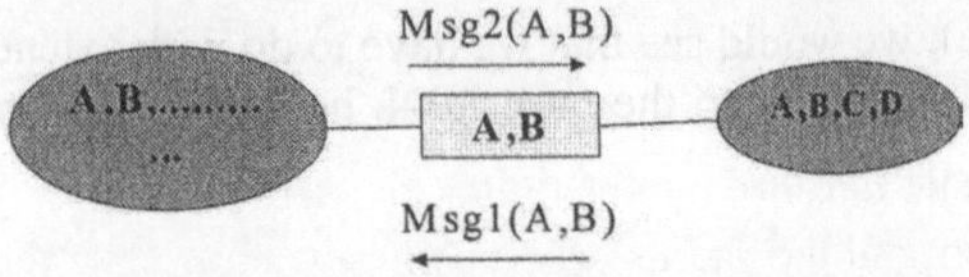

Fig. 6 "dynamic" Markov tree

Reasoning means now calculating margin of the variables of interest in this distribution. However, now we cannot rely on possibility of ignoring non-predecessor nodes. As a consequence, we can in fact calculate only the marginal of the leaf node using the procedure indicated in previous section, and also the joint probability distribution of the root and the leaf. Again, at each stage of computation only at most four nodes are engaged. To calculate margins of the remaining variables we need a trick that shall be called "dynamic Markov tree".

We shall distinguish four significant cases: (1) A pair of corresponding junction/branching (C,D in Fig.5b) nodes lies on a directed path between two nodes (A,B) of known joint distribution (at some level of collapsing) (2) A non-junction/non-branching node (C in Fig.5d) lies on a directed path between two nodes (A,B) of known joint distribution (at some level of collapsing). (3) A pair of corresponding junction/branching nodes (C,D in Fig.5a) lies on one of (branchless) paths between two corresponding junction/branching nodes (A,B) of known joint distribution (at some level of collapsing). (4) A non-junction/non-branching node (C,D in Fig.5c) lies on one of (branchless) paths between two corresponding junction/branching nodes (A,B) of known joint distribution (at some level of collapsing).

In any of these cases we can imagine that we transform for a moment the whole network into a Markov tree (as in Fig.6) such that we put the node or nodes with unknown marginal distributions (C,D) together with nodes of known distribution (A,B) into one hypernode (with potential equal to combination of the conditional distributions of B given A and D, C given A ,D given A as calculated during collapsing), and the remaining nodes of the network. Together with the nodes of known distribution (A,B) into another node. The nodes with known distribution (A,B) can serve as separator of the nodes with unknown margins from the rest of the network. The joint distribution of the separator (P(A,B)) is equal to the message from the remaining network "combined" with the potential of the small hypernode marginalized to the separator $(Msg2(A,B)*Pot(A,B,C,D)^{\downarrow A,B})$. As we know P(A,B) and $Pot(A,B,C,D)^{\downarrow A,B}$, we can easily calculate message Msg2(A,B) (by point wise division), and then derive P(A,B,C,D)=Msg2(A,B)*Pot(A,B,C,D), and hence we get P(C,D). So we can calculate stepwise all the distributions of nodes along a nesting hierarchy of nodes of SBN. At any stage no more than 4 nodes are engaged in the calculation so that the limitation of space needed is granted. Only one passage down the hierarchy is needed to propagate the marginal distribution of the root and the leaf to all the other nodes.

6. Final remarks

In this paper we have outlined a completely new method of reasoning in Bayesian networks. It is applicable to a more general class of networks then known reasoning methods: fusion of Pearl [1988], junction-tree method of Laurizen and Spiegelhalter [1988], hypertree method of Shafer [1996], edge reversal of Shachter [1990]. Contrary to these approaches it is always limited to consideration of at most 4 nodes at once. Also the change of the graph structure by adding new nodes in a way conforming to SBN requirements will not change the reasoning in any way.

Many Bayesian network learning methods can be cast to the new type of BN. The SBN can be learned in a manner proposed e.g. in [Cercone et al., 1997]. After defining a quality criterion, we can add stepwise oriented edges in such a way as to keep the SBN or extended SBN property. Another approach would be to start from a tree-like Bayesian network (as e.g. in [Cheng, 1997]) and then to add subsequent edges maximizing some quality criterion

References

[Cercone et al., 1997] Cercone N., Wong S.K.M., Xiang Y.: A 'Microscopic' study of minimum entropy search in learning decomposable Markov networks. *Machine Learning*, 1997, vol. 26, nr 1. .65-92

[Cheng et al., 1997] Cheng J., Bell D.A. and Liu W.: Learning belief networks from data: an information theory based approach. Proceedings of the Sixth ACM Int. Conf. on Information and Knowledge Management, 1997.

[Cooper, 1990] Cooper G. The computational complexity of probabilistic inference using Bayesian belief networks. Artif. Intell. 42,1990, 395-405

[Geiger et al., 1990] Geiger D., Verma T., Pearl J.: D-Separation: From theorems to algorithms. M.Henrion, et.al eds.. *Uncertainty in Artificial Intelligence* 5, Elsevier 139-148

[Klopotek, 2002] Klopotek M.A., Well-Structured Program Graphs and the issue of local computations. To appear in Proc. Intelligent Inf. Systems Conf., Sopot, 3-6 June 2002.

[Koller, Pfeffer, 1997] Koller D., Pfeffer A.: Object-Oriented Bayesian Networks. Proc. of the 13th Conf. on Uncertainty in Artificial Intelligence (UAI-97), 1997, 302-313

[Laurizen, 1988] Lauritzen, S.L., and Spiegelhalter, D.J. Local computations with probabilities on graphical structures and their application to expert systems. J. R. Statist. Soc. B-50(1988)157-224

[Pearl, 1988] Pearl J.: *Probabilistic Reasoning in Intelligent Systems: Networks of Plausible Inference*. Morgan Kaufmann, San Mateo CA, 1988

[Shachter, 1990] Shachter B.D.: Evidence absorption and propagation through evidence reversals. In M. Henrion, B.D. Shachter, L.N. Kanal, J.F. Lemmer (eds): *Uncertainty in Artificial Intelligence* 5, Elsevier Science Publishers B.V (1990), 173- 190

[Shafer, 1996] Shafer, G.: Probabilistic Expert Systems, SIAM CBMS-NSF Regional Conference Series in Applied Mathematics, Philadelphia, 1996, vol. 67

[Spirtes et al., 1993] Spirtes P., Glymour C., Scheines R.: *Causation, Prediction and Search*, Lecture Notes in Statistics 81, Springer-Verlag, 1993.

Machine Learning Methods for Improving Gender Recognition from Stop Consonants

Ewa Lukasik[1], Robert Susmaga[2]

Institute of Computing Science, Poznan University of Technology,
ul. Piotrowo 3a, 60-965 Poznan, Poland
e-mail: [1]Ewa.Lukasik@cs.put.poznan.pl, [2]Robert.Susmaga@cs.put.poznan.pl

Abstract: In the paper we present results of the extensive search for the best machine learning method enabling the recognition of data set with fuzzy boundaries between classes. The data under investigation were particular voiceless speech signals of non-stationary character: /p/, /t/ and /k/, carrying some information about gender of the speaker. The classification accuracy of 16 classifiers was compared, all working on the same attribute set consisting of cepstral coefficients. Reduced and extended (using feature construction methods) versions of attribute sets have also been considered. Surprisingly the best results have been observed for neural network and distance based classifiers and reached 87% of classification accuracy.

1. Introduction

Searching for the acoustic characteristics of stop consonants (voiced /b,d,g/ and voiceless /p,t,k/) has always been important research domain in speech processing. The goal was to improve still poor distinctions in this class of sounds in automatic speech recognition (ASR) systems. Stop consonants (known also as plosives) are dynamic, short, speaker and context dependent. Speaker variability elements that count are e.g. gender, accent, age or speech rate.

Voiceless stop consonants, on sight, could be treated as speaker invariable signals of non-stationary character – yet no tonal sound is emitted (such an approach was proposed e.g. in [11]). However, they are produced in the singular vocal tract and some differences are inevitable. Therefore it is interesting to define the degree of dissimilarity of speaker variability aspects or even to find some cues to speaker identification/verification (ASI/V) from stops.

Traditional ASR and ASI/V use similar techniques of pattern recognition. Front-end representation, feature (attributes) extraction and reduction, template matching, distance measures and stochastic models are common to both applications (although the template/models may employ different information in both cases). High degree of relevance to the sound characteristics and classification task on each stage is essential for the final performance of the classifier.

In this paper the possibility of gender recognition from voiceless stop consonants /p,t,k/ has been exploited. Gender is one of the main speaker variability factors, the distinction of which could help in both ASR and ASI/V processes. The goal of the work is to find out what is the influence of the classification method on the gender classification accuracy for a given set of attributes. We also try to answer the question if the machine learning methods are able to discover more information than may be driven from acoustic only features.

The work reported here is the part of the broader project accumulating the best of the methods used on all stages of the classification process. It joins activities that are currently conducted mainly in isolation and we expect it creates the synergy between seemingly different areas, that signal processing and machine learning seem to be now.

2. Characteristics of stop consonants

Stops are transient, non-continuous sounds, which are produced by a total obstruction of the oral tract followed by a sudden release of the pressure [7]. During the obstruction phase, no sound (voiceless stops: /p/, /t/, /k/) or only a small amount of low frequency energy due to the vibration of the vocal cords (voiced stops /b/, /d/, /g/) is radiated from the lips. Stops are made up of a sequence of acoustic events. The sequence of these events is following: a silence corresponding to the period of closure of the vocal tract, a burst corresponding to a sudden release of the air pressure (the spectral shape of the burst depends on the place of articulation), a friction noise followed by a period of aspiration, and finally, formant transition to the subsequent vowel. First three events are illustrated in Fig.1. The most characteristic information concerning the place of articulation is contained in the burst onset.

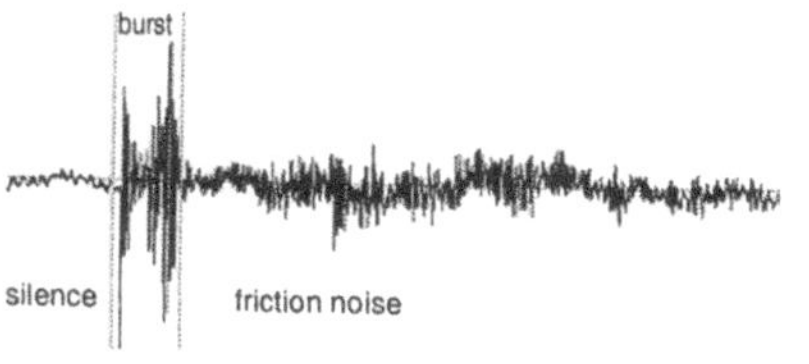

Fig. 1. Stages of the evolution of plosive /k/ in the male's utterance /Dominik/.

All stop characteristics are in fact influenced by the vowels that precede and follow it. The formant values at the release appear to provide a link between the characteristics of the burst spectrum and their ensuing development and in general are influenced by the subsequent vowel [6]. There probably the gender manifestation takes its origin.

3. Speech material

The data for experiments has been taken from speech database for Polish - CORPORA [3]. For the purpose of this work the extraction of stops has been performed manually, with the burst onset as the starting point and beginning of the transition as the final point. Although most of information characterizing plosives is contained in the burst onset we decided to take into account the following friction noise which slightly smoothes the spectrum but in this way segmentation (manual or automatic) becomes easier. It should be noted that each plosive comes form different, unrepeatable utterance. In this way we collected 854 observations: /p/ – 95 male, 129 female, /t/ – 98 male, 248 female, /k/ – 123 male, 161 female. The observation length varies from 80 to over 1200 samples, i.e. from 5 ms to almost 100 ms.

4. Methodology

It is important that machine learning tools may be applied only after the data receives the form of observations (objects) described by vectors of feature values (attributes). Usually this requires transforming the data (stored originally in time-domain) into alternative domains (e.g. frequency domain, time-scale domain etc.). Then actual classification may take place, which will be exploited here with a variety of machine learning algorithms.

4.1 Feature extraction

Transformation of the sounds into alternative domain has been performed using standard 'time to frequency' transformation method realized using DFT or DCT. In result we get data in the form of observations described by a number of coefficients that can be treated as attribute values. Depending on the factor analyzed, appropriate spectral scale should be used, for vocal tract characteristics being the intermediate scale, which can be achieved by cepstral smoothing performed by widowing the Fourier transform of the log spectrum of the spectrum (cepstrum). Each subsequent cepstral coefficient adds more details to spectrum envelope. In Fig. 2. spectral envelope using 15 and 25 coefficients is depicted and in Fig. 3 - averaged spectrum envelopes for male and female speakers. In our particular experiment first 25 cepstral coefficients were considered as 25 attributes of each of the 854 observations. 26th attribute describes the consonant (/p/,/t/,/k/). The data set created in this way will be further referred to as *Ceps25*.

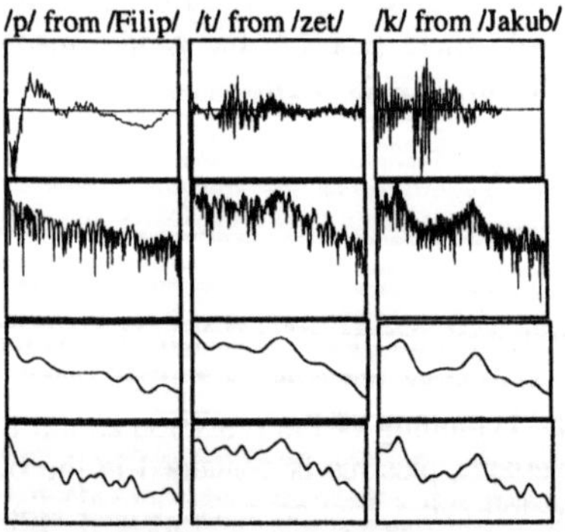

Fig. 2. Waveform, log spectrum, spectrum envelope from 15 and 25 cepstral coefficients for single utterances of male speaker M1.

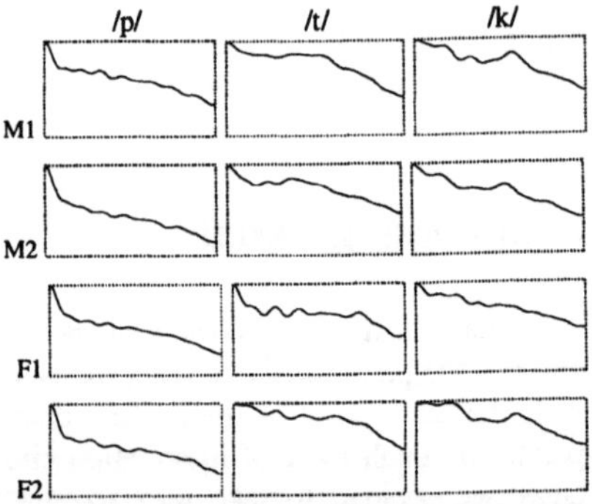

Fig. 3. Averaged spectrum envelope of all /p,t,k/ utterances of male (M1, M2) and female (F1, F2) speakers

4.2 Machine learning aspects

Our idea was not to focus on a single algorithm and 'tune' it to the data but rather to observe the general behavior of a variety of methods. Such an approach will certainly not produce the best possible classifier for the data. Instead, it will allow drawing conclusions regarding the methodologies utilized by the different algorithms, and will also give some insight into the structure of the data set itself.

As classifiers we employed the representatives of:

- distance-based methods (*ib*, *aha-ib*: variants of instance-based classifiers [1]) and *pebls*: [2]),
- decision trees, including classic approaches (*id3*, *c4.5* [13] and their variants: *sgidt*, *t2* [8]) as well as alternative ones (*lazy-dt* [8], *oc1* [12]),
- decision rules (*one-r* [5] and *c4.5-r* [13]),
- naive bayesian methods (*c-nbayes* and *d-nbayes* [9]),
- neural networks (*winnow* [10], *perceptron* [4]),
- decision graphs (*hoodg* [8]).

It must be stressed that the result of classification strongly depends on the selection of attributes that are taken into consideration during the classification process. This fact seems obvious as long as two different subsets of attributes are used and two different results are obtained. It is, however, less obvious in situations with shared attributes, e.g. when two sets of attributes differ in several attributes only. In particular, a removal of an attribute may result in an increase of properly classified observations. On the other hand the more non-linearity characterizes the borders between classes of objects the more difficult the classification becomes. Therefore the process of classification can be assisted by an introduction of attributes that are combinations (linear or non-linear) of the former ones.

5. Experiments and results[1]

During experiments we first considered data set with the original set of attributes (*Ceps25o-full*) and its reduced version (*Ceps25o-red*). Then we enriched this original data set with additional attributes constructed as non-linear combination of the original ones (*Ceps25e-full*). Finally, the enriched data set was reduced producing *Ceps25e-red*. Attribute selection in reduced sets was performed basing on the explicit information provided by the *c4.5* classifier. As far as the classifier validation test is concerned we applied the *N*-fold cross validation test (*N*-fold CV) with *N*=10. The general classifier validation experiments produced the results shown in Fig.4.

In evaluating the classifiers it must be stressed that the distance-based ones (*ib–pebls*) generally outperform the other approaches. Most decision tree building techniques could have failed because they partition the attribute space by axis-orthogonal cuts, which apparently fails to reconstruct the non-linear borders between classes.

---

[1] All computations have been performed in Poznań Supercomputing and Networking Centre

This concerns also the tree-derived methods of decision graphs (*hoodg*). As to rule generating algorithms the simpler approach (*one-r*) markedly failed in all cases, while the other one (*c4.5-r*) can be ranked in the middle. The naive bayesian approaches and the *perceptron* produce similar results on average, although the *perceptron* reacts differently to the variants of the data set. Above-average results can only be observed in case of the *oc1* (a tree generator that induces non-orthogonal cuts) and the *winnow* classifier (a neural network variant). This seems to be indicative of the much non-linearity characterizing the borders between classes. Additionally, relative good performance of the distance-based classifiers (as opposed to the border-reconstructing ones) indicates that the classes of objects form fuzzy and ambiguous 'clouds' in the attribute space rather than well-separated, distinct regions.

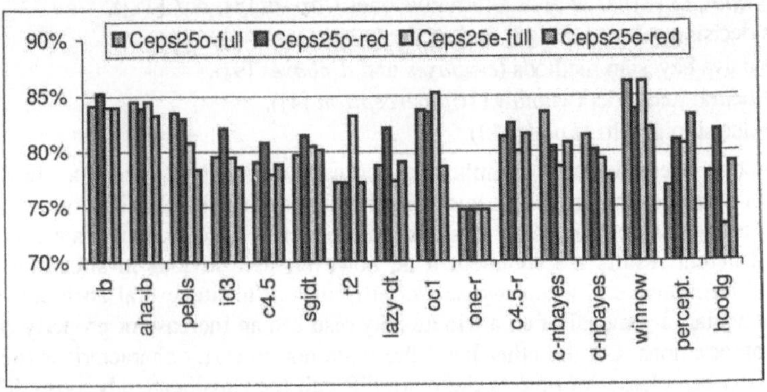

Fig. 4. Percentage of accurate classification rate for different classifiers / data sets

Another observation concerns the influence of attribute selection on the performance of classifiers. Removing some attributes from the original data table, i.e. forming *Ceps25o-red* (9 cepstral coefficients) out of *Ceps25o-full* (25 cepstral coefficients) helped most methods (but not *winnow* and the bayesian classifiers). This would suggest that only several cepstral coefficients prove useful for classification purposes. On the other hand, creating new attributes (the set *Ceps25e-full*) did not help many classifiers (it worked only with *t2* and *oc1*), which may indicate that the existing attributes are satisfactorily exploited. Similarly, reducing this extended set of attributes to *Ceps25e-red* produced a visibly better result only in case of one classifier (the *perceptron*).

Extensive search for optimal parameter values did not improve considerably the classification results: an average 3% increase of classification rate was observed. In particular the *ib* classifier applied to *Ceps25o-full* reached 87% accuracy. This means that revolutionary results are not to be expected here. It also means that approximately 85% of proper classification rate is probably the maximum that can be obtained from the cepstral-based data sets.

6. Conclusions

The research reported in this paper had to determine to what extent the method of classification could improve the classification rate of two-class data set, where the boundaries between classes are very indistinct. This is the case of voiceless plosive consonants /p/, /t/, /k/ uttered by male and female speakers, when gender is the object of recognition. Original set of attributes contained 25 cepstral coefficients, but both extended and reduced set of attributes were also considered. The maximum accuracy was 87%. Generally the best results have been obtained for distance measure based methods with slightly worse results for neural networks.

The data set studied was not very voluminous and slight decrease of the performance may be expected for larger sets. On the other hand, possible improvement may be searched for in other signal representations (e.g. wavelet packets) or acoustic and phonetic cues, that give hints for the attributes choice. The above paths will be explored in future work.

7. References

[1] Aha D.W. (1992), 'Tolerating noisy, irrelevant and novel attributes in instance-based learning algorithms', *International Journal of Man-Machine Studies*, **36**, pp. 267–287.
[2] Cost X. S., Salzberg S. (1993), 'A weighted nearest neighbor algorithm for learning with symbolic features', *Machine Learning*, **10**, pp. 57–78.
[3] Grocholewski S. (1997), 'CORPORA – Speech Database for Polish Difones', *Proc. EUROSPEECH'97*, Rhodes, Greece, pp. 1735-1738.
[4] Hertz J., Krogh A., Palmer R.G. (1991), *Introduction to the Theory of Neural Computation*, Addison Wesley.
[5] Holte R.C. (1993), 'Very simple classification rules perform well on most commonly used datasets', *Machine Learning*, **11**, pp. 63–90.
[6] Jackson P.J.B. (2001), "Acoustic cues of voiced and voiceless plosives for determining place of articulation", *Proc. of the CRAC*, Aalborg, Dennmark.
[7] Junqua J.C., Haton J.P. (1999), 'Robustness in Automatic Speech Recognition', *Kluwer Academic Publishers*, Boston, Dordrecht, London.
[8] Kohavi R., John G, Long R., Manley D., Pfleger K. (1994), 'MLC++: A Machine Learning Library in C++', in: *Proceedings of the Tools with Artificial Intelligence Conference*, IEEE Computer Society Press, pp. 740–743.
[9] Langley P., Iba W., Thompson K. (1992), 'An analysis of bayesian classifiers', in: *Proceedings of the 10th National Conference of Artificial Intelligence*, AAAI Press & MIT Press, pp. 223–228.
[10] Littlestone N. (1988), 'Learning quickly when irrelevant attributes abound: A new linear-threshold algoritm', *Machine Learning*, **2**, pp. 285–318.
[11] Lukasik E. (2000), 'Wavelet Packets based features selection for classification of voiceless plosives', *Proc. ICASSP 2000, IEEE Signal Processing Society*, pp. 689-692.
[12] Murthy S.K., Kasif S., Salzberg S. (1994), 'A system for the induction of oblique decision trees, *Journal of Artificial Intelligence Research*, **2**, pp. 1–33.
[13] Quinlan J.R. (1993), *C4.5: Programs for Machine Learning*, Morgan Kaufmann, CA.

The work has been supported by the Scientific Research Committee grant no 4 T11F 002 22

Sequential Classification

Agata Kołakowska, Witold Malina

Faculty of Electronics, Telecommunications and Informatics,
Technical University of Gdańsk, Poland
agatakol@eti.pg.gda.pl

Abstract. The following article describes an algorithm for constructing a decision tree classifier. It is a modified version of an algorithm in which one class was separated in every node of the tree. Now classes are divided into groups in every node. The proposed splitting method is based on Fisher criterion. The results of experiments on two real datasets are presented in comparison to the previous version of the algorithm.

1 Introduction

Sequential classification is one of possible approaches to pattern recognition. The idea of sequential (multistage) classifiers is to break up a complex decision into a collection of several simpler decisions. Such classifiers are usually represented as decision trees. One of their main advantages is that in different nodes of the tree objects are tested against certain subsets of classes and usually different subsets of features are used.

While constructing these classifiers it is difficult to ensure both high recognition rate and small size of the tree. Most of the decision tree construction procedures are top-down methods, in which the classes are divided into groups in every step. In these approaches the design of a decision tree consists of the following tasks: finding the decision rule for every node, deciding whether a node is terminal or not and finally assigning each terminal node a class label.

The most common way to find the decision rule is to look through a number of possible splits and choose the best one in some sense. Different split quality measures are known [4], i.e. entropy reduction, Gini index etc. We have decided to use Fisher criterion to solve this task.

2 Sequential algorithm

2.1 Fisher criterion for more than two classes

Fisher criterion, a classical method of linear discriminant analysis, is a well known feature extraction method used to solve problems of two classes of objects that have normal distributions. Some extensions of the criterion for many classes have been proposed.

We use the following form of a multiclass Fisher criterion:

$$F_\theta(d) = \frac{d^T B_\theta d}{d^T Ad} = \sum_{i=1}^{L} \frac{P_i[d^T(\mu_i - \theta)]^2}{d^T Ad} \tag{1}$$

where d is the discriminant vector being searched; μ_i, Σ_i, P_i are the mean vector, the covariance matrix and the a priori probability of class c_i; L is the number of classes; $B_\theta = \sum_{i=1}^{L} P_i B_{i\theta}$, $B_{i\theta} = (\mu_i - \theta)(\mu_i - \theta)^T$, θ is the mean vector of the selected class μ_k, $k = 1, 2 \ldots L$; A is the selected class covariance matrix, average covariance matrix or identity matrix.

The vector we are looking for is the one which maximizes $F_\theta(d)$, i.e. the eigenvector of the following matrix:

$$A^{-1}B_\theta \tag{2}$$

2.2 The algorithm for creating sequential classifier

The algorithm described below is a modified version of the algorithm presented in [1, 2]. The main difference is that classes are divided into groups. In the previous version only one class was removed from the set of classes in every step.

A discriminant vector for every class is found and classes are projected onto the discriminant vectors d as it is shown on Fig. 1.

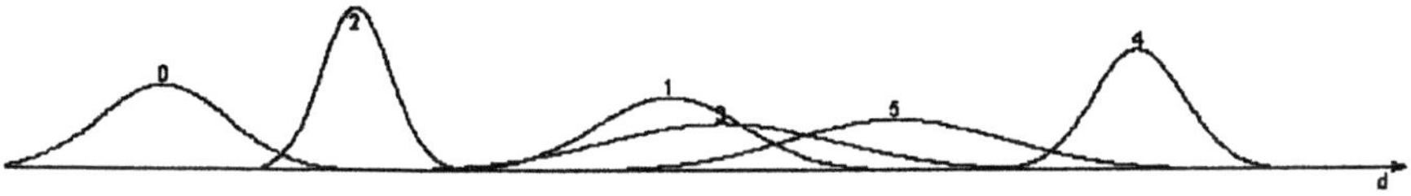

Fig. 1. Classes distribution after projection on a discriminant vector *d*

The distance between two groups is approximated by the distance between two neighbouring classes which are lying on the border between the two groups along vector d. The distance measure between two classes is defined in the following way:

$$F_l(c_L, c_R) = \frac{(m_L - m_R)^2}{s_L^2 + s_R^2} \tag{3}$$

where $m_i = d^T \mu_i$ and $s_i^2 = d^T \Sigma_i d$.

The best split on a given vector is the one which maximizes the following measure:

$$F_2(G_L,G_R) = \max_i F_1(c_i',c_{i+1}') \tag{4}$$

where c_i', c_{i+1}' are the neighbouring classes, $c_i \in G_L$, $c_{i+1} \in G_R$.

The best split over all vectors is the one which maximizes the following distance measure between two groups of classes G_L and G_R:

$$F_3(G_L,G_R) = \max_{d_1(c_i)} F_2(G_L,G_R) \tag{5}$$

If two or more splits have the same value of F_3 then we choose the split which leads to a more balanced tree. If for the distributions from Fig. 1 the distance between class 0 and 2 was the same as between class 2 and 1 we would choose the split between class 2 and 1.

It is worth noticing that two neighbouring classes are not necessary the closest in the sense of measure F_1, for example the distance $F_1(c_2, c_1) > F_1(c_2, c_3)$. But our experimental results convinced us not to take this into account. There was no significant difference in the error rate whereas calculating the distances only between neighbouring classes requires less computations.

After deciding what groups G_L and G_R will be created in the node we have to define the decision rule, i.e. a vector d and a threshold value. To do this we may either use the vector already found or treat the two groups as single classes and use a two-class Fisher criterion to separate them:

$$F(d) = \frac{[d^T(\mu_L - \mu_R)]^2}{d^T \Sigma d} \tag{6}$$

where μ_L and μ_R are the mean vectors of group G_L and G_R; Σ is the average covariance matrix of the two groups.

Both versions of the training algorithm are presented in the following procedure:

1. Assign $C \leftarrow$ set of classes.
2. If there is only one class in C go to step 8.
3. For every class c_i in C find the main discriminant vector $d_1(c_i)$ using criterion (1).
4. For every possible split calculate the distance between the two groups of classes using measure (5).
5. Select the split for which (5) is the highest.

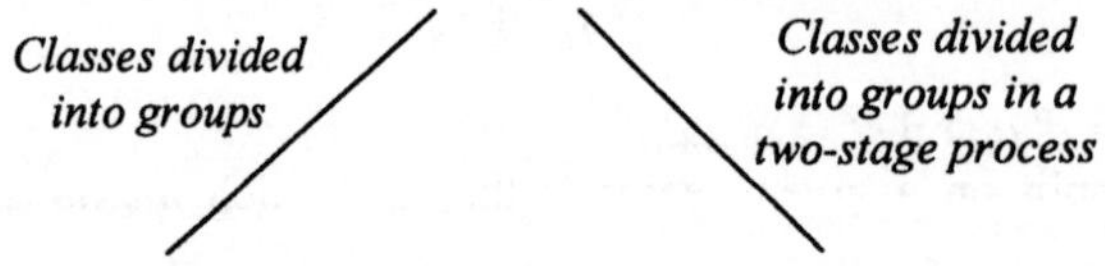

6. Define the decision rule using the vector on which the best split was found.

6a. Treating the two groups use criterion (6) to find the discriminant vector.

6b. Define the decision rule using the vector found in the previous step

7. Repeat procedure for group G_L and G_R.
8. Assign the terminal node the proper class label.

3 Experiments

The algorithm has been implemented and tested on artificial and real data. The first experiments were done on arificial datasets consisting of two-dimensional points of several classes. The results confirmed that the algorithm dividing classes into groups was better than the one separating one class in every step. Then the algorithms were tested on two real datasets which are described below.

3.1 Handwritten digits

The digits have been saved as binary bitmaps of size 32×32 pixels. An *m*×*m* grid has been placed on a digit. Every feature value represents the number of black pixels in a grid square. Using different sizes of the grid we have trained the classifier and classified the digits with different number of features.

Fig. 2. 4×4 feature grid placed on an example digit. The beginning of the feature vector for this digit is [0; 0.17; 0.43; 0.07; ...]

There are 2982 pictures in the dataset which are divided into two subsets. Half of the pictures have been used as a training set and half of them as a test set.

We have tested all three versions of the algorithm with all possible matrices. The best results for all algorithms were obtained using the average covariance matrix for 36 features (6×6 grid).

Table 1. Classification results for three types of algorithms

Type of training algorithm	Recognition rate [%]
One class separated in every step	89.4
Classes divided into groups in every step	90.0
Classes divided into groups in every node in a two-stage process	89.1

3.2 Satellite images

The next task was to recognize the type of soil on a satellite image [3]. Every feature vector represents a 3×3 pixel region. There are four values for each pixel representing intensities in four spectral bands. So the number of features is 36. The number of classes is six. Two separate datasets are given: a training set consisting of 4435 vectors and a test set with 2000 feature vectors.

Our sequential algorithm which divides classes into groups in every step results in a classifier which classifies correctly 84.4 % of the test elements.

Table 2 presents the results obtained using different methods [3].

Table 2. Comparison of classification results obtained for the satellite images dataset using different methods

Method		**Recognition rate [%]**
k-NN	*statistical*	90.6
LVQ	*neural network*	89.5
DIPOL92	*neural network*	88.9
RBF	*neural network*	87.9
ALLOC80	*statistical*	86.8
CART	*decision tree*	86.2
Backprop	*neural network*	86.1
Baytree	*decision tree*	85.3
NewID	*decision tree*	85.0
CN2	*rule induction*	85.0
C4.5	*decision tree*	85.0
Cal5	*decision tree*	84.9
Quadratic discriminant	*statistical*	84.5
Fisher sequential classifier	*decision tree*	**84.4**
AC2	*decision tree*	84.3
SMART	*statistical*	84.1
Logistic discriminant	*statistical*	83.7
Cascade	*neural network*	83.7
Linear discriminant analysis	*statistical*	82.9
Kohonen	*neural network*	82.1
CASTLE	*statistical*	80.6
Naive Bayes	*statistical*	71.3

More than half of the methods result in error rates lower than our algorithm. But it is worth emhasizing that there are only two linear classifiers: our Fisher sequential classifier and a classifier based on classical linear discriminant which appears to have lower classification accuracy. Moreover our classifier is almost as good as the one based on quadratic discriminant.

Interesting comparisons can be made among the decision tree classifiers. All of them perform at about the same level (CART is slightly better). But the exceptional fact about our classifier in that group is the tree size. We have created the smallest decision tree consisting of 11 nodes, whereas CART has used 66 nodes, Cal5 - 156 and AC2 - 116 nodes.

4 Conclusions

The experiments show that the algorithm works well in solving not only artificial two-dimensional problems for many classes but also real ones.

However it is obvious that it is not always possible to divide classes into groups with one hyperplane. So we are now implementing a modified version of the algorithm which directs a class to both son-nodes if it is necessary. Although the tree created in this way will be more complicated (more terminal nodes), it will be possible to approximate more complex decision boundaries.

References

[1] W.Malina: *Two-Parameter Fisher Criterion.* IEEE Trans. Systems, Man and Cybernetics, Vol. 31, No. 4, August 2001.

[2] A. Kołakowska, W. Malina: *Fisher sequential classifier.* 5th Conference Neural Networks and Soft Computing, Zakopane 6-10 czerwca 2000, str.227-232.

[3] D. Mitchie, D. J. Spiegelhalter, C. C. Taylor: *Machine Learning, Neural and Statistical Classification.* 1994.

[4] Safavian S.R., Landgrebe D.: *A Survey of Decision Tree Classifier Methodology.* IEEE Trans. Systems, Man, and Cybernet., Vol. 21, No. 3, May/June 1991.

Geometry and Logic in Pattern Classifiers

*,&Witold Pedrycz and #Nicolino Pizzi

*Department of Electrical & Computer Engineering
University of Alberta
Edmonton T6R 2T1 Canada
&Systems Research Institute, Polish Academy of Sciences
Warsaw, Poland
Institute for Biodiagnostics, National Research Council (NRC)
Winnipeg, MB, Canada

Abstract In this study, we discuss an important synergy emerging between the geometric representation of data and fuzzy logic in pattern classification. Next we show how this synergy is made operational and translates into a coherent architecture of a classifier. The crux of the proposed topology lies in a collection of simple linear classifiers (perceptrons) being combined into a logically coherent topology. In a nutshell: perceptrons come with simple geometrical interpretation while processing based on fuzzy operators (AND and OR logic units- fuzzy neurons) results in highly transparent and interpretable results. When combined together (forming a fuzzy adaptive logic network), they give rise to the computing construct that retains the advantages (processing and interpretability) of these two paradigms of information processing. We discuss a comprehensive development environment of adaptive logic networks and show their application to several classification problems.

Introduction

The synergy of fuzzy sets and neural network is a multifaceted endeavor. The commonly accepted point of view is about the coherent treatment of data and knowledge processing: neural networks concentrate on detailed numeric processing [3][4] whereas fuzzy sets focus on granular computing thereby being positioned at the logic end of processing [2][5][13][14][17][18][19][20][21][22]. This point of view has resulted in a vast array of topologies of neurofuzzy systems.There is also another stream of research of fuzzy neurocomputing in which we focus on the synergy between (fuzzy) logic and geometry. In this combination, geometric constructs are those of a low-end processing character operating at individual numeric entities. Fuzzy logic constructs operate at the higher-end of the processing spectrum. To some extent, this facet of synergy is visible in some existing constructs such as a network of experts [6][7][15] or adaptive logic networks [1].

In the developed neurofuzzy architecture, we exploit two classic constructs: a perceptron originating from the core studies on neural networks and a fuzzy logic processor [11][12] rooted in the realm of fuzzy sets and fuzzy logic.This organization of the material is as follows. First, we discuss the basic architecture by discussing its basic components and revealing how these two concepts of geometry and logic cooperate. This is followed by a discussion of learning in such networks. Several generalizations of the networks along with the underlying learning schemes are also studied.

The architecture of the network: merging geometry and logic

The geometry and logic are the two cornerstones of the proposed topology of the network. The geometry facet of the feature space is captured through a collection of perceptrons. It is obvious that the geometry of the perceptron governed by the expression

$$y = f(\sum_{i=1}^{n} w_i x_i + w_0) \tag{1}$$

(where "f " is a sigmoid function) revolves around a single hyperplane. The modifications of the weight vector (connections) **w** implies a certain position of the corresponding hyperplane in the feature space. More concisely, we have $y = f(\mathbf{x},\mathbf{w})$ with **w** denoting the connections of the perceptron. The combinations of the hyperplanes give rise to more general geometric constructs, refer to Figure 1. Usually these are formed by inserting an additional layer of units in which the results of computing produced at the first layer of the perceptrons become linearly aggregated. While this type of aggregation is commonly realized by multiplayer neural networks, it corresponds to an interesting and straightforward logical realization producing similar aggregation results.

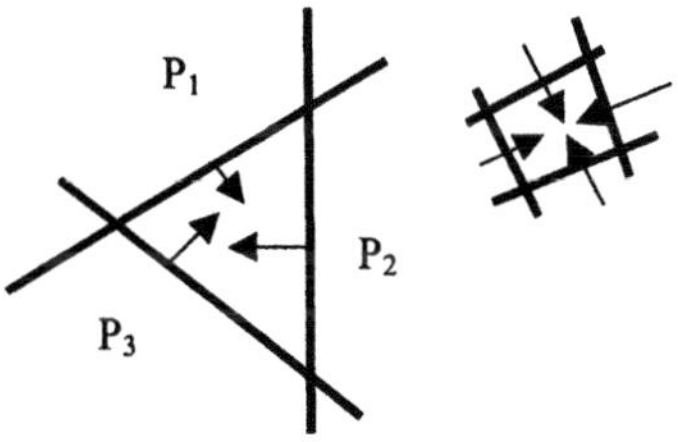

Figure 1. The geometry of perceptrons and their combinations along with their logic interpretations through building compound predicates

Put it differently: the geometric constructs of the perceptrons can be immediately captured and easily quantified in the language of logic. For instance, a convex region delineated by a collection of "c" perceptrons (namely a region of the feature space in which they generate high values of the output) can be written down as in the form of the following predicate

$$Q = P_1(\mathbf{x},\mathbf{w}_1)\ \&\ P_2(\mathbf{x},\mathbf{w}_2)\ \&\ \dots\ \&\ P_c(\mathbf{x},\mathbf{w}_c) \tag{2}$$

This predicate (Q) produces values close to one (meaning it becomes true) when all predicates are true (that is the corresponding perceptrons produce high outputs). In the above expression $P_i(\mathbf{x}; \mathbf{w}_i)$ denotes a truth value of the predicate and is equal to the output of this perceptron; $P_i(\mathbf{x}; \mathbf{w}_i) = f(\mathbf{x}, \mathbf{w}_i)$. The region formed by the perceptrons comes with an obvious logic interpretation. Usually the geometry of the landscape of the patterns in the feature approximated by the perceptrons is richer than a single convex region. As a matter of fact, we may encounter a family of disjoint regions. To capture this geometry, we take a union of the individual regions captured by the Q_is. To articulate the same observation in the language of logic, we write it down as follows

$$V = Q_1 \ or\ Q_2\ or \dots or\ Q_p \tag{3}$$

where V is a compound *or* predicate formed on a basis of Q_1, Q_2, and P_c. The perceptron governed by (1) produces values in [0,1]. The logic compatible with continuous truth values exploits fuzzy sets. The above predicates are realized in the form of logic neurons (AND and OR neurons). The two types of compound predicates map directly onto a network of logic neurons, a so-called logic processor cf. [8][9][10][11][12]. The overall network composed of two functionally distinct substructures is shown in Figure 2. We will be referring to it as a fuzzy adaptive logic network. It is worth stressing that the introductory idea of this nature has been originally introduced by Armstrong [1]. The logic aspect and the ensuing processing realized in terms of fuzzy neurons and logic processor have not been a part of the original proposal.

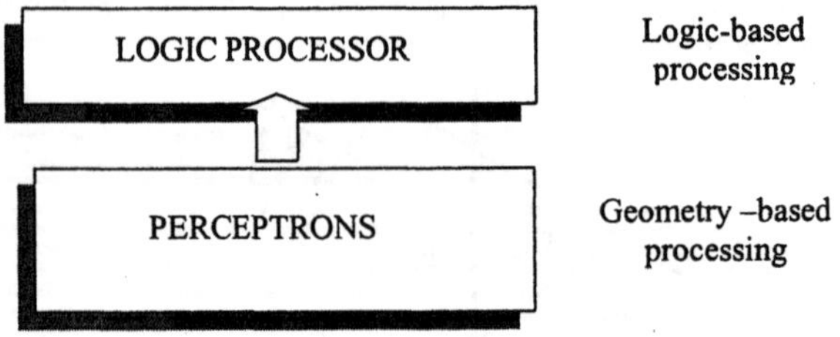

Figure 2. Fuzzy adaptive logic network: a general topology.

Summarizing, we note that each layer of the above network comes with a clearly defined functionality and a well defined delineated scope of geometric or logic processing.

It is of interest to contrast the proposed paradigm of processing and the resulting architecture with the well-known class of Takagi-Sugeno fuzzy models. Let us remind that in essence a TS model is a collection of "local" regression models confined to specific regions of the feature space where these regions are delineated by a collection of fuzzy sets defined in the individual feature spaces. In other words, the model comes as a collection of rules

- if $feature_1$ is A and $feature_2$ is B and ... then $y= a_0+a_1x_1+\ldots+a_nx_n$

The local models are "glued" together by the overlapping fuzzy sets standing in the conditions of the rules. More specifically, the level of activation of each rule μ_i is a weighting factor of the output of the linear expression (y_i) occurring in the conclusion part of the rule. Subsequently the aggregate $y^{\sim}$ is a weighted sum of the form $y^{\sim}= \Sigma\mu_i y_i/\Sigma\mu_i$. We note that the logic part of the model is associated with the feature space (in which we form a logic aggregate of the fuzzy sets) while the geometry of the construct manifests in the weighted average of the models. In the proposed approach, the aspects of logic and geometry are placed in a reversed order: first, in the feature space we consider the geometry of the perceptrons and then the aggregation comes with a strong logic flavor.

Fuzzy logic processing

There are two fundamental classes of logic-driven fuzzy neurons, cf. [8][9][10][11].

<u>OR neuron</u> The neuron processes n-inputs $\mathbf{x} = [x_1, x_2,\ldots, x_n]$ (where each input is in the unit interval) and completes an s-t composition operator of the form

$$y = OR(\mathbf{x}; \mathbf{w}) = \underset{i=1}{\overset{n}{S}}(w_i t x_i) \tag{3}$$

where $\mathbf{w} =[w_1 \; w_2 \; \ldots \; w_n]$ are adjustable weights (connections) confined to the unit interval. Owing to the type of the composition we note that if all weights are set to 1 then the output is just a standard OR combination of the inputs (OR gate). The higher the value of the connection, the more relevant the corresponding input. Observe that a

commonly used max-min composition is a special case of the operation introduced above.
AND neuron The neuron processes n-inputs $\mathbf{x} = [x_1, x_2, \ldots, x_n]$ (where each input is in the unit interval) and completes an t-s composition operator of the form

$$y = \mathrm{AND}(\mathbf{x}; \mathbf{w}) = \mathop{T}_{i=1}^{n} (w_i s x_i) \tag{4}$$

If all connections are set to zero, then we end up with the standard (nonweighted) combination of the inputs (AND gate).

The topology of the network, called here a fuzzy logic processor, reflects the form of the predicates. As a matter of fact, the considering (2) and (3), we note that first the results produced by the family of perceptrons are combined *and*-wise and this requires a collection of AND neurons whose outputs are combined *or*-wise. This or-wise combination gives rise to a layer of the OR neurons. Apparently the connections of all the neurons are calibrated to further incorporate the specificity of the data and impact coming from individual variables (outputs of the perceptrons) and the *and* predicates.

The learning scheme

The learning in the network considered here is parametric: we assume that the topology of the network has been given in advance while the parameters (connections) have to be optimized. The performance index Q assumes a standard form of a sum of squared errors between the output of the network and required target, that is

$$Q = \sum_{k=1,N} (\mathbf{target}(k) - \mathbf{y}(k))^T (\mathbf{target}(k) - \mathbf{y}(k)) \tag{5}$$

where **X** is a training data set formed by pairs of inputs and required outputs (targets) $X = \{\mathbf{x}(k), \mathbf{target}(k)\}$, k=1, 2, …, N. The updates of the connections (the logic processor as well as the collection of the perceptrons) are guided by the standard gradient-based update scheme that can be symbolically written down as

$$\mathbf{connections}(\mathrm{iter}+1) = \mathbf{connections}(\mathrm{iter}) - \alpha \nabla_{\mathbf{connections}} Q \tag{6}$$

with the term denoted as **connections** that captures all parameters of the network; *iter* denotes consecutive learning epochs and α stands for a positive learning rate.

An Illustrative experiment

In this section, we present a concise illustrative example to visualize the most essential feature of the network. We consider a nonlinear function $y = |\sin(2x_1)|\ |\cos(3x_2)|$ defined in the unit square (as shown in Figure 3). The training and testing set consist of 100 data points that were randomly drawn from this input space.

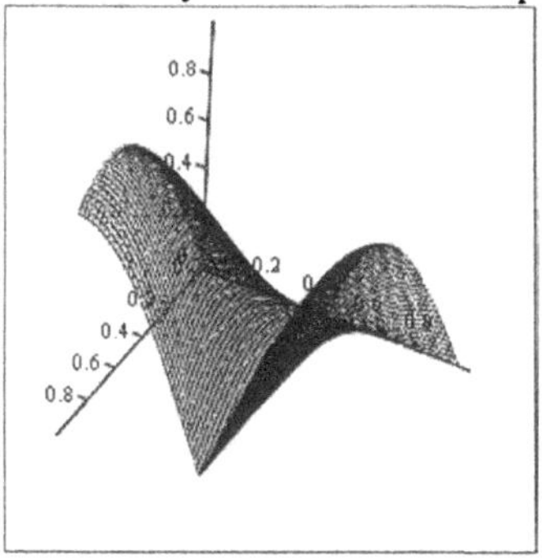

Figure 3. A nonlinear function to be approximated:

The training process was carried out for 2,000 epochs with the learning rate equal to 0.25. The results shown for the training and testing set are included in Table 1. The shadowed entries are those where the error (both for the training and testing) drops significantly in comparison to the rest of the table (in the range of 10-3 versus 10-2 for the smaller values of "p" (number of perceptrons) and the size of the hidden layer.

hidden/p	1	2	3	4	5	6	7
1	0.0501 0.0602	0.0500 0.6068	0.00487 0.05977	0.00486 0.05947	0.0489 0.0595	0.0487 0.0595	0.0487 0.0594
2	0.0493 0.0597	0.0294 0.0442	0.0485 0.0598	0.04875 0.05976	0.04881 0.05972	0.0488 0.0598	0.0487 0.0596
3	0.0493 0.0599	0.0286 0.0423	0.00171 0.00243	0.00179 0.00253	0.00275 0.00421	0.004179 0.006607	0.003234 0.005031
4	0.0496 0.0602	0.0279 0.0419	0.00141 0.00192	0.001421 0.001848	0.001129 0.001804	0.001250 0.001767	0.001403 0.002002
5	0.0499 0.0605	0.0275 0.0413	0.00148 0.00203	0.001145 0.001732	0.001244 0.001763	0.001275 0.001811	0.001395 0.002032
6	0.0504 0.0611	0.0277 0.0414	0.00146 0.00198	0.001437 0.001728	0.001262 0.001781	0.001256 0.001790	0.001371 0.001987

Table 1. Training and testing error of the network for different sizes of the layers; the entries in the table are a normalized performance index, namely Q/N

The minimal configurations leading to quite small error is (3,3) that is 3 perceptrons and 3 AND neurons.

Conclusions

The geometry and fuzzy logic are the two cornerstones of pattern recognition. We proposed a class of fuzzy adaptive logic networks in which the geometry of the feature space is captured through a collection of linear classifiers (perceptrons) while the aggregation of the results is realized in the logic framework of logic processors where all operations come with a clear semantics of *or* and *and*-like summarization. We discussed several interpretation issues of these networks and came up with illustrative examples.

Acknowledgments

Support from the Natural Sciences and Engineering Research Council of Canada (NSERC) and Alberta Software Engineering Research Consortium (ASERC) is gratefully acknowledged.

References

1. W.W. Armstrong, C. Chu, M.M. Thomas, Using adaptive logic networks to predict machine failure, Proc. World Congress on Neural Networks, Washington, DC, 1995, vol. II, 80-83.
2. B. Gabrys, A. Bargiela, General fuzzy Min-Max neural network for clustering and classification, *IEEE Trans. on Neural Networks*, Vol. 11, No. 3, pp. 769-783, 2000.
3. M.H. Hassoun, *Fundamentals of Artificial Neural Networks*, MIT Press, Cambridge, MA, 1995.
4. S.Haykin, *Neural Networks: a Comprehensive Foundation*, Macmillian College Publ, 1994.
5. H. Ishibuchi, K. Nozaki, N. Yamamoto, H. Tanaka, Selecting fuzzy if-then rules for classification problems using genetic algorithms", *IEEE Transactions on Fuzzy Systems*, vol. 3: 3, 1995, 260-270.
6. R.A. Jacobs, M.I. Jordan, S.J. Nowlan, G.E. Hinton, Adaptive mixtures of local experts, *Neural Computation*, 3, 1991, 79-87.
7. M.I. Jordan, R.A. Jacobs, Hierarchical mixture of experts and the EM algorithm, *Neural Computation*, 6, 1994, 181-214.
8. W. Pedrycz, Neurocomputations in relational systems, *IEEE Trans. on Pattern Analysis and Machine Intelligence*, 13, 1991, 289-296.
9. W. Pedrycz, *Computational Intelligence: An Introduction*, CRC Press, Boca Raton, FL, 1997.

10. W. Pedrycz, Conditional fuzzy clustering in the design of radial basis function neural networks, *IEEE Transactions on Neural Networks*, 9 no. 4,1998, 601- 612.
11. W. Pedrycz, F. Gomide, *An Introduction to Fuzzy Sets*, Cambridge, MIT Press, Cambridge, MA,
12. W. Pedrycz, A. Rocha, Knowledge-based neural networks, *IEEE Trans. on Fuzzy Systems*,1, 1993, 254-266.
13. W.Pedrycz, A.V. Vasilakos, Linguistic models and linguistic modeling, *IEEE Trans. on Systems Man and Cybernetics*, 1999, vol. 29, no. 6, 745-757.
14. W. Pedrycz, A. Bargiela, Granular clustering: a granular signature of data, *IEEE Trans. on Systems, Man, and Cybernetics –B*, 2002, to appear
15. V. Ramurthi, J. Ghosh, Structural adaptation in mixture of experts, *Proc. of ICPR*, 1996, pp. 704-708.
16. M. Russo, Genetic fuzzy learning, *IEEE Transactions on Evolutionary Computation*, 4(3), 2000, pp. 259-273.
17. P. K. Simpson, Fuzzy Min-Max neural networks – Part 1: Classification, *IEEE Trans. on Neural Networks*, Vol 3, No. 5, pp. 776-86, September 1992.
18. P. K. Simpson, Fuzzy Min-Max neural networks – Part 2: Clustering, *IEEE Trans. on Neural Networks*, Vol 4, No. 1, pp. 32-45, February 1993.
19. T. A. Sudkamp, R. J. Hammell II, Granularity and specificity in fuzzy function approximation, in Proc. *NAFIPS-98*, 105-109, 1998.
20. L. A Zadeh, Fuzzy sets and information granularity, In: M.M. Gupta, R.K. Ragade, R.R. Yager, eds., *Advances in Fuzzy Set Theory and Applications*, North Holland, Amsterdam, 1979, 3-18.
21. L. A. Zadeh, Fuzzy logic = Computing with words, *IEEE Trans. on Fuzzy Systems*, vol. 4, 2, 1996, 103-111.
22. L. A. Zadeh, Toward a theory of fuzzy information granulation and its centrality in human reasoning and fuzzy logic, *Fuzzy Sets and Systems*, 90, 1997, pp. 111-117.

Fuzzy Bayesian Classifier: a Multi-Agent System for Information Retrieval in the Web

José C Romero Cortés[1,2], Leonid B. Sheremetov[1,3]

[1] Center for Computing Research of the National Technical University, (CIC-IPN), Av. Juan de Dios Batiz Esq. Othon de Mendizabal s/n, 07738 Mexico, D.F.
[2] Metropolitan Autonomous University, Av. Sn Pablo 180, Acapotzalco, 02200, Mexico, D.F.
[3] Mexican Oil Institute, Eje Central Lazaro Cardenas 152, 07730, Mexico DF.
rcjc@correo.azc.uam.mx, sher@cic.ipn.mx

Summary. A fuzzy Bayesian approach helping an Internet user to filter Web pages is discussed. In the proposed approach, one page can be classified as having the continuous quality of being interesting, this means that a certain grade of membership can be associated with each page relative to a category of selection. Filtering is based on the evidences of the content of the page title, abstract or complete document. An example comparing crisp and fuzzy classifiers implemented as a part of multi-agent system to support information filtering and retrieval in the Web is discussed illustrating the proposed approach.

1 Introduction

The exponential growth of Internet requires tools and methodologies developed to manage this increasing and changeable bulk of information. One of them is information filtering focusing on searching, consulting and retrieving of useful information [1, 2]. The problem of Web search is translated into the problem of data mining without making an exhaustive revision taking a lot of user's time, which is in many cases restricted [3, 4]. A number of approaches to the discovering of pages of "interest" have been developed based on the frequencies of words, using nominal variables that correspond to the page titles (links, abstracts, articles, etc.) and ordinal variables that correspond to the classification categories of the pages [5, 7]. In these approaches, the arithmetic handling of the frequencies of key occurrences of words is used, which is computationally efficient but very empiric way of classification [2, 7, 9]. These approaches are close to the crisp Bayesian approach concerning the probabilities of accepting some page a posteriori, based on the existing evidence.

However, the fact that one page is interesting or important for the user corresponds to an event of fuzzy nature. Both, (i) the fact that the decision is subjective with a certain degree of uncertainty and (ii) the bad definition of the frontiers of the classification categories, deserve the fuzzy approach. Fuzzy Bayesian approach seeks that the subjectivity in the selection of the category to which a page belongs, be modeled using the fuzzy logic and the Bayes theorem. This focus is more natural considering the abundance of information that exist and the partiality that represent a training sample [2, 9]. Also the interest or importance of a document is of fuzzy nature, vague, ill defined and blurred. To implement information filtering and retrieval systems, agent technology recently has been used [10, 11].

In the present paper, the fuzzy Bayesian classifier is introduced. A prototype of Multi-Agent System (MAS) for information retrieval was developed, where the main agent, called Filter Agent, is based on the formal Bayesian approach. Discussion is illustrated with the example of crisp and fuzzy filtering.

2 Fuzzy Bayesian Classifier

The Bayesian crisp approach being applied to information retrieval in the Web, consists in taking a sample of pages of size n [1]. The user will classify each one of them in some of the mutually excluding and exhaustive categories. In the case of two categories, each page is "interesting" or "not interesting" based on the evidence, defined as a set of words composing for example, the page title. Based on this training and applying the theorem of Bayes, all the pages can be classified and filtered; only those of them that are of "interest" to the user being retrieved. The Bayesian theorem is defined as follows.

Let $H_1, H_2, ..., H_k$, be k mutually exclusive and exhaustive hypothesis. Also let $P(H_i \mid E)$ be the posterior conditional probability that H_i be true given the observed evidence E, with:

$$P(H_i \mid E) = \frac{P(E \mid H_i)P(H_i)}{\sum_{j=1}^{k} P(E \mid H_j)P(H_i)}, i = 1,2,...,k \tag{1}$$

The crisp Bayesian approach consists of acceptance (H_1) or rejection (H_2) of web pages according to the evidence (E) provided by the page title. The Bayesian rule of acceptance of the page is $P(H_1 \mid E) \geq P(H_2 \mid E)$.

The crisp Bayesian approach does not take into account the levels of vagueness, ambiguity and imprecision with which a user selects a web page. In this case, the hypothesis $H_i, ..., H_k$ as well as the evidence E are fuzzy for each web page [1, 12]. For managing the fuzzy nature of the filtering problem, a generalization of the crisp Bayesian approach for the fuzzy case is proposed by means of the application of the subsethood theorem, defined below.

Let A, B be two fuzzy subsets, then the subsethood measure $S(A,B)$ (the degree to which A is a subset of B) is defined as follows:

$$S(A,B) = \frac{M(A \cap B)}{M(A)}, \tag{2}$$

where *M(A)* is the count or the magnitude of the vector drawn from the origin to the fuzzy set *A*. As shown in [12], Bayesian theorem (1) is clearly deduced from (2). Let E be a fuzzy evidence, and let $H_j,...,H_k$, be *k* fuzzy hypothesis, then:

$$S(E,H_i)=\frac{S(H_i,E)M(H_i)}{\sum_{j=1}^{k}S(H_j,E)M(H_j)},i=1,2,...,k \tag{3}$$

where

$$\mathrm{S}(\mathrm{H}_i,E)=1-\frac{\sum_x \max[0,\mu_{H_i}(x)-\mu_E(x)]}{M(H_i)} \tag{4}$$

where $\mu_{H_i}(x)$, $\mu_E(x)$ are the membership degrees of the element x in the fuzzy sets H_i, E. The case, when *k*=2, represents only two fuzzy hypothesis: either accepting or rejecting a specific web page. For simplicity, this case is illustrated below by the example, though *k* hypothesis can be considered corresponding to the same number of classification categories [6, 8, 13], for example such categories could be *Excellent(*H_1*), Good(*H_2*), Regular(*H_3*), Bad(*H_4*)*, etc.

3 Fuzzy Classifier MAS: Implementation Details

According to our conceptualization, a Fuzzy Classifier MAS is composed of the following three types of domain agents: personal assistant (PA), search agent, and filter (crisp and fuzzy) agent. For the generation of the prototype system, the Component Agent Platform (CAP) based on the DCOM model has been used [15]. The CAP consists of the following types of agents: *Agent management system, Domain facilitator agent, Agent communication channel* and *Wrapper agent.*

Instead of implementing search agents as wrappers, which extract the URLs from the search engine responses [11], these agents use ActiveX controls such as *Microsoft Html Object Library* and *Microsoft Internet Control* to generate real queries to the search engines and to receive the answers. It also integrates a parser to store structured query information in the temporal database. The access to this database is provided by the Wrapper Agent. This temporary database contains all information delivered by the search services: URL, page title, page abstract/context, etc.; as well as the information obtained by the classifier at the next steps of the filtering process (probabilities, grades of membership, etc.).

The classification process contains two stages. At the first one, the training sample is generated (pages pertaining to this sample are marked in the database) and PA is invoked. The later calls the servlet which generates dynamically the page for the user to train the classifier. Being submitted, the training results arc stored in the database and PA's control (embedded in the page generated by the servlet) invokes the filter agent to finish the classification process.

To do this, it communicates to the SAS software [16] via another Wrapper Agent (a bridge containing the SAS's API) to calculate absolute and relative frequencies, cross tables, the posterior probabilities and membership functions. It is worth to mention that the software that is to be wrapped (SAS) may reside in a different machine. Calculations being completed, filter agent invokes once again the PA to deliver final results in the form of accepted and rated pages to the user (as in the former case, a servlet is invoked). All the communication between agents are coded in ACL agent communication language, which is supported inside the platform by the DCOM's ORPC protocol.

4 Crisp and Fuzzy Bayesian Classifiers: A Case Study

A number of experiments have been carried out with the developed MAS with both crisp and fuzzy classifiers. For the lack of space, for comparison we use the same example as discussed in [14] for the crisp case. For the search pattern "quality taguchi" the Google search engine generated 54 pages. Only page titles were used for classification, pages from 31 to 40 were used as a training sample, 6 of them were accepted and 4 rejected. Table 1 shows absolute frequencies and corresponding grades of membership for some words composing the titles of the pages.

Table 1. Words, their absolute frequencies and grades of membership for each hypothesis.

Words	Frequencies		Membership degrees	
	H_1	H_2	H_1	H_2
software	3	0	0.1071	0
design	2	0	0.0714	0
experiments	2	0	0.0714	0
....				
taguchi	1	0	0.0357	0
....				
videos	0	1	0	0.0588
Total	28	17		

Table 2 and Fig. 1 show the a posteriori probabilities and subsethoods for crisp and fuzzy classifiers respectively. As it can be seen from Table 2 and Fig. 1, the subsethoods are greater than the a posteriori probabilities for the majority of cases. For example, fuzzy classifier gives the acceptance (rejection) ratio of 1 for the cases when all the words of the title correspond to the accepted (rejected) words of the training sample, e.g. titles 50 and 1 respectively. In the opposite case, when the title contains the words not included in the sample, in the fuzzy case these pages are accepted with the 0.6 subsethood, which is not the case for the crisp classifier, e.g. titles 2, 3, and 30. The fuzzy conclusion seems more relevant because the only evidence is the percentage of accepted pages, which is 0.6 in this case. In the crisp case, the difference results from the approximate calculus of probabilities and the assumption of the independence of the words (see [7,11] for details). Finally, when the title combines accepted and rejected words or those found in the training sample and others no, fuzzy estimations are also more viable, e.g. title 5.

Table 2. Page titles with corresponding a posteriori probabilities and subsethoods.

Title	$P(H_1\|E)$	$P(H_2\|E)$	$S(E,H_1)$	$S(E,H_2)$
1.-No Title	0.1032	0.8968	0.0000	1.0000
2.-Links	0.5548	0.4452	0.6000	0.4000
3.-Lankar	0.5548	0.4452	0.6000	0.4000
4.-No Title	0.1032	0.8968	0.0000	1.0000
5.-Quality Improvement Software – FAQ	0.9117	0.0883	0.8033	0.1967
....				
30.-Six Sigma-Air academy Associates Public Workshops	0.3303	0.6697	0.6000	0.4000
31.-Quality manufacturing measurement videos team building planning production …	0.0027	0.9973	0.2500	0.7500
....				
50.-Taguchi	0.7137	0.2863	1.0000	0.0000

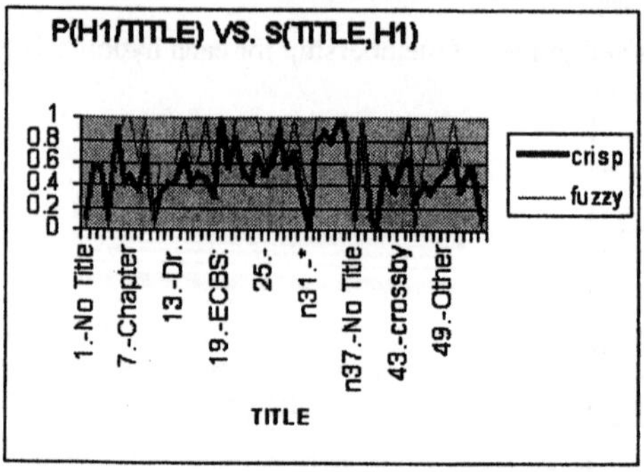

Fig. 1. Comparative results for the crisp and fuzzy classifiers.

5 Conclusions

The approach proposed in this paper captures the world complexity and tries to contribute to its ordering and organizing. It combines the fuzzy logic and the theorem of Bayes, which makes it a mathematical tool that classifies taking into account the expert's subjectivity, vagueness and imprecision. Fuzzy Bayesian approach in a natural way gives us the subsethood of the evidence for each hypothesis. Although the methodology proposed in this paper, is aimed and illustrated by the example from the filtering and retrieving of Web pages, the developed techniques and tools can work also for e-mail and usenet activities. The architecture of the MAS is scalable: different search engines can be accessed, meta search can be organized, another filtering techniques can also be implemented.

Acknowledgements

Partial support for this research work has been provided by the CONACyT, Mexico within the project 31851-A "Models and Tools for Agent Interaction in Cooperative MAS" and by the IPN within the project CGEPI 20010758.

References

1. Payne T. R. and Edwards P. (1995) Learning mechanisms for information filtering agents. Department of computing science. King's college. University of Aberdeen.
2. Quinlan, J. (1993) Learning logical definitions from relations. Machine Learning 5:239-266.
3. Berry M. and Linoff G. (2000) Mastering Data Mining, John Wiley & Sons,.
4. Fayyad, U. Piatetsky-Shapiro G., Smyth, P. Uthurusamy, R. editors, (1996) Advances in Knowledge Discovery and Data Mining, AAAI/MIT Press.
5. Balabanovic, M., Shoham Y., and Yun Y. (1995) An adaptative agent automated web browsing. Journal of image representation and visual communication 6(4).
6. Abd-Elrahman, A. M. (2000) On fuzzy Bayesian inference. International Data Analysis Conference, Innsbruck, Austria.
7. Mitchell, T. (1997) Machine Learning. Mc. Graw-Hill.
8. Yang, C. (1997) Fuzzy Bayesian Inference. Proceedings of IEEE International Conference on Systems, Man, and Cybernetics, Orlando, FL, USA.
9. Edwards P., Bayer D., Green C.L., and Payne T. (1996) Experience with learning agents with manage internet-based information. University of Aberdeen, Scotland, AB9 2UE.
10. Rennie J. and McCallum A. (1999). Using Reinforcement Learning to Spider the Web Efficiently, ICML'99.
11. Muller M. E. (1999) An Intelligent Multi-Agent Architecture for Information Retrieval from the Internet. Technical report, Institute for Semantic Information Processing, Univ. Osnabrück, available from http://www.aye-aye.de/martin/.
12. Kosko B. (1992) Neural networks and fuzzy systems: a dynamical systems approach to machine intelligence. Prentice Hall.
13. Manton K. G., Woodbury M. A. and Tolley H. D. (1994) Statistical applications using fuzzy sets. Wiley Series in Probability and Mathematical Statistics.
14. Romero J., C., (2000) Bayesian fuzzy agent to filter and recover information in Web pages. In Proc. of the International Congress in Computing. pp.472-480 (in Spanish).
15. Sheremetov, L. and Contreras M. (2001) Component Agent Platform. In Proc. of the CEEMAS'01, pp. 395-402.
16. Statistical Analysis System. (2001). Release 8.1.

Can Neural Networks Be Used to Define the Rules of Cardiovascular Disease Prevention in the Nutrition Domain?

Agnieszka Borowiec[1], Krzysztof Fronczyk[1], Bohdan Macukow[2], and Maciej Grzenda[2]

[1] National Institute of Cardiology, Department of Health Promotion, ul. Alpejska 42, 04-628 Warszawa, Poland
[2] Warsaw University of Technology, Faculty of Mathematics and Information Science, Pl. Politechniki 1, 00-661 Warszawa, Poland

Abstract. The primary objective of the work was to check the relation between household socio-economic characteristics and the corresponding food purchasing capabilities. The analysis has been based on the data collected in the national survey "Social Diagnosis 2000". In order to search for possible dependencies between variables gathered in the survey, different classification methods have been applied.

Statistic methods of logistic regression analysis and discriminant analysis have been applied to model the discussed relation. However, only limited prediction efficiency has been observed. Therefore, neural networks-based methods have been applied. Evolutionary construction of multilayer perceptrons has been used to select both network architectures and weights. The method developed and tested previously on numerous prediction and classification problems has been used to provide classification models for the data discussed. Multilayer perceptrons have been shown to provide more precise classification models. Results of the network construction are presented together with final discussion.

1 Introduction

Cardiovascular diseases remain in strong relation with improper nutrition [11]. However, the nutrition style may be resulted from social circumstances [12]. The purpose of our research was to test the relation between social data describing households and nutrition capabilities. Before applying neural networks, the quality of statistic models has been evaluated. Thus, results of different classification methods have been provided.

Our work has been based on the national survey "Social Diagnosis 2000". Each data pattern in the survey describes one household. It includes the information whether a household can afford to buy different food categories listed in the questionnaire. Thus, a vector of 13 binary variables has been obtained for each household. However, no sharp criterions can be adopted to describe each of 13 food categories. Thus, the answers in the survey are bound to reflect subjective opinions that are likely to depend on the expectations of each household. In addition there is no straightforward method for comparing different nutrition profiles. Two households that can afford to buy $n = 1, ..., 12$ categories out of 13 can have completely different nutrition profiles as the categories they prefer or are able to purchase food from can be completely different [12]. Thus, cluster analysis has been applied in order to determine typical groupings of households' profiles.

Therefore, standard statistic methods have been used in order to model the data available and evaluate the relation between social data and the corresponding cluster. Then evolutionary construction [5,9] of multilayer perceptrons [6] is used to build classification models serving to associate each household with its nutrition status. The results of the classification performed by the latter models have outperformed statistic methods.

The remainder of this work is organised as follows:

- section 2 describes in details the data set and the results of statistical analysis of the problem,
- neural networks-based approach is outlined in section 3 with the results listed in section 4,
- section 5 summarises the whole work.

2 Data set and statistic methods

The problem analysis is based on the data of the national research "Social Diagnosis 2000" - a survey of representative sample of 2756 Polish households. The survey was conducted in the year 2000. The data set includes thirteen variables concerning the capability of buying thirteen different food product categories by the households. In addition the set contains: income per month (continuous variable), number of household members (ratio variable), region (five dichotomous variables: central, north-west, north-east, south-west, south-east), size of village/town (six dichotomous variables: city over 500 thousands, city 200-500 thousands, city 100-200 thousands, city under 20 thousands, village), sex (dichotomous variable), age (continuous variable), years of education (ratio variable), employment status (four dichotomous variables: workers - only, farmers and agriculture workers - even if they work as workers too, proprietors - businessmen, not working - retired, pensioners or other), and marital status (dichotomous variable).

Cluster analysis has been used to determine data groupings. Two clusters have been observed. These correspond to the group of households that can afford to buy only basic food categories and the remaining group that can buy virtually all food categories. The impact of capability to buy many products like fish and vegetables on the prevention of cardiovascular diseases can not be underestimated [11]. Lack of some products available for the second group of households only may result in increased likelihood of cardiovascular diseases.

As a first step in the analysis we have performed several univariate Pearson χ^2-test to determine predictive variables of being a member of one of the nutrition clusters.

2.1 Discriminant analysis

Discriminant analysis [8] has been performed so as to determine the most important factors affecting the cluster each household belongs to. 18 variables have been included as independent variables to the analysis. Three of dichotomous variables: central region, village and workers could be omitted because some other variables in relation to them were considered.

Discriminant analysis using stepwise Wilks Lambda method has been performed. As a result of the analysis, the following variables have been selected as predictors: monthly income, years of education, marital status: married, employment status: businessmen, region: north-east, size of living place: city over 500 thousand, employment status, number of households members. The percentage of properly classified data patterns has been equal to 68%. All the data analysis was performed using SPSS (Statistical Program for Social Sciences) Version 10.0.

2.2 Logistic regression

In addition, multiple logistic regression [7] was performed using maximum likelihood estimation. Odds ratios (ORs) with 99% confidence intervals (Cls) were computed to show the association. The criterion for inclusion of variables in the logistic model was their association with being a member of one of the groups in the univariate analysis. Following the standard social sciences practice, basic demographic variables such as age, sex, were used in the model, although they were correlated with other potential predictors. Cluster membership was the dependent variable. The probability of belonging to one of clusters was modelled as a function of independent variables using logistic function.

Age and sex have not played any role in prediction, probably because of their correlation with income. Years of education, marital status, monthly family income, employment status (businessman), number of household members, living in north-east region, being retired, living in a city of population exceeding 500,000 citizens were associated with belonging to the one of clusters. Logistic regression analysis revealed that employment status (businessman) was the best predictor (odds ratio=3,52). 71.65% of data patterns have been properly classified by the logistic regression model.

3 Neural networks

In order to search for the mapping rule between household data and resulting nutrition status (cluster), multilayer perceptrons [6] have been applied. The primary objective was to check whether it is possible to properly classify the household data. Data clusters previously determined in the cluster analysis have been used. Neural networks have been used to classify each household data pattern into one of these two clusters. All the same, it has to be emphasised that this division is based on subjective opinions gathered in the survey. Multilayer perceptron has been applied as a representation of the classification model. Not only does it allow to model an arbitrary function, but also methods of its knowledge extraction exist [3].

In order to evaluate the generalisation abilities of the created networks the original data set has been randomly divided into the training set A_t and validation set A_v. Owing to the large number of data patterns, the training set and validation set have been composed of $card(A_t) = 2067$ and $card(A_v) = 689$ data patterns. Thus, the error rates Err_t and Err_v stand for the error measured on the training set and validation set, respectively. Both rates are computed in accordance with formula 1.

$$Err(s) := \sum_{z_i \in (A); i=1,\ldots,card(A)} \frac{\| d_i - \psi(F(z_i)) \|}{card(A)} * 100\% \tag{1}$$

$F(\cdot)$ stands for the mapping function realised by the network s, function $\psi(\cdot) : R \longrightarrow \{0,1\}$ is used to associate with each network output one of two valid data clusters, d_i is the valid cluster index for pattern z_i.

All the networks have been constructed and trained using evolutionary construction of multilayer perceptrons *ECoMLP* [5,9]. The method, described below selects network architecture and network weights at the same time. It is based on evolutionary programming (EP) [1,4] and self-adaptive control procedure [2]. As a consequence, the most crucial algorithm settings, namely weight mutation parameters, are selected in a self-adaptive manner. The method has been successfully applied for the short-term load forecast problem [5]. It has produced high quality prediction models. Overall results of the training have been better than results obtained using gradient-based training methods [10]. In addition tedious search for the optimal network architecture has been avoided.

Evolutionary construction of multilayer perceptrons *ECoMLP*

- $t := 0$,
- create initial population of MLPs
  $P(0) = \{s_i \in I \mid i = 1, ..., N\}$ satisfying the following assumptions:
  - fixed number of input layer nodes $card(L_0)$ and output layer neurones $card(L_M)$ defined by the problem,
  - random number of hidden neurones,
  - randomly chosen connection weights,
- in a sequence of generations construct consecutive populations $P(t)$ by:
  - applying standard EP selection and promoting the best $\frac{N}{2}$ networks to the next population, duplicating them and producing child subpopulation thereafter; the networks are evaluated in terms of their compliance with the optimisation criterion 1 i.e. the lower Err_t rate, the better the network,

- affecting child networks with mutation operator composed of:
  * hidden node mutation (add or delete neuron with p_a and p_d probability),
  * weight mutation in accordance with the learning rule of each individual (see below),
  * mutation of learning rule with probability of p_{lr},
- $t := t + 1$.

The weight mutation has been strictly based on the form of the *learning rule* controlling the behaviour of the mutation operator.

Learning rule and weight mutation

- let us define for each individual in the population $a_i \in P(t)$ learning rule (Met_i, Par_i) where:
  - $Met_i \in \{0, 1\}$ stands for mutation type, discrete or real,
  - Par_i is defined by $Par_i = (p_m)$ for discrete type and $Par_i = (p_m, \mu)$ for the real mutation type, respectively,
- mutate the weights of the network in accordance with the learning rule of the individual, using uniform distribution over a specified range of weights, in case of discrete mutation, or Gaussian distribution, otherwise; thus Par is used to store the distribution settings,
- mutate learning rules as well.

4 Results

In order to construct and evaluate MLP-based classification models numerous runs of *ECoMLP* have been performed. The results of the training show that there is only limited impact of reported household social profile on its nutrition status. The error rate $E_t(s_{max})$=25.64% that has been obtained for the best network in $P(2000)$ is lower than the corresponding error rate for both statistic methods. Still, it shows that numerous data patterns are unlikely to be properly classified. In spite of relatively large training set $(card(A_t)$=2067) and limited complexity of final networks composed of up to 10 neurones altogether, the validation error rate $E_v(s_{max}) = 29.75\%$ has been larger.

In other words only limited generalisation has been obtained. What is important, during the training it were the large network architectures that were proved inadequate and replaced in the selection process with more efficient structures of limited size. Once again, subjectivity of the survey answers has to be emphasised. The latter is characteristic for all the social data. In addition important factors not mentioned in the data set are bound to affect the food purchase. Last but not least, not only income but also other expenses like rents or education fees determine how much can be spent on food by a household.

5 Conclusions

Social data is frequently very subjective. Questionnaires do not always reveal all the truth about the situation of surveyed people. As a consequence, the relation between input data and measured characteristics is diminished. The purpose of this work was to check the possibility of automatic classification of household nutrition situation using a number of typical socio-demographic features as an input. Statistic methods have been shown to be unable to provide satisfactory interpretation of available data.

Neural networks based solutions have enabled additional improvement in the classification accuracy and outperformed statistical methods. Still, the results obtained show that only limited explanation of data available. As a consequence, there is a little chance for devising an expert system targeted at social welfare able to automatically predict social needs or expectations. Possible improvements can be based on defining more precise and less subjective questionnaires and adding new questions related to typical expenses of each household.

References

1. Bäck, T., Schwefel, H.P. (1993) An Overview of Evolutionary Algorithms for Parameter Optimization. Evolutionary Computation. MIT Press,**Vol. 1 No.1**, 1-23
2. Bäck, T. (1998) An Overview of Parameter Control Methods by Self-Adaptation in Evolutionary Algorithms. Fundamenta Informaticae. **35**, 51-66
3. Duch, W., Grabczewski, K. (1999) Searching for Optimal MLP. Proc. of the Fourth Conference Neural Networks and Their Applications. Zakopane, 65-70
4. Fogel, D.B. (1999) An Overview of Evolutionary Programming, The IMA Volumes in Mathematics and its Applications, ed. Williard Miller, **111**, 89-109
5. Grzenda, M., Macukow, B. (2001) Evolutionary Model for Short Term Load Forecasting. Proc. of MENDEL 2001 conference. Brno, 119-124
6. Haykin, S. (1999) Neural Networks: a Comprehensive Foundation, Prentice-Hall Inc., USA
7. Hosmer, D.W., Lemeshow, S. (1989) Applied Logistic Regression, John Wiley & Sons, USA
8. Klecka, W.R. (1980) Discriminant Analysis, Sage, London
9. Macukow, B., Grzenda, M. (2001) Towards the Evolution of Neural Networks. Opto-Electronics Review, **9(3)**, 316-319
10. Siwek, K. (2000) Load Forecasting Using Artificial Neural Networks, Phd thesis, Warsaw University of Technology (in Polish)
11. Stamler, J. (1999) Nutrition and Longevity: Multifaceted Improvements in Population Dietary Patterns to End the Cardiovascular Disease Epidemic. Nutrition, metabolism and cardiovascular diseases. **9(4) Suppl**, 37-51
12. Ross, E. et al. (1999) Gender, Socioeconomic Status and Family Status as Determinants of Food Behaviour. Social Science and Medicine. Vol. **46** No. **12**, 1519-1529

A Practical Approach To Image Reconstruction From Projections Using Neural Networks Structure

Robert Cierniak

Technical University of Częstochowa, Częstochowa, ul. Armii Krajowej 36, Poland

Summary. This paper presents a practical approach to the key problem in the computer tomography: image reconstruction from projections, using neural network. The two layer structure of the neural network is used, realizing the maximization of the energy, defined as difference between signal energy and its entropy. Some interesting results of the performed simulations are shown.

1 Introduction

Since Cormack's publication [1], image reconstruction from projections, the key task in the computer tomography, became one of the most appealing algorithmic problem. Recently, the most important reconstruction methods used in practice is the method with convolution and back propagation [4]. Other important investigated methods are those using Fourier inversion and an algebraic reconstruction technique (ART) [4][5].

It is possible that in the future the soft computing algorithms, thanks their specific properties, will be applied in computer tomography to solve mentioned nontrivial problem. One of the important and popular tool of the soft computing systems are neural networks. This paper presents an approach to image reconstruction from projections problem by using unsupervised neural network. The neural network structures in application to signal reconstruction based on the energy definition including the entropy term were studied in papers [2][3]. The criterion of the maximum entropy is met and has been endorsed by scientists representing different disciplines. In this paper a practical approach to construct neural network solving deconvolution problem [6] is applied and investigated. The advantages of presented definition of neural network have been demonstrated during computer simulations designed to prove the assumption that an appropriately constructed unsupervised neural network is able to reconstruct an image using projections.

2 Problem of the image reconstruction from projections

Computer tomography, which has its beginnings in the work of Allan M. Cormack, who in 1979 was awarded the Nobel Prize for medicine and physiology, has became a diagnostic method in medicine and in many other fields of science. This famous techniques is based on the well-known relation called the Radon transformation [6]:

$$p(s.\alpha)=\int_{-\infty}^{\infty}\int_{-\infty}^{\infty}\mu(s\cos\alpha-u\sin\alpha, s\sin\alpha+u\cos\alpha)ds\,du \tag{1}$$

where:

$\mu(x,y)$ — the distribution of the attenuation in an investigated cross-section of the body,

α — the angle of projection,

x, y — the co-ordinates of the examined object,

$s = x\cos\alpha + y\sin\alpha$ — the distance from the centre of rotation to the axis of the ray falling on the projection screen,

$u = -x\sin\alpha + y\cos\alpha$ — the distance between a given point on the investigated object with co-ordinates (x, y) and the centre of rotation, measured along the axis of the falling ray.

In practice the Radon transformation is realized by the projection using X-rays. Projections performed in this way may be subjected to the next phase of the signal processing: the values of the projection function $p(s,\alpha)$ passing through a fixed point (x,y) are accumulated to generate information about the attenuation coefficient $\mu(x,y)$ at this point. The accumulation given by the following expression is called the back-projection or Radon's back-projection operator:

$$\tilde{\mu}(x.y)=\int_{0}^{\pi}p(x\cos\alpha+y\sin\alpha.\alpha)d\alpha \tag{2}$$

where:

$\tilde{\mu}(x,y)$ — the image of the distribution of the X-ray attenuation in a section of the investigated body formed on the basis of the performed projections.

It is easy to show that the function $\tilde{\mu}(x,y)$ gives an image of the original distribution of the attenuation $\mu(x,y)$ in the investigated cross-section of the object. The relationship between the function and the attenuation coefficient is given by [4]:

$$\tilde{\mu}(x,y)=\int_{-\infty}^{\infty}\int_{-\infty}^{\infty}\mu(x',y')\frac{1}{\sqrt{(x-x')^2+(y-y')^2}}dx'dy' \tag{3}$$

The linear equation (4) has its discrete equivalent of the form:

$$\tilde{\mu}(i,j)\cong\sum_{k=1}^{K}\sum_{l=1}^{L}h_{ijkl}\,\mu(k,l) \tag{4}$$

where:

h_{ijkl} — gives the discrete impulse response of the signal, accountable for the geometric distortion of the original image and theoretically:

$$h_{ijkl}=\begin{cases}\pi & \text{dla } i=k \text{ i } j=l\\ \dfrac{1}{\sqrt{(i-k)^2+(j-l)^2}} & \text{dla } i\neq k \text{ lub } j\neq l\end{cases} \tag{5}$$

Existing methods of image reconstruction from projection apply different ways of filtering to avoid the effects of the geometrical distortion term, shown in equation (3) and (4).

The usage of neural networks could give a new impulse to the investigations of image reconstruction from projection. This is especially so given all the potential benefits that the application of artificial intelligence in this field of medical engineering could bring.

3 The neural algorithm of the image reconstruction from projections

In some publication [2][5] the methods of the distortion elimination from images using approach with the maximization of the entropy of the distorted images are presented. Let us define:

$$Ent(\mathbf{F})=-\sum_{i=1}^{I}\sum_{j=1}^{J}\chi(i,j)\ln(\chi(i,j)) \tag{6}$$

where: $Ent^S(\mathbf{F})$ —Shannon's entropy.

Function $\chi(i,j)$ could be interpreted as the probability measure proportional to intensity in the point of the image indexed by (i,j). In order to fulfil following constraints for probability measure:

$$\text{i.)}\ \forall i,j \quad 0 \le \chi(i,j) \le 1; \tag{7a}$$

$$\text{ii.)}\ \sum_{i=1}^{\mathrm{I}} \sum_{j=1}^{\mathrm{J}} \chi(i,j) = 1, \tag{7b}$$

it is proposed, to normalize the image intensity in its every point:

$$\chi(i,j) = \frac{\hat{\mu}(i,j)}{\sum_{i=1}^{\mathrm{I}} \sum_{j=1}^{\mathrm{J}} \hat{\mu}(i,j)} \tag{8}$$

It is proved that entropy from equation (6) has the maximum if:

$$\forall i,j \quad \chi(i,j) = \frac{1}{\mathrm{I} \cdot \mathrm{J}} \tag{9}$$

For many scientists an adoption of entropy function seems to be very attractive tool for the whole domain designated as the image reconstruction. Presented below neural network realizes the image reconstruction from projection using the maximum entropy criterion. Optimization taking advantage of the maximum entropy criterion in order to reconstruct discrete image can be formulated as the constraints [7]:

$$\begin{cases} \max\limits_{\mathbf{F}} Ent(\mathbf{F}) \\ \widetilde{\mathbf{F}} = \mathbf{HF} \end{cases} \tag{10}$$

The problem expressed in equation (10) can be reformulated using the energy function, as shown below:

$$\min_{\mathbf{F}} \left(-Ent(\mathbf{F}) + \mathrm{wsp} \sum_{i=1}^{\mathrm{I}} \sum_{j=1}^{\mathrm{J}} f\left(e_{ij}(\mathbf{F})\right) \right), \tag{11}$$

where:

$e_{ij}(\mathbf{F}) = \sum_{k=1}^{\mathrm{K}} \sum_{l=1}^{\mathrm{L}} h_{ijkl}\,\mu(k,l) - \widetilde{\mu}(i,j)$ — i-th row of matrix $\mathbf{HF} - \widetilde{\mathbf{F}}$,

wsp — suitable large positive coefficient,

$f(\bullet)$ — penalty function which takes the form:

$$f(e) = \frac{\partial f(e)}{\partial e} = p\mathrm{tgh}\left(\frac{e}{\lambda}\right), \tag{12}$$

where:

λ — slope coefficient.

Now we can start to construct a neural network realizing the deconvolution task of the equation (5). Let us formulate an energy expression to do it by minimizing the value of this function using neural network [3][7]. Energy expression could take a form:

$$E^t = -Ent\left(\mathbf{F}^t\right) + \text{wsp}\sum_{i=1}^{I}\sum_{j=1}^{J} f\left(e_{ij}\left(\mathbf{F}^t\right)\right) \tag{13}$$

In order to find a maximum of this function we determine derivation:

$$\frac{\mathrm{d}E^t}{\mathrm{d}t} = -\sum_{i=1}^{I}\sum_{j=1}^{J} \frac{\partial Ent\left(\mathbf{F}^t\right)}{\partial \mu^t(i,j)} \frac{\partial \mu^t(i,j)}{\partial t} +$$

$$+\,\text{wsp}\sum_{k=1}^{K}\sum_{l=1}^{L}\sum_{i=1}^{I}\sum_{j=1}^{J} \frac{\partial f\left(e_{kl}\left(\mathbf{F}^t\right)\right)}{\partial e^t_{kl}} \frac{\partial e^t_{kl}}{\partial \mu^t(i,j)} \frac{\partial \mu^t(i,j)}{\partial t}. \tag{14}$$

One can develop equation (14) and after some evolutions receive the appropriate form, ready to neural network implementation:

$$\frac{\mathrm{d}E^t}{\mathrm{d}t} = -\sum_{i=1}^{I}\sum_{j=1}^{J} \frac{\mathrm{d}\mu^t(i,j)}{\mathrm{d}t} z^t, \tag{15}$$

where:

$$z^t = \frac{\mathrm{d}\mu^t(i,j)}{\mathrm{d}t} = \frac{\partial Ent\left(\mathbf{F}^t\right)}{\partial \mu^t(i,j)} - \text{wsp}\sum_{k=1}^{K}\sum_{l=1}^{L} \frac{\partial f\left(e_{kl}\left(\mathbf{F}^t\right)\right)}{\partial e^t_{kl}} \frac{\partial e^t_{kl}}{\partial \mu^t(i,j)} \tag{16}$$

Index t means the dependence of the variable denoted by this symbol to time in the learning progress of the neural network.

4 Experiments and their results

The presented above neural network structure was tested next using mathematical model of the skull cross-section. During all simulations the image of this model was used with resolution 50×50 pixels. The progress in the reconstruction process is presented in Tab. 1. The first row in the table shows the number of realized iterations using described above the neural network algorithm of the image reconstruction from projections. The second row consists of images arisen during the reconstruction process on the output of the neural network.

Table 1. Process of the image reconstruction from projection using the mathematical model of the cross-section of the skull.

Number of iteration.	3	25	100	400	1000
View of the reconstructed image.	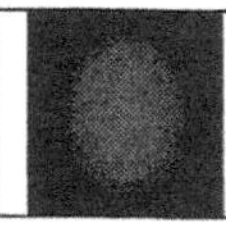	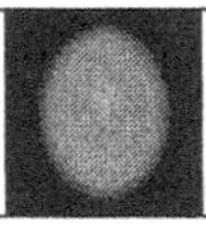		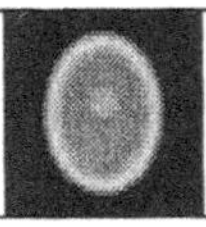	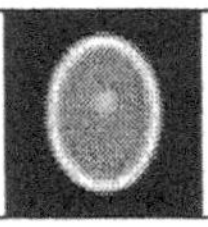

One can see above that after about one thousand iterations the results of the reconstruction process are stabilized on the satisfactory level. Therefore, one can say that at this moment the image is reconstructed and the process can be stopped.

5 Conclusion

The performed simulations demonstrated a convergence of the algorithm of image reconstruction from projections based on the neural network. The image of the cross-section of the investigated mathematical model, obtained after sufficient number of iterations is similar to the original image. Therefore, this method is acceptable from a diagnostic point of view.

Sizes of the processed image are not acceptable for a model of the more complicated mathematical object. The next step of investigations on the image reconstruction from projections using neural network could be an extension of the image sizes to apply in the simulations the standard mathematical model presented in literature [4].

References

[1] Cormack A. M., Representation of a function by its line integrals with some radiological application, J. Appl. Phys., vol. 34, pp. 2722-2727, 1963.

[2] Frieden B. R., Zoltani C. R., Maximum bounded entropy: application to tomographic reconstruction, Appl. Optics, vol. 24, pp. 201-207, 1985.

[3] Ingman D., Merlis Y., Maximum entropy signal reconstruction with neural networks, IEEE Trans. on Neural Networks, vol. 3, pp. 195-201, 1992.

[4] Jain A. K., Fundamentals of Digital Image Processing, Prentice Hall, New Jersey, 1989.

[5] Kaczmarz S., Angeneaherte Aufloesung von Systemen Linearer Gleichungen, Bull. Acad. Polon. Sci. Lett. A., vol. 35, pp. 355-357, 1937.

[6] Luo Fa-Long, Unbehauen R., Applied Neural Networks for Signal Processing, Cabridge University Press, 1998.

[7] Radon J., Ueber die Bestimmung von Functionen durch ihre Integralwerte Tangs gewisser Mannigfaltigkeiten, Berichte Saechsiche Akad. Wissenschaften, Math. Phys. Klass, vol. 69, pp. 262-277, Leipzig, 1917.

A Systolic Realisation of the Neuro-Tomograph

Robert Cierniak, Jacek Smoląg

Technical University of Częstochowa, Czestochowa ul. Armii Krajowej 36, Poland

Summary. This paper shows a systolic realization of the neural network structure used to solve the problem of the image reconstruction from projections. The theoretical analysis of the advantage of the systolic structure comparing with the sequential realization of the neural network is presented.

1 Introduction

This paper presents a practical approach to image reconstruction from projections problem by using unsupervised neural network. The neural structure called here the neuro-tomograph is based on the energy definition including the entropy term [2][3]. Unfortunately, direct parallel implementation of the structure with so high number of connections is impossible. Additionally, the simulations show that calculations performed in a sequent way are extremely time-consuming. The systolic realization of special defined neural network structure is proposed to take advantage of this approach in the problem of image reconstruction from projections.

2 Practical approach to the neuro-tomography

Because, for any given projection, the X-ray sensors are placed on the screen with raster Δ_s, it is possible that no ray passes through a given point of the image. To take this into account we will apply linear interpolation. This will ensure that the points which are outside of the rays falling directly on the sensors on the screen will be given a projection value according to the equation:

$$\tilde{p}(s,\alpha) \cong p(m,\alpha) + (s-m)\big(p(m+1,\alpha) - p(m,\alpha)\big) \qquad (1)$$

where:

$m = \mathrm{Trunc}(s)$ — the integer part of the variable s, where $s = i\Delta_s \cos\alpha + j\Delta_s \sin\alpha$; $-\mathrm{M} \le m \le \mathrm{M}-1$, where: M — is the radius of the circle defined by the tube around the investigated object.

In this way we can obtain the value of a given projection at every point of the discreet image. The results of the projections at each point are then collected to obtain values of the function $\tilde{\mu}(i,j)$. Aggregation is applied to all the projections passing through a given point, satisfying following expression:

$$\tilde{\mu}(i,j) \cong \Delta_\alpha \sum_{n=0}^{N-1} \tilde{p}(i\Delta_s \cos n\Delta_\alpha + j\Delta_s \sin n\Delta_\alpha, n\Delta_\alpha), \tag{2}$$

where: Δ_α — the angle, given in radians, by which the pair tube-screen is rotated after each projection;

$N = \mathrm{Trunc}(\pi/\Delta_\alpha)$ — the number of projections (integer value).

Image represented by $\tilde{\mu}(i,j)$ is a blurred version of the original discreet image $\mu(i,j)$. The unsupervised neural network structure presented below is designated to remove geometrical artefacts from this distorted image.

2.1 Neural network structure

A structure of the neural network realizing so formulated task is depicted in Fig. 1. Following this structure, Fig. 2 presents a chosen cross-section of neural network, what makes analysis of the algorithm details more clearly.

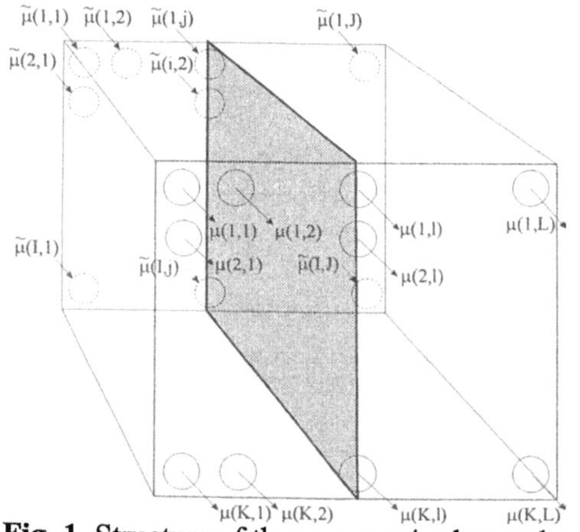

Fig. 1. Structure of the unsupervised neural network

The neural network presented above consists of two layers, with the same topology of neurons. In Fig. 2 one vertical cross-section through the neural network structure is depicted.

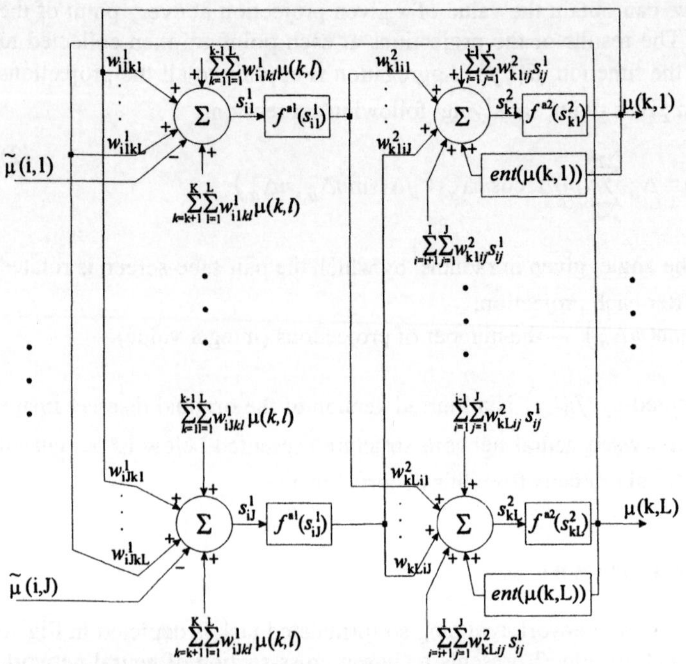

Fig. 2. Vertical cross-section of the neural network structure

All of the symbols which appear in the neural network structure are listed in order from the input to the output of the network.

I. layer

Weights of the connections:

$$w^1_{ijkl} = h_{ijkl}\,. \tag{3}$$

Weighting sum:

$$s^1_{ij} = e^t_{ij}(\mathbf{F}) = \sum_{k=1}^{K}\sum_{l=1}^{L} w^1_{ijkl}\,\mu^t(k,l) - \tilde{\mu}(i,j)\,. \tag{4}$$

Activation function:

$$f^{a1}\left(s^1_{ij}\right) = \frac{\partial f\left(e_{ij}\left(\mathbf{F}^t\right)\right)}{\partial e^t_{ij}}\,. \tag{5}$$

II. layer:

Weights of the connections:

$$w^2_{klij} = -\mathrm{K}\frac{\partial e^t{}_{kl}}{\partial \mu^t{}_{ij}} = -\mathrm{K}h_{klij}\,. \tag{6}$$

Weighting sum:

$$s^2_{ij} = \frac{\partial Ent\left(\mathbf{F}^t\right)}{\partial \mu^t(i,j)} + \sum_{i=1}^{I}\sum_{j=1}^{J} w^2_{klij}\,f^{a1}\left(s^1_{ij}\right). \tag{7}$$

Activation function:

$$f^{a2}\left(s_{ij}^{2}\right)=\mu^{t}(i,j)=\int_{0} s_{ij}^{2}\,\mathrm{d}t\,. \tag{8}$$

Additionally the following notation is used in the figure above:

$$ent\left(\mu^{t}(k,l)\right)=\frac{\partial Ent\left(\mathbf{F}^{t}\right)}{\partial\mu^{t}(k,l)}. \tag{9}$$

It is easy to find a numerical representation of all above mentioned functions. The performed in sequential way simulations demonstrated a convergence of the tested reconstruction algorithm. The only difficulty to use this method in practice is the number of the numerical calculations needed to lead the algorithm to solution with appropriate accuration.

3 Systolic realization of the neuro-tomograph

The main aim to apply presented below systolic realization of the neuro-tomograph structure will be to preserve the big advantage of the neural networks — parallel computations and make this algorithm possible to hardware implementation.

A direct hardware implementation could give the fantastic acceleration of the reconstruction process. In this case the time of calculations for one iteration of the algorithm is proportional to:

$$time\_consu\min g\_direct \sim 2\,. \tag{10}$$

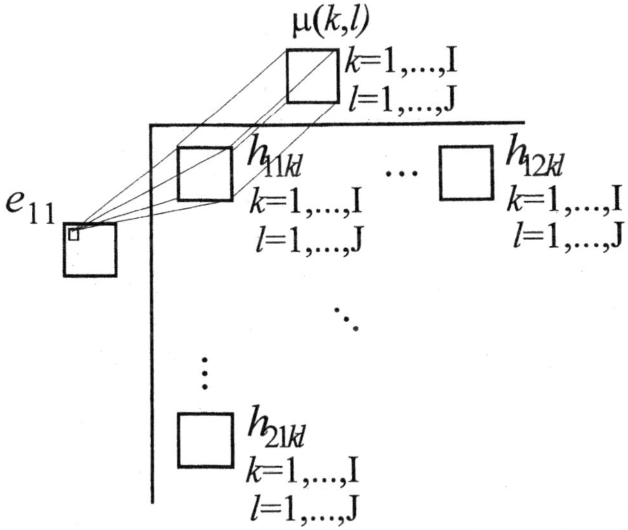

Fig. 3. Methodology of the computations in the neural reconstruction algorithm

Unfortunately, such physical realization of the presented in the previous sections neural network structure is absolutely non-realistic. The number of connections between layers is proportional to:

$$number\_of\_connection\_direct \sim (\mathrm{I})^4, \tag{11}$$

where: $\mathrm{I} \times \mathrm{J}$ — dimensions of the reconstructed image and $\mathrm{I} = \mathrm{J}$.

The calculation of the one neural network element e_{ij} being an output value for a neuron from first layer is explained in Fig. 3. Every element e_{ij} of this neural network is obtained in the same way. The only differences in this procedure described by (4) are matrices $\mathbf{W}_{ij}^1 = \left[w_{ijkl}^1\right]$.

Therefore, it is reasonable to consider a methodology to solve the problem of the very complex neural network structure. A possible technique appropriate in this implementation is the systolic approach to neural network hardware realization. An example of this realization for the first layer of the considered neural network is shown in Fig. 4.

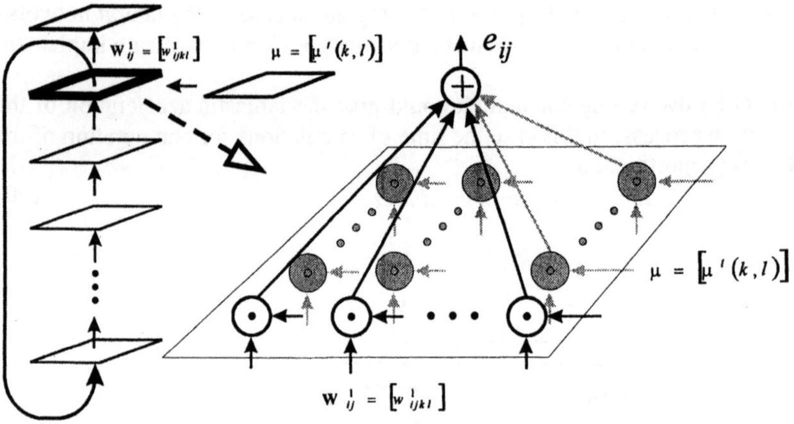

Fig. 4. A systolic realization of the neural reconstruction algorithm

One can see that every element of the array $\mathbf{e} = \left[e_{ij}\right]$ is obtained by multiplication — elements of array $\boldsymbol{\mu} = [\mu(k,l)]$ by elements of array $\mathbf{W}_{ij}^1 = \left[w_{ijkl}^1\right]$. This process is repeated $\mathrm{I} \cdot \mathrm{J}$-times, for each element e_{ij} separately using the same matrix $\boldsymbol{\mu}$ and changed at every time matrix $\mathbf{W}_{ij}^1$. In this realization desired number of connections in the first layer is given by:

$$number\_of\_connection\_systolic \sim (\mathrm{I})^2, \tag{12}$$

what is physically feasible, but the algorithm achieves the speed of one its iteration more less then before:

$$time\_consuming\_systolic \sim 2 \cdot I \cdot J\,. \tag{13}$$

The situation in the second layer of the neural network is similar.

4 Conclusions

The idea presented in this could give a new impulse in the investigation on the image reconstruction from projection. The main advantage of the neural network in this implementation is a parallel computation process. Theoretically, the systolic realizations of the neural network let partially prevent this very usable property and makes possible to implement the neural structure directly in the physically integrated circuit.

References

[1] Frieden B. R., Zoltani C. R., Maximum bounded entropy: application to tomographic reconstruction, Appl. Optics, vol. 24, pp. 201-207, 1985.

[2] Ingman D., Merlis Y., Maximum entropy signal reconstruction with neural networks, IEEE Trans. on Neural Networks, vol. 3, pp. 195-201, 1992.

[3] Jain A. K., Fundamentals of Digital Image Processing, Prentice Hall, New Jersey, 1989.

[4] Lipowska-Nadolska E., Morawski M., Tablice Systoliczne — Problemy wybrane, Akademicka Oficyna Wydawnicza PLJ, Warszawa, 1999.

[5] Luo Fa-Long, Unbehauen R., Applied Neural Networks for Signal Processing, Cabridge University Press, 1998.

[6] Radon J., Ueber die Bestimmung von Functionen durch ihre Integralwerte Tangs gewisser Mannigfaltigkeiten, Berichte Saechsiche Akad. Wissenschaften, Math. Phys. Klass, vol. 69, pp. 262-277, Leipzig, 1917.

[7] Smoląg J., *"Realizacje Sieci Neuronowych za pomocą Struktur Systolicznych"*, PhD dissertation, 1997.

An Investigation of Differential Skin Colonization of Neonates by Staphylococci, Using an Artificial Neural Network-based System

Diana R. Cundell[1], Les M. Sztandera[2], Alan Arbeter[3] and Jean M. Morrone[1]

[1]Biology Department, [2]Computer Science Department, Philadelphia University, Philadelphia, PA 19144, USA
[3]Department of Pediatrics, Albert Einstein Medical Center, Philadelphia, PA 19104, USA

Abstract. In this study, we designed an intelligent system to examine the influence of the demographic variables of gender, blood type, and race on the distribution of skin staphylococci bacteria on neonates up to 48 hours old. Bacterial samples were obtained from the axilla and groin of 200 babies, born over an 18-month period, and the staphylococci therein identified using standard microbiological techniques. The intelligent system created for the analysis of this real database was a supervised neural network program made up of a Multi-Layer Perceptron. Six skin staphylococcal species could be reproducibly classified, namely *S. aureus* (95.2%), *S. saprophyticus* (88.9%), *S. hominis* (84.2%), *Micrococcus* sp. (83.3%), *S. haemolyticus* (77.9%) and *S. epidermidis* (77.7%). The remaining three species, which constituted less than 3% of all isolates, were insufficient in number to assign to a class. Of the variables investigated, site of isolation had no effect on determining the staphylococcal distribution and the demographic variables, in order of importance, were found to be gender, blood type and race. These studies suggest that demographic variables are major factors influencing staphylococcal distribution. Such a system may, therefore, hold promise as a diagnostic tool.

1 Introduction

Human skin flora is composed of a limited number of bacterial species, which can tolerate this extreme environment, including diphtheroids, streptococci and staphylococci. More than 20 species of staphylococci are able to colonize human skin although most studies have isolated only 10 staphylococcal biotypes, namely *Staphylococcus aureus, S. epidermidis, S. hominis, S. haemolyticus, S. capitis, S. warneri, S. saprophyticus, S. cohnii, S. xylosus* and *S. simulans*. Although staphylococci can exist as commensals, permissive conditions and/or the presence of virulence factors can allow them to cause disease. Indeed, *S. aureus*, *S. epider-*

midis and *S. haemolyticus* are important agents in a variety of nosocomial infections, especially involving skin and soft tissues, and account for approximately 2/3 of all staphylococci in human clinical specimens.

Since many nosocomial infections are from the patients' endogenous skin flora, it is important to determine any host factors that might favor colonization by pathogenic staphylococci. As neonates are colonized by staphylococci within 8-12 hours of life, the pediatric nursery offers an ideal site in which to investigate factors influencing the colonization of human skin by staphylococcal species.

Our previous studies have suggested that the demographic variables of blood type, gender, age and race may be involved in staphylococcal host selection, and that such differential targeting may allow us to use these variables as a predictor of disease [1, 2].

2 Bacterial Sampling and Analysis Methodology

Collection of data was governed under the rules of a collaborative, expedited IRB agreement made between Philadelphia University and Albert Einstein Medical Center. Skin flora was obtained from the axilla and groin of healthy, term babies using a sterile cotton swab dipped in sterile normal saline (0.9%)and the staphylococcal species obtained isolated by culture on first staphylococcal isolation agar followed by subculture onto mannitol salt agar (both agars from Fisher Scientific, Pittsburgh, PA). Identification of strains of *Staphylococcus aureus* were made using standard microbiological techniques, namely yellow colonial pigmentation, β hemolysis of sheep blood agar, coagulation of plasma and the ability to turn mannitol salt agar yellow. Strains of coagulase negative staphylococci were typed using a commercially available biochemical kit.

2.1 An Artificial Neural Network Based System

In this research one of the most popular and successful neural network architectures, a Multi-Layer Perceptron (MLP) was used. An MLP network comprises a number of identical units organized in layers, with those on one layer connected to those on the next layer so that the outputs of one layer are fed-forward as inputs to the next layer.

The most important questions in determining a feed-forward neural network architecture are how to calculate the number of nodes in hidden layers, and how to calculate the number of hidden layers. Sztandera and Cios [3] addressed the problem of a dynamic generation of neural network architectures. The results presented here are based on outcomes obtained by the algorithm used to generate nodes and hidden layers until a learning task is accomplished. The algorithm operates on continuous data and equates a decision tree with a hidden layer of a neural network. A learning strategy used in this approach is based on minimization of the entropy function. This minimization of entropy translates into adding new nodes to the network until the entropy is reduced to zero. When the entropy is zero then all training examples are regarded as correctly recognized.

2.1.1 Fuzzy Entropy Measures

In general, a fuzzy entropy measure is a function f: P(X) → R, where P(X) denotes the set of all fuzzy subsets of X. That is, the function f assigns a value f(A) to each fuzzy subset A of X that characterizes the degree of fuzziness of A. Thus, f is a set-to-point map, or in other words, a fuzzy set defined on fuzzy sets.

One of the fuzzy entropy measures was proposed and investigated by Kosko [3]. He established that

$f(A) = (\Sigma count\ (A \wedge A^C))/ (\Sigma count\ (A \vee A^C))$, where Σcount (sigma-count) is a fuzzy cardinality.

2.1.2 A New Concept of Fuzzy Entropy

In our experiments we used fuzzy entropy suggested by Kosko and generalized fuzzy operations introduced by Dombi [3]. Generalized Dombi's operations form one of the several classes of functions, which possess appropriate axiomatic properties of fuzzy unions and intersections. The operations are defined below. From our experience the parameter □= 4 gives the best results [3].

Dombi's Fuzzy Union

$$\mu_{A \vee B}(x) = \{1 + [(1/\mu_A(x) - 1)^{-\Box} + [(1/\mu_B(x) - 1)^{-\Box}]^{-1/\Box}]\}^{-1}$$

Dombi's Fuzzy Intersection

$$\mu_{A \wedge B}(x) = \{1 + [(1/\mu_A(x) - 1)^{\Box} + [(1/\mu_B(x) - 1)^{\Box}]^{1/\Box}]\}^{-1}, \quad \text{where } \Box \in (0,\infty).$$

2.2 Feed-Forward Neural Network Architecture

The proposed algorithm generates feed forward network architecture for a given data set. The nodes and hidden layers are added until a learning task is accomplished. The algorithm operates on numerical data and equates a decision tree with a hidden layer of a neural network. A learning strategy used in this approach is based on achieving the optimal goodness function. This process of optimization of the goodness function translates into adding new nodes to the network until the desired values are achieved. When this is the case then all training examples are regarded as correctly recognized. The incorporation of fuzzy entropies into the algorithm seems to result in a drastic reduction of the number of nodes in the network, and in decrease of the convergence time. Connections between the nodes have a "cost" function being equal to the weights of a neural network. The directional vector of a hyperplane, which divides decision regions, is taken as the weight vector of a node.

The outline of the algorithm follows:

i) For a given problem with N samples, choose a random initial weight vector.
ii) Make use of learning rule: $\Delta w_{ij} = -\Box\, \partial f(F)/\partial w_{ij}$
where □ is a learning rate, f(F) is a fuzzy entropy function; and search for a hyperplane that minimizes the fuzzy entropy function: $\min f(F) = \Sigma N_r/N \text{ entropy}(L, r)$
where: L is a level of a decision tree, R is total number of nodes in a layer, r is number of nodes, f (F) is fuzzy entropy.
iii) If the minimized fuzzy entropy is not zero, but it is smaller than the previous value compute a new node in the current layer and repeat the previous step. Otherwise go to the next step.
iv) If there is more than one node in a layer compute a new layer with inputs from all previous nodes including the input data, then go to step ii). Otherwise terminate.

After applying the above described approach it was established that the first layer would contain 15 neurones, the second one 10, and the number of neurones in the third layer would be equal to the number of outputs (type of bacteria). Hyperbolic tangent was used as the function activating the first and the second layer. The linear function, on the other hand, is the activating function for the third layer.

3 Results

3.1 Gender, Blood Type and Race Distribution for the Six Output Classes of Staphylococcal Species within the Subject Database

A total of 392 bacterial isolates were recovered from the 200 babies, with between one and four separate staphylococcal species being isolated from each subject. Ninety-seven percent of the isolates of which belonged to the six major species used as output classes. The remaining 3 species of staphylococci, namely *S. capitis* (4 isolates recovered), *S. caprae* (5 isolates recovered) and *S. auricularis* (1 isolate) were too small to be assigned either individual classes or a combined class and were therefore removed from the database.

All six staphylococcal species output classes displayed differential distribution patterns from one another with respect to their input demographic variables, as is shown in Table 1. Gender appeared to play a role in determining the presence of three of the staphylococcal species with *S. hominis* and *S. aureus* being more frequently carried by males (57% and 54%, respectively) and *S. haemolyticus* by females (65%) than would be predicted from the general population (47% males, 53% females) (Table 1). Blood type also appeared to play a role in the distribution of three of the six staphylococcal species with *S. aureus* and *S. haemolyticus* being more prevalent on babies with blood type O (54% and 53%, respectively) and *Micrococcus* on babies with blood type A (50%) than the expected frequency of the general population (46%; Table 1). In addition, race appeared to influence the carriage of three species of staphylococci . *S. aureus* was found to be more often carried by Caucasians (32%) than the expected frequency for the subject population (20%) and was not isolated from any Hispanic subjects studied. A second staphylococcal species, *S. haemolyticus* was also more commonly isolated from Caucasian babies than the expected population frequency (30% compared with 20%). In contrast, there was an increase in the frequency of isolation *S. saprophyticus* from African American babies (76% compared with 64%), with the organism being absent in the skin flora of the Asian subjects studied.

3.2 Intelligent Artificial Neural Network-Based System as a Predictor of Staphylococcal Output Class

The novel neural system generated from the two hundred neonatal subject database was able to correctly classify 95.2% *S. aureus* (60/63), 88.9% of *S. saprophyticus* (16/18), 84.2% *S. hominis* (85/101), 83.3% of *Micrococcus* sp. (25/30), 77.9% *S. haemolyticus* (60/77) and 77.7% of *S. epidermidis* (80/103) isolates, respectively. This gave an overall prediction rate for the system of 83.1% (326/392).

The staphylococci incorrectly classified by the program were placed into the output groups as presented in the Table 2. This system is currently under development and, as such, no clinical evaluation of its efficacy at diagnosing staphylococcal distribution on data unseen by the system has yet been performed.

Discussion

These data suggest that, with training, staphylococcal distribution on healthy infants may be predicted with relative efficiency by inputting data for blood type, gender, and race into an artificial intelligence program. They reinforce our previous findings of a correlation between demographic variables and bacterial infection, and underline the importance of the fields of artificial intelligence as a powerful analytical tool allowing the dynamics between these factors to be interpreted. Such a system may, therefore, hold promise as a powerful diagnostic tool.

References

1. Cundell D.R., Silibovsky R.S., Sanders R. and Sztandera L.M. (2000) Analyzing putative correlates between age, blood type, gender and/or race with bacterial infection. *Artificial Intelligence in Medicine* **586**:1-5
2. Cundell D.R., Silibovsky R.S., Sanders R. and Sztandera L.M. (2001) An Intelligent Medical System to diagnose bacterial infection in hospitalized patients. *International Journal of Medical Informatics* **63**:31-40
3. Sztandera L. M. and Cios K. J. (1997), Ontogenic Neuro-Fuzzy Algorithm: F-CID3, *Neurocomputing*, **14**:383-402.

Table 1. Demographics distribution for the skin staphylococci recovered

Input	Frequency in each output class (%)						
	S. epi. (n=87)	*S. hom.* (n=82)	*S. haem.* (n=57)	*S. aur.* (n=50)	*S. sap.* (n=17)	*Micro.* (n=20)	Total babies (n=200)
Gender							
Male	41 (47%)	47 (57%)	20 (35%)	27 (54%)	8 (47%)	9 (45%)	93 (47%)
Female	46 (53%)	35 (43%)	37 (65%)	23 (46%)	9 (53%)	11 (55%)	107 (53%)
Blood Type							
A	27 (31%)	22 (27%)	17 (30%)	11 (22%)	4 (24%)	10 (50%)	61 (31%)
AB	3 (3%)	2 (2%)	3 (5%)	2 (4%)	1 (4%)	0 (0%)	6 (3%)
B	17 (20%)	17 (21%)	7 (12%)	10 (20%)	4 (24%)	5 (25%)	41 (20%)
O	40 (46%)	41 (50%)	30 (53%)	27 (54%)	8 (48%)	5 (25%)	92 (46%)
Race							
African-American	54 (62%)	50 (61%)	36 (63%)	31 (62%)	13 (76%)	13 (65%)	127 (64%)
Asian	7 (8%)	8 (10%)	5 (9%)	2 (4%)	0 (0%)	1 (5%)	16 (8%)
Caucasian	16 (18%)	18 (22%)	10 (18%)	16 (32%)	2 (12%)	6 (30%)	40 (20%)
Hispanic	10 (12%)	6 (7%)	6 (10%)	1 (2%)	2 (12%)	0 (0%)	17 (8%)

Table 2. Agreement matrix (contingency table) statistics

	Actual *S.aureus*	Actual *S. saprophyticus*	Actual *S.hominis*	Actual *Micrococcus*	Actual *S. haemolyticus*	Actual *S. epidermidis*	Total
Classified as *S.aureus*	60	0	0	0	0	0	60
Classified as *S.saprophyticus*	0	16	0	0	0	0	16
Classified as *S.hominis*	3	2	85	0	8	18	116
Classified as *Micrococcus*	0	0	0	25	0	0	25
Classified as *S. haemolyticus*	0	0	0	0	60	5	65
Classified as *S. epidermidis*	0	0	16	5	9	80	110
Total	63	18	101	30	77	103	392

Evolutionary Computing Techniques for Diagnosis of Urinary Tract Infections *in Vivo*, Using Gas Sensors

V.S. Kodogiannis [a], A.K. Pavlou [b], P. Chountas [a], A.P.F. Turner [b]

[a] Mechatronics Group, Dept. of Comp. Science, Univ. of Westminster, London, HA1 3TP, U.K

[b] Cranfield Biotechnology Centre, Cranfield University, Cranfield, MK43 0AL, UK

Summary. Recently, the use of smell in clinical diagnosis has been rediscovered due to major advances in odour sensing technology and artificial intelligence. It was well known that a number of infectious or metabolic diseases could liberate specific odours characteristic of the disease stage and among others, urine volatile compounds have been identified as possible diagnostic markers. A newly developed "artificial nose" based on chemoresistive sensors has been employed to identify *in vivo* urine samples from 45 patients with suspected uncomplicated UTI who were scheduled for microbiological analysis in a UK Public Health Laboratory environment. An intelligent model consisting of an odour generation mechanism, rapid volatile delivery and recovery system, and a classifier system based on a hybrid system of genetic algorithms, neural networks and multivariate techniques such as principal components analysis and discriminant function analysis-cross validation. The experimental results confirm the validity of the presented method.

Keywords: Neural networks, Genetic algorithms, Electronic noses, Microbial analysis.

1 Introduction

The 21st century is bringing new applications of intelligent diagnostic micro-array systems, able to monitor metabolic changes of human physiology and transform them to global patterns of diseases such as: diabetes, tuberculosis (TB), urinary tract infections (UTI) and gastrointestinal *Helicobacter pylori* (HP) related infections [1]. Since the report of an artificial electronic odour detection system by Persaud & Dodd [2], a substantial amount of research has been targeted on the development of integrated gas-sensing systems. In the past decade, experts have started to appreciate and mimic the sense of smell by developing the electronic nose (*e-nose*). The potential applications for the *e-nose* technology are very extensive. Those industries that are using or could use this technology include Food & Drink, Chemical, Petrochemical, Packaging, Pharmaceutical, Flavours & Fragrance, Environmental, Health and Security [3]. There have been an increasing number of attempts to apply artificial olfactory diagnostics in clinical practice [4]. The diagnosis of disease states is a primary pre-requisite of successful medical treatment and as such is a high priority in any area of clinical science. Microbial infections and related causes of illness seem to be one of the more common problems encountered in the world today. In many cases, infection with micro-organisms produces a change in the smell of a person, which can be especially noticeable on the breath, in the urine or the stools. However a critical step before introducing such "smart" devices into the clinic would be the *in vitro* static or dynamic headspace analysis of microbial volatile compounds, extracted from clinical isolates of UTI, HP and respiratory infections.

Detecting low numbers of bacterial species in clinical samples usually involves time consuming growth in selective media and subsequent isolation and identification by appropriate diagnostic procedures. Complex volatile mixtures are released during bacterial interaction with the host tissue or media, and chromatographic techniques have been used in the past to characterise those species on their gas profiles [5]. Recently some novel biomedical, gas-sensing applications have been reported, such as the diagnosis of leg-ulcer streptococcal [6] and respiratory infections [7] and rapid detection of bacterial clinical isolates *in vitro* using intelligent classification techniques [8].

UTI is a significant cause of morbidity with 3 million UTI cases each in the USA alone and thirty-one percent of nosocomial infections in medical intensive care units are attributable to UTI [9]. Approximately, 80% of uncomplicated UTI are caused by E.coli, and 20% by enteric pathogens such as *Enterococci, Klebsiellae, Proteus sp.*, coagulase(-) Staphylococci and fungal opportunistic pathogens such as *Candida albicans*. Current diagnostic techniques require 24-48 hrs to identify pathogenic species in urine midstream specimens ($\geq 10^5$ cml^{-1}) and apply antibiotic sensitivity tests. Despite the introduction of molecular tests, microscopy and culture remain the gold standard in every day clinical practice.

In the 1970s there were some early attempts to develop automated urine volatile analytical devices using advanced gas-chromatographic (GC) techniques and more than 200 volatile compounds were measured [10]. However lack of advanced computerised techniques to analyse specimen complexity and to detect consistent hidden diagnostic patterns, laborious techniques, high cost and the need for highly skilled personnel, prohibited those early attempts from reaching their diagnostic goal. The objectives of this study are to: i) Introduce the application of a gas-sensing device in a UK Public Health Laboratory environment by analysing 45 specimens of human urine by the application of an intelligent diagnostic model based on novel generation, detection, and rapid recognition of urinary volatile patterns within 5 hrs of receipt of specimens in the laboratory. ii) Combine classical NN techniques with advanced AI-based methodologies (GA's) to generate a powerful hybrid classification tool.

2 Experimental

Forty-five 5ml urine samples (following eukaryotic cell filtering extraction) were collected from randomly selected patients admitted in Gloucestershire PHLS and inoculated into specially made centrifuge bottles (50ml, Sterilin) each containing 95% BHI broth (Oxoid), 5% serum bovine (Oxoid), 0.70mg ml^{-1} of a series of amino acids (L-Leucine, L-Alanine, L-Serine, L-Valine, L-Asparagine, L-

Glutamine, L-Methionine, Sigma), 1mg ml^{-1} Urea (Sigma), 0.75mg ml^{-1} Lactose (Sigma), 0.1mg ml^{-1} Casein (Oxoid), 0.3mg ml^{-1} Acetylcholine (Sigma) to a final volume of 20ml per VGK and incubated aerobically for 5 hrs at 37°C. After 5 hrs of incubation to coincide with the logarithmic phase of growth, 45 VGK were placed in a 37°C water bath and directly connected with a specifically designed air-filtered sparging (bubbling) system as schematically shown in Fig. 1.

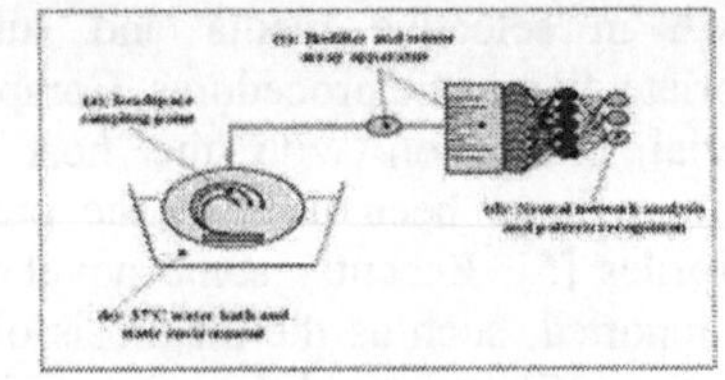

Fig. 1. Schematic representation of experimental apparatus

This consisted of Teflon tubing, a hydrophobic biofilter and an activated carbon filter to provide clean air-flow above the urine headspace.

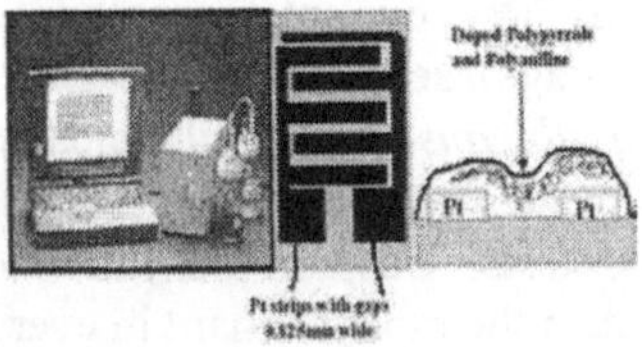

Fig. 2. The Bloodhound gas-sensing unit

A flow rate of 200ml min^{-1} was set automatically and environmental conditions at the sampling point were continuously monitored. The actual urine sampling time and baseline recovery per specimen was 3 min. A gas sensor array employed 14-electroconductive polymer chemoresistors produced by electropolymerisation of the corresponding monomers directly onto the sensor surface. Its structure is illustrated in Fig. 2.

A data capture software analysed complex volatile patterns liberated over the headspace of 45 UTI-VGK specimens and extracted multiple sensor parameters from each patient profile for further post-processing analysis. Thirty cases of UTI were identified from 45 randomly selected samples by standard microscopy and culture: 13 patients were infected with *E.coli* (e), 9 with *Proteus sp.* (p) and 8 with coagulase (-) *Staphylococcus sp.* (st). Two genetic training algorithms processed urine data through a parallel evolutionary succession process towards competent NN solutions. The first GA analysed patient data that had been randomly divided into a "training" group of 31 urinary samples (e: 9, p: 6, st: 5 and n: 11) and a group of 14 "unknowns" (e: 4, p: 3, st: 3 and n: 4, 31% of patient collected data). Fig. 3 displays a real time sensory response analysed by 4 extracted sensor features that describe sensor-volatile physicochemical interaction and pattern extraction: (a) Divergence: maximum step response, (b) Absorption: maximum rate of change of resistance), (c) Desorption: maximum negative rate of change of resistance and (d) Area under the curve. In order to improve the bacterial classification process fourteen conducting polymers and the above 4 features generated a set of 56 sensor parameters extracted from 14 gas-sensor responses. All sensors responses were pre-processed by using a suitable normalisation algorithm.

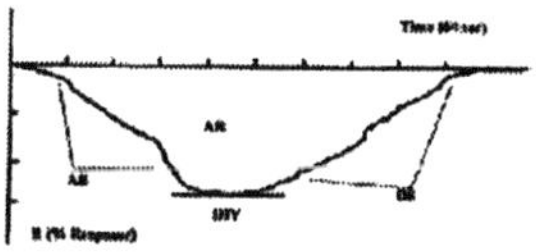

Fig. 3. Parameters measured for each sensor response

Sensor data processing employed a hybrid intelligent system of Genetic Algorithms, Back Propagation Neural Networks (GA-NN) and multivariate techniques such as non-parametric Principal Components Analysis (PCA), parametric Discriminant Function Analysis and cross validation (DFA-cv). An evolutionary process of 5 generations (3 NNs/generation) was carried out employing 1 crossover and a mutation rate of 0.5. Additionally the second GA performed a much broader evolutionary optimisation analysis of 100 generations. It also attempted to analyse the same amount of patient data but with a higher ratio of "unknown" proportion (42% of collected patient data) including 26 training samples (e: 8, p: 4, st: 4, n: 10) and 19 "unknown" UTI (e:5, p:5, st:4, n:5). A population of 600 NNs was evolved using an immigration mode, 2 crossovers and a mutation rate of 0.7 towards the "fittest" NN solution. Both "genetically" selected sensor parameters were also used to perform PCA and DFA-cv. PCA accomplished non-parametrically a significant dimension reduction by minimising minor UTI data variations so that information could be depicted on a few two-dimensional principal component score plots.

3. Results

Two parallel evolutionary algorithms selected 2 NN solutions. The first was a 3-layer (28-12-4) back-propagation NN that used an adaptive learning rate, a momentum of 0.42, an input pattern noise of 0.03 and achieved a 98% prediction rate. Thirteen out of 14 "unknown" UTI samples were identified correctly with a prediction output confidence ranging from 0.75 to 1.01. The intelligent system failed to characterise only one urine sample previously diagnosed with *E.coli* infection. However, this single pattern confusion was limited to the case of distinguishing between *E.coli* infection and normal urine. Both their prediction confidence outputs were very close-0.37 for *E.coli* and 0.43 for normal urine- but below a 0.5 test tolerance limit.

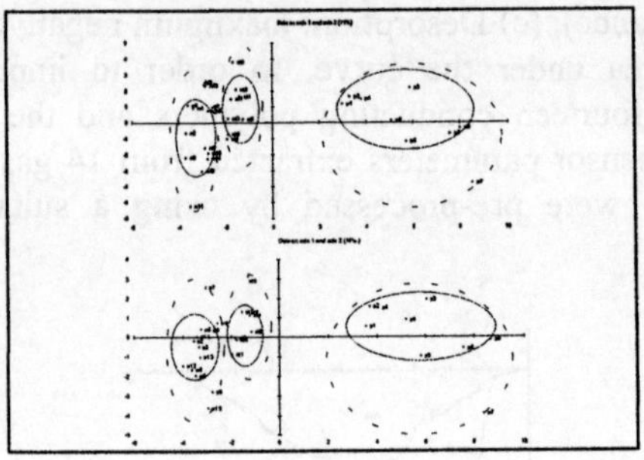

Fig. 4. Extraction of "genetically" selected sensor parameters and two-dimensional representations of PCA clustering between: a. normal urine (n), Proteus sp. (p) and Staphylococcus sp. (st) and b: E.coli (e), Proteus sp. (p) and Staphylococcus sp. (st). (Inner and outer circles divide most closely linearly discriminated patterns from the most drifted ones, respectively).

Twenty-eight "genetically" selected parameters performed PCA and DFA, which displayed two graphical cluster separations between *Proteus sp.*, *Staphylococcus sp.* UTI and normal samples. Cross-validation reclassified correctly 6 "unknown" patient samples (Figs. 4a & 5a). Furthermore by extracting all "genetically" selected sensor parameters that had been previously used as input neurones it was possible to reveal hidden non-linear patterns characteristic of each UTI group.

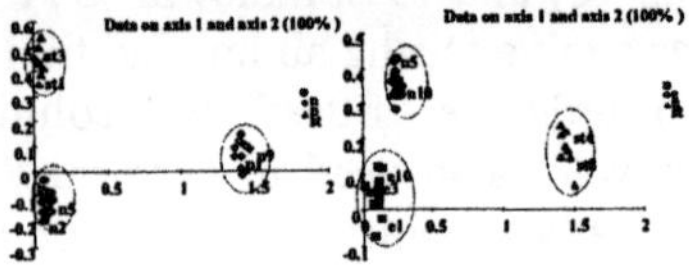

Fig. 5. DFA and 3-group separation between: a. normal urine (n), Proteus sp. (p) and Staphylococcus sp. (st) and b. normal urine, E.coli (e) and Staphylococcus sp. Cross-validation reclassified 6 (a) and 7 (b) "unknown" UTI cases.

Furthermore the second 3-layer NN (22-15-4) achieved a 95% prediction rate and recognised 18 out 19 "unknown". UTI cases. Only one normal patient sample had been mistaken for *E.coli* infection. A two-dimensional discrimination plot between 3 of the tested UTI groups (e, st, p) was produced by PCA. DFA also separated patient samples infected with *E.coli*, *Staphylococcus sp.* and normal urine samples. Cross validation recognised 7 "unknown" UTI cases (Figs. 4b & 5b).

4. Conclusions

It has long been recognised that analysis of urine may provide valuable clinical and physiological information. In this study we have demonstrated that the application of a novel diagnostic technique combining sensor technology with artificial intelligence may lead to rapid and accurate discrimination between different infective organisms in fresh samples of urine, based on the patterns of volatile compounds produced. We have investigated the hypothetical existence of 2 non-linear dynamical systems, in a move towards a novel diagnostic protocol: complex metabolic changes during active UTI and their expression as volatile pulses and the interaction of chemosensory surfaces and urinary volatile groups and their complex pattern recognition. To understand the complexity of *in vivo* UTI metabolic patterns and according to this hypothesis we developed a model, which has been applied successfully in this study. The above intelligent system introduces a unique biochemical "dialogue" with UTI pathogens and the disease itself *de profundis*. It sensed their active metabolic pulses and recognised complex profiles of such a dynamic physiological phenomenon.

References

1. Gibson, T.D., Hulbert, J.N, Prosser, O.C., Pavlou A.K (2000), Not to be sniffed at. Microbiology Today. **27**, 1, 14-17.
2. Persaud, K., Dodd, G.H. (1982), Analysis of discrimination mechanisms of the mammalian olfactory system using a model nose. Nature. **299**, 352-355.
3. Gopel, W. (1998), Chemical Imaging: I. Concepts and Visions for Electronic and Bioelectronic Noses. Sensors & Actuators B. **52**, 125-142.
4. Gardner, J.W., Shin, H.W., Hines, E.L. (2000), An electronic nose system to diagnose illness. Sensors & Actuators B. **70**, 19-24.
5. Davies, T., Hayward, N.J. (1984), Volatile products from acetylcholine are markers in the rapid urine test using headspace gas liquid chromatography. J. Chromatography. **307**, 111-121.
6. Parry, A.D. (1995), Leg ulcer odour detection identifies b-haemolytic streptococcal infection. J Wound Care. **4**, 404.
7. Hanson III, C.W., Steinberger H.A. (1997), The use of a novel electronic nose to diagnose the presence of intrapulmonary infection. Anaesthesiology. **87**, 3A, 269.
8. Pavlou A.K., Kodogiannis V.S., Turner A.P.F. (2001), Intelligent classification of bacterial clinical isolates *in vitro*, using electronic noses. Int. Conf. on Neural Net. & Expert Systems in Medicine and HealthCare, Milos Isl., Greece, 231-237.
9. Richards M.J., Edwards J.R., Culver D.H., Gaynes R.P. (1999), Nosocomial infections in medical intensive care units in the United States. National nosocomial infections surveillance system. Crit Care Med. **27**, 887-892.
10. Zlatkis A, Brazell R.S, Poole C.F. (1981), The role of organic volatile profiles in clinical diagnosis. Clin Chem. **27**, 789-797.

Neural Expert System for Pharmaceutical Formulation Development – Focus on Solid Dispersions

Aleksander Mendyk, Renata Jachowicz, Anna Błasiak

Department of Pharmaceutical Technology and Biopharmaceutics, Faculty of Pharmacy Jagiellonian University, Medyczna 9 St, Cracow, Poland.

Abstract.

Neural network-based expert system was created for improvement of pharmaceutical formulation development process. The knowledge database for this system was created from original, experimental data as well as from literature data. Different models for soluble and poorly soluble drugs were trained and tested. Best results were found when specific, pharmaceutical criterions were used to split base dataset in order to create more specialized neural models predicting behavior of some, well defined class of excipients. ANN function as a PharmCAD system (Pharmaceutical Computer Aided Design) was confirmed.

1 Introduction

Artificial neural networks (ANNs) are commonly known data-analysis tools capable to provide knowledge extraction from empirical data in the wide area of problems, among which there were successful medical and pharmaceutical applications [2,4,5]. Regarding this ANNs should be applied to optimization of pharmaceutical technological processes.

In order to ensure the optimum therapeutic effect of a drug it is necessary to prepare the proper dosage form for targeted and time release. The enhancement of the drug dosage form formulation is connected with the application of new auxiliary substances or with new technological possibilities. The use of solid dispersions (SDs) to increase the dissolution rate and the bioavailability of poorly soluble drugs in now well established. Many substances have been extensively studied with respect to carrier properties. Regarding large number of excipients it's hard to perform classical, combinatorial search for appropriate carrier and adjust its amount in the formulation. Physicochemical properties of excipient and drug define manner of their interaction, which is still not fully revealed. For now empirical knowledge and experience is the only way to perform formulation development.

2 Aim

The aim of this study was to enhance ability of ANNs to handle different drugs as well as different brands of carriers in one, simple neural expert system providing an aid in the search for new solid dispersion formulations.

3 Materials and Methods

3.1. Knowledge Database

Knowledge database was created from original, experimental data as well as from literature data describing dissolution test results for solid dispersions and physical mixtures. Dataset contained 272 formulations (approx. 3000 records), basing on 31 brands of drugs and 39 carriers in various binary and ternary (one drug and two carriers) combinations. A specific encoding system for drugs and carriers was applied, which was so-called ***Connectivity Index*** (CI) – a single value based on the chemical structure [2]. In case of unsatisfactory ANNs performance knowledge database was divided to reduce range of possible solutions. The reduction was performed according to the pharmaceutical state-of-the-art criterions like: drug solubility (one model for soluble and second for poorly soluble drugs) or brand of carrier (i.e. specific model for Macrogols-based solid dispersions).

3.2. Artificial Neural Networks

Classical backpropagation (BP) ANNs with momentum and delta-bar-delta modifications were chosen for this study. Fuzzy networks were also applied. Various architectures were studied – from single to 4 hidden layers in BP ANNs. All layers were fully interconnected. Hyperbolic tangent and so-called ***fsr*** (logarithm-based) [1] activation functions were applied. Input vector size was set to 16. As the input variables quantitative and qualitative composition with formulation preparation technology and dissolution test conditions were chosen. The only one output variable was defined as the amount of drug dissolved in the in vitro conditions at specified in the input time. Thus, ANN task was to predict drug dissolution time-profile in the in vitro conditions basing on the pharmaceutical formulation properties. MSE (mean squared error) and RMSE (root mean squared error) were chosen as the error measures. A classical 10-fold cross-validation scheme was applied in the best architecture search phase. Each training dataset was noised (amplitude ± 5%; 4 times more records), linearly scaled in the range

(0.2;0.8) and randomly presented to particular ANN. On-line performance criterion was learn error (RMSE) computed on the original (non noised) training dataset. Epoch parameter was set to 1. Maximum number of iterations was established by heavy numerical experimentation on 10 000 000. Nevertheless, some ANNs, like i.e. fuzzy nets, were trained up to 1 000 000 iterations. To prevent overfitting jog-of-weights technique was applied with patience criterion set on 300 000 iterations and noise amplitude set on 1% of each weight's value. About 70 architectures were trained to find the best one. To improve ANNs results average of the predictions of 8 best architectures for poorly soluble drugs dataset was computed. This procedure was based on the commonly known idea of experts committee [2]. Statistical significance of results was determined by t-Student test on $p<0.05$.

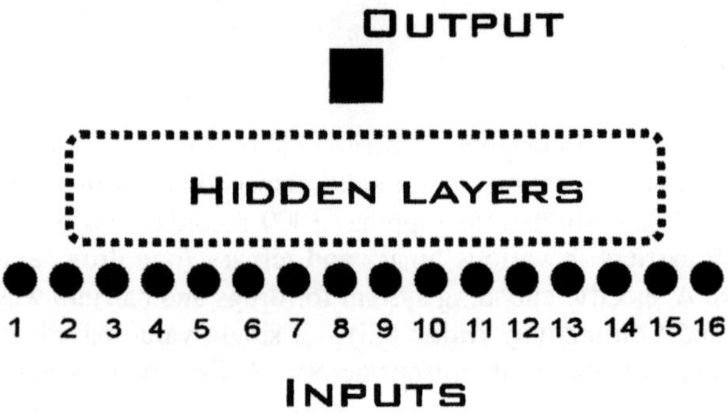

Fig. 1. General architecture layout of neural models for solid dispersions and physical mixtures. **Inputs:** 1. Drug molecular weight; 2. Drug CI; 3. Formulation type (solid dispersion or physical mixture); 4. Solid dispersion produced from physical mixture or not; 5. Preparation technology; 6. Solid dispersion cooling conditions; 7. Drug amount in the formulation; 8. Carrier 1 amount; 9. Carrier 2 amount; 10. Carrier 1 CI; 11. Carrier 2 CI. 12. Carrier 1 molecular weight; 13. Carrier 2 molecular weight; 14. Paddle or basket rounds per minute in the dissolution test; 15. pH of release media in the dissolution test; 16. Time of dissolution test. **Output:** amount of dissolved drug at specified in the input no 16 time.

3.3 Software and Hardware Environment

All computations were carried out with use of own-written ANNs simulator Nets2001 working under Windows 2000 Professional environment on the double-processor Pentium III 1GHz workstation.

4 Results and Discussion

Due to the unsatisfactory results of the whole dataset analysis (RMSE > 18) it was decided to create two separate neural models using drugs solubility as the splitting criterion. For that reason two different architectures were discovered to be the best ones for each model. For soluble drugs minimum error was found to be RMSE = 11.3, which was classified as the satisfactory value regarding maximum output value equal to 100. The architecture of this ANN consisted of 3 hidden layers with 15, 7 and 5 nodes in each layer respectively. Hyperbolic tangent was applied as an activation function (architecture named 15_7_5_hid_tanh). For poorly soluble drugs best architecture was found to have 3 hiden layers with 60, 20 and 8 nodes in each layer respectively and ***fsr*** as the activation function (architecture named 60_20_8_hid_fsr).

Higher error for poorly soluble drugs (Table 1) was the reason to use the experts committee in purpose to obtain better results. There was found statistically significant difference in MSE errors between original 60_20_8_hid_fsr and experts committee results.

Exemplary predictions of unknown for particular system formulations are shown on the Fig 2.

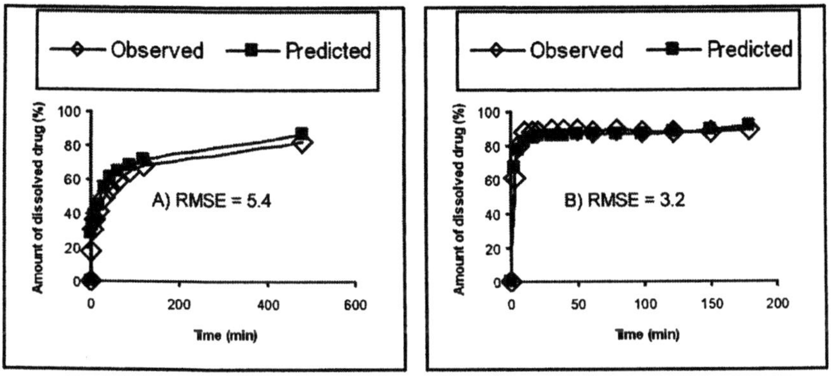

Fig. 2. Example of ANN results: A) ANN 15_7_5_hid_tanh, solid dispersion with 60% oxprenolol hydrochloride (soluble drug), 30% hydroxypropylcellulose and 10% ethylcellulose; B) ANN 20_7hid_tanh trained for Macrogols-based dataset, solid dispersion with 5% flurbiprofen (poorly soluble drug) and 95% Macrogol 20000.

Another experiment was carried out to find out whether more specialized neural models would have smaller errors of their predictions. Only Macrogols-based solid dispersions formulations were selected from the base dataset resulting in dataset containing 64 formulations (approx. 800 records). Best architecture was found to have two hidden layers with 20 and 7 nodes respectively and hyperbolic tangent as an activation function.

Table 1. Results of 10-fold cross-validation for various neural systems.

ANN model for:	Error (RMSE)
Soluble drugs	11.3
Poorly soluble drugs	15.5
Experts committee; poorly soluble drugs	14.4
Macrogols-based only; poorly soluble drugs	12.2

Smaller error (Table 1) is probably the result of the carrier class restriction to the Macrogols derivatives only. To ensure that, training of the best architecture 60_20_8_hid_fsr was performed for the whole poorly soluble drugs dataset excluding only test dataset containing the same formulations like in one of 10-fold cross-validation pairs in Macrogols-based dataset (test_file_no1). The results (Table 2) lead to the confirmation that restriction to the one chemical class of carrier improves results of predictions.

Table 2. RMSE errors for the best ANNs for specific problem trained on different datasets and tested on test_file_no1.

Macrogols-based training dataset ANN: 20_7_hid_tanh	All poorly soluble drugs training dataset without records in test_file_no1 ANN: 60_20_8_hid_fsr
6.6	22.5

To confirm expert system function of ANN it was attempted to predict completely unknown drug behavior in couple of formulations. It was done by extraction from base dataset for poorly soluble drugs all records describing formulations with indomethacin – a model drug selected for this experiment. As a result of this operation the training dataset was created which didn't contain any information about indomethacin (approx. 1900 records). Best architecture 60_20_8_fsr was trained on this dataset. RMSE for this dataset was found to be 16.13, which is not very much more than average results of expert committee (Table 1). The conclusion is that ANN is able to handle efficiently completely new drug data within limits of neural model accuracy. Results of numerical experiments like above, would provide valuable aid in the process of new formulation development saving the number of laboratory experiments.

5 Conclusions

Successful prediction of unknown qualitative and quantitative compositions of solid dispersion proves that ANN are capable to create representative model of various drugs and carriers mixtures prepared as a solid dispersion.

Different properties of drugs and carriers make difficult to create single, universal model for prediction of some solid dispersion dissolution properties. Thus, the solution may be more specialized models, though still universal in the meaning of some class of excipient (i.e. Macrogols or soluble drugs).

The neural network as the expert system is able to extract knowledge from empirical data and give an aid to make easier process of new pharmaceutical formulation development. Therefore, ANN models like shown above are called here PharmCAD systems (Pharmaecutical Computer Aided Design).

Acknowledgements

This work has been supported by Committee of Scientific Research, grant no. KBN 6 P05F 035 21.

References

1. Bilski J (2000) The backropagation learning with logarithmic transfer function. In: Rutkowski L, Tadeusiewicz R, (eds) Proceedings of the 5th Conference Neural Networks and Soft Computing pp. 71-76
2. Duch W, Korbicz J, Rutkowski T, Tadeusiewicz R (eds) Neural Networks (2000). In: Nałęcz M (ed). Biocybernetics and Biomedical Engineering. Vol. 6. Academic Publishing House EXIT, Warsaw
3. Kier LB, Hall LH, Murray WJ (1976) Molecular Connectivity II: Relationship to Water Solubiblity and Boiling Point, J. Pharm. Sci. 65
4. Mendyk A, Jachowicz R (2000) A simple approach to neural optimisation of pharmaceutical dosage form. In: Rutkowski L, Tadeusiewicz R, (eds) Proceedings of the 5th Conference Neural Networks and Soft Computing pp. 562-567
5. Osowski S (1996) Neural Networks in the Algorithmic Approach, WNT, Warsaw

Using Artificial Neural Network as a Tool for Epidemiological Data Analysis

Sebastian Polak[1], Aleksander Mendyk[2], Jerzy Brandys[1]

[1] Department of Pharmacoeconomics, Chair of Toxicology, Faculty of Pharmacy, Jagiellonian University, Cracow, Poland;

[2] Department of Pharmaceutical Technology and Biopharmaceutics, Faculty of Pharmacy, Jagiellonian University, Cracow, Poland;

Abstract. The importance of socio-economic part of medicine still increases. This study was performed to investigate abilities to use Artificial Neural Network as a tool for epidemiological data analysis. Back-propagation neural networks were simulated on own-written software. The sensitivity analysis results of created models suggest that ANN are able to discover most significant factors for studied output and as a consequence of this could be helpful for medical policy makers in decision process.

Introduction

In the past decade there has been a spectacular increase of interest in epidemiological data analysis. Large databases of potential helpful information are traditionally worked out with simple, statistical methods. Unfortunately, these techniques and statistical software usually require powerful computers - thus classical PC's are often unable to finish procedure.

At the same time there is a lot of papers describing use of Artificial Neural Network (ANN) in medicine. Most of them deal with medical decision supporting and medical diagnosis systems. There is a lack of papers and studies which show the ANN as a potential technology able to discover relationships in analysed epidemiological data. Thanks to its flexibility ANN could discover many unexpected and hidden relations and predict outcomes.

The aims of this work were:

1. to build a methodology which can help to make the most of extensive epidemiological databases

2. to create a model helpful in recognition of crucial factors for analysed variables

The data

The source of the data was National Centre for Health Statistics (NCHS), USA. The main used dataset was *The National Health and Nutrition Examination Survey Epidemiological Follow-up Study* (NHEFS).

Initial data required some pre-processing because of its errors. All blank fields and columns were removed. After pre-processing all 9281 records were described by 1425 variables (input vector). All fractions in learning set were rounded into the nearest integer. Predicted variable describes what was the cause of subject's death.

Table 1. Codes of output.

Nr of Cases	Code	Type of answer
815	-1	INAPPLICABLE
10	-7	REFUSED
130	-8	DON'T KNOW
6	-9	NOT ASCERTAINED
159	1	HEART ATTACK
146	2	OTHER HEART CONDITION
82	3	STROKE/SMALL STROKE/TIA/POSSIBLE STROKE
9	4	DIABETES
4	5	HIGH BLOOD PRESSURE
196	6	CANCER
15	7	KIDNEY CONDITION
66	8	PNEUMONIA OR FLU
39	9	OLD AGE
278	10	OTHER

All answers coded less than 0 (INAPPLICABLE, REFUSED, DON'T KNOW, NOT ASCERTAINED) were transformed into 0.

ANN simulator

Own-written simulator Nets2001 working under Windows 9x and NT environments.

Data pre-processing

To perform data pre-processing Phmc_app, own-written application, was designed to transform SAS-dedicated native files into the ASCII files formatted directly for the Nets2001 simulator. After Phmc_app, Split_file and/or Erase_0, own-created tools were applied for further data manipulation.

Methods

The back-propagation feed-forward neural networks were used in this study. In the first part of work all networks had 1425 input nodes (determined by the data) and one output node.

Error measures were RMSE (root mean squared error) and classification error (%) expressed as all errors and good positive classification (percentage of appropriately classified causes of death).

The number of hidden nodes was determined by trial and error. The activation function for each node in the network was hyperbolic tangent.

Notation of architecture name is formatted to describe number of hidden layers and nodes followed by activation function. (15_7 hid tanh means two hidden layers with 15 and 7 nodes respectively and hyperbolic tangent as activation function).

Results and discussion

As the graph presented on Figure 1 shows, the research was carried out simultaneously. Results of best architectures obtained using large dataset with 1425 inputs were as follows (Table 2).

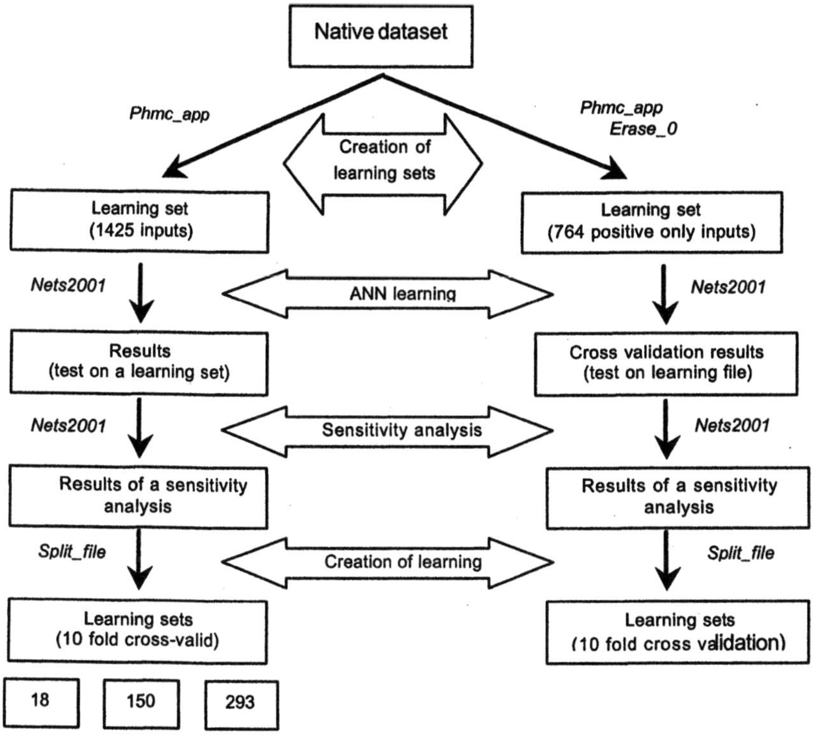

Fig. 1. Proceeding methodology

Table 2. Best architectures results (1425 inputs, test on a training set).

Architecture name	Max. number of iteration ($x10^6$)	RMSE	All errors	Good positive classific.
10 hid tanh_DTHCAUSE	15	0.23	3.6	75.15
15_7 hid tanh_DTHCAUSE	2	0.097	0.82	95.17

Next step was sensitivity analysis of all obtained models.

On this stage it is possible for health policy makers to discover relationships between demographic data (particular patient cause of death as an output for example) and use the results for financial planning (Table 3).

Second part of data sets was created by exclusion of training set records with outputs equal to zero. Results of best architectures tested on training sets shows Table 4.

Table 3. Examples of main variables obtained after sensitivity analysis of best model (1425 inputs).

Architecture name.	Number of input.	Code of input.
10hid tanh DTHCAUSE	1384	DOES SUBJECT HAVE FACILITY STAY DATA TAPE WITH A REPORTED CONDITION OF HEART ATTACK
	30	BROKEN/FRACTURED HIP REPORTED IN PREVIOUS INTERVIEW
	17	HEART ATTACK REPORTED IN PREVIOUS INTERVIEW
	173	WAS SUBJECT HOSPITALIZED FOR ANY OTHER HEART CONDITION
	583	DID SUBJECT RECEIVE PERSONAL INCOME FROM UNEMPLOYMENT
	585	DID SUBJECT RECEIVE PERSONAL INCOME FROM INTEREST EARNINGS

Table 4. Best architectures results (764 inputs, test on a training set).

Architecture name	Max. number of iteration ($x10^6$)	RMSE	All errors	Good positive classific.
5_3 hid tanh_DTHCAUSE	5	5.16	15.09	84.91
7_3 hid tanh_DTHCAUSE	5	5.18	16.90	83.10
10_5 hid tanh_DTHCAUSE	5	2.17	2.01	97.99

An example of decision-supporting ability of such neural model is the analysis of model responses after one variable change. A histogram of responses describes hypothetical distribution of death causes in case of prior nursing house admission reported or not. It is noticeable that only one variable modification gives different distribution of death causes, which could be a matter of discussion for policy makers in case of health care funds disposition.

Conclusions

The results of best architectures show that the Artificial Neural Networks are able to give valuable results in analysis of vast epidemiological data and could be used simultaneously with classical statistical methods. Sensitivity analysis of best created models (Table 3) demonstrates interesting medical relationships between cause of patient's death and demographic data (data mining).

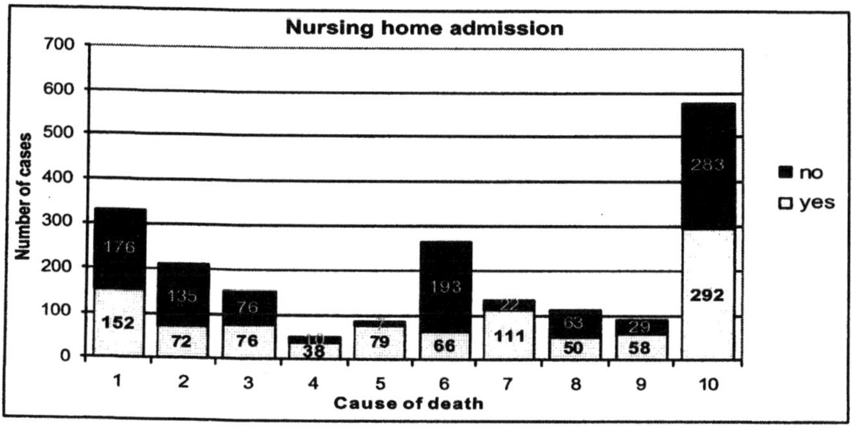

Fig. 2. Death cause distribution in numerical experiment with single modified value (10_5 hid tanh_DTHCAUSE).

In health policy systems, neural systems can provide a models for setting reasonable reimbursement plans, outcome expectations and health care resource allocation. It could be also helpful for insurance companies to select risk clients and adjust health insurance.

References

1. Osowski S. (1996) Neural network in algorithmic depiction. Scientific-Technical Publishing House, Warsaw (In Polish)
2. De Laurentis A., et al. (1999) A prognostic model that makes quantitative estimates of probability of relapse for breast cancer patients. Clinical Cancer Research vol. 5, 4133-4139
3. Plate T., Band P., Bert J., Grace J., (1997) A comparison between neural networks and other statistical techniques for modelling the relationships between tobacco and alcohol and cancer., Advances in Neural Information Processing, MIT Press, 967-973
4. Radensky P.W., Mango L.J., (1998) Interactive neural network-assisted screening:an economic assessment., Acta Cytologica, 42(1), 246-252
5. Walczak S., Scharf J.E., (2000) Reducing surgical patient costs through use of an artificial neural network to predict transfusion requirements., Decision Support Systems, 30, 125-138
6. Morrison J.R., Johnson J.D., Barnes J.H., Summers K., Szeinbach S.L., (1997) Predicting Total Health Care Costs of Medicaid Recipients: An Artificial Neural System Approach, 40, 191-197

A Neural Network Based Investigation of High Frequency Components of the ECG

Minija Tamošiūnaitė [1], Šarūnas Raudys [2]

[1] Vytautas Magnus University, Vileikos 8, Kaunas-3035, Lithuania,
[2] Institute of Mathematics and Informatics, Akademijos 4, Vilnius-2600, Lithuania

Abstract: New information retrieval method is applied to detect low amplitude high frequency components of electrocardiogram (ECG). The special neural network using similarities to prototype features is suggested. Prognosis error is chosen as similarity measure of a signal to a prototype. This measure is preferable in the case of a poor signal to noise ratio. New technique was successfully applied for classification of ECG recordings of myocardial infarction (MI) patients with the complication of ventricular fibrillation (VF) vs. the MI patients who have not had the VF, a problem where standard methods failed to provide satisfactory separation of pattern classes.

1 Introduction

Though the basic elements of ECG have been exhaustively explored during the one hundred year-history of clinical electrocardiography, the information content of the smaller details is still being debated. Among these are the T-wave alternans, QT dispersion, and cardiac late potentials [1, 2, 3, 4, 7]. The current study is focussed on the investigation of the late potentials (LP) - the low amplitude high frequency oscillations at the end of the QRS complex of an ECG [7].

A mechanism supposedly underlying the LP and ventricular fibrillation is called reentry, and includes circling of electrical activation around some obstacle for electrical conductivity (scar, etc.) [2]. Late potentials are hypothesized to be precursors of ventricular fibrillation (VF), the VF being life-threatening heart rhythm disturbance. The episodes of VF most often are caused by myocardial infarction [1, 3]. Reliable and inexpensive predictors of ventricular fibrillation are not discovered yet, though existence of late potentials in an ECG could be considered as a candidate feature to be included in the algorithm for the VF prediction.

Serious drawback for the practical usage of late potentials as the VF predictors is the difficulty to detect the phenomenon from the surface ECG. Amplitude of the LP is small and it interferes with muscular noise. LP are routinely traced high-resolution surface electrocardiograms, applying signal-averaging techniques. Currently the standard for LP detection is Simson method which is based on the analysis of duration of the QRS complex of a signal-averaged ECG and measurement of the amplitude in the terminal part of the complex in the 40-250

Hz frequency range [2, 7]. Nevertheless, the method fails to provide satisfactory separation between the two classes [1, 3], which may be due to the insufficiency of the method to grasp the entirety of the underlying electrophysiological model of LP.

In this paper a special robust to noise neural network based technique operating without signal averaging is introduced for LP-like phenomena detection. Specific autoregressive patterns are searched for at the end of the QRS complex, as well as further on, onto the T wave. The patterns of the ECGs of the patients who have had the MI complicated by the VF are compared to those with uncomplicated MI. It is supposed that LP like phenomena should be more probable in the VF group. The neural network-based method analyzed in this study fits the LP model more accurately than the one employed in Simson method. The current study extends and refines results of previous investigations described in [8].

2 Data Description

The investigation encompasses analysis of two segments of an ECG: the ST segment and the T wave (Fig. 1). The ST segment is situated directly after the QRS complex, and is the place where the oscillations of LP are most probable. The T wave represents recovery process following electrical activation and contraction of the heart, and may also possess traces of LP extending beyond the ST segment.

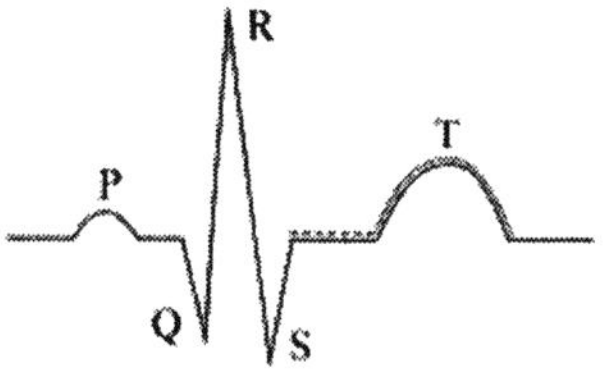

Fig. 1. ECG cycle with ST segment and T wave marked by dashed and dotted lines

The study was performed using ECG database collected at the Institute of Cardiology, Kaunas Medical University. Two pattern classes were created: myocardial infarction patients without complication of VF (MI group); MI patients with the complication of the VF (VF group). Parameters of the ECG records were as follows: 5 min., 2kHz sampling, 12 bits, 8 leads (I, II, V1-V6); ECGs recorded on the 7th-9th day after the MI. The lead V4, which otherwise is not widely used by cardiologists because of sensitivity to electrode position, was chosen for analysis. The LP-like oscillations of high frequency were supposed not to be sensitive to the small displacements of electrodes. Relatively low noise of the V4 lead provided advantage in the analysis of low amplitude details.

Two experiments were conducted: one with manually selected T waves and ST segments, five patterns of each kind picked from each ECG. The second experiment was conducted using automated segment selection with 45 patterns of each kind extracted from each ECG, and was directed towards investigation of impact of the increase in a number of ECG patterns on classification error. In the first experiment, 54 MI and 54 VF cases were analyzed. In the second experiment, the extended set of recordings, including 63 MI and 68 VF cases, was used. In the automated procedure one prototypical T wave was manually labeled in each ECG recording, and the rest waves were found by largest correlation match technique. The ST segments were defined to last 0.1 s. before the beginning of each T wave.

3 Description of the Network

The architecture of a neural network was proposed in [6] and is designed for classification of noisy signals with autoregressive structure. In the first layers of the network prototypical signals from both pattern classes are used to form informative features. The following layer produces a nonlinear feature transformation by *a priori* fixed algorithm. The output layer classifies the feature vectors. Training of each network layer is done separately. Search for unknown coefficients of the network is done as follows:

1. Choose *a priori* fixed moving average filter for isolation of the high frequency component from each signal (ST segment or T wave);
2. To characterize different types of electrical activation in the heart select several (say p) patients from both pattern classes as prototypical. Each *prototypical patient* is represented by *sets of five T waves or five ST segments.*
3. Use SLP to find coefficients of regressive model for prediction a middle value, x_j, of each elementary segment of the ECG signal $x_{j-L+1}, x_{j-L+2}\, x_{j-L+1} .. x_j\ x_{j+1}\ ..\ x_{j+L}$, where L denotes order of the model. $2L$ coefficients are obtained for each segment. In the current study the coefficients were averaged over the five segments representing the same patient to obtain the overall regression model, however other combinations are possible instead of averaging.
4. Use the *p prototypical regression models* from each class ($2p$ for two classes) in order to make prognosis along each single signal segment.
5. Calculate $2p$ *mean square prognosis errors* for each signal, according to $2p$ prototypical regression equations. Take the obtained errors as $2p$ *new features*.
6. To obtain the non-linear classification algorithm produce second-order polynomial features ($2\times2p$ features of the form x and x^2 were used in this study).
7. Train the single layer perceptron (SLP) classifier to discriminate the VF and MI pattern classes in the space of the $2\times2p$ features.
8. In order to make the final decision perform a majority voting procedure for the groups of 5 to 45 ST segments or T waves representing the same patient.

The steps 1-6 can be interpreted twofold: as training of the lower layers of the multilayer network, or as the feature extraction steps of the classification algorithm. The steps 7 and 8 represent tuning of the final decision-making unit.

Prognosis error was applied to form more robust to noise features than the regression coefficients themselves.

In the current study a 41 points triangular moving average filter was used in the first step. Performance of the network with several prototypical coefficient sets (p=5 to 15) was explored. Several types of regression models (denoted as L^{-1}-L) with parameter L varying between 2 and 7 were considered. To obtain low generalization error and speed up training process the data was rotated and scaled to have statistically uncorrelated features with identical variances (Chapter 5 in [5]).

In experiments with ECG data, the MI and VF classes were multiple times randomly divided into training and test sets: the training set consisted of 40 recordings, and the test set consisted of the rest of the available data. The division into two sets with consecutive training and testing of the neural network was repeated 20 times. The classification errors of each trial were averaged over 20 runs of the experiment.

4 Results and Discussion

The classification errors obtained in the test set during the first stage of experiments (i.e. 5 segments representing each record) are visualized in Fig. 2 in the form of histograms. For the ST segment in Fig. 2 (a) the average error of 20 experiments with different parameter values (number of prototypes and regression order) ranges between 31% and 37%. The error appeared neither to be significantly correlated with the order of the regression nor with the number of prototypes. For the T wave, Fig. 2 (b), the error varies between 38% and 44% for the same training parameter range. Excluding possibility that the standard deviation of the signal values, but not the autoregression pattern, has provided the differences between the two classes, classification according to standard deviation alone was performed and provided 43% of errors for the ST segments, and 48% of for the T waves (the errors shown by arrows in the histogram plots).

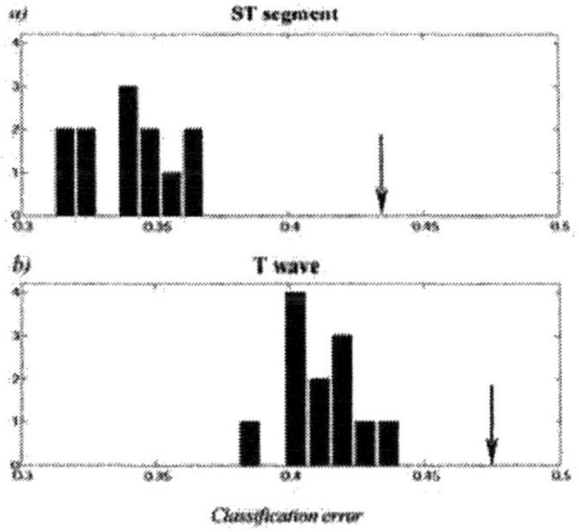

Fig. 2. Classification errors obtained analyzing ST segments (*a*) and T waves (*b*).

To give the better insight into the variations of error with model parameters, the corresponding relations for the ST segment are shown in Tab. 1. The standard deviations between the errors obtained in 20 different data set divisions range between 6 and 10%, thus diminishing the significance of the difference between the results provided using different models.

Table 1. Classification errors of the ST segments. Mean and standard deviations of 20 trials

# of prototypes vs. regression order		2^{-1}-2	3^{-1}-3	5^{-1}-5	7^{-1}-7
5	mean (std) %	35 (6)	33(9)	32 (7)	35 (6)
10	mean (std) %	31 (7)	34 (6)	36 (7)	37 (9)
15	mean (std) %	32 (10)	37 (6)	34 (9)	33 (7)

The percentage of errors of around 35% for the ST segment is a reasonable result for the task of detection of the trace of earlier ventricular fibrillation from the ECG recordings. The past VF episodes cannot be discovered by eye using the ECG analysis techniques employed by physicians. The classification result achieved by neural network is also better than the 42% of errors obtained using the Simson method for recognition of VF cases in the same data set. The results obtained both by the neural network method, and by the Simson method are comparable to the prognostic value of late potentials for VF described in literature, e.g. see [1, 2], though the results reported in different studies are not unanimous.

Classification of T waves has given 41% of errors on average. This is slightly better than the results obtained in [8] (47-48%) for the T wave. The increase in precision is reached by more careful filtering procedure applied in the first step of the algorithm. Nevertheless, the results for T are still worse than the ones obtained using ST segments, although, different discriminative power between the two classes in the ST and T cases according to standard deviation should be taken into account (see arrows in Fig. 2). Classification of the same classes according to regression coefficients (10th order) using both SLP and multi-layer perceptron provided notably worse results (e.g. 42 and 45% of classification errors for the ST segment).

In the second stage of experiments, relation between the number of employed segments and the classification error was investigated. The error decreased from 46% to approx. 37%, with the number of investigated segments increasing from 5 to 45, both in the ST segment and T wave classification, in 10 prototypes case. However, the error did not strictly decrease but rather fluctuated in the interval between 48 and 41% in the 5 prototypes case both for T and ST. In all cases the model structure 3^{-1}-3 was used. The non-strictly decreasing behavior of 5 prototype-case errors may reflect random influences upon the training and testing procedures (random division of data into the training/test sets, random initialization of the SLP, random initialization of clusterization procedure for prototype selection).

The results of the first stage of experiments indicate the advantage of classifying ST segments, but not T waves, when looking for signs of possibility of ventricular fibrillation. This is consistent with the LP hypothesis discussed earlier. However, the results of the second stage of experiments prompt for more careful explorations of the high frequency components beyond the QRS segment with possible prognostic value.

5 Conclusions

1. The neural network based on similarity-to-prototype features was able to separate the ECGs of patients who had suffered from the life threatening complication of the MI, the VF, from those who have not had the complication. The standard methods failed to provide separation between the two classes.
2. Both the ST segments and the T waves demonstrated ability to separate classes, though the ST segment revealed greater potential in VF prediction.
3. The classification error decreased with an increase in the number of waveform patterns from each ECG recording included into analysis.

Acknowledgements. The authors are thankful to Prof. Juozas Blužas and his research group from Institute of Cardiology, Kaunas, for the provided data sets and helpful discussions.

References

1. Bluzaite I., Brazdzionyte J. et al. (1997) Signal-averaged electrocardiogram. Pecularities of the first and recurrent myocardial infarction. J. Hong Kong Col. Cardiol. **5**, 119-125
2. Breithardt G., Cain M., et al. (1991) Standards for analysis of ventricular late potentials using high resolution or signal-averaged electrocardiography. Eur. Heart J. **12**, 473-480
3. Denniss A. (1992) Late potentials in the post-infarction period: correlations with programmed electrical stimulation. High-Resolution Electrocardiography. Futura Publishing Co., NY, 391-404
4. Klingenheben T., Hohnloser S. (1999) T wave alternans: what is the true practical clinical value? Card. Electrophysiol. Rev. **3**, 324-327
5. Raudys S. (2001) Statistical and Neural Classifiers: An integrated approach to design. Springer, London
6. Raudys S., Tamosiunaite M. (2000) Biologically inspired architecture of feedforward networks for signal classification. Advances in Pattern Recognition. LNCS **1876**, Springer, Berlin, 727-736
7. Simson M. (1981) Use of signals in the terminal QRS complex to identify patients with ventricular tachycardia after myocardial infarction. Circulation **64**, 235-242
8. Tamosiunaite M., Raudys S. (2001) A neural network based on ECG ST segment prediction accuracy for classification of ventricular fibrillation. Proc. of the 2nd Int. Conf. on Neural Networks and Artificial Intelligence ICNNAI'2001, October 2-5, 2001, Minsk, Belarus. Minsk, BSUIR, 100-103

Automatic Ischemic Stroke Segmentation Using Various Techniques

Andrius Usinskas[1], Erinija Pranckeviciene[2], Thomas Wittenberg[3], Peter Hastreiter[4], and Bernd F. Tomandl[4]

[1]Vilnius Gediminas Technical University, Vilnius, Lithuania (au@el.vtu.lt)
[2]Kaunas University of Technology, Kaunas, Lithuania
[3]Fraunhofer Institute for Integrated Circuits-Applied Electronics, Erlangen, Germany
[4]Neurocenter at the Clinics of the University Erlangen-Nuremberg, Erlangen, Germany

Abstract. Different methods of automatic segmentation of human brain ischemic stroke area in the computerized tomography scans are compared. Experts-radiologists performed the evaluation of segmentation techniques. A methodology of qualitative evaluation of the investigated methods is proposed. The best viability showed histogram, gray level co-occurrence matrix, mean and standard deviation methods, and supervised artificial neural network technique.

1 Introduction

Many image segmentation algorithms are developed for the solution of various image analysis tasks. The existence of a variety of approaches in medical image segmentation requires an investigation of their performance from the view of the doctor dealing with the particular problem.

Today, computer tomography (CT) is the modality of first choice for the examination of patients with acute stroke. Within the first hours after onset of the stroke appearance, the detection of ischemic regions in the brain using CT images is at the same time a very critical and a very difficult task. Later ischemic edema can be recognized as a hypodense area that is clearly visible. For scientific and medical studies dealing with ischemic stroke it is necessary and useful to calculate the volume of the stroke, since the patient status depends on the size and localization of the ischemic stroke. The manual calculation of the location and the volume of the stroke is very tedious and time consuming. In order to speed up possible early detection and diagnosis, it is important to find a better possible technique to segment the stroke in each CT slice.

Among the most successful methods of medical image segmentation mentioned in the survey on medical image analysis [1] are the methods based on boundary finding strategies using deformable models, intensity clustering techniques and a combination of both. The use of artificial neural networks for image segmentation and medical image analysis becomes promising research area [2]. Since no one algorithm can robustly segment a variety of relevant structures in medical images over a range of datasets [1], we investigate different image segmentation techniques for the brain CT image segmentation. In this study our aim is to show merits and disadvantages of the methods for automatic brain ischemic stroke recognition with the emphasis on the methods using artificial neural network.

A methodology of the qualitative segmentation evaluation is proposed based on ranking of processed images by experts-radiologists.

2 Methods of CT image segmentation

CT-scans from 3 different human heads with diagnosed ischemic stroke were analyzed. The first and the second scans included 16 slices, the third – 14 slices. All 46 images were made on a SOMATOM Volume Zoom (SIEMENS) at the Department of Neuroradiology at the University Hospital of the Friedrich Alexander University of Erlangen-Nuremberg, Germany. Size of slice images was 512×512 pixels, thickness – 8 mm. The images were converted from DICOM to BMP image format by cropping 4'096 possible gray levels (12 bit) to 100 gray levels (supported by 8 bit BMP).

The segmentation was performed using *a priori* information and without it. In the segmentation with the training set the features of sliding window such as mean and variance were used directly. The other preprocessed features of sliding window were histogram and gray level co-occurrence matrix. The methods without training were thresholding and iterated conditional modes algorithm. The novel approach utilizing a neural network to classify pixels according to region model was investigated. Training data – the stroke and non-stroke areas – were determined manually (fig. 1 a) as class *C*1 and class *C*2. The features calculated from these areas were a priori information for nearest neighbor classifier. The pixel values for the same area were the training set for artificial neural network

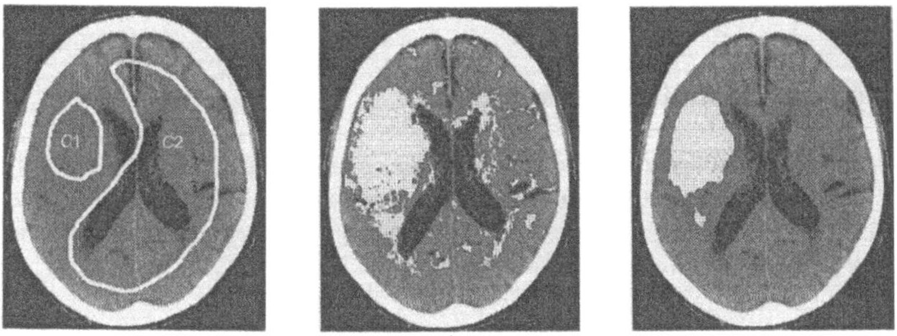

a b c

Fig. 1. Manually determined stroke and non-stroke areas as class *C*1 and class *C*2 (a), image segmentation using sliding 7×7 window (b), and 31×31 window (c)

2.1 Thresholding

The threshold operation changes pixel values depending on whether they are less or greater than the specified threshold producing binary image. If an input pixel value is less than the threshold, the corresponding output pixel is set to black, otherwise to white. The value of the threshold in the experiments was 25.

2.2 Artificial Neural Network (ANN) classification based on region model

In order to separate a patch of brain ischemic stroke area from the rest of the image we use a novel approach of the ANN training [3, 4]. It is based on the models (prototypes) of the regions of interest. The pixel from the region matching a prototype has high similarity value and low for other prototypes. By calculating the similarities of the pixels to the prototypes the entire image is transformed to the new feature space where the areas of interest separate better. Image features for the region prototypes were median and a histogram of a pixel intensity of the 10×10 neighborhood (block). The values of a block are denoted as $x = [x_1, \ldots, x_L]$, $L = M \times N$ where N is width and M is height of the block. $y_x = median(x)$ is a median of the vector. A histogram of the block is $n_x = [n_1/L, \ldots, n_l/L]$, where n_k, $k = 1$, l is a number of values falling in to the k-th bin and l is the number of bins. A multilayer perceptron is trained to approximate the function for region C:

$$y_x = f^C{}_{MLP}(n_x) \tag{1}$$

The learned relation serves as a prototype. A similarity measure of the pixel to the prototype is an absolute difference between the actual median value and MLP predicted value in the neighborhood of the pixel:

$$e^C{}_x = \left| y_x - f^C{}_{MLP}(n_x) \right| \tag{2}$$

The MLP with the one hidden neuron is trained to separate classes $C1$ and $C2$. New images are analyzed by calculating the similarity of pixels to prototypes (2) and classifying them to the stroke and non-stroke region.

2.3 Iterated conditional modes algorithm

The algorithm is an adaptive iterative averaging of the image luminance developed for gray image segmentation to obtain homogeneous image regions [5]. The ICM is based on a maximization of a probability density (criterion) function of the image model given real image data:

$$p(x_s \mid y_s, x_q, q \in N_8(s)) \propto \exp\left(-\sum_s \frac{(y_s - m_i)^2}{2\delta_i^2} - \sum_{x_s \in C} V_C(x) \right), \tag{3}$$

where s is the number of the current pixel and i is the number of the region. The x_s is the value of the pixel assignment to the region and y_s is the luminance value of the pixel s. The m_i and d_i are the mean value and the standard deviation of luminance of the region i. C is the clique of the pixel s, $V_C(x)$ is the potential function of the clique and $N_8(s)$ is 8 by 8 neighborhood of the pixel. Initial segmentation is obtained using the K-means clustering algorithm. The output image contains the large regions assigned mean luminance.

2.4 Image segmentation with training set

First of all it was necessary to choose the proper size of sliding window in order to find a better compromise between widow size and recognition accuracy (fig 2 b, c). We decided to use 21×21 sliding window for further stroke segmentations. So there were 26'966 positions of sliding window in the class $C2$, 3'314 positions of sliding window in the class $C1$, and 30'280 positions in total. As a classifier we used 3-nearest neighbor rule [6]. The nearest neighbor rule classifies x to the category C_n, where x_n is the nearest neighbor to x and x_n belongs to class C_n. according Euclidean distance. A mistake was made if C_n was not the same category. We chose the nearest 3 neighbors to assign every sliding window to one of the known class. In the following we describe each feature of the sliding window in more detail.

Mean of the sliding window is defined as:

$$F_1 = \frac{1}{21^2} \sum_{i=0}^{21^2-1} x_i , \tag{4}$$

where x_i is the value of the i-th pixel of the sliding window row.

The variance is defined as:

$$F_2 = \frac{1}{21^2-1} \cdot \sum_{i=0}^{21^2-1} (x_i - \mu). \tag{5}$$

The histogram is a function $H(i)$ of the number of occurrence of each gray level in the image: $H(i) = j$, where i – the gray level number [0, ..., 99], j – the number of i-th gray level occurrence [0, ..., 21^2].

The main part of the brain gray mass and stroke gray levels was in the range [0, ..., 49] of the histogram function so we used this range only for features extraction. There were 10 features at all. Each feature was the possibility of occurrence of 5 contiguous gray levels:

$$F_i = \frac{1}{21^2} \sum_{j=5(i-1)}^{5(i-1)+4} H(j) \tag{6}$$

where i – number of feature [1, ..., 10].

Gray level co-occurrence matrix represents an estimate of the probability that one pixel has intensity $L1$ and another – $L2$, where $L1$, $L2 \in [0; N_g-1]$, and N_g is the number of available gray levels in the image. According to [7] the 14 parameters can be extracted from above mentioned probability distribution characterizing image texture. Combining one feature with another, we found the six Haralick features best describing stroke and brain texture: contrast, sum of squares (variance), sum average, sum variance, sum entropy, and difference variance.

Continuing previous research on ANN utilization for image segmentation [8] we created multiple-layer feedforward ANN [9] from $21 \times 21 - 1 = 440$ inputs (an input as whole sliding window), 4 neurons in hidden layer and 1 neuron in the output (stroke/non-stroke). Transfer function of all neurons was Log-Sigmoid function. ANN learned by backpropagation Powell-Beale Restarts algorithm. Learning was stopped after 237 iterations.

3 Conclusions

We processed 46 CT images by the described methods. Radiologists from Vilnius, Kaunas (Lithuania), and Erlangen (Germany) assessed the results. The experts chose 3 best segmentation techniques for each CT slice. The results in table 1 show evaluation of each examined technique in percents.

Table 1. Evaluation of the methods for stroke image segmentation

Method	Evaluation, %
Thresholding	1
Artificial Neural Network based on the region model	1
Iterated Conditional Modes	13
Mean and standard deviation	18
Histogram	24
Gray level co-occurrence matrix	22
Supervised Artificial Neural Network	17

So the best viability showed methods were Histogram, Gray level co-occurrence matrix, Mean and standard deviation, and Supervised Artificial Neural Networks. Other methods can be utilized to solve this task too; therefore it must be discovered new better features for these methods. We found that the fastest method is thresholding. The slowest method was the histogram (tens of minutes), because there was a very large training set: 10×30'280 = 302'800, and it required processing of each sliding window position (more than 150'000). The largest memory utilization and the longest time were required for artificial neural network training. With the trained net segmentation lasts several seconds. Artificial neural network based on region model requires a small number of patterns to be trained. The performance of the net can be improved during the classification stage by retraining the net using the new examples it failed to classify correctly. Iterated conditional modes algorithm is very sensible to the contrast difference. It fails to identify an ischemic stroke area where it blends with the other parts of the image. According to the quality of the results and the time of performance the best method was based on the artificial neural network. As the result we offer:

1. To use artificial neural network, because when the network is trained it works fast even on old-type PCs such as 486 with 4 MB RAM.
2. To minimize the time of segmentation by keeping small quantity of features and reducing training set size.
3. To limit the area of interest by using thresholding technique.

For the first time the segmentation algorithms of the CT scans of brain ischemic stroke were investigated and assessed by Vilnius, Kaunas and Erlangen radiologists. The research is promising and indicates the need to expand the results in direction of the inclusion of more methods, more data and experts from different geographic regions.

4 Acknowledgements

Authors thank Kaunas University clinics head of tomography investigation MD Ph. D. A. Basevicius, Vilnius University hospital "Santariskiu clinics" doctor radiologist MD Ph. D. N. Valeviciene, professor I. Pitas of the Aristotle University of Thessaloniki for providing computer program of iterated conditional modes algorithm, and professor S. Raudys for the valuable ideas and consultations.

References

[1] J. S. Duncan and N. Ayache. *Medical image analysis: progress over two decades and the challenges ahead.* IEEE Transactions on Pattern Analysis and Machine Intelligence, 22(1):85-105, January 2000.

[2] K. Chen, D. Wang and X. Liu. *Weight adaptation and oscillatory correlation for image segmentation.* IEEE Transactions on Neural networks, 11(5):1106-1123, 2000.

[3] S. Raudys, M. Tamosiunaite, Biologically *Inspired Architecture of Feedforward Networks for Signal Classification.* In: Ferri, F.J., Inesta, J.M., Amin, A. and Pudil, P. (eds.), Advances in Pattern Recognition. Proceedings of the Joint IAPR International Workshops SSPR 2000 and SPR 2000, Alicante, Spain. Berlin: Springer, p. 727-736, 2000.

[4] M. Tamosiunaite, E. Pranckeviciene, *Application of the Biologically Inspired Network for Electroencephalogram Analysis*, in B. Reusch (Ed.): Computational Intelligence Theory and Applications, Lecture Notes in Computer Science No. 2206, Springer 2001.

[5] T. N. Pappas. *An adaptive clustering algorithm for image segmentation*, IEEE Transactions on Image Processing, 40(4):901-914, 1992.

[6] J. Schürmann. *Pattern Classification: A Unified View Of Statistical And Neural Approaches*. John Wiley & Sons, Inc., 1996.

[7] R. M. Haralick et al. *Textural features for image classification.* IEEE Transactions on System, Man, And Cybernetics, SMC-3(6):610-621, November 1973.

[8] A. Usinskas, R. A. Dobrovolskis. *Diagnosis Of Brain Ischemic Stroke With Personal Computer*. Medicina, 36(10):1144-1148, 2000 (in Lithuanian).

[9] S. Raudys. Statistical and Neural Classifiers: An Integrated Approach to Design (Advances in Pattern Recognition). Springer, 2001.

Simple Modification of Takagi-Sugeno Model

Bohdan Butkiewicz

Warsaw University of Technology, Institute of Electronic Systems, Nowowiejska 15/19, 00-665 Warsaw, Poland

Abstract. The Takagi-Sugeno model is very popular in fuzzy logic area. It can approximate different functions and physical processes. However, it is known that the model has one inconvenience. If simple triangular or trapezoidal membership functions are used for fuzzy sets then in intermediate area, described example by two fuzzy sets (conclusions of two rules) and two approximate functions used in these rules, the model can not approximate the process well. In the paper simple modification of the model is presented as one giving very good result.

1 Introduction

The idea of Takagi-Sugeno model [5] [6] seems very good. Many physical processes and other functions may be approximated by the use of Takagi-Sugeno model. A special case of this model [4], with linear functions for approximation, is used frequently. However, in some previous works, example Babuška [1] and Butkiewicz [2], it was shown that Takagi-Sugeno model has some inconvenience. If we make use of simple triangular or trapezoidal membership functions for fuzzy sets then in the intermediate area described by two fuzzy sets (conclusions of two rules) and two approximate functions used in these rules, the model will not approximate the process well. Good approximation is possible when one uses many fuzzy sets and membership functions with modified shapes. However, estimation of parameters of such model is complicated. Generally, the membership functions must be described by more parameters than uniform triangular or trapezoidal systems of functions. The case when conclusion functions have linear form is called Takagi-Sugeno-Kang (TSK) model [4]. In this case estimation of model parameters is easier and can be found in [3] [5]. Ying et al. in [7] [10] presented sufficient and necessary conditions for approximation of continuous function by Takagi-Sugeno fuzzy systems. It is also possible to use polynomial or spline functions as in traditional crisp (non fuzzy) solutions. Wang [8] [9] suggested another idea of exact approximation. In this case gaussian functions for membership and consequences are used.

2 Inconvenience of Takagi-Sugeno model

As it was mentioned above Takagi-Sugeno (TS) model has some inconvenience. Let us try to describe a physical process by the means of this model, and consider simple one-dimensional case when we approximate the function $y = f(x)$. Let us divide universum $\mathbf{X}$ in three parts (Fig. 1) by two fuzzy sets Small and Large, with trapezoidal membership functions. TSK model is built with two rules

if x is *Small* then $y_1(x) = a_1x + b_1$
if x is *Large* then $y_2(x) = a_2x + b_2$

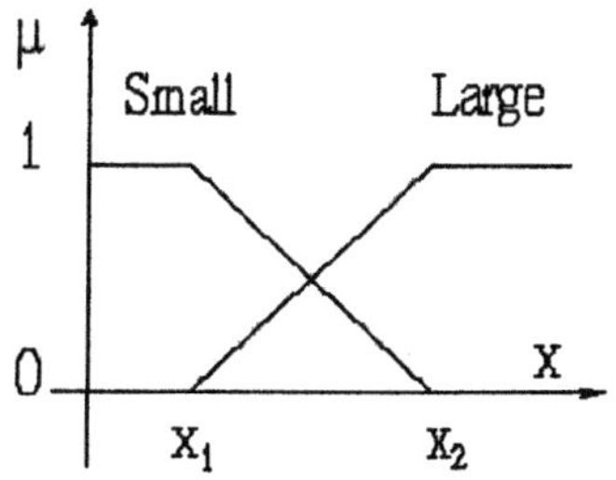

Fig. 1. Membership functions for simple TSK model

For any x the weights of rules in intermediate area are calculated as

$$w_1 = \mu_{Small}(x) = \frac{x_2 - x}{\Delta x} \qquad w_2 = \mu_{Large}(x) = \frac{x - x_1}{\Delta x} \tag{1}$$

where $\Delta x = x_2 - x_1$. Thus, the conclusion gives weighted mean

$$g(x) = \frac{w_1 y_1(x) + w_2 y_2(x)}{w_1 + w_2} \tag{2}$$

Suppose that parameters a_1, b_1 are estimated to fit values of $y(x)$ when $\mu_{Small}(x) = 1$ and a_2, b_2 are fit for $\mu_{Large}(x) = 1$. In intermediate area $[x_1, x_2]$ the model is described by function

$$g(x) = \frac{(\frac{x_2 - x}{\Delta x})(a_1x + b_1) + \frac{x - x_1}{\Delta x}(a_2x + b_2)}{\frac{x_2 - x}{\Delta x} + \frac{x - x_1}{\Delta x}} \tag{3}$$

After transformations one obtains

$$g(x) = \frac{a_2 - a_1}{\Delta x} x^2 + \frac{a_1x_2 - a_2x_1 + b_2 - b_1}{\Delta x} x + \frac{b_1x_2 - b_2x_1}{\Delta x} \tag{4}$$

It is a parabola, which passes by point of intersection of two lines approximating function $y(x)$ (Fig. 2). This parabola is always placed over or below the curve $y(x)$ if derivative of y changes its value smoothly. Thus, in this case, TSK model is worse than the simple crisp model with two linear functions. The same conclusion may be drawn when approximate functions $y_1(x), y_2(x)$ are nonlinear. It can be easily shown that in the two-dimensional case the situation is similar - TSK model is not good.

3 Modification of Takagi-Sugeno model

Inconvenience of the TS model shown in previous section does not disparage the general idea of TS model. The model can be easily corrected by through introducing only one additional parameter. Consider first TSK model. In intermediate area the approximate curve has a form of:

$$g(x) = A(x)x + B(x) \tag{5}$$

when A(x) and B(x) depends on a_1, a_2, b_1, b_2 and on the weights w_1, w_2 of rules

$$A(x) = \frac{a_1 w_1 + a_2 w_2}{w_1 + w_2} \qquad B(x) = \frac{b_1 w_1 + b_2 w_2}{w_1 + w_2} \tag{6}$$

The weights of rules in (1) depend linearly on x. Thus, after substitution, one obtains parabola (4). The parabola passes by end points of intermediate area $[x_1, x_2]$. Denote these points by $(x_1, y_1), (x_2, y_2)$.

Points $(x_1, y_1), (x_2, y_2)$ may be joined by chord. The chord is described by equation

$$h(x) = A_0 x + B_0 \tag{7}$$

when A_0, B_0 are equal

$$A_0 = \frac{y_2 - y_1}{x_2 - x_1} \qquad B_0 = y_1 - A_0 x_1 \tag{8}$$

New method consists of calculating weighted mean $u(x)$ of two functions: $g(x)$ describing TS model and $h(x)$ describing the chord (Fig. 2).

$$u(x) = \frac{g(x) + \lambda h(x)}{1 + \lambda} \tag{9}$$

where λ is constant non-negative. It will be desirable to obtain derivatives

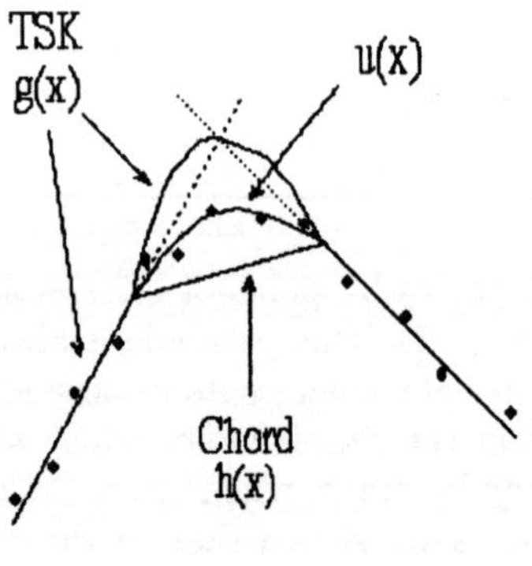

Fig. 2. Inconvenience of simple TSK model

of $u(x)$ at the ends of intermediate area equal inclinations of lines of TSK model

$$\left.\frac{du}{dx}\right|_{x_1} = a_1 \tag{10}$$

$$\left.\frac{du}{dx}\right|_{x_2} = a_2 \tag{11}$$

After substitution, from (10) one obtains

$$a_1 + 2(a_2 - a_1)\frac{x_1}{\Delta x} + (b_2 - b_1)\frac{1}{\Delta x} = a_1(\lambda + 1) \tag{12}$$

and as solution of equation (10)

$$\lambda_1 = \frac{2(a_2 - a_1) + b_2 - b_1}{a_1 \Delta x - \Delta y} = \frac{(g_1 - g_2)|_{x_1}}{(g_1 - g_2)|_{x_2}} \tag{13}$$

Similarly, from condition (11)

$$\lambda_2 = \frac{2(a_2 - a_1) + b_2 - b_1}{a_1 \Delta x - \Delta y} = \frac{(g_1 - g_2)|_{x_2}}{(g_1 - g_2)|_{x_1}} \tag{14}$$

Both conditions are contradictory. Comparing results one obtains interesting relation

$$\lambda_1 = \frac{1}{\lambda_2} \tag{15}$$

It would seem that a good choice of λ is geometrical mean $\lambda = \sqrt{\lambda_1 \lambda_2} = 1$, which means that $u(x)$ is an arithmetic mean for $g(x)$ and $h(x)$. In special case, when $\lambda = 0$, we have TSK model. For $\lambda \to \infty$ we obtain chord of arc. However, a better result could be obtained by changing experimentally λ or using least square error method or using the method described below in approximate way.

4 General case

Consider now TS model. In this case two lines $y_1(x)$, $y_2(x)$ are replaced by two functions $g_1(x)$, $g_2(x)$ approximating values of the process $f(x)$ correspondingly for $x < x_1$ and $x > x_2$. Thus, the equations (10) and (11) will change to the form

$$\left.\frac{du}{dx}\right|_{x_1} = \left.\frac{dg_1}{dx}\right|_{x_1} \tag{16}$$

$$\left.\frac{du}{dx}\right|_{x_2} = \left.\frac{dg_2}{dx}\right|_{x_2} \tag{17}$$

Of course, the only solution is $\lambda = 0$. Thus, condition for smooth change of derivative is not good. The problem can be solved approximately by using condition

$$f(x)\Big|_{x_1 + \Delta x/2} = u(x)\Big|_{x_1 + \Delta x/2} \tag{18}$$

However, a more convenient method could be suggested. Function $f(x)$ as physical process is frequently described by experimental values $f(x_k)$. Therefore, the point x_k in intermediate area may be chosen and condition (18) can be changed to the form

$$f(x_k) = u(x_k) \tag{19}$$

Of course, general methods like mean square approximation of all experimental data $\{f(x_k)\}$ $k = 1, ..., n$ by function

$$u(x) = \begin{cases} g_1(x) & \text{for } x \le x_1 \\ (g(x) + \lambda h(x))/(1+\lambda) & \text{for } x_1 < x < x_2 \\ g_2(x) & \text{for } x \ge x_2 \end{cases} \tag{20}$$

could be used. Now, points x_1, x_2 are not chosen arbitrarily and parameters of functions $g_1(x)$, $g_2(x)$ are not found separately, but three parameters x_1, x_2, λ together with parameters of functions $g_1(x)$, $g_2(x)$ are found by mean square method. Still second method is more complicated. Sometimes, from physical point of view, forms of functions $g_1(x)$ and $g_2(x)$ are known. Thus, its parameters and points x_1, x_2 may be found separately without big error. It is compromise between precision and transparency. Generally, the more precise the method is, the least transparent it is (see example Babuška [1]).

In multidimensional case it seems that reasonable solution can be found only when conclusions of the rules have form

$$y_i(x_1, x_2, ..., x_m) = a_{i0} + a_{i1}x_1 + a_{i2}x_2 + ... + a_{im}x_m \qquad i = 1, ..., n \tag{21}$$

Now, $h(x)$ is not the chord but a plane

$$h(x_1, x_2, ..., x_m) = a_0 + a_1 x_1 + a_2 x_2 + ... + a_m x_m \tag{22}$$

The value $u(\mathbf{x})$ may be found from (9) when now x is a vector $\mathbf{x} = (x_1, ..., x_m)$.

Least mean square error procedure may be used for estimation of model parameters as in conventional case.

5 Example

Here an example of modified TSK model is presented. Let us consider sintering process in metallurgy furnace. Details made from iron powder with some other components: copper, graphite, sulfide of manganin and slippery matters are pressed and later put into the furnace. Temperature inside the furnace attains 1110^0C. During sintering process (30 minutes in high temperature zone of the furnace) slippery matters evaporate so, the mass of details diminishes. The change of mass of detail after sintering process depends on the contents of copper in the powder. If the contents is small, the mass raises in consequence of chemical reactions with gases in the air environment inside the furnace. For larger contents the mass diminishes approximately linearly with percentage of copper. The best result for model parameters was obtained for $\lambda = 0.8$ (Fig. 3).

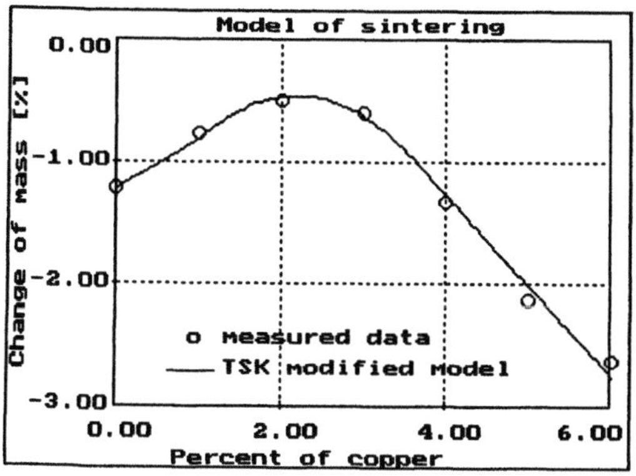

Fig. 3. Modified TS model of sintering

References

1. Babuška R., (2001) Construction of fuzzy systems - interplay between precision and transparency, European Symposium on Intelligent Technics (ESIT), Aachen, Germany, 445–452
2. Butkiewicz B. S., (2001) Inference in Fuzzy Models of Physical Processes, in Computational Intelligence Theory and Applications, Lecture Notes in Computer Science 2206, B. Reusch (ed.), Springer, Berlin, New York, 782–790
3. Kosko B., (1997) Fuzzy Engineering, Prentce-Hall Inc., London
4. Sugeno M., Kang G. T., (1988) Structure Identification of Fuzzy Model, Fuzzy Sets and Systems, **28**, 15–33
5. Takagi T., Sugeno M., (1985) Fuzzy Identification of Systems and its Application to Modeling and Control, IEEE Trans. on Systems, Man, and Cybernetics, **15**, No.1, 116–132
6. Takagi T., Sugeno M., (1983) Derivation of fuzzy control rules form human operator's control system, Proc. of IFAC Symp. on Fuzzy Information, Knowledge Representation and Decision Analysis, Marseilles, France, 55–60
7. Ying H., (1998) Sufficient condition on uniform approximation of multivariate functions by general Takagi-Sugeno systems, IEEE Trans. on Systems, Man, and Cybernetics, Part A: Systems and Humans, **28**, 515–520
8. Wang X. L., (1992) Fuzzy systems are universal approximators, Proc IEEE Int. Conf. on Fuzzy systems, San Diego (CA), 1163–1169
9. Wang X. L., Mendel J. M., (1992) Fuzzy basis functions, universal approximation, and orthogonal least-square learning, IEEE Trans. on Neural Network, **3**, No. 5, 807–814
10. Ying H., Ding Y., Li S., Shao S., (1999) Comparison of necessary conditions for typical Takagi-Sugeno and Mamdani fuzzy system as universal approximators, IEEE Trans. on Systems, Man, and Cybernetics, Part A: Systems and Humans, **29**, No. 5, 508–514

Applying Genetic Algorithm for Training Hybrid Neuro-Fuzzy Classifier – the *nfgClass* System

Piotr Grądzki

Systems Research Institute
Polish Academy of Sciences,
ul. Newelska 6, 01-447 Warsaw, Poland
E-mail: Piotr.Gradzki@ibspan.waw.pl

Abstract. The paper briefly presents the *nfgClass* system – the hybrid neuro-fuzzy-(genetic) classifier that can be applied for designing intelligent decision support systems. The learning abilities of the presented system can be substantially improved by applying a genetic algorithm as. In order to compare the performance of the systems trained with different learning algorithms, there were built two decision support systems for the glass identification problem and another two for the abalone species age problem. In both cases the first system was trained with conjugate gradient algorithm and the second one with the genetic algorithm.

1 Introduction

The traditional artificial intelligence systems, mainly based on the symbolic paradigm, showed to be efficient tools for solving exactly and completely stated problems. However, they were ineffective for solving the real life problems that are described or represented by the imprecise, incomplete, uncertain and linguistic knowledge or by large amounts of numerical data collected in databases.

The foregoing drawbacks of the symbolic paradigm based artificial intelligence systems have motivated many researches for creating new tools for designing intelligent decision support systems. As a result of those efforts the techniques named "computational intelligence" [1] have been developed. They have been worked out as a joint of three methodologies: artificial neural networks, fuzzy logic, and genetic algorithms. The artificial neural networks bring in the resulting system the ability for learning, generalising and processing large amount of numerical data; the fuzzy logic allows the follow-on systems to represent and process inexact and uncertain information); and the genetic algorithm – as a global optimisation tool – is used for strengthening the learning abilities of the resulting tool. Hence, as a result of joining the artificial neural networks, fuzzy logic, and genetic algorithms we get the system that is a synergistic combination of the three complementary technologies.

There are two directions of researches on systems that are built as a combination of neural networks and fuzzy logic based systems. The first one gives as results so-called fuzzy neural networks build of fuzzy neurons [4]. The results of the second research course are neuro-fuzzy systems [6] that use the artificial neural networks within the fuzzy logic systems framework. The most advanced types of the neuro-fuzzy systems are hybrid ones. In contrast to two other types of neuro-fuzzy system – the cascade and cooperative ones, where the separate parts corresponding to the neural network and fuzzy system can be extracted – in the hybrid system there cannot be distinguished separate parts corresponding to the constituent technologies.

The paper presents the *nfgClass* system [3] that can be used for designing the rule-based intelligent decision support systems. The *nfgClass* is the implementation of the hybrid neuro-fuzzy system. The proposed classifier has been successfully applied for building two decision support systems: one for the problem from the field of the forensic science and the second one for solving marine biology domain problem. In both cases, there has been performed a comparative analysis of the learning results obtained using the genetic algorithm and the conjugate gradient algorithm.

2 The Neuro-Fuzzy Classifier for Decision Support

2.1 The Neuro-Fuzzy Scheme for Knowledge Modelling

The *nfgClass* is a hybrid neuro-fuzzy system that has a feed-forward network-like structure. The structure of the system (Fig. 1) expresses the fuzzy rules base that models the process of decision-making. The network is build of three layers. The first one corresponds to the premises of the modelled fuzzy rules (the *fuzzy sets layer* in Fig. 1), the second layer represents the fuzzy rules themselves, and the last one (the *output layer*) is an implementation of the consequences of the fuzzy rules. The classifier has N numerical inputs. Each input attribute x_i (i=1,2,...,N) can be described by one *Small*-type, one *Large*-type and number of *Medium*-type fuzzy sets. The decisions generated by the proposed classifier have the form of possibility distribution over the set $Y=\{y_1, y_2,...,y_M\}$ of class labels. The possibility distribution is represented by fuzzy set B. The system models a set of R fuzzy rules, where the r-th one (r=1,2,...,R) has the form:

$$\text{IF } (x_1 \text{ is } A_{1r}) \text{AND} \ldots \text{AND } (x_r \text{ is } A_{Nr}) \text{THEN } (\textit{possibility distribution } B_r) \tag{1}$$

where A_{ir} is one of the *Small*, *Medium* or *Large*-type fuzzy sets for i-th input and r-th fuzzy rule. The aggregation of the fuzzy rules premises is performed with use of the *min*-operator. The number of nodes in the output layer is equal to the number M of class labels. The task of the output layer nodes is to perform rules aggregation. This operation is implemented with the *max*-operator. Thus, the *nfgClass* system generates decisions in the same way as in the Zadeh's compositional rule of inference [8].

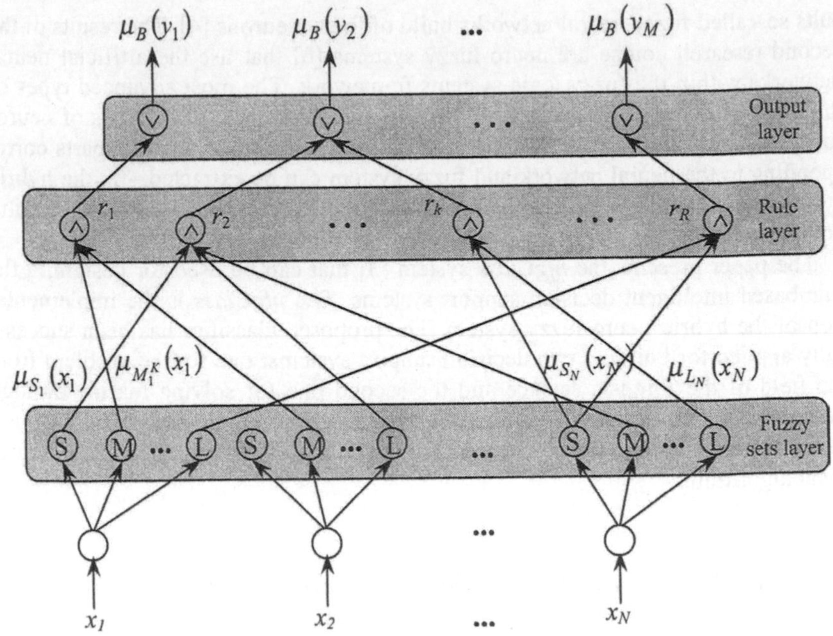

Fig. 1. Structure of the *nfgClass* system

There are five phases of designing the *nfgClass* system: 1) each input attribute is described by a number of fuzzy sets; 2) the initial fuzzy rules base is determined; 3) system training; 4) testing the system against test data; 5) pruning the system – removing "weak", superfluous fuzzy rules in order improve system's transparency.

The initial shapes of the fuzzy sets describing input attributes are determined using the *fuzzy c-means* algorithm [1]. For the phase 2, an algorithm, developed as an adaptation of the solution presented in [7], is applied. During the learning phase, the parameters of the membership function of the *Small*, *Medium*, and *Large*-type fuzzy sets describing the input attributes are tuned in order to minimize the cost function, defined as the mean square error Q:

$$Q = \frac{1}{KM}\sum_{k=1}^{K}\sum_{m=1}^{M}\left(\mu_{B^0}\left(y_m^{(k)}\right) - \mu_{B'}\left(y_m^{(k)}\right)\right)^2, \tag{3}$$

where the fuzzy set B' represent the desired possibility distribution over the set of class labels, and the fuzzy set B^0 - possibility distribution generated by the system. Then, the system is tested against the test data set in order to evaluate its accuracy. Finally, the analysis and reduction of the fuzzy rules base [3] is performed.

2.2 Learning with Genetic Algorithm

Genetic algorithms [5] have features that make them appropriate solution for improving learning abilities of the *nfgClass* system. Genetic algorithm uses only the fitness function – there is no need to calculate its the derivative. This is an important in case of dealing with non-differential functions, such as *min* or *max* operators. Furthermore, genetic algorithm starts searching the solution from a population of starting points and it uses a random number-based rules of selecting potential solutions. As, genetic algorithm searches the maximum of the fitness function *ff*, it is defined as:

$$ff = C - Q, \tag{4}$$

where C is a constant fulfilling the condition $ff>0$, and Q is a cost function (3). In the simulations presented below, the elitist strategy [5] was used and the crossover probability was set to 77% and the mutation probability was set to 0.7%.

3 Numerical Experiments

3.1 The Decision Support System for the Glass Identification Problem from the Forensic Science Field

One of the crucial phases of the criminal investigation is the identification of the evidences – such as pieces of glass – left at the crime scene. The Glass Identification Database was created by B. German from Central Research Establishment in Aldermaston. It consists of 214 instances, and 163 of them can be grouped into 2 classes (first: *float processed* – 82 samples; second: *non-float processed* – 81 samples). Each of them is described by 9 continuously valued attributes.

In the first phase of designing the decision support system, each input attribute was described by 3 adjectives: *Small*, *Medium*, and *Large* represented by appropriate fuzzy sets. Then the initial fuzzy rules base was created. – a set of 29 fuzzy rules was obtained. Afterwards, the training of the system was performed. Independently, the conjugate gradient algorithm (Fig. 2a) and genetic algorithm, with

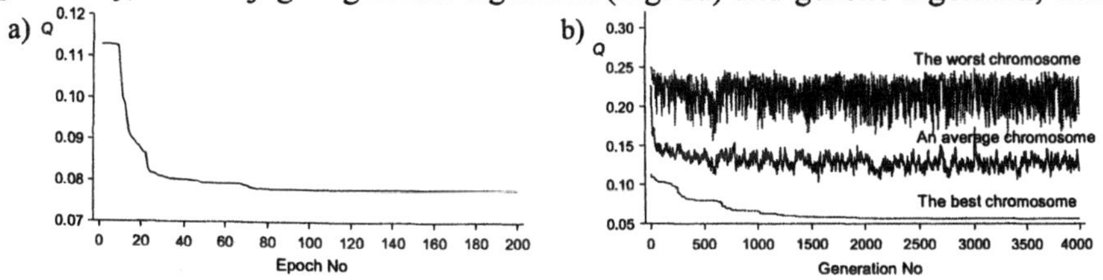

Fig. 2. Cost function versus epoch number (generation number) plot, a) conjugate gradient; b) genetic algorithm

population size set to 100 (Fig. 2b) were applied. Then, both systems were tested against test data set. After that, fuzzy rules analysis and reduction was performed. As a result, the systems containing only 2 fuzzy rules were received. Finally, both systems were once more trained and tested against the test data set. Table 1 contains the comparison of effectiveness of the systems trained by conjugate gradient and genetic algorithm.

Table 1. Accuracy of the decision support system

Learning algorithm	Number of rules	No. of correct decisions [%]	
		Learning data	Test data
Conjugate gradient	29	71.95	61.73
Genetic algorithm		86.58	70.37
Conjugate gradient	2	76.83	69.13
Genetic algorithm		81.70	75.31

3.2 The Decision Support System for the Abalone Species Age Problem from the Marine Biology Domain

The decision support system for evaluating the age of the abalone species upon their physical features was designed basing on the database created by Dr S. Waugh from the University of Tasmania. The database contain description of 4177 species and it is already divided into the learning set (3133 samples) and test set (1044 samples). Each sample is described by 1 nominal and 7 numerical attributes. All samples are divided into 3 classes.

Following the procedure described in section 2.1, the initial shapes of the fuzzy sets describing the input attributes were defined and the initial fuzzy rules base, containing 178 rules, was generated. Afterwards, the conjugate gradient algorithm (Fig. 3a) and genetic algorithm, with population size set to 20, (Fig. 3b) were ap-

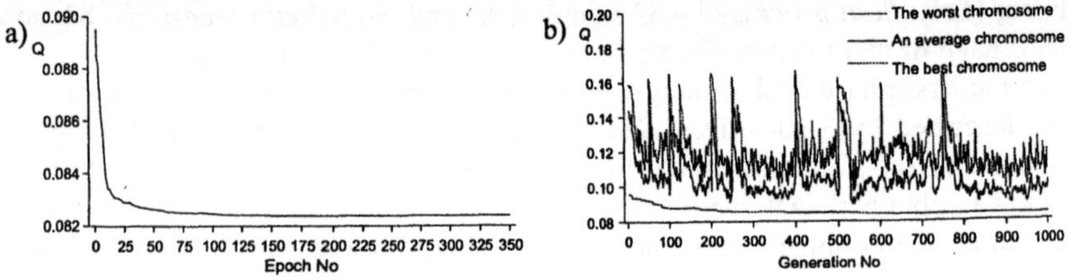

Fig. 3. Cost function versus epoch number (generation number) plot, a) conjugate gradient algorithm, b) genetic algorithm

plied separately.

Table 2. Accuracy of the decision support system

Learning algorithm	Number of rules	No. of correct decisions [%]	
		Learning data	Test data
Conjugate gradient	178	61.22	57.47
Genetic algorithm		62.30	58.43
Conjugate gradient	11	54.93	54.60
Genetic algorithm	8	64.06	60.25

Than, alike as in the glass identification problem case, both systems were tested, the analysis and reduction of fuzzy rules base was applied, and the final system was tuned. In this case, the best results for the system trained with conjugate gradient were achieved with 11 fuzzy rules, and for the second system for rules base containing 8 fuzzy rules. Table 2 contains the comparison of accuracy of the both system for both cases: working with full and the reduced fuzzy rules base.

4 Conclusions

The system briefly presented in the paper was successfully applied for designing two intelligent decision support systems. The learning abilities of the system have been substantially improved by applying a genetic algorithm. The consequence of this improvement was the enhanced system's accuracy. The decision support system for the glass identification problem generated 4.87% more correct decision for learning data and 6.18% for test data. In the second case the improvement was 9.13% for learning data and 5.56% for test data.

The results of the numerical experiments shown that the genetic algorithm used for training the *nfgClass* system brought significant improvement of accuracy of the system. Those results allow supposing that using more sophisticated techniques from the genetic algorithm's theory could give more improvements.

References

1. J. C. Bezdek, Pattern Recognition with Fuzzy Objective Function Algorithms, Plenum Press, New York, 1981.
2. J. C. Bezdek, What is computational Intelligence, in J. M. Zurada, R. J. Marks II an C. J. Robinson (Eds.), Computational Intelligence: Imitating Life, IEEE Press, pp. 1-12, 1994.
3. M.B. Gorzalczany, P. Gradzki, A Neuro-Fuzzy-Genetic Classifier for Rule-Based Intelligent Decision Support, Archiwum Informatyki Teoretycznej i Stosowanej, vol. 11, no. 3-4, pp225-247, 1999.
4. Sh. Horikawa, T. Furuhashi, Y. Uchikawa, On fuzzy modelling using neural networks with the back-propagation algorithm, IEEE Trans. on Neural Networks, 3(5), pp. 801-806, 1992.
5. Z. Michalewicz, Genetic Algorithms + Data Structures = Evolutionary Programs, Springer, Berlin, 1992.
6. D. Nauck, F. Klawonn, R. Kruse, Foundations of Neuro-Fuzzy Systems, J.Wiley&Sons, Chichester, 1997.
7. L. X. Wang, J. M. Mendel, Generating fuzzy rules by learning from examples, IEEE Trans. on System, Man and Cybernetics, vol. 22, no. 6, pp. 1414-1427, 1992.
8. L. A. Zadeh, Outline of a new approach to the analysis of complex systems and decisions processes, IEEE Trans. on Systems, Man and Cybernetics, vol. 3, no. 1, pp.28-44, 1973

Fuzzy Calculus by RBF Neural Networks

Vojislav Kecman[1], Zhenquan Li
School of Engineering, University of Auckland
Private Bag 92019, Auckland, New Zealand

Abstract. The paper presents novel modeling of fuzzy inference system by using the 'fuzzified' radial basis function (RBF) neural network (NN). RBF NN performs the mapping of the antecedent fuzzy numbers (a.k.a. membership functions, attributes, possibilities degrees) into the consequent ones. In this way, an RBF NN is capable of performing the rigorous calculus with fuzzy numbers. Prior the mapping, both the antecedents and the consequents are discretized and transferred into the n-dimensional and m-dimensional 'fuzzy' vectors. These vectors present the training inputs and outputs of an RBF NN and, in this way, an RBF network performs an exact $\Re^n \rightarrow \Re^m$ mapping. The generalization capacity of such a neural implementation is superior to the ability of the original fuzzy model.

1. Introduction

It is very well known that the radial basis function (RBF) neural networks (NNs) and fuzzy additive models (FAMs) are based on very similar, or sometimes even equal, underlying mathematics. This has been reinvented and shown by different authors independently many times (Jang, 1993; Kecman and Pfeiffer, 1994; see also Kecman, 2001). All these presentations show when and how the learning of fuzzy rules from numerical data is mathematically equal to the training of RBF, i.e., regularization, networks. The only numerical difference between these two models, which is the normalization that takes part in the FAMs due to the defuzzification step, is of lesser importance.

However, the main advantage of neural networks, their ability to learn from examples, is reduced by their black box behavior. Fuzzy logic theory on the other hand provides a mathematical strength to capture the uncertainties associated with human cognitive processes, such as thinking and reasoning, but fuzzy models are not able to learn. Hence, there is a natural idea to combine neural networks and fuzzy logic to overcome their shortcomings, and to retain their advantages. One possible implementation of such a network is given in (Li, Kecman, Ichikawa, 2002) where the NN of choice was the multilayer perceptron (MLP) network. The basic idea presented in that paper is further developed and enhanced, by applying the Gaussian functions as basis functions within the neural network, in this paper. In this way, the usually long learning time associated with MLP is avoided.

---

[1] Corresponding author. Email v.kecman@auckland.ac.nz

Recently, the so-called fuzzified neural networks (FNNs) have been attracting a lot of interest and many different structures have been proposed. See, for example, the following papers: Ishibuchi et al, 1993a; Ishibuchi et al, 1994; Hayashi et all, 1993; Ishibuchi et al, 1993b; Ishibuchi et al, 1995a; Ishibuchi et al, 1995b. There are also many other various approaches and papers on FNNs focusing on approaches as given in the first two papers. We do not list them here for the sake of brevity.

Here, we present an RBF NN which inputs are fuzzy numbers i.e., (fuzzy) vectors obtained after the discretization of antecedent attributes. We treat the classic FAM as a mapping of input attributes' shapes into the output attributes' forms. The detailed description of similar applications of RBF NNs in computer graphics is given in Kecman, 2001.

2. Fuzzified RBF network for a fuzzy number calculus

The basic disadvantage of the fuzzified MLP neural network (Li, Kecman, Ichikawa, 2002) stems from the gradient based learning that leads to usually very long learning times. Another shortcoming is that dimensionality of an input vector matters a lot in the case of MLP NN because it determines the dimensionality of the weight vector space v. The bigger the v, the longer the learning time as well as the more complex search space. In addition, the very learning depends upon too many random factors such as initialization of the weights and learning rates chosen. The application of radial basis functions resolves almost all of those crucial disadvantages in developing fuzzified NN models.

Usually, FNNs involve drawing conclusions from given inference rules and facts. In order to do that, the fuzzified RBF network should learn the given inference rules first, and then derive a proper conclusion for a given fact. Here, the learning of inference rules boils down to the learning of an exact mapping of antecedents into consequents. The inference rules can be written as

$$\begin{array}{l} \textit{Rule}\ 1\ \text{If}\ X_1\ \text{is}\ A_1^1\ \text{and}\cdots\text{and}\ X_k\ \text{is}\ A_k^1\ \text{then}\ Y_1\ \text{is}\ B_1^1\cdots\ Y_l\ \text{is}\ B_l^1, \\ \textit{Rule}\ 2\ \text{If}\ X_1\ \text{is}\ A_1^2\ \text{and}\cdots\text{and}\ X_k\ \text{is}\ A_k^1\ \text{then}\ Y_1\ \text{is}\ B_1^2\cdots\ Y_l\ \text{is}\ B_l^1, \\ \qquad\qquad\vdots\qquad\qquad\qquad\vdots\qquad\qquad\vdots\qquad\qquad\vdots \\ \textit{Rule}\ Rn\ \text{If}\ X_1\ \text{is}\ A_1^{I_1}\ \text{and}\cdots\text{and}\ X_k\ \text{is}\ A_k^{I_k}\ \text{then}\ Y_1\ \text{is}\ B_1^{o_1}\cdots\ Y_l\ \text{is}\ B_l^{o_l}. \end{array} \quad (1)$$

Where A_j^i and B_l^o are fuzzy numbers (a.k.a. membership degrees or attributes). The fuzzy model given by (1) will for any fact given as,

$$X_1\ \text{is}\ A_1^i\ \text{and}\cdots\text{and}\ X_k\ \text{is}\ A_k^j$$

produce the conclusion as:

$$Y_1\ \text{is}\ B_1^{o_{1i}}\cdots\ Y_l\ \text{is}\ B_l^{o_{li}}.$$

The model (1) consists of I^k rules providing that I fuzzy numbers (attributes) are associated with each universe of discourse ($Rn = I^k$). The fuzzy numbers A_j^i, B_l^o may have different shapes although triangles (i.e., B-splines of the 1st order), trapezoidals, singletons, B-splines of other orders (typically of the 2nd and 3rd order) and Gaussian RBFs are the most common ones. The very shape of the attributes does not play any important role for the approach taken here.

However, the inference scheme given above and embedded in fuzzy model can be looked at from a different angle that will be presented next. The inference rules can be considered as a mapping of input fuzzy numbers (shapes of input membership functions) into the output fuzzy numbers (into the shapes of the output membership functions). After a discretization of both the continuous antecedent fuzzy numbers (fuzzy numbers in the domain, if-part membership functions) and the consequent ones (fuzzy numbers in the range, then-part membership functions), the fuzzy model can also be treated as mapping of (fuzzy) vectors from an n-dimensional space into the (fuzzy) vectors in an m-dimensional space. n and m stand for the length of corresponding (fuzzy) vectors which depend only upon the rate of discretization of the corresponding original fuzzy numbers and upon the dimensionality of the input and output variables of the fuzzy model. (Thus, for example, if $k = 4$, meaning that the input to fuzzy model is 4-dimensional, and for triangular input membership functions the most common dimension of the input to the fuzzified RBF model will be $n = 4*3 = 12$, i.e., input vector to the fuzzified RBF model will be 12-dimensional. More explanation follows below).

Discretization, on its own, should be done in order to reproduce the true shape of fuzzy number. Hence, if the fuzzy numbers are the 0th order B-splines (rectangulars) only two points are relevant for capturing their shapes (namely, the left and the right corner). On the other side, three points (the left corner, the center and the right corner) will successfully reproduce the shape of triangular (1st order B-splines) membership function (fuzzy number). So will do the discretization of the trapezoidal fuzzy number into four elements vector. The Gaussian membership function obviously requires higher discretization rate in order to ensure proper reconstruction of its shape. (For such a function, as well as for the other more complex ones two coordinates, namely (x_i, μ_i) should be used). However, the rate of the discretization, as mentioned previously, does not introduce too high a numerical burden into the fuzzified RBF network. The reason is simple; the output o from an n-dimensional RBF (e.g., from the Gaussian RBF function as given in (2)) depends only upon the distance (i.e., upon the scalar value) between the data point $\mathbf{x}$ and the center of the RBF function $\mathbf{c}$,

$$o(\mathbf{x}) = \exp(-\frac{1}{2}(\mathbf{x}-\mathbf{c})^T \Sigma^{-1}(\mathbf{x}-\mathbf{c})) \qquad (2)$$

where $\mathbf{x}$ is the n-dimensional input vector (fact), Σ^{-1} is inverse of the shape (covariance) matrix Σ and it is usually diagonal matrix, i.e., $\Sigma^{-1} = diag(1/\sigma_1^2, 1/\sigma_2^2, ..., 1/\sigma_n^2)$ and the vector $\mathbf{c}$ is the center of the n-dimensional Gaussian basis function obtained after the discretization of the input fuzzy numbers. Note that $o(\mathbf{x})$ is a scalar value. Therefore, for the fuzzified RBF networks (same as it is the case with the standard FAMs), the basic cause of possible numerical difficulties may be the number of rules applied, and not the dimensionality of input variables. The basic steps in designing the fuzzified RBF network are:

i) the discretization of the antecedent and consequent fuzzy numbers, which
produce the centers $\mathbf{c}_i$ and the targets $\mathbf{d}_i$, (where $i = 1, Rn$) respectively,

ii) placement of the RBF basis functions' centers at the n-dimensional fuzzy vectors $\mathbf{c}_i$ obtained by discretization of the antecedent fuzzy numbers, and

iii) calculation of the output layer (fuzzy) weights of the fuzzified RBF network by standard learning procedure for the RBFs networks, which comprises the multiplication of the inversion of the so-called design matrix $\mathbf{G}$ (for details see Kecman, 2001) by the matrix $\mathbf{D}$ of discretized fuzzy vectors of consequent fuzzy numbers (targets $\mathbf{d}_i$), (see equation (3) below).

Here, the $\mathbf{G}$ matrix is a square (Rn, Rn) matrix where Rn stands for the number of rules and, this means that the fuzzified RBF network will find the interpolative solution of inference rules. The architecture of a fuzzified RBFs network for an $\Re^n \rightarrow \Re^m$ mapping is a standard RBF NN structure having an input, hidden and output layer. During the training the input vectors $\mathbf{x}$ represent the discretized antecedents of each particular rule, i.e., $\mathbf{x}_i = \mathbf{c}_i$, and in test and generalization phase it is equal to the, during the learning phase unseen, fact. Analogously, the desired vector $\mathbf{d}$ represents the discretized consequent of each corresponding rule. There are two sets of known, i.e., prespecified, parameters in a hidden layer of a fuzzified RBFs network. One, usually, calls them (fuzzy) weights or, just weights. They are the entries of a center matrix $\mathbf{C}$ (which are fuzzy vectors obtained after the discretization of antecedent fuzzy numbers), and elements of an inverse covariance matrix Σ^{-1}. The latter are, typically, the free design parameters. The hidden layer outputs y_r ($r = 1,\dots, Rn$, where Rn stands for the number of rules) are normalized.

The entries of an output layer weights matrix $\mathbf{W}$ are unknown and thus the very subjects of learning. However, (unlike in the fuzzified MLP networks and) when the HL parameters are prespecified, as it is the case here, the learning problem is linear and the solution is given as

$$\mathbf{W} = \mathbf{G}^{-1}\mathbf{D}. \tag{3}$$

where $\mathbf{D} = [\mathbf{d}_1^{\mathrm{T}}\ \mathbf{d}_2^{\mathrm{T}}\ \cdots\ \mathbf{d}_{Rn}^{T}]^T$ comprises all the desired output training vectors $\mathbf{d}_k = [d_{1k}\ d_{2k}, \dots, d_{mk}]^{\mathrm{T}}$, $k = 1, m$. Both $\mathbf{W}$ and $\mathbf{D}$ are (Rn, m) matrices. When the consequents are singletons, $m = 1$, and matrices $\mathbf{W}$ and $\mathbf{D}$ become the vectors $\mathbf{w}$ and $\mathbf{d}$ respectively.

In order to see the performance of a fuzzified RBF network, we use a 'simple' example when the FAM performs an $\Re^1 \rightarrow \Re^1$ mapping, and when the antecedents are triangles and consequents are either singletons or triangles. Such a choice will enable the visualization of the whole concept. However nothing (but dimensions), changes when an original fuzzy model represents an $\Re^p \rightarrow \Re^r$ mapping, or for the other selection of fuzzy numbers in original fuzzy model. The problem of an $\Re^1 \rightarrow \Re^1$ mapping is chosen for the sake of graphical presentation only.

Example 1: Develop fuzzified RBF network for modeling the Hermitian 1-dimensional function $y(x) = 11(1 - x + 2x^2)e^{-0.5x^2} + 5$. Use 20 rules.

i) Input fuzzy numbers are the 0th order *B*-splines (rectangulars), and the output attributes are singletons.

ii) Both the input and the output fuzzy numbers are the 1th order *B*-splines (triangles).

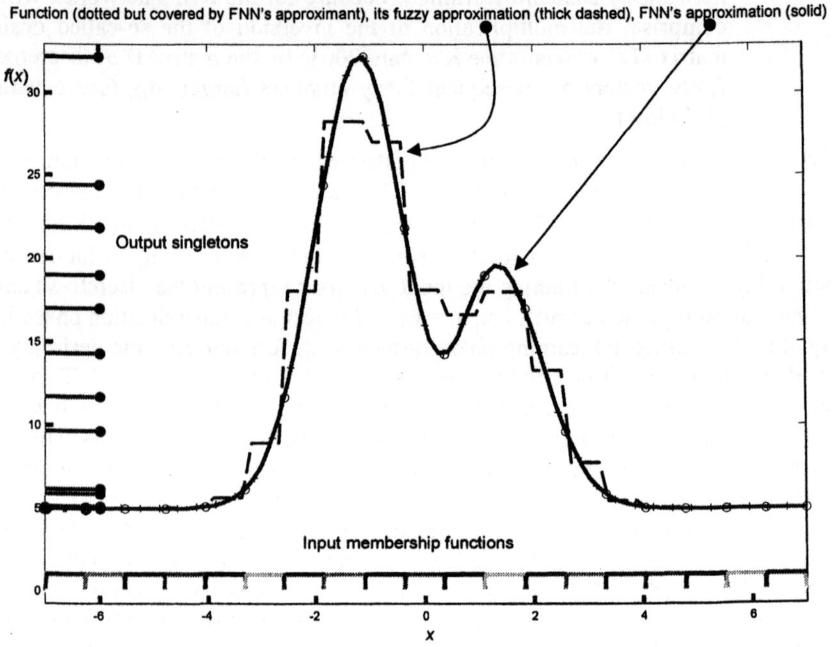

Figure 1 Approximation of Hermitian function (invisible for covered by FNN's approximant) by both a FAM (dashed, stepwise, curve) and fuzzified RBF NN (smooth solid curve). The original function is indistinguishable from its FNN's approximant. Input attributes are the 0th order *B*-splines (rectangulars) and the output ones are singletons. The inputs to the FNN are 2-dimensional (fuzzy) vectors, and the target values during the training i.e., the output are scalars.

Figs 1 and 2 show the modeling of a given function by classic FAM and by fuzzified RBF NN. The Hermitian function is chosen because it is a function possessing different dynamic properties over the domain, namely both the flat regions and the hairy (non-smooth) ones alternating each other. In both cases the fuzzified RBF NN produces much nicer approximations than the standard FAM.

3. Conclusions

The paper presents the basic idea and approach in a novel modeling of the fuzzy inference rules by the so-called fuzzified neural networks. Here, the RBF NN was used. Such a NN maps input fuzzy numbers into output ones (after both have been discretized). Such an approach is particularly attractive when the inputs to the fuzzy models are fuzzy facts rather than singletons (i.e., scalars). The resulting approximant to the original functional dependency between the input and the output variables is much smoother than the approximant obtained by classic FAMs. Such a modeling is possible even for very complex shapes of membership functions. For them, only the higher discretization rates (in order to reproduce their true shapes) should be used but this step does not affect the performance of the fuzzified RBF NN very much.

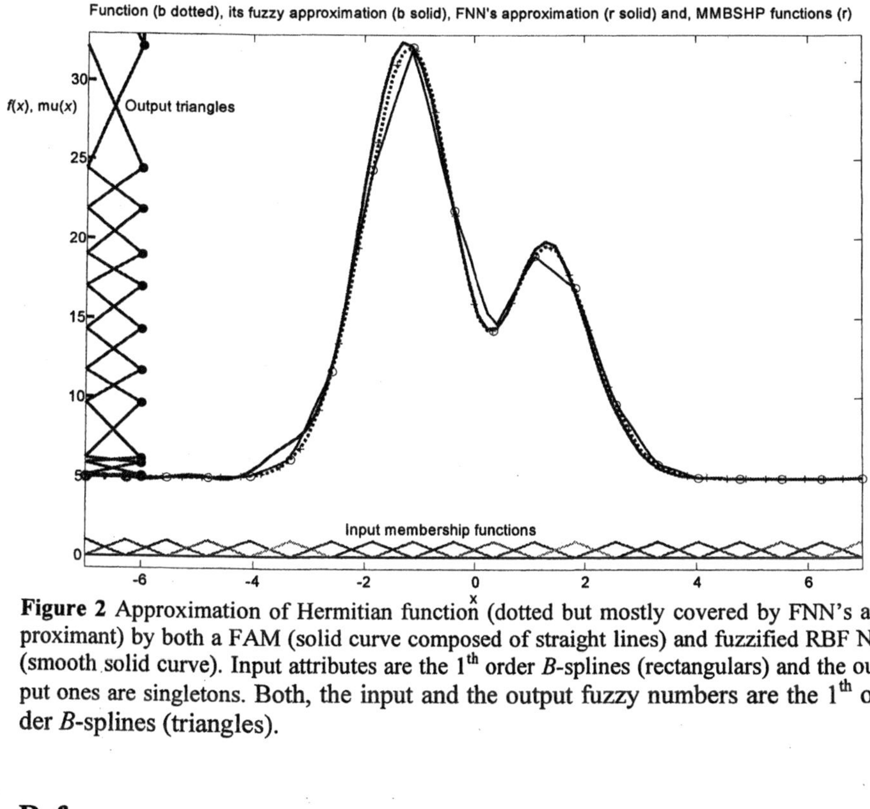

Figure 2 Approximation of Hermitian function (dotted but mostly covered by FNN's approximant) by both a FAM (solid curve composed of straight lines) and fuzzified RBF NN (smooth solid curve). Input attributes are the 1th order *B*-splines (rectangulars) and the output ones are singletons. Both, the input and the output fuzzy numbers are the 1th order *B*-splines (triangles).

References

Hayashi, Y., J.J Buckley and E. Czogala. Fuzzy neural network with fuzzy signals and weights. *Internat. J. Intelligent Systems* 8, pp., 527—537, 1993.

Ishibuchi, H., R. Fujioka and H. Tanaka. Neural networks that learn from fuzzy if-then rules. *IEEE Trans. Fuzzy system* 1(2), pp., 85—97, 1993a.

Ishibuchi, H. Okada and H. Tanaka. Fuzzy neural networks with fuzzy weights and fuzzy biases. *Proc. ICNN'93,* San Francisco pp., 1650—1655, 1993b.

Ishibuchi, H. Okada and H. Tanaka. Interpolatin of fuzzy if-then rules by neural net works. *International Journal of Approximate Reasoning* 10 (1), pp., 3—27, 1994.

Ishibuchi, H., K. Kwon and H. Tanaka. A learning algorithm of fuzzy neural networks with triangular fuzzy weights. *Fuzzy Sets and Systems* 71, pp., 277—293, 1995a.

Ishibuchi, H., K. Morioka and I.B. Turksen. Learning by fuzzified neural net works. *International Journal of Approximate Reasoning* 13, pp., 327—358, 1995b.

Jang, J.-S.R., Sun, T.-C., 'Functional equivalence between radial basis function net works and fuzzy inference systems', IEEE Trans. on NN, 4(1), pp. 156-159, 1993

Kecman V., Pfeiffer B-M., 'Exploiting the Structural Equivalence of Learning Fuzzy Systems and Radial Basis Function Neural Networks', 2-nd Europ. Congr. on Intell. Techn. and Soft Comput., EUFIT '94, Aachen, Vol. 1, pp. 58-66, 1994.

Kecman. V., 'Learning and Soft Computing, Support Vector Machines, Neural Networks, and Fuzzy Logic Models', The MIT Press, Cambridge, MA, USA, 2001.

Li, Z.Q., Kecman, V., Ichikawa, A., 'Fuzzified Neural Network Based on Fuzzy Number Operations', Fuzzy Sets and Systems, (to appear), 2002.

Extending Neuro-Fuzzy Classification to Semi-Supervised Learning

Aljoscha Klose[1], Daniela Girimonte[2], and Rudolf Kruse[1]

[1] University of Magdeburg, School of Computer Science, D-39106 Magdeburg, Germany
[2] Polytechnic of Bari, Electrotechnology and Electronic Dept., 70125 Bari, Italy

Abstract. Due to their rather intuitive and understandable application fuzzy *if-then* rules are a popular basis for classifiers. In many practical applications huge amounts of data are available for analysis. However, these are often unlabeled and the user must manually assign labels. The idea of semi-supervised learning is to use as much labeled data as available and try to additionally exploit the structure in the unlabeled data. In this paper we describe an approach to enable semi-supervised learning for (neuro-) fuzzy systems.

1 Introduction

With the advances in computer and sensor technology, today growing amounts of data are generated, collected, stored, and processed. However, transforming the data in the increasing number of archives into useful information and knowledge turns out to be fairly difficult. In reply to these challenges "Knowledge Discovery in Databases" or "Data Mining" has emerged as a new area of research [7]. The research in knowledge discovery in databases and data mining combines techniques from a variety of disciplines and brought up a number of analysis tools. Some well-known methods that are frequently used in data mining are, for instance, statistics (regression analysis, discriminant analysis etc.), time series analysis, decision trees, cluster analysis, association rules, inductive logic programming, or neural networks.

However, not all of these methods are equally appropriate for data mining. Hardly interpretable models like e.g. neural networks sacrifice the original goal of *understandable* patterns for prediction accuracy. We can often see that for practical purposes full precision is not necessary and may even be a waste of resources.

Due to their closeness to human reasoning, solutions obtained using fuzzy approaches are often easier to understand and to apply, as they allow what Zadeh so pointedly called *computing with words* [26]. Therefore, we expect fuzzy techniques to play a considerable role in data mining [14]. Good examples of models that gain their strengths by explicitly taking into account vagueness, imprecision or uncertainty are (possibilistic) graphical models [4] or fuzzy if-then rules.

Fuzzy if-then rules have become a popular approach to the important data mining task of classification. The use of linguistic variables eases the readability and interpretability of the rule base. There is a variety of methods that have been proposed to induce fuzzy rules from data. A common way are neuro-fuzzy systems which use learning algorithms derived from neural network theory to generate fuzzy rules [5,17,24]. Other approaches extract rules from decision trees [11]. Evolutionary algorithms are used in several promising approaches to learn both structure and parameters of fuzzy classifiers [6,9].

All these approaches have in common that they solve a ***supervised learning*** task, i.e. they induce the rules from a database of examples with known class labels. However, this need for labeled examples is a severe drawback in many practical applications. In contrast to the abundance of data available in the archives, labeling these data is a problem. Often, the labels for the training samples have to be assigned manually or determined by expensive analyses. Thus, labeling can become an at least tedious if not infeasible task when there are many objects—and *many* can easily mean tens of thousands. Typical examples of such domains include speech processing, object recognition or text classification.

There are algorithms, that can learn from data with unknown class labels, i.e. they perform ***unsupervised learning***. A well-known example is cluster analysis. Cluster analysis tries to find groups in the data such that objects in the same group are similar to each other. Fuzzy extensions of cluster analysis represent the clusters by multidimensional fuzzy sets and can better deal with partially overlapping clusters [10]. It is possible to use fuzzy clustering methods to extract fuzzy if-then rules from data [12]. However, the main problem of unsupervised learning is that it strongly depends on the given distance measures. It has usually problems in finding the right number of clusters. Usually, we cannot guarantee that clusters in the data space correspond to meaningful classes of objects.

As unsupervised learning does in many cases not yield satisfactory results, supervised learning is much more common in practice. If it is not possible to access the labels for all objects, one usually confines the examples to a certain—hopefully representative—fraction of the data and leaves the unlabeled data aside.

However, though unlabeled, the additional data might still bear valuable information on the true distribution of the objects in the input space. Thus, it is an appealing idea to use the remaining, otherwise discarded, data to support the learning of a classifier. This so-called ***semi-supervised*** learning could be expected to yield better generalization on unseen data with much less labeled examples.

In Sect. 2 we briefly review previous work on semi-supervised learning. However, most of these approaches deal with complex models like e.g. multidimensional cluster prototypes or support vector machines that are not easily interpretable and thus do give little insight into the data. Little has been done on the semi-supervised induction of more convenient models like fuzzy rules from data. In this paper we present our work to enable (neuro-) fuzzy classification to deal with partially labeled data.

In Sect. 3 we describe the well-known NEFCLASS system and its extension to allow semi-supervised learning. Sect. 4 summarizes our results.

2 Semi-Supervised Learning

The classical paradigms of machine learning can be separated into supervised and unsupervised approaches. Unsupervised learning techniques like cluster analysis seek for inherent structure in the distribution of the data, whereas supervised techniques try to generalize the regularities given by some labeled sample data.

The idea of exploiting both labeled and unlabeled data is not new, and early approaches date back to the 80's [20,23]. However, as argued above, with tremendously growing sizes of datasets in real-world applications labeling all of the data becomes more and more infeasible and the exploitation of additional unlabeled examples gets increasingly interesting. Thus a growing number of publications on semi-supervised learning can be observed over the past years.

There have been some proposals how to combine and thus exploit the benefits of both approaches. A number of approaches described in literature extend classically unsupervised cluster algorithms. Examples include semi-supervised agglomerative hierarchical clustering (ssAHC) [1], or semi-supervised prototype based fuzzy clustering [3,20]. Other semi-supervised algorithms extend traditionally supervised classifiers like e.g. support vector machines [2,8]. The modified algorithms solve the usual supervised task and introduce additional terms that e.g. measure cluster dispersion and thus take the unlabeled data into account. A review of semi-supervised approaches from a learning theoretic point of view can be found in [22].

Successful applications of these approaches are reported e.g. in the field of image processing [3] or text classification [18].

3 Semi-Supervised Learning with NEFCLASS

The implementation of our presented approach is based on the NEFCLASS model [15,16], a neuro-fuzzy model for data analysis. NEFCLASS can be viewed as a 3-layer feed-forward fuzzy neural network. The units in this network use t-norms or t-conorms instead of the usual activation functions in neural networks. The weights are fuzzy sets instead of real values. The first layer represents input variables, the third layer represents the output classes, and the units in the hidden layer represent fuzzy classification rules r of the form:

if A_1 is μ_1 **and** A_2 is μ_2 **and** ... **and** A_n is μ_n
then pattern $(A_1, A_2, \ldots, A_n)$ belongs to class c,

where the μ_k are fuzzy sets. The NEFCLASS rule base is learned from data by the *structural* approach of Wang and Mendel [25]. The fuzzy sets are fine-tuned in a second phase, with a backpropagation-like learning heuristic. NEFCLASS imposes several restrictions on the learning algorithm, e.g. membership functions must not pass their neighbors, must stay symmetrical, or membership degrees must add to 1 [16]. Thus the semantics of the linguistic terms are preserved.

Measuring Rule Set Quality for Partially Labeled Data

Given a class of classifier models, the task of any learning algorithm is to choose that instance that maximizes some objective function. We defined a measure based on the Minimum Description Length Principle (MDL) [21], that offers a well-founded method to assess the quality of rule bases with varying numbers of rules in the context of partially labeled data. MDL is equivalent to maximum likelihood for the estimation of models with a fixed number of free parameters, but additionally offers a possibility to compare objectively between models of different complexity and can thus help to prevent over-fitting.

To apply the MDL principle to our problem, we have to define an appropriate encoding scheme, that is used to transfer a message from an imaginary sender to an imaginary receiver. The *message* consists of the following parts:

- **the rule base (the *code*)**, e.g. the number of dimensions, the fuzzy sets on each axis (i.e. their parameters), the number of rules, the fuzzy sets used in a rule. This information is then used to encode
- **the data tuples (the *data* itself)**, e.g. the index of the rule that is used to encode this tuple, the exact values of the tuple using a rule specific code, and for misclassified data points the class label.

According to Shannon's coding theorem, the lengths in bits of the parts of a message are calculated as $-\log p_i$, where p_i is the probability of an instantiation i within all possible alternatives over some appropriately chosen probability distribution. As shown in [19], there are tight bounds between (neuro-) fuzzy classification systems and probabilistic classification approaches like Naive Bayes. We can use this interpretation of the fuzzy membership values as probability densities if we normalize the rule activations appropriately. Therefore, for every data point we transmit which rule is used to encode it (i.e. the rule with the highest activation). We can then exploit this knowledge to efficiently encode the tuple values, as higher probabilities (higher activations) have shorter codes. Additionally, we have to transmit whether the tuple belongs to the majority rule class.

In this way all the parts of the rule base are transmitted. Misclassified labeled tuples make the message longer, as the probability distribution of a

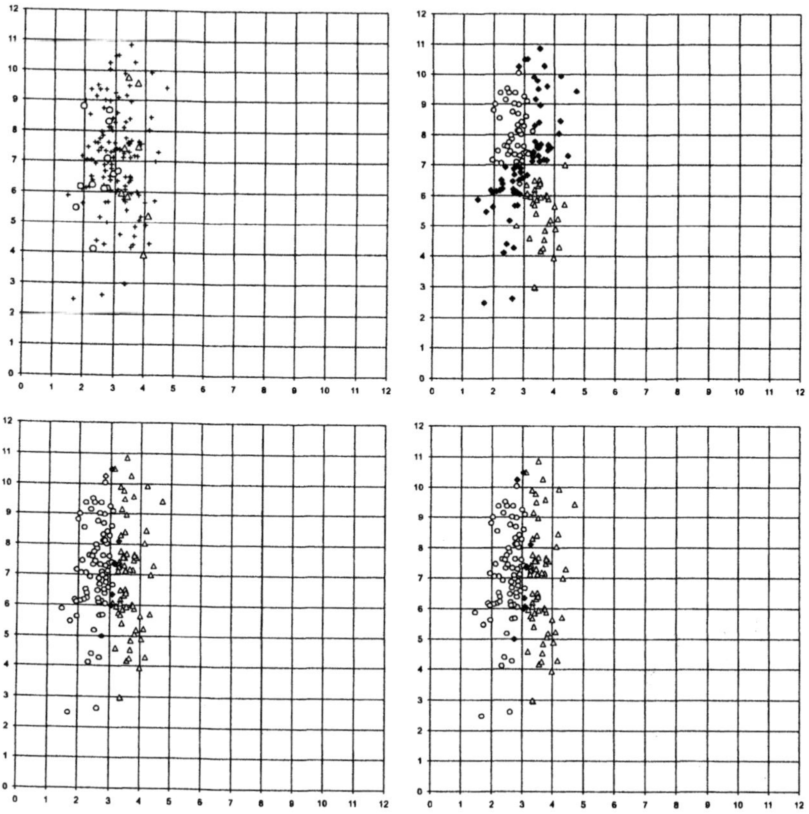

Fig. 1. (a) The 1st artificial dataset, classified (b) unsupervised, (c) supervised with NEFCLASS, and (d) semi-supervised with our approach.

rule becomes more heterogeneous. Unlabeled tuples are always assigned to the majority class and only their attribute values have to be transmitted. The better the fuzzy sets fit the real distribution of the data points the shorter the overall message length will be.

Unfortunately, the MDL based measure does not directly allow optimization methods like gradient descent or the backpropagation heuristics of the original NEFCLASS. In previous work we already successfully implemented simple evolutionary optimization of fuzzy sets [13]. Therefore, we extended this approach and implemented an evolutionary optimization for the fuzzy rule learning. Evolutionary algorithms can directly use the MDL measure as a fitness function. In the implementation of the evolutionary learning we roughly follow the "Pittsburgh-style" approach described in [6].

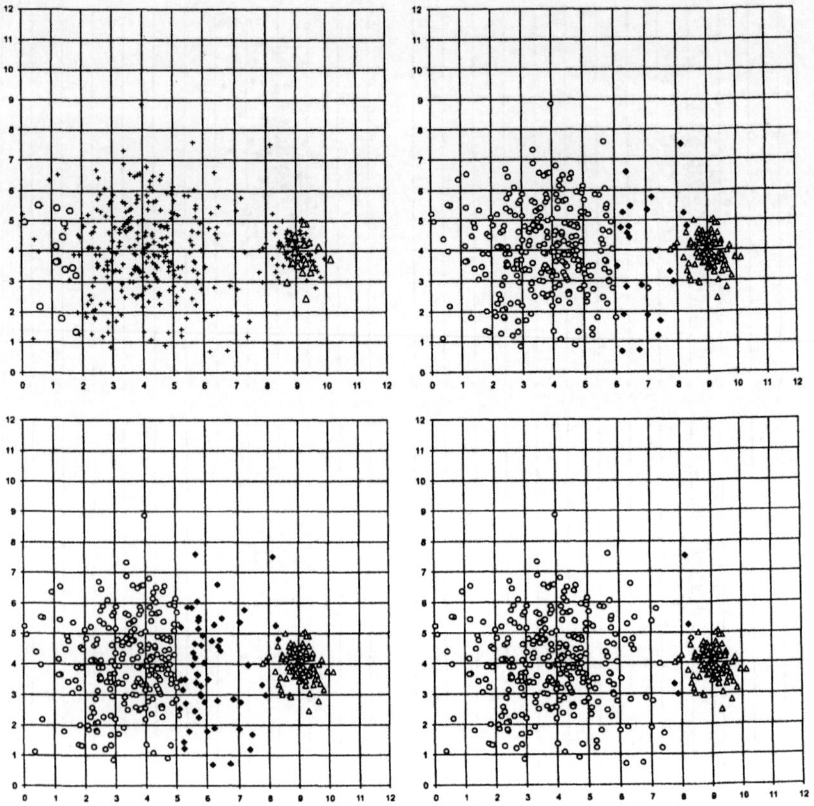

Fig. 2. (a) The 2nd artificial dataset, classified (b) unsupervised, (c) supervised with NEFCLASS, and (d) semi-supervised with our approach.

Empirical Results

In the following we present the results of applying our approach to artificial datasets. The datasets were generated to demonstrate the capabilities of our approach compared to the fully supervised NEFCLASS learning and completely unsupervised fuzzy rule induction with fuzzy cluster analysis.

The first dataset demonstrates how unsupervised learning fails due to the lack of guidance. The dataset has two clusters side by side, as can be seen in Fig. 1. The triangles and squares are the points with given class labels. The crosses are the additional data where the true label is hidden from the classifier. In (b) to (d), small black dots mark the misclassified points. The unsupervised FCM finds two clusters one on top of the other, which do not correspond to the underlying classes. Both, the supervised NEFCLASS and our semi-supervised modification succeed to learn from the few labeled examples to separate the clusters.

The second dataset depicted in Fig. 2 demonstrates a situation where unsupervised learning works better than supervised learning. There are two well separated clusters. The problem is that the given labels are not very representative for the classes. In practice this might be rather common, as manually given labels are often defined for the most different objects in the data. Using only the few labeled points, NEFCLASS splits the data in the middle between these and thus makes quite a lot of errors on the whole dataset. Our approach (1.5% errors) significantly outperforms both approaches in this example (NEFCLASS: 15.0% errors, FCM: 6.5% errors).

4 Conclusions

The state of the art in data mining is dominated by supervised approaches. However, in many real-world problems the assignment of labels for all objects is a severe problem and thus calls for semi-supervised methods.

Fuzzy set theory provides a method to formulate knowledge in a way that is interpretable to humans, and still allows efficient computations. Many problems have a certain robustness that allows a satisfying trade-off between performance and meaning, and are thus suited for fuzzy methods.

The authors presented an approach to induce fuzzy rules, that allows to exploit unlabeled training data that is often available, but rarely used in practice. The MDL based measure can be used to punish too complex rule bases. We successfully outperformed the unsupervised and supervised approaches in our examples. In our future work, we will apply the approach to more complex real-world problems.

References

1. A. Amar, N. T. Labzour, and A. M. Bensaid (1997): Semi-Supervised Hierarchical Clustering Algorithms. In 6th Scandinavian Conference on Artificial Intelligence (SCAI'97), pages 232–239, Helsinki, Finland
2. K. P. Bennett and A. Demiriz (1998): Semi-Supervised Support Vector Machines. In D. A. Cohn, M. S. Kearns, and S. A. Solla (Eds.): Advances in Neural Information processing Systems, pages 368–374. MIT Press, Cambridge, MA
3. A. M. Bensaid, L. O. Hall, J. C. Bezdek, and L. P. Clarke (1996): Partially Supervised Clustering for Image Segmentation. Pattern Recognition, 29(5):859–871
4. C. Borgelt and R. Kruse (2002): Graphical Models - Methods for Data Analysis and Mining. J. Wiley, Chichester
5. H. R. Berenji and P. Khedkar (1992): Learning and Tuning Fuzzy Logic Controllers Through Reinforcements. IEEE Trans. Neural Networks, 3:724–740
6. B. Carse, T. C. Fogarty, and A. Munro (1996): Evolving Fuzzy Rule Based Controllers Using Genetic Algorithms. Fuzzy Sets and Systems, 80:273–293
7. U. Fayyad, G. Piatetsky-Shapiro, P. Smyth, and R. Uthurusamy (Eds.) (1996): Advances in Knowledge Discovery and Data Mining. AAAI Press / MIT Press, Cambridge, MA

8. G. Fung and O. L. Mangasarian (1999): Semi-Supervised Support Vector Machines for Unlabeled Data Classification. Data Mining Institute, Technical Report 99-05
9. J. Hopf and F. Klawonn (1994): Learning the Rule Base of a Fuzzy controller by a Genetic Algorithm. In R. Kruse, J. Gebhardt, and R. Palm, (Eds): Fuzzy Systems in Computer Science, pages 63–73. Vieweg, Braunschweig
10. F. Höppner, F. Klawonn, R. Kruse, and T. Runkler (1999): Fuzzy Cluster Analysis. J. Wiley, Chichester
11. J. Jäkel, L. Gröll, and R. Mikut (1999): Automatic Generation and Evaluation of Interpretable Rule Bases for Fuzzy Systems. In Proc. CIMCA'99, pages 192–197, IOS Press, Amsterdam
12. F. Klawonn and R. Kruse (1997): Constructing a Fuzzy Controller from Data. Fuzzy Sets and Systems, 85:177-193
13. A. Klose, R. Kruse, K. Schulz, and U. Thönnessen (2000): Controlling Asymmetric Errors in Neuro-Fuzzy Classification. In Proc. ACM SAC'00, pages 505–509. ACM Press, New York
14. R. Kruse, C. Borgelt, and D. Nauck (1999): Fuzzy Data Analysis: Challenges and Perspectives. In Proc. 8th IEEE International Conference on Fuzzy Systems FUZZ-IEEE'99, Seoul, Korea. IEEE Press, Piscataway, NJ
15. D. Nauck and R. Kruse (1995): NEFCLASS – A Neuro-Fuzzy Approach for the Classification of Data. In Proc. ACM SAC'95, Nashville, Feb. 26–28, pages 461–465. ACM Press, New York
16. D. Nauck and R. Kruse (1997): A Neuro-Fuzzy Method to Learn Fuzzy Classification Rules from Data. Fuzzy Sets and Systems, 89:277–288
17. D. Nauck, F. Klawonn, and R. Kruse (1997): Foundations of Neuro-Fuzzy Systems. J. Wiley, Chichester
18. K. Nigam, A. McCallum, S. Thrun, and T. Mitchell (2000): Text Classification from Labeled and Unlabeled Documents using EM. Machine Learning, 39(2/3):103–134
19. A. Nürnberger, C. Borgelt, and A. Klose (1999): Improving Naive Bayes Classifiers Using Neuro-Fuzzy Learning. In Proc. 6th Int. Conf. on Neural Information Processing (ICONIP'99), pages 154–159, Perth, Australia
20. W. Pedrycz (1985): Algorithms of Fuzzy Clustering with Partial Supervision. Pattern Recognition Letters, 3:13–20
21. J. Rissanen (1983): A Universal Prior for Integers and Estimation by Minimum Description Length. Annals of Statistics, 11:416–431
22. M. Seeger (2001): Learning with Labeled and Unlabeled Data. Technical Report, Edinburgh University
23. D. M. Titterington, A. F. M. Smith, and U. E. Makov (1985): Statistical Analysis of Finite Mixture Distributions. J. Wiley, New York
24. N. Tschichold-Gürman (1995): Generation and Improvement of Fuzzy Classifiers with Incremental Learning Using Fuzzy Rulenet. In Proc. 1995 ACM Symposium on Applied Computing, Nashville, pages 466–470
25. L.-X. Wang and J. M. Mendel (1992): Generating Fuzzy Rules by Learning from Examples. IEEE Trans. Syst., Man, Cybern., 22(6):1414–1427
26. L. A. Zadeh (1996): Computing with Words. IEEE Transactions on Fuzzy Systems, 4:103–111

An ε-insensitive Learning in Neuro-Fuzzy Modeling

Jacek Łęski, Norbert Henzel

Institute of Electronics
Silesian University of Technology
Akademicka 16, 44-100 Gliwice. Poland

Abstract. The neuro-fuzzy modeling has an intrinsic inconsistency. It may perform thinking tolerant to imprecision, but neural networks learning methods are zero-tolerant to imprecision. Proposed method make it possible to exclude this intrinsic inconsistency of neuro-fuzzy modeling. This new method can be called ε-insensitive learning or εlearning, where in order to fit fuzzy model to real data, ε-insensitive loss function is used. Computationally efficient numerical method for the ε-insensitive learning is proposed. Finally, numerical example is given to demonstrate the improved generalization ability of obtained fuzzy model.

1 Introduction

The fuzzy modeling is based on the premise that human thinking is tolerant to imprecision, and the real world is too complicated to be described precisely [7]. Recently, fuzzy modeling plays an important role in many engineering fields, such as: pattern recognition, control, identification, data mining, and so on [1], [2], [4], [6]. In the neuro-fuzzy approach to the fuzzy modeling knowledge is acquired automatically by learning algorithms of neural networks. However, the neuro-fuzzy modeling has an intrinsic inconsistency. It may perform thinking tolerant to imprecision, but neural networks learning methods are zero-tolerant to imprecision, i.e., usually use the quadratic loss function, to match reality and a fuzzy model. In this case only a perfect matching between the reality and the model leads to a zero loss. Presented in this work approach to neuro-fuzzy modeling is based on the premise that human learning, as well as thinking, is tolerant to imprecision. Hence, zero loss for the difference between model and reality less than some pre-set value, noted ε, is assumed. If this difference is greater than ε, then the loss increases linearly. A learning method based on this loss function can be called ε-insensitive learning or shortly εlearning.

It is well-known in the approximation theory (Tikhonov regularization) and machine learning (statistical learning theory) that too precise learning on a training set leads to an overfitting (overtraining), which results in poor generalization ability. The generalization ability is interpreted as a production of reasonable decision for data previously unseen in the process of training [5]. Vapnik-Chervonenkis (VC) theory (or statistical learning theory) has recently emerged as a general theory for estimation of dependencies from a finite set of data. The most important in the VC-theory is Structural Risk Minimization (SRM) induction principle. The SRM principle suggest a tradeoff between the quality of an approximation and the complexity of the approximating function [5]. A measure of the approximation function complexity (or capacity) is called the VC-dimension. One of the simplest methods of control the VC-dimension is to change the insensitivity parameter ε and enforcing flatness of the approximating function by a regularization constant.

Recently, many authors (c.f. [1], [4], [6]) use fuzzy c-means to find clusters in the input space preserving similarity of input data, where each cluster corresponds to a fuzzy if-then rule in the Takagi-Sugeno-Kang form: IF $\mathbf{x}$ is $\mathbf{A}^{(i)}$, THEN $y = \mathbf{w}^{(i)T}\mathbf{x}'$; $i = 1, 2, ..., c$, where $\mathbf{x} \in \mathrm{I\!R}^t$ is the input variable, $y \in \mathrm{I\!R}$ is the output variable, $\mathbf{x}' \triangleq [\mathbf{x}^T, 1]^T$is the augmented input vector, $\mathbf{w}^{(i)} = [\widetilde{\mathbf{w}}^{(i)T}, w_0^{(i)}]^T \in \mathrm{I\!R}^{t+1}$ is the vector of consequent parameters of the i-th rule; $w_0^{(i)}$ denotes a bias of the i-th model. The antecedent fuzzy set of the i-th rule, $\mathbf{A}^{(i)}$ has a membership function $\mathbf{A}^{(i)}(\mathbf{x}) : \mathrm{I\!R}^t \to [0, 1]$. Usually, the Gaussian membership functions are used and their parameters are obtained from the fuzzy c-means clustering of the input space [1], [4].

For the input $\mathbf{x}$, the overall output of the fuzzy model is completed by a weighted averaging aggregation of outputs of individual rules, as [2], [6] $y = f(\mathbf{x}, \mathbf{w}) = \sum_{i=1}^{c} \overline{\mathbf{A}^{(i)}(\mathbf{x})}\, \mathbf{w}^{(i)T}\mathbf{x}'$, where $\overline{\mathbf{A}^{(i)}(\mathbf{x})}$ is the normalized firing strength of the i-th rule for the input $\mathbf{x}$, and $\mathbf{w} = [\mathbf{w}^{(1)T}, \cdots, \mathbf{w}^{(c)T}]^T$ denotes consequents vector. Defining $\mathbf{r}(\mathbf{x}') = [\overline{\mathbf{A}^{(1)}(\mathbf{x})}\mathbf{x}'^T, \cdots, \overline{\mathbf{A}^{(c)}(\mathbf{x})}\mathbf{x}'^T]^T$ the overall output of the fuzzy system can be written as $y = \mathbf{r}^T(\mathbf{x}')\,\mathbf{w}$.

Suppose we have the training set, $Tr^{(N)} = \{(\mathbf{x}_1, y_1), ..., (\mathbf{x}_N, y_N)\}$, where N is data cardinality, and each independent input datum $\mathbf{x}_i \in \mathrm{I\!R}^t$ has a corresponding dependent output datum $y_i \in \mathrm{I\!R}$. For fixed antecedents obtained via clustering of the input space, the LS solution to the consequent parameters estimation, minimizing the following criterion function $I(\mathbf{w}) = (\mathbf{y} - \mathbf{X}_r\mathbf{w})^T(\mathbf{y} - \mathbf{X}_r\mathbf{w})$ can be written in the matrix form, as $\mathbf{w} = (\mathbf{X}_r^T\mathbf{X}_r)^{-1}\mathbf{X}_r^T\mathbf{y}$, where $\mathbf{X}_r \triangleq [\mathbf{r}(\mathbf{x}_1'), \cdots, \mathbf{r}(\mathbf{x}_N')]^T \in \mathrm{I\!R}^{N \times c(t+1)}$ and $\mathbf{y} = [y_1, \cdots, y_N]^T \in \mathrm{I\!R}^N$.

The goals of this work are: to introduce a new tolerant to imprecision learning method, and to investigate the generalization ability of the fuzzy system obtained by means of this learning method for real-world high-dimensional data.

2 ε-insensitivity in neuro-fuzzy system learning

The problem of learning tolerant to imprecision can be presented as determining the consequent parameters $\mathbf{w}$, where in order to fit the fuzzy model to real data from the training set, ε-insensitive loss function is used. The

ε-insensitive loss function, for a vector argument, $\mathbf{g} = [g_1, \cdots, g_N]^T$ has the form [5]

$$\rceil \mathbf{g} \lceil_\varepsilon \triangleq \sum_{n=1}^{N} \rceil g_n \lceil_\varepsilon, \quad \rceil g_n \lceil_\varepsilon = \max(0, |g_n| - \varepsilon). \tag{1}$$

We seek a linear regression model $y = \mathbf{r}^T(\mathbf{x}')\,\mathbf{w}$, where $\mathbf{w}$ is obtained as a solution of the following problem

$$\min_{\mathbf{w} \in \mathbb{R}^{c(t+1)}} I(\mathbf{w}) \triangleq \sum_{n=1}^{N} \rceil y_n - \mathbf{w}^T \mathbf{r}(\mathbf{x}'_n) \lceil_\varepsilon + \frac{\tau}{2} \widetilde{\mathbf{w}}^T \widetilde{\mathbf{w}}, \tag{2}$$

where $\widetilde{\mathbf{w}}$ is the narrowed vector $\mathbf{w}$, with the components corresponding to the biases excluded, $\widetilde{\mathbf{w}} \triangleq \left[\widetilde{\mathbf{w}}^{(1)T}, \cdots, \widetilde{\mathbf{w}}^{(c)T}\right]^T$. The second term in (2) is related to minimization of the Vapnik-Chervonenkis dimension (complexity) of the regression model [5]. The parameter $\tau > 0$ controls the trade-off between the regression model complexity and the amount up to which errors are tolerated.

If we introduce a slack variables $\xi_n^+, \xi_n^- \geq 0$, then for all data $(\mathbf{x}_n, y_n)$ we can write

$$\begin{cases} y_n - \mathbf{w}^T \mathbf{r}(\mathbf{x}'_n) \leq \varepsilon + \xi_n^+, \\ \mathbf{w}^T \mathbf{r}(\mathbf{x}'_n) - y_n \leq \varepsilon + \xi_n^-. \end{cases} \tag{3}$$

Using (3) and $\widetilde{\mathbf{I}} = \operatorname{diag}\left(\left[\mathbf{1}_{t\times1}^T, 0, \cdots, \mathbf{1}_{t\times1}^T, 0\right]^T\right)$, the criterion (2) can be written in the form $I(\mathbf{w}) = \frac{1}{\tau} \sum\limits_{n=1}^{N} (\xi_n^+ + \xi_n^-) + \frac{1}{2}\mathbf{w}^T \widetilde{\mathbf{I}} \mathbf{w}$, and minimized subject to the constraints (3) and $\xi_n^+ \geq 0$, $\xi_n^- \geq 0$. The Lagrangian function takes the form

$$G = \frac{1}{2}\mathbf{w}^T \widetilde{\mathbf{I}} \mathbf{w} + \frac{1}{\tau} \sum_{n=1}^{N} (\xi_n^+ + \xi_n^-) - \sum_{n=1}^{N} \lambda_n^+ \left(\varepsilon + \xi_n^+ - y_n + \mathbf{w}^T \mathbf{r}(\mathbf{x}'_n)\right) \tag{4}$$
$$- \sum_{n=1}^{N} \lambda_n^- \left(\varepsilon + \xi_n^- + y_n - \mathbf{w}^T \mathbf{r}(\mathbf{x}'_n)\right) - \sum_{n=1}^{N} \left(\mu_n^+ \xi_n^+ + \mu_n^- \xi_n^-\right),$$

where $\lambda_n^+, \lambda_n^-, \mu_n^+, \mu_n^- \geq 0$ are the Lagrange multipliers. The following conditions for optimality we get by differentiating (4) with respect to $\mathbf{w}, \xi_n^+, \xi_n^-$ and setting the results equal to zero

$$\begin{cases} \frac{\partial G}{\partial \mathbf{w}} = \widetilde{\mathbf{I}} \mathbf{w} - \sum\limits_{n=1}^{N} (\lambda_n^+ - \lambda_n^-)\, \mathbf{r}(\mathbf{x}'_n) = \mathbf{0}, \\ \frac{\partial G}{\partial \xi_n^+} = \frac{1}{\tau} - \lambda_n^+ - \mu_n^+ = 0, \\ \frac{\partial G}{\partial \xi_n^-} = \frac{1}{\tau} - \lambda_n^- - \mu_n^- = 0. \end{cases} \tag{5}$$

The last two conditions (5) and the requirements $\mu_n^+, \mu_n^- \geq 0$ imply that $\lambda_n^+, \lambda_n^- \in \left[0, \frac{1}{\tau}\right]$. From the first condition (5), we obtain the support vector expansion: $\widetilde{\mathbf{I}}\mathbf{w} = \sum_{n=1}^{N} \left(\lambda_n^+ - \lambda_n^-\right) \mathbf{r}\left(\mathbf{x}'_n\right)$. For biases, the following condition is obtained, $\sum_{n=1}^{N} \left(\lambda_n^+ - \lambda_n^-\right) = 0$. Putting the conditions (5) in the Lagrangian we get $G = -\varepsilon \sum_{n=1}^{N} \left(\lambda_n^+ + \lambda_n^-\right) - \frac{1}{2} \sum_{n=1}^{N} \sum_{j=1}^{N} \left(\lambda_n^+ - \lambda_n^-\right) \left(\lambda_j^+ - \lambda_j^-\right) \mathbf{r}^T \left(\mathbf{x}'_n\right) \mathbf{r}\left(\mathbf{x}'_j\right)$ $+ \sum_{n=1}^{N} \left(\lambda_n^+ - \lambda_n^-\right) y_n$. Maximization of above Lagrangian with respect to λ_n^+, λ_n^- subject to constraints, $\lambda_n^+, \lambda_n^- \in \left[0, \frac{1}{\tau}\right]$ and $\sum_{n=1}^{N} \left(\lambda_n^+ - \lambda_n^-\right) = 0$ is the Wolfe dual formulation of (4). At the saddle point, for each Lagrange multiplier, the Karush-Kühn-Tucker (KKT) conditions must be satisfied

$$\begin{cases} \lambda_n^+ \left(\varepsilon + \xi_n^+ - y_n + \mathbf{w}^T \mathbf{r}\left(\mathbf{x}'_n\right)\right) = 0, \\ \lambda_n^- \left(\varepsilon + \xi_n^- + y_n - \mathbf{w}^T \mathbf{r}\left(\mathbf{x}'_n\right)\right) = 0, \\ \xi_n^+ \left(\frac{1}{\tau} - \lambda_n^+\right) = 0, \\ \xi_n^- \left(\frac{1}{\tau} - \lambda_n^-\right) = 0. \end{cases} \tag{6}$$

From (6) we see that the following conditions for λ_n^+ and λ_n^- are satisfied: (i) If $\lambda_n^{(\pm)} \in \left(0, \frac{1}{\tau}\right)$, then $\xi_n^{(\pm)} = 0$, (ii) If $\lambda_n^{(\pm)} = \frac{1}{\tau}$, then $\xi_n^{(\pm)} > 0$, (iii) If $\lambda_n^{(\pm)} = 0$, then $\xi_n^{(\pm)} < 0$. From the first two of the above conditions and (6) we can determine bias, $bias = y_n - \mathbf{w}^T \mathbf{r}\left(\mathbf{x}_n\right) - \varepsilon$, for $\lambda_n^+ \in \left(0, \frac{1}{\tau}\right)$ and $bias = y_n - \mathbf{w}^T \mathbf{r}\left(\mathbf{x}_n\right) + \varepsilon$, for $\lambda_n^- \in \left(0, \frac{1}{\tau}\right)$. Thus, we may determine bias by taking any $\mathbf{x}_n$ for which we have the Lagrange multipliers in open interval $\left(0, \frac{1}{\tau}\right)$. The bias is equal to $\overline{\mathbf{A}^{(1)}\left(\mathbf{x}\right)} w_0^{(1)} + \overline{\mathbf{A}^{(2)}\left(\mathbf{x}\right)} w_0^{(2)} + \cdots + \overline{\mathbf{A}^{(c)}\left(\mathbf{x}\right)} w_0^{(c)}$. Taking into account $\sum_{i=1}^{c} \overline{\mathbf{A}^{(i)}\left(\mathbf{x}\right)} = 1$, we see that $w_0^{(i)} = bias$, $i = 1, 2, ..., c$.

Computation of the parameters $\mathbf{w}$ leads to a quadratic programming (QP) problem. For a large training set standard optimization techniques quickly become intractable in their memory and time requirements. In [3] an alternative approach that determines the solution in classification problem is presented. In the next section this idea is used to solve the problem of fuzzy modeling with ε-insensitive learning.

3 Iterative QP solution

Regrouping the terms in (4) yields $G = \frac{1}{2}\mathbf{w}^T \widetilde{\mathbf{I}}\mathbf{w} + \sum_{n=1}^{N} \xi_n^+ \left(\frac{1}{\tau} - \lambda_n^+ - \mu_n^+\right)$ $+ \sum_{n=1}^{N} \xi_n^- \left(\frac{1}{\tau} - \lambda_n^- - \mu_n^-\right) + \sum_{n=1}^{N} \frac{\gamma_n^+}{2} \left(y_n - \mathbf{w}^T \mathbf{r}\left(\mathbf{x}'_n\right) - \varepsilon\right)^2$ $+ \sum_{n=1}^{N} \frac{\gamma_n^-}{2} \left(\mathbf{w}^T \mathbf{r}\left(\mathbf{x}'_n\right) - y_n - \varepsilon\right)^2$, where

$$\gamma_n^+ \triangleq \frac{2\lambda_n^+}{y_n - \mathbf{w}^T \mathbf{r}\left(\mathbf{x}'_n\right) - \varepsilon}, \qquad \gamma_n^+ \triangleq \frac{2\lambda_n^-}{\mathbf{w}^T \mathbf{r}\left(\mathbf{x}'_n\right) - y_n - \varepsilon}. \tag{7}$$

Condition for optimality we get by differentiating the above Lagrangian with respect to $\mathbf{w}$ and setting the results equal to zero

$$\mathbf{w} = \left(\mathbf{X}_r^T\left(\Gamma^+ + \Gamma^-\right)\mathbf{X}_r + \widetilde{\mathbf{I}}\right)^{-1}\left[\mathbf{X}_r^T\Gamma^+\left(\mathbf{y} - \varepsilon\mathbf{1}_{N\times 1}\right) + \mathbf{X}_r^T\Gamma^-\left(\mathbf{y} + \varepsilon\mathbf{1}_{N\times 1}\right)\right] \tag{8}$$

where $\Gamma^+ = \mathrm{diag}\left(\gamma_1^+, \gamma_2^+, ..., \gamma_N^+\right)$ and $\Gamma^- = \mathrm{diag}\left(\gamma_1^-, \gamma_2^-, ..., \gamma_N^-\right)$.

Expression (8) is the optimal solution. However, this solution is unconstrained and in order to satisfy the KKT conditions from the previous section, the special setting of the parameters λ_n^+ and λ_n^- is needed: if $\xi_n^+ < 0$ ($\xi_n^- < 0$), then $\lambda_n^+ = 0$ ($\lambda_n^- = 0$); if $\xi_n^+ = 0$ ($\xi_n^- = 0$), then $\lambda_n^+ \in \left(0, \frac{1}{\tau}\right)$ ($\lambda_n^- \in \left(0, \frac{1}{\tau}\right)$); if $\xi_n^+ > 0$ ($\xi_n^- > 0$), then $\lambda_n^+ = \frac{1}{\tau}$ ($\lambda_n^- = \frac{1}{\tau}$). Thus, Lagrange multipliers can be treated as a function of the slack variables. From the above rules we see that this function has a discontinuity at $\xi_n^+ = 0$ ($\xi_n^- = 0$). In [3] the following approximation of this function is proposed:

$$\lambda_n^+ = \begin{cases} 0, & \xi_n^+ < 0, \\ \beta\xi_n^+, & 0 \le \xi_n^+ < \frac{1}{\tau\beta}, \\ \frac{1}{\tau}, & \xi_n^+ \ge \frac{1}{\tau\beta}, \end{cases} \qquad \lambda_n^- = \begin{cases} 0, & \xi_n^- < 0, \\ \beta\xi_n^-, & 0 \le \xi_n^- < \frac{1}{\tau\beta}, \\ \frac{1}{\tau}, & \xi_n^- \ge \frac{1}{\tau\beta}, \end{cases} \tag{9}$$

where β is a big positive value, and

$$\xi_n^+ \triangleq y_n - \mathbf{w}^T\mathbf{r}\left(\mathbf{x}_n'\right) - \varepsilon, \quad \xi_n^- \triangleq \mathbf{w}^T\mathbf{r}\left(\mathbf{x}_n'\right) - y_n - \varepsilon. \tag{10}$$

From (8) we see that $\mathbf{w}$ depends on γ_n^+, γ_n^-, and from (7), (9), (10) that γ_n^+, γ_n^- depend on $\mathbf{w}$. In this case, the most popular algorithm for approximating the solution is the Picard iteration through (8) and (7), (9), (10). The procedure of seeking the optimal $\mathbf{w}$ can be called Iterative Quadratic Programming (IQP). For initialization we use $\gamma_n^+ = \beta$, $\lambda_n^- = 0$ for all n.

4 Numerical experiments and discussion

In the IQP method the parameter $\beta = 10^3$ and iterations were stopped as soon as the Euclidean norm in a successive pair of $\mathbf{w}$ vectors was less than 10^{-6}. Data originating from the Box and Jenkins work concerning the identification of a gas oven was used. To identify the model, the following vectors were used as input: $\mathbf{x}_n \triangleq [y(n-1), ..., y(n-4), x(n-1), ..., x(n-6)]^T$ and output $y_n \triangleq y(n)$. The learning set consists of the first 100 pairs of data, and the testing set consists of the remaining 190 pairs of data.

Parameters τ and ε were changed in the range from 0.01 to 0.5 (step 0.01), and from 0 to 0.2 (step 0.01) respectively. The number of if-then rules was changed from 2 to 6. After the training stage (neuro-fuzzy system design on the training set), the generalization ability of the designed model was determined as a root mean squared error (RMSE) on the test set. For each combination of the above parameters values, the training stage was repeated

Table 1. RMSE obtained for the testing part of the Box-Jenkins data.

c	2	3	4	5	6
RMSE for the zero-tolerant learning	0.3622	0.3785	0.4280	0.4159	0.5579
RMSE for ε-insensitive learning	0.3454	0.3679	0.3694	0.3842	0.5537
The insensityvity parameter ε	0.06	0.02	0.02	0.09	0.04
The regularization parameter τ	0.19	0.09	0.12	0.02	0.05

25 times for a different random initialization of the FCM method. Table 1 shows the lowest RMSE for each number of if-then rules. The values of τ and ε parameters for which the lowest RMSE was obtained as well as RMSE for zero-tolerant learning are also shown. It should be noted, that despite the number of if-then rules, the learning tolerant to imprecision leads to a better generalization comparing to the zero-tolerant learning.

5 Conclusions

In this work, a new approach to fuzzy modeling with learning tolerant to imprecision is presented. In this method of learning the ε-insensitive loss function is used. Numerically effective methods of design neuro-fuzzy system, called the iterative quadratic programming is also introduced. Learning tolerant to imprecision always leads to a better generalization comparing to the classical methods.

References

1. E. Czogała, J. Łęski (2000) Fuzzy and Neuro-Fuzzy Intelligent Systems. Physica-Verlag, Springer-Verlag Comp., Heidelberg.
2. J.-S.R. Jang, C.-T. Sun, E. Mizutani (1997) Neuro-fuzzy and Soft Computing. A Computational Approach to Learning and Machine Intelligence. Prentice-Hall, Upper Saddle River.
3. A. Navia-Vázquez, F. Pérez-Cruz, A. Artés-Rodríguez, A.R. Figueiras-Vidal (2001) Weighted Least Squares Training of Support Vector Classifiers Leading to Compact and Adaptive Schemes. IEEE Trans. Neural Networks, Vol. **12**, No. **5**, 1047-1059.
4. D. Rutkowska (2001) Neuro-Fuzzy Architectures and Hybrid Learning. Physica-Verlag, Springer-Verlag Comp., Heidelberg.
5. V. Vapnik (1998) Statistical Learning Theory. Wiley, New York.
6. L.-X. Wang (1998) A Course in Fuzzy Systems and Control. Prentice-Hall, New York.
7. L.A. Zadeh (1973) Outline of a new approach to the analysis of complex systems and decision processes. IEEE Trans. Systems, Man and Cybernetics, Vol. **3**, No. **1**, 28-44.

SOFT TECHNIQUES FOR BAYESIAN CLASSIFICATION

Robert Nowicki, Leszek Rutkowski

Department of Computer Engineering
Technical University of Czestochowa
Armii Krajowej Avenue 36
42-200 Częstochowa, Poland
Tel./fax: +48343250546
Email: rnowicki@kik.pcz.czest.pl

Abstract : In this paper we present a neuro-fuzzy classifier performing a Bayes decision function. The classifier is based on a neuro-fuzzy structure. The rough set theory is incorporated into this structure. It will be shown that a new hybrid system, i.e. rough-neuro-fuzzy classifier, is able to perform classification in the case of missing features.

1 Introduction

Soft computing techniques comprise fuzzy logic methods, rough sets, neural networks, evolutionary algorithms, probabilistic reasoning, Bayesian methods and statistical learning procedures (see e.g. Kecman [1]). According to Zadeh [14] "the constituent methodologies of SC are, for the most part, complementary and synergistic – rather than competitive. The principal thesis of soft computing is that in general it is advantageous to employ to constituent methodologies in combination rather than in a stand-alone mode."

In this paper we show that neuro-fuzzy systems are functionally equivalent to nonparametric classifiers based on the Parzen methods. Since nonparametric classifiers are asymptotically Bayes risk consistent we deduce that neuro-fuzzy classifiers reveal the same probability properties. Moreover, we incorporate the rough set theory to the neuro-fuzzy structure in order to deal with missing features.

2 Nonparametric function estimation

In this section the kernel methods for nonparametric function estimation (see e.g. [4], [9], [10]) are presented. In the next section we will show similarities between nonparametric methods and neuro-fuzzy systems.

Density estimation

Let $\mathbf{X}^1,\ldots\mathbf{X}^N$ be sequence of independent, identically distributed random variables taking values in $\Re^n$ and having a probability density function f. The Parzen-Rosenblatt estimate of f is given by the formula (see [4])

$$\hat{f}_N(x)=\frac{1}{N\sigma_N^n}\sum_{k=1}^{N}K\left(\frac{\mathbf{x}-\mathbf{X}^k}{\sigma_N}\right) \tag{1}$$

where K is an appropriately chosen function fulfilling the conditions:

$$\sup_y\left|K(\mathbf{y})\right|<\infty \tag{2}$$

$$\int_{\Re^n}\left|K(\mathbf{y})\right|d\mathbf{y}<\infty \tag{3}$$

$$\lim_{\|\mathbf{y}\|\to\infty}\|\mathbf{y}\|^n\left|K(\mathbf{y})\right|=0 \tag{4}$$

$$\int_{\Re^n}K(\mathbf{y})d\mathbf{y}=1 \tag{5}$$

In equation (4) symbol $\|\cdot\|$ stands for the Euclidean vector norm. Sequence σ_N is a function of N and satisfies the conditions

$$\lim_{N\to\infty}\sigma_N=0 \quad\text{and}\quad \lim_{N\to\infty}N\sigma_N^n=\infty \tag{6}$$

We assume that the function K is of the form

$$K(\mathbf{x})=(2\pi)^{-\frac{1}{2}n}e^{-\frac{1}{2}\|\mathbf{x}\|^2} \tag{7}$$

where $\|\mathbf{x}\|^2=\mathbf{x}^T\mathbf{x}$. Then we can rewrite estimator (1) as follows

$$\begin{aligned}\hat{f}_N(\mathbf{x})&=\frac{1}{(2\pi)^{\frac{1}{2}n}N\sigma_N^n}\sum_{k=1}^{N}\exp\left(-\frac{\left(\mathbf{x}-\mathbf{X}^k\right)^T\left(\mathbf{x}-\mathbf{X}^k\right)}{2\sigma_N^2}\right)\\&=\frac{1}{(2\pi)^{\frac{1}{2}n}N\sigma_N^n}\sum_{k=1}^{N}\prod_{i=1}^{n}\exp\left[-\frac{1}{2}\left(\frac{x_i-X_i^k}{\sigma_N}\right)^2\right]\end{aligned} \tag{8}$$

Regression estimation

The procedure (1) can be easily extended to estimate a regression function based on the sample $\{(\mathbf{X},Y),(\mathbf{X}^1,Y^1),\ldots,(\mathbf{X}^N,Y^N)\}$ of i.i.d. random variables. The estimator of the regression function

$$R(\mathbf{x})=E[Y\mid\mathbf{X}=\mathbf{x}] \tag{9}$$

takes the form

$$\hat{R}_N(\mathbf{x}) = \frac{\sum_{k=1}^{N} Y^k K\left(\frac{\mathbf{x} - \mathbf{X}^k}{\sigma_N}\right)}{\sum_{i=1}^{n} K\left(\frac{\mathbf{x} - \mathbf{X}^k}{\sigma_N}\right)} \tag{10}$$

Applying kernel (7) to (10) one gets

$$\hat{R}_N(\mathbf{x}) = \frac{\sum_{k=1}^{N} Y^k \prod_{i=1}^{n} \exp\left[-\frac{1}{2}\left(\frac{x_i - X_i^k}{\sigma_N}\right)^2\right]}{\sum_{k=1}^{N} \prod_{i=1}^{n} \exp\left[-\frac{1}{2}\left(\frac{x_i - X_i^k}{\sigma_N}\right)^2\right]} \tag{11}$$

Nonparametric classification

Let $\{(\mathbf{X}, Y), (\mathbf{X}^1, Y^1), \ldots, (\mathbf{X}^N, Y^N)\}$, be a sequence of i.i.d. pairs of random variables; Y takes the values from the set; $S = \{1, \ldots, M\}$, whereas $\mathbf{X}$ takes the values in $\Re^n$. The problem is to estimate Y from $\mathbf{X}$ and the learning sequence $\mathbf{V}^N = (\mathbf{X}^1, Y^1), \ldots, (\mathbf{X}^N, Y^N)$. Suppose that p_m and f_m, $m = 1, \ldots, M$, are the prior class probabilities and the class conditional densities, respectively. We define the Bayes discriminate function

$$g_m(\mathbf{x}) = p_m f_m(\mathbf{x}) \tag{12}$$

Let

$$T_m^k = \begin{cases} 1 & \text{if} \quad Y^k = m \\ 0 & \text{if} \quad Y^k \neq m \end{cases} \tag{13}$$

for $k = 1, 2, \ldots, N$ and $m = 1, 2, \ldots M$. The Bayes discriminate function can be rewritten as follows

$$g_m(\mathbf{x}) = f(\mathbf{x}) E\left[T_m^k \mid \mathbf{X}^k = \mathbf{x}\right] \tag{14}$$

where $f(\mathbf{x}) = \sum_{m=1}^{M} p_m f_m(\mathbf{x})$.

We consider a procedure classifying every $\mathbf{x}$ to a class m, $m \in S$, which maximizes $\hat{g}_{Nm}(\mathbf{x})$, where $\hat{g}_{Nm}(\mathbf{x})$ is the following estimate of the Bayes discriminate function

$$\hat{g}_{Nm}(\mathbf{x}) = \frac{1}{(2\pi)^{\frac{1}{2}n} N\sigma_N^n} \sum_{k=1}^{N} T_m^k \prod_{i=1}^{n} \exp\left[-\tfrac{1}{2}\left(\frac{x_i - X_i^k}{\sigma_N}\right)^2\right] \tag{15}$$

Alternatively one can take the estimate of $E[T_m^k \mid \mathbf{X}^k = \mathbf{x}]$, i.e.

$$\hat{R}_{Nm}(\mathbf{x}) = \frac{\sum_{k=1}^{N} T_m^k \prod_{i=1}^{n} \exp\left[-\tfrac{1}{2}\left(\frac{x_i - X_i^k}{\sigma_N}\right)^2\right]}{\sum_{k=1}^{N} \prod_{i=1}^{n} \exp\left[-\tfrac{1}{2}\left(\frac{x_i - X_i^k}{\sigma_N}\right)^2\right]} \tag{16}$$

3 The neuro-fuzzy methods for classification

The neuro-fuzzy architectures realise the fuzzy inference on the basis of the fuzzy IF-THEN rules in the form

$$R^k : \text{IF } \mathbf{x} \text{ is } A^k \text{ THEN } y \text{ is } B^k \tag{17}$$

where $\mathbf{x} \in \mathbf{X}$, $y \in \mathbf{Y}$ are the input and output linguistic variables, respectively. In the case of independent features rule (17) takes form

$$\begin{aligned} R^k : \text{IF } x_1 \text{ is } A_1^k \text{ AND } x_2 \text{ is } A_2^k \text{ AND} \ldots \\ \ldots \text{AND } x_n \text{ is } A_n^k \text{ THEN } y \text{ is } B^k \end{aligned} \tag{18}$$

The common method of fuzzification is the singleton fuzzification

$$\mu_{A'}(\mathbf{x}) = \begin{cases} 1 & \text{if } \quad \mathbf{x} = \bar{\mathbf{x}} \\ 0 & \text{if } \quad \mathbf{x} \neq \bar{\mathbf{x}} \end{cases} \tag{19}$$

where $\bar{\mathbf{x}} = [\bar{x}_1, \bar{x}_2, \ldots, \bar{x}_n]^T$ is the crisp input vector, and A' is the fuzzy set in the premise in the form: $\mathbf{x}$ is A'.

The inference process is performed by the composition inference rule. The fuzzy set B'^k, which is the result of the inference process on the basis of the k-th rule, is defined by

$$B'^k = A' \circ (A^k \to B^k) \tag{20}$$

When we use the *sup-T* definition of the fuzzy sets composition we can describe the membership function of B'^k fuzzy set as

$$\mu_{B'^k}(y) = \sup_{\mathbf{x} \in \mathbf{X}} \left\{ \mu_{A'}(x) \overset{T}{*} \mu_{A^k \to B^k}(\mathbf{x}, y) \right\} \tag{21}$$

where $\overset{T}{*}$ depicts any *T-norm*, e.g. minimum operation.

In the case of the singleton fuzzification (19), the equation (21) takes the following form

$$\mu_{B'^k}(y)=\mu_{A^k\to B^k}(\overline{\mathbf{x}},y) \tag{22}$$

The relation between A^k and B^k, which the membership function is denoted as $\mu_{A^k\to B^k}(\mathbf{x},y)$, is defined by one of many definitions of fuzzy implication. The common ones belong to Mamdani approach. They include Mamdani relation

$$\mu_{A^k\to B^k}(\mathbf{x},y)=\min\{\mu_{A^k}(\mathbf{x}),\mu_{B^k}(y)\} \tag{23}$$

and Larsen relation

$$\mu_{A^k\to B^k}(\mathbf{x},y)=\mu_{A^k}(\mathbf{x})\cdot\mu_{B^k}(y) \tag{24}$$

Combining (23) or (24) with height defuzzifier [6] we obtain the following description of neuro-fuzzy system

$$\overline{y}=\frac{\sum_{k=1}^{N}\overline{y}^k\cdot\mu_{A^k}(\overline{\mathbf{x}})}{\sum_{k=1}^{N}\mu_{A^k}(\overline{\mathbf{x}})} \tag{25}$$

where we define fuzzy set A^k as Cartesian product

$$\mu_{A^k}(\mathbf{x})=\prod_{i=1}^{n}\mu_{A_i^k}(x_i) \tag{26}$$

so

$$\overline{y}=\frac{\sum_{k=1}^{N}\overline{y}^k\cdot\prod_{i=1}^{n}\mu_{A_i^k}(\overline{x}_i)}{\sum_{k=1}^{N}\prod_{i=1}^{n}\mu_{A_i^k}(\overline{x}_i)} \tag{27}$$

and in the case of Gaussian membership function we have got

$$\overline{y}=\frac{\sum_{k=1}^{N}\overline{y}^k\cdot\prod_{i=1}^{n}\exp\left[-\left(\frac{\overline{x}_i-\overline{x}_i^k}{\sigma_i^k}\right)^2\right]}{\sum_{k=1}^{N}\prod_{i=1}^{n}\exp\left[-\left(\frac{\overline{x}_i-\overline{x}_i^k}{\sigma_i^k}\right)^2\right]} \tag{28}$$

Comparing (28) with (16) it turns out that they are functionally equivalent. A similar observation has been made in [2] and [13]. It should be noted that procedure (16) is asymptotically Bayes risk consistent under some mild conditions imposed on σ_N. Consequently the neuro-fuzzy system also reveals the same property.

The knowledge of fuzzy classification system is represented by a set of K rules in the form

$$R^k : \text{IF } \mathbf{x} \text{ is } A^k \text{ THEN } \mathbf{x} \in c^k \tag{29}$$

where $\mathbf{x} = [x_1, x_2, \ldots, x_n]^T$ is the vector of object or state features (properties). The notation $\mathbf{x} \in c^k$ means that object $\mathbf{x}$ belongs to the class k. In the specific case of independent features where $A^k = A_1^k \times A_2^k \times \ldots \times A_n^k$ we can express rule (29) in form

$$\begin{aligned} R^k : \text{IF } x_1 \text{ is } A_1^k \text{ AND } x_2 \text{ is } A_2^k \text{ AND} \ldots \\ \ldots \text{AND } x_n \text{ is } A_n^k \text{ THEN } \mathbf{x} \in c^k \end{aligned} \tag{30}$$

Rules in the form (17) and (18) are different than rules in the form (29) and (30), but it is easy to associate the output value (25) of the neuro-fuzzy architecture with the membership of the object $\mathbf{x}$ to the classes.

4 Classification in the case of missing features

Let us suppose that we have got some universe of objects or states $\mathbf{X}$. Each object $\mathbf{x}$ in universe $\mathbf{X}$ is described by a set of properties or features $Q = \{x_1, x_2, \ldots, x_n\}$. From these properties standpoint some objects are undistinguished, i.e. they have the same values of all properties from set Q. The sets of undistinguished objects in a given set of features are called abstraction classes, and denoted as $[\mathbf{x}]_{\tilde{Q}}$. $\tilde{Q}$ is the equivalent relation specified in the universe $\mathbf{X} \times \mathbf{X}$ by the set of features Q.

For each set A of objects $\mathbf{x}$ in the space $\mathbf{X}$ and any set of features Q, the $\tilde{Q}$-lower approximation of A is defined [5] as

$$\underline{\tilde{Q}}A = \{\mathbf{x} \in \mathbf{X} : [\mathbf{x}]_{\tilde{Q}} \subseteq A\} \tag{31}$$

and the $\tilde{Q}$-upper approximation of A is given by

$$\overline{\tilde{Q}}A = \{\mathbf{x} \in \mathbf{X} : [\mathbf{x}]_{\tilde{Q}} \cap A \neq \varnothing\} \tag{32}$$

We assume that we do not have information about all features from the set $Q = \{x_1, x_2, \ldots, x_n\}$ but only the information about features from a subset $P \subset Q$. Then, set of unknown features is expressed as $U = Q \setminus P$. We can describe these subsets as $P = \{p_1, p_2, \ldots, p_{n_P}\}$, $U = \{u_1, u_2, \ldots, u_{n_U}\}$. Obviously $P \cup U = Q$ and

$n_P + n_U = n$. Therefore we cannot realise fuzzy classification on the basis of the fuzzy sets $A^k \subseteq X_1 \times X_2 \times \ldots \times X_n$ used in rule (29). It is possible to perform fuzzy classification based on the features from subset P and it should be assumed something about unknown features from subset U .

We can derive [3] the following equations

$$\mu_{\overline{P}A^k}(\mathbf{x}) = \prod_{i \in P} \mu_{A_i^k}(x_i) \cdot \sup_{x_i \in Q \setminus P} \left\{ \mu_{A_i^k}(x_i) \right\} \tag{33}$$

$$\mu_{\underline{P}A^k}(\mathbf{x}) = \prod_{i \in P} \mu_{A_i^k}(x_i) \cdot \inf_{x_i \in Q \setminus P} \left\{ \mu_{A_i^k}(x_i) \right\} \tag{34}$$

where $\mu_{\overline{P}A^k}$ and $\mu_{\underline{P}A^k}$ are membership functions corresponding to P-upper and P-lower approximations of fuzzy sets A^k, respectively. The values of $\mu_{\overline{P}A^k}$ and $\mu_{\underline{P}A^k}$ are applied as firing level of particular rules in neuro-fuzzy system described by formula (28).

5 Conclusions

In the paper we have applied basic soft techniques for classification. The rough-neuro-fuzzy classifier has been derived. Functional similarities between nonparametric methods and neuro-fuzzy systems assure nice probabilistic properties of these systems. It should be noted that the results of the paper are applicable to other neuro-fuzzy structures (see [6], [7], [8], [11] and [12]).

References

[1] V. Kecman, "Learning and Soft Computing", MIT, Cambridge, 2001.

[2] L. I. Kuncheva, "On the Equivalence Between Fuzzy and Statistical Classifiers", International Journal of Uncertainty, Fuzziness and Knowledge-Based Systems, v. 4, No. 3, 1996, pp. 245-253.

[3] R. Nowicki, L. Rutkowski, "Rough-Neuro-Fuzzy System For Classification", Proc. of FSKD'02 Singapure, 2002.

[4] E. Parzen, "On estimation of a probability density function", Annals of Math. Statistics, v. 33, pp. 1065-1076.

[5] Z. Pawlak, „Rough sets", International Journal of Information and Computer Science, Vol. 11, No. 341, 1982.

[6] D. Rutkowska, R. Nowicki, „New neuro-fuzzy architectures", Proc. Int. Conf. on Artificial and Computational Intelligence for Decision, Control and Automation in Engineering and Industrial Applications, ACIDCA'2000, Intelligent Methods, Monastir, Tunisia, March, 2000, pp. 82-87.

[7] D. Rutkowska, R. Nowicki, L. Rutkowski, "Neuro-fuzzy architectures with various implication operators", The State of the Art in Computational Intelligence - Proc. Intern. Symposium on Computational Intelligence (ISCI 2000), Springer-Verlag, Kosice, Slovakia, August/September 2000, pp. 214-219.

[8] D. Rutkowska and R. Nowicki, "Implication – based neuro-fuzzy architectures", International Journal of Applied Mathematics and Computer Science, No.4, 2000, pp. 675-701.
[9] L. Rutkowski, "Identification of MISO non-linear regressions in the presence of a wide class of disturbances", IEEE Trans. Information Theory, v. IT-37, 1991, pp. 214-216.
[10] L. Rutkowski, Multiple Fourier series procedures of non-linear regressions from noisy data. – IEEE Trans. Signal Processing, v. 41, No. 10, 1993, pp. 109-118.
[11] L. Rutkowski, "New Soft Computing Techniques For System Modelling, Pattern Classification and Image Processing", Springer-Verlag (to be published).
[12] L. Rutkowski, K. Cpałka, „Flexible Neuro-Fuzzy Systems", IEEE Trans. Neural Networks, (submitted for publication).
[13] L.-X. Wang, "Adaptive Fuzzy Systems and Control", PTR Prentice Hall, Englewood Cliffs, New Jersey, 1994.
[14] L. A. Zadeh, New Frontiers in Fuzzy Logic and Soft Computing, Proc. of Fourth Conference „Neural Networks and Their Application", Zakopane, May 18-22, 1999, pp. 1-4.

Gradient Descent Based Optimization of Transparent Mamdani Systems

Andri Riid and Ennu Rüstern

Tallinn Technical University, Department of Computer Control, Ehitajate tee 5, Tallinn 19086, Estonia. E-mail: andri@dcc.ttu.ee

Abstract. The tradeoff between accuracy and interpretability in fuzzy modeling has shifted into focus in last few years. This paper aims at improving accuracy of linguistic models while maintaining a good interpretability. A new gradient-based method, extended version of Jager approach, is proposed for the optimization of transparent Mamdani systems. The advantage of Mamdani systems if compared to 0th order TS systems in Jager approach is that their interpolation properties allow one to obtain less complex models without loss of accuracy. Several modeling examples confirming the advantages of the chosen algorithm are included.

1 Introduction

Many papers have been written about neuro-fuzzy systems. Most of these address the optimization of fuzzy systems based on gradient descent (GD) method. Perhaps the earliest work in this research line is [1] that considers 0th order TS systems with symmetric triangular antecedent membership functions (MFs). Later contributions include [2] that extends the method on various types of fuzzy systems including 1st order Takagi-Sugeno (TS) systems. The hybrid learning rule, proposed by Jang [3] combines gradient descent with least-squares estimator for consequent parameters and outperforms the previous approaches in terms of approximation error.

What is common to mentioned approaches is that no attention is paid to semantic properties of fuzzy systems, thus the obtained models and controllers are non-transparent to interpretation and it can be claimed that the basic feature that distinguishes fuzzy systems from other nonlinear approximators (e.g. neural networks) is sacrificed to approximation accuracy.

Jager's work, where GD is applied to 0th order TS systems in a manner that maintains a fuzzy partition on antecedent variables, is an interesting exception. The importance of the approach is that it guarantees distinguishability of input MFs that, as has been shown in [4], is the important precondition for transparency. The algorithm, published in Ph.D. thesis [5] is, however, not well known with the exception of [6] and [7] (in the latter an extension for 1st order TS systems is given). In this paper we propose a further extension of Jager algorithm for Mamdani systems, to minimize the existing gap between transparency and accuracy in fuzzy modeling.

2 System Definition

We consider a MISO Mamdani system with the following rule base

IF x_1 is A_{1r} AND… AND x_i is A_{ir} … AND x_N is A_{Nr} THEN y is B_{1r}, (1)

where A_{ir} and B_{jr} the linguistic labels of ith input variable x_i and output variable y ($i = 1 \dots N$), respectively, associated with the rth rule ($r = 1 \dots R$).

Numerical mapping of input-output variables of (1) (in discrete form) is obtained by applying the inference function (2),

$$y = Y_{cog}(F(y)) = \sum_{q=1}^{Q} F(y_q) y_q \Big/ \sum_{q=1}^{Q} F(y_q) \tag{2}$$

where y_q is output value at q^{th} discretization interval and Y_{cog} denotes center-of-gravity defuzzification function.

$F(y)$ in (2) is given by (3), assuming product-product-sum inference.

$$F(y) = \sum_{r=1}^{R} \left(\prod_{i=1}^{N} \mu_{ir}(x_i) \right) \gamma_r = \sum_{r=1}^{R} \tau_r \gamma_r , \tag{3}$$

where μ_{ir} and γ_r are normal and convex antecedent and consequent membership functions (MFs), having one-to-one correspondence with respective linguistic labels in (1) and τ_r is the activation degree of the rth rule. (2) and (3) yield

$$y = \sum_{r=1}^{R} \tau_r \sum_{q=1}^{Q} \gamma_r(y_q) y_q \Big/ \sum_{r=1}^{R} \tau_r \sum_{q=1}^{Q} \gamma_r(y_q) . \tag{4}$$

According to [7], such system is transparent (i.e. fully interpretable) if antecedent and consequent MFs satisfy (5) and (6), respectively. S_i is the number of MFs defined per i^{th} input variable.

$$\forall x_i \in X_i : \sum_{s=1}^{S_i} \mu_i^s(x_i) \le 1 , \tag{5}$$

$$\mathrm{Y}_{cog}(\gamma_r(y)) = \int_{y_{min}}^{y_{max}} y\gamma_r(y)dy \Big/ \int_{y_{min}}^{y_{max}} \gamma_r(y)dy = \mathrm{core}(\gamma_r(y)) \tag{6}$$

If consequent MFs, γ_r, of the system are symmetrical (6) and triangular i.e.

$$\gamma_r(y) = \max\left(0, \min\left(\frac{2b_r - 2y + s_r}{s_r}, \frac{2y - 2b_r + s_r}{s_r} \right) \right), \tag{7}$$

where b_r and s_r are the center and spread of the triangle, it can be shown [8] that the inference function (4) of a Mamdani system with (7) reduces to (8).

$$y = \sum_{r=1}^{R} \tau_r b_r s_r \Big/ \sum_{r=1}^{R} \tau_r s_r \tag{8}$$

Note that if $\forall r\ (s_r = \xi)$, where ξ is arbitrary constant, (8) further reduces to the inference function of a 0th order TS system which implies that a Mamdani system with symmetrical triangular consequent MFs is, in fact, a 0th order TS system if the supports s_r are all equal.

To satisfy (5), Jager definition of fuzzy sets [4] is used in the following (a_i^s is the center of sth MF of the ith antecedent variable)

$$\mu_i^s(x_i) = \max\left(0, \min\left(\frac{x_i - a_i^{s-1}}{a_i^s - a_i^{s-1}}, \frac{a_i^{s+1} - x_i}{a_i^{s+1} - a_i^s}\right)\right) \tag{9}$$

3 The Algorithm

Gradient descent method minimizes the objective function E:

$$E = \frac{1}{2}\sum_k^K \varepsilon(k) = \frac{1}{2}\sum_k^K (y(k) - \tilde{y}(k))^2 , \tag{10}$$

where $\tilde{y}(k)$ is the kth reference value and $y(k)$ is obtained by applying the inference function (8) with the kth given input pattern. The update rules based on (8) and (10) have the following form.

$$b_r(l+1) = b_r(l) - \eta_b \frac{\partial E}{\partial b_r(l)} = b_r(l) - \frac{\eta_b}{2}\sum_{k=1}^K \frac{\partial \varepsilon(k)}{\partial b_r(l)} , \tag{11}$$

where η_b is the learning rate of b_r. To compute the derivatives in (10) and similar expressions for other adaptable parameters s_r and a_i^s we apply the chain rule

$$\frac{\partial \varepsilon}{\partial b_r} = \frac{\partial \varepsilon}{\partial y}\frac{\partial y}{\partial b_r} , \tag{12}$$

$$\frac{\partial \varepsilon}{\partial s_r} = \frac{\partial \varepsilon}{\partial y}\frac{\partial y}{\partial s_r} , \tag{13}$$

$$\frac{\partial \varepsilon}{\partial a_i^s} = \frac{\partial \varepsilon}{\partial y}\frac{\partial y}{\partial a_i^s} = \frac{\partial \varepsilon}{\partial y}\left(\frac{\partial y}{\partial \mu_i^{s-1}}\frac{\partial \mu_i^{s-1}}{\partial a_i^s} + \frac{\partial y}{\partial \mu_i^s}\frac{\partial \mu_i^s}{\partial a_i^s} + \frac{\partial y}{\partial \mu_i^{s+1}}\frac{\partial \mu_i^{s+1}}{\partial a_i^s}\right). \tag{14}$$

Once the partial derivatives are obtained, the following update rules can be written:

$$b_r(l+1) = b_r(l) - \eta_b (y(k) - \tilde{y}(k)) \frac{\tau_r(k) s_r(l)}{\sum_{r=1}^R \tau_r(k) s_r(l)} \tag{15}$$

$$s_r(l+1) = s_r(l) - \eta_s (y(k) - \widetilde{y}(k))(b_r(l) - y(k)) \frac{\tau_r(k)}{\sum_{r=1}^{R} \tau_r(k) s_r(l)} \tag{16}$$

$$\text{if } a_i^{s-1} < x_i < a_i^s \tag{17}$$

$$a_i^s(l+1) = a_i^s(l) - \eta_a \frac{(y(k) - \widetilde{y}(k))}{a_i^s(l) - a_i^{s-1}(l)} \cdot \frac{1}{\sum_{r=1}^{R} \tau_r(k) s_r(l)} \cdot$$

$$\cdot \left[\frac{\mu_i^s(x_i(k))}{\mu_i^{s-1}(x_i(k))} \sum_{r'=1}^{R(\mu_i^{s-1})} \tau_{r'}(k) s_{r'}(l)(b_{r'}(l) - y(k)) - \sum_{r'=1}^{R(\mu_i^s)} \tau_{r'}(k) s_{r'}(l)(b_{r'}(l) - y(k)) \right]$$

$$\text{if } a_i^s < x_i < a_i^{s+1} \tag{18}$$

$$a_i^s(l+1) = a_i^s(l) - \eta_a \frac{(y(k) - \widetilde{y}(k))}{a_i^{s+1}(l) - a_i^s(l)} \cdot \frac{1}{\sum_{r=1}^{R} \tau_r(k) s_r(l)} \cdot$$

$$\cdot \left[\sum_{r'=1}^{R(\mu_i^s)} \tau_{r'}(k) s_{r'}(l)(b_{r'}(l) - y(k)) - \frac{\mu_i^s(x_i(k))}{\mu_i^{s+1}(x_i(k))} \sum_{r'=1}^{R(\mu_i^{s+1})} \tau_{r'}(k) s_{r'}(l)(b_{r'}(l) - y(k)) \right]$$

where $r' = 1 \ldots R(\mu_i^s)$ refers to rules having A_i^s in their premise.

Note that if $\forall r$ ($s_r = \xi$), the resulting (15), (17) and (18) constitute the original Jager algorithm for 0th order TS systems.

4 Experimental Results

In the examples below the proposed algorithm is used to model highly nonlinear functions in comparison with ANFIS and the original Jager algorithm.

In order to ensure a good initial configuration of the model, the centers of consequent MFs are determined with a one-step least squares procedure [3], i.e. the model is initialized as a 0th order TS system. The obtained consequent singletons are then converted into symmetrical triangles. To stabilize the learning process, variable learning rate and heuristic step size adjustment strategy [3] are utilized.

First test system is the function

$$y = 0.6\sin(\pi x) + 0.3\sin(3\pi x) + 0.1\sin(5\pi x) \tag{19}$$

Test data set is obtained by discretizing the input variable $x = [-1,1]$ with the step 0.01 that results in 201 training samples. Additionally, two-input single-output fuzzy system from [9], depicted in Fig. 2, right, is identified from 441 training samples with 18, 36 and 66 rules. The results in terms of approximation error obtained with 200 training epochs are depicted in Fig. 1, right and Table 1.

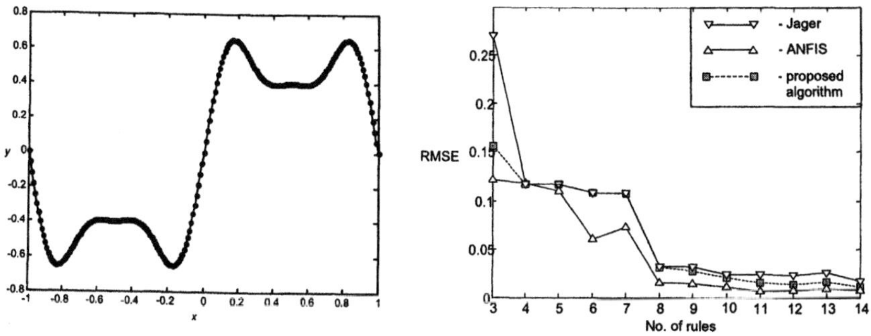

Fig. 1. Training data (left) and modeling root-mean-square-errors (RMSE) (right).

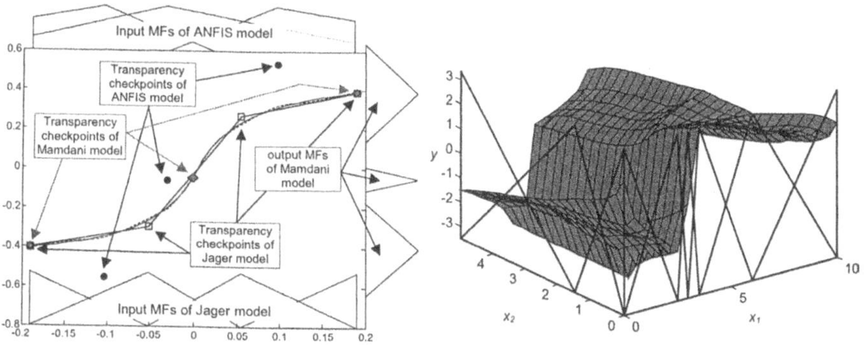

Fig. 2. Interpolation/approximation properties of fuzzy systems (left) and two-input test system (right).

We see that the proposed algorithm consistently outperforms Jager algorithm and while not being real contender to ANFIS makes a good attempt at it. It can be observed, however, that the excellent approximation properties of ANFIS generally come at the expense of transparency. Considering the curve in Fig. 2, left, application of ANFIS results in very low error, Transparency checkpoints (one for each rule, see [8]) that are not situated on the actual system output, however, indicate strong non-transparency. Linguistically such system would be impossible to interpret correctly. Jager's transparent 0th order models, on the other hand, generally require more rules for faithful tracking and even then, linear interpolation does not always provide smoothness. The advantage of a Mamdani system is that while preserving transparency, its interpolation properties allow more efficient approximation.

Table 1. Modeling RMSEs of two input test function.

R	Initial error	ANFIS	Jager	proposed algorithm
6×3	0.5538	0.1594	0.2479	0.1790
9×4	0.2891	0.1178	0.1710	0.1416
11×6	0.1858	0.0780	0.0811	0.0589

5 Conclusions

The neuro-adaptive learning techniques [10] provide a method for the fuzzy modeling procedure to learn information about a data set, in order to compute the membership function parameters that allow the fuzzy system to track the given input/output data. The learning method works similarly to that of neural networks.

Modeling theory and praxis have proven that approximation error cannot be the only criterion for finding a "best" model. It is theoretically possible to formulate a model that fits any given (finite) learning data set with very high accuracy – according to the rule "the more complicated the model is, the more accurately it will fit the given data." For noisy data, this means that, at a certain point in modeling, the model begins to fit the noise (overfitting), which results in poor performance on new data.

Although overfitting is less potent danger in fuzzy modeling (the parameters of fuzzy systems have physical meaning that serves the same purpose as regularization in neural networks), approximation error still does not provide full information about the “goodness” of the model, because the linguistic properties of fuzzy systems (such as interpretability) and accuracy, are generally contradictory requirements.

In present work we have extended the neuro-fuzzy approach onto Mamdani fuzzy systems in order to minimize the gap between interpretability and accuracy in fuzzy modeling.

References

1. Nomura, H., Hayashi, I., Wakami, M. (1992) A learning method of fuzzy inference by descent method. Proc. 1st IEEE Int. Conf. on Fuzzy Systems, pp. 485-491, San Diego, CA, USA.
2. Guely F., Siarry, P. (1993) Gradient descent method for optimizing various fuzzy rule bases. Proc. 2nd IEEE Int. Conf. Fuzzy Syst., pp. 1241-46, San Francisco, CA, USA.
3. Jang, J.-S.R. (1993) ANFIS: Adaptive-network-based fuzzy inference system. IEEE Trans. Systems, Man and Cybernetics, **23**(3), 665-685.
4. Valente de Oliveira, J. (1999) Semantic constraints for membership function optimization. IEEE Trans. Systems, Man and Cybernetics Part A, **29**(1), 128-138,
5. Jager, R. (1995) Fuzzy Logic in Control. Ph.D. dissertation. Technical University of Delft, Delft, Holland.
6. Abonyi, J., Nagy, L., Szeifert, F. (1998) Indirect Model Based Control Using Fuzzy Model Inversion. Proc. IEEE Int. Conf. Intelligent Syst., pp. 951-956, Vienna, Austria.
7. Abonyi, J., Andersen, H. et al. (1999) Inverse fuzzy-process-model based direct adaptive control. Mathematics and Computers in Simulation, **51**(1-2), 119-132.
8. Riid, A., Rüstern, E. (2000) Transparent fuzzy systems and modeling with transparency protection. Proc. IFAC Symp. on Artificial Intelligence in Real Time Control, pp. 229-234. Budapest, Hungary.
9. Riid, A. (2002) Transparent Fuzzy Systems: Modeling and Control. Ph. D. dissertation. Tallinn Technical University, Tallinn, Estonia.
10. Jang, J.-S. R., Sun, C.-T., Mizutani, E. (1997) Neuro-Fuzzy and Soft Computing. Prentice Hall.

A Neural Network Equivalent to a Neuro-Fuzzy System for Classification

Danuta Rutkowska

Department of Computer Engineering, Technical University of Częstochowa, Armii Krajowej 36, 42-200 Częstochowa, Poland

Summary. The paper presents a neural network that is equivalent to a connectionist neuro-fuzzy system designed for classification problems. The neural network is a single-layer network that contains classical neurons with a specific activation function. The weights of the linear part of the neurons as well as the nonlinear functions have an interpretation related to the corresponding neuro-fuzzy system. Examples of classification problems solved by means of this network are illustrated.

Keywords. Neural networks, neuro-fuzzy systems, classification

1 Introduction

Neural networks are widely used as classifiers; see e.g. [5]. However, neural networks work as a "black box", which means that they produce classification results but do not explain their performance. Thus, we do not know the rules of classification. Neural network weights have no physical interpretation.

Fuzzy and neuro-fuzzy systems can also be employed in order to solve classification problems; see e.g. [4]. The systems of this kind are rule-based systems that realize fuzzy IF-THEN rules.

In this paper, it is shown that a neuro-fuzzy classifier which satisfies some assumptions is equivalent to a classical single-layer neural network. It is worth emphasizing that this neural network represents and realizes fuzzy IF-THEN rules for classification. The weights of this network have an interpretation with regard to membership functions of fuzzy sets applied in the fuzzy rules.

Results of classification examples illustrate that the assumptions required to obtain the equivalent neural network are easy to fulfill.

2 A neuro-fuzzy classifier

A neuro-fuzzy system for classification can be presented in the form of the connectionist network shown in Fig.1.

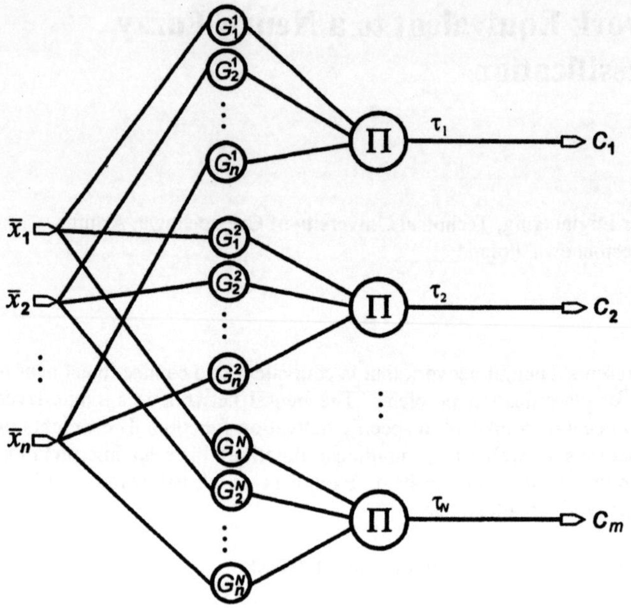

Fig.1. A neuro-fuzzy system for classification

The classifier illustrated in Fig.1 reflects the following fuzzy classification rules:

$$R^{(k)}: \textbf{IF} \quad x_1 \text{ is } G_1^k \quad \text{AND} \ \ldots \ \text{AND} \quad x_n \text{ is } G_n^k \quad \textbf{THEN} \quad \mathbf{x} \in c_l \tag{1}$$

where $\mathbf{x} = [x_1, \ldots, x_n]^T$, and x_i, for $i = 1, \ldots, n$, are linguistic variables, c_l, for $l = 1, \ldots, m$, are classes, N denotes the number of rules $R^{(k)}$, for $k = 1, \ldots, N$.

In Fig.1 each rule is associated with one class. It is easy to notice that $m \leq N$. Thus, more than one rule can be assigned to the same class.

The crisp input values, presented in Fig.1, constitute the input vector $\bar{\mathbf{x}} = [\bar{x}_1, \ldots, \bar{x}_n]^T$. The output values, τ_k, for $k = 1, \ldots, N$, represent degrees of rule activation (see, e.g. [4]), expressed as follows:

$$\tau_k = \prod_{i=1}^{n} G_i^k(\bar{x}_i) \tag{2}$$

where

$$G_i^k(x_i) = \exp\left[-\left(\frac{x_i - \overline{x}_i^k}{\sigma_i^k}\right)^2\right] \tag{3}$$

is the Gaussian membership function, characterized by the center and width parameters, $\overline{x}_i^k$ and σ_i^k, respectively.

The neuro-fuzzy network portrayed in Fig.1 performs a classification task based on the values of τ_k, for $k = 1,\ldots,N$. Each input vector $\overline{\mathbf{x}} = [\overline{x}_1,\ldots,\overline{x}_n]^T$ is classified to the class c_l (where $l = 1,\ldots,m$), which is associated with the maximal degree of rule activation, that is $\max_k \{\tau_k\}$.

3 Assumptions

Let us assume that the width parameter, σ_i^k, of the Gaussian membership function defined by Equation (3), is the same for each $i = 1,\ldots,n$, which means that

$$\sigma_i^k = \sigma^k \tag{4}$$

for $k = 1,\ldots,N$.

In addition, let us consider normalized vectors $\overline{\mathbf{x}} = [\overline{x}_1,\ldots,\overline{x}_n]^T$ and $\overline{\mathbf{x}}^k = [\overline{x}_1^k,\ldots,\overline{x}_n^k]^T$. In this case

$$|\overline{\mathbf{x}}| = \sqrt{\sum_{i=1}^{n} (\overline{x}_i)^2} = 1 \tag{5}$$

and

$$\left|\overline{\mathbf{x}}^k\right| = \sqrt{\sum_{i=1}^{n} \left(\overline{x}_i^k\right)^2} = 1 \tag{6}$$

It will be shown in the next section that the neuro-fuzzy classifier illustrated in Fig.1 can be presented in the form of classical neural network if the assumptions (4)-(6) are fulfilled.

4 The neural network equivalent to the neuro-fuzzy classifier

The neuro-fuzzy classifier portrayed in Fig.1 is mathematically described by Equation (2). If assumption (4) is satisfied, the degree of rule activation, τ_k, for $k = 1,\ldots,N$, can be expressed based on Equations (2) and (3) as follows:

$$\tau_k = \prod_{i=1}^{n} \exp\left[-\left(\frac{\bar{x}_i - \bar{x}_i^k}{\sigma^k}\right)^2\right] \tag{7}$$

It is obvious that Equation (7) can be rewrite in the following way

$$\tau_k = \exp\left\{\sum_{i=1}^{n}\left[-\left(\frac{\bar{x}_l - \bar{x}_l^k}{\sigma^k}\right)^2\right]\right\} \tag{8}$$

and subsequently as:

$$\tau_k = \exp\left\{-\frac{1}{\left(\sigma^k\right)^2}\left[\sum_{i=1}^{n}(\bar{x}_i)^2 - 2\sum_{i=1}^{n}\bar{x}_i\bar{x}_i^k + \sum_{i=1}^{n}\left(\bar{x}_i^k\right)^2\right]\right\} \tag{9}$$

If assumptions (5) and (6) are fulfilled, then Equation (9) takes the form:

$$\tau_k = \exp\left\{-\frac{2}{\left(\sigma^k\right)^2}\left[1 - \sum_{i=1}^{n}\bar{x}_i\bar{x}_i^k\right]\right\} \tag{10}$$

which is a mathematical description of the network presented in Fig.2, where

$$w_i^k = \bar{x}_i^k h^k, \qquad w_0^k = -h^k$$

and

$$h^k = 2/\left(\sigma^k\right)^2$$

The network shown in Fig.2 is a classical single-layer neural network. However, the nonlinear function, which is usually the sigmoidal function in neural networks, in this case is the exponential function, $f(x) = \exp(x)$.

A similar network, but supplemented by an additional layer to perform a defuzzification operation, is considered in [2].

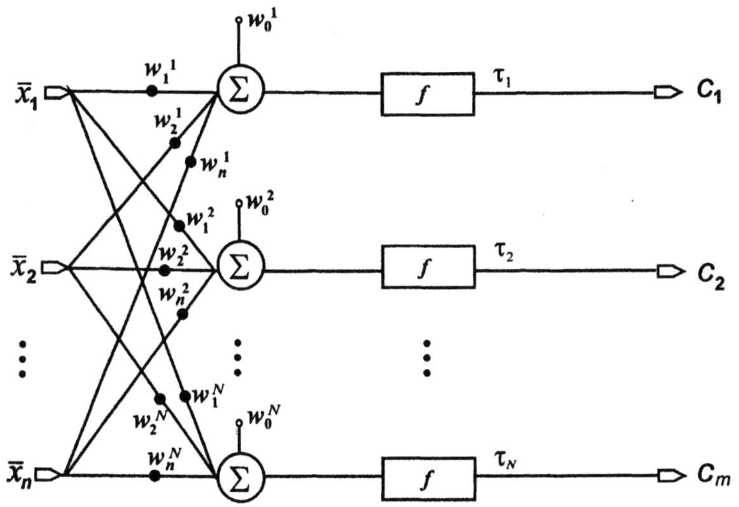

Fig.2. The neural network equivalent to the neuro-fuzzy classifier

5 Classification examples

The well-known IRIS classification problem [1] has been solved by use of the network proposed in this paper. The data were normalized, so assumption (5) was satisfied. At first, the network was composed of three neurons representing 3 rules (one rule for each class of iris species: Sestosa, Versicolor, and Virginica). The vectors of centers were also normalized according to assumption (6). The centers were determined as the centers of the ranges of the labeled data (normalized) associated to each class. The width parameters of the membership function (3) were chosen as equal to the half of the ranges. In order to fulfill assumption (4), the maximum of those values were taken as the width parameter.

The IRIS data set includes 150 data items (50 for each class) which contain measurements of four features of the iris flowers: sepal length, sepal width, petal length, petal width. Thus, the network with 4 inputs was employed.

The network composed of 3 neurons performed the classification with several mistakes. Thus, the network architecture was extended to include more neurons which realized additional rules formulated based on the mistakes. The membership functions of the fuzzy sets applied in these rules were characterized by very small width parameters. The center parameters were the same as the components of the input vectors which caused the misclassifications. In this way, the network containing 9 neurons was created. This network performed the IRIS classification task without any mistakes.

Let us notice that using the method described above, in order to determine the parameters of the membership functions, we find the weights of the network without applying a learning algorithm usually employed to neural networks.

Similarly, the weights can be chosen for other classification problems, for example medical diagnosis tasks. However, the network usually contain more neurons. The network composed of 16 neurons can solve (without any mistake) the problem of two-class diagnosis (positive and negative) of tumor in the mucous membrane of the uterus [4]. The classification is performed based on the data containing records of 9 attributes for 65 women (52 sick and 13 healthy).

Of course, it is possible to use a classical learning method. However, in this case it is necessary to split the data into learning and testing sequences.

6 Conclusions

The single-layer neural network, proposed in this paper for classification, has the following features:

- Each neuron represents one fuzzy IF-THEN rule
- The number of neurons equals to the number of rules in the rule base
- Weights of the neurons have an interpretation concerning parameters of the membership functions of the corresponding neuro-fuzzy system
- It is easy to modify the network architecture when a rule is added or removed (by addition or removal, respectively, the neuron that represents this rule)

Thus, in contrast to classical neural networks, the network proposed in this paper does not work as a "black box". This network is a rule-based neural network.

Single-layer neural networks can contain many neurons, so it is no problem to increase the number of rules in order to achieve better performance of the classifier. In this way, it is easy to incorporate a learning from mistakes [3], by formulating new rules to avoid the mistakes. This method was applied in the classification problems depicted in Section 5.

It is worth emphasizing that, in contrast to classical learning of neural networks, the method proposed in this paper allows the network to work without mistakes (based on the data set) and do not lose its generalization ability.

References

1. Fisher R.A. (1936) The use of multiple measurements in taxonomic problems, Ann. Eugenics, 7, 179-188.
2. Rutkowska D. (2000) Neural network architecture of fuzzy systems, In: Hampel R., Wagenknecht M., Chaker N. (eds.), Fuzzy Control Theory and Practice, Physica-Verlag, Springer-Verlag, Heidelberg, New York, 277-286.
3. Rutkowska D., Starczewski A. (2001) A neuro-fuzzy classifier that can learn from mistakes, Proc. 10th International Conference on System-Modelling-Control, Zakopane, Poland, 189-194.
4. Rutkowska D. (2002) Neuro-Fuzzy Architectures and Hybrid Learning, Physica-Verlag, Springer-Verlag, Heidelberg, New York.
5. Żurada J. M. (1992) Introduction to Artificial Neural Systems, West Publishing Company, New York.

Compromise Weighted Neuro - Fuzzy Systems

Leszek Rutkowski, Krzysztof Cpałka

Technical University of Częstochowa, Department of Computer Engineering
Al. Armii Krajowej 36, 42 – 200 Częstochowa, Poland

Summary. In the paper we present new neuro – fuzzy systems. They are called the AND–type fuzzy inference systems (NFIS). Based on the input – output data we learn not only parameters of membership functions but also a type of the systems and aggregating parameters. We propose the weighted T-norm and S-norm to neuro – fuzzy inference systems.

1. Introduction

In the literature two approaches have been proposed to design neuro – fuzzy systems. The first approach, called Mamdani method, uses "engineering implications" for inference (see Mendel [2]) and disjunction to aggregate individual rules. In the Mamdani approach the most widely used operators measuring the truth of the relation between input and output are the following:

$$I(a,b) = T\{a,b\} \overset{e.g.}{=} \min\{a,b\} \tag{1}$$

The aggregation is performed by an application of S-norm:

$$S\{a_1, a_2, \ldots, a_n\} = S\{\mathbf{a}\} = a_1 \overset{S}{*} a_2 \overset{S}{*} \ldots \overset{S}{*} a_n = \overset{n}{\underset{i=1}{S}}\{a_i\} \overset{e.g.}{=} \max_{i=1,\ldots,n}\{a_i\} \tag{2}$$

The other paradigm applies fuzzy implications for inference and conjunction for aggregation. For example we use an S-implication:

$$I(a,b) = S\{1-a,b\} \overset{e.g.}{=} \max\{1-a,b\} \tag{3}$$

For NFIS with a logical implication the aggregation is realized by a T-norm:

$$T\{a_1, a_2, \ldots, a_n\} = T\{\mathbf{a}\} = a_1 \overset{T}{*} a_2 \overset{T}{*} \ldots \overset{T}{*} a_n = \overset{n}{\underset{i=1}{T}}\{a_i\} \overset{e.g.}{=} \min_{i=1,\ldots,n}\{a_i\} \tag{4}$$

It should be noted that the aggregation of antecedents in each rule is performed by the same formula (4) for both Mamdani and logical – type systems. Various structures of NFIS are discussed in [3] and [4].

In this paper we propose a new class of neuro – fuzzy inference systems characterized by automatic determination of a fuzzy inference (Mamdani / logical and disjunction / conjunction) in the process of learning. Consequently, the structure of the system is determined in the process of learning. We refer to this class as to AND-type fuzzy systems.

Moreover we introduce softness, weights and parameterised families of triangular norms to AND-type neuro – fuzzy inference systems.

2. Flexibility in NFIS

2.1. NFIS realized by compromise implication

Following by Yager and Filev [7] we propose a compromise fuzzy implication given by:

$$I(a,b) = N(\lambda)T\{a,b\} + \lambda S\{N(a),b\} \tag{5}$$

where $\lambda \in [0,1]$, $N(\lambda) = 1-\lambda$, and based on implication (5) we derive a compromise neuro – fuzzy system. It includes Mamdani – type, logical – type, more Mamdani – type than logical – type and more logical - type than Mamdani – type fuzzy inference systems. Moreover, the parameter λ, determining a type of the system, can be found in the process of learning.

2.2 NFIS realized by soft T–norms and S–norms

The soft versions of operators (4) and (2) have been proposed by Yager and Filev [7]. They are defined as follows:

$$\tilde{T}\{\mathbf{a};\alpha\} = (1-\alpha)\frac{1}{n}\sum_{i=1}^{n} a_i + \alpha T\{\mathbf{a}\} = N(\alpha)\text{avg}(\mathbf{a}) + \alpha T\{\mathbf{a}\} \tag{6}$$

and

$$\tilde{S}\{\mathbf{a};\alpha\} = (1-\alpha)\frac{1}{n}\sum_{i=1}^{n} a_i + \alpha S\{\mathbf{a}\} = N(\alpha)\text{avg}(\mathbf{a}) + \alpha S\{\mathbf{a}\} \tag{7}$$

where $\alpha \in [0,1]$. In the same spirit we define softening of "engineering implication" (1) and logical "fuzzy implication" (3).

2.3. NFIS realized by parameterised families of T–norms and S–norms

Most fuzzy inference structures studied in the literature employ Mamadani, product, Łukasiewicz or drastic triangular norms. In this paper we apply the Dombi family [1] of the parameterised triangular norms:

$$\vec{T}_D\{\mathbf{a};p\} = \left(1 + \left(\sum_{i=1}^{n}\left(\frac{1-a_i}{a_i}\right)^p\right)^{\frac{1}{p}}\right)^{-1} \tag{8}$$

$$\vec{S}_D\{\mathbf{a};p\} = 1 - \left(1 + \left(\sum_{i=1}^{n}\left(\frac{a_i}{1-a_i}\right)^p\right)^{\frac{1}{p}}\right)^{-1} \tag{9}$$

where $\vec{T}_D, \vec{S}_D$ stands for the T-norm and S-norm of a Dombi family parameterised by $p \in [0, \infty)$. The parameter p can be found in the process of learning. Obviously formula (8) defines the "engineering implication". Combining (9) and (3) we get the fuzzy S-implication generated by the Dombi family.

2.4. NFIS realized by T-norms and S-norms with weighted arguments

We propose the weighted T-norm:

$$T^*\{a_1, a_2; w_1, w_2\} = T\{1 - w_1(1 - a_1), 1 - w_2(1 - a_2)\} \tag{10}$$

For a moment we interpret parameters a_1 and a_2 as antecedents of a rule. The weights w_1 and w_2 are corresponding credibilities of the both antecedents. Observe that:

$$T^*\{a_1, a_2; 1, 1\} = T\{a_1, a_2\} \tag{11}$$

and

$$T^*\{a_1, a_2; 0, w_2\} = T\{1, 1 - w_2(1 - a_2)\} = 1 - w_2(1 - a_2) \tag{12}$$

The S-norm corresponding to the T-norm (10) is defined as follows:

$$S^*\{a_1, a_2; w_1, w_2\} = S\{w_1 a_1, w_2 a_2\} \tag{13}$$

The weights w_1 and w_2 can be found in the process of learning subject to the constraint $w_1, w_2 \in [0,1]$. One may apply the weighted T-norm for selection of significant inputs.

3. Compromise weighted NFIS

In this paper, we consider multi - input, single - output NFIS mapping $\mathbf{X} \to \mathbf{Y}$, where $\mathbf{X} \subset \mathbf{R}^n$ and $\mathbf{Y} \subset \mathbf{R}$.

The fuzzifier performs a mapping from the observed crisp input space $\mathbf{X} \subset \mathbf{R}^n$ to the fuzzy sets defined in $\mathbf{Y}$. The most commonly used fuzzifier is the singleton fuzzifier which maps $\bar{\mathbf{x}} = [\bar{x}_1, \ldots, \bar{x}_n] \in \mathbf{X}$ into a fuzzy set $A' \subset \mathbf{X}$ characterized by the membership function:

$$\mu_{A'}(\mathbf{x}) = \begin{cases} 1 & \text{if} \quad \mathbf{x} = \bar{\mathbf{x}} \\ 0 & \text{if} \quad \mathbf{x} \neq \bar{\mathbf{x}} \end{cases} \tag{14}$$

The fuzzy rule base consists of a collection of N fuzzy IF - THEN rules in the form:

$$R^{(k)}: \text{IF } \mathbf{x} \text{ is } A^k \text{ THEN } y \text{ is } B^k \tag{15}$$

where $\mathbf{x} = [x_1, \ldots, x_n] \in \mathbf{X}$, $y \in \mathbf{Y}$, $A_1^k, A_2^k, \ldots, A_n^k$ are fuzzy sets characterized by membership functions $\mu_{A_i^k}(x_i)$, whereas B^k are fuzzy sets characterized by membership functions $\mu_{B^k}(y)$, respectively, $k = 1, \ldots, N$.

The fuzzy inference determines a mapping from the fuzzy sets in the input space $\mathbf{X}$ to the fuzzy sets in the output space $\mathbf{Y}$. Each of N rules (15) determines a fuzzy set $\overline{B}^k \subset \mathbf{Y}$ given by the compositional rule of inference:

$$\overline{B}^k = A' \circ \left(A^k \to B^k\right) \tag{16}$$

where $A^k = A_1^k \times A_2^k \times \ldots \times A_n^k$.

Fuzzy sets $\overline{B}^k$, according to the formula (16), are characterized by membership functions expressed by the sup-star composition:

$$\mu_{\overline{B}^k}(y) = \sup_{\mathbf{x} \in \mathbf{X}} \left\{ \mu_{A'}(\mathbf{x}) * \mu_{A_1^k \times .. \times A_n^k \to B^k}(\mathbf{x}, y) \right\} \tag{17}$$

where $*$ can be any operator in the class of T-norms. It is easily seen that for a crisp input $\overline{\mathbf{x}} \in \mathbf{X}$, i.e. a singleton fuzzifier (14), formula (17) becomes:

$$\mu_{\overline{B}^k}(y) = \mu_{A_1^k \times .. \times A_n^k \to B^k}(\overline{\mathbf{x}}, y) = I\left(\mu_{A^k}(\overline{\mathbf{x}}), \mu_{B^k}(y)\right) \tag{18}$$

where $I(\cdot)$ is an "engineering implication" or fuzzy implication.

The aggregation operator, applied in order to obtain the fuzzy set B' based on fuzzy sets $\overline{B}^k$, is the T-norm or S-norm operator, depending on the type of fuzzy implication.

The defuzzifier performs a mapping from a fuzzy set B' to a crisp point $\overline{y}$ in $\mathbf{Y} \subset \mathbf{R}$. The COA (centre of area) method is defined by following formula:

$$\overline{y} = \frac{\int_{\mathbf{Y}} y \mu_{B'}(y) dy}{\int_{\mathbf{Y}} \mu_{B'}(y) dy} \quad \text{or by} \quad \overline{y} = \frac{\sum_{r=1}^{N} \overline{y}^r \cdot \mu_{B'}(\overline{y}^r)}{\sum_{r=1}^{N} \mu_{B'}(\overline{y}^r)} \tag{19}$$

in the discrete form, where $\overline{y}^r$ denotes centres of the membership functions $\mu_{B^r}(y)$, i.e. for $r = 1, \ldots, N$:

$$\mu_{B^r}(\overline{y}^r) = \max_{y \in \mathbf{Y}} \left\{ \mu_{B^r}(y) \right\} \tag{20}$$

For other definitions of defuzzifier the reader is referred to [2].

Now we propose new structure of NFIS. The novel system is characterized by:

- soft strength of firing controlled by parameter α^{τ},
- soft implication controlled by parameter α^{I},
- soft aggregation of the rules controlled by parameter α^{agr},
- weights in antecedents of the rules $w_{i,k}^{\tau} \in [0,1]$, $i = 1, \ldots, n$, $k = 1, \ldots, N$,
- weights in aggregation of the rules $w_k^{\text{agr}} \in [0,1]$, $k = 1, \ldots, N$.

Moreover we assume that fuzzy norms in connection of antecedents, implication and aggregation are parameterised by parameters p^{τ}, p^{I}, p^{agr} respectively. The weighted soft NFIS of the AND-type is presented below:

$$\tau_k(\bar{\mathbf{x}}) = \left(\begin{array}{c} (1-\alpha^{\tau})\text{avg}\left(\mu_{A_1^k}(\bar{x}_1),\ldots,\mu_{A_n^k}(\bar{x}_n)\right) + \\ +\alpha^{\tau}\vec{T}^{*}\left(\mu_{A_1^k}(\bar{x}_1),\ldots,\mu_{A_n^k}(\bar{x}_n)\ ; w_{1,k}^{\tau},\ldots,w_{n,k}^{\tau}, p^{\tau}\right) \end{array} \right) \tag{21}$$

$$I_{k,r}(\bar{\mathbf{x}},\bar{y}^r) = \left(\begin{array}{c} (1-\alpha^{I})\text{avg}\left(\tilde{N}_{1-\lambda}(\tau_k(\bar{\mathbf{x}})), \mu_{B^k}(\bar{y}^r)\right) + \\ +\alpha^{I} \left(\begin{array}{c} (1-\lambda)\vec{T}\left(\tau_k(\bar{\mathbf{x}}), \mu_{B^k}(\bar{y}^r)\ ; p^{I}\right) + \\ +\lambda\vec{S}\left(1-\tau_k(\bar{\mathbf{x}}), \mu_{B^k}(\bar{y}^r)\ ; p^{I}\right) \end{array} \right) \end{array} \right) \tag{22}$$

$$\text{agr}_r(\bar{\mathbf{x}},\bar{y}^r) = \left(\begin{array}{c} (1-\alpha^{\text{agr}})\text{avg}\left(I_{1,r}(\bar{\mathbf{x}},\bar{y}^r),\ldots,I_{N,r}(\bar{\mathbf{x}},\bar{y}^r)\right) + \\ +\alpha^{\text{agr}} \left(\begin{array}{c} (1-\lambda)\vec{S}^{*}\left(I_{1,r}(\bar{\mathbf{x}},\bar{y}^r),\ldots,I_{N,r}(\bar{\mathbf{x}},\bar{y}^r)\ ; w_1^{\text{agr}},\ldots,w_N^{\text{agr}}, p^{\text{agr}}\right) + \\ +\lambda\vec{T}^{*}\left(I_{1,r}(\bar{\mathbf{x}},\bar{y}^r),\ldots,I_{N,r}(\bar{\mathbf{x}},\bar{y}^r)\ ; w_1^{\text{agr}},\ldots,w_N^{\text{agr}}, p^{\text{agr}}\right) \end{array} \right) \end{array} \right) \tag{23}$$

$$\bar{y} = \frac{\sum_{r=1}^{N} \bar{y}^r \cdot \text{agr}_r(\bar{\mathbf{x}},\bar{y}^r)}{\sum_{r=1}^{N} \text{agr}_r(\bar{\mathbf{x}},\bar{y}^r)} \tag{24}$$

Compromise operator in formula (22) is defined as follows:

$$\begin{aligned} \tilde{N}_{\nu}(a) &= (1-\nu)N(a) + \nu N(N(a)) \\ &= (1-\nu)N(a) + \nu a \end{aligned} \tag{25}$$

where $\nu \in [0,1]$, for details see [5].

4. Simulation results

Compromise Weighted NFIS, described by formulas (21) - (24), is simulated on *Human Operation at a Chemical Plant* problem [6].

We deal with a model of an operator's control of a chemical plant. The plant produces a polymer by the polymerisation of some monomers. Since the start-up of the plant is very complicated, a men has to make the manual operation at the plant. The 3 continuous attributes are available for control: monomer concentration, change of monomer concentration and monomer flow rate. We used the compromise weighted NFIS with probabilistic (experiment 1 and 2, see Table 1) and Dombi (experiment 3 and 4, see Table 1) triangular norms, Gaussian membership functions and four rules.

In the learning process the parameter λ reached the value equal 0 and the system become of a Mamdani type. The performance of the control system was

0.0063. The results of the simulations are summarized in Table 1. The values of weights after learning process reflects Fig. 1.

Table 1. Experimental results

Experiment number	Name of flexibility parameter	Initial values	Final values after learning	RMSE (learning sequence)
1	ν	0.5	0.0000	0.0079
2	ν	1	-	0.0170
3	ν	0.5	0.0000	0.0068
	p^{τ}	10	9.2563	
	p^{I}	10	9.9971	
	p^{agr}	10	9.8426	
	α^{τ}	1	0.9523	
	α^{I}	1	0.9826	
	α^{agr}	1	0.9717	
4	ν	0.5	0.0000	0.0063
	p^{τ}	10	9.3821	
	p^{I}	10	9.9935	
	p^{agr}	10	9.7992	
	α^{τ}	1	0.9416	
	α^{I}	1	0.9901	
	α^{agr}	1	0.9658	
	$\mathbf{w}^{\tau}$	1	Fig. 1	
	$\mathbf{w}^{agr}$	1	Fig. 1	

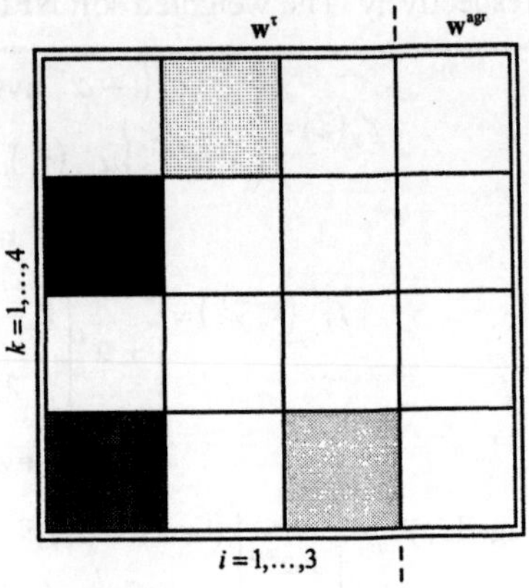

Fig. 1. Weights representation in the chemical plant problem $w_{i,k}^{\tau} \in [0,1]$, $w_{k}^{agr} \in [0,1]$, $i=1,\dots,3$, $k=1,\dots,4$ (dark areas correspond to low values and vice versa)

References

[1] E. P. Klement, R. Mesiar, E. Pap, *Triangular Norms*, Kluwer Academic Publishers, Netherlands 2000.

[2] J. M. Mendel, *Uncertain Rule-Based Fuzzy Logic Systems: Introduction and New Directions*, Prentice Hall PTR, Upper Saddle River, NJ, 2001.

[3] D. Rutkowska, *Neuro – Fuzzy Architectures and Hybrid Learning*, Springer-Verlag 2001.

[4] L. Rutkowski, *New Soft – Computing Techniques For System Modelling, Pattern Classification and Image Processing*, Springer (to be published).

[5] L. Rutkowski, K. Cpałka, "A General Approach to Neuro - Fuzzy Systems", *The 10th IEEE International Conference on Fuzzy Systems*, Melbourne 2001.

[6] T. Takagi and M. Sugeno, "Fuzzy identification of systems and its application to modelling and control," *IEEE Trans. Syst., Man, Cybern.*, vol. 15, pp. 116-132, 1985.

[7] R. R. Yager, D. P. Filev, *Essentials of Fuzzy Modeling and Control*, John Wiley&Sons, 1994.

A Fuzzy Relational System with Linguistic Antecedent Certainty Factors

Rafał Scherer and Leszek Rutkowski

Department of Computer Engineering
Częstochowa University of Technology
Al. Armii Krajowej 36, 42-200 Częstochowa, Poland
rscherer@kik.pcz.czest.pl, lrutko@kik.pcz.czest.pl

Abstract In this paper, we describe a new relational fuzzy system with linguistic antecedent certainty factors. This is achieved thanks to fuzzy sets placed in a relation matrix linking antecedent and consequent fuzzy sets. Expert uncertainty about antecedent fuzzy linguistic values, now can be expressed in the form of linguistic values, e.g. *roughly, more or less*. Some numerical simulations of the new fuzzy model are also given.

1 Introduction

The power of fuzzy systems stems from their ability to process natural language expressions. We can model nearly any term using different shapes of fuzzy sets and various modifiers, i.e. fuzzy hedges. They transform original fuzzy linguistic values (primary terms e.g. *small, big*) into new, more specific fuzzy sets like *very fast* or *quite slow flow*. Thanks to them, we can make expert statements more precise. The concept of fuzzy hedges is well established in the literature. In general, they can be divided into powered and shifted hedges. Powered hedges model adverbs e.g. *very* by powering membership functions, whereas shifted hedges model adverbs by moving points of membership functions.

In this paper, we present a different view on linguistic hedges. Instead of modifying antecedent or consequent linguistic values, we introduce additional fuzzy sets. In our approach (Section 3), we use a fuzzy relational system with linguistic values defined on a unitary interval. They are elements of a fuzzy relation matrix connecting antecedent or consequent linguistic values. Section 4 is concerned with the neuro-fuzzy structure of the new model, and finally numerical simulations of the system are provided in the Section 5.

2 Fuzzy Linguistic and Relational Systems

We consider a fuzzy system with the N-dimensional input $\mathbf{x}$, and a scalar output $y \in \mathrm{Y}$. We denote by A a collection of K linguistic terms A^k defined on $\mathrm{X} \in \mathbb{R}^N$, i.e.

$$A = \{A^1, A^2, \dots, A^K\} \tag{1}$$

having membership functions $\mu_{A^k}(\mathbf{x})$ for $k = 1, \dots, K$. Output variable y has a set of M linguistic values B^m, defined on $\mathrm{Y} \in \mathbb{R}$, i.e.

$$B = \{B^1, B^2, \dots, B^M\} \tag{2}$$

having membership functions $\mu_{B^m}(y)$ for $m = 1, \dots, M$. Sets (1) and (2) are related to each other to a certain degree by a $K \times M$ relation matrix $\mathbf{R}$. Having given vector $\overline{A}$ of K membership values $\mu_{A^k}(\overline{\mathbf{x}})$ for a crisp observed input value $\overline{\mathbf{x}}$, vector $\overline{B}$ of M crisp memberships μ_m is obtained through a fuzzy relational composition

$$\overline{B} = \overline{A} \circ \mathbf{R} \tag{3}$$

implemented element-wise by a generalized form of *sup-min* composition, i.e. *s-t* composition

$$\mu_m = \mathop{\mathrm{S}}_{k=1}^{K} \left[\mathrm{T}\left(\mu_{A^k}(\overline{\mathbf{x}}), r_{km}\right) \right] \tag{4}$$

The crisp output of the relational system is computed by the weighted mean

$$\overline{y} = \frac{\sum_{m=1}^{M} \left\{ \overline{y}^m \mathrm{S}_{k=1}^{K} \left[\mathrm{T}\left(\mu_{A^k}(\overline{\mathbf{x}}), r_{km}\right) \right] \right\}}{\sum_{m=1}^{M} \mathrm{S}_{k=1}^{K} \left[\mathrm{T}\left(\mu_{A^k}(\overline{\mathbf{x}}), r_{km}\right) \right]} \tag{5}$$

where $\overline{y}^m$ is the centre of gravity (centroid) of the fuzzy set B^m.

3 A New System with Fuzzy Certainty Factors

In this section, we propose a new fuzzy relational system by adding fuzzy sets to the relation matrix $\mathbf{R}$. In this case, the relation matrix contains fuzzy sets C_{km} defined on a unitary interval

$$\mathbf{R} = \begin{bmatrix} C_{11} & C_{11} & \cdots & C_{1M} \\ C_{21} & C_{22} & \cdots & C_{2M} \\ \vdots & \vdots & C_{km} & \vdots \\ C_{K1} & C_{K2} & \cdots & C_{KM} \end{bmatrix} \tag{6}$$

Then, if we define several fuzzy linguistic values on unitary interval (e.g. see Fig. 1), an expert can express his uncertainty concerning antecedent terms by a linguistic description. In SISO systems, or MISO systems with multidimensional antecedent fuzzy sets, the expert can define rules similar to the following exemplary ones

$$\begin{aligned} &R^1 : \text{IF } \mathbf{x} \text{ is exactly } A^1 \text{ THEN } y \text{ is } B^1 \\ &R^2 : \text{IF } \mathbf{x} \text{ is more or less } A^1 \text{ THEN } y \text{ is } B^2 \\ &R^3 : \text{IF } \mathbf{x} \text{ is roughly } A^1 \text{ THEN } y \text{ is } B^3 \end{aligned} \tag{7}$$

Rules (7) do not modify antecedent values. The membership degree of an antecedent fuzzy set is divided into several intervals by fuzzy sets C_{km}. Instead of defining many antecedent sets we use a smaller number of input fuzzy sets and several sets C_{km}. Every fuzzy set A^k has up to M defined linguistic values C_{km}. In Fig. 1 there is also the set *not at all*, which meaning is similar to the standard hedge *not*. It is activated when its input fuzzy set A^k is not active.

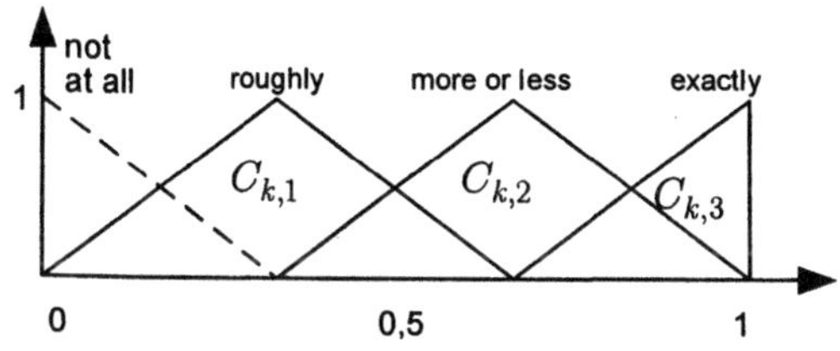

Fig. 1. Example of fuzzy linguistic values, expressing uncertainty in rule antecedents. The set *not at all* is optional, replacing standard hedge *not* in a rule antecedent.

The inference in this system is similar to the *sup-min* composition, but min operation is replaced by a membership degree $\mu_{C_{km}}(\tau^k)$, where τ^k is the membership degree of the k-th multivariate input fuzzy set. The vector of crisp memberships is obtained by

$$\mu_m = \mathop{S}_{k=1}^{K} \left[\mu_{C_{km}} \left(\mu_{A^k} (\overline{\mathbf{x}}) \right) \right]. \tag{8}$$

Eq. (8) reflects fuzzy hedge modifier operation. For example instead of quadratic function for concentration operation *very*, we use a fuzzy set *exactly* (Fig. 1). Interpretation and operation of the sets in Fig. 1 is different from standard linguistic hedges. For example, standard fuzzy hedge more or less dilates an input fuzzy set, whereas ours *roughly*, *more or less* divide membership degree range into several intervals.
The overall system output is also computed through a weighted average

$$\overline{y} = \frac{\sum_{m=1}^{M}\left\{\overline{y}^{m} \mathop{\mathrm{S}}_{k=1}^{K}\left[\mu_{C_{km}}\left(\mu_{A^k}\left(\overline{\mathbf{x}}\right)\right)\right]\right\}}{\sum_{m=1}^{M} \mathop{\mathrm{S}}_{k=1}^{K}\left[\mu_{C_{km}}\left(\mu_{A^k}\left(\overline{\mathbf{x}}\right)\right)\right]}. \tag{9}$$

Graphical inference (without defuzzification) in the new system is in Fig. 2. The example is based on rules (7).

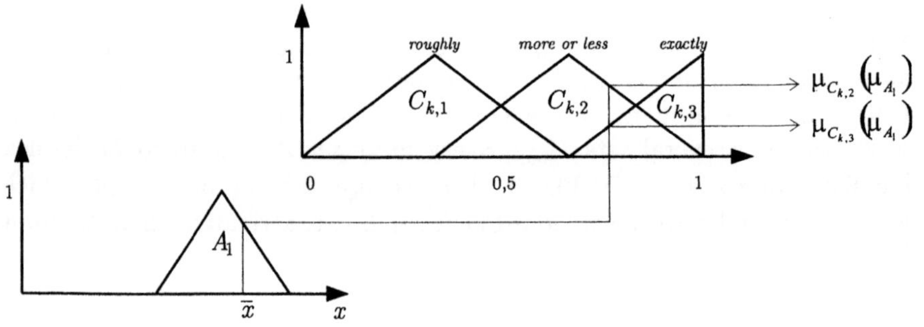

Fig. 2. Graphical inference of the new system on the basis of the exemplary rules (7).

4. Neuro-Fuzzy Structure of the New System

In this section we present (Fig. 3) the neuro-fuzzy structure of the new system. The first layer consists of K input multivariate fuzzy membership functions. The second layer is responsible for the composition of certainty values and membership values from the previous layer. Finally, the third layer defuzzifies M output values through the center average method. All parameters of the neuro-fuzzy system can be tuned by the backpropagation algorithm.

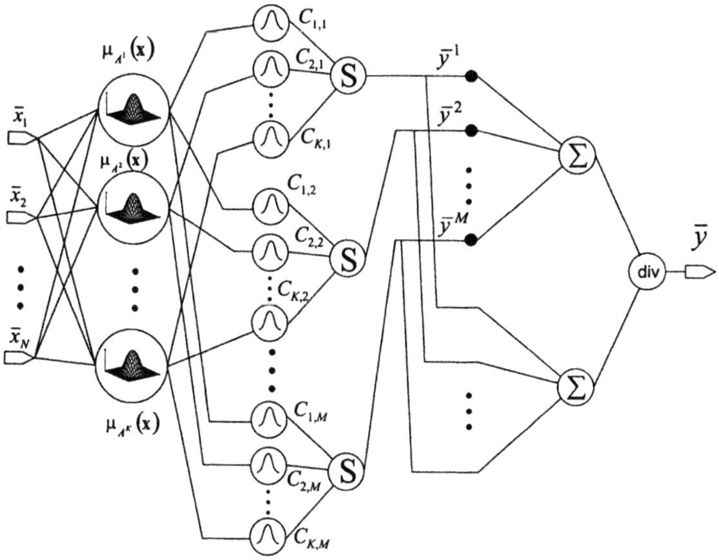

Fig. 3. The neuro-fuzzy structure of the relational system with fuzzy certainty degrees in antecedents

5 Numerical Simulations

In this section we test our systems on the well-known problem of a truck backer-upper nonlinear control [16]. The goal is to train a fuzzy model on a 282-element data set to park a truck. A fuzzy model generates the right steering angle of the truck on the basis of the truck position, expressed by an angle and a distance from the loading dock. We do not use distance from the truck and the loading dock, assuming that the truck always has enough space to park. The truck moves backward every time by a fixed distance.

As a reference point we used the Mamdani singleton rule-based fuzzy system with algebraic Cartesian product and 6 rules. The relational system had 6 multidimensional input Gaussian fuzzy sets, 3 output singleton fuzzy sets and 18 Gaussian sets in the relation R. Systems were trained only by the backpropagation algorithm, which changed input and output fuzzy set widths and centers and relation R elements. In case of relational systems with fuzzy certainty degrees, the widths of Gaussian fuzzy sets in relation R were fixed to 0.6. This value was picked by successive simulations to be the best. The systems were initialized randomly. Learning errors during training for all systems for 50,000 iterations are shown in Fig. 4 a) and b).

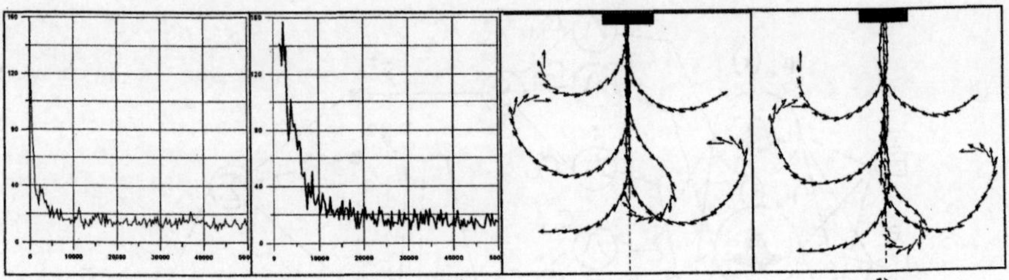

Fig. 4. Learning error for a) Mamdani system, b) relational system with fuzzy certainty degrees. Truck trajectories for c) Mamdani system, d) relational system with fuzzy certainty degrees.

Both systems give good steering trajectories. The relational system with fuzzy certainty degrees performs slightly worse, but paying this small price an expert can linguistically express his uncertainty for a given antecedent term.

6 Conclusions

We have proposed a new fuzzy model with fuzzy sets linking antecedent and consequent fuzzy sets. These linking fuzzy sets are elements of the relation. Thus, we can model descriptions like IF x is *roughly fast* THEN .... Our approach does not involve standard fuzzy hedges, so input and output linguistic values remain intact. This improves the transparency of the model.

Numerical simulations showed reliable behaviour of the new system. Its performance is comparable with the popular singleton model, but the new system allows expressing expert's uncertainty regarding input linguistic variables.

References

[1] Babuska R., Fuzzy Modeling For Control, Kluwer Academic Press, Boston, 1998.

[2] Branco P.J.C, Dente J.A., A Fuzzy Relational identification Algorithm and its Application to Predict the Behaviour of a Motor Drive System, *Fuzzy Sets and Systems*, vol. 109, pp. 343-354, 2000.

[3] Ischibuchi H., Nakashima T., "Effect of Rule Weights in Fuzzy Rule-Based Classification Systems", *IEEE Transactions on Fuzzy Systems*, vol. 9, no. 4, pp.506-515, 2001.

[4] Ishibuchi H. and T. Nakashima, "Effect of Rule Weights in Fuzzy Rule-Based Classification Systems", IEEE Transactions on Fuzzy Systems, vol. 9, no. 4, pp.506-515, 2001.
[5] Jager R., *Fuzzy Logic in Control,* Thesis Technische Universiteit Delft, 1995.
[6] Nauck D. and R. Kruse, "How the Learning of Rule Weights Affects the Interpretability of Fuzzy Systems", Proceedings of 1998 IEEE World Congress on Computational Intelligence, FUZZ-IEEE, Alaska pp. 1235-1240.
[7] Pedrycz W., *Fuzzy Control and Fuzzy Systems,* 2nd extended edition, John Wiley & Sons Inc., New York, Chichester, Toronto, Brisbane, Singapore 1993.
[8] Piegat A., "Fuzzy Modeling and Control", Physica Verlag, Heidelberg New York, 2001.
[9] Rutkowska D., Piliński M., Rutkowski L.: Neural Networks, Genetic Algorithms and Fuzzy Systems, PWN, Warsaw (1997)
[10] Setness M., Babuska R., Fuzzy Relational Classifier Trained by Fuzzy Clustering, IEEE Transactions on Systems, Man and Cybernetics – Part B: Cybernetics, Vol. 29, No. 5, October (1999)
[11] Wang L.-X., Adaptive Fuzzy Systems And Control, PTR Prentice Hall, Englewood Cliffs, New Jersey, 1994.

Interval Type 2 Neuro-Fuzzy Systems Based on Interval Consequents

Janusz Starczewski and Leszek Rutkowski

Częstochowa University of Technology, Department of Computer Engineering,
Al. Armii Krajowej 36, 42-200, Częstochowa, Poland

Abstract. There are several ways to synthesize fuzzy systems and neural networks. The so-called neuro-fuzzy systems exhibit advantages of both techniques, namely learning abilities of neural networks and natural language description of fuzzy systems. Recently the concept of type 2 fuzzy sets, i.e. fuzzy sets with fuzzy membership grades, was introduced to fuzzy inference systems. This paper presents a new neuro-fuzzy system of type 2 derived under the assumption that the rule antecedents are characterized by interval fuzzy membership grades and the consequents are intervals. An application for the checking of the driver's steering behaviors is given as an example.

1 Introduction

The idea of describing higher order of fuzziness was introduced by Zadeh [11]. His concept was to associate elements of fuzzy sets not with the precise membership grades but with their fuzzy membership grades. Therefore a fuzzy set of type 2 in the universe of discourse $X \subset R$ is defined as the following set of pairs $\{x, \mu_{\tilde{A}}(x)\}$ and denoted symbolically as

$$\widetilde{A} = \int_{x \in X} \mu_{\tilde{A}}(x) / x \tag{1}$$

where x is an element of the fuzzy set, and its fuzzy membership grade $\mu_{\tilde{A}}(x)$ is a fuzzy set of type 1, or more precisely the fuzzy subset of the unit interval $[0,1]$

$$\mu_{\tilde{A}}(x) = \int_{u \in [0,1]} f_x(u) / u \tag{2}$$

where f_x is called a secondary membership function.

Generally operations on type 2 fuzzy sets rely on the use of Zadeh's extension principle [11]. Depending on several assumptions, mainly as to the shapes of secondary MF, specific simplified operations may be found [1, 3, 5, 10].

This work concerns type 2 fuzzy sets with interval membership functions (MF), which are described by fuzzy membership grades of the following form

$$\mu_{\tilde{A}}(x) = \int_{u \in [0,1]} \begin{Bmatrix} 1 & \text{for } \hat{\mu}_A(x) \le u \le \breve{\mu}_A(x) \\ 0 & \text{otherwise} \end{Bmatrix} / u = \left[\hat{\mu}_A(x), \breve{\mu}_A(x)\right] \tag{3}$$

where $\hat{\mu}_A(x)$ and $\breve{\mu}_A(x)$ are lower and upper membership grades respectively.

In a fuzzy inference system (FIS) employing interval type 2 fuzzy sets we make use of smart intersection established on upper and lower bounds of fuzzy membership grades [11, 1, 4]. Namely if we assume an interval shape of the secondary MF, the intersection of sets may be facilitated by consideration of just two non-fuzzy functions: upper and lower MF. In this situation traditional T-norms compute separately upper and lower MF of the resultant type 2 fuzzy set

$$\begin{aligned} \breve{\mu}_B &= \mathop{\mathrm{T}}_{n=1}^{N} \breve{\mu}_{A_n}(x_n) \\ \hat{\mu}_B &= \mathop{\mathrm{T}}_{n=1}^{N} \hat{\mu}_{A_n}(x_n) \end{aligned} \tag{4}$$

In the sequel this will be used for computing the Cartesian product and in the inference rule.

2 Type 2 FIS Based on Interval Consequents

Generally the type 2 FIS may be considered as a weighted collection of several subsystems of type 1 [3]. Unfortunately the number of the embedded type 1 subsystems is strongly increasing with the dicretization density. Utilizing the interval character of secondary MF the interval model may consist of only two embedded subsystems and the output type reduction switching mechanizm [4, 10].

The quickest way to present the interval type 2 FIS based on interval consequents is to create a connectionist structure of the system as in Fig. 1, known as the neuro-fuzzy system. Note that if interval consequents are normal (i.e. are intervals in the domain of elements and equal to crisp one in the domain of memberships) every extended T-norm inference rule lead to this structure. Only activation degrees are computed according to T-norm formulas (4) for each rule k.

As we have mentioned the key to build a connectionist structure of type 2 FIS is an algorithm of simplified type reduction (Liang et.al.) [4]. This algorithm computes bounds of the rectangular type reduced set of type 1, which we call the maximal and the minimal intermediate outputs of the system.

1. calculate an initial average $y'_{\max}$ of consequents $\bar{y}^1_{\min}, \bar{y}^1_{\max}, \bar{y}^2_{\min}, \bar{y}^2_{\max}, \ldots, \bar{y}^K_{\min}, \bar{y}^K_{\max}$ weighted by their average activation degrees $\mu_{B^k} = \left(\breve{\mu}_{B^k} + \hat{\mu}_{B^k}\right)/2$; $k = 1,2,\ldots,K$
2. $\forall k = 1,\ldots,K$ if $\bar{y}^K_{\max} > y'_{\max} \Rightarrow \mu_{B^{k,\max}} = \breve{\mu}_{B^k}$, else $\mu_{B^{k,\max}} = \hat{\mu}_{B^k}$; if $\bar{y}^K_{\min} > y'_{\max} \Rightarrow \mu_{B^{k,\min}} = \breve{\mu}_{B^k}$, else $\mu_{B^{k,\min}} = \hat{\mu}_{B^k}$
3. find nearest $\bar{y}_{nrst} = \min\limits_{k=1,\ldots,K} \left(\bar{y}^k_{\max}, \bar{y}^k_{\min}\right) : \left\{\bar{y}^k_{\max} > y'_{\max}, \bar{y}^k_{\min} > y'_{\max}\right\}$

4. calculate an average $y'_{\max}$ as in step 1 using new weights $\mu_{B^k,\max}$ and $\mu_{B^k,\min}$
5. if $y'_{\max} \leq \overline{y}_{nrst} \Rightarrow$ the output is $y'_{\max}$, else go to step 2

The procedure obtaining minimal intermediate output proceeds according to the same algorithm when we change $y'_{\max}$ for $y'_{\min}$, the minimum operator in step 3 for the maximum, and when we reverse the direction of inequalities in step 2 and 3. Obtained intermediate outputs are actually bounds of the normal and rectangular type reduced set of type 1. Hence the defuzzification by the center of area method reduces to an average of intermediate outputs.

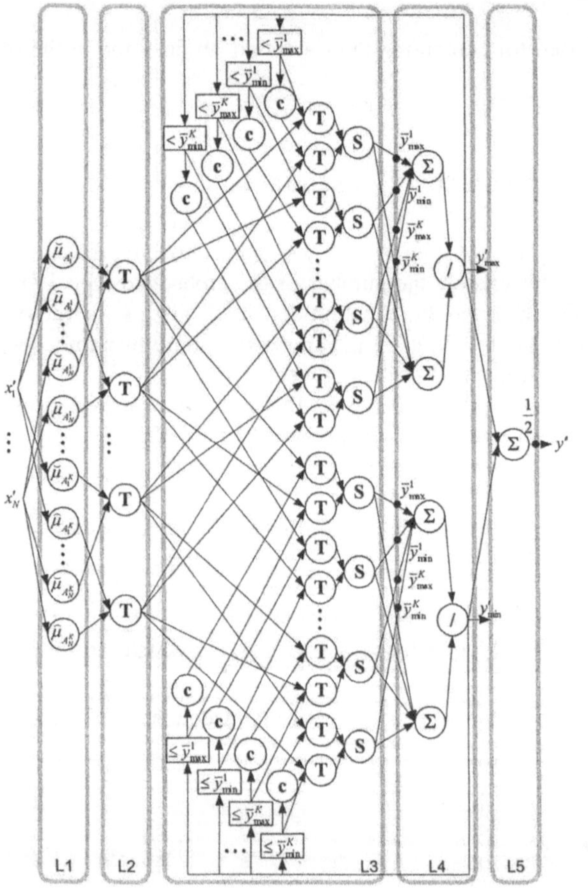

Fig. 1. Interval type 2 neuro-fuzzy system based on interval consequents. L1 layer calculates upper and lower grades of compatibilty between premises (singleton fuzzification is used) and antecedents. L2 layer realizes the Cartesian product and inferencing producing upper and lower membership grades of conclusions. L3 layer embodies two switches controlled by one-or-zero comparators. This layer switches between upper and lower memberships of conclusions in order to obtain the maximal and the minimal intermediate output values in the L4 layer according to the algortithm. L5 layer calculates the overall output as an average of intermediate outputs

A simple example of inferencing and the type reduction is presented in Fig. 2. The exemplary FIS realizes two inputs – one output mapping with the use of two rules.

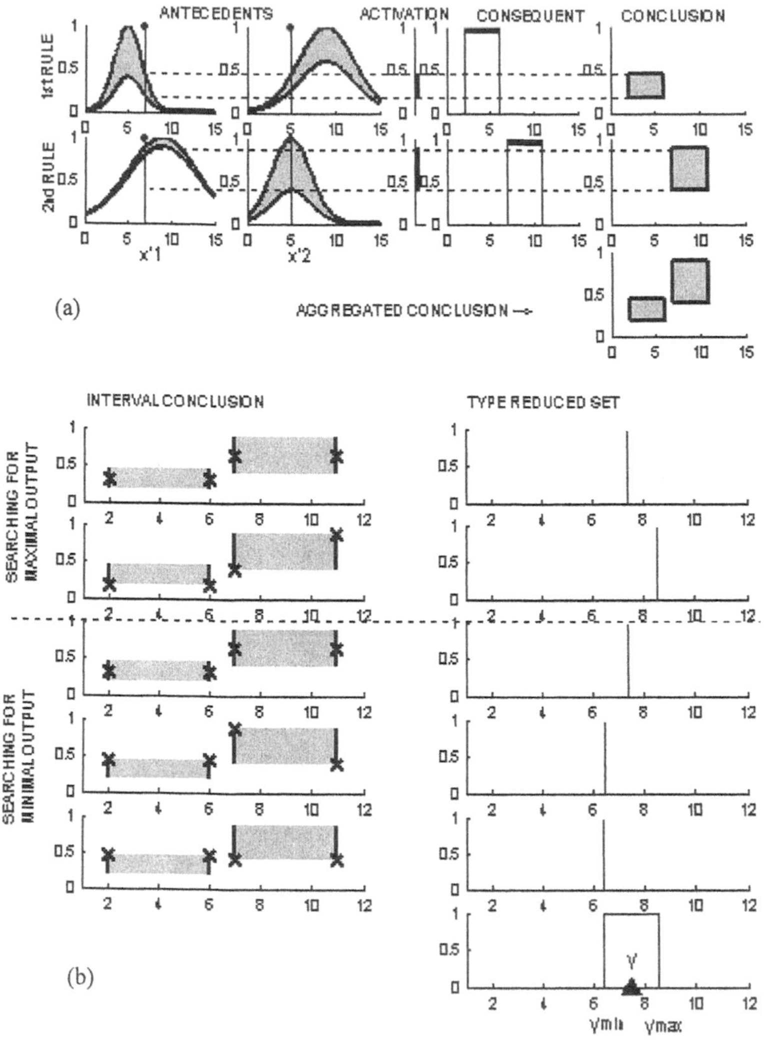

Fig. 2. Interval type 2 inferencing based on interval consequents. **(a)** two singleton premises are mapped by the upper and lower antecedents' MF; the minimum Cartesian product of the obtained interval compatibility degrees constitutes activation degrees; any extended T-norm rule produces conclusions. **(b)** type reduction of aggregated conclusions; chosen points dentoted by x

Depending on the fuzzy form of consequents, the structures of neuro-fuzzy systems may differ significantly in construction. What is more, not every combination of rule relations, methods of Cartesian product, shapes of secondary MF and finally type reduction methods lead to achieve a "flat" architecture of neuro-FIS.

3 Type 2 FIS Checking Driver's Behavior

The objective was to build a system which verifies drivers' behaviors. Our motivation was that a fuzzy inference system would signal all steering mistakes made by tired drivers or even correct the direction of a moving vehicle in situations when drivers fell asleep or were unconsious. As all drivers know, it is very important to move between the boundaries of a trafic lane. This interval translates itself into the interval of the turning angle. In fact it is sufficient to apply a standard fuzzy system of type 1 to deal with the problem of mobile steering [6]. But in our problem we need to know the interval of all posible turning angles, and when the driver's behavior exceeds this interval, the error should be signalized.

Fig. 3 (a) presents a typical vehicle with a torsional front axle during a right turn maneuver on a r radius circle. The output parameter of the system is the turning angle θ of the front center of the vehicle.

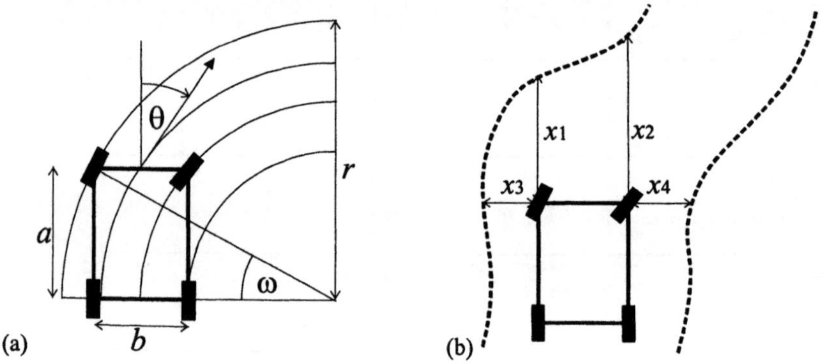

Fig. 3. Four-wheels vehicle. **(a)** motion parameters. **(b)** sensory data

The technical limitation of the vehicle is its minimal turn radius $r_{\min}$, i.e. the radius of the circle described by the front outer wheel. So the tangent of the boundary turning angle of this wheel is

$$\tan \omega_{bound} = 1 \Big/ \sqrt{\left(r_{\min}/b\right)^2 - 1} \tag{5}$$

where b is the wheel base of the vehicle. This concludes that the minimal distance indicated by the front sensors, necessary for full turn negotiating, is

$$x_{fbound} = \sqrt{2ba/\tan \omega_{bound} + b^2 - a^2} - b \tag{6}$$

while a is the wheel base.

Sensory data used for learning, shown in Fig. 3 (b) were generated randomly. Distances x_1, x_2 were generated as 13 tan(*rand*) + x_{fbound}, where the *rand* variable was a random value uniformly distributed in $[0,\pi/2]$. For simplicity a constant road width was assumed, where $x_3 + x_4 = reminder$. The dividing point between two sensory variables x_3 and x_4 was chosen at random with uniform distribution.

Desired output values were calculated in the folowing way. Supposing that $x_2 > x_1$ the vehicle should turn right. Henceforth the tangent of the minimal turning angle of the outer wheel is such a value that the vehicle being in the constant turn does not exceed road boundaries

$$\tan \omega_{\min} = 2ba/\left(x_2^{\,2} + a^2 + 2bx_2\right) \tag{7}$$

The tangent of the maximal turning angle of the outer wheel was determined with the assumption that the turning vehicle should not cut in, i.e. in this situation the right-rear wheel should not exceed the boudaries

$$\tan \omega_{\max} = 2bx_4/\left(x_4^{\,2} + b^2 + 2ax_4\right) \tag{8}$$

In the case of $x_1 > x_2$ the vehicle must turn left and equations (8) and (7) are still valid, when we change x_2 for x_1 and x_4 for x_3.

The tangent of the maximal or minimal turning angle of the middle-front of the vehicle is scaled with the following trigonometric dependence

$$\tan\theta = \pm 2\Big/\left(\frac{2}{\tan\omega} + \frac{a}{b}\right) \tag{9}$$

while the minus sign is allowed for θ oriented clockwise.

It is important to bear in mind the technical limitation $|\tan\omega_{\min}| \le \tan\omega_{bound}$. Moreover we have chosen a parameter of the front sensors' insensibility called *myopia* such that if x_1 (or x_2) $> myopia \cdot x_{fbound}$, then $\tan\theta_{\min} = 0$.

For such an established task we have used interval fuzzy inference systems with 42 rules of type 2 (extended algebraic product as the Cartesian product and height type defuzzification is used). The backpropagation method was used to tune system parameters with comparing intermediate output values with corresponding desired pairs $(\theta_{\min}, \theta_{\max})$. All used learning rates were set to 0.25 and the motion parameters were set as follows: $b = 2{,}6$, $a = 1{,}8$, $reminder = 1.6$, $r_{\min} = 4.5$, $myopia = 10$. Each epoch consisted of 100 iterations of the learning algorithm.

To minimize the number of the redundant rules we have fixed the partition of the input space in the way depicted in Fig. 4. The initial consequent centers were set to zero.

In the first 40 epochs only the centers of consequent fuzzy sets were trained as in the typical type 1 fuzzy system. This initial type 1 tuning may be considered as a "launching" procedure of type 2 systems. From the 41st epoch two interval systems of type 2 were trained as it is shown in Fig. 5. One of them had singleton consequents (for details see [10]). In this case the consequent centers and height parameters of the lower MF of antecedents were tuned. The other type 2 system had interval consequents established by center and deviation parameters. Hence consequent centers and consequent deviations and height parameters of the lower antecedent MF were tuned. It should be noted that the root mean squared error (RMSE) gives not sufficient information about mistakes made by drivers. Only if the overall system output exceeds the desired interval, it would cause an accident. Thus we made use of a "bounded" root mean squared error (BRMSE), which bases on only positive error between the overall output and the maximal desired output and between the minimal desired output and the overall output.

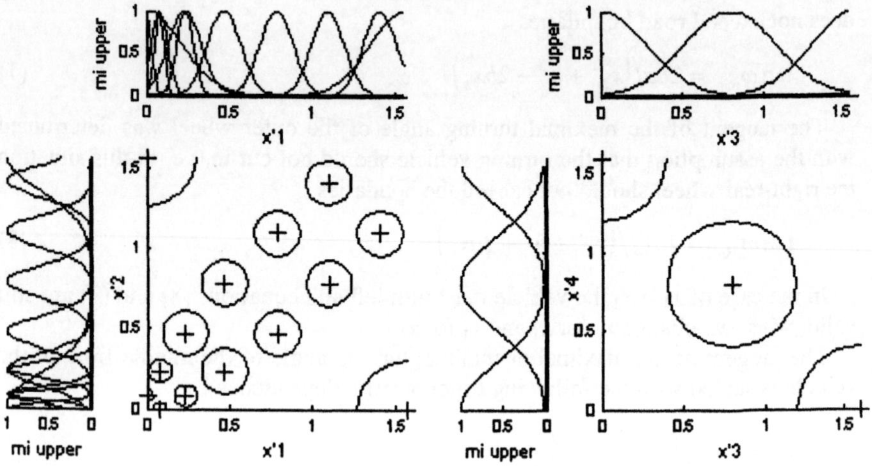

Fig. 4. Partition of the input space. Antecedents are depicted by upper MF (*solid gaussian curves*) with means (+) and standard deviations (equal to *circle* radiuses)

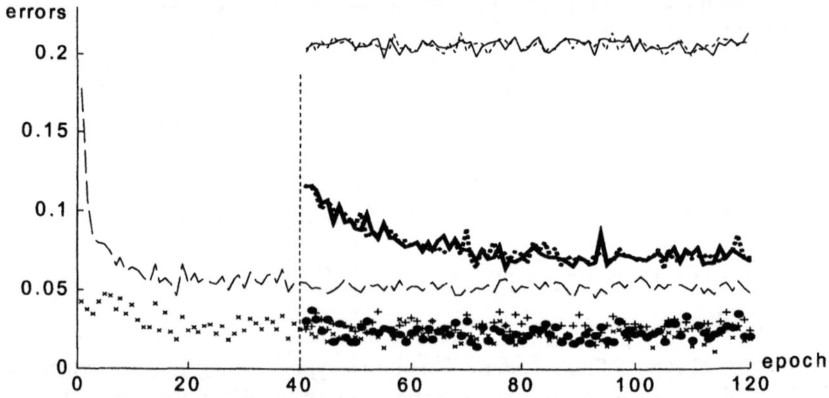

Fig. 5. Error rates: RMSE (*thin dashed line*) and BRMSE (*crosses*) of the "launching" type 1 neuro-fuzzy system, minimal and maximal output RMSEs (*thin solid and dotted lines*) and BRMSE (*pluses*) of the type 2 interval system with singleton consequents, minimal and maximal output RMSEs (*thick solid and dotted lines*) and BRMSE (*dots*) of the type 2 interval system with interval consequents. All curves were depicted as average error rates of 6 independent random designs

In Fig. 5 the fuzzy system of type 1 was tuned with the use of the mean value of desired bounding outputs. This system outperforms type 2 fuzzy systems both in learning speed and in learning accuracy. But in our problem it is important to achieve low level of out of the "bound" error. If we succeeded with lowering the learning RMSE of the type 2 FIS to the RMSE of the type 1 FIS, stabilized checking BRMSE of the type 2 FIS would be lower than BRMSE of type 1 FIS. Nevertheless among type 2 interval FIS, system based on interval consequents performs better than system based on singleton consequents presented in [10].

4 Concluding Remarks

In this paper the new connectionist structure of the type 2 fuzzy inference system has been created. The type 2 FIS does not outperform traditional type 1 systems when using only overall output. The main applicability arises from employing the bounding outputs both in learning and testing. Accordingly one interval stated application is proposed.

References

1. Gorzałczany M. (1989) An Interval-Valued Fuzzy Inference Method – Some Basic Properties, Fuzzy Sets and Systems **31**, 243-251
2. John R. I., Czarnecki C. (1998) A Type 2 Adaptive Fuzzy Inferencing System, IEEE FUZZ Proc., Man and Cybernetics, 2068-2073
3. Karnik N. N., Mendel J. M. (1998) An Introduction to Type-2 Fuzzy Logic Systems, Univ. Southern California, Report
4. Liang Q., Mendel J. M. (2000) Interval Type-2 Fuzzy Logic Systems, IEEE FUZZ Conf., San Antonio, TX
5. Mendel J. M. (2001) Uncertain Rule-Based Fuzzy Logic Systems: Introduction and New Directions, Prentice Hall PTR, Upper Saddle River, NJ
6. Ng K. C., Trivedi M. M. (1998) A Neuro-Fuzzy Controller for Mobile Robot Navigation and Multirobot Convoying, IEEE Trans. Cybernetics, **28**, NO. 6, December, 829-840
7. Rutkowski L. (to be published) New Soft Computing Techniques for System Modelling, Pattern Classification and Image Processing, Springer
8. Rutkowski L., Starczewski J. (2000) From type-1 to type-2 fuzzy inference systems - part 1, Proc. V Conference on Neural Networks and Soft Computing, Zakopane, Poland, June 6-10, 46-51
9. Rutkowski L., Starczewski J. (2000) From type-1 to type-2 fuzzy inference systems - part 2, Proc. V Conference on Neural Networks and Soft Computing, Zakopane, Poland, June 6-10, 52-64
10. Starczewski J., Rutkowski L. (2002) Connectionist Structures of Type 2 Fuzzy Inference Systems, Lecture Notes in Computer Science **2328**, 617-624
11. Zadeh L. A. (1975) The Concept of a Linguistic Variable and its Application to Approximate Reasoning – I, Information Sciences **8**, 199-249

Generation of Fuzzy Neural Network Structure

Zbigniew Świątnicki[1], **Vladimír Olej**[2]

[1] Department of Logistic Management, Logistics Institute
Military University of Technology
Kaliskiego 2, 00-908 Warsaw, Poland
zswiat@wat.waw.pl

[2] Department of Information Systems, School of Finance
Matej Bel University
Tajovského 10, 974 01 Banská Bystrica, Slovak Republic
olej@financ.umb.sk

Abstract. A genetic method to generate a fuzzy neural network, which has both structure and synapse weights adequate for a given task is proposed.

Keywords. Optimization, fuzzy neural networks, genetic algorithms.

1 Background

Genetic algorithms (GAs) [1,2,3,4] are robust adaptive optimization methods based on biological principles. They represent an efficient technique of learning based on the dynamics of the evolution. Fuzzy neural networks (FNNs) employing basic fuzzy logic operations are introduced in [5]. In the learning process (by GAs), they afford for shortening the time of method convergence towards the global maximum. Crisp numbers express input and output values of FNNs. Input values in the FNNs formulation can be realized as fuzzy sets, outputs as membership function values of the given fuzzy set.

The paper presents a possibility of exploitation of GAs for optimization of the FNN structure and its application to pattern recognition. Generally, there can be several approaches to generation structure of neural networks (NNs) based on GAs. Two of them are used most frequently. In the first approach, NNs are only generated from a genotype while in the second approach two genotypes are used. These methods [6 to 9] make use of GAs to determine: synapse weights NNs, where their structure is known in advance; NNs structure and synapse weights.

2 State of the Art in Neural Networks and Fuzzy Neural Networks

This proposal belongs to the second group of methods. These make use of GAs to determine structure and synapse weights NNs (FNNs). It is possible to characterize it in the following way: It can work with general NNs (FNNs). It does not have any limitation for synapse weights between neurons. The synapse weights have one of the following three values (**R**, 0 and –**R**) where **R** is a set of real numbers for NNs or they are from the interval [0,1] for FNNs. The type of each synapse is determined by its direction. The direction of a synapse can be defined as a forward character (the synapse goes out of the neuron and its type is 1), or as a backward character (the synapse goes into the neuron and its type is -1), or cannot be defined (the synapse is not created and its type is 0). In a NN (FNN) the neuron is represented by a genotype. The NNs and FNNs are created by an input as well as by a hidden and an output layers. There can be more hidden layers. Every layer contains some neurons that are connected by some synapses. Every synapse has its weight and every neuron has its threshold. The input neuron IN_i is connected to a neuron of the hidden layer (summation fuzzy neuron for FNNs [5]) H_j. The synapse weights between the input layer neuron IN_i and the hidden layer neuron H_j are v_{ij}. These weights obtained in the learning process by GAs acquire values from the set of real numbers **R**. The synapse weights between the hidden layer neuron H_i and the output layer (logical fuzzy neuron for FNNs [5]) OUT_j are w_{ij}. These weights obtained in the learning process by GAs acquire values from the interval $w_{ij} \in [0,1]$.

3 Methodology – Genetic Algorithms

Genes describe every living organism. They can stay in several forms - alleles. The set of alleles of a living organism is called a genotype. Fitness η evaluates genotypes with regard to their adaptation to the environment in which they live. In general, genotypes are represented like allele strings. Length l of a genotype expresses the number of alleles in it and it is constant. In a GA, there are M individuals available. These M individuals create a population. Genetic algorithms modify a population by a time step t. The set of individuals of the population at the time t is expressed as $\beta(t)$. The size of $\beta(t)$ is constant and equal to M. Distributed genetic algorithms (DGAs) [10] make use of GAs. Their task is to divide the population between defined numbers of independent GAs. All independent GAs works in a distributed system with the same task and with their own population (Fig. 1).

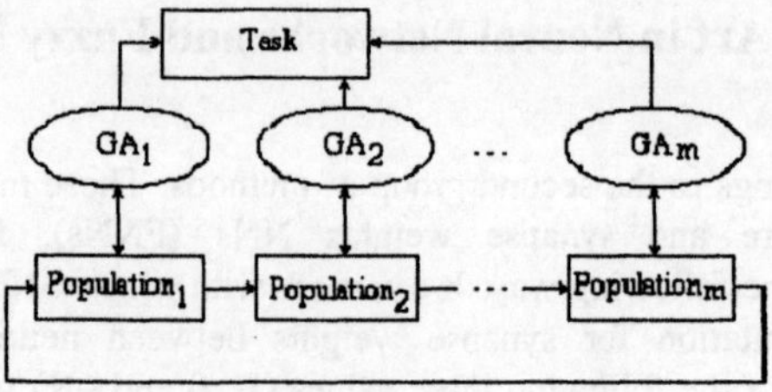

Fig. 1. Realization of DGAs

A DGA provides the exchange of the population parts between individual GAs. The conditions of this exchange (the number of individuals, the method of choice of individuals, etc.) are predetermined by the user. The fitness η is evaluated at every GA independently of the other GAs. It affords for decreasing the time consumption of the convergence towards the global maximum. The DGA can be expressed as follows:

Initialization: Let t := 0. Create m independent GAs. For each GA choose M_{max} individuals from all possible genotypes α and create populations $\beta_1(0)$, $\beta_2(0)$, ... , $\beta_m(0)$.

Generation updating: By means of genetic operators (selection, crossing, mutation), from populations $\beta_1(t)$, $\beta_2(t)$, ... , $\beta_m(t)$ create the following populations $\beta_1(t+1)$, $\beta_2(t+1)$, ... , $\beta_m(t+1)$. Then t := t + 1.

Choice of individuals: From each population $\beta_1(t)$, $\beta_2(t)$, ... , $\beta_m(t)$ select the individuals with the highest fitness η and create sets $\beta'_1(t)$, $\beta'_2(t)$, ... , $\beta'_m(t)$, for which $\beta'_i(t) \subset \beta_i(t)$, $0 \leq i \leq m$.

Exchange of individuals: Insert the set $\beta'_i(t)$ into the population $\beta_{(i+1) \bmod m}(t)$.

Stop condition: If $t \geq t_{max}$, or the number of generations, the defined fitness η etc. is achieved, then stop DGA; otherwise continue from the second step. Consider genotype $G_i \in \beta(t)$ with the highest fitness η the most suitable.

4 Algorithm for Optimization of Fuzzy Neural Networks Structure

A DGA is used for generation and an optimization of FNNs structure. Its goal was an identification of input patterns and it made possible to decrease the time of computing because the generation and an optimization of FNNs structure are time consuming. Creation of the final phenotype, i.e. the FNN structure depends on a correct choice of rules. The rules are responsible for division of neurons. This formal description can be expressed as follows

$$G = \{R_1, R_2, \dots, R_i, \dots, R_u\}, \tag{1}$$

where R_i is the ith rule of genotype G; $R_i = \{D_1, D_2, \dots, D_j, \dots, D_v\}$ and D_j is the jth description of the ith rule; $D_j = \{g_1, g_2, \dots, g_k, \dots, g_w\}$ and g_k is the kth gene of the jth description. For example, the jth description of the ith rule can be defined as follows

$$D_j = \{P_r, P_s, RP, \text{Threshold}, \text{Weight}\}, \tag{2}$$

where P_r, $P_s \in <0,u>$ determines a creation of a neuron according to the rules. If it equals 0 then the neuron is not created; $RP \in <1,s>$ is a relative position and defines the number of directions where the neuron can be located; Threshold and Weight $\in <-\mathbf{R},\mathbf{R}>$ where **R** is a set of real numbers for NNs or it is from the interval [0,1] for FNNs. Then a maximal fitness η for input patterns can be defined this way

$$\eta = \rho * \sigma + \tau * \gamma - \nu * \delta, \tag{3}$$

where ρ can be defined as (the number of outputs of FNN - 1) * (the number of outputs of FNN) * (the number of patterns); σ is the number of correct classifications of input patterns; τ is the number of outputs of FNN; γ is the number of outputs of FNN, where the deviation is smaller than the predetermined limit for all patterns; ν is 1/ (the number of patterns); δ is the error that is the sum of errors of actual values on the FNN output from the required values for all patterns and the FNN output.

The algorithm of generation of FNN structure consists of three parts. The first part creates a defined number of neurons in general, the original genotype G can be divided into two new genotypes (P_r, P_s). If $P_r \neq 0 \wedge P_s \neq 0$, then two genotypes can be created from the genotype G; If $(P_r = 0 \wedge P_s \neq 0) \vee (P_r \neq 0 \wedge P_s = 0)$, then one genotype can be created from the genotype G; If $P_r = 0 \wedge P_s = 0$, then no genotype can be created from the genotype G.

The number of divisions is computed from the number of all neurons. It guarantees, that the FNN structure can consist of any number of neurons. The new genotypes become the original genotype in the next step of the algorithm. A fitness η is obtained when the division is finished. If fitness η is zero, then a genotype has not been created and the generation of the FNN structure finishes. If fitness η is not zero, then an arrangement of created neurons begins on an area.

The second part arranges the created neurons on area d * d, where d provides that two neurons do not have the same position. The greatest problem is to determine distance v_d between two neurons which can be expressed as $v_d = (d / s_d)$, where s_d is the number of neurons really created. Every neuron has an information about its position. An arrangement of created neurons depends on the size d. In the third part, connection of neurons is realized. It is dependent on a step of branching k. On this basis, the size of the neuron surrounding where the search will take place can be defined. The search will be realized around all neurons. A forward synapse has a value equal to 1 and a backward synapse has a value equal to –1. If both values are not found, then the research continues. The algorithm generates the first neuron in the input layer, then in the hidden or the output layer, next it creates synapses, and it finishes by determining the synapse weights. Values of synapses weights are obtained from variable Weight defined for each neuron.

5 An Example of Application for Pattern Recognition

The created FNN structure is going to be tested and evaluate after the third part of algorithm. On the basis of variable Weight and a list of synapses for each neuron the threshold for a neuron is calculated. Next, the fitness η of the FNN is calculated after a determination of the thresholds of individual neurons. Let the FNN structure be created according to Section 2. The input patterns for FNN are Q, D, G, A and the noisy input patterns are Q', D', G', A' (Fig. 2). These patterns are represented by some fuzzy sets ***Q, D, G, A, Q', D', G', A'***. Next, let us consider the FNN which is composed of the input layer $IN = \{IN_1, IN_2, \dots, IN_{in}\}$, the hidden layer $H = \{H_1, H_2, \dots, H_h\}$ and the output layer $OUT = \{OUT_1, OUT_2, \dots, OUT_{out}\}$ with these parameters: $in = 64$, $out = 4$, $d = 50$ and $k = 7$.

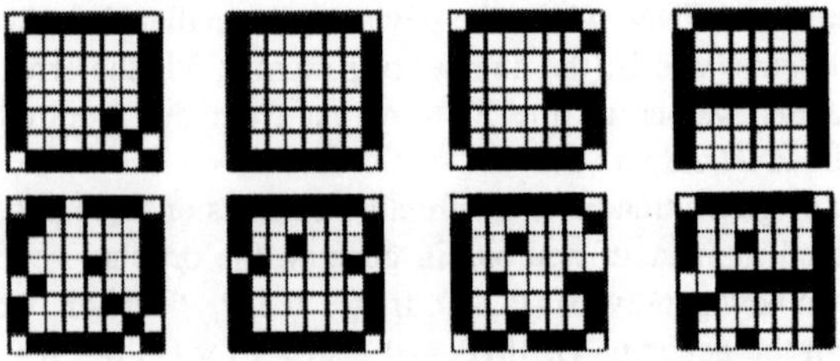

Fig. 2. Input patterns for fuzzy neural network

From the values of a membership functions μ of outputs $OUT = \{OUT_1, OUT_2, OUT_3, OUT_4\}$ it follows, as we can see in Table 1: if input FNN is Q (Q'), then output OUT_1 represents the degree of membership in fuzzy sets ***Q (Q')*** with value $\mu_Q = 0.81$ ($\mu_{Q'} = 0.87$), output OUT_2 represents the degree of membership to fuzzy sets ***D (D')*** with value $\mu_D = 0.21$ ($\mu_{D'} = 0.28$) etc.

Table 1 Values of fuzzy neural network outputs for input patterns

Input Pattern	OUT_1		OUT_2		OUT_3		OUT_4	
	μ_Q	$\mu_{Q'}$	μ_D	$\mu_{D'}$	μ_G	$\mu_{G'}$	μ_A	$\mu_{A'}$
Q (Q')	**0.81**	**0.87**	0.21	0.28	0.18	0.24	0.31	0.29
D (D')	0.23	0.18	**0.91**	**0.83**	0.26	0.31	0.19	0.33
G (G')	0.18	0.27	0.32	0.29	**0.78**	**0.86**	0.32	0.22
A (A')	0.21	0.19	0.25	0.37	0.16	0.14	**0.85**	**0.81**

6 Conclusion

The paper proposed a new approach with features described in Section 3 and Section 4 to design the FNN having almost arbitrary synapses using an optimizing method, DGA. The method changes the structure of the FNN dynamically according to a DGA. A FNNs is assumed to be a virtual living thing, which has genes of genotypes representing synapse weights between its neurons. Several initial FNNs generated randomly are removed or reproduced according to their fitness η, and one of the best FNNs is obtained as the result of generation iterations.

References

1. Holland J. H. (1975) Adaptation in Natural and Artificial Systems. University of Michigan Press, Ann Arbor
2. Spiessens P. (1988) Genetic Algorithms. AI MEMO, No. 88-19, Vrije Universitiet Brussel
3. Hoffmeister F., Back T. (1990) Genetic Algorithms and Evolution Strategies. Similarities and Differences. Proc. of 1st Workshop on Parallel Problem Solving from Nature, Dortmund, Germany, 455–469
4. Goldberg D. E. (1989) Genetic Algorithms in Search, Optimization, and Machine Learning. Addison – Wesley, Reading, MA
5. Lehotský M., Olej V., Chmúrny J. (1995) Pattern Recognition Based on the Fuzzy Neural Networks and their Learning by Modified Genetic Algorithms. Neural Network World, **5**, No.1, 91–97
6. Nagao T., Agui T., Nagahashi H. (1993) A Genetic Method for Optimalization of Asynchronous Random Neural Networks and its Application to Action Control. Proc. of International Joint Conference on Neural Networks '93, Nagoya, Japan, 1–4
7. Adeli H., Hung S. L. (1995) Machine Learning – Neural Networks, Genetic Algorithms, and Fuzzy Systems. John Wiley and Sons, Inc., New York
8. Buckley J. J., Hayashi Y. (1993) Hybrid Neural Networks can be Fuzzy Controllers and Fuzzy Expert Systems. Fuzzy Sets and Systems, **60**, 135–142
9. Godjevac J. (1994) Comparison Between Classical and Fuzzy Neurons. Proc. of 2nd European Congress on Fuzzy Intelligent Technologies, **1**, Aachen, Germany, 1326–1332
10. Olej V. (1997) Realization of Distributed Genetic Algorithms and Evolution Strategies. Artificial Intelligence and Information - Control Systems of Robots '97, World Scientific Publishing Co. Pte. Ltd., Printed in Singapore by Uto-Print, editor Ivan Plander, 277–285

Regularization Background of Clustering Algorithms

Piotr Boguś[1], Katarzyna Lewandowska[1], Francesco Masulli[2,3]

[1]Department of Physics and Biophysics, Medical University of Gdańsk, Dębinki 1, 80-211 Gdańsk, Poland, gogo@amedec.amg.gda.pl, kale@amedec.amg.gda.pl
[2]INFM National Institute for Physics of Matter, Via Dodecaneso 33, 16146 Genova, Italy
[3]Department of Computer Sciences, University of Pisa, Corso Italia 40, 56125 Pisa, Italy, masulli@disi.unige.it

Abstract: The paper presents the hard, fuzzy, possibilistic and maximum entropy principle clustering algorithms from the regularization theory point of view. The differences between the objective functions lay in the choice which their term is treated as the standard term and which as the regularization term.

1. Introduction

Let us define a set $\mathbf{\Omega} = \{\mathbf{x}_i;\ i = 1, \ldots, n\}$ of n data vectors and a set of c clusters associated to the set of their centroids $\mathbf{Y} = \{\mathbf{y}_j;\ j = 1, \ldots, c\}$. An unsupervised learning machine for Vector Quantization (VQ) or Clustering [1,5] is a mapping $F(\mathbf{x}, \mathbf{Y}) : \mathbf{\Omega} \to J$, where J is the set J={1,... , c}. We denote E_{ij} as the distortion (also called distance, local energy, loss, error) associated to pattern $\mathbf{x}_i$ when mapped to the index j and $p_{ij} = p(\mathbf{x}_i \in \text{cluster}_j)$ as the probability that the data point $\mathbf{x}_i$ belongs to the cluster j (it can be also considered as the fuzzy or possibilistic degree of membership in the cluster). The empirical risk is then the expectation of the distortion (or total cost function , averaged energy), i.e.:

$$< E >= \sum_{i=1}^{n} \sum_{j=1}^{c} p_{ij} E_{ij} \tag{1}$$

The hard c-means (HCM) algorithm is an algorithm of clustering [1,5] that has been proposed as an approximate implementation of the likelihood maximization data set based on mixture density model. In [1], it has been demonstrated that HCM algorithm can be also obtained by optimization of the objective function (1) where E_{ij} is Euclidean distance $E_{ij} = |\mathbf{x}_i - \mathbf{y}_j|^2 = d_{ij}$ and assumes that probability (membership values) which associates data point $\mathbf{x}_i$ to cluster j are

$$\forall_{ij} \quad p_{ij} = \begin{cases} 1 & \text{if } x_i \in j \\ 0 & \text{if } x_i \notin j \end{cases} \tag{2}$$

The clustering problem in the HCM setting is often ill-posed in the sense of Hadamard [6,7,12], especially when the "right" number of classes is unknown [15]. In particular HCM is a subject to the problem of local minima and shows a strong dependency from the outliers.

In order to obtain more robust clustering algorithms and transform the clustering into a well-posed problem, it is possible to apply regularization approach, by adding a "regularization" term $\lambda\|\mathbf{Pf}\|^2$ to the empirical risk in (1). It measures the costs of the error connected with a solution of the operation $\|\mathbf{Pf}\|^2$ which contains some "a priori" information on the problem. As shown by Miyamoto et al [11], some efficient clustering algorithms, proposed in the recent literature as implementation of other theoretical point of views, can be enclosed in the common framework of the application of the regularization theory.

In Sects 3,4,5 we discuss the fuzzy c-means [1,3,4], the possibilistic c-means [3,9,10] and the maximum entropy based clustering algorithms and in Sect. 5 we propose a common background for clustering methods.

2. Fuzzy Approach to Clustering

The fuzzy c-means (FCM) algorithm of clustering [1,3,4] performs the fuzzy partition of the data set. Assume that each element of the data set Ω is a data vector $x_i \in R^P$ and that the c clusters are represented by centroids $y_j \in R^P$. Let V_{nc} denotes a set of real valued matrices. The fuzzy c-partition of the data set Ω is any matrix $v \in V_{nc}$ with the following properties:

$$\forall_{ij} \quad v_{ij} \in \langle 0,1 \rangle \tag{3}$$

$$\forall_i \quad \sum_{j=1}^{c} v_{ij} = 1 \tag{4}$$

$$\forall_j \quad 0 < \sum_{i=1}^{n} v_{ij} < n \tag{5}$$

The fuzzy c-means algorithm of clustering is considered as an optimization of the objective function

$$J_m(v, Y) = \sum_{i=1}^{n} \sum_{j=1}^{c} (v_{ij})^m E_{ij} \tag{6}$$

where m is a weighting exponent, $m \in <1,\infty)$. The FCM algorithm can be formulated as an iteration schema of calculations of the fuzzy cluster centroids

$$\mathbf{y}_j^t = \frac{\sum_{i=1}^{n} (v_{ij}^{t-1})^m \mathbf{x}_i}{\sum_{i=1}^{n} (v_{ij}^{t-1})^m} \tag{7}$$

for j=1,.....,c where new matrix v_{ij} is calculated by

$$v_{ij} = \frac{1}{\sum_{s=1}^{c}\left(\frac{d_{ij}}{d_{is}}\right)^{\frac{2}{m-1}}} \qquad (8)$$

3. Possibilistic Approach to Clustering

Possibilistic approach to clustering [3,9,10] relaxes the probabilistic constraint (4) according to which the sum of the membership values of a data point in all the classes must be equal to one. The set of constraints, which is chosen in possibilistic approach, is limited to (3) and (5). The objective function is

$$J_m(v,Y) = \sum_{i=1}^{n}\sum_{j=1}^{c}(v_{ij})^m E_{ij} + \sum_{j=1}^{c}\eta_j\sum_{i=1}^{n}(1-v_{ij})^m \qquad (9)$$

where η_j are positive numbers. The first term demands that a distance from a point to a centroid of a cluster must be as low as possible. The second term forces v_{ij} values to be the greatest as possible. In [10] there is an alternative formulation of possibilistic approach with an objective function

$$J_m = \sum_{j=1}^{c}\sum_{i=1}^{n} v_{ji}E_{ji} + \sum_{j=1}^{c}\eta_j\sum_{i=1}^{n}(v_{ji}\ln v_{ji} - v_{ji}) \qquad (10)$$

and for which in general iteration schema we obtain the solution

$$v_{ji} = \exp\left(-\frac{E_{ji}}{\eta_j}\right). \qquad (11)$$

4. Maximum Entropy Approach To Clustering

The usage of maximum entropy approach to broad class of problems was firstly proposed by Jaynes [8]. For clustering the maximum entropy principle MEP appears in the papers of Rose and al. [13,14]. An entropy of a system which consists on n data points divided between c clusters is as following

$$H(p_{11},p_{12},\ldots,p_{nc}) = -\sum_{i=1}^{n}\sum_{j=1}^{c} p_{ij}\ln p_{ij} \qquad (12)$$

We maximize the entropy using Lagrange multipliers method under normalization and constant averaged energy constraints using Lagrange function which can be presented in the form

$$L = \frac{1}{\beta}\sum_{i=1}^{n}\sum_{j=1}^{c} p_{ij} \ln p_{ij} + \sum_{i=1}^{n}\sum_{j=1}^{c} p_{ij} E_{ij} + \sum_{i=1}^{n} \lambda_j \left(\sum_{j=1}^{c} p_{ij}\right) \tag{13}$$

As the solution we obtain the Gibbs distribution in the form

$$p_{ij} = \frac{\exp(-\beta E_{ij})}{\sum_{j=1}^{c} \exp(-\beta E_{ij})} \tag{14}$$

The parameter β can be interpreted as a fuzziness control parameter. For $\beta = 0$ each point $\mathbf{x}_i$ is equally associated with all clusters. As β increases the associations become less fuzzy and for $\beta = \infty$ each point $\mathbf{x}_i$ belongs to exact one cluster with probability 1. We define the cost function called the free energy

$$F = \sum_{i=1}^{n}\sum_{j=1}^{c} E_{ij} = -\frac{1}{\beta} \ln Z \tag{15}$$

where Z is the total partition function. Eventually the solution of minimization of <E> is performed by using so-called deterministic annealing on F as first proposed by Rose et al. [13,14]. In this method for each value β we perform a minimization of F starting at $\beta = 0$. The deterministic annealing process is in fact tracking of the global minimum while increasing β. There is not need to specify number of clusters. At $\beta = 0$ there is only one cluster and then during annealing the "natural" clusters differentiate. Technically the algorithm uses the iterations

$$\mathbf{y}_j^{new} = \frac{\sum_{i=1}^{n} p_{ij}^{old} \mathbf{x}_i}{\sum_{i=1}^{n} p_{ij}^{old}} \quad \text{for all } j \tag{16}$$

with using the equation (14) for calculating of probabilities.

5. Regularization Background of the Clustering Algorithms

Developing the Miyamoto et al. idea [11], we can consider [3,11] the general objective function in the form with the regularization term R

$$J = \sum_{i=1}^{n}\sum_{j=1}^{c} v_{ij} d_{ij} + R \tag{17}$$

where the standard term is an energy (error function). In such a schema, for HCM clustering algorithm we have R=0, for possibilistic approach

$$R = \sum_{j=1}^{c} \eta_j \sum_{i=1}^{n} v_{ji} \ln v_{ji} - \sum_{j=1}^{c} \eta_j \sum_{i=1}^{n} v_{ji} \tag{18}$$

while for MEP approach an entropy starts to play a role of regularization term and

$$R = \frac{1}{\beta}\sum_{i=1}^{n}\sum_{j=1}^{c} v_{ij}\ln v_{ij} + \sum_{i=1}^{n}\lambda_j \left(\sum_{j=1}^{c} v_{ij}\right). \tag{19}$$

The above presented schema interprets MEP as the minimization of the energy with an entropy constraint on probability distribution.

Find that while assuming for all j that $\eta_j=1/\beta$ the regularization term for possibilistic approach will be in the form

$$R = \frac{1}{\beta}\sum_{j=1}^{c}\sum_{i=1}^{n} v_{ji}\ln v_{ji} - \frac{1}{\beta}\sum_{j=1}^{c}\sum_{i=1}^{n} v_{ji} \tag{20}$$

and appears similar to this for MEP approach. Let us perform the manipulations

$$\sum_{j=1}^{c}\sum_{i=1}^{n}(v_{ji}\ln v_{ji} - v_{ji}) = \sum_{j=1}^{c}\sum_{i=1}^{n} v_{ji}(\ln v_{ji} - 1) = e\sum_{j=1}^{c}\sum_{i=1}^{n}\frac{v_{ji}}{e}\ln\left(\frac{v_{ji}}{e}\right)$$

where e is a natural logarithm base. Let us introduce the new coefficients $u_{ji}=v_{ji}/e$ and modify multipliers $\eta_j=\eta_j/e$ (or $\beta=\beta/e$). Then for possibilistic approach

$$R = \sum_{j=1}^{c}\eta_j\sum_{i=1}^{n} v_{ji}\ln v_{ji} - \sum_{j=1}^{c}\eta_j\sum_{i=1}^{n} v_{ji} = \sum_{j=1}^{c}\eta_j\sum_{i=1}^{n} u_{ji}\ln u_{ji} \tag{21}$$

or using $\eta_j=1/\beta$ assumption

$$R = \frac{1}{\beta}\sum_{j=1}^{c}\sum_{i=1}^{n} v_{ji}\ln v_{ji} - \frac{1}{\beta}\sum_{j=1}^{c}\sum_{i=1}^{n} v_{ji} = \frac{1}{\beta}\sum_{j=1}^{c}\sum_{i=1}^{n} u_{ji}\ln u_{ji} \tag{22}$$

Using an objective function for possibilistic approach in the form above corresponds to the minimization of the Lagrange function in MEP without a normalization condition. Such a posed problem gives a question: how to understand the entropy without the normalization condition for probabilities? Anyway MEP optimization problem without the normalization condition gives

$$u_{ji} = \exp\left(-1 - \frac{E_{ji}}{\eta_j}\right) = \frac{1}{e}\exp\left(-\frac{E_{ji}}{\eta_j}\right) \quad \text{and} \quad v_{ji} = \exp\left(-\frac{E_{ji}}{\eta_j}\right)$$

and this solution is similar to one obtained for possibilistic approach (see (11)).

In turn the FCM algorithm of clustering corresponds to, so called, nonlinear regularization, where the v_{ij} raising to a power m introduces a nonlinearity in the „error" term of objective function (1). Making an assumption $\beta=2/(m-1)$ and expressing an energy in logarithm way $E_j(\mathbf{x}_i) \equiv \log(E_j^{\beta}(\mathbf{x}_i))$ one can find that the solution of the MEP (14) can be presented

$$u_j(\mathbf{x}_i) = \frac{\exp\left(-\frac{2}{m-1}\log E_j^{\beta}(\mathbf{x}_i)\right)}{\sum_{k=1}^{c}\exp\left(-\frac{2}{m-1}\log E_k^{\beta}(\mathbf{x}_i)\right)} = \frac{1}{\sum_{k=1}^{c}\left(\frac{E_j^{\beta}(\mathbf{x}_i)}{E_k^{\beta}(\mathbf{x}_i)}\right)^{\frac{2}{m-1}}} \tag{23}$$

in the form of FCM solution (8). Find that for $\beta=2/(m-1)$ when $\beta \to \infty$ then $m \to 1$ and when $\beta \to 0$ then $m \to \infty$. This give us the possibility of performing the deterministic annealing for FCM by going with m from ∞ to 1 (see e.g. [2]).

6. Conclusion

In the paper, we have presented the objective function approach to some clustering algorithms. The regularization background of those algorithms should lead us to better understanding the nature of clustering schemas. The FCM algorithm, possibilistic algorithm and MEP based algorithm can be considered from the common objective function schema as the different types of regularization for the hard classic c-means algorithm.

References

[1] J.C. Bezdek, Pattern Recognition with Fuzzy Objective Function Algorithms. Plenum Press, 1987, Second Edition.

[2] J.C. Bezdek and N.R. Pal. Two Soft Relatives of Learning Vector Quantization. Neural Networks, Vol. 8, No. 5, 1995, pp. 729-743.

[3] P. Boguś, F. Masulli, Fuzzy and Possibilistic Approaches to Clustering, Colloquia in Artificial Intelligence, Second Polish Conference on Theory and Applications of Artificial Intelligence, Łódź, 28-30.08.1998.

[4] P. Boguś, A.M. Massone, F. Masulli, A. Schenone, Interactive Graphical System for Segmentation of Multimodal Medical Volumes Using Fuzzy Clustering, Machine Graphics & Vision, 7(4), 765-780, 1998.

[5] R. Duda, P. Hart, Pattern Classification and Scene Analysis, New York, Wiley Interscience, 1973.

[6] F. Girosi, M. Jones, T. Poggio. Regularization Theory and Neural Networks Architectures. Neural Computation, Vol. 7, No. 2, March 1995, pp. 219-269.

[7] S. Haykin. Neural Networks. A Comprehensive Foundations. Macmillan College, 1994.

[8] T. Jaynes, Information Theory and Statistical Mechanics, Physical Review, 106, 620-630, 1957.

[9] R. Krishnapuram, J.M. Keller, A Possibilistic Approach to Clustering, IEEE Transactions of Fuzzy Systems, 1(2), 98-110, 1993.

[10] R. Krishnapuram, J.M. Keller, The Possibilistic C-Means Algorithm: Insights and Recommendations, IEEE Transactions of Fuzzy Systems, 4(3), 385-396, 1996.

[11] S. Miyamoto, M. Mukaidono. Fuzzy C-Means as a Regularization and Maximum Entropy Approach. Proceedings of the Seventh International Fuzzy Systems Association World Congress. IFSA'97 Prague, Czech Republic, June 25-29, 1997. Academia, Prague 1997. Volume II, pp. 86-92.

[12] T. Poggio, F. Girosi. Networks for Approximation and Learning. Proceedings of the IEEE, Vol. 78, No. 9, 1990, 1481-1497.

[13] K. Rose, E. Gurewitz, G.C. Fox, Statistical Mechanics and Phase Transitions in Clustering, Physical Review Letters, 65(8), 945-948, 1990.

[14] K. Rose, E. Gurewitz, G.C. Fox, A Deterministic Annealing Approach to Clustering, Pattern Recognition Letters, 11, 589-594, 1990.

[15] Smyth, P. Clustering using Monte Carlo Cross-Validation, Proceedings of the Second International Conference on Knowledge Discovery and Data Mining, AAAI Press: Menlo Park, CA. August 1996.

Simulated Annealing C-Means Clustering Algorithm Convergence Proof

Piotr Boguś[1], Anna Maria Massone[2,3], Francesco Masulli[2,4]

[1]Department of Physics and Biophysics, Medical University of Gdańsk, Dębinki 1, 80-211 Gdańsk, Poland, gogo@amg.gda.pl
[2]INFM National Institute for Physics of Matter, Via Dodecaneso 33, 16146 Genova, Italy
[3]Institut of High Energy Physics, Université de Lausanne Bâtiment des Sciences Physiques CH-1015 Dorigny, Switzerland, AnnaMaria.Massone@iphe.unil.ch
[4]Department of Computer Sciences, University of Pisa, Corso Italia 40, 56125 Pisa, Italy, masulli@disi.unige.it

Abstract. The paper presents a simple proof of convergence for the simulated annealing c-means (SACM) algorithm. This proof supports the excellent experimental performances shown by this algorithm that are also due to an accurate modeling of clusters making use of the Mahalanobis distance.

1 Introduction

Many iterative algorithms have been proposed for the solution of the clustering problem. Most of them, such as the classical hard c-means (HCM) algorithm, can be trapped in local maxima. To avoid this problem, many clustering algorithms have been proposed [1, 3, 8, 12, 13, 14, 15]. In particular, two interesting approaches to clustering are based on simulated and on deterministic annealing schema [2, 15, 16]. Simulated annealing is a global search technique derived by statistical physics, which is based on Metropolis algorithm [10]. In simulated annealing we simulate the behaviour of a real thermodynamically system which is first heated over the phase transition point and next slow cooling in the sequence of equilibrium states.

Simulated annealing has been applied to the solution of many optimisation problems, including clustering [2,7,11,16]. The Simulated Annealing Clustering Algorithm (SACM) proposed by our group in [2] permits to apply a global search technique to search for minima of the HCM functional, using an accurate membership function based on the Mahalanobis distance. The paper shows a simple convergence proof for the SACM algorithm, based on the method proposed in [9, 16].

In the next two sections we introduce the clustering problem and the HCM. In Sec. 3 we present the SACM. In Sec. 4 we sketch the technique for convergence proof, and in Sec. 5 we apply it to the SACM, showing in such a way the convergence property of this algorithm.

2 Formulation of Clustering Problem

In the classical clustering problem we consider the set (training set) $\Omega = \{x_i; i = 1,...,I\}$ of I data vectors and the set $C = \{c_j; j = 1,...,C\}$ of C clusters. We denote

$$p_{ij} = p(x_i \in c_j)$$

as the probability that the data point $\mathbf{x}_i$ belongs to the cluster j. Note that p_{ij} can be interpreted in many ways, for example, as memberships values u_{ij}. For each I, usually the normalization condition holds:

$$\sum_{j=1}^{C} p_{ij} = 1$$

Generally the state of the system is given by the set of p_{ij}, where i =1,... , n and j =1, ... , c. We introduce the distortion or loss function

$$E_{ij} = E(x_i \in c_j)$$

due to the association data point $\mathbf{x}_i$ to cluster j. Then the empirical risk or total averaged energy is

$$< E >= \sum_{i=1}^{n} \sum_{j=1}^{c} p_{ij} E_{ij}$$

3 Hard C-Means Algorithm of Clustering

The classical hard c-mean (HCM) algorithm of clustering (Duda & Hart 1973 [5]) maximizes the likelihood of a mixture density model of the data set (see [2, 5]).

Let us define $D_j(x_k)$ as the Euclidean distance between the sample i-th and the center of cluster j-th. Then, the HCM while maximizes the likelihood function, minimizes at the same time an empirical risk defined as [1]:

$$J_w = \sum_{k=1}^{n} \sum_{j=1}^{c} u_{jk} D_j^2(x_k) \tag{1}$$

where

$$u_{jk} = \begin{cases} 1 & \text{if} \quad D_j(x_k) = \min_{1 \le p \le c} D_p(x_k) \\ 0 & \text{otherwise} \end{cases} \tag{2}$$

Note that, in the HCM, E_{ik} is usually defined as the as the square of the Euclidean distance between the sample i-th and the center of cluster j-th.

4 Simulated Annealing C-Means Algorithm of Clustering

The simulated annealing c-means algorithm of clustering SACM presented in [2] considers the application of Euclidean and Mahalanobis distances.

J_w is defined as in the form as in (1), while the distance $D_j(x_k)$ can be the Euclidean distance

$$D_j(x_k) = E_j(x_k) = \|x_k - y_j\| \quad (3)$$

or the more accurate Mahalanobis distance

$$D_j^2(x_k) = M_j^2(x_k) = |\Sigma_j|^{1/d} (x_k - y_j)^t \Sigma_j^{-1} (x_k - y_j), \quad (4)$$

with Σ defined as the cluster covariance matrix.

The SACM algorithm was defined as following:

1. Assign the number of clusters.
2. Initialize T_{start} and randomly the centers of clusters.
3. Evaluate the cost function J_w using (1) (using Euclidean or Mahalanobis distance).
4. **Do until** ΔJ_w decreases
   a) randomly generate new cluster centers;
   b) update the membership values of all samples to all clusters using;
   c) evaluate the covariance matrices (only for Mahalanobis distance);
   d) evaluate the cost function J_w using (2) and corresponding equation (3) or (4);
      (i) if $\Delta J_w < 0$ accept the new centers;
      (ii) otherwise generate a random number R and accept the new center only if $R < P(\Delta J_w)$, where $P(\Delta J_w)$ is given by

$$P(\Delta J_w) = \exp\left(-\frac{\Delta J_w}{T}\right)$$

5. Update T using a procedure which based on the following equation in each step s

$$T^{(s+1)} = \eta T^{(s)}$$

where η is the control parameter.

Note that SACM algorithm does not request the calculation of the inverses of the covariance matrixes, such as methods based on direct likelihood maximization.

The comparison of experimental results obtained for classical hard c-means HCM [1, 5], deterministic annealing algorithm [14, 15] DA and simulated annealing c-means SACM algorithm are presented in Tab. 1. The algorithms were tested on the classical Anderson's IRIS Plants database [5, 6]. IRIS contains the data of three classes, each of 50 instances in R^4 (with four fathers). Typical reported error rates for IRIS are: 0-5 mistakes for supervised classifier and 10-15 for unsupervised classifiers. In the experiment each clustering algorithm was applied 12 times and we apply Euclidean and Mahalanobis distances.

Table 1. Error rates (number of mistakes)

	max	min	mean
HCM-Euclid	30	16	19.3
DA-Euclid	17	16	16.1
SACM-Euclid	17	14	15.6
HCM-Mahala	46	8	29.9
DA-Mahala	10	8	8.5
SACM-Mahala	11	3	7.7

5 Convergence of Simulated Annealing Algorithm

Let us denote

- π – assignments (distributions) of data vectors in clusters,
- Λ – the set of all possible assignments,
- $P_{rt}(T)$ – the probability of generating distribution π_t from distribution π_r at temperature T,
- $p_{rt}(T)$ – the probability of accepting distribution π_t once it has been generated from distribution π_r at temperature T,
- J_r – the objective function corresponding to distribution π_r.

Theorem: A simulated annealing algorithm converges to the solution if the following conditions are satisfied [9,16]:

1) function $P_{rt}(T)$ is independent of T,
2) $P_{rt} = P_{tr}$ for all $\pi_r, \pi_t \in \Lambda$,
3) if $J_r \le J_t \le J_u$ then $p_{ru}(T) = p_{rt}(T)p_{tu}(T)$ for all π_r, π_t and $\pi_u \in \Lambda$,
4) if $J_r \ge J_t$ then $p_{rt}(T) = 1$ for all $\pi_r, \pi_t \in \Lambda$,
5) if $J_r < J_t$ then $p_{rt}(T) > 0$ for all $\pi_r, \pi_t \in \Lambda$ and $T>0$,
6) if $J_r < J_t$ then $\lim_{T\to 0} p_{rt}(T) = 0$ for all $\pi_r, \pi_t \in \Lambda$.

This theorem can be used to proof the convergence of any simulated annealing algorithm.

6 Convergence of Simulated Annealing C-Means Algorithm of Clustering

We can now show that the simulated annealing c-means SACM algorithm presented in chapter 3 converges. We consider all conditions of the theorem of Sec. 4 in turn.

Condition 1 – the function $P_{rt}(T)$ should be independent of T: in the SACM algorithm we randomly generate new centers (see steps 2. and 4.a. of algorithm description in chapter 4). Hence the probability of generating the new assignment having an old assignment is independent of T.

Condition 2 – $P_{rt} = P_{tr}$ for all π_r, $\pi_t \in \Lambda$: we randomly generate all assignments from the same uniform probability distribution.

Condition 3 – if $J_r \le J_t \le J_u$ then $p_{ru}(T) = p_{rt}(T)p_{tu}(T)$ for all π_r, π_t and $\pi_u \in \Lambda$: to examine this condition let us consider all the possibilities as in the tab. 2 (see [16]) so we have

Table 2. Particular cases of the inequality $J_r \le J_t \le J_u$

Case		p_{rt}	p_{tu}	p_{ru}
1	$J_W^r < J_W^t < J_W^u$	$\exp(-(J_W^t - J_W^r)/T)$	$\exp(-(J_W^u - J_W^t)/T)$	$\exp(-(J_W^u - J_W^r)/$
2	$J_W^r = J_W^t < J_W^u$	1	$\exp(-(J_W^u - J_W^t)/T)$	$\exp(-(J_W^u - J_W^r)/$
3	$J_W^r < J_W^t = J_W^u$	$\exp(-(J_W^t - J_W^r)/T)$	1	$\exp(-(J_W^u - J_W^r)/$
4	$J_W^r = J_W^t = J_W^u$	1	1	1

Case 1: $$p_{ru}(T) = \exp(-(J_W^u - J_W^r)/T) = \exp(-(J_W^u - J_W^t + J_W^t - J_W^r)/T) = \\ = \exp(-(J_W^u - J_W^t)/T) \cdot \exp(-(J_W^t - J_W^r)/T) = p_{rt}(T)p_{tu}(T).$$

Case 2: $$p_{ru}(T) = \exp(-(J_W^u - J_W^r)/T) = 1 \cdot \exp(-(J_W^u - J_W^t)/T) = p_{rt}(T)p_{tu}(T), \\ \text{hence } J_W^r = J_W^t.$$

Case 3: $$p_{ru}(T) = \exp(-(J_W^u - J_W^r)/T) = \exp(-(J_W^t - J_W^r)/T) \cdot 1 = p_{rt}(T)p_{tu}(T), \\ \text{hence } J_W^t = J_W^u.$$

Case 4: $$p_{ru}(T) = 1 = 1 \cdot 1 = p_{rt}(T)p_{tu}(T).$$

Condition 4 – if $J_r \ge J_t$ then $p_{rt}(T) = 1$ for all π_r, $\pi_t \in \Lambda$: this condition is satisfied by algorithm step 4.d.(i).

Condition 5 – if $J_r < J_t$ then $p_{rt}(T) > 0$ for all π_r, $\pi_t \in \Lambda$ and $T>0$: this condition is satisfied by algorithm steps 4.d.(ii).

Condition 6 – if $J_r < J_t$ then $\lim_{T\to 0} p_{rt}(T) = 0$ for all π_r, $\pi_t \in \Lambda$: find that we have that

$$\lim_{T\to 0} p_{rt}(T) = \lim_{T\to 0} \exp(-(J_W^t - J_W^r)/T) = 0.$$

7 Conclusions

In [2] we proposed the simulated annealing c-means (SACM) algorithm making use of an accurate modeling of clusters based on the Mahalanobis distance. SACM avoids the expensive calculation of the inverses of the covariance matrixes (that, moreover, can be ill conditioned), such as it happens for methods based on likelihood maximization. This paper presents a proof of convergence for SACM algorithm proposed in [2]. With together the usage of the Mahalanobis distance, this proof supports the excellent experimental performances of the algorithm.

References

1. J. C. Bezdek, Pattern Recognition with Fuzzy Objective Function Algorithms, second edition, Plenum Press, 1987

2. P. Boguś, A.M. Massone, F. Masulli, A Simulated Annealing C-Means Clustering Algorithm, R. Parenti, F. Masulli (eds.), Proceedings of the third International ICSC Symposia on Intelligent Industrial Automation IAA'99 and Soft Computing SOCO'99, June 1 – 4 1999, Genova, Italy, ICSC Academic Press, pp. 534-540, 1999.
3. P. Boguś, A.M. Massone, F. Masulli, A. Schenone, Interactive graphical system for segmentation of multimodal medical volumes using fuzzy clustering, Machine GRAPHICS & VISION, vol. 7, no. 4, pp. 781-791, 1998.
4. P. Boguś, Simulated Annealing in Clustering. Colloquia in Artificial Intelligence, Proceedings of CAI 2000 Third Polish Conference on Theory and Applications of Artificial Intelligence, Łódź, October 5-7, pp. 67-84, 2000.
5. R. Duda, P. Hart, Pattern Classification and Scene Analysis, New York, Wiley Interscience, 1973.
6. R. A. Fisher, The use of multiple measurements in taxonomic problems, Annual Eugenics, vol. 7, no. 2, pp. 179-188, 1936.
7. S. Geman, D. Geman, Stochastic relaxation, Gibbs distributions, and the Bayesian restoration of images, IEEE Transactions on Pattern Analysis and Machine Intelligence, vol. PAMI-6, no. 6, pp. 721-741, 1984.
8. R. Krishnapuram, J. M. Keller, A Possibilistic Approach to Clustering, IEEE Transactions on Fuzzy Systems, vol. 1, no. 2, pp. 98-110, 1993.
9. P. J. M. van Laarhoven, E. H. L. Aarts, Simulated Annealing: Theory and Applications, D. Reidel Publishing Co., Dordrecht, Holland, 1987.
10. N. Metropolis, A.W. Rosenbluth, M.N. Rosenbluth, A.H. Teller, and E. Teller, Equation of state calculations for fast computing machines, Journal of Chemical Physics, vol. 21, pp. 1087-1092, 1953.
11. S. Kirkpatric, C.D. Gelatt, Jr., M.P. Vecchi, Optimization by simulated annealing, Science, vol. 220, pp. 671-680, 1983.
12. F. Masulli, P. Boguś, M. Artuso, A. Schenone, The Maximum Entropy Principle and Its Application to the Segmentation of Multivariate Medical Images, In R. Tadeusiewicz, L. Rutkowski, J. Chojcan (eds.), Proceedings of the Third Conference „Neural Networks And Their Application", Kule (Poland), 14 X -18 X 97, Polish Neural Networks Society, Częstochowa, pp. 285-291, 1997.
13. F. Masulli, M. Artuso, P. Boguś, A. Schenone, Application of Possibilistic Clustering to the Segmentation of Multivariate Medical Images, In: P. Blonda, M. Castellano, A. Petrosino (eds.), Proceedings of the Second Italian Workshop on Fuzzy Logic, Bari, Italy, 19-20 March 1997, World Scientific, pp. 105-112, 1998.
14. Rose, E. Gurewitz, G. C. Fox, Statistical Mechanics and Phase Transitions in Clustering, Physical Review Letters, vol. 65, no. 8, pp. 945-948, 1990.
15. K. Rose, E. Gurewitz, G. C. Fox, A deterministic annealing approach to clustering, Pattern Recognition Letters, vol. 11, pp. 589-594, 1990.
16. S. S. Selim, K. Alsultan, A simulated annealing algorithm for the clustering problem, Pattern Recognition, vol. 24, no. 19, pp. 1003-1008, 1991.

Learning by Constraint Relaxation

John Day

Department of Computer Science, Florida Institute of Technology,
Melbourne, Fl 32901 USA
jday@csihq.com

Summary. We present a soft computing approach to text processing and propose a constraint theoretic approach for machine learning called learning by constraint relaxation (LCR). Words do not convey exact meanings but act as soft constraints over possible meanings. LCR is based on this principle: a failure to recognize is an opportunity to learn. A rule-making language, RML, has been implemented to facilitate problem representation and experimentation with constraint relaxation problems. LCR has been used to extract knowledge from texts containing medical descriptions and informatics codes.

1 Introduction

The principles of soft computing can be applied to solving AI problems by using a variety of paradigms and techniques borrowed from many areas of computer science and mathematics. These areas include statistics, neural nets, decision theory, and probability, logic, linguistics, and software engineering. The approaches are different in each area, but in them we seek a common theme, which allows us to unify our approach.

In this paper we propose a new unifying approach: learning as a kind of constraint satisfaction problem (CSP). Specifically, a kind of deductive learning takes place when a CSP is solved, using the principle "use knowledge to find more knowledge". Furthermore, inductive learning takes place when a partial constraint satisfaction problem (PSCP) is solved by relaxing a constraint, using the principle "a failure to recognize is an opportunity to learn".

Many current ML techniques, such as Naïve Bayes, assume complete feature independence. Although these techniques are surprisingly successful, it is clear that there is additional relational knowledge, based on constraints, that should be exploited.

Newer techniques, such as co-training [2] are emerging which do exploit these relationships. It is possible to understand co-training in terms of "co-constraints", the idea that solutions to constraint solutions involve combinations of one or more domain variables. This extends the idea of two training domains in the co-training setting to any arbitrary number of co-constrained domains in the LCR theory.

2 Constraint Satisfaction Problems (CSP)

Constraint satisfaction problems have been formally defined [6] as a 3-tuple (X,D_i,C) where X is a set of n variables $x_1, x_2, \ldots x_n$, where Di is a collection of domains D_1, $D_2, \ldots D_n$, representing the domain of each variable in X.

C is a finite set of constraints that, in effect, specify which relationships of variables to domain values are acceptable. We introduce the term co-constraint to denote the involvement of two or more variables in a constraint expression. For example, using domains X,Y, and Z of integers, we say the constraint expression $x_1 + y_1 + z_1 < 20$ is co-constrained over X,Y, and Z. A solution S to a constraint satisfaction problem is a set of assignments to each variable in X, which satisfy all of the constraints.

A constraint satisfaction problem may be over-constrained, such that no solution may be found. Freuder (1989) [5] has defined a class of partial constraint satisfaction problems (PCSP) where solutions are obtained by weakening (or "relaxing") one or more constraints, subject to minimizing the cost of constraint failure. The approach for solving over-constrained constraint problems is similar to solving an over-constrained system of linear equations. There are many possible solutions, but the "best" solution is one that minimizes a cost or maximizes a reward in an optimal sense.

2.1 The Meanings of Words as Soft Constraints

It is a common misconception that the words of a text actually contain the meaning that they appear to convey.

The truth is that the words in the text are merely *constraints* on the actual meaning intended by an author. The true meaning of the text, when it is read, is an interpretation, which exists only in the mind of the reader. The words themselves are merely indices for the meanings and associations known by the reader.

The structure and ordering of the words in the text constitute a constraint satisfaction problem, whose solution will have some probability of being interpreted by the reader as the same message intended by an author.

It is not always possible to verify that the reader has interpreted a text correctly, even if the reader claims to have "understood" the text in the sense of satisfying the underlying constraint satisfaction problem. This is because an absolutely correct solution depends on the author and reader agreeing on the common domain definitions. If the domains differ, then the reader's solution may be inconsistent with respect to the author's intended meaning.

Even if the author-reader domain definitions are identical, multiple consistent solutions may exist, so a reader's interpretation of the text might be consistent but different from the solution intended by the author.

This is an insight into the constraint-theoretic nature of word meanings. We observe that humans are remarkably successful in conveying meaning to each other in written and spoken language. The question remains: how can we apply the constraint-theoretic view to text extraction in a useful way?

2.2 Learning as Constraint Satisfaction

The constraint satisfaction paradigm provides a way to solve problems that are relational in nature and that are solved by assigning values to variables in some optimal way. Barták [1] has described a variety of applications in computer science and engineering that have been approached as CSP problems.

But CSP has not been viewed, heretofore, as a learning paradigm. However, if we accept the definition of learning given in the introduction, then it is reasonable to view the changes to the CSP variables as a kind of machine learning, in a form ready made for analyzing and solving learning problems.

2.3 Deduction as Simple Constraint Satisfaction

Let us consider the solutions of constraint satisfaction problems as a kind of learning, specifically, a kind of *deductive learning.*

For example, the sentence "**Roses are red**" matches the constraint pattern "**?flower are ?color**"[1], where the match variables are constrained by *domain membership*. We assume that '**roses**' and '**red**' are already recognized as members of the '**?flower**' and '**?color**' domains, respectively.

What is learned? One or more sets of values, which satisfy the given constraints. It is deductive in nature because the values are clearly entailed by the constraints, which can be verified in the manner of a proof. We have learned a new instance of concepts we already knew.

It is thus useful to think of a CSP solution as a kind of logical deduction, implied by its constraints.

This kind of solution is a "sound and complete" deduction, provided it is consistent with all of the constraints.

2.4 Induction as Partial Constraint Relaxation

The concept of "inductive learning" w.r.t. to PCSP involves satisfying constraints by containing "open" values, in other words, an assignment which fails because of a symbol which has not been seen previously seen and is not recognized.

It is at this point that we apply the "induction step", according to the principle "a failure to recognize is an opportunity to learn". The induction step consists of "relaxing" the constraint by enlarging the domain to contain the previously unrecognized values.

What has been learned? Answer: the values induced by relaxing the constraint(s).

---

[1] In our rule-making language (RML), words preceded by '?', '*', or '+' are interpreted as match variables for exactly one word, zero or more words, or one or more words, respectively.

How good is this learning? Answer: It depends almost entirely on the number and nature of the co-constraints. To see this, consider a system of unary constraints, where there are no co-constraints. Then any domain value must be admitted, valid or not.

Co-constraints are the relationships which allow us to distinguish valid solutions from meaningless or nonsensical solutions.

3 RML, a Rule-making Language

RML is a scripting language similar to Python and Perl, developed by the author [3] to manipulate text strings for knowledge extraction and for constraint experimentation. It is based on the principle "everything is a string" and has facilities for pattern matching, text/HTML/XML report markup language and built-in relational methods language functions.

Constraints in RML are represented by pattern-matching templates. These templates are simple RML strings consisting of a sequence of fixed words and constraint variables. RML uses a recursive symbolic pattern matching algorithm with backtracking, which treats character string pattern matching as a constraint satisfaction problem.

The pattern-matching algorithm is an extension of an algorithm developed by Winston and Horn [7]. Words in an input string are recursively unified with words and variables in one or more pattern templates.

Variable prefixes (Table 1) serve to identify variables and constrain the number of words to be unified with each variable. Optional suffixes (Table 2) further constrain words to simple numeric or list types or allow user-written predicates written in RML or C to constrain the match in any arbitrary fashion.

Table 1. RML MATCH() constraint variable prefixes

Prefix	Behavior
?x	Match exactly one delimited word
+x	Match one or more delimited words
*x	Match zero or more delimited words

Table 2. RML MATCH() constraint variable suffixes

Suffix	Behavior
?x^#	Constrains ?x to be a fixed-point or integer number
?x^*L*	Constrains ?x to be a member of list *L*
?x:(*expr*)	Constrains match to depend on the evaluation of *expr* (any Boolean-valued RML expression or function)

Note: ?x^L is just a shorthand expression for ?x:(x in L). Similarly, ?x^# is just a shorthand notation for ?x:(ISNUM(x))

Armed with this knowledge, let us examine an actual RML rule, in which many of the above mechanisms have been embedded. This rule will recognize sentences like "101 Dalmation puppies" or "The number of Dalmation puppies is 100" and fire rule action map.dogs() which prints "We have 100 Dalmation puppies" on the console:

```
def map.dogs.1(q,k,a) log 'We have',q,k,a; enddef

set animals = ['dog' 'cat' 'horse' 'fish' 'puppies'],
    species = ['dalmation' 'mutt' 'bassett' 'trout'
               'siamese'],
    rule.animals.1 = {* Toy rule for quantifying
                         animals *}
[
    # ACTION
   "map.dogs.1('?qty', '?kind', '?animal')"

    # DISJUNCTIVE PATTERNS
   '?qty^# ?kind^species ?animal^animals '
   'The number of ?kind^species ?animal^animals is
         ?qty^# '
]; {* end rule.animals.1 *}
```

3.1 LCR Example

LCR has been used to extract knowledge from medical texts and has been used to learn encodings for medical informatics applications [4].

In the following example (Table 3) we see the learning of concepts related to medical descriptions of medications. We begin with a handful of vocabulary and one rule, enough to recognize the three phrases in the test set.

Running the algorithm on the test set induces words in each domain when the corresponding constraint is relaxed. In the last example, two constraints were relaxed, causing "garbage" to be learned, underscoring the importance to maintain sufficient constraints while relaxing constraints for induction.

Table 3. LCR example

```
Training set (extracted collocations):
      TYLENOL capsule 250mg
      CODEINE tablet 10 mg
      ADVIL caplet 500 mg
Lexicon:
      Drugname: [Tylenol->1,codeine->2, advil->3]
      Dosage_form: [capsule->1, tablet->2, caplet->3]
      Dosage_measure: [mg->1]
Deduced rule:
    ?drugname  ?dosage_form  +dosage
Test set collocations:
      ACETOMETAPHINE capsule 1000mg
      TYLENOL pill 250mg
```

```
        TYLENOL liquid 1 oz
        XYZ ABC 1000 mm ("garbage")
Running algorithm
  Relax drugname:      -> learned "acetometaphine"
  Relax dosage_form:    -> learned "pill"
  Relax dosage_meaure: -> learned "liquid"
                        -> learned "oz"
  Relax all variables: -> learned ???? GARBAGE!
```

The quality of LCR learning is measured by its accuracy and completeness. We shall see that this depends on the number and consistency of the constraints applied. Generally, it is safe to relax only one constraint at a time. In any case, sufficient constraints must remain to insure that only valid concepts are learned.

The necessary conditions for LCR include a dependency on the consistency of semantic meanings in words and a requirement to satisfy all crucial constraints while relaxing one, or more, constraints that admit learning.

4 Conclusion

We have presented a novel approach to text extraction by posing learning problems as constraint satisfaction problems.

Two types of knowledge are extracted:

- Constraint pattern sets, which are schemas for sentences or phrases, with keywords represented as variables constrained to a specific domain
- Lexicon entries tagged by part of speech and other encoded attributes

LCR is based on two general learning principles:

"Use knowledge to find more knowledge"

"A failure to recognize is an opportunity to learn"

References

1. Barták, R.: Constraint Programming: In Pursuit of the Holy Grail. In: Proceedings of Week of Doctoral Students. Charles University, Prague (1999).
2. Blum, A., Mitchell, T.: Combining labeled and unlabeled data with co-training. In: Proceedings of Conference on Learning Theory. (1998).
3. Day, J.C.: RML Reference Manual, Computer Science Innovations, Melbourne, Fl. http://www.csi.cc/rml (1994).
4. Friedman C, Wyatt J.: Evaluation Methods in Medical Informatics. New York: Springer-Verlag, (1997).
5. Freuder, E.: Partial constraint satisfaction. In: Proceedings of the International Joint Conference on Artificial Intelligence. (1989) 278-283.
6. Montanari, U.: Networks of constraints: Fundamental properties and applications to picture processing. Information Science, Vol 7, (1974) 95-132.
7. Winston, P.H., Horn, Horn, B.K.P.: Lisp, Third Edition. Addison-Wesley. (1988).

Forests of Decision Trees

Krzysztof Grąbczewski and Włodzisław Duch

Department of Informatics, Nicholas Copernicus University, Grudziądzka 5, 87-100 Toruń, Poland. http://www.phys.uni.torun.pl/kmk

Abstract. In many cases it is better to extract a set of decision trees and a set of possible logical data descriptions instead of a single model. Methods for creating forests of decision trees based on Separability of Split Value (SSV) criterion are presented. Preliminary results confirm their usefulness in understanding data structures.

1 Introduction

Recent trends in computational intelligence (CI) and data mining prove that understanding of data becomes increasingly more important. Especially in medicine CI expert systems always provide some explanations of diagnoses inferred by decision support tools. Human experts may not be satisfied with a single description of the problem they examine, even if it is quite accurate. Different experts may stress different factors in their evaluations of the problem, corresponding to different models of the data they are used to.

One of the most attractive ways to describe the classification process is to use logical rules, which can be easily extracted from decision trees. Usually data mining systems provide their users with just a single set of rules (the one that seems to be the most precise). At best several sets of rules with increasing accuracy are provided [1]. However, many sets of rules with similar complexity and accuracy may exist, using for example different feature subsets, bringing more information of interest to the domain expert. Therefore methods that are aimed at finding many different descriptions of the same data are worth investigation.

We have augmented our decision tree based on the *Separability of Split Value* (SSV) criterion [2,3] with the capability to generate forests of trees, instead of single trees. The algorithms have been tested on several datasets coming from the UCI repository of machine learning problems [4].

2 SSV Criterion

The SSV criterion is one of the most efficient among criteria used for decision tree construction [2,3]. It's basic advantage is that it can be applied to both continuous and discrete features, which means that methods based on it can operate on raw data without the need for any data preprocessing. The *split* value (or *cut-off point*) is defined differently for continuous and discrete features. In the case of continuous features the split value is a real number, in other cases it is a subset of the set of alternative values of the feature. The best split value is the one that separates the largest number of pairs of objects from different classes, so for both types of features *left side* (*LS*) and *right side* (*RS*) of a split value s of feature f for a given dataset D can be defined:

$$\mathrm{LS}(s,f,D) = \begin{cases} \{x \in D : f(x) < s\} & \text{if } f \text{ is continuous} \\ \{x \in D : f(x) \notin s\} & \text{otherwise} \end{cases} \tag{1}$$

$$\mathrm{RS}(s,f,D) = D - \mathrm{LS}(s,f,D)$$

where $f(x)$ is the f's feature value for the data vector x. The *separability of a split value* s is defined as:

$$\mathrm{SSV}(s) = 2 * \sum_{c \in C} |LS(s,f,D) \cap D_c| * |RS(s,f,D) \cap (D - D_c)| \tag{2}$$

$$- \sum_{c \in C} \min(|LS(s,f,D) \cap D_c|, |RS(s,f,D) \cap D_c|) \tag{3}$$

where C is the set of classes and D_c is the set of data vectors from D which belong to class $c \in C$. Similar criterion has been used for design of neural networks by Bobrowski *et al.* [5].

Among all the split values that separate the maximal number of pairs of vectors from different classes the one which separates the smallest number of pairs of vectors belonging to the same class. For every dataset containing vectors which belong to at least two different classes, for each feature which has at least two different values, there exists a split value with largest separability. When the feature being examined is continuous and there are several different split values with maximal separability close to each other, the split value closest to the average of all of them is selected. To avoid such situations it is good to examine split values that are natural for a given dataset (i.e. centered between adjacent feature values that occur in the data vectors). If there are non-maximal (regarding separability) split values between two maximal points or if the feature is discrete, then the best split value is selected randomly.

Decision tree is constructed recursively by searching for best splits. At each stage when the best split is found and the subsets of data resulting from the split are not completely pure (i.e. contain data belonging to more than one class) each of the subsets is being analyzed the same way as the whole data. The decision tree built this way gives maximal possible accuracy (100% if there are no contradictory examples in the data) which usually means that the created model overfits the data. To remedy this a cross validation training is performed to find the optimal pruning parameters for the tree. Optimal pruning produces a tree that generalizes well the patterns used for tree construction.

3 Construction of Forests

There are two ways to generate forests of trees, or more generally different models of the data, related to the variance due to the data sample and the variance due to the flexibility of the data model itself. The simplest way of finding multiple solutions to a problem is to apply a data mining technique to different samples of data depicting the same problem. Most computational intelligence methods, including decision trees, are not quite stable, for some data sets small perturbations of the training data may lead to remarkably different results [6]. It can be easily seen in cross validation tests, where each training pass is performed for different data selection. In section 4 we present some examples of application of this method.

Another possibility of forest generation is to explore beam search strategy which looks for the best tree. In each of beam search stages there is a beam of n decision trees (search states). Each stage adds a single split to the trees in current beam, so very simple trees in first beams and more complex structures in next stages are created. The usual technique to search for the best tree is to build the shortest tree with maximal accuracy possible (the first final state found), and then prune it to obtain good generalization (pruning is determined in SSV empirically by means of cross validation). This method has proven to be quite accurate, but it is justified strictly in the case of the shortest tree, other trees may require different pruning parameters. To find a forest all trees that appear in a beam at any stage of the search process are ordered by their estimated accuracy. To estimate the accuracy a cross validation on the training data is performed and a validation error is assigned to each beam position which is a pair (s,p) where s is search stage (beam index) and p is the position in that beam (the states in a beam can be sorted by the errors for the training set). The precise algorithm goes as follows:

- Perform n-fold cross validation for the training set. For each part:
  - Run beam search process (do not stop when first final state is found - stop when all the states in current beam are final);
  - for each pair (s,p) where $s \in \{1,\dots,m\}$, m is the number of search stages (the number of beams generated), $p \in \{1,\dots,k_s\}$, k_s is the number of states in sth beam, calculate the validation error $E_V = E_{TRN} + nE_{TST}$, where E_{TRN} and E_{TST} are the numbers of misclassified samples in the training and test (validation) parts, respectively.
- Run beam search for the whole training data.
- Assign an average validation error to all pairs (s,p) that correspond to some states in the generated beams.
  - Discard the pairs that do not correspond to a state in any of cross validation parts (the idea is that such search states are not common and would not generalize well);
  - When calculating the average values remove the maximal and the minimal ones.
- Sort all the beam states positions with increasing average validation error.
- Present a required number of leading states as the forest.

4 Results

We have applied the above algorithm to three real life datasets from the UCI repository [4]. In all the three cases we have found some sets of logical rules describing the data. The rule sets (in fact decision trees) which after sorting got to the beginning of the state list were very similar to the best known logical description of that data. In addition some alternative sets have been found for each analyzed dataset.

The hypothyroid dataset was created from medical tests screening for hypothyroid problems. Since most people were healthy 92.5% of cases belong to the normal group, and 8% of cases belonging to the primary hypothyroid or compensated hypothyroid group. 21 medical facts were collected in most cases, with 6 continuous test values and 15 binary values. A total of 3772 cases are given for training (results from one year) and 3428 cases for testing (results from the next year). Thus from the classification point of view this is a 3 class problem with 22 attributes.

The forest search algorithm pointed to the following rules as the first (the best) one (all values of continuous features are multiplied here by 1000):

1. if TSH $> 6.05 \wedge$ FTI $< 64.72 \wedge$ thyroid surgery = no then primary hypothyroid
2. if TSH $> 6.05 \wedge$ FTI $> 64.72 \wedge$ thyroid surgery = no $\wedge$ on thyroxine = no $\wedge$ TT4 < 150.5 then compensated hypothyroid
3. else healthy

These rules are 99.79% accurate (8 errors) on the training data and 99.33% accurate (23 errors) on the test data.
The second set of rules in the forest gives accuracy of 99.76% (9 errors) and 99.36% (22 errors) on training and test sets respectively:

1. if TSH $> 6.05 \wedge$ FTI < 64.72 then primary hypothyroid
2. if TSH $> 6.05 \wedge$ FTI $> 64.72 \wedge$ thyroid surgery = no $\wedge$ on thyroxine = no $\wedge$ TT4 < 150.5 then compensated hypothyroid
3. else healthy

These sets of rules occur several times in the forest, since they can be obtain in several different ways (equivalent forms). At the fifth position in the forest there is another (slightly simpler) set of rules (99.52% on training, 98.89% on test)

1. if TSH $> 6.05 \wedge$ FTI $< 64.72 \wedge$ thyroid surgery = no then primary hypothyroid
2. if TSH $> 6.05 \wedge$ FTI $> 64.72 \wedge$ thyroid surgery = no $\wedge$ on thyroxine = no then compensated hypothyroid
3. else healthy

Further positions bring even more simple rules. For instance the 13th set, with training accuracy 99.50% and test accuracy 98.92% is:

1. if TSH $> 6.05 \wedge$ FTI < 64.72 then primary hypothyroid
2. if TSH $> 6.05 \wedge$ FTI $> 64.72 \wedge$ thyroid surgery = no $\wedge$ on thyroxine = no then compensated hypothyroid
3. else healthy

The Wisconsin breast cancer dataset contains 699 instances, with 458 benign (65.5%) and 241 (34.5%) malignant cases. Each instance is described by 9 attributes with integer value in the range 1-10 and a binary class label. For 16 instances one attribute is missing. The meaning of features is: F_2 = Uniformity of Cell Size, F_3 = Uniformity of Cell Shape, F_5 = Single Epithelial Cell Size, F_6 = Bare Nuclei, F_8 = Normal Nucleoli. Some of the rule sets chosen for the forest are presented below.

1. if $F_3 < 2.5$ then benign	95.6% accuracy (25 err. + 6 unclass.)
2. if $F_6 < 2.5 \wedge F_5 < 3.5$ then benign	95.0% sensitivity
3. else malignant	95.9% specificity

1. if $F_3 < 2.5$ then benign	95.0% accuracy (35 err.)
2. if $F_5 < 2.5 \wedge F_8 < 2.5$ then benign	93.8% sensitivity
3. else malignant	95.6% specificity

1. if $F_3 < 2.5$ then benign	95.1% accuracy (34 err.)
2. if $F_5 < 2.5 \wedge F_2 < 2.5$ then benign	95.9% sensitivity
3. else malignant	94.8% specificity

1. if $F_3 < 2.5$ then benign	95.1% accuracy
2. if $F_5 < 2.5 \wedge F_6 < 2.5$ then benign	95.0% sensitivity
3. else malignant	95.2% specificity

1. if $F_3 < 2.5$ then benign	95.1% accuracy
2. if $F_6 < 2.5 \wedge F_3 < 4.5$ then benign	94.2% sensitivity
3. else malignant	95.6% specificity

The Ljubljana breast cancer data contains 286 cases, of which 201 are no-recurrence-events (70.3%) and 85 are recurrence-events (29.7%). There are 9 attributes with 2-13 different values each. This is a difficult and noisy data. In our forest two rule sets occur at the beginning:
75.5% accuracy (70 errors), probably due to small sample and without real meaning, 30.5% sensitivity, 94.5% specificity:

1. if breast = left $\wedge$ inv-nodes > 2.5 then recurrence-events
2. else no-recurrence-events

Quite understandable rule making 68 errors, 31.8% sensitivity, 95.0% specificity:

1. if deg-malig $> 2.5 \wedge$ inv-nodes > 2.5 then class recurrence-events
2. else no-recurrence-events

Further some more detailed rules can be found. First of them stands at position 22 and gives 76.92% accuracy (66 errors), 47.1% sensitivity, 89.6% specificity:

1. if deg-malig $> 2.5 \wedge$ inv-nodes > 2.5 then class recurrence-events if deg-malig $> 2.5 \wedge$ inv-nodes $< 2.5 \wedge$ (tumor-size = 30-34 $\vee$ tumor-size = 25-29 $\vee$ tumor-size = 50-54) then class recurrence-events
2. else no-recurrence-events

Although the overall accuracy may be similar different sets of rules may have significantly different values of sensitivity and specificity.

5 Discussion

Medical datasets often contain small number of examples (sometime 100 and less) with relatively large number of features. In such cases many data mining systems may find solutions which are precise but not meaningful according to the experts' knowledge. In large spaces with sparse samples it is quite likely that several different logical expressions may accidently classify some data well. Such a case is evident in the Ljubliana cancer data. Providing experts with several alternative descriptions gives more chance that they will find interesting explanations in common with their experience and will notice new regularities in the data that may give them a better understanding of the problem.

Forests consist of trees which very often differ in their decisions (different samples are misclassified by different trees). It will be very interesting to see the results obtained using trees from the forest as committees. In such a case the committee of decision trees can give answers which may be interpreted as probabilities of object's belonging to a given class. Of course it can also yield better classification accuracy, but even if it does not, it provides an interesting solution to the problem of combining the comprehensibility of decisions with high accuracy and confidence.

Another possible extension of this work is to add a method to automatically detect how many trees give interesting results and should be kept in the forest. This can be done by means of forest committees. One also can use methods to evaluate statistical significance [7] of the differences among classification accuracies of trees to select the trees that give insignificantly different results.

Acknowledgments: Support by the Polish Committee for Scientific Research, grant 8 T11C 006 19, is gratefully acknowledged.

References

1. Duch W, Adamczak R. and Grąbczewski K. (2001) Methodology of extraction, optimization and application of crisp and fuzzy logical rules. *IEEE Transactions on Neural Networks* **12**: 277-306
2. Grąbczewski K, Duch W. (1999) A general purpose separability criterion for classification systems, *4th Conference on Neural Networks and Their Applications*, Zakopane, Poland, pp. 203-208
3. Grąbczewski K. Duch W. (2000) The Separability of Split Value Criterion, *5th Conference on Neural Networks and Soft Computing*, Zakopane, Poland.
4. Blake, C.L, Merz, C.J. (1998). UCI Repository of machine learning databases http://www.ics.uci.edu/ mlearn/MLRepository.html. Irvine, CA: University of California, Department of Information and Computer Science.
5. Bobrowski L, Krętowska M, Krętowski M. (1997) Design of neural classifying networks by using dipolar criterions. *3rd Conf. on Neural Networks and Their Applications*, Kule, Poland
6. Breiman, L. (1998): Bias-Variance, regularization, instability and stabilization. In: Bishop, C. (Ed.) Neural Networks and Machine Learning. Springer, Berlin, Heidelberg, New York
7. Dietterich T. (1998) Approximate Statistical Tests for Comparing Supervised Classification Learning Algorithms, *Neural Computation* **10**, 1895-1923

Agent Populations as Computational Intelligence

Marek Kisiel-Dorohinicki, Grzegorz Dobrowolski, and Edward Nawarecki

Department of Computer Science
University of Mining and Metallurgy, Kraków, Poland
e-mail: {doroh,grzela,nawar}@agh.edu.pl

Abstract. The paper deals with agent-based architectures of hybrid soft-computing systems, which should exhibit intelligent behaviour at a population level. Three levels of complexity of such systems are distinguished together with their potential advantages. The considerations are illustrated by prototypical realisations of *evolutionary multi-agent systems* dedicated to multiobjective optimisation, data classification, and time-series prediction.

1 Introduction

More and more results in the field of soft computing are reported recently that in their core are based on combining different ideas and methods. Hybrid systems that put together elements of fuzzy logic, neural networks, evolutionary computation and other approaches by the effect of synergy exhibit some kind of intelligent behaviour [1], which is sometimes called *computational intelligence* (CI) as opposed to rather symbolic artificial intelligence.

The idea of building such systems can be essentially ordered and enriched using the notion of an intelligent agent. Conceptual relation between particular soft computing techniques and agents or their populations forms a base for distinguishing various levels of architectural design. It can be foreseen that the proposed approach can not only give a universal platform for cooperation of different known methods but also magnify their solving abilities up to gaining *computational intelligence* at a level of agent populations.

2 Agent-based architectures of CI systems

Let us start from enumeration of the most important features of *multi-agent systems* (MAS) that are currently adopted by community of researchers [4] and can be even regarded as defining ones for the term:

- a set of agents and a sub-system called environment constitute a multi-agent system;
- agents perform (characteristic of them) actions that result in changes of themselves or the environment;

- some of agents' actions (elementary) form mechanisms regarded as specific to multi-agent systems in general, i.e. communication, negotiation, exchange of resources etc.;
- if there is a structure embedded in the environment (a graph) reflecting spatial phenomena of a system, it forms a base for migration of agents;
- an agent treated as a *black box* (observed from outside) may have some human features attributed, like autonomy, intelligence, etc.

With two additional assumptions:

- a number of agents in a system is relatively large,
- there are some mechanisms incorporated in a system for *generation and removal of agents* that cause the number of agents changes dynamically

we obtain a very interesting type of considered systems, which may be called a *mass multi-agent system* [3]. Such systems may be used for simulation of problems that are distinguished due to their granularity in the sense of existence of a large number of similar objects that manifest some kind of autonomy, but also as a platform facilitating realisation of problem-solving techniques – these may be called *multi-agent computational systems* (MACS) and will constitute a base for further considerations.

From a multi-agent perspective, three types of architectures of computationally intelligent systems may be distinguished. They show consecutive levels of increasing complication that nevertheless may be organised and utilised thanks to incorporation of soft computing methods into well-cooperating capsules — agents.

Figure 1a presents an example of a traditional approach – an evolutionary decision system that uses a fuzzy rule base and inference machine. Each individual represents here a rule (or a group of them), the evolving population – a knowledge base that refines itself to give the sought-after result of inference. Everything may be encapsulated in a single agent utilising this hybrid mechanism to better adapt to the environment it lives in.

An evolutionary multi-agent system (EMAS) depicted in figure 1b can be regarded as a next step of complication. Here evolutionary processes work at a population level – agents are able to reproduce (generate new agents) and may die (be eliminated from the system) on the base of adequately combined evolutionary operators. Evaluation of agents behaviour and selection mechanisms lead to arising the best fitted population with respect to the goal of the system. The result is formed as a simple composition of results obtained by particular agents. The architecture of EMAS is homogeneous, which means that agents are identical in the sense of an algorithm and built-in actions.

So described EMAS may be considered a new soft computing technique for problems that are being solved by searching some space for elements of the given features. Population of agents is assigned as a means for the search there. Let us investigate what opportunities are hidden behind the proposed approach:

- local selection allows for intensive exploration of the search space, like in parallel evolutionary algorithms,
- the way phenotype (behaviour of an agent) is developed from genotype (inherited information) depends on its interaction with the environment,
- the behaviour of agents can be dictated by their various internal mechanisms uniform or not across the population,
- self-management of the population (with respect to the size or other indexes) is applicable if appropriate selection mechanisms are used,
- the appropriately defined environment should facilitate effective implementation of EMAS based on a distributed computer architecture.

The highest level of complication is exemplified in figure 1c. Agents are heterogeneous in this case. Some of them may use a neural network, others – evolutionary algorithm etc. The global goal is attained as a consequence of negotiation among the agents. Variety of techniques and protocols can be applied for that purpose. It can be said that this kind of systems closely approaches typical multi-agent ones operating in the network environment.

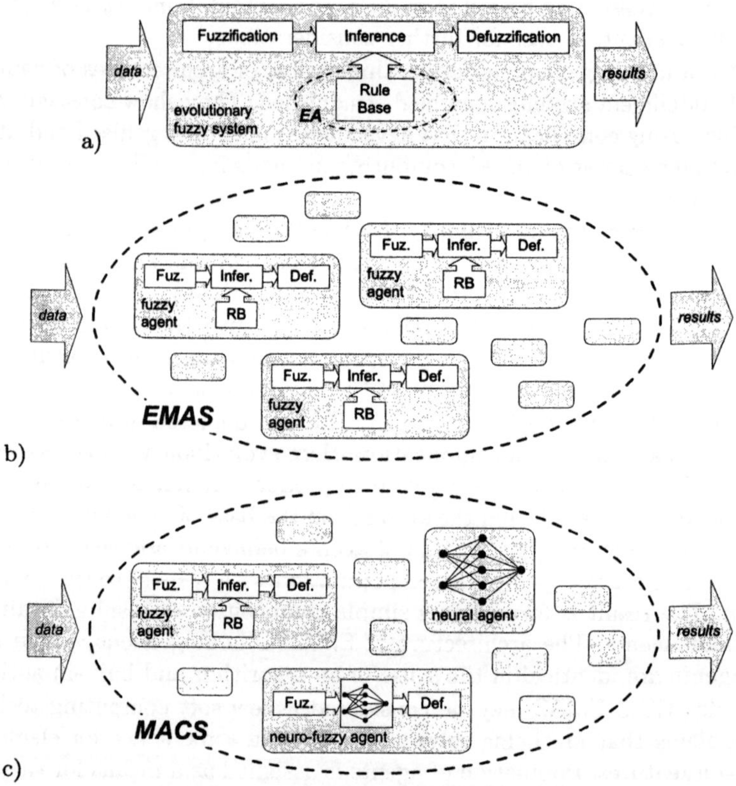

Fig. 1. Architectures of CI systems: a hybrid system in a single agent (a), a population of homogenous agents (b), a population of heterogeneous agents (c)

The terse description of the idea of computational intelligence using as a warp the multi-agent paradigm is attempted to be clarified in the next sections. They include descriptions of three systems developed that can be located somehow in the considered sequence of architectures.

3 EMAS for multiobjective optimisation

The particular EMAS should search for a set of points which constitute the approximation of the Pareto frontier for a given multicriteria optimisation problem [5]. The population of agents represents feasible solutions to the problem defined by a system of objective functions. Energetic reward/punishment mechanism prefers non-dominated agents via *domination principle* forcing dominated agents to give a fixed amount of their energy to the encountered dominants. This may happen when two agents communicate with each other and this way obtain the information about their quality. The flow of energy connected with the *domination principle* causes that dominating agents are more likely to reproduce whereas dominated ones are more likely to die.

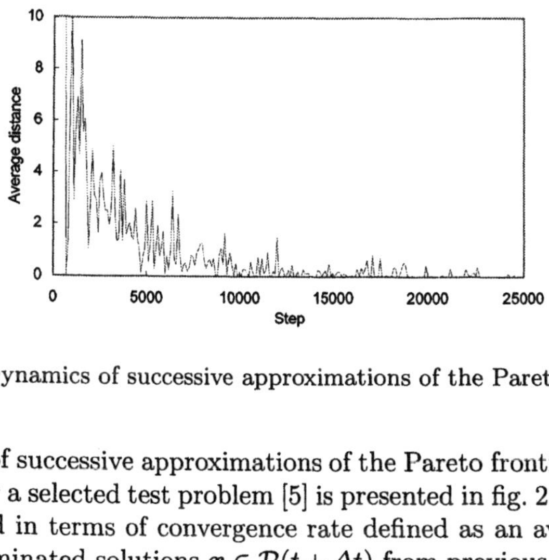

Fig. 2. Dynamics of successive approximations of the Pareto frontier

Dynamics of successive approximations of the Pareto frontier $\mathcal{P}(t)$ in time intervals Δt for a selected test problem [5] is presented in fig. 2. The dynamics is characterised in terms of convergence rate defined as an average distance of new non-dominated solutions $x \in \mathcal{P}(t+\Delta t)$ from previous approximation $\mathcal{P}(t)$.

4 Fuzzy EMAS for data classification

The goal of this particular system is data classification, which means that it should assign membership classes to supplied data sets – vectors of attributes, possibly describing some domain-specific objects, events or phenomena. Of course before the system is able to give correct answers it should be given a

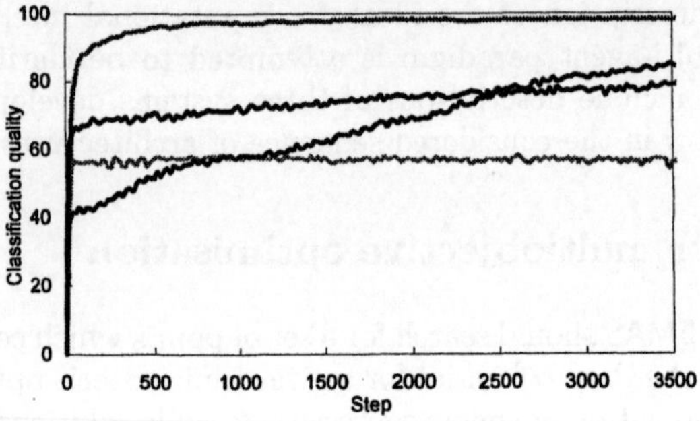

Fig. 3. Classification quality during learning phase for four data sets

representative set of examples: selected vectors of attributes with appropriate class membership assigned. The system consists of two kinds of agents, namely *classifier* and *supervisor* agents [7]. Classifier agents consist of one or more fuzzy classifiers and carry out the classification of incoming data. Supervisor agents are responsible for distributing the data, collecting answers of classifier agents, and generating the whole system's response.

Data sets used in the tests [7] are available from *UCI Machine Learning Repository*. Figure 3 shows the system's classification quality during learning phase. One may notice that for most data sets the systems learns quite quickly, but for some of them a longer learning phase is needed.

5 Neural EMAS for time-series prediction

In this case the goal of the system is *prediction* (or *forecasting*), i.e. generation of information about possible future development of some process from data about its past and present behaviour. Subsequent elements of the sequence(s) to be predicted are supplied to the system, where they become available for all agents. Agents perform analysis of incoming data and give predictions of the next-to-come elements of input. To model the characteristics of a signal agents use artificial neural networks [6] – in the particular case multi-layer perceptrons, which are supervisory trained using the comparison between values predicted and received as an error measure. The networks are also a subject of generational evolutionary optimisation [2].

Figure 4 shows the results of experiments [2] with weather data from the Biological Station Mountain Lake (University of Virginia), namely the temperature measured at about 2.5 m above the ground every 30 minutes during 7 years. In the first plot the prediction error in consecutive steps of the system activity is presented – one may notice that it is mostly below 10%, which is not a bad result considering complexity of the time-series. In the second plot the number of hidden neurons in all networks in the system (mean and standard deviation) is also presented.

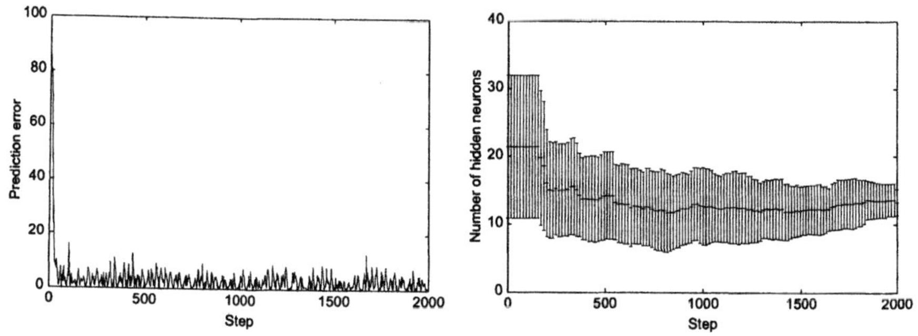

Fig. 4. Weather time-series prediction error and average number of hidden neurons

6 Concluding remarks

The idea of building computational intelligence using the framework of multi-agent systems together with strong suggestion of awaited benefit is presented in the paper. It is justified by two facts:

- results of agent technology (theoretical foundation, methods of design and specification, even some programming tools) can be utilised,
- some systems of the discussed type has been already built and tested and seem to be promising.

The most complicated (heterogeneous) architectures are now the subject of the studies. The main question is whether similar results can be obtained on the basis of simpler architectures — this requires extended simulation experiments for a representative set of test cases.

References

1. P. Bonissone. Soft computing: the convergence of emerging reasoning technologies. *Soft Computing*, 1(1):6–18, 1997.
2. A. Byrski, M. Kisiel-Dorohinicki, and E. Nawarecki. Agent-based evolution of neural network architecture. In M. Hamza, editor, *Proc. of the IASTED Int. Symp.: Applied Informatics*. IASTED/ACTA Press, 2002.
3. G. Dobrowolski, M. Kisiel-Dorohinicki, and E. Nawarecki. Some approach to design and realisation of mass multi-agent systems. In R. Schaefer and S. Sędziwy, editors, *Advances in Multi-Agent Systems*. Jagiellonian University, 2001.
4. J. Ferber. *Multi-Agent Systems. An Introduction to Distributed Artificial Intelligence*. Addison-Wesley, 1999.
5. M. Kisiel-Dorohinicki, G. Dobrowolski, and E. Nawarecki. Evolutionary multi-agent system in multiobjective optimisation. In M. Hamza, editor, *Proc. of the IASTED Int. Symp.: Applied Informatics*. IASTED/ACTA Press, 2001.
6. T. Masters. *Neural, Novel and Hybrid Algorithms for Time Series Prediction*. John Wiley and Sons, 1995.
7. A. Niemiec, R. Pajak, and M. Kisiel-Dorohinicki. Agent-based fuzzy classifier system. Accepted for publication in *Intelligent Information Systems XI – Proc. of IIS 2002 Conference*.

Conditional Belief Functions Versus Proper Belief Functions

Mieczyslaw Alojzy Klopotek[1,3] and Slawomir Tadeusz Wierzchon[1,2]

[1] Institute of Computer Science, Polish Academy of Sciences, Warszawa, Poland
[2] Department of Computer Science, Bialystok University of Technology, Poland
[3] Institute of Computer Science, University of Podlasie, Poland

Abstract. Dempster-Shafer conditional belief functions are generally not usable because composition of conditional belief functions is not granted to yield joint multivariate belief distribution, as some values of the belief distribution may be negative [1,3]. The paper proposes a framework, within which a sufficient condition for non-negativity of the graphoidally represented belief function is defined.

1 Introduction

The Dempster-Shafer Mathematical Theory of Evidence (MTE) is a well known extension of classical probabilistic methods of representation of and reasoning with uncertain knowledge. It has been applied in integration of knowledge from heterogeneous sources for object identification, technical diagnosis under unreliable measuring devices, medical applications, network reliability computation, reliability in real-time X-ray radioscopy and ultrasounds, multisensor image segmentation, safety control in large plants, map construction and maintenance, just to mention a few. For a recent review of definitions of fundamental concepts and reasoning methods within MTE see [4,5], for a review of learning methods consult [1,5], for a review of interpretations of MTE see [5],

MTE generalizes probability theory in that the basic probability mass (m) is assigned not only to elementary events, but also to sets of events.

$$\sum_{A \in 2^{\Xi}} m(A) = 1, \quad m(\emptyset) = 0$$

Based on this, belief (Bel), plausibility (P) and commonality (Q) are defined:

$$Bel(A) = \sum_{B \subseteq A} m(B), \quad Pl(A) = 1 - Bel(\Xi - A), \quad Q(A) = \sum_{A \subseteq B} m(B)$$

If m is non-negative everywhere, then we talk about proper belief ect. When only Q is non-negative everywhere, we speak about pseudo-belief etc.

One can combine evidence from independent sources E_1, E_2 via the combination operator $\oplus$: (c - normalizing constant)

$$m_{E_1,E_2}(A) = m_{E_1} \oplus m_{E_2}(A) = c \cdot \sum_{B,C;A=B \cap C} m_{E_1}(B) \cdot m_{E_2}(C)$$

Consider a mass function m defined over the set $\Xi = \Xi_1 \times ... \times \Xi_n$ that is over a multidimensional set of variables $X = \{X_1, ..., X_n\}$. Thus, elements of Ξ are n-dimensional vectors. Let q be a subset of these variables. For the set A of elements from Ξ let $A^{\downarrow q}$ be the set of projections of vectors of A onto the subspace spanned by the set of variables q. Then define $m^{\downarrow q}(C) = \sum_{A; C=A^{\downarrow q}} m(A)$. $Bel^{\downarrow q}$, $Pl^{\downarrow q}$, $Q^{\downarrow q}$ are defined accordingly. Under multivariate settings, conditional mass, belief, plausibility, commonality are defined as follows: Let Bel be a belief function defined for the set of variables X and let q be a subset of this set. Then $Bel^{|q}$ is any pseudo-belief function fitting the equation

$$Bel = Bel^{|q} \oplus Bel^{\downarrow q}$$

The analogy between MTE and probability theory is obvious. It goes further in that both possess the so-called graphoidal properties [3], so that compact representation of multivariate Bel in terms of a belief network, exploiting conditional independence of variables (analogous to probabilistic conditional independence) is possible [5].

However, a widespread usage of conditional belief functions is hampered because composition of conditional belief functions is not granted to yield proper multivariate belief distribution, as some values of the belief distribution may turn out to be negative [1,3]. We explain this problem in detail in Section 2. Section 3 proposes a framework, within which a sufficient condition for non-negativity of the graphoidally represented belief function is defined. Section 4 contains some concluding remarks.

2 The Problem

Let us illustrate the problem of well-formedness of graphoidal decomposition in MTE with Bayesian networks. Table 1a) gives marginal distribution of X_1, table 1b) table 1c) - some conditionals. For these definitions, $m_{X_1} \oplus m_{X_2|X_1} \oplus m_{X_3|X_2}$ and $m_{X_1} \oplus m_{X_2|X_1} \oplus m_{X_3|X_1} \oplus m_{X_4|X_1}$ are proper belief functions (with non-negative values of m). But the function $m = m_{X_1} \oplus m_{X_2|X_1} \oplus m_{X_3|X_2} \oplus m_{X_4|X_3}$ is not a proper belief function, as visible in table 2. It is easily checked that all marginals over each individual variable of $m = m_{X_1} \oplus m_{X_2|X_1} \oplus m_{X_3|X_2} \oplus m_{X_4|X_3}$ are identical.

Also the function $m = m_{X_1} \oplus m_{X_2|X_1} \oplus m_{X_3|X_1} \oplus m_{X_4|X_1} \oplus m_{X_5|X_1}$ is not a proper belief function as visible in the table 2

Hence, in MTE, sample generation from a network and the development of learning algorithms identifying graphoidal structure from data, reasoning from sample data, understanding of causality and of mechanisms giving rise to belief distributions is hampered. For this reason, known sample generation algorithms do not use conditional belief functions [2] and therefore (1) conditional independence between variables cannot be pre-specified for the sample and (2) a single generator pass may fail to generate a single sample element.

Table 1. a) Sample marginal distribution b), c) sample conditional distributions

(a)

X_1	m_{X_1}
{a}	0.4
{b}	0.4
{a,b}	0.2

(b)

X_i	X_{i+1}	$m_{X_{i+1}\|X_i}$
{a} ×	{a}	0.293333
{a} ×	{b}	-0.126667
{a} ×	{a,b}	-0.166667
{b} ×	{a}	-0.126667
{b} ×	{b}	0.293333
{b} ×	{a,b}	-0.166667
{a,b} ×	{a}	0.3
{a,b} ×	{b}	0.3
{a,b} ×	{a,b}	0.4

(c)

X_1	X_i	$m_{X_i\|X_1}$
{a} ×	{a}	0.166667
{a} ×	{b}	-0.0833333
{a} ×	{a,b}	-0.0833333
{b} ×	{a}	-0.0833333
{b} ×	{b}	0.166667
{b} ×	{a,b}	-0.0833333
{a,b} ×	{a}	0.35
{a,b} ×	{b}	0.35
{a,b} ×	{a,b}	0.3

Table 2. $m = m_{X_1} \oplus m_{X_2|X_1} \oplus m_{X_3|X_2} \oplus m_{X_4|X_3}$ (left) and $m = m_{X_1} \oplus m_{X_2|X_1} \oplus m_{X_3|X_1} \oplus m_{X_4|X_1} \oplus m_{X_5|X_1}$ (right)

X1	X2	X3	X4	m
		....		...
{a} ×	{b} ×	{a} ×	{a}	9.40444e-05
{a} ×	{b} ×	{a} ×	{b}	-2.91556e-05
{a} ×	{b} ×	{a} ×	{a,b}	-3.82222e-05
		....		...

X1	X2	X3	X4	X5	m
		....			...
{a} ×	{b} ×	{b} ×	{b} ×	{a,b}	-0.000107315
{a} ×	{b} ×	{b} ×	{a,b} ×	{a}	0.0022038
{a} ×	{b} ×	{b} ×	{a,b} ×	{b}	-0.000107315
		....			...

3 The Solution

In our solution to the problem of well-formedness of belief functions composed from conditional belief functions we impose the restriction that in the Bayesian network no two parents of a node are directly connected.

The fundamental idea behind the approach is to replace the conditional belief function with a special conditional probability function while splitting some values of variables into subvalues. These subvalues take care of differences between belief distributions for subsets and supersets of elementary values of variables. The proper generation of samples is run with these special conditional probability functions in a very traditional way, and after completion of sample generation the split values are again joined.

The main difficulties we encounter with handling conditional belief functions is that the conditional independence in MTE is radically different from probabilistic independence and that the conditional mass functions m take negative values.

To overcome negativeness, we assume that the conditional belief functions are represented in terms of so-called K functions as introduced in [1]. Given that X is the set of all variables in the conditional belief function and q the set of conditioning variables, we have:

$$K_{|q}(A) = \sum_{B; A^{\downarrow q} \subseteq B^{\downarrow q}, A^{\downarrow X-q} = B^{\downarrow X-q},} m(B)$$

For example, given m in table 3 (a) we get K in table 3 (b): K-function is

Table 3. A conditional mass function m (a) and its corresponding cumulative mass function K (b).

(a)

X1	X2	m
{a} ×	{a}	0.166667
{a} ×	{b}	-0.0833333
{a} ×	{a,b}	-0.0833333
{b} ×	{a}	-0.0833333
{b} ×	{b}	0.166667
{b} ×	{a,b}	-0.0833333
{a,b} ×	{a}	0.35
{a,b} ×	{b}	0.35
{a,b} ×	{a,b}	0.3

(b)

X1	X2	K
{a} ×	{a}	0.516667
{a} ×	{b}	0.266667
{a} ×	{a,b}	0.216667
{b} ×	{a}	0.266667
{b} ×	{b}	0.516667
{b} ×	{a,b}	0.216667
{a,b} ×	{a}	0.35
{a,b} ×	{b}	0.35
{a,b} ×	{a,b}	0.3

nonnegative. For any level of conditioning variables the conditioned variables form a probability distribution.

Now we extend the set of values of every variable. If the set S is a set of values of an attribute, then we define the function $MY()$ as $MY(S) = S$ and $SU()$ as $SU(S) = \emptyset$. Let us define the concept of a V-expression as follows. S is a V-expression. For any V-expression V for any proper non-empty subset $s \subset MY(V)$ we define V-expressions $s©V$ and $s@V$ and define functions $MY(s©V) = MY(s@V) = s$, $SU(s©V) = SU(s@V) = V$. The only element of the set $\{S\}^n$ is a V(n)-expression. $MY(S^n) = S$ and $SU(S^n) = \emptyset$. For any V-expression V for any proper non-empty subset $s \subset MY(V)$, V(n)-expressions are elements of the set: V_n=$\{s©V, s@V\}^n$-$\{s©V\}^n$ and for every $v_n \in V_n$ $MY(v_n) = s$, $SU(v_n) = V$. Thus each V(n)-expression is a vector of n V-expressions.

Let X_j be a node in the belief network with n successors and let $\pi(X_j)$ be the set of its predecessors in the network. Let $K_{X_j|\pi(X_j)}$ be the K-function associated with this node. We transform it into a conditional probability function by replacing X_j with X'_j taking its values from the set of V(n)-expressions over the set of values of X_j, and every variable $X_i \in \pi(X_j)$ is replaced with X''_i taking its values from the set of V-expressions over the set of values of X_j. $P(x'_j|x''_{i1}, \ldots, x''_{ik})$ is calculated as follows:

1. If $SU(x''_{i1}) = \ldots = SU(x''_{ik}) = \emptyset$ then for any subset of values s from the domain of X_j $\sum_{x'_j; MY(x'_j)=s} P(x'_j|x''_{i1}, \ldots, x''_{ik}) = K_{X_j|\pi(X_j)}(x'_j|x''_{i1} \ldots, x''_{ik})$.
2. If $SU(x'_j) \neq \emptyset$ then $P(x'_j|x''_{i1}, \ldots, x''_{ik}) = P(SU(x'_j)^n|x''_{i1}, \ldots, x''_{ik})$.
3. If $x''_{il} = MY(x''_{il})©SU(x''_{il})$ then
$P(x'_j|x''_{i1}, \ldots, x''_{il}, \ldots, x''_{ik}) = P(x'_j|x''_{i1}, \ldots, SU(x''_{il}), \ldots, x''_{ik})$
4. If $x''_{il} = MY(x''_{il})@SU(x''_{il})$ let x^*_{il} denote either x''_{il} or $SU(x''_{il})$ and otherwise let x^*_{il} denote only x''_{il}. if $x''_{il} = MY(x''_{il})@SU(x''_{il})$ let x^+_{il} denote either $MY(x''_{il})$ and otherwise let x^+_{il} denote only x''_{il}. Then
$P(x'_j|x^+_{i1}, \ldots, x^+_{ik}) = average_{x^*_{i1}, \ldots, x^*_{ik}}(P(x'_j|x^*_{i1}, \ldots, x^*_{ik}))$

To meet the well-formedness criterion, $P(x'_j|x''_{i1},\ldots,x_{ik})''$ has to be non-negative everywhere. If X_j is a parent of another node in the network on the $h-th$ outgoing edge, then the respective x''_j acts as the $h-th$ element of the vector x'_j. With such a transformed probability distribution we generate the sample and then replace all the V- and V(n) expressions V with $MY(V)$.

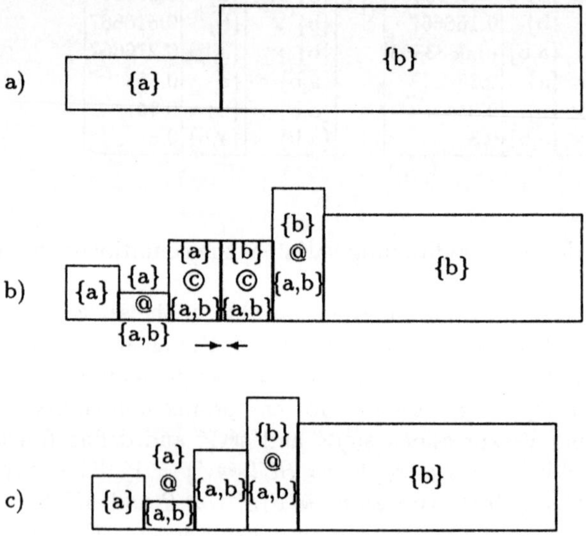

Fig. 1. An illustration of the merging process of the values of variable X1 with the domain {a,b}. (see the text for explanations)

If X_j is the conditioning variable in the $n-th$ branch then the composite (vector) values act as if they were the nth component of the vector. After random generation the variable values collapse back to what they were before. Figure 1 provides an insight into the background idea of the process of transformation of K distributions into $P(|)$ distributions in case of a single successor. The idea is that of splitting a conditional distribution into parts that compensate one another to achieve the original distribution. With more (say n) successors one shall imagine a multidimensional ($n+1$-dimensional picture with independent splits for each successor. Out of the 2^n parts resulting from splitting, only one will merge with the neighboring value of the conditioning variable. To illustrate the merging process of the values of a variable consider the variable X1 with the domain {a,b}. In Figure 1a) a symbolic representation of the original conditional distribution of $K(X2|X1=\{a\})$ (to the left) and $K(X2|X1=\{b\})$ (to the right) is visible. In Figure 1b) in the neighboring region of X1={a} and X1={b} the distributions of $K(X2|X1=.)$ tend to get to a balance (equal to the $K(X2|X1=\{a,b\})$), hence are denoted $K(X2|X1=\{a\}©\{a,b\})$ and $K(X2|X1=\{b\}©\{a,b\})$. As a "side-effect" the distributions of areas further away change so as to compensate so that proper distribution of the region is reestablished: $K(X2|X1 = \{a\}) = 0.5 \cdot (K(X2|X1 = \{a\}©\{a,b\}) + K(X2|X1 = \{a\}@\{a,b\}))$ and $K(X2|X1 = \{b\}) = 0.5 \cdot (K(X2|X1 = \{b\}©\{a,b\}) + K(X2|X1 = \{b\}@\{a,b\}))$. In Figure 1c) subpopulations in neighboring regions with identical distributions of $X2$. $X1$={a}©{a,b} and $X1$={b}©{a,b} are merging: The conditional distribution is kept $(K(X2|X1 = \{a\}©\{a,b\}) = K(X2|X1 = \{b\}©\{a,b\}) = K(X2|X1 = \{a,b\}))$, but the objects acquire "double identity" with respect to X1: their X1 value is equal to the set {a,b}.

4 Concluding Remarks

The proposed method of creation of conditional belief functions implies a new sample generation procedure for MTE that has several significant advantages:

- A single sample object is generated in a single generator cycle (earlier generators [2] required 1 to n passes because of contradictions in component belief functions)
- The conditional independence structure can be pre-specified for the generated sample
- As a result a sufficient well-formedness criterion for conditional belief functions is developed ensuring that the joint belief distribution represented by a set of conditional belief functions really exists.

To verify the above sample generation algorithm, and hence the well-formedness criterion, a program has been implemented allowing to generate the sample from conditional belief functions and to test MTE conditional independence properties of the sample. The independence test is based on a previously elaborated layered independence test [1]. The PC algorithm of Spirtes/Glymour/Scheines has been successfully tested for multivariate belief distributions for samples generated by our approach [1,5]

References

1. Klopotek M.A.: *Methods of Identification and Interpretations of Belief Distributions in the Dempster-Shafer Theory* (in Polish). Publisher: Institute of Computer Science, Polish Academy of Sciences, Warsaw, Poland, 1998.
2. Moral S, Wilson N. Importance sampling Monte-Carlo algorithm for the calculation of Dempster-Shafer belief, Proc. 6th Int.Conf. IPMU'96, Granada 1-5.7.1996, Vol. III, pp. 1337-1344
3. Shenoy P.P.: Conditional Independence in Valuation-based Systems. *International Journal of Approximate Reasoning*, 10, 203-234, 1994.
4. Wierzchon S.T.: *Methods of Representation and rocessing of Uncertauin Information in the Dempster-shafer Theory* (in Polish), Publisher: Institute of Computer Science, Polish Academy of Sciences, Warsaw, Poland, 1996,
5. Wierzchon S.T., Klopotek M.A.: *Evidential Reasoning. An Interpretative Investigation.* University of Podlasie Publishing House, Siedlce, 2002.

Transformation Distances, Strings and Identification of DNA Promoters

Maciej Marczak[1], Włodzisław Duch[2], Karol Grudziński[2], and Antoine Naud[2]

[1] Systems Research Institute, Polish Academy of Sciences, Warsaw, Poland
[2] Department of Informatics, Nicholas Copernicus University, Grudziądzka 5, 87-100 Toruń, Poland. www.phys.uni.torun.pl/kmk

Abstract. Computational intelligence methods usually work in vector spaces and are not able to deal with objects that have complex structures. Methods based on similarity may be applied in structural domains. Similarity may be defined by minimal cost needed to transform one object into another. The costs of the substitution operations that such transformation is composed from may be treated as adaptive parameters. For strings this leads to a generalization of edit (Levenshtein) distance. This distance is computed using dynamic programming method and applied to the problem of identifying DNA gene promoter sequences.

1 Introduction

Neural networks and other computational intelligence (CI) methods assume very simple vector space paradigm for representation of knowledge. Artificial intelligence (AI) deals with symbolic representation of knowledge that usually cannot be represented in such way. In effect AI and CI became widely separated, with AI community focusing on modeling of complex knowledge and inductive symbolic machine learning approaches, and CI community focusing on pattern recognition problems. Both approaches are insufficient in many situations and a new learning paradigm is needed [1]. Complex systems, such as commercial organizations, chemical molecules or molecular biology objects (DNA sequences, genes, proteins) cannot be easily accommodated in AI or CI knowledge representation frameworks.

A general framework for processing of structural data, based on recurrent neural networks and hidden Markov models, has been introduced [2], but it is rather difficult to implement and use. The two most common knowledge representation schemes in AI are based on the state or the problem description [3]. The goal is also a state or a simple problem that has known solution. A set of operators is defined, transforming the initial object (state, problem), into the final object (goal). Each operator has some costs associated with its use. Solutions are represented by paths in the search graph. The best solution has lowest costs of transforming the initial object into the final object.

This seems to be a very good model for CI methods applied to complex objects. It is used in this paper for DNA sequences, but the method is quite general and may be applied to arbitrary complex objects, as long as transformation operators and associated costs may be defined. Evaluation of similarities between objects should be done efficiently, therefore we have developed a method based on dynamic programming [4]. Members of the same class (cluster) should have high internal similarity, while those from different classes (clusters) should differ significantly. This may be achieved by adapting costs of operations that are performed on objects. Experimental results for the identification of promoter sites in DNA strings are given in the third section. A short discussion closes this paper.

2 Transformation distances

Comparison of two objects is done using similarity or equivalently distance measures. A set of operators should be given, with associated costs of using each operator. In case of strings such operators are substitutions of single letters or substrings by other substrings, including an empty substring (representing deletion). In case of numerical values shift operators may change one value into another at the cost proportional to the numerical difference between the values. The set of operators should be complete, i.e. for every pair of objects a transformation that changes one of the objects into another should exist.

A transformation T is defined by a finite sequence of operators $T = \prod_i \hat{\Omega}_i$. Transformation $T O_i$ always creates a single object O_j, but for every pair of objects O_i and O_j many transformations connecting these objects (i.e. changing one object into the other) may exist. The cost of the transformation $W(T)$ is a sum of the costs of all the operations $W(T) = \sum_i W(\hat{\Omega}_i)$. These costs will be called below the operation (or substitution) weights.

The edit distance of two strings S_1 and S_2, is defined as the minimum number of single-letter insertions, deletions and substitutions required to transform S_1 into S_2. Each of these operations has its own weight. Efficient sequential and parallel algorithms for computing the edit distance between two strings exist, based on the idea of dynamic programming. A distance $D(O_i, O_j)$ between a pair of objects O_i, O_j is equal to the minimum weight of all transformations connecting these objects. At first sight calculation of such distances may look like an NP-complete problem. One of us has proved [4] that it is equivalent to the generalization of the edit distance (Levenshtein distance). An efficient algorithm based on dynamic programming was found to calculate these distances, with the complexity of the order of $O(|O_i| \times |O_j|)$, where $|O_i|$ is the length of the object O_i, i.e. it distance from an empty object.

A String Transformation System (STS) is a triple (O, S, W), where:
O – a set of objects, which are finite sequences of features
S – a set of elementary substitutions, which are finite pairs of sequences of features
W – a normalized weight function, assigning to all substitutions weights.

Normalization means that the sum of weights for all elementary substitutions is equal to one. This condition may be replaced by fixing the value of one, frequently used substitution. String Transformation Systems may be treated as a special case of the general Transformation Systems described in [1,5]. Sets of substitutions, each with its own weight, create multi-letter substitutions, e.g. $(abdc, cg)$, $(a, atccg)$, $(daac, \emptyset)$, where $\emptyset$ is a null string. In this case the edit distances are computed using the dynamic programming [6].

3 Classification of complex objects

The ability to calculate distances or similarities between complex objects allows to use the powerful similarity-based approaches for calculation of classification probabilities [7]. Consider a two-class problem with a set of $C+$ training cases from the first class and $C-$ training cases from the second class. For all objects belonging to these sets the distance matrix $D_W(O_i, O_j)$ is computed. This matrix depends on the set of weights $\{W_i\}$ assigned to the elementary substitutions Ω_i. Classification probabilities $p(C_i|\mathbf{X}; W)$ depend on the distances, therefore they also depend on the choice of substitutes and their weights. In supervised learning these weights are optimized using the error function:

$$E(W) = \sum_{\mathbf{X}} \sum_{i} (p(C_i|\mathbf{X}; W) - P_i(\mathbf{X}))^2 \quad (1)$$

where $P_i(\mathbf{X})$ is the true probability of assigning the vector $\mathbf{X}$ to the class C_i, known for the training set vectors. This error function should be minimized in respect to parameters W and all other parameters and procedures used to calculate the $p(C_i|\mathbf{X}; W)$ probability [7]. In an ideal case distances between all objects in the $C+$ class should be zero, and the same for the distances inside $C-$ class. A set of weights and substitutions that achieve this explains the class structure, but for real life data this situation will rarely be possible.

The disadvantage of error function minimization is the need to recalculate all lowest-cost distances. Below a computationally less expensive approach is followed. Objects will be represented in vector spaces reflecting their structural relations. Some minimal transformations connect only one pair of objects, while some may connect many. Among all transformations with minimal cost for every pair of objects O_i and O_j those that connect the largest subset are called Primary Transformations (PTs). They represent the most probable hypothesis or the most useful transformations.

For every object O two vectors defining its relations with all objects from its own class and from all other classes are created:

$$V^+(O) = [v_1^+, \ldots, v_n^+], V^-(O) = [v_1^-, \ldots, v_n^-], \quad (2)$$

where v_i^+ (similarly v_i^-) is the number of S_i substitutes ($i = 1 \ldots n$) in the primary transformations that connect this object with all others in the $C+$ set. These vectors provide structural representation of object relations. This representation depends on the choice of the elementary substitution set S and the choice of weights W. For the string objects a simple set of letter substitutions (identity substitutions $s \leftrightarrow s$ plus symbol removal/addition $s \leftrightarrow \theta$ substitutions) and constant weights lead to quite good results. Thus for n symbols objects are represented by two vectors in the $3n$-dimensional space. In this space the difference of the two vectors $X(O) = V^+(O) - V^-(O)$ may be used with the linear discriminiation to define a separating hyperplane W_R:

$$O_i \in C^+ \Leftrightarrow X(O_i) \cdot W_R > 0; \quad O_i \in C^- \Leftrightarrow X(O_i) \cdot W_R < 0 \quad (3)$$

for all O_i objects in the training set. Once the $X(O)$ vectors are defined any method of classification may be used, in particular linear discrimination or a Support Vector Machine approach. Of course there is no guarantee that this representation will lead to a separable problem.

4 Experiments with promoters

A site on a DNA string to which RNA polymerase will bind and initiate transcription is called a promoter. These sites contain signals that are used to regulate gene expression. *Escherichia coli* is a well-known bacterium with 4.6 million bases in its genome. A small number (106) of short DNA subsequences (57 nucleotides) have been identified, exactly half of them containing the promoter signals. The task is to distinguish between these sequences. The data contains strings of the type ... tttatattttcgcttgtcaggccg ... The data is available from the UCI repository [8].

Since 4 letters, a, c, t, g are present in the string a naive way to change them into numerical values is to replace them by 1, 2, 3 ,4. In the STS approach structural representation of strings described above is defined in 12-dimensional space (4 symbols, 3 transformations: identity and $s \leftrightarrow \theta$. For example, the value of the first feature for object O is equal to the number of $a \leftrightarrow a$ substitutions in the primary transformation connecting this object to all others from the $C+$ class. Classification procedures applied directly to promoter data work in 57-dimensional space.

STS results were compared with the results of the nearest neighbor methods with various distance functions and optimization of k, the number of neighbors taken into account during classification. Using the leave-one-out method with k=1 and Euclidean distance (the most common k-NN variant) gives only 70.8% correct answers. Optimization of k indicates best solution for $k = 18, 19$, increasing accuracy to 84.0%. Other distance function improve results significantly, with the best results obtained using probabilistic, data dependent Value Difference Metric [7] that was computed separately for the 105 training vectors in each partition of the leave-one-out procedure, and applied to the one test vector. Optimizing k allows to reach 91.5% of accuracy with this method.

Table 1. Classification results for the promoters data with different distance functions.

Method	Leave-one-out accuracy %	No. of errors
ID3 [9]	82.1	19
Euclides, k=19	84,0	17
Manhatan, k=19	85,9	15
Canberra, k=33	87,7	13
STS, k=1	90,6	10
Value Difference Metric, k=7	91,5	9
MLP [9]	92.5	8
STS, k=9	94,3	6

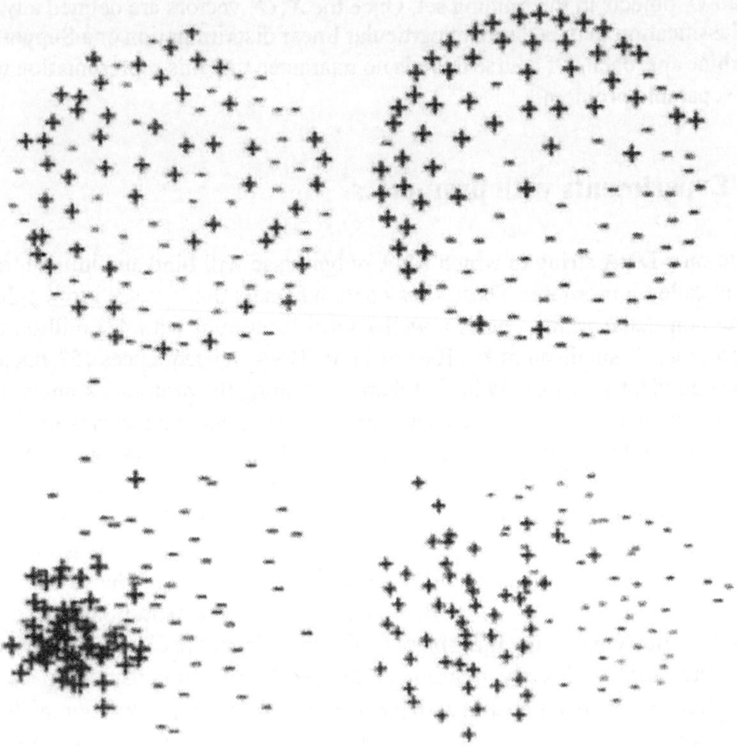

Fig. 1. MDS representation of the original (Euclidean) DNA string distances (top-left) and 3 representations of the same data shown using transformation distances with different costs of substitutions. Promoter instances are marked as +, remaining as −.

Turning to the STS approach, the simplest set of substitutions with equal costs leads to the distance matrix that has been used in the kNN procedure, giving in the leave-one-out test 90,6% accuracy for k=1. Several methods for adjusting costs of substitutions were tried, resulting with results reaching 94.3% accuracy in the kNN leave-one-out procedure (corresponding to about 6 errors). Similar results are achieved with linear discrimination using $V^+ - V^-$ matrix. Table 1 contains comparison of results obtained on this dataset. Towell *et. al* [9] report that adding domain knowledge and refining it with the neural network they obtained 4 errors only. Knowledge-based support vector machine has been used on this data recently, making 5 errors [10]. We have not used any additional information to improve the results.

Multidimensional scaling technique allows to visualize relations between data objects [11]. In our case original space has 57 dimensions. Ideal transformation distance should lead to two well separated small clusters. Clusterization is positively correlated with the accuracy of classification. Several examples of the effects of transformation distances with different substitution costs are shown in Fig.1. In all cases configuration obtained from the principal component analysis was taken for the start of the MDS procedure. Transformation distances improve the clusterization of sequences taken from promoter and the non-promoter DNA quite clearly.

5 Conclusions

Although the research reported here is still in the preliminary stage it offers a relatively easy extension of computational intelligence methods to complex domains where problems cannot be easily represented in the vector space as a set of a fixed number of features. Our preliminary results are very encouraging and it is obvious that many methods may be used in connection with the transformation distances. Full optimization of costs of all operations may become difficult, requiring global optimization, therefore methods should be thought in which efficient gradient techniques are applicable. Numerous extensions and applications of the approach described here are planned in the near future.

Acknowledgments: Support by the Polish Committee for Scientific Research, grant 8 T11C 006 19, is gratefully acknowledged.

References

1. Goldfarb, L, Golubitsky O. (2001) What is a structural measurement process? Faculty of Computer Science, U.N.B., Technical Report TR01-147
2. Frasconi P, Gori M, Sperduti A. (1998) A General Framework for Adaptive Processing of Data Structures. IEEE Transactions on Neural Networks **9**, 768-786
3. Rich E, Knight K. (1991) Artificial Intelligence. 2nd ed, McGraw-HillInc, New York.
4. Marczak, M. (2001) Zastosowanie uogólnienia odległości Levenshteina w systemie transformacji symbolicznych. Analiza Systemowa w Finansach i Zarządzaniu, Wybrane problemy, Vol.3, IBS PAN Warszawa
5. Goldfarb, L. Nigam, S. (1994) The unified learning paradigm: A foundation for AI. In: V.Honovar, L.Uhr, Eds. Artificial Intelligence and Neural Networks: Steps Toward Principled Integration. Academic Press, Boston
6. Gusfield D. (1997) Algorithms on Strings, Trees, and Sequences: Computer Science and Computational Biology. Cambridge Univ Press, Cambridge, UK
7. Duch, W. (2000) Similarity base methods: a general framework for classification, approximation and association. Control and Cybernetics **29**, 937-968
8. Blake, C.L, Merz, C.J. (1998). UCI Repository of machine learning databases http://www.ics.uci.edu/ mlearn/MLRepository.html. Irvine, CA: University of California, Department of Information and Computer Science.
9. Towell, G, Shavlik, J, Noordewier, M. (1990) Refinement of Approximate Domain Theories by Knowledge-Based Artificial Neural Networks. In: Proc. 8th National Conf. on Artificial Intelligence (AAAI-90), Boston, MA, p. 861-866
10. Fung, G, Mangsarian, O.L, Shavlik, J, (2001) Knowledge-BasedSupport VectorMachineClassifiers. Data Mining Institute Technical Report 01-09, Univ. of Wisconsin, 2001
11. Naud A. (2001) Neural and statistical methods for the visualization of multidimensional data. PhD Thesis, Dept. of Informatics, N. Copernicus University http://www.phys.uni.torun.pl/kmk/publications.html

Solving Stochastic Shortest Path Problem Using Monte Carlo Sampling Method: A Distributed Learning Automata Approach

M. R. Meybodi and Hamid Beigy

Soft Computing Laboratory
Computer Engineering Department
Amirkabir University of Technology
Tehran, Iran
meybodi@ce.aku.ac.ir *beigy@ce.aku.ac.ir*

Abstract. In this paper, we introduce a Monte Carlo simulation method based on distributed learning automata (DLA) for solving the stochastic shortest path problem. We give an iterative stochastic algorithm that finds the minimum expected value of set of random variables representing cost of paths in a stochastic graph by taking sufficient samples from them. In the given algorithm, the sample size is determined dynamically as the algorithm proceeds. It is shown that when the total sample size tends to infinity, the proposed algorithm finds the shortest path. In this algorithm, at each instant, DLA determine which edges to be sampled. This reduces the unnecessary sampling from the edges which don't seem to be on the shortest path and thus reduces the overall sampling size. A new method of proof (different from [2,3]) is used to prove the convergence of the proposed algorithm. The simulations conducted confirm the theory.

1 Introduction

The deterministic shortest path problem has been studied extensively and many algorithms reported in the literature. In this problem, one looks for a path joining source and destination nodes while minimizing sum of costs of the traversed edges. However, there are many applications in which cost of edges are random variables [1]. These graphs called *stochastic graphs* and can be defined by a triple $G =< V, E, Q >$, where $V = \{1, 2, \ldots, n\}$ is set of nodes, $E \subset V \times V$ is set of edges, and $n \times n$ matrix Q is the probability distribution describing the statistics of edge costs. In particular, cost C_{ij} of edge (i, j) is assumed to be a random variable with q_{ij} as its probability density function. It is assumed that the distribution q_{ij} is not known a priori.

The path π_i from source node v_s to destination node v_d in the stochastic graph G is defined as an ordering $\pi_i = \{i_1, i_2, \ldots, i_{m_i}\}$ ($\pi_i \subset V$) in such a way that $i_1 = v_s$ and $i_{m_i} = v_d$ are source and destination nodes, respectively and $(i_j, i_{j+1}) \in E$ for $1 \leq j < m_i$. Assume that there are r paths $\Pi = \{\pi_1, \pi_2, \ldots, \pi_r\}$ between source node v_s and destination node v_d. The shortest path is defined as a path with minimum expected cost. In other word, the shortest path π^* has the expected cost $C_{\pi^*} = \min_{\pi_i \in \Pi}\{C_{\pi_i}\}$, where $C_{\pi_i} = \sum_{j=1}^{m_i-1} C_{i_j i_{j+1}}$ and C_{ij} are the expected cost of path π_i and edge (i,j), respectively. It is evident that when enough samples are taken from edges of the graph, the estimated cost of paths approach to their expected value, but the ways to sample, number of samples, and distribution of sampling are important and must be addressed.

DLA is a network of automata which collectively cooperate to solve a particular problem. In DLA, the number of actions for any automaton in the network is equal to the number of outgoing edges from that automaton. When an automaton selects one of its actions, another automaton on the other end of edge corresponding to the selected action will be activated. At any time only one automaton in the network will be active. Formally, a DLA with n learning automata (LA) can be defined by a graph (A, E), where $A = \{A_1, A_2, \cdots, A_n\}$ is the set of automata and $E \subset A \times A$ is the set of edges in the graph in which an edge (i,j) corresponds to action α_j of automaton A_i. Two DLA based algorithms for finding shortest path in stochastic graph are reported in the literature [2,3]. In [2], DLA is introduced and applied to the shortest path problem. In order to compute the probability of path π being the shortest ($p(\pi)$), a DLA is constructed from given graph. Each LA in this DLA updates its action probability vector using L_{R-I} reinforcement scheme [4] until the shortest path is found. In [3], another DLA based algorithm which is faster than the algorithm reported in [2] is given. That is, it requires fewer number of samples taken from the edges of the graph in order to decide which path from source to destination is shortest. The main difference between algorithms reported in [3] and the one reported in [2] is the definition of dynamic threshold. In [2], the dynamic threshold is the average cost of sampled paths whereas in the algorithm given in [3] the dynamic threshold is defined to be the minimum of average cost of sampled paths taken. It has been shown that both algorithms find the shortest path in a stochastic graph with probability as close as to unity.

In this paper, we introduce a Monte Carlo simulation method based on DLA for solving the stochastic shortest path problem. We give an iterative stochastic algorithm that finds the minimum value of set $\{C_{\pi_1}, \ldots, C_{\pi_r}\}$ of random variables representing the expected cost of paths in a stochastic graph by taking sufficient samples from them. In this algorithm, the sample size is determined dynamically as the algorithm proceeds. It is shown that when the total sample size tends to infinity, the proposed algorithm finds the shortest path. In this algorithm, at each instant, DLA determine which edges to be sampled. This reduces the unnecessary sampling from the edges which don't seem to be on the shortest path and thus reduces the overall sampling size. A new method of proof (different from [2,3]) is used to prove that if each LA used in DLA uses the L_{R-I} learning algorithm, the given algorithm finds the shortest path with probability as close as to the unity. The convergence proof reported in [2,3] is based on Martingle theorem whereas the convergence proof reported in this paper is based on sampling theory. The simulation results show that the proposed algorithm performs better in comparing to algorithms reported in [2,3] for some of the graphs and perform worse for some other.

The rest of the paper is organized as follows: Section 2 presents the proposed Algorithm. Simulation results and discussion are given in section 3 and section 4 concludes the paper.

2 Proposed Algorithm

In this section, we propose an algorithm based on DLA for finding shortest path in a stochastic graph. In this algorithm, the stochastic graph plays the role of random environment for DLA. The output of DLA is a sequence of actions that represent a particular path in the graph. The environment uses the length of this path to produce its response. This response causes the actions along this path be *rewarded* or *penalized*. In the proposed algorithm, at first a network of LA which is isomorphic to the input graph is created. In this network each node is a LA and each outgoing edge of this node is one of the actions of this LA. The algorithm then traverse the graph (as described later) until the shortest path is found. For the sake of simplicity, we use notations shown in figure 1 to describe the algorithm. The action probability vector for automaton A_j is shown by $p^j = (p^j_1, p^j_2, \cdots, p^j_{r_j})$ where p^j_m denotes the probability of selecting action α_m, that is, edge (j, m). For simplicity in the presentation of algorithm, the actions of an automaton are shown by the indices of adjacent automata. For example, the set of actions of automaton A_2 in figure 1 is represented by $\{\alpha_5, \alpha_6\}$. The variable $AvgCost(k)$ stores the average taken over the cost of the paths traversed up to time k and T denotes the dynamic threshold. Now, we give a general description of the proposed algorithm. In the first step, the source automaton A_s chooses one

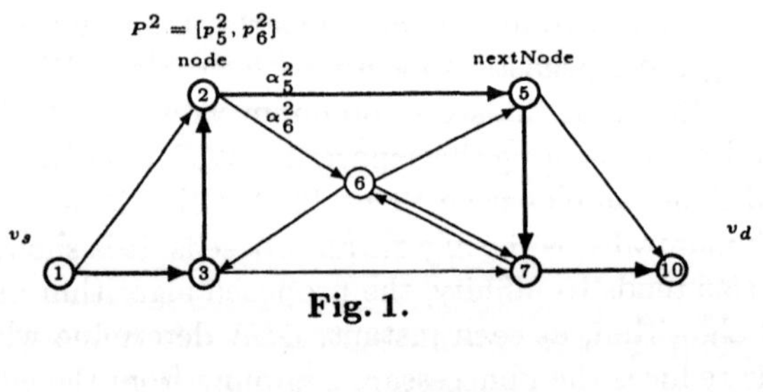

Fig. 1.

of its actions, say α_m. This action activates automaton A_m on the other end of edge (s, m). The process of selection of an action and activating an automaton is repeated until destination automaton A_d is reached or for some reason moving along the edges of the graph is not possible or the number of visited nodes exceeds the number of nodes in the graph. After the A_d is reached, the length of the traversed path and average cost of sampled paths ($AvgCost$) are computed. Then $AvgCost$ is compared with a *dynamic threshold* (described later) and depending on the result of comparison, the value of dynamic threshold is updated. Dynamic threshold T at instant k is the minimum of sequence $\{AvgCost(0), \ldots, AvgCost(k-1)\}$. At the beginning of algorithm, the dynamic threshold is set to average cost of some random generated paths. If $AvgCost$ is less than T, then T is set to $AvgCost$ and all the selected actions of automata along the traversed path are rewarded. If $AvgCost$ is grater than T, then T remains unchanged and all the selected actions of automata along the traversed path are penalized. Updating of action probability vectors are done according to the L_{R-I} algorithm in the direction from A_d to A_s. In updating phase the step lengths of automata at instant k along the traversed path are updated according to the following equation.

$$a_k = \frac{a}{b + \epsilon k} \quad \text{for } k > 1 \text{ and } b \geq 1 > a/\epsilon > 0 \tag{1}$$

The process of travelling from A_s to A_d is repeated until the stopping criteria is reached which at this point the path last travelled has minimum expected length among all the paths from source to destination. The algorithm stops if the product of the probability of choosing the edge of the traversed path, called *path probability*, is greater than a certain threshold. Updating the step length of L_{R-I} scheme according to equation (1) decreases the risk of convergence to non–optimal action [5]. In order to excludes loops from the traversed paths, the algorithm meets every node along a path being traversed at most once. To implement this, if an LA chooses action α_k from the list of its actions, then all unactivated LAs will disable action α_k (but not removed) in their list of actions. When travelling again from source to destination node, all the disabled actions will be enabled.
The main contribution of this paper is summarized by the following theorem.

Theorem 1. If $q(n)$ evolves according to the given algorithm, then the proposed algorithm converges to the shortest path with a probability as close as to unity for graphs with unique shortest path.

Sketch of Proof This theorem is proved in two steps. In the first step, it is shown that every edge in the graph will be sampled infinitely often with probability 1. In the second step, it is first shown that the dynamic threshold is a decreasing function with respect to time and then shown that the dynamic threshold converges to its minimum with probability 1. That is the algorithm finds the path with minimum expected cost with probability as close as to unity. The detailed proof is given in [6].

3 Experiments

In order to study the feasibility of the proposed algorithm, experiments are conducted on stochastic graphs given in figures 2 through 4. These graphs are borrowed from [7]. Graph 1, which is shown in figure 2 is a graph with 4 nodes, 5 arcs, $v_s = 1$, and $v_d = 4$. Graph 2 that is shown in figure 3 is a graph with 10 nodes, 23 arcs, $v_s = 1$, and $v_d = 10$. Graph 3, which is shown in figure 4 is a graph with 15 nodes, 42 arcs, $v_s = 1$, and $v_d = 15$. To compare the performance of the proposed algorithm and the algorithm reported in [2,3], three sets of experiments are conducted on the above mentioned graphs and the results are summarized in table 1. The proposed algorithm will be terminated when the probability of traversed path is greater than 0.9 or 900,000 paths are traversed. The algorithm is executed 100 times and the results are summarized in two tables. The average number of iterations for converged runs and the percentage of converged runs are given in the first table. The second table for each algorithm, shows the total number of samples taken from all edges in the graph and also the total number of samples taken from the edges along the shortest path. The simulation results show that the proposed algorithm performs better in comparison with algorithms reported in [2,3] for some of the graphs and performs worse for some other graphs. It seems that the graph on which the proposed algorithm is tested plays a major rule on the rate of convergence. For more experimentation refer to [6].

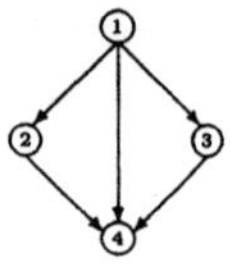

Fig. 2. Graph 1

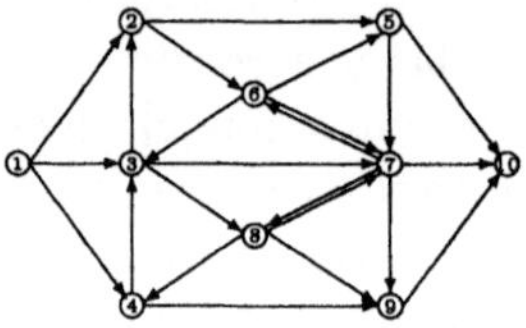

Fig. 3. Graph 2

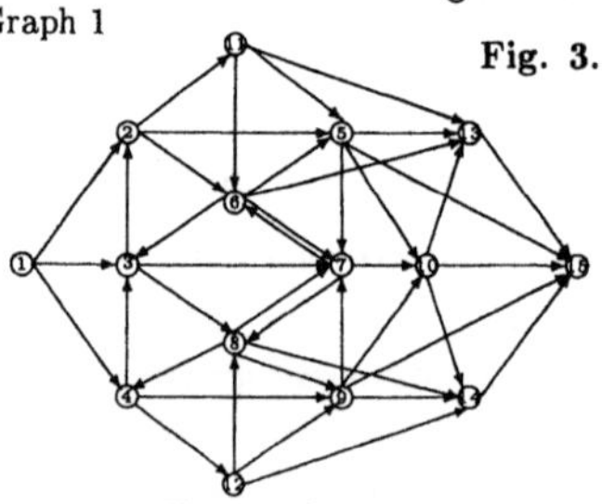

Fig. 4. Graph 3

4 Conclusion

In this paper we have studied the problem of determining the optimal path in a stochastic network. The algorithm presented provides policy which can be used to determine a path from source to destination node with minimal expected cost. This algorithm is an adaptive procedure based on distributed learning automata. A new method of proof (different from [2,3]) is used to prove the optimality of the proposed algorithm. It seems the graph on which the algorithm is tested plays a major rule on the rate of convergence.

Table 1. The simulation results of Algorithm($\epsilon = 0.01$)

a	Graph 1		Graph 2		Graph 3	
	Avg. Iterations	Runs Converged	Avg. Iterations	Runs Converged	Avg. Iterations	Runs Converged
0.0060	851	100	2400	99	39782	98
0.0061	871	100	2414	100	26325	96
0.0062	847	100	2445	99	26987	98
0.0062	829	100	2253	99	32155	100
0.0063	834	100	2218	99	37585	100
0.0064	833	100	2650	99	33275	98
0.0065	843	100	2475	100	27847	99
0.0066	812	100	2360	99	22688	99
0.0068	810	100	2177	99	20344	97
0.0069	805	100	2149	100	27161	97
0.0070	794	99	2377	98	22996	99

a	Graph 1		Graph 2		Graph 3	
	Avg. Samples	Shortest Path	Avg. Samples	Shortest Path	Avg. Samples	Shortest Path
0.0060	1700	999	9017	4177	141293	35170
0.0061	1740	997	9113	4246	92689	53560
0.0062	1692	978	9074	4307	97396	30580
0.0062	1658	964	8416	3951	114157	28713
0.0063	1666	968	8269	3867	110175	29526
0.0064	1664	960	9614	4465	135480	42219
0.0065	1686	962	9137	4257	99022	25870
0.0066	1624	938	8662	4169	81898	23655
0.0068	1620	931	8075	3795	72277	22654
0.0069	1610	925	8050	3807	95517	30237
0.0070	1572	899	8534	4106	83126	22952

References

1. Polychronopoulos, G. H. and Tsitsiklis, J. N. (1996): Stochastic Shortest Path Problems with Recourse. Newtorks, 27,133–143
2. Meybodi, M. R. and Beigy, H. (2001): Solving Stochastic Shortest Path Problem Using Distributed Learning Automata. Proc. of 6th Annual Int. Computer Society of Iran Computer Conference CSICC-2001, Iran, 70–86
3. Beigy, H. and Meybodi, M. R. (2001): A New Distributed Learning Automata Based Algorithm For Solving Stochastic Shortest Path Problem, Tech. Rep. TR-CE-2001-006, Computer Eng. Dept., Amirkabir Univ. of Tech., Tehran, Iran
4. K. S. Narendra and K. S. Thathachar (1989): Learning Automata: An Introduction, New York: Printice-Hall.
5. Najim, K. and Pozyak, A. S. (1994): Learning Automata: Theory and Applications, Oxford: Pergamon press
6. Meybodi, M. R. and Beigy, H. (2001):A Sampling Method Based on Distributed Learning Automata for Stochastic Shortest Path Problem, Tech. Rep. TR-CE-2001-007, Computer Eng. Dept., Amirkabir Univ. of Tech., Tehran, Iran
7. Alexopoulos, C. (1997): State Space Partitioning Methods for Stochastic Shortest Path Problems, Newtorks, 30, 9–21

Visualization of Large Data Sets Using MDS Combined with LVQ.

Antoine Naud and Włodzisław Duch

Department of Informatics, Nicholas Copernicus University,
Grudziądzka 5, 87-100 Toruń, Poland.
www.phys.uni.torun.pl/kmk

Abstract. A common task in data mining is the visualization of multivariate objects using various methods, allowing human observers to perceive subtle inter-relations in the dataset. Multidimensional scaling (MDS) is a well known technique used for this purpose, but it due to its computational complexity there are limitations on the number of objects that can be displayed. Combining MDS with a clustering method as Learning Vector Quantization allows to obtain displays of large databases that preserve both high accuracy of clustering methods and good visualization properties.

1 Introduction

Visualization helps in data exploration by providing the user an idea about clusters in data and their mutual relations, shows outliers and allows for rough classification of data. A very popular way to visualize data is based on self-organizing topographic feature maps (SOM) [1], known also as the Kohonen networks. SOM is so popular because the method may be applied to very large databases and provides clusterization as well as visualization at the same time. Unfortunately SOM networks are among the worst classifiers, as found in empirical studies [2]. There are many better clustering methods than SOM, for example methods based on dendrograms. We have compared SOM visualization using simplexes (up to dimension 20), hypercubes and points on the hypersphere, with a method that preserves correct topographical relations among multidimensional objects [3,4]. These results clearly show that minimization of a quantitative measures for the distortions of original data topography, i.e. the multidimensional scaling technique [5,6], generates maps that preserve both local and global features in a better way than SOM does.

Unfortunately MDS requires difficult minimization of cost function that is based on distances among the represented multidimensional objects. For N objects $N(N-1)/2$ distances enter the cost function, and if maps are 2-dimensional they have $2N-3$ adaptive parameters (position (x,y) of an arbitrary point and the rotation angle, or y coordinate of a second point, may be fixed).

The MDS-based interactive software developed by one of us [7] performs a mapping of multivariate data from a high-dimensional space (D-dimensional space, $D \gg 3$) to data points in a lower d-dimensional space ($d \ll D$). Usually $d = 2$ in order to allow visualization by scatterplots, but higher d values may be useful for dimensionality reduction. The MDS dimensionality reduction is such that similar (or close, in the sense of some distance measure in the D-dimensional space) multivariate objects are mapped on representative points close to each other in the d-dimensional representation space. The mapping should preserve topography of data vectors. Linear projections are often not able to preserve topography; such mappings have to be non-linear. Topography preservation may be unreachable in the whole feature space if the analyzed multivariate data is intrinsically high dimensional and cannot be imbedded in a lower dimensional space without much distortion.

Combination of this algorithm with clusterization methods have several advantages. First, hierachical clusterization methods or any other clusterization may be used. Second, information about the cluster centers may be displayed on the map and combined with MDS information, giving more details than dendrograms typically used to display clusters. Third, multi-level mapping, starting from large clusters and creating smaller ones, may help to find a better MDS solution since initially smaller number of points are mapped. Fourth, it may be applied to large datasets, and thus be competitive to SOM, providing good clusterization and visualization.

The process that combines clusterization with dimensionality reduction is described below. We have used Learning Vector Quantization (LVQ) for clusterization [1] but any other algorithm can be used. Since it is not clear how accurate are the maps created in this way, we have compared them to the original, fully optimized maps in the third section. A short discussion concludes this paper.

2 Combining MDS with LVQ

A direct visualization by MDS of large datasets may be unpracticable due to the limitation on the number of simultaneously mapped objects. Various approaches have been proposed to tackle this problem. Our approach is similar to the so-called *frame method* [8]. It proceeds as follows: First build (by some heuristics) a smaller dataset (called the basis B), designed as a first approximation of the original large dataset. Then map the Basis using standard MDS. Finally add to the mapped Basis all the remaining cases from the original dataset. Let us denote D the dataset to be visualized and N_D the number of cases in this dataset. Let B denote the basis and N_B be the size of the basis, $N_t = N_m + N_f$ is the total number of points considered during the mapping, $F = \{P_i, i = 1, N_f\}$ the set of known data points and by $M = \{P_i, i = 1, N_m\}$ the set of new data points. In Chang and Lee [8] the basis B is build by selecting a subset of points from D, as a result the final display highly depends on which points are selected. We prefer to use a clustering technique on the dataset in order to obtain N_B cluster centers that more uniformly represent the data. For the final step, we use *relative MDS* [13], where each new data is individually added to the mapped Basis using an algorithm that is much less time consuming than the full Stress minimization. The general process proposed for mapping large datasets is shown in figure 1.

Relative MDS mapping differs from standard MDS in this respect that during minimization of the topography distortion measure (called "Stress") only the points from M set are allowed to move while the points from F set are kept fixed. This is

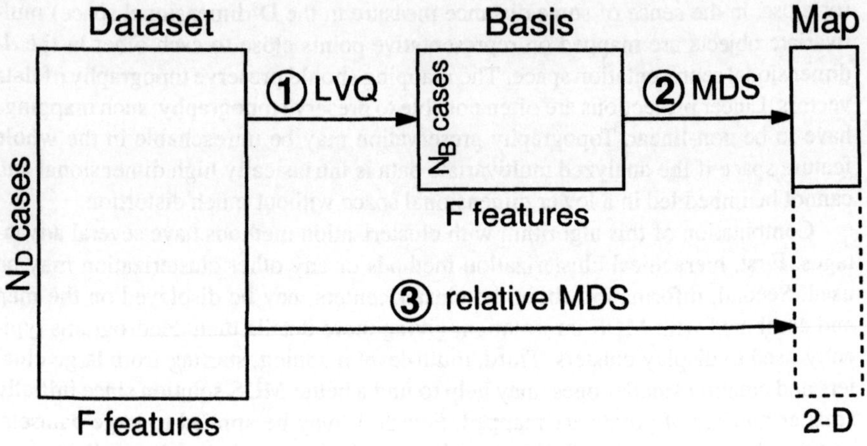

Fig. 1. Process used for the visualization of large datasets: ① – cluster the data using LVQ to form the so-called Basis, ② – Map the Basis using standard metric MDS, ③ – Add the remaining Dataset cases to the mapped Basis using relative MDS.

achieved by modifying the Stress function so that it sums only over the distances that change during mapping, i.e. the distances between the added and the basis points, and the added points interpoint distances. The original Stress function:

$$S(\mathbf{x}) = \sum_{ij}^{N_D} w_{ij} \cdot \left(\hat{d}_{ij} - d_{ij}\right)^2 \tag{1}$$

is redefined as:

$$S_r(\mathbf{x}) = \sum_{i=1}^{N_D} \sum_{j=1}^{N_B} w_{ij} \cdot \left(\hat{d}_{ij} - d_{ij}\right)^2 \tag{2}$$

In relative mapping, the order in which the data are added does not influence the final result because each case is added independently from the other added cases. Relative mapping can also be seen as an alternative to methods designed for the purpose of giving generalization capability to Sammon mapping, such as the ANN Sammon mapping [9], Neuroscale [10] or incremental scaling [11].

3 Visualization of the `Satimage` dataset

It is interesting to see where a new data points "falls" among known cases, discover the class of its neighbors (classified or labeled), and to get an insight on how a classifier would evaluate this new data. `Satimage` dataset comes from the Landsat MSS imagery, it consists of four digital images of the same scene in different spectral bands. This dataset is often used to perform comparison of classifiers, and it is part of the UCI repository [12]. The dataset is made of $N_D = 4435$ cases with 36 numerical features in the range 0 to 255. Each case stands for one pixel in the image, the pixels are attributed to 6 classes standing for different soil types photographed.

The visualization of the N_D cases has been performed by clustering the data into N_B cluster centers. As we are interested in determining the optimal size for the basis, we performed a series of mappings with different values for N_B and compared the resulting displays visually and by means of the final Stress. The following different values were chosen: $N_B = 50, 100, 200, 300, 400, 500, 600, 700, 1000, 1200, 1300$ and 2000. The final Stress values obtained for each Basis size N_B are presented in Fig. 2, as well as the final Stress obtained when mapping directly the entire dataset. As can be expected, the final Stress values decrease when the Basis size increases. The curve decreases towards the lowest Stress S_0 obtained when mapping all the N_D dataset cases in one MDS run, but the convergence seems to reach a plateau at a higher level than S_0.

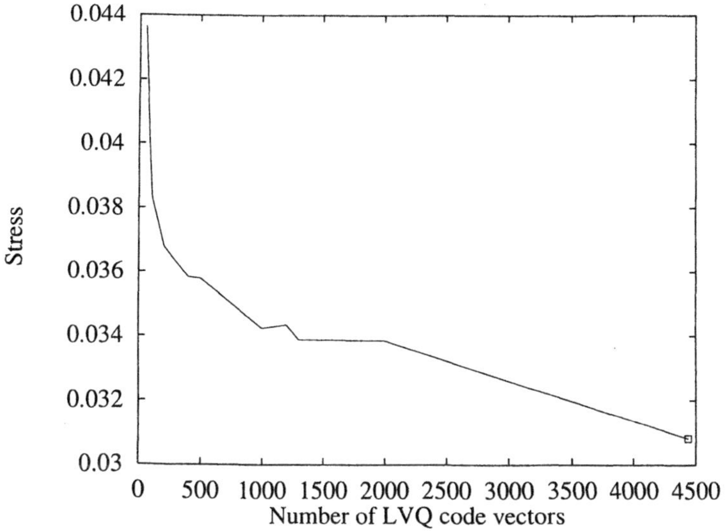

Fig. 2. Final Stress values obtained for various Basis sizes N_B (LVQ code vectors). The whole dataset map lowest Stress is marked by a little square on the right side.

The entire mapped `Satimage` dataset is shown in figure 3 for different values of N_B. A Basis size of $N_B = 100$ code vectors is certainly too low for it induces artifacts (hole effects). A Basis size of $N_B = 1000$ cluster centers gives already a fairly good display because the obtained configuration does not differ very much from the one obtained by direct mapping of the whole dataset. However the display obtained when mapping the whole dataset in one MDS run (d) is better, because the separation of classes `grey soil`, `very damp grey soil` and `red soil` is enhanced. The Basis size $N_B = 1000$ can be considered as optimal, as can be observed on the curve of Fig. 2 where the "speed" of Stress decrease slows down.

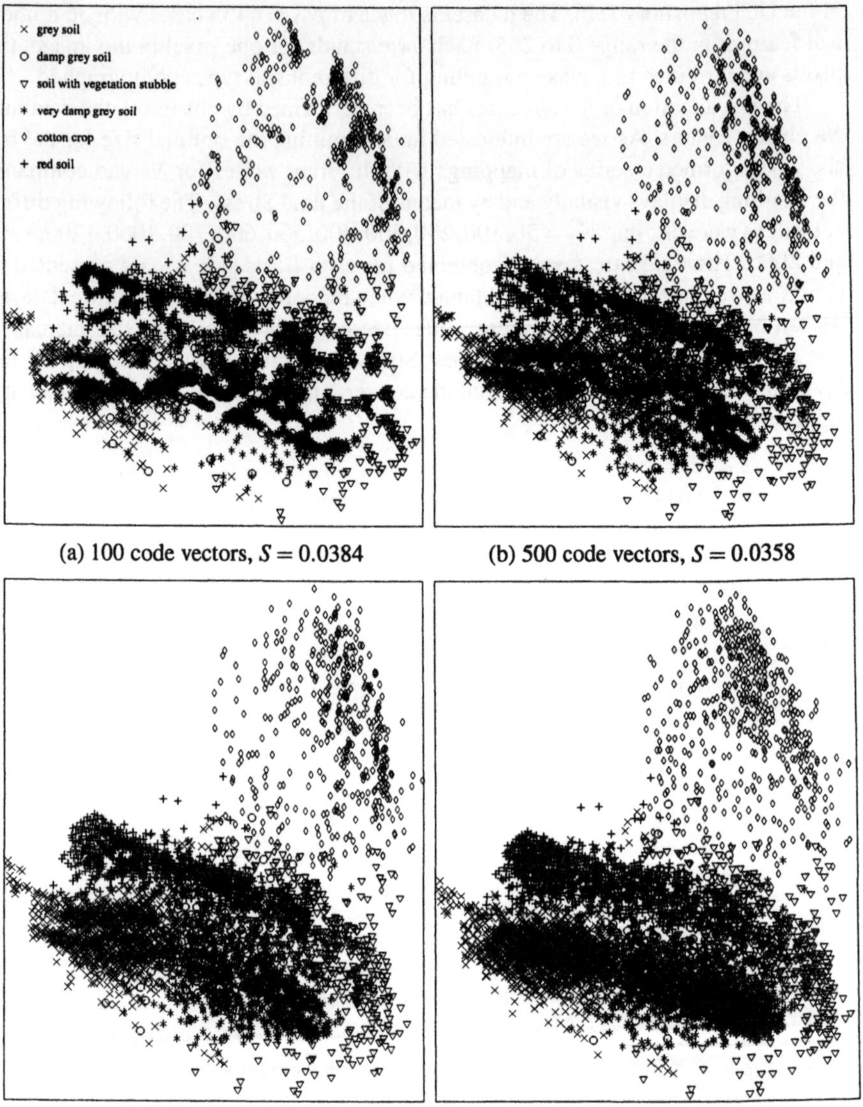

(a) 100 code vectors, $S = 0.0384$ (b) 500 code vectors, $S = 0.0358$

(c) 1000 code vectors, $S = 0.0342$ (d) whole dataset (4435 cases), $S_0 = 0.0308$

Fig. 3. Visualization of `Satimage` dataset obtained using various Basis sizes N_B (LVQ code vectors) and by direct mapping of the whole dataset.

4 Discussion

The main advantage of MDS dimensionality reduction is that the topographical distortions induced can evaluated by the value of the Stress function reached during minimization. In this paper we have shown that the main disadvantage of MDS, its computational complexity, may be removed by mapping smaller number of cluster centers and adding the remining points using relative maping. Interactive zooming on interesting areas of the input space [13] allows for exploration of the neighborhood of the case under inspection. Since there may be some uncertainty in the input one may generate a number (for example 100) of vectors drawn from a Gaussian distribution centered at this vector. The class of these additional points is determined using neural or other classification systems and corresponding points added (using relative mapping) to the map. Visual inspection of such map allows estimating the probability of misclassification, proportional to the number of points from alternative classes.

Acknowledgments: Support by the Polish Committee for Scientific Research, grant 8 T11C 006 19, is gratefully acknowledged.

References

1. Kohonen T. (1995) *Self-Organizing Maps.* Springer-Verlag, Heidelberg Berlin
2. D. Michie, D. J. Spiegelhalter, and C. C. Taylor, editors. *Machine Learning, Neural and Statistical Classification.* Ellis Horwood, New York, 1994.
3. Duch W, Naud A. (1996) Multidimensional scaling and Kohonen's self-organizing maps. In *Proc. 2nd Conf. "eural Networks and their Applications", Szczyrk, Poland,* Vol. I, pp. 138–143
4. Duch W, Naud A. (1996) On global self-organizing maps. In *Proc. 4th European Symposium on Artificial Neural Networks, Brugges,* pp. 91–96
5. Kruskal J. B. (1964) Non metric multidimensional scaling : a numerical method. *Psychometrika* **29**, 115–129
6. Sammon J. W. (1969) A nonlinear mapping for data analysis. *IEEE Transactions on Computers* **5**, 401–409
7. Naud A. (2001) Neural and statistical methods for the visualization of multidimensional data. PhD Thesis, Dept. of Informatics, Nicholas Copernicus University, Poland. http://www.phys.uni.torun.pl/kmk/publications.html
8. Chang C. L, Lee R. C. T. (1973) A heuristic relaxation method for nonlinear mapping in cluster analysis. *IEEE Transactions on Systems, Man, and Cybernetics* **3**, 197–200
9. Kraaijveld M. A, Mao J, Jain A. K. (1995) A nonlinear projection method based on Kohonen's topology preserving maps. *IEEE Transactions on Neural Networks,* **6**, 548–559.
10. Tipping M. E. (1996) *Topographic mappings and feed-forward neural networks.* PhD thesis, Aston University, Birmingham, UK
11. Basalaj W. (1999) Incremental multidimensional scaling method for database visualization. In *Proceedings of Visual data Exploration and Analysis VI, SPIE,* Vol. **3643**, 149-158
12. Blake, C.L, Merz, C.J. (1998). UCI Repository of machine learning databases http://www.ics.uci.edu/ mlearn/MLRepository.html. Irvine, CA: University of California, Department of Information and Computer Science.
13. Naud A, Duch W. (2000) Interactive data exploration using MDS mapping. In: 5th Conf. on Neural Networks and Soft Computing, Zakopane, Poland, pp. 255-260

Controlling the Asymptotic Level Density for Quantization Processes with Self-Organizing Maps

Ewa Skubalska-Rafajłowicz[1]

Institute of Engineering Cybernetis, Wrocław University of Technology,
Wybrzeże Wyspiańskiego 27, 50 370 Wrocław, Poland.
Email: raf@ldhpux.immt.pwr.wroc.pl

Abstract. We analyze different methods of controlling magnification factor in the relation between the density of the input vectors and the asymptotic density of the quantizers. We also propose a new method of modeling the one-dimensional self-organizing process and examine some properties of the method. Empirical studies show strong influence of the learning rate strategies on the observed magnification factor of the vector quantization process.

1 Introduction

Several design algorithms have been developed for vector quantization [3], [19],[17], [11], [18] [15]. The most widely used method for designing vector quantizers is the generalized Lloyd algorithm, known also as LBG scheme [9], [17]. An alternative is Kohonen's learning algorithm [7], [8], which can be seen as a generalization of the LBG method [9], [14].

The mechanism of the self-organizing maps SOM proposed by Kohonen leads to ordering (by linear topology for the cluster units) of multidimensional space which "tend" to approximate the density function of the input vectors. In further studies [12], [14], [18] it was established, that this is true only for uniform density of data in one dimension. In univariate case the density of the SOM output units in the input space is proportional to the α-th power of the input probability density (if the number of units goes to the infinity), where $\alpha = 2/3 - 1/3(n^2 + (n+1)^2)$ and n is number of neighbors in Kohonen's algorithm. If $n = 0$, the algorithm is equivalent to LBG method with $\alpha = 1/3$ in one dimension.

In this paper we shall analyze different methods of controlling magnification factor of the relation between the density of the input vectors and the asymptotic density of the quantizers.

Nonlinear weight adjustments proposed in [18] allow to obtain (in one dimension) the density of output units, which asymptotically is uniform or proportional to the input probability density $f(x)$ [18]. The adaptive learning step adjustments proposed in [1] leads to the similar results, however only simulations confirm possibility of controlling the magnification factor.

We also propose a new method of modeling the one-dimensional self-organizing process and examine some properties of the method. Empirical studies show strong influence of the learning rate strategies on controlling the magnification factor of the vector quantization process.

We confine mainly to the scalar case and one dimensional topology of the self-organizing network, because for this case some theoretical results concerning with asymptotic properties of the quantizers exist. However, results which address to the multi-dimensional problems are also indicated.

2 Vector quantization

Vector quantization technique encode data using only a finite set vectors (quantizers, reference vectors) $w = (w_1, w_2, \ldots, w_N)$. Each data vector x is described by the closest reference vector $w_{s(x)}$ for which the distortion error $||x - w_{s(x)}||^\beta$ is minimal. Usually $||\cdot||$ is Euclidean metric and $\beta = 2$. When the probability distribution of input data is described by $f(x)$, then the average distortion is determined by

$$\int ||x - w_{s(x)}||^\beta f(x) dx \tag{1}$$

and has to be minimized through an optimal choice of reference vectors $w_1, w_2, \ldots, w_N$.

Designing a good set of quantizers is the main problem in vector quantization and requires the minimization of (1), which has many local minima.

It is known, that an asymptotic density distribution of the quantizers $Q(x)$ that is proportional to $f(x)^\alpha$, with $\alpha = d/(d+\beta)$ is optimal for the task of minimizing the average β- distortion measure (1) in d dimensions [19].

3 SOM related learning algorithms

3.1 Kohonen learning algorithm

Kohonen learning algorithm [8] is as follows:

Step 1. Initialize weights: real numbers from the unit interval: $w_1, w_2, \ldots w_N$

Step 2.Present a new input signal x and calculate distance of x to all N units: $|x - w_i|, \;\; i = 1, \ldots, N$. Find a winner unit s, i.e., $s = arg \min_i |w_i - x|$.

Step 3. Update weights as follows

$$\begin{gathered} w_i(t+1) = w_i(t) + \eta(t) \cdot h_{ci}(t)\, [x - w_i(t)], \\ i = 1, 2, \ldots, n, \;\; t = 1, 2, \ldots \end{gathered} \tag{2}$$

where $\eta(t) \in (0,1)$ is decreasing learning rate (a scalar-valued adaptation gain) and $h_{ci}(t)$ is a neighborhood function.

Step 4. Adjust parameters η and σ. Go to Step 3.

Neighborhood function can be defined as: $h_{si} = 1$, if $|s - i| \leq n$ and $h_{si} = 0$ otherwise. A proper form for h_{si} might be of Gaussian type:

$$h_{si}(t) = h_0(t) \exp(-|s-i|^2/\sigma(t)^2) \tag{3}$$

where $h_0(t)$ and $\sigma(t)$ are suitable chosen decreasing functions of time.

The asymptotic results on the magnification factor of the stationary map [12], [14] were obtained with the assumptions that (close to the equilibrum configuration) $\eta(t) = \eta$ and $h_{si}(t) = h_{si}$ are constant.

3.2 Concave model of weight adjustments

In the paper [18] the following method of weight adaptation was proposed:

$$w_i(t+1) = w_i(t) + \eta \cdot h_{si} \cdot (x - w_i(t))^{\kappa}, \quad i = 1, \ldots, N, \tag{4}$$

where $\kappa > 1$ is odd integer.

The asymptotic density $Q(x)$ has been shown [18] to be proportional to $f(x)^{2/(\kappa+2)}$ (assuming that the learning rate η is a small constant).

3.3 Convex model of weight adjustments

Adapt the weight

$$w_i(t+1) = w_i(t) + \eta \cdot h_{si} \cdot (x - w_i(t))^{1/\kappa}, \ i = 1, \ldots, N, \tag{5}$$

where $\kappa \leq 1$ is some constant odd integer [18].

The asymptotic density $Q(w)$ has been shown [18] to be proportional to $f(t)^{2\kappa/(2\kappa+1)}$ when the learning rate η is a small constant.

3.4 Adaptive learning step adjustments

The adaptive learning step adjustments proposed in [1] leads to the following learning algorithm:

$$w_i^{new} = w_i + \eta \cdot P(w_s)^{-m} \cdot \frac{1}{|x - w_s|^{dm}} h_{si} \cdot (x - w_i), \quad i = 1, \ldots, N, \tag{6}$$

where d is real dimension of the data, m is a real number and $P(w_s)$ is the probability of the event that w_s is the best matching unit. There is supposition that the result is valid also with multi-dimensional data.

Numerical simulations indicate that the asymptotic density $Q(x)$ is of the form $f(x)^{2/3(1+m)}$, if the learning rate η is a small constant [1].

3.5 Neural gas

In [11] a neural network is proposed which, instead of Kohonen neighborhood function h_{si}, utilizes a neighborhood ranking $\{w_{i_1}, w_{i_2}, \ldots, w_{i_N}\}$ of the reference vectors being closest to x, i.e.,

$$||w_{i_k} - x|| \leq ||w_{i_{k+1}} - x||,\ k = 1, 2, \ldots, N-1.$$

Unit $w_{i_1} = w_s$ is the best matching unit, i.e., a winner. The learning rule is as follows:

$$w_i(t+1) = w_i(t) + \eta h_\lambda(k_i(x, w)) \cdot (x - w_i(t)),\ i = 1, 2, \ldots, N, \tag{7}$$

where $k_i(x, w))$ is a distance from x to the unit w_i and h_λ is 1 for zero and decays to zero for increasing k_i with the characteristic decay parameter λ. If $\lambda \to 0$, the learning rule becomes equivalent to on-line LGB method [14], [11]. In case of a small decay constant $\lambda \to 0$ and a small constant η an asymptotic density distribution of reference units is proportional to $f(x)^{d/d+2}$. Thus, "neural-gas" network has the same asymptotic property as LBG scheme [9].

3.6 Gaussian learning step adjustments

We propose another learning algorithm with adaptive learning rate

$$w_i(t+1) = w_i(t) + \eta \cdot \exp[-|x - w_i(t)|^2/(2\sigma_i^2)] \cdot h_{si} \cdot (x - w_i),\ \ i = 1, \ldots, N, \tag{8}$$

where $\sigma_i = 1/2 \cdot (w_{i+1} + w_i)\sigma_0(t)$ if $x \geq w_i$ and $\sigma_i = 1/2 \cdot (w_{i-1} + w_i)\sigma_0(t)$ if $x \leq w_i$.

$\sigma_0(t)$ is a parameter of the learning process. Moreover, we assume that $\sigma_0(t) \geq 1/2$.

The algorithm should be used when all weights are ordered, i.e.,
$w_1 \leq \ldots \leq w_N$ or $w_1 \geq \ldots \geq w_N$.
In such a case (and also with $h_{si} = 1$, $i = 1, \ldots, N$) only the best matching unit and its neighbors are learned efficiently.

The method is similar to the maximum entropy approach (see for example [4], [5]), but it corresponds to a stochastic gradient descent on the another cost function

$$-\sum_{i=1}^{N} \int f(x)\sigma_i^2 \exp[-|x - w_i|^2/(2\sigma_i^2)]\ dx \tag{9}$$

We propose the generalization of the method to the multi-dimensional case using any space-filling-curve based transformation of the data [16]. There are strong connections between space-filling curves and self-organizing maps with linear topology. In his work [7] Kohonen indicates that linear SOM produce approximations of space-filling curves, which mimick probability measures induced by data.

4 Results of simulations

To examine the properties of the learning algorithm with Gaussian learning step adjustments (8) (with $\sigma_0 = 1/2$), we carried out a series of simulations for the normal probability density $f(x)$ with mean $m = 0.5$ and variance $\sigma^2 = 0.01$. The starting state for each simulation was $N = 100$ reference vectors drawn at random according to the input distribution $f(x)$. In the case of normal distribution $N(m, \sigma^2)$ resulting f^α is also normal $N(m, \sigma^2/\alpha)$. Thus, the observed magnification factor was estimated by

$$0.01 \cdot \left[\sum_{i=1}^{N} (w_i - N^{-1} \cdot \sum_{j=1}^{N} w_j)^2 / (N-1) \right]^{-1} \tag{10}$$

The magnification factors α produced during the learning process by algorithm (8) with $\sigma_0 = 0.5$ and constant learning rates $\eta = 0.01$, 0.1 and 0.5 are given in Table 1. Estimated magnification factors α of the quantization process obtained by algorithm (8) with $\eta = 0.5$ and with different constant values σ_0 are shown in Table 2.

Table 1. Estimated magnification factor of the quantization process obtained by algorithm (8) with $\sigma_0 = 0.5$ during the learning process

number of iterations	1000	10 000	100 000	200 000	300 000	400 000	500 000	2500 000
$\eta = 0.01$	0.88	0.87	0.83	0.80	0.78	0.77	0.75	-
$\eta = 0.1$	0.95	0.90	0.75	0.68	0.64	0.61	0.60	-
$\eta = 0.5$	0.90	0.79	0.65	0.60	0.53	0.47	0.46	0.35

Table 2. Estimated magnification factors α of the quantization process obtained by algorithm (8) with $\eta = 0.5$ and with different constant values σ_0

σ_0	1.5	1.0	0.8	0.6	0.5
α	1.02	0.63	0.53	0.40	0.35
α/σ_0	0.67	0.63	0.66	0.66	0.70

Conclusions. The simulations indicate that learning algorithm (8) and variants of Kohonen's one behave similarly from the point of view of controlling the magnification factors.

The simulation results indicate that the magnification factor α of the quantization process obtained by algorithm (8) depends linearly on the values σ_0, i.e., $\alpha \cong 0.66 \cdot \sigma_0$.

Moreover, there are some gaps in the theoretical analysis of the asymptotic properties of magnification factors of the vector quantization process obtained by different models of the self-organization.

References

1. H. U. Bauer, R. Der, M. Herman, Controlling the magnification factor of self-organizing feature maps *Neural Computation*, vol.8, 757–771, 1996.
2. E. Erwin, K. Obermayer, K.L. Schulten, Self-organizing maps: ordering, convergence properties and energy function, *Biol. Cybern.*, vol.67, 47–55, 1992.
3. A. Gersho, R.M. Gray, *Vector quantization and Signal Compression*, Kluwer Academic Publisher, Boston, 1993.
4. T. Heskes, B. Kappen, Self-organization and parametric regression, *Poc. I-CANN95,* Paris, France, 81–86, 1995.
5. T.Heskes, Transition Times in Self-Organizing Maps, *Biological Cybernetics*, vol.75, 49–57, 1996.
6. T. Kohonen, Self-organizing formation of topologically correct feature maps, *Biol. Cyb.*, vol.43, 59–69, 1982.
7. T. Kohonen, Self-organizing maps, *Proc. of the IEEE* **78**, 1464–1480 (1990).
8. T. Kohonen, *Self-organizing maps*, Berlin, Heidelberg Springer Verlag (1995).
9. Y.Linde, A. Buzo, R.M. Gray, An algorithm for vector quantizer design, *IEEE Transactions on Communication*, vol.28, 84-95, 1980.
10. S.P. Luttrell, Code vector density in topographic mappings: scalar case, *IEEE Trans. on Neural Networks* , vol.2, 427–436, 1991.
11. T.M. Martinetz, S.G. Berkovich, K.J. Schulten, Neural-gas network for vector quantization and its application to time-series prediction *IEEE Trans. on Neural Networks*, vol.4., 558–559 (1993).
12. H. Ritter, K.L. Schulten, On the stationary state of Kohonen's self-organizing sensory mapping, *Biological Cybernetics*, vol.54, 99–106, 1986.
13. H. Ritter, K.L. Schulten, Convergence properties of Kohonen's topology conserving map: Fluctuations, stability, and dimension detection, *Biolgical Cybernetics*, vol.60, 59–71, 1988.
14. H. Ritter, Asymptotic level density for a class of vector quantization processes, *IEEE Trans. on Neural Networks* **2**, 173–175 (1991).
15. E. Skubalska-Rafajłowicz, Applications of the Space-Filling Curves with Data Driven MeasurePreserving Property, *Nonlinear Analysis, Theory, Methods & Applications*, vol.30(3), pp .1305–1310, 1997.
16. E. Skubalska-Rafajłowicz, Space-Filling Curves and Kohonen's 1-D SOM as a Method of a Vector Quantization with Known Asymptotic Level Density, Proc. of the 3rd Conf. *Neural Networks and Their Applications*, Kule 1997, pp .161–166.
17. E. Yair, K. Zeger, A. Gersho, Competitive learning and soft competition for vector quantizer design , *IEEE Trans. on Signal Processing* **40**, 294–309 (1992).
18. Y. Zheng, J.F. Greenleaf, The effect of concave and convex weight adjustments on self-organizing maps, *IEEE Trans. on Neural Networks* **7**, 87–96 (1994).
19. P.L. Zador, Asymptotic Quantization Error of Continuous Signmals and the Quantization Dimension, *IEEE Trans. on Information Theory* **28**, 139–149 (1982).

Formal Neuro-Immune Network

Alexander Tarakanov[1], Georgy Penev[1], Kurosh Madani[2]

[1] St.Petersburg Institute for Informatics and Automation of Russian Academy of Sciences (SPIIRAS) – 14-th Line, 39 – 199178 ST-PETERSBURG – RUSSIA
[2] Intelligence in Instrumentation and Systems Lab. (I^2S) - SENART Institute of Technology - University PARIS XII, Avenue Pierre POINT, F-77127 LIEUSAINT - FRANCE

Abstract. The paper presents an attempt to introduce a new formal notion of Neuro-Immune Network (NIN) based on a rigorous mathematical basis. This notion is inspired by a biological phenomenon of reciprocal impact between the neural and immune systems. The paper considers examples of NIN including a possible application to intrusion detection in computer networks.

1 Introduction

All biological systems on the levels of cells and bio-molecules can be regarded as sophisticated information processing systems. However, only neural and immune systems possess extraordinary capabilities of "intellectual" processing that includes memory, ability to learn, to recognize, and to make decisions how to treat any unknown situation.

The possibilities of the neural system as a biological prototype has been already intensively used in computer science based on the mathematical and software models of Artificial Neural Networks (ANN) and their hardware implementation in neural computers [3, 9, 14]. However, the bio-molecular principles of information processing by the immune system and their importance for the modern computer science have been appreciated only recently in a new computational technique, called the Artificial Immune System (AIS) [4]. A rigorous mathematical basis of AIS has been proposed in the publications [10-12] based on a biological prototype of immune network [8] and on the notions of Formal Protein (FP) and Formal Immune Network (FIN). This paper introduces a new formal notion of NIN as a combination of FIN and ANN inspired by biological prototype of neuro-immuno-modulation [1, 6]. The underlying premise, evidenced by this prototype, is that the immune system activity effects on neural functions and behavior, and vice versa. Thus the brain and immune system represent a single, integrated system.

In this work we present the simplest version of NIN that includes only one neuron and one immune cell. They effect one another by secreting special proteins. For this purpose we take traditional model of the neurons as a summation with a threshold, according to [14], and modify it by adding possibilities to secrete and bind proteins and change the threshold. We consider a model of the proteins as FP coded by a real unit vector, according to [10]. We consider two examples of NIN including a possible application to intrusion detection in computer networks.

2 Definitions and Mathematical Formalization of NIN

2.1 Artificial Neuron

According to [14], let us define an Artificial Neuron (AN) as a tuple given by relation (1), where n is a number of the inputs, $X= [x_1,...,x_n]^T$ is a vector of the inputs, $U= [u_1,...,u_n]^T$ is a vector of the weights, h is a threshold of excitation, and $z=\{0,1\}$ is an output. Upper case "^{T}" is a usual designation for transposing operation so that X is column-vector while X^T is string-vector.

$$\mathrm{AN} = < n, X, U, h_0 , z >, \tag{1}$$

A neuron operates as following: if $u=X^TU$ designate the weighted sum of the inputs, then the output of the AN satisfies to the following condition: *if* $u>h_0$ *then* $z=1$ *else* $z=0$.

2.2 Formal Protein

According to [10], any unit vector P with n real-valued components $P= [p_1,..., p_n]^T$ and with $PP^T=1$, can be considered as a special kind of FP with $n-1$ links. Let us call, for convenience, any unit vector of dimension n as FP of dimension n.

Binding energy between any pair $\{P, R\}$ of such FPs, of the dimensions n_P and n_R, correspondingly, can be defined by a bilinear form expressed by (2), where W is a matrix of dimension $n_P{\times}n_R$. Let us call this matrix as binding matrix. It is known (e.g. see [7]), that extreme values of the bilinear form (2) are determined by the so-called Singular Value Decomposition (SVD) of the matrix (relation (3)), where s_i are singular values; P_i and R_i are left and right singular vectors; r is rank of the matrix. Such SVD exists for any real rectangular matrix.

$$w = - P^T WR, \tag{2}$$

$$W = s_1 P_1 R_1^T + ... + s_r P_r R_r^T \, , \tag{3}$$

Let us consider binding as recognizing between FPs. Then binding energy can be viewed as a numerical measure of the recognition: the lower this energy is – the better is recognition, and vice versa. At the same time, if matrix W is given, then the pair of the FPs with extreme recognition ability is corresponded to the first singular vectors P_1 and R_1 of this matrix, while the maximal singular value s_1 determines the minimal binding energy: $w^* = -P_1^T MR_1$ and $w^* \leq w(P,R)$, $\forall P,R : P^T P = R^T R = 1$. Such rigorous mathematical properties of the binding energy between the FPs that are based on the bilinear form (2) and the SVD (3) provides the computational basis for developing a rigorous FIN approach to pattern recognition [13]. Finally, let us define binding as the event, when $w \leq w_h$, where w_h is a given threshold of binding.

2.3 Formal Cell

Let us define a Formal Cell (FC) as a tuple expressed by relation (4), where *P* (FP-messenger) and *R* (FP-receptor) are unit vectors of the dimensions n_P and n_R, and FS is any formal set.

$$\text{FC} = < n_P,\ n_R,\ P,\ R,\ FS > \tag{4}$$

Let us consider two special cases of the FC: *B-cell* (or formal B-cell), where *FS* is empty set, and *N-cell* (or formal neuron), where FS is modified artificial neuron. Behavior of such cells is defined by the following additional rules.

B-cell $= < n_P,\ n_R,\ P,\ R >$; *if R is bound then B-cell secretes P.*

N-cell $= < n_P,\ n_R,\ P,\ R,\ n_N,\ X,\ U,\ h,\ z >$; $P = f(u, h)$, $h = \{h_0, h_1\}$;

N-cell secretes P for any X; if R is bound then $h = h_1$ *else* $h = h_0$.

2.4 Neuro-Immune Network

Let us define Neuro-Immune Network (NIN) as the tuple expressed by relation (5), where n_N, n_P, n_R are dimensions of the vectors *X, P, R,* correspondingly, *W* is a binding matrix of the dimension $n_P \times n_R$, and w_h is a threshold of binding.

$$\text{NIN} = < n_N,\ n_P,\ n_R,\ W,\ w_h,\ B\text{-}cells,\ N\text{-}cells > \tag{5}$$

2.5 NIN Operation Trough An Academically Example

To show how above defined NIN operates, let us consider unit vectors relative to the two dimensional space. Then any vector can be represented as depending on one angle, for example: $P(\varphi) = [\cos\varphi, \sin\varphi]^T$. Let this angle to have only one of six following discrete values: $\varphi_0 = 0$, $\varphi_1 = \frac{\pi}{2}$, $\varphi_2 = \pi$, $\varphi_3 = -\frac{\pi}{2}$, $\varphi_4 = \frac{\pi}{4}$ and $\varphi_5 = -\frac{3\pi}{4}$. This leads to exactly six types of the FPs: P_0, P_1, $P_2 = -P_0$, $P_3 = -P_1$, P_4 and $P_5 = -P_4$. Let us consider now, the following NIN that includes such FPs:

$$\text{NIN} = < n_N{=}2,\ n_P{=}2,\ n_R{=}2,\ W,\ w_h = -1,\ B\text{-}cell,\ N\text{-}cell >$$

with

$$W = \begin{bmatrix} -1 & 0 \\ 0 & -1 \end{bmatrix}; \text{ B-cell: } P_B = P_4, R_B = P_1;$$

$$\text{N-cell: } X = [x_1, x_2]^T, x_1 = \{0,1\}, x_2 = \{0,1\}, U = [2, 1]^T, u = 2x_1 + x_2,$$

$$P_N = [\cos\varphi, \sin\varphi]^T, \ \varphi = \frac{\pi}{2}u, \ R_N = P_5, h = \{0, 3\}.$$

Table 1. Table of the NIN states for all inputs

x_1x_2	u	P_N	$R_B=P_1$ binds P_N ?	B-cell secretes P_4?	$R_N=P_5$ binds P_4?	h	z
00	0	P_0	no	no	no	0	0
01	1	P_1	no	no	no	0	1
10	2	P_2	no	no	no	0	1
11	3	P_3	yes	yes	yes	3	0

According to (2), the binding energy between any pair of FPs $\{P_i, P_j\}$ of such NIN is given by: $w = \cos(\varphi_i - \varphi_j)$. According to the threshold w_h, only three pairs of the FPs are able to be bound: $\{P_0, P_2\}$, $\{P_1, P_3\}$, $\{P_4, P_5\}$. Hence, the NIN works as shown in Tab. 1. According to the first and the last columns of the Tab. 1, the N-cell of the considering NIN realizes the well-known XOR (eXclusive OR) function. It's known also that no one single-layer ANN (perceptron) is able to realize this function [14].

3 Application To Intrusion Detection

To validate the above exposed concept, we have used a numerical experiment staged by [13] using a fragment of the database of [2], as shown in Tab. 2. The fragment presents 106 records (column "#") on the 15 intrusion types (short names in column "Sign") and a normal behavior (*norm*) of the network connection. The fragment utilizes 33 characteristics (columns "1",...,"33") for the network connection records, including lengths (number of seconds) of the connection (column "1"), number of data bytes from source to destination (column "2"), from destination to source (column "3"), and so forth (to column "33").

Using the idea of the so-called shape space [5] and the SVD (3), these data were represented by the FIN as two values of the binding energy between FPs [13]. These values are shown in Tab. 2 (columns "w_1" and "w_2") and represented geometrically in Fig. 1 as points that form clear groups (classes) in the shape space. Such classes (rounded in Fig. 1 for the sake of obviousness) correspond to the normal behavior and the intrusion types. In other words, we have obtained a classification of the intrusions by the unsupervised learning.

Table 2. Intrusion records fragment

#	Sign	1	2	...	33	w_1	w_2
1	ap2	906	57964	...	0	-0.044	-0.018
10	ap2	903	87164	...	0.04	-0.046	0.026
45	norm	0	223	...	0	-0.216	0.065
48	norm	1	3170	...	0.13	-0.014	-0.004
97	snm	0	105	...	0	-0.132	-0.014
106	xsn	50	226		0	0.114	-0.088

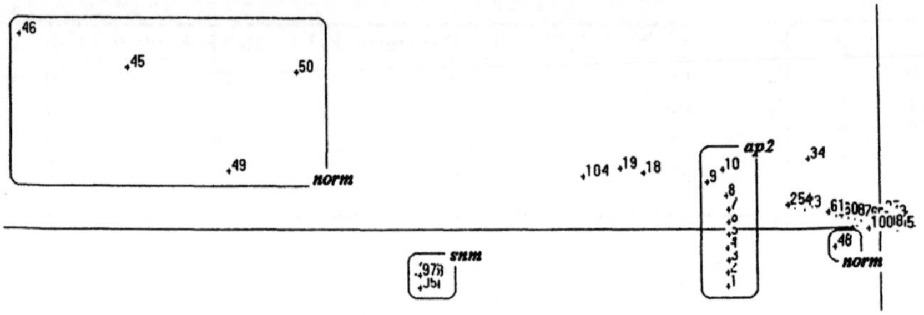

Fig. 1. Intrusion records in the FIN shape space

Using such classification, let us define the following NIN to detect the intrusion apache2 (*ap2*) by separating it from the normal behavior (*norm*) of the network connection: NIN = < $n_N=33$, $n_P=2$, $n_R=2$, W, $w_h=-1$, *B-cell*, *N-cell* >, where matrix W and *B-cell* are the same as in the previous example, s_5 and A_5 are fifth singular value and singular vector of a matrix 106×33, and *N-cell* is as follows:

$$N\text{-}cell\colon X=[x_1, \ldots, x_{33}]^T,\ \ U=\frac{1}{s_5}A_5,\ R_N=P_5,\ h=\{h_0, h_1\},$$

$$h_0=-0.14,\ h_1=-0.04;\ \ if\ u>h_1\ then\ P_N=P_1\ else\ P_N=P_0,$$

Such NIN works as usual AN if $u\leq h_1$. In such case N-cell detects the intrusion *ap2* when the weighted sum of the inputs is greater than the usual threshold h_0 : *if* $u>h_0$ *then* $z=1$ *else* $z=0$. But when the sum exceeds the second threshold h_1 (when the point that corresponds to the current input X in the shape space arranges righter than the outlined region of *ap2* in Fig. 1), then the NIN blocks the detection of the intrusion *ap2*. It worth noting another feature of the NIN of this example. In fact, we used the parameters of some FP A_5 to assign the weight coefficients U of the neuron. This fact shows a possibility of using NIN as a mean of training ANN.

4 Conclusion

As shown by Tarakanov et al. [10-13], the developing FIN approach to pattern recognition gives rather fine classification thus focusing attention on the most dangerous situations, which is beyond the possibilities of the traditional statistics. On the other hand, a growing need to overcome main disadvantages of the neural networks' models, such as spurious patterns, non-localized errors, etc., is well recognized. These factors prevent the proliferation of neurochips in those fields where the cost of a single error is too high (e.g. aviation, medicine, information security). Therefore, the authors hope that the NIN has the potential for combining advantageous and overcoming disadvantageous of ANN and FIN in large-scale control and computer networks.

Acknowledgements

A.Tarakanov acknowledges the supports of the EU (project IST-2000-26016), the USAF (project BASIS), and the EOARD (project 2200p).

References

1. Ader R, Felten D, Cohen N (eds) (2000) Psycho-neuro-immunology. Academic Press, New York
2. Bay SD (1999) The UCI KDD archive [http://kdd.ics.uci.edu]. University of California, Dept. of Information and Computer Science, Irvine, CA
3. Chebira A, Madani K, Mercier G (1997) Multi-neural networks hardware and software architecture: application to divide to simplify paradigm DTS. LNCS Vol. 1240, Springer Verlag, 1977, pp. 841-850.
4. Dasgupta D. (1999) Artificial Immune Systems and their Applications. Springer.
5. DeBoer RJ, Segel LA, Perelson AS (1992) Pattern formation in one and two-dimensional shape space models of the immune system. J Theoret Biol 155: 295-333
6. Hori T, et al. (1995) The autonomic nervous system as a communication channel between the brain and the immune system. Neuroimmunomodulation 2: 203-215
7. Horn R, Johnson C (1986) Matrix analysis. Cambridge University Press
8. Jerne NK (1974) Towards a network theory of the immune system. Ann Immunol (Inst. Pasteur) 125C: 373-389
9. Krogh A, Vedelsby J, Neural network ensembles, cross validation, and active learning. In: Tesauro G (ed) Advances in neural information processing systems 7. MIT Press, pp 231-238
10. Tarakanov A (1999) Formal peptide as a basic agent of immune networks: from natural prototype to mathematical theory and applications. In: Proc. 1st int. workshop of central and eastern Europe on multi-agent systems (CEEMAS'99). St.Petersburg, Russia, pp 281-292
11. Tarakanov AO (2001) Information security with formal immune networks. In: Gorodetsky VI, Skormin VA, Popyack LJ (eds) Information Assurance in Computer Networks (Lecture Notes in Computer Science). Springer, Berlin, pp 115-126
12. Tarakanov A, Dasgupta D (2000) A formal model of an artificial immune system. BioSystems 55(1-3): 151-158
13. Tarakanov A, Skormin V (2002) Pattern recognition by immunocomputing (accepted to the 2002 Congress on Evolutionary Computation. Honolulu, USA)
14. Wasserman P (1990) Neural computing. Theory and practice. Van Nostrand Reihold, New York

Memory Management in Artificial Immune System

Krzysztof Trojanowski[1)], Sławomir T. Wierzchoń[1,2)]

[1)] Institute of Computer Science, Polish Academy of Sciences

01-237 Warszawa, ul. Ordona 21

e-mail: {trojanow,stw}@ipipan.waw.pl

[2)] Department of Computer Science, Białystok Technical University

15-351 Białystok, ul. Wiejska 45[a]

Abstract: *In this paper an idea of the artificial immune system was used to design an algorithm for non-stationary function optimization. The unknown and varying in time optimum is treated here as an antigen and the aim of the system is to produce antibodies. Three different strategies awarding memory cells are investigated.*

Keywords: Clonal Selection, Apoptosis, Immune Memory, Non-stationary Optimization

Introduction

The vertebrate immune system offers an interesting metaphor for solving complex tasks from the field of optimisation, data analysis or anomaly detection – consult (Hofmeyr, 1999) and (Wierzchoń, 2001a) for extensive review of its architecture and algorithms used. An exciting property of the system is its adaptability: it can learn the structures of the antigens, and remember those structures, so that future response to the antigens can be much faster. The term antigen refers to a plethora of enemy substances and organisms, e.g. bacteria or viruses that invade the body. The agents responsible for the detection and elimination of the antigens are lymphocytes, or white blood cells. We distinguish two main classes of lymphocytes, called B-cells and T-cells, respectively, that cooperate in the detection of antigens. In an optimization task we refer to the algorithms used by B-cells only. A recognition process relies upon establishing chemical bonds between antibodies (receptors) located on the surface of B-cell and antigens. If the strength of the bond, called the *affinity*, exceeds a pre-specified threshold, a B-cell is activated. Activated lymphocytes are stimulated to divide and also to produce free antibodies. The process of choosing most activated cells together with their cloning is said to be *clonal selection*. The diversity of the immune system is maintained through two important mechanisms: *somatic mutation* (the clones are subjected intensive genetic mutations during their reproduction) and *apoptosis* (roughly 5% of B-cells are replaced every day by new cells). But the antibodies can also recognize other antibodies. This mechanism of reciprocal recognition and stimulation of the antibodies by antigens as well as other antibodies can be used to explain emergence of the immune memory (Jerne, 1974).

When searching for an optimum in changing environment the current optimum is treated as an antigen, which should be matched by antibodies. The process of new optimum identification is equivalent to the primary immune response while its repeated identification, when environment changes periodically – to the secondary response. Obviously this last phenomenon can be observed only if our optimizer is able to organize a kind of memory. This is the subject of our study.

The first attempt to employ artificial immune system to time-dependent optimization was done by Gaspar and Collard (1999). They restricted to a simple model, called pattern tracking, in which the affinity of an antibody is measured in terms of Hamming distance to a bit-string which represents the current optimum and which changes periodically. More precisely, the antigen was represented by a bit-string of length $l = 40$. Every $t = 50$ iterations the bit-string was replaced by other string located at increasing Hamming distance in order to make its identification more difficult. Wierzchoń (2001b) proposed a more realistic environment with a single peak moving randomly around the square of size 100×100. This experiment was motivated by the study described in (Grefenstette, 1992). When the peak moved periodically, the secondary immune response was pretty observed. Later, Trojanowski and Wierzchoń (2002) used an immune algorithm on more complicated environment observing the emergence of immune memory. In present study we investigate different strategies leading to the immune memory formation.

Optimisation of non-stationary functions

In this paper we use the algorithm tested already by Wierzchoń (2001b). It is a binary immune system and its pseudocode is given in Figure 1.

1. *Fitness evaluation*. For each individual or antibody p in the population P of binary strings compute its fitness i.e. the value of the objective function f_p. Define the string with highest fitness to be the antigen.
2. *Clonal selection*. Choose n antibodies with highest fitness to the antigen.
3. *Somatic hypermutation*. Make c_i mutated clones of i-th antibody. The clone $c_{(i)}$ with highest fitness replaces original antibody if $f_{c(i)} > f_i$.
4. *Apoptosis*. Replace d weakest antibodies by randomly generated strings.

Figure 1. Frame immune algorithm used in the experiments described later.

Step 2 of this algorithm can be realized in many ways. In our case we tested three methods (called exogenic activation) of searching for the highest fitness. The first method used fitness values of antibodies without any changes, the second and the third - fitness values modified with a normalized *success register* value. The success register is a kind of counter attached to every antibody, which is incremented every time the antibody is the best among all other antibodies in the population. This kind of prize is awarded every iteration. Formulas of individual evaluation functions for the three methods are presented below:

$$f_1'(X) = f(X),$$
$$f_2'(X) = f(X) + 5 * NormSuccR * f(X),$$
$$f_3'(X) = f(X) + 10 * NormSuccR * f(X),$$

where: $f(X)$ is a fitness value of an antibody X, *and NormSuccR* is a normalized value of success register, and it is a value from the range [0, 1].

Results of experiments

We performed three groups of experiments with two types of environments. Our test-bed was a test-case generator proposed by Trojanowski and Michalewicz (1999). The generator creates a convex search space, which is a multidimensional hypercube. It is divided into a number of disjoint subspaces of the same size with defined simple unimodal functions of the same shape but possibly different value of optimum. In case of two-dimensional search space we simply have a patchy landscape, i.e. a chess-board with a hill in the middle of every field. Hills do not move but cyclically change their heights what makes the landscape varying in time. The goal is to find the current highest hill.

In our experiments there was a sequence of fields with varying hills' heights. Other fields of the space were static. We did experiments with two-dimensional search space where the chess-boards were of size 4 by 4, i.e. with 16 fields, and of size 6 by 6, i.e. with 36 fields. Thus the search spaces consisted of 15 local optima and one global optimum in the first case, and of 35 local optima and one global optimum in the second case. We tested four shapes of the sequence of non-stationary fields presented in Figure 2. In the figure, values in cells are weights of unimodal functions of the respective fields, which control heights of the hills. In other words the function located at the (i,j)-field is of the form $f_{ij}(x,y) = w_{ij} \cdot g(x-a_i, y-b_j)$, where g is a fixed unimodal function and (a_i, b_j) is the center of this field. Lower index at the value in the cell represents the position of the field in the sequence of presented optima.

The environments #1 and #3 (left part of Figure 2) were test-beds for experiments with cyclic changes, while the environments #2 and #4 (right part of Figure 2) were test-beds for experiments with both cyclic and acyclic[1] changes. The aim

[1] Results for all environments can be found in the full paper located at the url: http://www.ipipan.waw.pl/~stw/ais.

of these experiments was to trace efficiency of primary (acyclic changes) and secondary (cyclic changes) immune response to the antigens (i.e. current optima). For experiments with cyclic changes a single epoch obeys 5 cycles of changes. In all the experiments each antigen has been presented through 10 iterations. Thus, in case of the environment #1 a single epoch took 200 iterations, in case of the environment #2 - 400 iterations, in case of the environment #3 - 300 iterations, and in case of the environment #4 - 600 iterations. Experiments with non-cyclic changes were based on the environments #2 and #4 and a single epoch included just one cycle of changes and took 80 and 120 iterations respectively.

0.1	0.1	0.1	0.5_4
0.1	0.1	0_3	0.1
0.1	0.5_2	0.1	0.1
1_1	0.1	0.1	0.1

0.546_5	0.100	0.100	0.146_4
0.100	0.500_6	0.500_3	0.100
0.100	0.546_2	0.146_7	0.100
1.000_1	0.100	0.100	0.000_8

					1_6
				0.65_5	
			0.25_4		
		0.0_3			
	0.25_2				
0.65_1					

1_{12}					0_6
	0.47_{11}			0.07_5	
		0.65_{10}	0.25_4		
		0.5_3	0.5_9		
	0.65_2			0.25_8	
0.47_1					0.07_7

Figure 2. Environments #1 (top left), #2 (top right), #3 (bottom left) and #4 (bottom right) - shapes of the sequence of non-stationary fields in testing environments.

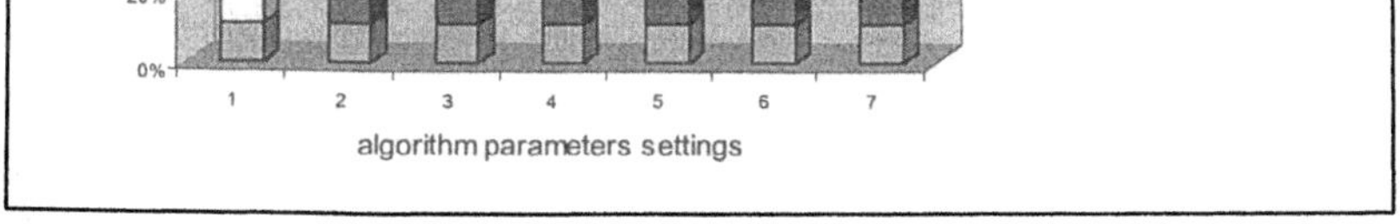

Figure 3. Division of population into activated and washed out individuals. Individuals that do not belong to any of the two subgroups are supposed to form an immune memory.

For the six environments described above we did series of experiments by changing the parameters n (defined in step 2 of the algorithm in Figure 1) and d (defined in step 4) – see Figure 3.

For the results estimation we used two measures proposed by Trojanowski and Michalewicz (1999): Accuracy and Adaptability. *Accuracy* is a difference between the value of the current best individual in the population of the "just before the change" generation and the optimum value averaged over the entire run. *Adaptability* is a difference between the value of the current best individual of each generation and the optimum value averaged over the entire run. For both measures the smaller values are the better results.

Exemplary results for cyclic environments are presented in Fig. 4 (env. #1) and Fig. 5 (env. #2) (please, visit the url mentioned in the footnote for a full set of results).

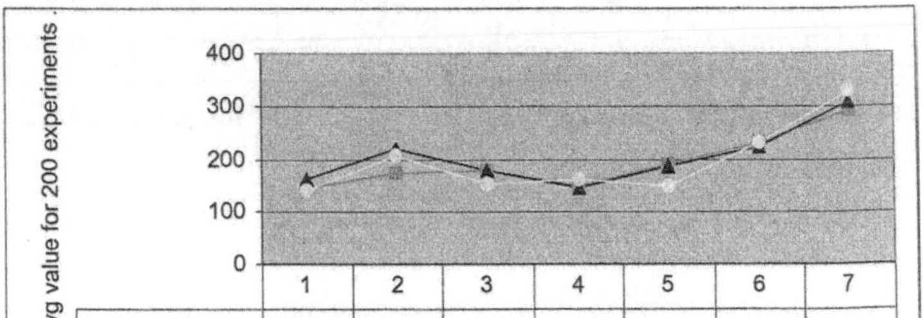

	1	2	3	4	5	6	7
fitness	145.921	173.657	179.452	147.754	191.244	230.404	288.925
succ reg 1	162.846	217.557	176.17	146.653	185.688	221.86	305.869
succ reg 2	141.402	206.203	152.061	162.976	147.766	229.274	326.568

Figure 4. Results for experiments with 7 types of parameter settings and three types of memory management performed with environment #1 (cyclic changes).

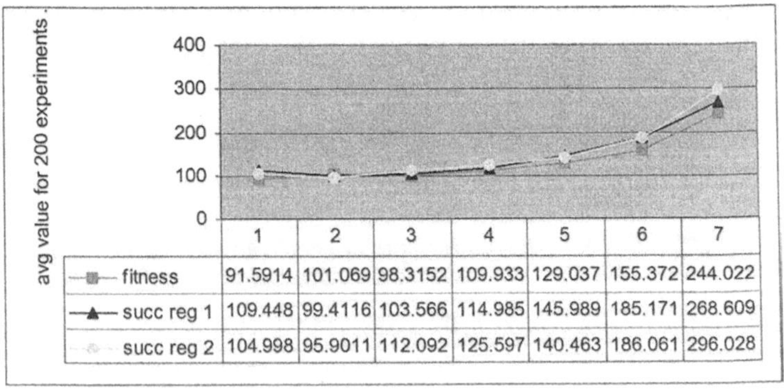

	1	2	3	4	5	6	7
fitness	91.5914	101.069	98.3152	109.933	129.037	155.372	244.022
succ reg 1	109.448	99.4116	103.566	114.985	145.989	185.171	268.609
succ reg 2	104.998	95.9011	112.092	125.597	140.463	186.061	296.028

Figure 5. Results for experiments with 7 types of parameter settings and three types of memory management performed with environment #2 (cyclic changes).

Conclusions

Although for different types of environments, different strategies won the competition, presence of memory – i.e. a gap between the group of stimulated and deleted antibodies (defined in Figure 3) – does not guarantee conclusively better results, than in case where there is no gap (i.e. in the first setting of the parameters). Table 1 summarizes the cases, where memory improved the algorithm.

	Cyclic changes				Non-cyclic changes	
	Env. #1	Env. #2	Env. #3	Env. #4	Env. #2	Env. #4
Fitness	-	-	-	+	+	+
Succ reg 1	+	+	+	-	-	+
Succ reg 2	-	+	+	+	-	-

Table 1. Table of cases, where presence of memory gave better results, than its absence.

Number of cases, where memory improved algorithm results is just a little bigger, than the number of cases, where the results got decreased. That observation indicates, that: (a) the memory emerges indeed, (b) it improves algorithm behaviour, but current form of its management is rather insufficient. In further research we will work on searching other methods of memory management, more resistant to side effects of exogenic activation and apoptosis that corrupt memory content.

References

Gaspar, A., Collard, Ph. (1999) From Gas to artificial immune systems: Improving adaptation in time dependent optimization. *Proc. of the 1999 Congress on Evolutionary Computation*, Washington DC, IEEE Publishing, 1859-1866

Grefenstette, J. (1992) Genetic algorithms for changing environments. In: R. Manner, B. Manderick, eds., *Parallel Problem Solving from Nature 2*, Elsevier, 465-501

Hofmeyr, S.A. (1999) An interpretative introduction to the immune system. Technical Report, Dept. of Computer Science, University of New Mexico, Albuquerque, NM

Jerne, N.J. (1974) Towards a network theory of the immune system. *Ann. Immunol. (Inst. Pasteur)*, 125C: 373-389

Wierzchoń, S.T. (2001a) *Artificial Immune Systems. Theory and Applications* (in Polish). Warszawa EXIT

Wierzchoń, S.T. (2001b) Artificial immune systems in action: Optimization of non-stationary functions (in Polish). *Proc. of the Workshop "Artificial Intelligence"*, SzI'2001, Siedlce, Poland, 97-106

Trojanowski,K., and Michalewicz, Z. (1999) Searching for optima in non-stationary environments, *Proc. of the 1999 Congress on Evolutionary Computation*, Washington DC, IEEE Publishing, 1843-1850

Trojanowski, K., and Wierzchoń, S.T. (2002) Searching for memory in artificial immune system. In: M.A. Kłopotek, S.T.Wierzchoń, M.Michalewicz, eds, *Intelligent Information Systems 2002*. Physica-Verlag (in print)

A Software Platform for Evaluation of Neural Algorithms for Stereo Image Processing

Bogusław Cyganek, Jan Borgosz

Department of Electronics and Computer Science
University of Mining and Metallurgy
Al. Mickiewicza 30, Kraków, 30059, Poland
E-mail: {cyganek,borgosz}@uci.agh.edu.pl

Abstract. The paper presents a software platform for implementation and evaluation of different neural algorithms for stereo image processing. The described program constitutes a self-contained image evaluation and testing module but also it can be used as a library that can be a part of a bigger image processing software. Thanks to its flexible and object oriented design it can be easily extended to comprise any new neural method. Presented techniques and solutions can also guide other researchers facing similar problems in image processing.

1 Introduction

Scientific papers are full of descriptions of different image processing methods, however their implementation, evaluation and testing can pose a real problem. This is due to strong dependence on operating systems and programming platforms. There exist many commercial-scientific software packages – nevertheless they are oriented rather toward math computations, at the same time rarely offering any satisfactory solution for utilization of strict operating system and computer features that are necessary for image processing. It is an organization of image storage, change of image formats, results data post-processing and representation, just to mention few. Things go even worse when testing time demanding algorithms, such as those based on neural networks. One solution is to develop own image processing platform that can be flexible enough for implementation and efficient testing of new algorithms. The same software modules can be also used in real applications thus providing what has been coined in Object-Oriented Programming community as software reusability [7][10][11].

The paper describes software platform for evaluation of stereo image methods. The platform is built up from two modules: the first one is responsible for user interface in Win32 environments [8], the second comprises all blocks responsible for image loading and storage, format transformations and stereo processing algorithms. Moreover, the latter is basically platform independent.

2 Description of the Software Platform

2.1. Image Representation

A flexible data structure for image representation is crucial for efficient image processing and computations of disparity maps. There must be a trade off between different input formats of images and their internal representation. Further, considering allowable size of images and time complexity of algorithms, it has been chosen that images will be represented internally as square matrices, programmatically denoted by the base template class `TImageFor<T>` [10][7], where `T` stands for a given data type chosen for representation of a single pixel. The class notation used hereafter comes from Taligent® [11]. Fig. 1 depicts the class hierarchy for digital image representation that was chosen in our software platform.

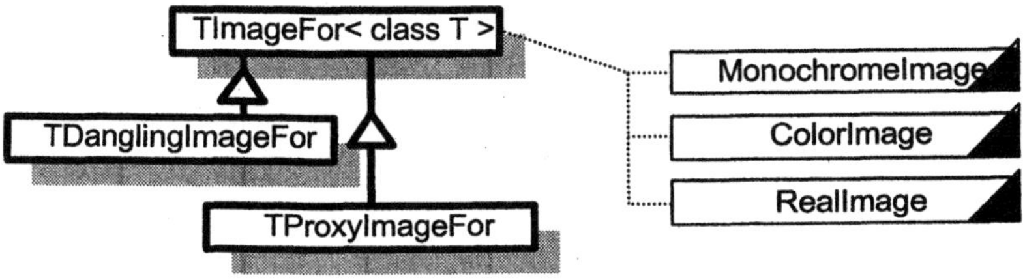

Fig. 1. The class hierarchy for a digital image representation

The three instances of the base class in Fig. 1 are as follows: `MonochromeImage` for monochrome pixels of one-byte depth, `ColorImage` for color pixels of three-bytes depth, and `RealImage` for pixels in floating point format suitable for precise computations such as the convolution.

There are two derived template classes: `TDanglingImageFor` and `TProxyImageFor`. The former is used when at each pixel it is necessary to store a different length list of values rather than a single value. The latter approximates image-in-image concept that enables operations on a part of a given image as if it were a separate image by itself – however, the underlying data storage in this case is only one. This feature creates a data abstraction that facilitates uniform treatment of all images despite of their real representation.

2.2. Stereo Processing Modules

The stereo processing module, represented by the class hierarchy in Fig. 2, is the most important part of our evaluation platform. Due to its uniform interface, each stereo algorithm can be used basically in the same manner, at the same time hiding all implementation details. Such an approach contributes to the platform independence and allow for easy addition of new classes implementing another stereo methods.

The principal abstract base class `TTwoMonochromeImageProcessor` exposes the following interface method:

```
virtual MonochromeImage * operator() (
          const MonochromeImage & leftImage,
          const MonochromeImage & rightImage );
```

It is implemented in the form of the binary call operator [10], that takes two image references as its input, and outputs a pointer to the (orphan) outcome image. In the case of stereo processors the outcome image is simply a disparity map.

The three classes: `TAddGenerator`, `TSubtractGenerator`, and `TXORGenerator` are used simply to add, subtract or exclusively-or the two input images.

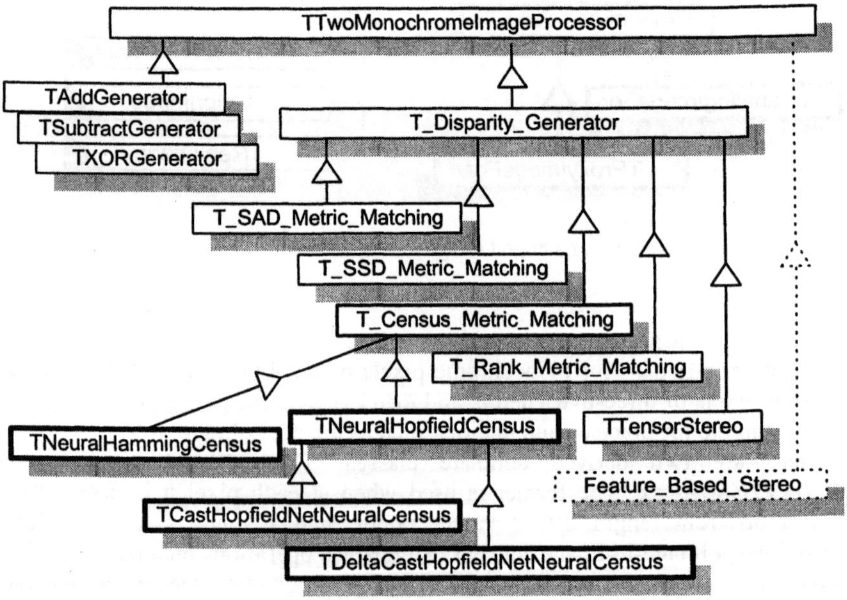

Fig. 2. The class hierarchy for stereo processing modules

The derived class named `T_Disparity_Generator` builds a foundation for all point-oriented stereo processing algorithms [1][9]. All its derivatives are just specializations for a given point-oriented stereo method. These are: `T_SAD_Metric_Matching` that uses the *Sum-of-Absolute-Differences* measure, `T_SSD_Metric_Matching` with the *Sum-of-Square-Differences* measure, `T_Census_Metric_Matching` that relies on the *Census* measure,

`T_Rank_Metric_Matching` with the *Rank* measure [3][4]. At the same time `T_Census_Metric_Matching` is a base for all neural oriented stereo methods, such as `TNeuralHopfieldCensus` that implements the Hopfield neural network and its derivatives `TCastHopfieldNetNeuralCensus` and `TDeltaCastHopfieldNetNeuralCensus` that implement modified versions of the Hopfield net [5][6][2]. The class `TNeuralHammingCensus` implements the Hamming neural network which structure is depicted in Fig. 6.

It can be easily observed that all neural network classes are derived from the common base class that one of the tasks is to preprocess input images with the *Census* filter. It has been shown that the format of the signal applied to the input layer of a neural network for image processing is crucial for proper results, and that preprocessing images with the *Census* filter fulfills this requirement [1][2][4].

There are also two classes for the tensor based stereo methods. The first one, named `TTensorStereo`, implements the point-oriented version of this method. The second, `Tensor_Based_Algorithm`, implements the disparity-oriented version of the tensor stereo method [1].

2.3. User Interface and its Functionality

Fig. 3 depicts the user interface of the presented stereo image processing platform. Visible are different kinds of windows, such as: input stereo pair, disparity map, binary representation of an image, etc. User interface was implemented with the Microsoft's Visual C++ 6.0 and the Microsoft Foundation Classes 4.2 library.

Fig. 3. View of the user interface

3 Experiments and Conclusions

Fig. 4 and Fig. 5 depict exemplary disparity maps obtained by means of the Hamming neural network run on the presented evaluation platform.

a b c d

Fig. 4. Experimental results obtained by means of the software platform and Hamming neural network: (**ab**) "Pentagon" stereo pair, (**c**) disparity map obtained with window 11×11, (**d**) disparity map obtained with window 15×15

a b c d

Fig. 5. Experimental results obtained by means of the Hamming neural network: (**ab**) "Corridor" stereo pair, (**c**) disparity map with window 5×5, (**d**) disparity map 11×11

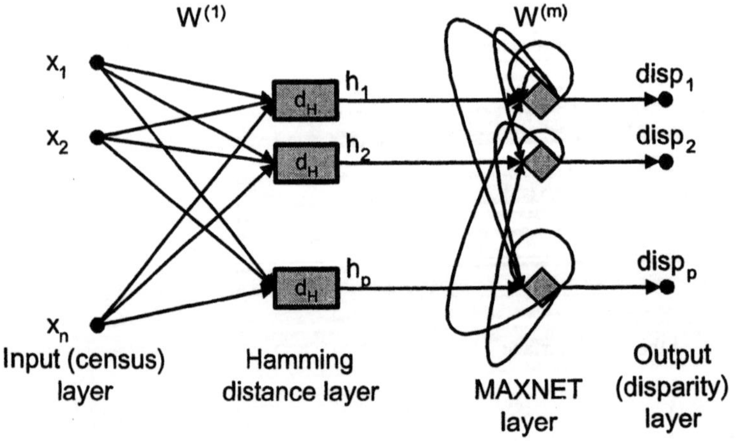

Fig. 6. The Hamming neural network used in experiments

Fig. 6 shows the Hamming neural network employed in experiments that were performed with help of the described evaluation platform. Details of the stereo matching with the Hamming neural network can be found in [2]. Execution times for disparity maps in Fig. 4(cd) were 48.03 and 90.11 seconds, respectively, on the IBM PC® machine with Pentium® 800MHz.

The presented solution of the evaluation platform for stereo image processing confirmed to be very useful and easily extensible. At the other side, execution times have been verified to be much shorter than those of corresponding implementations of stereo algorithms run with commercially available scientific packages. Simultaneously, a researcher has a freedom of easy addition of almost any new ideas, such as for example neural network with different activation functions for each neuron.

It is strongly recommended to properly design all software modules prior to the programming of a framework. Especially important is a choice of interface methods of each class. Also, it was verified that usage of the design patterns can greatly help and clarify the structure of the whole software.

The paper has been sponsored by the Polish Scientific Committee grant no. 10.10.120.311.

References

1. Cyganek B. (2001) Stereo matching with tensor representation of local neighborhood. Ph.D. thesis (in Polish). University of Mining and Metallurgy, Kraków, Poland,
2. Cyganek B. (1999) Neural Networks Application to The Correlation-Based Stereo-Images Matching, 5th International Conference EANN '99, Warsaw, Poland, 17-22
3. Cyganek B., Borgosz J. (2001) A Comparative Study of Performance and Implementation of Some Area-Based Stereo Algorithms, 9th International Conference on Computer Analysis of Images and Patterns CAIP'2001, Warsaw, Poland, 709-716
4. Cyganek B., Borgosz J. (2001) An Experimental Comparison of Area-Based Stereo Algorithms, EURASIP Conference: ECMCS 2001, Budapest, Hungary
5. Cyganek B., Korohoda P., Borgosz J. (1999) Matching Stereo-Images with Cellular Neural Networks, Fourth Conference on Neural Networks and Their Applications, Zakopane, Poland
6. Cyganek B., Korohoda P. (1999) Improved Neural Network for Fast Extraction of Information from Stero-Images, Fourth Conference Neural Networks and Their Applications, Zakopane, Poland
7. Gamma E., Helm R., Johnson R., Vlissides J. (1995) Design Patterns. Elements of Reusable Object-Oriented Software. Addison-Wesley
8. Richter J. (1999) Advanced Windows. The Developer's Guide to the Win32® API for Windows NT™. Microsoft Press
9. Scharstein D. (1999) View Synthesis Using Stereo Vision. Lecture Notes in Computer Science 1582, Springer-Verlag
10. Stroustrup B. (1998) The C++ Programming Language. 3rd edition, Addison-Wesley
11. Taligent (1995) Taligent Guide to Designing Programs. Addison-Wesley

Sequential Analysis of Medical Images Using Neural Networks

Marek Czeleń, Grzegorz Wojtas, Zbigniew Mikrut[1]

Institute of Automatics, University of Mining and Metallurgy
Mickiewicza 30, 30-059 Kraków, Poland
e-mail: zibi@biocyb.ia.agh.edu.pl

Abstract. A problem frequently encountered in the analysis of medical images is reaching a correct and reliable diagnosis of the examined organ, particularly by persons with little experience, e.g. first year medical students. That fact has become an inspiration for construction of an assisting program, based on application of three neural networks: 1) moving the attention point along the selected object, 2) elaborating the diagnosis for the area in the current viewport, 3) reporting the end of the examination.
In the present work a summary is done for almost a hundred of experiments, testing the efficiency of all those neural networks in the analysis of raw medical images. The final version of the algorithm uses *backpropagation* type networks: it operates on square areas which are 31x31 pixels in size for the first and third networks and 91x91 pixels in size for the second (diagnosing) network. The achieved level of correct recognition (about 80%) is a very good result, if one takes into account rather low quality (dynamic range) of the analysed images and the observed natural interferences.

1 Introduction

With the increasing presence of the equipment for digital recording and visualisation of medical images more and more needs are expressed, concerning not only the quality increase of the registered images but also their intelligent analysis. Such systems are narrowly specialised applications, the role of which is to suggest the answer, leaving the final decision to the human staff. Most of such applications performs an overall analysis of the selected object, applying various preprocessing methods, segmentation, detection and classification of preselected features, both by neural [3, 8] and non-neural [5] methods.

An interesting alternative is provided by a sequential object analysis, for which a distant and unequal led ideal is the human vision system. It seems the neural networks are one of the few possibilities for realisation of that technique [6, 1]. This concerns both implementation of moving the so called "attention point" and the analysis (diagnosing) of the currently "seen" image window.

In order to preserve a consistent approach to the problem for the present study it was decided that *raw data* or slightly preprocessed medical image data will be

[1] The work was partially supported by the Polish Committee for Scientific Research under grant No. T11E 007 17.

used as input. It reflects the authors' belief that an adequately complicated neural network will be able to extract the interesting image areas by itself. Other concepts of recognition based on raw images can be found in papers [7, 2, 4].

The material selected for the study consisted of ERCP[1] X-ray images, registered for several patients (see Fig. 3). The task for the created application was a preliminary examination of the pancreatic duct area preselected by the human operator. During the pancreas area tracking the application should be able to provide a current diagnosis, looking for the following pathological changes:

- branches characteristic for the acute pancreas inflammation
- swellings and constrictions characteristic for the pancreas cancer
- presence of cysts.

2 Methods and Experiments

In order to select an appropriate form of the input data and the neural network structures, several experiments have been carried out, during which the networks were learned and their structure was being adjusted. Therefore it is not possible to strictly divide the description of the study into the classical stages, i.e. design of the input data form, choice of the network structure and the experiments themselves. The concepts presented below are results from positively completed tests.

2.1 Task Distribution

The artificial neural networks operating on raw images are able to perform well in only one learned task. That is a limitation for the sequential image analysis procedure, because for a complete analysis of the pancreatic duct image in each step it is necessary to determine the motion direction, elaborate the local diagnosis and possibly evaluate the condition for the algorithm termination. Therefore it has been decided that three independent networks will be used:

1) the first network determined the motion direction for the "focus of attention" point using a small (31x31 pixels) area of the image, what was equivalent to determination of a new actual position
2) the second network elaborated the local diagnosis at the actual position using a bigger image area than the previous network (91x91 pixels), which was reduced to the area 31x31 pixels in size
3) the third network, operating on the same image area as the diagnosing network, determined whether any part of the pancreatic duct can be seen. It was one of the conditions required for program termination, in the case when all the objects has been analysed or in a situation when the first network lost the tracked object.

---

[1] Endoscopic Retrograde CholangioPancreatography

2.2 Construction of the Learning Sequences

During the construction of the learning sequences the main objective was to ensure that they are properly representative. For the network setting the motion direction the images and the respective motion directions have been selected in such a way that the direction distribution was reasonably uniform or the forward motion was slightly preferred. Obviously the images should be consistent (non-contradicting) what has been finally ensured by proposing a concept of "virtual vehicle" (see sect. 2.4).

Another problem was the necessity of making a decision concerning the choice of the algorithm used for determination of the motion direction for the "narrow" and "wide" objects (see Fig. 3a and 3b respectively). When the pancreatic duct is narrow, then bright areas can be seen on both sides. On the other hand when it is wide, then the bright area can be detected on one side only. Frequently other objects are visible in the image window, which can interfere in the process of direction determination (e.g. in almost every image a duodenoscope tube - a device for dosage the contrast medium - can be seen). Such situations have also been taken into account during the construction of the learning sequence.

It was also ensured that the numbers of images representing particular diseases (pathological conditions) were approximately the same. The images have been registered at different angles, so that after the learning stage the network would be able to carry out a proper evaluation. In the construction of the learning set for the network responsible for analysis termination both the images containing parts of the pancreatic duct and images without such parts have been taken into account. The ratio of the respective images was kept close to the 1:1.

2.3 Preprocessing

The ERCP image express particularly low dynamic range (see Fig. 1 upper row). The preliminary experiments have shown that the neural network was not able to correct the dynamic range on its own, and - what is a consequence of the above - that execution of a simple preprocessing essentially affects the obtained results. From several examined methods of contrast enhancement based on the histogram analysis one was selected, consisting of histogram stretching to the full brightness range accompanied by aggregation of 10% brightest and 10% darkest pixels. Several examples of application of the above mentioned operation are shown in Fig.1.

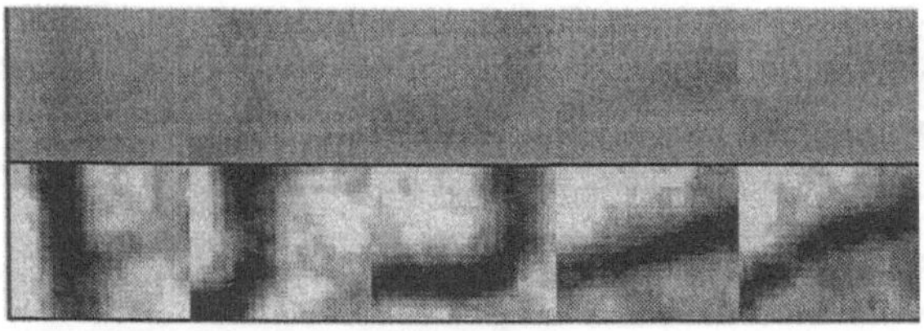

Fig. 1. Image contrasting using the histogram analysis

2.4 Moving the Focus of Attention

The best results have been obtained by implementing the "virtual vehicle" concept, in which the window to be analysed behaves like a small vehicle, moving along the pancreatic duct as if it was a road. During consecutive steps the window is turned in such a way that its centre is kept in the same location, while the lateral edge (with respect to the motion direction) is kept parallel to the segment connecting the actual analysis window centre with its previous location (Fig.2)

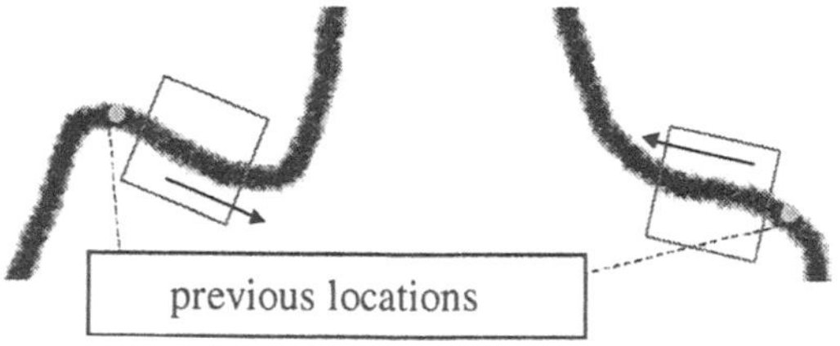

Fig.2. The virtual vehicle concept

For such a situation the network "sees" similarly oriented images and is able to determine the direction of motion for the attention point with its proper orientation ("forward" direction). The rotation angle is determined using the actual and previous location of the window centre by the program. Therefore the neural network should be able to recognise relative direction (with respect to the previous motion direction) within the [-90,90] degrees.

The tests have not confirmed the utility of methods based on the *log-polar transform* and similar concepts. It was a direct consequence of considerable information averaging near the edges of the input image area, what is an advantage only when the tracked object is within the window. The attempts of application of *"receptor fields"*, detecting lines of various inclinations have lead to better results than the transforms mentioned above, but still the results were worse then for the pure contrast enhancement. An attempt of applying a Kohonen network, as a feature detecting network, did not work at all. Also the combining of contrasted image with the information taken from the receptor field or with the Kohonen network did not improve the correctness of the network operation (see Tab. 1).

3 Results and Discussion

The structures of all the networks tested are listed in Table 1, while several examples of analysis are presented in Fig.3.

In the cases when the pancreatic duct was located too close to other objects entering the "region of interest" of the direction determining network or when it crossed other objects (Fig.3a) the network was not able to determine properly the motion direction because the information about context (surrounding) was not sufficient. Possible extension of the window on one hand would increase the amount of available information, but on the other hand it would complicate the analysis by introducing more visible organs.

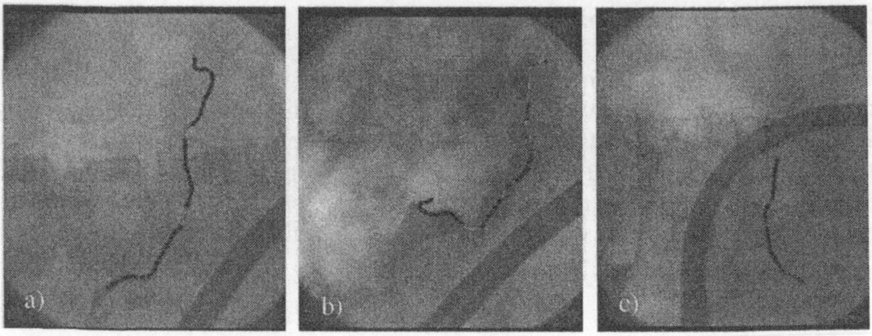

Fig. 3. **(a)** Analysis of a regular pancreas; NN diagnosis: 84.6% of the pancreas length does not exhibit any pathological changes. **(b)** Pancreatic duct with cysts; NN diagnosis: 38.5% of the pancreas length exhibits cysts, 22.9% exhibits constrictions. **(c)** Regular pancreatic duct; NN diagnosis: 78.1% of the pancreas length does not exhibit pathological changes.

Table 1. Summary of data representations and network architectures tested (X)

Data representation	Network structure [type, inputs, structure]	NN 1	NN 2	NN 3
Log-Polar	Bp, (8x5), (100:100:2)	X		
	Bp, (12x6), (100:100:8)	X		
Retina	Bp, (68), (15:15:5)	X		
	Bp, (130), (15:15:5)	X		
	Bp, (68), (100:100:16)	X		
Square window	Bp, (31x31), (15:15:5)	X		
of analysis	Bp, (31x31), (100:100:2)	X		
	Bp, (31x31), (100:100:5)	*X*		
	Bp, (31x31), (25:25:5)		*X*	
	Bp, (31x31), (10:2)			*X*
Receptor fields	Bp, (var), (15:15:5)	X		
Hybrid net-	Kh, (31x31), (5:5) + Bp, (25), (15:15:5)	X		
work	Kh, (31x31), (5:5) + Bp, (25), (5:5:5)	X		
	Kh, (31x31), (5:5) + Bp, (31x31+5), (15:15:5)	X		

Bp – backpropagation
Kh – Kohonen SOM

The pancreases of regular shapes are better suited for the analysis than the pathological ones (see Fig. 3). Particularly difficult cases are the ducts with cancer symptoms, because the constrictions in their sections are seen as discontinuities, what may lead to errors in the procedure of determination of motion direction.

For the diagnosing network the interference from another objects (e.g. the spine) has lead to erroneous detection of branching. However the network used for determination of the conditions of analysis termination correctly reported the fact of absence of the pancreatic duct on its ends or in the case of deviation from the proper route within the duct area. The errors were generated mainly on discontinuities, which the network was not able to distinguish from the situation when two various objects were present.

4 Conclusions

The obtained results prove that the analysis of raw images using neural networks is possible and effective. The diagnostic recognition level about 80% presents a very good result, if the low quality of the ERCP images and the presence of natural interference are taken into account. The result is comparable to the 85% recognition level reported in the paper [5], whereas it should be mentioned that in the cited work structural descriptions (grammars) have been applied to a preselected (binary) object.

The presented method can be also applied to the analysis of medical images containing objects of classes similar to the ERCP images, e.g. coronary vessels or eyeball vessels. Having this in mind refinement of the whole algorithm is planned, by introduction of feedback worked-out in the diagnosing network. The feedback's task would include a temporary reduction of the step length between consecutive attention shifts (at present the step length is constant) in order to provide a possibility of more detailed analysis by the recognising network in the cases which are difficult to diagnose. That would be a next step towards the functional similarity of the proposed algorithm to the movements of the human eyeball, executed during realisation of the diagnostic task, which have been registered in our Biocybernetic Laboratory.

References

1. van de Laar P., Heskes T., Gielen S. (1997) Task-Dependent Learning of Attention. Neural Networks vol.10 no 6, Pergamon
2. Lindblad T., Lindsey C., Padgett M., Vanyachine A., Zanevsky I. (1998) Digital X-Ray image processing using biologically inspired methods. Proc. IJCNN, Anchorage, Alaska.
3. Mikrut Z., Tadeusiewicz R. (2000) Neural Networks applied to digital image processing and recognition, in: Biocybernetics and Biomedical Engineering, Vol. 6, Ed. Nałęcz M. AOW EXIT, Warsaw (in Polish)
4. Neubauer C. (1998) Evaluation of Convolutional Neural Networks for Visual Recognition. IEEE Trans. Neural Networks, Vol. 9, No. 4
5. Ogiela M., Tadeusiewicz R. (2000) Syntactic Pattern Recognition for X-Ray Diagnosis of Pancreatic Duct. Eng. in Medicine and Biology, IEEE Magazine, **19**, 6.
6. Postma E., Herik H., Hudson P. (1997) SCAN: A Scalable Model of Attentional Selection. Neural Networks vol.10 No. 6, Pergamon
7. Sjostrom P. J., Wahlberd L.U. (1999) Automated cell recognition and counting based on combination of artificial neural networks and standard image analysis methods. Proc. 3rd Int. Conf. Cognitive and Neural Systems, Boston
8. Żurada J. M. (1992) Introduction to artificial neural networks. West Publ., St. Paul New York.

Medical Image Recognition Based on Fractal Features

Edward Kacki[1], Marcin Janaszewski[2]

[1]Technical University of Lodz , Skorupki 6/8, 90-924 Lodz, Poland
email: ekacki@ics.p.lodz.pl
[2] The College of Computer Science, Rzgowska 17a, 93-008 Lodz, Poland
email: janaszm@leo.wsinf.edu.pl

Abstract. The article presents a new method of feature extraction from an image represented as a digital bit-mapped display in grey scale. The method is based on an idea of fractal model of nature and processes carried out in it. The results of three recognition experiments of different kinds of medical images were included. Fractal and traditional features were evaluated, by the Fisher coefficient, in each experiment. Extracted features were recognised by the use of: sigmoidal neural network, neuro-fuzzy system, k-nearest neighbour method and the nearest mode algorithm. The authors presented the discussion of obtained results, tips concerning fractal features extracting, the comparison of effectiveness and the properties of recognition the method used.

1 Introduction

The natural objects are not as ideal fractals as Cantor dust or Sierpinski triangle, because they do not show similarity in each scales. They are often multifractal objects, that is they consist of some fractals, between which, there is not any self-similarity relation. Objects often reveal only partial similarity. Searching for similarity in objects shown on images had been carried out before in order to perform image compression [1]. The algorithm presented here is based on the fractal image compression method. The base difference between the presented approach and the image compression is followed by different goals of self-similarity searching. In the author's approach the searching is carried out to determine the feature vector, which describes the degree of self-similarity in different scales of investigated image. Moreover, a special emphasis is put on acceleration of fractal feature extraction algorithm.

2 Fractal method of feature extraction (FM)

Fractal method may by used for squared images, of which the side, expressed in pixels, is the power of 2. In the paper, an image is treated as a matrix in which the element from the i-th row and the j-th column represents a grey level of image pixel from the i-th row and the j-th column. The grey levels belong to range <0,255>.

The fundamental element of fractal features extraction is an operation called by authors "similarity testing", which may be presented in a few stages:

1. Cutting out, from a tested image, two subimages, from which the one is called a range and appointed by the letter *P*. The second one called a domain is appointed by the letter *D*. A domain can not be larger than a range.
2. Diminishing the domain *D* to the range size, by averaging of the neighbouring pixels. The diminishing is done only when the domain is larger than the range. In this way, by the domain diminishing a new matrix *D'* is obtained.
3. Calculating by the method of last squares the best affine mapping:

$$(\bar{a},\bar{b}) = \min_{(a,b)\in R^2} \|P-(aD'+b)\| \tag{2.1}$$

Where: $\|*\|$- is Euclidean norm

4. Calculating an error *Err(P, D)* which characterizes a degree of similarity between the domain *D* and the range *P*. The calculation is based on the following formula:

$$Err(P,D) = \frac{1}{\overline{\overline{P}}}\|P-(aD'+b)\| \tag{2.2}$$

Where: $\overline{\overline{P}}$ - elements number of matrix *P*

Stage 1 should be explained here. Especially the way of domains and the ranges choice. The Ranges' choice is carried out by the means of quaternary division of an image. The first two hollow of the division and the way of range numbering is shown on the Fig 2.1, where the following symbols were introduced:

P_{ik}- *k*-th range in *i*-th hollow, $i = 1, 2,\ldots,\log_2(\textit{image side})-1$, $k=1,2,\ldots,4^i$; *i* - single-digit number. Each range in *i*-th hollow has equal side $(bo)/2^i$.

$P_{ik} \in \boldsymbol{P_i}$; $\boldsymbol{P_i}$ - Is a set of all ranges from hollow *i*.

The way of domains choice was presented, for 8*8 pixels image, on the Fig 2.2. Each blank represents one pixel of the tested image. The following domains are chosen by a gradual frame shifting per 1 pixel. The upper left pixel of D_{jl} domain is situated in $l/(bo)$ row and $l\%(bo)$ column. $j = 1, 2,\ldots,\log_2(bo)-1$; $l = 1,2,\ldots,((bo-bd_j) + 1)^2$; *j* - single-digit number.

Where: *bo* - size of the image side, measured in pixels.

bd_j - size of the domain side from *j*-th hollow, measured in pixels. $bd_j = bo/2^j$

A C_{ij} feature of the tested image is formed in two stages:

Stage 1:

$$E_{ijk} = Err(P_{ik}, D_{jl}) \quad \overline{D_{jl}} \in D_j \quad for\ k = 1,2,\ldots,4^i \tag{2.3}$$

Where: $\overline{D_{jl}}$ -The first found domain which fulfils the following condition:

$$Err(P_{ik},\overline{D_{jl}}) < AErr \tag{2.4}$$

Where: *AErr* - an acceptable error. It is a parameter of the algorithm.
In case where there is no domain, in D_j set, which fulfils the (2.4) condition:

$$E_{ijk} = \min_{D_{jl} \in D_j} \{Err(P_{ik}, D_{jl})\} \tag{2.5}$$

Stage 2:

$$C_{ij} = \frac{1}{\overline{\overline{P_i}}} \sum_{k=1}^{\overline{\overline{P_i}}} E_{ijk} \tag{2.6}$$

For: $i = 1, 2, ..., \log_2(bo)-1$; $j = 0, 1, ..., i$;
$\overline{\overline{P_i}}$ - the number of elements in P_i set.

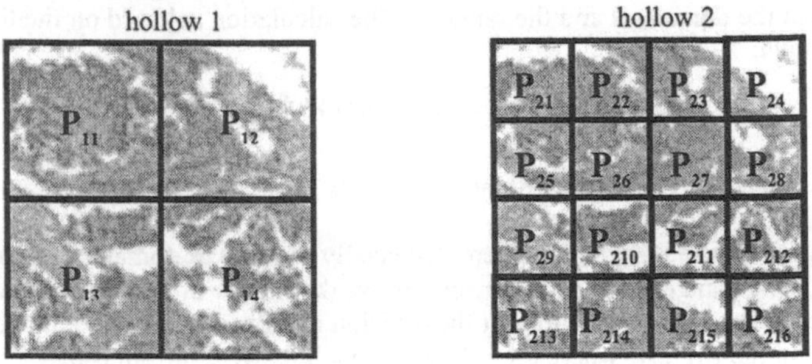

Fig. 2.1. The first two hollows of quaternary division of an image

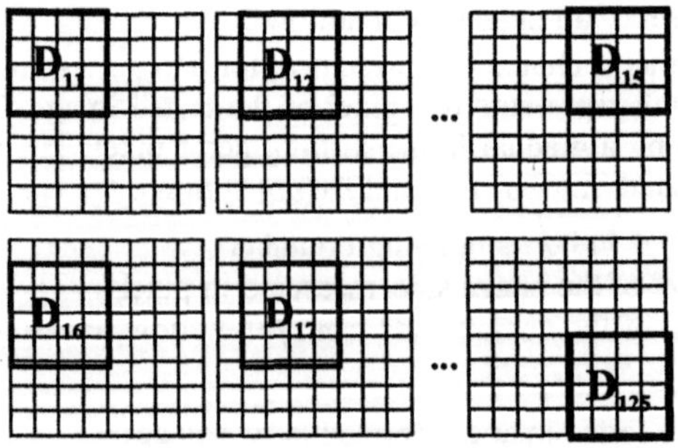

Fig. 2.2. The way of the domain choice, shown for the first hollow and the image of the size 8*8 pixels

3 Computer investigations

The above described algorithm was implemented by the use of Visual C++ tool. In order to test the fractal features usefulness, the three recognition experiments of different types of medical images were carried out. The first experiment concerned textures recognition, which were visualised by means of magnetic resonance topograph in Medical Physics Department, University of Dundee, Scotland, and which are used as a research material[4] for COST B11[3] project. The second experiment concerned microscope images represented in different phases of angiosarcoma. The third concerned of brain sections recognition. All recognised sections came from the same brain and were made by the use of magnetic resonance tomography. In each experiment a large number of fractal features, for different values of domain hollow, range hollow and acceptable error, were extracted. For the comparison of the recognition quality of fractal features with the recognition quality of different well known features, 280 features were extracted on the basis of an image histogram, absolute gradient values, Run-length matrix, co-occurrence matrix for four directions and five distances between image pixels, and autoregressive model. The extraction was carried out by means of MaZda[4] application. All extracted features were evaluated by the means of Fisher coefficient (*F*). In the first two experiments three training sets were constructed. The first, fractal set (FS), included two best fractal features (in the sense of *F* factor evaluation). The second, MaZda set (MS), included two best features extracted by the use of MaZda. The last one, MaZda and Fractal set (M&FS), included the best fractal feature and the best feature extracted with MaZda. In the third experiment only FS was constructed. Each experiment tested each training set by the means of the cross validation and the following recognition methods: nearest neighbour (k-NN)[11], nearest mode (NM)[11], sigmoidal neural network (SNN)[7], neuro-fuzzy system (NF)[10]

4 Results

1. The long time feature extraction, especially for the large hollows, was obtained. This restricts the application of the fractal feature extraction method to images smaller than 512*512 pixels. Therefore, the acceleration of the method seems to be worth considering.
2. The results of the first experiment show that for the grain textures the small domains hollow 0 and 1 and the small ranges hollow 1 and 2 should be used.
3. The second experiment shows that for images which have small, not repeating irregularities (the second experiment) it would be the best option to extract features for high domains hollow and high ranges hollow. For images, whose size is 128*128 pixels, the domains hollow: (3, 4, 5) and the range hollows: (4, 5, 6) should be used. For images, which have different sizes the hollows should be chosen in such a way, that domains should have 32*32 pixels or 16*16 pixels and ranges should have16*16 or 8*8 or 4*4 pixels.

4. The results of the third experiment show that for images which have big areas of similar grey levels small ranges hollow should be used, similar to those applied for grain textures.
5. If small values of domains hollow and ranges hollow:1, 2, 3 are used, then high value of acceptable error *AErr* (5, 20) should be applied. Doing so, will accelerate the feature extraction without the loss of the recognition quality.

In the first experiment, the best results, 100% of good recognitions, were obtained for M&FS and for each recognition method but for NFS. Such a good result was also obtained for MaZda set and NM, k-NM methods. In the second experiment, the best results, 90% of good recognitions, were obtained for M&FS and neural systems (SNN and NFS).In the third experiment, the best results, 95% of good recognitions, were obtained for NFS. A little worse result 91% was achieved after applying k-NM method.

5 Main conclusions and observations

Conclusions and observations referred to fractal method of feature extraction:

1. The information about self similarity obtained in small hollows could be used to accelerate the feature extraction in higher hollows. The next idea of acceleration is based on splitting of fractal feature extraction into stages. At the first stage, every eighth domain is tested. At the second stage, every fourth domain is tested, at the third, every second domain is tested and finally at the fourth all domains are tested. Additionally, the information about domains tested in the earlier stages could be used in all the following stages. The features extracted in each stage could be applied in the recognition tasks. Moreover, one can write a parallel algorithm easily (Simultaneously calculating a few values of E_{ijk}).

2. In the carried out experiments, the combination of the fractal features with MaZda features gave no worse but often better results. Therefore, the fractal features carry additional information about image properties, which is not represented among the best MaZda features. Experiments revealed that the information carried by fractal features may be useful in medical image recognition. Fractal features should be used especially in difficult tasks, where traditional features do not give good results. The authors suggest the application of the multistage recognition. At the first stage the traditional features should be recognised, by the means of a method, where the discarding of patterns is possible. At the second stage the discarded patterns should be recognised by the means of fractal features.

The conclusions referring to the applied recognition methods:

1. The carried out experiments showed that methods in which the discarding of patterns is possible do not always give smaller loss of coefficient than methods which do not have discarding mechanism (DM). Howbeit, the k-NN and NM methods which used DM always obtained smaller or equal error coefficient (defined as a ratio of the value of correctly recognised objects and values of all ob-

jects from testing set) in comparison with the same methods without the mechanism. In that case, the methods which have DM should be applied in difficult pattern recognition tasks, especially in such cases where costs of making mistakes are very high. The additional advantage of methods, which have DM, is the possibility of discarding new cases which are not represented in the training set. The advantage has a special meaning in the medical application, because the new cases, which were not represented in the training set, should be discarded and examined seperately to avoid expensive mistakes.

2. The best recognition results were obtained for k-NN and SNN. It should be emphasized here that, in a few cases, SNN gave little worse results than k-NN algorithm. It is the result of a different DM applied in the mentioned methods. The discarding mechanism used in SNN, discards features more frequently, which makes the method safer. On the other hand, unnecessarily discarded features may appear. Therefore, such a DM should be applied in tasks where high values of loss function appear. Recognition results obtained in the second experiment show that there are recognition tasks in which neural systems (SNN and NFS) may give better results than minimum-distance methods as k-NM algorithm and methods based on patterns as NM methods. Indeed, there are tasks in which classes are only slightly discriminated by minimum-distance dependences and the calculated patterns do not represent features of individual classes. In such situations good classes discrimination may be realised by different dependences, which can be proved by SNN and NFS.

References

[1] Fisher Y.: Fractal Image Compression, SIGGRAPH'92 Course Notes, 1992.

[2] Hayes D. F.: Atlas of breast cancer, London Mosby-Wolfe, 1995.

[3] Internet 2001, http://phase.pki.uib.no/~costb11/

[4] Internet 2001, http://www.eletel.p.lodz.pl/cost/download.html.

[5] Internet 2001, http://www.eletel.p.lodz.pl/cost/materialy.html

[6] K•cki E., Janaszewski M.: Neural network in extremal temperature determination at cyclic heating, Procedings of the fourth conference Neural network and Their Aplications in Zakopane, pp.673-679, Poland 1999.

[7] Masters T.: Neural networks in practice, Warsaw, WNT, 1996. (In Polish)

[8] Materka A., Strzelecki., M., Lerski R., Schad L.: Feature evaluation of texture test objects for magnetic resonance imaging, Procedings of the fifth conference Computers in Medicine in Lodz, pp 101-107, Poland 1999.

[9] Rubens R. D., Fogelman I.: Bone metastases. Diagnosis and treatment. London: Springer-Verlab, 1991

[10] Rutkowska D., Pili•ski M., Rutkowski L.: Neural networks, genetic algorithms and fuzzy systems, Warsaw, PWN, 1997. (In Polish)

[11] Tadeusiewicz R., Flasi•ski M.: Pattern recognition, Warsaw, PWN, 1991. (In Polish)

[12] Trojani M.: A colour atlas of breast histopatology, J. B. Lippincott Company, Philadelphia, 1991.

Improving Image Database Summarization by Automatic Image Feature Selection Using GA

Zoran Stejić[1], Eduardo M. Iyoda[1], Yasufumi Takama[1,2], and Kaoru Hirota[1]

[1] Dept. of Comp. Intel. and Systems Science, Tokyo Institute of Technology
4259 Nagatsuta, Midori-ward, Yokohama 226-8502, Japan
[2] PREST, Japan Science and Technology Corporation (JST), Tokyo, Japan

Abstract. The problem of image feature selection is addressed, within the framework of the image classification and image database summarization applications. The existing image classification methods, as well as the *image database summarization method* proposed by Stejić et al. (2001), require manual selection of image features used for the classification, which makes these methods difficult to design, domain-dependent, and non-optimal. We extend the original image database summarization method by the automatic feature selection procedure, based on genetic algorithm. The proposed method is evaluated through comparison with the original one, on two image databases, each with 1000 photographs, partitioned into 10 semantic categories. The proposed automatic feature selection procedure improves the performance over 11% in average. The proposed method enables the user an easy access to the image database contents, by bridging the gap between a *large number of images* in a database, and a typically *small number of semantic categories* those images represent. Furthermore, through the proposed automatic feature selection procedure, the method is able to adapt to the *diverse content* and *dynamic nature* of the image databases, typical for the Internet.

1 Introduction

During the last decade, exponential growth in the amount of digital images on the Internet, in various image collections and databases, is making the problem of accessing image data increasingly important [5]. On one hand, *image retrieval methods* enable the user to find a specific image, or a group of images, in a database [5,11], while on the other hand, *image classification methods* assist the user in browsing, i.e., non-directed exploration of the image database contents [3,8,10,9].

The *image database summarization method* [6] differs from the image classification methods, since, rather than assigning one of the predefined semantic categories to each database image, it aims to: (1) discover the *semantic categories dominating the database*; (2) identify a *small number of representative images* within each category; and (3) based on the representative images, *name each category.* The result is a rough, keyword-based summary, providing a user with an abstract overview of the image database contents.

The image database summarization method, as well as the existing image classification methods, require manual selection of image features used for image classification, which makes these methods difficult to design, domain-dependent, and non-optimal (Section 2).

We address this problem, and propose the automatic image feature selection procedure, based on genetic algorithm (GA). The proposed procedure is incorporated in the image database summarization method. The extended database summarization method is evaluated through comparison with the original one, on two image databases, each with 1000 photographs, partitioned into 10 semantic categories.

Section 2 surveys the existing research dealing with the semantic image classification and database summarization. Section 3 presents the proposed GA-based automatic image feature selection procedure. Finally, Section 4 describes the experiments used for the performance evaluation of the proposed method.

2 Related Works

The existing methods for semantic image classification are described considering: (1) the *classification problem* addressed; (2) the *classification method* applied to the problem; and (3) the choice of *image features* used for the classification. Majority of the existing classification methods address the 2-category, i.e., binary classification problem, including indoor/outdoor [8,9], city/landscape [10,9], and sunset/mountain-forest [9] scene classification. Methods used to perform the classification include k-nearest neighbor (k-NN) [8,10], Singular Value Decomposition (SVD) [3], and binary Bayesian classifiers [9]. Image features employed for the classification are color [3,8,10,9], shape [10,9], and texture [8,10,9].

The *image database summarization* method [6] is different from the image classification methods both in the nature of the problem addressed, and in the method applied to solve it. Namely, rather than assigning one of the predefined semantic categories to each database image, the objectives are: (1) to discover the *semantic categories dominating the database*; (2) to identify a *small number of representative images* within each category; and (3) based on the representative images, to *name each category*. The result is a rough, keyword-based summary of the image database contents. In [6], four classification problems are addressed, containing between 2 and 8 image categories, ranging from natural scenes to artificial objects. In the *image classification step*, agglomerative hierarchical clustering is used to discover the dominant image categories, while in the *image category naming step*, representative images within each category are identified and named through a combination of k-nearest neighbor (k-NN), majority classifier, and feed-forward neural network (3-layer perceptron) techniques. Color image features are used. For further details, please refer to [6].

Regardless of the classification method applied, the choice of image features is crucial for the success of the classification, and strongly depends on the database contents. For different image categories, features having sufficient discriminatory power can be very different [8,10,9]. Furthermore, "it is quite difficult to predict the performance of a feature or feature combination" [8], on a particular classification problem.

Despite this fact, most of the existing image classification methods rely on manual approaches in choosing the image features. Depending on the classification problem, features are *a priori* selected based on various heuristics, e.g., "(color) seems to be effective and efficient for content-based image retrieval" [3], or "city images usually have strong vertical and horizontal edges due to the presence of man-made objects" [9]. In [10], a heuristic procedure is proposed to "qualitatively measure the saliency of a feature towards a classification problem, based on the plot of the intra-class and inter-class distance distributions." Even though this approach can be used to determine the discriminative power of individual image features, it still involves a human judgment, and its application to feature combinations is not considered.

The heuristics-based, manual approaches to image feature selection, that all of the existing image classification methods rely on, have the following three drawbacks: (1) **difficult design**: with the increase in the (a) number of images, (b) variety of content (i.e., number of image categories), and the (c) number of image features, manually selecting optimal features or feature combinations, based on heuristics, becomes increasingly difficult; (2) **domain dependence**: fixed selection of image features, done *a priori*, means that each new database, or addition of new images/image categories to the existing database, requires feature selection to be re-done; and (3) **non-optimality**: heuristics in no way guarantee the optimality of the selected features, with respect to a given classification problem.

The three drawbacks are especially emphasized in the case of image databases typical for the Internet, which are characterized by: (1) *large scale*: exponentially increasing over the last decade; (2) *diverse content*: ranging from drawings to photographs, with a variety of motives, in color or grayscale; and (3) *dynamic nature*: with images being constantly added and removed.

3 GA-Based Automatic Feature Selection Procedure

The purpose of the automatic image feature selection procedure is to find a (sub-)optimal combination of image features, among arbitrarily many features or feature representations, and take the burden of the feature selection off the user. The procedure is expected to improve the performance of the image database summarization method, i.e., the image classification and image category naming steps.

Input of the proposed procedure is a classified set of images, the *training set*. Each image is partitioned into 2×2 equal blocks and, from each block, color (*color moments* [7]), shape (*edge-direction histogram* [1]), and texture

(*texture neighborhood* [4]) features are extracted. An *image vector* is defined as *weighted concatenation* of the 12 (4 blocks × 3 features) feature vectors: $\boldsymbol{f}_{\text{image}} \equiv [w_1 \cdot \boldsymbol{f}_1, w_2 \cdot \boldsymbol{f}_2, \dots, w_{12} \cdot \boldsymbol{f}_{12}]$, such that $w_i \in \mathbf{R}, \sum_{i=1}^{12} w_i = 1$.

Output of the proposed procedure is an optimal assignment of *feature weights*, $w_1, w_2, \dots, w_{12}$, to feature vectors. The resulting feature weights are used to construct the image vectors of the database images, by transforming, i.e., scaling, the corresponding feature vectors. Optimal assignment is the one resulting in the highest classification precision (Section 4). To find the optimal assignment, genetic algorithm (GA) is employed.

Solving a problem using genetic algorithm requires specification of: (1) chromosome coding, (2) fitness measure, and (3) GA parameters [2].

A *chromosome* represents a 12-D weight vector $\boldsymbol{w} \equiv (w_1, w_2, \dots, w_{12})$, containing the 12 feature weights, i.e., real-valued genes. Each chromosome, i.e., the corresponding weight vector, is used to scale the feature vectors and construct the image vectors of the training set images. Then, classification step is applied to the resulting image vectors. *Fitness* of a chromosome is defined as the average classification precision (Section 4).

Conventional *GA parameters* [2] are adopted: selection is roulette-wheel; crossover is uniform, with probability 0.6; mutation is standard, with probability 0.01; population size is 50 chromosomes; length of the evolution is 500 generations.

4 Experiments

The proposed method is systematically evaluated on two image databases, totalling 2,000 images: (1) *Corel-1000-A database*, which contains 1,000 color photographs partitioned into 10 categories, including both natural scenes and artificial objects [11]; and (2) *Corel-1000-B database*, which contains 1,000 color photographs partitioned into 10 categories, showing natural scenes [6]. Both test databases originate from *Corel Corporation*'s "Corel Gallery 3.0", a well-known image collection, used for the evaluation of the image classification methods [11,6].

The proposed automatic image feature selection procedure is expected to improve the performance of the image classification and the image category naming steps, compared with the original image database summarization method [6]. As in [6], evaluation is done separately for the classification and category naming steps.

Image classification step is evaluated through the average classification precision. Classification precision for a given category of images is defined as the ratio of the number of correctly classified images, over the total number of images in that category [6]. Table 1 (*Classification Precision* column) shows the average classification precision of the proposed method, compared with the original one, on the two test databases. In the classification step, the proposed feature selection procedure brings *over 11% increase in the average classification precision*, compared with the original method.

Image category naming step is evaluated in the same way as the image classification step, through the average classification precision. Table 1 (*Naming Precision* column) shows the average classification precision of the proposed method, compared with the original one, on the two test databases. In the category naming step, the proposed feature selection procedure brings *over 20% increase in the average classification precision*, compared with the original method.

Table 1. Comparison of the proposed method to the original image database summarization method, on the Corel-1000-A and Corel-1000-B test databases

Database	*Classification Precision (%)*		*Naming Precision (%)*		*# Identified and Named Categories*	
Corel-1000-A	48	59	45	72	8 / 10	9 / 10
Corel-1000-B	37	49	37	57	7 / 10	9 / 10
Method	Original	Proposed	Original	Proposed	Original	Proposed

The overall performance of the proposed method is evaluated by integrating the classification and category naming steps, and computing the number of *correctly identified and named* image categories, as a fraction of the total number of categories contained in each test database [6]. As Table 1 shows, the proposed method correctly identified and named 9 out of 10 image categories for both test databases, outperforming the original method.

The proposed automatic image feature selection procedure brings the following advantages, compared with both the existing image classification methods, and the original image database summarization method (Section 2): (1) *easy design*: image feature selection, a crucial step for the performance of the method, is done automatically; (2) *domain independence*: automatic feature selection can easily adopt to a new database, or addition of new images/image categories to the existing database, without loss in the performance of the method; and (3) *optimality*: the proposed procedure, due to GA properties [2], is guaranteed to converge to a (sub-)optimal solution (i.e., selected features). The three advantages are especially emphasized in the case of image databases typical for the Internet, which are large in scale, diverse in content, and dynamic in nature.

5 Conclusion

The problem of image feature selection is addressed, within the framework of the image classification and image database summarization applications The genetic algorithm-based, automatic image feature selection procedure is proposed, and incorporated in the image database summarization method [6].

The proposed method is evaluated through comparison with the original one, on two image databases, each with 1000 photographs, partitioned into 10 semantic categories. The proposed automatic feature selection procedure improves the performance over 11% in average.

The proposed method enables the user an easy access to the image database contents, by bridging the gap between a *large number of images* in a database, and a typically *small number of semantic categories* those images represent. Furthermore, through the proposed automatic feature selection procedure, the method is able to adapt to the *diverse content* and *dynamic nature* of the image databases, typical for the Internet.

References

1. Brandt, S., Laaksonen, J., Oja, E. (2000): Statistical shape features in content-based image retrieval. In: Proceedings of the 15th International Conference on Pattern Recognition (ICPR-2000). Barcelona, Spain, 1066–1069
2. Goldberg, D. E. (1989): Genetic Algorithms in Search, Optimization and Machine Learning. Addison-Wesley, Reading, MA
3. Huang, J., Kumar S. R., Zabih, R. (1998): An automatic hierarchical image classification scheme. In: Proceedings of the 6th ACM International Multimedia Conference (MM'98). Bristol, UK, 219–228
4. Laaksonen, J., Oja, E., Koskela, M., Brandt, S. (2000): Analyzing low-level visual features using content-based image retrieval. In: Proceedings of the 7th International Conference on Neural Information Processing (ICONIP'00). Taejon, Korea, 1333–1338
5. Smeulders, A. W. M., Worring, M., Santini, S., Gupta, A., Jain, R. (2000): Content-based image retrieval at the end of the early years. IEEE Transactions on Pattern Analysis and Machine Intelligence **22**(12), 1349–1380
6. Stejić, Z., Iyoda, E. M., Takama, Y., Hirota, K. (2001): Automatic textual summarization of image database contents using combination of clustering and neural network techniques. In: Proceedings of the 2nd International Conference on Intelligent Technologies (Intech'01). Bangkok, Thailand, 233–239
7. Stricker, M., Orengo, M. (1995): Similarity of color images. In: Proceedings of IS&T and SPIE Storage and Retrieval for Image and Video Databases III. San Jose, CA, USA, 381–392
8. Szummer, M., Picard, R. W. (1998): Indoor-outdoor image classification. In: Proceedings of the IEEE International Workshop on Content-based Access of Image and Video Databases (in conjunction with ICCV'98). Bombay, India, 42–51
9. Vailaya, A., Figueiredo, M., Jain, A. K., Zhang, H. J. (2001): Image classification for content-based indexing. IEEE Transactions on Image Processing **10**(1), 117–130
10. Vailaya, A., Jain, A. K., Zhang, H. J. (1998): On image classification: city images vs. landscapes. Pattern Recognition **31**(12), 1921–1936
11. Wang, J. Z., Li, J., Wiederhold, G. (2001): SIMPLIcity: Semantics-sensitive Integrated Matching for Picture LIbraries. IEEE Transactions on Pattern Analysis and Machine Intelligence **23**(9), 947–963

System Identification Using Delaunay Tessellation of Self-Organizing Maps

Janos Abonyi and Ferenc Szeifert

University of Veszprem, Department of Process Engineering, P.O. Box 158, H-8201, Hungary // www.fmt.vein.hu/softcomp, abonyij@fmt.vein.hu

Abstract. The Self-Organizing Map (SOM) is a vector quantization method which places prototype vectors on a regular low-dimensional grid in an ordered fashion. A new method to obtain piecewise linear models of dynamic processes is presented. The operating regimes of the local linear models are obtained by the Delaunay tessellation of the codebook of the SOM. The proposed technique is demonstrated by means of the identification of a pH process.

1 Introduction

Artificial neural networks have successfully been used to build models directly based on process data. The Self-Organizing Map is one of the most popular neural network models. The SOM algorithm performs a topology preserving mapping from high dimensional space onto a two dimensional grid of neurons so that the relative distances between data points are preserved. The net roughly approximates the probability density function of the data and, thus, serves as a clustering tool [1]. It also has the capability to generalize, i.e. the network can interpolate between previously encountered inputs. As SOM provides a compact representation of the data distribution, it has been widely applied in analysis and visualization of high-dimensional data [1].

In this paper a new method to use SOM for the identification of dynamic systems is presented where SOM is used to partition the input space of piecewise linear models. As the input–output map of such a model is piecewise linear, local linearization and inversion algorithms can be easily derived and the model is computationally cheap to evaluate [2]. This partitioning is obtained by the Delaunay tessellation of the neurons (also called codebook) of the SOM. A similar approach based on the application of Voronoi diagrams of SOM has already been suggested in the context of time series prediction [3]. Furthermore, the Delaunay-based multivariable spline approximation from scattered samples of an unknown function has proven to be an effective tool for classification [4]. Recently, Delaunay Networks were introduced to represent interpolating models and controllers [5]. Usually, the identification of these models is divided into two tasks: structure identification that generates the partition of the input space and parameter identification of the local models. To obtain a suitable partition iterative model building algorithms have been worked out [4,6], where in every iteration an additional node is inserted into the model by a forward selection algorithm and the parameter vector is re-estimated by standard least-squares method.

The aim of the paper is to present a new, one-step approach for the identification of such piecewise linear models. The main idea is to quantize the available input-output data to get a set of neurons and use the obtained neurons (codebooks) as model parameters. The paper is organized as follows. Section 2 presents the structure of the problem of the identification of piecewise linear models based on Self-Organizing Maps (SOM). Section 3 presents the Delaunay tessellation based identification of the model. A detailed case study is given to illustrate the proposed approach on the modeling performance in Section 4. The process under study is a pH neutralization reactor. Conclusions are given in Section 5. The proposed approach has been implemented in MATLAB and the software can be downloaded from www.fmt.vein.hu/softcomp.

2 Self-Organizing Map of Dynamical Systems

The Nonlinear AutoRegressive with eXogenous input (NARX) model establishes a nonlinear relation between the past inputs and outputs and the predicted output: $y(k+1) = f\big(y(k), \ldots, y(k-n_y), u(k-n_d), \ldots, u(k-n_u)\big)$. Here, n_y and n_u denote the maximum lags considered for the output, and input terms, respectively, $n_d < n_u$ is the discrete dead time, and f represents the mapping of the model. Our goal is to develop a data-driven algorithm for the identification of this model in the form $y_k = f(\boldsymbol{z}_k)$, where $y_k = y(k+1)$, $\boldsymbol{z}_k = [z_{k,1}, \ldots, z_{k,n}]^T$ is based on the measured input and output data,$\boldsymbol{z}_k = [y(k), \ldots, y(k-n_y), u(k-n_d), \ldots, u(k-n_u)]$, and the y_k output of the model is identical to the one-step ahead prediction of the output of the system, $y_k = y(k+1)$, where $k = 1, \ldots, N$ denotes the index of the k-th input-output data-pair, $\mathbf{x}_k = [\mathbf{z}_k^T, y_k]$.

The piecewise linear models are special case of operating regime based models. If we denote the input space of the model by $T : \boldsymbol{z} \in T \subset \mathcal{R}^n$, the piecewise linear model consists of a set of operating ranges $T_1, T_2, \ldots, T_s$ which satisfy $T_1 \cup T_2 \cup \cdots \cup T_s = T$ and $T_j \cap T_i = \oslash$ when $i \neq j$. Hence, the model can be formulated as **If** $z_k \in T_i$ **then** $y_k = [\boldsymbol{z}_k^T 1]\boldsymbol{\theta}_i$ where $\boldsymbol{\theta}_s$ denotes the parameter estimate vector used in the ith local model.

The SOM algorithm performs a topology preserving mapping from high dimensional space onto map units so that relative distances between data points are preserved. The map units, or neurons, form usually a two dimensional regular lattice. Each neuron i of the SOM is represented by an l-dimensional weight ($l = n+1$), or model vector $\boldsymbol{m}_i = [m_{i,1}, \ldots, m_{i,l}]^T$. These weigh vectors of the SOM form a codebook. The neurons of the map are connected to adjacent neurons by a neighborhood relation, which dictates the topology of the map. The number of the neurons determines the granularity of the mapping, which affects the accuracy and the generalization capability of the SOM.

SOM is a vector quantizer, where the weights play the role of the codebook vectors. This means, each weigh vector represents a local neighborhood of the space, also called Voronoi cell. The response of a SOM to an input $\boldsymbol{x}$ is determined by the reference vector (weight) $\boldsymbol{m}_i^0$ which produces the best match of the input $i^0 = \min_i \|\boldsymbol{m}_i - \boldsymbol{x}\|$, where i^0 represents the index of the Best Matching Unit (BMU). During the iterative training of SOM, the SOM forms an elastic net that folds onto "cloud" formed by the data. The net tends for approximate the probability density of the data: the codebook vectors tend to drift there where the data are dense, while there are only a few codebook vectors where the data are sparse. The training of SOM can be accomplished generally with a competitive learning rule as $\boldsymbol{m}_i^{(k+1)} = \boldsymbol{m}_i^{(k)} + \eta \Lambda_{i^0,i}(\boldsymbol{x} - \boldsymbol{m}_i^{(k)})$ where $\Lambda_{i^0,i}$ is a spatial neighborhood function and η is the learning rate. Usually, the neighborhood function is $\Lambda_{i^0,i} = \exp\left(\frac{\|\boldsymbol{r}_i - \boldsymbol{r}_i^0\|^2}{2\sigma^{2(k)}}\right)$ where $\|\boldsymbol{r}_i - \boldsymbol{r}_i^0\|$ represents the Euclidean distance in the output space between the i-th vector and the winner. Both the neighborhood function and the learning rate should be scheduled during learning to achieve good modeling performance [1].

3 Delaunay Tessellation based Modeling

In the proposed framework, the operating regions are simplices defined by characteristic points (also called nodes) $\boldsymbol{p}_j = [p_{j,1}, p_{j,2}, \ldots, p_{j,n}]^T$, with $j = 1, \ldots, n_p$, where n_p is the number of nodes. To get a unique and efficient partition, the input space is partitioned by Delaunay tessellation of the characteristic points. In the following, some definitions are given as they are necessary for understanding this method. An *n-polytope* is the smallest convex set containing a finite set of points in $\mathbb{R}^n$. An *n-simplex* is a polytope containing $n+1$ linearly independent points in $\mathbb{R}^n$. The *Delaunay tessellation* of a set of points is a set of n-simplices such that the circumsphere of each simplex does not contain other points in its interior. For example, in two dimensions, three points form a simplex obtained by Delaunay triangulation if and only if the circle that is determined by these points does not contain any other point of that set. Consequently, the bounding spheres of the simplices are as small as possible, and the obtained triangles are as equilateral as possible. It has been proven that among all mappings with a given bound on their second derivative, the piece-wise linear approximation based on the Delaunay triangulation (also called Delaunay tessellation) has the smaller worst case error of all triangulations [7]. The simplices are represented by the *connectivity matrix* $\mathrm{V} = [v_{s,j}]$, whose sth row contains the indices of the points that form simplex T_s: $T_s = \mathrm{conv}(\boldsymbol{p}_{v_{s,1}}, \ldots, \boldsymbol{p}_{v_{s,n+1}})$. For $\boldsymbol{z} \in T_s$, the membership function $A_i(\boldsymbol{z})$ is defined through the barycentric coordinates

$b_s = [b_{s,1}, \dots, b_{s,n+1}]$ of z: $b_s = \mathcal{Z}_s^{-1} z'$, where z' is the extended regression vector, $z' = [z_1, \dots, z_n, 1]^T$, and

$$\mathcal{Z}_s = \begin{bmatrix} p_{v_{s,1}} & \cdots & p_{v_{s,n+1}} \\ 1 & \cdots & 1 \end{bmatrix}.$$

Because of the piecewise linear nature of the model, the model response can be computed by linear interpolation of the $d = [d_1, \dots, d_i \dots, d_{n_s}]^T$ parameters assigned to each characteristic point, p_i, $y = \sum_{j=1}^{n+1} b_{s,j} d_{v_s,j}$.

The barycentric coordinates can also be used to determine in which simplex the observation is. If $z \in T_s$ all the barycentric coordinates of z are positive: $b_{s,k} > 0, \forall k = 1, \dots, n+1$. The main idea of the paper is to quantize the available $x = [z^T y]^T$ input-output data to get a set of n_r prototypes $\mathcal{M}$=$\{m_1, \dots, m_{n_r}\}$ and use the obtained codebooks as model parameters, $p_i = [m_{i,1}, \dots, m_{i,n}]^T$, and $d_i = m_{i,n+1}$.

4 Application to a pH process

The prediction of the pH (the concentration of hydrogen ions) in a continuous stirred tank reactor (CSTR) is a well-known benchmark problem with nonlinear dynamics. The dynamic model for the pH in the tank is given in [8]. As the process can be modeled as a first-order dynamic system [8], the model has the following form: $pH(k+1) = f(pH(k), F_{NaOH})$. The SOM of the process is shown in Fig. 1 where a 6×6 map has been used to map the typical operating points of the process. The neurons of SOM containing

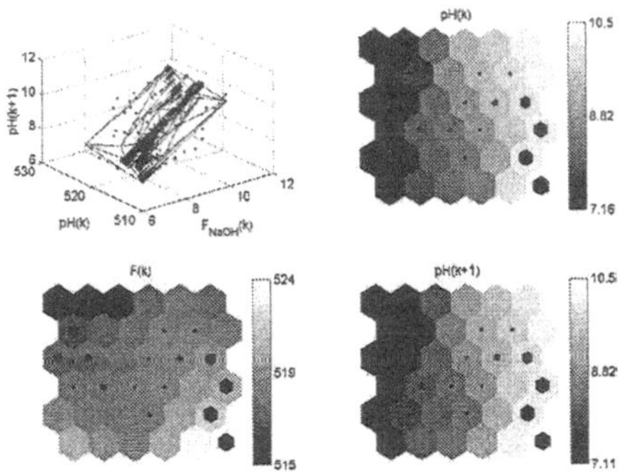

Fig. 1. SOM of the pH process

steady state operation data are marked by black hexagons with proportional size to the number of steady state data in the operating regions of the neurons. It can be seen in Fig. 1 that the s-shaped titration curve, also shown in Fig. 2, has also an s-shape rotated in the two-dimensional grid of SOM. This fact nicely illustrates the distance preserving mapping property of SOM. The resulting Delaunay tessellation based input partitions are shown in Fig. 2 along with the steady state behaviour of the process and the obtained model. As the model is piece-wise linear, every simplex defines a local linear dynamic model. Hence it is possible to extract knowledge about the dynamic properties of these local models. As an example of knowledge extraction, the stability of the local models is evaluated [9,2] and depicted in Fig. 2. Unstable simplices are denoted by dashed-dotted lines (– · –). One can see that the model correctly represents the dynamic properties of the system as it contains stable local models in the steady state region of the process and the steady state behaviour of the local models are near to the steady state (titration) curve of the process.

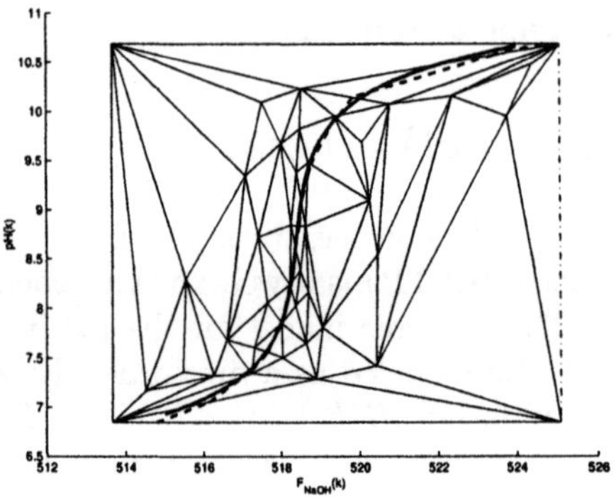

Fig. 2. Delaunay input partition of the model, stable simplex (—),unstable simplex (– · –), steady-state of the model (– –), steady-state of the process (—).

Recurrent simulation with a separate validation data set was used to evaluate the differences in the modeling performance of the models. The performance was measured by the mean squared prediction error (MSE). The results show that the models are much more accurate than the linear model with $MSE = 0.777$. When the operating regions are constructed by Voronoi diagram of the codebook, the parameters of the local are identified by standard least squares (LS) method ($MSE = 0.245$). In case of Delaunay tessellation, there is no need to re-estimate the parameters of the local models as the $\boldsymbol{d}$ vector is determined directly from $\mathcal{M}$ ($MSE = 0.140$). However, it is possible to use SOM only for the partitioning the input space. In this case $\boldsymbol{d}$ is re-estimated based on the baricentric coordinates of $\boldsymbol{z}_k$ by standard LS method. It is interesting to see that because of the large number of neurons the SOM initialized Delaunay Network model can be overparameterized and the LS estimated model could have bad generalization properties ($MSE = 0.205$).

5 Conclusions

A new piecewise linear modeling framework has been developed which employs non-overlapping operating regimes obtained by the Delaunay triangulation of the codebook of Self-Organizing Maps. For sake of illustration, in this paper the proposed approach has been applied to an easily visualizable first-order system (pH reactor). However, the presented tools can be applied for higher-order multi-input multi-output processes in a straightforward manner. Our further research is to show that as obtained the model can be easily incorporated into model based control algorithms.

Acknowledgement

The financial support of the Hungarian Ministry of Culture and Education (FKFP-0073/2001) and the Hungarian Science Foundation (OTKA T 0373600) are greatly acknowledged. Janos Abonyi is grateful for the financial support of the Janos Bolyai Research Fellowship of the Hungarian Academy of Science.

References

1. T. Kohonen, The self-organizing map, Proceedings of the IEEE 78(9) (1990) 1464–1480.
2. J. Abonyi, R. Babuska, F. Szeifert, Fuzzy modeling with multivariate membership functions: Gray-box identification and control design, IEEE Trans. on Systems, Man, and Cybernetics, Part B. 31(5) (2001) 755–767.
3. J. Principe, L. Wang, M. Motter, Local dynamic modleing with Self-Organizing Maps and applications to nonlinear system identification and control, Proceedings of the IEEE 86(11) (1998) 2241–2258.
4. D. Cubanski, D. Cyganski, Multivariable classification through adaptive Delaunay-based c^0 spline approximation, IEEE Transactions on Pattern Analysis and Machine Intelligence 17 (1995) 403–417.
5. T. Ullrich, H. Tolle, Delaunay-based local model networks for nonlinear system identification, in: IASTED International Conference Applied Modelling and Simulation, Banff, Canada, 1997.
6. M. Brown, T. Ullrich, Comparison of node insertion algorithms for delaunay networks, in: Proceedings of IMACS 2nd MATHMOD Conference, Wienna, 1997, pp. 445–780.
7. S. M. Omohundro, The Delaunay triangulation and function learning, in: Technical Report 90-001, International Computer Science Institute Berkeley, California, 1989.
8. N. Bhat, T. McAvoy, Determining model structure for neural models by network stripping, Computers and Chemical Engineering 16 (1992) 271–281.
9. J. Abonyi, R. Babuška, H. Verbruggen, F. Szeifert, Incorporating prior knowledge in fuzzy model identification, International Journal of Systems Science 31 (5) (2000) 657–667.

Neural Network Reactive Navigation and Control of Wheeled Mobile Robot

Zenon Hendzel

Rzeszow University of Technology, Department of Applied Mechanics and Robotics, zenhen@prz.rzeszow.pl, 35-959 Rzeszow , Powstancow Warszwy 8 Poland

Abstract. A neural net real-time obstacle avoidance and control approach for mobile robot has been developed and numerically implemented. A collision-free path is calculated using an efficient neural net motion planer. The output of the navigation level is fed into a neural net tracking controller that takes into account the complete dynamics of the mobile robot. The proposed neural reactive navigation approach is based on the coordination of elementary behaviors. To avoid the convex obstacles the neural navigator fuses a 'reaching the middle of a collision-free space' behavior and a 'goal-seeking' behavior. A 'wall-following' behavior was conducted too, which can be applied to avoid the concave obstacles. The structure of the neural-net controller for nonholonomic mobile robot is derived using a filtered error approach. The effectiveness of the proposed method is numerically verified by a series of experiments on the emulator of wheeled mobile robot Pioneer-2DX.

1. Introduction

Trajectory tracking control implies an a priori trajectory design to be given for the entire robot operation. Expansion of the range of robot tasks and an increase in robot autonomy created a need to generate trajectories on-line; for example, robots need to adjust trajectories on-line to avoid collisions with obstacles in the workspace while approaching a given goal point. There are a lot of studies on trajectory generation for robots using various approaches e.g. [1,2,6,7]. The artificial potential field method is a popular tool for on-line trajectory generation with inherent collision avoidance [1,2]. A detailed presentation of the potential fields method appears in [6]. A comprehensive overview of the reactive navigation, robot behavior and behavior-based control field we can find in the book [1]. Several neural network models e.g. [2,3,5,7] were proposed to generate real-time trajectories. In this paper, inspired by Braitenberg's principles [1] a neural network approach is proposed for collision-free trajectory generation in unknown environment. A strategy of reactive navigation is developed including three main agents: 'reaching the middle of a collision-free space' behavior, a 'goal-seeking' behavior and a 'wall-following' behavior. The output of the navigation level is fed into a neural net tracking controller that takes into account the complete dynamics of the mobile robot. The structure of the neural-net controller for nonholonomic mobile robot is derived using a filtered error approach.

2. Model of a mobile robot

In this paper, a nonholonomic differential-drive mobile robot is considered [4]. The mechanical structure of the mobile robot, like Pioneer-2DX, is shown in figure 1.

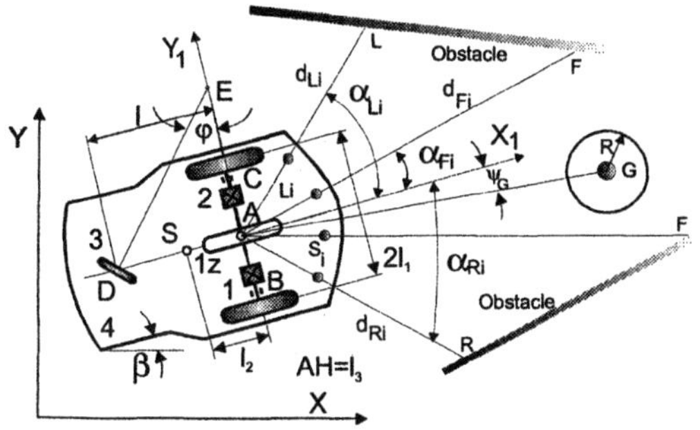

Fig. 1. Robot modeling

Presented robot has two degrees of freedom. Tacking α_1,α_2 - angles of the self-turn of the propel wheels as independent coordinates, then from velocity vectors of points A, B and C, we receive

$$\begin{bmatrix} \dot{\alpha}_1 \\ \dot{\alpha}_2 \end{bmatrix} = \frac{1}{r}\begin{bmatrix} 1 & l_1 \\ 1 & -l_1 \end{bmatrix}\begin{bmatrix} u_v \\ u_\beta \end{bmatrix} \tag{1}$$

where $r_1 = r_2 = r$ is radii of the wheels, u_v is the translational velocity of point A of robot and u_β is the angular velocity of the frame. In the word coordinates a posture is defined as $[x_A, y_A, \beta]^T$, where (x_A, y_A) is the position of the point A, and β is the heading angle of the robot with respect to absolute coordinates (x, y). The mobile robot's kinematics is defined by a Jacobian matrix $J(\beta)$ that transforms velocities $u_B = [u_v, u_\beta]^T$ expressed in mobile base coordinates to velocities expressed in Cartesian coordinates

$$\begin{bmatrix} \dot{x}_A \\ \dot{y}_A \\ \dot{\beta} \end{bmatrix} = \begin{bmatrix} V_{Am}\cos(\beta) & 0 \\ V_{Am}\sin(\beta) & 0 \\ 0 & \omega_m \end{bmatrix} \begin{bmatrix} u_v \\ u_\beta \end{bmatrix} \tag{2}$$

with the maximum linear V_{Am} and angular ω_m speeds.

3. Overview of the navigator

Described mobile robot is equipped with eight an ultrasonic sensor ring as depicted in Fig.1. The radius of the sensors s_i, is L_i and sensors are divided into three group. A group is composed of three, two and three neighboring sensors, gives a distance to the obstacle d_{Li}, d_{Fi}, d_{Ri}, in its field of view , where $d_{min} \le d_{(.)} \le d_{max}$ and each sensor covers an angular view which are oriented by angles $\alpha_{Li}, \alpha_{Fi}, \alpha_{Ri}$ respectively. A navigation task is defined as navigating the mobile robot from a start coordinate to its goal without colliding with the obstacles in between. With considering the vehicle dynamics, it is assumed that the current configuration of the mobile robot is generated at each time step, based on the environment information, $d_{(.)}$. In this research, three navigation task is discussed: 'reaching the middle of a collision-free space' behavior , 'goal-seeking' behavior and a 'wall-following' behavior .

4. Neural net coordinate systems and navigation task

Diagram of the navigator and controller architecture is depicted in figure 2a. The selected method consists in reaching the middle of a collision-free space. The used navigator is build with neural network based on a linear neurons. Let the inputs variables of the neurons are respectively the normalized measured distances on the right $d_R^n = d_R / (d_R + d_L)$, on the left $d_L^n = d_L / (d_R + d_L)$ and in the front $d_F^n = d_F / \eta$, with $d_L = min(s_2, s_3)$, $d_F = min(s_4, s_5)$, $d_R = min(s_6, s_7)$ and η is a distance beyond which the obstacle are not taken into account. Then, using equation (1), vector u_B of linear and angular velocities of the wheels can be described such as

$$\begin{bmatrix} u_v \\ u_\beta \end{bmatrix} = \frac{r}{2} \begin{bmatrix} 1 & 1 \\ l_l^{-1} & -l_l^{-1} \end{bmatrix} \begin{bmatrix} w_{11} & w_{12} & w_{13} \\ w_{21} & w_{22} & w_{23} \end{bmatrix} \begin{bmatrix} d_L^n \\ d_R^n \\ d_F^n \end{bmatrix} \tag{3}$$

where $w_{ij} = const$ are the weights of input signals as shown on the figure 2b. The output variables of the net u_v and u_β are multiplying coefficients applied to the maximum linear and angular speeds (2), where $|u_v| \le 1, |u_\beta| \le 1$.

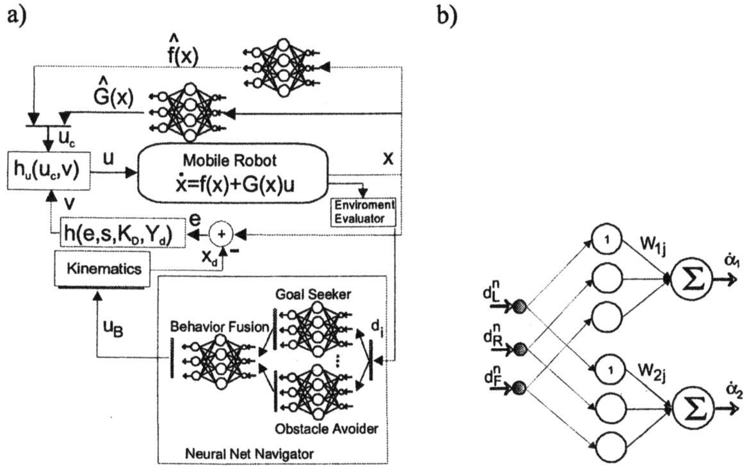

Fig. 2 a). Navigator and controller b). Neural network as approximator

The output of the network (4) and equations (1), (2) generating desired trajectory for the tracking control. In the, 'goal-seeking' behavior the robot is attracted by the goal. The actions u_v and u_β are generated by similar scheme. The normalized vector u_B can be described such as

$$\begin{bmatrix} u_v \\ u_\beta \end{bmatrix} = \frac{r}{2} \begin{bmatrix} 1 & 1 \\ l_1^{-1} & -l_1^{-1} \end{bmatrix} \begin{bmatrix} w_{11} & w_{12} \\ w_{21} & w_{22} \end{bmatrix} \begin{bmatrix} \psi_G \\ d_{AG} \end{bmatrix} \tag{4}$$

where ψ_G is the angular deviation needed to reach the goal, d_{AG} is the distance between the point A of the robot and the goal, as shown on the figure 1. For the 'wall-following' behavior, e.g. for following the wall to the right of the robot, the algorithm generates a desired trajectory such as the robot should follows the current contour (wall). The auxiliary velocity vector u_B is given by

$$\begin{bmatrix} u_v \\ u_\beta \end{bmatrix} = \frac{r}{2} \begin{bmatrix} 1 & 1 \\ l_1^{-1} & -l_1^{-1} \end{bmatrix} \begin{bmatrix} w_{11} & w_{12} \\ w_{21} & w_{22} \end{bmatrix} \begin{bmatrix} d_{RF} - d_0 \\ d_F \end{bmatrix} \tag{5}$$

where $d_{RF} = min(d_R, d_F)$, d_0 is a fixed distance to the wall.

5. The robot tracking control system

Following the motion planning procedure described in section 4, the trajectory tracking problem is posed as follows [4]. Given a desired trajectory $x_d(t)=\left[\alpha_{id},\dot{\alpha}_{id}\right]^T$, i=1,2 a state error vector as $e = x - x_d$ and a filtered error $s=\left[\Lambda^T, 1\right]e$, find a control torque u such that $\lim_{t\to\infty} s = 0$. Dynamic equations of motion can be written in state space [3,4,5], $\dot{x} = f(x,a)+G(x,a)u$ .The control action

$$u=\hat{G}^{-1}(x,\hat{a})\left[-\hat{f}(x,\hat{a})+v\right], \qquad v=-K_D s - Y_d \tag{6}$$

would bring the s to zero exponentially for any positive K_D, where v and Y_d are auxiliary signals [3]. The estimates in (6) will be constructed by neural network approximator. To control that system we used an adaptive controller, where $\hat{f}(x,\hat{a})$ and $\hat{G}(x,\hat{a})$ in (6) are replaced by neural net $\hat{f}(x,\hat{W}_f)$ and $\hat{G}(x,\hat{W}_G)$ and an adaptive law for updating the weights $\hat{W}_f$ and $\hat{W}_G$ [5].

6. Simulation results

To illustrate the performance of the proposed algorithms for path planning and control, first it was build simulator of the mobile robot and workspace in Matlab/Simulink. The weights of the neural nets , in all experiments, was adjusted by experimentation to get the best trajectory generation. An example of the resulting navigation 'reaching the middle of a collision-free space' behavior and control is shown in figure 3a. The impacts of the sensors is depicted in figure 3b.

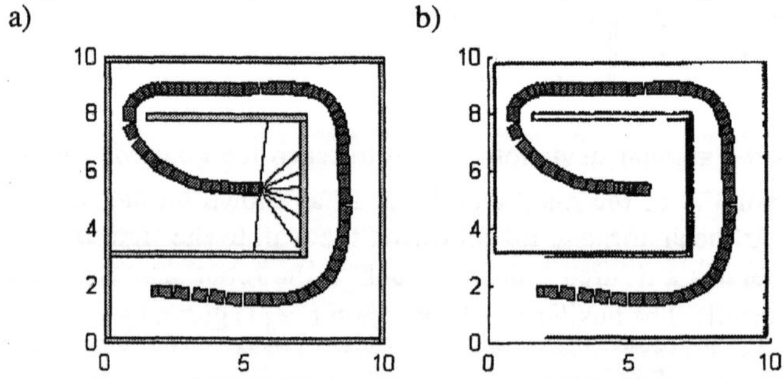

Fig.3 a).Reaching the middle of a free space b). Impact of the sensors

The figure 4 presents an experimental example of elementary behaviors: 'wall following' behavior, 'goal-seeking' behavior and finally the coordination of elementary behaviors which is shown additionally. This experimental showed efficiency for the proposed solution.

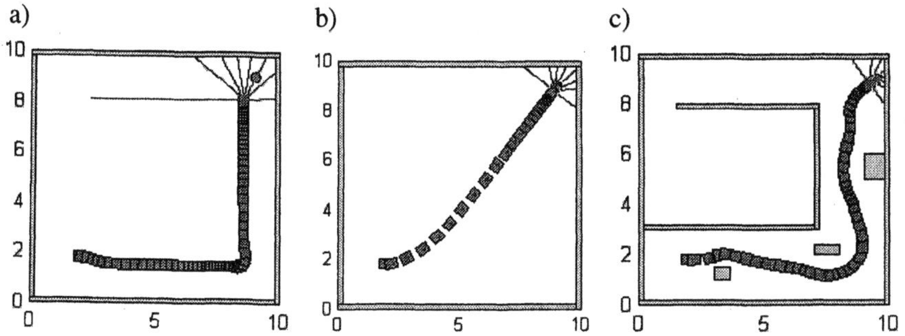

Fig.4.Behaviors:a).Wall following b).Goal seeking c). Fusion of behaviors

7. Conclusion

A complete algorithm for motion planning of mobile robot is developed. A collision-free path and control is calculated using neural-net path planner and neural-net controller respectively. The numerical experimental results obtained with emulator of mobile robot Pioneer-2DX confirmed also the effectiveness of the proposed path planning and control strategy.

References

[1] Arkin R.C. (1998) Behavior-Based Robotics, The MIT Press

[2] Berenstain J.,Koren J. (1989) Real-Time Obstacle Avoidance for Fast Mobile Robots, IEEE Transaction on Systems, Man, and Cybernetics, Vol.19, No.5, 1179-1186

[3] Giergiel J., Hendzel Z., Żylski W. (2000) Adaptive Fuzzy Controller of Wheeled Mobile Robot, Proc. of the 5-th Conference Neural Networks and Their Applications, Zakopane, 395-400

[4] Giergiel J., Hendzel Z., Żylski W. (2000) Kinematics, Dynamics and Control of Wheeled Mobile Robots, AGH Press, Kraków (in Polish)

[5] Hendzel Z, Żylski W. (1997) Neural Net Mobile Robot Controller, CAE-Techniques, Proceedings of 3rd International Scientific Colloquium, Rzeszów, 361-368

[6] Latombe J.C(1991) Robot Motion Planning, Kluwer Academic Publishers

[7] Zalzala A.M.S., Morris A.S. (1996) Neural Networks for Robotic Control, Ellis Horwood

Training of Neural Network Wiener Models with Recursive Prediction Error Algorithm

Andrzej Janczak

University of Zielona Góra, Institute of Control and Computation Engineering
ul. Podgórna 50, 65-246 Zielona Góra, Poland
E-mail: A.Janczak@issi.uz.zgora.pl

Abstract. Identification of the Wiener system consisting of a linear dynamics in series with a static nonlinearity is considered. A recursive prediction error training algorithm for a recurrent neural network Wiener model is proposed. The gradient of the model output w.r.t. parameters of its linear part is computed with the sensitivity method. The proposed algorithm has superior convergence properties in comparison with gradient methods such as the sensitivity method or the truncated backpropagation through time. Its performance is illustrated with a simulated example of a pneumatic valve.

1 Introduction

Neural networks of both the feedforward and recurrent types are widely used in nonlinear system identification and modelling. While different nonlinear model structures can be represented by neural networks, models capable to approximate large classes of nonlinear systems such as the nonlinear autoregressive with exogenous input (NNARX) and nonlinear output error (NOE) are the most common. Two examples of other useful models which have not so general nature are Wiener and Hammerstein models. A characteristic feature of both of them is their predefined internal structure consisting of a linear dynamics and a static nonlinearity. Different methods are available for identification of Wiener systems including correlation methods [1], parametric regression [2–5], nonparametric regression [6,7], and nonlinear optimization both based on parametric [8,9] or neural networks [10–13] models.
Gradient descent type methods are commonly used for training neural models. A method used for feedforward networks is called the backpropagation or the recursive backpropagation in its on-line version. For recurrent neural networks, computation of the gradient is more complicated and the corresponding methods are known as the real time recurrent learning, called also the dynamic backpropagation or sensitivity method (SM), and the backpropagation though time. All these methods have the linear convergence rate and can be quite slow in many practical cases. A faster convergence rate can be achieved with methods which rely on a second-order approximation of the optimization criterion to determine the search direction. An alternative to the gradient descent methods is the prediction error (PE) or its pattern

version – the recursive prediction error (RPE). The PE and RPE algorithms have superior convergence properties in comparison with the gradient descent methods as they use the approximate Hessjan to compute the search direction. Properties of the PE and RPE algorithms for different neural network models were discussed in [14–16]. The RPE algorithms for Wiener models with a known static nonlinearity or the nonlinear model approximated with a piecewise linear function were also analyzed by Wigren [8,9].
The present study extends the RPE algorithm to training a recurrent neural Wiener model with one layer of nonlinear nodes. The gradient of the model output w.r.t. parameters of its linear part is computed with the SM. The approximating capabilities of the RPE algorithm are illustrated with a simulated data set. Finally, the convergence properties of the RPE are compared with the SM and combined RPE & SM examples.

2 The neural network Wiener model

The SISO Wiener system is composed of a linear dynamic element followed by a static nonlinear element. This nonlinear structure can be represented by a neural network model of a layered architecture, shown in Fig. 1. The first hidden layer, consisting of a single linear recurrent node, forms a linear dynamic element model. The other hidden layer of nonlinear nodes and a linear output node, are used as a model of the nonlinear element, and form a structure of a single input single output multilayer perceptron (MLP). Although the neural network model of the nonlinear element can contain more than one layer of nonlinear nodes, no other structures are considered in this work, as from the universal approximation property of the MLP, it follows that one hidden layer of nonlinear nodes is enough to approximate any continuous function to any degree of accuracy. An alternative to the recurrent neural network structure of Wiener model, discussed here, is a purely feedforward neural network model. Its obvious advantage of a feedforward nature is partly cancelled by the necessity of modelling both the nonlinear element and its inverse. The recurrent neural network Wiener model containing M nonlinear nodes is described by

$$\hat{y}(n) = \hat{f}[s(n), \mathbf{w}], \tag{1}$$

$$\hat{f}[s(n), \mathbf{w}] = \sum_{j=1}^{M} w_{2M+j}\varphi[x_j(n)] + w_{3M+1}, \tag{2}$$

$$x_j(n) = w_j s(n) + w_{M+j}, \tag{3}$$

$$s(n) = -\sum_{m=1}^{na} a_m s(n-m) + \sum_{m=1}^{nb} b_m u(n-m), \tag{4}$$

where $u(n)$ is the input signal at time n, $s(n)$ is the linear dynamic model output, $\hat{y}(n)$ is the model output, $\hat{f}(\cdot)$ is the steady state characteristic of

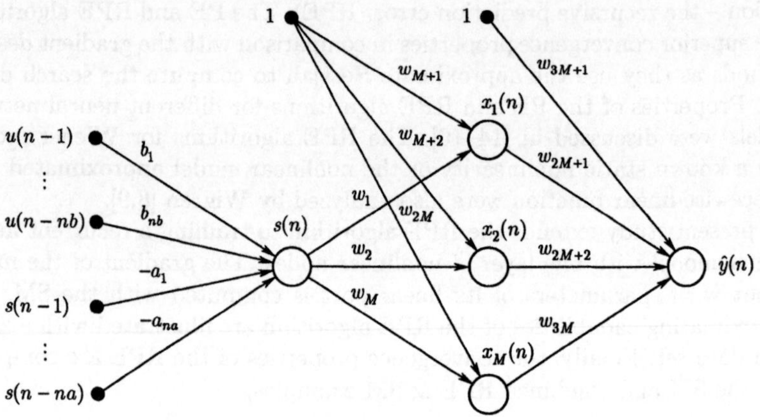

Fig. 1. The neural network Wiener model

the model, $x_j(n)$ is the activation of the j-th nonlinear node, $\varphi(\cdot)$ is the nonlinear activation function, a_m and b_m are parameters of the linear dynamic model, and $\mathbf{w} = [w_1\ w_2 \ldots w_{3M+1}]^T$ is the vector of weights and biases of the nonlinear element model.

3 Recursive prediction error learning algorithm

The identification problem can be formulated as follows. Given a set of input and output data $Z^N = \{[u(n), y(n)],\ n = 1, \ldots, N\}$ and a candidate neural network Wiener model, estimate parameters of the model so that the predictions $\hat{y}(n|\Theta)$ of the system output are close to to the system output $y(n)$ in the sense of the following mean square error criterion

$$V_N(\Theta, Z^N) = \frac{1}{2N} \sum_{n=1}^{N} \left[y(n) - \hat{y}(n|\Theta)\right]^2. \tag{5}$$

A solution of this problem, for nonlinearly parameterized models, is a gradient technique based on approximation of the Hessjan known as the prediction error method. The PE method is a batch optimization method of a Gauss-Newton type. The RPE algorithm is a recursive counterpart of the PE method. Both the PE and RPE algorithms are guaranteed to converge to a local minimum of $V_N(\Theta, Z^N)$ with probability one as $N \to \infty$ [15]. Given the gradient

$$\Psi(n, \Theta) = \left[\frac{d\hat{y}(n, \Theta)}{d\Theta}\right]^T \tag{6}$$

of the model output with respect to the parameter vector

$$\Theta = [a_1 \ldots a_{na}\ b_1 \ldots b_{nb}\ \mathbf{w}^T]^T, \tag{7}$$

the RPE algorithm can be expressed as [15,16]

$$\mathbf{K}(n) = \frac{\mathbf{P}(n-1)\mathbf{\Psi}(n)}{1+\mathbf{\Psi}^T(n)\mathbf{P}(n-1)\mathbf{\Psi}(n)}, \tag{8}$$

$$\mathbf{\Theta}(n) = \mathbf{\Theta}(n-1) + \mathbf{K}(n)[y(n) - \hat{y}(n|\mathbf{\Theta}(n-1)], \tag{9}$$

$$\mathbf{P}(n) = \mathbf{P}(n-1) - \mathbf{K}(n)\mathbf{\Psi}^T(n)\mathbf{P}(n-1). \tag{10}$$

It is well-known that numerical difficulties may occur in recursive computation of the matrix $\mathbf{P}(n)$. Theoretically matrix $\mathbf{P}(n)$ should be always positive definite but, due to the finite world length of the computer, the matrix $\mathbf{P}(n)$ may loose its positive semidefinition property. Rapid reduction of the matrix $\mathbf{P}(n)$ caused by processing very accurate measurements or a linear dependence of some elements of the vector $\mathbf{\Psi}(n)$ are two typical sources of such problems. To avoid them, discrete square root filtering techniques are used in practice [17].

4 Gradient computation

All the considered algorithms require calculation of the gradient $\mathbf{\Psi}(n)$ of the model output w.r.t. its parameters

$$\mathbf{\Psi}(n) = \left[\frac{\partial\hat{y}(n)}{\partial a_1} \cdots \frac{\partial\hat{y}(n)}{\partial a_{na}} \frac{\partial\hat{y}(n)}{\partial b_1} \cdots \frac{\partial\hat{y}(n)}{\partial b_{nb}} \frac{\partial\hat{y}(n)}{\partial w_1} \cdots \frac{\partial\hat{y}(n)}{\partial w_{3M+1}}\right]^T. \tag{11}$$

Although the model (1) – (4) is a recurrent one due to the difference equation (4), calculation of the gradient does not require much more computation than in the case of the pure static model. The only difference is in calculation of the partial derivatives of the model output w.r.t. the parameters of the linear dynamic model. This can be done with the SM simulating the following set of linear difference equations [12,13]

$$\frac{\partial s(n)}{\partial a_k} = -s(n-k) - \sum_{m=1}^{na} a_m \frac{\partial s(n-m)}{\partial a_k}, \; k = 1,\; 2, \ldots, na, \tag{12}$$

$$\frac{\partial s(n)}{\partial b_k} = u(n-k) - \sum_{m=1}^{na} a_m \frac{\partial s(n-m)}{\partial b_k}, \; k = 1,\; 2, \ldots, nb, \tag{13}$$

Then, the partial derivatives of the model output w.r.t. the parameters a_k and b_k are

$$\frac{\partial\hat{y}(n)}{\partial a_k} = \frac{\partial s(n)}{\partial a_k}\frac{\partial\hat{y}(n)}{\partial s(n)}, \tag{14}$$

$$\frac{\partial\hat{y}(n)}{\partial b_k} = \frac{\partial s(n)}{\partial b_k}\frac{\partial\hat{y}(n)}{\partial s(n)}, \tag{15}$$

where

$$\frac{\partial \hat{y}(n)}{\partial s(n)} = \sum_{j=1}^{M} w_j w_{M+j} \varphi'[x_j(n)]. \tag{16}$$

Finally, the partial derivatives of the model output w.r.t. the parameters of the nonlinear element model can be calculated according to the well-known backpropagation rules.

5 Simulation example

As a source of simulated data for testing the RPE algorithm and comparing it with the SM and RPE & SM, a model of a pneumatic valve was used [8]. In this model, the pneumatic control signal applied to the stem is used as the input $u(n)$, and the flow through the valve as the output $y(n)$. It is assumed that the model output is additively disturbed by white Gaussian noise $e(n)$ with the standard deviation of 0.01 A sequence of 10000 pseudorandom numbers, uniformly distributed in $[-1, 1]$ was used as the model input. Based on the simulated input-output data, the model (1) – (4) containing 10 nonlinear nodes of the hyperbolic tangent activation function was identified with the RPE, SM, and RPE & SM algorithms. The obtained results are illustrated in Fig. 2 and 3. To compare estimation accuracy, the mean sum-squared parameter estimation error $Jd(n)$ of the linear dynamic model, and the mean sum-squared estimation error $Js(n)$ of the nonlinear element model are employed.

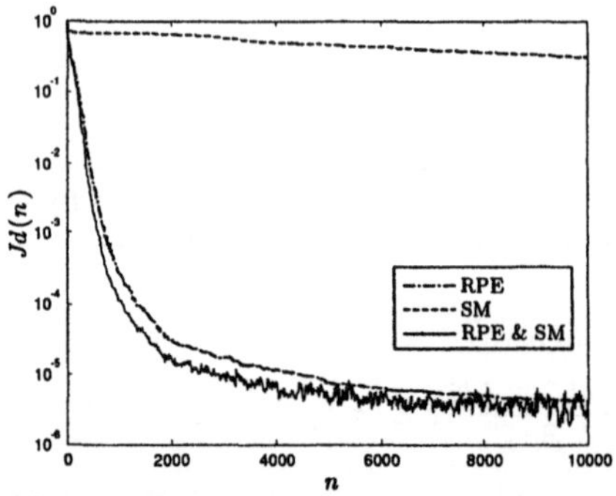

Fig. 2. Convergence of the linear element model

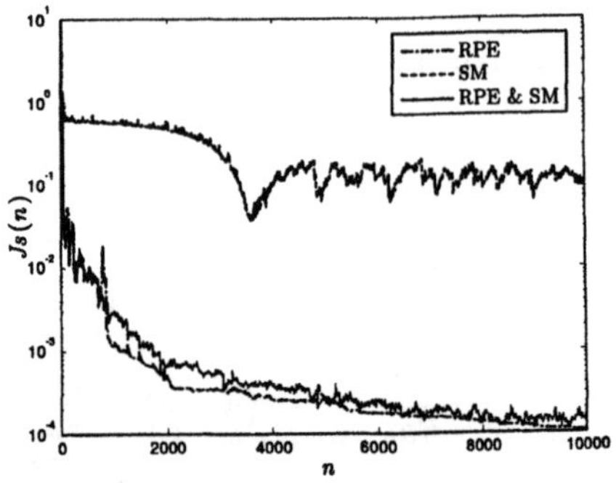

Fig. 3. Convergence of the nonlinear element model

6 Conclusions

The RPE identification algorithm has been extended to training the recurrent neural network model. Calculation of the gradient is performed with the SM method and it does not require much more computation than the backpropagation. In comparison with gradient descent methods, the RPE algorithm has much better convergence properties at the expense of a higher computational complexity. The presented approach can be very useful for systems disturbed additively at their outputs by white noise disturbances. Note that in such cases, the gradient descent algorithms require a small step size to achieve convergence to a local minima of the performance function.

References

1. Billings S. A, Fakhouri S. Y. (1982) Identification of systems containing linear dynamic and static nonlinear elements. Automatica. **10**, 15–26.
2. Janczak A. (2001) On identification of Wiener systems based on a modified serial-parallel model. Proc. ECC'01, Porto, Portugal. 1852–1857.
3. Kalafatis A. D., Wang L., Cluett W. R. (1997) Identification of Wiener-type nonlinear systems in a noisy environment. Int. J. Control. **66**, 923–941.
4. Marciak C., Latawiec K., Rojek R., Oliveira G. H. C. (2001) Adaptive least-squares parameter estimation of OBF-based Wiener models. Proc. 7th IEEE Conf. MMAR'2001, Międzyzdroje, Poland. 965–969.
5. Pearson R. K., Pottmann M. (2000) Gray-box identification of block-oriented nonlinear models. J. Process Control. **10**, 301–315.
6. Greblicki W. (1994) Nonparametric identification of Wiener systems by orthogonal series. IEEE Trans. Automat. Contr. **39**, 2077–2086.
7. Greblicki W. (1997) Nonparametric approach to Wiener system identification. IEEE Trans. Circuits Syst. I. **44**, 538–545.
8. Wigren T. (1993) Recursive prediction error identification algorithm using the nonlinear Wiener model. Automatica. **29**, 1011–1025.
9. Wigren T. (1994) Convergence analysis of recursive identification algorithms based on the nonlinear Wiener model. IEEE Trans. Automat. Contr. **39**, 2191–2206.
10. Al-Duwaish H., Karim M. N., Chandrasekar V. (1996) Use of multilayer feed-forward neural networks in identification and control of Wiener model. IEE Proc. Control Theory Appl. **143**, 255–258.
11. Janczak A. (1995) Identification of a class of nonlinear systems using neural networks. Proc. 2nd Int. Symp. MMAR'95, Międzyzdroje, Poland. 697–702.
12. Janczak A. (1997) Identification of Wiener models using recurrent neural networks. Proc. 4th Int. Symp. MMAR'97, Międzyzdroje, Poland. 727–732.
13. Janczak A. (1998) Recurrent neural network models for identification of Wiener systems. Proc. CESA'98 IMACS Multiconference, Nabeul-Hammamet, Tunisia. 965–970.
14. Billings S. A, Jamaluddin H. B., Chen S. (1992) Properties of neural networks with application to modelling non-linear dynamical systems. Int. J. Control. **55**, 193–224.
15. Chen S., Billings S. A. (1992) Neural networks for nonlinear dynamic system modellinig. Int. J. Control. **56**, 319–346.
16. Nørgaard M., Ravn O., Poulsen N. K., Hansen L. K. (2000) Neural Networks for Modelling and Control. Springer, London.
17. Kaminsky P. G, Bryson A. E., Schmidt S. F. (1971) Discrete square root filtering: A survey of current techniques. IEEE Trans. Autaomat. Control. **AC-16**, 727–735.

Dynamic GMDH Type Neural Networks

Marcin Mrugalski, Eugen Arinton, Józef Korbicz

University of Zielona Góra, Institute of Control and Computation Engineering,
ul. Podgórna 50, 65–246 Zielona Góra, Poland, fax: +48 68 3254615,
e-mail: {M.Mrugalski,E.Arinton,J.Korbicz}@issi.uz.zgora.pl

Summary. This paper presents a new identification method based on Artificial Neural Networks (ANNs) which can be used for both static and dynamic systems. In particular, a Group Method of Data Handling (GMDH) type neural network with dynamic neurons is considered. The final part of this work contains an illustrative example regarding an application of the proposed approach to the real system identification task.

1 Introduction

In recent years, there has been a growing interest in applying ANNs to dynamic system identification [1,7,8]. They enable to model the behaviour of complex systems without a priori information about the system structure or parameters. Other advantages of neural networks over conventional identification methods include simplicity of implementation, generalization abilities and good approximation properties. On the other hand, there are no efficient algorithms for selecting structures of classical ANNs and hence many experiments should be carried out to obtain an appropriate configuration. To tackle this problem the GMDH approach can be employed [3,4]. The concept of this approach is based on iterative processing of a operation defined sequence leading to the evolution of the resulting structure. GMDH network is a combination of the black box concept as a study of input and output, the neural approach that utilizes the concept of threshold logic and connectionism, the inductive approach and the probabilistic approach. Another problem arises from the identification of dynamic systems. One of the most interesting solutions is based on the application of various dynamic neuron models [5]. The dynamics is introduced to this neuron in such a way that the neuron activity depends on its internal states. It is achived by an introduction of a linear dynamic system - Infinite Impulse Response (IIR) filter - to the neuron structure.

The paper is organized as follows. Section 2 presents the structure of the GMDH type neural network. In Section 3 the dynamic neuron model with IIR filter is described. The final part of this work contains an illustrative example, which confirms the effectiveness of the proposed approach.

2 Synthesis of the GMDH type neural networks

A successful identification depends on a proper selection of the model structure. One way to solve this problem is to use the so-called GMDH type neural networks. The concept of the synthesis of this kind of network is based on the iterative processing of a defined sequence of operations leading to the evolution of the resulting structure. The process is completed when the optimal degree of complexity is achieved.

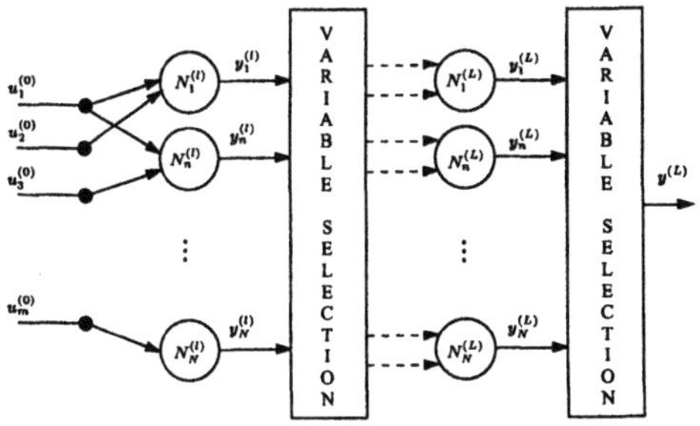

Fig. 1. Synthesis of the GMDH type neural network

The GMDH neural network is constructed through the connection of a given number of the elementary neurons (Fig. 1). It is assumed that at least two input signals $u_1, ..., u_m$ constitute the stimulation which results in the formation of the output signal $y_n^{(l)}$:

$$y_n^{(l)} = f(u) = f(u_1^{(l)}, \ldots, u_m^{(l)}). \tag{1}$$

The GMDH approach allows much freedom in defining a neuron activation function f. In most cases it has a non-linear character. From the practical point of view the equation (1) should be not too complex because it may complicate the learning process and extend the computation time. The number of neurons N in the first layer of the network depends on the number of external inputs m. In a general case, a network of m inputs is built up from p input neurons $(m > p)$ N new elements are formed this way, where N has a form:

$$N = \frac{m!}{p!(m-p)!}. \tag{2}$$

The output of the neuron may become the input to other neurons in the next layer. The definition of the quality index $Q(y_m^{(l)})$ of the neurons is a preliminary task in designing a GMDH type network. In this work, this quality index has the following structure:

$$Q(y_n^{(l)}) = \frac{\sum_{k=1}^{n_t} (y_n^{(l)}(k) - y(k))^2}{\sum_{k=1}^{n_t} y^2(k)}, \tag{3}$$

where n_t is the number of validation data points, $y(k)$ is the k-th scalar measurement of the system output, and $y_n^{(l)}(k)$ is the neuron output. During the training the GMDH network the number of layers suitably increases. Each time when a new layer is added, new neurons are introduced. The selection of best performing neurons for their processing accuracy is realized before the formed layer is added to the network. The remaining neurons are removed. One of the most interesting ways of performing the selection procedure is called an optimal population method. This approach is based on rejecting the neurons for which the defined quality index is larger than an arbitrarily determined threshold e_h. Usually e_h is determined separately for each layer. In the described way neurons that model the searched input-output relation accurately are included in each layer. The selection methods plays a role of a mechanism of the structural optimization at the stage of construing a new layer of neurons. To avoid the problem of overfitting, the identification data, i.e. the experimental input-output data is divided into two sets, namely the identification and validation sets. This means that the first set is used to estimate the parameters of the neurons, and the second one is used to select best performing neurons. Finally, when additional layers do not improve the performance of the network, the synthesis process is stopped. To obtain the final structure of the network, all unnecessary neurons are removed, leaving only those which are relevant to the computation of the model output.

3 Dynamics in GMDH neural networks

One of the most interesting ways of introducing dynamic properties into the GMDH network is to use a dynamic neuron model [5]. Dynamics in these neurons is realized by the introduction of a linear dynamic system - an IIR filter. In this way, each neuron in the network reproduces the output signal based on his past values of the inputs and outputs. Such a neuron model (Fig. 2) consists of two submodules, the filter module and the activation module. The behaviour of the filter module is described by the following equation:

$$\begin{aligned}\widetilde{y}(k) = &- a_1\widetilde{y}(k-1) - \ldots - a_n\widetilde{y}(k-n) \\ &+ \mathbf{v}_0^T\mathbf{u}(k) + \mathbf{v}_1^T\mathbf{u}(k-1) + \ldots + \mathbf{v}_n^T\mathbf{u}(k-m),\end{aligned} \tag{4}$$

where $a_1, a_2, \ldots, a_n$ denotes the feedback filter parameters, n denotes filter order, $\mathbf{v}_0^T, \mathbf{v}_1^T, \ldots, \mathbf{v}_n^T$ is the input vector to the filter module where m is the number of inputs to the dynamic neuron. The filter output is used as the input for the next module, namely the activation module. The activation module can be described by:

$$y(k) = f(\widetilde{y}(k)). \tag{5}$$

The main objective is to estimate the parameters $a_1, a_2, \ldots, a_n$ and parameter vectors $\mathbf{v}_i^T$, $i = 0, \ldots, m$.

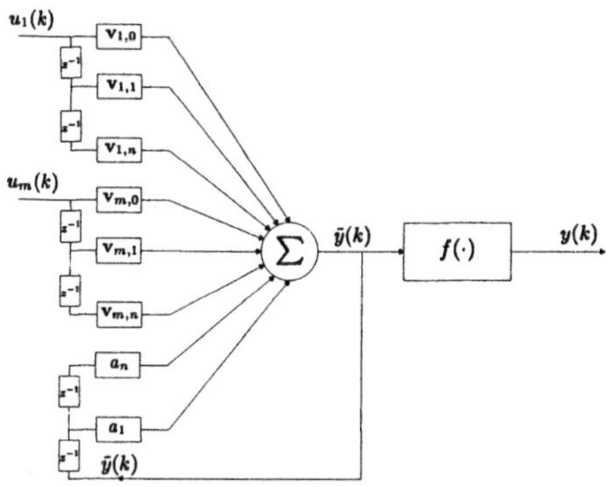

Fig. 2. A dynamic neuron model

The main advantage of the GMDH neural network is that their can be applied to systems with a large number of input. This usually causes various problems while using classical perceptrons. On the other hand, this can be viewed as the main drawback to the GMDH neural networks. This is because their application is limited to systems for which the number of inputs is greater than three. To overcome, this problem it is possible to decompose the IIR filters in a way shown in Fig. 3. As can be observed, as a result of such a decomposition a greater number of input variables can be obtained.

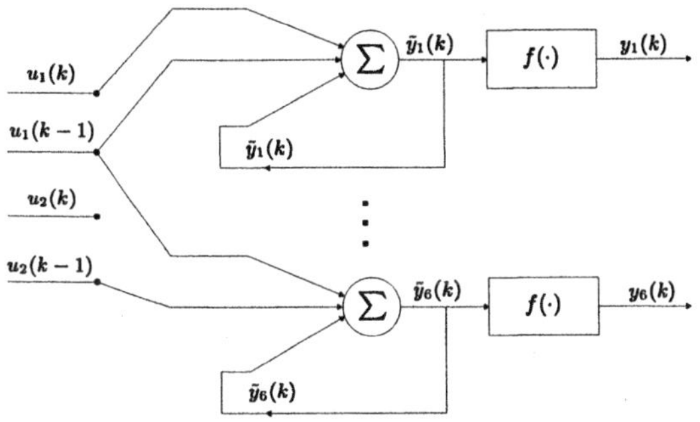

Fig. 3. Decomposition of the IIR filters for $m = 2$ and $n = 1$

4 Simulation example

The purpose of the present section is to show the effectiveness of the proposed approach. In particular, the real data from an industrial plant were employed to identify the non-linear dynamic model of chosen parts of the plant. The plant to be considered is the evaporation station at the Lublin Sugar Factor S.A. [2]. The Fig. 4 shows the scheme of the plant with all the available process variables.

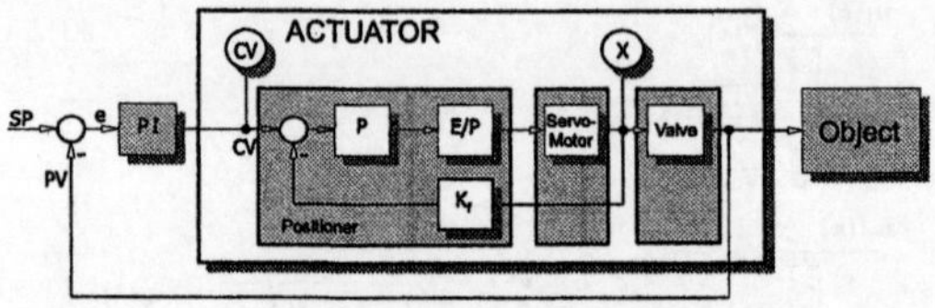

Fig. 4. A scheme of the system being considered

Based on the observation of the process variables and the knowledge about the process the model can be expressed as:

$$P_v = g(C_v, X), \tag{6}$$

where $g(\cdot)$ denotes the modelled relationship, P_v is the juice flow at the outlet of the evaporator, C_v is the control value, X stands for servomotor rod displacement. The data used for the identification and validation sets were collected in November 2001. The data were, of course, appropriately filtered, moreover offset levels were removed. It should be also pointed out that these data sets were scaled for the purpose of neural networks designing. For the hyperbolic tangent neurons this range way $[-1, 1]$. To perform such a transformation, the linear scaling can be used. The quality indexes (3) for the GMDH static and dynamic models, obtained with the application of the outer-bounding ellipsoids algorithm [6], are given in Table 1.

Table 1: Quality indexes for the identification and validation data sets

GMDH	Identification	Validation
Static	0.0971	0.0787
Dynamic	0.0659	0.0377

The system and the dynamic model output for the validation data set are shown in Fig. 5.

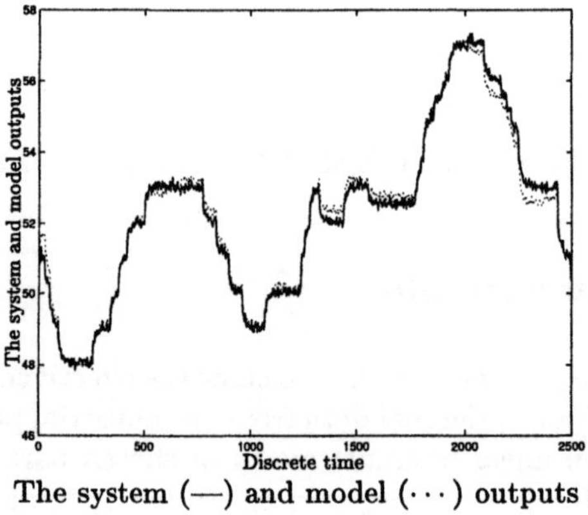

Fig. 5. The system (—) and model (···) outputs signals

The comparative study performed shows that the dynamic GMDH model is superior to the static model. From the results presented in Table 1. it can be seen that the introduction of the dynamic neurons has significantly improved modelling performance. Moreover, as can be seen from Fig. 5, the approximation abilities of the model resulting from the proposed approach are satisfactory.

5 Conclusions

The objective of this paper was concerned with modelling of an industrial process, especially obtaining dynamical models directly from observed data. To tackle this problem, the dynamic GMDH type neural network was employed. The main advantage of the presented approach, comparing to the classical neural networks, is that in the GMDH networks have a structure that grows to fit the particular task being considered. This enables them to perform better than networks with fixed structures. Another advantage of the presented approach is that due to the application of dynamic neurons the network has a smaller number of free parameters to obtain comparing to other networks. Moreover, the results obtained with dynamic GMDH network are better than in the static case.

Acknowledgements

This work was supported by the EU FP 5 Research Training Network project DAMADICS and in part by the State Committee for Scientific Research (KBN) in Poland.

References

1. Duch W., Korbicz J., Rutkowski L., Tadeusiewicz R. (2000) Biocybernetics and Biomedical Engineering 2000. Neural Networks. Academic Publishing House, Exit, Warsaw (in Polish)
2. Edelmayer A. (2000) Research of quantitative and qualitative FDI methods based on data from Lublin Sugar Factory. Proc. IFAC Symp. SAFEPROCESS'2000. Budapest, Hungary, 331–358
3. Farlow S. J. (1995) Self-organizing Methods in Modelling. GMDH-type Algorithms. Marcel Dekker Inc., New York
4. Ivakhnenko A. G., Muller J. A. (1995) Self-organizing of nets of active neurons. System Analysis Modelling Simulation. **20**, 93–106
5. Korbicz J., Patan K., Obuchowicz A. (1999) Dynamic neural networks for process modelling in fault detection and isolation systems. Int. Appl. Math. and Comp. Sci. **9**(3), 519–546
6. Mrugalski M., Witczak M. (2002) Parameter estimation of dynamic GMDH neural networks with the bounded-error technique. Jour. Appl. Comp. Sci. (in print).
7. Patton R. J., Chen J. (1999) Robust Model-Based Fault Diagnosis For Dynamic Systems. Kluwer Academic Publ, London
8. Pham D. T., Xing L. (1995) Neural Networks for Identification, Prediction and Control. Springer Verlag, London

Generalized Spectrum Analysis by Means of Neural Networks

Dariusz Grabowski[1], Janusz Walczak[1]

[1] Silesian University of Technology, ul. Akademicka 10, 44-100 Gliwice, Poland
dgrabows@polsl.gliwice.pl, jwalczak@polsl.gliwice.pl

Abstract. The problem of determination of generalized signal spectrum using neural networks has been investigated. The paper contains the formalization of the problem and is focused on building of a neural network that may be used to calculate coefficients of the generalized Fourier series for various base functions. The theoretic considerations have been illustrated by an example of analysis of a signal belonging to the Hilbert space of signals with finite energy for Laguerre's base and a wavelet base.

1 Introduction

The assignment of a finite or infinite sequence of real or complex numbers to a function $f(\cdot)$ is called a discrete representation of a signal described by this function [4, 9]. The coefficients of Fourier series are the usual example of a discrete representation for periodic signals. In general, the creation of a discrete representation is closely related to the problem of the best approximation [9]. In Hilbert spaces of signals H with the defined norm $\|\cdot\|_H$ and scalar product $(\cdot,\cdot)_H$ the generalized Fourier series of a signal f:

$$f(t) \cong \sum_{h\in N} F_h e_h(t), \tag{1}$$

is solution to the problem of the best approximation:

$$\min_{\{F_h\}} \| f(t) - \sum_{h\in N} F_h e_h(t) \|_H . \tag{2}$$

The Fourier series is convergent to the function f in the sense of the norm $\|\cdot\|_H$. The countable bases $\{e_h\}$, $h\in N$ always exist in separable Hilbert spaces [9] and in that case the coefficients of Fourier series (Eq. 1) are determined by:

$$F_h = (f, e_h)_H, \qquad f, e_h \in H, h \in N . \tag{3}$$

It follows that there are many discrete representations of the given function f according to the base taken into consideration. The discrete representations are real or complex functions of a discrete variable $F_h(h)$, $h \in N$ and are alternatively called generalized signal spectrums [4, 9].

The space of periodic signals L_T^2 as well as the space of signals with finite energy L^2 belong to the Hilbert spaces that are the most commonly used in engineering. In that case the generalized spectrums are expressed by the following formula:

$$F_h = (f, e_h)_{L_T^2} = \frac{1}{T} \int_0^T f(t) e_h(t)\, dt, \qquad f, e_h \in L_T^2,\ h \in N, \tag{4}$$

$$F_h = (f, e_h)_{L^2} = \int_0^\infty f(t) e_h(t)\, dt, \qquad f, e_h \in L^2,\ h \in N. \tag{5}$$

The banks of base functions $\{e_h\}$, that are employed in computations of generalized spectrum, are created on the ground of the theory of orthogonal polynomials [4] and methods of wavelet analysis [8].

The contemporary realizations of systems used for determination of generalized signal spectrum based on microprocessors are called analyzers of generalized spectrum, Fig. 1. The application of recurrent neural networks to realization of generalized spectrum analyzer has been proposed in the paper.

The research on many phenomena of nature involves application of generalized signal spectrums [8, 9]. These kinds of spectrums are used in telecommunication [4, 9], geophysics and seismology [2], medicine [7], image processing [1], optics [10], electrical systems diagnosis [5], etc.

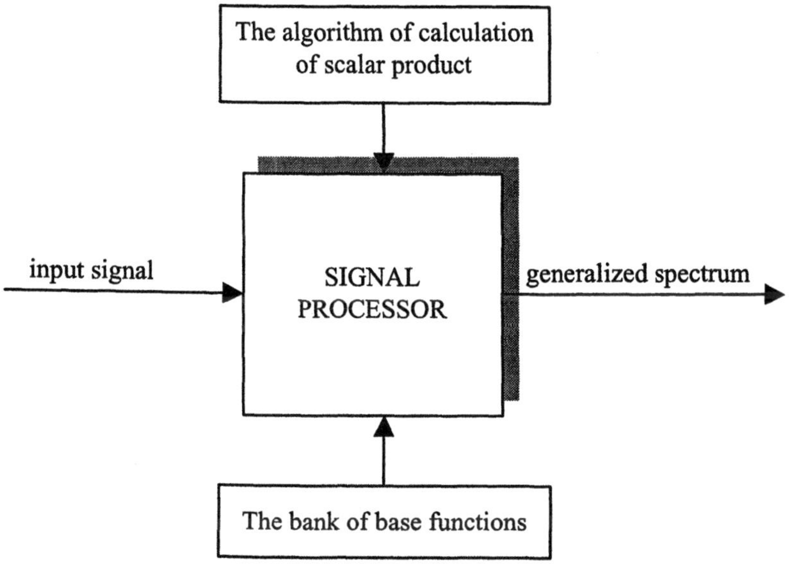

Fig. 1. The block diagram of the generalized spectrum analyzer

2 Neural generalized spectrum analyzer

The problem of generalized spectral analysis consists in determination of the vector **F** of coefficients F_h for finite number ($K+1$) of base functions assuming that ($M+1$) samples of an analyzed function f_i as well as base functions e_{ih} are given. In that case the solution to the problem of the best approximation (see Eq. 2) for K and M large enough and for RMS norm is equivalent to minimization of the following energy function:

$$J(\mathbf{F}) = \frac{1}{2}(\mathbf{EF} - \mathbf{f})^T (\mathbf{EF} - \mathbf{f}), \tag{6}$$

where:

$$\mathbf{F} = [F_h], \quad \mathbf{E} = [e_{ih}], \quad \mathbf{f} = [f_i], \qquad h = 0,1,\ldots,K, \quad i = 0,1,\ldots,M. \tag{7}$$

The energy function may be associated with a recurrent neural network [3, 6]. The dynamic of this network is described by the following differential equation:

$$\frac{d\mathbf{F}}{dt} = -\mu \nabla J(\mathbf{F}) = -\mu\, \mathbf{E}^T (\mathbf{EF} - \mathbf{f}), \tag{8}$$

where: μ - the vector of learning rates.

The block diagram of the neural network has been shown in the Fig. 2. The input data for the neural network consists of samples of the analyzed function and the base functions taken into account.

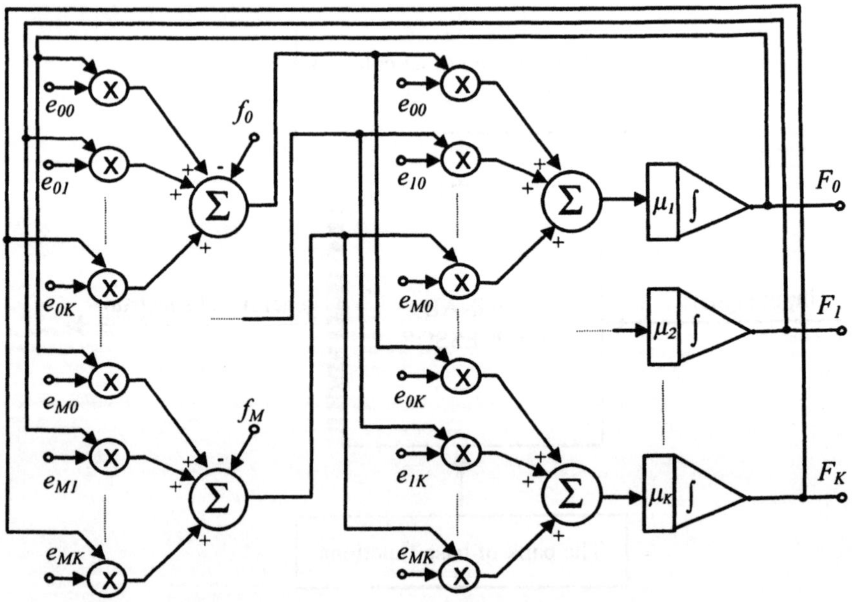

Fig. 2. The bloc diagram of the neural generalized spectrum analyzer

3 Example

The following signal belonging to the Hilbert space L^2 has been analysed in order to verify the proposed method of generalized spectrum analysis:

$$f(t) = \sin(\omega_0 t)e^{-\alpha t}, \qquad \omega_0 = 0.628\, rad/s, \quad \alpha = 0.1, \quad t \in R_+ . \tag{9}$$

The generalized spectrum analysis has been carried out for Laguerre's base (Fig. 3):

$$e_h(t) = \frac{1}{h!} e^{-t/2} L_h(t), \qquad h \in N, \tag{10}$$

where $L_h(t)$ - Laguerre's polynomials, as well as for the wavelet base (Fig. 4):

$$e_h(t) = \psi_{pq}(t) = 2^{-p/2}\psi(2^{-p}t - q), \qquad h, p, q \in N, \tag{11}$$

with the mother function $\psi(t)$ expressed by:

$$\psi(t) = (1 - t^2)\, e^{-t^2/2} . \tag{12}$$

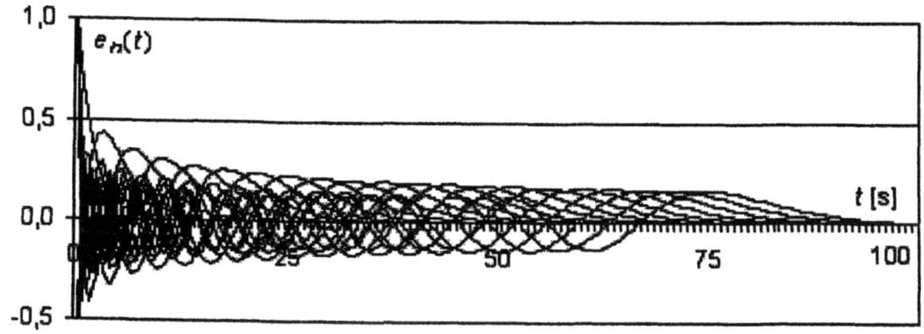

Fig. 3. The Laguerre's base for $K = 20$

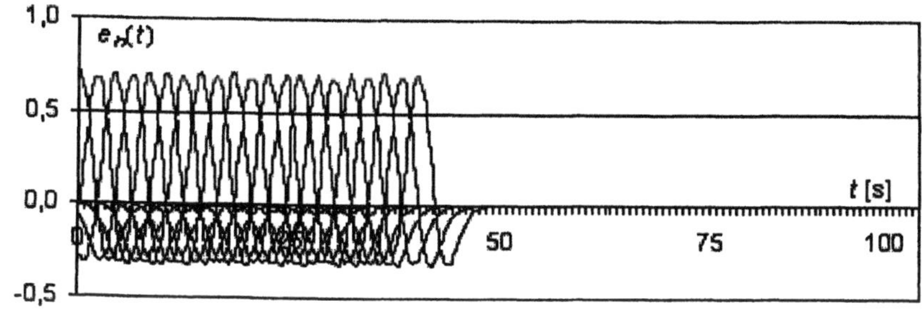

Fig. 4. The wavelet base of Mexico Hat type for $K = 20$ and p=1

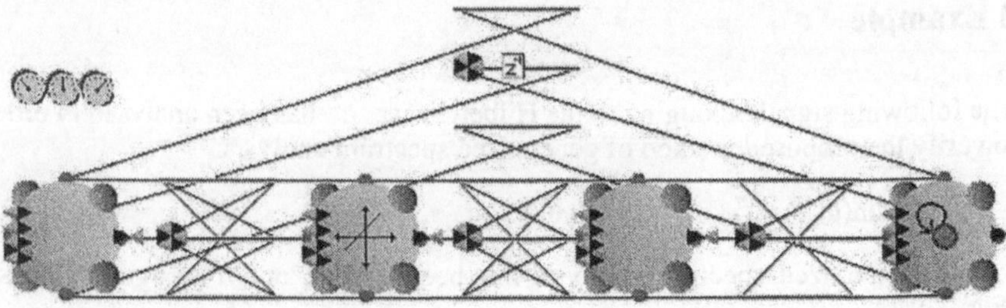

Fig. 5. The realization of the neural generalized spectrum analyzer in *NeuroSolutions*

The simulations of the neural network in the Fig. 2 have been carried out by means of *NeuroSolutions*™, Fig.5. The spectrums calculated by the neural network for Laguerre's and the wavelet bases are shown in the Fig. 6. The simulation has been carried out assuming that the number of base functions is equal to 21 and the number of samples is equal to 128. The quality of approximation may be evaluated on the base of Fig. 7 and Fig. 8.

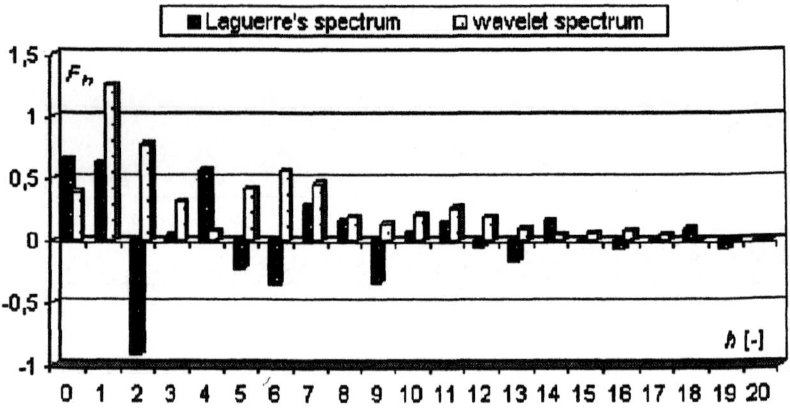

Fig. 6. The spectrum obtained for Laguerre's and wavelet bases

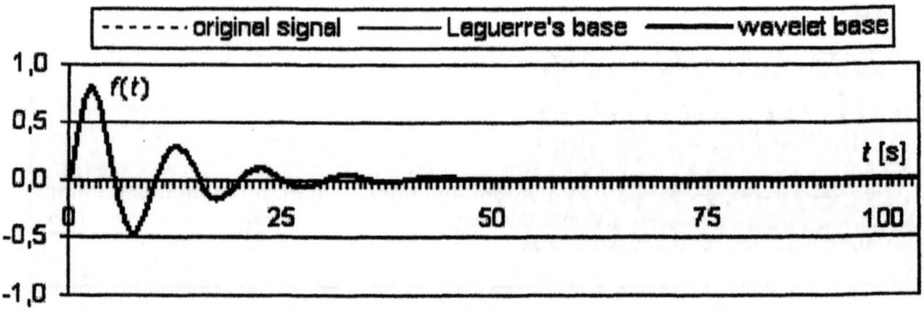

Fig. 7. The original signal and signals synthesized using calculated spectrums

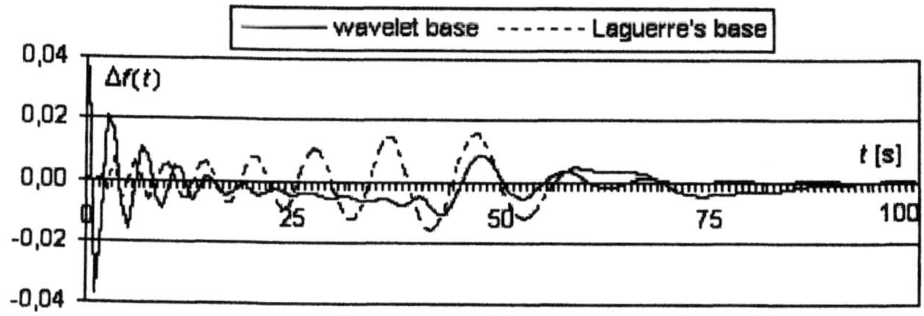

Fig. 8. The error of approximation for wavelet and Laguerre's bases

4 Conclusions

The proposed neural approach proved to be an effective way of generalized signal spectrum determination. The investigations have confirmed that analysis of signals belonging to the space L_T^2 of periodic signals requires a few steps of learning while analysis of signals belonging to the space L^2 of signals with finite energy needs a few thousands of steps assuming zero initial conditions. The global convergence of the algorithm of generalized spectrum analysis is the advantage of the proposed solution.

References

1. Ayer S, Schroeter P, Brigger P (1994) Time-varying motion estimation using orthogonal polynomials and applications. Proceedings of 12-th International Conference on Pattern Recognition, Jerusalem, Israel, pp 409–414
2. Boyce JF, Murray LR (1989) Signal analysis in seismic studies. Advances in Electronics and Electron Physics 77: 209–318
3. Cichocki A, Unbehauen R (1993) Neural networks for optimization and signal processing. J.Wiley, New York
4. Harmuth HF (1992) Transmission of information by orthogonal functions. Springer-Verlag, New York
5. Juszczyk W, Zajac M (1994) Fault diagnosis methods in selected synchronous drive system. Proceedings of 9-th Symposium on Basic Problems in Power Electronics and Electromechanics, Wisla, Poland, pp 170–175 (in Polish)
6. Mandziuk J (2000) Hopfield neural networks. Exit, Warsaw (in Polish)
7. Philips W, Jonghe G (1992) Data compression of ECGs by high degree polynomial approximation. IEEE Trans. Biomedical Eng. 39: 330–337
8. Popularkis AD (1996) The transforms and applications handbook. CRC and IEEE Press, Boca Raton, Florida
9. Soliman SS, Srinath MD (1998) Continuous and discrete signals and systems. Prentice-Hall, Upper Saddle River, New Jersey
10. Yaroslavsky L, Eden H (1996) Fundamentals of digital optics. Digital signal processing in optics and holography. Birkhauser, Boston

Wavelet Network for Recursive Function Learning

Zygmunt Hasiewicz

Wrocław University of Technology, Institute of Engineering Cybernetics, Janiszewskiego 11/17, 50-372 Wrocław, Poland, e-mail: zhas@ict.pwr.wroc.pl

Abstract. We present a wavelet neural network for recovering non-linear functions from random data. The network has modular architecture and exploits a father wavelet as activation function. Synaptic weights of the net are trained according to simple recursive rules and yield consistent estimates of function values on a pre-defined grid of points. The weights are then applied for reconstruction of the underlying non-linearity.

1 Introduction

This contribution deals with employing wavelet neural networks for recovering non-linear characteristics and belongs to the stream originated by Zhang and Benveniste in [7] and next developed in [5], [1], [8], [6] and [3], among others. The strength of wavelet networks lies in their versatile and powerful modeling capabilities, well recognized in the literature, thus providing great potential to achieve satisfactory performance. We propose a class of networks based on father wavelets with compact support which play the role of activation functions. The networks possess simple modular structure, easy to expand. The training process is an extremely easy recursive procedure.

2 Problem Statement

We consider the standard task of recovering a non-linear function $R(x)$ from the set of training data $\{(x_k, y_k)\,;\ k = 1, 2, ..., N, N+1, ...\}$ where

$$y_k = R(x_k) + z_k \tag{1}$$

We assume that $\{x_k\}$ is random and is a sequence of independent and identically distributed (i.i.d.) random variables for which there exists a probability density function $f(x)$. In turn, $\{z_k\}$ is an i.i.d. random process such that $E\, z_k = 0$, $var\, z_k = \sigma_z^2 < \infty$. By assumption, processes $\{x_k\}$ and $\{z_k\}$ are mutually independent. The aim is to recover the non-linearity $R(x)$ in an interval $[a, b]$. We assume that $|R(x)| \leq M_R$ and $\delta \leq f(x) \leq M_f$, some $M_R, M_f, \delta > 0$, for $x \in [a, b]$.

3 Wavelet Module

Let $\varphi(x)$ be a scaling function (father wavelet) of a multiresolution analysis (see, e.g., [4]) with compact support $[s_1, s_2]$,

$$\operatorname{supp} \varphi(x) = [s_1, s_2]$$

Consider the wavelet neural module (WNM) as in Fig. 1, where the wavelet block (WB) is as in Fig. 2. The wavelet block WB, with $2(n_{\max} - n_{\min} + 1)$

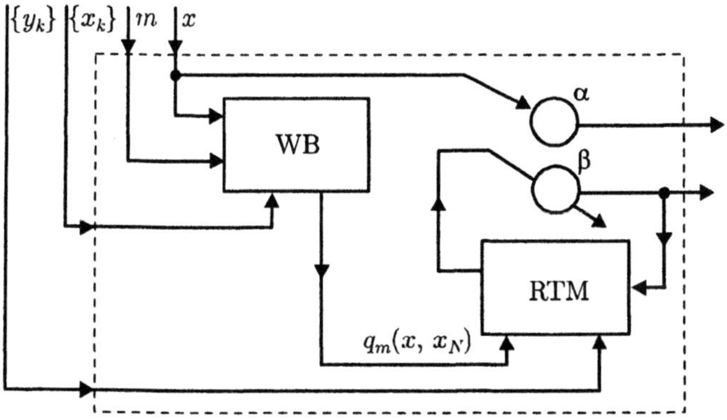

Fig. 1. Wavelet neural module (WNM)

activation functions φ, produces the quantity

$$q_m(x, v) = 2^m \sum_{n=n_{\min}}^{n_{\max}} \varphi(2^m x - n)\varphi(2^m v - n)$$

where the shift weights $n_{\min}$ and $n_{\max}$ depend on the input (activation) point x and the scale parameter m as follows

$$\begin{aligned} n_{\min} &= n_{\min}(x; m) = \lfloor 2^m x - s_2 \rfloor + 1 \\ n_{\max} &= n_{\max}(x; m) = \lfloor 2^m x - s_1 \rfloor \end{aligned} \tag{2}$$

Note however that for each point x and each scale m we have

$$n_{\max} - n_{\min} = \lfloor s_2 - s_1 \rfloor = const$$

Based on $q_m(x, v)$ and the training data $\{(x_k, y_k)\,;\ k = 1, 2, ..., N, N+1, ...\}$, the synaptic weights α and β are trained in the module WNM, according to the chosen point x. We simply put (see Fig. 1)

$$\alpha = x \tag{3}$$

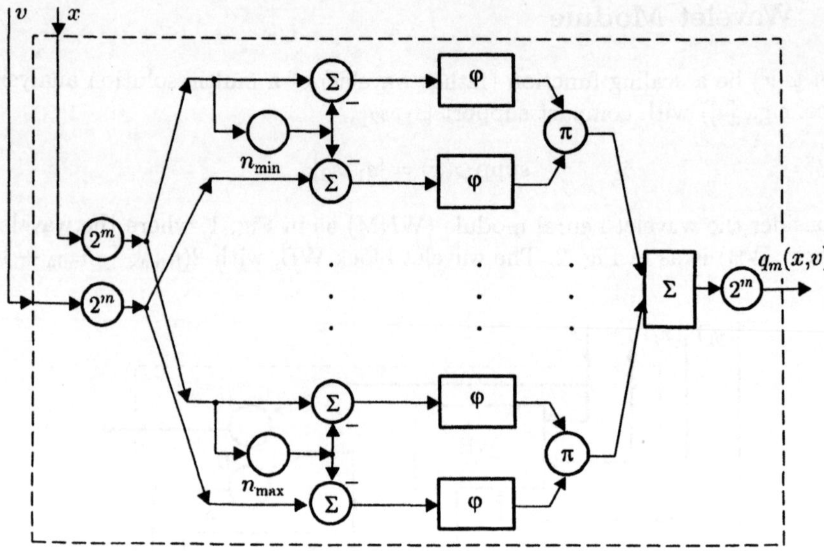

Fig. 2. Wavelet block (WB) with the scale factor m

whereas β is updated due to the recursive training procedure of the form

$$\beta_N = \beta_{N-1} + \gamma_N \, q_m(x, x_N) \left(y_N - \beta_{N-1} \right) \tag{4}$$

completed by the recursive training module RTM, where γ_N is a positive number sequence tending to zero.

The following facts take place. Their proofs are here omitted for brevity.

Theorem 1. *If γ_N is such that $0 < \gamma_N \le N^{-\tau}$, $0 < \tau \le 1/2$, and the scale parameter m is fitted to the number of training data N, i.e. $m = m(N)$, in such a way that $m(N) \to \infty$ and $\gamma_N 2^{m(N)} \to 0$ as $N \to \infty$ then*

$$\beta_N \to R(x) \quad \textit{in mean square}$$

as $N \to \infty$ for arbitrary initial β_0, provided that $R(x)$ and $f(x)$ are continuous functions at point x.

Theorem 2. *If $R(x)$ is at least Lipschitz regular around x, $f(x)$ is continuous at x, γ_N is selected as in Theorem 1 and the wavelet module WNM is calibrated according to the rule*

$$m(N) = \lfloor -(1/3) \log_2 \gamma_N \rfloor$$

then asymptotically

$$\beta_N = R(x) + O\left(\gamma_N^{2/3}\right) \quad \textit{in mean square}$$

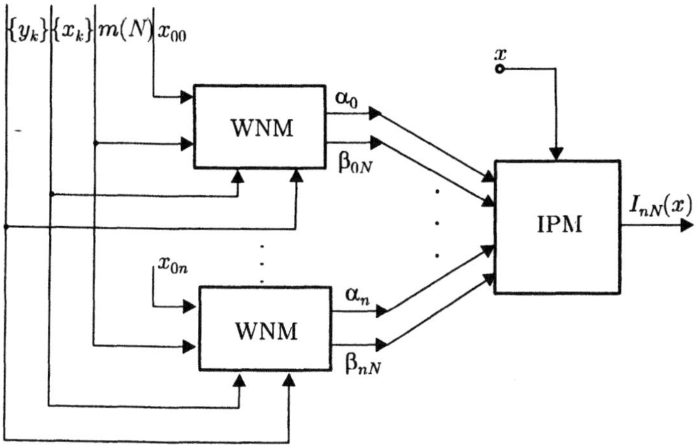

Fig. 3. Wavelet network for recursive function learning

For $\gamma_N = CN^{-\tau}$ $(C > 0,\ 1/2 \geq \tau > 0)$ *and accordingly*

$$m(N) = \lfloor (\tau/3) \log_2 N \rfloor \tag{5}$$

we get

$$\beta_N = R(x) + O\left(N^{-(2/3)\tau}\right) \quad \textit{in mean square}$$

4 Function Learning

Consider the structure shown in Fig. 3. The structure consists of multiple of wavelet neural modules WNM, activated by a collection $x_{00}, x_{01}, ..., x_{0n}$ of pre-selected estimation points in $[a, b]$, and the module IPM with the activation input x realizing the interpolation process on the basis of the worked-out synaptic weights $(\alpha_i = x_{0i}, \beta_{iN})$ for $i = 0, 1, ..., n$, according to the formula (Lagrange interpolation polynomial)

$$I_{nN}(x) = \sum_{i=0}^{n} \beta_{iN} W_i(x)$$

where

$$W_i(x) = \frac{(x - \alpha_0) \dots (x - \alpha_{i-1})(x - \alpha_{i+1}) \dots (x - \alpha_n)}{(\alpha_i - \alpha_0) \dots (\alpha_i - \alpha_{i-1})(\alpha_i - \alpha_{i+1}) \dots (\alpha_i - \alpha_n)}$$

Assume that estimation points x_{0i} form an equidistant grid on $[a, b]$, i.e.

$$\alpha_i = x_{0i} = a + ih_n\,,\ i = 0, 1, ..., n$$

where $h_n = (b - a)/n$. Taking advantage of Theorems 1 and 2, one can ascertain the following.

Theorem 3. *If the density $f(x)$ is continuous at the grid points $x_{00}, \dots, x_{0n}$, the non-linearity $R(x)$ is at least $n+1$ times differentiable on $[a,b]$, i.e. $R(x) \in C^p[a,b]$, $p \geq n+1$, and the wavelet modules WNM are calibrated according to the rule (5) (for γ_N selected as $\gamma_N = CN^{-\tau}$, $0 < \tau \leq 1/2$) then for each point $x \in [a,b]$ it holds that*

$$I_{nN}(x) = R(x) + O(d_n + s_{nN}) \quad \textit{in mean square}$$

where

$$d_n = \left[(b-a)^{n+1} / \left((n+1)\, n^{n+1}\right)\right]^2$$

$$s_{nN} = \left[(n+1)\,(n-1)!\right]^2 N^{-(2/3)\tau}$$

are the deterministic and stochastic part of the error.

5 Example

Using the Haar scaling function in the wavelet block WB in Fig. 2, i.e.

$$\varphi(x) = I_{[0,1]}(x) = 1(x) - 1(x-1)$$

where $1(x)$ is the perceptron (step) activation function, we get (see (2))

$$[s_1, s_2] = [0, 1]$$

$$n_{\min} = n_{\max} = \lfloor 2^m x \rfloor$$

and

$$q_m(x,v) = 2^m I_{[\lfloor 2^m x\rfloor/2^m, (\lfloor 2^m x\rfloor+1)/2^m]}(v)$$

Accordingly, the training procedure (4) takes the form

$$\beta_N = \beta_{N-1} + \gamma_N\, 2^m I_{[\lfloor 2^m x\rfloor/2^m, (\lfloor 2^m x\rfloor+1)/2^m]}(x_N)\left(y_N - \beta_{N-1}\right)$$

Observe that the innovation component is activated (differs from zero) only if the actual observation x_N falls in the appropriate neighbourhood of x.

6 Conclusions

The proposed wavelet net for non-linearity recovering is composed of standardized (identical) modules (Fig. 3) which are easy to train and work autonomously (in parallel). Hence, the net can be readily expanded (in order to increase precision; Theorem 3) without any revision (retraining) of the already existing part of the net. Training of the net is a recursive on-line process which can be stopped and restarted at any time.

References

1. Delyon, B., Juditsky, A., Benveniste, A. (1995) Accuracy analysis for wavelet approximations. IEEE Trans. Neural Networks **6**, 332-348
2. Hasiewicz, Z. (1999) Composite neural networks for non-linearity recovering. Proc. 4th Conf. Neural Networks and Their Appl., 123-128
3. Hasiewicz, Z. (2000) Modular neural networks for non-linearity recovering by the Haar approximation. Neural Networks **13**, 1107-1133
4. Mallat, S. (1998) A Wavelet Tour of Signal Processing. Academic Press, San Diego
5. Pati, Y. C., Krishnaprasad, P. S. (1993) Analysis and synthesis of feedforward neural networks using discrete affine wavelet transformations. IEEE Trans. Neural Networks **4**, 73-85
6. Zhang, Q. (1997) Using wavelet network in non-parametric estimation. IEEE Trans. Neural Networks **8**, 227-236
7. Zhang, Q., Benveniste, A. (1992) Wavelet networks. IEEE Trans. Neural Networks **3**, 889-898
8. Zhang, J., Walter, G. G. et al. (1995) Wavelet neural networks for function learning. IEEE Trans. Signal Proc. **43**, 1485-1496

Interpolation and Approximation of Models

Bruno Pelletier

ONERA-CERT, DTIM, 2, Avenue Edouard Belin, 31055 Toulouse Cedex, France

Abstract. A global approach may not be well suited for the approximation of complex and high-dimensional input-output mappings, inadequacy being defined in terms of complexity and/or accuracy. In this paper, a global modelling method from a set of locally optimal simpler models is presented. Theoretical aspects of interpolation and approximation of models are addressed. The method has been applied to the remote sensing of ocean color from space where it has shown good results in comparison with global approaches based on multilayer perceptrons and radial basis functions networks.

1 Introduction

If neural networks have shown good abilities in classification and input-ouput mappings approximation, complexity control of neural architectures is still an open problem. Several approaches have been studied as regularization, network growing[1][2] and network pruning[3][4]. But in the case of the modelling of a complex phenomenon with a large number of input variables, a near optimal neural network may remain complex or inaccurate. This might be a consequence of adopting a global approach of the problem. There is therefore an interest in constructing a global model from a set of local models, locality being defined on a proper subset of the input space. This is the case for example when a phenomenon may be seen as a continuous non-stationary random process where each density at any time may be approximated by an element of a given class of models. The same may also occur in function approximation where some variables have been recognized as playing the role of parameters. In such cases, it is assumed that the input space may be split into subsets of homogeneous variables, the influences of which in the studied phenomenon are different.
This paper aims at presenting a global modelling methodology where a global model is being constructed from a set of local models, namely small neural networks, which implies performing interpolation or approximation of models. A problem that arises is the continuity of a family of local optimal models. For example, let us consider the case of the approximation of a parameterized function $f(x;\theta)$ by an element $\hat{f}(x;\rho)$ of a parametric family of models. If $\hat{f}(x;\rho(\theta))$ is an optimal approximation of $f(x;\theta)$ for each θ, the continuity of $\hat{f}(x;\rho(\theta))$ with respect to θ is not guaranteed. However, there exists a class of problems for which the continuity is ensured. Among them is the problem of the remote sensing of ocean color from space which has stimulated this

research. More precisely, it is wished to recover the phytoplankton concentration in the ocean from top of atmosphere reflectances measurements. This class of problems is formally stated in the next section and theoretical aspects of the method are presented. Experimental results are presented in the last section. This method has shown for this complex inverse problem many much better results than global approaches involving multilayer perceptrons and radial basis functions networks.

2 Methodology

Let us consider the following classification problem. Let $\{(\mathbf{U}_i, y_i), i = 1...N\}$ be a set of joint observations of a random vector $\mathbf{U} \in \mathcal{R}^{n+d}$ together with a class label $y_i \in \{y_k, k = 1...M\}$. Let us further assume that the d last components of the random vector $\mathbf{U}$ have been recognized as playing a deterministic role. Thus $\mathbf{U}$ may be seen as a random process $\mathbf{X}(\theta)$ where $\mathbf{X}$ is formed with the n first components of $\mathbf{U}$ and θ with the d last. Let us also assume the following properties for the random process :

1. For each $\theta \in \mathcal{D} \subset \mathcal{R}^d$, $\mathbf{X}(\theta)$ is drawn independantly and uniformly according to a probability law of the set $\mathcal{P}(\theta) = \{p_i(\theta), i = 1...M\}$.
2. Secondth order statistics are sufficient for modelling the density of a class : $p(\mathbf{X}|y_i; \theta)$.
3. The random process is continuous, that is each realization of the random process is a continuous function of θ.

A global classifier model assigning a label y^k to each realization of X may be taken as a standard classifier whose parameters depend continuously on θ. Basic to a standard classifier is a model of the probability density of $\mathbf{X}(\theta)$.

2.1 Local probability density modelling

The second property of the random process $\mathbf{X}(\theta)$ allows us to optimally model the probability density of each class $p_i(\theta)$ by a standard ellipsoidal kernel $\mathcal{K}$ parameterized by its mean vector $\mu = \left(\mu^1, ..., \mu^n\right)^t \in \mathcal{R}^n$ and its covariance matrix Σ where the dependence on θ has been ommited. The covariance matrix Σ may be written as $T^{-1}(T^{-1})^t$ where $T = \{T_{ij}\}$ stands for an upper triangular matrix with strictly positive diagonal elements. Each kernel is an element of an $\frac{n(n+3)}{2}$-dimensional family which will be denoted by $\mathcal{F}$. Let $\rho = \left(\mu^1, ..., \mu^n, T_{11}, T_{12}, ..., T_{nn}\right)^t$ be an $\frac{n(n+3)}{2}$-dimensional parameter vector for this family. The local probability density model of $\mathbf{X}(\theta)$ may be written as follows :

$$\hat{p}(\mathbf{X};\theta) = \frac{1}{M}\sum_{i=1}^{M}\mathcal{K}(\mathbf{x};\hat{\rho}_i(\theta)) \tag{1}$$

where $\hat{\rho}_i(\theta)$ is an optimal parameter vector for the ith class probability density model. An estimate $\hat{y}$ of the class label y can be a real function of $\mathbf{x}$ which may be taken as the conditional mean of y given $\mathbf{X}$ ie :

$$\hat{y} = E[y|\mathbf{X}] = \frac{\sum_{i=1}^{M} y^i \mathcal{K}(\mathbf{x}; \hat{\rho}_i(\theta))}{\sum_{i=1}^{M} \mathcal{K}(\mathbf{x}; \hat{\rho}_i(\theta))} \tag{2}$$

which amounts to be a normalized radial basis functions neural network[5].

2.2 Global modelling

The problem adressed here is the construction of a global model given a set of locally optimal models. A local model for a given θ is in fact optimal iff the probability density of $\mathbf{X}(\theta)$ is optimally modelled, which is also optimal iff the probability density of each class is optimally modelled because of the class independance property. Thus this problem may be seen as an interpolation or approximation problem in the set $\mathcal{F}$ and may be stated as follows. Given a set $\mathcal{D}_m = \{(\theta_k, \hat{\rho}(\theta_k)), k = 1...N_\theta\}$ of optimal parameter vectors $\hat{\rho}(\theta_k)$ corresponding to a given θ_k, the problem is to find an application $f : \theta \mapsto \rho = f(\theta)$ such that an error criterion $\mathcal{E}$ defined on the kernel parameter space is being minimized. For this problem, the application assigning to each θ the optimal parameter vector $\hat{\rho}(\theta)$ of a kernel is continuous with respect to θ. A standard error criterion is the mean square error :

$$\mathcal{E} = \frac{1}{2} \sum_{i=1}^{N_\theta} d(\rho_i - f(\theta_i))^2 \tag{3}$$

where d is a distance between the true parameters and the approximated ones. The expression of the distance d depends on two a priori choices :

- The choice of a parameter vector for the family $\mathcal{F}$. In fact, every one-to-one transformation of ρ would be an allowable choice.
- The choice of a metric tensor on the parameter space to define distances between points which need not be euclidean.

The choice of a parameter vector influences in a large amount the result of this second modelling process, especially when dealing with linear interpolation. This choice may be avoided by taking into consideration the intrinsic geometry of the family $\mathcal{F}$. This point of view allows us to define distances in $\mathcal{F}$ independently of the parameterization which is used. More precisely $\mathcal{F}$ may be endowed with the Fisher information metric the components of which are defined as follows :

$$g_{ij} = E[\frac{\partial \log p(x;\rho)}{\partial \rho^i} \frac{\partial \log p(x;\rho)}{\rho^j}] \tag{4}$$

where ρ^i stands for the ith component of ρ[6]. Let G be the metric tensor in matrix form. For the purpose of the approximation of f by a function $\hat{f}(\theta;\eta)$ parameterized by a vector η, the previously defined metric induces a metric $\tilde{G}$ on the η parameter set. In such a case, the steepest descent direction for a function $\mathcal{E}(\eta)$ has the following expression :

$$-\hat{\nabla} = -\tilde{G}^{-1}\nabla\mathcal{E} \tag{5}$$

where $\nabla\mathcal{E}$ stands for the standard gradient of $\mathcal{E}$. This expression may be used in an adaptive algorithm for the optimization of the approximant $\hat{f}(\theta;\eta)$.
For the purpose of interpolation it is possible to consider geodesics on $\mathcal{F}$ parameterized by arclength and defined by the connection induced by the metric tensor G. In such a case, a gaussian kernel is a convenient choice for the tensor matrix may be written as follows :

$$G = diag(\Sigma^{-1}, A_1 + \Sigma_1, ..., A_n + \Sigma_n) \tag{6}$$

where Σ_k has the following expression :

$$\Sigma_k = \begin{pmatrix} \Sigma_{kk} & ... & \Sigma_{kn} \\ ... & ... & ... \\ \Sigma_{nk} & ... & \Sigma_{nn} \end{pmatrix} \tag{7}$$

and $A_k = \{A_{ij} : i,j \geq k\}$ a matrix the same size as Σ_k with $A_{ij} = \frac{1}{T_{kk}^2}$ if $i = j = k$ and 0 otherwise. Thus analytical expressions for the geodesics may be derived.
It is to be noted that this method, since taking into account the intrinsic geometry of a family of models, should perform better or equal than the same computations would when performed on a given parameter space with euclidean metric, provided the sample set $\mathcal{D}_m$ contains enough information for the description of the studied phenomenon. For example, when performing linear interpolation on a coarse grid of the θ-space, it may occur that the application f is locally linear on a given subset of the θ-space for a given parameterization of $\mathcal{F}$. Thus standard interpolation in this parameter space with euclidean metric would perform better than the above method on this subset. But first, this behaviour is only local and second, both methods should agree on this subset as soon as the grid becomes finer.

3 Simulation results

The problem addressed here is to recover the phytoplankton concentration y in the ocean from measurements $X^i, i = 1...n$ of top of atmosphere (TOA) reflectances at several wavelengths λ_i. The part of the incident light beams which has penetrated the ocean and latter reaches a remote satellite sensor has been "colored" by the composition of the ocean. Thus TOA reflectances measurements contain information about the phytoplankton content. The viewing geometry of an observed zone is described by three angles, namely θ_s the sun zenith angle, θ_v the viewing zenith angle and $\Delta\phi$ the azimuthal difference angle. Let $\theta = (\theta_s, \theta_v, \Delta\phi)^t$ be the geometrical parameter vector. Each TOA reflectance measurement at a given wavelength depends continuously on the phytoplankton concentration y, the geometrical parameters θ and on a large number of parameters as wind speed and direction, atmosphere composition... which induce a dispersion of measurements in the reflectances space. Thus, the remote sensing of phytoplankton content is an inverse problem and reflectances measurements may be seen as realizations of a continuous random process $\mathbf{X}(\theta)$.

A wide simulated data set of 7 million points has been generated for five different wavelengths, seven phytoplankton concentrations and various values of other parameters. On figure 1.A is plotted the estimated phytoplankton concentration versus sample number obtained with a multilayer perceptron of 200 neurons on the hidden layer. The input samples were composed of the first four principal components of the reflectances vectors, normalized to mean 0 and variance 1 together with the geometrical parameters. Similar results were obtained using radial basis functions networks of different sizes. The very poor quality of those approximations illustrates the fact that a global approach fails on this complex problem where it may not have been appearent on the graph of figure 1.A that the true function to be approximated is in fact a step function, with respect to the sample number, with 7 levels corresponding to the 7 concentrations.

It has been shown experimentally in a second time that secondth order statistics were sufficient for modelling the probability density of each class of $\mathbf{X}|y,\theta$. A set of locally optimal models has been constructed for θ taking values on a regular grid of the θ space. The local models kernels parameters were computed with principal component analysis for each class. The mean square error of those models for the estimated concentration is less than $1e^{-5}$ for concentrations ranging from 1 to 15mg/m3 on a large domain of the θ-space which means that the classes are perfectly separated. A global model has been constructed by linear interpolation of the immediate neighbours of a given point on the grid of the θ space. Two methods have been tested. First, euclidean linear interpolation in the natural parameter space of a gaussian kernel family. Results are shown in figure 1.B. Secondly, linear interpolation on $\mathcal{F}$ from two neighbours connected by a geodesic has been done showing quite similar but less stable results because of numerical problems. The fact is that the θ space grid is too coarse for an interpolation scheme to be accurate on the whole domain. But the simulation of such a phenomenon is very time consuming, namely several months on a hundred of machines. The coarseness of the θ grid is easily seen with geodesic distances in $\mathcal{F}$ where kernels are relatively dispersed. In fact, both interpolation methods give accurate results as soon as this dispersion is not strong enough. Anyway, this two steps modelling method gives many much better results than a direct global approach of the problem.

4 Conclusion

A global modelling method from a set of locally optimal models has been presented together with theoretical aspects of interpolation and approximation of models. It has been applied to a particularly complex inverse problem showing good results in comparison with standard global approaches as multilayer perceptrons and radial basis functions networks. This modelling approach might be a promising direction for the elaboration of complex models from a set of simpler ones. For this purpose, a much more deeper insight in the instrinsic geometry of a set of models would be helpful, mainly because distances are defined independently of the parameterization.

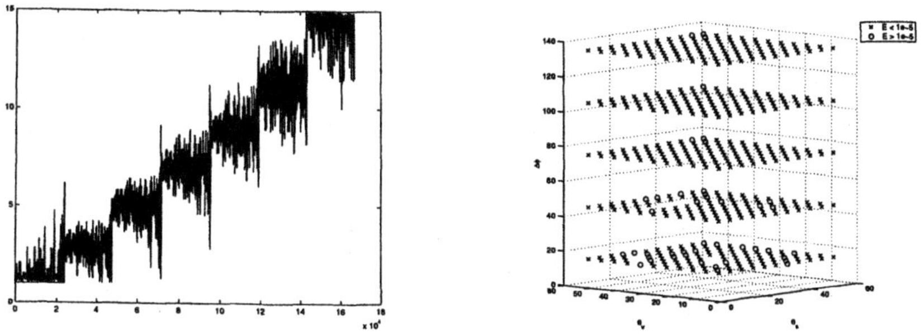

Fig. 1. A. Estimated concentration with MLP. B. Errors of interpolated models.

References

1. Fahlman, S.E., C. Lebiere (1990) The cascade-correlation learning architecture. Advances in Neural Information Processing Systems. **2**, 524-532
2. Lee, T.-C., A.M. Peterson, J.J-C. Tsai (1990) A multilayer feed-forward neural network with dynamically adjustable structures. IEEE Int. Conf. on Systems, Man and Cybernetics, 367-369
3. LeCun, Y., J.S. Denker, S.A. Solla (1990) Optimal brain damage. Advances in Neural Information Processing Systems, **2**, 598-605
4. Weigend, A.S., D.E. Rumelhart, B.A. Huberman (1991) Generalization by weight-elimination with application to forecasting. Advances in Neural Information Processing Systems, **3**, 875-882
5. Poggio T., F. Girosi (1990) Networks for approximation and learning. Proc. of the IEEE, **78**, 1481-1497
6. Amari S.I., (1985) Differential-geometrical methods in statistics. Springer, Lecture Notes in Statistics, **28**, Berlin

Wavelet Network Estimating Regression Function

Przemysław Śliwiński

Wrocław University of Technology, Institute of Engineering Cybernetics, Janiszewskiego 11/17, 50-372 Wrocław, Poland, e-mail: slk@ict.pwr.wroc.pl

Abstract. In the paper we propose the wavelet network estimating the regression function from the set of learning pairs. The entire framework (consisting on the network architecture, learning algorithm and pruning procedure) is derived from the theory of non-parametric estimation of the regression function.

1 Introduction

Wavelet networks are the feed-forward networks with wavelet functions as the neuron activation functions. They were primarily proposed by Zhang and Benveniste [16], however, the idea of implementing non-parametric estimation algorithms in a form of neural networks can be found in the papers of Specht [10] and [11] ; see also [1] and [7]. Wavelet networks have been already applied to recover non-linearities [8], [14], [15], estimate density functions [4], in prediction [13] and system identification [3].

In the paper we consider the properties of the wavelet network developed according to the recent results concerning the wavelet estimation of the regression function (see e.g. [2], [5], [6], [9]).

2 Theoretical background

Consider a problem of estimating a regression function $R(x)$ from the set of data $\{(x_k, y_k)\}_{k=1}^{N}$, where

$$y_k = R(x_k) + z_k,$$

under the following assumptions:

A1. Input signal x_k is stationary random white and uniformly distributed in the unit interval, $x_k \sim U[0,1]$.

A2. The function $R(x)$ is bounded in that interval.

A3. External additive random disturbance z_k is stationary white and zero-mean, independent of the input x_k.

Remark 1. The assumption **A2** is very weak and satisfied in all practical situation. Observe that $R(x)$ can be smooth or have jumps (i.e. it can be discontinuous as well).

Wavelet estimate. The wavelet estimate of $R(x)$ can have the following form

$$\hat{R}_N(x;K) = \sum_{n=0}^{2^M} \hat{\alpha}_{Mn,N} \cdot \varphi_{Mn}(x) + \sum_{m=M}^{K-1} \sum_{l=0}^{2^m} \hat{\beta}_{ml,N} \cdot \psi_{ml}(x) \tag{1}$$

In the estimate, $\varphi_{Mn}(x)$ and $\psi_{ml}(x)$, $M, m, n, l \in \mathbf{Z}$, are scaled and translated Haar wavelet functions $\varphi(x)$ and $\psi(x)$, respectively

$$\varphi_{Mn}(x) = 2^{\frac{M}{2}} \varphi\left(2^M x - n\right) \quad \text{and} \quad \psi_{ml}(x) = 2^{\frac{m}{2}} \psi\left(2^m x - l\right)$$

and $K \in \mathbf{Z}$ is the scale parameter corresponding to the estimate accuracy; M is an arbitrary constant not greater then K. The coefficients $\hat{\alpha}_{Mn,N}$ and $\hat{\beta}_{ml,N}$ are the following sample means

$$\hat{\alpha}_{Mn,N} = \frac{1}{N} \sum_{k=1}^{N} y_k \varphi_{Mn}(x_k) \quad \text{and} \quad \hat{\beta}_{ml,N} = \frac{1}{N} \sum_{k=1}^{N} y_k \psi_{ml}(x_k). \tag{2}$$

It was shown that for assumptions **A1-A3** (see [9]):

Lemma 1. *If the following conditions hold*

$$K = K(N) \to \infty \quad \text{and} \quad 2^{K(N)}/N \to 0 \quad \text{with} \quad N \to \infty \tag{3}$$

then the estimate $\hat{R}_N(x; K(N))$ *converges to* $R(x)$ *in the integrated mean square sense:*

$$MISE\hat{R}_N(x; K(N)) = \mathrm{E} \int_0^1 \left[\hat{R}_N(x; K(N)) - R(x)\right]^2 dx \to 0 \text{ with } N \to \infty \tag{4}$$

Moreover:

Lemma 2. *The error* $MISE\hat{R}_N(x;K)$ *can be disassembled into the following two parts:*

$$MISE\hat{R}_N(x;K) = O\left(2^{-K}\right) + O\left(2^K/N\right) \tag{5}$$

The first component of (5) corresponds to the bias (systematic) error and is of deterministic nature (namely, it is the error of approximation of $R(x)$ by the wavelet expansion for the scale parameter K), the latter is the variance error and is a consequence of the randomness of the learning set.

Remark 2. The convergence (4) holds for all estimation algorithms exploiting orthogonal expansions (see [1] and [7]), however, the decomposition (5) is (under assumption **A2**) unique for wavelet-based algorithm only.

3 Wavelet network

From the Lemma 1 we conclude that the estimate (1) converges to arbitrary bounded (e.g. smooth or discontinuous) function $R(x)$. However, to assure the convergence, the complexity of the estimate (controlled by the parameter K) should grow to infinity with growing N (see (3)). Clearly, these requirements cannot be fully satisfied in practical implementations[1].

In our framework we consider wavelet network with fixed size, i.e. implementing the estimate (1) with fixed parameter K.

Network architecture. The wavelet network is the feed-forward one-and-half layer network. An example for $K = 3$ is presented on Fig. 1. For scales $m = 0, \ldots, 2$ each sum in (1) is implemented by modules of neurons with appropriate activation functions φ or ψ. The elements with labels $\hat{\alpha}_{00}, \hat{\beta}_{00}, \ldots, \hat{\beta}_{23}$

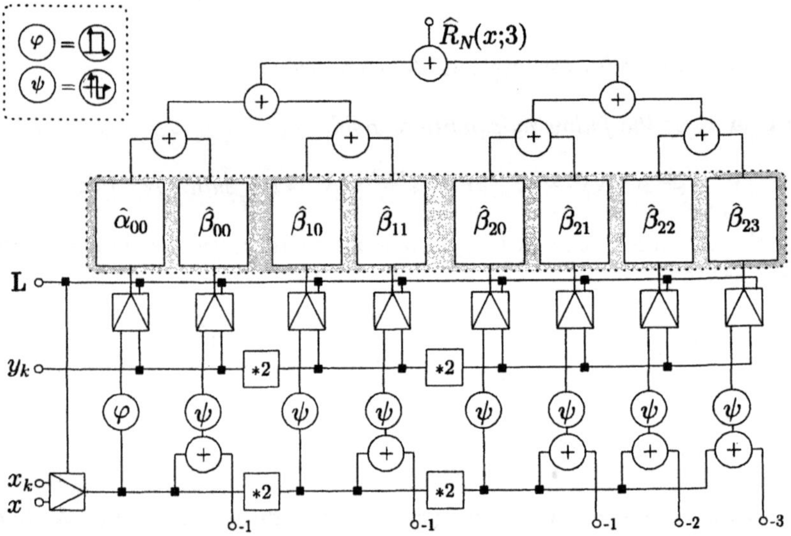

Fig. 1. Wavelet network for $K = 3$. By activating the input **L** one can learn the network *in situ*. The picture in the upper left corner illustrates that the activation functions of the wavelet neurons are extremely simple in implementation

are simple processors (arithmetic units) implementing the learning algorithm and pruning procedure described below.

[1] Hasiewicz in [5] showed that this issue can be partialy overcame and proposed *modular wavelet networks*. Like our network, they assemble modules corresponding to each value of m. However, in case of new incoming measurements, they can be enlarged by adding new modules without re-learning of the existing part.

Learning algorithm. The networks weights are equal to the coefficients $\hat{\alpha}_{Mn,N}$ and $\hat{\beta}_{ml,N}$; therefore as the learning algorithm we propose the recursive version of the equations in (2)

$$\hat{\alpha}_{Mn,N} = \frac{N-1}{N}\hat{\alpha}_{Mn,N-1} + \frac{1}{N}y_N\varphi_{Mn}(x_N)$$
$$\hat{\beta}_{ml,N} = \frac{N-1}{N}\hat{\beta}_{ml,N-1} + \frac{1}{N}y_N\psi_{ml}(x_N)$$

with the initial conditions $\hat{\alpha}_{Mn,0} = \hat{\beta}_{ml,0} = 0$.

Notice the simplicity of the algorithm. It requires only elementary arithmetic operations and has computational complexity of order $O(N)$.

Pruning procedure. The Lemma 2 says that the wavelet network of fixed size can estimate an arbitrary $R(x)$ with the finite accuracy only since for large number of learning pairs the overall error approaches the first component, independent of N

$$MISE\hat{R}_N(x;K) = O\left(2^{-K}\right) \quad \text{for large } N$$

In turn, for small sets of learning pairs, the error (5) depends only on the second component

$$MISE\hat{R}_N(x;K) = O\left(2^{K}/N\right) \quad \text{for small } N$$

Thus we can expect rather poor performance of the network for small sets of learning pairs. Exploiting once again the results of estimation theory we propose the procedure of adaptation of the network size to the number of learning pairs (i.e. a *regularization algorithm*; see e.g. [12]). Since the network is of fixed size, the procedure should prune (deactivate) these net modules for which the error introduced by the variance is greater than the reduction of the bias component (cf. (5)), i.e. for which

$$2^{-m} \le 2^m/N$$

Finally, we prune (by simple zeroing of respective weights) these modules (corresponding to the scale m) for which the following inequality holds

$$N \le 2^{2m}$$

Large size networks. For large networks (i.e. for large parameter K) one can prove the following lemma (see [9]).

Lemma 3. *If the scale parameter $K(N)$ is selected according to the rule*

$$K(N) = \left\lceil \frac{1}{2}\log_2 N \right\rceil \tag{6}$$

then the asymptotic rate of convergence (4) is of order

$$MISE\hat{R}_N(x;K(N)) = O\left(N^{-1/2}\right) \tag{7}$$

The convergence rate in (7) is guarantied for all bounded functions $R(x)$ with finite (but not known) number of discontinuities. It is worth to mention that this property of wavelet networks is unique amongst all feed-forward networks (cf. Remark 2).

4 Conclusions

The results presented in the paper draw to the conclusion that the wavelet-based estimates of the regression function can be easily implemented as a wavelet neural networks (estimates based on Haar wavelet functions are well-disposed to hardware realizations due to simplicity of activation functions). Moreover:

- The network can effectively estimate any functions met in practical applications.
- The properties of the network are independent of the distribution of the external disturbances z_k.
- The learning algorithm is simple and fast. It can be implemented within the network structure.
- The pruning procedure is automatic (controlled by the size of the learning pairs only).

References

1. Gałkowski K., Rutkowski L. (1994) Realizacja algorytmów rozpoznawania i nieparametrycznej estymacji za pomocą sieci neuronowych. In *Proceedings of First National Conference Neural Networks and Their Applications.* 237–242, Częstochowa.
2. Härdle W., Kerkyacharian G. *et al.* (1998) *Wavelets, Approximation, and Statistical Applications.* Springer-Verlag, New York.
3. Hasiewicz Z. (1996) Non-parametric system identification by probabilistic neural network using multiresolution approach. In *Proceedings of Second National Conference Neural Networks and Their Applications.* 206–211, Szczyrk.
4. Hasiewicz H. (1997) Wavelet neural network for density estimation. In *Proceedings of Third Conference Neural Networks and Their Applications.* 136–141, Kule.
5. Hasiewicz Z. (2000) Modular neural networks for non-linearity recovering by the Haar approximation. *Neural Networks.* **13**, 1107–1133.
6. Hasiewicz Z. (2001) Non-parametric estimation of non-linearity in a cascade time series system by multiscale approximation. *Signal Processing.* **81**, 1107–1133.
7. Pawlak M. Rafajłowicz E. (1996) Slowly expanding orthogonal neural net for uniformly distributed input patterns — part 1 and 2. In *Proceedings of Second National Conference Neural Networks and Their Applications.* 365–376, Szczyrk.

8. Śliwiński P. (1999) Self-organizing wavelet neural network – the data driven approach. In *Proceedings of Fourth Conference Neural Networks and Their Applications.* 153–158, Zakopane.
9. Śliwiński P. (2000) *Non-linear system identification by wavelets.* PhD dissertation, Wrocław University of Technology, Institute of Engineering Cybernetics.
10. Specht D. (1990) Probabilistic neural network. *Neural Networks.* **3**, 109–118.
11. Specht D. (1991) A general regression neural network. *IEEE Transactions on Neural Network.* **2**, 568–576.
12. Vapnik V. N. (1995) *The Nature of Statistical Learning Theory.* Springer-Verlag, New York.
13. Zhang B. L., Coggins R. *et al.* (2001) Multiresolution forecasting for futures trading using wavelet decompositions. *IEEE Transactions on Neural Networks.* **12**, 765–775.
14. Zhang J., Walter G. *et al.* (1995) Wavelet neural networks for function learning. *IEEE Transactions on Signal Processing.* **43**, 1485–1497.
15. Zhang Q. (1997) Using wavelet network in nonparametric estimation. *IEEE Transactions on Neural Networks.* **8**, 227–236.
16. Zhang Q., Benveniste A. (1992) Wavelet networks. *IEEE Transactions on Neural Networks.* **3**, 889–898.

Dynamic Programming with NAR Model versus Q-learning - Case Study

Jarosław Chrobak and Andrzej Pacut

Warsaw University of Technology Nowowiejska 15/19, Warsaw 00-665, Poland, jchrobak@ia.pw.edu.pl, apacut@ia.pw.edu.pl

Abstract. Two approaches to control policy synthesis for unknown systems are investigated. An indirect approach is based on adaptive identification of a neural network model in the NAR form (nonlinear autoregresion model) followed by application of the dynamic programming to this model. A direct approach consists of Q-learning with the use of a lookup table. Both methods were applied to optimization of a stock portfolio problem and tested on Warsaw Stock Exchange data.

1 Introduction

Synthesis of control policy for an unknown time-varying system can be approached either indirectly, i.e. by the model identification followed by control synthesis for the identified system, or by a direct estimation of the control policy, without the use of a model. In this paper we study both methods as applied to a problem of optimization of a stock investment policy understood as a strategy of investing a capital into a stock of several companies to make the maximal profit. Verification of both approaches is based on Warsaw Stock Exchange (WSE) records of 1994–1998. We focus on three companies: BSK (a bank), Żywiec (a brewery) and Optimus (a computer company). The problem is formulated in details in Sec. 2. The indirect control synthesis is presented in Sec 3, and Sec. 4 is devoted to the direct control synthesis. In Sec. 5 we compare the results for both approaches and draw final conclusions.

2 Problem Formulation

Suppose a certain initial capital c_0 is to be invested into the stock market among m chosen companies. We assume that after each "investment period" the entire resulting capital have to be reinvested. Denote by $c(t)$ the capital reinvested at the end of t-th period and by $u_k(t)$, $k = 1, \dots, m$, its fraction invested at this time into the k-th company, $\sum_{k=1}^{m} u_k(t) = 1$. Capital distribution at the moment t can thus be described by a vector $u(t) = [u_1(t) \;\cdots\; u_m(t)]^T$. Vector u was chosen as decision variable (control). The problem we consider is to find the optimal investment policy that maximizes our capital $c(t)$.

The structure of the considered control system is shown in Fig. 1. Note that the controlled object can be divided into two parts, namely the stock

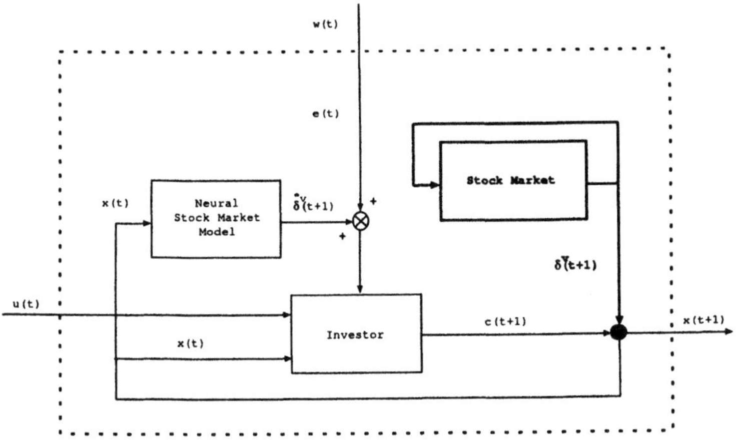

Fig. 1. Control structure. The object can be partitioned into a stock market part (bold lines) and the investor part

market part and the investor part. The stock market part is related to a subsystem with unknown dynamics which can be interpreted as a price setting process at Warsaw Stock Exchange. The investor part is a subsystem of known dynamics that represents an influence of both the stock market part and the investment decisions $u(t)$ on the individual invested capital $c(t)$. Since we consider investors whose actions do not influence the stock prices ("small investors"), we assume that the stock market part is uncontrollable but observable.

We will analyze a discrete-time model of the market share prices $v_1, \ldots, v_m$ of m companies. By $v_k(t)$, $t = 0, 1, \ldots$, we denote the opening price of k-th chosen company share at t-th session. Moreover, let define the relative increases of the share prices as $\delta_k^v(t) = (v_k(t) - v_k(t-1)) \;/\; v_k(t-1)$. On the basis of historical data analysis we decided to bound the daily share value variations to 10 percent, so the relative price increases take values from $[-0.1, 0.1]$. Wherever their quantization is necessary, each relative price increase is quantized into $d_x = 21$ levels, thus leading to a rectangular grid of $d_x^m = 9261$ values.

Let define state vector for the considered system as

$$x(t) = [c(t)\; \delta_1^v(t) \cdots \delta_m^v(t)]\,. \tag{1}$$

We assume that investment decision (control) $u(t)$ is chosen according to some stationary control policy μ, i.e. $u(t) = \mu(x(t))$. Moreover, we assume that the control values are at all times bounded to a simplex $U = \{u \geq 0 : \sum_{k=1}^{m} u_k = 1\}$ where for vectors an inequality denotes simultaneous inequalities for all coordinates. Whenever the control quantization is necessary, a uniform grid is made within this simplex. We used 11 levels for each control variable thus getting 66 discrete control values.

Taking into consideration the assumption that the whole capital is reinvested, the capital at the $t+1$-st control stage can be expressed by the recurrent formula

$$c(t+1) = c(t) \sum_{k=1}^{m} u_k(t)(1 + \delta_k^v(t+1)), \quad c(0) = c_0, \tag{2}$$

where c_0 is the initial capital.

The goal of the decision process is to find the optimal stationary investment policy μ^* which fulfills the state and control constraints and maximizes the quality index

$$J(x(0)) = \mathcal{E}\left\{ \lim_{T\to\infty} \sum_{t=0}^{T} \alpha^t g(x(t), u(t), x(t+1)) \mid S \right\} \tag{3}$$

where S denotes the system and control constraints $S : \{u(t) = \mu(x(t)),$ $x(t+1) = f(x(t), u(t), w(t)), t = 1, 2, \ldots\}$, α is the discount factor, $g(x(t), u(t), x(t+1)) = \ln(1 + u^T(t)x_{2,m+1}(t+1))$ is a reward for the transition from state $x(t)$ to state $x(t+1)$ under control $u(t)$, and $x_{2,m+1}$ is a state subvector consisting of entities from 2 to m. Therefore, $\mu^*(x) = \arg\max_{u\in\mathcal{U}} J(x)$ for any x, where $\mathcal{U}$ is the set of admissible control sequences u. Such formulation is quite standard and the details can be found e.g. in [2].

Classic optimal feedback control of a time-invariant plant requires that the plant to be controlled is known. Typically, we assume knowledge of the state equations. Unfortunately, in the problem we investigate the state equations are not known. Consequently, they must either be identified on the base of observations and then the control policy established for the identified system (the indirect method), or the control policy has to be derived directly from the observation of the system behavior (the direct method).

3 Indirect Control Synthesis

The optimal control synthesis problem can be approached with the dynamic programming, by solving the Bellman equation which can be for any $x(t)$ written as

$$J^*(x(t)) = \max_{u\in\mathcal{U}} \mathcal{E}\left\{g(x(t), u, x(t+1)) + J^*(x(t+1)) \mid x(t)\right\}. \tag{4}$$

One may pursue the idea of separating the system equation estimation from the control. The system equation estimation can be based on the data available before the current control generation step, and the control is calculated on the basis of estimated model rather than the real system. This is a reason why such the approach may be labelled the indirect control synthesis.

We first describe the models used for system estimation and then discuss the control algorithm. The dynamics of δ^v is approximated by NAR model

$\hat{\delta}^v(t+1) = \mathcal{M}(\delta^v(t))$, with a nonlinearity in the form of a neural network. In this case, from (2) we obtain

$$c(t+1) = c(t) \cdot \left[\sum_{k=1}^{m} u_k(t)(1 + \hat{\delta}_k^v(t+1) + e_k(t)) \right] . \tag{5}$$

where $e(t)$ is a white noise vector characterized by a known distribution.

Model estimation We experimented with several discrete-time, nonlinear models. The models were set up with the use of a multilayer perceptron networks. The simplest structure we considered was the NAR(1) model (first order nonlinear autoregresion model [4])

$$\hat{y}(t) = h(y(t-1)) + e(t) \tag{6}$$

where h is a nonlinear function, y is the share price increase vector, and $\{e(t)$ is an m-dimensional Gaussian white noise of zero mean and diagonal covariance matrix of diagonal elements $\sigma_1^2, \ldots, \sigma_m^2$. We also experimented with NAR(2) and NAR(3) structures.

In all cases, function h was approximated by a two layer perceptron network with the sigmoidal hidden layer and a linear output layer. Hiperbolic tangens function was used as the activation function of hidden neurons. The input variables were pre-scaled to the interval $[-0.9, 0.9]$ to achieve faster estimation convergence. The simplest gradient descent algorithm was sufficient to achieve a decent convergence speed. Learning speed coefficient was being set separately for each network weight with the help of delta-bar-delta algorithm [3]. The initial weights were selected randomly. Several models with different number of neurons in hidden layer were performed and tested.

The best results were achieved for the NAR(1) model with 5 hidden neurons. Mean square error of this model was approximately equal 0.04 while a mean square error of the worst model was about 0.06. The NAR(1) model with 5 hidden neuron was next used as a basis of the optimal investment policy generation described in the next paragraph.

Control The Bellman equation was solved for J^* with the use of successive approximations in the following form

$$\hat{J}^+(x(t)) = \max_{u \in \mathcal{U}} \mathcal{E} \left\{ g(x(t), u, x(t+1)) + \alpha \hat{J}(x(t+1)) \mid x(t) \right\} \quad \forall x(t) \tag{7}$$

where the approximation $\hat{J}^+$ replaces $\hat{J}$ at each iteration.

The optimal investment policy generation algorithm was implemented in the following way: the investment policy was calculated with the help of successive approximations method (7) and used without changes during 10 next decision steps. The share price model was estimated adaptively before each investment policy calculation. A window consisting of the last 50 management moments was used as a training set for the model estimation process. The window was shifted during the investment process in such a way that the last data in the window is followed by the moment of the new investment policy calculation.

4 Direct Control Synthesis

In a direct control synthesis based on dynamic programming in unknown environment, the optimal control is established directly rather than through the estimated model. We implemented here the Q-learning method [5] in its lookup-table form. The look-up table results from the discretization of both arguments of Q-function. We used 3, 5, or 7 discretization points for each state variable, and all 66 points of the discretized control space. This leads to the lookup tables of 1782, 8250, and 22638 points, respectively. The TD(0) algorithm for Q-learning [1] can be written in the form

$$\begin{aligned}\hat{Q}^{+}(x(t),u(t)) &= \hat{Q}(x(t),u(t)) + \\ &+ \gamma \cdot \Big(g(x(t),u(t),x(t+1)) + \max_v \hat{Q}(x(t+1),v) - \hat{Q}(x(t),u(t))\Big)\end{aligned} \tag{8}$$

where $\hat{Q}^{+}$ replaces $\hat{Q}$ after each iteration. The optimal policy μ^{*} is established as the value which maximizes the Q-function, namely

$$\mu^{*}(x(t)) = \arg\max_{u\in\mathcal{U}} Q(x(t),u) \quad \forall x(t).$$

Notably, not all the state-control pairs are "visited" if the approximation is too fine. The reason is too small a set of historical data. In fact, we run into such a problem for all cases except for the 3-level state discretization.

The direct synthesis algorithm was implemented in the similar manner as the indirect synthesis one (see Sec. 3).

5 Testing and Conclusions

A testing procedure was applied to both control strategies. We started the testing with the initial capital of 10000 PLN and assumed that no additional capital can be later added and that the entire capital is to be invested at all times. The investment policies were evaluated for the capitals accumulated by the end of the testing periods. The results are presented in Fig. 2.

Two methods testing was applied, forward testing and backward testing. The forward testing uses the results from the 10-moment window in that the control policy was applied. In the backward testing we apply the policy in 10 moments that precede the moment of the policy calculation. The goal of the backward testing is to check the best possible (yet not causal) solution

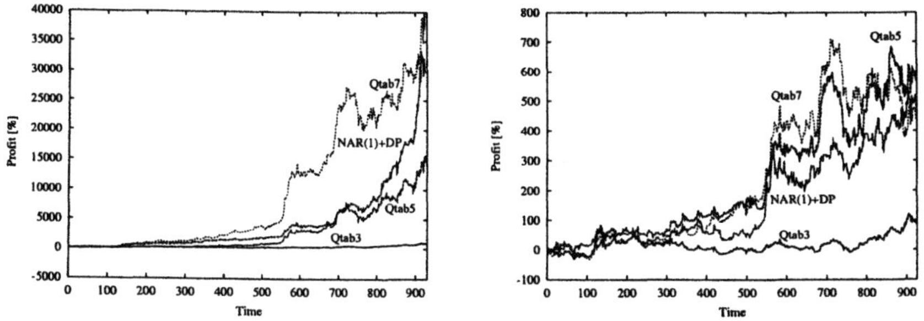

Fig. 2. Investments results. Each sound investment policy calculation method should provide much better performance for forward (left) than backward (right) testing. It can be seen that for Q-learning algorithm the 3-level share increase discretization is too coarse to achieve a good performance

obtainable for the data. The forward testing is used to obtain causal measure of control quality. For the forward testing the best result was obtained for the strategy produced by Q-learning algorithm with five discrete values of share price increase - the profit of about 600%. The worst result was obtained for the strategy of the same algorithm but with three discrete values of price increase - the profit below 100%. The way of state space discretization has thus significant influence on the strategies quality. To give some insight into the behavior of the WSE in the investigated period we may say that the increase of the overall stock exchange indexes (WIG, WIG20) at this time was about 50%.

Both direct and indirect control synthesis methods produce comparable results but indirect control synthesis is significantly more time consuming. It is caused by computationally expensive model estimation procedure and successive approximation algorithm. We must stress that each of the considered method leaded to financial profit.

This work was supported by grant No. 7 T11A 022 20 of the Committee for Scientific Research of Poland

References

1. D.P. Bertsekas and J. Tsitsiklis, *Neuro-Dynamic Programming*, Athena Scientific, Belmont, Mass., 1996.
2. D.P. Bertsekas, *Dynamic Programming and Optimal Control*, Athena Scientific, Belmont, Mass., 1995.
3. S. Haykin, *Neural Networks - A Comprehensive Foundation* Macmillan College Publishing Company, 1994.
4. K.S. Narendra, *Neural Networks for Control: Theory and Practice*, Proceedings of the IEEE, Vol. 84, No. 10, pp. 1385-1407, 1996.
5. C.J.C.H. Watkins and P. Dayan, *Technical Note: Q Learning*, Machine Learning, Vol. 8, pp. 279-492, 1992.

Evaluation of Economic Effectiveness of Provinces with Rough and Fuzzy Sets

Marcin Korzeń, Andrzej Piegat
Faculty of Computer Science and Information Systems
Technical University of Szczecin
E-mail: mkorzen@wi.ps.pl , Andrzej.Piegat@wi.ps.pl

Abstract

The paper presents the problem of influence evaluation of people living in provinces of a country on their production value. The production in a given province depends on a number of economic factors, but not only. It also depends on features of people (not only of managers) such as: organizational cleverness, diligence, and ingeniousness, local patriotism, engagement, and education level. Authors applied 2 methods for the economic effectiveness evaluation of provinces based on rough and fuzzy sets which enables to compare their advantages and deficiencies.

1. INTRODUCTION

The gross production y [PLN/1 inhabitant] of a province can be influenced by a number of factors from which the authors took into account the following ones:

x_1 - fixed assets [PLN/1 inhabitant],
x_2 - indirect capital consumption [PLN/1 inhabitant]
x_3 - employee rate in the country population [%]
x_4 - unemployment rate [%]
x_5 - average month salary [PLN]
x_6 - investment outlays [PLN/ 1 inhabitant]
x_7 - innovation activity outlays [PLN/1 inhabitant]
x_8 - economic effectiveness of the country inhabitants [low, mean, high].

Values of the country production y and of other factors x_1 - x_7 (inputs) influencing the production are published in Poland by Main Statistic Office [1]. Value of the factor x_8, of the country economic effectiveness is not known. Knowledge of this factor is very important, because it enables to evaluate how effective inhabitants of a province use means and possibilities, which they have at disposal. It also enables to compare provinces. Depending on the comparison result the country government may award more financial means to a province of high effectiveness and less means to a province of low effectiveness. Input/output scheme of the production system of a province is presented in Fig.1.

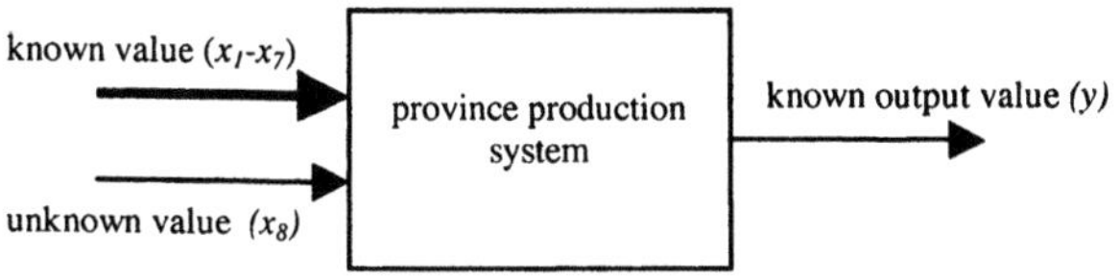

Fig.1.Input/output scheme of the province production system (meanings of variables x_i are given on page 1).

In terms of the system theory problem of evaluation of the economic effectiveness of provinces is a problem of evaluation of one of the system inputs (x_8), given the output y - and the input (x_1-x_7) - values. For evaluating the input x_8 the authors proposed a method, which idea is presented in Fig.2.

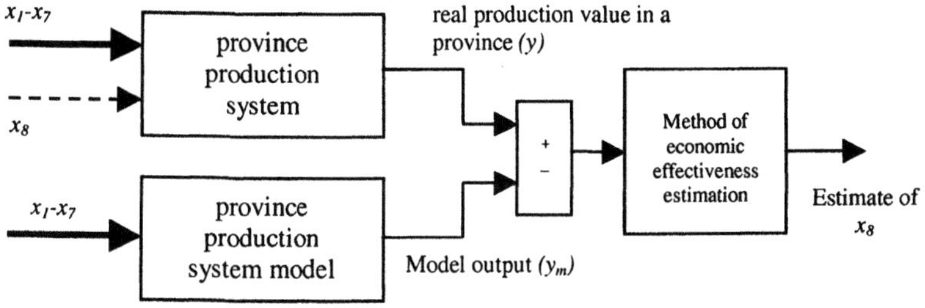

y - real production value in a province [PLN/1 inhabitant],
y_M - mean production of similar provinces (achieved at values of economic factors x_1-x_7 which are similar to values of the given province)
x_8 - economic effectiveness of the province.

Fig.2. Scheme of information processing in the evaluation method of economic effectiveness (province evaluation)

The first method of province evaluation bases on comparison of production y of a province and of the mean production y_M achieved by similar provinces, that is provinces having similar values of economic factors x_1 - x_7 (without factor x_8 - economic effectiveness). Method 1 requires detecting classes of similar provinces. For evaluation of the effectiveness x_8 of provinces according to the method the authors applied rough sets [3], a theory which idea was created by prof. Zdzisław Pawlak [3].

Investigations of the province effectiveness were made by M. Korzeń in the frame of his dissertation opened on Faculty of Computer Science and Information Systems of Technical University of Szczecin and conducted under scientific tutelage of Andrzej Piegat as a professor conferring the degree.

2. EVALUATION OF THE PROVINCE ECONOMIC EFFECTIVENESS WITH APPLICATION OF ROUGH SETS

Investigation of economic effectiveness of provinces in Poland was realized using statistic data [1] from year 1996. In that year Poland was partitioned into 49 provinces, which is a sufficient number of examples at 7 conditional attributes x_1 -x_7. Examples of primary statistic data used in investigations are shown in Tab.1.

Province	Fixed assetes X_1	Indirect capital consumption X_2	Employee rate in the country population X_3	Unemploy-ment rate X_4	Average month salary X_5	Investments outlays X_6	Innovation activity outlays X_7	Gross product Y
Warszawskie	43 864,00	21 517,70	49,71	4,10	1 130,61	4 419,00	244,25	18 833,00
Bialskopodlaskie	23 728,00	6 982,54	44,13	11,90	737,74	930,00	13,58	5 879,50
....	....	....	....	....	....	....	....	....
Zamojskie	22 113,00	6 498,88	48,63	12,40	718,15	748,00	53,65	5 504,00
Zielolonogórskie	24 040,00	9 526,99	34,52	15,30	742,41	1 233,00	182,67	8 163,80

Tab.1. Examples of primary values of explanatory variables x_1 -x_7 and the explained variable y of the province effectiveness problem.

All variables of the problem were normalized to interval [0,100] and next discretized as follows:

$(1 \leq x_i < 25.75)$ = small (1), $(25.75 \leq x_i < 50.5)$ = mean (2),
$(50.5 \leq x_i < 75.25)$ = large (3), $(75.25 \leq x_i < 100)$ = very large (4).

After normalization and discretization of primary data a secondary information table, Tab.2, was obtained.

Prov.\ attr. no.	X1	X2	X3	X4	X5	X6	X7	Y
Warszawskie	4	4	4	1	4	4	1	4
Bialskopodlaskie	2	1	3	2	1	1	1	1
....								
Zamojskie	1	1	4	2	1	1	1	1
Zielonogórskie	2	1	1	3	1	1	1	1

Tab.2. Normalized and discretized information table of the evaluation problem of economic effectiveness of provinces.

In information table of the problem, Tab.2, 32 elementary conditional sets E_i were determined, sets of provinces with identical discrete values of conditional attributes (x_1-x_7). Examples of indiscernible provinces are:

E_2 = *{Bialskopodlaskie, Białostockie, Chełmskie, Łomżyńskie}*,
E_6 = *{Częstochowskie, Nowosądeckie, Siedleckie, Skierniewickie, Tarnowskie}*,
E_9 = *{Gorzowskie, Pilskie, Zielonogórskie}*.

Next, a search was made to detect absolute reducts [2] of the complete, 7-element set of conditional attributes $\{x_1, x_2, \ldots, x_7\}$. Two 6 - element absolute reducts were detected:

$RED_{ab1}(P) = \{x_1, x_2, x_3, x_4, x_5, x_7\}$, $RED_{ab2}(P) = \{x_1, x_2, x_3, x_4, x_6, x_7\}$.

After detecting absolute reducts a research was made to detect relative reducts (in relation to the concept family D*). Two 4-element relative reducts were detected:

$RED_{rel1}(P) = \{x_1, x_3, x_4, x_7\}$, $RED_{rel2}(P) = \{x_1, x_2, x_4, x_6\}$.

The both relative reducts gave high approximation quality γ of the concept family:

$\gamma_{REDrel1} = \gamma_{REDrel2} = 0.959$.

Cardinality of positive regions of the both reducts was identical as cardinality of the positive region of the full 7-element set P of conditional attributs and was equal to 47 provinces at universum U containing 49 provinces. However, a research shown that the second relative reduct had higher significance σ of its attributes:

$\sigma_1(x_1, x_3, x_4, x_7\} = 0.106,$ $\qquad\qquad$ $\sigma_2(x_1, x_2, x_4, x_6) = 0.170.$

Moreover, the second relative reduct generated smaller number of decisional rules than the first one (24 versus rules). Therefore in next steps an rough model of the economic effectiveness of provinces with following variables was determined: $y = f(x_1,x_2,x_4,x_6)$ -

production = *f* (fixed assets, indirect capital consumption, unemployment rate,investment outlays).

Decisional rules of the rough set model of provinces production are given in Tab.3.

Lp.	X1	X2	X4	X6	Y1	supp.	strentgh	cert.	abstr. classes
1	4	4	1	4	4	1	0.02	1	1
2	2	1	2	1	1	5	0.1	1	2 3 6 23 42
3	1	2	2	1	2	1	0.02	1	4
4	2	2	3	1	1	1	0.02	1	5
5	1	1	3	1	1	2	0.041	1	7 15
6	1	1	2	1	1	9	0.18	1	8 25 33 35 36 37 38 43 48
7	2	2	4	1	1	1	0.02	1	9
8	2	2	2	2	2	1	0.02	1	10
9	2	1	3	1	1	7	0.14	1	11 13 19 28 29 34 49
10	2	1	3	2	1	1	0.02	1	12
11	3	2	1	2	2	1	0.02	1	14
12	3	1	3	1	1	2	0.041	1	16 30
13	2	1	4	1	1	3	0.061	1	17 26 39
14	2	2	1	2	2	1	0.02	1	18
15	3	4	3	2	2	1	0.02	1	20
16	2	2	2	1	2	1	0.02	1	21
17	3	1	2	2	1	1	0.02	1	22
18	1	2	3	1	2	1	0.02	0.5	24
19	3	2	2	3	1	1	0.02	1	27
20	3	4	3	3	4	1	0.02	1	31
21	3	2	1	3	3	1	0.02	1	32
22	1	1	4	1	1	3	0.061	1	40 45 46
23	3	2	2	2	2	2	0.041	1	41 47
24	1	2	3	1	1	1	0.02	0.5	44

Tab.3. Decisional table of the rough set model of province production with quantitative indexes characterizing particular rules.

The rough set model of the province production can graphically be shown in form of 3-dimensional sections, Fig.3.

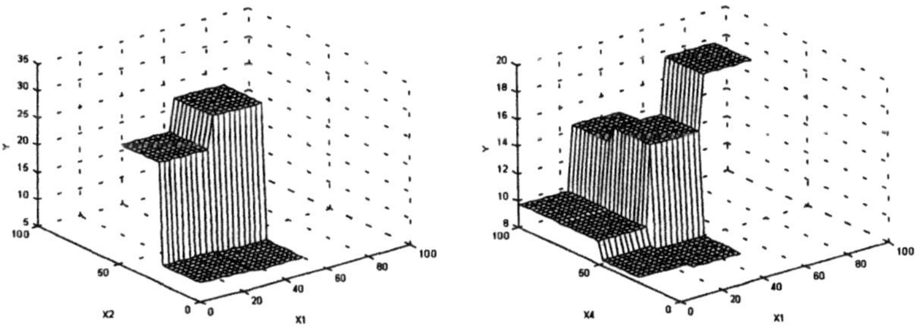

Fig.3. 3-dimensional cuts of the 5D-model surface of the province production in subspaces: $\{X_1,X_2\}$ *at* $x_3 = 30$, $x_4 = 1$, and $\{X_1,X_4\}$ at $x_2 = 1$, $x_3 = 1$.

Rectangular sectors of the rough model surface are situated on the level of the mean production value y_M of particular classes of similar provinces, which are determined by antecedents of rules. Using the mean production values y_M, the difference $e = y_M - y$ for each province in the given class can be calculated (y- real production of a province).

Positive value of the difference e testifies to over-average effectiveness and negative value to low economic effectiveness of a province. Three qualitative evaluations of the province effectiveness were applied: ($e = y - y_M < -2$) = low effectiveness, ($-2 \le e < 0$ and $0 < e < 2$, without $e = 0$) = mean effectiveness, ($e = 0$) = undetermined effectiveness, ($e \ge 2$) - high economic effectiveness.

Modeling results of the province production and evaluation of the province economic effectiveness are given in Tab.4.

Prov.No.	y	ym	e=ym-y	Eval.
1	100	100	0	*
2	3.789	8.003	-4.214	L
3	16.23	8.003	8.225	H
.....				
47	39.02	38.43	0.5871	M
48	1	8.321	-7.321	L
49	20.76	15.63	5.125	H

Tab.4. Modeling results of the province production y_M and evaluation of the economic effectiveness of particular provinces in Poland in 1996 (L - low, M - mean, H -high, the sign "*" refers to undetermined effectiveness, to provinces, which do not have any similar ones to be compared with, which are singletons in their classes.

Classification of Polish provinces (by the province number) in respect to their economic effectiveness, resulting from the rough set model is given below:

high-effective provinces: *{3, 8, 11, 17, 24, 29, 35, 38, 42, 43, 45, 49}*,
mean-effective provinces: *{7. 13, 15, 16, 26, 30, 34, 37, 40, 41, 47}*,
low-effective provinces: *{2, 6, 19, 23, 25, 28, 33, 36, 39, 44, 46, 48}*,
provinces of undetermined effectiveness:*{1, 4, 5, 9, 10, 12, 14, 18, 20, 21, 22, 37,31,32}*.

3. EVALUATION OF THE PROVINCE ECONOMIC EFFECTIVENESS WITH FUZZY SETS

The rough set model of the province production ca be treated as a fuzzy model with crisp functions of membership $\chi(x_1, x_2, \dots, x_7)$ to hyper-rectangular sectors of the input space of the problem. Output y of the rough set model is calculated from formula (1).

$$y(x_1,x_2,\dots x_n) = \frac{\sum_{i=1}^{n} \chi_i(x_1,x_2,\dots x_n)\cdot y_i}{\sum_{i=1}^{n} \chi_i(x_1,x_2,\dots x_n)} \qquad (1)$$

where:

$$\chi_i(x_1,x_2 \dots x_n) = \begin{cases} 1 & for\ (x_1,x_2\dots x_n)\ that\ lie\ in\ sector\ i \\ 0 & else; \end{cases} \qquad (1')$$

$y_i = \frac{1}{n}\sum_{y_k \in K_i} y_k$, y_i - mean production of provinces that belong to sector i,

K_i - set of production values y_k of provinces, which belong to sector i.

Crisp membership functions χ_i to sectors can be replaced by fuzzy membership functions μ_i, e.g. with Gaussian functions (2), [4]:

$$\mu_i(x_1, x_2, \dots x_n) = e^{-\sum_{j=1}^{n}\frac{(x_j - x_{ji})^2}{(2a_{ji})^2}} \quad , \; i=1 \dots m; \qquad (2)$$

where: x_{ji} - j-th center-coordinate of the i-th membership function,
a_{ji} - width of the i-th membership function.

Output y of a fuzzy model can be calculated from formula (3).

$$y = \frac{\sum_{i=1}^{m} y_i \mu_i(x_1, x_2, \dots x_n)}{\sum_{i=1}^{m} \mu_i(x_1, x_2, \dots x_n)} \qquad (3)$$

Rule base of the fuzzy model transformed from the rough set model is given by (4):

1) IF $(x_1 \approx x_{11})$ AND, ... , AND $(x_n \approx x_{n1})$ THEN $(y \approx y_1)$
2) IF $(x_1 \approx x_{12})$ AND, ... , AND $(x_n \approx x_{2n})$ THEN $(y \approx y_2)$ (4)
... ...
m) IF $(x_1 \approx x_{1n})$ AND, ... , AND $(x_n \approx x_{nm})$ THEN $(y \approx y_m)$.

In Fig.4 surfaces of particular rules of the resulting fuzzy model surface in the subspace $X_1 * X_4$ are presented.

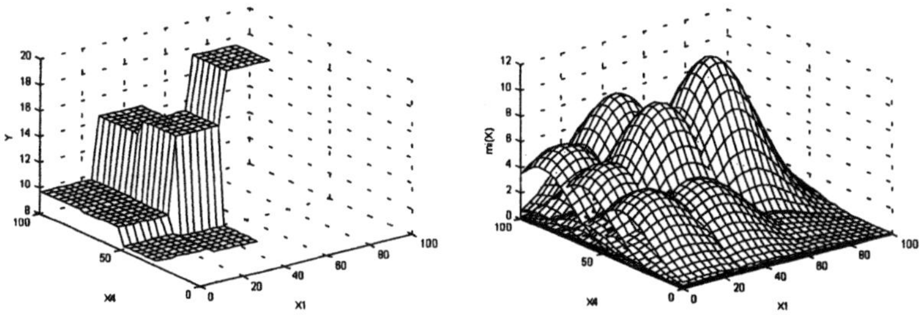

Fig. 4. Membership functions to particular input space sectors multiplied by conclusions y_i of corresponding rules (a) and the resulting fuzzy model surface of the province production y_M in the subspace $X_1 * X_4$ of the problem.

In Fig. 5 and 6 intersections of the rough set model and of the fuzzy model surfaces are presented, which enables their comparison.

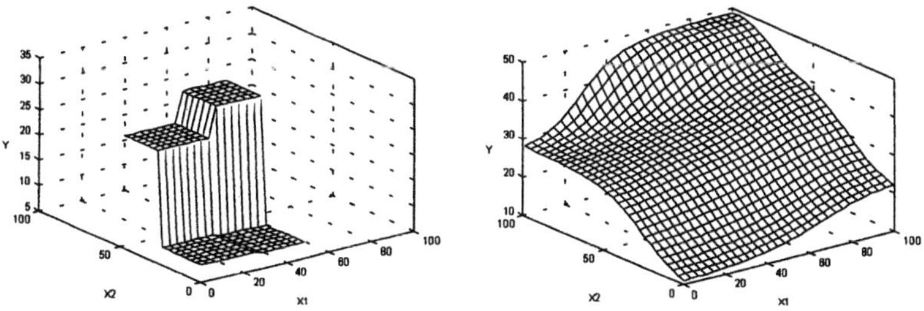

Fig.5. Comparison of 3-dimensional cuts $y_M = f(x_1, x_2)$ at $x_4 = 30$ and $x_6 = 1$ of 5-dimensional surfaces of the rough set model (a) and of the fuzzy model (b) of the province production in Poland in 1996.

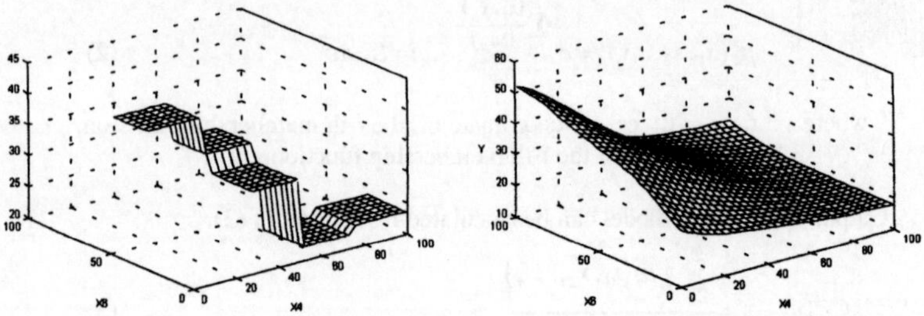

Fig.6. Comparison of 3-D cuts $y_M = f(x_4, x_6)$ at $x_1 = 30$ and $x_2 = 30$ of 5-D surfaces of the rough set model (a) and of the fuzzy model (b) of the province production in Poland in 1996

In Tab.5 evaluation results of the province effectiveness achieved with use of the rough set model and of the fuzzy model $y_M = f(x_1, x_2, x_4, x_6)$ are given.

Prov.no.	y	y_{rough}	e_r=y-y_{rough}	rough eval.	y_{fuzzy}	e=y-y_{fuzzy}	fuzzy eval.
1	100	100	0	*	100	0.0114	M
2	3.79	8	-4.21	L	7.21	-3.42	L
3	16.2	8	8.23	H	12.8	3.43	H
4	27	27	0	*	27.9	-0.887	M
5	22.1	22.1	0	*	24.5	-2.37	L
6	5.39	8	-2.61	L	9.89	-4.5	L
7	8.43	9.61	-1.18	M	10.4	-1.93	M
8	12.8	8.32	4.52	H	13	-0.185	M
9	23.5	23.5	0	*	20.2	3.28	H
10	35.8	35.8	0	*	34.9	0.923	M
11	18.1	15.6	2.48	H	16.5	1.59	M
12	17.7	17.7	0	*	18	-0.244	M
13	16.7	15.6	1.11	M	16	0.703	M
14	46.7	46.7	0	*	41.8	4.97	H
15	10.8	9.61	1.18	M	11.9	-1.08	M
16	21.4	19.8	1.66	M	18.4	3.02	H
17	18.2	14.5	3.74	H	15.2	2.98	H
18	42.1	42.1	0	*	43.4	-1.31	M
19	12.2	15.6	-3.48	L	10.7	1.49	M
20	48.2	48.2	0	*	48.2	-0.00773	M
21	33.1	33.1	0	*	21.4	11.6	H
22	22.1	22.1	0	*	27.9	-5.84	L
23	3.64	8	-4.37	L	12.8	-9.19	L
24	28.6	25.8	2.8	H	17.9	10.7	H
25	2.83	8.32	-5.49	L	4.92	-2.09	L
26	14.1	14.5	-0.345	M	14.1	0.0241	M
27	21.3	21.3	0	*	30.9	-9.6	L
28	7.1	15.6	-8.53	L	12.4	-5.29	L
29	18	15.6	2.39	H	17.1	0.942	M
30	18.1	19.8	-1.66	M	19.6	-1.47	M
31	95.8	95.8	0	*	85.5	10.3	H
32	57.1	57.1	0	*	46.2	10.9	H
33	2.24	8.32	-6.08	L	6.31	-4.06	L
34	16.5	15.6	0.901	M	11.9	4.63	H
35	18.9	8.32	10.6	H	11.9	6.99	H
36	4.18	8.32	-4.15	L	5.88	-1.7	M
37	8.81	8.32	0.491	M	8.94	-0.13	M
38	12.9	8.32	4.53	H	10.1	2.78	H
39	11.1	14.5	-3.39	L	11.6	-0.564	M
40	9.08	9.68	-0.602	M	9.6	-0.526	M
41	37.8	38.4	-0.587	M	35.5	2.38	H
42	11	8	2.97	H	12.5	-1.52	M
43	11.2	8.32	2.87	H	12.1	-0.935	M
44	23	25.8	-2.8	L	17.2	5.84	H
45	12.6	9.68	2.96	H	9.36	3.28	H
46	7.32	9.68	-2.36	L	12	-4.65	L
47	39	38.4	0.587	M	37.6	1.38	M
48	1	8.32	-7.32	L	5.73	-4.73	L
49	20.8	15.6	5.12	H	14.7	6.09	H

Tab.5. Modeling results of the province product y_M and effectiveness evaluation of particular provinces in Poland (L-low, M-mean, H-high) based of the rough set- and the fuzzy model.

Below the fuzzy model classification of polish provinces in respect of their economic effectiveness is given:

high-effective provinces: *{3, 9, 14, 16, 17, 21, 24, 31, 32, 34, 35, 38, 41, 44, 45, 49},*
mean-effective provinces: *{1, 4, 7, 8, 10, 11, 12, 13, 15, 18, 19, 20, 26, 29, 30, 36, 37, 39, 40, 42, 43, 47},*
low-effective provinces: *{2, 5, 6, 22, 23, 25, 27, 28, 33, 46, 48}.*

4. CONCLUSIONS

To evaluate the province effectiveness a model is required that would approximate information samples of the problem. The model can be constructed both with rough and fuzzy sets. Surface of the rough set model changes rapidly. It consists of local hyper-rectangular submodels and is, from its nature, more "rough" than surface of a fuzzy model, which is smooth and is of more global character that surface of a rough set model. On the other hand, advantage of a rough set model is the fact that its local submodels, representing particular rules, are created only in these sectors of the input space where information samples exist. Therefore a rough set model does not contain "empty" rules, which often occur in fuzzy models. The rough set theory also enables easy determining insignificant inputs and their removal from the model (decreasing the model dimensionality), which is much more complicated in a fuzzy model. This is why a combination of the both modeling methods can scientifically be very attractive. And the authors of the paper propose such approach.

In the first step of the approach a rough model of the problem is constructed, the number of inputs is reduced and active regions of the reduced input space are detected. The rough set model provides us with rough knowledge of causalities existing between dependent and independent variables of the problem. In the second step, on the bases of the rough set model, a more accurate fuzzy model is created.

In the problem under consideration an important point of the fuzzy model was also its ability of evaluation of these 14 provinces that had not been evaluated by the rough set model because they were singletons in their classes. The fuzzy model could evaluate them owing to the smooth and more global character of its surface. The more precise fuzzy model evaluated 12 provinces differently than the rough set model did. However, in 11 cases the difference was the smallest possible one (1-class difference). It testifies to satisfactory accuracy of the rough set model.

5. BIBLIOGRAPHY

[1] *The Statistical Yearbook 1997*, The Main Statistical Office, Warsaw, Poland

[2] Mrożek A., Płonka L. (1999), *Data analysis by rough set method*, The Academic Publishing Office PLJ, Warsaw, Poland

[3] Pawlak Z. (2001), *Data analysis - the rough set perspective*, chapter in *Fuzzy models and their application*, edit. Chojcan J., Łęski J., Technical University of Śląsk - Publishing, Gliwice, Poland

[4] Piegat A. (2001), *Fuzzy modeling and control*, A Springer-Verlag Company, Heidelberg-New York

Evolutionarily Developed Neural Networks for Investment Strategies Construction

Janusz Morajda

Cracow University of Economics, Dept. of Computer Science, ul. Rakowicka 27, 31-510 Kraków, Poland; eimorajd@cyf-kr.edu.pl

Abstract. The study presents the idea of feedforward evolutionary neural network that utilizes (instead of classical training) a specific evolutionary procedure for network development. This procedure is responsible for network evolving, connections selection and weight values determination. Basic features of such networks and the algorithm of network development are submitted. Such a network has been applied to a problem of construction of investment strategy for Polish stock index WIG 20. The evolutionary network development process has been characterized and discussed. Relatively good results of application of generated by the network investment strategies have been obtained for the test data.

1 Introduction

Neural networks as well as evolutionary algorithms turned out to be applicable and effective tools in modeling complex, noisy and nonlinear systems, not excluding financial markets. Financial applications of such methods focus mainly on time series predictions and investment decision support [1, 2, 3].

A common approach utilizes multilayer perceptron or other type of feedforward network that is trained on selected learning data (usually with backpropagation algorithm) and afterwards generates forecasts or transaction signals. A great many variations of methods based on various types of neural networks have been developed and published [3]. Other techniques exploits evolutionary algorithms or fuzzy logic for decision rules development [1, 4]. A number of hybrid approaches have been also developed. The most popular hybrid methods in the financial field concern utilization of genetic algorithms for neural network design or input variable selection [2] (then the network usually undergoes classical training process).

Although many applications of computational intelligence techniques in financial markets have been reported as successful, no universal method has been established and commonly accepted as the most effective one. Consequently there is ongoing need for developing and testing new approaches to the problem of financial forecasting and decision support. The study, for this task, proposes evolutionary developed neural networks that can be regarded as a kind of evolutionary artificial neural networks (EANNs) [6].

2 The concept of evolutionarily developed neural networks

Proposed here evolutionarily developed neural networks (EDNN) process the data analogously to typical feedforward neural networks, however there are some crucial differences between them. The basic features of EDNN are as follows:

- **Neuron (cell) model** – classical (based on McCulloch and Pitts idea); in presented research hyperbolic tangent transfer function has been applied.
- **Data processing** – feedforward, starting from input cells (these cells only deliver an input pattern and do not process data) – see figure 1.
- **Training** – no training process is performed – weights of connections between cells are established once and they do not undergo any further modifications[1]; however, these connections and their weights (beginning from the second layer) are determined with utilization of specific evolutionary process of network development (see below) that uses a learning data set.
- **Network structure** – the network consists of a basic layer of ordered neurons (cells) and some "genetic" layers that can be treated as subsequent populations of neurons created in turn by a specific genetic algorithm used for the network development process. The connections leading to particular neuron are unknown *a priori* and are established by genetic selection while the neuron is being created. EDNN structures include much more cells than classical neural networks (a number of several thousands or more).
- **Network development** – at first, the basic layer with randomly determined values of weights is created. Next layers are developed in turn in evolutionary process that utilizes information included in learning data set. While a new neuron of such a layer is being created, it is being connected with a number of best evaluated cells belonging to previous layers. Then this neuron itself undergoes genetic evaluation on the basis of its output signals accuracy. Evaluation is performed for all learning (or validation) patterns with utilization of corresponding actual outputs of the system being modeled.
- **Cell evaluation criterion** – there is no need to use error function – a criterion based on the ultimate goal, the network is created for, can be applied.
- **Network output** – there is no pre-defined network output – each cell both performs data processing and generates output signals; however, when the network creation is completed, the ultimate output (outputs) are selected as the best evaluated network cells.

The structure of EDNN is depicted on figure 1, and the algorithm of evolutionary network development is presented below.

Let **j** denotes the number of currently considered neuron, and **l(j)** – the number of layer where the neuron **j** is placed. Let the algorithm parameters are denoted as follows: **I** – the number of inputs (input cells **j** = 1, 2, ..., **I** belong to the basic layer 1), **L** – the number of cells in the basic layer, **v** – the size of connections window in the basic layer, **b** – the number of being selected best evaluated cells,

[1] Nevertheless further weight tuning with a gradient method can be applied.

t – number of connections of each neuron in genetically created layers (2, 3, ...), **m** – number of cells in each "genetic" layer, **N** – total number of cells.

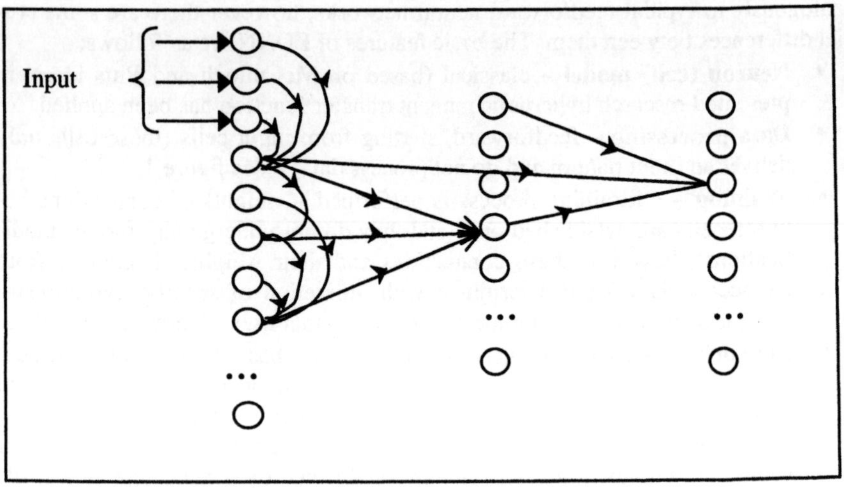

Fig. 1. The structure of EDNN. Basic layer, containing input cells and a number of data processing neurons, is depicted on the left side. Moving to the right, there are evolutionarily developed "genetic" layers. The data flow is directed from the top (input) to the bottom in the basic layer and then to the right through next layers.

The algorithm of network development process consists of the following steps:

Step 1. For each data processing neuron **j** in the basic layer (**j** = **I**+1, ..., **L** in turn):

- set connection with previous **v** cells (**j**-1, ..., **j**-**v**), or cells 1, 2, ..., **j** if **j**-**v** < 1
- for these connections determine weight values as random numbers from the selected range [-**a**, **a**] (where **a** > 0) and immediately rescale proportionally all weights (analyzing the input data set) so that the "working" area of transfer function is placed around 0.5 and –0.5 (in case of hyperbolic tangent); such operation prevents from decaying or overvaluing signals in large networks.

Step 2. Evaluate all cells in the basic layer (**j** = **I**+1, ..., **L**) on the basis of their signal accuracy according to accepted criterion, and then: **j** ← **L**+1 , **l**(**j**) ← 2

Step 3. Find the set **B** of **b** best evaluated neurons in layers 1, ..., **l**(**j**)-1

Step 4. Select the **t** cells from the set **B** using the roulette rule (i.e. method where selection probability is proportional to evaluation measure); this procedure is equivalent to selection operation in a classical genetic algorithm.

Step 5. Locate the cell **j** in layer **l**(**j**) and connect it with **t** cells selected in step 4. This is equivalent to genetic crossover operation (with **t** parents), as **t** cells "create" a new neuron **j** and pass to it their signals.

Step 6. Set the weights of connections as positive values proportional to evaluation measures of selected **t** cells. Then rescale all these weight values analogously to such operation in step 1.

Step 7. Evaluate the cell **j**.
Step 8. **j** ← **j**+1 , if ((**j**-**L**) mod **m**) = 1 then **l**(**j**) ← **l**(**j**)+1
Step 9. If **j** > **N** then establish ultimate network output as the best evaluated cell in the whole network and **STOP**, else go to step 3.

The operation of fully developed network begins from activating input neurons by input signals, then output signals of all cells are calculated in sequence (in order as the cells were created). The signals of the best cell (see step 9) are treated as ultimate network outputs.

Note that the connections and their weights were selected with utilization of learning data that determined cells evaluation, so the network can be susceptible to overfitting. Careful parameter selection should prevent it. There is also possibility of application of independent validation to cell evaluation. However, before putting into practice, the network should be tested using an independent test set.

3 Problem formulation

The considered problem deals with decision support concerning investments in Polish stock index WIG 20. Knowing forecasts of change between current and next-day close-session index quotations, an active investment strategy can be applied. Let us consider a strategy that assumes buying index (opening or preserving long position) when an increase of index value is forecasted, and selling it short (opening or preserving short position) in the opposite case.

The described above EDNN has been applied to this task, with assumption that positive output signal represents the index buy recommendation (long position), while negative signal implies short-selling decision (short position).

Six input variables have been (arbitrarily) selected: last logarithmic daily rate of return, difference of last two rates of return, index volatility as the mean of absolute values of last 10 return rates, 5-day trend indicator, 10-day *momentum* technical indicator, and 10-day *outbuying/outselling* technical indicator. All the input variables have been normalized.

The learning set consists of 1164 patterns (each of them includes 6 input values and corresponding future return rate – necessary for cell evaluation) from the period from 24th May 1994 (index value = 1245.4) to 25th February 1999 (index = 1243.3). The test set includes 682 patterns from 5th March 1999 (index = 1260.1) to 26th November 2001 (index = 1265.5).

The EDNN parameters (see section 2) were selected as follows: **I** = 6, **L** = 2000, **v** = 200, **b** = 50, **t** = 20, **m** = 200, **N** = 6000. So the network has 21 layers with 2000 cells in the basic layer and 4000 cells in 20 "genetic" layers.

The cells evaluation measure was the cumulative rate of return achieved by a particular cell for the learning set (learning data period) as a result of application of active investment strategy based on cell output signals[2]. Although financial

[2] Cells that have generated extremely bad results with negative return rate can be also well evaluated, but possible connections from them to other cells must have negative weights.

markets should be considered as nonstationary systems, the positive correlation between such return rates in in-sample and out-of-sample periods can be often observed. This fact allows to make presumption that well evaluated (in the sense of cumulative return rate) cells in the learning period will be also effective during the future operation.

4 Results

Figure 2, presents a typical process of EDNN development (it took about 270 s of processing time on Pentium III 800 MHz). The chart, for successively created network layers, shows averaged evaluation measure (rate of return) for learning period, and corresponding return rate values for test period.

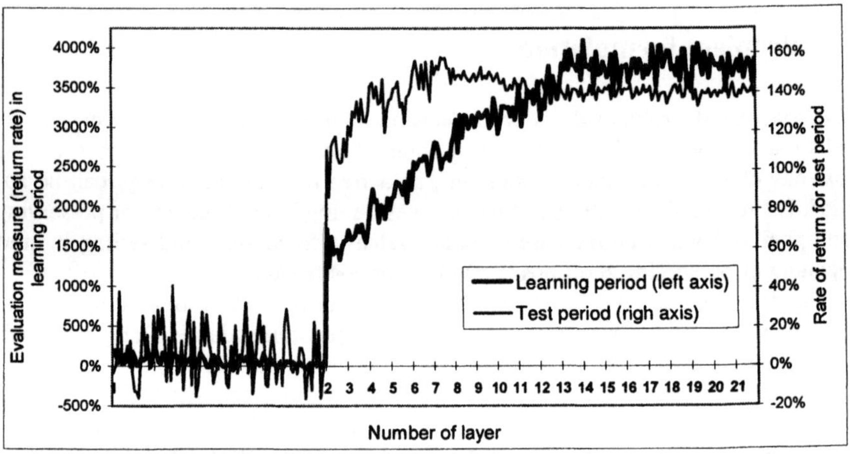

Fig. 2. Evaluation measure (cumulative rate of return) for successive cells in the EDNN for learning and test data. For better visualization, particular points on the chart represent average values from 20 cells, so individual cells may give outlying results. The horizontal axis represents successively created network cells (that process data in the same sequence).

The analysis of network development process (thick line) indicates that evaluation measure increases (first rapidly, then nearly linearly) achieving saturation state (typical for genetic optimization) at around 14th layer. The return rate in the test period behaves similarly at the beginning, however it achieves maximum in 7th layer, and then certain decrease (indicating slight data overfitting) and stabilization is observed. It suggests need for applying validation to prevent overfitting.

Next, the method has been assessed according to its effectiveness in the test period. In order to avoid accidental influence of randomly generated basic layer weights, the process of network development has been repeated 10 times, starting from different sets of weights in the first layer. Each network has been estimated according to the cumulative rate of return obtained as a result of application of network output signals in the test period (containing data not used at the stage of network development). The results are presented in table 1. Two strategies have been considered: strategy A – based on signals of the best cell of EDNN and strategy B – based on summarized signal of 5 best cells ("committee decision").

Table 1. Rates of return in % obtained by EDNN in the test period.

Strategy	Cumulative rates of return [%] for EDNNs 1-10										Mean	Std. dev.
A	160.0	41.3	186.9	96.9	45.1	107.6	66.6	220.7	158.6	17.9	**110.2**	**68.7**
B	109.0	80.3	178.5	97.3	41.2	24.6	66.6	62.7	122.7	75.2	**85.8**	**44.0**

All obtained return rates in test period are positive and in most cases fairly good. The application of strategy A is on average more profitable than B, but can be regarded as more risky (due to higher value of standard deviation).

The similar research concerning the same problem and the same data sets has been performed with utilization of Bayesian neural networks trained with back-propagation (with use of program *Neural Connection 2.1*) and obtained mean rate of return (for 100 different initial weight sets) for the test period was 75,8% (with standard deviation 48,4%). In comparison, the EDNN method has provided better results and can be regarded as a relatively effective tool in considered issue.

5 Final remarks

The EDNN networks proved to be effective tools in the financial decision support task and can be also useful in similar problems. Consequently, further research on the issue is worth performing. Various EDNN modifications can be considered, including network evolving (or re-development) during performance stage, incorporating mutation operator, or final weight tuning with classical learning methods.

References

1. Bauer R. (1994) Genetic Algorithms and Investment Strategies. Wiley, New York
2. Morajda J. (1999) Applications of Neural Networks in the Financial Markets – Selected Aspects. Proc. of the 4th Conf. "Neural Networks and Their Applications", Zakopane
3. Refenes A. P. (1995) Neural Networks in the Capital Markets. Wiley, Chichester
4. Rutkowska D., Piliński M., Rutkowski L. (1997) Neural Networks, Genetic Algorithms and Fuzzy Systems. PWN Warszawa-Łódź (in Polish)
5. Tadeusiewicz R. (1993) Neural Networks. AOW RM Warszawa (in Polish)
6. Yao X. (1995) Evolutionary Artificial Neural Networks. Encyclopedia of Computer Science and Technology, Marcel Dekker Inc., New York.

Credit Granting Procedure: Multilayer Perceptron and Classification Tree

Dorota Witkowska
Iwona Staniec

Technical University of Lodz
90-361 Lodz, Piotrkowska 266, Poland

Keywords: firm classification, artificial neural networks, classification tree.

Abstract: In the paper we discuss the results of the firm classification. For the purpose of the analysis we apply artificial neural networks and classification trees. In our investigation we use statistical data concerning 115 small enterprises that applied for a credit in two regional banks in Lodz. The aim of our research is to analyze the efficiency of above mentioned methods in the credit granting procedure.

1. Introduction

Traditionally credits are granted on the basis of credit scoring patterns using past experiences of the credit officers. This approach suffers, however, from: high costs of training of credit officers, frequent incorrect decisions made by credit officers, and different decisions made by different credit officers for the same case. These difficulties suggest the need to improve credit management decision that can be considered as classification problem.

2. Classification methods

For the purpose of classification numerous statistical methods and artificial neural networks (ANN) can be used. In our research we employ: artificial neural networks such as multilayer perceptron (MLP) that is trained applying backpropagation algorithm, and classification tree.

Classification tree is a very comfortable tool for the decision processes analysis, especially when these processes are characterized by certain degree of complexity. Classification trees are used for the cases or objects classification on the basis of one or more independent variable measurements. Leaves of the tree are related to classes that objects belong to. The branches represent values of features used for classification. Nodes represent semi sets, which are subject to the further partitions. The classification rules are defined in nodes. The characteristic features of classification trees are hierarchical nature and elasticity.

The classification tree creation is the process of the recurrent partition of the training set into semi sets to obtain homogenous - in terms of the objects membership - classes. In practice one is aiming to create classification tree with the lowest possible number of nodes, that is to obtain the simplest classification rules. The decision tree construction consists of four stages: (1) definition of the classification accuracy measure, (2) selection of the partition method, (3) selection of the "halt rule", and (4) selection of the classification tree structure.

3. Data description

In our investigation, we use data regarding 115 small companies that applied for a credit in the period from 1994 to 1997 in two regional banks in Lodz (75 firms in one of the banks and 40 in another). The value of the credit varied from $140 to $1600 of monthly credit repayments, which have to be paid in the period not longer than 5 years. To consider a company as a potential borrower, credit offices evaluate the economic and financial situation of companies and, applying credit-scoring method, they decide if the credit is to be allowed.

It is worth mentioning that banks are not allowed to inform about their clients. Thus we obtain only limited data that let us to describe each enterprise by nine variables: (a) - the gross profit, (b) - the net profit, (c) - the average net monthly profit, (d) - the monthly repayment of the credit, (e) - the value of maximal monthly interest, (f) - the average monthly repayment of the credit and the interest, (g) - the monthly liabilities to other banks and institutions, (h) - the residual monthly profit, (i) - the decision about allowing the credit (i=0 or i=1).

To employ supervised learning methods of classification it is necessary to divide the all inestigated cases into two separable sets i.e. training and testing sets. The parameters of neural networks and classification tree are estimated on the basis of the same data. The training set contains 75 firms (that applied for a credit in the "first" bank) or 85 elements (- i.e. 75 enterprises from the "first" bank and 10 from the "second" bank). The testing set contains 40 or 30 firms respectively (i.e. enterprises applied for a credit in the "second" bank).

4. Numerical experiments

All enterprises (89 firms that obtained credits and 26 that were rejected by the bank experts) are classified employing STATISTICA™ v. 5. 5.

Efficiency of classification is evaluated by comparison of our solutions to the credit granting decisions (since the banks are not willing to inform if their decisions were correct). The accuracy of classification is usually measured in terms of classification errors. The percentage general classification error can be defined as:

$$E = \frac{K}{N} \cdot 100\% \qquad (1)$$

where: K is the number of misclassified firms, N is the number of all firms.

We may also consider the p-class classification error that is defined as follows:

$$E_p = \frac{K^*_p}{N_q} \cdot 100\% \tag{2}$$

where: K^*_p is the number of firms that originally belong to the class q but they are classified to the class p with $p \neq q$, N_q is the number of firms originally belonging to the class q $(p, q = 1, 2)$.

Let us assume that the class p=1 contains creditworthy clients (i.e. enterprises that obtained the credit) and the class p=2 includes uncreditworthy clients. Considering the bank point of view, the error of the first kind E_1 is the most important. Since it informs about the percentage share of misclassified to the class p=1 clients (i.e. firms that should not obtain the credit) in the total number of the enterprises evaluated by the bank as uncreditworthy firms. The error of the second kind E_2 describes the share of enterprises that will not obtain the credit, though they are the creditworthy firms, in the total number of creditworthy firms.

The results of numerical experiments - in terms of classification errors - are presented in tables. The numbers in parenthesis (below values of the first and the second kind errors) denote the position of the enterprise in the whole set of investigated firms. Experiments are provided for two training and testing sets structures, i. e. 75/40 and 85/30.

4.1. Back propagation algorithm

MLP experiments are described by the network topology (for instance the network denoted as 8-3-1 contains eight input variables, three hidden neurons and one output variable), and the number of iterations provided for the ANN training.

Table 1. Classification errors: MLP trained using back-propagation algorithm

Network topology	Number iteration	Training set 75 elements			Testing set 40 elements		
		E	E_1	E_2	E	E_1	E_2
8-3-1	10 000	1.33	0	1.82 (57)	10.0	0	11.76 (76, 82, 87, 96)
8-5-1	10 000	0	0	0	7.50	0	8.82 (76, 87, 96)
8-5-1	15 000	0	0	0	7.50	0	8.82 (76, 87, 96)
8-5-1	25 000	0	0	0	7.50	0	8.82 (76, 87, 96)

Source: Authors' calculations.

Analyzing the results of the MLP training for 75 elements (Table 1), one can notice that 8-5-1 networks learn to recognize all enterprises that applied for the credit. The network 8-3-1 misclassifies the firm denoted as (57). During testing procedure, all networks generate the errors of the first kind equal to zero and, regardless the number of iterations, for the networks 8-5-1 the general classification error is 7.5%. In all experiments the same enterprises, i.e.: (76), (87) and (96), are misclassified. The network 8-3-1 also misrecognized the firm (82).

Analyzing the results of the MLP training for 85 elements (Table 2) one can notice that, regardless the network topology, all networks misclassify firms denoted as: (43), (57), (76), (82), (87) as well as (96) and generate errors of the second kind in the testing set.

Table 2. Classification errors: MLP trained using back-propagation algorithm

Network topology	Number iteration	Training set 85 elements			Testing set 30 elements		
		E	E_1	E_2	E	E_1	E_2
8-3-1	10000	4.71	5.00 (43)	4.62 (57, 76, 82)	6.67	0	8.33 (87,96)
8-5-1	10000	4.71	5.00 (43)	4.62 (57, 76, 82)	6.67	0	8.33 (87,96)
8-5-1	15000	4.71	5.00 (43)	4.62 (57, 76, 82)	6.67	0	8.33 (87,96)
8-5-1	25000	4.71	5.00 (43)	4.62 (57, 76, 82)	6.67	0	8.33 (87,96)

Source: Authors' calculations

4. 2. Classification Tree

The tree identification procedure seems to be suitable since it does not require data preprocessing to find out sufficient features. As one can notice (Table 3), the most important, in terms of the credit grating decisions, variables are: (h) the residual monthly profit - 100, (c) the average net monthly profit - 61, (b) the net profit - 57, and (a) the gross profit - 55.

Table 3. Discriminant variable ranking (0=low; 100=high)

Features	Rank	Features	Rank	Features	Rank	Features	Rank
(h)	100	(b)	57	(g)	20	(f)	5
(c)	61	(a)	55	(e)	7	(d)	2

Source: Authors' calculations

We consider two variants of the classification tree (i.e. one - and two - nodes tree). On the basis of cost analysis (Table 4), the two - nodes tree is selected.

Table 4. Statistics evaluated for investigated trees

Symbol of the classification tree	Number of nodes	Cost SK.	Std. deviation	Error cost	Node complex
T1*	2	0.02667	0.0186	0.026	0.00
T2	1	0.26667	0.0510	0.266	0.24

Source: Authors' calculations

Note: The select tree is denoted by *.

At the beginning of the tree creation process all objects are temporally assigned to the source node, i.e. to the class of firms that obtained the credit. Subsequently the source node (i.e. node No. 1) is divided into two new nodes (Figure 1). The objects, for which the residual monthly profit is not greater than 491,84, are assigned to the node No. 2, and qualified as incredible clients. The number of such cases is 22. The remaining cases are assigned to the node No. 3, i.e. to the group of creditworthy firms. Thus during classification procedure we obtain 53 firms that are recognized as credible clients.

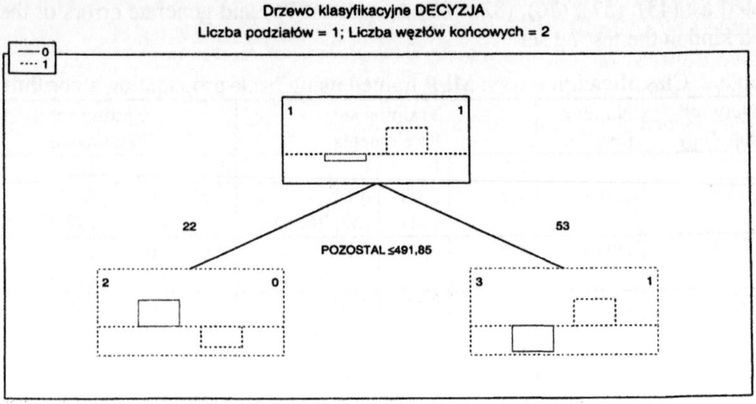

Fig. 1. The selected classification tree
Source: Authors' calculations

Table 5. Classification errors: classification tree

Training set 75 elements			Testing set 40 elements		
E	E1	E2	E	E1	E2
2.67%	0	3.63% (57, 74)	10%	0	11.76% (76, 82, 87, 96)

Source: Authors' calculations

In the training set two companies are misclassified. While in the test set four companies are misclassified. In both sets the rejected (by the bank experts) cases are properly identified, all misclassifications concern firms that obtained credits. Therefore we can say that the credit officers were more optimistic.

Comparing the results that we obtain using MLP and classification tree we notice that the same enterprises are misrecognized, and MLP classification is slightly more accurate.

Employing the training set that includes 85 elements we find out that the same discriminant variables are essential in the credit granting procedure as we observed for the previously presented experiment. But the values of variable rank are usually bigger, i.e.: (h) the residual monthly profit - 100, (c) the average net monthly profit - 70, (b) the net profit – 67, and (a) the gross profit - 65.

Since the same features are used for partition in both experiments, we obtain the same results of classification (compare Tables 6 and 5). Analyzing the classification errors generated by MLP and classification tree for the training and testing sets structure 85/30 we can see that the errors are the same for both methods though MLP misclassifies the firm (43) and the classification tree – the firm (74).

Table 6. Classification errors: classification tree

Training set 85 elements			Testing set 30 elements		
E	E1	E2	E	E1	E2
4.7%	0	6.15% (57, 74, 76, 82)	6.67%	0	8.33% (87, 96)

Source: Authors' calculations

It is worth adding that in previously provided research (Witkowska et al., 2001) the clients denoted as: (57), (76), (87) and (96) were always misclassified. Thus it seems that the credit officers applied different rules to evaluation these firms.

5. Conclusion

Taking into account the results of our experiments, it is visible that MLP and classification tree generate similar classes. Both methods "learn from the experience". Thus the data sets that are used for training are extremely important. It is necessary to have the wide representation of all probable cases that requires a huge number of observations. In our investigation we use the limited data regarding 115 firms applying for a credit in two banks.

Our research shows that classification trees as well as MLP can be successfully used as an alternative methods of classification, especially when it is impossible to fulfil the assumptions that are required by other methods. There are two major classification tree advantages:

- the tree graph represents all information in straight manner, immediate and easy to interpretation;
- large elasticity of trees permits to evaluate the influence of each variable.

It is worth mentioning that, regardless the structure of the training and testing sets, we obtain the same results of classification.

References

Wilson R. L., Sharda R., (1994) Bankruptcy Prediction Using Neural Networks, Decision Support Systems, 11, 545 - 557.

Witkowska D., Kamiński W., Staniec I.: Credit granting procedure: artificial neural networks, discriminant analysis, k-means method, IFAC Symposium on Modeling and Control of Economic Systems, Klagenfurt, Austria, September 6-8, 2001, s. 239-241.

Reliability Analysis of Structures by Neural Network Supported Monte Carlo Methods

Joanna Kaliszuk[1] and Zenon Waszczyszyn[2]

[1] Department of Civil and Environmental Engineering, University of Zielona Góra, ul. Prof. Z. Szafrana 2 , 65-516 Zielona Góra, e-mail: j.kaliszuk@uz.zgora.pl
[2] Institute of computer Methods in Civil Engineering, Cracow University of Technology, ul. Warszawska 24, 31-155 Kraków, e-mail: zenwa@twins.pk.edu.pl

Abstract. A forward neural network is used for generating samples in the Monte Carlo Methods. The patterns for network training and testing are computed by a FE program. A high numerical efficiency of the proposed approach is demonstrated on example of a plane multistorey elastoplastic frame.

1. Introduction

The assessment of structural reliability needs the probabilistic analysis [3]. Complexity of analysis can be overcome by computer simulations and especially by those associated with Monte Carlo methods [2, 6]. The simplest, classical (crude) Monte Carlo method (CMC) corresponds to generating samples which are then randomly selected and examined whether they fulfill the reliability criteria. The Importance Sampling Monte Carlo simulation (ISM) is a more advanced method and it needs a smaller number of random trials than CMC to estimate the probability of reliability [6].

In structural engineering the samples are usually computed by the Finite Element Method (FEM) programs [4, 5]. A great number of samples is needed in the MC simulation so application of FEM program is numerically inefficient for large scale problems because of high computational time. That is why in [4] neural networks are suggested for generating samples for the MC simulation.

In the paper the idea taken from [7] is developed and examined on an example of a plane elastoplastic frame with random yield points of frame members. The FEM program [6] is used for computing patterns corresponding to the ultimate loads of the frame. A simple back-propagation neural network trained on such patterns enables us to quickly generate samples for the MC simulation.

2. Structural failure, reliability and Monte Carlo simulation

Stationary type structural problems are analyed and the probability of failure for a fixed time is defined by the following relationship:

$$\bar{p}_f = \text{Prob}\{G(\mathbf{X}) \equiv R - S \leq 0\} = \int_{G(\mathbf{X})\leq 0} f(\mathbf{X})\, d\mathbf{X} \tag{1}$$

where: p_f – probability of failure, R – resistance of structure, S – actions (loads) applied to structure, $\mathbf{X} = [\mathbf{X}^R, \mathbf{X}^S]$ – vector of random variables. The complement of p_f is the probability of reliability $p_r = 1 - p_f$ that the structure will not fail.

The Monte Carlo simulation corresponds to computation of integer in Eq.(1). Following the law of large numbers the Classical Monte Carlo (CMC) estimator of the probability of failure is:

$$\bar{p}_f = \frac{1}{N}\sum_{i=1}^{N} I(\mathbf{X}_i) \qquad I(\mathbf{X}_i) = \begin{cases} 1 & \text{for} \quad G(\mathbf{X}_i) \le 0 \\ 0 & \text{for} \quad G(\mathbf{X}_i) > 0 \end{cases} \tag{2}$$

In order to improve the CMC computational efficiency the Importance Sampling MC method (SMC) is recommended [6], associated with the following estimator:

$$\bar{p}_f = \frac{1}{N}\sum_{i=1}^{N} K(\mathbf{X}_i) \qquad K(\mathbf{X}_i) = \begin{cases} f(\mathbf{X}_i)/g(\mathbf{X}_i) & \text{for} \quad G(\mathbf{X}_i) \le 0 \\ 0 & \text{for} \quad G(\mathbf{X}_i) > 0 \end{cases} \tag{3}$$

where: $f(\mathbf{X})$ – probability density function, $g(\mathbf{X})$ – importance sampling function.

3. Computing of patterns by FEM and generating of samples by a neural network

The only possibility for generating samples for the MC simulation is the use of Finite Elements Method (FEM) programs in order to compute values of the resistance function $R = R(\{X_j\}_p)$, where: X_{jp} – selected components of the state vector $\mathbf{X}_p$ for patterns $p = 1,\ldots, P$. In a special case of plane, elastoplastic frames the structural resistance corresponds to the ultimate load factor $R_p = P_{ult}(\{X_j\}_p)$ and the function of action is related to the load factor, i.e. $S = P$. The pairs of patterns $\{(\mathbf{X}_p, R_p)\}$ are used for the training and testing of a forward neural network. The trained network is used for computing samples R_i for values of inputs $\{\mathbf{X}_i\}$ randomly selected from sets of variables generated according to assumed distribution of probability density functions.

4. Reliability of a plane elastoplastic frame

A two bay four-storey frame, taken from [5], was used as an example to present the numerical efficiency of the discussed approach. The frame data, shown in Fig.1, was analysed by the FE program ELPLAF-v1 basing on [7].

Perfect elastoplastic material, distributed yielding zones and the second order geometrically nonlinear theory were assumed. The ultimate load corresponds to the limit load of the frame global buckling $P_{ult} = P_{L\,buckling}$. The computation were carried out for two inputs $X_1 = R_c$ and $X_2 = R_b$, where: R_c, R_b – yield points of the frame columns and beams, respectively. The normal probability function for both the yield points was assumed with the mean value $\mu = 240$ MPa and standard deviation $\sigma = 24$ MPa. The values of the frame ultimate load were computed as the

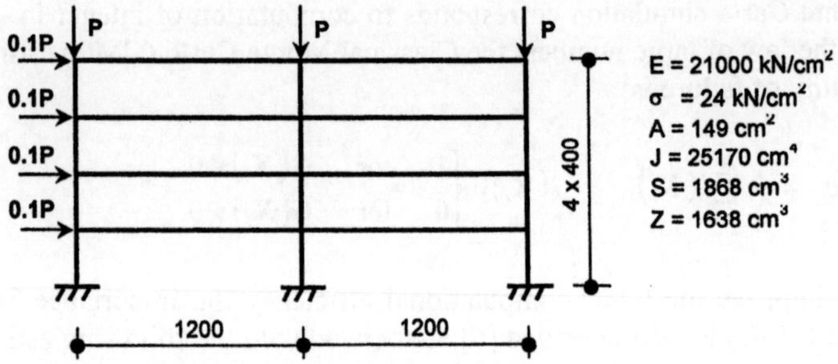

Fig. 1. Data for the considered elastoplastic frame

neural network output $y = R = P_{\text{ult}}\ (R_c, R_b)$. The ultimate load for mean yield points was $R_0 = P_{\text{ult}}\,(\mu, \mu) = 1042.3$ KN and then the patterns were computed for $R_c, R_b \in [\mu - 3\sigma, \mu + 3\sigma]$, corresponding to regular mesh of 16×16 points which gave $L = 256$ patterns for the network training . $T = 100$ testing inputs were randomly selected points at the above defined input domain.

A very simple network BPNN + M : 2 –3 –1 was trained by the BP + Momentum learning method and then tested using the MATLAB Neural Network Toolbox [1]. The following errors are listed in Table 1:

$$\text{avr}\, ep = \frac{1}{V}\sum_{p=1}^{V} ep \qquad \max ep = \max\left\{ep \,\middle|\, p = 1,\dots,V\right\} \quad \text{for} \quad ep = \left|\frac{1 - y_{(p)}}{t_{(p)}}\right| \cdot 100\%$$

$$RMS = \sqrt{\frac{1}{V}\sum_{p=1}^{V}\left(t_{(p)} - y_{(p)}\right)^2} \tag{4}$$

where: $V = L, T$ – number of patterns for the network training and testing, respectively, t_p, y_p – output values for known and neurally computed outputs for the p-th pattern. The regression coefficient r was computed for the set full set of pairs $\{t_p, y_p\}$, where $p = 1,\dots, L+T$.

Table 1. Errors of neural approximation

Process	*avr ep* [%]	*max ep* [5%]	*RMSE*	*r*
Training	0.379	2.128	0.004822	0.9996
Testing	0.387	1.118	0.004760	0.9980

Three cases of MC simulation were analyzed. They are put together in Table 2. In case 1 two random variables were considered, i.e. $X_1 = R_c$, $X_2 = R_b$ and in case 2 and 3 only one random variable was assumed, i.e. either R_c or R_b are taken into account.

Table 2. Simulation cases of random variables

Case	Random variable	*PDF*	Mean value μ	Standard dev. σ
1	S [kN]	*Log-N*	6.592	0.2
	R_c [MPa]	*N*	240	24
	R_b [Mpa]	*N*	240	24
2	S [kN]	*Log-N*	6.592	0.2
	R_c [MPa]	*N*	240	24
3	S [kN]	*Log-N*	6.592	0.2
	R_b [Mpa]	*N*	240	24

The results of computation of the probability of failure p_f by formulae (2) and (3) are shown in Table 3. In all the three cases the (SMC) method gave acceptable value of p_f for significantly lower number of simulation than CMC. The simulation by SMC was performed for the importance sampling function $g\ (\mathbf{X}_i)$ with the normal PDF of parameters μ= 1042.3 kN and σ= 165 kN.

Table 3. Estimation of the frame failure probability by Monte Carlo simulations

Number of simulations	Case 1		Case 2		Case 3	
	CMS	SMS	CMS	SMS	CMS	SMS
50	0.0200	0.0502	0.0200	0.0553	0.0000	0.0333
100	0.0400	0.0493	0.0400	0.0501	0.0400	0.0371
1000	0.0500	0.0539	0.0670	0.0556	0.0550	0.0420
2000	0.0585	0.0573	0.0590	0.0533	0.0420	0.0415
5000	0.0552	0.0570	0.0622	0.0537	0.0446	0.0425
10000	0.0555	0.0558	0.0586	0.0541	0.0420	0.0415
50000	0.0578	0.0562	0.0546	0.0563	0.0418	0.0417
100000	0.0551	0.0558	0.0550	0.0550	0.0416	0.0416

CMS crude Monte Carlo simulations , SMC Important Sampling Monte Carlo simulations

In Fig.2 there are shown the points on the (R, S) plane corresponding to 10000 trials of the CMC and IMC simulations. They are related to Cases 1 and 3.

These figures correspond to Fig.3 where the probability of the frame reliability p_r is shown as a function of the load factor P for the three considered cases. It is visible that Cases 1 and 2 coincide. Another situation takes place in Case 3 in which the yield point of beams is fixed, i.e. R_c = 240 MPa . That is why at P_{ult}= 1042 kN the ultimate load reaches the value 1042 kN and probability of reliability falls down to zero, i.e. $p_r\,(P{=}1042) = 0$.

The reliability curve $p_r\,(P)$ enables us to estimate the value of the load factor P at the assumed probability of the frame reliability. For instance in Fig.3 it is shown that for p_r = 0.9 the corresponding load equals P = 927 kN for Cases 1 and 2 , and P = 1023 kN for Case 3 of random variables selection, respectively.

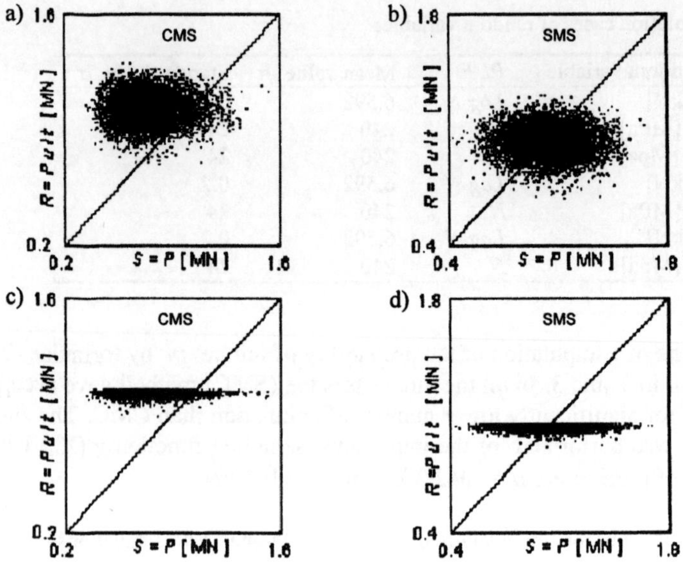

Fig. 2. Monte Carlo simulations for 10000 trials: **a, b)** Case 1, **c, d)** Case 3

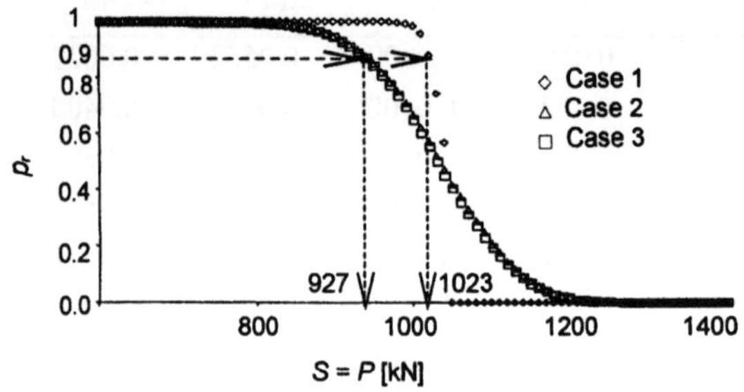

Fig. 3. Reliability curves $p_r(P)$ of the elastoplastic frame for three cases of the random variables selection

The computations were performed on PC AMD A1000 under Windows 98. During the computations the CPU time was evaluated. It was stated that the time of computation of a single pattern by the FE program was in-between 10.2 to 83.2 sec., on average about 32 sec. (2077 sec. for generating 67 patterns). The projection of this time for generating 1000 samples for the MC simulation gives $32\text{x}1000 = 3.2 \text{ x } 10^4$ sec.

The CPU time needed for evaluation of one point at the probability curve in Fig.2., using the neural network for generating 100 000 samples, was 1.2 sec. for CMC and 1.8 sec. for SMC. That means that the neural network needs the CPU time of order 10^{-4} lower than using the FE program for generating 1000 samples.

A simple model of frame was applied in [5] for computation of the ultimate load of the frame shown in Fig.1. Due to the assumption of plastic hinges and geometrically linear theory the time of computation of p_r at 1000 samples was about 0.6 x 10^4 sec. In [4] the CPU time for 100 000 MC simulations was about 10 sec. but the network was of structure 2-6-1 and the frame was bigger than the frame in Fig.1.

5. Some conclusions

1. Application of neural networks for generating samples for the MC simulation can significantly shorten the CPU time needed for computation of the probability of reliability of the frame considered.
2. In the paper a comparatively simple example of a plane elastoplastic frame has been discussed. The proposed approach can be applied to the analysis of other types of structures, (e.g. plates and shells) and other random variables (e.g. changes of member cross-sections, local and global structural imperfections).
3. A more realistic evaluation of advantages of the approach for engineering design purposes needs a much more extended numerical analysis of various structures as well as it certainly will depend on types and number of random variables.

Acknowledgement. Financial support by the Polish Committee for Scientific Research, Grant No 8 T07E 020 22 "Applications of artificial neural networks in the analysis of steel structures" is gratefully acknowledged.

References

1. Denmuth H., Beale M. (1998) Neural network toolbox for use with Matlab, User's Guide, Version 3. The Math Works
2. Marek P, Brozzetti J, Guštar M (2001) Probabilistic assessment o structures using Monte Carlo Simulation engineers. TERECO, ITAM CAS CR Prague
3. Murzewski J. (1989) Reliability of engineering structures (in Polish). Arkady Warszawa
4. Papadrakakis M, Papadopoulos V., Lagaros N.D. (1996) Structural reliability analysis of elastic-plastic structures using neural network and Monte Carlo simulation. Computer Methods in Applied Mechanics and Engineering, 136: 145-163
5. Pulido J.E., Jacobs T.L., Prates de Lima E.C. (1992) Structural reliability using Monte Carlo simulation with variance reduction techniques on elastic-plastic structures. Computers & Structures, 43: 419-430
6. Rubinstein RY (1981) Simulation and the Monte Carlo method. John Wiley & Sons, New York
7. Waszczyszyn Z., Pabisek E. (2002) Elastoplastic analysis of plane steel frames by a new superelement. Archives of Civil Engineering, (in press).

BP Neural Network Computation of Response Spectra Using a Subpicture Idea

Krystyna Kuźniar

Pedagogical University of Cracow, ul. Podchorążych 2, 30-084 Kraków, Poland
e-mail: kkuzniar@wsp.krakow.pl

Abstract. The paper deals with an application of neural networks for computation of response spectra on the fourth floor of a prefabricated medium height building under seismic-type excitations. The subpicture idea from picture transmission is also adapted to this problem. Both the training and testing patterns were formulated on the basis of measurements performed on an actual structure. Neurally evaluated spectra were compared with spectra computed on the basis of experimental data. The main advantage of the neural approach with the subpicture idea is that the prediction of building response spectra can be performed using very simple neural networks and without analysis of structural motion equations.

1 Introduction

The technical state of real buildings subjected to seismic-type (paraseismic) excitations can be estimated on the basis of dynamic responses of buildings. Both seismic-type excitations and dynamic responses are described by response spectra very often. The main problem discussed in the paper was formulated for the neural mapping of a response spectrum from excitation into a response spectrum from a selected building floor vibrations. The subpicture idea from picture transmission technique [3] was applied. In this field of knowledge, pictures are subdivided into frames (subpictures) and each frame is transmitted separately. In the paper an analogous idea has been introduced for response spectra.

2 Measurements on an actual building

The analysis concerns a medium height (5-storey), prefabricated, residential building BSK type i.e. a typical building with load-bearing walls erected using block technology. The building is founded directly on the ground using concrete strip footings. The plan and vertical section of a segment of the building are shown in Fig. 1.

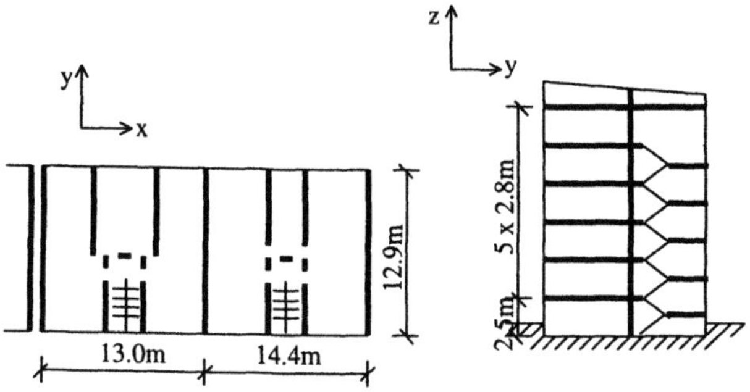

Fig. 1. Plan and vertical section of the building BSK type

Full-scale tests were conducted. The explosions in a nearby quarry were the sources of building vibrations. The measurements were performed many times [1,2]. Data for the analysis have been completed as pairs: excitation-response. From among many experimental tests, sixteen measurements of horizontal vibrations in transverse direction of building (y) were taken into consideration. The seismographs were located on the ground and on the fourth floor of the building. From each of the records of displacements in time domain, both with respect to excitations and responses, the displacement response spectrum (S_d) was computed. A fraction of critical damping $\varphi = 2\%$ was assumed [1]. In Fig. 2 there are shown selected displacement response spectra from an excitation record on the ground level and from the corresponding response record on the fourth floor level, respectively.

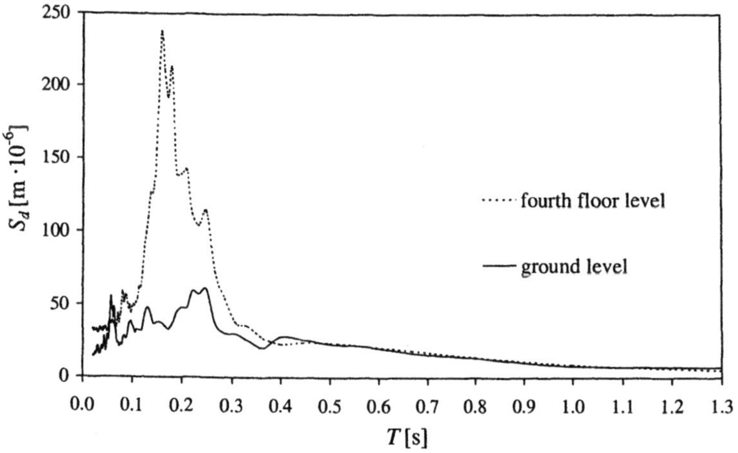

Fig. 2. Displacement spectra recorded on the ground level and on the fourth floor level

3 Neural network computation of response spectra

The paper deals with an application of neural technique for evaluation of a relation between the response spectrum on a ground level and response spectrum on the fourth floor level. These spectra were subdivided into segments for this purpose. Each part of the excitations response spectra was mapped into a corresponding value of response spectra from records on the building fourth floor. The vibration periods (T_i) were taken from the range 0.02 – 1.3sec. with the step 0.25Hz. Thus 198 discrete values of displacement response spectrum $S_d(T_i)$ were obtained from each of the analysed records (both on the ground level and on the fourth floor level).

The following input vector was proposed:

$$\mathbf{x}_{(6x1)} = \{ S_{dg}(T_{i-2}), S_{dg}(T_{i-1}), S_{dg}(T_i), S_{dg}(T_{i+1}), S_{dg}(T_{i+2}), T_i \} \tag{1}$$

where: T_{i-2}, T_{i-1}, T_i, T_{i+1}, T_{i+2} – successive vibration periods, i = 3, ..., 196; S_{dg} – displacement response spectrum from excitation record (on the ground level).

The corresponding value of displacement response spectrum from record on the fourth floor was expected as the output of neural network:

$$\mathbf{y}_{(1x1)} = \{ S_{df}(T_i) \} \tag{2}$$

where i = 3, ..., 196 for each of sixteen excitation-response analysed pairs.

Back-propagation neural networks with Resilient back-propagation learning method were formulated. The SNNS program, Version 4.2 [4] was used. The sigmoid activation function was applied, so all the input and output parameters were scaled to the range [0.1, 0.9].

Because of network approximation, the network error (Mean Square Error *MSE*) was computed:

$$MSEV = \frac{1}{V}\sum_{p=1}^{V}(y_p - \hat{y}_p)^2 \tag{3}$$

where: V – number of patterns, y_p and $\hat{y}_p$ – values of pth pattern computed on the basis of recorded vibrations and neurally predicted, respectively.

Relative errors were also computed:

$$e_p = \left|1 - \frac{\hat{y}_p}{y_p}\right| \cdot 100\%, \qquad e_{avr} = \frac{1}{V}\sum_{p=1}^{V} e_p, \qquad e_{\max} = \max_p e_p \tag{4}$$

From the experimental data P = 3104 patterns were arranged in sixteen groups of measurements results (194 patterns in each group). In the first step of analysis, every measurement was taken as the learning set and the testing set was composed of the remaining patterns. The networks of structure $6-5-1$ were formulated. The main goal of this stage was to select patterns with smallest network learning error (*MSEL*), smallest network average and maximal testing errors (*MSET*) and smallest number of learning epochs. Such patterns were taken as the learning patterns in the next step of analysis with learning set composed of $n_L = 2, 3, 4, 5$ and 8 measurements in sequence. The errors corresponding to the training and testing processes for 5 and 8 measurements taken for learning are collected in Table 1.

Table 1. Errors of neural networks of structure $6-5-1$

n_L	Number of patterns		*MSEL*	Number of	*MSET*		e_{avr} [%]		Correlation
	L	*T*		epochs	average	max	*L*	*T*	coefficient
5	970	2134	0.00010	3000	0.00072	0.00217	5.2	9.2	0.687
8	1552	1552	0.00007	3000	0.00065	0.00161	3.8	8.1	0.791

In Fig. 3 the relative average errors computed for each of the measurements are presented for networks mentioned in Table 1.

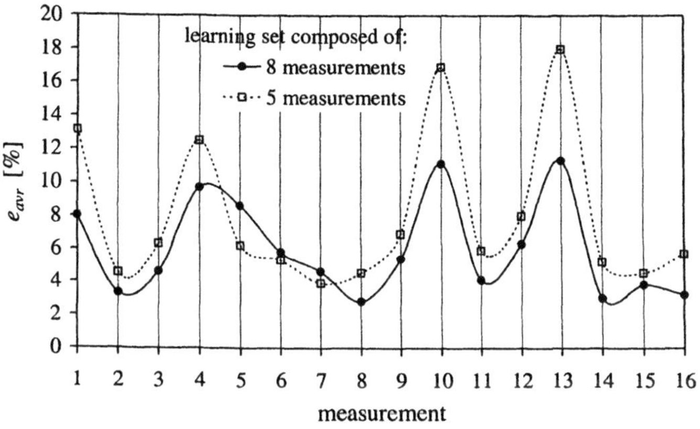

Fig. 3. Relative average errors computed for each of measurements

In Fig. 4 the Success Ratio as the function $SR(e_p)$ [%] is presented for the prediction of displacement response spectra on the fourth floor of the building using the neural networks mentioned above. This function enables us to evaluate what percentage of patterns gives the neural prediction with the error not greater than an e_p[%].

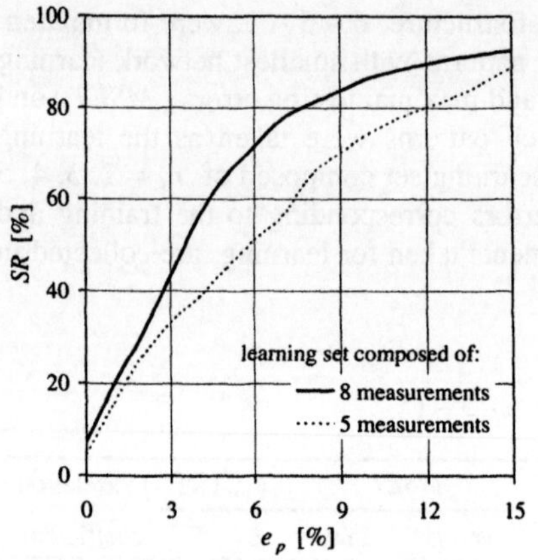

Fig. 4. Success Ratio *SR* vs. relative error e_p for the neural prediction of response spectra

a)

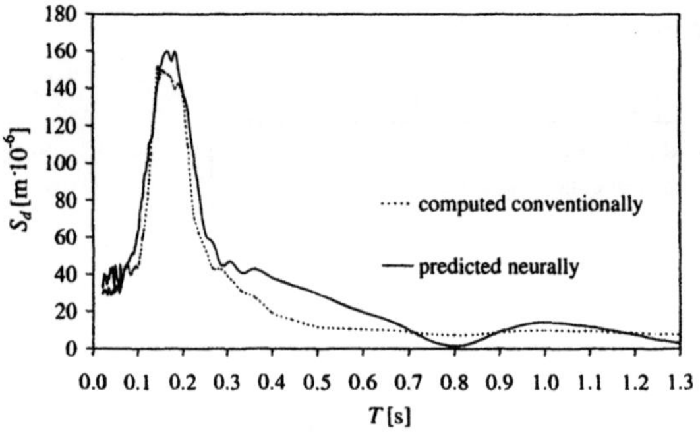

b)

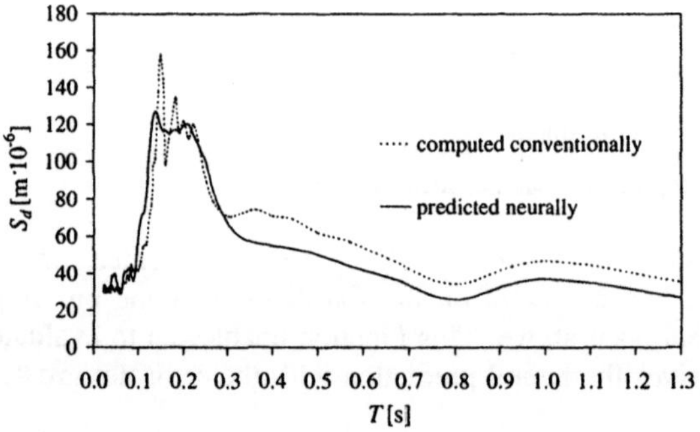

Fig. 5. Comparison of displacement response spectra on the fourth floor of the building computed conventionally and predicted neurally

In Fig. 5 there are shown some examples of comparison of conventionally computed and neurally predicted displacement response spectra on the fourth floor of the building, using the network with training set composed of 50% of all patterns (8 measurements). It was stated (cf. Table 1, Fig. 4, Fig. 5) that the neurally predicted displacement response spectra were very close to the corresponding spectra computed conventionally.

4 Conclusions

- The main advantage of the neural approach with the subpicture approach is that the prediction of building response can be performed using very simple networks and without analysis of motion equations of the considered structure.
- Application of very simple BP network with training set composed of 50% of all patterns enables us to predict the spectra with satisfactory accuracy.
- The neurally predicted displacement response spectra on the fourth floor of the building are very close to spectra calculated conventionally.

Financial support by the Polish Committee for Scientific Research, Grant No 8 T07E 028 20 "Application of neural networks in problems of response spectra, response simulation and identification of dynamic parameters of structures" is gratefully acknowledged.

References

1. Ciesielski R., Kuźniar K., Maciąg E., Tatara T. (1995) Damping of Vibration in Precast Buildings with Bearing Concrete Walls. Arch. Civil Eng. **41**, 3, 329-341
2. Ciesielski R., Kuźniar K., Maciąg E., Tatara T. (1992) Empirical Formulae for Fundamental Natural Periods of Buildings with Load Bearing Walls. Arch. Civil Eng. **38**, 4, 291-299
3. Osowski S. (1996) Neural Networks – An Algorithmic Approach (in Polish). Wydawnictwa Naukowo-Techniczne, Warszawa
4. Zell A. ed. (1998) SNNS – Stuttgart Neural Network Simulator. User's Manual, Version 4.2

Neural Networks in Updating of Dynamic Models with Experimental Verification

Bartosz Miller[1] and Leonard Ziemiański[1]

[1]Rzeszów University of Technology, ul. W.Pola 2, 35-959 Rzeszów, Poland

Abstract. This paper presents the application of artificial neural networks in updating of dynamic models of engineering structures. There are presented examples of updating of two models: a model of a beam hung on two strings and a model of a portal frame. There are used multi-layer feed-forward networks and networks with radial basis function, the input vectors consist of preprocessed data obtained from the measurements done on a laboratory models of considered structures.

1 Introduction

The detailed analysis of engineering structures requires very precise dynamic models of considered structures. The intensive technical progress enables the application of very complicated models with the very large number of degrees of freedom (DOF). However, the increase in the number of DOF is not sufficient for obtaining the high fidelity of reproduction of the dynamic behaviour of real structures. Some parameters of the models have to be tuned in order to achieve a good agreement between the results of measurements done on a real structure or its laboratory model and numerical simulations performed on a dynamic model. The process of modifying the dynamic model is called *updating* [1].

Many different approaches to model updating have been developed [1]:

- direct techniques based on modal data,
- iterative techniques based on modal data,
- iterative techniques based on frequency domain data.

Direct methods require mode shape information and they reproduce the measured data exactly. The main drawback of this methods is that the responses of all degrees of freedom are needed. Iterative methods improve the correlation between the measured data and the analytical model by using penalty function. In penalty function mode shape and eigenvalue or Frequency Response Function (FRF) data directly without extracting the eigenfrequencies and eigenforms can be involved. The penalty functions are generally nonlinear of the parameters and so iterative procedure is required.

This paper presents the application of Artificial Neural Networks (ANNs) [2,3] as the tool for the dynamic model updating. The input vector of the networks consists of preprocessed FRF defined as a ratio of two signals: the response of a structure and an excitation force. The output vector consists of updated values of selected model parameters.

2 The updating procedure and models under the study

The process of model updating consists of four steps:

- the numerical simulations — responses of a structure to a known excitation are calculated; by the introduction of changes in values of selected model parameters the whole set of responses is obtained, each pair composed of the calculated response and corresponding value of model parameter form one learning or testing pattern,
- the network learning — an ANN is used to predict the values of parameters being updated using structure's responses as input vectors; the learning and testing sets are obtained from numerical simulations done in the previous step,
- the prediction of updated parameters — the values of parameters are obtained from the ANN using the response measured on a real structure or its laboratory model as input vector,
- the updated model — updated values of parameters are applied to the model.

The models of two structures are under the study: the model of an aluminium beam hung on two elastic strings and the model of a portal frame. Both models are built using Finite Element Method (FEM). The model of the aluminium beam is shown in Fig. 2a, it consists of 24 Timoshenko beam elements and it has 50 DOF. The laboratory model of the beam is shown in Fig. 1a.

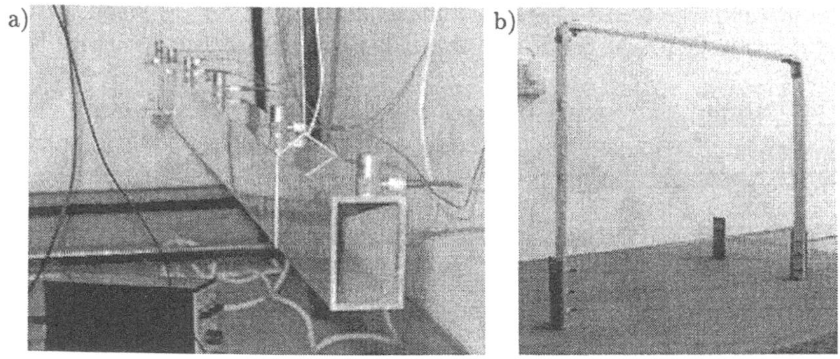

Fig. 1. The laboratory models. (**a**) The beam. (**b**) The portal frame

Finite element model of the portal frame is shown in Fig. 2b, it consists of 12 frame elements and it has 33 DOF. The laboratory model is shown in Fig. 1b.

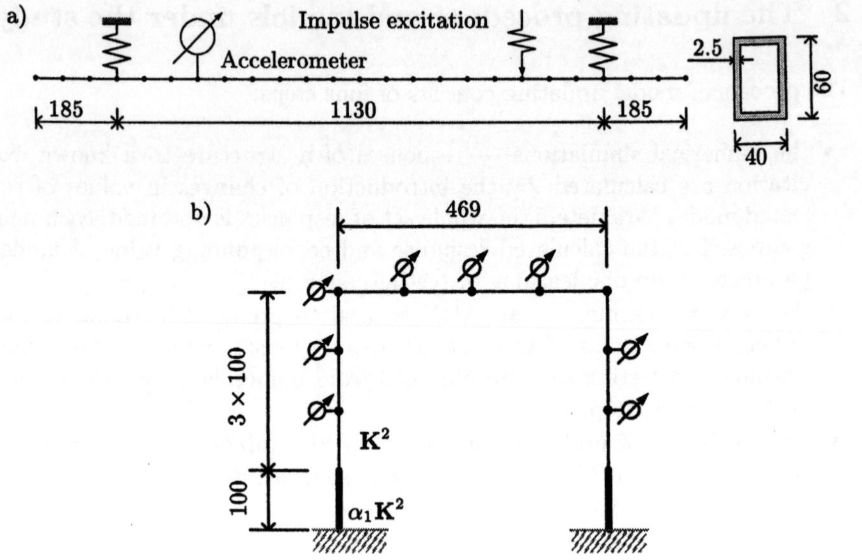

Fig. 2. The finite element models. (**a**) The model of the aluminium beam. (**b**) The model of the portal frame

The vibrations of the laboratory model of the beam were excited by an impulse excitation. Two signals were measured: the reference and the response signal. The reference signal was measured by the force sensor built into the hammer, the response signal was measured by the accelerometer on the beam. FRF is defined as the ratio of the response and the reference signals (both expressed in frequency domain and as absolute values). In case of the measurements of the frame only the responses of the structure were measured.

The learning and testing patterns were obtained from numerical simulations with different values of selected model parameters. The parameters which were changed during the updating were chosen according to the following rules:

- from among all model parameters they are determined with the highest error,
- the measured structure responses are sensitive to these parameters changes.

3 The updating of dynamic model of the beam

The updating of Young's modulus of the beam is presented in previous papers by the same authors [4–6]. This paper deals with the updating of the model of undamaged and damaged beam using eigenfrequencies as input information.

The input vector consisted first five eigenfrequencies. There were used networks taught using the Levenberg-Marquardt algorithm (LM) and networks with Radial Basis Function (RBF). The networks had five inputs, one hidden layer with no more than 10 neurones and they predicted the value of the shape ratio k_s of the Timoshenko beam for the undamaged cross-section or for the cross-section with partially or completely removed upper and lower flanges. For the undamaged beam additionally the mass density was predicted by the networks.

The parameters of the model (mass density, shape ratio of the undamaged cross-section — marked '0', shape ratio of the cross-section with removed half of the thickness of both flanges — marked 'o', and shape ratio of the cross-section with completely removed flanges — marked '.') were determined using the measurements done on the beam without damage ('0000000'), with damage located in place corresponding to the location of 19th finite element of the dynamic model ('0000o00') and with flanges removed in place corresponding to the location of 17th, 18th and 19th finite elements of the dynamic model ('00...00'). Other four examples of damaged beam were used for testing of the updated model. The results are shown in Table 1.

Table 1. The errors of the eigenfrequencies prediction by the updated model for the undamaged and damaged beam

Damage	ω_1	ω_2	ω_3	ω_4	ω_5	RMSE $\times 10^{-3}$
0000000	1.1%	0.7%	0.3%	-0.2%	-0.7%	6.8
0000o00	0.7%	-0.0%	-0.6%	-0.0%	0.0%	4.1
000oo00	0.5%	-0.3%	-0.3%	0.7%	1.4%	7.7
00ooo00	0.4%	-0.3%	0.5%	1.6%	1.5%	10.0
00oo.00	2.4%	-0.9%	0.1%	1.6%	1.3%	15.0
00o..00	2.4%	-0.1%	1.2%	1.6%	-0.4%	14.0
00...00	-1.1%	-1.2%	0.6%	0.6%	-1.1%	9.4

0 — undamaged part of the beam.
o — the part of the beam with removed half of the thickness of both flanges.
. — the part of the beam with completely removed both flanges.

The results of updating are very good, the fidelity of reproduction of eigenfrequencies by the updated model is very high. The maximal error equals approximately 2.5%, in comparison with the measurements accuracy of about 1% the 2.5% error should be considered as very small. The model of the beam should be admitted as properly updated in the range of first five eigenfrequencies.

4 The updating of dynamic model of the portal frame

The application of eight accelerometers allowed to measure not only eigenfrequencies but also eigenforms of the laboratory model of portal frame. The comparison of measured and calculated eigenforms was used as a test of updated model quality.

Two parameters of the model were updated: multiplayers α_1 and α_2 used for calculating the element stiffness matrices of the lowest elements of the model from the formula $\mathbf{K}^1 = \alpha\mathbf{K}^2$, where $\mathbf{K}^2$ is stiffness matrix of above-situated element, α_1 was used for the left and α_2 for the right post.

The input vector of the networks updating the model consisted of first four eigenfrequencies, the networks had one hidden layer with up to 10 neurones and two outputs. Levenberg-Marquardt learning algorithm was used. The results of updating are shown in Table 2.

Table 2. The errors of the eigenfrequencies prediction by the updated model of the portal frame

Eigen-frequency	Measured value	Calculated value	Relative error
ω_1	27.00	27	0.0%
ω_2	81.50	85	-4.3%
ω_3	169.75	169	-0.4%
ω_4	176.50	177	-0.3%

RMSE= 23×10^{-3}

The differences between the eigenfrequencies obtained from the updated model and the measured ones are very small, only for the second eigenfrequency the difference is higher than 1%. Considerably higher error of second eigenfrequency prediction is caused by the measurement error: while 1st, 3rd and 4th eigenfrequencies are measured with accuracy of approximately 1%, the accuracy of the 2nd one is lower and equals approximately 5% [6]. The results obtained from the updated model are of the same accuracy as the measurements.

Fig. 3 presents the comparison of eigenforms obtained from calculations and from measurements, the differences between measured and calculated forms are small, so taking into account the comparison of eigenfrequencies and eigenforms there should be admitted that the model of portal frame is properly updated in the range of first four eigenfrequencies.

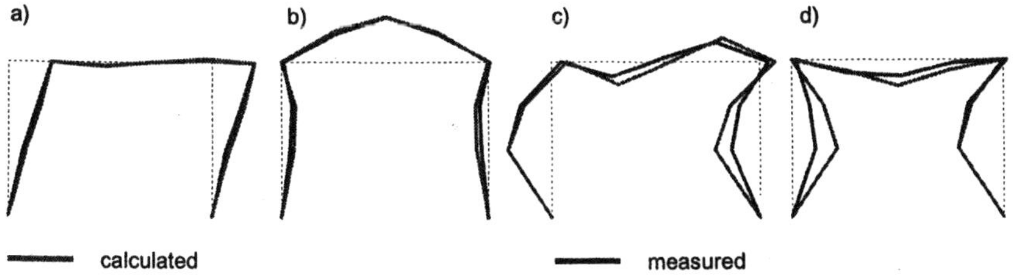

Fig. 3. Eigenforms obtained from numerical calculations and from measurements. (**a**) 1st eigenform. (**b**) 2nd eigenform. (**c**) 3rd eigenform. (**d**) 4th eigenform

5 Conclusions

The results of numerical simulations using models updated be neural networks show the compatibility with the results of experimental measurements. Neural networks can be successfully applied in updating with limited number of input data and the updated models, thanks to the constant physical interpretation of model improvements, can be used in variety of problems including the location and assessment of damages of the considered structure.

References

1. Friswell M.I., Mottershead J.E. (1996) *Finite Element Model Updating in Structural Dynamics*, Kluwer Academic Publishers, Dordrecht
2. Haykin S. (1999) *Neural networks. A comprehensive foundation*, Prentice Hall, Upper Saddle River, 2nd ed.
3. Waszczyszyn Z., Ziemiański L. (2001) *Neural Networks in Mechanics of Structures and Materials – New Results and Prospects of Applications* in Computers&Structures 79:2261–2276
4. Miller B., Ziemiański L. (2001) *Updating of Mathematical Models Using Neural Networks*, Proceedings of 2nd European Conference on Computational Mechanics, vol I, 386–387, Kraków
5. Miller B., Ziemiański L. (2001) *Updating of a Dynamic Model of an Aluminium Beam Using Neural Networks (in polish)*, Proceedings of VI School of Modal Analysis, Kraków
6. Miller B. (2002) *Updating of Mathematical Models of Engineering Structures (in polish)*, PhD dissertation, Rzeszów University of Technology, Rzeszów

A Fuzzy Neural Network for the Analysis of Experimental Structural Mechanics Problems

Ewa Pabisek, Magdalena Jakubek and Zenon Waszczyszyn

Institute of Computer Methods in Civil Engineering, Cracow University of Technology, Warszawska 24, 31-155 Kraków, Poland, e-mail: zenwa@twins.pk.edu. pl

Abstract. A simplified neuro-fuzzy network is formulated. The membership functions of the network weights are computed on the base of learning the single patterns. The network is applied to the interval analysis of two problems from experimental structural mechanics.

1. Introduction

Results of tests on material models can be noisy, incomplete and inconsistent. Another aspect is a limited number of tests because of various difficulties and costs of arrangement of experiments on laboratory specimens or full scale structures. That is why fuzzy variables and a possibility approach seem to match better the nature of experimental results than using crisp variables [5] . This concerns also fuzzy neural networks.

There are three possibilities to formulating fuzzy networks. The first one corresponds to the neural network with crisp parameters (called for short NN weights) and performing computations on interval variables [8]. Much advanced are NNs with crisp inputs and outputs but their processing is performed on fuzzyfied variables with fuzzy reasoning rules, cf. fuzzy inference systems [4]. The third class is associated with full fuzzification of transmitted signals, NN weights and neurons of a fuzzy NN [2]. A more numerically efficient approach depends on joining simple membership functions of signals and NN parameters with interval arithmetics [7].

In the paper a simplified approach, proposed in [6] is discussed. The main idea lies in the formulation of NN weights on the basis of weight values, computed for single patterns taken each after the other from the training pattern set. Crisp type neurons are used for the transformation of interval values for fixed α - cuts, transmitted through NN.

The above mentioned approach is developed in the paper. The corresponding neuro-fuzzy network approach is applied to the estimation of the stress intensity factor related to fracture toughness of dense concrete.

2. A fuzzy neural network

The idea of a fuzzy NN, proposed in [6], is shown Fig. 1 where a schematic algorithm is shown. It corresponds to a standard multi-layered, forward neural network and the training set of patterns:

$$\mathcal{L} = \{(x, t)^{(p)} \mid p = 1,\ldots, L\} \tag{1}$$

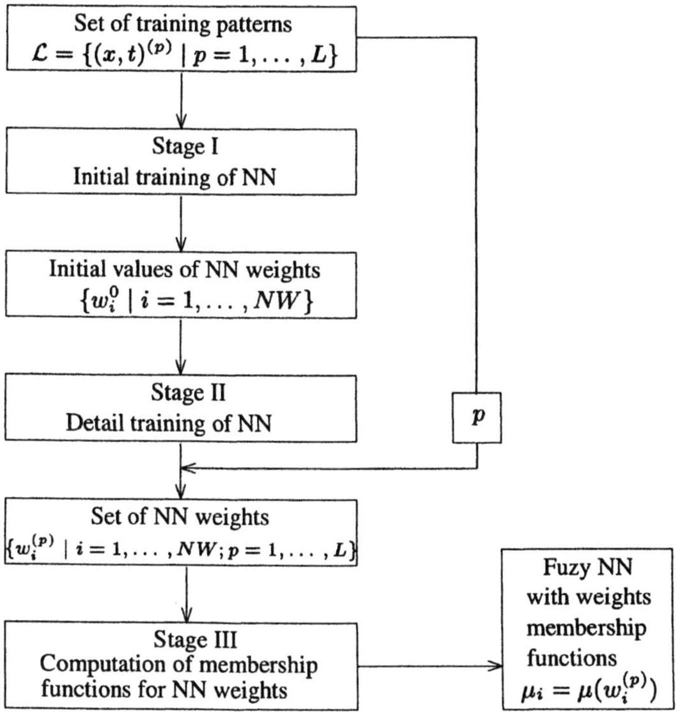

Fig. 1. Schematic algorithm of a fuzzy NN formulation

Let as assume that the network was designed using a corresponding cross-validation procedure and a subset selected from (1). The formulated network is then trained on set (1) at Stage I of the algorithm shown in Fig. 1. A set of NN weights (both synaptic weights and biases) is collected as a set of initial value weights $W^o = \{w^o{}_i \mid i = 1,\ldots, NW\}$, where: NW – number of NN weights.

The weights $w^o{}_i$ are assumed as initial weights to learn weights corresponding to each pattern of the training set (1). At Stage II the network is trained L times for a sequence of single patterns $p = 1,\ldots,L$. After this training a set of weights is completed, i.e. $\mathcal{W} = \{W_i\} = [w_i{}^{(p)} \mid i = 1,\ldots,NW;\ p = 1,\ldots, L]$.

The membership functions for the NN weights $\mu_i = \mu(W_i)$ are computed at Stage III. In [6] the triangular membership functions were assumed. In Fig.2a a triangular shape of MB function (t) is shown for the weight w (index i is ommited). The distances $3\sigma_L$ and $3\sigma_R$ are measured from the mean value $\overline{w}$, where: σ_L, σ_R – standard deviations of patterns p that are smaller or greater than

$\overline{w}$, respectively. The interval values of α-cut $[w^L, w^R]_\alpha$ are depicted in Fig. 2a as w^L_α, w^R_α.

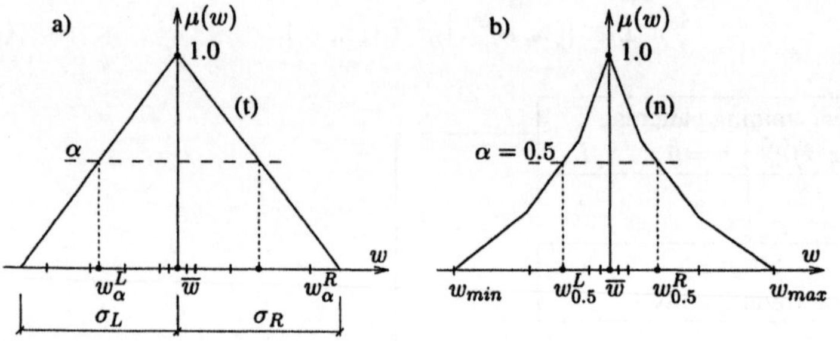

Fig. 2. Shapes of membership functions for NN weights: a) triangular MF (t), b) nonlinear MF (n)

The other method of formulation of a nonlinear MF (function (n) in Fig. 2b) lies in on computation of the discrete cumulative functions for the ranges $w_{min} \leq w^{(p)} < \overline{w}$, $\overline{w} \leq w^{(p)} \leq w_{max}$. Numbers of patterns w^L_α, w^R_α are computed from inequalities $(1-2K/L) \leq \alpha < (1-2(K-1)/L$, where: $K = k^L_\alpha, k^R_\alpha$ – numbers of weight values on the left or right hand sides of $\overline{w}$, respectively. In case of $\alpha \in (K-1, K)$ the values w^L_α, w^R_α are computed by linear interpolation in the range (w^{K-1}, w^K).

After the membership functions are formulated for each NN weight the fuzzy network is ready for operation. The network can be used for interval values of inputs $[x^L_j, x^R_j]_\alpha$ for both fuzzy type variables, i.e. $(x^L_j \neq x^R_j)_\alpha$, and for crisp inputs, i.e. $x^L_j = x^R_j$ for each α-cut. In general the outputs are computed as intervals $[y^L_m, y^R_m]_\alpha$ for both the fuzzy and crisp inputs. They are computed by means of interval arithmetic manipulations for fixed α-cuts.

3. Estimation of dense concrete fracture toughness

Dense concrete (of $\rho > 2600$ kg/m^3), used in special structures, is brittle. Estimation of the concrete fracture toughness is made on the basis of laboratory tests on especially prepared specimens. In Fig. 3 the so-called Model II is shown as well the equilibrium path during the specimen loading. On the basis of experimental results the stress intensity factor K_{IIC} is computed [ ]:

$$K_{IIC} = \frac{5.11 P_Q}{2BW} \sqrt{\pi a} \left[\mathrm{MN/m}^{3/2}\right] \tag{3}$$

where all variables and parameters are shown in Fig. 3.

In Table 1 experimental results are given for selected tests, performed at the Institute of Building Materials and Constructions of Cracow University of Tech

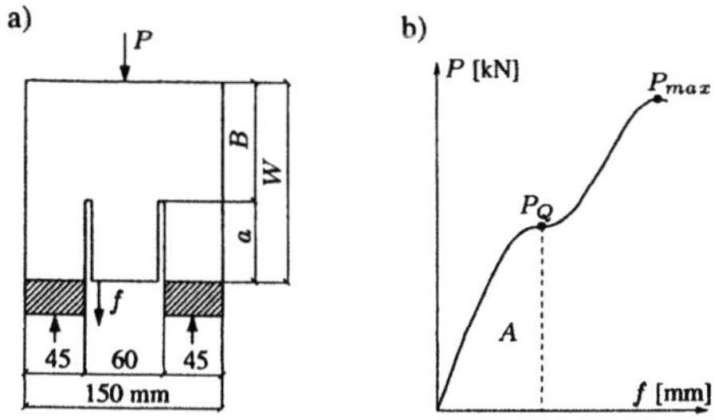

Fig.3. a) Model II of concrete specimens, b) Force–displacement curve

nology for data: $a = 60$ mm, $B = 90$ mm and $W = 150$ mm (Tests I performed in 1998, test II in 1991, cf. references in [9]). 9 concretes of strength f_c were used and from each of them 6 specimens were made. The first five concretes of Nos 1-5 (Tests I) were used for the network training, the four next concretes of Nos 6-9 (Tests II) were explored for the fuzzy NN testing.

Table 1. Stress intensity factor K_{IIC} for Tests I and Tests II

Tests	I					II			
No. of concrete	1	2	3	4	5	6	7	8	9
f_c [Mpa]	25.8	30.1	35.1	36.6	40.2	27.2	30.2	35.5	41.0
K_{IIC} [MN/m$^{2/3}$]	2.36	2.70	2.84	3.00	3.32	2.38	2.71	2.94	3.29
	2.48	2.82	2.92	3.35	3.72	2.19	3.20	2.89	3.20
	2.62	3.00	2.97	3.30	3.25	3.25	3.12	3.12	3.86
	2.52	2.65	3.10	3.12	3.82	2.66	3.37	2.85	4.35
	2.48	2.90	3.05	3.05	3.42	2.55	2.05	3.04	3.29
	2.63	2.69	3.00	3.46	3.35	2.34	2.79	2.96	3.20
mean K_{IIC}	2.52	2.79	2.82	3.21	3.48	2.56	2.87	2.97	3.53

The network was designed as a very simple network BPNN: 1-3-1, with one input $x = f_c$ and one output $y = K_{IIC}$. The sigmoidal neuron NN was trained by Levenberg-Marquardt learning method [1]. After a rapid training process the error of Stage I was $RMSE \approx 0.8 \cdot 10^{-2}$ and for Stage II $RMSE\ (p) < 1 \cdot 10^{-6}$ for each pattern p.

In Fig. 4 the MF functions (t) and (n) are shown for selected concretes. The concretes of Nos 1, 5, 6 and 9 are considered as corresponding to minimal and maximal values of strentgh f_c . Concretes 1 and 5 were used for training of neuro-fuzzy NN, concretes 6 and 9 were used for testing of the trained network . It is visible that the crisp values corresponding to the cut $\alpha = 1$ are close to mean values of stress intensity factors computed on the base of measurements (they are marked at the top of figures with $*$ among other 6 specimens marked with $\Diamond$). The coincidence of mean values $*$ and $\Diamond$ is very good for the training patterns. In case of training patterns the maximal errors between $*$ and $\Diamond$ are 12.5 % for mean values of specimens made of concretes Nos 6–9, used as testing patterns.

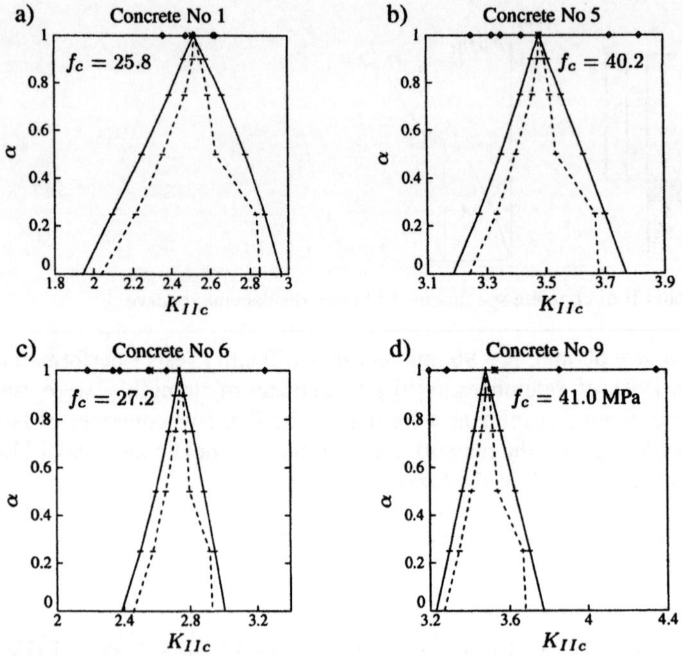

Fig. 4. Membership functions for stress intensity factor K_{IIC} for concretes of selected strength f_c

In the next Fig. 5 there are shown intervals for all the concretes. The intervals correspond to the cuts $\alpha = 0.5$, 1.0 for the nonlinear MS functions (n), cf. Fig.2b. It is visible that the experimental dispersion of six points, corresponding to concretes of the same strength, is different but all the six measurements are covered by the intervals $\alpha = 0.5$ for concretes Nos 1–4 and 8 .

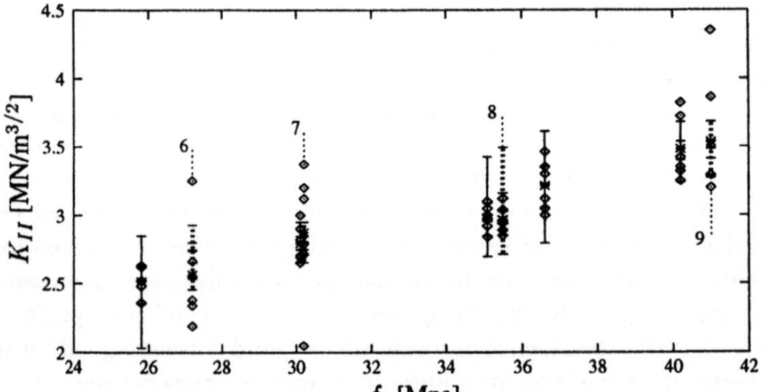

Fig.5. Estimating intervals for cut $\alpha = 0.5$ for concretes of Tests I and II

4. Final remarks and some conclusions

1. A simplified neuro-fuzzy network can be easily formulated using the algorithm schematically presented in Fig.1. The neural weight membership functions are formulated on the base of weights computed for single patterns taken from the training set.
2. The network can be applied for both crisp and interval inputs mapping into interval outputs.
3. The network has been examined on an example of identification of the stress intensity factor associated with fracture toughness of dense concretes.
4. The intervals of parametric estimation of characteristics of of semi-rigid steel connections were successfully computed in [3] using the above discussed neuro-fuzzy network.

Acknowledgement. Financial support by the Polish Committee for Scientific Research, Grant No 8 T07E 020 22 "Applications of artificial neural networks in the analysis of steel structures" is gratefully acknowledged.

References

1. Denmuth H, Beale M (1998) Neural network toolbox for use with MATLAB, User's Guide, Version 3, The Math Works
2. Hayashi Y, Buckley JJ, Czogala E (1993), Int. J. Intell. Systems, 7:527-537
3. Jakubek M, Pabisek E, Waszczyszyn Z (2002) Estimation of parameters of characteristics of steel semi-rigid connections (in Polish), Proc. 48th Polish Conf. Civil Eng., Zakopane, Poland
4. Jang J-ShR, Sun Ch-T, Mizutani E (1997) Nero-fuzzy and soft computing. Prentice-Hall, Upper-Hall Saddle River, NJ
5. Muhanna RL, Mullen RL (2001) Uncertainty in mechanics, problems – interval-based approach. J. Eng. Mech., 127: 357-566
6. Ni SH, Lu PC, Yuang CH (1996) A fuzzy neural network approach to evaluation of slope failure potential. Microcomputers in Civil Eng., 11: 59-66
7. Rajasekaran S, Febin MF, Ramasaeny JV (1996) Artificial fuzzy neural net works in civil engineering. Comp. Stru., 61: 291-302
8. Yager RR (1991) Modelling and formulating fuzzy knowledge base using neural network. Techn. Rep. No. MIT-1111, Machine Intell. Institute, Iona College
9. Waszczyszyn Z, Słoński M (2000) Analysis of some problems of experimental mechanics and biomechanics by means of the ANFIS neuro-fuzzy system. J. Teoret. Appl. Mech., 38:429-445

Neural Network Identification of a Circular Hole in the Rectangular Plate

Grzegorz Piątkowski[1] and Leonard Ziemiański[1]

Department of Structural Mechanics, Rzeszów University of Technology, W. Pola 2, 35-114 Rzeszów, Poland

Abstract. Numerical tests have been carried out for 2D plates with internal defects in a form of circle hole. An identification procedure of the defect based on neural network analysis of eigenfrequencies is presented [1]. The position of the hole has been searched. The Backpropagation (BP) Artificial Neuron Networks (ANN) with one hidden layer, trained with the Levenberg-Marquardt (LM) learning algorithm have been applied [2]. The single networks and the cascade sets of BP neural networks have been used [1,3].

1 Description of numerical model

Numerical models of rectangle plates with a circle hole have been considered. The geometry of plate is presented in Fig.1. The position of the void's centre is defined by two parameters, which are OY and OZ coordinates.

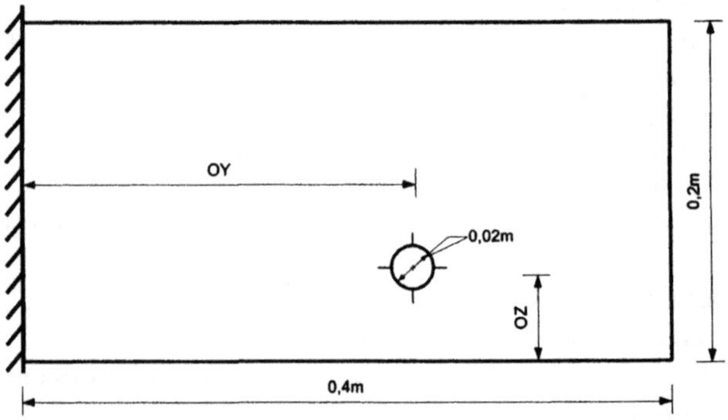

Fig. 1. Scheme of plate. Main dimensions

The location of the hole with constant radius of $0.02m$ has been changed in wide range:

- OY coordinate: $0.05m \div 0.35m$
- OZ coordinate: $0.05m \div 0.10m$ - due to symmetry of the plate there were taken into consideration the holes with centres under or at the axis of symmetry of the plate

The coordinates have been changed with step of $0.01m$. The number of 186 different positions (31 in horizontal and 6 in vertical direction) of hole's centre have been obtained in that way.

For each location of a void the FEM model of plate has been build using Adina system. Numerical models have been build with 2D solid plane stress elements [4]. Quadrilateral, eight nodes elements were preferred. Elements meshes were generated automatically on the basis of sets of solid geometry faces.

An isotropic linear elastic material model has been used. The plate has the following material properties: Young's modulus $E = 215GPa$, Poisson's ratio $\nu = 0.3$, density $\rho = 7850kg/m^3$.

The eigenproblem was solved with subspace-iteration method of frequency calculation. The number of 10 frequencies (see Table 1) and corresponding mode shapes were calculated.

Table 1. Calculated eigen-freqeuncies for uniform plate

Number	1	2	3	4	5
ω $[rad/s]$	883.701	3207.51	3371.12	7062.61	9038.84
Number	6	7	8	9	10
ω $[rad/s]$	9330.39	11246.5	11719.0	12528.7	12731.1

2 Hole position identification on the basis of eigenfrequency analysis

2.1 Eigenfrequencies only

Values of eigenfrequencies of plate with the hole were used as input vector for neural networks. Attempts of the void's position identification on the basis of various number of eigenfrequencies have been carried out, for example first seven (1-2-3-4-5-6-7) or only first three (1-2-3) eigenfrequencies.

The coordinates OY and OZ of centre of the hole were scaled to range $0.1 \div 0.9$ and were used as output vectors for neural networks training.

The total number of 186 patterns, corresponding to different considered location of the holes' centres were to use.

It was decided that 70% of patterns would be used for learning and the remaining 30% for testing in training process.

Standard networks Results in the form of set of statistical parameters such as linear correlation coefficient R^2, standard deviation δ and mean square error MSE are presented in Table 2. These are the best results achieved from neural networks of given architecture. The number of used frequencies is the same as the number of neurons in input layer. Regardless of the number of used frequencies and of used architecture of networks the OZ coordinate was identified with bigger error than OY coordinate.

Table 2. Example results. Identification based on ω. Standard network

Used frequencies	Hidden Layer	Statistical parameter	Identification of OY coordinate		Identification of OZ coordinate	
			Learn	Test	Learn	Test
1-2-3-4-5-6-7	5	R^2	1.000	0.999	0.999	0.997
		δ	0.00376	0.00593	0.00883	0.0169
		MSE·10^3	0.0141	0.0350	0.0688	0.306
1-2-3	7	R^2	0.998	0.999	0.968	0.968
		δ	0.0109	0.00914	0.0496	0.0485
		MSE·10^3	0.118	0.0822	2.46	2.31

Cascade networks In order to improve the accuracy of the OZ coordinate identification, the number o cascade networks were built and tested [1,3]. The output of the first network was the OY coordinate scaled to the range $0.1 \div 0.9$. This value was added to the input vector used in the first network. This extended vector was the input to the second network in cascade which identified the OZ coordinate.

The cascade networks had architectures which were analogous to previously used standard networks. Moreover the use of the same input vectors allowed to compare results of the identification of the voids' locations.

In every tested case the improvement of both coordinates identification was reached. Please compare the Table 2 with the Table 3.

As one can see at histograms presented in Fig. 2 the error of OY coordinate identification was decreased from a level of $\pm 5\%$ which was reached for standard networks to the level of $\pm 1\%$. Such high precision was achieved for every of tested cases.

Presented results point at the fact that the separation of coordinates identification allow the exact determination of the OY coordinate. The recognition of the OY coordinate was not disturbed like it was in the case of use of the standard networks.

Table 3. Example results. Identification based on ω. Cascade network

Used frequencies	Hidden Layer	Statistical parameter	Identification of OY coordinate		Identification of OZ coordinate	
			Learn	Test	Learn	Test
1-2-3-4-5-6-7	5	R^2	1,000	1,000	0,996	0,991
		Std	0,00035	0,00060	0,018	0,0266
		MSE·10^3	0,00012	0,00037	0,323	0,708
1-2-3	7	R^2	1,000	1,000	0,968	0,967
		Std	0,00051	0,00076	0,0495	0,0534
		MSE·10^3	0,00026	0,00058	2,450	2,910

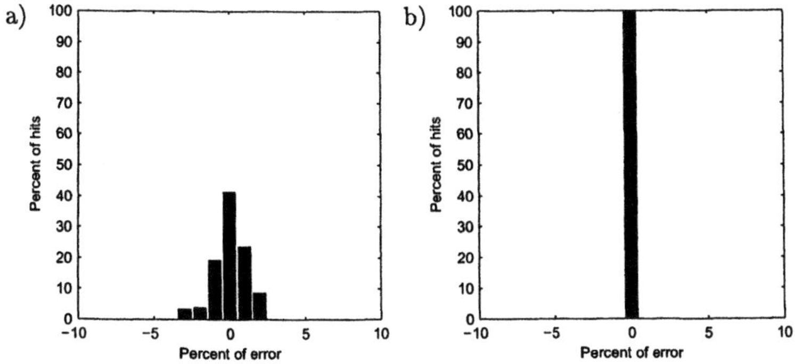

Fig. 2. Identification of OY coordinate - comparison of neural training results a) standard network 3-7-2, b) cascade network 3-7-1

2.2 Change of eigenfrequency values

With relation to previous task the eigenfrequencies of the uniform plate without a hole were computed. Relative changes of the eigenfrequencies were used as the input vector for neural networks. The relative changes $\Delta\omega_i$ were calculated as follows:

$$\Delta\omega_i = \frac{\omega_i - \omega_i^o}{\omega_i^o} \tag{1}$$

where: the ω_i^o are values of eigenfrequencies for uniform plate and the ω_i values corresponding to the plate with the hole.

The number of learning and testing patterns was the same as in the previous step.

Results Results achieved for standard networks are put together in Table 4, when results for cascade networks are in Table 5.

Table 4. Example results. Identification based on $\Delta\omega$. Standard network

Used frequencies	Hidden Layer	Statistical parameter	Identification of OY coordinate		Identification of OZ coordinate	
			L	T	L	T
1-2-3-4-5-6-7	5	R^2	0.999	0.999	0.997	0.989
		δ	0.00581	0.00534	0.0162	0.0276
		$MSE \cdot 10^3$	0.0335	0.0288	0.26	0.764
1-2-3	7	R^2	1.000	1.000	0.978	0.956
		δ	0.0053	0.00523	0.043	0.054
		$MSE \cdot 10^3$	0.0279	0.0269	1.85	3.04

Like for networks described at point 2.1 the results for the cascade networks are significantly, better than for the standard networks. The MSE error and the standard deviation δ for learning as well as for testing process are smaller at least about a order of magnitude. The OZ coordinates identification by the second network of cascade still have a certain error but this error is distinct smaller than for identification with standard networks.

Table 5. Example results. Identification based on $\Delta\omega$. Cascade network

Used frequencies	Hidden Layer	Statistical parameter	Identification of OY coordinate		Identification of OZ coordinate	
			U	T	U	T
1-2-3-4-5-6-7	5	R^2	1.000	1.000	1.000	0.999
		δ	0.00019	0.00027	0.00563	0.00965
		$MSE \cdot 10^3$	0.00003	0.00007	0.00315	0.0925
1-2-3	7	R^2	1.000	1.000	0.985	0.970
		δ	0.0007	0.00059	0.0349	0.0471
		$MSE \cdot 10^3$	0.0005	0.00037	1.62	2.18

Figure 3 presents graphical comparison of the MSE errors obtained from identification process for variety of neural networks. The networks in this comparison had the same architectures but used the input vectors were prepared in different ways. The values of eigenfrequencies (ω) or the relative changes of the eigenfrequencies ($\Delta\omega$) were used as the input vector for neural networks. As one can see the MSE is significantly smaller in second case for every network.

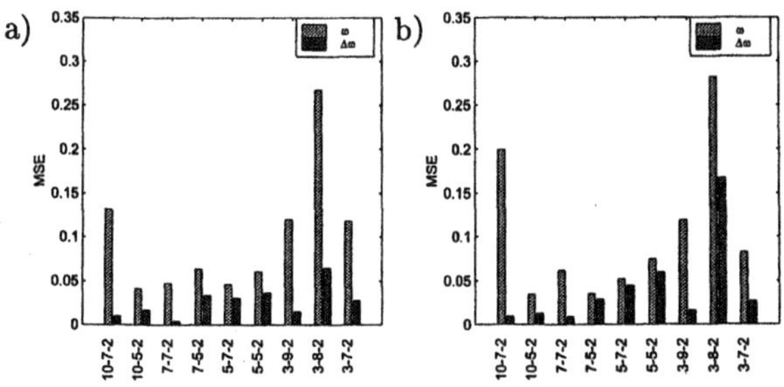

Fig. 3. The MSE errors of OY coordinate identification. Standard networks a) Learning, b) Testing

3 Final remarks

On the basis of achieved results the following conclusions can be expressed:

- artificial neural networks make it possible to use the analysis of eigenfrequencies for a hole's position searching in tested plates,
- better results were achieved for neural networks trained with relative changes of the eigenfrequencies,
- application of cascade networks can improve accuracy of neural identification in both analysed ways of input vectors preparation,
- even networks trained with small input vector (only three first eigenfrequencies) can identify the hole's location with $\pm 5\%$ level precision.

References

1. Waszczyszyn Z., Ziemiański L. (2001) *Neural Networks in Mechanics of Structures and Materials – New Results and Prospects of Applications* in Computers&Structures 79:2261–2276
2. Haykin S. (1999) *Neural networks. A comprehensive foundation*, Prentice Hall, Upper Saddle River, 2nd ed.
3. Piątkowski G., Ziemiański L. (2001) *Wave Propagation And Neural Networks As A Tool For Damage Detection In Rods*, Proceedings of 2nd European Conference on Computational Mechanics, vol. I, 392–393
4. ADINA System Online Manuals (2001), Theory and modeling guide, ADINA R&D Inc., Watertown

Neural Analysis of Concrete Shrinkage

Anna Urbańska[1], Zenon Waszczyszyn[2]

[1] Department of Civil and Environmental Engineering, University of Zielona Góra, ul. Prof. Z. Szafrana 2 , 65-516 Zielona Góra, e-mail: a.urbanska@uz.zgora.pl

[2] Institute of computer Methods in Civil Engineering, Cracow University of Technology, ul. Warszawska 24, 31-155 Kraków, e-mail: zenwa@twins.pk.edu.pl

Abstract. Results of tests on laboratory specimens were selected from the data bank described in [4]. The tests on concrete plates concerning the shrinkage strains up to 435 days at nearly stationary humidity and temperatures were accepted as a data to compare the experimental results with the Eurocode 2 recommendations [3]. The comparison was made by means of three neural networks: BPNN-Rprop, RBFNN and ANFIS. It was stated that the RBFNN approximation is close to EC curves.

1. Introduction

The paper deals with application of neural networks to compare the results of new laboratory tests [4] and EC-2 recommendation. Three measured factors, i.e. time in days, humidity and temperature, are accepted as input variables. The experimental results which are a basis for the paper are selected from a very rich data bank discussed in [4]. The data are restricted to tests on concrete plates made of two concretes but, according to conclusions in [3], the concrete strength in not the principle characteristic for the shrinkage phenomenon. This question is also discussed in the paper.

2. Experimental data

The experimental data correspond to tests on laboratory specimens, performed in the Institute of Building Materials and Structures of Cracow University of Technology. The results of tests on concrete plates were selected from the experimental data bank described in [3]. The tests were carried out on plates of dimensions 600×600×100 mm made of two concretes, i.e. concrete A of strength f_{cm} = 13.7 MPa and concrete B of strength f_{cm} = 26.3 MPa. The shrinkage strain ε_{cs} was measured at nine points on the plate surface, during the period up to 435 or 1035 days. The humidity *RH* [%] and temperature *T* [°C] were also measured in the days of shrinkage strains measurements. In what follows the data sets were completed from measurements up to 435 days, i.e. *PA* = 3753 measurements for concrete A and *PB* = 3234 measurements for concrete B.

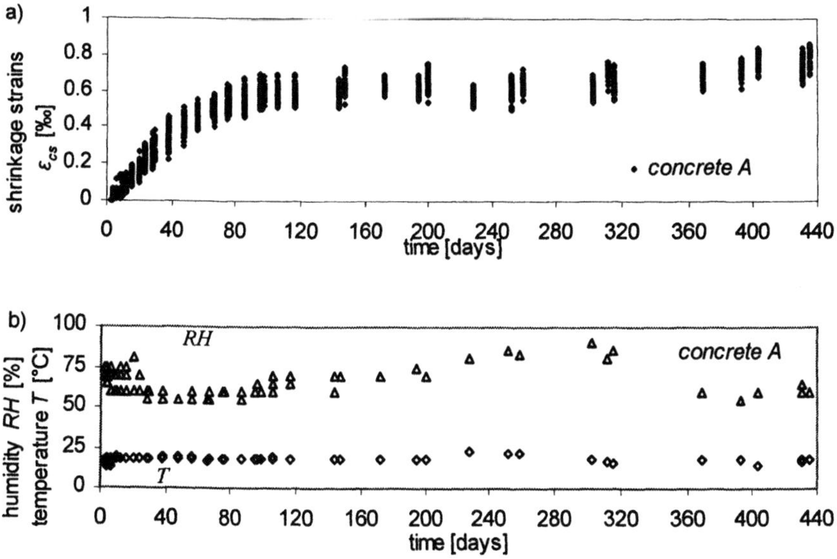

Fig. 1. Results of measurements for concrete A, a) shrinkage strains ε_{cs},
b) humidity *RH* and temperature *T*

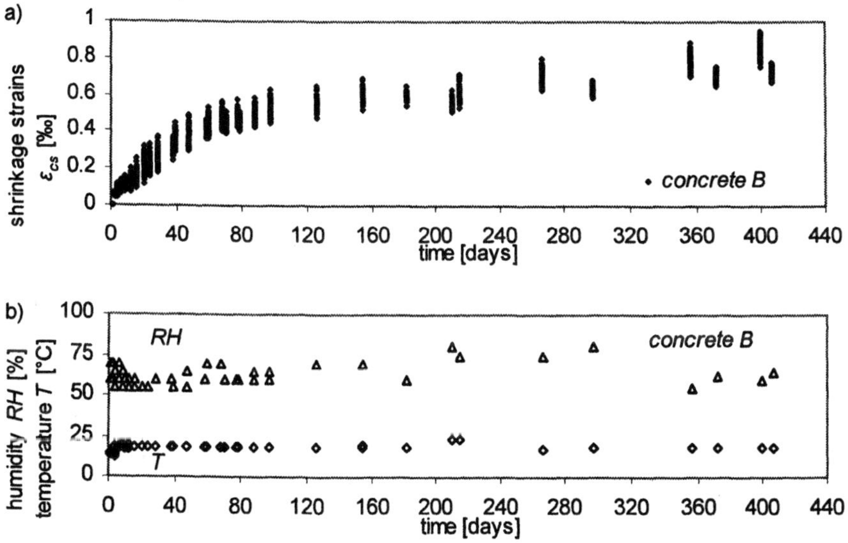

Fig. 2. Results of measurements for concrete B, a) shrinkage strains ε_{cs},
b) humidity *RH* and temperature *T*

In Figs 1 and 2 distribution in time of measured values of shrinkage strains ε_{cs} humidity *RH* and temperature *T* is shown for concretes A and B, respectively.

Measurements were performed frequently in the first period (0, 120) days and then the distance of the measurement time was 20 to 80 days. The range of humidity was RH = [55, 90]% for concrete A and RH = [55, 80]% for concrete B. More stable temperature was in concrete A , on average $T_{avr} \approx 18^{\circ}$C.

3. EC-2 approximation of shrinkage strains

Eurocode 2 (EC-2) recommends the following relationship for shrinkage strain function $\varepsilon_{cs}\,(t - t_s, RH, f_{cm})$:

$$\varepsilon_{cs}\,(t - t_s) = \varepsilon_s\,(f_{cm}) \cdot \beta_{RH} \cdot \beta_s\,(t - t_s) \qquad (1)$$

where: $\varepsilon_s\,(f_{cm}) = [160 + \beta_{cs} \cdot (90 - f_{cm})\,] \cdot 10^{-6}$, $\beta_{RH} = -1.55\,[1 - (RH / 100)^{3}$], $\beta_{sc}\,(t - t_s) = [(t - t_s) / (0.035\, h_0^2 + t - t_s)]^{0.5}$ are functions with the following coefficients: β_{sc} – coefficient associated with the type of cement, t_s – age of concrete in days at the beginning of shrinkage, , h_0 – notional size in mm .In Figs. 1 and 2 the EC-2 curves were depicted, computed according to values of parameters specified in [3]. For all the concrete plates the following values of parameters were assumed: t_s = 2 days, h_0 = 85.71 mm, T_{avr} = 18°C. Other parameters were accepted to be different for two concretes: a) concrete A : β_{sc} = 9, RH_{avr} = 65.3%, b) concrete β_{sc} = 11, RH_{avr} = 62.6%.

4. Neural simulation

In Fig.3 the results of shrinkage strain measurements were gathered for both types of concrete. The EC-2 curves, depicted for concretes A and B, were computed for data discussed above in Point 3. The curves EC(A) and EC(B) practically coincide. That is why the whole set $P = PA+PB$ = 3753 + 3234 = 6987 patterns was used for the neural networks training and testing. The training set, composed of L = 3500 patterns was randomly selected. The remaining T = 3487 patterns were used for the network testing.

Three neural networks were applied: 1) BPNN with Rprop learning 2) ANFIS (Adaptive Neuro-Fuzzy System), 3) RBFN (RBF Neural Network). The MATLAB Neural Network Toolbox [1] was used for the BPNN and RBFN training and the MATLAB Fuzzy Toolbox [2] was explored for ANFIS. Three input variables were assumed as components of the input vector $\boldsymbol{x} = \{t, RH, T\}$ and the scalar output was $y = \varepsilon_{cs}$.

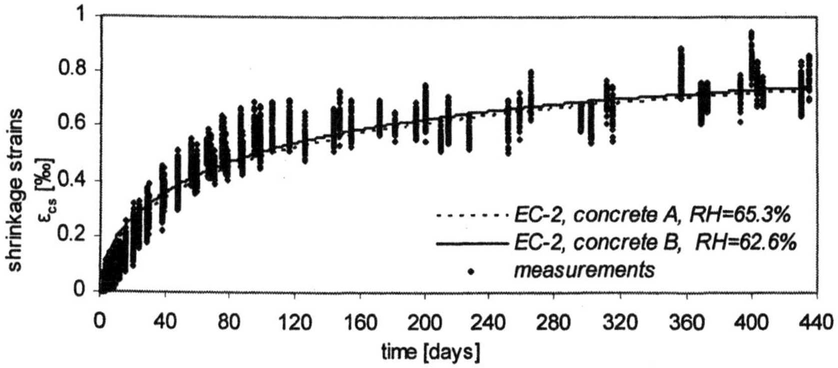

Fig. 3. Measure shrinkage strains for plates made of concrete A and B and corresponding EC(A) and EC(B) curves

After extensive numerical experiment the BP neural network was designed as BPNN : 3–60–1 and trained by means of Rprop needed 500.epochs. The RBNN was associated with 3 Gaussian functions for the spread parameter $sp = 1$. The 27 Gaussian membership functions were automatically selected by simulator [1]. The network Root-Mean-Square-Error was about $RMSE(L) \approx RMSE(T) \approx 3 \cdot 10^{-3}$.

In Table 1 errors of the RBFN and EC-2 approximations are put together with respect to the following measures

$$RMSE = [\ \frac{1}{V}\sum_{p=1}^{V}\sum_{i=1}^{3}\left(t_i^{(p)} - y_i^{(p)}\right)^2\ ]^{1/2} \tag{2}$$

where: $V = L, T, P$ – number of patterns of the training and testing and full sets, respectively $e_p = |1 - y_p / t_p| \cdot 100\%$ – relative error the p-th pattern; t_p , y_p – computed and experimental values of the output variable. The values of regression coefficients r are computed for the sets of pairs : $\{(y_p , t_p) \mid p = 1 ,..., P\}$ for RBFN *Learning* and *Testing* respectively.

Table 1. Errors of neural approximation

Aproximation	*RMSE* × 10 $^{-3}$	Relative errors [%]		Regression
		avr e_p	max e_p	coefficient *r*
RBFN *Learning*	0.0334	8	47.1	0.987
RBFN *Testing*	0.0334	8	44.8	0.987

In Fig. 4a the comparison of experimental shrinkage strains and computed by RBFN are shown for the training set of patterns. In Fig.4b the experimental results are compared with results by EC-2 computed for the shrinkage of plates made of concrete A.

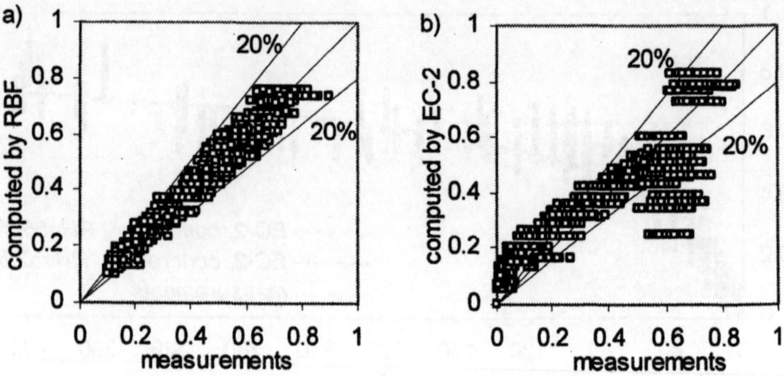

Fig. 4. Comparison of experimentally measured and computed shrinkage strains.

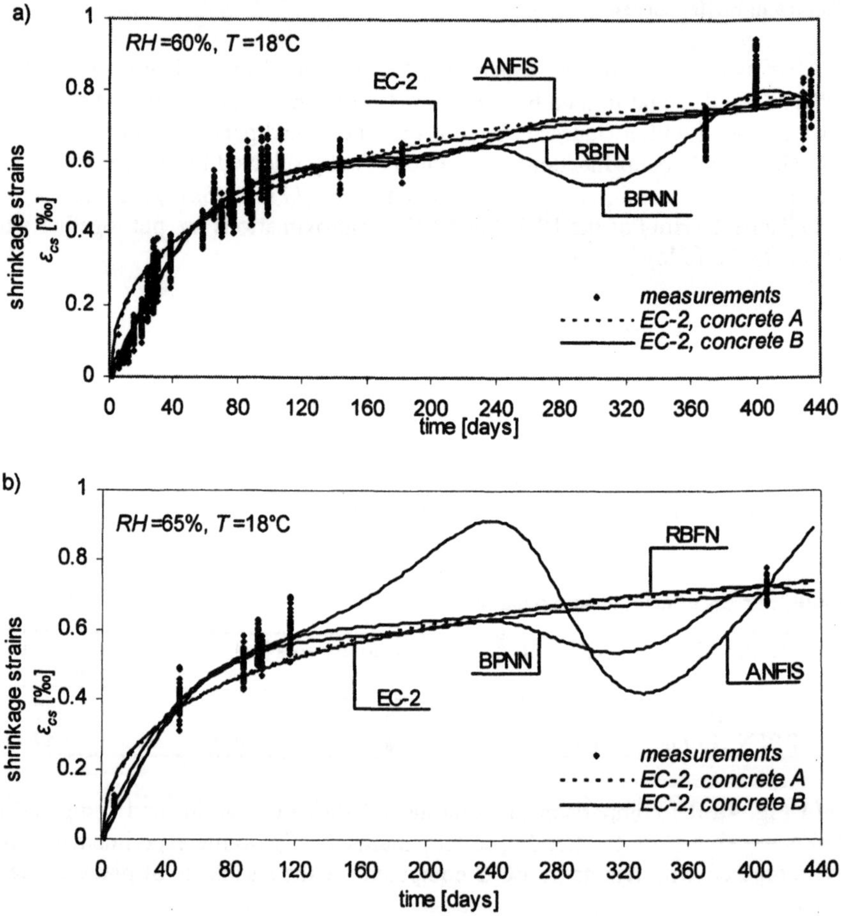

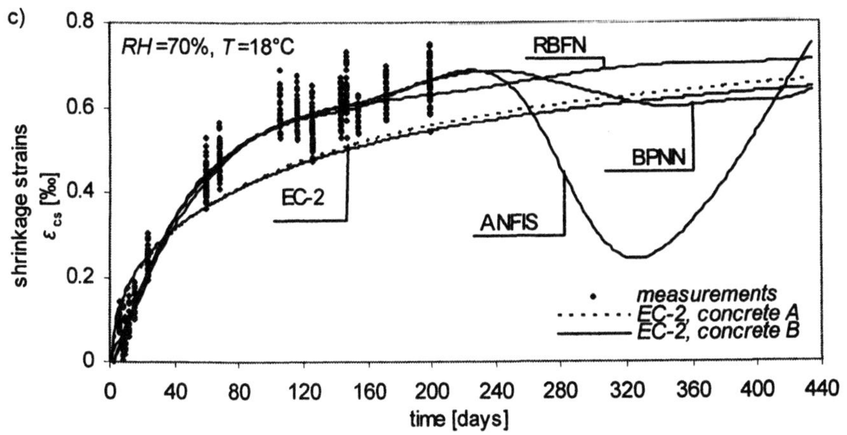

Fig. 5. Neural vs. EC-2 approximations for different values of average humidity: a) $RH = 60$ %, b) $RH = 65$ %, c) RH=70%.

In Fig 5 the generalization properties of the three considered neural networks are shown. The computations were performed for the fixed values of humidity *RH* 60, 65, 70%. In figures the experimental points associated with these and the RBF approximation seems to match better to physically reasonable generalization.

5. Conclusions

1. RBFN approximation of shrinkage strains has better generalization properties than BPNN and ANFIS
2. For lower humidities the RBFN approximation quite well correlates with EC-2 approximation
3. For short term shrinkage the EC-2 approximation overestimate the neural approximation.

References

[1] Denmuth H, Beale M (1998) Neural network toolbox for use with Matlab, User's Guide, Version 3. The Math Works

[2] Denmuth H, Beale M (1998) Fuzzy logic toolbox for use with Matlab, User's Guide, Version 3. The Math Works

[3] ENV 1992-1-1 : (1992) Eurocode 2, Design of concrete structures, P.1: General rules and rules for buildings

[4] Ligęza W, (2002) Redistribution of internal forces in braced concrete plate elements (in Polish), Dept. Civil Eng., Cracow Univ. of Technology, Monograph No 277.

Short-Term Load Forecasting For Energy Markets

Witold Bartkiewicz, Bożena Matusiak

University of Łódź, Department of Computer Science,
Rewolucji 1905r Str. 39, 90-214 Łódź, Poland

Abstract. The problem of the application of neural predictors for Short-Term Load Forecasting (STLF) for energy transactions planning in utility is discussed. The conditional expected value of the energy demand approximated by the neural network forecast does not necessarily indicate the optimal size of the order, according to the financial regulations associated with energy markets. Two approaches to the solution of this problem are presented. The first one is based on GANN - hybrid neural-genetic STLF system, trained with the financial cost function. The second approach rely on determining of the sources of uncertainty for classical neural predictor.

1 Introduction

In recent years neural networks became one of the most useful tools in Short-Term Load Forecasting (**STLF**) [1][3][5]. Neural network applications in STLF and other forecasting problems are in most cases focused on single point predictions. Their performance is typically assessed on the basis of technical considerations (statistical tests of fitting error), without the discussion of the impact of the errors on the uncertainty of the decision processes associated with the obtained forecasts.

In this paper the problem of the application of neural network predictors for short-term energy transactions planning in power distribution company is discussed. Because of the energy market regulations and prices resulted from the participation of the company in exchange and balancing markets, the optimal size of the order can substantially differ from predicted expected value of the conditional target distribution of the energy demand. It means that the forecasting models based on statistical mean squared error, evaluate inappropriate aspects of this problem. We investigate two approaches for relating neural STLF systems and decision analysis models.

The first approach is based on replacing the square error function for the neural network training by the financial cost function resulted from market prices of the energy. Because we expect that in the future complexity of the optimization problem in case of full treatment of the cost analysis, will restrict the possibility of application of the gradient learning methods, the model is trained using genetic algorithm.

The second approach is based on determining the sources of uncertainty of the neural predictor. It is possible for neural network trained with square error function to assess the variance of the prediction around new data point. It allows to estimate the entire distribution of the forecasted energy demand, and calculate correction for neural network output according to the financial conditions on the market.

2 STLF and energy transactions planning

Short-term energy transactions planning in polish utilities is associated with participation in Day Ahead Market (DAM) on Polish Power Exchange, and Balancing Market (BM) - nation wide market for handling imbalances between the supply and demand of the energy. According to the market regulations the distribution company should prepare for a given day k the timetable of energy purchases for all 24 hours. The deadline for declaration of the orders to the market operator is 10 a.m. on a previous k-1 day. Taking into account, that the plan of transactions must be prepared earlier, based on information from at least a day k-2, this process requires two-day ahead hourly energy demand forecasts.

In our case the STLF system is developed from 24 neural networks according to the equations:

$$\begin{aligned} ED_k(t) = f(&ED(t)_{k-7}, ED(t-2)_{k-2}, ED(t-1)_{k-2}, ED(t)_{k-2}, \\ &ED(t+1)_{k-2}, TMIN_k, TMAX_k, d_{1k}, \dots, d_{6k}) \end{aligned} \tag{1}$$

where $ED_k(t)$ denotes the energy demand at hour t in k-th day, $TMIN_k$, $TMAX_k$ - temperature forecasts for day k, $d_{1t}, \dots, d_{6t}$ - type of the week-day coding variables.

The model for each hour is consisted of multilayered perceptron network (MLP) with one hidden layer, structure {13-10-1} and logistic transfer functions.

The estimates of the energy demand given by the output of the regression-type models like (1) are uncertain. Errors in the forecasts and resulting inappropriate setting by the distribution company of the contracted amount of energy cause the imbalance between the demand and the supply. It is settled by the purchasing or selling of the additional energy on the balancing market. The energy transaction planning process requires of the consideration of three following price elements [9]:

- market price - the price of the energy on the DAM market (r_M),
- incremental price - the price of the receiving of the additional energy required for balancing the order with the actual demand. It is paid by the distribution company to the market operator $r_I > r_M$,
- reductive price – the price of the resignation of the receiving energy required for balancing the order, paid by the market operator to distributor $r_R < r_M$.

It can be shown [8], that taking to the account above financial conditions optimal size of the order y^* is given by the equation:

$$F_{ED}(y^*) = \frac{r_I - r_M}{r_I - r_R} \tag{2}$$

where $F_{ED}(\cdot)$ denotes the cumulative probability function of the energy demand (*ED*) distribution. The optimum value according to the financial criterion, given by (2) can substantially differ from expected value of the demand provided by the output of neural network model, trained with sum-of-squares error function. Only if the price ratio on the right side of (2) is equal 0.5 (it means that the financial risk of the prediction error is the same in plus and in minus) and distribution of the demand is symmetric both results are the same.

3. Neural-genetic (GANN) model trained with financial cost function

The financial environment can be included into the forecasting process by the replacement of the statistical square error function used during the neural network training stage, by the goal function resulted from underlying decision situation. According to the energy market prices discussed in previous chapter the cost associated with the single transaction for a given order size y can be expressed by:

$$c(y) = yr_M + \max(ED - y, 0)r_I - \max(y - ED, 0)r_R \tag{3}$$

The goal function for training the model can be developed by summing over the training set the cost terms (3) for the neural network outputs $f(\mathbf{x}, \mathbf{w})$ (1), and training values of the energy demand *ED* [7][8]:

$$E = \sum c(f(\mathbf{x}, \mathbf{w})) \tag{4}$$

where $\mathbf{x}$ denotes inputs, and $\mathbf{w}$ weights of the network.

Taking into account the possibility of future extension of the model we have decided to train the neural network with genetic optimization scheme, because it is almost independent on complexity of the underlying decision problem. Cost function (4) is inconvenient for gradient neural network learning scheme, because it is nondifferentiable, but it is relatively simple, and it is possible to write appropriate weights changing equations. Further extension of the cost analysis model (e.g. including hedging strategy, hour-ahead energy market, etc.) will require application of the more complex goal functions, for which the gradient approach will not be applicable.

The basic parameters of the genetic algorithm were set as follows:

- population of chromosomes with real coding (set of 100 randomly generated chromosomes in the first step),
- tournament selection,
- one point crossover with a probability of crossing equal 0,8
- irregular mutation with a probability of mutation equal 0,007
- limit of generations from 500 up to 30000 epochs.

4. Correction of the forecasts based on assessment of the model variance

It is visible from (2) that the estimation of the optimal size of the energy order according to the financial conditions requires determination of the cumulative probability distribution function of the predicted energy demand $F_{ED}(\cdot)$. Neural network trained with classical square error function approximates the expected value of the predictive energy demand distribution. Assuming that residual factors of the model are normally distributed (it generally holds in our case - see [4]), the distribution of the predicted distribution is also normal with probability density $N(f(\mathbf{x},\mathbf{w}),\sigma_y(x))$. Value $\sigma_y(\mathbf{x})$ denotes the standard deviation of the model output around new data point for a given $\mathbf{x}$ (so called prediction variance or error bar of the model). In this case equation (2) has a unique solution:

$$y^* = F^{-1}_{N(f(\mathbf{x},\mathbf{w}),\sigma_y(x))}\left(\frac{r_I - r_M}{r_I - r_R}\right) \tag{5}$$

or alternatively:

$$y^* = f(\mathbf{x},\mathbf{w}) + \sigma_y(\mathbf{x})F^{-1}_{N(0,1)}\left(\frac{r_I - r_M}{r_I - r_R}\right) \tag{6}$$

where F^{-1} is inverse of the cumulative probability function of the normal distribution. As it is visible from (6) it is possible to obtain the optimal size of the order from the forecast of energy demand given by neural network model, trained with square error function, by addition of the simple correction resulted from uncertainty of the model (given by its variance), and financial risk of the prediction.

The problem of determining of the neural network output variance for a given input have been discussed in many papers in context of estimation of the prediction intervals (error bars) for the forecasts (in STLF see e.g. [2][5-6]). Commonly two main sources of the prediction uncertainty are considered:

$$\sigma_y^2(\mathbf{x}) = \sigma_w^2(\mathbf{x}) + \sigma_\varepsilon^2(\mathbf{x}) \tag{7}$$

Table 1. Financial costs of the forecasting errors for selected hours (PLN)

	Hour	6	12	17	18	24
C_I=0,82	ANN	12224	21461	24341	19827	11409
	GANN	9998	16996	21774	18309	10991
	ANN_ADJ	9029	14007	15080	15252	11213
C_{II}=0,24	ANN	17302	26359	28262	30230	20791
	GANN	14909	23476	28615	28476	14584
	ANN_ADJ	14034	21736	24900	23409	13183
C_{III}=0,5	ANN	21167	34340	37799	35856	23020
	GANN	22363	37959	48121	44495	24623
	ANN_ADJ	21170	34328	37775	35869	23062

where $\sigma_w^2(\mathbf{x})$ denotes model variance associated with weights uncertainty resulted from the sampling error of the training set, and $\sigma_\varepsilon^2(\mathbf{x})$ denotes the random component variance. In our case $\sigma_w^2(\mathbf{x})$ is assessed using bootstrap approach, and input dependent target noise variance $\sigma_\varepsilon^2(\mathbf{x})$ is estimated by additional neural network (for more detailed information see [6]).

5. Simulations and discussion of the obtained results

At this time the energy market in Poland is dominated by the segment of long- and medium- term contracts between the producers and distributors of the energy. Because of this the volume of transactions on the power exchange is rather low. Also the balancing market in Poland is at relatively early stages of its development. The transactions with physical delivery and settlements ran last year in September. The real prices of the energy both in the DAM and balancing market cannot be at this time regarded as representative.

From this reasons presented in this paper methods have been tested using simulated market prices coefficients. As it was mentioned in chapter 2 the optimal size of the order depends on the price ratio on the right side of equation (2). The simulations contained performance analysis for three values of this ratio: C_I=0,82; C_{II}=0,24; C_{III}=0,5. The first case represents situation when costs of overestimation of the order volume are much higher then underestimation. The second one concerns the opposite situation. The last coefficient represent situation when costs of both errors are more or less the same.

Results (for several selected hours) of the performance analysis in terms of the financial costs associated with forecasting errors of each discussed method are presented in Table 1. The used abbreviations: ANN denotes “pure” neural network model, GANN - hybrid neural-genetic model described in chapter 3, ANN_ADJ – neural predictor with financial adjustment described in chapter 4. The data about energy demands and prediction errors came from one of the polish distribution companies. The costs in Table 1 were calculated for one year long set of data.

Both discussed methods gave significant savings of the costs of the transactions in first two cases. Simulations showed that the costs associated with the neural prediction adjustment given by (6) are almost for all cases lower that for GANN model. It is not surprising that in case III where costs of the underestimation and overestimation of the energy demand are the same, the best results were achieved by the standard neural network predictor. In this case square error function correctly evaluates the financial aspects of the problem. Deterioration of the results for ANN_ADJ model is insignificant, but for GANN is very clear.

In conclusion generally ANN_ADJ model is more reliable in our problem then GANN. It is also more flexible regarding to the changes of the prices of the energy on the market. It does not require retraining of the whole model, like in case of GANN. But for more complex decision problems the simple and elegant solution like the given by (6) may be not applicable.

References

1. Bardzki W., Bartkiewicz W., Gontar Z., Zieliński J.S.(1998) Short-term electrical load forecasting in transformation period (Case Study). Proc. of the Intl. ICSC/IFAC Symp. on Neural Computation (NC '98), Vienna, Austria, Sept. 22-26, 324 – 328
2. Bartkiewicz W. (2000) Confidence intervals prediction for the short-term electrical load neural forecasting models, Elektrotechnik und Informationstechnik. 1(117), 8-12
3. Bartkiewicz W, Gontar Z., Zieliński J.S. (2000) Neural-Heuristic approach to short-term load forecasting problems. Proc. of the II International ICSC Symp. on Neural Computation, NC'2000, Berlin, Germany, May 21-26, 740-744
4. Bartkiewicz W. (2000) Distribution of the residuals of neural predictor for short-term electrical load forecasting problems, Proc. of the V Polish Neural Networks Society Conf.: Neural Networks and Soft Computing, Zakopane, June 6 – 10, 112-117
5. Bartkiewicz W., Gontar Z., Zieliński J.S., Bardzki W. (2000) Uncertainty of the short-term load forecasting in utilities. Proc. of the Intl Joint Conference on Neural Networks (IJCNN 2000), Como, Italy, July 24-27, vol. VI, 235-240
6. Bartkiewicz W. (2001) Error bars for short-term load forecasting neural networks models. Proc of X-th Intl. Conf. on Present-Day Problems of Power Engineering (APE '01), Gdańsk - Jurata, June 6-8, vol. III, pp. 75-82
7. Matusiak B. (2000) Hybrid Neural – Genetic System for Energy Transaction Planning. Proc. of the III Conf. on Theory and Applications of Artificial Intelligence (CAI 2000), Łódź, Poland, October 5-7, 41-48
8. Matusiak B., Bartkiewicz W. (2001) Linking neural predictors with decision models: The short-term load forecasting case study. Proc of X-th Intl Conf. on Present-Day Problems of Power Engineering (APE '2001), Gdańsk - Jurata, Poland, June 6-8, vol. III, 109-116
9. Rules of the Balancing Market 2000 in Poland ver. 1.0., PSE S.A., Warsaw, (in Polish)

Systolic Architecture for Higher Order Neural Networks

Jarosław Bilski, Jacek Smoląg

Department of computer Engineering, Technical University of Częstochowa,
Al. Armii Krajowej 36, 42-200 Częstochowa, Poland,
e-mail: bilski{jsmolag}@kik.pcz.czest.pl

Abstract. The higher order neural networks extend classical neural networks structures. In this case we can apply fewer number of layers and neurons to achieve the same results as classical feedforward neural networks. The paper describes the idea of the systolic architecture for higher order neural networks. The systolic architecture for the recall phase is presented and the computational performance is analysed. The number of iteration strongly depends on the network order and number of layer inputs but it does not depend on number of neurons.

1. Introduction

The higher order neural networks have bigger abilities than classical neural networks. Their neurons operate based on the following equation

$$y = f(s)$$

where

$$s = w_0 + \sum_{i_1=1}^{n} w_{i_1} x_{i_1} + \sum_{i_1,i_2=1}^{n} w_{i_1 i_2} x_{i_1} x_{i_2} + \sum_{i_1,i_2,i_3=1}^{n} w_{i_1 i_2 i_3} x_{i_1} x_{i_2} x_{i_3} + \ldots$$

or

$$s = w_0 + \sum_{k=1}^{N} w_k \prod_{i \in P} x_i$$

Model of this neuron is shown in Fig. 1. Several results concerning learning of the higher order neural networks have been presented in [1, 2]. This structure requires a lot of computation for each neuron. In [3, 4, 5, 6] various systolic architectures for

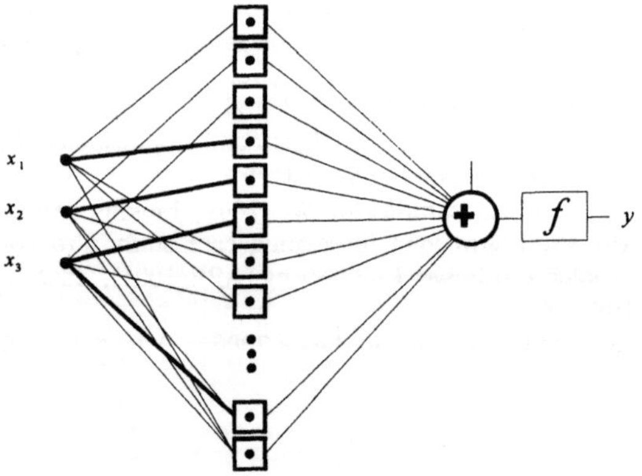

Fig. 1 Model of higher order neuron

implementation of neural networks and learning algorithms have been studied. In this paper systolic techniques are applied to the high order neural network realisation.

2. Systolic architecture

Systolic arrays are the simplest regular, modular structures with only local interconnections [3]. Systolic architecture of higher order neuron consists of two parts: multiplier part and accumulation part. The aim of first the part is calculation of required products of inputs. It is obtained by using special ring systolic array with FIFO memory. The other part multiplies products from the first part by appropriate weights and next accumulate results (see Fig.2).

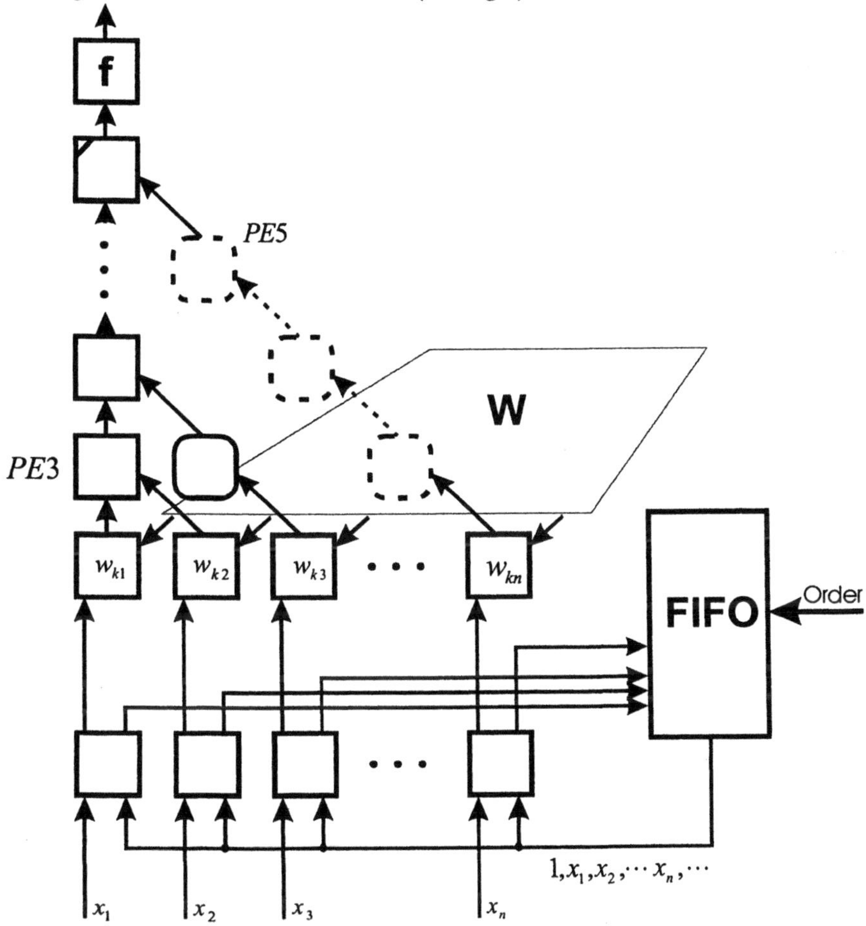

Fig. 2. Systolic architecture of one higher order neuron

All processing elements of one higher order neuron in systolic architecture are presented in Fig. 3. The way of preparing elements in weight matrix is depicted in Fig. 4.

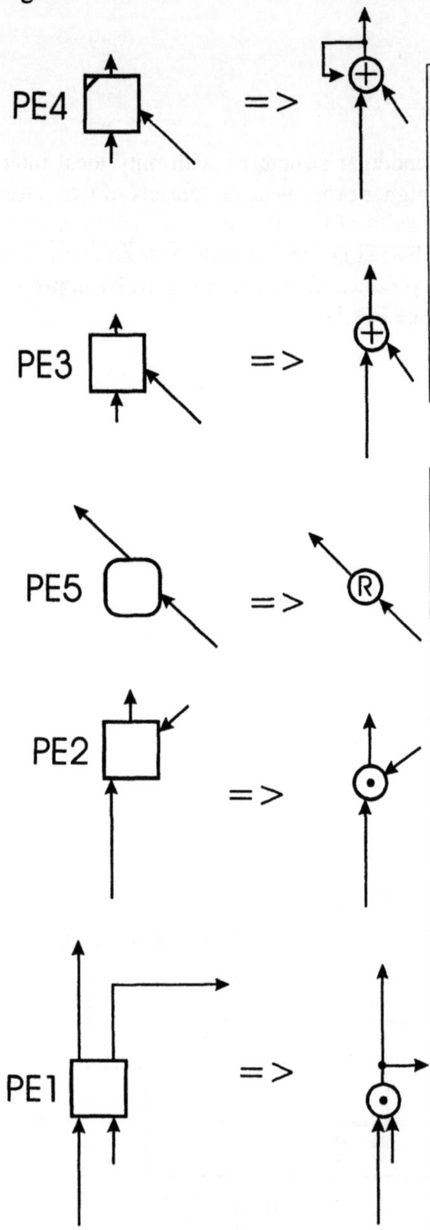

Fig. 3. Higher order neuron processing elements

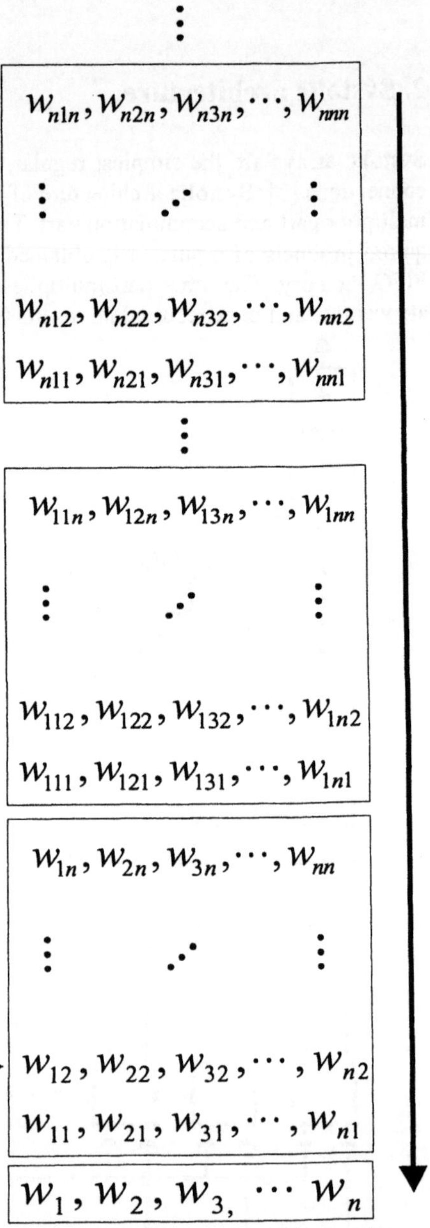

Fig. 4. The form of weight matrix

One layer of the high order neural network is shown in Fig. 5. It is easy to observe that the number of time cycles for this layer is the same as for a single neuron. It is because the multiplier part is common for all neurons and the accumulation parts operate parallel. It causes an important advantage; the number of time cycles does not depend on number of neurons in a single layer. Of course complexity of systolic architecture increases.

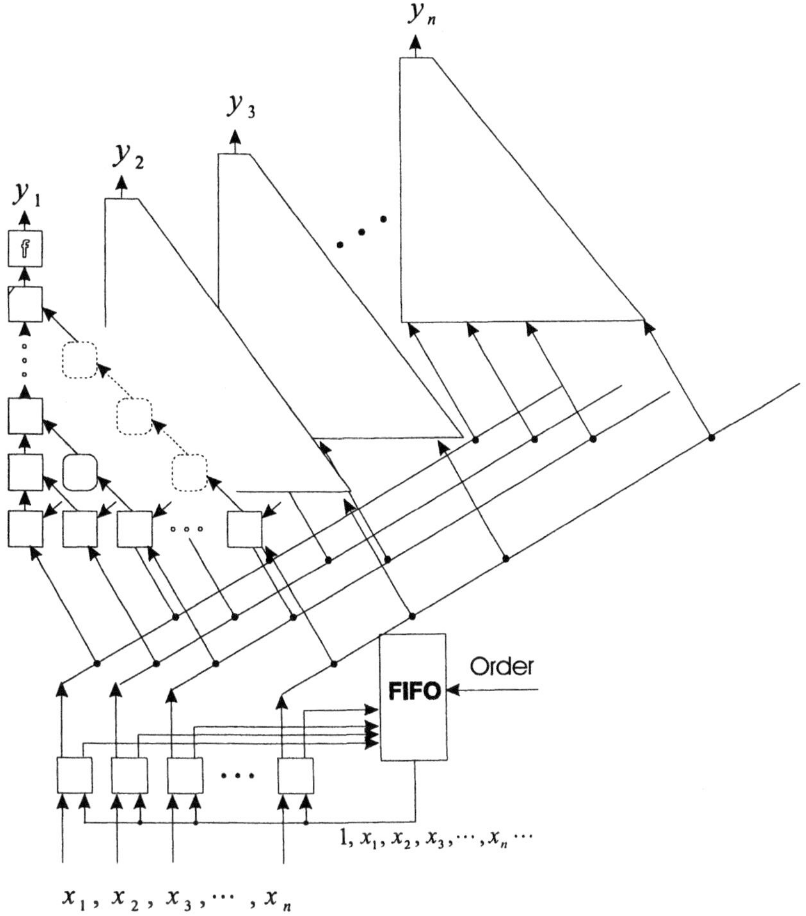

Fig. 5. One higher order neural network layer

3. Conclusion

In this paper we analysed the computational performance of the high order neural network systolic implementation versus classical serial implementation. Number of time cycles in classical (serial) and systolic implementations are given by

$$OPS_{serial} = \sum_{i}^{N} (1+i)n^{i}$$

$$OPS_{systolic} = 1 + n + \sum_{i}^{N} n^{i-1}$$

respectively, where N is an order and n is a number of inputs.

Fig. 6 presents number of time cycles in classical and systolic implementations of single high order neuron

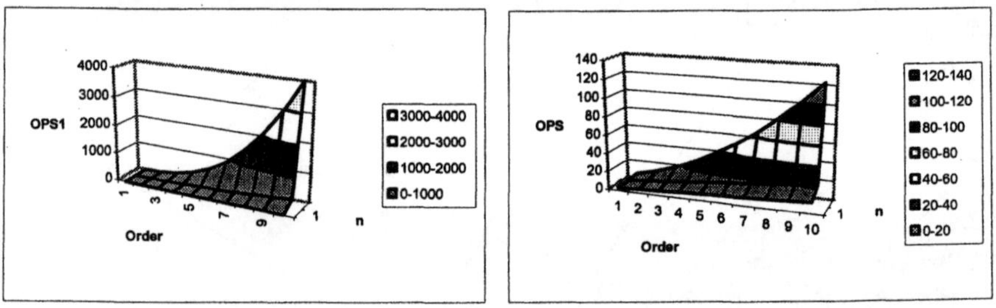

Fig. 6. Number of time cycles in a) classical (serial) and b) systolic implementation

while Fig. 7 shows performance factor. It can be noted that number of time cycles in systolic implementation does not depend on number of neurons in neural network layer.

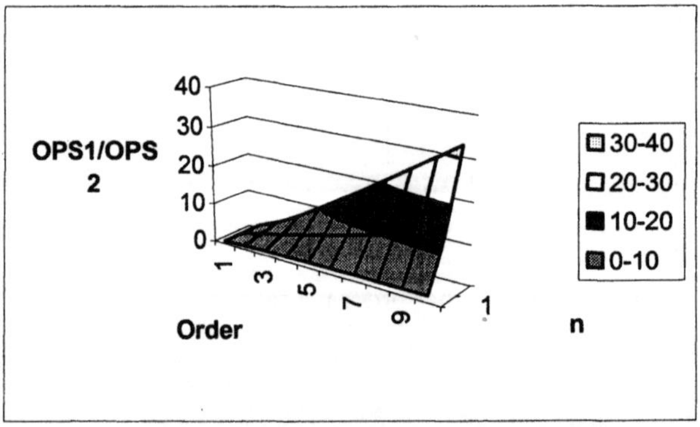

Fig. 7. Performance factor for systolic architecture

We observed that systolic implementation outperforms classical one.

References

[1] M. Güler, E. Sahin (1994) A Binary-input Supervised Neural Unit that Forms Input Dependent Higher-order Synaptic Correlations, Proc. Of World Congress on Neural Networks, III, pp.730-735

[2] M. Güler (1994) The neuron as a computational unit, Hints from Life to AI, METU

[3] S. Y. Kung (1988) VLSI D Array Processors, Prentice Hall

[4] S. Y. Kung (1993) Digital Neural Networks, Prentice Hall

[5] J. Smoląg, L. Rutkowski, J. Bilski (1999) Systolic array for neural networks, IV KSNiIZ, Zakopane, pp. 487-497

[6] Smoląg J., Bilski J. (2000) A systolic array for fast learning of neural networks, VNNSC Zakopane, pp. 754-758

Decomposition and Argument Reduction of Neural Networks

P. Buciak[1], T. Łuba[1], H. Niewiadomski[1], M. Pleban[1], P. Sapiecha[1], H. Selvaraj[2]

[1] Department of Electronics and Information Technology, Warsaw University of Technology Nowowiejska 15/19, 00-665 Warsaw, Poland, luba@tele.pw.edu.pl
[2] Department of Electrical and Computer Engineering, University of Nevada, Las Vegas, Las Vegas, NV USA 89154, salvaraj@ee.unlv.edu

Abstract. The article presents methods of dealing with huge data in the domain of neural networks. The decomposition of neural networks is introduced and its efficiency is proved by the authors' experiments. The examinations of the effectiveness of argument reduction in the above filed, are presented. Authors indicate, that decomposition is capable of reducing the size and the complexity of the learned data, and thus it makes the learning process faster or, while dealing with large data, possible. According to the authors' experiments, in some cases, argument reduction, makes the learning process harder.

Keywords. Neural networks, decomposition, back propagation, argument reduction, control systems.

1. Introduction

Often, in the area of neural networks, computers have to deal with unmanageable amount of information, stored in decision tables of many inputs and outputs [9, 20]. The more complex such a function is, the more difficult it is to achieve satisfactory training results. So the objective is to reduce the number of inputs and outputs in such a way, that no information is lost. Hence, in such cases the application of decomposition seems to be a natural approach.

Generally speaking, decomposition appears as a fundamental problem of great importance for a wide spectrum of scientific fields: knowledge discovery, machine learning, artificial intelligence, logic synthesis, computer-aided design of very large integrated circuits [2].

In this paper, we will focus on decomposition of multiple-valued functions based on the graph coloring heuristics. In gradient decent methods the goal is to find the structure of a neural network suitable for given data. However, some research in this field has been done, but currently there is a lack of general method.

The decomposition method of decision tables based on graph coloring heuristics generalizes the decomposition of Ashenhurst, Curtis, Łuba, Perkowski/Wang [1, 3, 16].

2. Decomposition of MVL Functions

This section contains the formulation of several basic ideas related to functional decomposition [7, 8, 17, 20]. Let C_i and D be finite sets for all $i \in \{1, 2, ..., n\}$. *The multiple-valued function F* is defined as a mapping $F(X_1, ..., X_n) : C_1 \times ... \times C_n \rightarrow D$. Every element of the domain $C_1 \times ... \times C_n$ is called *a minterm* (*sample* or *object*). A listing of minterms with the value of the function is called *a decision table* (or *truth table* in binary case). Decision tables do not include minterms for which the function values are not specified. For the sake of clarity this unspecified set of minterms will be called *Don't Care Set* (*DC*). There, the functions with non-empty *DC*-set will be called *the partial functions*. Let F be a multiple-valued function representing functional dependency $Y = F(X)$, where X is the set of *input variables* and Y is the set of *output variables*. Let the partition of input variables into two disjoint sets: *the free set A* and *the bound set B* be given. We say that there exists *a*

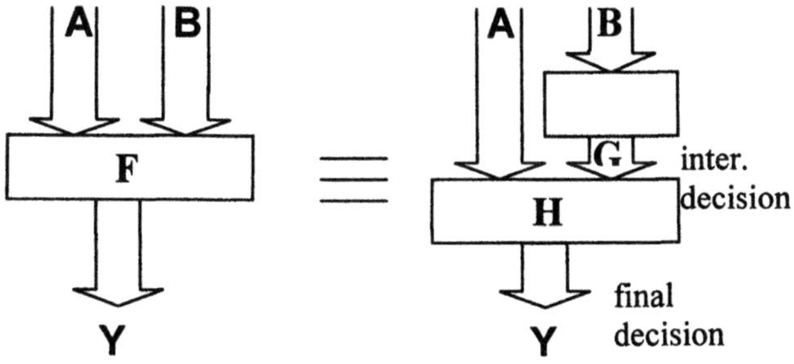

Fig. 1. Decomposition Scheme

functional decomposition of F if $F(X) = H(A, G(B))$. More precisely speaking, G and H denote functional dependencies $Y = H(A, Z)$ and $Z = G(B)$. Function $H(A, G(B))$ is called a simple disjoint decomposition of function F. The structure of decomposed decision function is shown in fig. 1. It is necessary to emphasize that the function after decomposition is equivalent to one before decomposition, as decomposition is a method which helps to structure a decision table.

The interpretation of the presented scheme is as follows. At the beginning, the intermediate decision is taken on the basis of attributes from subset B. Then consequently, the final decision is taken with respect to both intermediate decision and attributes from subset A. The fundamental problem is then, given a function F and the partition of the set of input variables into sets A and B, to find the functions G and H, such that $F = H(A, G(B))$. To solve this problem, let us first introduce some useful concepts.

The decomposition chart of the function F consists of a two dimensional matrix with columns indexed using the values of the bound set variables and rows indexed using the values of the free set of variables. Elements of the matrix $m_{i,j}$ are the values assumed by the function F for the vectors constructed from i-th row and j-th column. *The column multiplicity* of the matrix is denoted by $\nu(B|A)$.

Theorem 1 *Let $F : [m]^n \rightarrow [m]^k$, $F = \{f_i\}_{i \in [k]}$ be a group of finite functions, where $f_i : [m]^n \rightarrow [m]$. Let A and B be a pair of disjoint subsets of variables Var(F). Then:*

$F(A, B) = H(A, G(B)) \Leftrightarrow \nu(B|A) \leq d^j$,

where:

$G = \{g_k(A)\}_{k=1,...,j}$ for $g_k : [m]^{Card(A)} \rightarrow [d]$ and

$H = \{h_l(G(A), B)\}_{l=1,...,n}$ for $h_l : [u]^{j+Card(B)} \rightarrow [m]$,

$u = max\{d, m\}$

Proof See [7, 17].

This theorem suggests that the fundamental problem of a partial finite function decomposition is nothing but finding an expansion of the function for which $\nu(B|A)$ has the least value, and this problem can be reduced to a graph coloring problem [14, 17]. Its objective is to color all the vertices of the graph with a minimal number of colors, in such a way, that no two adjacent vertices (in our case columns, that are contradictory), are assigned the same color. Even though the above-mentioned problem is in general NP-hard, many heuristics have been invented (e.g. Seq. Algorithm, Seq. Algorithm with Ordering, Maximal Independent Sets Algorithm), which solve it in polynomial time [12].

Example 1.

Let us decompose function F given in table 1 in conformity with Algorithm 1.

Table 1. Decision table of function F

B			A		F
x_1	x_2	x_3	x_4	x_5	
0	0	0	0	0	0
2	0	2	2	0	2
1	1	1	0	0	0
1	1	1	1	1	1
0	0	0	1	1	1
2	2	2	2	0	2
1	1	2	1	1	1
1	0	1	0	0	1
1	1	1	2	0	1
1	1	2	0	0	2

Table 2. Decomposition chart

A \ B	000	101	111	112	202	222
00	0	1	0	2	-	-
11	1	-	1	1	-	-
20	-	-	1	-	2	2

The decomposition chart of function F is constructed in table 2.

Afterwards the graph $G_{F(A,B)}$ (fig. 2) of incompatible columns is created and coloring algorithm is executed. For instance columns 000 and 101, in contrast to columns 112 and 202, are incompatible and consequently they are colored with different numbers.

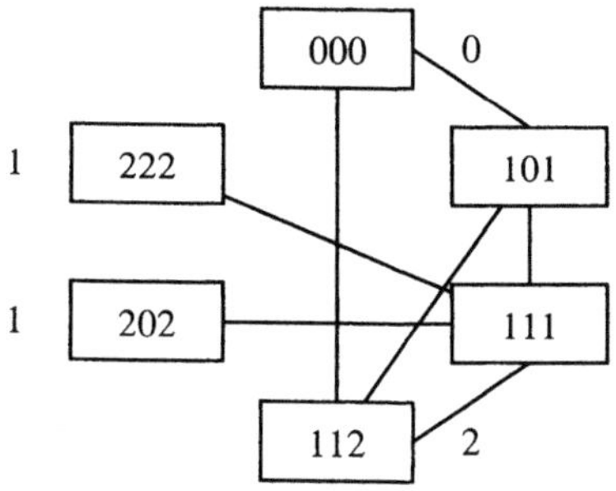

Fig. 2. Incompatibility graph

Table 3. Function G

B			G
x_1	x_2	x_3	
0	0	0	0
1	0	1	1
1	1	1	0
1	1	2	2
2	0	2	1
2	2	2	1

Table 4. Function H

A		G	H
x_4	x_5		
0	0	0	0
0	0	1	1
0	0	2	2
1	1	0	1
1	1	2	1
2	0	0	1
2	0	1	2

Finally decision tables for functions G and H (respectively table 3 and 4) are derived from previously colored graph $G_{F(A,B)}$.

3. Argument reduction

Is a procedure of elimination of redundant inputs of the system. Theory and algorithms can be found in [11, 15].

4. Experimental results

The main objective of our experiments was the analysis of the influence of decomposition and argument reduction on neural network training process. Then, instead of one large network, the decision tables (and therefore neural networks) were decomposed into five sub-networks connected in a way presented in fig. 3 (the number of neurons is limited because of clarity). We tried to train two architectures of neural networks: the first one, which consisted of single neural network and the second – composed of five neural networks connected in a serial way.

Table 5. The training results (data without argument reduction)

# of	Original network		Decomposed network (into 5 blocks)		
patterns	Mean Square Error	# of error pat.	Sub-net's name	Mean Square Error	# of error pat.
			G1	0.0045	23
			G2	0.0012	4
1102	1.650	1102	G3	0.0005	0
			G4	0.0015	1
			H	0.1127	119
			G1	0.0128	167
			G2	0.0143	183
4369	2.355	4369	G3	0.0017	0
			G4	0.0062	3
			H	0.2397	310
			G1	0.0286	636
			G2	0.0875	1911
17688	6.089	17688	G3	0.1742	20
			G4	0.1047	82
			H	1.6148	2350

Table 6. The training results (data after argument reduction)

# of	Original network		Decomposed network (into 5 blocks)		
patterns	Mean Square Error	# of error pat.	Sub-net's name	Mean Square Error	# of error pat.
			G1	0.140	6
			G2	1.515	49
1091	21.81	1091	G3	2.406	76
			G4	0.481	10
			H	22.88	12437
			G1	0.851	119
			G2	0.875	67
4275	24.51	4275	G3	3.090	407
			G4	0.480	6
			H	24.59	56820
			G1	1.796	1361
			G2	1.310	1389
16356	25.23	16356	G3	1.376	213
			G4	1.167	64
			H	25.39	239554

For decomposition and reduction we applied our software *HOSEA* [9, 13, 14]. Neural networks simulations were performed on Stuttgart Neural Network Simulator (*SNNS*) [19].

The data set consisted of 17688 disjoint 4-valued patterns of 60 inputs and 24 outputs and was acquired as a result of air pollution measurements of a power plant (unfortunately, the name and location can not be disclosed due to official restrictions). In order to find out how the results of our approach depend on the size of a pattern set, smaller training sets were prepared, using selection with equal probability from original pattern set.

The effects of training with Scaled Conjugate Gradient [4, 21] algorithm are presented in table 5, 6. The time of training was limited to 3600 seconds.

It is necessary to emphasize, that networks before and after decomposition are equivalent in information sense, as the decomposition methodology, what has been already stated, does not lose information.

We can see that, after applying the decomposition, the mean square error as well as the number of erroneous patterns and bits decreased considerably. It is important to point out that before the application of the decomposition the data were too complex to be trained effectively. However, after the decomposition of the data, we achieved a reasonable training results. As it is shown in table 5, the most difficult problem was to properly learn the *H* sub-network. The reason of that is the difficulty of the intermediate decision encoding.

Another interesting observation is the fact, that argument reduction decreased significantly the effectiveness of learning. At first sight it seems to be counterintuitive, but it may be explained by the form of the data after reduction. In our case the number of neural network's inputs was decreased, but the size of the data (compare the first column of tables 6 and 5) remained almost the same, what had a negative impact on training process. According to our results, the efficiency of training may be improved after argument reduction only if the degree of freedom of neural network and the size of data are diminished in comparative degree.

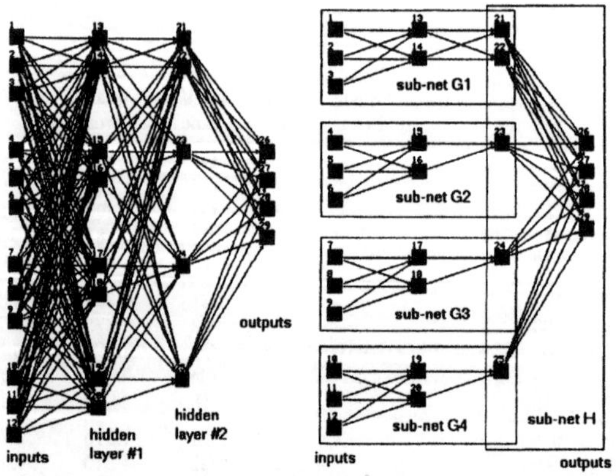

Fig. 3a, 3b. The network before and after decomposition

5. Conclusions

The decomposition allows processing of data which, in the original form, are not suitable for data mining, because of its huge size. It proved to be very effective, as the number of mistakes was kept at a reasonable level. The influence of argument reduction strategy was also examined. The experiments shown, that it is not a general approach and in some cases it can even make training impossible.

References

[1] R. L. Ashenhurst, The Decomposition of Switching Functions, *Proc. Int. Symp. of Theory. of Switching*, 1957.

[2] S. Chang, M. Marek-Sadowska, T. Hwang, Technology mapping for TLU FPGA's based on decomposition of Binary Decision Diagrams, *IEEE Transaction on Computers*, vol. 15, No. 10, 1996.

[3] H. A. Curtis, *A New Approach to the Design of Switching Circuits*, Princeton, N.J., Van Nostrand, 1962.

[4] S. Y. Kung, *Digital Neural Networks*, PTR Prentice Hall, 1993.

[5] Y. Lai, K. Pan, M. Pedram, OBDD-based functional decomposition: algorithms and implementation, *IEEE Transaction on Computers*, vol. 15, No. 8, 1996.

[6] Y. Lai, M. Pedram, S. Vrudhula, EVOBDD-based algorithms for integer linear programming, spectral transformation, and functional decomposition, *IEEE Transaction on Computers*, vol. 13, No. 8, 1994.

[7] T. Łuba, Decomposition of multiple-valued functions, *Proc. IEEE-ISMVL*, USA, 1995.

[8] T. Łuba, C. Moraga, S. Yanushkevich, M. Opoka, V. Shmerko Evolutionary Multi-Level Network Synthesis in Given Design Style, *Proc. IEEE-ISMVL*, Portland, Oregon, USA, 2000.

[9] T. Łuba, H. Niewiadomski, H. Pleban, H. Selvaraj, P. Sapiecha, Functional decomposition and its application in design of digital circuits and machine learning, *IASTED Inter. Conf. On Applied Informatics*, Innsbruck, Austria, 2001.

[10] T. Masters, *Neural Networks in Practice*, Prentice-Hall, 1996.

[11] Z. Pawlak, Rough Sets: Theoretical Aspects of Reasoning About Data, Kluwer, 1991

[12] M. Perkowski, R. Malvi, S. Grygiel, M. Burns, A. Mishchenko, Graph coloring algorithms for fast evaluation of Curtis decompositions, *DAC*, 1999.

[13] P. Sapiecha, H. Selvaraj, M. Pleban, Decomposition of Boolean Relations and Functions in Logic Synthesis and Data Analysis, *The Second International Conference on Rough Sets and Current Trends in Computing*, Banff, Canada, 2000.

[14] H. Selvaraj, H. Niewiadomski, M. Pleban, P. Sapiecha, Decomposition of Digital Circuits and Neural Networks, Proc. SCI 2001, US, 2001.

[15] A. Skowron, C. Rauszer, The discernibility matrices and functions in information systems in: R. Slowinski (Ed.), Intelligent Decision Support. Handbook of Applications and Advances on the Rough Set Theory, Kluwer, 1992

[16] C. Yang, V. Singhal, M. Ciesielski, BDD decomposition for efficient logic synthesis, International Conference on Computer Design, 1999.

[17] W. Wan, M. Perkowski, A New Approach to the Decomposition of Incompletely Specified Multi-Output Function Based on Graph Coloring and Local Transformations and Its Application to FPGA Mapping, Proc. Euro-DAC'92.,1992.

[18] D. de Werra, Heuristics for Graph Coloring, Computational Graph Theory, Tinhofer, Mayr, Noltenmeier, Syslo (Eds.), Springer-Verlag, New York, 1990.

[19] http://www-ra.informatik.untuebingen.de/SNNS/

[20] B. Zupan, M. Bohanec, J. Demšar, I. Bratko, Feature transformation by function decomposition, IEEE Expert, Special Issue on Feature Transformation. 1997.

[21] J. M. Żurada, Introduction to Artificial Neural Systems, West Publishing Company, St. Paul, 1992.

Traffic Flow Simulation - Cellular Automata with Fuzzy Rules Approach

Marcin Burzyński[1], Waldemar Cudny[1,2], and Witold Kosiński[3]

[1] Institute of Environmental Mechanics and Applied Computer Science
Bydgoszcz University, ul. Chodkiewicza 30, 85-064 Bydgoszcz
email marcinb@ito.pl

[2] Institute of Fundamental Technological Research, IPPT PAN
Polish Academy of Sciences, ul. Świętokrzyska 21, 00-049 Warszawa
email wcudny@ippt.gov.pl

[3] Research Center, Chair of Artificial Intelligence
Polish-Japanese Institute of Information Technology
ul. Koszykowa 86, 02-008 Warszawa, *email wkos@pjwstk.edu.pl*

Abstract. A discrete automaton model with fuzzy rules to simulate one–way traffic flow is introduced. Results of simulations are consistent with the so-called fundamental diagram (flow versus density), as is observed in the real free–way traffic. Fuzzy controller approach makes possible to include driver's individual characteristics and provides a new point of view in the further traffic flow research.

1 Introduction

Modelling traffic transport problem is very interesting and important for its dynamics and serious dramatic consequences in real life. We focus on the cellular automata approach (CA) instead of on the classical ones (the kinetic theory of vehicular traffic [13], or fluid–dynamics approach [14]) because of one important property of cellular automata, namely the lack of stability, i.e. very small changes in transition rules or states can have very dramatic consequences [2]. Finally, in the contrast to the differential equation approach, the biggest advantage of CA is that each cell of the automaton can reflect individual object characteristics. Recently the cellular automaton approach is chosen more often in different area, e.g. for biological models [9], modelling spread and movement of an oil slick [8], simulation of behaviour of vivid entities population and modelling predator-prey systems [1,3,5] and to model physical problems like heat conductivity [4].

We develop cellular automaton transition rules by a fuzzy controlling decision process, and call them *Fuzzy Rules*. We claim that those rules describe the way in which a driver behaves in the reality, hence they are more suitable than the classical deterministic transition rules.

Fuzzy transition rules and a more complex set of states of cells lead to the model which cannot be classified as a classical cellular automata [10], and it is more correctly to place it between cellular automaton and multiagent simulations.

2 Model

Used model is similar to that introduced by Nagel and Schreckeberg [6,7]. However, some crucial details are changed: we use rules based on a fuzzy controller instead of probabilistic rules and some driver's individual characteristic are included in our model.

Lattice. The computional model is defined on a 1D Cartesian lattice of the linear size L and with periodic boundary conditions. Each cell can be empty or occupied by a single car. Each cell is described by the set of parameters as follows: $F = 0$ or 1, this parameter determines whether the cell is empty or it is occupied by a car. $V = 0$ or 1 to 7, it is spot speed of the car. $V_{max} =$ 0 or 1 to 7, it is maximal speed that car can develop. $N = 0$ or 1 to number of cars.

Neighborhood . Due to the driver's observation direction, we define asymmetric neighborhood of a cell a_n as the set of cells $\{a_{n+1}, a_{n+2}, ..., a_{n+7}\}$.

Time evolution of model. Cells are updated synchronously by each car translation based on the distance S proportional to the calculated velocity V; due to the unit time interval in most cases $S = V$. The main advantage of the synchronous approach is the easy way to implement the model on Beowulf Computer Cluster what is needed for more complex models.

Fuzzy controller. We use a Mamdani Controller [12] to control the output variable A which is the acceleration and the slowing down (the negative acceleration) of a car. There are two input variables: the distance D to a nearest car and the spot speed V. All three variables are regarded as linguistic variables to which fuzzy sets are attached. Parameters of triangular membership functions of sets A, D, V (see Fig. 1) and a rule matrix have been chosen arbitrarily to avoid a car crash (see Table 1).

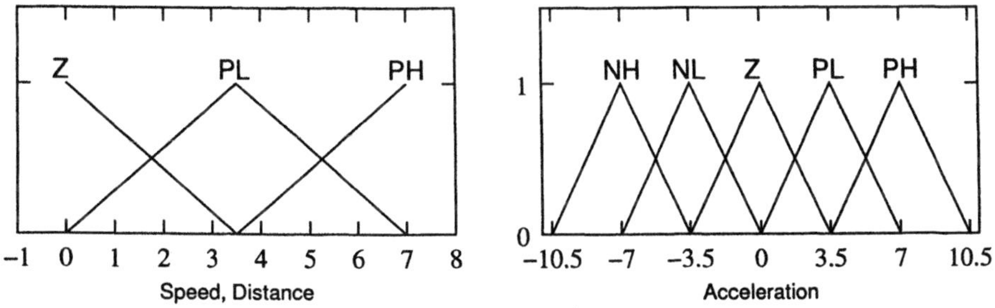

Fig. 1. Fuzzy sets of input and output variable

Notice the rule matrix is symmetric. Both the control and detection processes are simplified to be linear. In further research we are going to include nonlinear detection process (based on driver's utility function [11]) and then we will be able to use all advantages of fuzzy controlling. Moreover, different rules can be used, e.g. Takagi–Sugeno–Kondo. Having a set of training data an adaptation module could be constructed and then added to the system.

Table 1. Rule Matrix

		Speed		
		Z	PL	PH
	Z	*Z*	*NL*	*NH*
Distance	PL	*PL*	*Z*	*NL*
	PH	*PH*	*PL*	*Z*

Transition Rules. The dynamics in one iteration is realized as follows:

- Choose a cell,
- If it is empty do nothing,
- If the cell is occupied by a car:
  - Detect distance D to the next car,
  - If there is no car in neighborhood:
    - Acceleration $A = 1$, $V = V + A$,
    - If $V > V_{max}$, $V = V_{max}$,
    - Car translation $S = V$,
    - Car is advanced to site $b_{n+S} = a_n$,
  - There is a car in the neighborhood:
    - Send D, V to Fuzzy Controller,
    - Controller will calculate acceleration A,
    - $V = V + A$,
    - If $V > V_{max}$, $V = V_{max}$,
    - If $V < 0$, $V = 0$,
    - Car translation $S = V$,
    - If $S > D$, considered car crashes into the next car, cells occupied by cars that crashed are updated to empty site: $a_n = 0$ and $a_{n+S} = 0$,
    - If $S \leq D$, car is advanced to site $b_{n+S} = a_n$,
- Repeat for all cells,
- When it is done:
  - Primary Array = Secondary Array,
  - Secondary Array = 0 (each cell is updated to empty cell).

Implementation. The model was implemented in ANSI Cage. All simulations runs have been carried out on workstation powered by Duron 1 GHz processor, 192 MB PC100 SDRAM. Linux Mandrake 8.1 has been chosen as an operation system for its stability. Program was compiled by "gcc" version 2.96, with "-O1" parameter. Main program was run by BASH script for multiply call with the same or different sets of input parameters. When size of automaton is $L = 10^4$, the number of iteration is $I = 10^4$ or more and due to averaging of results many simulations has to be done. It is obviously that the used hardware configuration cannot longer satisfy requirements of the time efficiency. That is why we consider to implement our model on Cluster of Workstation (COW) using LAM Library (parallel processing environment). LAM is using Message-Passing Interface (MPI) which is easy to implement.

3 Simulations

Initial parameters. Most of simulations were performed on lattices of 1000 cells. The number of iterations was $I = 10^4$. We have also examined dynamics of automata with the lattice of 10^4 sites. All initial parameters were input through script file.

Parameters of Mamdani controller. At this stage of research we have decided to apply the same fuzzy sets' parameters to every car. It is obvious that to distinguish drivers' characteristics in our further models one has to use an independent set of fuzzy sets' parameters for each driver.

Initial state of automaton. Initial conditions are generated randomly. Therefore automaton initial state of cells is prepared before starting the simulations. Special stand-alone program was written to prepare *cell population.* First, we choose car density. Second, we initiate a set of parameters that denote a discrete distribution of the maximal car speed. The last two parameters are: the size of automata and a boolean parameter that controls whether the spot speed of a car is chosen randomly from $\langle 0; V_{max} \rangle$ or it is set to zero.

Measured Variables. As it was said our model based on an 1D automaton with periodic boundary conditions, it means the traffic simulation was performed in a long closed loop and on a single lane. The total number N of cars in the automaton cannot change during one simulation, thus it is possible to define constant system density

$$\rho = N/L. \tag{1}$$

This is a drastic simplification of the problem, because the constant number of cars is not usually possible in the real traffic flow. Thus, to reflect real conditions, number of cars should be measured and averaged on a fixed site over a time period.

The flow rate is measured as follow:

- A continuous set of sites is chosen arbitrary, let us call it Tunnel.
- Before first iteration will be done, we detect and save configuration of the Tunnel,
- After iteration t_i we detect a new configuration and compare to the previous one,
- If any new car appears (therefore we need cars to be numbered) we set $n(t) = 1$, else $n(t) = 0$.

The flow rate is defined by

$$q = \frac{1}{I} \sum_{i=1}^{I} n(t_i). \tag{2}$$

4 Results

The main object of our study is the fundamental diagram. Performed simulations' results are consistent with Schreckenberg's model [6] and real measurements [16].

Distribution of maximal speed V_{max} can change the fundamental diagram. As it is shown on Fig. 2 there are two maxima instead of one. It is evident there are no the same fancy for a maximal speed among drivers. A number of drivers with high speeds or idlers can change dramaticly the traffic flow dynamics. Therefore we notice a need to examine relationships between the preferable maximal speed and the fundamental diagram.

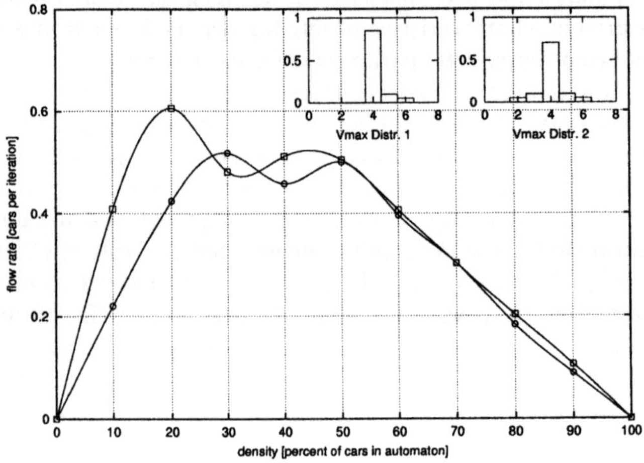

Fig. 2. Fundamental diagrams (flow rate versus density). Curve(□): number of iterations $I = 10^4$, size of automaton $L = 10^4$, V_{max} distribution 1. Curve (∘): $I = 10^4$, $L = 10^3$, V_{max} distribution 2 .

5 Conclusions

At the present we are at an early stage with our research. Introduced model is simple but implemented procedures, fuzzy transition rules and type of data that described a single driver make it promising as a starting point for more sophisticated simulations. We are going to develop driver's characteristics by adding a new parameter to characterize the individual minimal safety distance to the next car. We suspect the fuzzy controller reflects correctly the way in which decisions are made by a driver; it is obvious, however, that there are differences among drivers [11]. Hence a different controller can be used, for example, based on Takagi–Sugeno–Kondo rules which possess fuzzy premise parts and functional consequent ones. Now the output (defuzzification) is calculated as the center of the gravity of the fuzzy consequent part.

According to the cellular automaton character, it is possible the model's dynamics becomes more dramatic by applying different decision unit to each driver. A number of papers have been written about single lane traffic simulation, therefore it is a time to examine dual carriage-way model. All those features cause that a single workstation cannot longer manage simulation of more complex models. Hence we are going to implement our model on parallel computers.

References

1. Burzyński, M. (2001): Symulowanie układu drapieżca-ofiara za pomocą automatu komórkowe. M.Sc. Thesis, Akademia Bydgoska im. Kazimierza Wielkiego, Wydział Matematyki, Techniki i Nauk Przyrodniczych, Bydgoszcz
2. Kułakowski, K. (2000): *Automaty komórkowe.* "jak", Kraków
3. Droz, M., Pekalski A. (2000): Coexistence in predator-prey system. to be published in *Phys. Rev. E.*
4. Nagórski, Z. (2001): *Modelowanie przewodzenia ciepła za pomocą arkusza kalkulacyjnego, MRS+Excel->KM3R.* Oficyna Wydawnicza Politechniki Warszawskiej, Warszawa
5. Lipowski, A. (1999): Oscillatory behavior in a lattice prey-predator system. *Physical Review E*, **60** (5), 5179-5184
6. Nagel, K., Schreckenberg M. (1992): A cellular automaton model for freeway traffic. *J. Phys. I France*, **2**, 2221-2229
7. Schadschneider, A., Schreckenberg, M. (1993): Cellular automaton models and traffic flow. *J. Phys. A: Math. Gen.* **26**, 679-683
8. Karafyllidis, I. (1997): A model for the prediction of oil slick movement and spreading using cellular automata. *Environment International*, **23** (6), 839-850
9. Ermentrout, G. B., Edelstein-Keshet, L. (1993): Cellular automata approaches to biological modeling. *J. Theor. Biol.*, **160**, 97-133
10. Wolfram, S. (Fall 1983): Cellular automata. *Los Alamos Science*, **9**, 2-21
11. Wang, X., Wang, F. (2000): A driver's Utility Function and its Properties. UCI-ITS-WP-0014, Institute of Transport Studies and Department of Civil & Environmental Engineering University of California.
12. Łachwa, A. (2001): *Rozmyty świat zbiorów, liczb, relacji, faktów, reguł i decyzji.* EXIT, Warszawa
13. Prigogine, I., Herman, R. (1971): *Kinetic Theory of Vehicular Traffic.* Elsevier, New York
14. Lighthill, M. J., Whitman, G. B. (1955): *Proc. R. Soc. Lond.*, **A 229**, 317
15. Piegat, A. (1999): *Modelowanie i sterowanie rozmyte.* EXIT, Warszawa
16. Hall, F. L., Brian, L. A., Gunter, M. A. (1986): *Transport Rev.*, **A 3** ,197

An MLP Predictor of ELF Environmental Magnetic Fields Pollution

G. Capizzi[1], S. Coco[1], C. Giuffrida[1], A. Laudani[1], G. Pappalardo[2], R. Pulvirenti[1]

[1]DEES - University of Catania, V. A. Doria 6, Catania, Italy 95125, e-mail: capizzi@dees.unict.it

[2]DMI - University of Catania, V. A. Doria 6, Catania, Italy 95125

Abstract. In this paper an MLP neural network is presented aimed to predict ELF environmental magnetic field pollution originating from electric devices. The inputs to the neural network are measured values of the three components of the ELF stationary magnetic field taken at accessible points lying on a regular grid enclosing a current free region. The MLP NN predicts magnetic field values at points internal to the grid. The neural network training is performed off-line by using polynomial harmonic functions. In order to validate the procedure a simple case study is illustrated concerned with the neural prediction of ELF magnetic field intensity within a current free parallelepiped region, surrounded by active conductors carrying assigned currents.

1 Introduction

There is wide concern about the Extremely Low Frequency (ELF) electromagnetic emissions originating from electric devices, whose effects on human health are not fully understood and perhaps potentially dangerous. For this reason continuous monitoring of levels of human exposition to ELF fields is performed by extensive measurements in regions of interest taken at few accessible points. However, it is difficult to reconstruct the complete field behavior from the measured data, since a suitable inverse modeling, depending on the peculiar field structure, is necessary. In the simplest cases, when a direct model of the electromagnetic problem is available (position and emission features of all electromagnetic sources and their interactions with the environment are known), a direct computation of fields is carried out. On the other hand, when the problem does not lend itself to easy direct modeling, an inverse approach must be taken; this leads to a strong need for extensive experimental data whence an empirical model for prediction can then be derived heuristically. In this latter case, the inverse problem can be treated by using Artificial Neural Networks (ANN) thanks to their generalization capabilities and accuracy of results with respect to conventional inverse modeling techniques. In this way prediction can be performed from scarce experimental data even in the presence of noise.

In this paper we present an MLP neural network to predict ELF environmental magnetic field pollution originating from electric devices. The inputs to the neural network are measured values of the three components of the ELF stationary magnetic field taken at accessible points lying on a regular grid enclosing a current free region. The MLP NN predicts magnetic field values at points internal to the grid. The neural network training is performed off-line by using polynomial harmonic functions.
The paper is structured as follows: in Section 2 the neural model adopted is illustrated; in Section 3, in order to validate the procedure, a simple case study is illustrated concerning the neural prediction of ELF magnetic field intensity within a current free parallelepiped region, surrounded by active conductors carrying assigned currents; the authors' conclusions follow in Section 4.

2 The neural model

In current free regions, each component B_k (k = x, y, z) of the ELF stationary magnetic field is harmonic, i.e. governed by the Laplace equation subject to assigned boundary conditions:

$$\nabla^2 B_k = 0$$

Unfortunately for the purpose of monitoring ELF magnetic field pollution it is practically impossible to know with adequate detail the required boundary data so to solve directly the above problem in an analytical or numerical way.
However, boundary data can be related to the values of the magnetic field components in the interior region by using the Green's function G(Q;P) for the considered domain Ω:

$$B_k(P) = \oint_{\partial\Omega} \left(-\frac{\partial G(Q;P)}{\partial n} \right) \cdot B_k(Q) d\Omega$$

This integral expression highlights that each field component B_k in the generic point P internal to the domain depends solely on P, the values of B_k on the boundary surface and the Green's function. The latter, unfortunately, is generally not analytically known, except for a few simple domain shapes like spheres etc. But, for a quick and easy execution of measures, more practical shapes should be chosen, such as regular parallelepipeds on whose external surfaces grids of measure points are easily positioned. For these reasons, our approach employs a supervised ANN, which allows us to predict ELF magnetic field intensity only from a few data taken at the surface of the region of interest, which is likely to have a practical shape for measurements [1][2]. The domain shapes considered in this work are of parallelepipedal type, due to their practical convenience in setting up the measure points on their surface, positioned according to a regular grid. An example of such a grid is shown in figure 1. The neural predictor is based on a Multi Layer Perceptron (MLP) network, whose input/output schematisation is shown in fig. 2.

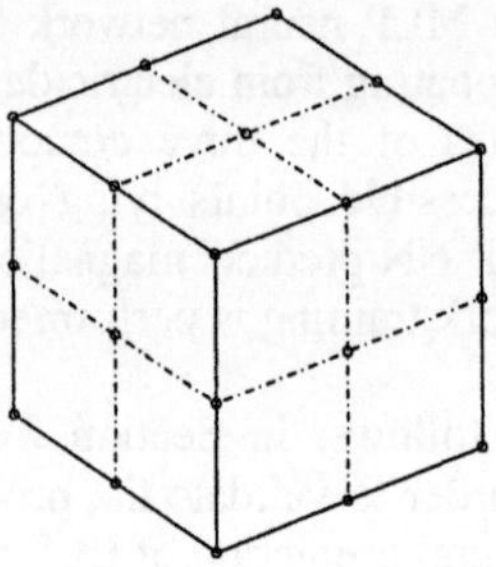

Fig. 1. Grid of measure points positioned on a parallelepiped surface

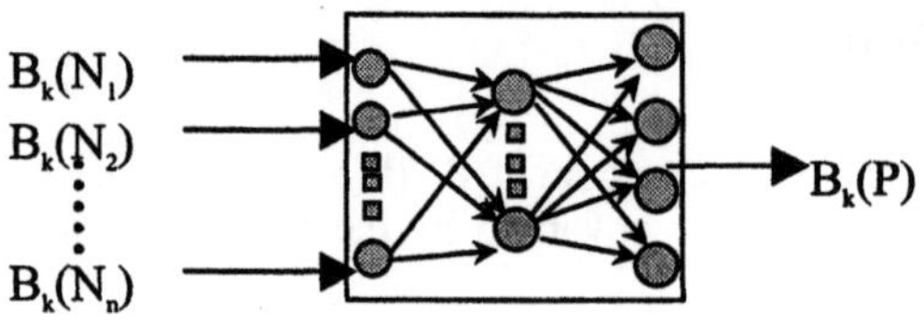

Fig. 2. Input/output schematisation of the ELF magnetic field predictor

The neural network structure has as inputs the values of the magnetic field components on the surface $\partial\Omega$, and as output the values of the magnetic field intensity at an arbitrarily chosen point P internal to Ω.
After extensive experimental work, the network architecture giving the best performance was devised. This architecture is fully interconnected and composed by a 3 neurons hidden layer with hyperbolic tangent activation function, and an output layer with one neuron and a linear activation function.
Contrary to conventional usage, this neural predictor is not trained by experimental data. Instead, training data are computed from a class of suitably selected harmonic functions, which match the typical field behaviour observed in neighborhood of electrical devices.
A further advantage of this off-line training is its modularity with respect to the harmonic functions degree and flexibility in pattern generation, allowing us to reduce effectively the number of training functions required to reach a target precision. The network is actually trained by using several subclasses of polynomial harmonic functions in 3D space $\wp(x, y, z)$, in accordance with the scheme illustrated in Table 1. The training set is generated by suitably choosing a few values for each coefficient in the normalized range (-1, 1) and by imposing to them the Laplacian constraint $\nabla^2 \wp(x, y, z) = 0$.
The techniques due to Nguyen and Widrow [4] are followed to initialise the neural network weights and biases, and the classical Levenberg-Marquardt algorithm [3]

has been used to speed up training with respect to conventional gradient descent back-propagation.

Table 1. Classes of harmonic functions employed for training.

Polynomial harmonic functions	Number of functions used for training
$A + Bx + Cy + Dz$	625
$Exy + Fxz + Gyz$	125
$Mx^2 + Ny^2 + Oz^2$ $(M + N + O = 0)$	375
$A+Bx+Cy+Dz+Exy+Fxz+Gyz+Mx^2+Ny^2+Oz^2$ $(M+N+O=0)$	1125
$Hx^3+Sxy^2+Uxz^2$ $(6H+2S+2U=0)$	1029
$Ly^3+Qx^2y+Vyz^2+Wxyz$ $(6L+2Q+2V=0)$	7203
$Pz^3+Rx^2z+Ty^2z$ $(6P+2R+2T=0)$	1029
$Hx^3+Sxy^2+Uxz^2+Pz^3+Rx^2z+Ty^2z+Ly^3+Qx^2y+Vyz^2+Wxyz$ $(6H+2S+2U=0;\ 6L+2Q+2V=0;\ 6P+2R+2T=0)$	9261
$A+Bx+Cy+Dz+Exy+Fxz+Gyz+Mx^2+Ny^2+Oz^2+Hx^3+Sxy^2+Uxz^2+$ $Pz^3+Rx^2z+Ty^2z+Ly^3+Qx^2y+Vyz^2+Wxyz$ $(6H+2S+2U=0;\ 6L+2Q+2V=0;\ 6P+2R+2T=0;\ M+N+O=0)$	10290

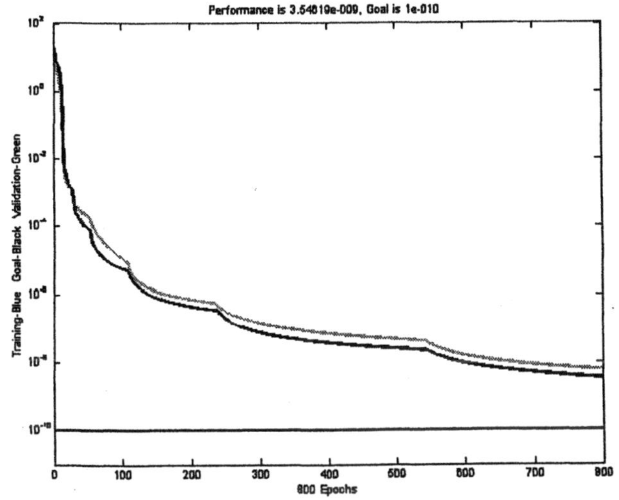

Fig. 3. Validation and training error history.

The network's generalization ability has been improved by using early stopping technique, which avoids overfitting. Obtained results are very favourable, since validation error (error evaluated by using unknown patterns during training) and training error show a very similar behaviour, and no significant overfitting occurred. The observed mean square error (MSE) for both validation and training, after 800 epochs, is shown in Figure 3; its asymptotic value is about 10^{-8}. After training, testing data were generated by selecting harmonic functions different from those employed for training. In figure 4 some target and predicted values are shown for several test harmonic polynomial functions. The MSE observed value is about 10^{-5}, which makes the target and predicted values nearly indistinguishable in the plot.

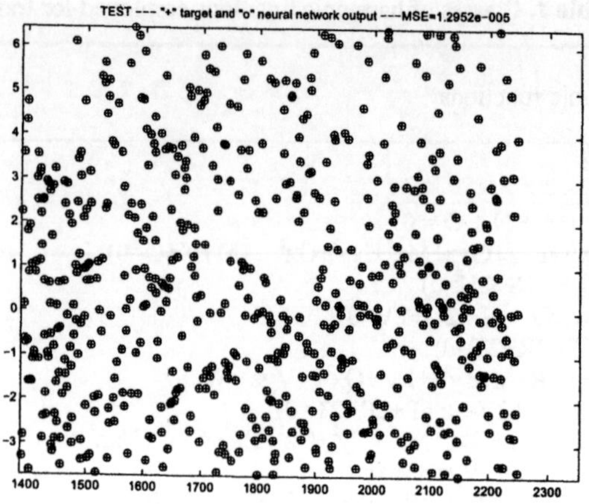

Fig. 4. Comparison between target and predicted output for several test harmonic polynomial functions.

3 Results

Several experiments for the validation of the trained MLP network have been carried out. Hereafter, a simple case study is illustrated concerning the neural prediction of the ELF magnetic field intensity within a current free parallelepiped region, completely surrounded by active conductors carrying assigned currents.
This case was chosen because the problem is amenable to analytical solution and therefore a comparison with predicted values can be carried out easily. First the magnetic field distribution generated by the above conductors was analytically computed; in particular the values of the magnetic field intensity at several test points within the parallelepiped were considered as references to carry out the comparison. Then for such a configuration a suitable number of measurement points for each B_k component were selected on the parallelepiped boundary. The prediction was performed at the same points previously considered as reference inside the parallelepiped. In this experiment it has been found that 50 points on the boundary are sufficient to guarantee the desired precision in the prediction (relative error less than 10%). Table 2 reports the values of the modulus of magnetic field at the test point P(1.75,1.45,1.25).

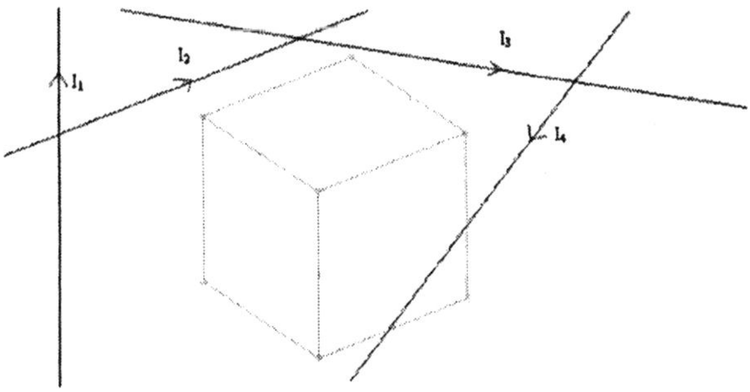

Fig. 5. The parallelepiped region sorrounded by active conductors used for validation

Table 2. Comparison between computed and measured value

Analytically Computed (mT)	ANN predicted value (mT)
91.3	98.7

4 Conclusions

Unlike other neural predictors, the one here illustrated is based on an off-line training employing polynomial harmonic functions, suitably chosen to represent typical ELF environmental magnetic field behaviour originating from electric devices. The MLP neural predictor implemented gave very favourable results when used in practical problems concerning the ELF magnetic field prediction in current free regions from few measurements taken on a regular grid on the surface of the parallelepiped.

5 References

[1] Capizzi G., Coco S., Laudani A., Pappalardo G., Pulvirenti R. (2001) Prediction of ELF Environmental Magnetic Fields by Artificial Neural Networks. Proceedings of EANN 2001, Cagliari, Italy, July 16-18.

[2] Coccorese E., Martone R., and Morabito F. C. (1994), A Neural Network Approach for the Solution of Electric and Magnetic Inverse Problems, IEEE Transactions on Magnetics, Vol. 30, N° 5, Sep. 1994.

[3] Hagan M.T. and Menhaj M. (1994) Training Feedforward Networks with the Marquardt Algorithm. IEEE Transactions on Neural Networks, vol. 5, no. 6.

[4] Nguyen D. and Widrow B. (1990). Improving the learning speed of 2-layer neural networks by choosing initial values of the adaptive weights. Proceedings of the International Joint Conference on Neural Networks. vol. 3, 21-26.

Forecasting of Meteorologic Data by Artificial Neural Networks

H. Kerem Cigizoglu

İstanbul Technical University, Civil Engineering Faculty, Division of Hydraulics, Maslak, 80626, İstanbul, TURKEY

Abstract. The forecasting of the meteorologic data carries significance for meteorology and water resources engineering. The forecasting of rainfall particularly is complicated because the data is intermittent, i.e. the observed time series data contains zero values as well as the positive non-zero observations. The available meteorologic models having physical basis are difficult to establish since they require tremendous amount of data for calibration. In this study artificial neural networks are employed to forecast the rainfall data using with and without periodic components. The forecasting results are evaluated in terms of mean square error (MSE) and the total rainfall for the testing period. It is shown that the forecasted series capture the general behaviour of the observed one and compare well in terms of the rainfall total.

1 Introduction

The problem of flooding is as old as time. However, while natural flooding of large areas did not create situations more dangerous than others in a prehistoric world, the expansion of human activity and the aggregation of people in larger and larger urbanised areas has made more and more preventing damages caused by floods as well as control and management of flood waters a problem of vital necessity. There are several ways of approaching the precipitation forecasting problem, which may be roughly categorised into stochastic and deterministic. Traditionally, hydrologists are more familiar with the stochastic models, while meteorologists tend to determine precipitation either on the basis of images extrapolation (radar and satellite) or by means of atmosphere dynamics models. A detailed description of available stochastic models is given in [1].

In several countries weather forecasts based upon Mesoscale Atmospheric Models are available which generally extend the forecast horizon to 72 hours. Unfortunately the precipitation forecasts provided by these models are not usable within the frame of rainfall-runoff models, given the size of the Mesoscale model meshes which, in the best cases are of 50•50 km2, and consequently the average precipitation over the mesh is totally unrealistic at the sub-catchment scale.

Simpler approaches are therefore required in the form of `conceptual` solutions or `black-box` modeling techniques. Neurocomputing provides one possible answer to the problematic task sediment transfer prediction. Many of the available techniques for time series analysis assume linear relationships among variables. In the real world, however temporal variations in data do not exhibit simple regularities and are difficult to analyse and predict accurately. Linear recurrence and their combinations for describing the behaviour of such data are often found to be inadequate. It seems necessary that nonlinear models such as artificial neural networks (ANN's), which are suited to complex nonlinear models, be used for the analysis of real world temporal data. These tools contain no preconceived ideas about the manner in which a model ought to be structured or work. It also provides a flexible approach, with the power to provide different levels of generalization, and can produce a reasonable solution from small data sets. The modeller has control over the data inputs and irrelevant variables can be identified or removed during the model building process.

There are numerous studies related to the application of ANN`s to various problems frequently encountered in water resources. The nonlinear ANN approach was shown to provide a good representation of the rainfall-runoff relationship [2]. Neural network methodology was employed to forecast daily runoff as a function of daily precipitation, temperature, and snowmelt [3]. Other recent applications of ANNs are remote sensing of hydrological processes [4], classification of river basins [5], estimation and forecasting of sediment concentration data [6] and [7].

2 The structure of the ANNs

Multi layer feedforward networks consist of a set of sensory units (source nodes) that constitute the input layer, one or more hidden layers of computation nodes, and an output layer of computation nodes. The input signal propagates through the network in a forward direction, on a layer-by-layer basis. These neural networks are commonly referred to as multilayer perceptrons (MLPs).

Many procedures are discussed in the literature for the training of neural networks. Error back propagation is one of the most commonly used procedures. The method is generally an iterative nonlinear optimization approach using a gradient descent search method. Error back propagation provides a feed forward neural network, giving the capacity to capture and represent relationships between patterns in a given data sample.

The neural network employed in this study possessed a three-layer learning network consisting an input layer, a hidden layer and an output layer. Error back propagation is used as training procedure throughout the study. The equations related to this training procedure are available in all standard ANN text books [8].

3 Analysis of data

In this study 8 hour rainfall data (three measurements per day each representing the total of the 8 hour long rainfall, unit=mm) of a station (station No. 976) on Arac in West Black Sea Region of Turkey are used. The observation period starts at 1th January of 1995 and ends at 24th May of 2001 (totally 7000 values). The maximum and minimum measurements in this period are 44.3 mm and 0 mm, respectively.

4 Application of ANNs to the data

The application of the ANNs to forecast the rainfall consists of two steps. The premiere step is the training of the neural networks. The second step is the testing of trained ANNs by applying to the data which is not used during training. The back propagation method is employed to train the ANNs for multilayer perceptrons. The determination of the number of hidden layers and the number of nodes both in input layer in each hidden layer providing the best training and testing results are the primary considerations in training and testing procedures.

The optimum learning, η, and the momentum, α, rates are found after trying various values and observing the mean square error (MSE) produced at the end of the testing stage. It is seen that picking high values like 0.5 and 0.9 for η and α throw the network into oscillations or saturate the node outputs. Saturation occurs when the net input to the function producing node output is a large value (either positive or negative) and variations in the input thus have little effect on the output (Eberhart and Dobbins, 1990). It is seen that η and α should be decreased if the number of input and output layers are increased. The iteration number, on the other hand, increases by decreasing η and α values. In this study 0.04 and 0.02 values are found adequate for η and α , respectively. The testing stage results using these parameter values are presented in detail in the following part of the study.

4.1. Forecasting of rainfall data using the past data

Initially the first 6500 rainfall values (each value is the total of 8 hours) between 01.01.1995 and 08.12.2000 are considered for training the neural networks. The last 500 values (period between 09.12.2000 and 24.05.2001) are than examined for testing purpose. Different numbers of input values are considered and the best result (lowest MSE during the testing stage) is obtained for 6 inputs in other words the last consecutive 6 (t-6, .., t-1) rainfall values constituted the input layer. In order to determine the hidden layer number and the hidden layer node number simulations are carried out for one, two and three hidden layers with various hidden layer nodes. Employing more than one hidden layer did not increase the forecasting accuracy in terms of MSE. Similarly 3 hidden neurons provided the best forecasting result during the testing stage. The forecasted values are presented in Fig.1. The MSE of the testing period and the total forecasted rainfall are 2.30 and 280mm, respectively. The forecasted total rainfall is 2.8% more than the observed 272mm.

Then the study is repeated by incorporating the periodic component values $\cos(2\pi i/365)$ and $\sin(2\pi i/365)$ into the input layer increasing the input layer node number to 8. Here i represents the day of the year (time t). For this case The MSE is 2.25. The forecasted total, 270 mm, is 0.8% less than the observed one. It is obvious that considering periodic components increases the forecasting performance. Examining Figs. 1 and 2 it can be said that some high values are underestimated but in general ANN forecasts capture the general structure of the observed series.

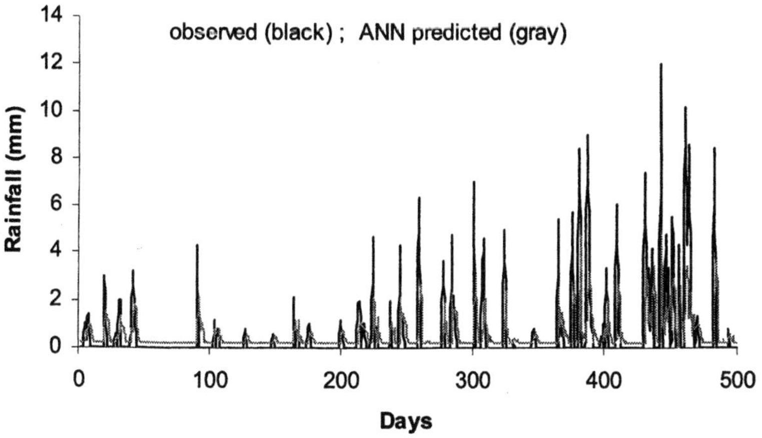

Figure 1. The forecasted rainfall values for the time t using the last 6 (t-6, t-5, t-4, t-3, t-2, t-1) values as input.

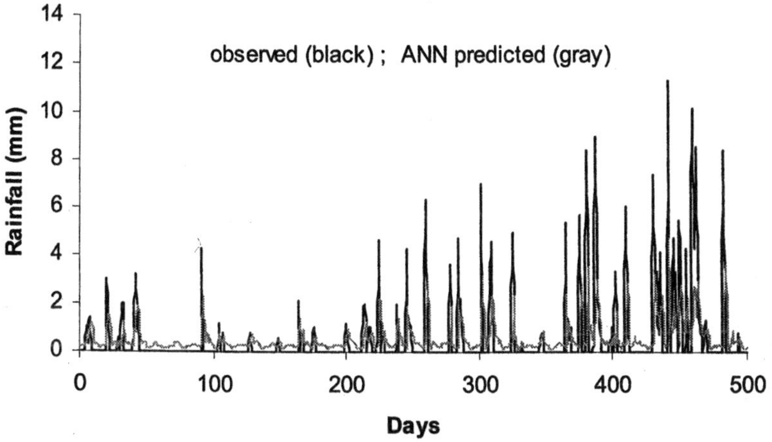

Figure 2. The forecasted rainfall values for the time t using the last 6 (t-6, t-5, t-4, t-3, t-2, t-1) values and periodic components as input.

5 Conclusions

In the presented study ANNs are employed to forecast the rainfall values at the present time using the past future rainfalls. It is seen that the ANN predicted totals are quite close to the observed values. The incorporation of periodic components into the input layer of ANNs provides improvement in the forecasting accuracy. Considering the complexity of the available rainfall forecasting techniques the obtained results carry important significance.

References

1. Foufoula-Georgiou E., Georgakakos K.P. (1991) Hydrologic Advances in Space-Time Precipitation Modeling and Forecasting. In D.S. Bowles and P.E.O'Connell (eds.), Recent Advances in the Modeling of Hydrologic Systems, 47-65.
2. Minns A.W., Hall, M.J. (1996) Artificial neural networks as rainfall runoff models, Hydrological Sciences Journal 41: 399-417.
3. Tokar A.S., Johnson, P.A. (1999) Rainfall-runoff modelling using artificial neural networks, Journal of Hydrologic Engineering 4: 232-239.
4. Islam S., Kothari, R. (2000) Artificial neural networks in remote sensing of hydrologic Processes, ASCE Journal of Hydrologic Engineering 5:138-144.
5. Thandaveswara, B.S., Sajikumar, N. (2000) Classification of river basins using Artificial Neural Networks, ASCE Journal of Hydrologic Engineering 5: 290-298.
6. Cigizoglu, H.K. (2002a) Suspended sediment estimation and forecasting using artificial neural Networks, Turkish Journal of Engineering & Environmental Sciences, 26,1.
7. Cigizoglu, H.K. (2002b) Intermittent river flow forecasting by artificial neural networks, XIV. International Conference on Computational Methods in Water Resources, Delft, Netherlands, 23-28 June.
8. Eberhart, R.C., Dobbins, R.W. (1990) Neural network PC tools: a practical guide, San Diego: Academic Press, 414p.

Artificial Neural Network Predictive System for Oxygen Steelmaking Converter

Jan Falkus, Piotr Pietrzkiewicz, Wojciech Pietrzyk, and Jan Kusiak

Akademia Górniczo-Hutnicza, Mickiewicza 30, 30-059 Kraków, Poland

Abstract. The main objective of the paper is the presentation of the static control model of steelmaking converter process based on the artificial neural network approach. The results of classical mass and energy balance as well as regression models are also presented. The developed artificial neural network predicts the temperature of the liquid metal and the volume of necessary oxygen blow. The ANN was trained and tested with the real industrial data measured in one of the Polish steel plants. The comparison of the ANN results with the classical calculations is presented.

1 Introduction

The oxygen converter process is currently a prevailing steelmaking aggregate producing approximately 80% of the total world steel market. For this reason, any improvement of the technology of this process leads to significant economical savings. Because the rafination cycle of an individual heat in a converter is very dynamic and lasts from 16 to 20 minutes, the proper control of this process is very important.

A general control system of the converter process can be simply described as a two-step algorithm. The first step consists of the off-line static control, which precedes the heat. Its goal is determination the input parameters of a heat. When the blow is started, there is a dynamic step, which depends on the measured parameters supplying the information on current carbon content and temperature of a liquid metal.

The main goal of the paper is to present the static model of the oxygen converter process based on the artificial neural network technique. The developed artificial neural network predicts the temperature of the liquid steel and the amount of the oxygen blow. The obtained results were compared with these obtained from the classical approaches: mass and energy balance as well as the regression analysis models. Those models relate the output variable: metal bath temperature or the volume of oxygen blow with such input variables as the mass of the input hot metal, scrap, iron ore, etc.

2 Mass and energy balance of the oxygen converter process

The process consists of two basic stages. At the first one the furnace is simply charged with the hot pig iron, scrap and iron ore with fluxes, such as burnt and dolomite lime. The second stage is the oxygen injection at high flow rate during which gases, such as CO and CO_2, and iron oxide fumes (Fe_2O_3) exit from the mouth of furnace. At turndown, liquid steel and slag are the remaining products of the process.

It is important to determine exact amount of each charged material and the volume of oxygen blow, to obtain desired temperature of the metal bath and as the consequence, the required chemical composition of steel. In the industrial practice, the calculations are based on the mass and energy balance of the converter process. Such model can be easily explained, because it takes into consideration the balance of all input and output mass and energy streams. This model requires following input and output variables:

- mass of input materials: pig iron, scrap, lime dolomite, coke and all of the remaining charge materials used in the heat, etc.,
- chemical composition of all input materials,
- chemical composition, weight of metal bath and slag,
- input and output temperatures of metal bath.

These data are applied in the mass-energy balance model, which relates them with the output variables. However, the estimation of these parameters is difficult and very often inaccurate, because of the lack of information concerning the metal losses associated with vaporization of the melted steel and out-of-control removal of the metal from converter. All of these disturbances are of random character and are the source of the inadequate results of calculations. Some statistical estimations concerning the magnitude of the above mentioned losses can be made on the basis of the observation of all heats within a campaign.

The heat balance is also calculated on the basis of the material balance. The oxidation reactions occurring during the blow produce more energy than required to simply raise the temperature of the hot metal, from about 1350°C to the desired turndown temperature, and to melt the fluxes. Most of the excess heat is used to increase the amount of steel produced by melting cold scrap and by reducing iron ore to metal. Some heat is also lost by conduction, convection, and radiation to the surroundings. Comparison of the sum of input energy and heat removal allows the estimation of the value of wasted energy during the converter process. The energy input must be equal to the energy output. This main assumption allows to calculate the temperature of the liquid metal after primary oxygen blow [1].

The developed model based on the data obtained from one of the Polish steel plants predicts the temperature of the metal bath. It was assumed in the model, that the value of heat waste is proportional to the input heat stream. The proportionality coefficient was considered as an optimization parameter of the mean square error between the calculated and measured values of the metal bath temperature. The similar approach based on the mass and energy balance was used next for the model predicting the oxygen blow volume, according to stoichiometry of reactions taking place in a converter and the final composition of the liquid metal and slag.

The simulation was carried out for one selected converter campaign. The obtained accuracy expressed by the root mean square values for the temperature and the oxygen blow volume are 90.5°C and 1230 m^3, respectively.

3 Regression analysis of the converter process

One of the common tools used in the statistical modelling of the industrial processes is the multiple linear regression analysis. The main purpose of the multiple linear regression is to establish the model, which gives the quantitative relationship between the process input variables (the predictor variables) and the output variable. The oxygen converter model has to predict either the temperature of the metal bath or the volume of oxygen blow for the given values of the input variables.

The data for the converter registered in the real industrial process include 47 variables. Because, the data are very noisy and many of variables show the low correlation to the output signal, the data set was preliminary filtered before the regression analysis. As the result, the data set consisted of 21 input variables describing the steelmaking process.

The regression analysis was performed using two basic methods: standard multiple linear regression and the backward stepwise regression. The first one takes into consideration all 21 input variables of the model and includes them into the final model. On the other hand, the backward stepwise regression technique starts with all the terms and removes the least significant terms until all the remaining terms are statistically significant. The backward stepwise regression analysis eliminated 12 variables, which have low correlation with the output signal. The final regression models have 9 input variables: mass and temperature of the hot pig iron, phosphorus contents, the mass of scrap (5 values describing different scrap), coke mass and volume of the oxygen blow (or temperature).

The objective of the analysis is to model the temperature of the metal bath and the volume of oxygen blow. The data set consists of 1446 records. The predictive abilities of the elaborated backward stepwise regression models are presented in Fig.1 (temperature of metal bath)and Fig.2 (volume of the oxygen blow).

4 ANN model of the oxygen converter process

The artificial neural networks become more and more common in solving engineering problems in the field of metallurgy and materials science. The earlier positive experience in an application of the ANN to the different fields of metallurgy [2] - [6], as well as chosen publications [7] - [10] encouraged Authors to undertake an attempt of using the ANN approach to the modelling of the oxygen converter process. Two different ANN models were developed. First predicts the metal bath temperature and the second one the necessary volume of the oxygen blow. The industrial converter process data set of 1446 heats was divided to the training (723 records), validation (361 records) and testing (362 records) sets. The Statistica^{TM} Neural Networks package was used. The network variables have been normalized.

The MLP models for the temperature of the metal bath and the volume of the oxygen blow had the topologies of 10:7:1 and 10:5:1, respectively. The input variables were the same as in the regression analysis.

The big influence on the quality of the converter process has the condition of the converter lining. Therefore, an additional variable describing the wear of the convertor lining has been included in the next step of the ANN modelling. Because, it is difficult to define precisely the state of the converter lining, the whole campaign was divided into three stages, and the stage number was implemented as the additional input variable. The topologies of the two considered models were 11:6:1 (for temperature prediction) and 11:5:1 (for oxygen volume).

The obtained results for temperature and oxygen blow predictions for both considered models are presented in Fig. 1 and Fig. 2.

5 Results and conclusions

The mass and energy balance requires the consideration of all variables describing the converter process. Some of them, as for example the value of the liquid metal mass after the main blow, are not precise and can be a source of significant errors. The biggest error in the calculations of the model of the consumption of the oxygen during the blow is caused by the fact, that the level of the oxidation of slag (the content of FeO and Fe_2O_3 in the slag) and the amount of losses of iron resulting from the vaporization process are difficult to measure.

The evaluation of the accuracy of developed models (mass and energy balance model, regression model and ANN model) of the converter process is possible by the comparison of the percentage of heats by means of errors of calculated process variables (metal bath temperature and oxygen blow volume).

The results presented in Figures 1 and 2 show that the ANN model predictions are more accurate than these obtained from the mass - energy balance model. The ANN models which takes into consideration the wear of the converter lining give slightly better results. The ANN models give similar results to the multiple linear regression equation. However, the ANN model seems to be more flexible to the description of phenomena occurring in the process, which are highly non-linear. At that stage of research, it is difficult to show, that the control system based on the ANN model is better. All presented models were based on the noisy data obtained from the industry. The fur-

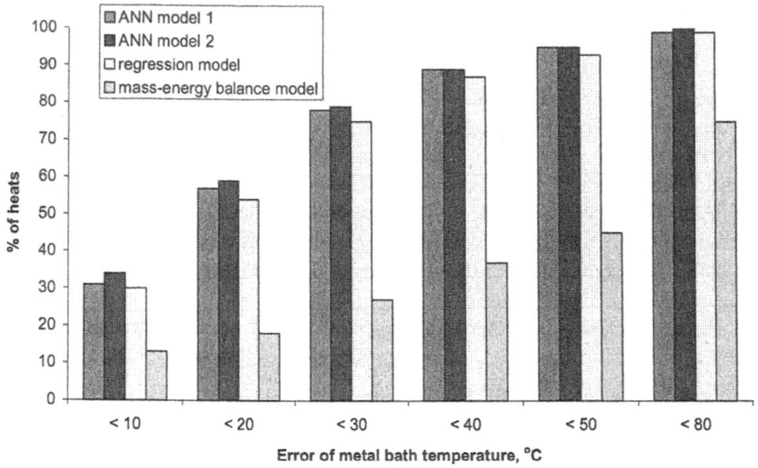

Fig. 1. The comparison of prediction errors of the metal bath temperature.

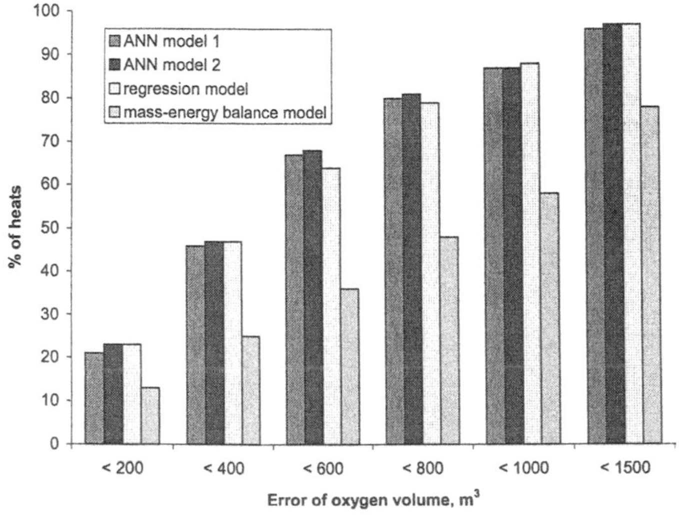

Fig. 2. The comparison of prediction errors of the oxygen blow volume.

ther research will focus on the fuzzy ANN approach, because, most of the industrial measurements parameters are not reliable and difficult to quantify.

Acknowledgments The financial assistance of the Polish Scientific Committee (KBN), project No 7T08B 06220, is fully acknowledged.

References

1. Kruciński, M., Falkus, J. (1988) Steel metallurgy - calculus and laboratory. Manuscript No. 1140 AGH, Kraków (in Polish).
2. Falkus, J., Pietrzkiewicz, P. (2001) Neural networks in statical controlling of oxygen converter process. Proc. Conf. "High Technologies in Advanced Metal Science and Engineering". St. Petersburg, Russia.
3. Roberts, S.M., Kusiak, J., Liu, Y.L., Forcellese, A., Withers, P.J. (1998) Prediction of damage evolution in forged aluminium metal matrix composites using a neural network approach, J. Materials Processing and Technology, 80-81, 507–512.
4. Roberts, S.M., Kusiak, J. (2001) The application of artificial intelligence to the constitutive and microstructural behaviour of nickel-base superalloys. Proc. Conf. ESAFORM2001, Liege, 441–444.
5. Kusiak, J., Svietlichnyj, D., Pietrzyk, M. (2001) Application of Artificial Neural Networks in the On-Line Control of Hot-Flat Rolling Processes. Int. J. Engineering Simulation, 1, 3, 17–23.
6. Pietrzyk, M., Kusiak, J., Roberts, S.M. (2001) A history dependent constitutive model for the hot forming of Waspaloy. Proc. Conf. ECCM-2001, Krakow, CD-ROM.
7. Chen, J. (2001) A predictive system for blast furnace by integrating a neural network with qualitative analysis. Eng. Appl. of Artificial Intelligence, 14, 77–85.
8. Keuthen, M., Seeliger, A., Thornton, S.G. (1995) Neural net process condition prediction in steelmaking. EUFIT'95, Aachen.
9. Singh, H., Sridhar, N.V., Deo, B. (1996) Artificial neural nets for prediction of silicon content of blast furnace hot metal. Steel Research, 11, 65, 521–527.
10. Yun, S.Y., Chang, K.S., Byun, S.-M. (1996) Dynamic prediction using neural network for automation of BOS process in steel industry. Iron and Steelmaker, 37-42.

Evaluation of a Helicopter Model Using Generalized Back Propagation Through Time

Krzysztof Fujarewicz

Silesian University of Technology, Akademicka 16, 40-100 Gliwice, Poland

Summary. This paper deals with a problem of evaluation of nonlinear model of the helicopter. The plant is an educational apparatus with two degree of freedom. Whereas the theory of linear identification is well established, there are several possible approaches to identification or evaluation of nonlinear plants. Here so called Generalized Back Propagation Through Time Method (GBPTT) is utilized. This method, derived originally for recurrent neural networks, can be used for any nonlinear dynamical system given as a block diagram. The method is fully structural and, in addition, mnemonic. The results of applying of GBPTT for the helicopter shows that obtained model outperforms the model achieved by separate measurements or estimation of its parameters.

1 Introduction

The plant – an educational model of the helicopter produced by Humusoft, Praque – which mathematical model is identified in this paper, is presented schematically in Fig. 1. From the control theory point of view it is multidimensional and nonlinear. It has two inputs: voltages on both motors, and two outputs: signals proportional to azimuth angle φ and elevation angle ψ.

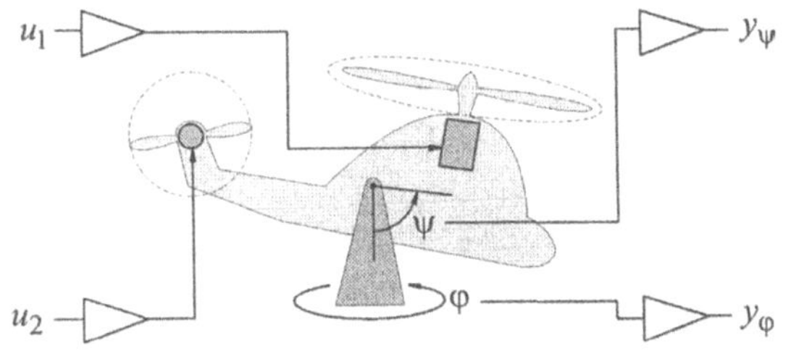

Fig. 1. Educational model of the helicopter

In this paper GBPTT method, described in [4, 7, 8], is utilized. Standard BPTT is the off-line algorithm which depends on "unfolding" in time discrete time neural network and applying BP algorithm to obtained static (feed-forward) network. Such procedure has some disadvantages: requires, mentioned above, unfolding in time (which may be very difficult in case of more complicated dynamical neural network), and works only with discrete in time neural networks.

GBPTT method does not have these disadvantages. It does not require "unfolding in time" and it can be applied for both discrete and continuous in time systems. Moreover, it can be applied not only to neural networks, but to every nonlinear dynamical system (also containing neural networks) and can be used for solving identification as well as suboptimal control problems. GBPTT is a method of sensitivity analysis but differs from method known from literature [3, 14] in different definition of the sensitivity function. In this method so called input-output sensitivity function is searched. This function denotes the sensitivity of the output signal of the system at particular time moment on variation of input signal at certain previous moment. Most of problems of identification and suboptimal control of nonlinear dynamical systems can be reformulated to the task of finding the input-output sensitivity function. GBPTT is also structural and mnemonic. It is assumed that the system is given in structural form – as a block diagram. The method describes how to transform this block diagram in order to obtain a structural sensitivity model. The input-output sensitivity function can be obtained using the sensitivity model but computational cost can be strongly decreased by using so called transposition in time of sensitivity model. GBPTT method also describes how to transpose in time sensitivity model. Both transformations: building the sensitivity model and its transposition in time consist in applying several simply rules of the block diagram transformations. Hence the GBPTT method can be referred to as a fully mnemonic method. In work [7] this method has been used to identification of counterflow heat exchanger and in [8] it has been applied for solving optimal control problem of the heat exchanger.

In Section 2 of this work a phenomenological model of the helicopter will be presented. In Section 3 the GBPTT method will be applied to identification of simplified helicopter model. A block diagrams of the helicopter model and the identification experiment will be drawn. Then the sensitivity model and sensitivity model transposed in time of the identification experiment will be constructed. It will be also explained how they can be used to generate partial derivatives of performance index with respect to identified parameters. Finally, Section 4 will present the results of identification of the helicopter model.

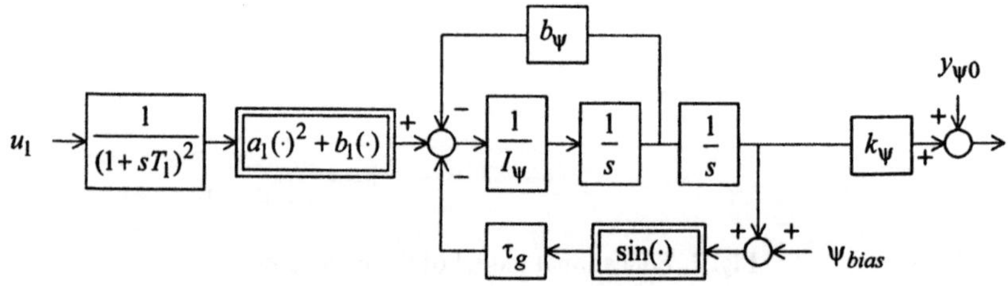

Fig. 2. A block diagram of first main channel of the helicopter model

2 The Model

The block diagram of the simplified phenomenological model of the first main channel (from u_1 to y_ψ) is presented in Figure 2. In this diagram first two elements (on the left side) describe the dynamics of the main motor with the propeller, while the rest of the block diagram is the model of the body dynamics around the horizontal axis. The parameters are described below:

T_1 – time constant of the second order inertia modelling the main motor,

a_1, b_1 – parameters of the nonlinear function of the propeller torque,

I_ψ – moment of inertia of the body around the horizontal axis,

b_ψ – viscous friction coefficient,

$\tau_g = mgl$ – coefficient of the torque originating from the body mass,

k_ψ, y_ψ – parameters of the angle sensor,

ψ_{bias} – angular shift of the centre of gravity.

Although the model from Fig. 2 is only the part of the whole phenomenological model, in this work, due to space limitations, we will focus only on identification of this subsystem. There are additional reasons of such an approach. First channel of the model is, from the control point of view, the most difficult – for high values of the angle ψ model of this channel is unstable. Moreover, the cross-couplings appearing in the model are relatively weak (for example gyroscopic effect vanish for $\psi = \pi/2$), hence the fact that whole system is multidimensional is not the main problem of the control task.

Since parameters ψ_{bias}, k_ψ and y_ψ are measured with high accuracy only remaining six parameters from listed above will be identified. Let us define the vector of these parameters

$$p = [T_1, a_1, b_1, I_\psi, b_\psi, \tau_g]^T \tag{1}$$

3 Evaluation of The Helicopter Model Using GBPTT Method

In this Section we will make use of GBPTT method. Readers not familiar with this method can find its description in one of the following works [4, 7, 8].

The identification experiment is done in system presented in Fig. 3.a. Our goal is to minimize following performance index

$$J = \frac{1}{2}\int_0^T e^2(t)\mathrm{d}t \tag{2}$$

where T is the duration of the identification experiment. To minimize performance index (2) using gradient method we have to calculate the gradient $\nabla_p J$.

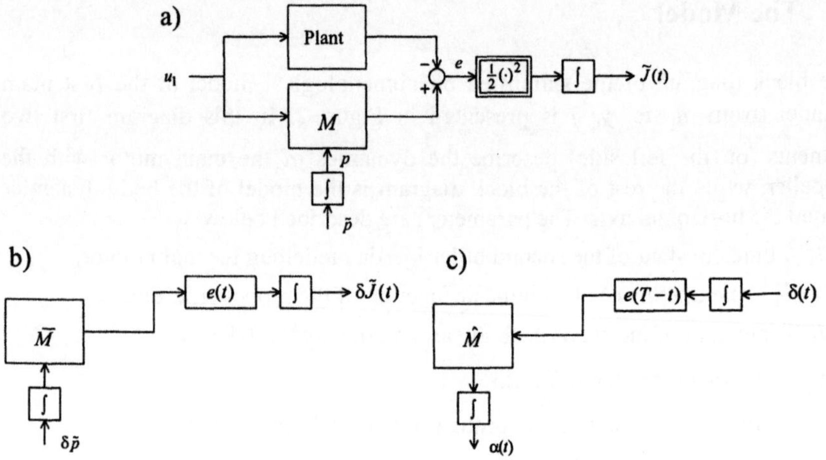

Fig. 3. A block diagram of identification experiment (a), its sensitivity model (b) and sensitivity model transposed in time (c)

In block diagram from Fig. 3.a there are additional elements and additional signals $\tilde{p}(t), \tilde{J}(t)$. Signal $\tilde{p}(t) = p\delta(t)$, where $\delta(t)$ is the Dirac impulse, are non-zero only at moment $t = 0$. Hence "signal" p is constant. On the other hand it is obvious that $\tilde{J}$ satisfies relation $\tilde{J}(T) = J$.

Thanks to these modifications problem of finding the value of gradient $\nabla_p J$ is now reformulated [6] to task of finding input-output sensitivity function

$$S_{\tilde{p}(0)}^{\tilde{J}(T)} = \nabla_p J \tag{3}$$

In order to calculate function (6) structural sensitivity model (Fig. 3.b) has to be constructed. The sensitivity model should take into account only variation of parameter vector p, so the plant can be omitted. After transposition in time sensitivity model takes form presented in Fig. 3.c. On picture 3 elements denoted by $\bar{M}, \hat{M}$ are sensitivity model of the helicopter and its transposition in time respectively. They can be easily constructed on the fully mnemonic way using several simply rules of the GBPTT method.

The system from Fig. 3.c stimulated at moment $t = 0$ by a Dirac impulse produces on its outputs signal $\alpha(t)$. This signal is equal at moment $t = T$ to searched function (3), which is used during iterative minimization of performance the index (2).

4 Results

The duration of the identification experiment was $T = 25[s]$. The input signal u_1 was chosen as a piece-constant. Its value changes for every 5 second and takes in successive time periods following values: 0.5, 0.7, 0.6, 0.4, 0.3[MU], where MU is a "machine unit". In addition, the physical helicopter model was inclined to guarantee its stability. This made possible identification in open-loop configuration. The response of the plant is presented in Fig. 6.a using dashed line. Solid line indicates the response of the phenomenological model (Fig. 2) with parameters obtained by measurements or estimation. It can be seen that both responses differ each other considerably. The performance index (2) equals 0.49[$\mathrm{MU} \cdot \mathrm{s}$]. The result obtained after application of the GBPTT method is shown in Fig. 6.b. (solid line). The performance index decreased and reach value about 0.0026[$\mathrm{MU} \cdot \mathrm{s}$].

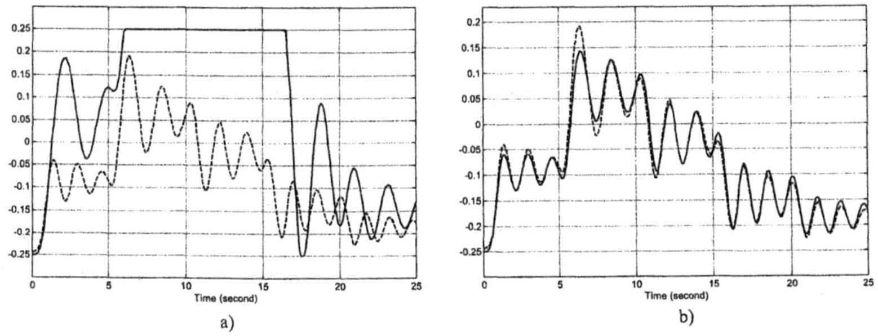

Fig. 4. a) Results of identification by separate measurement of parameters, solid line–the model, dashed line–the plant, b) results of identification by using GBPTT

5 Conclusion

In this paper the simplified phenomenological model of the helicopter is identified. The plant is an educational helicopter model. The identification problem is solved using so called Generalized Back Propagation Through Time method. This method differs from standard BPTT algorithm and its advantages are as follows: it can be applied not only for neural network, it does not require "unfolding in time" and in contrary to standard BPTT it can be used for continuous in time systems. This method, after reformulating of an original problem (of identification or suboptimal control) into task of finding so called input-output sensitivity function, is fully structural and mnemonic.

Presented in this paper identification result confirm that GBPTT is the universal and very useful method which can be utilized in many practical problems of nonlinear identification. Moreover, thanks to the form of input-output sensitivity function, which is calculated in GBPTT method, optimal control problems can be solved as well.

Acknowledgement

This work has been supported by Polish Scientific Committee (KBN) under grant 8 T11A 012 19.

References

1. Ahmed, M. S. (1994) Block partial derivative and its application to neural-net-based direct-model-reference adaptive control, IEE Proc.-Control Theory Appl., **141**, 305-314
2. Baldi, P. (1995) Gradient descent learning algorithm overview: A general dynamical systems perspective, IEEE Trans. Neural Networks, **6**, 182–195
3. Cruz, J. B. (Ed.) (1973) System sensitivity analysis, Benchmark papers in electrical engineering and computer science, Dowden, Hutchinson & Ross, Inc., Stroudsburg
4. Fujarewicz, K. (1999) Optimal control of nonlinear systems using generalized back propagation through time, Proc. Eighteenth IASTED Conference Modelling, Identification and Control, Innsbruck, Austria, 468–471
5. Fujarewicz, K. (1999) Systems transposed in time and their application to gradient calculation in dynamical systems containing neural nets, Proc. Fourth Conference - Neural Networks and Their Applications, Zakopane, Poland, 395–400
6. Fujarewicz, K. (1999) Control of certain nonlinear systems using neural networks - Ph.D. thesis, Silesian University of Technology
7. Fujarewicz, K. (2000) Identification of heat exchanger using generalized back propagation through time, Proc. Nineteenth IASTED Conference Modelling, Identification and Control, Innsbruck, Austria, 267–273
8. Fujarewicz, K. (2000) Identification and suboptimal control of heat exchanger using generalized back propagation through time, Archives of Control Sciences, **10**(XLVI), No. 3–4, 167–183
9. Kailath, T. (1980) Linear Systems, Prentice-Hall, Inc., Engelwood Cliffs, N.J.
10. Narendra, S. N., Parthasarathy, K. (1991) Gradient methods for the optimization of dynamical systems containing neural networks, IEEE Trans. Neural Networks, **2**, 252-262
11. Pearlmutter, B. A. (1995) Gradient calculations for dynamic recurrent neural networks: A survey, IEEE Trans. Neural Networks, **6**, 1212–1228.
12. Wan, E., Beaufays, F. (1996) Diagrammatic derivation of gradient algorithms for neural networks, Neural Computation, **8**, no. 1, 182–201
13. Werbos, P. J. (1990) Backpropagation through time: what it does and how to do it, Proc. IEEE, **78**, 1550–1560
14. Wierzbicki, A. (1977) Models and sensitivity of control systems, WNT, Warsaw, 1977
15. Williams, R., Zipser, D. (1989) Learning algorithm for continually running fully recurrent neural networks, Neural Computation, **1**, 270–280

Correction of Non-linear Dynamic Properties of Temperature Sensors by the Use of ANN

Lidia Jackowska-Strumiłło

Computer Engineering Department, Technical University of Lodz,
Al. Politechniki 11, 90-924 Lodz, Poland, e-mail: lidia_js@kis.p.lodz.pl

Abstract. The paper presents a new method for correction of dynamic errors by means of Artificial Neural Networks (ANNs), in which an inverse dynamic model of the sensor is realised by a neural corrector. Feedforward multilayer ANNs and a moving window method were applied. The proposed correction technique has been evaluated experimentally for small platinum RTD immersed in oil. The obtained results were compared to classical, linear correction method. Different multilayer perceptron networks were applied as neural correctors. The ANN approach significantly improved correction performance for the sensor exhibiting non-linear behaviour.

1. Introduction

Temperature sensors working in hard environmental conditions have usually poor dynamical properties and their application is limited to measurements of slow temperature changes. Additionally, dynamical behaviour of all temperature sensors depend strongly on their construction and working conditions that may vary in time during the process. Therefore correction of temperature sensors dynamical errors is an important and a complex problem. In traditional methods, the model of the corrector is designed on the basis of the sensor's model, obtained from the laws of thermokinetic [2, 5]. For a wide class of multilayer temperature sensors in a cylindrical sheath, for which a heat flow has only one, radial direction, a transfer function of the thermal conversion stage is given by:

$$G_T(s) = \frac{\Theta_T(s)}{\Theta_O(s)} = \frac{\prod_{j=1}^{m}(1+s\tau_j)}{\prod_{i=1}^{n}(1+sN_i)} \qquad (1)$$

where: $\Theta_O(s), \Theta_T(s)$ – are the Laplace transforms of temperature changes correspondingly in the medium surrounding the sensor and in the sensing element evoked by the change of the temperature Θ_O, N_i – is thermal time constants, and τ_j – are zeros, which are also thermal time constants [2, 5].

Application of the above linear model is limited to small temperature ranges and there is a wide class of industrial sensors and applications, for which this model is not correct. In these cases application of Artificial Neural Networks (ANN) presented in the paper is a good alternative solution.

2. Dynamic errors correction

Generally, dynamic error correction may be realised by the use of series, parallel, series-parallel or closed loop method [6]. In series correction method, which is considered in the paper, corrector module is connected to the output of the sensor. An ideal corrector should estimate an inverse model to the sensor. However, in real systems this condition is not fulfilled and the role of the corrector is to improve the system dynamics. The method of determination of the corrector's model is shown in Fig.1. The role of the optimisation procedure is to choose the proper corrector's model structure and to adjust its parameters for the given optimisation criteria.

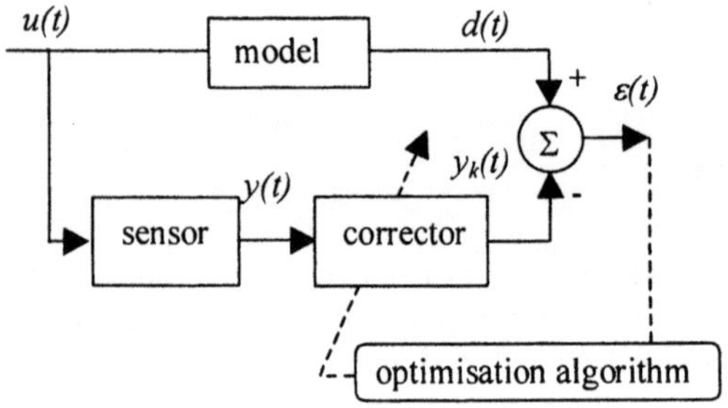

Fig. 1. Method of determination of optimal corrector's parameters [6].

2.1. Correction in linear system

For linear systems, two corresponding transfer functions $G_T(s)$ for the sensor and $G_K(s)$ for the corrector are used to calculate the overall transfer function $G_{TK}(s)$ of the system $G_{TK}(s) = G_T(s)\,G_K(s)$. Then the output signal of the corrector $y_K(t)$ may be calculated from the equation (2), which describes the correction algorithm, which may be realised using the computer:

$$y_K(t) = L^{-1}\{y(s)G_K(s)\} = \frac{d}{dt}\int_0^t y(\tau)h_K(t-\tau)d\tau \,, \tag{2}$$

where: $h_K(\tau)$ – is the corrector's step response.

In classical correction method the model of the corrector is designed on the basis of the sensor's analytical model. There is a wide class of temperature sensors, for which dynamic model of the sensor in the form of a transfer function of inertial element of the first or the second order is sufficiently accurate. In these cases parameters of the model can be estimated by the use of LSE algorithm and application of classical correction method gives good results. For the first order model, $G_T(s) = K/(1+sN_T)$ the transfer function of the corresponding corrector transfer function equals [5]:

$$G_K(s) = \frac{K_K(1+sN_K)}{1+s\frac{N_K}{k}} \tag{3}$$

where: $k > 1$ – is the finite correction coefficient.

For properly designed corrector, for $N_K = N_T$, the resulting time constant of the system is k-times smaller than the sensor's time constant.

The most popular criteria of corrector's parameters determination is criteria of mean sum square error (MSSE) minimisation. For the system in Fig.1, when the sensor's input signal and the noise generated at the corrector's input are not correlated, a total MSSE of the system can be evaluated from the equation [6]:

$$\overline{\varepsilon^2} = \int_0^\infty S_{uu}(\omega)\left|1 - G_{TK}(j\omega)\right|^2 d\omega + \int_0^\infty S_{zz}(\omega)\left|G_K(j\omega)\right|^2 d\omega = \overline{\rho^2} + P_z \tag{4}$$

where: $S_{uu}(\omega), S_{zz}(\omega)$ - density of the power correspondingly of the input signal and of the noise.

The first dynamic component of the error $\overline{\rho^2}$ decreases with the increase of correction coefficient k and equals zero for an ideal corrector, while the second component P_z, depending on the noise, increases with the increase of k. The error function described by the equation (4) has always one minimum [6].

2.2. Correction by the use of ANN

In ANN-based correction method, artificial neural network fulfils the role of the corrector. Dynamic model of the corrector, which implements an inverse model of the sensor, is built by observing interdependence between sensor's input and output signals. A general discrete-time model of the corrector can be described by a non-linear difference equation [4]:

$$y_k(k+1) = f[y(k), y(k-1), \ldots, y(k-n+1)] \tag{5}$$

Corrector structure described by this equation was realised by different multilayer perceptron networks and the so-called *moving window* method [1]. The effect of dynamical modelling by a static network structure has been obtained by extending the network's input vector to the current and a number of past samples of the system states. For the considered problem the backpropagation training algorithm with Levenberg-Marquardt optimisation algorithm was used to minimise the sum square error cost function [1]. Increasing the number of neurons in the hidden layer of the neural corrector improves the quality of inverse function approximation, but also increases the error component depending on noise. A minimum of MSSE or SSE errors for testing data sets were the criteria for choosing the optimal network structure.

3. Experimental results

Verification of ANN based correction method was performed experimentally for small industrial, resistance temperature sensor, Pt100, in a steel sheath with the diameter of 4 mm. A series of identification experiments was performed by the use of the step response method for different step magnitudes. The sensor was plugged into thermostat fulfilled by oil that features high viscosity and its output signal was register by computerised measuring system [3]. The obtained experimental data, shown in Fig.2, was the basis for designing of classical and neural correctors.

Table 1. Sensor's substitute time constant (N) and root-mean-square error of approximation (ε) for different step magnitudes (ΔT).

No	ΔT [°C]	N [s]	ε [s]
1	14.0	12.5	0.3
2	34.0	16.3	2.2
3	57.2	15.2	3.9
4	76.5	16.5	4.0
5	95.6	16.1	4.2
6	123.3	16.2	4.1
7	173.4	16.9	8.0

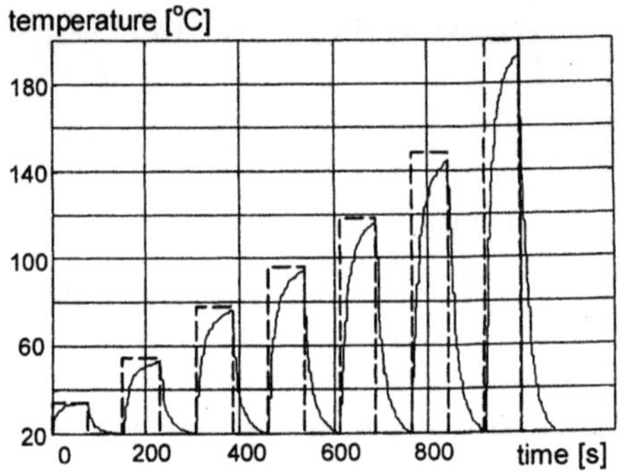

Fig. 2. Experimental data for networks training and testing: temperature interrogation – dashed line, sensor's output – solid line.

For each from the seven step responses sensor's substitute time constant (N) and root-mean-square error of approximation (ε) for different step magnitudes (ΔT) were computed. The results are shown in table1. Quality of approximation decreases with the increase of ΔT. The obtained results showed, that inertial model of the first order is not suitable in these working condition. Increase of the order of the model has not brought better results also. Model described by equation (1) has resulted in satisfactory approximation accuracy but only for one step magnitude, because the sensor that works in such conditions occurs to be a non-linear dynamic element. For the step magnitude 57.2 °C the following time constants were estimated: $N_1 = 22\ s$, $N_2 = 6\ s$, $\tau = 12\ s$.

In ANN based approach from the seven step responses, six were used as the data for the networks training and one was used for the networks testing. Different feedforward networks were tested as the correctors. The main criteria considered by choosing the best network structure was minimum of sum square error (SSE), computed for the testing data. Also maximum absolute error and SSE for the training data were taken under consideration. The best results were obtained for the two-layer perceptron network with the structure (6-15-1), i.e., six inputs, 15 neurons with sigmoidal activation function in the hidden layer and one output (position 7 in table 2). The network's input vector consists of actual value of the signal from the sensor's output y(k) and five consecutive signal samples from the past. The corrected temperature value $y_K(k+1)$ is computed at the network output.

Table 2. Sum square errors for training and testing data sets and maximum absolute errors for testing data sets for different MLP network structures and initial weights values sets.

No	network structure	initial set No	learning epochs	SSE (training)	SSE (testing)	maxE (testing)
1	(10-20-1)	1	300	0.160	0.030	0.094
2	(10-20-1)	1	400	0.063	0.024	0.058
3	(10-20-1)	1	468	0.020	0.028	0.11
4	(10-20-1)	2	574	0.020	0.012	0.056
5	(8-18-1)	3	464	0.020	0.019	0.065
6	(8-15-1)	4	800	0.022	0.009	0.032
7	(6-15-1)	5	435	0.020	0.007	0.031
8	(6-12-1)	6	1000	0.049	0.022	0.045

Results of correction procedures are shown for two step responses in Fig.3.

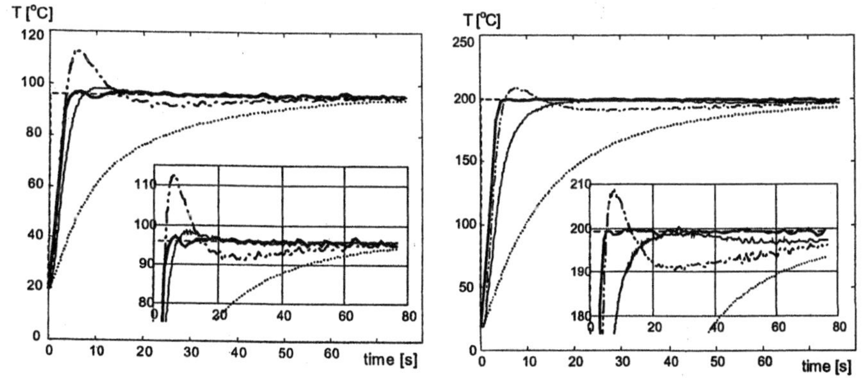

Fig. 3. Comparison of classical and neural correction methods: interrogating signal - dashed line; sensor's output – dotted line; classical correction for the model (3), $N_K = 15\ s$, $k = 10$ – dashed–dotted line; classical correction for the model (1), $\tau_{1K} = 22s$, $\tau_{2K} = 6s$, $N_{1K} = 12\ s$, $N_{2K} = 2\ s$ – thin solid line, neural correction – thick solid line.

To minimise the influence of noise, moving average filter was applied before the corrector in classical method and after the neural network in the ANN based method. To compare the quality of applied correction, and time $t_{0,05}$ for dynamic errors of normalised step responses were computed and shown in table 3.

Table 3. Mean-sum-square-errors (MSSE) and times $t_{0,05}$, after which dynamic error became to be less then 5% of signal value in steady state for normalised step responses, for different correction methods, step magnitudes ΔT and signal to noise ratios (SNR).

correction method	ΔT [°C]	SNR [dB]	MSSE [-]	$t_{0,05}$ [s]
	14.0	33	0.08	55.5
sensor without corrector	76.5	48	0.10	57.4
	173.4	55	0.11	62.6
classical correction,	14.0	33	0.03	64.7
1st order inertial model,	76.5	48	0.03	34.9
N_K=15s, k=10	173.4	55	0.03	30.1
classical correction,	14.0	33	0.02	47.6
model given by eq.(1),	76.5	48	0.03	6.3
τ_{K1}=22s,τ_{K2}=6s, N_{K1}=12, N_{K2}=2s	173.4	55	0.04	11.8
neural correction,	14.0	33	0.03	51.7
MLP ANN (6-15-1)	76.5	48	0.01	4.4
	173.4	55	0.01	4.4

5. Conclusions

Application of ANN based correction method is especially superior to traditional methods in measurement environments, in which sensors dynamic behaviour is non-linear. Results obtained for neural correction are comparable to classical methods in small temperature ranges and significantly better for wide temperature ranges.

References

[1] Haykin S. *Neural Networks: a comprehensive foundation* – 2nd ed. Prentice Hall, 1999.

[2] Jackowska-Strumillo L.: Sankowski D., McGhee J., Henderson I.A.: *Modelling and MBS experimentation for temperature sensors.* Meas., Vol.**20**, No.1, pp.49-60, 1997.

[3] Jackowska-Strumiłło L.: *Computerised System for RTD Dynamics Identification.* Int. IMEKO Seminar on Low Temperature Thermometry and Dynamic Temperature Measurement. Wrocław, (1997), pp. D-(25-30).

[4] Jackowska-Strumiłło L.: *ANN based correction of dynamic errors in temperature measurements.* Fifth Conference „Neural Networks and Soft Computing" – Zakopane, June 6-10, 2000, pp. 681-686.

[5] Michalski L., Eckersdorf K., McGhee J.: *Temperature Measurement.* John Wiley and Sons Ltd., Chichester, 1991.

[6] Sydenham P.: *Handbook of Measurement Science.* John Wiley &Sons Ltd., 1982.

Short-term Weather Forecasting with Neural Networks

Marcin Jaruszewicz[(1)] and Jacek Mańdziuk[(1,2)]

[(1)] Faculty of Mathematics and Information Science
Warsaw University of Technology, Plac Politechniki 1, 00-661 Warsaw, Poland
e-mail: mandziuk@alpha.mini.pw.edu.pl, jaruszewicz@data.pl
[(2)] Corresponding author

Abstract
A method of short-term weather forecasting based on artificial neural networks is presented. Each training sample consist of a date information combined with meteorological data from the last three days gathered at the meteorological station in Miami, USA. The prediction goal is the next day's temperature. Prediction system is built based on multilayer perceptron network trained with backpropagation algorithm with momentum.
The *average prediction error* of the network on the test set equals 1.12°C. The *average percentage predictio n error* is equal to 5.72%. The results are very encouraging and provide a promise for further exploration of the issue. The so-called *correlation ratio* δ between predicted and real changes (trends) is equal to 0.7136. Relatively high value of δ additionally confirms good quality of presented results.
Experimental results of application of the Principal Component Analysis method at the stage of pre-processing of the input data are also presented. In that case the average prediction error and the average percentage prediction error are equal to 2.76°C and 15.28%, respectively.

1. Introduction

Weather forecast is one of the most challenging, though very interesting, tasks in a field of prediction. Conventional methods are based on solving a large and quite complicated set of differential equations which describes an approximate model of a climate. In order to complete such task in a reasonable time very powerful computers have to be used, and the more precise results are expected the more computers' power and time is required.

Due to the above reasons several attempts have been made in order to apply other approaches to the problem. Some of them are based on artificial intelligence systems, and in particular artificial neural networks [1]. Simple architecture and the power of parallel information processing provide a tempting alternative to classical methods and opens an opportunity to output encouraging, high quality results in a relatively short time. A neural network after appropriate training is able to produce weather predictions almost instantaneously - only a few matrix operations are necessary. On the other hand neural networks, as oppose to the exact differential equations – based methods, provide only approximate solutions and therefore – in practice – bottom limits on the possible prediction error exist.

One of the key factors in effective design of neural networks-based systems trained in a supervised manner is the quality (reliability) and completeness of the training data (past observations).

In Poland, meteorogical data is collected by the IMGW [2] which also sends this data out to other meteorological centres in the world. One of such centers with a huge database (storing the data collected by many meteorogical stations all over the world) opened for the public access is maintained by Forecast Systems Laboratory (FSL) [3]. Unfortunately, after closer examination it appeared that in several cases the data stored in the FSL database was not complete and consequently not useful for our purpose. Based on the completeness criteria the data collected by the University of Miami, Florida, USA was finally chosen as the source of training and testing data for our prediction system.

2. System's architecture

Prediction system was built based on a multilayer perceptron network. Two different learning algorithms were applied and tested. At first, standard backpropagation method [4-5] with momentum was used. Each network's input sample was composed on 17 variables: two describing the date of an observation (day and month), and 15 describing the weather data - temperature, pressure, dev point temperature, wind direction and wind speed - from the last three days preceding the prediction date. The network had one hidden layer composed of 10 neurons. The output layer was composed of one neuron predicting temperature value.

In the other training method, meteorological data was pre-processed by the Principal Component Analysis (PCA) method [6]. After applying the PCA, the size of the input sample was reduced from 17 to 10 orthogonal, uncorrelated components. Network's architecture was analogous to the previous case, with the exception that the size of the input layer was equal to 10 and the hidden layer size was reduced to 4. Standard backpropagation with momentum was used for the training.

In both cases the input data was normalized and scaled to the range (-1, 1). All neurons except these in the input layer had the following sigmoidal activation (transfer) function:

$$f(x)=\frac{2}{1+e^{-x}}-1 \tag{1}$$

For input layer neurons identity activation function ($f(x)=x$) was used. Initially, all weights in the network were randomly chosen from the range (-0.01, 0.01).

3. The principal component analysis

The PCA method defines transformation matrix from the set of input vectors composed of (possibly) correlated components to another set of vectors composed of orthogonal and uncorrelated components. PCA saves the most relevant information from the multidimensional dataset and at the same time reduces its dimension. Some information – statistically irrelevant - is therefore discarded.

In short, the PCA transformation is based on the following autocorrelation matrix:

$$\mathbf{R}_{xx} = \frac{1}{n}\sum_{k=1}^{n}(\mathbf{x}_k \mathbf{x}_k^{T}), \tag{2}$$

where n is the number of vectors in the input set, $\boldsymbol{X}_k$ is the k-th vector. Eigenvectors of matrix $\boldsymbol{R}_{xx}$ corresponding to eigenvalues sorted in the decreasing order point out the principal components. The first principal component is responsible for the highest percentage of the variance of the sample [6], the second one – for the next highest variance, and so on. By choosing the required number of principal components one is able to build matrix $\boldsymbol{W}$ of the PCA transformation:

$$\mathbf{W}=[\mathbf{w}_1,\mathbf{w}_2,\ldots,\mathbf{w}_M]^{T}, \tag{3}$$

where M is the required number of components and w_k (for $k=1,\ldots,M$) are the principal components itself.

In the neural networks framework the PCA matrix can be also build in alternative way, using a two layer feed-forward network trained by Sanger's formula. The input and output layer sizes are equal to the dimensions of the input vectors respectively in the initial dataset and in the transformed one. Learning epochs are repeated for all vectors from a dataset as long as the weights are changing. Weights are updated according to the following formula:

$$\Delta w_{i,j} = \eta[y_i x_j - y_i \sum_{h=1}^{i} w_{j,h} y_h], \tag{4}$$

where η is the learning rate, $w_{i,j}$ is the weight from the j-th neuron in the input layer to the i-th neuron in the output layer. After appropriate learning period a set of weights between layers provides an estimation of the PCA transformation matrix.

4. Weather prediction results

As mentioned previously the weather data was collected for the area of Miami, FL, USA. The dataset consisted of 942 observations from the period 1998-2000. Variability of the average daily temperature is presented in Fig.1. The average temperature is equal to 21.8°C with the minimum of 3.2°C and the maximum of 28.8°C. Seasonal oscillations are clearly visible. In the sample there also exist some number of (statistically) extreme values. These outliers as well as the structure of the temperature data are presented in Fig. 2. It is important to note that outliers were *not* discarded from the training/testing data.

Since the original size of the dataset (942 samples) was relatively small for our purpose, the dataset was artificially doubled by adding to each sample a small amount of Gaussian noise (not exceeding 0.01%). The dataset of 1884 observations was divided in two disjunctive sets: learning set composed of 95% of the samples and test set composed of the other 5% of the samples. All samples from learning set were presented to the network 400'000 times in both PCA algorithm and backpropagation method.

In case of using the backpropagation algorithm *without PCA* the *average prediction error* was equal to 1.12°C. The respective *average percentage error* – calculated as the mean value of all percentage errors within the test set - was equal to 5.72% (see Table 1). Additionally, the *average comparative error* defined as:

$$\varepsilon = \frac{\sum_{i=0}^{N}(P_i^t - R_i^t)}{\sum_{i=0}^{N}(R_i^{t-1} - R_i^t)} \tag{5}$$

and the *correlation ratio* between predicted and real changes:

$$\delta = \frac{\sum_{i=0}^{N}(R_i^t - R_i^{t-1})(P_i^t - R_i^{t-1})}{\sqrt{\sum_{i=0}^{N}(R_i^t - R_i^{t-1})^2 (P_i^t - R_i^{t-1})^2}}, \tag{6}$$

were calculated. In the above equations N denotes the size of the test set, P_i^t and R_i^t are the i-th predicted and real values at time t, resp. The ε coefficient was equal to 0.7736 (according to [7] acceptable weather prediction methods are characterised by $\varepsilon < 1.0$). The correlation ratio δ was equal to 0.7136. Relatively high value of δ additionally confirms good quality of presented results.

The experiment was repeated several times with various initial weights. The results are repeatable with relatively low variance (below 10%).

Table 1. Results for backpropagation without PCA algorithm.

Error	Value [°C]	Value [%]
Average	1,12	5,72
Minimum	0,00	0,00
Maximum	4,40	41,59

In case the PCA was initially used for pre-processing the data (and reducing the input dimension from 17 to 10) the average error was equal to 2.76°C, i.e. 15.28% of the real value (see Table 2).

Table 2. Results for backpropagation with PCA pre-processing algorithm.

Error	Value [°C]	Value [%]
Average	2,76	15,28
Minimum	0,02	0,1
Maximum	10,4	98,08

Therefore, one of the main qualitative conclusions is that the backpropagation alone outperformed the backpropagation with PCA support. Several other experiments with different number of principal components, including the case of all components – i.e. without compression, showed that usability of PCA in weather prediction seems to be doubtful. The possible reason for such a property may be very complex mutual relations (dependencies) between individual factors in the meteorological data.

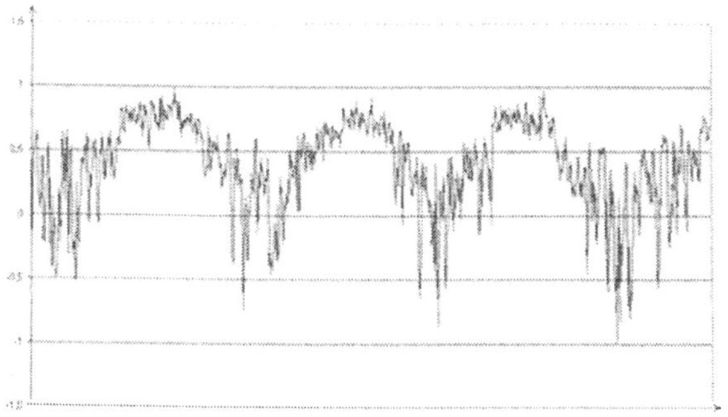

Fig.1. Variability of the daily temperature in Miami, USA – days of 1998-2000.

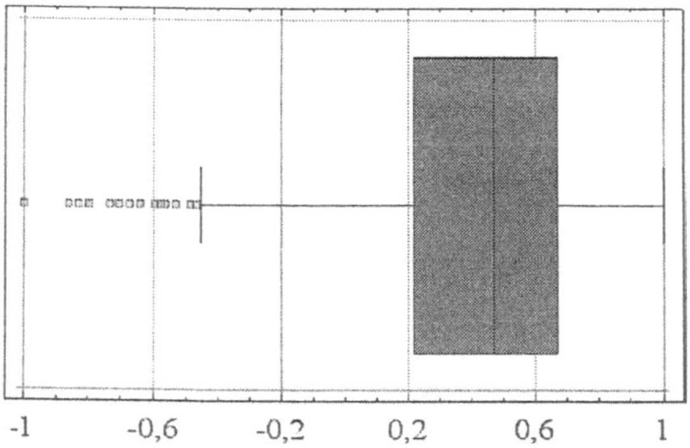

Fig.2. Statistic variability of the temperature in Miami, USA – standard box and whisker plot. The central box covers the middle 50 percent of the data. The sides of the box are the lower and upper quartiles, and the vertical line drawn through the box is the median. The whiskers extend out to the lower and upper values range of the data. Small boxes are outliers.

5. Conclusions

An approach to the weather forecasting problem based on artificial neural networks is presented. Obtained results - with an average error of 5.72% (1.12°C) and high correlation between predicted and real changes - are very encouraging and provide a promise for further exploration of the issue, e.g. by applying more sophisticated learning algorithms like the variable metric method or combining our approach with expert systems. One of the important conclusions of this piece of research is problematic applicability of the PCA method as a supporting tool for data pre-processing in the problem considered. This issue deserves further investigation, however an *ad-hoc* explanation may be a very high complexity and correlation of meteorological data which prevents dimensionality reduction and efficient orthogonalisation.

References

[1] D. Silverman, J. Dracup, Artificial Neural Networks and Long Range Precipitation Prediction in California, *J. of Applied Meteorology*, 31(1), 2000, 57-66

[2] http://www.imgw.pl

[3] http://raob.fsl.noaa.gov

[4] P.J. Werbos, Beyond regression: new tools for prediction and analysis in the behavioral sciences, *Ph.D. thesis, Harvard University, Cambridge, MA, USA*

[5] D.E. Rumelhart, G.E. Hinton, R.J. Williams, Learning Representations by Back-Propagating Errors, *Nature*, 323, 1986, 533-536

[6] Osowski Stanisław: Neural networks in information processing, *OWPW*, Warsaw 2000.

[7] Zbigniew Sorbjan: Fundaments of numerical weather prediction, WPW 1975.

Method for Detection of Wheat Grain Damage with Application of Neural Networks*

Aleksander Kubiak[1], Zbigniew Mikrut[2]

[1]Food Engineering Department, University of Warmia and Mazury, Oczapowskiego 7, 10-725 Olsztyn, Poland
e-mail: akubiak@uwm.edu.pl
[2]Institute of Automatics, University of Mining and Metallurgy, Mickiewicza 30, 30-059 Kraków, Poland
e-mail: zibi@biocyb.ia.agh.edu.pl

Abstract. In the present paper the application of *backpropagation* type neural networks to assessment of wheat grain quality is described. The contours of whole and broken grains have been extracted using the log-polar transform, precisely normalised and then used as input data for the neural network. The network optimisation has been carried out and then the results have been analysed in the context of response values worked-out by the output neurones. By evaluation of the obtained results it has been found that correct recognition of the grain quality is possible on the 97% level for the learning set, and 94% level for the test set. The achieved recognition level allows the utilisation of the proposed method in industrial devices dedicated to grain quality evaluation.

1 Introduction

The assessment of wheat grain quality is being done at all the stages of its production, processing and storage. Small grains and impurities are removed using mechanical sieves. Still such a procedure does not guarantee an efficient removal of all the broken grains. Considerable quantity of damaged grains in the wheat affects its quality as a seed, and also as a material for further processing. The quality evaluation of food and agricultural products is done mainly by their visual inspection, carried out by qualified experts. When analysis of huge number of samples is required such evaluation is expensive, time-consuming and subjective.

Computer image analysis is one of the fields which enable an objective evaluation of grain materials. It has been applied for quality assessment of edible beans[1], rice [7], pistachio nuts [3] as well as wheat grain [4]. The classification systems used for qualitative evaluation of the examined samples are mainly based on the analysis of geometrical parameters of the studied objects (length, width, area, circumference, shape coefficients) [4]. Multidimensional databases describ-

* This work was partially supported by the University of Mining and Metallurgy grant No. 10.10.120.39.

ing the shapes of the studied objects are used for classification based on statistical methods [6], fuzzy sets [1], genetic algorithms [2] and neural networks [3].

Taking into account the fact that the geometrical parameters used up to date do not fully reflect the shape of the studied objects, in the present work the *log-polar transform* [8] of the outlines of whole and broken grains has been used as a form of input data for the neural network. One version of the method (so called log-Hough transform) proved to be quite efficient as a preprocessing algorithm for shapes recognised by use of a Kohonen network [5]. In the present work *back-propagation* type networks have been used for the task of recognition of whole and broken wheat grains.

2 The Research Material and Preprocessing

The research material consisted of samples of wheat grains (whole and broken), belonging to two wheat varieties: one Polish Gama variety and one German Estica variety. The grain images, registered using a CCD camera and an image acquisition module, have undergone preprocessing by binarisation, dilation, erosion and hole filling[1]. The binarised wheat grain images have been transformed to the log-polar representation and edge-detection has been carried out.

The most important stage of the preliminary processing was a versatile normalisation of the grain image edges in the log-polar space. The well-known properties of replacement of rotation and magnification operations in the Cartesian space by translations along respective directions in the log-polar space has been used [10]. In particular [5]:

- the object has been centered by iterative calculation of the gravity centre
- the angular position has been normalised by analysis of edge function derivative, attenuated by exponential function
- the object's edge has been iteratively shifted along the "radius" axis, what is equivalent to magnification normalisation in the Cartesian space (see Fig. 1).

The normalised vector representations of the studied wheat grains has been used as input data for a *backpropagation* type neural network, implemented using the NeuralWare Professional II+ software.

The network's input data have been divided into two sets: the learning set consisting of a proportional number of the input data, representing both the whole and broken grains of both wheat varieties, and a test set, consisting of the remaining data (see Table 1).

Taking into account the greater diversity of the broken grain shapes in relation to the whole grains, the vectors representing the broken grains of Estica variety have been placed twice in the learning sequence: in the beginning and in the middle, in order to achieve a better learning by the network. The learning sequence thus consisted of 500 data samples. For testing of the trained network both learning and test sets have been used, consisting of 400 and 513 elements respectively.

[1] using the Lucia D ver.3.5 package (Laboratory Imaging Ltd., Prague, Czech Republic).

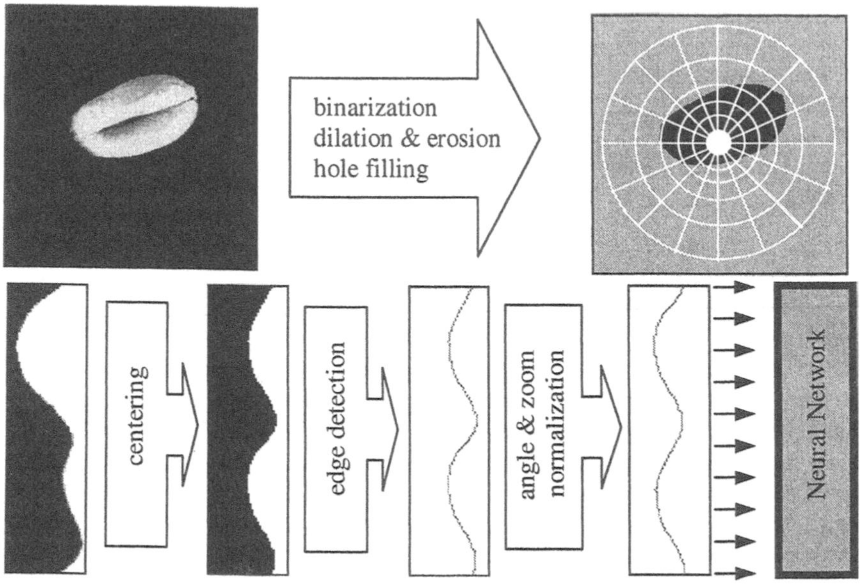

Fig. 1. Upper row: preprocessing of the image of the whole grain in Cartesian space, below: normalisation in log-polar domain. Dimension of the log-polar images is 40x144 pixels.

Table 1. Structure of the data in the learning and test sets

	Learning set		Test set		Total	
Variety	Whole	Broken	Whole	Broken	Whole	Broken
Estica	100	100	48	185	148	285
Gama	100	100	189	128	289	228
Total	200	200	237	313	437	513

3 Neural Network

The neural network used in experiments consisted of 3 layers. The input layer was formed by 144 neurones, reflecting the number of the input vector components. The number of neurones in the hidden layer has been determined experimentally, by testing 80 networks of various number of elements in the hidden layer.

The network's output layer consisted of two neurones, one for each class to be recognised (whole, broken). Consecutive network's learning cycles have been carried out for various values of the learning coefficients and the momentum parameter. For selected networks the learning process has been also carried out for various starting values of "random seed" parameter, which affects the selection sequence for presentations of the learning set elements.

The best results have been obtained for a network containing 15 neurones in the hidden layer. The remaining parameters have been set as follows: learning rate for the hidden layer 0.3, learning rate for the output layer 0.15, the momentum parameter 0.3, Delta learning rule and sigmoidal transfer function. The number of presentations was set to 200000.

4 Results of the Study

After completion of the learning process the neural network of the 144-15-2 structure has been tested - using both the learning and test sets. The learning set has been used in order to determine the reliability with which the network recognises the whole and broken grains used in the networks learning, and to propose some additional parameters which might be helpful in increasing the percent recognition level. The recognition results for the wheat grains have been analysed by two methods:

- "threshold" recognition: the output values produced by neurones of the network's output layer have been compared to a certain "threshold value". In the cases when the value of the neurone's answer has been greater than the threshold value the output values has been regarded as a correct recognition (otherwise it was regarded as a rejection)
- so called *recognition reliability* Delta [9] has been determined: the difference of the values produced by the output layer neurones has been calculated and then it was compared to a certain, predetermined value. In cases when the difference was greater than the given value the neurone's answer was taken into account, otherwise it was rejected.

In the test carried out both methods of neurone response classification have been taken into account. Both threshold and difference values have been preliminarily determined from the intersection point of the cumulative histograms of individual neurone's responses for the *learning* set (Fig. 2). The recognition results for the learning and test sets for selected threshold and reliability values are presented in Tables 2,3.

Table 2. Recognition results (%) for the learning set using threshold and difference (Delta)

Threshold	Rejected	Total	Whole	Broken	Delta	Rejected	Total	whole	Broken
0.4	0.00	96.50	96.50	96.50	0.4	2.25	96.67	96.48	96.87
0.5	0.00	96.50	96.50	96.50	0.5	3.75	96.88	96.92	96.84
0.6	0.25	96.49	96.50	96.48	*0.6*	*5.75*	*97.61*	*97.89*	*97.33*
0.7	2.25	96.67	96.48	96.87	0.7	8.00	97.55	97.81	97.30
0.8	*5.00*	*96.84*	*96.37*	*97.33*	0.8	12.00	97.73	98.27	97.21
0.9	11.00	96.63	96.04	97.21	0.9	29.00	98.24	98.48	98.03

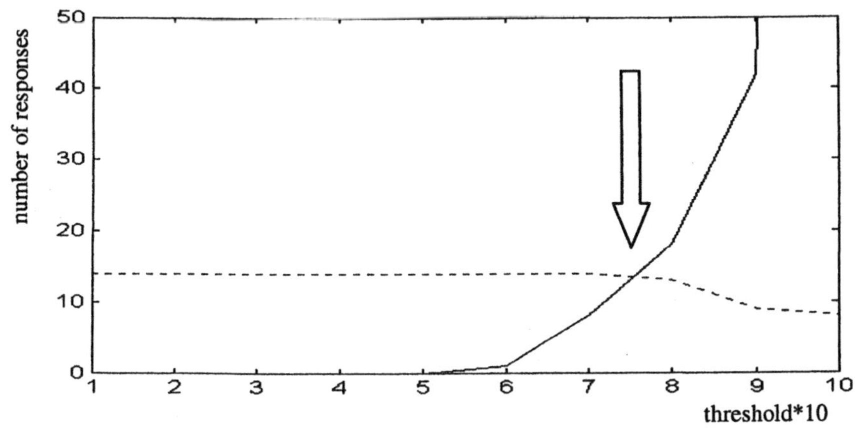

Fig. 2. Cumulative histograms of correct responses (solid line, cumulation from 1 to 10) and wrong ones (dotted line, cumulation from 10 to 1).

Table 3. Recognition results (%) for the test set using threshold and difference (Delta)

Threshold	Rejected	Total	Whole	Broken	Delta	Rejected	Total	Whole	Broken
0.4	3.27	92.10	100.00	86.58	0.4	4.36	91.25	94.78	88.51
0.5	3.27	92.10	100.00	86.58	0.5	7.45	91.75	95.09	89.12
0.6	5.64	93.06	100.00	88.00	*0.6*	*10.54*	*92.28*	*95.45*	*89.71*
0.7	6.54	93.38	100.00	88.51	0.7	12.54	92.72	96.28	89.85
0.8	*12.36*	*94.19*	*100.00*	*89.71*	0.8	16.90	93.22	96.17	90.73
0.9	18.36	94.88	100.00	90.73	0.9	33.64	95.07	96.32	94.06

5 Discussion and Summary

The recognition level for the learning set was 96%, while the network has recognised 96.5% of the whole grains and 95.5% of the broken grains. The recognition level for the test set was 89.1% total and 94.5% and 83.7% for the whole and broken grains respectively.

From the results presented in Tables 2 and 3 it can be seen how grain quality recognition level for the learning set is changing depending on the threshold or Delta value. This was used to determine the threshold value as 0.8 and then the recognition level was found to be 96.4% and 97.3% for the whole and broken grains respectively. The results have been obtained with rather low percentage of rejection cases which was equal to 5%. For the same learning set a similar effects has been obtained for Delta value equal to 0.6 and then the recognition levels were 97.9% and 97.3% for the whole and broken grains respectively.

For the test set the networks has recognised - for the same values of threshold and Delta values - 100% of the whole grains and 89.7% of broken grains for the threshold value equal to 0.8. For the Delta value equal to 0.6 the network has recognised correctly 95.4% and 89.7% of the whole and broken grains respectively. The rejection levels for the above mentioned threshold and Delta values were respectively 12.4% and 10.5%.

By evaluation of the obtained results it has been found, that by making use of the threshold or Delta values it is possible to recognise correctly the wheat grain quality with recognition level exceeding 90% (94.2% for threshold value equal to 0.8 and 92.3% for Delta=0.6). In this application the above mentioned rejection rates are meaningless because during industrial testing we can easily resize the set of grains to be recognised. Taking into account the fact that in the research material two wheat varieties were present, often exhibiting quite considerable diversity within each wheat variety, and between the varieties, such a recognition level should be regarded as high, what makes a good prospect for application of the object edge normalisation method in the log-polar space and the neural networks in industrial devices for wheat grain quality assessment.

References

1. Chtioui Y., Panigrahi, S., Backer L. F. (1999) Rough sets theory as a pattern classification tool for quality assessment of edible beans. Trans. of the ASAE, vol. 42(4):1145-1152
2. Chtioui Y., Bertrand D., Barba D. (1998) Feature selection by genetic algorithm. Application to seed discrimination by Artificial Vision. J. Sci. Food Agric, **76**, 77-86
3. Ghazanfari. A., Irudayara J., Kusalik A. (1996) Grading pistachio nuts using neural network approach, Trans. of the ASAE, vol. 39(6):2319-2324
4. Kubiak A., Fornal Ł. (1994) Interaction between geometrical features and technological quality of polish wheat grain. Polish Journal of Food and Nutrition , 7/48, 3, 160-167
5. Mikrut Z. (2001) Recognition of objects normalised in Log-polar space using Kohonen networks. Proc. of the 2nd Int. Symp. Image and signal processing and analysis, Pula, Croatia
6. Ohsawa R., Tsutsumi T. H. et al. (1998) Quantitative evaluation of common buckwheat (Fagopyrum esculentum Moench) kernel shape by elliptic Fourier descriptor. Euphtica, **101**, 175-183
7. Sakai N., Yonekawa S., Matsuzaki A. (1996) Two dimensional image analysis of the shape of rice and its application to separating Varieties. Journal of Food Engineering, **27**, 397-407
8. Schwartz E. L. (1977) Spatial mapping in the primate sensory projection: analytic structure and the relevance to perception. Biological Cybernetics, **25**, 181-194
9. Tadeusiewicz R., Mikrut Z. (1994) Neural Networks applied to visual pattern recognition – a comparative study. Appl. Math. and Comp. Sci., vol. 4 No. 3, 397-411
10. Weiman C. F. R. (1989) Polar exponential sensor arrays unify iconic and Hough space representation. SPIE vol. 1192: Intelligent robots and computer vision VIII

The WWW Based Data Mining Toolbox Architecture

Lukasz Kurgan [1,2], Krzysztof J. Cios [1,2,3,4] and Michael Trombley [1]

[1] Dept. of Computer Science and Engineering, University of Colorado at Denver
[2] Dept. of Computer Science, University of Colorado at Boulder
[3] University of Colorado Health Sciences Center, Denver
[4] 4cData, LLC, Golden, CO, U.S.A.
emails: lkurgan@carbon.cudenver.edu, Krys.Cios@cudenver.edu, mptrombl@ouray.cudenver.edu

Abstract. This paper presents the Data Mining (DM) toolbox architecture based on cutting edge World Wide Web (WWW) technologies. The DM toolbox is used to discover new and useful knowledge by integrating results generated by multiple DM tools. The proposed architecture allows submission of data to the DM toolbox and generation of results that combine knowledge generated by several different DM tools. The DM toolbox dynamically finds DM tools that are relevant to a specific data mining task, submits the data to the tools, receives results of their analysis, and combines the results to generate a final report. The proposed architecture will increase the usability of DM tools, helping achieve a more consistent and better integrated Data Mining and Knowledge Discovery (DMKD) process.

1 Introduction

1.1 The KD Process

Knowledge Discovery (KD) is a nontrivial process of identifying valid, novel, potentially useful, and ultimately understandable patterns from large collections of data [7]. DM is just one of the KD steps concerned with the generation of knowledge from data. In practice, DM, KD, and DMKD are used synonymously to describe the same process.
Several DMKD process models were proposed. They include: the six-step model by [4, 5], the five-step model by [3], and the nine-step model by [8]. For an extensive discussion of the above models see [5].

1.2 The DM Toolboxes, Tools, and Methods

To define an architecture for a DM toolbox, we first define the difference between DM methods and tools. The DM method is an implementation of a DM algorithm. The DM tool is a DM method that can communicate and operate within the DMKD framework. In other words, a DM tool is a highly interoperable DM method that works within the framework.
A DM toolbox consists of several DM tools that are used in tandem to discover new and useful knowledge from data. The DM toolbox user would submit his data to the toolbox, and receive the combined knowledge discovered by all the DM tools that would be used by the toolbox. The most important feature of the proposed architecture is the ability of the DM toolbox to dynamically select and use only those DM tools that are relevant to a specific data analysis task, requested by user. The goal for the proposed architecture is to increase usability, user friendliness, and applicability of the DM tools that will be used. The proposed architecture will also increase consistency, and integration of the DMKD process model.

1.3 XML: Key Ingredient for Building DM Toolboxes

XML (eXtensible Markup Language) is a standard proposed by the WWW Consortium [1]. XML is a markup language for documents that contain structured or semi-structured information that uses custom-defined tags. Structured information consists of content and context. XML is a standard to identify structures in documents by enabling users to define tags (element names) that are used to describe context of the data. As such, XML is one of the best mediums for building data integration systems [12]. XML technology is widely used in industry to transfer and share information in a platform-independent way. Most of the current database management systems already support the XML standard.

From the DM point of view, XML can help in solving multiple problems:

- building standard data and knowledge repositories that would enable sharing of both data and the discovered knowledge between different DM tools that work on different software platforms. XML is able to help with both creation of such repositories and communication between them and the DM tools.
- implementing communication protocols between DM tools. By using standardized communication protocols, different DM tools, say, developed by different companies, could be integrated to generate broader, more understandable and accurate, data models.

To summarize, XML and XML-based technologies provide a wide range of tools that can help in transforming DM methods into tools, and integrating these tools into DM toolboxes.

2 XML-based Technologies

XML, along with other technologies that are built on top of XML constitute core technologies for the proposed DM toolbox architecture.

2.1 Communication Protocols

XML-RPC (XML-Remote Procedure Call) [19] is a very simple XML and HTTP based protocol. It allows for making procedure calls and transmittal of complex data structures between programs running on disparate operating systems, and in different environments. XML-RPC implementations are available for virtually all operating systems, programming languages, dynamic and static environments. SOAP (Simple Object Access Protocol) [14] is another platform-independent and popular XML and HTTP based protocol. SOAP is a superset of XML-RPC, but they are not fully compatible. SOAP is mostly used for accessing services, objects, and servers over the Internet.

SOAP and XML-RPC are two communication protocols that are not only platform-independent and loosely coupled, but also seamless in terms of implementation. They can be used for communication between different DM tools, and between DM tools and knowledge repositories. The proposed DM toolbox can use these protocols to access all XML compatible DM tools over the Internet. Such architectures support ease of development, distribution and customization since both protocols are open source, Internet based, and have strong industry support.

2.2 Predictive Data Models Language

PMML (Predictive Model Markup Language) [13] is the XML-based language for defining predictive data models, which was developed by the Data Mining Group [6]. It allows for vendor-independent defining and sharing of data models between PMML compliant applications. PMML is a unified language for storing knowledge generated by different DM methods, and thus helps in removing incompatibilities caused by using proprietary formats. The PMML currently supports several DM models like decision trees, naive Bayesian models, regression models, sequence and association rules, neural networks, and center- and distribution-based clustering algorithms [6]. For details on PMML see [10]. Products from many major vendors like IBM, Oracle, SPSS, NCR, Magnify, Angoss and others already currently support PMML. The usability of XML for storing, retrieving and using the domain knowledge via the use of PMML is described in [2].

2.3 Service Description and Discovery Tools

WSDL (Web Services Description Language) [18] is the XML based format for describing web based services. WSDL allows the description of services and their messages regardless of what message formats or network protocols are used for communication. Most commonly, WSDL is used in conjunction with SOAP, HTTP, and MIME. WSDL provides an interface definition, abstract semantics and implementation definitions, and end points and network addresses, where the described web service can be invoked.

UDDI (Universal Description Discovery and Integration) [15] is a platform-independent framework based on XML, SOAP, HTTP and Domain Name System (DNS) protocols. UDDI is an industry initiative that serves the purpose of describing, discovering and integrating web-based services. It defines an API for publishing and searching web services, and can be applied to both XML and non-XML services. UDDI has strong industry support; currently over 300 companies support the UDDI initiative.

3 The DM Toolbox Architecture

3.1 Overview

The idea of implementing DM toolboxes arises from a simple observation that no single DM tool performs well on all types of data. There are many DM software implementations of DM methods available. Comparison of 43 existing implementations of DM methods was done in [9]. The proposed DM toolbox architecture tries to solve the problem of integration of available DM tools [9].

The main idea behind the proposed architecture is that a DM toolbox would consist of DM tools that would be published as web services [5]. Currently, several programming platforms already offers tools for publishing software as web service, providing WSDL description for it, and enabling SOAP based communication between the published services.

The DM toolbox architecture will use:

- UDDI to publish, find, and use DM tools that are published as web services. We envision that because of very strong industry support, DM researchers and companies will publish their software online and use UDDI to advertise it
- WSDL to describe formal DM tools and toolboxes
- SOAP as the protocol for interactions within a toolbox
- XML as the universal data format. XML can be used directly for storing data, and by using the PMML standard it can be also used to store discovered knowledge
- Internet as the communication medium

The proposed architecture implements the DM toolbox as a web client that accesses DM tools that are published as web services using a UDDI service, WSDL description mechanism, and SOAP as the communication protocol. The execution model of the proposed architecture consists of the following steps:

- The toolbox accepts the data from the user
- The toolbox checks availability and description of online-enabled DM tools (published as web services) using UDDI
- The toolbox invokes the tools that can provide meaningful results for currently processed data
- The toolbox serves data or portions of user data to the chosen DM tools for processing
- The chosen tools process the data, and return results to the toolbox
- The toolbox analyses and integrates the results and serves them back to the user. The results can be stored in a repository that uses a PMML language model, which will help to integrate knowledge coming from different sources.

The detailed execution model of the proposed architecture is shown in Figure 1 (black arrows denote the runtime communication, gray arrows denote the design-time or dynamic communication).

Using the proposed architecture, the DM toolbox can access and use several DM tools that are published as web services. The toolbox is able to process and integrate results sent back from the tools and store them in the knowledge base. We think that the proposed architecture will be widely accepted because of several factors:

- ease of developing web services, using SOAP protocol and UDDI; see implementation example below

- flexibility and wide applicability of the proposed architecture. The architecture can work cross-platform, uses popular Internet based protocols, supports distribution and is powered by dynamic finding of all DM models applicable to a specific task
- use of open standards that have broad industry support

The DM toolbox architecture is shown in Figure 2.

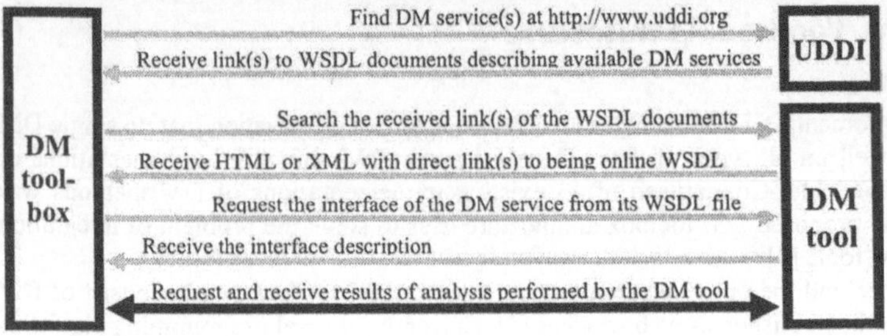

Fig. 1. The detailed execution model of the proposed DM toolbox architecture

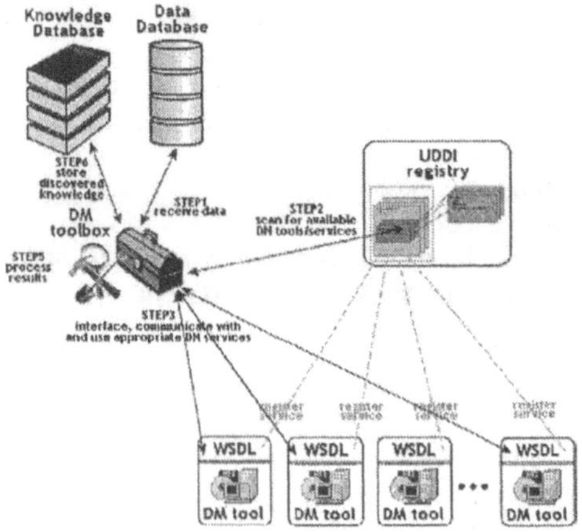

Fig. 2. DM toolbox architecture using Internet via HTTP, XML, SOAP and UDDI

3.2 Implementation

Web services are commonly implemented in any of several different programming languages, on many different platforms, and using a wide variety of application development tools. For the purpose of this demonstration, a sample web service was generated using C# and Visual Studio .Net. The DMServices web service was implemented with four methods that take and return string collections, but actually have no other functionality. They are simply to illustrate the process of finding and accessing web services through UDDI. The service was registered in the UDDI registry at run time using techniques described in [11]. The building and consequent registration of web services is not the topic of this paper.

In order to dynamically locate a web service, UDDI provides a framework for simplifying the discovery process [16]. Two key structures are the tModel and businessService. Often, the tModel for a service is equivalent to the service's WSDL document. The businessService is an XML-based structure used to represent details of the service in UDDI. How and where the service is accessed is provided in a structure known as the bindingTemplate, and is nested within the businessService. An example of the businessService for the DMServices web service is shown in Figure 3.
Using the XML structures defined by UDDI [16], we created a user interface for finding web services based on user-provided search strings for the service name and description. We again used C#, Visual Studio .Net, and the UDDI SDK 1.75 [17]. The development tools used allowed us to quickly develop an interface between the software and the UDDI registry, but are by no means the only way to do so.

```
<BusinessService (...)>
  <name>DMServices
  </name>
  <description (...)>Provides some DM functions.
  </description>
  <bindingTemplates>
    <bindingTemplate (...)>
      (...)
      <accessPoint URLType=
       "http">http://isl2.cudenver.edu/DM.asmx
      </accessPoint>
      (...)
      <tModelInstanceDetails>
        <tModelInstanceInfo tModelKey="...">
          (...)
        </tModelInstanceInfo>
      </tModelInstanceDetails>
    </bindingTemplate>
  </bindingTemplates>
  (...)
</BusinessService>
```

Fig. 3. A portion of the businessService XML description of the DMServices web service.

Using our tools, we simply took the user's input string(s), searched across all business listings, inspecting the service names and descriptions associated with each business for a match to the user's input. As matching services were discovered, we set a boolean flag to display the resulting matches in a tree structure for the user to explore. The primary functionality can be seen in the code snippet of Figure 4.

```
Regex nameRegex = new Regex(".*" + textBox1.Text +
".*",RegexOptions.IgnoreCase);
Regex descRegex = new Regex(".*" + textBox2.Text +
".*",RegexOptions.IgnoreCase);
FindBusiness fb = new FindBusiness();
fb.Name = "%"; // Wildcard to search across all business names
try {
     BusinessList bl = fb.Send();
     treeView1.Nodes.Clear();
     if (bl.BusinessInfos.Count == 0)
       treeView1.Nodes.Add("No services found!");
     foreach (BusinessInfo bi in bl.BusinessInfos) {
       GetBusinessDetail gbd = new GetBusinessDetail();
       gbd.BusinessKeys.Add(bi.BusinessKey);
       BusinessDetail bd = gbd.Send();
       foreach (BusinessEntity be in bd.BusinessEntities) {
         TreeNode businessNode = new TreeNode(be.Name);
         foreach (BusinessService bs in be.BusinessServices) {
           bool nameMatch = false;
           bool descMatch = false;
           if (nameRegex.Match(bs.Name).Success)
             nameMatch = true;
           foreach (Description d in bs.Descriptions) {
             if (descRegex.Match(d.Text).Success)
                                    descMatch = true;
...}...
```

Fig. 4. Example of the UDDI search code

Finally, in Figure 5, we show our tool and the results it found in the UDDI using the service description search string "data mining". As one can notice, two results were found. This is because we registered our service under two names, showing the possibility that more than one service may easily be found to perform a desired task.

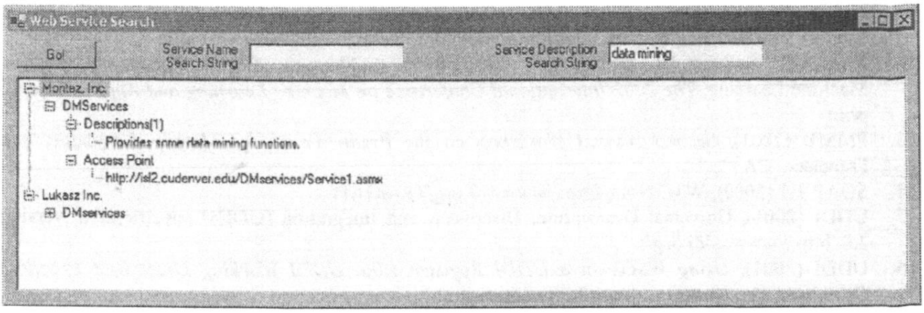

Fig. 5. Sample output for performing a search for data mining web services using UDDI

4 Conclusions

This paper presents a web-based architecture for a DM toolbox, which uses XML based technologies like XMP-RPC, SOAP, PMML, WSDL, and UDDI. The architecture uses

SOAP and XML-RPC for communication between the toolbox and DM tools used by it, UDDI for dynamic searching and accessing of the tools, and PMML as the standard for storing discovered knowledge. The architecture has several advantages, like using open standards that have broad industry support, ease of development, flexibility, wide applicability, and support for distribution. We think that there is a strong need for a tool that aims to integrate DM solutions since, for the last several years, the DMKD community has generated solutions that were not applicable in a broad context.

XML based technologies make it possible to build DM toolboxes that can dynamically integrate multiple DM tools, to build standardized knowledge repositories, and to communicate and interact between different DM tools. Development of such toolboxes will result in wider applicability of DM products.

References

1. Bray, T., Paoli, J., & Maler E., (2000) Extensible Markup Language (XML) 1.0 (Second Edition), W3C Recommendation, http://www.w3.org/TR/2000/REC-xml-20001006
2. Büchner, A.G., Baumgarten, M., Mulvenna, M.D., Böhm, R., & Anand, S.S., (2000) Data Mining and XML: Current and Future Issues, *Proc. of the First International Conference on Web Information Systems Engineering (WISE'00)*, 127-131, Hong Kong
3. Cabena, P., Hadjinian, P., Stadler, R., Verhees, J., & Zanasi, A. (1998), *Discovering Data Mining: From Concepts to Implementation*. Perentice Hall
4. Cios, K.J., Teresinska, A., Konieczna, S., Potocka, J., & Sharma, S. (2000) , Diagnosing Myocardial Perfusion from PECT Bull's-eye Maps - A Knowledge Discovery Approach, *IEEE Engineering in Medicine and Biology Magazine*, Special issue on Medical Data Mining and Knowledge Discovery, 19(4), 17-25
5. Cios, K. J., & Kurgan, L. (2002), Trends in Data Mining and Knowledge Discovery, In: Pal N.R., Jain, L.C. and Teoderesku, N. (Eds.), *Knowledge Discovery in Advanced Information Systems*, Springer, in print
6. DMG (2001), The Data Mining Group, http://www.dmg.org/
7. Fayyad, U.M., Piatesky-Shapiro, G., Smyth, P., & Uthurusamy, R. (1996), *Advances in Knowledge Discovery and Data Mining*, AAAi/MIT Press
8. Fayyad, U.M., Piatetsky-Shapiro, G., & Smyth, P. (1996), Knowledge Discovery and Data Mining: towards a unifying framework, *Proceedings of the Second International Conference on Knowledge Discovery and Data Mining (KDD96)*, Portland, OR
9. Goebel, M., & Gruenwald, L. (1999), A Survey of Data Mining Software Tools, *SIGKDD Explorations*, 1(1), 20-33
10. Grossman, R.L., Bailey, S., Ramu, A., Malhi, B., Hallstrom, P., Pulleyn, I., & Qin, X. (1999), The Management and Mining of Multiple Predictive Models Using the Predictive Modeling Markup Language, *Information and Software Technology*, 41(9), 589-595
11. Januszewski, K. (2001), Web Service Description and Discovery Using UDDI, Part I, MSDN Library, http://msdn.microsoft.com/library/default.asp
12. Kurgan, L., Swiercz, W., & Cios, K.J. (2002), Semantic Mapping of XML Tags using Inductive Machine Learning, *The 2002 International Conference on Machine Learning and Applications*, in print
13. PMML (2001), *Second Annual Workshop on the Predictive Model Markup Language*, San Francisco, CA
14. SOAP 1.1 (2000), W3C Note, http://www.w3.org/TR/SOAP/
15. UDDI (2001), Universal Description, Discovery, and Integration (UDDI) specification, version 2.0, http://www.uddi.org/
16. UDDI (2001), *Using WSDL in a UDDI Registry 1.06: UDDI Working Draft Best Practices Document*, http://www.uddi.org/bestpractices.html
17. UDDI SDK (2001), Microsoft UDDI Software Development Kit 1.75, http://msdn.microsoft.com/downloads/default.asp?URL=/downloads/sample.asp?url=/msdn-files/027/001/814/msdncompositedoc.xml
18. WSDL (2001), Web Services Description Language (WSDL) 1.1, W3C Note, http://www.w3.org/TR/wsdl
19. XML-RPC (2001), UserLand Software, Inc., http://www.xmlrpc.com/

Concept of Neural Model of the Sea Bottom Surface

Jacek Łubczonek[1], Andrzej Stateczny[1]

[1] Maritime University of Szczecin, Wały Chrobrego 1/2, Szczecin, Poland

Abstract. This paper presents concept of neural model of the sea bottom surface, which could be implemented in marine numerical maps. The model consists of self-organizing network and set of trained networks used in surface approximation. Self-organizing networks firstly solves problem of division of data points into training subsets. Secondly it classifies any input data to one of approximating network. Set of approximating networks is used to calculate depth value at any coordinates of point within surface domain. An example illustrates reconstruction of surface based on neural model of bottom surface.

1 Introduction

Artificial neural networks are good alternative to traditional methods of surface modeling. One of the main advantages of neural networks is replacing traditional database to trained net, what simplifies algorithm of depth value calculation at any coordinates within domain of surface modeled. The main limitation of neural network used in surface modeling is often big size of training data set. Currently the number of data points obtained during hydrographic survey can reach up to 100 000 or more. So, it is rather impossible to train the network from whole data set. The simplest way to solve this problem is to divide original data points set into smaller subsets, which could be trained separately. This technique was already applied in [1]. The main idea of this technique was to divide original domain of bottom surface into set of overlapping rectangular subdomains. It allowed creating subsets of data points referring to each subdomain, which finally were used to train network. Such solution increased computational efficiency of training algorithms and ensured surface approximation within its entire large domain.

These results were motivation to build the neural model of the sea bottom for large and often irregular domain of bottom surface. Such model should calculate depth value within border of any type of waterway – at open sea or inland-restricted areas. This work focused more on role of self-organized network; assessment of various types neural networks used in surface approximation was already presented in [1][7][8].

2 Neural Networks and Traditional Methods of Surface Modeling

At present there are many interpolation methods, which are used in surface modeling. Applying them, the bottom surface model is created by calculating depth value in each interpolation knots of regular grid. These methods are often time-consuming, because each time an interpolation algorithm must seek certain number of the nearest points to the knots being interpolated using proper technique of points seeking [4]. For example having 10000 knots the interpolation algorithm must be run the same times.

Neural networks, in contrast to the traditional methods, realize in other way depth calculation. Set of data points can be used to train the network. Having trained network covering domain of bottom surface it is possible to calculate unknown depth value at any points. Of course, when big set of data points is divided into subsets, there should be created set of trained networks. Schematically it was illustrated in figure 1, where the input vector represents coordinates of any data points (x,y) and the output signal is the depth value (z).

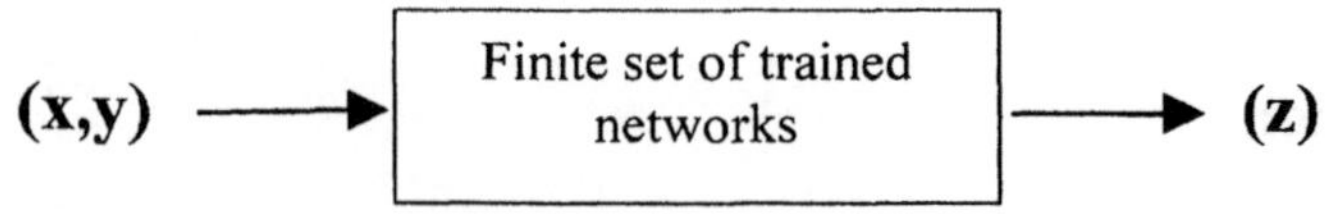

Fig. 1. Calculation of depth value using neural network.

3 Neural Model of Bottom Surface

Self-organizing network creates basic structure of proposed neural model. This kind of network was used to create training subsets and to classify input vector to proper trained network from the whole set. Training subsets were created after automated division by self-organizing algorithm two-dimensional input space into clusters of data points. For this aim k-means algorithm were used. Neurons (t_i) were organized after presenting n vector (x_n) from set of data points according to WTA algorithm [5]

$$t_i(n+1)=t_i(n)+\eta[x_n-t_i(n)] \tag{1}$$

Value of learning factor η decreased in k-th iteration [3]

$$\eta=(\eta_o/K)(K-k),\ k=1,2,3...,\tag{2}$$

where η_o=0.5 and K=4000.

For better organization of neurons conscience mechanism was used [5]. There was applied variable potential of neurons (p_M), which changed according to power function:

$$p_M(k)=p_{max}(p_{min}/p_{max})^{k/K}, \tag{3}$$

where p_{max}=0.7 and p_{min}=0.1.

After neurons' organization each cluster domain was spread to overlap in some part neighboring clusters. To do this there was defined the new radial subdomain, which center coordinates were the same as organized neuron position. Its radius was equaled

$$R=R_c+R_s, \tag{4}$$

where R_c denotes distance from neuron to the furthest point P in data cluster; R_s equals average distance to the nearest 40 points calculated from P. Data points gathered within border of radial subdomain created one training subset. It was illustrated in fig. 2, where set of data points was divided into four clusters (they were separated by dashed lines). There is an example of one radial subdomain with center situated in neuron of cluster no 1. Data points lying within this domain created the training subset.

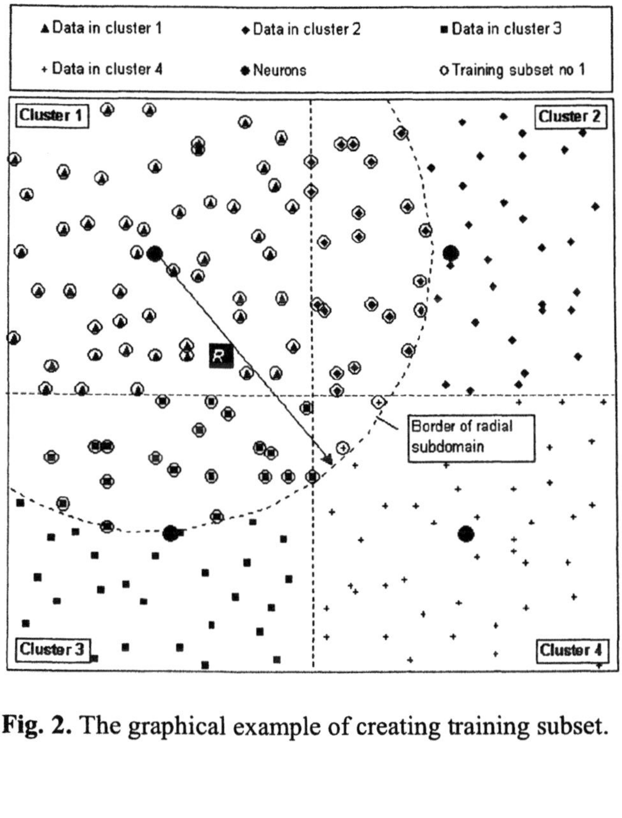

Fig. 2. The graphical example of creating training subset.

Having data point subsets there was performed network training (for surface approximation we can use e.g. multilayer perceptron or RBF networks). In that way there was created finite set of trained networks, where each one corresponded to one organized neuron. During depth computation the next task realizing by self-organized network was classification of input vector to neuron with biggest activation. It allowed to choose proper trained network from the whole set. The complete scheme of neural bottom model with *n* neurons of self-organized network is shown in fig. 3.

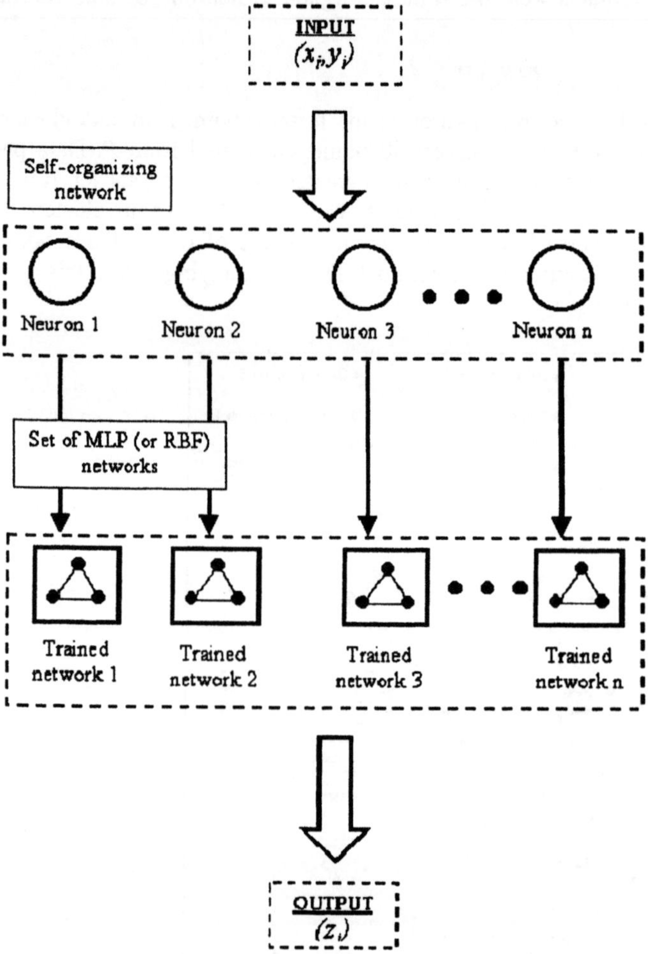

Fig. 3. Scheme of bottom surface model.

4 Example of Surface Modeling

Neural model of surface was used to approximate many types of surfaces. Here is showed one example of surface modeling from scattered data (fig. 2) generated from mathematical surface. Domain of this surface is 100 meters square; approximate range of depth values (Z) is [0, -38.5].

Firstly four neurons were organized using k-means algorithm with conscience mechanism. After that there was created four training data subsets. For surface approximation was used multilayer perceptron. Its structure was: one hidden layer; 30 hidden neurons with sigmoid transfer function. Network was trained separately for each data subset by quasi-Newton algorithm.

According to the scheme in figure 3 our neural model of bottom surface consisted of 4 neurons of self-organized network and four trained MLP networks. Reconstruction of surface compared with mathematical surface was showed in fig. 4. We can note that the shape of surface modeled was almost identical compared with its mathematical representation.

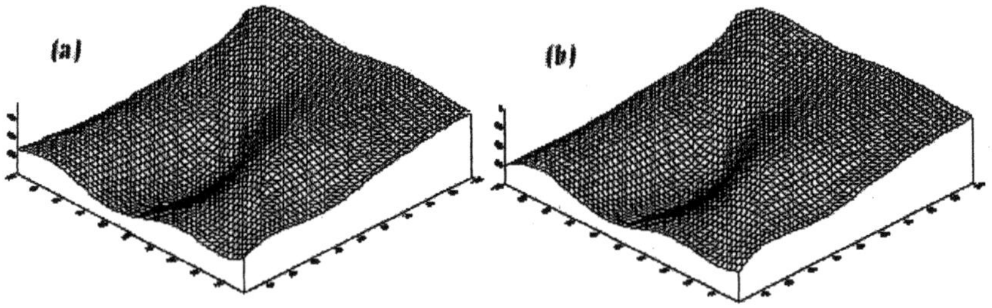

Fig. 4. Comparison of surface shapes (a) mathematical model, (b) approximated surface based on neural model.

Calculated RMS error (5) in the knots of 1m grid was equaled 0.08m.

$$RMS = \sqrt{\frac{1}{N}\sum_{i=1}^{N}(z_i - Z_i)^2} \qquad (5)$$

where z_i - calculated depth value in i-th knot,
Z_i - mathematical depth value in i-th knot,
N – number of grid knots (N=10000).

5 Sum-up

The main aim of this work was to show concept of neural model of sea bottom surface. The work showed that applying self-organizing network we could create training subsets equally spaced over the domain of surface being modeled. In that way there was possible to create set of trained network used in surface approximation. Presented scheme of surface model allows apply neural networks theoretically for any set of data points and shape of surface domain.

Practically the model could be a part of marine numerical maps [2][6][9]. It could be used to calculate depth value in knots of regular grid to generate three (or two) dimensional view of bottom surface; to calculate depth for current vessel position (coordinates); to model hydrodynamic phenomena; to process bathymetric data in navigational information systems.

References

1. Balicki J, Kitowski Z, Stateczny A (1999) Artificial neural networks for modelling of spatial shape of sea bottom. IV Conference of Neural Networks and Their Applications, Zakopane, pp. 637-643
2. Bojarowski K, Szacherska M, Stateczny A (1997) Spatial information system for maritime navigation. 5th Bilateral Meeting Poland-Italy, Monselice
3. Duch W, Korbicz J, Rutkowski L, Tadeusiewicz R (2000). Biocybernetic and biomedical engineering 2000 (vol 6 Neural networks). Academic Publishing House, Warsaw (in Polish)
4. Łubczonek J (2000) A comparison of selected methods of surface modelling: an example of seabed surface. Research Bulletin No 59, Maritime University, Szczecin, pp. 74-79
5. Osowski S (1996) Neural networks in algorithmic form. Scientific Technological Publishers, Warsaw (in Polish)
6. Stateczny A, Łubczonek J (2001) Spatial sea chart – new possibilities of presenting navigational information. Ist International Congress of Seas and Oceans (vol 1), Międzyzdroje, pp. 523-528
7. Stateczny A (1999) Spatial model of shape of sea bottom - as layer three-dimensional numerical sea chart. IX Scientific Technological Conference of Spatial Information Systems, Warsaw, pp. 317-323 (in Polish)
8. Stateczny A (2000) The neural method of sea bottom shape modelling for spatial maritime information system. In: CA Brebbia & J. Olivella (eds) Marine Engineering and Ports II. WIT Press Southampton, Boston
9. Weintrit A (1997) Electronic navigational chart. Maritime University, Gdynia (in Polish)

Systolic Simulation of Hamming Neural Network

Jacek Mazurkiewicz[1]

[1] Institute of Engineering Cybernetics, Wroclaw University of Technology, Poland
50-372 Wroclaw, ul. Janiszewskiego 11/17, e-mail: jmazur@ict.pwr.wroc.pl

Abstract. The paper describes the systolic simulation of Hamming net algorithm. Systolic arrays creation methodology is based on Data Dependence Graphs analysis. The proposed implementation is focused on completely digital circuits. Input data is passed through the neurons in a time share basis, weights are stored in digital shift registers and no separate thresholds are used. The architecture provides massive parallelism and reprogrammability. The efficiency of proposed simulation is discussed based on implementation quality criteria for array architecture.

1 Introduction

The Hamming net implements the optimum minimum error classifier when bit errors are random and independent. The performance of the Hamming net is proved in problems such as character recognition, recognition of random patterns and bibliographic retrieval.

2 Hamming Net Description

The feedforward Hamming net maximum likelihood classifier for binary inputs corrupted by noise is presented at Fig. 1. The Lower Sub Net calculates N minus the Hamming distance to M exemplar patterns, where N is the number of elements in one pattern. The upper sub net selects that node with the maximum output. All nodes use threshold logic nonlinearities, where it is assumed that the outputs of these nonlinearities never saturate. Thresholds and weights in the Maxnet are fixed. All thresholds are set to zero and weights from each node to itself are 1. Weights between nodes are inhibitory with a value of $-\varepsilon$, where $\varepsilon < 1/M$ [1]. The connection weights and offsets of the lower sub net are assigned as [2]:

$$w_{ji} = \frac{x_i^j}{2} \qquad \Theta_j = \frac{N}{2} \tag{1}$$

for $0 \le i \le N-1$ and $0 \le j \le M-1$, Θ_j - the threshold in that node, w_{ji} - the connection weight from input i to node j in the lower sub net.
The connection weights in the upper sub net (Maxnet) are fixed as:

$$w_{lk} = \begin{cases} 1 & if \quad k = 1 \\ -\varepsilon & if \quad k \neq 1 \end{cases} \tag{2}$$

for $0 \leq l, k \leq M$ and $\varepsilon < 1/M$, w_{lk}- the weight from node k to node l in the upper sub net and all thresholds in this max net are kept zero.

The outputs of the lower sub net are obtained with unknown input pattern as:

$$\mu_j = \sum_{i=0}^{N-1} w_{ji} x_i - \Theta_j \tag{3}$$

for $0 \leq i \leq N-1$ and $0 \leq j \leq M-1$.

The inputs of the Maxnet are initialized with threshold logic nonlinearities:

$$y_j(0) = f_t(\mu_j) \tag{4}$$

for $0 \leq j \leq M-1$. The Maxnet does the maximization:

$$y_j(t+1) = f_t\left(y_j(t) - \varepsilon \sum_{k \neq j} y_k(t)\right) \tag{5}$$

for $0 \leq j, k \leq M$. This process is repeated until convergence. [2]

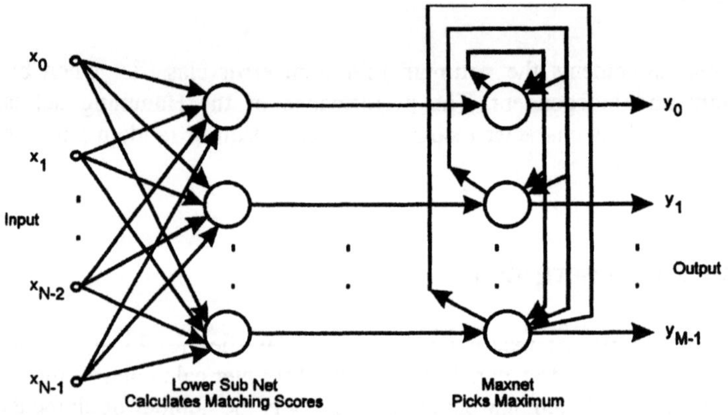

Fig. 1. Hamming neural network

3 Data Dependence Graph for Hamming Neural Network

A Data Dependence Graph is a directed graph that specifies the data dependencies of an algorithm. Nodes represent computations and arcs specify the data dependencies between computations (Fig. 2.). Each node in Data Dependence Graph responsible for Lower Sub Net multiplies the input signal x_i and corresponding weight w_{ji} which is stored in local memory unit. The product of multiplication is passed to the nearest neighbor on the right hand. The input signals x_i are passed to the nearest bottom neighbors. The μ_i nodes collect the partial products and calculate the global value of coproduct (3). The last *N-1* columns of nodes on the right are responsible for Maxnet. They transmit step by step the partial results among the neurons which belong to the Maxnet. and they calculate the output value (5) [5].

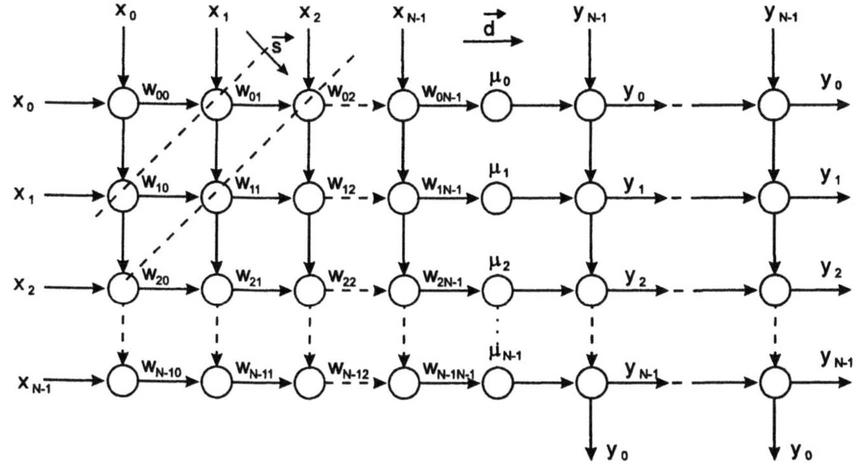

Fig. 2. Data Dependence Graph related to Hamming neural network

4 Data Dependence Graph Mapped into Systolic Array

4.1 Elementary Processors Assignment

Mathematically, a linear projection is often represented by a *projection vector* $\vec{d}$. Because the Data Dependence Graph of a locally recursive algorithm is very regular, the linear projection maps an n-dimensional Data Dependence Graph onto an *(n-1)* dimensional lattice of points, known as processor space. It is common to use a linear projection for processor assignment, in which nodes of Data Dependence Graph along a straight line are projected to an elementary processor in the processor array (Fig. 2.). [4]

4.2 Schedule Assignment

A schedule function represents a mapping from the n-dimensional index space of the Data Dependence Graph onto a 1-D schedule (time) space. Linear scheduling is very common for schedule assignment (Fig. 2.). A linear schedule is based on a set of parallel and uniformly spaced hyperplanes in the Data Dependence Graph. These hyperplanes are called *equitemporal hyperplanes* - all the nodes on the same hyperplane are scheduled to be proceed at the same time. A linear schedule can also be represented by a *schedule vector* $\vec{s}$, which points in the direction normal to the hyperplanes. It is necessary to avoid the violation of precedence relations specified by the dependence arcs. For systolic design, the schedule vector $\vec{s}$ in the projection procedure must satisfy the following two conditions: causality condition and positive pipeline period (6). [6]

$$\vec{s}^T\vec{e} > 0 \quad \text{and} \quad \vec{s}^T\vec{d} \neq 0 \tag{6}$$

$\vec{e}$ - represents any of the dependence arcs in the Data Dependence Graph

5 Proposal of Systolic Realization

The Hamming net algorithm is modified for convenience to implement in a parallel systolic architecture. For that the following changes are made: the inputs are considered binary - 0 and 1 - instead of 1 and -1, the weights are made 1 and 0 instead of +0,5 and –0,5 corresponding to a pattern. This will avoid the subtraction of the threshold $\Theta_j = 0,5 * N$ after the summation. The weights are obtained by the following algorithm.

$$w_{ji} = x_i^j \quad for \quad 0 \le i \le N-1 \quad and \quad 0 \le j \le M-1 \tag{7}$$

The activation function of the lower sub net is updated as follows:

$$y_j(k) = \begin{cases} y_j(k-1) - 1 & if \quad (x_i \oplus w_{ji}) = 1 \\ y_j(k-1) & if \quad (x_i \oplus w_{ji}) = 0 \end{cases} \tag{8}$$

$y_j = y_j(N)$ for $0 \le i \le N-1$ and $0 \le j \le M-1$ and $0 \le k \le N$.

It is possible to constitute the maximization network with a layer of up counters, whose outputs are changed with the following algorithm:

$$y_j(k) = \begin{cases} y_j(k-1) + 1 & if \quad AND\{O_i\} = 0 \\ y_j(k-1) & if \quad AND\{O_i\} = 1 \end{cases} \tag{9}$$

O_i - the output vector, obtained from the MSBs - sign bits - of these counters

5.1 Elementary Processor Realization

The Fig. 3 presents the parallel implementation of the algorithm for Hamming net using only digital circuits. The input vector corrupted by noise is applied to the input register when *ILP - Input Load Pulse* - is present. The down counter is cleared by this signal. The input data is applied sequentially to each processing element with the *Shift Control Pulse SP'*, which is derived from *SP* and *LCP - Load Counter Pulse*: *not(LCP) & SP*. At the same time the weight register is also shifted once by the same signal. The content of the down counter is updated according to the (8) with the presence of the pulse *CP'*, which is derived from *CP* and *ILP*: *not(ILP) & CP*.

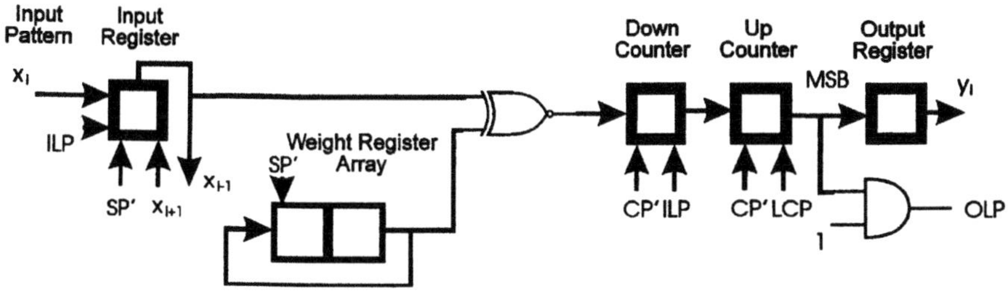

Fig. 3. Single slab implementation of Hamming network

The data obtained in each register after N steps will be negative. They are transferred to the up counters when *LCP* signal is present. *LCP* signal is applied only after N shift operations of the input register and weight registers are performed. The MSBs of the register contents will be the sign bits, which will be 1 for all the data at this stage. The MSBs give the output vector O_j for $0 \leq j \leq M - 1$. The up counters constitute the Maxnet, which will count up when *CP'* signal is present. The operation of the up counter is stopped by a control signal *OLP - Output Load Pulse* - derived from the output vector O_j. When any one of the sign bits of the registers becomes 0 (its content becomes positive) *OLP* stops the operation of the up counter and thereby the neuron with the largest activation function wins the competition. The output pattern is the inverted output of the vector O_j which is obtained when *OLP* signal is present.

6 Efficiency of Hamming Net Systolic Implementation

6.1 Computation Time

This is time interval between starting the first computation and finishing the last computation of problem [2]:

$$T = \max_{\vec{p},\vec{q} \in L} \left\{ \vec{s}^{T} (\vec{p} - \vec{q}) \right\} + 1 \tag{10}$$

where L is the index set of the nodes in the Data Dependence Graph. In the presented architecture the schedule vector is defined as: $\vec{s} = [1 , 1]$. In fact the Data Dependence Graph for this algorithm is combined by two independent structures of operations. We can notice this observation at (Fig. 1.). The first part of Data Dependence Graph is responsible for Lower Sub Net calculation. This part is spread on *N* elements in horizontal point of view. The second part guarantees the data communication within Maxnet. Here we have *N-1* elements in horizontal axis. The total computation time for retrieving algorithm taking into account the computation time for Lower Sub Net and the computation time for Maxnet can be calculated as (τ - processing time for elementary processor):

$$T_{systol} = (4N-3)\tau \qquad (11)$$

6.2 Processor Utilization Rate

Lets define the speed-up factor as the ratio between the sequential computation time and the array computation time, then the utilization rate is the ration between the speed-up factor and the number of processors [2]. If we assume that all elementary processors need the same time-period to proceed their calculations the speed-up and utilization rate factors can be estimated as:

$$speed-up = \frac{(2N-1)N}{4N-3} \qquad utilization\ rate = \frac{(2N-1)}{4N-3} \qquad (12)$$

7 Conclusions

The Hamming net algorithm is modified suitably for the systolic implementation. The systolic algorithm for the computation of the activation values of the lower sub net is developed. The upper sub net which acts as a maximization network is constructed by using simple counters. The main advantage of the proposed architecture is that it can be easily extended to larger networks. This work has been supported by Wroclaw University of Technology grant No. 342926.

References

1. Ferrari A., Ng Y. H. (1992). A Parallel Architecture for Neural Networks, Parallel Computing'91, Elsevier Science Publishers B. V., 283–290
2. Kung S. Y. (1993). Digital Neural Networks, PTR Prentice Hall
3. Mazurkiewicz J. (1998). A Processor Pipeline Architecture for Hopfield Neural Network, II SCANN'98 Conference on Artificial Neural Networks, Trnava, 158–163
4. Mazurkiewicz J. (2001). Efficiency of Systolic Simulator Based on Elementary Processors with Switched Functions for Hopfield Neural Network, VII MENDEL 2001 Conference on Soft Computing, Brno, 349-354
5. Mazurkiewicz J. (2001). SIMD-type Simulator for Recurrent Neural Nets, 35th MOSIS'01 Conference Modelling and Simulation of Systems, Ostrava, vol. 1, 173-180
6. Shiva S. G. (1996). Pipelined and Parallel Computer Architectures, HarperCollins
7. Zhang D. (1999). Parallel VLSI Neural System Design, Springer-Verlag

Neural Network Simulation of Energy Transfer Processes in a Membrane Protein System

Petr V. Nazarov[1], Vladimir V. Apanasovich[1], Vladimir M. Lutkovski[1], Marcus A. Hemminga[2], Rob B. M. Koehorst[2]

[1] Department of Systems Analysis, Faculty of Radiophysics, Belarusian State University, Skaryna Ave 4, Minsk 220050, Belarus. E-mail: lutkovski@bsu.by
[2] Laboratory of Biophysics, Wageningen University, Dreijenlaan 3, 6703 HA, Wageningen, The Netherlands. Website: http://ntmf.mf.wau.nl/hemminga/

Abstract. The method of the direct application of an artificial neural network for modelling of a complex system is developed with the purpose of speeding up the optimisation procedure for determination of system parameters. The method provides a significant decrease in simulation time. Moreover the artificial neural network produces a smooth approximation of stochastic simulation results and consequently it reduces the level of stochastic errors. The developed algorithm is applied to model the fluorescence resonance energy transfer within a system of M13 major coat protein mutants embedded in a membrane.

1. Introduction

Computer modelling has become a standard method for the parameter determination and study of complex systems and processes. Especially in systems that cannot be described by a set of analytical equations Monte Carlo simulation provides a general approach to such a problem. However, computer simulation has several weak points. One of them is the high time cost of its realisation, which makes it difficult to use an optimisation technique for the determination of model parameters. At the same time, it is known that it is possible to approximate any existing smooth function using an artificial neural network (ANN) with a sufficient number of layers and neurons [3, 5, 1].

In this paper we propose to apply an ANN to reproduce a simulation model. This makes it possible to use the ANN to fit the model parameters to an experimental data set, and to strongly speed up the fitting procedure. Here we demonstrate the application of this idea to the simulation model of energy transfer processes between fluorophores in a membrane protein system.

2. Theory

Let us consider the following problem. A system Θ has a set of input parameters P, and a set of output values F. Some input parameters are known (P_0) and others should be defined (P_X), so that P=[P_0, P_X]. In this case, the system described performs the following operation:

$$\Theta(P_0, P_X) = F\ . \tag{1}$$

Usually the determination of the unknown parameters P_X is carried out in the following way:

1. A set of F is obtained experimentally.
2. A model Ξ of system Θ is created. It performs the operation:

$$\Xi(P_0, P_X) = F^* \tag{2}$$

3. An initial estimation is made for P_X.
4. An optimisation algorithm, using a variation of parameters P_X, is executed to minimize the error $\|F^*-F\|$.

This very general algorithm is represented in Fig.1.

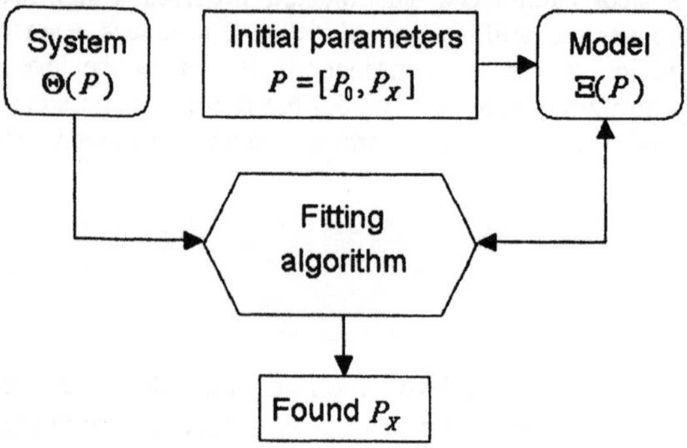

Fig.1. Methodology of parameter determination

The most crucial problem of this scheme is the time-consuming operation (2). In some cases this approach is not useful at all, because the time of optimisation becomes non-realistic. To significantly speed up the algorithm, we propose the application of an ANN that replaces model (2).

Continuous functions can be uniformly well approximated by linear combinations of sigmoidal functions, as was independently shown by Cybenko [3], and Hornik, Stinchcombe, and White [5]. The error in the approximation of functions by an ANN is bounded [1]. For our case this means that it is possible to replace the operation (2) by a neural network transform

$$\boldsymbol{\Psi}(P_0, P_X) = F^*\ . \tag{3}$$

The computation time needed for transform (3) is much less than for operation (2). The suggested neural network approach to modelling is illustrated in Fig. 2. In this scheme the generation of a representative training set is the most time-consuming procedure. To be sure the training set is representative we used the following algorithm.

Two subsets of training pairs are taken: a deterministic and a stochastic one.

Step 1. The generation of a "boundary" parameters set. For each parameter 3 values are taken: minimal, average and maximal. Then all possible combinations of these values are generated which provides the first training subset. For example, for a system with 4 input parameters this gives 3^4=81 training pairs in this subset.
Step 2. The generation of a primary training subset. In this step input parameters are randomly selected within a certain range. In our numerical experiments we take up to 5000 of training pairs.
Step 3. The determination of similar training pairs. Due to the random selection of parameters, some training vectors can be close to each other. Their use for training does not lead to an increase of precision, only to an increase of training time.

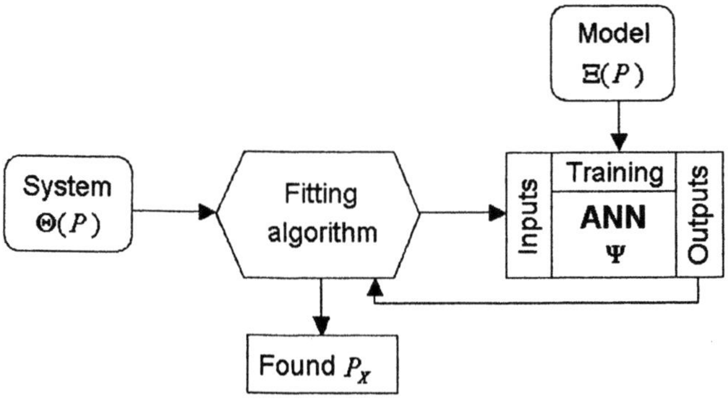

Fig.2. The direct application of an ANN to modelling

The method described is used for the simulation of dipole-dipole energy transfer processes between membrane proteins.

3. Model Description

The fluorescence resonance energy transfer (FRET) method has been applied to several problems in biology as a means of estimating intra- and intermolecular distances in macromolecular systems. Especially it has been used for the determination of the conformation and association of proteins embedded into a phospholipid bilayer. [6] The idea of FRET spectroscopy consists of labelling macromolecules with fluorescent probes of two types: donors with a relatively long lifetime of the excited state and acceptors with a short lifetime. The emission spectrum of the donor and the absorption spectrum of the acceptor should overlap. The donors are excited by a light source and some of them transfer excitation energy to the acceptors. From the resulting emission spectra, it is possible to define an efficiency of the energy transfer processes using Föster's theory [4]. The experimental system consists of mixed lipid vesicles of *dioleoyl phosphatidylcholine* (DOPC) and *dioleoyl phosphatidylglycerol* (DOPG) with inserted major coat proteins of the M13 bacteriophage [7]. In this system there are two types of proteins – wild, containing only one *tryptophane* amino acid (donor) and mutant proteins, containing both *tryptophane* and *AEDANS* (acceptor).

Because of its complexity in these reconstituted protein-lipid systems, the problem of determining the association and conformation of the M13 coat protein cannot be solved analytically. All analytical solutions that are known today have very serious simplifications and limitations. Therefore we used a simulation model. In this model a biological membrane is approximated by a two-dimensional periodic structure with a hexagonal packing of the lipids in which proteins are randomly distributed (Fig. 3 **a**). The area occupied by each protein on the membrane surface is assumed to be equal to that of a lipid. The distance between two nearest molecules on the grid is 5.6 Å and the thickness of the lipid bilayer is 30 Å. M13 coat protein mutants are approximated by hexagonally situated rods with a constant location of the donor (D) and variable location of the acceptor (A) (Fig. 3 **b**).

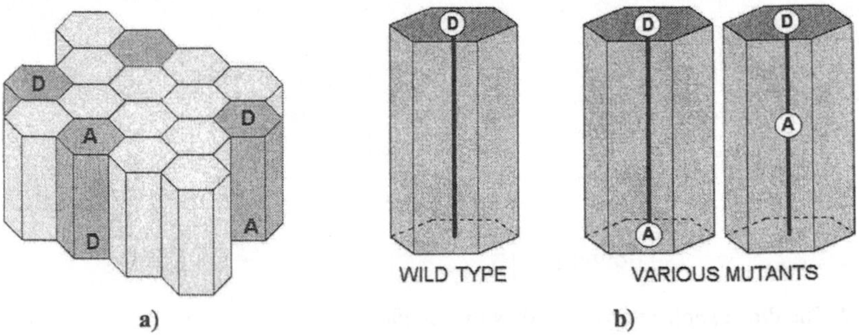

Fig 3. Model of a membrane (**a**) and membrane proteins (**b**) with fluorescent labels

The input parameters of the model are:
1) Concentrations of wild-type proteins and mutants.
2) Location of the acceptor in the protein.
3) Coefficient of protein-protein association (the probability that a selected protein is located in immediate proximity to another one).
4) Föster distance (the photophysical parameter, which describes the intensity of energy transfer [4]).

The intensity of fluorescence and energy transfer efficiency are taken as output values. Because of the simulation nature of the model, the resulting output contains stochastic errors. Therefore simulations are run several times to reduce these errors. This results in an increase of calculation time. In our numerical experiments one complete calculation takes up to 2 min.

4. Results

A three-layer perceptron is used to reproduce the described simulation model. Some statistic experiments are conducted to define the optimal number of neurons in hidden layers. This number depends on the number of variable input parameters. So, for 3 variable parameters the ANN should have 10-12 neurons in hidden layers, for 4 parameters 14 and for 5 parameters – 16. These values were experimentally obtained. In our case the application of a larger number of neurons does not lead to a decrease of the error for a test set.

The ANN is trained by the Back Propagation Error algorithm with the Levenberg-Marquardt optimisation technique [2]. To avoid overtraining after each 10 epochs, the ANN is tested on a set of control input-output pairs (200 elements). If the results of testing did not improve for a certain time, the training procedure is stopped. All calculations were made in MATLAB® 6.1 with the Neural Networks Toolbox on a PC with Intel Pentium III-850 CPU. The time costs of the ANN method application are shown in Table 1.

Table 1. The time costs of the ANN method

Task	3 variable parameters	4 variable parameters
Training subset 1 generation	30 min	90 min
Training subset 2 generation	12 hr	22 hr
Training	6 min	12 min
ANN simulation	$5{\cdot}10^{-4}$ s	$8{\cdot}10^{-4}$ s

The average time of the calculation conducted by the simulation model is 48 sec. To obtain the same result by the ANN calculation it takes about $6{\cdot}10^{-4}$ s, depending on the number of neurons in the hidden layers. This means that the calculation is speeded up by approximately a factor of 10^5.

After execution of the training procedure the mean relative square error on the training set varied from 0.8 to 1.2% depending on the task. The resulting errors on the test input-output set varied from 0.9 to 1.5%. To prove the quality of the method used, comparison were made using the simulation model and the ANN. One result is represented in Fig 4, which shows an excellent agreement.

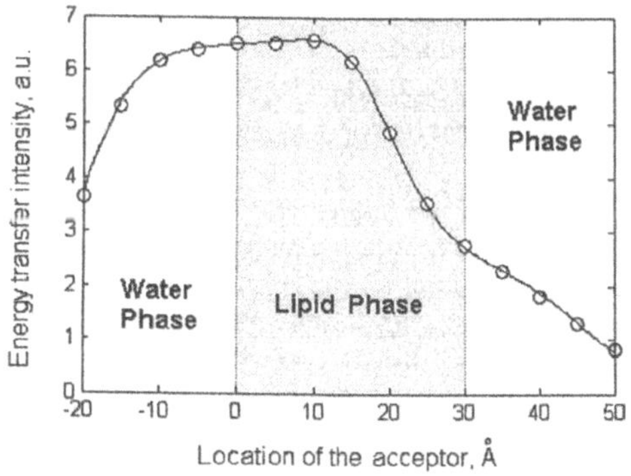

Fig. 4. The dependence of the energy transfer intensity on the location of the acceptor label (assuming no protein aggregation). The circles show the computer-simulated values, and the line shows the neural network approximation

Fig. 4 shows that an ANN is able to build a smooth interpolation of the dependences of fluorescence intensity from input parameters of the model. Due to high speed of the ANN calculation it is possible to obtain smooth dependences. These dependences are quite complex and so they hardly can be described by a single analytical function with physically meaningful parameters. Moreover an ANN approximation of a model allows calculating numerical values of derivatives and hence it allows using a gradient fitting technique.

5. Conclusions

The use of a trained ANN in the modelling presented here results in a gain in computing time by a factor of 10^5. This allows using optimisation technique to determine parameters of the system considered. Moreover the ANN produces a smooth approximation of the results of a stochastic simulation. Thus it decreases the level of stochastic errors. Due to this smooth dependency it is possible to use a standard optimisation technique, such as gradient search, for parameter determination.

The imperfections of described algorithm are the following. It works only when the number of variable parameters is quite small (in our experiments – up to 5). Furthermore ANN approximation of a system may contain some inaccuracies.

Nevertheless, the method of ANN modelling can be used as a very good tool for determination of initial estimations of parameters. It is not limited to biophysical problems, and can be applied to any situation where the scheme from Fig.1 can be used.

References

1. Barron AR (1993) Universal approximation bounds for superpositions of a sigmoidal function. IEEE Trans on Inform Theory, 39:3:930-945
2. Bishop M (1997) Neural Networks for Pattern Recognition. Clarendon Press, Oxford
3. Cybenko G (1989) Approximations by superpositions of a sigmoidal function. Math Contr Signals Syst, 2:304-314
4. Föster T (1948) Intermolecular energy migration and fluorescence. Ann Phys 2:55-75
5. Hornik K, Stinchcombe M, and White H (1989) Multilayer feedforward networks are universal approximators. Neural Networks, 2:359-366
6. Koppel D, et al. (1979) Intramembrane Position of Membrane-Bound Chromophores Determined by Excitation Energy Transfer. Biochemistry 18:5450-5457
7. Spruijt R, et al. (2000) Localization and rearrangement modulation of the N-terminal arm of the membrane-bound major coat protein of bacteriophage M13. Biochim Biophys Acta 1509:311-323

Neural Network Modifiers of Nonlinear Dynamical Systems

Andrzej Ossowski

Institute of Fundamental Technological Research
Polish Academy of Sciences,
Ul. Świętokrzyska 21, 00-049 Warsaw, Poland
aossow@ippt.gov.pl

Abstract: The general concept of modification of non-linear dynamical system with bounded controls has been formulated. The method of Lyapunov functions has been applied to solve the problem of modification of system stability properties. It has been shown that optimal modifying feedback controls can be realized by neural networks. In particular, ternary neural networks can be considered as optimal modifiers of affine control systems. General structures and fundamental properties of such networks have been described.

1. Introduction

Many real systems important for science and technology can be modeled by finite dimensional systems of (non)linear ordinary differential equations

$$\dot{\mathbf{x}} = \mathbf{F}(\mathbf{x}, \mathbf{u}), \qquad (1)$$

where $\mathbf{x} \in R^n$ is the state vector, $\mathbf{u} = [u_1, \dots, u_m] \in U \subset R^m$ is the vector of bounded controls and U is a compact region. If a real system is designed in such a way that the free system (i.e. system (1) with $\mathbf{u} \equiv \mathbf{0}$) meets certain requirements then any non-vanishing vector control $\mathbf{u}(t)$ applied to the system makes it possible to change its dynamics. Therefore one can pose the problem of optimal modification of dynamical properties of the system (1) in order to improve system performance according to certain criteria [1,2]. The optimal modifying control is usually assumed in the form of a state feedback $\mathbf{u} = \mathbf{u}(\mathbf{x})$. Then the dynamics of the modified system is described by the autonomous differential equations $\dot{\mathbf{x}} = \mathbf{F}(\mathbf{x}, \mathbf{u}(\mathbf{x}))$. A particular form of the optimal feedback is dependent on many factors and especially on the modification aim and the applied method of analysis of the problem.

In this work we consider the problem of optimal modification of stability properties of dynamical systems [1,2]. The method of optimal Lyapunov functions is applied to study the problem in the case of multidimensional analytical systems. We show that ternary neural networks can be considered as optimal modifiers of affine control systems.

This work is supported in part by KBN, grant nr 8T12C 046 21

2. Modification of stability properties

To study the problem of modification of stability properties we assume that $\mathbf{F(0,0)=0}$ and system (1) with $\mathbf{u} \equiv \mathbf{0}$ (i.e. the autonomous system $\dot{\mathbf{x}} = \mathbf{F}(\mathbf{x},0) = \mathbf{F}_0(\mathbf{x})$) is locally *asymptotically stable* in a neighbourhood X of the unique stationary point $\mathbf{x} = \mathbf{0}$. We also assume that there exists a region $X_0 \subset X$ such that any system trajectory $\mathbf{x}(t)$ starting from any $\mathbf{x}_0 \in X_0$ belongs to X_0.

It is logical to require that system modification realised by a feedback control $\mathbf{u} = \mathbf{u}(\mathbf{x})$ improves convergence of system trajectories starting from X_0. To realise such a modification a suitable quality (stability) index should be introduced. We can do that e.g. by applying the method of *Lyapunov functions* which seems to be the most adequate for the analysis of stability modification problems [1,2].

3. Lyapunov approach to stability modification

The Lyapunov approach presented in this work is based on the concept of a stability index which enables to formulate sufficient stability conditions for (non)linear dynamical systems. It is proved (e.g. in [1,2]) that stability properties of system (1) can be characterized by the index given by the following formula

$$\gamma(\mathbf{S}) = -\sup_{\mathbf{x}\in X_0} \inf_{\mathbf{u}\in U} \left[\frac{\mathbf{x}^T\mathbf{S}\mathbf{F}(\mathbf{x},\mathbf{u})}{\mathbf{x}^T\mathbf{S}\mathbf{x}} \right] \tag{2}$$

where $\mathbf{S}$ is a positive definite $n \times n$ matrix. Indeed, if the index is positive then the following estimate is valid for any $t \geq t_0$

$$\|\mathbf{x}(t)\|_{\mathbf{S}} \leq \|\mathbf{x}(t_0)\|_{\mathbf{S}} \exp[-\gamma(\mathbf{S})(t-t_0)] \tag{3}$$

and the quadratic form $V_{\mathbf{S}}(\mathbf{x}) = \mathbf{x}^T\mathbf{S}\mathbf{x} = \|\mathbf{x}(t)\|_{\mathbf{S}}^2$ is a Lyapunov function of the system. This means that $\gamma(\mathbf{S})$ is the index of exponential convergence of system trajectories in $X_0 = \{\mathbf{x}\colon \|\mathbf{x}(t)\|_{\mathbf{S}}^2 \leq c^2\}$ and the value

$$\delta(\mathbf{S},\mathbf{x},\mathbf{u}) = -\left[\frac{\mathbf{x}^T\mathbf{S}\mathbf{F}(\mathbf{x},\mathbf{u})}{\mathbf{x}^T\mathbf{S}\mathbf{x}} \right] \tag{4}$$

can be interpreted as the local exponential rate of convergence near $\mathbf{x}$.

If the set of admissible controls U is compact and $\mathbf{F}$ is a continuous function, then there always exists an optimal feedback control $\mathbf{u}(\mathbf{x}, \mathbf{S})$ maximising local exponential rate of convergence $\delta(\mathbf{S},\mathbf{x},\mathbf{u})$. Hence, the stability index of the optimal closed-loop system of modification is given by the following formula

$$\gamma(\mathbf{S}) = -\sup_{\mathbf{x}\in X_0} \left[\frac{\mathbf{x}^T\mathbf{S}\mathbf{F}(\mathbf{x},\mathbf{u}(\mathbf{x},\mathbf{S}))}{\mathbf{x}^T\mathbf{S}\mathbf{x}} \right]. \tag{5}$$

Let us denote by γ_0 (**S**) index (5) for $\mathbf{u} \equiv \mathbf{0}$. It is clear that γ_0 (**S**) determines stability properties of the autonomous system $\dot{\mathbf{x}} = \mathbf{F}_0(\mathbf{x})$ in the region X_0. Since the autonomous system is stable by assumption, the stability condition $\gamma_0(\mathbf{S})>0$ should be satisfied. We assume that γ_0 (**S**) can be calculated or empirically estimated for a class S of positive definite matrices **S** for which the autonomous system is exponentially stable in X_0. This task is feasible particularly in the case of linear or quasi-linear dynamical systems. Suitable class S of matrices for such systems can be easily generated by using the Lyapunov matrix equation [1].

4. Discrete neural realisation of optimal modifiers

In many practical cases the modification problem can be solved analytically. If the model of a real system is given then the optimal form of feedback control **u**(**x**, **S**) can be determined from the infinium (2) for a wide class of functions **F**(**x**,**u**). However, in the general case, when the set of admissible controls U is a compact region in R^m, it may be difficult to realize practically exactly optimal modification by using a computer system because the optimal modifier has to solve in real time the optimality problem over $\mathbf{u} \in U$ for any actual state $\mathbf{x}(t)$. Furthermore, if the model of the system is not known exactly the above optimization cannot be performed directly at all. For these reasons it is logical to look for quasi-optimal but feasible in real time solutions to the problem.

In order to generate efficient controls in real time it is possible to apply an appropriate *neural network* (with $m + n$ inputs, one or two *hidden layers* and one output) that enables to predict efficiency of any control $\mathbf{u} \in U$ for any actual state $\mathbf{x}(t)$ of the system. Optimal weights of *sigmoid* neurons and the network structure are determined by using standard method of *supervised learning* by examples of the form (**x**, **u**, δ(**S**,**x**,**u**)),where (**x**, **u**) , δ are input and output data, respectively. We denote such a network by N(**S**,**F**).

Values of the local exponential rate of convergence δ(**S**,**x**,**u**) can be get from numerical simulations of system (1) or measurements performed on the real system. Indeed, it is easily to deduce from (3) that the local exponential rate of convergence near the point **x** of the system with control **u** can be estimated from the following formula

$$\delta(\mathbf{S},\mathbf{x},\mathbf{u}) \approx \frac{1}{T}\ln\left[\frac{\|\mathbf{x}(t)\|_{\mathbf{S}}}{\|\mathbf{x}(t+T)\|_{\mathbf{S}}}\right], \tag{6}$$

where $\mathbf{x} = \mathbf{x}(t)$ and $\mathbf{x}(t+T)$ are the subsequent states measured/calculated with the sampling period T. The period T should be relatively short in comparison to natural time constants of the system.

There is no problem to generate any number of learning examples. To do that, random constant controls $\mathbf{u}_j \in U$ can be applied to the system starting from certain initial states $\mathbf{x}_j \in X_0$ in subsequent sampling periods. Since input data $(\mathbf{x}_j, \mathbf{u}_j)$, $j \in J$ should be representative, it is important to ensure uniformity of the distributions of points $\mathbf{x}_j \in X_0$ and $\mathbf{u}_j \in U$. Then *back propagation* techniques and *cumulative delta modification* can be applied to find optimal neurons weights. Validation of the learned network $N(\mathbf{S},\mathbf{F})$ can be performed by using additional examples generated. First of all, the basic condition $\delta(\mathbf{S},\mathbf{x},\mathbf{0}) \geq \gamma_0(\mathbf{S})$ should be checked for different $\mathbf{x}_j \in X_0$. If necessary, further learning can be performed with the same or decreased sampling period.

One way of designing efficient sub-optimal modifiers is to apply discrete controls [3]. Since the region of admissible controls U is compact, any control vector $\mathbf{u} \in U$ can be approximated with the assumed accuracy $\varepsilon > 0$ by a vector from a suitable finite set $\{\mathbf{u}_1,...,\mathbf{u}_k\}$. In each sampling instant the discrete modifier has to decide merely which constant control of $\mathbf{u}_1,...,\mathbf{u}_k$ should be applied to the system within the subsequent sampling period in order to achieve maximal local exponential rate of convergence. The neural network $N(\mathbf{S},\mathbf{F})$ enables to make the correct decision in real time. The discrete controls $\mathbf{u}_1,...,\mathbf{u}_k$ can be chosen from learning examples in such a way that the global stability index (5) of system (1) in the domain X_0 approaches its maximum i.e. $\forall(\mathbf{x} \in X_0)\ \exists\ (i \in \{1,...,k\})$ such that $\delta_i = \delta(\mathbf{S},\mathbf{x},\mathbf{u}_i) \geq \delta(\mathbf{S},\mathbf{x},\mathbf{u}_j)$ for $j \in J$ in a fixed neighborhood of $\mathbf{x}$.

5. Optimal modification of analytical systems

Of particular interest are dynamical systems (1) with a function $\mathbf{F}(\mathbf{x}, \mathbf{u})$ analytical with respect to control components $u_1,...,u_m$. In such a case the system dynamics can be approximately described by the equations of the following form

$$\dot{\mathbf{x}} = \mathbf{f}_0(\mathbf{x}) + u_1\mathbf{f}_1(\mathbf{x}) + \cdots + u_m\mathbf{f}_m(\mathbf{x}) + \Sigma_{i=1}^{k}\Sigma_{j=1}^{k} u_i u_j \mathbf{f}_{ij}(\mathbf{x}) + \cdots \tag{7}$$

where $|u_i| \leq \alpha$, $i=1,...,m$; $|u_1|+...+|u_m| \leq \beta \leq m\ \alpha$. The control bounds are usually assumed in order to limit each control component as well as the total control "power" [4, 5]. If only terms linear with respect to controls u_i are taken into account in (7) we have the so-called *affine* control system. In particular,, if $\mathbf{f}_0$ is a linear state function (i.e. equal to $\mathbf{A}_0\mathbf{x}$, where $\mathbf{A}_0$ is a stable real $n \times n$ matrix) and the functions $\mathbf{f}_1,...,\mathbf{f}_m$ are constant the model is said to be *linear*.

If the model (7) is known then one can try to find exact optimal controls directly from (2). This is not always feasible and/or sensible in practice. Sometimes it may be better to apply certain suboptimal but relatively simple controls. In particular, if one consider only the affine part of system (7) with the assumed control bounds then one can easily deduce from (2) that some optimal controls are the bang-bang controls of the following form

$$u_i = -\ \alpha\ \mathrm{sign}\ [\ \mathbf{x}^T\mathbf{S}\ \mathbf{f}_i(\mathbf{x})\ ]. \tag{8}$$

while the remaining controls should be equal to zero [1,2,4,5]. It can be expected that such a control will be efficient also for analytical system (7) with higher order terms. Thus ternary (discrete) modifying controls are naturally distinguished in the class of analytical systems (7). There are at most 3^m different ternary control vectors for systems (1) satisfying the assumed bounds. Since the switching surfaces $\{\mathbf{x} : \mathbf{x}^T\mathbf{S}\ \mathbf{f}_i(\mathbf{x})=0\}$, $i=1,...,k$ divide the space X_0 into disjoint regions that correspond to different optimal ternary controls, the modification problem of analytical systems can be treated as pattern classification and neural networks can be successfully applied.

There is no problem with generation of learning examples ($\mathbf{x},\mathbf{u},\delta$). Indeed, according to our assumptions, the free system $\dot{\mathbf{x}} = \mathbf{f}_0(\mathbf{x})$ is stable, locally in a neighborhood of the origin $\mathbf{x} = \mathbf{0}$ and $\mathbf{f}_0(\mathbf{0}) = \mathbf{0}$. Hence, the system (7) remains stable for any controls of sufficiently small amplitude $\alpha > 0$ (see [3]). Therefore we can perform empirical investigations of real analytical systems without the risk of stability loss.

6. Application of ternary neural networks

There is an attractive possibility to realise completely hardware neural feedback systems for stability modification of analytical systems. Indeed, given system (7) let us consider the layer consisting of k identical networks $N_i(\mathbf{S},\mathbf{F}) = N(\mathbf{S},\mathbf{F})$, $i=1,\ldots,k$ with the input signals ($\mathbf{x}$, $\mathbf{u}_i$) and outputs δ_i, respectively. To realise a hardware system of modification it suffices to design a neural network that generates on the output the proper control $\mathbf{u}_i \in \{\mathbf{u}_1,\ldots,\mathbf{u}_k\}$ maximising the local index $\delta(\mathbf{S},\mathbf{x},\mathbf{u})$.

In our further consideration it is convenient to assume, without any loss of generality, that the control amplitude $\alpha = 1$. We apply standard neural sigmoid cells with the output $y = \mathrm{sign}[w_1 x_1 + w_l\, x - p]$, where $w_1,\ldots,w_l$ and p are the input weights and output, respectively. It can be easily proved that the decision process and control generation can be realised by the ternary neural network shown in fig.1.

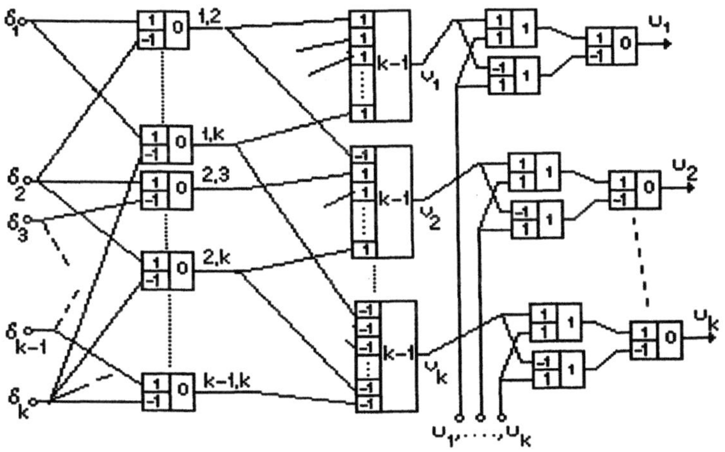

Fig1. The ternary neural system of stability modification

The first layer of the neurons compares the predictions of the local stability inices $\delta(\mathbf{S}, \mathbf{x}, \mathbf{u}_i)$ proposed by k input networks $N(\mathbf{S},\mathbf{F})$ for the actual state $\mathbf{x}$

and selected discrete controls $\mathbf{u}_1,...,\mathbf{u}_k$. The second layer decides which of the controls $\mathbf{u}_1,...,\mathbf{u}_k$ should be put at the system input. The signals v_i $i=1,...,k$ are equal to 1 (or -1) if the corresponding controls u_i are to be bang-bang (or switched off). Finally, the output controls of the network are generated by the output layer of independent comparators (each composed of the three cells) as is shown in fig.1.

It is interesting to notice that the neural network under consideration are usually dependent on the system dynamics as well as the choice of a Lyapunov function i.e $N=N(\mathbf{S},\mathbf{F})$. Therefore, additional optimization of the network over $\mathbf{S} \in S$ (i.e. Lyapunov function optimization [1,2,4,5]) can be performed in order to achieve further improvement of stability properties of the system.

7. Conclusions

The general conception of stability modification in dynamical control systems has been described in this paper. The possibility of application of neural network software as well as hardware neural realisation of optimal systems of modification have been studied.

References

[1] Ossowski A.(1998), Active Parametric Modification of Linear Vibrating Systems, Smart Structures, 3. High Technology Vol. 65. NATO Science Series,.

[2] Ossowski A.(2001), Intelligent control of stable smart structures, AI-MECH2001, Methods of Artificial Intelligence in Mechanics and Mechanical Engineering, pp. 183-190, November 13-15, Gliwice 2001.

[3] Ossowski A., Święcicka A.(2001), Multiple-valued Logic Feedback Controllers of Dynamical Systems, pp. 66-75, Communications of the 10th International Symposium, Intelligent Information Systems X, June 17-21, Zakopane 2001.

[4] Ossowski A.(2000), Stability and Control of Smart Structures, p. 249-260, Polish-Ukrainian Transactions, Theoretical Foundations of Civil Engineering, Warsaw, June 2000.

[5] Ossowski A.(2000), Neural Network Controller Stabilisation of Multidimensional Linear Systems, p. 149-152, International Conference-Mechatronics 2000, Warsaw, September 2000.

Probabilistic-Fuzzy Method of Ship Manoeuvre Safety Assessment in a Restricted Area

Zbigniew Pietrzykowski

Maritime University of Szczecin,
Wały Chrobrego 1/2, 70-500 Szczecin, Poland

Abstract. A probabilistic-fuzzy method for determining a navigational safety indicator relating to a ship manoeuvring in a fairway is presented. The notion of fuzzy event probability has been used. Navigational accident threat has been defined as a fuzzy event. On the basis of the probabilistic risk analysis and elements of fuzzy logic the traditional approach takes into account both safety failure and uncertainty associated with the threat estimation. The probability is determined by two different approaches. The calculation results are presented.

1. Introduction

The analysis of navigational safety in open and restricted areas plays an important role in the prevention of accidents at sea. In the case of restricted areas, such as fairways, harbour entrances and basins, turning basins, the analysis may concern the existing, newly designed or modernized (extended) fairway elements.

In order to assess navigational risk in restricted areas the most frequently used are methods of quantitative analysis based on probabilistic methods. One approach in such cases utilises data from simulated passages conducted by navigators. On the basis of estimated density distribution function of the random variable 'distance from danger' the probability of a ship's deviation outside the boundaries of the fairway can be determined. This event is considered as a navigational accident.

This classical approach does not take into account situations when, for instance, the ship approaches one fairway limit too close. Such situations may result in an accident. Among others, this refers to areas that are difficult to navigate in, where dangerous situations happen although few accidents have occurred.

2. Probabilistic-fuzzy method of determining navigational safety indicator

The fuzzy event probability refers to a situation where there exist uncertainties of both fuzzy and probabilistic type [1, 5, 6]. Such a case occurs when we attempt at determining the probability of a navigational threat situation in restricted area traffic, namely in a fairway. The value of this probability makes up an significant indicator of navigational safety.

A navigational threat NT is understood as a situation where an undesired event such as an accident may occur together with associated losses. The degree of threat may be interpreted as navigational situation assessment in the assumed evaluation scale. This degree describes a current state of a ship-environment system on the basis of knowledge, experience and skills of navigators. It also reflects navigators' opinion concerning a possibility of a navigational collision. The distance between the ship and danger (fairway limit) is a basic parameter taken into account in navigational situation assessment. Consequently, navigational threat can be interpreted as a fuzzy event, described by the membership function which represents degrees of membership of the distance from danger to the corresponding fuzzy set. The determination of the probability that navigational threat will appear comes down to the determination of fuzzy event probability.

This approach is an extension of the method presented in [2, 7] used for assessing a dangerous ship manoeuvre situation in a restricted area. A dangerous situation means a system state which due to no action or inadequate action taken may change into a state of safety failure. The term "dangerous situation" is assumed to be described by the membership function of the fuzzy set 'dangerous situation', which roughly corresponds to the fuzzy set "dangerous distance".

Comparing the notions presented above and taking into account the fact that navigational threat exists not only in the case of dangerous navigational situations, one can state that the term 'navigational threat seems to represent a broader notion. Hence the probability of the fuzzy event "navigational threat" more widely defines the level of navigational safety of a ship manoeuvring in a restricted area.

3. Description of the method of determining navigational threat probability

The determination of navigational safety indicator consists in computing the probability of fuzzy event 'navigational threat'. In stage one, simulated or field studies are performed, consisting of a series of trials in which navigators handle a ship through a fairway. In the trials, the fairway is divided into sections defined by lines perpendicular to the fairway centre line [3].

In stage two, the trials of reliable size, guaranteeing a preset level of confidence, are followed by the estimation of random variables density functions, the variables being the distances of ship's points to the starboard side and port side from the fairway centre line. The estimation is performed separately for particular sections. When the phenomenon model (type of distribution) is determined, its parameters are estimated.

The two stages are identical to those in the probabilistic method, in which the probability of collision, understood as ship's deviation outside an allocated manoeuvring area, is calculated. For instance, the probability of grounding for the starboard side from the fairway centre line in its i-th section is described by the equation:

$$P_{ais} = \int_{x=d\max}^{+\infty} g_{is}(x)d(x) \tag{1}$$

where:

$g_{is}(x)$ density function of random variable x of the maximum distance of ship's extreme points to the starboard side from the fairway centre line in the i-th section,

d_{max} distance from the fairway centre to the fairway border (half of the fairway width).

The third stage consists in the determination of the probability of fuzzy event 'navigational threat'. Two basic approaches to the determination of fuzzy event probability are applied: Zadeh's approach and Yager's approach [5, 6]. In the former the probability of a fuzzy event occurrence is a real number in the [0, 1] interval. The latter uses a fuzzy set.

Assuming that we know the density distributions of random variable x for, respectively, extreme starboard ($g_{is}(x)$) and port ($g_{ip}(x)$) positions of ship water plane points as well as their corresponding functions of membership to sets 'navigational threat' $\mu_{NTis}(x)$ and $\mu_{NTip}(x)$, in Zadeh's approach the probability that a navigational threat will occur can be expressed by the equations:

$$p(NT_{is}) = \int_{x=-\infty}^{\infty} \mu_{NTis}(x) g_{is}(x)d(x) \tag{2a}$$

$$p(NT_{ip}) = \int_{x=-\infty}^{\infty} \mu_{NTip}(x) g_{ip}(x)d(x) \tag{2b}$$

The determination of the probability, following Yager's approach, requires that the fuzzy set has to be described as the sum of its α-cuts. This requires that α values are determined for discrete values of x – distance from danger. To determine the α values, it is necessary to apply the discretisation step Δx. The values of membership function $\mu_{NT}(x)$ can be set as those for α-cuts ($\alpha_i=\mu_{NT}(x_i)$).

Accounting for the fact that the membership functions are monotonic, the probability of events $NT_{\alpha i}$ for given α_i-cuts ($\alpha_i=\mu_{NT}(x_i)$) in i-th section on both port and starboard sides can be calculated using these equations:

$$P_{NTis\alpha_i} = \int_{x=x_i}^{\infty} g_{is}(x)d(x) \tag{3a}$$

$$P_{NTip\alpha_i} = \int_{x=-\infty}^{x_i} g_{ip}(x)d(x) \tag{3b}$$

Then the probability of a fuzzy event 'navigational threat for the i-th section and for the two fairway sides is described by these equations:

$$p(NT_{is}) = \sum_{\alpha\in[0,1]} \alpha / P_{NTis\alpha_i} \tag{4a}$$

$$p(NT_{ip}) = \sum_{\alpha\in[0,1]} \alpha / P_{NTip\alpha_i} \tag{4b}$$

With a small discretisation step Δx the membership function describing a fuzzy set of the probability of fuzzy event 'navigational threat' can be reproduced on the basis of the determined α-cuts.

4. Research

The research featured the following: a fairway bend, 150m wide at the bottom, 600 m radius (Fig. 1), divided into 25-metre sections. The ship was a loaded tanker with 40000 DWT capacity, length overall L=196m, beam B=28m and draft T=11m. In the experimental studies a ship-handling simulator working in real time was used. The navigators - ship's captains and pilots were told to carry out a series of simulated passages, handling the ship through a part of the fairway.

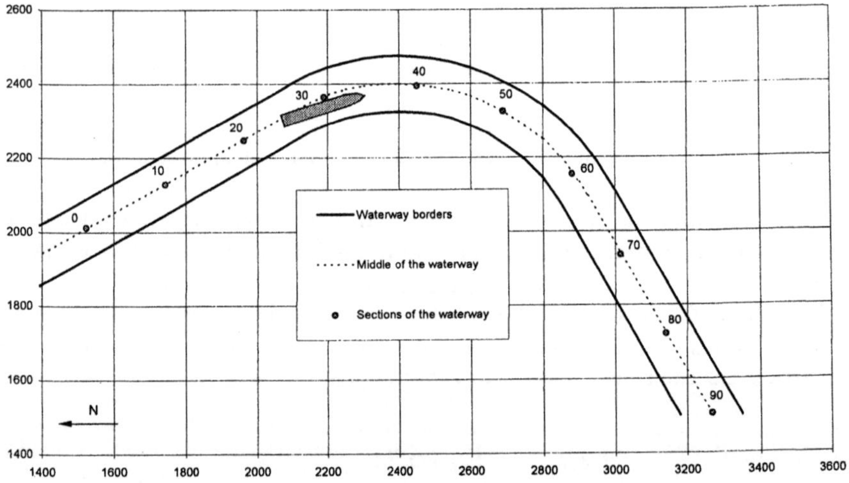

Fig. 1. The area of the bend divided into sections

Two random variables were defined in each section: maximum distance of ship's points to the starboard and port side from the fairway centre line. After a series of simulated trials, parameters of the density functions of the mentioned random variables were estimated. It was assumed that the normal distribution well describes the distribution of ship's points to the starboard and port side of the fairway centre line, which had been confirmed by relevant statistical tests [3].

The expert studies aimed at determining the membership function to a set 'threat situation' for the starboard and port sides of the fairway in each of the sections, $\mu_{NTis}(x)$ and $\mu_{NTip}(x)$, respectively. The basic criterion chosen for assessing a navigational threat was the distance of the extreme port and starboard points of the water plane from the fairway centre line. Data from the questionnaires using the method of psychological scaling [5] was used to specify degrees of membership to the sets 'navigational threat'.

A modified form of the function of membership to the set 'dangerous situation' for both fairway sides, as it is known in the literature [4], was used. Then the function parameters x_0 and x_1 were estimated. For example, for i-th section of the starboard side it has this form:

$$\begin{cases} \mu_{NTis}(x) = 1 - \exp(-((x - x_o)/x_1)^2) & \textit{for} \quad x > x_0 \\ \mu_{NTis}(x) = 0 & \textit{otherwise} \end{cases} \tag{5}$$

5. Results

In order to determine the navigational safety indicator – probability of fuzzy event 'navigational threat' in the analysed fairway – the previously estimated distributions of random variable x (distance from danger) and the membership functions of the fuzzy set 'navigational threat' were used. To compare the results, the defuzzification method of the centre of gravity was applied in case of Yager's approach. The results for the chosen fairway sections are shown in Tables 1 and 2. Besides, they are presented against the values of probability of collision determined by the probabilistic method.

Table 1. Assessment of ship manoeuvring safety in a restricted area, fairway port side

Section number	probability of collision P_a	probability of navigational threat p(NT) Zadeh's approach	Yager's approach
30	3.7139e-014	1.3693e-001	2.5931e-001
55	4.3536e-003	1.8794e-001	1.5436e-001
75	2.5991e-002	3.1693e-001	2.3268e-001

Intuitively one can state that the probability of a navigational threat *p(NT)* is higher than the probability of a collision P_a. This results from the fact that situations of threatened safety were taken into account, which led to collision avoidance. The difference between the values of fuzzy probability in the two approaches might be due to discretization.

Table 2. Assessment of ship manoeuvring safety in a restricted area, fairway starboard side

Section number	probability of collision P_a	probability of navigational threat p(NT) Zadeh' approach	Yager's approach
30	2.3560e-010	2.7298e-001	3.5751e-001
55	1.8835e-002	3.3693e-001	2.3728e-001
75	4.0033e-003	1.4355e-001	1.3137e-001

6. Conclusions

The presented method, using the concept of fuzzy event probability, allows to determine the probability of a navigational threat. Thus a complex assessment of navigational safety level is possible for a ship manoeuvring in a restricted area.

The method combines the probability of collision (probabilistic method) with the probabilities of situations considered as more or less dangerous, although creating navigational threat. Besides, the method enables the comparison of safety levels in analysed parts of a restricted area.

The method has a practical significance as it allows for the quantitative determination of the probability of navigational threat situation. It takes into account navigator's intuitive judgement of navigational threat resulting from his or her knowledge, experience and skills. Finally, it significantly supplements the range of a navigational safety indicators used so far.

References

[1] Driankov, D., Hellendorn, H., Reinfrank, M. (1993) An Introduction to Fuzzy Control. Springer, Berlin

[2] Gucma, L., Pietrzykowski, Z. (2001) Probabilistic-fuzzy method of ship manoeuvre risk assessment. Safety and Reliability International Conference KONBIN, Szczyrk, Vol. 3: 107-116

[3] Iribarren, J.R. (1999) Determining the horizontal Dimensions of Ship Manoeuvring Areas. PIANC Bulletin No 100, Bruxelles, pp 5-25

[4] James, C. (1986) Modelling the Decision Process in Computer Simulation of Ship Navigation. The Journal of Navigation Vol. 39: 32-48

[5] Kacprzyk J. (1986) Fuzzy sets in systems analysis. PWN, Warszawa (In Polish)

[6] Rommelfanger, H. (1994) Fuzzy Decision Support Systems, Springer, Berlin (In German)

[7] Pietrzykowski, Z., Gucma, L. (2001) Theoretical foundations of the probabilistic-fuzzy method for assessment of dangerous situation of a ship manoeuvring in a restricted area. Annual of Navigation No 3/2001, Gdynia, pp 111-125

Irregular Shape Particle Size Analysis Using Neural Network Approach

Edward RÓJ

Fertilizers Research Institute, 24-110 Puławy, ul. Aleja 1000-Lecia PP13a

e-mail: eroj@atena.ins.pulawy.pl

Abstract:

Granular materials of irregular shape occur in great variety in nature and in different branches of industry. Chemical engineering processes as catalysis, adsorption, heat exchange and many others using the granular materials are of great practical value. Also many commercial products are of granular type and that is why the characteristics of the granular material is so important. In the paper an optical method, combined with neural network approach, developed for irregular shape particle size analyzing has been presented. The method relies on determination of a relative volume and relative surface of sample particles using grid and random secant methods, respectively. Some experimental data obtained for ammonia synthesis catalyst has also been compared with sieve analysis method results.

1 Introduction

Particles of irregular shapes are very commonly used in various branches of chemical engineering processes. Any bed formed with the particles can be characterized by particle size distribution and by particle mean diameter. The two parameters are used, for example, in pressure drop calculations, heat and mass transfer coefficient determination and many other applications. There are different advanced commercial methods developed for characterization of the particle size ranged 0.04-2000 μm. As it can be seen most of them are developed for small diameter particles. In many industrial applications there are used particles of higher dimensions than the range given above, i.e. 1-50 mm or even more, and for them most popular is sieve analysis method. Usually there are two parameters used for particle characterization: particle size distribution and particle mean diameter. The particle size distribution is necessary to calculate the particle mean diameter of a bed consisting of a mixture of particles of different shapes or size. In the paper an optical method combined with neural network approach is applied to solve the problem of particle characterization particularly for a particle diameter ranged above 1 mm. The suggested method can use taken or scanned pictures of the analyzed particles and the pictures may be then processed using any image analysis techniques [3, 6, 7, 8]. Some experiments carried out with samples of catalyst for ammonia synthesis have proved that results obtained using the suggested method is comparable with sieve analysis method [4]. However, in general, the proposed method is cheaper, and can be applied even for higher particle dimensions than it was mentioned above.

2 Determination of relative volume and relative surface of irregular shape particles

To determine a relative volume and relative surface of any irregular shape particle, optical methods developed for metallurgy industry have been adopted. The adopted optical methods are designed for particle characterization. The methods are based on analysis of two dimensional pictures of the analyzed particles, and using Cavalieri-Haquert principle and Saltykov-Smith method [5, 4], a relative volume and relative surface of any particle can be determined. To estimate a relative particle volume the grid method has been applied. The method requires to count all grid knots placed inside the particle's contour, Fig.1. The following relationship can be used to find an estimator of the relative volume:

$$V_V = \frac{\sum_i V_i}{V_c} = \frac{N}{N_s} \tag{1}$$

For determination of the relative surface a random secant method has been used developed by Saltykov and Smith-Gutman [5]. The method relies on measurement a number of particle contour intersections with reference to the total length of the grating plate lines. The relationship allowing to find the estimate of the relative surface can be presented as follows:

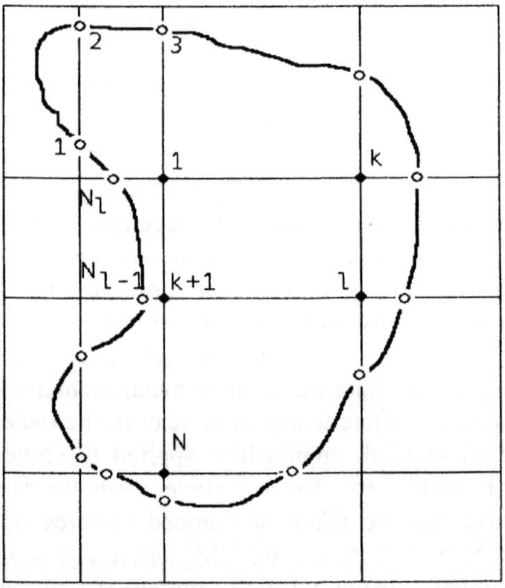

Fig. 1. Principle of grid knot and secant method for particle size analysis

$$S_v=2\ N_l/L \tag{2}$$

Practically, to find estimates of the relative volume and relative surface of any particle, the only thing which is to be done, there is a calculation of all grid knots and a particle contour intersections with an reference grid for all particles placed in a field of view. Furthermore, the methods mentioned above lead to calculation every particle's length of perimeter and its surface. Final result is an average value for the two parameters obtained for all analyzed particles. Having obtained a relative volume value and relative surface value the specific surface value can be calculated as a quotient of relative surface and a relative volume of the tested particles according to the relationship [2]:

$$S_0 = \frac{S_v}{V_v} \tag{3}$$

and the surface mean diameter

$$d_p = \frac{6}{S_0} \tag{4}$$

If the fraction by weight or volume is x_i, then

$$S_0 = \sum_i x_i S_{0i} = 6\sum_i \frac{x_i}{d_{pi}} \tag{5}$$

or

$$d_p = \frac{1}{\sum_i \frac{x_i}{d_{pi}}} \tag{6}$$

On the other hand, combining equations (1), (2) and (3) the surface mean diameter for i-th fraction can be calculated as:

$$d_{pi} = 3\frac{L}{N_s}\frac{N}{N_l} \tag{7}$$

Using the equation (6) a surface mean diameter can be calculated for any bed of particle of non-uniform size and irregular shapes. The same method allows to calculate a particle size distribution [1, 2].

However, to solve the task and apply the above equations, it is necessary to extract properly the contour of each particle, particular in case, if the particles are in touch with each other or light reflexes make distortion of the particle texture. In that case an appropriate technique should be use to segment the edges of any particle. There are many techniques used in image processing technology which might be useful to solve the problem [6, 7, 8]. A neural network approach has been used to find the solution for purpose of the paper.

3 Segmentation of the particle image using neural networks approach

Image segmentation problem is very important particularly in case of the images are affected by noise or separation the particular particle edges is hard or sometimes even impossible. In that case an advanced techniques for segmentation textured images should be used [3, 6, 7, 8]. If the segmentation problem is solved then it is possible to proceed to final calculations of a particle size analysis.

There are different methods which can be applied to solve the problem. Many of them there are neural minimal distance based methods which in some circumstances are highly accurate. Another approach, textured image segmentation, Bayesian approaches capitalizing on computational efficiency of multiresolution representations have received much attention. Many of the researches have been based on multiresolution stochastic models which use the Gaussian pyramid image decomposition. Also, there are reports of attractable snakes based on the greedy algorithm for contour extraction [6]. The algorithms were computer implemented and successfully applied for data segmentation analysis. Some interesting results have been obtained for modeling of highly intertwining data set at subclass level using minimum cross-entropy approximation [8]. The technique derives on approximation of the probability density function of the data sets in the subspace partitions by considering both the interclass and interclass properties of the data points.

In the considered case the simplest approach has been applied using one of the neural minimal distance methods which is the natural way of neural network computation. There is a standard neural network of MLP type. The output function of a neuron govern the equation:

$$f(R \cdot X) = f\left(0{,}5\left(\|R\|^2 + \|X\|^2 - \|R - X\|^2\right)\right) = f\left(I_m - D(R, X)\right) \tag{8}$$

where f – is a transfer function, R – is a reference vector, D – is distance.

For normalized input vectors any monotonically growing functions evaluate the influence of reference vectors **R** on classification probability p_i. If the classes are assigned as $C_i=1,\dots,N_c$, then the probabilities generated by the layer output can be formulated as [3]:

$$P(C_i|X;M) = \sum_j W_{ij} h_j(X) \tag{9}$$

$$p_i = p(C_i|X;M) = \frac{P(C_i|X;M)}{\sum_j P(C_j|X;M)} \tag{10}$$

where W_{ij} – the weights between output node; they are equal to $W_{ij}=S(C_i,C_j)/C_j$, and S is a matrix estimating similarity between the output classes, and M is a model. So that the neural network generates probabilities which can be used to extract existing classes among input data. In the considered case two classes have been considered using image pixel features. As an input vector the following features have been defined: entropy, contrast and difference distribution entropy [7]. The three features have been used as an neural network input. Training data were prepared using some selected pictures belonged to a background, and to a particle surface and to a contour of particles. The MLP network dimension is 3x4x2.

4 Experimental results

A catalyst for ammonia synthesis of granulation 1.6-3 mm and consisting of five fractions has been analyzed. Below, in Fig. 2, there is an image of the catalyst sample after processing using the neural based method. All intermediate gray shades have been reduced to only two: white and black colors, a) and b). In the last image b) there are presented extracted edges. The edges as well as entire particle images are necessary to apply the grid and secant methods for particle size analysis. Some experimental results are shown in Table 1.

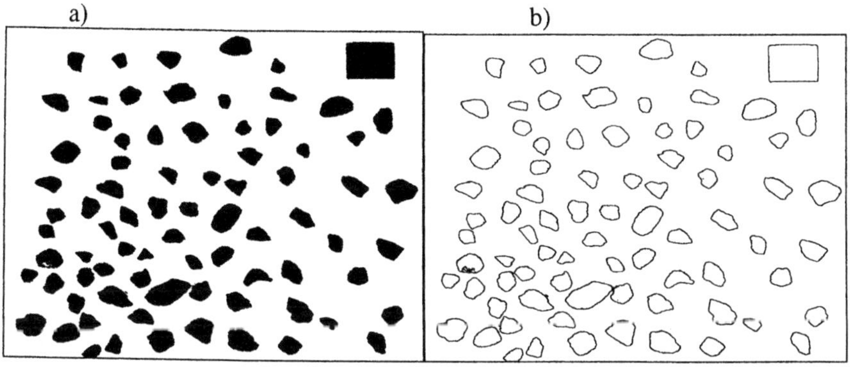

Fig. 2. Image of ammonia catalyst particles a) and edge extracted picture b)

Table 1. Granular bed analysis results using an optical and sieve analysis methods

sieve dimension, mm	>1.6	1.6-2.0	2.0-2.5	2.5-3.1	>3.1
weight fraction	10.3	21.6	28.8	27.9	11.4
d_{pi}, mm, optical method	1.31	1.60	2.06	2.31	2.43
d_{pi}, mm sieve analysis method	1.32	1.80	2.25	2.82	3.50

5 Conclusions

A method comprising an optical method derived from metallurgy and neural network approach have been applied for irregular shape particle size analysis. Obtained data have proved that this approach may be considered as a complement method to the commonly used sieve analysis method. Results obtained by the developed method are in general below the results obtained by the sieve analysis and fit better to pressure drop experimental results. There are well developed image processing techniques which might be applied to enrich the classification methods. Further studies should be continued to develop more reliable and fast methods in image analysis techniques to combine them into developed methodology.

References

1. Bobrowski, D. (1980), Probabilistic in technical applications, WNT, Warszawa
2. Carman A.C. (1956) Flow of gases through porus media, London Butterworth Scientific Publications
3. Duch, W., Grudziński, K. (1999), The weighted k-NN with selection of features and its neural realization, Proceedings of the Fourth Conference "Neural Networks and Their Applications", Częstochowa
4. Rój E. (2001), Determination the particle mean diameter of a packed bed using optical method. Inż. Chem. i Proc., 22, 3E,1231-1236
5. Ryś, J. (1970), An introduction to quantity metallography, Śląsk Publishing House, Katowice
6. Strumiłło, P., Szczypiński, P.,et al.(1997), A computer program for analysis of X-ray images of wheat grains. Scientific Works, Electronics, Łódź Technical University (In Polish)
7. Strzelecki, M. (1997), Segmentation of textured biological images using multilayer perceptron neural networks. Scientific Works, Electronics, Łódź Technical University (In Polish)
8. Zhu, Q. (1998), Minimum Cross-Entropy Approximation for Modeling of Highly Interwining Data Sets at Subclass Levels. Journal of Intelligence Information System 11, 139-152

NEURAL CLASSIFIER FOR BOTTOM SEDIMENTS

Dariusz Szulc[1], Mariusz Wąż[2]
[1,2] Naval University of Gdynia 69 Śmidowicza Str., 81-103 Gdynia, Poland

Summary

The article presents the application of neural networks for classification of bottom sediments by means of broadband analysis of hydroacoustical signals. The results of detection of five classes of sediments using a multilayer perceptron with back-propagation have been described below.

Introduction

The approaches for the application of neural networks in acoustical classification of sea bottom have been known in which the input values for the neural network were the chosen parameters of the bottom echo envelope, for example the echo energy or signal duration. However, in this work a different approach have been proposed which depends on directly applying the values from an appropriate fragment (corresponding to a given layer) of an echo signal.

For the initial broadband analysis of hydroacoustical signal reflected from the sea bottom the time delay spectrometry method have been applied. It allows to isolate the borders between the deposited sediments and separate the portions of the signal passing through the layers.

For the classification of the sea bottom type multilayer perceptron with back-propagation have been applied with the following structure:

- the input layer containing 20 neurons, which corresponds to 20 samples of the signal in case of each type of sediment layer,
- three hidden layers having 15, 15 and 10 neurons each,
- the output layer of 5 neurons, which should contain the proper values for the corresponding bottom type, coded by means of, so called, 1 of 5 code: [1 0 0 0 0] for the first type, [0 1 0 0 0] for the second one and so on.

The output layer presents the probability of classifying the given signal for the appropriate class of sediments. Such way of output information coding allowed, for real neural network output values, to apply the following decision rule: it is considered that the neural network has assigned the m-th bottom class to the signal if the value of the m-th neuron in the output layer is the highest of all 5 of them.

A characteristic curve for all hidden layers has been assumed to be similar to the logistic differentiable sigmoidal function based on the tangent hyperbolic function:

$$\varphi(\varepsilon) = \frac{2}{1+\exp(-2\varepsilon)} - 1$$

therefore, each of the neurons was calculating the following function:

$$y = \frac{2}{1+\exp(-2\sum_{i=1}^{n}(w_i x_i + Z))} - 1$$

where: n-number of inputs for a given neuron.

For neurons in the output layer the linear activation function has been assumed to be equal to the total input of the neuron. So, they were calculating the following function:

$$y = \sum_{i=1}^{n}(w_i x_i + Z)$$

In the model for the neural sea bottom classifier the supervised learning has been utilized, by means of presenting an adequate learning set containing the chosen input signals and corresponding to them reference outputs (for example [1 0 0 0 0], [0 0 0 1 0]). The accuracy (correctness) that must be achieved in the learning process of the network is assumed by determining the size of the allowed error Δ. This error is defined as the measure of the difference between the output signal (which can consist of a number of values – here 5), determined by the network after a given step, and the reference output.

The mean square error has been used in the neural network:

$$\Delta = \frac{1}{5}\sum_{j=1}^{5}\delta_j^2$$

where, δ_j - errors in particular outputs of the network.

For the modification of the weights and thresholds in the process of network learning delta rule has been applied. It has been slightly changed so that it not only took into account the error made by a neuron and the input value x_{ij} in the current learning step but also to a certain degree the error and the input value in the previous step.

For the implementation of the backpropagation of errors the Levenberg-Marquardt algorithm, which was available in the used programming environment, has been used.

Classification of the sediment layers with the application of neural networks

Before the application of registered hydroacoustical signals to the input layer of the network they were subjected to additional preprocessing in a number of stages.

Stage One

For the distinction of the layers in the sediments the reflected signals were composed in the linear scale. This allowed to strongly expose the maximum values corresponding to the transfer of the signal from one layer to another. Unfortunately, because of the high dynamics, such signal is not suitable for the further analysis and it was necessary to transform it to the logarithmic scale. A sample run of the signal at one of the measuring point is presented on figure 1.

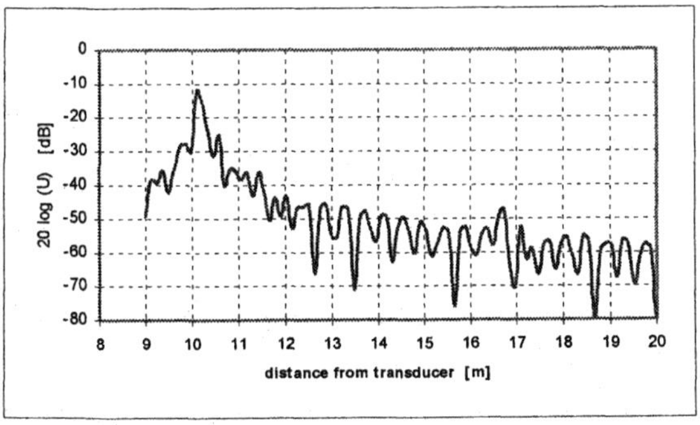

Figure 1. The spectrum of signal reflected from the bottom at a measuring point

The acoustical data have been collected at each of the measuring point. The signal run presented above is representative for one of the registered groups.

Stage Two

Basing on the relationship between the number of the sample and the depth of the layer in the bottom from each of the runs the fragments have been selected corresponding to singular, homogenous layers of the sediment. As a result 5 sets (their portions corresponding to different layers) have been selected and treated later as 5 separate bottom classes used for training and testing of the neural network. The information regarding the set sizes and names (types of layers in the bottom) are presented in the table 1.

Tab. 1. Information on the classes of bottom sediments used in the neural network

Class number	Measuring point	Layer type	Depth of layer from – to [m]	Number of signals
1	I	Sand	0 – 0.6	29
2	I	Slime and slit	0.6 – 1.8	29
3	II	Slimy sand	0 – 1.1	34
4	II	Slit	1 – 9.5	34
5	III	Clay	0.1 – 0.7	29

Stage Three
In the neural network 20 input neurons have been used so each signal presented to the network consisted of 20 values.

Stage Four
Before the beginning of the training process, each of the five sets of signals has been divided into the training set and testing set. An experiment has been conducted in which 60% of signals from all sets were the training set and the remaining 40% were the testing set.

Stage Five – training and testing of the neural network.
In the process of training, the data from the training set were presented to the input layer of the neural network in an alternating way, that is one signal from the first set (first class – bottom type) and then one signal form the second set (class 2), one from the third, fourth and fifth and then again one from the first and so on for all the signals in the training set. Afterwards, when the network has reached in the learning phase the training level not higher then the assumed threshold (set experimentally at 0.05) the testing phase has been started.

The results
The neural network has been applied in three tasks:

1. Basing on the training set it has learned to recognize the signals
   2a. The test phase has been conducted basing on the testing set
   2b. For the whole set of signals the efficiency of the constructed neural network has been analyzed for the classification of bottom sediments

Task 1.
60% of the signals coming from the different sediment layers have been input into the neural network along with the corresponding correct answers. For the successive signals, if the learning error was smaller then the assumed threshold the signal was counted as correctly recognized. The percentage results for the training set are presented in figure 2.

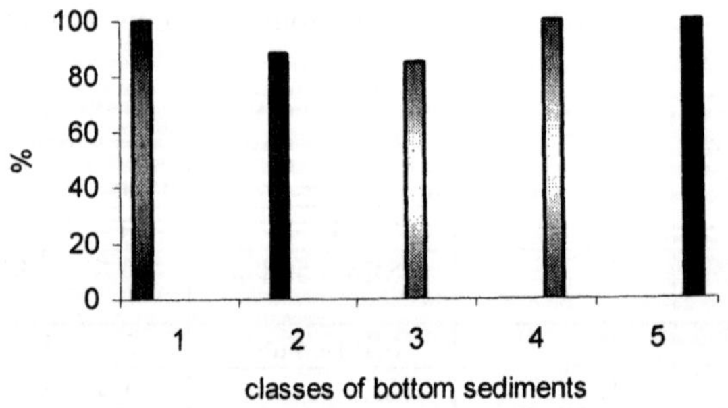

Figure 2. The presentation of the network learning for classification of signals to the particular sediment class for 60% of the training set

From the above results it can be inferred that the neural network has learned to properly recognize the I, IV and V class of sediments.

Task 2a.

After the termination of the learning process the testing set (40% of all signals) has been presented into the input layer of the neural network. The percentage results have been shown in the figure 3.

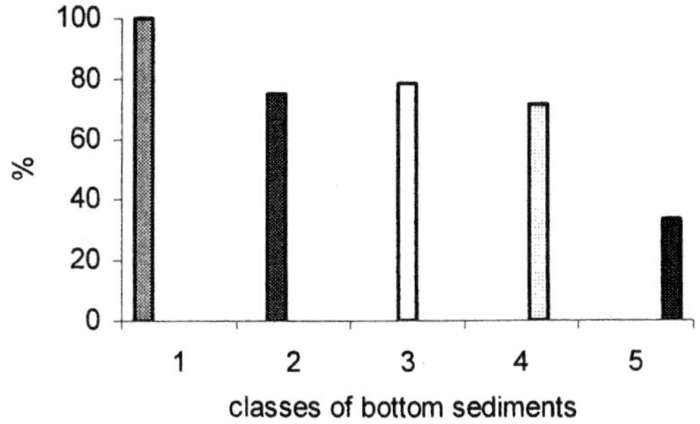

Figure 3. The presentation of the percentage distribution of signal classification to the successive classes of sediments for 40% of the training set

The obtained results of the application of neural network indicate that for the classes I-IV the efficiency of classification oscillates from 100% for the first class to 71.43% for the fourth one. Unfortunately, the fifth class of sediment was recognized only in 33.33%.

Task 2b.

In this task both sets have been combined into one a complete set of acoustical signal responds from the particular sediment layers and then it was presented to the neural network. As a result the final results of the classification efficiency were obtained. The percentage results are shown on figure 4.

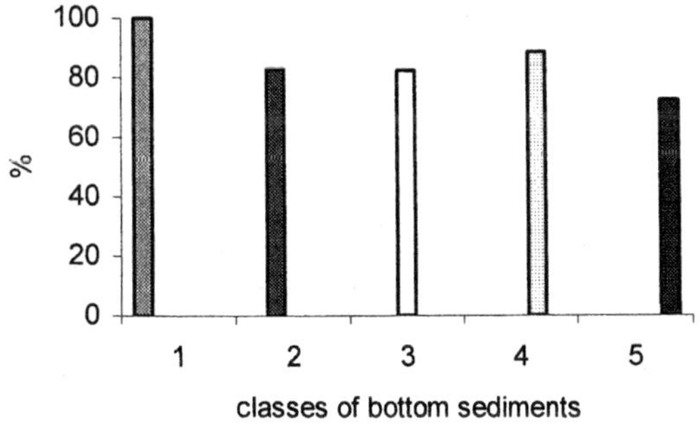

Figure 4. The column presentation of the percentage distribution of the classification of successive sediment classes to the complete signal set.

Table 2 presents the summery of the effectiveness of the neural network in which the percent share of the properly classified signals have been indicated for 60% and 80% - percentage sizes of the training sets.

Tab. 2. The summary of the results of the application of the neural network

	60%	80%
Zu	85,81	85,16
Zt	68,75	71,88
Zp	90,24	94,51

where:

Z_u - properly classified signals from the training set
Z_t - properly classified signals from the testing set
Z_p - proper classification of signals from the combined, complete set

Conclusions

The applied multilayer perceptron with backpropagation of error yields fine expected results in the process of classification of bottom sediments. In order to increase its efficiency it would be necessary to increase the size of the signal training set and then conduct further optimization of the neural network.

References

[1] Korbicz J., Obuchowicz A., Uciński D. (1994), Artificial Neural Networks. Basics and Applications RM Academic Publishing House, Warsaw (In Polish)

[2] Osowski S. (1996), Neural Networks in Algorithmic Expression, WNT, Warsaw (In Polish)

[3] Tadeusiewicz R. (1993), Neural Networks, RM Academic Publishing House, Warsaw (In Polish)

[4] Watkins C. D., Sadun A., Marenka S. (1995), Modern Methods of Picture Transformation, WNT, Warsaw (In Polish)

PERFORMANCE OF ROC CURVES AND LVQ NEURAL NETWORKS IN DETECTION OF MIDDLE CEREBRAL ARTERY SPASM

Miroslaw SWIERCZ[1], Zenon MARIAK[2], Jaroslaw KREJZA[3]

[1] Faculty of Electrical Engineering, Bialystok Technical University, ul. Grunwaldzka 11/15, 15-893 Bialystok, Poland, e-mail: mswiercz@cksr.ac.bialystok.pl

[2] Department of Neurosurgery, [3] Department of Radiology, Medical Academy Bialystok, ul. M. Curie-Sklodowskiej 24 a, 15-276 Bialystok, Poland

Abstract. Transcranial color-coded Doppler ultrasonography (TCCD) is used by radiologists for detection of middle cerebral artery spasm. In this study, TCCD examination was performed in 100 patients, refereed by neurosurgeons for arterial angiography. Angiographic images were used to establish the four-grade scale of spasm, which was combined with TCCD blood flow measurements. The overall performance of TCCD in detection of MCA narrowing was estimated by means of Receiver Operating Characteristics (ROC). The ROC analysis proved very high efficiency (over 90%) of TCCD for detection of moderate-to-severe spasm. The multi-parameter classification of TCCD data was also performed by LVQ networks. LVQ networks showed very good accuracy (80-95%), not only for binary outcome, but also for classification of TCCD data in a multi-grade scale of spasm.

1 Introduction

The practical use of transcranial Doppler ultrasonography (TCD) in diagnosis of cerebral vasospasm is based on the phenomenon of increasing blood flow velocity with vessel narrowing [1]. The most commonly used threshold value of velocity in the middle cerebral artery (MCA), which discriminates vasospasm from a normal stet of the artery, is 120 cm/s [4]. Due to other findings [5], a critical velocity value for confirming vasospasm would be 200 cm/s, and for excluding this condition – 120 cm/s; the thresholds for individual patients fall within this range.

However, the increased flow in the vessel is a result of a variety of factors (not only the vasospasm) [4], so a unique blood velocity threshold, common for a wide population, does not exist. Besides, TCD ultrasonography can cause errors in blood flow measurements, because it is not possible to control the angle between the interrogated vessel and the ultrasound beam. The more advanced method, i.e. transcranial color-coded Doppler ultrasonography (TCCD), enables visualization of examined vessels and angular correction of the measurement of blood flow [3].

In the paper, overall diagnostic performance of TCCD examination was assessed with the Receiver Operating Characteristics (ROC) methodology. This method allowed establishing threshold values of blood velocities, which yielded the maximal efficiency of the test. The TCCD data classification task was also solved with the Learning Vector Quantization (LVQ) neural networks, which were able to create decision boundaries in the multidimensional space of blood flow parameters, measured with transcranial color-coded Doppler ultrasonography.

2 Materials, methods and techniques

2.1 Transcranial color-coded Doppler ultrasonography (TCCD) and digital subtraction angiography (DSA)

The ultrasound scanner (SSA 140 A, Toshiba Medical Systems), equipped with a 2.5 MHz 90° phased-array probe was used for examination of intracranial cerebral arteries. One hundred consecutive patients (54 men and 46 women), routinely refereed by neurosurgeons for intra-arterial digital radiography, received TCCD examination immediately before angiograms. For each patient, only data from middle cerebral arteries (MCAs) were taken to further analysis. The mean (Vm), peak-systolic (Vps) and end-diastolic (Ved) velocities were calculated by tracing the maximum frequency envelope of the Doppler waveform. Due to non-perpendicular position of the probe, the angular correction algorithm was applied to improve the accuracy of measurements.

Selective intra-arterial digital subtraction angiography (DSA) was performed via the femoral artery Saldinger approach in both internal carotid arteries or in at least one vertebral artery. To quantify the degree of vasospasm, the M1 segment of MCA was measured at its point of maximal reduction and compared with the normal section of the artery, adjacent to the narrowed segment.

Angiographic vasospasm was graded as: none, mild (equal or less than 25% of vessel caliber reduction), moderate (between 25% and 50% of reduction) and severe (more than 50% of reduction). To facilitate classification, the angiograms were reviewed by two neuro-radiologists, unaware of ultrasound findings.

2.2 Learning Vector Quantization (LVQ) neural networks

Learning Vector Quantization is a classification network, which assigns vectors to one of several classes [2], defined by a user; so the training of the LVQ network is performed in a supervised mode. The network consists of two layers: an input, competitive layer, which assigns the input vectors to a certain number of subclasses and an output, linear layer, which transforms the competitive layer's output subclasses into target classes, determined by the user.

In each step of the training process, the winning neuron with the weights w_w, is characterized by the smallest Euclidean distance to the processed input vector x:

$$w_w = \arg\min_{w_i,\ i\in\overline{1,S1}} \{\|w_i - x\|\} \tag{1}$$

where $S1$ is the number of competitive neurons in the input (Kohonen) layer.

If the winner belongs to the same class as the training vector x, it is moved towards this vector; if it belongs to another class – is repulsed from the vector x:

$$w_w' = w_w + \alpha\,(x - w_w) \quad or \quad w_w' = w_w - \gamma\,(x - w_w) \tag{2}$$

where α is the attraction and γ - the repulsion coefficient.

The competitive layer splits the input space into $S1$ subclasses, which in turn are combined by the linear layer into $S2$ user-defined target classes. The decision boundaries, separating different classes, may form the shapes in a multidimensional space, which are more complicated than ordinary hyperplanes.

In the classification mode, the competitive layer computes the distance between an input vector to each neuron, and again, the nearest processing element is declared to be a winner. The output of this neuron is set to "1", while the outputs of all the other neurons are set to "0".

2.3 Receiver Operating Characteristics (ROC curves)

There are two types of errors for binary classification problems [2]: false positive (a classification of positive, given to an example, which is actually negative), and false negative (a negative classification of an example, which is actually positive).

The term 'sensitivity', *Se*, (or power) of the test denotes the probability of the true positive classification. The term 'specificity', *Sp*, is the probability of a true negative classification. For a certain decision threshold, these values can be presented in a form of a confusion matrix.

In signal detection theory, the plot of *Se* versus 1–*Sp*, as the decision threshold is varied, is known as the 'Receiver Operating Characteristic', or ROC curve [2]. In radar applications, the ROC curve is used to measure how well a receiver can detect signal from noise. In medical field, the ROC curve measures the ability to distinguish positive from negative examples.

The ROC plot spans from the lower left (0; 0) to he upper right (1; 1) corner of the unit square. The area under the ROC curve (A_z) is a global summary statistics of diagnostic accuracy, based on all possible cut-off values [6]. For perfect discrimination, the ROC plot passes through the coordinates (0; 1), what corresponds to Se = 100% and Sp = 100% for each threshold value ($A_z = 1$). The straight line from coordinates (0; 0) to (1; 1) means that the test is unable to discriminate between classes (A_z is 0.5) [6]. The tests of $0.5 < A_z \le 0.7$ are less accurate; moderately accurate show $0.7 < A_z \le 0.9$, and highly accurate have $0.9 < A_z < 1$.

3 Results

Out of 200 examined middle cerebral arteries, TCCD data from 158 arteries in 99 patients were of satisfactory quality to be included in ROC analysis and construction of LVQ networks. In this group, mild vasospasm was angiographically detected in 17 arteries, moderate spasm in 19 arteries and severe spasm in 9 MCAs. Primarily selected four grades of spasm were re-grouped, and the experiments were performed for two classification problems:

a) detection of any grade of vasospasm, i.e. discrimination of the normal artery state from any narrowing of its diameter;
b) detection of moderate-to-severe spasm, i.e. the condition of more than 25% of MCA narrowing.

Figure 1 shows the ROC curves, when the peak-systolic velocity Vps was used for detection of all vasospasms (a) and the moderate-to-severe spasm (b). Some arbitrary values of velocities are located on the ROC plots, what enables both the sensitivity and the specificity for these thresholds to be delineated.

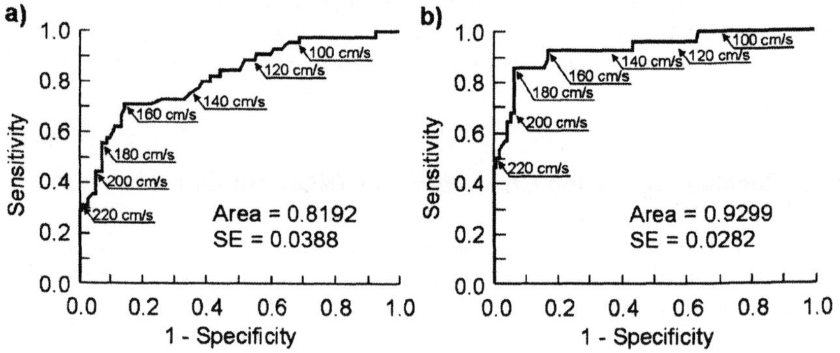

Fig. 1. ROC curves for MCA spasm detection, using peak-systolic velocity, Vps. (a) Detection of any vasospasm. (b) Detection of moderate-to-severe spasm

Table 1 shows the parameters, resulting from ROC curves, which can be used to evaluate diagnostic performance of TCCD examination. The most commonly used coefficient, the area A_z, is very high for moderate-to severe spasm and about 12% lower for all vasospasms. The difference is statistically significant, as assessed with a non-paired *t*-test. The table also contains values of the partial area under the ROC curve, corresponding to high sensitivity ($Se \geq 80\%$).

Table 1. Diagnostic performance of TCCD ultrasonography in detection of middle cerebral artery spasm (SE is the standard error of the mean)

Velocities	All vasospasms		Moderate-to-severe spasm	
	$A_{z\,total}$ (SE)	$A_{z\,partial}$	$A_{z\,total}$ (SE)	$A_{z\,partial}$
Peak-systolic	0.8192 (0.0388)	0.0820	0.9299 (0.0282)	0.1591
Mean	0.8220 (0.0404)	0.0776	0.9375 (0.0341)	0.1569
End-diastolic	0.8117 (0.0427)	0.0697	0.9408 (0.0359)	0.1576

The peak-systolic velocity (Vps) performs best as a single diagnostic parameter in detection of both selected groups of vasospasms. The highest efficiency of the test for detection of moderate-to-severe spasm (92%) was identified for Vps = 182 cm/s, which threshold corresponds to *Se* = 86% and *Sp* = 93%. For detection of any spasm grade, almost the same Vps threshold was shown to be optimal, but the associated efficiency was reduced to 85% (*Se* = 55% and *Sp* = 91%).

In the next experiments, diagnostic performance of TCCD was assessed by the LVQ net-based classification of a set of velocities (Vps, Vm, Ved), which characterize blood flow condition for a patient. Fig. 2 shows the projection of a data set for moderate-to-severe spasm onto the plane, spanned on Vps and Vm velocities. One can see that data assigned to specific grades of vasospasm occupy overlapping regions in the input space; so no a specific triple (Vps, Vm, Ved) exists, which could separate the regions assigned to different spasm grades.

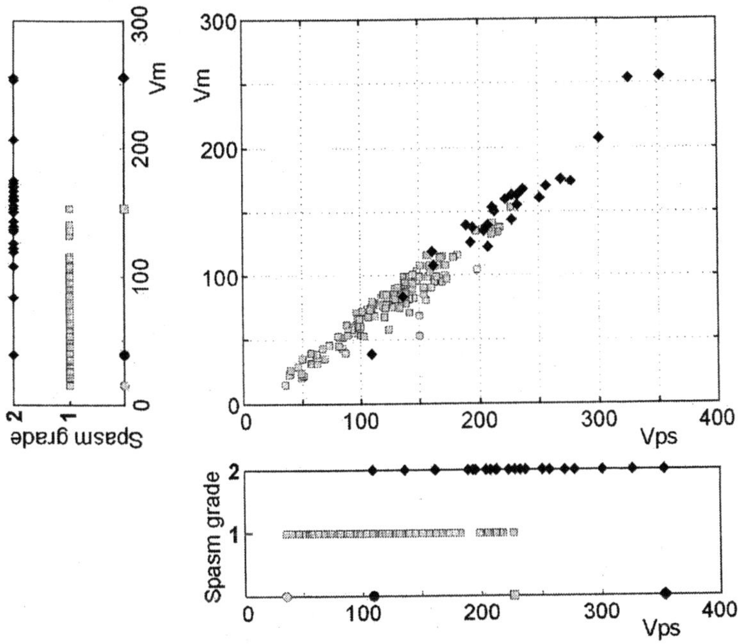

Fig. 2. Projection of TCCD data onto the Vps-Vm plane and distribution of blood flow velocities for moderate-to-severe vasospasm

Table 2 shows the performance of two LVQ architectures in detection of any spasm and moderate-to-severe spasm, presented in a form of confusion matrices. The rows in Table 2 represent class, computed by an LVQ network and columns – the actual class, determined from angiographic examination. Both LVQ networks had 3 inputs and 2 outputs (representing the spasm grade in '*1 of N*' code). Classification accuracies, obtained for simple LVQ networks are similar to the areas under ROC curves, but higher for more complex structures.

Table 2. Diagnostic performance of two LVQ architectures, trained for binary classification

Class 1 – no spasm			Class 2 – any grade of vasospasm		
8 neurons in Kohonen layer Overall classification rate = 0.7957			16 neurons in Kohonen layer Overall classification rate = 0.8757		
	Class1_act	Class2_act		Class1_act	Class2_act
Class1_lvq	0.9469	0.3556	Class1_lvq	0.9292	0.1778
Class1_lvq	0.0531	0.6444	Class1_lvq	0.0708	0.8222
Class 1 – no spasm + mild spasm			Class 2 – moderate-to-severe vasospasm		
8 neurons in Kohonen layer Overall classification rate = 0.8467			16 neurons in Kohonen layer Overall classification rate = 0.9209		
	Class1_act	Class2_act		Class1_act	Class2_act
Class1_lvq	0.9077	0.2143	Class1_lvq	0.9846	0.1429
Class1_lvq	0.0923	0.7857	Class1_lvq	0.0154	0.8571

4 Conclusions

Performance of the transcranial color Doppler ultrasonography (TCCD) in diagnosis of advanced MCA narrowing is very high, as estimated with the area under the ROC curve and LVQ classifiers. For diagnosis of any MCA narrowing, this performance is acceptable for clinical purposes.

The ROC analysis, presented above, evaluates the overall accuracy of binary classification, based on a single parameter, which characterizes the blood flow in MCA. The LVQ network is a much more sophisticated tool, which is able to take into account individual variabilities of flow velocity in examined vessels and solve a pattern recognition task, which result does not depend on any decision threshold.

References

1. Aaslid, R., Huber, P., Nornes, H. (1984) Evaluation of cerebrovascular spasm with transcranial Doppler ultrasound. Journal of Neurosurgery **60** 37-41
2. Kohonen, T. (1987) Self-Organization and Associative Memory, 2nd edition. Springer-Verlag, Berlin
3. Krejza, J., Mariak, Z., Melhem, E.R., Bert, R. (2000) A guide to the identification of major cerebral arteries with transcranial color Doppler sonography. AJR Am. J Roentgenology **174** 1297-1303
4. Ohkuma, H., Manabe, H., Tanaka, M. et al. (2002) Impact of cerebral microcirculatory changes on cerebral vasospasm after aneurysmal subarachnoid hemorrhage. Stroke **31** 1621-1627
5. Sloan, M.A., Wozniak, M.A., Macko R.F. (1999) Monitoring of vasospasm after subarachnoid hemorrhage, in: V.L. Babikian, L.R. Wechsler, eds., Transcranial Doppler ultrasonography. Butterworth-Heinemann, Boston 109-127
6. Zweig, M.H., Campbell, G. (1993) Receiver operating characteristics (ROC) plots: a fundamental tool in clinical medicine. Clin. Chem. **39**, 561-577

Neural Network Approach to Acoustic Detection of Number of Vehicles

Tomasz Walkowiak, Pawel Zogal

Institute of Engineering Cybernetics, Wroclaw University of Technology,
ul. Janiszewskiego 11/17, 50-372 Wroclaw, Poland
e-mail: twalkow@ict.pwr.wroc.pl, pzogal@medcom-online.de

Abstract. The paper reports results of applying a perceptron neural network to determine the number of sound sources on a scene monitored by an array of linearly spaced microphones. The standard techniques for solving this problem were found inadequate in the presence of normal disturbances (such as produced by wind). The paper proposes an indirect application of a perceptron neural network, to analyze the results of the MUSIC beam forming technique. The method is experimentally shown to deal with this problem. Field experiments included scenes with zero, one or two moving vehicles proved the system effectiveness.

1 Introduction

Detecting the number of sound sources is an integral part of many sound tracking and recognition systems. Many of such systems especially those dealing with vehicles have military background, however police or traffic inspection could also benefit from those. An example of an application is a passive sonar that detects and tracks submarines without an earlier ping or an intelligent mine [10]. The idea behind the latter example is to actively neutralize enemy objects that happen to be in range of such a mine. One has to assume that such a system requires both object recognition and tracking as missile homing systems have quite narrow angular range. A civil application might be a traffic data collection or movement control of a robot.

Detecting the number of sound sources using a microphone array is a complicated task, especially in a noisy environment which is almost the case in real life applications. Unfortunately most of the work in this area focuses on angular localization with the number of sources already known. The basics and main methods can be found in [2,4,7]. Nowadays, most of the work focuses on modifications of those basic algorithms in order to achieve better resolution or less computational cost [5,6]. The most known methods of determining the number of sound sources use either the information theory [9] or some heuristic algorithms [2] or finally – neural networks [3]. The last approach seems to be most promising at the moment.

2 Background

The input data are the sounds emitted by military vehicles such as BWP, BRDM, T72 tank or the Gozdzik assault gun in a military filed. The sources of those sounds are mainly the engines, tracks and wheels of those vehicles. Their characteristics depend on many factors such as speed of a vehicle, environmental conditions and surface type. However, a priori knowledge of those characteristics is not needed. Besides that, inspected vehicles have particular routes and speeds in certain range [10]. The experiments were repeated at two different locations, at dissimilar weather conditions. The most important assumptions concerning the data collected (and thus heavily affecting the developed system) are:

- most of the signal energy is concentrated in the 50-200Hz band;
- the vehicles move around with speeds ranging from 0 to 30 km/h (in most of the cases it's around 15 km/h);
- the area can be treated as flat and without any obstacles obscuring sound propagation and producing unwanted reverberations;
- there are no more than 2 vehicles in the acoustic field at a time as the available measurement systems consisted of only 4 microphones and although it would theoretically allow detection of 3 sources, the environmental noises make it impossible.

The mentioned factors allow us to assume that the vehicle are far field point sources which implies that the sound wave coming to the measure point is flat.

3 System Architecture

The structure of our system can be divided into 6 blocks connected sequentially (i.e. the output of the 1st block serves as the input into the 2nd one). Those blocks are: data acquisition, preprocessing, short time Fourier transform, MUSIC algorithm [4,7], feature extraction and finally the neural classifier.

3.1 Data Acquisition

The sounds were gathered using 4 Brüel & Kjær 4188 microphones. The sensors were placed in an ULA (uniform linear array) configuration with 60cm span. The microphones were connected to 4 Brüel & Kjær 2671 preamplifiers. Next, the 4 signals were gathered in a 4 channel NEXUS 2693A0S4 amplifier. Finally, the data was converted into digital form using a PC and a dSpace DSP set. Used format was 16bit and 5kHz sampling. Apart proper sounds, some additional information which included real number and positions of the vehicles was stored as well. This was needed for further off-line processing (e.g. system learning, efficiency measuring).

3.2 Preprocessing

Gathered data files were further processed in order to standardize the input. First thing done in this stage is the removal of the constant component in each of 4 signals. The purpose of such action is to have 0 mean signals. Next step was the power normalization. Power of a measured signal is dependent mainly on the distance between the vehicle and the microphone array. Since our task is to determine the number of sound sources and not their positions, we want to keep the features used in the final classification independent of actual distance from the array. As far as removing the constant component is a local operation on each of the 4 signals, power normalization must be done globally because relations between each signals may contain useful information. This process consists in dividing all signals by a constant depending on signal's power. In our case it's a power of a 1s recording given by the following equation:

$$\sigma = \sqrt{\frac{5000}{K} \sum_{i,j} x_{ij}^2} \tag{1}$$

Where K is the number of samples in a file and x_{ij} is a j-th sample in the i-th channel. 5000 stands for used sampling frequency.

3.3 Short Time Fourier Transform

Next stage of the system is the short time Fourier transform [8] of the signals acquired. The complex number representation is needed in further processing – the MUSIC algorithm. The signal was transformed using 1024 samples window and Hann window function. The span between windows was 50 samples. The values were chosen arbitrary. The 1024 window size was chosen to get the high frequency resolution and fast processing (the fast Fourier transform [4] requires power of 2 window size), however only 51 bands below 250Hz were kept in further processing, as there was almost no signal energy above that level.

3.4 MUSIC Algorithm and the Pseudo-spectrum Concept

The MUSIC algorithm has been first presented in [7]. The data model comprises the one assumed in this system. Having an ULA microphone array with M omnidirectional sensors which is pinged by a set of N ($N<=M$) narrowband zero-mean, far-field signals (N – signal sources). Assuming that the received signals are $\mathbf{Y}(t)$, the spatial covariance matrix can be presented as:

$$\mathbf{R} = E[\mathbf{Y}(t)\mathbf{Y}^H(t)] \tag{2}$$

According to [3] eigenvectors corresponding to N largest eigenvalues span the signal subspace which is orthogonal to the noise subspace which is spanned by the rest of the eigenvectors. In our case we don't know the number of the sources N, so we are unable to form the definite signal subspace matrix. On the other hand decomposition of matrix **R** gives information on the eigenvalues ($\lambda_{i,f}$) which can be interpreted as the powers of consecutive potential sound sources. Since *N* is unknown the assumption is, that there are *M* pseudo-sources some of which correspond to the real sources and the remaining ones to noise. Decision on the real number of sources is taken by the neural classifier. One has also to admit that preceding considerations are about narrow-band sources, however in this case the moving vehicles are rather wide-band emitters. The proposed solution is introduction of pseudo-spectra of the pseudo-sources. A pseudo-spectrum is a set of *k*-th eigenvalues in all processed bands (e.g. 1st pseudo-spectrum comprises of largest eigenvalues of the estimate of the covariance matrix **R** in each band). In case of this system, there are 4 pseudo-spectra. As one can see on the attached figure, noise pseudo-spectra have common structure (i.e. follow the 1/f pattern [8]) and contain much less energy than the pseudo-spectra associated with real sources.

3.5 Feature Extraction

The feature vector used in further processing was based on pseudo-spectra described in the previous section. However, using all data contained would imply too much complexity, so we decided on deriving some measures describing the pseudo-spectra. The first class of such measures used is connected with the power of the sources whereas the second one deals with the structure of each pseudo-source. The power of a pseudo-source is expressed in the following equation:

$$P_i = \sum_f \lambda_{i,f} \tag{3}$$

The measure describing the structure is the relation between the power below 50Hz and the whole P_i:

$$K_i = \frac{\sum_{f<50Hz} \lambda_{i,f}}{P_i} \tag{4}$$

The choice of 50Hz boundary was empirically. As one can see on attached graphs, many pseudo-sources corresponding to noise have 1/f structure with the majority of power concentrated in the bands below 50Hz. The final feature vector consisted of 8 components: $\{\ \log(P_1),\ldots,\log(P_4),\log(K_1),\ldots,\log(K_4)\ \}$. The logarithmic vector space was dictated by the fact that most relations between powers are either divisions or multiplications. Having logarithmized the vector space, one has addition/subtraction relations which are more convenient for neural networks.

3.6 Signal Classification

The final part of the system is the neural network classifier. It has the MLP (multi layer perceptron) architecture with 8 input neurons which correspond to the components of a single feature vector, 22 hidden layer neurons and 2 output neurons. The number of neurons in the hidden layer was chosen experimentally. Such network produced best results and higher numbers didn't give any improvement. The log-sigmoid was used as a transfer function in both hidden and output layer. Besides that, the output values above the 0.5 threshold were considered as 1s and below the mentioned level as 0s. The output coding was 0,0 for no vehicles; 1,0 for one vehicle and 1,1 for two sources. The network presented above was trained using the Levenberg-Marquardt [1] algorithm which gave the fastest convergence.

4 Obtained Results

The experiments conducted aimed at the choice of the number of neurons in the hidden layer and testing of logarithmic and linear vector space. The comparison criterion was of course the final performance. The detailed results are presented in the tables below. The best performance was reached with 22 hidden neurons. As we assumed, logarithmic vector space improved the classification. One has to denote that the presented system has 0.5s resolution whereas in [3] and [10] signal classification is done on a 4s chunk. After averaging the results over 8 frames which gives the same 4s resolutions, system performance rises considerably.

Table 1. Performance comparison

	heuristic algorithm [10]			NN from [3]			this system		
no. of vehicles	% of responses that: n=0	n=1	n=2	n=0	n=1	n=2	n=0	n=1	n=2
0	81%	3%	16%	98%	1%	0%	88%	11%	1%
1	5%	89%	6%	1%	86%	13%	2%	86%	12%
2	11%	12%	76%	7%	22%	72%	0%	23%	76%

Table 2. System performance after result averaging over 8 frames (4s)

no. of vehicles	% of responses that: n=0	n=1	n=2
0	96%	4%	0%
1	0%	93%	7%
2	0%	17%	83%

5 Conclusions and Future Work

This paper presented a neural network approach to detection of vehicles based on acoustic information. The performance of the system is tightly coupled with the temporal resolutions. The efficiency was ranging between 80% (0.5s chunks) to 90% (4s chunks). One should consider those results satisfactory as it's physically impossible to reach 100% efficiency (e.g. 2 vehicles of the same type passing each other) without additional information. The neural classifier used in the system showed good generalization ability. The training set consisted of 6 minutes of recording, whereas the test set comprised of 20 minutes. Presented system was implemented in the MATLAB environment and despite this fact a PC Pentium III 500MHz machine processed 67 minutes of 4 channel recording in 60 minutes which gives near real-time speed.

Future work can be divided into 2 aspects: efficiency improvement and speed up. The latter one can be easily done with implementing the system in a C/C++ environment taking into account particular processor optimization. Apart that, some parts can be easy parallelized (FFT, eigenvalue decomposition). Efficiency can be improved by coupling the system with visual or seismic data processing.

References

1. Bishop Ch. (1995) Neural Networks for Pattern Recognition. Clarendon Press, Oxford
2. Blesler Y., Macovski A. (1986) Exact Maximum Likelihood Parameter Estimation of Superimposed Exponential Signals in Noise. IEEE Trans. on Acoustics, Speech and Signal Processing **34**, 1081-1089
3. Caban D., Walkowiak T. (1999) Application of Neural Networks to Determine the Number of Acoustic Sources. 5th International Conference on Soft Computing, Mendel '99, Brno, Czech Republic, June 9-12, 329-332
4. Johnson, D.H., Dudgeon D.E. (1993) Array Signal Processing: Concepts and Techniques. Prentice Hall, Englewood Clifs, New York
5. Luo F.L., Unbehauen R. (1998) Applied Neural Networks for Signal Processing. Cambridge University Press
6. Moulines E., Cardoso J-F. (1991) Second-order versus fourth-order MUSIC algorithms: an asymptotical statistical analysis. Int. Sig. Proc. Workshop on Higher Order Statistics, Chamrouse, France
7. Schmidt R.O. (1979) Multiple emitter location and signal parameter estimation. Proc. RADC Spectrum Estimation Workshop, Rome, 243-258
8. Smith S. W. (1999) The Scientist and Engineer's Guide to Digital Signal Processing. California Technical Publishing
9. Wang H., Kaveh K. (1999) Coherent Signal-Subspace Processing for the Detection and Estimation of Angles of Arrival of Multiple Wide-Band Sources. IEEE Trans. on Acoustics, Speech and Signal Processing **33**, 823-831
10. Zamojski W. et al. (1999) A System for Recognition and Tracking of Moving Objects on the Basis of Acoustic Information. Reports of the Institute of Engineering Cybernetics, Wroclaw University of Technology, PRE 17/99, Wroclaw, Poland (In Polish)

Druck: Strauss Offsetdruck, Mörlenbach
Verarbeitung: Schäffer, Grünstadt

GPSR Compliance

The European Union's (EU) General Product Safety Regulation (GPSR) is a set of rules that requires consumer products to be safe and our obligations to ensure this.

If you have any concerns about our products, you can contact us on ProductSafety@springernature.com

In case Publisher is established outside the EU, the EU authorized representative is:

Springer Nature Customer Service Center GmbH
Europaplatz 3
69115 Heidelberg, Germany

Batch number: 10725962

Printed by Printforce, the Netherlands